CITIES OF THE AMERICAN WEST

• JOHN W. REPS •

CITIES OF THE AMERICAN WEST

A History of Frontier Urban Planning

• PRINCETON UNIVERSITY PRESS •

Copyright © 1979 by Princeton University Press
Published by Princeton University Press, Princeton, New Jersey
In the United Kingdom: Princeton University Press, Guildford, Surrey

All Rights Reserved

Library of Congress Cataloging in Publication Data will be
found on the last printed page of this book

Publication of this book has been aided by a grant from the
Amon Carter Museum of Western Art

Printed in the United States of America by Princeton
University Press, Princeton, New Jersey

Designed by Frank J. Mahood

The Amon Carter Museum was established in 1961 under the will of the late Amon
G. Carter for the study and documentation of westering North America. The program of the Museum, expressed in publications, exhibitions, and permanent collections, reflects many aspects of American culture, both historic and contemporary.

To the Memory of Three Gifted Teachers   THOMAS W. MACKESEY

Who Helped Me Learn and with Gratitude   ALBERT S. CARLSON

to Cornell and Dartmouth Where They Taught   WALTER CURT BEHRENDT

CONTENTS

PREFACE •————————————————————————————————————

Chicago in 1893 throbbed with excitement and activity. South of its business district the gleaming white buildings of the World's Columbian Exposition soared above the waters of Lake Michigan. The exposition's elaborately designed complex of structures, built to celebrate the discovery of America four centuries earlier, had been in the making for several years. Now it stood as a magic city for all to admire. Visitors from throughout the country and, indeed, from all over the world, filled its exhibits, jammed the Midway amusement district leading inland from the fair's lakeside site, and crowded the city's hotels and shops.

It was a proud year for the city that had begun its existence on the western frontier barely six decades before. Indians then had camped where now towered the young skyscrapers of Chicago's Loop district. The very site of the fair not long ago had been an unsightly swamp bordering an expanse of prairie stretching south and west. Now, with a population of more than one million, Chicago ranked second in size among the nation's cities. Its rapid growth, substantial improvements, and success in winning from its eastern competitors the honor of sponsoring the fair symbolized the coming of age of the American West.

Among the visitors Chicago welcomed that summer were members of the American Historical Association. Like so many other scholarly, professional, business, and fraternal groups, this organization had chosen the city as the place for its annual meeting. Joining his colleagues was a young historian from the University of Wisconsin who came to present an address entitled "The Significance of the Frontier in American History."

If the location was appropriate, so was the time. Frederick Jackson Turner opened his remarks with a quotation from an obscure bulletin issued two years earlier by the superintendent of the census: "Up to and including 1880 the country had a frontier of settlement, but at present the unsettled area has been so broken into by isolated bodies of settlement that there can hardly be said to be a frontier line. In the discussion of its extent, its westward movement, etc., it can not, therefore, any longer have a place in the census reports."[1]

This short statement, Turner asserted, marked "the closing of a great historic movement," for, he continued, "the existence of an area of free land, its continuous recession, and the advance of American settlement westward, explain American development." Turner then proceeded to trace the movement of the frontiers of the Indian trader, the rancher, and the farmer and to summarize their influence on national legislation, land policy, and the growth of democratic institutions.

It was the frontier that had shaped the American character, which Turner described as "that coarseness and strength combined with acuteness and inquisitiveness; that practical, inventive turn of mind, quick to find expedients; that masterful grasp of material things, lacking in the artistic but powerful to effect great ends; that restless, nervous energy; that dominant individualism, working for good and for evil, and withal that buoyancy and exuberance which comes with freedom."[2] "Now," he concluded, "four centuries from the discovery of America, at the end of a hundred years of life under the Constitution, the frontier has gone, and with its going has closed the first period of American history."[3]

In his analysis Turner quoted approvingly from a guide for western settlers published in 1837. Its author described how the frontier was first occupied by the trapper and hunter with a crude cabin and small garden, then by the farmer, and finally by "men of capital and enterprise" who typically transformed the "small village" of the previous occupants into "a spacious town or city" with "substantial edifices of brick, . . . colleges and churches."[4] Turner evidently felt that this description of what he called the "modes of advance" of the frontier accurately characterized the settlement of the American West.

This concept of a neat progression in the sequence of settlement that only in its last stage resulted in the creation of towns and cities does not fit many of the facts of western American history. Turner either did not know or failed to appreciate that, in much of the West, the founding of towns preceded rural settlement or took place at the same time that agricultural or range lands were being opened for farming or ranching.[5]

It is this urban frontier of the American West that we shall explore—a frontier of Spanish *pueblos*, of mining camps, of railroad communities, of Mormon settlements, of speculative towns, of agricultural marketing centers, of coastal, lake, and river ports, of military posts that were transformed into urban places, and of capital cities. The establishment of urban communities, whatever their origins, stimulated rather than followed the opening of the West to agriculture. As vanguards of settlement, towns led the way and shaped the structure of society rather than merely responding to the needs of an established agrarian population for markets and points of distribution.

A major focus of this study is the physical patterns on which the towns and cities of the trans-Mississippi West grew. Contrary to the Turnerian thesis, these urban centers did not take shape through a process of gradual and random incremental growth that transformed a crossroads hamlet into a town and then perhaps to a major city. Instead, the typical procedure involved the selection of a promising site by an individual, group, church, railroad, corporation, or governmental agency. The tract was then surveyed into streets, blocks, lots, and open spaces. Only after this initial design was determined were houses, shops, mills, churches, stores, and public buildings erected on predetermined locations. The western frontier thus had its origins in hundreds and thousands of planned communities.[6]

Most of the incremental growth that did take place in western cities occurred only well after their founding. If their initial platted area proved insufficient in size to accommodate an increased population, "men of capital and enterprise" seized the opportunity to profit by speculative additions to these growing communities. In a number of cases, however, the municipality itself responded to this need for expansion by having land within its political jurisdiction or ownership laid out in new streets and building sites. One example of this process of continuing planning was, as we shall see, Los Angeles, the West's largest metropolis.

Whether undertaken by private initiative or under municipal direction, such additions to the urban fabric were normally also planned in the sense that, prior to land sales, some individual or public official determined the width and orientation of streets, the size and shape of blocks, the dimensions of the lots, and what if any sites were to be set aside for such purposes as parks, schools, and churches. In many cases the original townsite plat was simply extended; in others a new and sometimes contrasting pattern was stamped on land adjacent or close to the initial settlement.

There were, of course, variations on this procedure. The earliest mining camps did develop more or less spontaneously, although clearly not as the logical result of earlier pioneer or farming settlement. Even in such towns as these, however, efforts were quickly made to bring some necessary degree of order through surveys of streets, adjustments in property claims, and reservations of locations for cemeteries, schools, courthouses, and town halls. Several of the later mining towns were actually laid out in advance of occupancy and thus in design were usually indistinguishable from settlements having more conventional origins.

That most of the towns in the American West were planned does not imply that they were well designed. Urban planning is a sophisticated art and science, whose mastery one would not expect to find among those assigned to or attracted by the frontier. Until well into our own era America had relatively few skilled practitioners in this field. In the American West they were almost totally absent, and by default the tasks of laying out towns and future cities were carried out by land surveyors, engineers, military officials, speculative real estate developers, or complete amateurs. Only late in the nineteenth century were persons with some claim to professional competence available for urban planning activities in the West. Some of the earlier planners were talented; most were not, but good or bad, the results of their work provided the physical patterns that the towns of the region followed as they began to grow.

One unifying theme running through the diverse strains of western cities is the prevailing use of the gridiron street system with its rectangular blocks and lots. While we may think of this as typically American, it has been the plan-form used in all great periods of mass town founding in the past: Mediterranean colonization by the Greeks and Romans; medieval urban settlement in southwestern France, Poland, and eastern Germany; Spanish subjugation of Latin America; and English occupation of Northern Ireland.

If gridiron towns were pervasive in the West, the region differed little in this respect from that part of the country east of the great plains. For here, too, the majority of towns laid out both during the colonial era and years of independence followed this pattern. Easy to design, quick to survey, simple to comprehend, having the appearance of rationality, offering all settlers apparently equal locations for homes and business within its standardized structure, the gridiron or checkerboard plan's appeal is easy to understand.

That the plan can also be monotonous, inappropriate for hilly terrain, lacking in focal points for important buildings, monuments, or open spaces, and hazardous because of too-frequent street intersections have become painfully obvious with the passing of years. These shortcomings could hardly have been given much consideration by those responsible for planning the towns of western America, and given the circumstances under which they worked it is not difficult to see why. The founders of towns were limited both in time and experience, and if they had reflected at all on the consequences of their choices they would doubtless have felt such considerations as beauty, safety, and convenience in design of towns to be outweighed by more practical and mundane matters.

Although Turner failed to appreciate the importance of town founding and urban planning in the settlement of the frontier, he called attention to one aspect of western settlement that deserves emphasis because of its impact on the direction our own investigation will follow. After tracing the movement of the line of settlement from the Atlantic seaboard into the Midwest and across the Mississippi, Turner pointed out how the "gold discoveries had sent a sudden tide of adventurous miners" to California, where their settlements, along with those of early pioneers in Oregon and the Mormons in Utah, created a pattern of several detached frontiers.

Turner spelled out the consequences: "As the frontier has leaped over the Alleghanies, so now it skipped the Great Plains and the Rocky Mountains; and in the same way that the advance of the frontiersmen beyond the Alleghanies had caused the rise of important questions of transportation and internal improvement, so now the settlers beyond the Rocky Mountains needed means of communication with the East, and in the furnishing of these arose the settlement of the Great Plains and the development of still another kind of frontier life. Railroads, fostered by land grants, sent an increasing tide of immigrants into the far West."[7]

In this analysis Turner overlooked a far older frontier that was also detached from the main line of settlement moving westward through the Mississippi Valley. This consisted of the crescent of Hispanic towns, forts, missions, and ranchos extending from Texas through New Mexico and Arizona and curving up the Pacific Coast to San Francisco Bay. This aspect of western settlement lay almost neglected by American historians until the early years of the present century, when Herbert Eugene Bolton would begin a lifetime of studies of what he termed the Spanish Borderlands.

The presence of these several detached frontiers on the Pacific Coast, in the Willamette Valley of Oregon, within the Great Basin kingdom of the Mormons in Utah, and especially the Spanish Southwest, poses problems for the modern historian in organizing his material. If the western movement of this country had been a steady progression past the valley of the Mississippi, through the Great Plains, into the Rockies, and beyond to the Pacific Coast, both a chronological and a regional approach could be combined. History refused to fall into such neat patterns, and the reader of this book must be prepared for a more peripatetic journey through the enormous region and its towns and cities that we shall explore together.

A word of explanation is in order concerning the manner in which we approach our subject. I have chosen to begin with a summary of the westward movement of urban settlements having Anglo-American or French backgrounds, although many communities of Hispanic origins in Texas, the Southwest, and California began their existence earlier. This will bring us in time to the period of the Mexican War and geographically to the eastern edge of the region with which we shall be concerned—the vast area extending from the plains of Texas, Oklahoma, Kansas, Nebraska, and the Dakotas to the Pacific Coast.

Chapters 2, 3, and 4 deal with the location, form, and growth of Hispanic towns. Under different geographic, social, and political influences from those that prevailed east of the Mississippi, Spanish and Mexican colonists had created urban physical patterns and ways of town life substantially unlike those of Anglo-American origins. By the 1820s these two traditions of town planning came into conflict as eastern settlers pushed into Texas. Shortly before midcentury other Americans from the East leap-frogged the intervening plains and mountains to begin large-scale Anglo settlement in California. The Hispanic urban culture that had slowly developed over the years was absorbed and eventually almost replaced in the process. Chapters 5, 6, and 8 describe how this took place in Texas, New Mexico, Arizona, and California.

Chapters 9 and 10 are devoted to the establishment of an important and fascinating isolated frontier—that of the Mormons in the Great Basin of Utah and its bordering lands. This is followed by an examination in Chapter 11 of another and even more distant, detached region of towns and small cities in Oregon and Washington.

Two states of the central plains, Kansas and Nebraska, were opened for colonization a few years before the Civil War. Scores of planned communities resulted and are dealt with in Chapters 12 and 13. Just before the last decade of the century portions of Oklahoma became available for white settlement on a large scale, and the process of initial urbanization is described in Chapter 19.

Many of the American West's most important cities owed their origins to the discovery of gold, silver, copper, or other minerals. While the mining camps themselves more often than not faded into obscurity once the deposits of ore had been exhausted or were no longer profitable to mine, the chief supply centers for the mining frontier, such as Sacramento or Denver, continued to grow with the diversification of their economic base or with their designation as capital cities. Chapters 7, 14, and 15 follow the frontier of the miner in rough chronological order from California and Nevada to Colorado, and to Idaho, Montana, and South Dakota.

Equally important as creators of towns and cities were the transcontinental railroads and their connecting lines that thrust across the plains and into the mountains following the Civil War. Chapters 16, 17, and 18 record how urban settlements were planned by the great railroad corporations and how existing communities were re-shaped by this new means of transportation. The final chapter surveys the urban West at the end of the nineteenth century and examines its achievements, shortcomings, and consequences.

Several hundred illustrations drawn from more than eighty collections accompany the text. They have not been added as embellishment but have been used as essential historical evidence. They are of several types: military surveys, early manuscript or printed plats prepared as legal records of townsite designs, plans or views used for promotional purposes, less formal sketches or drawings by early residents or visitors, illustrations originally appearing in travel accounts or other published works, and official surveys to record existing conditions for local, state, or federal officials.

A special effort has been made to include a large number of bird's-eye views or high-level panoramic depictions of cities in which American lithographic artists excelled during the period from 1850 to 1900. In the Notes on the Illustrations, located at the end of the volume, I have provided information on the surveyors, artists, printers, and publishers of these graphic documents. The location of the originals of all plans, maps, or views reproduced herein is also noted.

For reasons beyond the control of the author, production of this book has been subject to frequent delays and has required five years from the time the manuscript was completed. During that period books and articles have appeared dealing directly with or touching on the subjects considered in this volume. While it has been possible to incorporate some of this scholarly research in footnotes, some major studies are recognized only by entries in the bibliography, and citations of a few very recent publications have had to be omitted.

Sources used are listed in a long bibliography arranged by chapters. Doubtless a number of potentially useful manuscripts, books, articles, public records, and other materials have been overlooked, and it is inevitable that in a work of this scope errors will appear that have escaped the efforts of both author and editor to eliminate. I hope that despite such shortcomings the reader will find my study as rewarding to read as I found it to write and that scholars will be tolerant of what they may detect as mistakes in fact or believe to be flaws in interpretation.

ACKNOWLEDGMENTS

This book was conceived by Mitchell A. Wilder, Director of the Amon Carter Museum of Western Art in Fort Worth, Texas. Throughout the eight-year period of research and writing for what became a much more elaborate and time-consuming study than either of us had originally anticipated, his encouragement was both stimulating and unfailing. I am grateful to him, the directors of the museum, and to its efficient staff for providing the financial aid, travel arrangements, and research assistance necessary to carry out this work.

During the first two years of research I was fortunate to have Ian Stewart as a research assistant through the generosity of the directors of the Amon Carter Museum who provided funds for that purpose. Mr. Stewart compiled an extensive bibliography of relevant sources, aided in securing photographs of maps, plans, and views, and on two trips to Arizona and New Mexico and to the Pacific Northwest gathered material in the field that proved extremely helpful. Without his aid my study would have taken much longer to complete.

The staff of Olin Library and the Fine Arts Library at Cornell University offered almost daily assistance in meeting a variety of requests for information and in finding material in collections under their direction. I am also indebted to the administration of Olin Library for allowing me to occupy a faculty study whose privacy and proximity to the library stacks provided ideal working conditions.

More than one hundred museums, libraries, historical societies, public offices, universities, and individuals supplied photographs of graphic materials in their collections. Most of them are identified at the beginning of the Notes to the Illustrations. I am deeply obligated to all of them for their cooperation.

A grant to the Amon Carter Museum by the National Endowment for the Arts made possible the publication of an exhibition catalog describing and illustrating a large number of nineteenth-century city views. Many of these plates appear in this book as well, and the additional cost of color reproduction has been underwritten by the Amon Carter Museum.

Several graduate students at Cornell produced research papers on Western city planning in one or more courses taught by me during the years this book was in preparation. While their names appear in footnotes and the bibliography, I would like to list them here because of the special help and intellectual stimulation their studies brought to my own work: Steven Andrachek, Robert Craig, Margaretta Darnell, Barbara Dittrich, Daniel Garr, Howard Iber, Ellen Lamb, Robert Miller, Stephen Morris, Kenneth Nicolay, Deborah Pokinski, Joan Sears, and Steven Sher. Garr's study grew to become his Ph.D. dissertation, a major resource on which I have drawn extensively and which is separately discussed in the appropriate chapters.

Richard Hugh Munn typed the manuscript with care and skill. Ronnie C. Tyler, Director of Publications for the Amon Carter Museum, read the manuscript initially and offered many useful suggestions. He also undertook the laborious task of verifying the sources of all graphic materials and securing permissions for their reproduction. As on two previous occasions, I have been fortunate to have Gail Filion as my editor. The imprint of her careful and sensitive editorial hand is on every page. I wish to acknowledge my debt to her while at the same time indicating that whatever errors remain are my responsibility.

•CITIES OF THE AMERICAN WEST•

Cities on the Way West: The Beginning of Urbanization in the Ohio and Mississippi Valleys

THE new nation that emerged from the long years of the Revolution, while still largely agricultural already possessed an urban base from which its cities on the eastern seaboard would grow and expand.[1] Internal colonization of the Ohio and Mississippi valleys created additional urban settlements, and to these would be added by annexation other towns and small cities founded by the French. With rare exceptions all of these towns had been deliberately planned, and their designs offered ample precedents from which frontier town founders in the West could draw as the mainstream of American migration penetrated the older Hispanic domain or ventured into regions inhabited by Indians or completely unoccupied.

Figure 1.1 shows the settlement pattern of the eastern United States early in the nineteenth century. While west of the Ohio-Indiana boundary the white population was then still sparse, elsewhere villages, towns, and cities dotted the landscape. Even west of the Mississippi, in Louisiana and for a short distance up the Missouri River, a traveler on the frontier would have encountered a number of communities.

With a handful of exceptions—Boston, Annapolis, and Washington are the most important—virtually all of these towns and cities had been laid out in some version of the gridiron plan with straight streets intersecting at right angles to form rectangular blocks. These in turn had been divided into tiers of rectilinear lots. There were variations on this general theme. Savannah's grid, for example, was interrupted by a large number of open squares. The original plan of Philadelphia incorporated a central square at the intersection of its two main streets plus four others, one in each of the quadrants of the town. In New York an extension plan prepared in 1811 by commissioners appointed by the state legislature proposed a large parade ground that broke the linear grid extending up Manhattan Island to 155th Street. Baltimore had several open spaces incorporated in its grid street system, the most imposing being the cross-shaped Mount Vernon Place on the axis of Charles Street, where the first monument to George Washington was begun in 1815.[2]

Many foreign visitors remarked on the widespread use of the rectilinear plan in American cities. When the young Englishman Francis Baily arrived in Philadelphia in the spring of 1796, he was at first captivated by this approach to urban planning: "That perfect regularity in which [Philadelphia] . . . is built, is said not to be approved of by some; but it is what I most admire; indeed, it accords so much with the ideas of the Americans in general, that it is a practice which is almost universally adopted in laying out their new towns, and in improving their old ones."[3]

Philadelphia's plan that Baily so admired is reproduced in Figure 1.2. The city then served as one of the three principal gateways used by foreign immigrants bound for the first American West beyond the Allegheny Mountains. From Philadelphia persons heading west traveled by Forbes's Road to Pittsburgh and then usually continued their trip by boat down the Ohio River. A second frontier highway, Braddock's Road, connected Baltimore to Pittsburgh. The other major route westward led from New York up the Hudson to Albany, then across New York State to Buffalo by road or, after 1825, by the Erie Canal. From Buffalo the traveler could proceed by water on Lake Erie or could follow a wagon road along the southern shore of the lake to northern Ohio and beyond.

While Baily praised Philadelphia's four-square order, he also liked the quite different design prepared for the nation's projected new capital by Pierre Charles L'Enfant, a French artist who had served in the American Revolution and whom George Washington had retained in 1791 to plan the city that would bear his name.[4] In the fall of 1796 Baily arrived in Georgetown and immediately went to inspect the site of the federal city to which the seat of government was to move from Philadelphia four years later.

In his journal Baily recorded these impressions: "The President's House and the Capitol are situated upon two eminences; and other different rising grounds in the site are fixed on, with an intention of erecting obelisks, statues, &c., to eminent men. These eminences communicate with each other by means of streets proceeding from one to the other, like radii from a centre."

Doubtless Baily saw in Washington a copy of the official plan of the proposed city reproduced in Figure 1.3. This engraving had been published four years earlier and was used in the periodic auctions of town lots. Baily appreciated an important feature of Washington's novel design, observing that the "general mode of laying out a town by means of streets crossing each other at right angles and at certain distances, without any regard to the position of the ground, will be avoided."[5]

It was a lesson that few planners of towns in the American West were ever to learn. The elaborate baroque design of Washington that L'Enfant had devised, and his attempt to fit a street system to a site rather than the reverse, was to have few imitations in the trans-Mississippi

Figure 1.1 Map of the United States: 1813

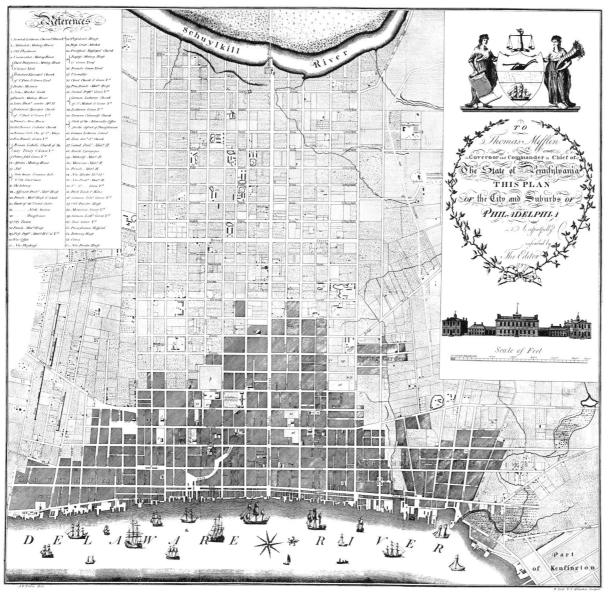

Figure 1.2 Plan of Philadelphia, Pennsylvania: 1794

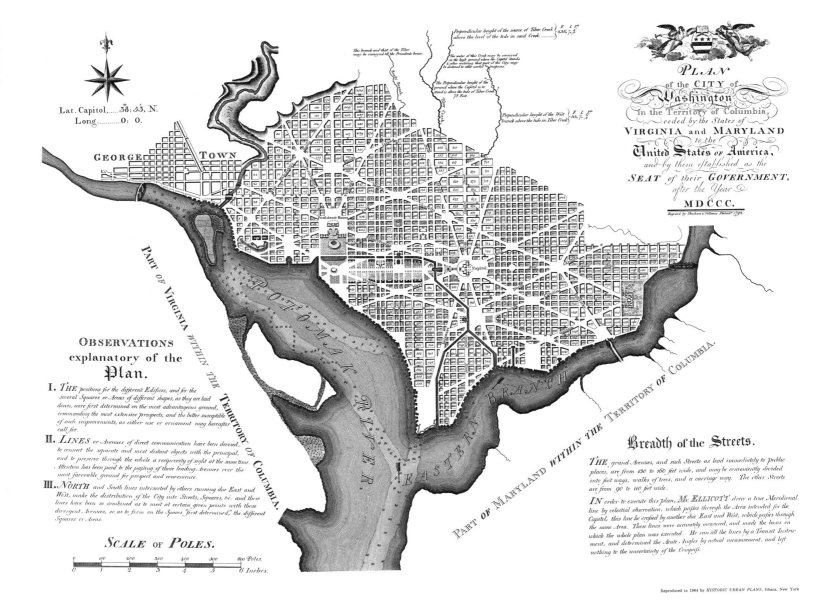

Figure 1.3 Plan of Washington, D.C.: 1792

West although rather half-hearted and unskillful use of some of Washington's design elements would be later incorporated in the city plans for Buffalo, Detroit, Indianapolis, and Madison.

After Baily had visited Philadelphia, Washington, New York, and Baltimore, he set out for Pittsburgh, which might be regarded as the first town of the old West. It had grown up at the point of land where the Allegheny and Monongahela rivers join to form the Ohio and where the French had established Fort Duquesne. After the fort fell to the British in 1758 and was renamed Fort Pitt, its strategic location attracted a few settlers, and a tiny grid of four blocks was surveyed facing the Monongahela.

In 1784 John Penn and his son, descendants of William Penn, the founder and planner of Philadelphia, decided to prepare a plan for a much larger town. They extended the little settlement on the Monongahela side of the point by running new streets parallel and perpendicular to the few then existing. At the northern edge of the now enlarged grid they reserved a square for the courthouse using the same pattern as the central square at Philadelphia with Market and Fourth Streets entering the square at the midpoints of its sides.

Along the Allegheny the Penns laid out Penn and Liberty Streets parallel to the water, and they divided this strip of land by a series of short cross-streets terminating at the river bank. It was this town that Baily described in the fall of 1796 as containing "about four hundred houses" and "laid out nearly on Penn's plan, though the streets do not cross each other at right angles."[6]

It was a clumsy piece of design. As John Melish noted critically in 1806, "the plan was meant to accommodate the town to both rivers, but it is by no means so well designed as it might have been. The streets are generally too narrow, and they cross one another at acute angles, which is both hurtful to the eye and injurious to the buildings."[7] Figure 1.4 shows the street pattern of Pittsburgh a few years later when an addition along the Allegheny created still another orientation for the grid streets of the town. In the later, trans-Mississippi West there would be numerous examples of such hasty, careless, and unskillful planning where sharply angled street intersections and jogs resulted from each landowner's following his own inclinations in the subdivision of property without any overall direction.

Planned with far greater care was a series of towns founded in western Pennsylvania by public initiative at the end of the eighteenth century. One of these appears in Figure 1.4 located opposite Pittsburgh on the north side of the Allegheny and taking its name from that river. In

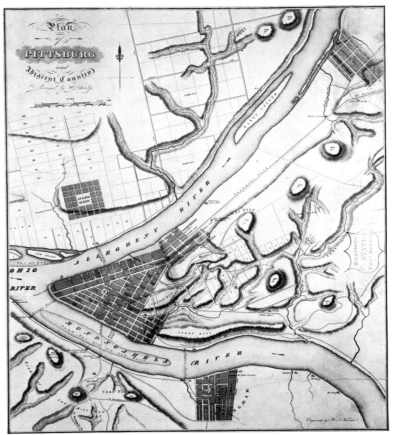

Figure 1.4 Plan of Pittsburgh, Pennsylvania: ca. 1815

1787 the legislature authorized the planning of a town on this location which the Commonwealth had retained in public ownership. The statute specified that sites should be reserved for a courthouse, jail, market, cemetery, and a common pasture of 100 acres.

David Redick's plan for Allegheny, which he surveyed the following year, showed no originality in the design of the street system, but he was extremely generous in making his central square equal in area to one-ninth of the entire town. The common and burying ground provided additional open space. Redick reserved land for these purposes on all four sides of the community.

Twenty-five miles down the Ohio River at the mouth of Big Beaver Creek the state of Pennsylvania owned another extensive tract of land. In 1791 the legislature directed that this should be laid out as a town surrounded by outlots of from five to ten acres in size. Daniel Leet planned Beaver in a gridiron of straight streets forming 64 blocks. At the center, where the two main 100-foot streets met, he reserved four blocks for a public square, and he set aside one block at each corner of the town for other public uses.

Later in the decade the Pennsylvania legislature authorized the creation of four other towns in the northwest corner of the state. Andrew Ellicott, who had surveyed the boundaries and recorded the topographic features for Washington, D.C., was retained to plan the new communities. In 1794 and 1795 Ellicott laid out Waterford, Franklin, and Warren. Although he used a basic gridiron pattern for all three communities, he recognized changes in topography by bending the grid where necessary to fit the irregular sites. He also carefully provided reservations for several public squares in each town.

The isolated locations of these towns and conflicts over land titles hindered their growth, but Ellicott's fourth planned town enjoyed greater success. This was Erie, surveyed in 1795 on a nearly level site where a peninsula created a natural harbor in the middle of the strip of land giving Pennsylvania an outlet to Lake Erie. Figure 1.5 is a plan of the town published in 1836 but showing Ellicott's original design. It consisted of three identical sections, each with an elongated public square at its center. Beyond the town Ellicott provided larger outlots for farm and garden purposes. Along the shore Ellicott set aside spaces for docks, wharves, and other facilities needed for port activities.[8]

While Erie eventually became an important transfer point between land and water transportation routes, it was Buffalo at the eastern end of the lake, and easier to reach by land through central New York, that developed as the dominant lake port. Andrew Ellicott's brother, Joseph, planned the town in 1804 while he was the land agent in western New York for the Holland Land Company. L'Enfant's design for Washington obviously influenced Joseph Ellicott more than it had his brother, for Buffalo combined a series of radial boulevards with an underlying grid system, as one can see in Figure 1.6. Here, too, outlots in a variety of shapes and sizes provided a range of choices for potential land purchasers.[9]

The plan for the other major Lake Erie port of this period was less elaborate and more typical of the towns that were to be founded in central and northern Ohio. This was Cleveland, established by General Moses Cleaveland in 1796, when he led a surveying party in the employ of the Connecticut Land Company to define the bounds of the tract its leaders had purchased from Connecticut after that state had relinquished its claim to political jurisdiction over the northeastern corner of Ohio.

Near the center of what came to be known as the Western Reserve Cleaveland selected a town site at the mouth of the Cuyahoga River. The plat by Seth Pease, one of the surveyors, is reproduced in Figure 1.7. At the center Cleaveland and Pease placed a public square of 10 acres, ran four main streets outward from the midpoints of each of its sides, and surveyed other streets parallel to these to form an oddly asymmetric grid with a few irregularly curving streets leading down the steep bank to the river.

Francis Baily did not follow this northern route west but instead proceeded down the Ohio River from Pittsburgh. From the western line of Pennsylvania to the mouth of the Muskingum River he passed by the first portion of the federal public domain that the Continental Congress in 1785 had ordered surveyed into townships each six miles square. Alternate townships were to be divided into 36-mile-square sections with sections 8, 11, 26, and 29 to be reserved in federal ownership and section 16 to be set aside to provide for the support of schools. The remaining land was to be put up for sale in an effort to raise funds for the support of the central government and to encourage western settlement.[10]

The area of the first seven ranges of townships surveyed under the Land Ordinance of 1785 is shown in Figure 1.8. By the time Baily floated by in the winter of 1796-97 the ordinance had been amended to provide for local federal land offices in the area that politically had been organized as the Northwest Territory under an act of 1787. The township surveys of the federal public domain were later extended westward and, except for a few areas, eventually covered the entire country.

This great grid imposed on the continental landscape was to have a significant influence on the planning of towns. As entire townships and the mile-square sections were further subdivided by their original owners, smaller rectangular tracts were created. When these were acquired by town promoters it seemed natural for them to lay out streets parallel to their borders. Often these tracts lay at section or township boundaries along which the earliest rural roads were usually located. Here one might find a small cluster of houses forming a crossroad ham-

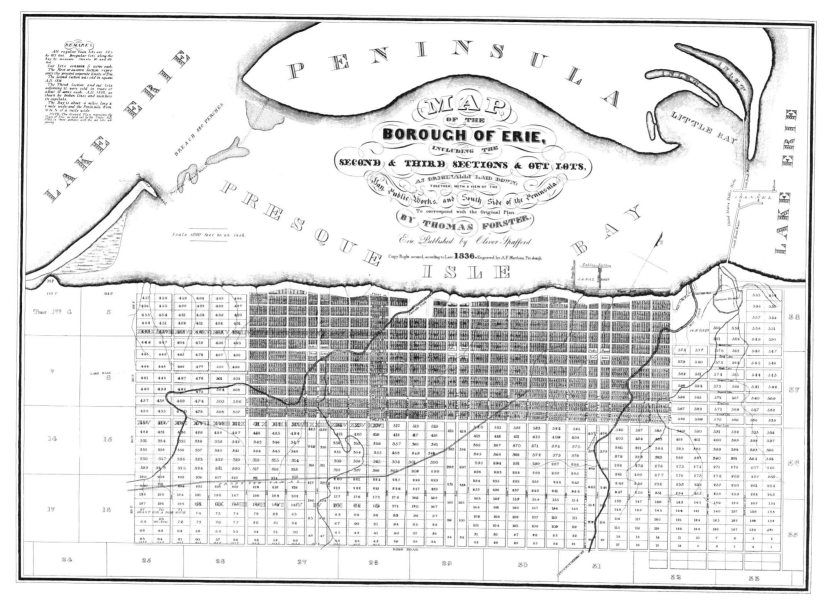

Figure 1.5 Plan of Erie, Pennsylvania: 1836

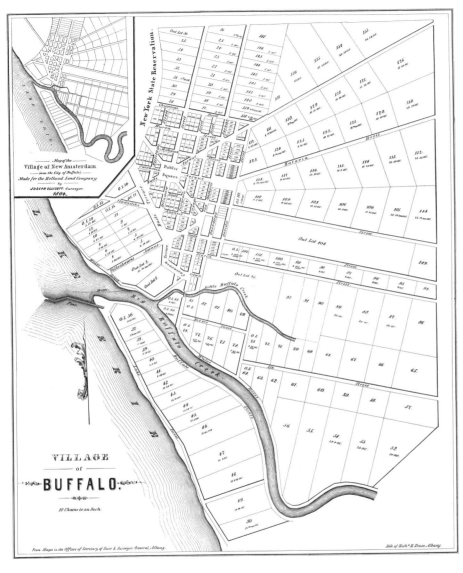

VILLAGE
of
BUFFALO.

10 Chains to an Inch

From Maps in the Offices of Secretary of State & Surveyor General, Albany.

Lith of Rich. H. Pease, Albany

Figure 1.6 Plans of Buffalo, New York: 1804 and 1851

let or village. As the settlement grew, additional streets were surveyed parallel with the first to form expanding gridiron towns.

Later federal legislation in the nineteenth century provided for half-sections of land to be claimed for townsite purposes if the tracts had not already been acquired for agricultural use. Such land could be purchased at the minimum price and, in theory, was to be held in trust by the officials of the municipality or, if it was not incorporated, by the judges of the county court for disposal to residents under regulations adopted by the state in which the site was located. In practice the law was an open invitation for speculators to acquire land at a bargain price and sell it for whatever the market might command.[11]

The earliest of the many planned Ohio towns, however, was settled at the eastern edge of an enormous tract of land purchased from the federal government in 1787 before it had been surveyed into townships. A group of New England army veterans constituting the Ohio Company of Associates initiated this venture. The location selected for their town of Marietta can be seen in the lower left corner of Figure 1.8. In the spring of the following year Rufus Putnam supervised its planning on a site at the mouth of the Muskingum River, where he found several of the strange geometric earthworks of the vanished Ohio Mound Builders.

Putnam skillfully incorporated these ditches, mounds, and earthen platforms into the design of his town. In Figure 1.9, the first printed plan of Marietta, the darker portions indicate the location of these curious works erected by earlier occupants of the Ohio Valley.[12] While Putnam's plan represented no great achievement in urban design otherwise, his retention of these man-made features of the site was commendable. In the later settlement of the Far West other founders of towns would unfortunately largely disregard topography either through carelessness or in a deliberate attempt to impose the works of man upon nature.

While Baily merely noted that Marietta "consists of about one hundred houses agreeably situated," he apparently did not disembark to inspect the peculiar feature of its site.[13] Nor was he aware that this town, unlike most others along the Ohio, had resulted from a planned colonization movement whose members shared the costs and received land in proportion to their investment. He did, however, furnish a valuable account of a more typical example of proposed urban development.

One of his companions whom he had met on the trip "had planned out a town which he meant to lay out, as soon as he arrived on the

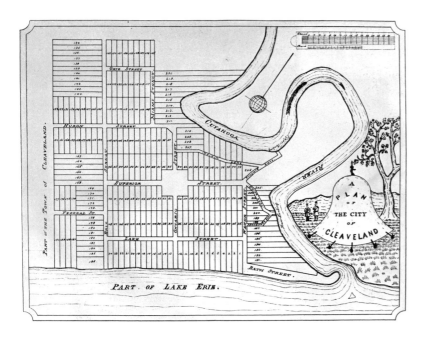

Figure 1.7 Plan of Cleveland, Ohio: 1796

spot'' where he had purchased land earlier from Judge John Cleves Symmes. Symmes had also obtained land in wholesale quantities from Congress in what is now southwestern Ohio. Baily's friend told him how he proposed to promote his project. ''In order to found a colony at first, he holds out an encouragement to settlers by giving them a town lot and four acres of ground for nothing, except on condition that they shall build a house on the town lot, and cultivate the ground. This he does only to the first twelve or twenty that may offer themselves, and after the place is once settled it increases very fast; for it must be observed that it is not so much the *present* advantage which land speculators look to, as the rise which is almost sure to take place in consequence of an increase of settlements; and in order to manage this concern to the best advantage, the landholders will always take care and not sell all their lands *contiguous to each other*, but only at *certain distances*, so that the whole face of it may be cultivated, and the intermediate uncultivated parts consequently rise in value.''[14]

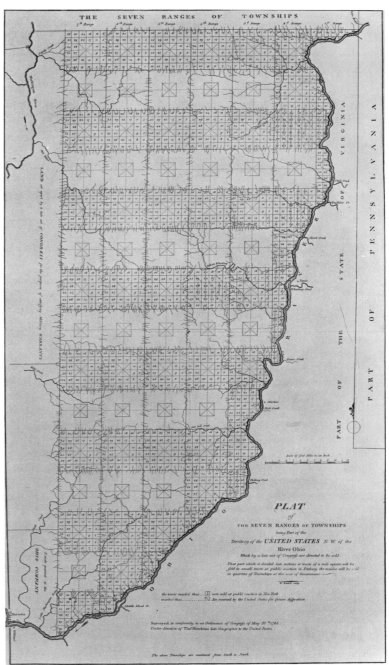

Figure 1.8
Map of the Townships Surveyed in Eastern Ohio: 1796

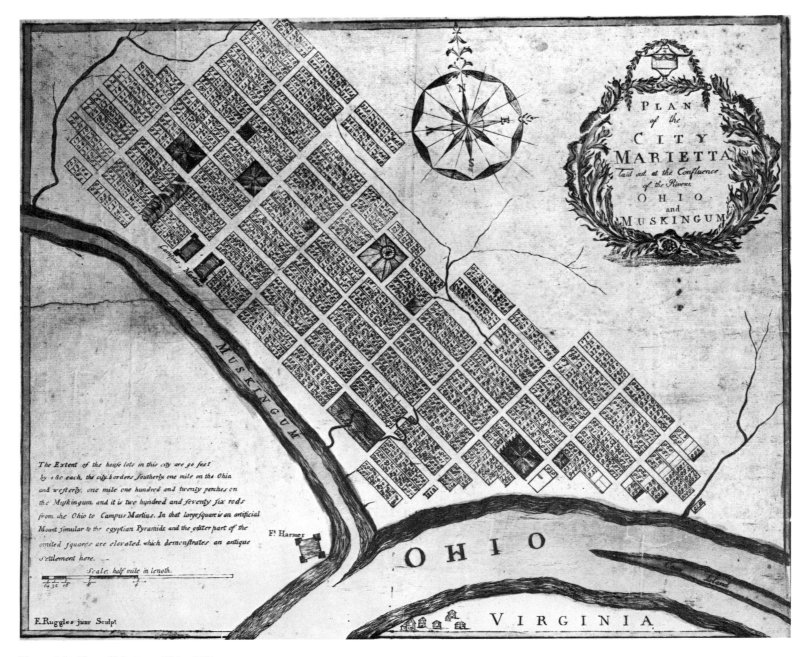

Figure 1.9 Plan of Marietta, Ohio: 1789

Some days later Baily visited the site, the present town of Waynesville, Ohio, with his friend. "The town he had laid out at right angles, nearly on Penn's plan, with a square in the middle, which he told me, with a degree of exulting pride, he intended for a court-house, or for some public building for the meeting of the legislature; for he has already fallen into that flattering idea which every founder of a new settlement entertains, that his town will at some future time be the seat of government."[15]

The same techniques of townsite promotion would be used again and again throughout the West after being tested and refined in the Ohio and Mississippi valleys. While not all of these speculative ventures proved successful, most were profitable enough to repay the promoter for his time and investment, and many turned out to be enormously profitable.

Certainly the development of Cincinnati, on a portion of Symmes' Purchase, from a small village to a thriving city in a few short years must have stimulated the hopes of all landowners that they could duplicate such an achievement. When Baily arrived there in April, 1797, the town was still in its infancy, consisting of "about three or four hundred houses, mostly frame-built." Yet already it had become "the grand depot for the stores which come down for the forts established on the frontiers; and here is also the seat of government for the territory."[16]

The town had been surveyed in 1788 by John Filson and Israel Ludlow. The first printed plan of the community showing their work was published in 1815 and is reproduced in Fig. 1.10. In its checkerboard of square blocks Cincinnati differed little from other frontier settlements, but Filson and Ludlow included in its design a number of marketplaces, a commons or public landing at the riverbank, a tiny public square near its western boundary, and a courthouse site of more generous size at the northern edge of development.

Baily found little of this to his liking. The vigorous advocate of the gridiron system a few months earlier had by now become its severest critic. "I have taken occasion to express my approbation of the American mode of laying out their new towns . . . but I think that oftentimes it is a sacrifice of beauty to prejudice, particularly when they persevere in making all their streets cross each other at right angles *without any regard to the situation of the ground.*"

The young Englishman felt that "both utility and beauty" might be combined "with a little attention" and "avoid that disgusting appearance which many of the new towns in America make." He suggested

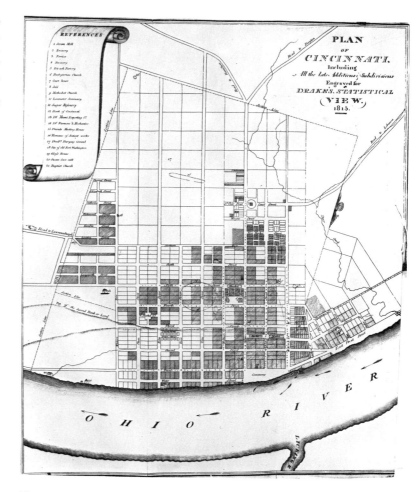

Figure 1.10 Plan of Cincinnati, Ohio: 1815

that as at Washington the planners should "fix upon all the eminences . . . as so many central spots from which streets [could] . . . proceed like rays from a centre." The minor streets could then be made "subservient to these, and suitable to the other irregularities of the ground." The new towns would thus "preserve an uniformity, a cleanliness, and aggreable prospect through the whole," which the undeviating gridiron plan seldom achieved.[17]

Others in the Northwest Territory thought as Baily did and attempted to apply some of these principles to the towns for whose planning they were responsible. Judge Augustus Brevoort Woodward in 1807 directed the replanning of the fire-destroyed old French town of Detroit into a pattern as eccentric as its originator. His design for the central portion of a 10,000-acre tract, all of which he expected to be developed according to his plan, is shown in Figure 1.11. Its basic unit consisted of a triangle divided into eight blocks arranged around a smaller triangular space intended for parks, markets, schools, churches, or other civic purposes. These units were linked together by an intricate pattern of radial streets leading to large circular or rectangular open spaces.

Woodward apparently was more influenced by his fascination with geometry than he was with trying to express in his plan any features of the generally flat terrain on which Detroit stood. As a former resident of Washington he undoubtedly was strongly influenced by the radial avenue system in that city. Whether or not his novel design would have proved beneficial will never be known, for after his departure from the Detroit scene in 1824 portions of his plan were abandoned and a more conventional grid substituted. Only the southern half of Grand Circus, the Campus Martius (now Cadillac Square), and a few of the radial streets remain in downtown Detroit as reminders of one of the planners of the American West who dared to break with established tradition and lay out a town of distinctive design.[18]

Indianapolis represented another departure from rigid gridiron planning, and the design of this planned capital can also be traced to that of Washington. Alexander Ralston, who had helped Andrew Ellicott in his surveys for the national capital, laid out this town in 1821 on a site almost in the center of the new state of Indiana. When Indiana was admitted to the Union in 1816 the federal government offered four sections of land still in the public domain for its seat of government. One commission appointed by the legislature selected the location, and a second commission retained Ralston to prepare a town plan.

The results of Ralston's work can be seen in Figure 1.12. He proposed to locate the governor's house at the center surrounded by a circular street set within a square formed by four blocks. From its corners Ralston led four diagonal streets outward to the corners of the townsite, slashing through the centers of some of the blocks formed by the underlying grid of streets. On two sides of the central focal point of the city

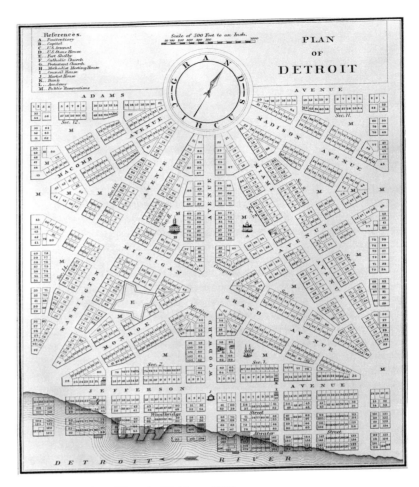

Figure 1.11 Plan of Detroit, Michigan: 1807

Ralston provided blocks for the courthouse and the capitol, both fronting on Washington Street. Ralston also reserved two markets and six triangular sites for churches.

While there was a mechanical quality to this symmetrical layout, Ralston's design recognized at least one topographic feature. In the southeast quadrant a stream ran diagonally through the town, and here the planner interrupted the grid street pattern and placed two streets on either side of the watercourse. It seems likely that Ralston intended this area to be developed for industrial purposes with the stream used to provide water power for mills and as a convenient method to dispose of industrial waste.[19]

While several other towns in the Northwest Territory broke with the gridiron tradition—Sandusky being the most important in Ohio—it was a rare community that its founders did not lay out with straight streets intersecting at right angles.[20] Dayton, founded in 1795, Chillicothe, planned a year later, and Zanesville, dating from 1799, were all early Ohio settlements whose designs followed this tested pattern. When Joel Wright received instructions from the state legislature to plan a new capital city for the state in 1812, he responded with the design shown in Figure 1.13. Nothing in this plan in any way distinguishes it from the dozens of other existing or proposed settlements that by that time had begun to fill in the blank spaces on the map of Ohio.[21]

South of the Ohio River in Kentucky the principal inland town was Lexington, first settled in 1779 shortly after Harrodsburg and Boonesborough were established as the earliest Kentucky "stations" or quadrangles of log cabins surrounded by a stockade. Francis Baily, who followed the river route west, did not visit Lexington, but a later English traveler, James Silk Buckingham, described it as having a "perfectly regular" plan with "streets running in parallel lines, and being crossed by others at right angles. In the centre of the town is a public square, and in the center of this, surrounded by trees and lawn, is the spacious Court-House, surmounted by a lofty spire."[22]

In Tennessee there were few nucleated settlements. Of these the most important were Nashville, on the Cumberland River near the center of the modern state, and Knoxville, located on the Holston and French Broad rivers, which unite to form the Tennessee River in the western foothills of the Great Smoky Mountains. Nashville was first formally platted in 1784 when Thomas Malloy surveyed 200 acres of land in a little grid of streets centered on a courthouse square and with its other blocks laid out in one-acre lots.[23]

When Baily returned to the East from New Orleans he journeyed through Tennessee, reaching Nashville in August, 1797. He found it a community of "about sixty or eighty families; the houses (which are chiefly of logs and frame) stand scattered over the whole site of the town, so that it appears larger than it actually is." Baily ended his jour-

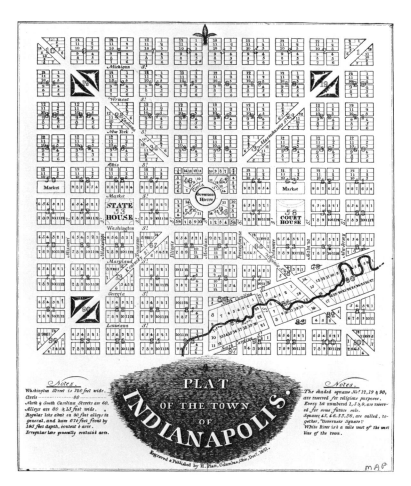

Figure 1.12 Plan of Indianapolis, Indiana: 1821

nal with his arrival at Knoxville, which, however, he did not describe. It had been planned in 1791 by Charles McClung as the capital of the Territory South of the River Ohio on land owned by his father-in-law, James White. McClung surveyed a checkerboard of sixteen square blocks formed by five straight streets running in one direction crossed

Figure 1.13 Plan of Columbus, Ohio: 1817

by five others. Half of one of the blocks at the center of town was reserved for a courthouse and jail, and on an adjoining block Governor William Blount erected his two-story frame mansion from which he conducted the business of territorial government.[24]

Lexington was soon to be overtaken in importance by another early Kentucky settlement, which Baily reached on April 11, 1797. This was Louisville at the falls of the Ohio River. George Rogers Clark planned this settlement in 1779 with three streets running parallel to the water crossed by 12 shorter thoroughfares leading to the bank of the river. In his original plan he reserved for public use a tier of 12 half-blocks along the southern border of the town and a much wider strip of equal length between the Ohio River and the first east-west street. Unfortunately, the town was forced to sell this common land to extinguish a claim by the former owner of the townsite on whose land Clark had unwittingly settled his followers.[25]

Clark later founded a second but far less successful town on the Indiana side of the river. The location of Clarksville can be seen in Figure 1.14, which shows in 1824 the plans of Louisville, Shippingsport, and Portland on the Kentucky shore and Jeffersonville, a few miles east of Clarksville in Indiana. All of these communities, then contesting for the canal that would make the Ohio safer for navigation and bring prosperity to the town or towns through which it passed, echoed Louisville in their orthogonal street patterns.

The first design of Jeffersonville, however, had been substantially different. It had been planned in 1802 following a suggestion made by Thomas Jefferson that, to avoid yellow fever, the new towns of the country should be laid out with half of their area preserved as open space. Jefferson summarized his notion in a letter to a friend: "Take, for instance, the chequer board for a plan. Let the black squares only be building squares, and the white ones be left open, in turf and trees. Every square of houses will be surrounded by four open squares, and every house will front an open square."[26]

The original plan of Jeffersonville is reproduced in Figure 1.15 showing how its proprietor had followed the president's suggestion but with the added and rather confusing feature of a second grid of streets placed at a 45°-angle from the first so that the open squares were each cut into four triangular spaces by these diagonals. Some years later when land speculation drove up the price of lots, the proprietor regretted his generosity in dedicating so much of Jeffersonville's site to public use.

In 1816 the Indiana legislature received a petition to allow the town to be replatted, and in the following year the governor approved a statute permitting officials to replan the town so as to eliminate the diagonal streets, enlarge all of the blocks, and survey the open squares into lots. Titles were adjusted so that existing land owners were given lots of equal size, and America's first comprehensive urban redevelopment project was completed.[27]

It would not be the only time that deviations from gridiron planning on the American frontier were modified or completely eliminated. Jackson, the capital of Mississippi also followed Jefferson's system of alternating open blocks with those divided into building sites, but successive encroachments on the public squares and their subdivision into lots soon obliterated its original design of 1822. The even more unusual plan of Circleville, Ohio, established in 1810 with its eight radial streets and circular boulevard forming a cobweb pattern, was replatted gradually from 1838 to 1856 to wipe out all traces of its novel street system. Much later in California the four diagonal streets extending outward from the central diamond-shaped public square of Brawley were subsequently reduced in length to bring the town more into conformity with the prevailing grid pattern so typical of the trans-Mississippi west.[28]

As Baily noted in his journal, "Louisville is the last place of any consequence which you pass in going down the Ohio."[29] Owensboro on the Kentucky side was not settled until a few years after Baily made his trip, Evansville near the southwestern corner of Indiana was not founded until 1816, and Paducah, fifty miles from the mouth of the Ohio in western Kentucky, did not begin its existence until a decade later. Nor was there yet any settlement at the confluence of the Ohio and Mississippi rivers, although an unsuccessful attempt would be made in 1818 to establish a town on this site at the southern tip of Illinois where Cairo was eventually planned during the orgy of land speculation that seized the country in the 1830s.[30]

Down the great Mississippi only few towns existed before 1800. Baily drifted by New Madrid on the Missouri bank, a town founded in 1789 by an American group in what was then Spanish territory. Baily observed that its "original plan . . . was according to that of Penn," but that the river had already eroded so much of the bank that the fort built in the center of the town at the water's edge had "long since been buried under its waters."[31]

Early in May, 1797, Baily floated past the Chickasaw Bluffs at the southwestern corner of Tennessee where the town of Memphis would be laid out in 1819 by William Lawrence in an elongated grid of streets with four public squares and a promenade between the town and the water. While in 1830 Memphis's population was only 663, by midcen-

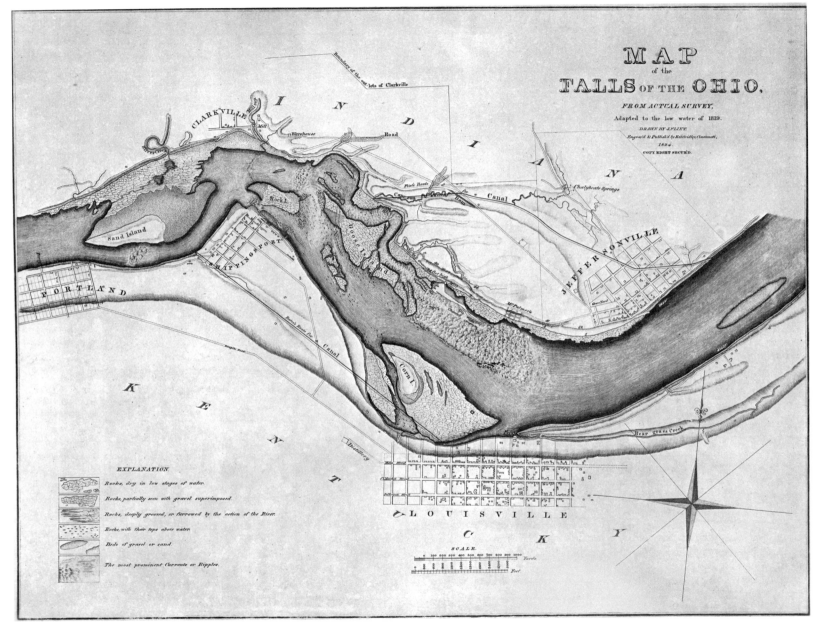

Figure 1.14 Map of Louisville, Kentucky and Vicinity: 1824

tury it had nearly 9,000 inhabitants and was one of the leading cotton-shipping centers of the South.[32]

At Walnut Hills near the location later to be selected by Newlet Vick in 1811 for his town of Vicksburg, Baily came in sight of the Spanish Fort Nogales. It was, as he noted, "a beautiful situation for a town." At the time of his visit, however, it consisted only of the Spanish military fortification with a "few houses . . . scattered around it."[33]

More impressive, although still small, was the town of Natchez, which at the time of Baily's visit was in the process of being transferred from Spanish to American control. A map of the town and fort in that period is reproduced in Figure 1.16, but Baily's description indicates the civil settlement could not have been as compactly developed as this drawing suggests. He recorded that Natchez "is situated upon a high hill, which terminates in a bluff at the river, and consists of about eighty or ninety houses scattered over a great space of land. The streets are laid out upon a regular plan; but there is so much ground between most of the houses, that it appears as if each dwelling was furnished with a plantation. There is a fort . . . but it is in a ruinous condition, and could not be defended against a regular attack."[34]

Baton Rouge, later to become the capital of Louisiana, received only passing mention by Baily although his boat stopped there for the night. Perhaps he was already anticipating the sight that would greet him when he landed in New Orleans, the only truly urban center he encountered on his long journey from the East. The city was then nearly 70 years old, having been planned in 1722 by Adrien de Pauger under the supervision of Jean Baptisti, Sieur de Bienville, as the chief French town for the lower Mississippi Valley.

Reproduced in Figure 1.17 is a plan of New Orleans as it existed in 1815 following a period of substantial expansion after the Louisiana Purchase in 1803 brought it under American jurisdiction. By that time a number of *faubourgs* or suburbs had been laid out by plantation owners up and down the river on either side of the original French community whose outlines can be seen in the center of the drawing.

Noting that New Orleans "is laid out upon Penn's plan; that is, with the streets, (which are rather narrow) crossing each other at right angles," Baily observed that not all the blocks formed by the "fifteen rows of streets from north-east to south-west, and seven rows in the opposite direction" had yet been fully developed. He commented with approval on the "public square, which is left vacant . . . for the purpose of beauty and ornament . . . to expose to view a church which stands at the farther end of it."

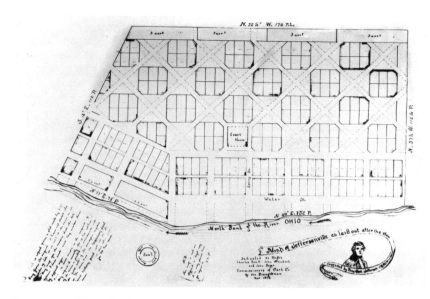

Figure 1.15   Plan of Jeffersonville, Indiana: 1802

Neither the church nor such other buildings as the "plain edifice" serving as the government house or the "very plain edifice" housing the Ursuline Convent impressed the visiting Englishman. More to his liking was the levee along the Mississippi, which he described as being "of considerable width in some places" and forming in New Orleans "a handsome raised gravel walk, planted with orange-trees; and in the summer-time [serving] for a mall, and in an evening . . . a fashionable resort for the beaux and belles of the place." Baily also admired the houses whose "upper part is sometimes furnished with an open gallery, which surrounds the whole building. . . . It affords an agreeable retreat in the cool of the evening in this warm climate." He estimated that the city contained "about a thousand houses," probably an overly generous figure in 1797, although seven years later its population was about 12,000 and was steadily growing.[35]

In the upper part of the Mississippi Valley the earliest towns were also of French origin. Most of these could be found on either side of the river in the area of settlement extending a hundred miles or so south from the mouth of the Illinois River. Cahokia, the most northerly, grew

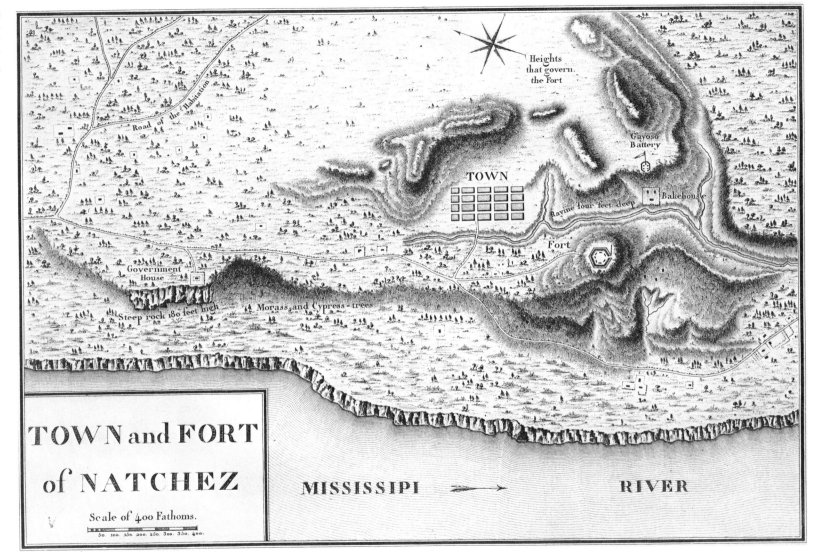

Figure 1.16 Map of Natchez, Mississippi and Vicinity: 1796

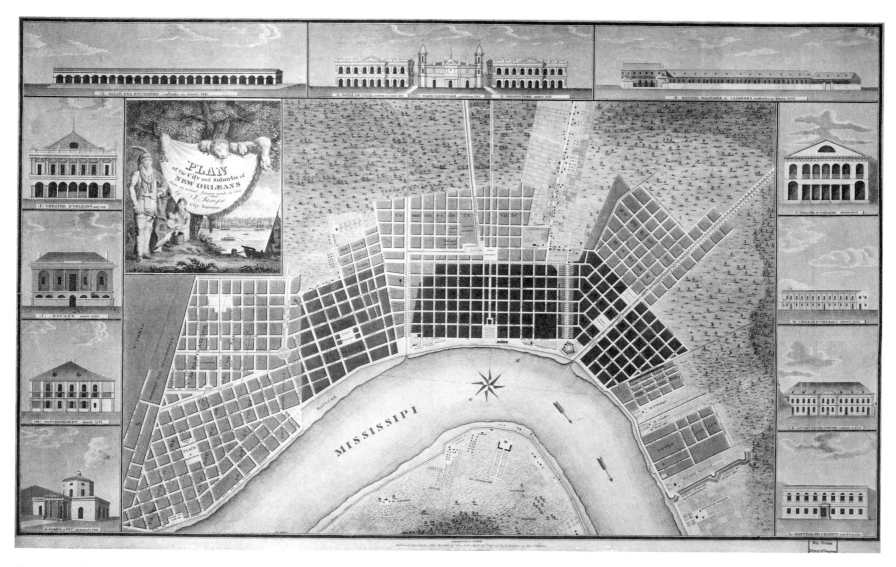

Figure 1.17   Plan of New Orleans, Louisiana: 1815

up near a mission established in 1699. South of this were Prairie du Rocher and then Kaskaskia, the plan of which as surveyed in 1765 is reproduced in Figure 1.18. Across the river Ste. Genevieve stood on a high bluff, relocated here in 1784 from its original site chosen in 1732 on the floodplain below. On its new location, selected when Spain controlled the western side of the Mississippi, the town was planned around a large public square whose edges provided the orientation for the narrow streets forming a nearly symmetrical gridiron pattern.[36]

St. Louis, the most important of the French towns in this region, was laid out by Pierre Laclede in 1764 to provide a base for his fur-trading enterprise of Maxent, Laclede and Company. Laclede planned a linear grid settlement with the principal streets running parallel to the river and a series of short cross-streets intersecting these as shown in Figure 1.19.

The town's initial growth was rapid as many of the French farmers and inhabitants of the little villages on the east bank of the Mississippi moved to St. Louis when the English established control over their former homes. What Laclede and the new residents of the city did not know then was that France had secretly transferred jurisdiction over the west bank to Spain. Under Spanish rule, St. Louis languished, but following the Louisiana Purchase it began a long period of growth and expansion to become the chief gateway to this vast area added to the United States.[37]

St. Louis and indeed most of the central Mississippi Valley enjoyed a substantial land boom during the early decades of the nineteenth century. Dozens of new towns were hastily laid out, promoted with extravagant advertising, and described by their sponsors as the coming metropolitan centers of the country, if not the world.

Timothy Flint, who lived in the region for ten years beginning in 1815, recorded that he had read more than one hundred such advertisements for speculative new communities in which "art and ingenuity have been exhausted in devising new ways of alluring purchasers, to take lots and build." The inflated claims for the advantages of each town included "the fine rivers, the healthy hills, the mineral springs, the clear running water, the eligible mill-seats, the valuable forests, the quarries of building-stone, the fine steam-boat navigation, the vast country adjacent, the central position, the connecting point between the great towns, the admirable soil, and last of all the cheerful and undoubting predictions of what the town must one day be."[38]

Local newspapers often aided town promoters by giving space to such wildly unrealistic claims, but at least one journal could not resist the opportunity to poke fun at these promotional exaggerations. Announcing that the town of "Ne Plus Ultra" had been located a hundred miles north of St. Louis, the *Missouri Gazette* for July 17, 1818, soberly described its main street as one mile wide with a canal down its center connecting the Missouri to the Mississippi. Its city blocks were each 160 acres in area, and a 100-acre mound 500 feet high was to be raised in the center of the town. The town was to have unrivaled transportation facilities, for "the great western road from the seat of government, across the Rocky mountains to the Pacific Ocean, opening a direct communication with China, must pass through this city, and the great northern road from the Gulf of Mexico to the new world lately discovered, by way of the north pole, must inevitably pass through this great city destined to be the capital of the western empire, or perhaps the world."[39]

A few of these new cities of the West fulfilled their promoters' promises. St. Louis itself grew with amazing speed. In 1840 James Silk Buckingham criticized the narrow streets of the old French portion of the town but quickly added that "the American portion of the city is as regularly laid out, and as well executed, as any town of similar size in the Union." He described a series of handsome buildings: the courthouse, many churches, the Jesuit University of St. Louis, large business structures, and elegant mansions.

From the Illinois side of the river, he "had a fine view of the city . . . with its sweeping line of shore crowded with steamboats . . . and the long rows of white stone buildings rising above these, in gradual ascent towards the upper part of the town." It was, Buckingham concluded, "altogether an imposing and beautiful picture."[40] Three and a half decades later St. Louis presented the even more impressive sight seen in Plate 1 showing the city from a point above where Buckingham stood in an earlier year.

Chicago underwent an even more dramatic growth, for until 1830 only Fort Dearborn occupied its site. In 1827 Congress granted to the state of Illinois alternate mile-square sections of land along the projected route of a canal to connect Lake Michigan with the Mississippi by way of the Illinois River. Three years later the Canal Commissioners directed their engineer, James Thompson, to lay out 240 acres of one of its sections immediately west of the fort so that the proceeds from land scales could be made available for the canal project.

Figure 1.20 shows Chicago in 1834 with Thompson's original plan occupying that portion divided by the fork in the Chicago River. In the modern city this area is bounded by Madison, Desplaines, Kinzie, and State Streets. It was this unimaginative design that established the be-

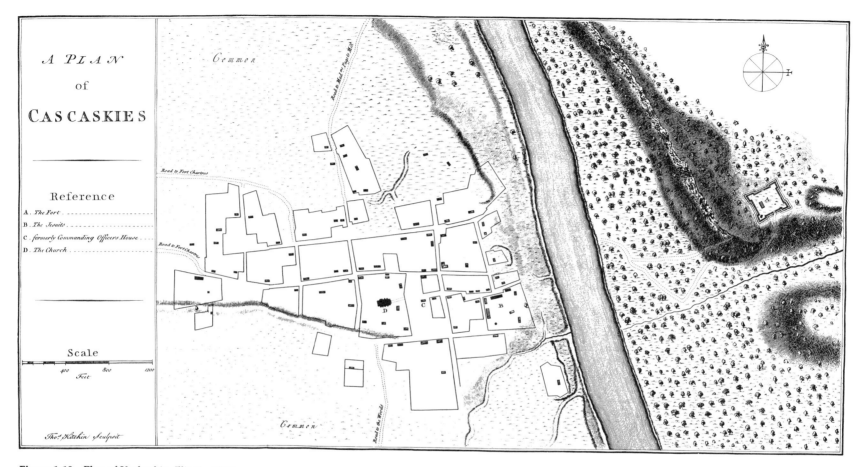

Figure 1.18 Plan of Kaskaskia, Illinois: 1765

ginning of Chicago's almost unending and relentless gridiron pattern as the Canal Commissioners continued to sell off land in their alternate sections and as purchasers of other sections from the government land office filled in the intervening spaces with continuations of Thompson's north-south and east-west streets.

Immediately south of the area first platted by Thompson lay the section in the township reserved under the government land system for school purposes. In 1833 school officials divided this into blocks and lots and put them up for auction. They retained only four 4-acre plots for school locations, and these sites together with a single block in

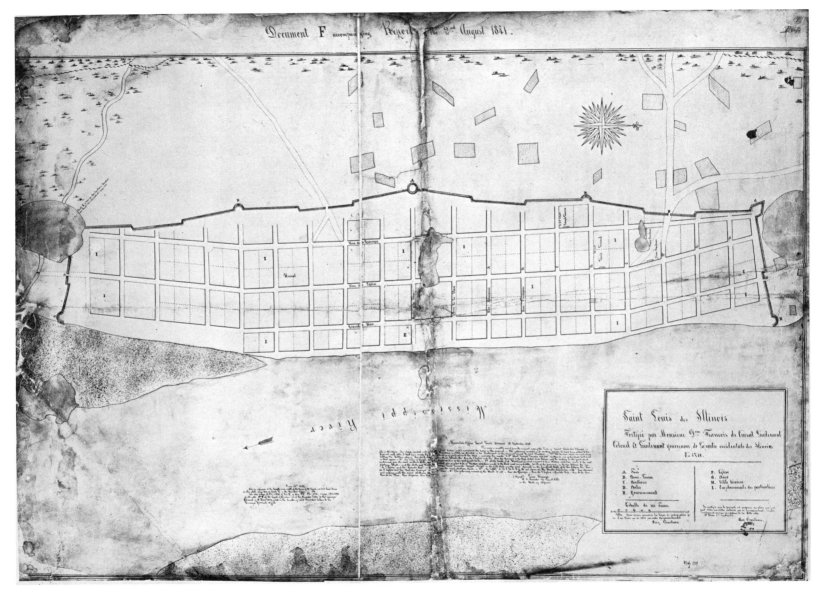

Figure 1.19   Plan of St. Louis, Missouri: 1780

Thompson's grid constituted the only public squares or open spaces of the city.[41]

In this casual manner state, city, and school officials lost their opportunities to plan wisely for the future and to realize the true value of the public land over which they exercised responsibility. Reviewing these events near the turn of the century, the Chicago historian Joseph Kirkland harshly but justifiably criticized this policy, which, as we shall see, was also to be followed later in such cities as Los Angeles, San Diego, and San Francisco:

"The sale of the school section was the greatest administrational blunder—or crime—in our annals." Kirkland observed that in 1892, as now, the 5,000 lots were "among the most valuable . . . for . . . building purposes. . . . Suppose these to have been leased instead of sold . . . they would now constitute an educational 'foundation' beside which Oxford, Edinburgh and Cambridge, Harvard, Yale, Cornell and Columbia, all shrink to insignificance. At a rough guess the sum may be placed at $100,000,000."[42]

Soon Chicago became a center for speculation in town lots. As Buckingham recorded in 1840, "in the mania for planning cities, and buying and selling house-lots, which then prevailed all over the United States, Chicago held a distinguished place." Buckingham stated that lots "in streets not yet marked out, except on paper, were sold from hand to hand at least ten times in the course of a single day, and at every new sale with a large advance of capital, so as to cost the evening purchaser, at the very least, ten times as much as the price paid by the morning buyer for the same spot!"[43]

The land boom continued, broken only by short periods of depression. By the end of the century Chicago, like St. Louis, was a densely built-up community with towering office buildings, smoky industrial plants, a bustling waterfront, and with a vast grid of streets clutching in their geometric grasp tens of thousands of houses stretching outward on the flat prairie land. Figure 1.21 shows the city in 1892, but its truly urban character had been firmly established several decades earlier.

Both St. Louis and Chicago demonstrated the potential financial rewards that successful town promotion and real estate development could bring. Many of the speculative town founders in the Far West gained their initial experience in these cities or in other eastern and midwestern communities that grew with such speed during the first half of the nineteenth century. In creating the cities of the West, real estate speculators, developers, and investors would apply the same techniques that had proved so effective in these rising urban centers.

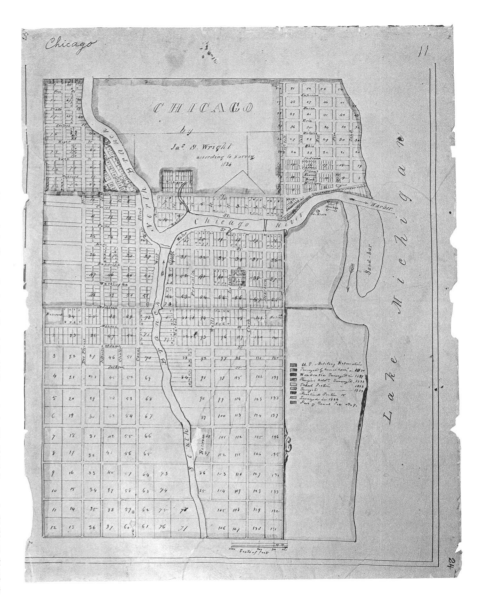

Figure 1.20 Plan of Chicago, Illinois: 1834

The thrust of western urbanization continued at a remarkable pace. Writing in 1825 Timothy Flint recalled that ten years earlier Cincinnati "was the only place that could properly be called a town" between eastern Ohio and Natchez. It had doubled in size since, and "numerous cities and towns, over an extent of two thousands of miles, are emulating the growth of this place. The banks of the Ohio are destined shortly to become almost a continued village."[44]

The same process occurred on the upper Mississippi and the lower Missouri rivers. As Buckingham steamed up the Mississippi from St. Louis in 1840 he passed dozens of river settlements. He estimated the population of Alton, Illinois, then only 25 years old, at 3,000. On the Missouri side of the river he observed several new communities: Clarkesville, Louisiana Laventon, and Hannibal. The latter town, where Mark Twain was then a lad of five, was to become the most important of these river communities.

In 1869, as the view reproduced in Plate 2 reveals, Hannibal was spreading westward from the river following extensions of its original checkerboard street system that had been surveyed around a public square four blocks up the slope from its busy steamboat landing. The Hannibal and St. Joseph Railroad, completed ten years earlier, linked the town with the Missouri River, and residents proudly claimed that their little city would become the eastern terminus of the trancontinental rail route leading across the plains and mountains to the Pacific.

Continuing his voyage up the river Buckingham visited Quincy, Illinois, with its "good landing" and "a population of 3,000 inhabitants." As he "ascended the hill from the landing" he was "agreeably surprised to find a large and pretty town occupying the level plain above." At its center he entered "a square as large as Russell or Grosvenor Squares in London, with a hotel, occupying more ground than the Clarendon." Quincy had been founded less than twenty years earlier, but its progress convinced Buckingham that it "can hardly fail to become a town of considerable size and importance."[45]

North of Quincy opposite the southeastern corner of Iowa stood Nauvoo, a town that the Mormon prophet, Joseph Smith, planned in 1839. Buckingham was forced to abandon his projected trip above Quincy, but we shall later return to Nauvoo when we follow the Mormons west and examine the towns for which they were responsible.

Buckingham's objective had been the Saint Anthony Falls on the Mississippi in Minnesota. Between Quincy and the northern border of Illinois he would have seen a number of relatively new communities: Rock Island on the Illinois side of the Mississippi near the mouth of the canal from Chicago; and Burlington, Davenport, and Dubuque, among others on the Iowa bank. Urban settlement at the Mississippi Falls in Minnesota, however, had barely begun. A number of squatters had built cabins and begun to farm some of the land around Fort Snelling, but it was not until 1847 that a group of them filed official land claims and had a portion of the site platted as the town of St. Paul.[46]

The American Fur Company established a trading post at this site, and regular steamboat service began. Two years later when the territory of Minnesota was created with St. Paul as the seat of government the town's population was 840. Across the river and a few miles away was the village of St. Anthony where another 250 settlers lived. Between the two little communities a new town was established a few years later on a portion of the Fort Snelling reservation that speculators persuaded the government to sell. Using the Sioux Indian word for "water" and the Greek word for "city," one of its residents suggested the name of Minneapolis.

The best locations for mills were in this newest community, but St. Paul remained the most important of the three towns throughout the boom years of the 1850s when thousands of settlers streamed into the new territory. The town as John Stanley sketched it in 1853 is shown in Figure 1.22. It was this little community that two years earlier Governor Alexander Ramsay predicted would become "the great Capital of the Northwest."[47]

The prophecy would come true for the Twin Cities of St. Paul and Minneapolis, but they had a great deal of competition. One authority states that during the years 1855 through 1857 townsite promoters laid out no fewer than 700 projected towns in the territory. A member of the legislature is reported to have introduced a measure in 1857 that would have reserved one-third of the land in the territory for agriculture before it was completely platted into townsites or surveyed for roads.[48]

Urbanization of Wisconsin had taken place even earlier. When it was admitted to statehood in 1836 at least a dozen towns were large enough, or thought they were, to compete for the prestige and certain prosperity of becoming the capital city. When the legislature reached a deadlock on the issue, one of its members and a future governor, James Duane Doty, slipped away with his surveyor and platted three new towns. One of them, Madison, whose plan is shown in Figure 1.23, ultimately won enough votes to become the capital. Doty's promotional techniques included the thoughtful provision of a deed to a choice corner lot in his new town for each of his fellow legislators.[49]

In the trans-Mississippi West, as will be seen, this kind of controversy over the location for the seat of government was repeated almost endlessly with the creation of new territories and states. Not all of them

THE CITY OF CHICAGO.

Figure 1.21 View of Chicago, Illinois: 1892

Stanley. Del.

Sarony, Major & Knapp, Lithᵣ 449 Broadway. N.Y.

Figure 1.22   View of St. Paul, Minnesota: 1853

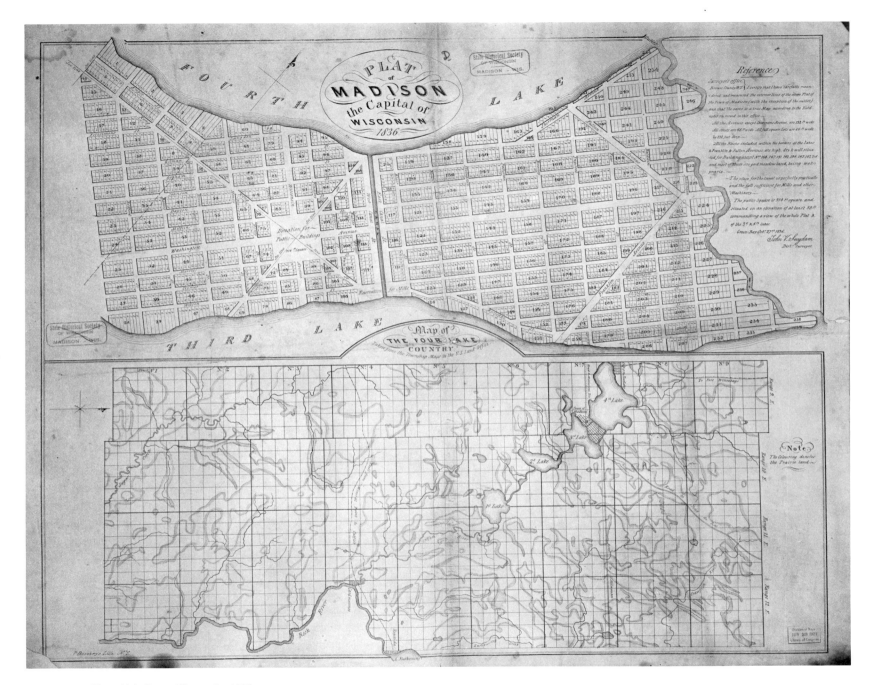

Figure 1.23 Plan of Madison, Wisconsin: 1836

would produce a capital city so well planned as Doty's. The great square for the public buildings occupied a rise in the ground between Madison's two lovely lakes. Leading to it Doty laid out not only two very wide thoroughfares entering its sides but diagonal streets extending from its corners. The radial thoroughfare running to the west led to the site reserved for the state university, thus providing major focal points of architectural interest at either end.[50]

In the early years of the nineteenth century the most westerly urban centers were located along the Missouri River from its mouth to a point some miles above where that stream bends sharply to the north to form what is now the eastern border of Kansas. A few miles west of the river's mouth stood St. Charles, which had grown up around a French fur trading post and mission. La Charette, another 50 miles upstream, was the last white settlement Lewis and Clark passed through in 1805 on their epic journey of discovery. Six years later Henry Brackenridge noted in his journal that it consisted of "about thirty families."[51] By that time the frontier of settlement extended much further up the river. Brackenridge saw several little clusters of houses, and at a point beyond the mouth of the Mine River that he estimated to be two hundred river miles from the Mississippi he passed by "a flourishing settlement . . . but one year old, but . . . increasing rapidly" and consisting "of seventy-five families."[52]

When Missouri became a state in 1821 there were a number of little towns on both sides of the Missouri River. Franklin, located near the center of the state, then consisted of more than a hundred log cabins, thirteen stores, four taverns, two mills, two blacksmith shops, and a post office. The pride of the town were two brick buildings, although it could also boast of several frame dwellings of sawn lumber.[53] Franklin then overshadowed Boonville, a little hamlet of eight houses located on the opposite bank of the Missouri.

It was from Franklin that William Becknell in 1821 led a party of merchants to distant Santa Fe. His venture proved so profitable that trade with the new republic of Mexico via the Santa Fe Trail attracted dozens of others who plodded the long, dry miles to the Southwest each year. While Franklin enjoyed an immediate boom as the jumping-off point for the Santa Fe trade, its place was taken after 1825 by the newly planned town of Independence located not far from the western border of Missouri on rising ground six miles south of the Missouri River.[54]

When Charles Joseph Latrobe visited Independence in 1832, he found it a community "full of promise, like most of the innumerable towns springing up in the midst of the forests in the West, many of which, though dignified by high-sounding epithets, consist of nothing but a ragged congeries of five or six rough log-huts, two or three clapboard houses, two or three so-called hotels, alias grogshops; a few stores, a bank, printing office, and barn-looking church. It lacked, at the time I commemorate, the last edifices, but was nevertheless a thriving and aspiring place."[55]

By midcentury the appearance of Independence had improved substantially. Not only had the town prospered from the Santa Fe trade but through its streets were passing many of the Forty-Niners bound for California or groups of more serious-minded settlers headed for Oregon. The fur trade of the upper Missouri River had also benefited the merchants of the town, and around its courthouse square, shown in Figure 1.24 stood sturdy structures of brick or stone, and many other streets of the town were as regularly planned and as well developed.

A few miles to the west, two other communities could be found. One was Westport on the north bank of Brush Creek. The other was called Kansas or Westport Landing and occupied a small strip of low-lying land along the Missouri near the mouth of the Kansas River where a townsite company organized by John C. McCoy had surveyed a street and a few lots in 1839. This little waterfront community is shown in Figure 1.25 as depicted early in the 1850s. By this time the merchants of

Figure 1.24 View of the Courthouse Square in Independence, Missouri: 1855

above. The early name given to this area—Quality Hill—suggests that here could be found the better residences of the now rapidly growing community whose occupants could look down on the transportation and mercantile center along the waterfront.

Following the Civil War and with the coming of railroads Kansas City built a new business district on its more elevated portion, eventually expanded to absorb its old rival, Westport, and stretched its rectilinear network of streets in all directions. The city of that period appears in Figure 1.26 as seen from the Kansas side of the river in 1869. While steamboat travel was then still important, it would shortly be superseded by the rail lines that made Kansas City, with Omaha, one of the two principal gateways to the Far West across the many bridges that would be added to the one shown in the view linking the two sides of the Missouri River.[58]

All this, however, was to take place well after the pioneering days of settlement in that immense region stretching beyond the Missouri. West of Kansas City in 1845 only tiny pockets of white settlement existed: forts, trading posts, temporary camps, Indian agent compounds, and a few mission stations.[59] Trails connecting these establishments were few in number and hazardous to traverse. While such explorers as Meriwether Lewis and William Clark, Zebulon Pike, Stephen H. Long, and John Charles Frémont had begun to map the region, much of it remained largely uncharted. Most authorities regarded the Great Plains as an uninhabitable desert. It was to this region also that most of the surviving Indians who had formerly occupied the southeastern part of the country had been moved. Beyond their reservations in Kansas and Oklahoma roamed the yet unconquered tribes of Dakotas, Pawnees, Arapahos, Kiowas, Apaches, and Comanches.

Yet well before the momentous decade of the 1840s when several vectors of settlement would be thrust deep into the West, Anglo-American urbanization on a substantial scale had begun in Texas. The creation there of dozens of new towns in the years following Mexican independence was only the latest episode in a long series of urban planning achievements along the northern rim of Spain's former realm.

In these Spanish borderlands, towns were founded in response to orders and directives from military, religious, and civil officials acting under centralized royal authority. A series of detailed regulations specified how towns were to be designed and the manner in which land in and around them was to be distributed. Private speculation in land was limited or non-existent. The pace of change was slow, and most townspeople lacked the initiative, incentive, or ability to move.

Figure 1.25 View of Kansas City, Missouri: 1855

Kansas were also sharing in the trade to Santa Fe, a town that had then come under American jurisdiction.[56]

It was in front of this rather forlorn cluster of buildings that Senator Thomas Hart Benton in 1853 mounted a rock by the river to address a handful of citizens gathered at this western outpost of the state Benton represented. Pointing to the hills above the town he grandly proclaimed his belief in the future that lay ahead: "There, gentlemen, where the rocky bluff meets and turns aside the sweeping current of this mighty river; here, where the Missouri, after pursuing its southward course for two thousand miles, turns eastward to meet the Mississippi, a large commercial and manufacturing center will congregate, and another generation will see a great city on these hills."[57]

Benton's prophecy was soon to be realized. Steamboats began to use the landing at Kansas with increasing frequency, and although the citizens of Independence constructed a mule-drawn railroad between that town and its river landing six miles to the north, Kansas (soon to attach the word "City" to its name) came to dominate the region. Its increased population required an expansion of McCoy's town, and construction crews set to work cutting roads up the steep bluffs to the level land

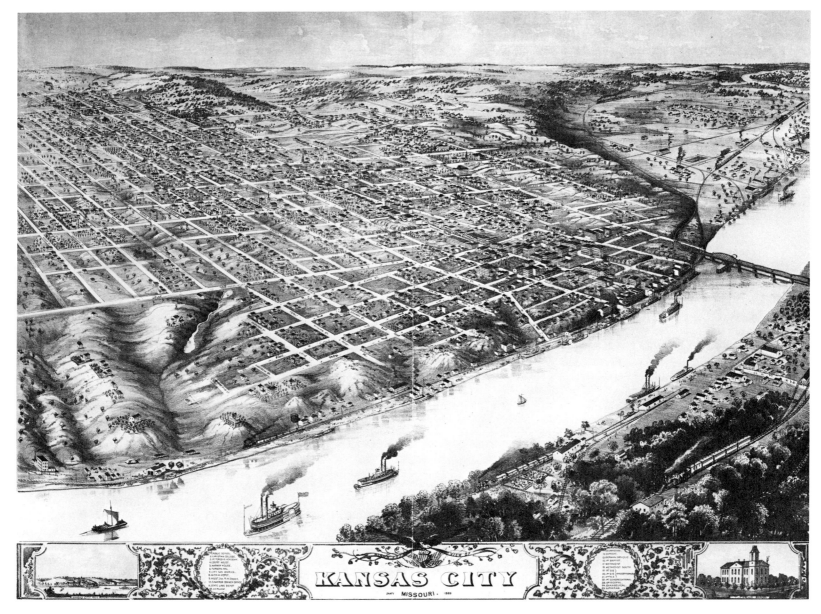

Figure 1.26 View of Kansas City, Missouri: 1869

All this was in sharp contrast to the Anglo-American tradition, where, with the exception of a few planned cities on public land, private developers determined the location and design of communities, and profits from land sales lined the pockets of individual speculators and investors. Mobility, both social and physical, characterized the Anglo-American urban frontier. Unsuccessful towns could be and often were discarded like a threadbare suit of clothes.

Centralized planning was resisted. As Timothy Flint observed in 1825 when he contemplated the progress of urbanization in the Ohio and Mississippi valleys, "every thing, with us, must be free, even to the advancement of a town. Nothing will grow vigorously in our land from artificial cultivation." In America, Flint noted with pride, "nothing is forced," and the "magnificent result is only the development of our free and noble institutions, upon a fertile soil."[60]

These two approaches to urbanization would eventually clash as the mainstream of the American westward movement flowed into Texas, the Southwest, and California. It is to the beginning of that older tradition in the lands under Spanish control that we now turn.

II

Spanish Settlements in the Southwest:
Evolution of Policy, Elements of Colonization, and
the First Towns in New Mexico

Iɴ the vast region of the American West the first communities founded by Europeans resulted from Spain's attempts to secure control over this northern frontier of an expanding and profitable colonial domain. From the beginning of the seventeenth century until the empire came to an end more than two hundred years later this area was to be the setting for countless efforts to establish civil, religious, and military settlements stretching from eastern Texas westwards to the Pacific and then north along the coast to San Francisco Bay.

In this arid crescent of Spanish territory some of the greatest cities of the modern West began their existence as modest colonial communities: San Antonio, Albuquerque, Tucson, San Diego, Los Angeles, and San Francisco. Others, not so large but important nonetheless, shared the same traditions: Laredo, Santa Fe, Santa Barbara, and Monterey, among them. Still others, such as Sonoma, California, and Gonzales, Texas, developed in much the same fashion under the rule of an independent Mexico, which carried on many of the urban policies established by its former rulers.

By the time the first towns were begun in this portion of the American West, Spanish colonial urban planning policies and techniques had become firmly established. At least in theory little was left to chance; official rules and regulations governed virtually every aspect of urbanization. Those laws relating to town planning and design were among the most specific and widely accepted. Because this legal basis for urban development was so important throughout Hispanic America, its origins and growth require extensive explanation.

Columbus began the tradition when, on his second voyage to America, he founded the town of Isabella on the northern coast of Hispaniola. It could scarcely have occurred to him that this short-lived settlement would be but the first of hundreds of communities that would be required to subjugate a new continent. He doubtless intended this town to serve only as a convenient base on the way to what he believed was the nearby coast of China.[1]

The first permanent Spanish town in the Western Hemisphere dates from 1502 when Governor Nicolás de Ovando supervised the planning of Santo Domingo on the west side of the Ozama River at its mouth on Hispaniola's south coast. This replaced a settlement founded six years earlier on the other side of the river, which had been destroyed by a hurricane.

Spanish officials furnished Ovando a set of instructions prepared in 1501, one part of which dealt with town founding: "Because it is necessary to establish some towns in the Island of Española and as it is not

possible to render specific instructions from here, examine the locations and situations of said Isle; and in conformity with the quality of the Land and the people now resident in those towns which now exist, establish towns in those places which seem proper to you."[2]

Ovando's accomplishments in the planning of Santo Domingo could scarcely have been guided except in the most general way by these vague admonitions. He or some unknown person under his direction worked out the exact details of urban design when he laid out the new town in the pattern shown in Figure 2.1, a view published in 1599 but based on earlier drawings.[3] It was this town that the historian Gonzalo Fernández de Oviedo y Valdés, once a resident of Santo Domingo, could describe in 1526 as "superior in general" to any town of Spain. The design, Oviedo asserted, was even better than Barcelona's "because the many streets are more level and wide and incomparably straighter." This was possible because "the city was founded in our own time" and "there was opportunity to plan the whole thing from the beginning. It was laid out with ruler and compass, with all the streets being carefully measured. Because of this, Santo Domingo is better planned than any town I have seen."[4]

By 1513 the Spanish had planned sixteen other towns on the island, fourteen of them founded by Ovando before he returned to Spain in 1509 to report his accomplishments.[5] Santo Domingo's role as the most important early settlement in the West Indies, Ovando's descriptions of it, and, later, Oviedo's words of praise for its wide, straight streets and orderly layout, can scarcely have been overlooked by officials in Spain now concerned with shaping a set of policies for further exploration, conquest, and settlement.

Thus when Pedrarias Dávila received his instructions from Ferdinand V in 1513 before setting out for the new colonial domain overseas he found among them two fairly specific directives governing the selection of sites for towns and how they should be planned. These may have guided him when he founded Panama City six years later. They read, in part, as follows: "let the city lots be regular from the start, so that once they are marked out the town will appear well ordered as to the place which is left for a plaza, the site for the church and the sequence of the streets; for in places newly established, proper order can be given from the start, and thus they remain ordered with no extra labor or cost; otherwise order will never be introduced."[6]

Similar individual instructions may have been furnished other leaders of expeditions sent out from Spain, but by 1521 Charles V issued a *cédula* or royal decree establishing certain general requirements for the

Figure 2.1 Plan of Santo Domingo, Dominican Republic: 1586

founding of new towns.[7] There is also evidence to suggest that some kind of prototype town plan had been prepared by the Council of the Indies, established in 1524 with its offices in Seville. Two years after that date Bartolomé de Celada reported that he had laid out the Villa de la Frontera de Cáceres in Honduras. In his account he stated that he had "ordered . . . according to the custom of these monarchs and lords . . . a plan be made conforming to that of Seville, immediately marking off on it lots for the church and for the plaza, for the hospital, for the Governor, and for myself."[8]

What Ovando began a quarter of a century earlier as a novel enterprise had thus quickly evolved into a fairly routine activity governed by a set of increasingly specific regulations and, probably, by a model plan that the founders of towns in the new world were expected to follow. As the pace of colonization and urbanization quickened, these rules and guides were doubtless further refined by officials studying official reports and personal accounts flowing back to the homeland or from firsthand descriptions provided by those returning from tours of duty in the expanding colonial empire.

Before the death of Charles V this accumulated experience and documentation of town planning must have been extensive, including information on the following major cities, among many others: Balboa, Santiago de Cuba, Campeche, Guadalajara, Cartagena, Quito, Guayaquil, Buenos Aires, Lima, Bogotá, and Santiago.[9]

In 1560 the emperor's successor, Philip II, ordered that these town planning regulations and the multitude of orders, laws, and resolutions governing all other aspects of colonization should be printed. A decade later he directed that work should begin on the codification of these laws and that obsolete and conflicting sections be eliminated. This apparently proved more difficult than was anticipated, and it was not until more than a century later that the task was completed and published in 1681 as the Recopilación de Leyes de los Reynos de las Indias.[10]

The town planning sections of these Laws of the Indies, however, all date from 1573.[11] In that year Philip issued a long and detailed royal ordinance governing the founding of towns, drawing to some extent on earlier directives given to the leaders of colonization groups but adding many new and highly detailed provisions.[12] These regulations of 1573 remained in effect during the entire period of Spanish colonial town planning in America. They are found, for example, virtually unaltered in the 1781 edition of the Laws of the Indies.[13] The laws were thus in force and, in theory, governed the layout of all Spanish towns in the

United States except for St. Augustine, which had been founded in 1565, eight years prior to their proclamation.

In preparing this remarkable document Spanish officials almost certainly consulted historical and theoretical works on urban planning and studied examples of town development in Spain and elsewhere in Europe as well as examining colonial experience in the New World. They produced a fascinating combination of theory and practice.

Several treatises on urban design were available for their use. Many of the town planning principles set down by Leon Battista Alberti in his *De Re Aedificatoria* in 1485 closely parallel portions of the Laws of the Indies. Volumes on Roman castrametation or the art of military encampment also existed, such as that by Guillaume du Choul published in 1555. It was translated from the original Italian into Spanish in 1579 and would have been especially interesting to those in Spain aware of the numerous Roman settlements in their country. Machiavelli's *Arte della Guerra* of 1521 with its model encampment plan showing a central square or plaza, a pattern of gridiron streets, and a rectangular perimeter was surely known in Spain almost from the date of its publication.

The *Ten Books of Architecture* by Vitruvius, written about 30 B.C. and rediscovered early in the fifteenth century, also contained many suggested principles concerning site selection for new towns and how they should be planned. His proposal that streets should "be laid down on lines of division between the quarters of two winds" is echoed in the Laws of the Indies' prescription that the corners of town plazas should face the cardinal points of the compass from which the four principal winds were believed to blow.[14]

There were practical examples of town planning in Spain itself and in the areas of Europe under its control. Foncea and Puerto Real were Spanish new towns that had been surveyed in a rectangular pattern prior to American colonization. Philippeville, in what is now southern Belgium, had been planned under the Spanish by Sebastian van Noyen in 1555 and named for Philip II. Its plan consisted of a series of ten radial streets extending diagonally from a central square to the five bastions at the points of its pentagonal perimeter to the midpoints of the curtain walls. While this radial plan differed substantially from the normal pattern prescribed by the Laws of the Indies, it did incorporate the central plaza or square so characteristic of Spanish colonial planning.[15]

Hieronimo Marino's plan for Vitry-le-François, founded in 1545 by order of Francis I, must have been well known in Spain as a result of the intermittent conflicts between that country and France. The view

Figure 2.2   Plan of Vitry-le-François, France: 1634

edge when he carried out the royal directions to plan new settlements on the Island of Hispaniola.[16]

The regulations of 1573, therefore, could well have been based on a number of sources. They are remarkable nonetheless for their detail, for the fact that they pulled together a great body of accepted theory and practice in town planning, and for the length of time they remained in effect as guides to the design of hundreds of urban settlements. Let us now examine their provisions.

The laws specified that founders of new towns should select elevated sites that could be easily fortified and near "fertile . . . land for farming and pasturage; fuel and timber." To be avoided were lagoons and marshes "in which poisonous animals and corruption of air and water breed." The site was to be vacant—one that could "be occupied without doing harm to the Indians and natives or with their free consent."

The starting point of the survey was to be the plaza. This was to be located near the harbor in the case of a port city or, for an inland town, at the center of the community. The regulations specified "an oblong shape" with the length "being equal to at least one and a half times its width." Such proportions were held to be "the best for festivals in which horses are used and any other celebrations which have to be held."

The size of the plaza was to vary with the number of residents, but officials responsible for town planning were advised that these new towns were "bound to grow" and "therefore the plaza is to be planned with reference to the possible growth of the town." In any event the plaza was not to be "smaller than two hundred feet wide and three hundred feet long nor larger than eight hundred feet long and three hundred feet wide." The regulations suggested that "a well proportioned medium size plaza is one six hundred feet long and four hundred feet wide."

Following the peculiar and mistaken Vitruvian principle, the regulations required that "the four corners of the plaza are to face the four points of the compass, because thus the streets diverging from the plaza will not be directly exposed to the four principal winds." The surveyors were to work carefully and "by means of measuring by cord and ruler" lay out the "squares, streets and building lots."

The laws described the street system in considerable detail: "From the plaza the four principal streets are to diverge, one from the middle of each of its sides and two streets are to meet at each of its corners." The plaza, therefore, was to be the point from which no fewer than 12 streets would lead outward. Despite the specificity of this regulation,

reproduced in Figure 2.2 shows its central square at the intersection of the four principal thoroughfares, its orthogonal pattern formed by straight streets intersecting at right angles, and its rectangular boundaries.

One other urban settlement is of particular importance in the development of the Laws of the Indies. This is Santa Fe, a siege town founded by Ferdinand and Isabella in 1492 as part of their successful attack on Granada, the last Moorish stronghold in Spain. A modern aerial photograph showing its plan appears in Figure 2.3. The gridiron street system and central plaza were features that were to be repeated almost endlessly throughout the colonial domain that was discovered by Columbus the year Santa Fe was founded. The connection between this plan, the layout of Santo Domingo a decade later, and the eventual codification of town planning practice will doubtless always remain a matter of speculation. We do know, however, that Ovando had first-hand familiarity with the Santa Fe design, since he was present at the siege of Granada. Consciously or not, he surely drew on that knowl-

Figure 2.3   Vertical Aerial Photograph of Santa Fe, Spain: 1958

the great majority of Spanish colonial towns were not planned in this manner, nor was the plaza always oblong.[17]

Additional streets were to be laid out and "so planned that even if the town should increase considerably in size it would meet with no obstruction which might disfigure what had already been built." Nowhere do the laws require straight streets intersecting at right angles, but this is clearly implied and was doubtless so well understood that it was not considered necessary to make this explicit. Exact street widths were not specified, only that "in cold climates the streets shall be wide; in hot climates narrow."

Climate also seemed to be a consideration in the provision requiring that "the whole plaza and the four main streets diverging from it shall have porticoes." Other "smaller, well proportioned plazas" were to be provided "on which the main church, the parish church or monastery shall be built." Each of these uses was to receive "an entire block so that no other structure can be built next to them excepting such as contribute to their commodiousness or beauty."

In inland towns the church was not to be located on the main plaza "but at a distance from it in a situation where it can stand by itself, separate from other buildings so that it can be seen from all sides. It can thus be made more beautiful and it will inspire more respect." At port cities the church was to be located where it could be seen from the harbor. Apparently this did not preclude a location on the main plaza, where, in fact, many if not most churches were actually built, whether in a port or inland settlement.

Building lots were to be distributed according to a precise system. Sites fronting the main plaza were to be assigned "for the church, Royal and Town house, [and] also shops and dwellings for the merchants." These structures were "to be the first erected." A customhouse was also to be built between the church and the plaza. Two hospitals were to be constructed as well—one "for the poor and sick of non contagious diseases" located "next to the church forming its cloister." The other hospital for those with contagious diseases was "to be built in such a place that no harmful wind passing through it, may cause harm to the rest of the town." An elevated location for this structure was recommended.

Similar care was to be taken in the siting of "slaughter houses, fisheries, tanneries, and all such like productive of garbage." For inland towns built along rivers, these occupations were to be "relegated to the river bank . . . situated below the town."

After the sites for these uses and activities had been determined "the remaining building lots" were to be "distributed by lottery." Additional lots were to be held in royal ownership for distribution "to settlers who may come later." Settlers were also to receive farm parcels, their occupancy being determined by drawing lots. These were to be located beyond a town common "of adequate size" so that even if growth of the settlement occurred "there would always be sufficient space for its inhabitants to find recreation and for cattle to pasture without encroaching upon private property."

Land remaining beyond the common was reserved to the crown for future grants to later settlers. Any land suitable for irrigation was "to be distributed to the first settlers . . . by lottery." As soon as town lots and farming plots were assigned, the settlers were to plant crops and build their houses having first joined in erecting "some kind of palisade or . . . ditch around the main plaza so that the Indians cannot do them harm."

During the course of construction no natives were to be admitted to the town. The purpose of this instruction was to impress the Indians with the power of the Spanish. When they were finally allowed to visit the new town the natives would "be filled with wonder and will realize that the Spaniards are settling there permanently and not temporarily. They will consequently fear the Spaniards so much that they will not dare to offend them and will respect them and desire their friendship."

In addition to these sections of the laws governing town planning and land distribution there were others prescribing the system of local government.[18] The jurisdiction of the elected council and various public officials included not only the town proper but the surrounding farm lands, common, and adjacent area. Generally the total area involved in such a royal grant was square in shape, each side just over five and one-quarter miles long and consisting of nearly 28 square miles of territory. The entire urban-rural community was commonly known as a *pueblo* or, less commonly in the area with which we are concerned, a *villa*.[19] In addition to performing the usual functions of local government the officials of the *pueblo* had the responsibility of managing farm tracts known as *propios*. These lands were rented to settlers, and the revenues derived from this source constituted the principal source of municipal funds.[20]

The sections of the Laws of the Indies just examined applied only to civil communities, but two other forms of Spanish colonial settlements played a major role in colonization. In what is now the United States, missions and *presidios*, or forts, were far more numerous than municipalities and probably of greater importance. While in theory *pueblos*,

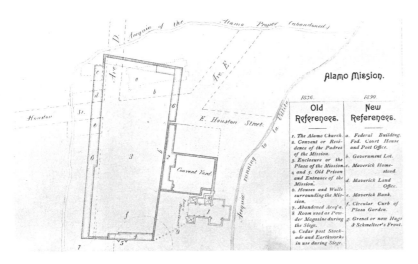

Alamo Mission.

Old References.	New References.
1836.	1890.
1. The Alamo Church.	a. Federal Building, Fed. Court House and Post Office.
2. Convent or Residence of the Padres of the Mission.	b. Government Lot.
3. Enclosure or the Plaza of the Mission.	c. Maverick Homestead.
4 and 5. Old Prison and Entrance of the Mission.	d. Maverick Land Office.
6. Houses and Walls surrounding the Mission.	e. Maverick Bank.
7. Abandoned Aceq'a.	f. Circular Curb of Plaza Garden.
8 Room used as Powder Magazine during the Siege.	g. Grenet or now Hugo & Schmeltzer's Front.
9. Cedar post Stockade and Earthworks in use during Siege.	

Figure 2.4 Plan of Mission San Antonio de Valero, San Antonio, Texas: 1836

missions, and *presidios* were established for different purposes and took different forms, in practice the distinction between them was not always so clear-cut.

Under Spanish colonial policy missions were intended to become self-governing civil settlements once their Indian inhabitants had been converted to Christianity, learned useful trades, and adjusted to European social and political institutions. At that time the mission chapel would become the parish church, the mission fathers would move on to new areas to repeat the process of "reducing" other tribes to the true faith, and the Indian residents would be accorded all the rights of Spanish citizenship.[21]

The physical form of the mission did indeed often resemble an urban settlement, and many of the missions exceeded the *pueblos* or civil settlements in size and population. That tireless Jesuit missionary and frontier explorer, Father Eusebio Francisco Kino, in 1703 described his mission of Nuestra Señora de los Dolores as having not only "a well-built and spacious church" but "a water-powered mill, carpenter and blacksmith shops, oxen for ploughing, cultivated land, productive gardens, a vineyard sufficient for mass-wine, trees that supply us with

abundant Castilian fruit, and so on."[22] In this communication Kino constantly refers to his missions of northern Mexico and southern Arizona as urban settlements. He mentions, for example, that on March 13, 1687, "I founded my first town, namely that of Nuestra Señora de los Dolores, and then I turned my attention to many others." Two of these he lists were in Arizona: "San Francisco Javier del Bac, and . . . San Gabriel del Guébavi," both categorized as being two of the several "recently established towns."

The typical mission complex stood in the middle of extensive farm fields, orchards, and pastureland. Usually the buildings were enclosed by an adobe wall. Inside the quadrangle formed by the wall was a variety of buildings housing the granary, shops, modest huts for the Indians, and other structures in addition to those related to the church and its monastic buildings. Unfortunately, few drawings or plans of entire missions seems to have survived if, indeed, they were ever prepared. Reproduced in Figure 2.4, however, is an attempt by a nineteenth-century historian to reconstruct the general pattern of mission San Antonio de Valero, only the church of which has survived and is known to us as the Alamo in San Antonio. A description of this large group of structures in 1745 provides additional details:

"The Indian pueblo, where the neophytes lived, consisted of two rows of small huts built on either side of an *acequia* [water ditch]. These were built of adobe bricks and were generally roofed with straw. Along each row of houses there was a sort of street. The missionaries lived in their small friary, a two-story structure of stone and mortar, with three living cells on the second floor and offices and other rooms on the first. Next to the friary there was a large gallery where the Indian women worked at the looms to make the cloth for their dresses; then followed a granary for the mission corn and other grains, and beyond there were several rooms which were used as offices." The same account also mentions a blacksmith shop and a carpenter shop.[23] Doubtless there were also buildings for a school and an infirmary, two of the structures noted at Mission San Luis Rey in California by Duflot de Mofras in 1844.[24] Because at San Antonio a *presidio* existed near the mission, there would have been no guardhouse or quarters for a small detachment of soldiers that was usually quartered at more isolated missions to provide some military protection for the mission fathers.[25]

Secularization of the missions and their conversion to civil communities did eventually occur, but, within the limits of the United States at least, the results were scarcely what had been envisaged. In California, members of the Franciscan order steadfastly resisted efforts to remove them from control of the missions, and it was not until the Mexican period of administration that this occurred. The results were chaotic. In some cases a typical *pueblo* plan for a plaza and house lots was prepared and sites assigned to the Indian residents, as at missions San Luis Rey and San Luis Obispo. At mission San Juan Bautista the plaza was apparently laid out in front of the mission church with that structure and a long arcaded building forming one of its sides. The California Indians, however, could not adapt themselves to their new status, and the flood of Americans following the Mexican War and the California gold rush proved their final undoing.[26]

Towns such as Santa Clara, shown in Figure 2.5 as it appeared in 1856, did indeed develop around the old missions, and the space in front of the church often, as in this case, became a plaza resembling the pattern prescribed by the Laws of the Indies.[27] The house lots and other building sites, however, quickly passed into the hands of the new settlers, and in the flood of Anglo migration the half-educated, outnumbered, and unsophisticated Indians were soon engulfed or cut adrift. In 1852 Benjamin Davis Wilson described the condition of Indians in the vicinity of the southern California former missions. He found them "in their straggling huts of brush or tule, trying to get a meagre subsistence out of the small patches not yet taken up by the whites—ill clothed, in filth and wretchedness, without food half the year, save what is stolen. If there be savages among these southern Indians, a Mission is now the place to seek them, where riot and debauchery reign supreme."[28]

The third type of settlement used in Spanish colonization—the *presidio*—was closely related to *pueblos* and missions. These forts were intended to safeguard the occupants of religious and civil communities of the region from Indian attack or invasion by other colonizing powers. In turn, the missions and the *pueblos* were expected to produce food and other supplies for soldiers of the garrison. The task of defending the frontier against Indian attack—the principal function of the *presidio* garrison—was made easier by the work of the missionaries and the gathering of the natives into the mission settlements where their activities could be observed and directed. Civilians at the *pueblos* were also expected to be available in case of attack to bolster the military capacity of soldiers at the forts.

Plans of the *presidios* were not governed by the Laws of the Indies. Instead, each was designed for its individual site and according to the judgment of its founding military commander. This resulted, as will be seen, in considerable variety of physical forms. A number of early plans, maps, and views of Spanish *presidios* have fortunately survived, many of which are reproduced in subsequent chapters.[29]

Although the *presidio* itself was normally a walled compound of compact dimensions whose occupants were subject to military discipline, outside the walls of the *presidio* could often be found houses and farms of some soldiers and of other settlers attracted to the relative security of the location. In the late eighteenth century, and perhaps earlier, the distinction between *presidios* and *pueblos* was further blurred as a matter of policy. Royal regulations issued in 1772 for the *presidios* of Texas, Arizona, New Mexico, and California as well as those of northern Mexico specifically encouraged civil settlement. The King's orders were clear and specific:

"With the justified aim that protection by well-regulated presidios will foment settlement and commerce in the frontier area, and that the strength of the presidios likewise will be augmented by a great number of inhabitants, I order the commandant-inspector, captains, officers, and other persons on no pretext to impede or dissuade people of good reputations and habits from entering and settling in their districts; and when their presidio is no longer large enough to contain the incoming families, they are to expand it on one side, the work to be done in common since it redounds to the benefit of all. At the same time I order the captains to distribute and assign lands and town lots to those that ask them, with the obligation that they cultivate them and that they keep horses, arms, and munitions for use in expeditions against enemies when necessity demands it and they are so ordered." A further provision prohibited any military commander from "molesting of merchants selling goods . . . or of artisans who wish to work at the presidios."[30]

The predominantly military character of the *presidios* thus underwent a gradual change. Lands around the forts were surveyed and granted to both civilians and soldiers, many of whom were accompanied by their families. This combination of municipal and garrison community developed at Tubac, Arizona, and at such places as San Diego, Santa Barbara, and Monterey, in California, and at Goliad, Texas, among others.

If individual missions, *pueblos*, and *presidios* often resembled each other in physical form and essential functions, the distinction between them became even less clear when several of these religious, civil, and military settlements grew up in proximity to one another. Santa Fe, which we will presently examine, was not only a *villa* and a *presidio*, but a center of missionary activities as well. At San Antonio, Texas, the *presidio* and the *pueblo* were literally within a stone's throw of one

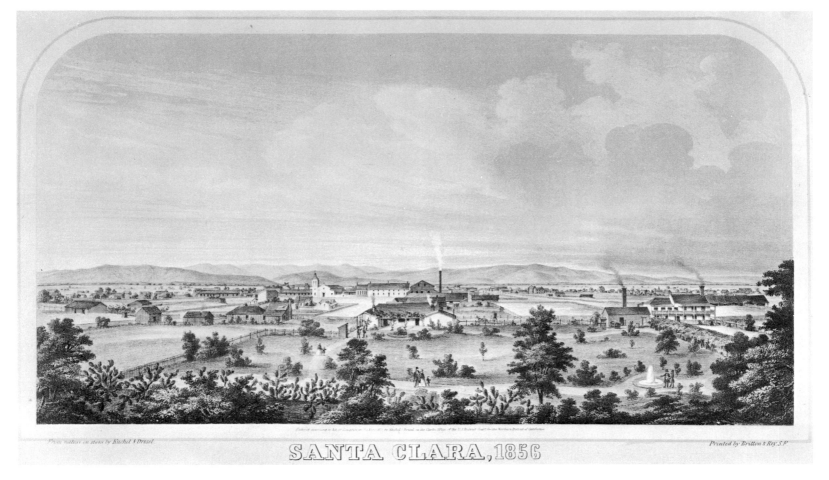

SANTA CLARA, 1856

Figure 2.5 View of Santa Clara, California: 1856

another. Across the river a few hundred feet away stood the mission San Antonio de Valero, while four other missions could be found within a few miles south of the most concentrated point of Spanish settlement. At what is now San Francisco the *presidio* occupied a site at the mouth of the Golden Gate, a few miles away lay the mission, and roughly midway between by the early years of the nineteenth century the *pueblo* of Yerba Buena developed on a cove inside San Francisco Bay. The three types of Spanish colonial settlement were thus intimately related and, often, physically contiguous. In this and subsequent chapters we shall see how these three elements of colonization, singly or together, began the urbanization of the American Southwest.

That vast region served as the setting for extensive exploration before Spain seriously attempted permanent settlement. It lay at the fringe of the Spanish domain, which in the northern hemisphere centered on

Mexico City. It required a century of expansion from this core of Hispanic America before these northern borderlands attracted the attention of would-be settlers. Until the end of the sixteenth century the borderlands were traversed only by occasional explorers seeking civilizations like those of the Aztec or the Inca or by a few venturesome and dedicated missionaries thrusting into the unknown in search of souls for the true faith.[31] Coronado's explorations beginning in 1539 are the best known, but many others preceded and followed him during the sixteenth century, as the Spanish attempted to learn more about the nature of the land and people over which they claimed dominion.

The frontier of settlement in Mexico moved northward in midcentury with the discovery of silver deposits in what became the province of Nueva Galicia. A few years later Nueva Vizcaya was created as a province, extending colonization still further toward what is now the northern part of Mexico. In these lands the Spanish encountered Indians quite different in character from the urbanized Aztecs, who, after an initial period of resistance, had adapted themselves to many of the customs of their conquerors. The warlike northern tribes had never been subjugated by native leaders such as Montezuma, and they strongly resisted Spanish frontier expansion. This circumstance more than anything else stimulated the development of the mission system as an instrument in colonization. If missionaries could pacify the Indians through religious instruction and conversion, the role of the *conquistador* would be made immensely easier. Royal support for mission activities may have been a religious duty, but it served as well—and quite consciously—as an important element in territorial expansion.

Thus, when Juan de Oñate in 1595 succeeded in gaining authorization for settling in the valley of the Rio Grande in what is now New Mexico, the king agreed to provide at royal expense five priests and a lay brother to accompany the expedition. The terms of the agreement clearly indicated that this was to be more than a venture in further exploration. Article 1 stipulated that Oñate's purpose was "settlement and pacification." Article 2 provided for a system of municipal government in accordance with the Laws of the Indies, leaving it to Governor Oñate to declare "whether the pueblo that is to be settled is to be a city, town, or village."[32]

A proposal by Don Pedro Ponce de León for a similar project delayed Oñate's expedition, but finally, in January, 1598, he left his base at San Gerónimo leading a column of 129 soldiers, some of them with their families, 83 wagons, and 700 head of cattle. Two months later ten Franciscans joined the party, which on the last day of April reached the Rio Grande across from what is now El Paso, Texas. There Oñate and Father Alonso Martínez claimed the land for God and King Philip.[33] The region through which they had passed and the much larger and less known area that lay ahead can be seen in Figure 2.6, a map published nearly a century later showing the place names assigned by the Spanish to Indian towns and to their own new settlements.

Crossing the river, Oñate led his men slowly northward, pausing from time to time to treat with the Indians. The reception by the natives was generally friendly, but as the party moved north they found many of the Indian *pueblos* deserted by their occupants for fear they would be harmed by the invaders. On July 7 Oñate, with the aid of two Mexican Indians who served as interpreters, arranged a council with seven chiefs of the region. He explained that his group had come for peaceful purposes, that his king across the sea was a powerful monarch who now claimed the land, and that the Spaniards would protect the Indians from their enemies if they would submit to Spanish civil rule and the Christian religion. It seems doubtful if the Indians understood all the implications of this proposal, but they signified their willingness to obey and knelt to kiss the hands of Oñate and Father Martínez.[34]

After some further exploration of the region, the governor selected the Indian *pueblo* of Caypa for his base, renaming it San Juan de Los Caballeros. The name, according to a curious epic poem composed by one of the soldiers present and published in 1610, was "in memory of those noble sons who first raised in these barbarous regions the bloody tree upon which Christ perished for the redemption of mankind."[35] San Juan occupied a site on the east bank of the Rio Grande about 25 miles northwest of the location later selected for Santa Fe.

Oñate regarded this as only a temporary headquarters. Nearby he began the development of a new town. Our only knowledge of this is a tantalizing reference, dated September 9, 1598, to "the city of San Francisco de los Espanoles, which is under construction."[36] For some reason Oñate abandoned this project and some time in 1599 or early 1600 moved his entire company a short distance away on the west side of the Rio Grande to occupy the Indian *pueblo* of Yuqueyunque at the mouth of the Chama River.

Under its new name of San Gabriel this town served as the capital of New Mexico for the next decade.[37] In 1601 a witness described the place as "consisting of approximately four hundred houses." With its former occupants peacefully evacuated to San Juan the Spaniards found it "unnecessary" to build "houses or fortification." The only changes made by Oñate's company according to another observer was to build

Figure 2.6 Map of New Mexico and Adjoining Regions: ca. 1688

"doors and windows in them in the Spanish custom." Although Oñate "wanted a town established" the soldiers and settlers refused to do so because of "their dissatisfaction at remaining and their desire to abandon the land because of the great privations they were suffering."[38]

Increasing discontent bordering on mutiny threatened the success of the colonizing venture. Following his success in a bloody battle with the residents of the *pueblo* of Ácoma, who showed the first sign of hostility to the conquerors of their land, Oñate led an exploring party as far east as Kansas. During his five-month absence some of the settlers deserted and on their return to Mexico aired their discontent with their former leader and the country they had abandoned. The next few years saw a series of investigations of Oñate and his administration, a tentative and reluctant decision by Viceroy Luis de Velasco to discontinue further efforts at colonization, the resignation of Oñate in 1607, and, eventually, an order by the crown that New Mexico was to be held and that all expenses of this effort were to be born by the royal treasury. Early in 1609 Velasco appointed Don Pedro de Peralta as royal governor to carry out this order.[39]

Peralta's orders of March 30, 1609, instructed him to "inform himself of the actual condition of the settlements, endeavoring first of all to found and settle the villa that has been ordered built, so that they may begin to live with some order and decency." Peralta was to establish a municipal government whose officials were authorized to grant "each resident two lots for house and garden, two contiguous fields for vegetable gardens, two others for vineyards and olive groves, and in addition four *caballerías* [one *caballería* = 105.7 acres] of land." These land grants required continuous settlement for ten years; if, during that period, the settler absented himself for more than "four consecutive months without permission" the city officials could grant the land to another person. For the city itself the viceroy directed Peralta to "mark out six districts" with "a square block for government buildings and other public works."[40]

After Peralta's arrival in New Mexico in 1609 or, more likely, in the next year, he selected a site for the new capital. His choice fell on a location 25 miles southeast of San Gabriel, away from the concentration of Indian towns along the Rio Grande, and sheltered on the north by mountains. On the north bank of a river flowing westward to the Rio Grande he then proceeded to lay out the new town, naming it Santa Fe.[41]

It is an exasperating fact that very little is recorded about the town or its plan for the first century and a half of its existence. The viceroy, the Marquis of Guadalcázar, reported to the king in May, 1620, that the Franciscans had established a monastery in the town, the only community of Spaniards in New Mexico, and that "the villa of Santa Fé . . . contains fifty residents." He regarded the situation as "unpromising."[42] Father Alonso de Benavides, writing in 1630, indicated that by that time the population had increased to "about two hundred and fifty," but with wives, children and servants the total population was nearly one thousand. He mentioned that after his arrival in January, 1626, he "started the construction of the church and friary," probably referring to the Chapel of San Miguel located to the south of the Santa Fe River in the *barrio de Analco* which developed as the Indian quarter.[43]

The earliest known survey of the oldest capital city in the United States is reproduced in Plate 3, a drawing prepared in 1766 by Lt. Joseph de Urrutia who served under Captain Nicolás de Lafora, cartographer for the Marqués de Rubí when de Rubí carried out his exhaustive inspection of the *presidios* on the northern frontier of the Spanish colonies. While in the period intervening since Peralta prepared the original plan of Santa Fe many changes had doubtless taken place, the general pattern of the settlement more than a century and a half earlier probably followed that shown in Urrutia's survey.

Peralta evidently attempted to follow certain provisions of the Laws of the Indies, but he deviated from them in several instances. The length of the plaza, for example, was more than twice its width, and its corners did not face the cardinal points of the compass as stipulated by the regulation. Nor did Peralta provide streets entering the midpoints of the plaza on its east and west sides. He did, however, place the church and monastery of San Francisco (identified on the drawing with the letter "A") slightly away from the plaza, as the laws recommended.

The northern side of the western half of the plaza was occupied by the Governor's Palace (marked on the Urrutia drawing with the letter "B"). This was part of a walled compound with towers at its corners stretching northward to encompass the *cuarteles* or barracks for the *presidio* garrison. The *presidio* site also apparently extended one block to the west to what is now Grant Avenue.[44]

The streets of Santa Fe followed the gridiron system suggested by the Laws of the Indies, although to reconstruct the complete system of thoroughfares from Urrutia's map requires some imagination. Long before he prepared his survey, buildings had encroached into the street right-of-way. A series of documents dating from 1715 records how certain residents petitioned Governor Juan Ignacio Flores Mogollon to reestablish the older property lines, his investigation of the problem, and his orders attempting to adjust and reconcile the conflicting interests of the encroaching property owners and the rights of the municipality.[45]

Difficulties in preserving order and regularity of streets and property boundaries may have begun earlier, but they were complicated by the Indian occupancy of Santa Fe during the years 1680-1693 following the Pueblo Revolt that drove the Spanish out of New Mexico. When Governor Diego de Vargas fought his way into Santa Fe in 1693 he found the churches destroyed, council houses erected in the plaza, and other adobe structures built by the Indians enclosing its east, south, and west sides. These were demolished in the process of reconstructing the town according to its original plan.[46]

The governor's palace survived the Indian occupancy, but it was in a very poor state of repair. In 1708 the governor, the Marqués de la Peñuela, planned to tear it down and build a new official residence, but action by the viceroy spared the building. It was eventually repaired and, as further reconstructed in subsequent years, stands today on its original site.[47] Less controversial was the logical decision to rebuild the parish church on the site assigned by Peralta and used for that purpose almost from the founding of the town until the Pueblo Revolt. Begun in 1714, the church soon provided an effective termination of the vista eastward from the plaza, along the *calle de San Francisco*, the town's principal thoroughfare.[48]

Urrutia's map shows another significant addition to the architectural fabric of Santa Fe. This is the Chapel of Our Lady of Light, identified with the letter "C" by Urrutia and facing the governor's palace from the south side of the plaza. Under construction by 1760, *La Castrense*, as it was known, served as the chapel for the *presidio* garrison, but almost exactly a century after its completion it was sold by church authorities and pulled down to make way for small shops.[49]

While this chapel was still under construction, Pedro Tamarón y Romeral, bishop of Durango, visited the city. He admired the new church, but he was clearly not much impressed by the town, whose population, he was told, consisted of "379 families of citizens of Spanish and mixed blood, with 1285 persons." All the buildings, he noted, including the churches, were built of adobe, and he suggested that "there was need of a stone fort" since "there is no fortress . . . nor any formal presidio building." Santa Fe, he commented, "is a very open place" with "the houses . . . far apart."[50]

Far more critical in his assessment of conditions at Santa Fe was Father Francisco Atanasio Dominguez, who conducted an extensive visit to New Mexico in 1776. After describing in considerable detail the various churches and their possessions he turned his attention to the town. In reading the following account one should keep in mind that civil and ecclesiastical authorities in the Spanish colonies occasionally differed on even the most trivial matters and often were at odds on major issues. Father Dominguez's devastating description of Santa Fe may thus have been colored by some feelings of hostility toward the military and municipal officials responsible for conditions in the frontier capital.

While admitting that "the location, or site, of this villa is . . . good," Dominguez stated that Santa Fe's "appearance, design, arrangement, and plan do not correspond to its status as a villa nor to the very beautiful plain on which it lies, for it is like a rough stone set in fine metal." Comparing it to Tlatelolco, a suburb of Mexico City, "with its streets, well-planned houses, shops, fountains . . . [which] lift the spirit by appealing to the senses," he found Santa Fe "the exact opposite, for in the final analysis it lacks everything. Its appearance is mournful because not only are the houses of earth, but they are not adorned by any artifice of brush or construction."

Dominguez found only "a semblance of a street in this villa. It begins on the left facing north shortly after one leaves the west gate of the cemetery of the parish church and extends down about 400 or 500 varas" (1200 to 1500 feet). Referring to this thoroughfare as "this quasi-street," he commented that it lacked "orderly rows, or blocks, of houses." He noted that on the north side of the plaza stood "the government palace . . . with its barracks, or quarters for the guard" facing the military chapel.

On the east and west sides of the plaza "are houses of settlers, and since there is nothing worth noting about them, one can guess what they are like from what has been seen." Then Dominguez penned his final critical observation: "The government palace is like everything else here, and enough said."[51]

Dominguez's description of Santa Fe in 1776 and the Urrutia survey a decade earlier do not seem completely compatible. While Urrutia's drawing certainly does not depict a settlement of substantial order and regularity, neither does it show the degree of disorganization that Dominguez implies where he does not explicitly condemn. Unfortunately, Lafora's report of the Rubí expedition that Urrutia accompanied fails to provide verbal details of the town. Lafora states only that "the map I drew [of Santa Fe] shows its layout."[52]

Perhaps in the ten years after Urrutia prepared his drawing major changes had taken place, with further encroachments on streets and additional deterioration of buildings. Certainly Santa Fe did not impress Governor Juan Bautista de Anza when he received the appointment as governor in 1777, a year after Dominguez visited the town. His proposal to remedy conditions in Santa Fe may well have been the first suggested urban renewal project in the United States. Writing in 1782, Father Juan Agustín de Morfi provides the details:

"In 1779 Governor . . . Anza wished to give a new form to the Villa and for this purpose to move it to the south bank of its river, razing all the buildings of the old settlement." Not surprisingly, most of the residents opposed such drastic action. Anza's arguments of "the disasters and inconveniences which injured them" failed to win them over. Twenty-four citizens went to Mexico, complained to Anza's superiors, and in 1780 "they won an order that the governor should not proceed in moving the Villa until there be demonstrated the conveniences which from that should ensue."[53]

Thwarted in his plans for Santa Fe, Anza did carry out extensive improvements elsewhere in New Mexico. His orders from Teodoro de Croix, commander general of the newly created Interior Provinces of New Spain, included a directive aimed at reorganizing the pattern of settlement along the Rio Grande valley. Anza was to gather together the scattered Spanish families then living in hamlets or on farms into little "pueblos in good order, walled, close to the fields of labor, and filled with fifty families each."[54]

Two of the settlements to which Anza directed his attention had previously been founded as Spanish *pueblos*. One was Santa Cruz, established by Governor Vargas in April, 1695, with the imposing name of Villa Nueva de Santa Cruz de la Cañada on a site about 25 miles northwest of Santa Fe.[55] Whether this new town was laid out according to the Laws of the Indies or was simply a new name for the existing Indian *pueblo* that the Spanish occupied is not known. In 1776 Dominguez described it as a little group of eight houses around the church and monastery, with a number of other houses and farms scattered along the river valley. Morfi, on the other hand, states that "in 1762 it had two hundred and forty-one families and one thousand five hundred Spanish souls," but added the comment that it "extended along the two margins" of the river "the space of some leagues." Bishop Tamarón in 1760 observed that while the population was more than 1500 "the settlers are scattered over a wide area," and "there is no semblance of a town." No plans of this settlement have survived, and we can only speculate on what Anza accomplished in 1779, when, according to Morfi, he "reduced it to the regular form."[56]

What was destined to be a far more important city has an almost equally obscure early history. This was Albuquerque, founded by Governor Francisco Cuerbo y Valdez in 1706 on the east side of the Rio Grande 60 miles southwest of Santa Fe. The governor described the location as "a good place as regards land, water, pasture, and firewood." He obviously intended the new town to be an important place, giving to it the title of *villa*. Of greater interest is the governor's statement in the certification of founding sent to the viceroy and the king that in establishing the settlement he "bore in mind that which his Majesty provides in his royal laws in *título* seven, book four of the *Recopilación*," a reference to the town planning sections of the Laws of the Indies.[57]

Albuquerque must have resembled Santa Cruz in its early years. Dominguez observed, "the villa itself consists of twenty-four houses near the mission. The rest of what is called Albuquerque extends upstream to the north, and all of it is a settlement of ranchos on the meadows of the . . . river for the distance of a league from the church to the last one upstream."[58] Morfi commented that "the settlement is scattered throughout the entire breadth of the valley," and then added the same cryptic statement he had made about Santa Cruz: "In 1779 the governor, Don Juan Bautista de Anza, reduced it to the regular form."[59]

What this "regular form" may have consisted of is unknown, for descriptions, plans, or views of Albuquerque dating before the middle of the nineteenth century have not survived if they were ever prepared. The view reproduced in Figure 2.7 was not drawn until 1856, but it doubtless conveys something of the appearance of the city as it existed during the final years of Spanish rule. The author of the work in which this appeared found the town "irregularly laid out and badly built." The plaza was "some two or three acres in extent . . . into which the principal streets lead." He observed that the houses of Albuquerque were "generally grouped about without order, and the best are but indifferent mud buildings, some of the more humble ones being partly in ruins."[60]

A suggestion of Albuquerque's original plan of 1706 or, perhaps, Anza's modification of it, is provided by a modern sketch map of this portion of the city, now known as Old Town, reproduced in Figure 2.8. As a subsequent chapter will note, the center of the contemporary city developed two miles away in the vicinity of the railroad station when the Atchison, Topeka, and Santa Fé line reached the area in 1881. While this event caused a sharp drop in property values and activities in the original settlement, it eventually made possible the preservation and restoration of many of the older buildings, including the church of San Felipe de Nerí that was begun in 1706.

This sketch may be compared with the view reproduced in Figure 2.9 showing old Albuquerque in 1886 as seen from the southeast. Quite obviously many changes had taken place in the town since its founding or Anza's efforts to replan it in 1779, but this portion of a much larger bird's-eye view suggests how the town might have appeared in its early days when it served as one of the outposts on the Spanish colonial frontier.

While Santa Fe, Santa Cruz, and Albuquerque represented the only attempts made by Spain to establish true cities in New Mexico, many small hamlets or villages could be found strung along the Rio Grande valley by the end of the eighteenth century. Some of these *plazas*, as they were called, probably resulted from Anza's efforts to carry out his instructions for the better defense of the province by gathering settlers together in fortified places. A common form for such a *plaza* consisted of a quadrangle of houses linked together by party walls, and with doors and windows opening only on the side facing the open square thus enclosed.[61]

A modern aerial photograph of the best preserved of these little settlements appears in Figure 2.10. This is Plaza del Cerro at Chimayó, a few miles east of Santa Cruz. Earlier known as Plaza San Buenaventura, this settlement probably assumed its present form some time prior to 1750. Others existed at such places as Truchas, Las Trampas, Taos, Ojo Caliente, and Cebolleta.[62] Similar but smaller settlements consisting of dwellings and miscellaneous buildings housing two or more generations of a single extended family also existed. Some of these were built as far north as southwest Colorado in the nineteenth century by settlers moving beyond the original confines of the Spanish colonial domain. One such *plaza* or fortified *hacienda* was Madrid Plaza, whose dwellings, store rooms, and cattle sheds enclosed the corral.[63] Either for one or several families, the *plaza* form of settlement proved popular. One early historian of New Mexico, writing in 1812, asserted that there were then ''102 settlements of Spaniards'' located in such fortified villages.[64]

Although Albuquerque would eventually outstrip Santa Fe in size and population, the older capital remained by far the most important city of the region until well into the nineteenth century. It retained the basic form established by Peralta, but with two significant changes. One was the enlargement and formal arrangement of the *presidio* complex. Completed sometime in the early 1790s, this took the form of an

Figure 2.7   View of Albuquerque, New Mexico: 1856

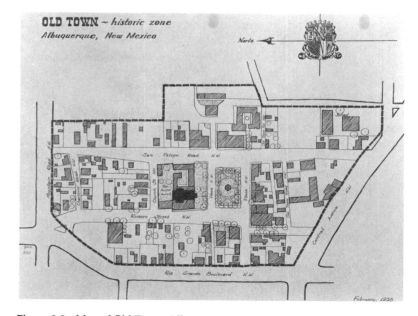

Figure 2.8   Map of Old Town, Albuquerque, New Mexico: 1958

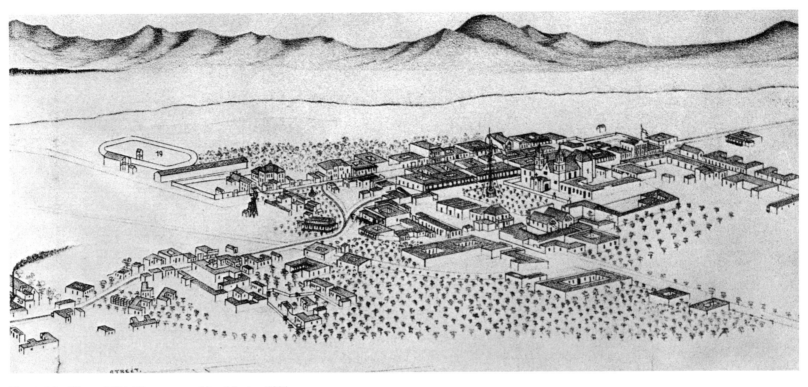

Figure 2.9 View of Old Albuquerque, New Mexico: 1886

immense quadrangle of barracks around a parade ground measuring more than 900 by 1200 feet located to the northwest of the *plaza*.

The other modification in the original plan was the gradual filling in by buildings of the entire eastern half of the *plaza* so that its shape became a square instead of an elongated rectangle. Both these changes can be seen in the first detailed survey of the city reproduced in Figure 2.11. This was prepared during the Mexican War by Lt. J. F. Gilmer in 1846, following American occupancy of the city. Other additions to the town can be noted: the church of Our Lady of Guadalupe to the southwest, Fort Marcy on a commanding height overlooking the town from the northeast and built for the American garrison, and many houses along the streets of the town and the roads leading to it.

Santa Fe had obviously benefited from the opening of trade with the United States following Mexican independence. But just as Urrutia's map may present a false impression of order in the previous century, Gilmer's neat military survey may imply a greater regularity and more imposing character than when the town was seen from eye level. Certainly the following description by an observer who entered Santa Fe on June 30, 1846, is anything but enthusiastic:

"Riding ahead, I passed several hills, and overlooked then at once the beautiful wide valley . . . in which *Santa Fe*, the celebrated capital of New Mexico, lies. My expectations of seeing a fine city had already been cooled down by previous accounts of travellers, and by the sight of the Mexican country towns through which we had passed. How-

Figure 2.10
Aerial View of Plaza
del Cerro, Chimayo,
New Mexico: 1971

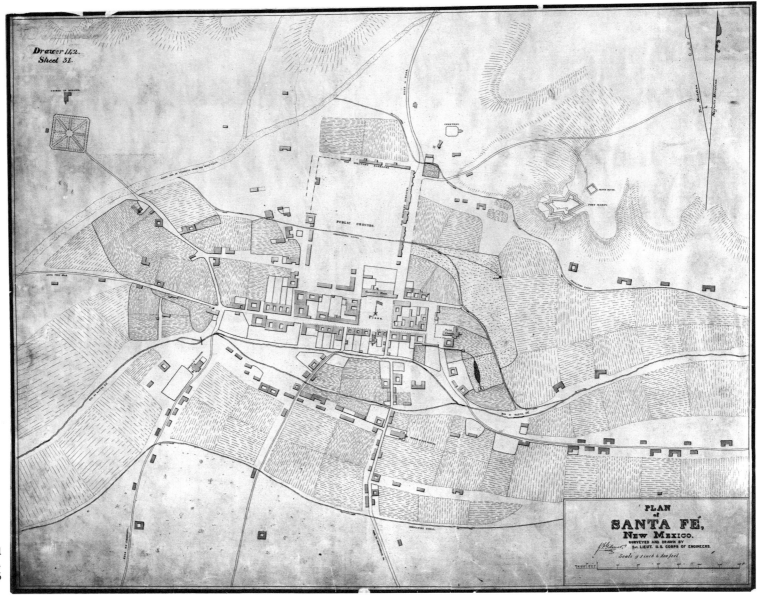

Figure 2.11
Plan of Santa Fe,
New Mexico: 1846

Figure 2.12   View of Santa Fe, New Mexico: 1848

ever, when I perceived before me that irregular cluster of low, flat roofed, mud built, dirty houses, called Santa Fe, and resembling in the distance more a prairie-dog village than a capital, I had to lower them yet for some degrees."

Entering the town, he noted that "all the houses . . . are built of adobes, but one story high, with flat roofs; each house in a square form, with a court or open area in the centre. The streets are irregular, nar-row, and dusty. The best looking place is the 'plaza'; a spacious square, one side of which the so-called palacio, the residence of the Governor, occupies. The palace is a better building than the rest; it has a sort of portico, and exhibits two great curiosities, to wit: windows of glass, and festoons of Indian ears."[65]

A view of Santa Fe at that time is reproduced in Figure 2.12 showing the city from the south. In the foreground is the Indian *barrio* on the

Figure 2.13   View of San Francisco Street, Santa Fe, New Mexico: 1866

south bank of the river. Beyond, marked by the overly large American flag, is the *plaza*, with the old *presidio* quadrangle to the north. A second flag high atop the hill to the right flies from the newly erected Fort Marcy.

The military events of 1846 thus brought to a formal end the long but not very impressive record of Hispanic town planning in New Mexico. Growth of Santa Fe and Albuquerque and the founding of many new settlements after that date would be largely governed by new and foreign attitudes toward the nature and form of urban communities. Nevertheless, much of the original character of early Santa Fe remained nearly unchanged. The view in Figure 2.13, published in 1866, reveals the appearance of San Francisco Street leading eastward from the plaza to its terminus at the church, which three years later was to be replaced by the present and more imposing Cathedral of St. Francis. There is little in this scene that would not have been familiar to an eighteenth-century visitor.

All this would soon change—a process that was to be repeated in the other parts of the American west where Spain and then Mexico established urban settlements. In the chapters to follow we shall see the results of these colonization efforts in Texas, Arizona, and California, and how these towns, too, ultimately were modified by the rapid westward movement of people from another culture who brought with them divergent attitudes toward patterns for cities that modified or replaced the older designs stemming from the ancient Spanish Laws of the Indies.

III

Spanish Towns of the Texas Frontier

THE first Spanish settlements in Texas were closely related to colonization efforts in New Mexico. The supply and communications line to that northern outpost of empire followed the route used by Oñate, crossing the Rio Grande at what came to be called El Paso del Norte, now Ciudad Juarez, Mexico. There in December, 1659, Father García de San Francisco de Zúñiga established the first of several missions, naming it Nuestra Señora de Guadalupe de El Paso. The Pueblo Revolt of 1680 in New Mexico and the mass evacuation of settlers from that region substantially increased the population on the right bank of the Rio Grande. A town, *presidio*, and several Indian settlements were founded in the vicinity to accommodate and protect the refugees from New Mexico. By the end of the seventeenth century the area included six missions, four *pueblos* of Spaniards, and the *presidio* of El Paso. Two missions could be found on the north side of the river below what is now El Paso, Texas: Nuestra Señora de la Concepción de Socorro and Corpus Christi de la Isleta del Sur.[1]

The major thrust of Spanish colonization into Texas, however, did not occur here but well to the south and east. Motivations for settlement in that more distant region were mixed. Religious officials wanted to found missions where their obligations to Christianize the Indians might be fulfilled. Individuals and officers of the Crown alike were intrigued by rumors of great and wealthy kingdoms beyond the unknown lands to the northeast of Mexico. Perhaps most important of all, the area lay between the Spanish colonial domain and the territory claimed by or potentially open to occupation by other European powers.

The bewildering sequence of settlement founding, movement, abandonment, and re-establishment of missions, *presidios*, and civil communities in Texas resulted mainly from Spanish reaction to French colonization activities. Herbert Bolton's thesis that the Spanish borderlands were a defensive frontier, expanding and contracting in a series of protective moves when threatened by other nations, is nowhere better sustained than in Texas.[2] Like a chess player, the Spanish crown advanced and withdrew its missions, *presidios*, and *pueblos* as if they were bishops, castles, and pawns threatening to check or stalemate the opposition on a great, continental playing board. The end game was not to be reached for many decades, and then not until both of the original opponents had surrendered their places to others.

At the beginning, however, France made the first move in 1682 with La Salle's bold sortie down the Mississippi to its mouth, where he named the region Louisiana and claimed the land for the French king he so honored. The next year La Salle returned to France to report this event. There also was the former Spanish governor of New Mexico, Diego Dionisio de Peñalosa, who had defected to France and was urging the establishment of a French base on the western side of the Gulf of Mexico. La Salle received authorization to begin a settlement near the mouth of the Mississippi and set out in 1684 with four ships and a party of 300 colonists.

Whether through design or a navigator's error, La Salle and his group landed at Matagorda Bay, more than two-thirds of the distance beyond the Mississippi toward what is now the Mexican boundary on the Gulf. One ship had already been captured by pirates, another was wrecked attempting a landing, and a third sailed for France shortly after discharging its cargo of supplies and passengers.

La Salle supervised the construction of Fort St. Louis at the head of Lavaca Bay and then set out westward. He reached the lower Pecos River, nearly 300 miles from his base, before returning to find that disease had severely reduced the strength of the garrison and that its members were at the point of mutiny. The wreck of the remaining ship during a storm eliminated any further thoughts of exploration, conquest, or permanent colonization. The murder of La Salle in 1687 by some of his own men on the party's desperate march to the Mississippi and, eventually, Canada, brought the venture to a tragic end.[3]

Spain could not be sure, however, that Louis XIV did not intend to pursue an expansionist policy. Intelligence reports as early as 1678 informed them of Peñalosa's attempts to promote French settlement on the western Gulf, and in 1689, two years after La Salle's death, a Spanish exploring party led by Alonso de León reached Fort St. Louis. León's report confirmed the stories of the French expedition. It also contained recommendations for founding a line of *presidios* and several missions in Texas to establish Spanish control of the frontier. These suggestions reached the viceroy at the same time as rumors of further French colonization attempts. León received orders to return to the area, and in 1690 he and Father Damian Massanet founded the mission of San Francisco de los Tejas about seven miles west of the Neches River near the modern town of Weches. This location was less than a hundred miles from the border of what was to become the state of Louisiana.[4] The first Spanish settlement in East Texas thus lay well over three hundred miles from the nearest Spanish source of supply or military power.

León reported his accomplishments to the viceroy, including further information learned from the Indians about French activity to the east.

He pointed out that *presidios* and civil settlements would be needed to control the region of East Texas and to serve as supply points on the long route from Mexico. Father Massanet's suggestions to the viceroy differed somewhat. He advocated founding seven more missions and at least one civil settlement. The latter he proposed to be located with one of the missions on the Guadalupe River roughly halfway between his new mission among the Tejas Indians and the Mexican frontier. He opposed the creation of a *presidio* in the Tejas area, believing that the Indians were peaceful and that the soldiers of such a garrison might molest them and interfere with the work of the missionaries. It was this recommendation that the viceroy decided to follow, although he elected to postpone any attempt at civil settlement on the Guadalupe until receiving approval from Spain.[5]

A second mission founded five miles east of Mission San Francisco by Father Jesús María in the fall of 1691, and named Santisimo Nombre de María, was destroyed a few months later by a flood on the Neches River. This disaster was followed by others. The natives proved unwilling converts, an epidemic swept the area killing many of the Indians and at least one of the missionaries. A crop failure caused by the flood and a subsequent drought caused great hardships. Authorities in Mexico failed to provide expected supplies. In the face of increasing Indian intractability Father Massanet changed his previous position and requested the viceroy either to establish a *presidio* or to allow the missionaries to withdraw. Before a party of soldiers could be sent to escort the priests to safety, the Indians began to harrass the mission. On the night of October 25, 1693, Mission San Francisco was put to the torch by Father Massanet, who then fled with his followers to the southwest on the long march to Mexico. The first and brief period of Spanish settlement in East Texas thus ended in complete failure.[6]

Concern for French influence in the lower Mississippi Valley and along the coast of the Gulf of Mexico led to the Spanish settlement of Pensacola in November, 1698. The move proved to have been made just barely in time, for two months later Pierre, Sieur d'Iberville, arrived with a fleet of five vessels obviously intending to settle at the same place. After a polite but strained exchange of messages the French fleet sailed westward to Biloxi Bay to establish a fort. In 1701 Iberville returned, and a year later, on Mobile Bay, constructed Fort Louis, in whose shadow he laid out a little town.[7]

This time there could be no doubt of French intentions to establish control of the mouth of the Mississippi. To nervous officials in Mexico and in Spain itself it seemed more than likely this rival power would seek to expand westward into Texas as well. Their apprehensions appeared to be confirmed in 1713 when Louis Juchereau de St. Denis planted the trading post of Natchitoches on the Red River in what is now western Louisiana. St. Denis then had the temerity to appear the next year at the Rio Grande *presidio* of San Juan Bautista proposing the opening of trade between Louisiana and Mexico.[8]

The ponderous colonial bureaucracy surrounding the viceroy eventually produced a response to this flood of unwelcome news. On April 24, 1716, a column of 25 soldiers, 40 men, women, and children, 8 Franciscan priests, and 3 lay brothers crossed the Rio Grande to begin the re-occupation of Texas.[9] Their orders called for the establishment of several missions and a military outpost. By the end of the following year six missions and a *presidio* in various stages of construction testified to the will and energy of this group. The *presidio* founded by the military leader, Domingo Ramón, was named Nuestra Señora de los Dolores de los Tejas and occupied a site about thirty miles east of the Neches River near the present town of Douglas.[10] On the east bank of the Neches a site was found for the first mission, which took its name in part from the abandoned settlement dating from 1690: San Francisco de los Neches. Nearer the *presidio* and located between the Neches and the Sabine Rivers were four other missions: Nuestra Señora de la Purísima Concepción, San José de los Nazones, Nuestra Señora de Guadalupe de los Nacogdoches, and Nuestra Señora de los Dolores de los Ais. East of the Sabine and midway to Red River—only a few miles from the French inland post of Natchitoches—stood a sixth mission, San Miguel de los Adaes.[11]

Founding missions and a *presidio* was one thing; keeping them supplied, and the missions protected from both Indians and the French, was another. Ramón and the missionaries wrote the viceroy asking for additional soldiers and for items that could be used as gifts to the Indians, who were already receiving such favors from the French in what was to become a competition between the two powers to secure native cooperation.

The new viceroy, the Marqués de Valero, received an offer from Father Antonio de Sanbuenaventura y Olivares to locate a mission on the San Antonio River. Father Olivares suggested that a few soldiers would also be needed, and that some farmers and craftsmen at the site would be helpful as well. The viceroy's advisers urged him to accept this offer but proposed also that a *presidio* be founded with the mission on the San Antonio River and that a second stronghold be established on the coast at Espíritu Santo (Matagorda) Bay. Accepting the advice,

Valero named Martín de Alarcón to carry out this plan to create an intermediate base between Mexico and the East Texas settlements.[12]

While Alarcón received his appointment as captain-general and governor of Texas in December, 1716, it was not until April, 1718, that he set out on his expedition. The viceroy had instructed him to recruit 50 married soldiers, a carpenter, mason, blacksmith, and a weaver and with livestock and supplies to proceed to the San Antonio River. With Father Olivares, Alarcón was to found one or two missions and assign ten soldiers as a mission guard. Two towns were eventually to be settled in the region through which the San Antonio, Guadalupe, and Colorado rivers flowed, but for the time being only one was to be established near the missions on the San Antonio. He was then to proceed to East Texas.[13]

Impatient with the time taken by Alarcón in preparing for the expedition, Olivares was not on the best of terms with the governor, but with his missionaries he met Alarcón on May 1 at the San Antonio River, and the two men immediately selected a site for the mission a short distance from the west bank of the river at the San Pedro Springs. Five days later, as Alarcón's chaplain records, "the governor, in the name of his Majesty, took possession of the place called San Antonio, . . . and it was given the name of villa de Bejar." Apparently neither the town nor the *presidio* was surveyed at this time, since the account states only that "this site is henceforth destined for the civil settlement and the soldiers who are to guard it."[14]

Even the site of the mission, San Antonio de Valero, on the banks of San Pedro Creek was not firmly fixed, since it was shortly to be moved twice before a permanent location was found.

Alarcón then departed for East Texas. He found conditions far from promising. Ramón and some of his men had been ill, several of the soldiers had deserted, the missionaries found the Indians as reluctant as ever to live under mission supervision, and there were rumors that the French post at Natchitoches was to be strengthened. Ramón had moved the *presidio* closer to the mission of San Francisco de los Texas, thus abandoning whatever work had previously been accomplished in erecting suitable fortifications on the original site. All this Alarcón reported to his superiors on his return to Mexico in January, 1719.[15]

The precariousness of the Spanish position was demonstrated in June, 1719, when eight French soldiers appeared at the mission of San Miguel de los Adaes and captured the single soldier stationed there and a lay brother who was in charge in the absence of the mission priest. The war between France and Spain, begun in January of that year and

including a French attack on Spanish Pensacola in mid-May, had come to Texas. The episode has a comic opera air. Officials in Spain had apparently neglected to inform the viceroy of the war. The only effective defenders at San Miguel proved to be a flock of chickens. Frightened by the strangers, they clucked and flapped their wings in flight. This startled the French captain's horse, who reared and threw his rider. In the confusion the lay brother escaped to Mission Dolores spreading the alarm and the story that 100 French soldiers were marching to Natchitoches and that the Spanish were to be driven out of Texas.

Ramón led a retreat to Mission San Francisco on the Neches River. Although two missionaries returned to Mission Concepción for a time, by the middle of July all the Spaniards had withdrawn still further to a camp on the Trinity River. When no reinforcements arrived by the beginning of fall the entire party began the long march westward to the new mission of San Antonio de Valero, which they reached by December.[16]

In Mexico City the viceroy, the Marqués de Valero, already had begun plans for strengthening Texas. News of the abandonment of the East Texas missions and *presidio* provided added motivation. He appointed an experienced soldier, the wealthy José Virto de Vera, Marqués de Aguayo, to assemble an army, secure Matagorda Bay by the construction of a *presidio*, restore the missions in East Texas, and build a second *presidio* on the frontier between Texas and Louisiana.[17]

Aguayo ultimately succeeded in raising a force of 500 men; 6 cannon; 800 mules loaded with arms, clothing, and food; 4,000 horses; 600 head of cattle; and 900 sheep. All this took time, and it was not until the spring of 1721 that this impressive array of men, supplies, and livestock arrived at the San Antonio River. Aguayo had previously reinforced that settlement with a detachment of 84 soldiers in 1719 and in late 1720 or early 1721 a still larger force of 116 men.[18]

By that time a second mission had been established by the missionaries who had evacuated their establishments in East Texas. This had been accomplished with the permission of Aguayo in 1720, and its name, San José y San Miguel de Aguayo, was selected in his honor. Captain Juan Valdez and Father Antonio Margil chose a site three leagues, or roughly 7½ miles south of mission San Antonio de Valero on the east bank of the San Antonio River. In the presence of the Indians Captain Valdez turned the land over to the Franciscans. Plans were made for the *plaza mayor*, a public square more than 300 feet square, streets of uniform width on which the Indians were to build their houses, and for a church, hospital, jail, and cemetery.[19]

From San Antonio Aguayo dispatched a force of 40 men under Captain José Domingo Ramón to take possession of Espíritu Santo (Matagorda) Bay, which the Spanish feared might be occupied by the French. Ramón reported his unopposed occupation of the area early in April, 1721. A month later Aguayo began his march to the east. Movement of such a force proved slow and difficult; it took 16 days to cross the Trinity River, and not until the end of July did the column reach the site of the first mission of San Francisco de los Tejas abandoned in 1693.[20]

Aguayo proceeded slowly to the west bank of the Neches River and made camp near the site of Ramón's temporary *presidio* of 1716. There he received a visit from Louis St. Denis, then commander of the French fort at Natchitoches. St. Denis informed Aguayo that France and Spain had negotiated a truce, but Aguayo responded that while he would not initiate any hostilities he was determined to carry out his orders to re-establish the missions and erect *presidios*. By the end of August this had been accomplished, although Aguayo shifted the sites for two of the missions.[21]

We can only assume that each mission took the usual form of an enclosed square or *plaza* on which fronted the church and other buildings. No plans or other graphic evidence of their form seem to have survived. For the *presidios*, however, our information includes precise drawings of their layout. First to receive attention was the *presidio* de Los Dolores de los Tejas, which was ordered rebuilt on its old site a mile and a quarter from Mission Concepción on August 15.[22]

Aguayo described this event in a later report sent to the king: "Having re-established five missions, building anew the churches and living quarters of the padres, I built in the center of them a presidio for their protection (drawing plans for the fortification to meet the needs of the twenty-five men designated as its garrison)."[23] Figure 3.1 reproduces its plan as published in Mexico City a year later. The site was on a hill overlooking a branch of the Angelina River. It took the form of a square stockade 60 *varas* (about 165 feet) on each side, with two projecting bulwarks at opposite corners. Four short, diagonal streets led from the square parade ground to the bulwarks and the other two corners of the fortification. A single gate at the northeastern corner opened to a street separating the stockade from the barracks, officers' quarters, storehouses, and magazine.

The second *presidio* erected by Aguayo was far more impressive. On the road to Natchitoches, only about 18 miles from the French fort, and a short distance beyond the easternmost mission, Morfi tells us "the

marquis established the presidio, the foundations of which gave considerable trouble, it being necessary to dig them with bars in the solid rock."[24]

The plan of this fort appears in Figure 3.2, following the description provided by Father Juan Antonio Peña, the chaplain of the expedition: "On the top of . . . [an] elevation, which commanded the whole plain his lordship laid out and began at once to build the fortification. He gave it the form of a hexagon, making each side about fifty-five yards long. He left three bastions unconstructed and made the other three smaller than he had planned. These he placed at the alternate corners so that each should protect two sides of the fort."[25]

Aguayo designed the Presidio of Nuestra Señora del Pilar for a garrison of 100 men. Thirty-one had brought their families with them, and Aguayo intended, as Morfi observes, that "these, and such others as might come later, should gradually form a settlement, without causing new expense to the royal treasury." They were to have ample protection. The stockade constructed of pointed logs was eight feet high, the bastions were "protected by earthworks," which were to "be replaced by stone defenses." In each bastion Aguayo installed "two small cannon mounted in such a manner as to protect two curtains."[26]

Los Adaes *presidio* became the capital of Spanish Texas from which 13 colonial governors administered the province until 1773. Although no *pueblo* or *villa* was ever formally established as a civil settlement, the community functioned as a trading point, market town, and supply base as well as a fortress. A few earthen mounds on the site about two miles northeast of Robeline, Louisiana, are the only remains of Aguayo's accomplishment in asserting Spanish hegemony over the region.

Aguayo founded two other *presidios* before his work was done and he returned to Mexico to receive from the king the rank of field marshal as a reward for his accomplishments. Reaching San Antonio in January, 1722, after terrible hardships, he determined to relocate that *presidio* on a new site between San Pedro Creek and the west bank of the San Antonio River. Morfi tells us that "the ground being thickly covered by trees, he had it cleared and the necessary timber for the church, storehouse, and soldiers' quarters fashioned." Then, "after a considerable number of mud bricks had been made, he outlined a square seventy-three varas [200 feet] on each side, and had four bastions built, one on each corner."[27] Figure 3.3 shows Aguayo's design for this fort, with a gate at the south opposite the military chapel. Three rows of buildings, the outermost forming the curtain walls, surrounded the

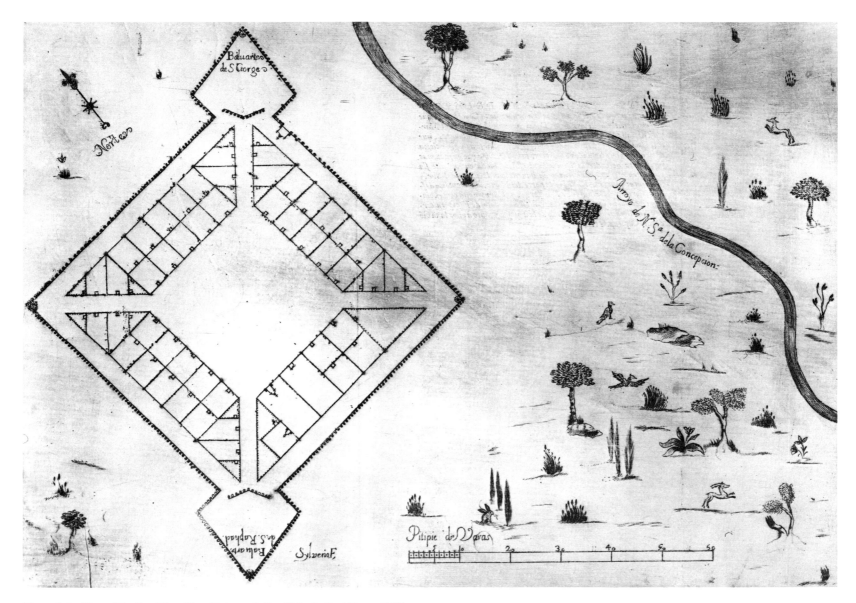

Figure 3.1   Plan of the Presidio of Los Dolores de Los Tejas in East Texas: 1722

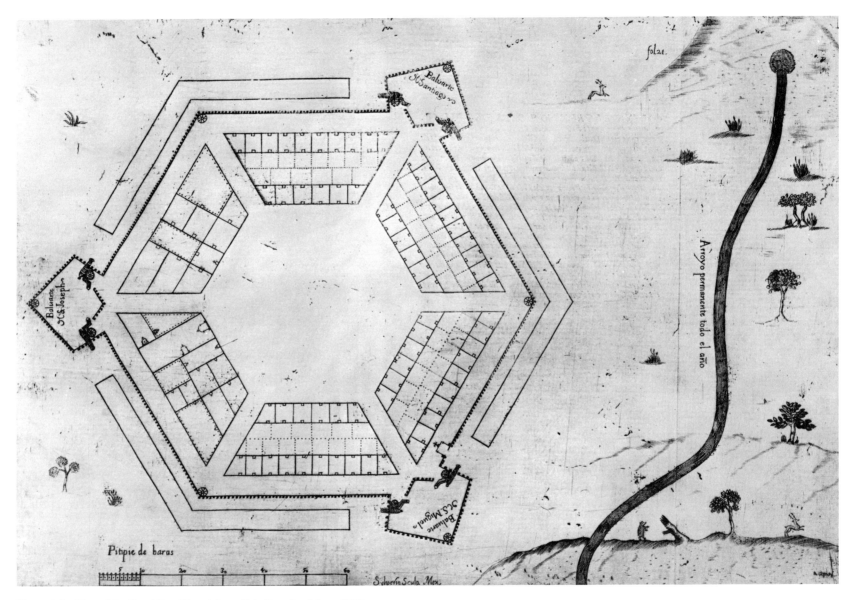

Figure 3.2 Plan of the Presidio of Los Adaes, Robeline, Louisiana: 1722

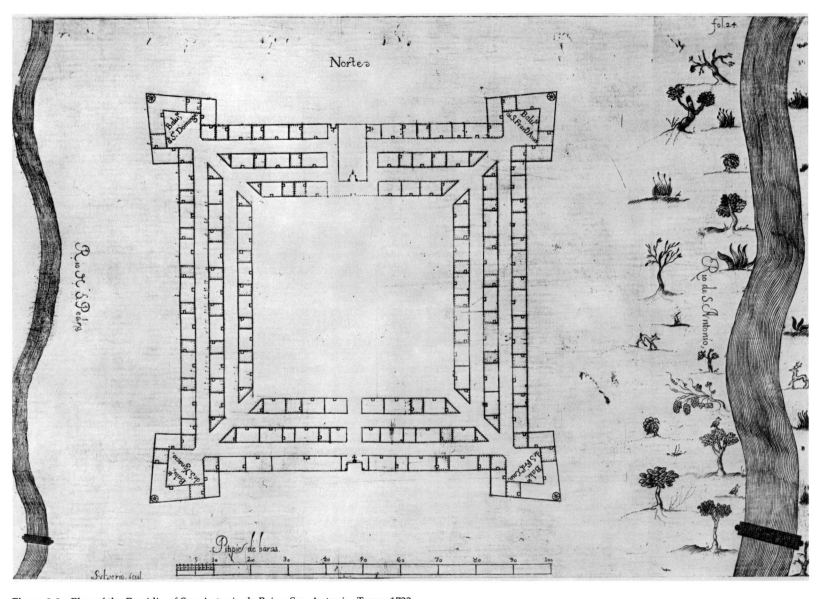

Figure 3.3 Plan of the Presidio of San Antonio de Bejar, San Antonio, Texas: 1722

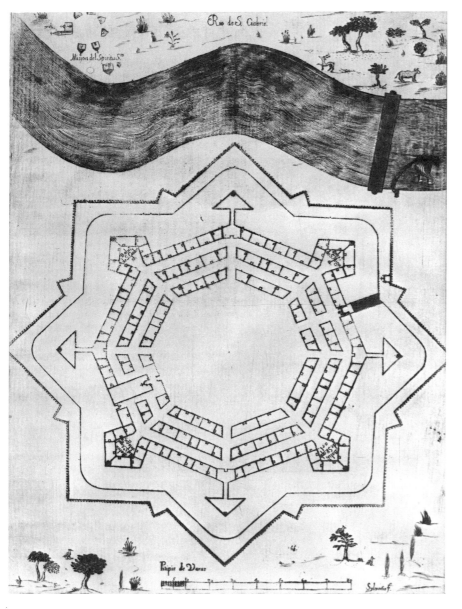

square parade ground, with short diagonal streets leading from it to the bulwarks at the four corners. Probably the outer walls were of adobe. Although in the course of construction rain ruined 30,000 adobe bricks, the governor "immediately ordered twenty-five thousand more made," paying "out of his own pocket" the "forty laborers" set to work on this project.[28]

At San Antonio Aguayo also founded a third mission, the short-lived San Francisco Xavier de Nájera. The chosen location lay about two and a half miles south of the Mission San Antonio de Valero, which by that time had been moved to a second site on the east bank of the San Antonio River, and which in 1727 was to be shifted "two gun shots" to the south to its present site.[29] Within a few years the new mission failed for lack of funds, and the Indians came under the jurisdiction of Mission San Antonio de Valero.[30]

Aguayo then set out for the Gulf coast to lay out the most elaborate of the four *presidios* he founded. Again, we turn to Morfi for some details of its location and design: "The second day after Easter, April 6, the lines for the fort were laid down on the same spot where La Salle had constructed his. While excavating the foundations, nails, firelocks, and fragments of guns were found, and the place where the artillery had been buried and the powder burned was discovered. The foundations for the new structure were dug in fifteen days. These formed an octagon, with a moat all around and four bastions, to which was added a tower. Each curtain was forty-five varas [124 feet] in length."[31]

The plan of this imposing fortification as published later that year is reproduced in Figure 3.4. Aguayo selected an equally impressive name: Presidio de Nuestra Señora de Loreto en la Bahía del Espíritu Santo. La Bahía is the mercifully shortened title by which it was known, both at this site and at its other two locations.

Aguayo clearly intended this spot to be a major colonial settlement. He established a garrison there of 90 soldiers, and across the Garcitas Creek he founded still another mission known as Nuestra Señora del Espíritu Santo de Zúniga. Its location can be seen in the upper left corner of the *presidio* plan. Further, on his return to Mexico, Aguayo recommended to the king that 400 families—half from the Canary Islands or Cuba and an equal number of native Mexicans—be sent immediately to settle at La Bahía, San Antonio, and in East Texas. Unless this was done, he asserted, "it will be most difficult if not impossible, for that province to be self-supporting."[32] He found a sympathetic reader, for the king issued a *cédula* on May 10, 1723, ordering the transfer of 200 families from the Canary Islands for that purpose. Although this was not carried out, a second order issued February 14, 1729, in-

Figure 3.4 Plan of the Presidio of Loreto en la Bahia del Espiritu Santo, Matagorda Bay, Texas: 1722

creased the number to 400 families.[33] It was a partial execution of this royal decree that led to the formal establishment of the first civil settlement in Texas at San Antonio.[34]

Aguayo's settlement pattern of missions and *presidios* soon underwent substantial modifications. At La Bahía lax military discipline, Indian hostilities, and crop failures led Governor Pérez de Almazán to relocate both the fort and the mission in 1726. The spot selected lay on the Guadalupe River about 50 miles northwest of the end of Matagorda Bay.[35]

More drastic changes soon occurred. Viceroy Juan de Acuña, Marqués de Casafuerte, concerned over the mounting costs of maintaining the *presidios* on the northern frontier, appointed General Pedro de Rivera in 1724 to inspect the entire region and report on what adjustments might be made. Rivera's tour required three and a half years. After leaving Texas he submitted his report to Casafuerte in 1728. The report recommended reduction of the garrisons at Los Adaes, La Bahía, and San Antonio, and the abandonment of Los Dolores de los Tejas.[36]

Casafuerte implemented these recommendations the following year. His order closing the *presidio* of los Tejas, issued in April, 1729, caused consternation in the missions located between the Neches and Sabine rivers because this would deprive them of protection from Indian attacks and make maintenance of mission discipline virtually impossible. Protests from mission authorities were to no avail, but a request to relocate missions Concepción, San Francisco, and San José on the Colorado River, well to the west of their existing locations, received approval. By mid-1730 this had been accomplished, but a year later all three were withdrawn further westward to the San Antonio River near the existing *presidio* and mission settlements.[37] Fourteen years of patient, if largely ineffective work was thus abandoned.

Although Rivera severely criticized Aguayo's earlier accomplishments, the two men agreed on one matter—the absolute necessity of attracting civilian settlers to Texas. Rivera earlier had "pointed out how important it was to settle twenty-five families in the . . . presidio of San Antonio" in a communication to Viceroy Casafuerte. In his report of 1728 this point came up again: "I now repeat this recommendation, supporting my statement with the reason that moved me to insist upon the plan. The location being so fertile and pleasant, as I have described it, it is particularly suited for the settlement of twenty-five families, who would fully protect the land and induce others to imitate them in settling such other sites as many seem convenient."[38]

Rivera's proposal was merely the latest of many similar plans that had been advanced over the years for civil settlement in Texas.[39] And although they were accepted, it required three years to put them into effect. Casafuerte first learned of Spain's approval of the policy when at the end of 1729 he received word that families from the Canary Islands would be sent to Veracruz by way of Havana and that they were to be escorted to La Bahía, San Antonio, and Los Adaes.

The viceroy turned to Rivera for advice, and on January 16, 1730, the general submitted a long report suggesting possible settlement locations. When news came that the Canary Islanders had landed at Havana, Rivera proposed moving them to San Antonio. Casafuerte's other advisers concurred. The viceroy then asked Aguayo for suggestions concerning the exact location at San Antonio most appropriate for a municipality.[40]

Aguayo replied in a long communication accompanied by the map reproduced in Figure 3.5. For a man with Aguayo's military experience and firsthand familiarity with the area, this map is a curious piece of work. It contains many errors, and even the compass directions are incorrect since north is to the left rather than as shown on the drawing. The loop in the San Antonio River opposite Mission San Antonio de Valero is shown extending to the west rather than eastward. The *presidio* had been located by Aguayo almost directly west of the loop between the river and San Pedro Creek, and, by 1730 when Aguayo prepared this sketch from memory, Mission San José had been moved from the location shown to the other side of the river. The other principal element, identified as Villa de San Antonio de Casafuerte, represented Aguayo's proposal to locate the civil settlement on the eastern bank of the San Antonio River. When Rivera examined this map he pointed out its flaws and proposed that the new town should be located "a musket shot" west of the *presidio* on a low, flat hill that he had earlier earmarked as a desirable spot for a town.[41]

Casafuerte accepted this recommendation as well as Rivera's other suggestion, made earlier, that it would be better to people Texas with settlers from Mexico than from Spain or the Canary Islands. The viceroy accordingly wrote the king advising him to discontinue recruitment of additional families. It is difficult to understand the motives for this action. Its effect was to stop what promised to be a successful attempt at providing perhaps two thousand settlers so badly needed for the underpopulated province. Fifteen of the promised 400 additional families were detained in Cuba, and only a little group of less than 60 persons from the Canary Islands were brought from Cuba to Mexico and then escorted to San Antonio.[42]

The long march began on November 15, 1730, and it was not until March 9 of the next year that the settlers reached their destination.

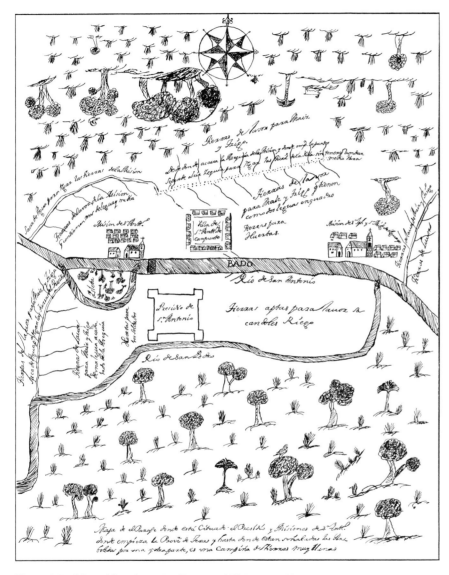

Figure 3.5 Map of San Antonio, Texas and Vicinity: 1730

Viceroy Casafuerte had issued long and highly detailed orders covering all aspects of the project, listing the supplies to be furnished the party, directing them to be given temporary lodging in the *presidio* until they could construct their own accommodations.

Most important for our inquiry were the instructions issued to the governor or, in his absence, the captain of the *presidio* for the selection of the site and planning of the town. The location west of the *presidio* recommended by Rivera was to be used. On this spot the official in charge was ordered to "survey the land, lay off the streets, the town blocks, the main plaza, and the site for the church, the priest's house, the public hall, and the other buildings shown in the map which is sent with these instructions."[43]

The map referred to appears in Figure 3.6. The instructions that it accompanied required that all land grants be made in accordance with the Laws of the Indies, and it is evident that the laws also governed most features of the proposed town plan. The orientation of the streets so that the corners of the rectangular blocks faced the cardinal points of the compass were as specified in the laws. So, too, was the dimension of the plaza, which, if the bordering streets were included, measured exactly 400 by 600 Spanish feet mentioned in the laws as appropriate for "a well proportioned medium size plaza." The plan also showed an arcade (*portales*) around the plaza as called for in the laws.

The drawing prescribed a uniform street width of 40 feet (about 37 English feet, the Spanish "pie" or foot being approximately 11.1 inches). Blocks of three different dimensions were to be used. The two largest blocks, each 320 feet square, faced the ends of the plaza. That at the northeast was intended for the church, and the one opposite for the "Royal Palace" or government building. Four smaller blocks, 240 feet square, also faced the plaza, one of which was to be occupied by the grain market. Additional blocks of this size and others 240 by 320 feet were to be laid out, and one block given to each family.

The instructions specified that the surveyor should then lay out the commons, the pasture lands, and the farm tracts. The entire unit would consist of a series of great squares. The inner square for the town itself was to have the church door as its center and to measure 2186 *varas* (about 6,000 feet) on each side (1093 *varas* in each direction from the church). The surveyor was to mark this boundary between the town and the commons with a plowed furrow "in order that willows and other trees may be planted to mark out the four sides of the area of the inner town. They will serve not only to beautify it, but as soon as they grow to the height of a man their branches will furnish shade to the

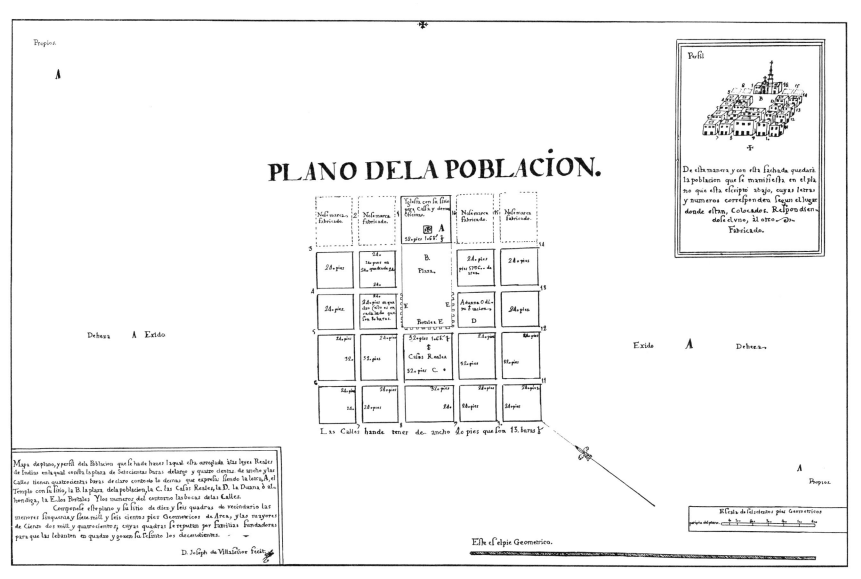

Figure 3.6   Plan of San Antonio. Texas: 1730

settlers.'' The outer boundary of the commons was to lie 1,093 *varas* beyond this point on each side. The sides of the square for the pasture lands were to be surveyed parallel to these lines 2,186 *varas* farther away, and the farm fields were to occupy the area an equal distance beyond. The entire urban-rural unit would thus have an area of just under 12 square miles, the outer boundaries being a square slightly under 3½ miles on each side.[44]

It should have been obvious to the viceroy and his advisers that, if the town lands had been surveyed in this manner, their boundaries would have encroached on the domain of Mission San Antonio de Valero as well as on the site of the *presidio*. This issue became more of a problem when Captain Juan Antonio Pérez de Almazán, the commander of the *presidio*, decided that the site designated for the town west of the fort was unsuitable because the lands could not easily be irrigated. He selected as a substitute location the land immediately to the east of the *presidio* and including the area within the eastward loop of the San Antonio River.

The common, pasture, and farm lands could not be located as prescribed in the instructions, and these outlying portions of the settlement were surveyed instead in a roughly triangular pattern with the approximately north-south alignment of the San Antonio River as the base. The specified distances between the boundaries of the town, the commons, the pastures, and the farms were increased, however, to provide the same area of land for each purpose as described in the instructions.[45]

Almazán also found it necessary to modify substantially the design of the town itself when on July 2, 1731, he assembled the settlers for this purpose. The plan sent from Mexico showed the church facing southwest from one end of the elongated plaza. The captain felt the best site for this structure was immediately to the east of the *presidio*, and therefore the plaza could not extend westward without encroaching on the fortifications. His solution was to turn the church in the other direction so that its entrance was on the east side, lay out the plaza in this direction and place the church almost adjacent to the *presidio*.

In the report describing what he accomplished Almazán stated that he laid out a plaza 200 by 133⅓ *varas* (555 by 370 feet) east of the church, two blocks facing the plaza on both it north and south sides, and three streets leading to the plaza on those two sides. The northeastern block was set aside for the *aduana* or grain market. Other blocks were then surveyed 80 *varas* or 222 feet on each side, with all the streets made 13⅓ *varas* or 37 feet wide. Opposite the church, occupying the entire block at

its western and shorter side, he provided a site for the *casa real* or government house.[46]

It is not entirely clear if Almazán used an east-west orientation or the northeast-southwest axis for the plaza prescribed by his instructions. His statement seems to indicate the latter, but this appears at variance with all subsequent maps, plans, and surveys of the town. The only detailed eighteenth-century plan of the new *villa* reveals other departures from the captain's instructions and his report of how he planned San Antonio.

This is reproduced in Figure 3.7, a manuscript map drawn about 1777. The drawing reverses conventional orientation, for north is at the bottom, and the church thus faces east to the plaza. Here the plaza appears as a square, about 80 *varas* or 222 feet on each side including the boundary streets. The streets scale approximately 10 *varas* in width, or less than 28 feet. Most of the blocks appear to be about 60 *varas* square, or 166½ feet on each side. The smaller blocks around the edges of the town are shown one-half or one-fourth this size. If this drawing is an accurate representation of the town at the time it was made, one possible explanation for these discrepancies is that major changes and adjustments to the town plan were carried out some time between 1731 and 1777. The only other possibility is that it represents a proposed replanning of the community.

Some weight is given to this latter view by the description written by Morfi, probably late in 1777, to whose manuscript *History of Texas* this map is attached: ''On the west bank of the San Antonio river . . . is situated the villa of San Fernando and the presidio of San Antonio de Béxar, with no other division between them than the parochial church. . . . The town consists of fifty-nine houses of stone and mud and seventy-nine of wood, but all poorly built, without any preconceived plan, so that the whole resembles more a poor village than a villa, capital of so pleasing a province. . . . The streets are tortuous and are filled with mud the minute it rains.''[47] Certainly this scornful description and the neat regularity of the drawing do not correspond.

A second map of the area that was eventually to become the city of San Antonio is reproduced in Figure 3.8, a general survey of the *presidio* and *villa* on the west bank of the San Antonio River opposite Mission San Antonio de Valero east of the loop in the river. It also shows the other four missions, two on each side of the river, south of the first three establishments. The parochial church can just be discerned standing in the center of what appears to be a large quadrangle. This was in reality divided into two plazas, that of the *presidio* on the lower or west-

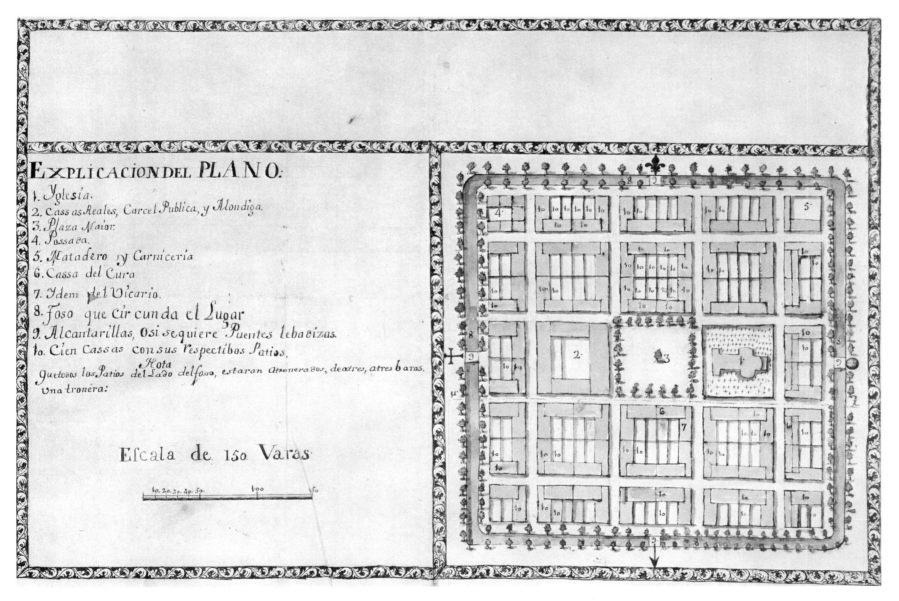

Figure 3.7 Plan of San Antonio, Texas: ca. 1777

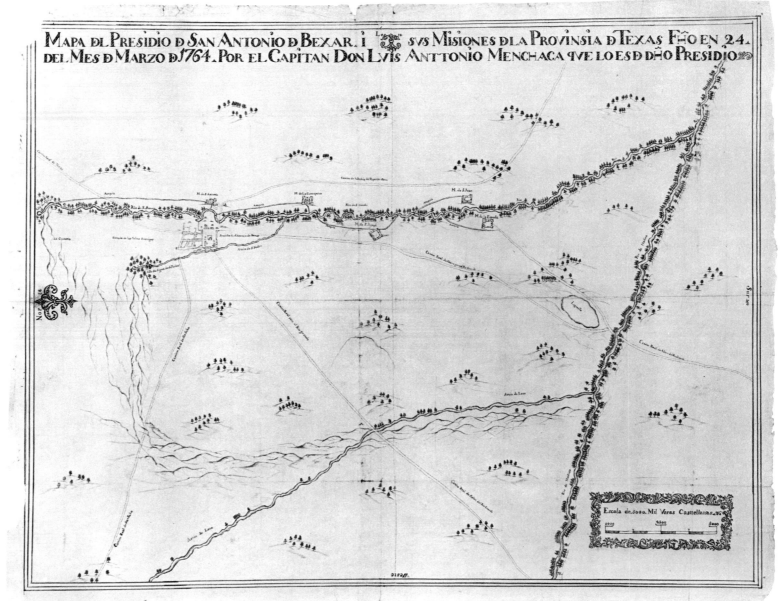

Figure 3.8
Map of
San Antonio,
Texas and
Vicinity: 1764

ern side, and that of the *villa* to the east. Most of the houses in this combined military and civil community seem to have been located to the north of the *presidio*, where structures can be seen clustered among three roughly parallel, north-south streets crossed by two others, with a third extending only halfway to the east. It seems likely that this area was occupied by married soldiers and civilians attracted to the San Antonio region rather than by the members of the fifteen Canary Island families and their descendants living on lots in the *villa* planned by Almazán.

The only other eighteenth-century map of San Antonio dates from 1767. Reproduced in Plate 4, it shows in more detail the immediate vicinity of the *presidio*, *villa*, and the oldest mission—incorrectly identified as "Mission de San Joseph" east of the river loop. While it is helpful in showing the relationship between the civil and the military settlements, this map introduces a further doubt about the details of the original town plan. The letter "D" identifies the "Plaza de la Villa," but here we see it with its longer dimension on the north-south axis! Whatever was first planned or had occurred later, however, the approximate size and shape of the two plazas shown here was to persist in future years.

Small as it was, San Antonio enjoyed the status of the most important settlement in the vast province of Texas. It was an almost empty honor, for there existed few competitors. In East Texas the *presidio* of Los Adaes and the three remaining missions of the area formed a second nucleus of settlement. The third could be found on the Guadalupe River, where the *presidio* of La Bahía and its associated mission had been relocated in 1726 from their original sites on the coast.

The bulk of the population residing in the San Antonio area was Indian. In 1740 more than 800 of them lived in the five missions.[48] Soldiers and their families, the Canary Islanders, and the Spanish missionaries could not have numbered more than 200. Population at the other settlements must have been well below this figure. Frequent defections by the Indians individually and, occasionally, in large groups reduced the population in the missions and native *pueblos* from time to time. This problem was particularly acute in the East Texas missions where few Indians could be persuaded or coerced into living under mission supervision.

A more serious Indian problem was the constant harrassment of these frontier settlements by various tribes of Apaches. In the mid-1740s the residents of San Antonio ventured out to their farm fields only in large groups. Indian raids on the mission lands to kill and steal livestock were common. Horses had been introduced to North America by the Spanish, and the Apaches soon recognized their utility as transportation for war parties that could strike swiftly and withdraw to safety. Guns provided by both the Spanish and the French made the Indians an even greater menace.[49] Punitive forays by Spanish soldiers brought temporary relief, but Indian hostility remained a constant threat.

Attempts to pacify the Indians through missionary activity in the region north of the San Antonio met with little success. On the San Xavier River (now the San Gabriel) missionaries of the College of Santa Cruz established a provisional mission in 1746. Late in the next year they succeeded in obtaining approval from the viceroy to found three missions under the protection of a detachment of soldiers: San Francisco Xavier de Horcasitas, San Ildefonso, and Nuestra Señora de la Candelaria. The missionaries also advocated the establishment of a civil settlement, but this was never approved. In 1751 the *presidio* of San Francisco Xavier was formally established in the area with a garrison of 50 soldiers. This venture proved short-lived. Indian attacks and hostilities between the missionaries and the *presidio* commander caused the abandonment of the site and a temporary relocation of mission activities to the San Marcos River in 1755. Two years later the soldiers and missionaries were withdrawn from this location as well.[50]

While the San Xavier settlements passed through their brief and bleak existence on the edge of the northern frontier, a whole series of new missions and civil settlements was being successfully planted along the valley of the lower Rio Grande under the skillful direction of José de Escandón. In 1746 Viceroy Revilla Gigedo directed him to explore the hitherto unsettled region from Tampico, Mexico, to the mouth of the San Antonio River, an area to become known as Nuevo Santander.[51] His exhaustive tour of inspection of the new colony was followed by a detailed report containing a series of recommendations.

Escandón proposed to take 500 families from the settled parts of Mexico and to settle them in 14 new towns. A number of missions would also be established. His plan called for two of these towns to be located north of the Rio Grande: the Villa de Vedoya composed of 50 families and located on the lower Nueces near what is now Corpus Christi; and the Villa de Balmaceda with 25 families on the lower San Antonio River to the site of which would be moved the *presidio* and mission of La Bahía. Shortage of funds and the hostility of Indians at the Nueces River site prevented Escandón from carrying out these proposals except for the transfer of the two La Bahía settlements. In all other respects his colonization efforts that began in December, 1748, succeeded admirably. Seven years after he had prepared the map in Figure 3.9 to accompany his report he stated that he had founded 1 city,

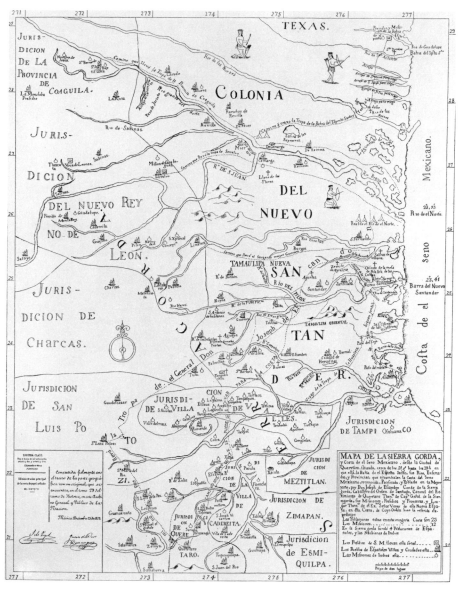

Figure 3.9 Map of the Northeastern Part of Mexico and the Adjoining Area in Texas: 1755

17 *villas*, 3 military settlements, 2 mining camps, and 15 missions.

Settlers flocked to join the expedition. Nearly 700 families and 750 soldiers moved northward in a huge column. On Christmas Day, 1748, Escandón laid out his first *villa*, Santa María de Llera, for 67 families. At suitable intervals and on favorable sites, other towns were surveyed on the march to the Rio Grande during the spring of 1749. Along the south bank of that river Escandón planned the *villas* of Reynosa and Camargo. A year later an aide planned Revilla (now Guerrero) further upstream.

The plan of Reynosa as drawn at the time of its founding is reproduced in Figure 3.10. Virtually identical designs were used for at least 14 other towns founded by Escandón or at his orders.[52] If his proposals for towns on the lower Nueces and San Antonio rivers had materialized, they doubtless would have taken this form. At Reynosa, as at most of his towns, Escandón planned a square plaza 124 *varas* (345 feet) on each side. The eight streets entering its corners were 12 *varas* (33⅓ feet) wide. Their extension to the limits of the town created blocks of two sizes. Those fronting the plaza measured 100 by 200 *varas* (278 by 556 feet). The four corner blocks were twice this size. All lots measured 20 by 100 *varas* (55½ by 278 feet).[53]

It is possible that an identical or similar plan was used in 1755 when Tomás Sánchez, after securing approval from Escandón, settled with a few families north of the Rio Grande, where he had previously pastured his cattle. Escandón designated this as the *villa* de Laredo, and later that year he reported that 13 families with a population of 62 persons were living at this location in Texas. Escandón authorized this settlement only after directing Sánchez first to examine the site on the Nueces River that he had originally proposed for a town. The Laredo grant was made after Sánchez reported the Nueces River location to be unfavorable. Although Laredo may have consisted mainly of a series of farms, it seems likely that Escandón would have insisted on some kind of town survey.

This is strongly implied in a report submitted by Tienda de Cuervo in 1757 following his tour of inspection of Nuevo Santander. In describing conditions at Laredo he used the designation of "town" or "town of Laredo" at least six times. It then consisted of 11 families with 85 persons.[54] The only graphic record of Laredo during this period is so small in scale that it is difficult to judge if the buildings in the little settlement followed some kind of formal town design. This is reproduced in Figure 3.11, a small section of an enormous map of the new province drawn in

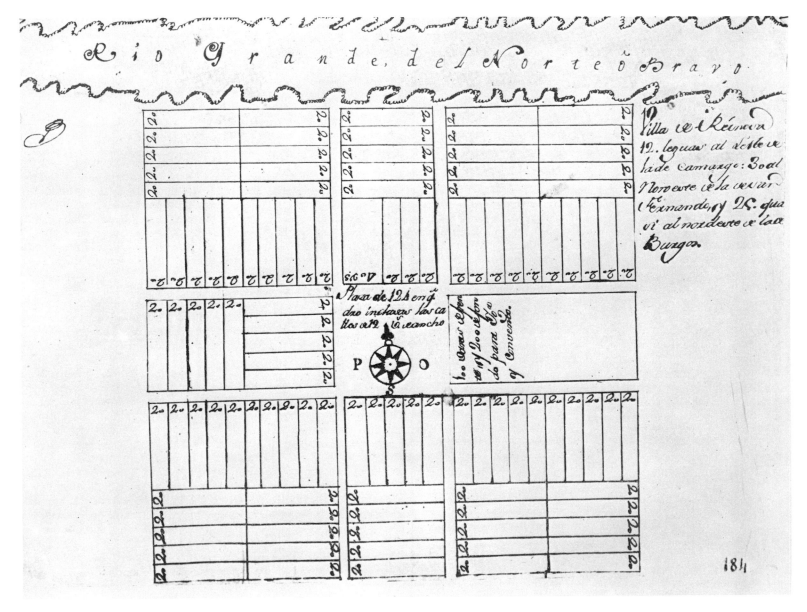

Figure 3.10 Plan of Reynosa, Tamaulipas, Mexico: 1751

1758. At the left appears a sketch of the Rancho de Dolores, ten leagues down the Rio Grande. This, too, Escandón had founded at the time he established Laredo. The drawing indicates that Dolores then had 30 houses and 111 inhabitants. Laredo consisted of only 12 houses and 84 persons, although it continued to bear the more exalted title of *pueblo*.

Laredo may have been given a more precise layout in 1767 when a royal commission arrived in the province to confirm land ownership of individual settlers who until that time held their property only under provisional title. New surveys of the towns were carried out, streets were reduced in width from 12 to 10 *varas*, and sites for public buildings facing the plaza were designated. Laredo, the first settlement visited by the commission, probably was thus surveyed either on a new plan or one that followed the street, block, and lot lines made in 1755.[55]

Escandón's original settlement program included moving the mission and *presidio* at La Bahía and combining them with a civil settlement. He was able to accomplish only the first part of this project when in 1749 he transferred the existing settlements westward to the San Antonio River near the present town of Goliad. Nearby, a second mission, Nuestra Señora del Rosario, was begun 5 years later.[56] Within a few months after the new site was selected the *presidio* consisted of a single barrack 20 feet wide and 70 feet long, a stable, 40 temporary houses for the soldiers and their families, and a more substantial structure for the captain.[57] Twelve years later it was described as being laid out in a square 76 *varas* (210 feet) on each side, stockaded on the north, and with the chapel, guardhouse, barracks, captain's quarters, and several houses nearly completing the enclosure.[58]

The only drawing of the *presidio* of La Bahía on this, its third site is reproduced in Figure 3.12, another of the valuable graphic records of Spanish colonial settlements prepared by Joseph de Urrutia in 1767. The main elements previously described can be clearly seen, and it is obvious from the number of soldiers' houses (identified with the letter "D") that the post had a substantial civil population living in or near the rectangular garrison. Slightly more than a decade later Morfi put the population at "515 persons, including all ages and both sexes and counting the members of the garrison stationed there as well."[59]

One other major Spanish colonization project in the eighteenth century began in 1757 when Colonel Diego Ortiz Parilla led a column of 61 soldiers and missionaries 130 miles northwest of San Antonio with orders to establish a *presidio* and two missions. This action culminated years of discussion about further efforts to pacify the Apaches and secure the outer frontier of Texas. On the north bank of the San Sabá River, Parilla laid out the Presidio de San Luis de las Amarillas. A few miles downstream on the south side of the river the Franciscans began construction of mission Santa Cruz de San Sabá.[60]

By the spring of 1758 more than 300 persons were living in the *presidio*, of which 237 were women and children. The mission compound, on the other hand, was nearly deserted, since the Apaches stubbornly refused to live under religious supervision in an Indian *pueblo*. In March a series of attacks—not by the Apaches but by their more warlike neighbors to the north, the Comanches—culminated in the destruction of the mission and the massacre of its inhabitants.[61]

A campaign of reprisal against the Indians led by Parilla in 1759 ended in failure. In 1762 missionary activity was transferred to the upper Nueces at a site some 85 miles south of San Sabá and about the same distance west of San Antonio where two missions were founded.[62] The San Sabá *presidio*, however, was allowed to remain, and its new commander, Felipe de Rábago y Terán, began to strengthen it on his arrival in 1760. A year later he reported to the viceroy that he had replaced the rotted stockade, built a stone blockhouse, and dug a moat around the perimeter.[63]

Rábago may have exaggerated the improvements he accomplished, for when the Marqués de Rubí visited the *presidio* in July 1767 on his long tour of inspection of the Spanish northern frontier, he found the fort poorly located and inadequately designed. In a secret message to the viceroy he stated that it was beyond a doubt the worst *presidio* he had seen.[64]

Rubí had not yet visited the Texas *presidios* of San Antonio, Los Adaes, and La Bahía, and it may be that he was totally unprepared for the rather primitive military installations on the borderlands frontier. The plan of the *presidio* of San Sabá drawn at the time of Rubí's inspection and reproduced in Figure 3.13 suggests that, whatever its faults, it was better designed to withstand attack than any of the others in Texas. The northwest corner contained the commander's quarters, chapel, and guardhouse located near the circular tower protecting the principal gate. A smaller tower rose from the southeast corner. Two outlying walls provided access to the river, and the large parade ground was completely enclosed by barracks forming the defensive wall. An elevation of the north side of the fort from the interior can be seen at the top of the drawing.[65]

Renewed Indian attacks and an epidemic in 1768 led Rábago to abandon the fort, and although it was subsequently reoccupied for a time under a new commander, by the summer of 1770 the *presidio* of San

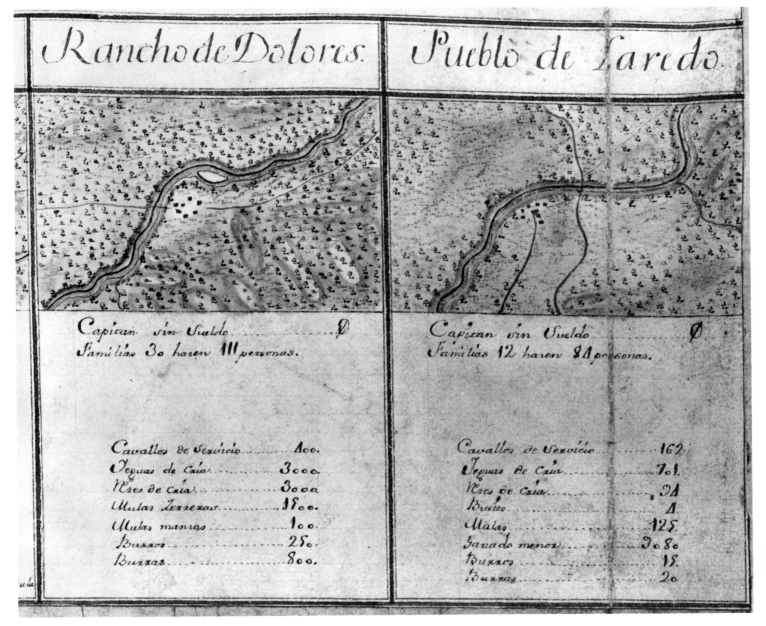

Figure 3.11
Plans of Dolores and
Laredo, Texas: 1758

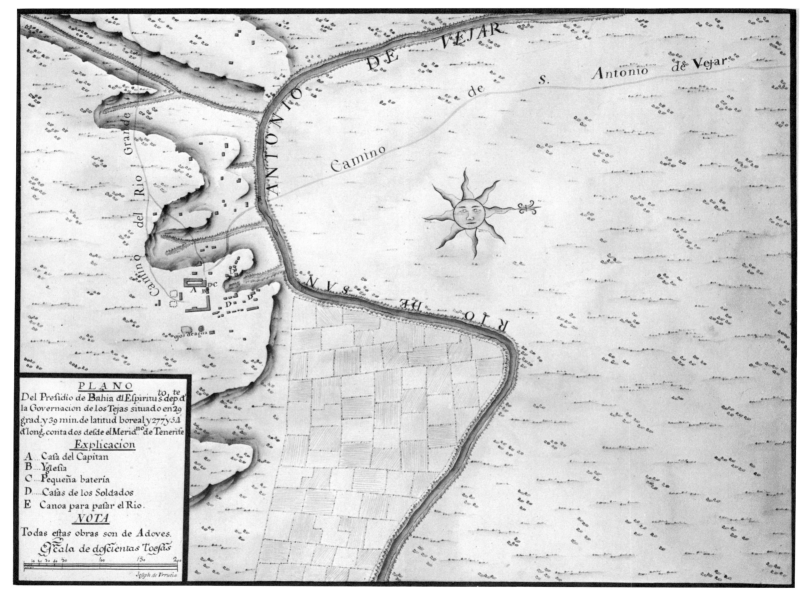

Figure 3.12 Plan of the Presidio of Bahia del Espiritu Santo near Goliad, Texas: 1767

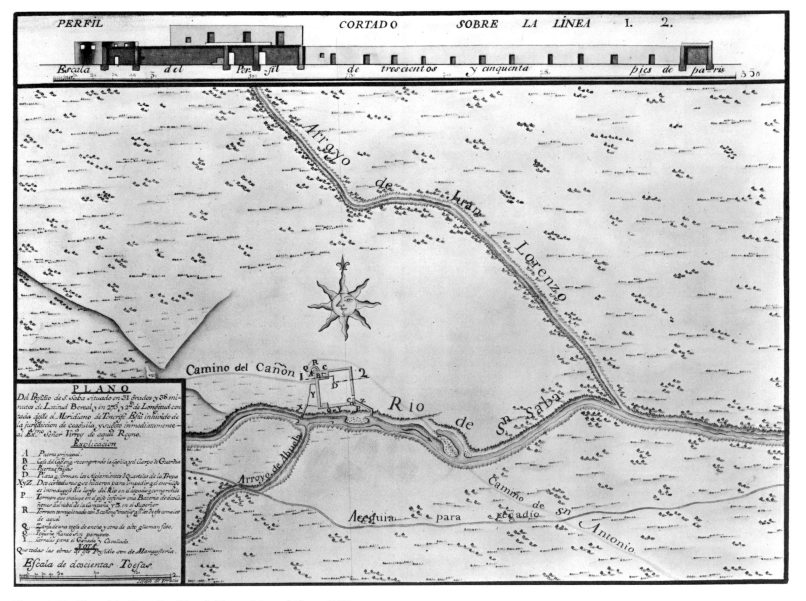

Figure 3.13 Plan of the Presidio of San Sabà near Menard, Texas: 1767

Sabá lay deserted. Visited over the years by occasional explorers and passed in 1849 by wagon trains bound for the California gold fields, the old *presidio* finally became the temporary home of pioneers moving into this part of Texas in the 1860s. After the town of Menard was platted in 1864, a mile downstream and across the river, stones quarried for the fort were hauled away and used in the construction of a courthouse, jail, and school.[66] Today the fort has been partly restored on its original foundations and stands in the Texas State San Sabá Historic Park as a mute reminder of a colonization effort that failed more than two centuries ago.[67]

The withdrawal from San Sabá marked the beginning of a general retrenchment of Spanish colonial activities in Texas and the Southwest—a period that was to witness in California the last northward thrust of a dying empire. The Marqués de Rubí concluded his tour of inspection in 1768 with a lengthy report and a series of recommendations on how the military defenses of the borderlands should be organized. In 1772 King Charles III incorporated them in his Royal Regulations for Presidios, which reduced the number of forts along the frontier and required the relocation of many others. The decree established a cordon of military posts in an east-west line from Altar, near the Gulf of California, to La Bahía. Except for this latter *presidio* the only other fort within what is now the United States was Tucson. San Antonio and Santa Fe lay well to the north of the presidial cordon. In these two places and at a few other points military posts were to be retained, but the effect of the king's decree was to signal a drastic consolidation of resources and a falling back to the Rio Grande as the real frontier of New Spain.[68]

Rubí seriously considered proposing the abandonment of San Antonio with its five missions, *villa*, and *presidio* but reluctantly concluded that too much money and effort had been expended on these settlements to justify such drastic action.[69] That is precisely what he did recommend, however, for the *presidio* of Los Adaes and the missions in East Texas. There were few logical arguments against such a move. Mission activity there had proved an almost total failure. At the time of Rubí's visit in 1767 not a single Indian was converted to Christianity or even under instruction. Only thirty Spanish families lived in the vicinity of the *presidio*, and the importance of this as a military post had been almost totally eliminated when Louisiana passed to Spanish control in 1762.[70]

The Baron de Ripperdá, governor of Texas in 1773, journeyed to Los Adaes that spring to carry out the new policy. Determined to waste no time, he ordered the evacuation of all residents within five days. On June 25 most of the angry and resentful settlers began the long march to San Antonio, where they had been promised land. Some refused to obey orders and vanished before the march began. Others dropped out on the way. Most of the defectors gathered at El Lobanillo, the ranch of Antonio Gil Ybarbo, who vigorously opposed the policy of evacuation.

At San Antonio the evacuees petitioned to be allowed to return to East Texas, and with the support of Ripperdá their case was put before the viceroy by Ybarbo. Surprisingly, Viceroy Antonio María Bucareli y Ursua granted their request, and although this was later partially rescinded, the matter was eventually left in Ripperdá's hands with the understanding that no settlement would be made within 100 leagues (250 miles) of Natchitoches, the French outpost in western Louisiana. The initial approval had included a stipulation that the settlement would be made in accordance with the Laws of the Indies, and although no plan of the settlement has apparently survived it was under these regulations that Nuestra Señora del Pilar de Bucareli temporarily joined the small number of Spanish civil communities in Texas.[71]

On the west bank of the Trinity River, where the road to Los Adaes crossed the stream, Ybarbo in the fall of 1774 staked out a plaza. Doubtless the streets and house lots were also planned at this time according to the provisions of the laws. The first chapel was replaced two years later by a more substantial church 25 *varas* (70 feet) long. A little more than a year after its founding Ripperdá reported that the town consisted of a number of huts, 20 houses of hewn timber, and a guardhouse. Two years later he found more than 50 houses in the town, and a number of farms and corrals in the vicinity. Adding to its growth were the persons who had refused to leave East Texas some years earlier and who now moved to the new and apparently permanent town. A census in 1777 revealed the population to consist of 125 men, 87 women, 128 children, and 5 slaves.

Bucareli's life proved short. Comanche raids in 1778 terrorized the settlers. Requests for an armed guard of soldiers were refused. Ybarbo, without authorization from the governor, began to move the settlers eastward toward their former homes where they proposed to settle in the area occupied by friendly Indians. A flood in February, 1779, following a disastrous fire the previous month convinced those remaining that they, too, should join their friends in yet another search for a permanent home.

Sometime in March or April, Ybarbo led his followers to the now deserted mission of Nuestra Señora de Guadalupe de los Nacogdoches near the Angelina River. Although re-settlement in this region was clearly in violation of the Royal Decree in 1772 and the subsequent orders to evacuate East Texas, this re-occupation of the region was eventually approved, and Ybarbo in October 1779 received a commission as captain of the militia and lieutenant governor of the *pueblo* of Nacogdoches.[72]

In view of Ybarbo's previous action in planning Bucareli according to the Laws of the Indies it seems likely that he also surveyed the new site in much the same manner. One of the early plats of Nacógdoches dates from a much later period—1846—and is reproduced in Figure 3.14. The "public square" probably was the plaza of 1779. Eight streets leading from its four corners provided the basis for the familiar gridiron pattern of streets, blocks, and lots where the settlers began to erect their dwellings. The large Washington Square and the site of Nacogdoches University represents a later addition to the town begun in 1845.

Four years later, in 1783, a census of Texas showed that the population of Nacogdoches had reached 349. At that time there were 1,248 persons residing at the San Antonio *presidio* and *villa*. At the *presidio* of La Bahía there were 454 persons, most of whom must have been civilians or the families of soldiers stationed at the fort.[73] When Francisco Xavïer Fragoso passed through Nacogdoches on September 23, 1788, he noted that the town consisted of 80 or 90 houses, although he placed the population at only around 250 persons.[74] By 1803 when the population of San Antonio was estimated at 2,500, Nacogdoches was said to have 770 residents. It had then outstripped La Bahía, whose population was thought to be 618.[75]

These three settlements and the surviving missions represented all that the Spanish had been able to accomplish in more than a century of colonizing activities. In the waning years of the empire new efforts were to be made, stimulated by fear of American penetration following the Louisiana Purchase in 1803. A series of proposals for new civil settlements was made by officials and advisers. Perhaps the most elaborate was put forward in 1805 by Governor Manuel Antonio Cordero, who outlined a program of founding towns according to the Laws of the Indies on the Brazos, Trinity, Colorado, San Marcos, and Guadalupe rivers to form a string of settlements along the road from San Antonio to Nacogdoches.[76]

Only two new towns were begun as a result of this proposal. The settlers for the Villa de Salcedo set out from San Antonio in December, 1805, bound for a location on the east bank of the Trinity River opposite the abandoned town of Bucareli. On January 23 the first house lot was conveyed to one José Luis Durán. The town probably was laid out according to the Laws of the Indies, for detailed instructions to this effect had been given to the settlers. The first residents were joined by others from Louisiana, and in the fall of 1809 the population was 101.[77]

News of the new community of Salcedo reached Louisiana and resulted in a flood of applications from residents for permission to settle in Texas, some of them including proposals for founding other new towns. Spanish officials viewed these requests with some suspicion, believing that opening Texas to settlement in this way would only weaken their already tenuous control over the region. Instead, Governor Cordero recruited 16 families from Nuevo Santander in December, 1807, and had them escorted to the San Marcos River, where the Villa de San Marcos de Neve was laid out. Although no plat of the town exists, this also probably followed the Laws of the Indies pattern.

San Marcos enjoyed only a brief existence. A flood in the summer of 1808 caused much destruction, the hardships of frontier life proved too much for many of the settlers, and the Indians continually raided the tiny community. In 1812 the place was abandoned.[78] Trinidad de Salcedo lasted perhaps a year longer, but by 1813 it too stood deserted.[79]

In 1810, a few years after the founding of these short-lived communities, another new town was planned on the southern border of Texas some 30 miles above Laredo. The governor of Coahuila, Antonio Cordero y Bustamente, ordered the commander of the nearest *presidio* in Mexico to establish the *villa* of Palafox on the left bank of the Rio Grande. One Manuel Garza owned the chosen site, and Juan José Díaz, commander of the Presidio del Rio Grande, found it necessary to condemn the land in order to secure proper title. Garza received another large tract in the vicinity as payment.

The plan reproduced in Figure 3.15 shows the design for the town surveyed under Díaz' direction: a square plaza 100 *varas* (277½ feet) on each side, excluding the 13-*vara* (36 feet) streets entering the plaza at each corner. It seems likely that this drawing was intended only to indicate the size and shape of the plaza and the location of the earliest buildings erected facing it, for one of the few surviving records of the town reveals that as early as 1814 there were 36 heads of households residing in the community, while an official census two years later recorded the population as 277 persons.[80]

It proved easier to settle Palafox than to maintain its existence. A series of Comanche raids in 1818 caused its abandonment for 8 years. Although many of the original settlers returned in 1826 to re-occupy the town and resume their farming and ranching activities, they once again

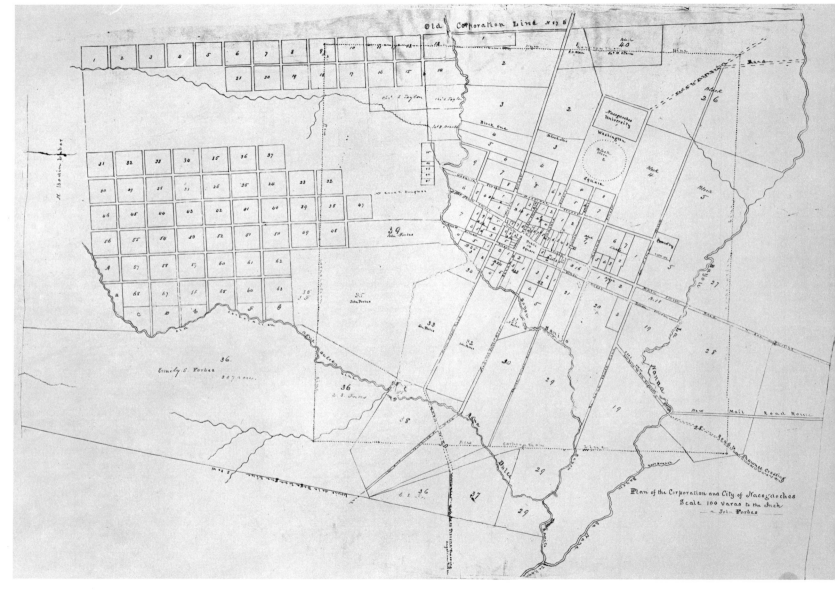

Figure 3.14 Plan of Nacogdoches, Texas: 1846

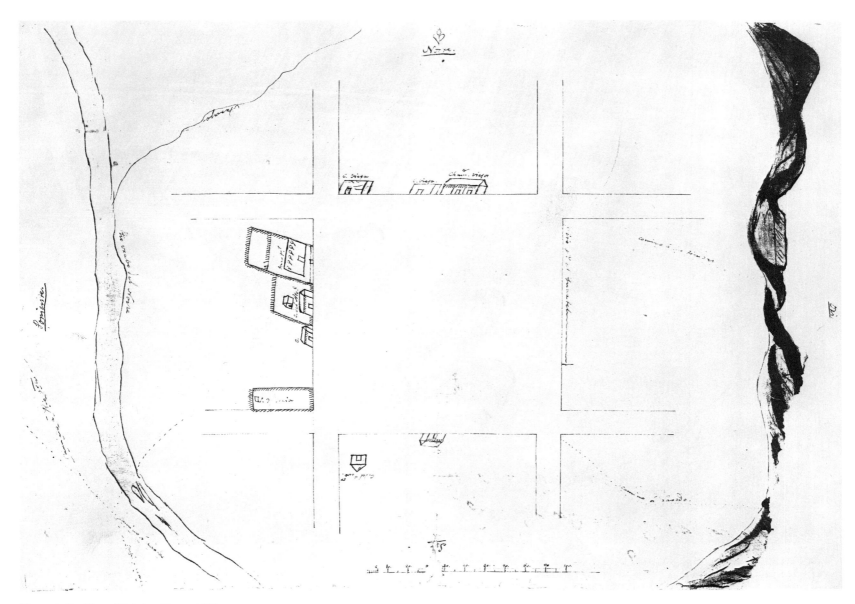

Figure 3.15 Plan of Palafox, Texas: 1824

Figure 3.16 View of Champ d'Asile, Texas: 1830

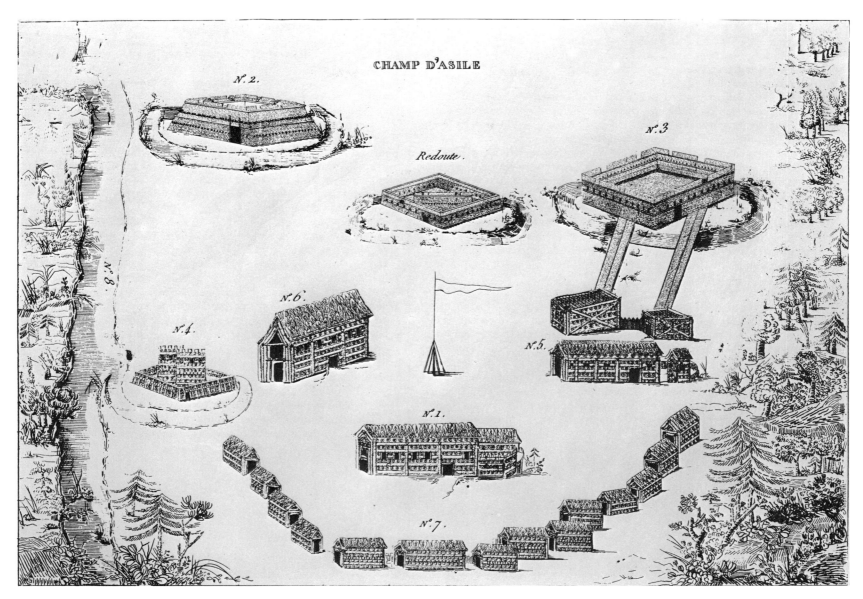

Figure 3.17 View of Champ d'Asile, Texas: 1819

found it necessary to evacuate their homes when the Indians soon renewed their attacks. Before the end of the decade the little *villa* had been sacked and destroyed, and no further attempt was made to establish an urban community in this desolate and uninviting portion of the Rio Grande valley.

One other town passed through a brief existence before the end of the Spanish period in Texas. This was Champ d'Asile or Aigleville, a bizarre community with an unusual plan and one begun under equally strange circumstances. In January, 1818, a group of French Napoleonic exiles landed on Galveston Island. There they were joined by their leader, General Charles Lallemand, who, with other former officers, led the party 50 miles up the Trinity River. The general announced that it was his purpose to found a peaceful agricultural community where all land would be held in common. It is more likely that he intended to establish some kind of military base from which exiled French officers and their families could gradually expand their holdings in territory so ineffectively controlled by the now crumbling Spanish empire. Perhaps they dreamed of an even greater future—of an empire of their own in America with a Bonaparte on its throne.[81]

It was a romantic vision; equally so is the view reproduced in Figure 3.16 purporting to show the progress of construction. In the background one can see a massive fort, one of several such structures described by a young Frenchman who participated in the project: "We constructed two earthen forts, each 640 feet around, with eight-foot parapets and twelve-foot ditches surrounded by cut logs, a square, wooden fort twenty feet on a side, and another fort which was not finished, a small wooden redoubt, another called a traverse, a third which was not completed; a covered runway, a hospital, a store, a bakery, and nineteen wooden cabins to serve as living quarters, one of which was for the commander-in-chief, etc."[82]

These buildings appear in the curious view of Champ d'Asile reproduced in Figure 3.17. It was published in France the year after the project began as an illustration in a book describing the colony. It was already out of date. The Spanish had learned of the French invasion and had begun to mobilize, food ran short at the new town, promised supplies never arrived, and by the end of the summer the entire company retired to Galveston Island.[83]

Texas did not seem to be a region in which towns and cities could thrive. Certainly Spanish colonial policy had produced little in the way of urban life. Civil settlements and presidial towns were few in number and small in size. Secularization of the missions in the latter part of the eighteenth century proved as disastrous for the Indian neophytes in Texas as it was to be in California some decades later.[84] Although some of the mission lands, such as those at La Bahía, were to be incorporated into later towns, the Texas mission system itself did not result in the creation of permanent towns for Indians as contemplated by Spanish law and practice.

It was, therefore, a largely pastoral Texas over which an independent Mexico assumed jurisdiction when that new nation began its existence in 1821. Mexican colonization policies adopted after that year changed this situation swiftly and irrevocably. In deciding to open the Texas borders to settlement from abroad the Mexican government achieved in a few years what Spain had labored unsuccessfully to accomplish for more than a century.

This decision, however, brought to Texas a predominantly English-speaking population with cultural and political backgrounds quite different from those who previously had inhabited the land. The clash of these two cultures as it affected the planning of towns will be examined in a later chapter after an exploration of Spanish and Mexican colonial planning accomplishments in Arizona and California.

IV

Expansion of the Spanish Borderlands: Urban Settlement
of Arizona and California in the Hispanic Era

THE northward thrust of Spanish colonization from Mexico took three directions. In New Mexico, north of the base of colonial empire, settlement efforts were under way by the beginning of the seventeenth century. A century later the Spanish moved eastward into Texas in response to real or fancied threats to that frontier by the French. The region to the northwest of Mexico, however, lay almost neglected until well after the middle of the eighteenth century. To the Spanish communities of this area and their later development under Mexican rule, we now turn.

Before 1751 the only Spanish settlements of this region within what is now the United States consisted of three missions on the southern edge of modern Arizona. The Jesuit missionary, Father Eusebio Francisco Kino, founded them as the northern outposts of a mission chain in what was then called Pimería Alta—the southwest corner of Arizona and the adjoining portion of the present Mexican state of Sonora.[1] Two of them, San Gabriel del Guevavi and San Cayetano del Tumacácori, occupied sites on the upper reaches of the Santa Cruz River just north of the modern Mexican border. The third, San Xavier del Bac, lay some 50 miles downstream near what was later to become the city of Tucson. By 1700 or shortly thereafter Kino's fellow Jesuits were building mission churches and compounds, attempting to convert the Pima Indians to Christianity, and introducing them to the town-like life of mission *pueblos*.[2]

Kino's death in 1711 ended further plans for expansion of mission activity in this area, and while these and other missions to the south were maintained, the Jesuits shifted much of their attention and resources to the Baja California peninsula, where a new string of missions were gradually developed.[3] It was not until after the Pima revolt of 1751 that Spanish officials authorized the establishment of a *presidio* in Arizona at a location a few miles north of Tumacácori.

The map reproduced in Figure 4.1 shows this new settlement, San Ignacio de Tubac, in 1766, 14 years after its founding. The fort itself occupied an elevation commanding the river valley below it to the east. It took the form of a rectangle enclosing the mustering ground and incorporating the headquarters of the commander, barracks for the soldiers, and storehouses.

South of the fort one can see a number of structures. Although the legend does not identify them, these houses and other buildings belonged to families of soldiers and, probably, civilian settlers who farmed the lands lying between the river and the irrigating ditch running along the base of the slope. At the time Urrutia drew this map the population of the garrison and the adjoining community numbered perhaps 500.[4] The drawing suggests that the settlements south of the fort may have consisted of a central plaza and a system of lanes or streets laid out in the traditional rectilinear patterns. So well established was this civil settlement at Tubac that it remained even after the *presidio* was moved northward in 1776 near the mission of San Xavier del Bac. Sometime later it achieved the status of a municipality with its own governing body and a large belt of surrounding land under its jurisdiction.[5]

It was from the *presidio* of Tubac that Juan Bautista de Anza set out in 1774 to open a supply route to California. Following the success of this undertaking he led a party of colonists in the fall and winter of 1775-76 to begin the settlement of San Francisco. By the time Anza arrived on his first journey to California there were already two *presidios* and five missions established, for Spain had at last mobilized some of its resources in a determined effort to secure effective control over the Pacific Coast.

Early Spanish voyages along the California coast had produced some knowledge of its geography; Sebastián Vizcaíno, for example, had landed at Monterey Bay in December, 1602, and reported that it was "the best port that could be desired, for besides being sheltered from the winds, it has many pines for masts and yards." Proceeding inland, his party found "a climate and soil like those of Castile," much game, and Indians who "appeared to be a gentle and peaceable people."[6] Earlier, Juan Rodríguez Cabrillo had commanded an expedition that sailed from Acapulco in 1542, charted San Diego Bay and mapped other parts of the California coast. Both explorers, as did others, somehow missed San Francisco Bay, the finest natural harbor on the coast. Its narrow entrance flanked by two headlands was discovered only later, after colonization had already begun along the shores of San Diego and Monterey bays.

Three remarkable men of New Spain planned and carried out the initial phase of California settlement. Two of them, José de Gálvez as *visitador* or inspector general and Viceroy Francisco de Croix, dispatched to the king early in 1768 a long proposal for the administrative reorganization of the northern borderlands and the extension of settlement into Alta California. They supported their argument by pointing out that recent Russian, Dutch, and English explorations of the Pacific Coast posed the threat that these powers might establish colonies of their own in the region.[7]

This possibility had long concerned Spain, and intelligence reports reaching the crown that Russia was planning settlements on the North American coast were already under study when the Gálvez and Croix

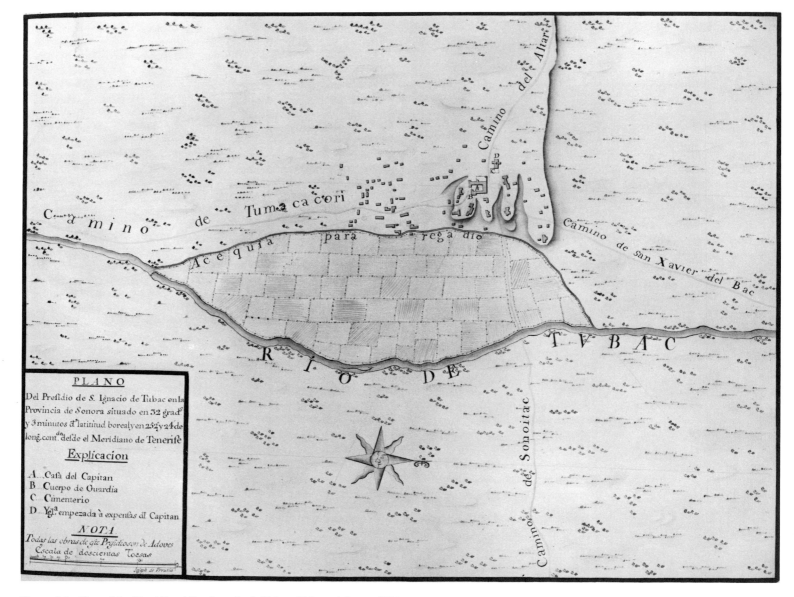

Figure 4.1 Plan of the Presidio of San Ignacio de Tubac, Tubac, Arizona: 1766

dispatch arrived. Once again Spain began a major colonization effort in a defensive move to secure its borders as it had earlier in Texas. By October, 1768, word reached the viceroy that Charles III had approved the occupation of Alta California, and later that month Gálvez conferred with the third person who was to play a major role in the settlement of California, Father Junípero Serra, the new Father-President of the Franciscans who had recently taken over the Baja California missions following the expulsion of the Jesuit Order. With Croix's full support the two men organized an expedition during the remaining months of the year.

Their immediate destination was San Diego Bay. Two ships sailed from La Paz early in 1769, while another party, including Governor Gaspar de Portolá and Serra, set out overland in March. By the end of June Portolá and Serra reached their goal only to find that scurvy and other diseases had taken a severe toll of the party that had arrived earlier by ship. Some days later on July 16 Serra raised a cross on a little hill to mark the site of the first mission, San Diego de Alcalá, and the few healthy members of the party began the construction of a *presidio*. By October this consisted of some "modest buildings, surrounded by a palisade of logs capable of being easily defended in case of need."[8]

Two days before the dedication of the mission Portolá departed with a few men to find Monterey Bay as instructed by Gálvez. He arrived at his destination in October but failed to recognize it as the splendid harbor described by Vizcaíno. Before he turned back, however, he sent Sergeant José de Ortega northward on a reconnaissance trip, and it was Ortega who first saw San Francisco Bay and reported to his commander that they had stumbled on what one member of the party described as a port so large that "not only all the navy of our most Catholic Majesty but those of all Europe could take shelter there."[9]

On their return trip to San Diego, Portolá and Father Juan Crespí erected crosses at Monterey Bay and the smaller Carmel Bay immediately to the south to mark their discoveries. The next year they returned, decided that Monterey Bay must after all be the great harbor Vizcaíno referred to, and in the summer of 1770 founded the mission and *presidio* of San Carlos Borromeo.[10] The next year Serra moved the mission site to the nearby Carmel Valley and also established two other missions—San Antonio de Padua, some 55 miles southeast of Monterey and 12 or 13 miles inland, and San Gabriel Arcángel near the modern city of Pasadena. In 1772 Serra founded the mission of San Luis Obispo a few miles inland on a site roughly halfway between the San Carlos and San Gabriel missions. Serra thus began what was eventually to become an extensive chain of mission complexes stretching

northward from San Diego to and even beyond San Francisco Bay.[11]

At the southern edge of Monterey Bay the expedition's engineer, Miguel Costansó, surveyed the outline for the royal *presidio* as shown in Figure 4.2. This took the form of a square about 225 feet on each side with protruding bastions at each corner. In the modern city this site, about a mile east of the present *presidio*, is bounded by Fremont, Abrego, Webster, and Estero Streets.[12]

During the first years of Monterey, virtually everyone lived within the stockaded walls of the *presidio* whose population included not only the governor and the military garrison but families of the soldiers and probably a number of civilian settlers as well. Two views of the *presidio* in 1792 show its central plaza and the chapel (Figure 4.3) and the much more imposing sight of the enclosure as seen looking toward Monterey Bay (Figure 4.4).

Six years later Captain George Vancouver of the English navy described the *presidio* as consisting of "a parallelogram or long square, comprehending an area of about 300 yards long by 250 yards wide," indicating that Costansó's original fort had been substantially enlarged. Vancouver noted that "the several buildings for the use of the officers, soldiers, etc., and for the protections of stores and provisions, are erected along the walls on the inside of the inclosure, which admits of but one entrance for carriages or persons on horseback; . . . this is on the side of the square fronting the church."[13]

While work was progressing on the construction of the Monterey *presidio* further explorations of San Francisco Bay were carried out. Pedro Fages and Father Crespí in 1772 and Fernando de Rivera y Moncada and Father Francisco Palóu in 1774 visited the area and reported favorably on what they observed.[14] In 1775 Viceroy Antonio María Bucareli y Ursua, who had succeeded Croix, ordered Anza to proceed from Tubac to California with a party of colonists to be settled on the shores of the bay.

In March 1776 Anza and Father Pedro Font selected the sites for the *presidio* and, some distance to the west, a mission. Font recorded his prophetic vision of the future, remarking that if the area "could be well settled like Europe there would not be anything more beautiful in all the world, for it has the best advantages for founding in it a most beautiful city, with all the conveniences desired, by land as well as by sea, with that harbor so remarkable and so spacious, in which may be established shipyards, docks, and anything that might be wished."[15]

Shortly after the middle of June Lt. José Joaquín Moraga set out from Monterey leading a party of "sixteen . . . soldiers, all married and with large families, seven colonists likewise married and with families, some

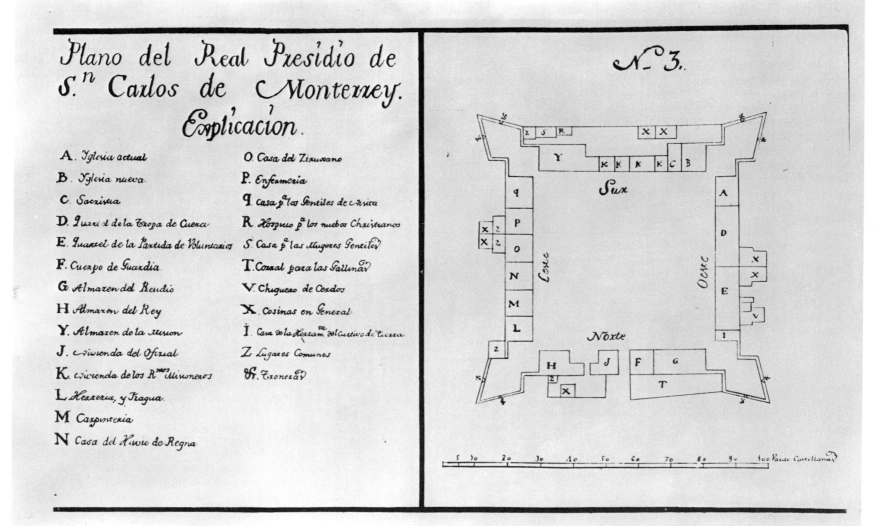

Figure 4.2   Plan of the Presidio of San Carlos de Monterey, Monterey, California: ca. 1771

Figure 4.3 View of the Presidio, Monterey, California: ca. 1792

Figure 4.4 View of the Presidio, Monterey, California: ca. 1792

workmen and servants of the foregoing, herdsmen, and muleteers driving the Presidio cattle and the pack train with provisions and utensils necessary for the journey."[16] Moraga fixed on the exact location for the *presidio* and set his group to cutting wood and constructing a chapel and a storeroom. Moraga's drawing of the *presidio* is reproduced in Figure 4.5 showing a rectangle about 310 by 333 feet with projecting bastions at two opposite corners. In the usual fashion the buildings were located around the perimeter facing a central parade ground or plaza. Those structures identified with the number "10" were designated as dwellings for the soldiers and citizens, indicating that the settlement was intended to combine both military and civil functions.

When Captain George Vancouver visited the San Francisco *presidio* in 1792 he noted that only three of the four sides had been enclosed by a wall "about fourteen feet high, and five feet in breadth . . . formed by uprights and horizontal rafters of large timber, between which dried sods and moistened earth were pressed as close and as hard as possible." The garrison then consisted of 35 soldiers "who, with their wives, families and a few Indian servants, composed the whole of the inhabitants." Most of the buildings were of wood with roofs of thatch. Vancouver found the chapel "distinguishable from the other edifices, by being whitewashed with lime made from sea-shells."[17]

Perhaps Vancouver's visit caused some uneasiness about the vulnerability of the *presidio*, for two years later the Spanish constructed a fort on a point of land commanding the narrow entrance to the bay below and to the east of the *presidio*.[18] Even with this added protection, San Francisco as a military base could have offered little more than token resistance to a determined enemy, and the early accounts of the *presidio* and fort contain frequent comments about the dilapidated conditions of both and the ease with which they might be attacked.

The view of the *presidio* in 1816, reproduced in Figure 4.6, may be a reasonably fair representation of its appearance in that year, but 11 years later one visitor who first saw it from the water referred to the *presidio* as a mere "cluster of houses which all of us took for a farm," before finally realizing that this and the fort below was all there was to Spanish San Francisco.[19]

The mission of San Francisco de Asis—later known simply as Mission Dolores—had also been dedicated in 1776 on a site several miles east of the *presidio*. Its first buildings were "all of wood with roofs of tule thatch."[20] Vancouver in 1792 found the mission buildings "more finished, better contrived [and] . . . larger" than those of the *presidio* although arranged on only two sides of what was intended to be a fully

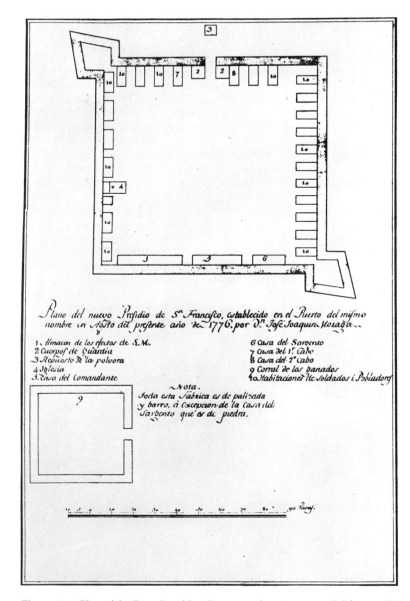

Figure 4.5   Plan of the Presidio of San Francisco, San Francisco, California: 1776

Lith. de Langlumé e de l'Abbaye N.4.

Lith. par V. Adam d'après Choris.

Vue du Presidio s.ᵗ Francisco.

Figure 4.6   View of the Presidio of San Francisco, San Francisco, California: 1816

enclosed quadrangle.[21] By 1816, however, the quadrangle had been completed with the addition of "a large church and a row of fairly large buildings, serving as store-houses and dependencies." Beyond this complex were "the dwellings of the Indians . . . laid out in regular order and cut by straight streets, made at equal distances."[22]

The Spanish founded a fourth *presidio* in 1782 when Governor Felipe de Neve and Captain José de Ortega supervised the construction of the rectangular enclosure shown in Figure 4.7 at the foot of a hill not quite a mile from the shore of the Santa Barbara channel. Its design was similar to the simple rectangle with two projecting bastions used earlier at San Francisco.[23] Slightly more than one mile northeast and inland from this settlement the mission of Santa Barbara was founded in 1786, the tenth of such establishments in California and one destined to become one of the largest and most successful.[24]

The *presidio* of Santa Barbara included, as did the others at San Diego, Monterey, and San Francisco, a substantial civilian component. Three years after its founding its population of 203 included 47 women.[25] As the population increased many of the residents moved outside the presidial enclosure to build their houses on small, palisaded plots. A. Duhaut-Cilly in 1827 noted that "around the fortress are grouped, without order, sixty to eighty" such dwellings. By that time the population probably exceeded 700.[26] The location of these buildings southeast of the *presidio* can be seen in the map of Santa Barbara and vicinity in 1853 reproduced in Figure 4.8. This also shows the site of the mission somewhat removed from the civil and military settlement, which in those early years of American rule remained little changed from its conditions under Spanish and then Mexican control.

After 1772 all of the California *presidios* were subject to new royal regulations governing the affairs of military establishments in the Interior Provinces—a new administrative unit consisting of the northern provinces of Mexico and Texas, New Mexico, Arizona, and California. A section of these regulations directed *presidio* commanders to promote civil settlement and to enlarge the military compound if necessary to accommodate population growth. Commanders were ordered "to distribute and assign lands and town lots to those that ask them," with preference to be given to soldiers completing their ten-year enlistments or retiring and to families of soldiers who had died in service.[27] While this new rule merely formalized a practice that had been followed at some of the Spanish *presidios*, it represented something of a change in policy. The theoretical difference between a *presidio* and a *pueblo* or *villa*, not always very clear in reality, thus became further narrowed. Al-

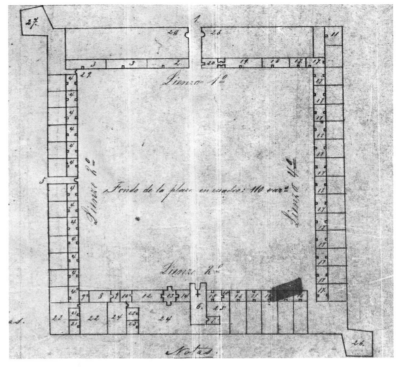

Figure 4.7 Plan of the Presidio of Santa Barbara, Santa Barbara, California: 1788

though the settlers in and near a *presidio* remained under military government, they obtained rights in land, engaged in civilian occupations, and—as we shall see—eventually gained the privileges of self-government as a civil community.

Purely civil settlements, however, were not neglected. When Bucareli appointed Neve to the governorship of California in 1774 one of the major problems he faced was the food supply of the colony. The missions then established could barely support their own population. Some crops were raised near the *presidios* at San Diego and Monterey, but they were insufficient to feed the garrisons. The land route from New Mexico was long and dangerous. Virtually all supplies arrived by

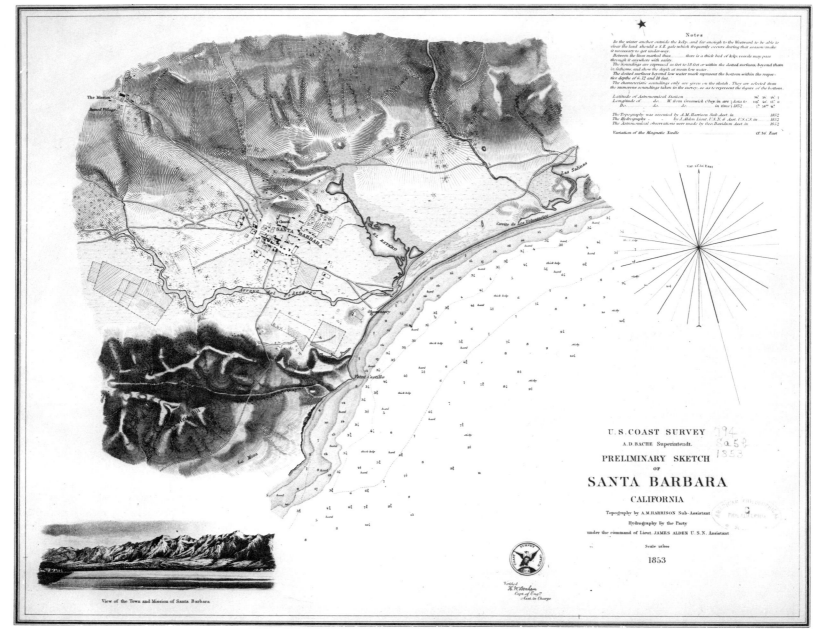

View of the Town and Mission of Santa Barbara

sea from the Mexican port of San Blas, far down the coast. The threat of starvation was very real if unfavorable winds delayed or wrecked the supply ships. Both Bucareli and Neve realized that farming communities were essential to the success of colonization. Sharing this concern was Teodoro de Croix, nephew of the former viceroy, who served as commandant general of the Interior Provinces and was Neve's direct superior.[28]

Soon after his arrival Neve began an examination of possible sites for *pueblos* that could serve as farming communities, thereby reducing the costs and uncertainties of supplying Alta California. An additional benefit would be to augment the number of Spanish settlers who could be called into militia service if needed. On his journey north to Monterey from the former capital of Loreto in Lower California, Neve in the winter of 1776-77 passed through and noted favorably the valley of the Porciúncula River halfway between San Diego and Santa Barbara. Later, on a tour of inspection from Monterey to San Francisco, he returned via the Santa Clara Valley, where he found another attractive site on the east bank of the Guadalupe River eight miles upstream from its mouth at the southern end of San Francisco Bay. All this he reported to the viceroy in June, 1777, by a letter that also requested Bucareli to furnish 40 to 60 settlers to begin a town.[29]

Without waiting for a reply to what he probably realized was an impossibly large number of civilian recruits, Governor Neve acted on his own. From the *presidios* at San Francisco and Monterey he selected nine soldiers with farming experience, recruited another five settlers, and directed Lt. José Moraga to lead them and their families—a total of 68 persons—to the site on the Guadalupe River some three miles from the new Mission Santa Clara. On November 29, 1777, Moraga designated the location for the *pueblo* of San José de Guadalupe, "marking out for them the plaza for the houses and distributing the houselots among them. He measured off for each one a piece of land for planting. . . .They also proceeded to build a dam to take the water from the Guadalupe River . . . to irrigate the fields."[30]

The drawing reproduced in Figure 4.9 shows the general design for the new community. The town proper is represented by the single, detached square at the top. The other 21 rectangles designate the bounds of the farm fields. These had to be newly surveyed a year after the town's founding because the original agricultural tracts were found to be subject to flood, as indeed were the house lots as well.[31]

Figure 4.9 was drawn by Lt. Moraga to record ownership of land in the *pueblo*, which he formally conveyed to the first settlers in September, 1783.[32] At that time he also marked (apparently rather vaguely) the boundaries of the *propios*, or lands that could be rented by the municipality, and the *ejidos*, or common lands to be used in making future grants for house lots (*solars*). This action was not popular with the padres of nearby Santa Clara mission who maintained that the *pueblo* lands encroached on their property. Serra, who had in 1773 advocated additional civil settlement in California but who now opposed the establishment of *pueblos*, sought to have Neve's action overruled in Mexico. This controversy continued for some years, long after both men had vanished from the California scene, but eventually the location and extent of the San José *pueblo* lands were sustained.[33]

Frequent floods continued to plague the town. In 1787 permission was granted to move to another location, but for some reason this was delayed until ten years later. In 1797 a new site within the four-league grant was selected slightly more than a mile south of the original settlement, and the next year a new allocation of land took place. No plan or survey of this second San José has been found, and the only detail of its design that is mentioned in the fragmentary records of that period is the fact that between the house lots there was reserved a space of 10 *varas* (28 feet) "for a division or street."[34]

The new survey included a plaza, for in 1798 an adobe town hall stood at its center at about the intersection of Post and Market Streets in the modern city.[35] If the 10-*vara* streets had originally been arranged in a rectangular grid, encroachments on the right-of-way or changes in their alignment over the years must have largely obscured any resemblance to an orderly Laws of the Indies community. One visitor in 1841 found the place "a sleepy village of perhaps one hundred and fifty inhabitants, and with no regular streets."[36] Five years later another observer, while estimating the population at "some six or eight hundred," described the streets as "irregular, every man having erected his house in a position most convenient to him."[37]

Nevertheless, San José had fulfilled the function intended by Neve. Despite floods and other difficulties, the *pueblo* farm lands in 1781 produced enough grain to meet all the needs of the *presidios* of Monterey and San Francisco.[38] The yield of crops doubtless increased in subsequent years as the population grew to 80 in 1790 and more than doubled to 165 by the turn of the century.[39]

Even before founding San José Governor Neve had begun to draft a more ambitious program for promoting settlement in California. At the request of Commandant General Croix in August, 1777, Neve prepared a series of progressively more detailed reports containing his proposals

Opposite: **Figure 4.8**   Map of Santa Barbara, California and Vicinity: 1853

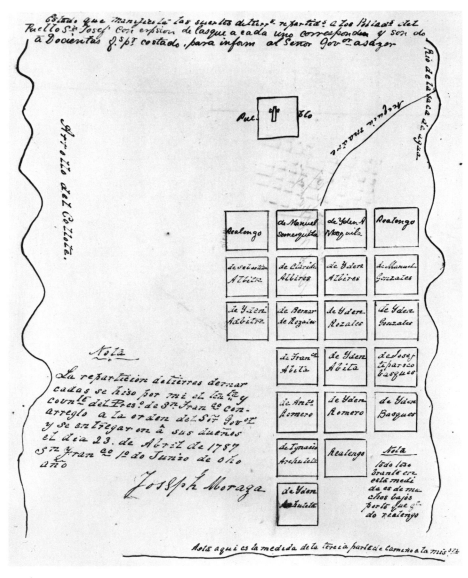

Figure 4.9 Plan of San José, California: 1787

for reorganizing the system of government. By June, 1779, Neve completed a draft of a *reglamento* for California—in effect, a constitution or organic law by which the province was to be governed and a statement of policies to be followed. Croix forwarded the document to Viceroy Martín de Mayorga for approval, and on January 1, 1781, it was put in effect. Endorsement by the crown followed in October of that year, and it was under this *reglamento* that California was to be governed through the remaining years of Spanish and then Mexican rule. Its provisions with respect to *pueblo* land grants had an even longer life, since they were recognized as binding after California came under American control.[40]

Title 14 dealt at length with the founding of new civil settlements to "encourage tilling, planting and stockraising, and in succession the other branches of industry, so that in the course of a few years their produce may suffice to supply the Post-Garrisons with victuals and horses . . . thus freeing the Royal Treasury from the forced costs which it is now under to meet these ends."[41] Neve cited the *pueblo* of San José as having already been founded for this purpose, and "the building of another is determined upon."

Each *pueblo* settler was to be paid 3½ *reales* (about $116) each year for the first two years and slightly less than half this amount annually for three more years. Rations, tools, and livestock were also to be provided each settler, with additional animals, "one Forge . . . six Crowbars, six iron Spades and the necessary tools for Carpentry and Wagonmaking" to the community in common.

The Laws of the Indies were to be followed in planning towns, with building lots and streets arranged around a *plaza* and farming tracts 200 *varas* (555 feet) square. Settlers were to be free of taxes for 5 years subject to certain obligations. They were to "build their houses as best they may, and dwell in them," construct irrigation ditches, build a granary by the third year and "the Royal Buildings within four years," breed specified numbers of livestock, keep their cattle branded, and maintain "two horses, a saddle complete, firelock and other arms" so that they might "defend their respective districts" if so ordered by the governor.[42]

Neve supplemented these general regulations with more specific directions governing the founding of the second *pueblo* in California. The governor and Croix had corresponded frequently about this matter for more than two years, a party of settlers had assembled in Loreto, and in the spring of 1781 Neve traveled south from Monterey to Mission San Gabriel to plan the town and meet the new arrivals. Sub-lieutenant José

Dario Argüello led the 11 families to the selected spot, and on September 4 the colonists were set to work at El pueblo de la Reina de los Angeles—the Town of the Queen of the Angels.[43]

The governor's instructions for how the town should be planned and the land divided had been prepared a week before. They specified that the farm tracts were to be 200 *varas* square as provided in his earlier *reglamento*. Each family was to receive four such tracts, two capable of being irrigated and two others. They were to be separated from the town lots by a tract of land 200 *varas* wide. Beyond the farming tracts *propios* (municipal land to be rented), *realengos* (land for future settlers), and common pasture and grazing lands were to be reserved as called for by the Laws of the Indies. Settlers were to draw lots to determine which tracts they were to receive. The pattern of these farm fields and their location with respect to the *pueblo* are shown in Figure 4.10 as drawn in 1786. The four rectangles indicated as measuring 100 by 300 *varas* were not mentioned in the instructions, and their use is a matter of conjecture.

For the design of the town Neve specified that the plaza was to measure 75 by 100 *varas* (208 by 277 feet). He followed the provisions of the Laws of the Indies exactly in requiring that "from said plaza four main streets shall extend, two on each side; and besides these, two other streets shall run by each corner." The orientation of the plaza and the *pueblo* was also to follow the prescriptions of the Laws: "The four corners [of the plaza] shall look towards the four cardinal points, for the reason that said streets being prolonged in this manner . . . shall not be exposed to the four winds, which would be a great inconvenience."

Town building lots were to be 20 by 40 *varas* (55½ by 110 feet), and as many of these were to be marked out as there were farm tracts capable of being irrigated. Strangely omitted were any specifications for street widths. The only other detail in Neve's instructions dealt with sites for public buildings: "The front of the Plaza looking towards the East shall be reserved to erect at the proper time the Church and Government Buildings and other public offices." The remaining lots on the plaza were to "be allotted to settlers."[44]

The earliest plat showing Los Angeles as laid out in general conformity to these instructions appears in Figure 4.11. José Argüello used two scales when he prepared this drawing in 1793. The *suertes*, now neatly arranged in a grid four parcels wide by nine long, are drawn only one-eighth of their actual size compared to the town itself at the upper left. That portion of the drawing indicates that, while most of Neve's specifications had been followed, some variations had been introduced.

The streets marked "o" at the northeastern end of the plaza enter, not at the corners, but about 10 *varas* (28 feet) toward the main streets located at the middle of the three sides of the plaza then enclosed by building lots. The corresponding streets at the southwestern corner of the plaza had been omitted where smaller lots had been assigned for various public buildings. The vacant spot beyond to the south was doubtless intended as the location for the church. Possibly other streets had been surveyed or staked out to form a gridiron pattern outside of the area depicted, for three years earlier a census of the settlement revealed that it then consisted of 39 households with a population of 141, and other fragmentary accounts of that period refer to houses on streets other than those fronting the plaza.[45]

The plan of the town underwent a major change in 1818. Four years before, the foundations of a church had been constructed to front on the plaza. In 1815 flood waters reached the site, and it was decided to move the church to higher ground a short distance to the south. Here, on its present site, the parish church was finally constructed, and a new plaza was created in front of it, replacing the original civic square. This project took many years. New lots were granted over the years, one house in the middle of the plaza had to be removed in 1825, and in 1838 the council was forced to order the demolition of another structure that encroached on one of its sides. The plaza thus gradually took its present slightly irregular form: 134 *varas* (378 feet) on the north, south, and west, and only 112 *varas* (308 feet) along its eastern side.[46]

During the nineteenth century Los Angeles continued to grow and change. By 1810 the population approached 400, and in 1827 when A. Duhaut-Cilly visited the town he "counted eighty-two houses composing the Pueblo" and estimated the population at "one thousand inhabitants, including in this number two hundred Indians, servants or laborers."[47] In 1835 Los Angeles succeeded in becoming the capital of California. Although it enjoyed this status for only a year before Monterey recaptured its position, Los Angeles enjoyed a temporary land boom. The area under municipal ownership and control was vast; the territorial legislature in 1834 had fixed the boundaries at "two leagues to each of the four winds, measuring from the center of the plaza." Instead of the normal four square leagues of a Spanish or Mexican *pueblo*, this action extended the municipal domain to 16 square leagues, or over 100 square miles.[48]

Land ownership records were fragmentary and conflicting. No map of the town existed, and the *ayuntamiento*, or council, could find no one able to prepare an accurate survey. Two street commissions appointed

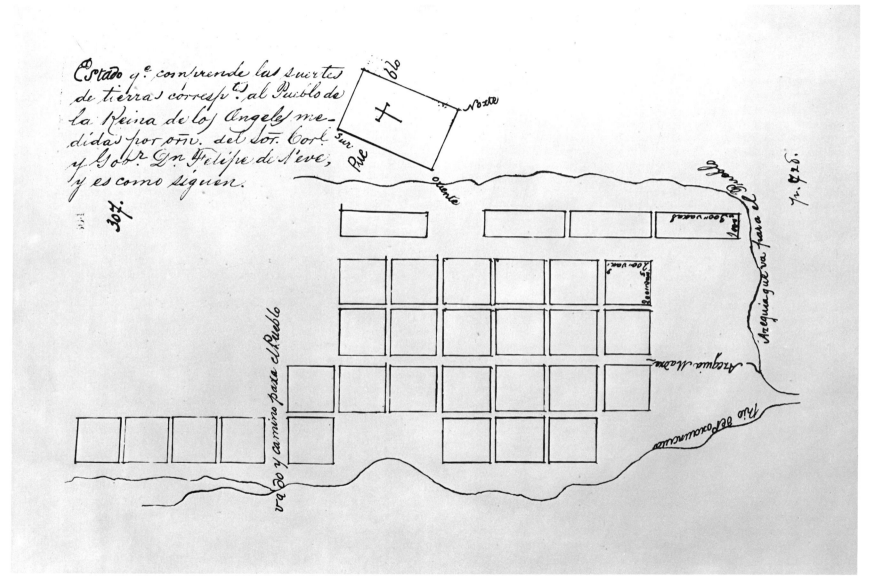

Figure 4.10 Plan of Los Angeles, California: 1786

in 1836 "to report a plan for repairing the monstrous irregularity of the streets brought about by ceding house lots and erecting houses in this city" had to abandon their work because of the inadequacy of records and surveys.[49] An attempt to widen all streets to 15 *varas* (41½ feet) failed because the *syndic* (city attorney), noting that the Laws of the Indies specified that in warm climates the streets should be narrow, ruled "the instructions given the Syndic are absolutely opposed to this law and are prejudicial to the aspect of the town."[50]

In 1845, two years before Los Angeles was finally occupied by American forces, the *ayuntamiento* made another attempt to bring order to the town. A series of ordinances prescribed that houses were to be whitewashed and shingled, buildings on the main streets that remained incomplete were to be finished on penalty of fine or confiscation, lots occupied only by ruined walls were to be improved within two months, and revenues from fines were to be applied to improving conditions in the city and making it more attractive.[51]

William Rich Hutton depicted Los Angeles at the end of its Spanish and Mexican era in the two drawings reproduced as Figures 4.12 and 4.13 when he visited the town in the summer of 1847. Six months earlier Edwin Bryant described the community in these unflattering words: "Its streets are laid out without any regard to regularity. The buildings are generally constructed of adobes one and two stories high, with flat roofs. The public buildings are a church, quartel, [barracks] and government house. Some of the dwelling-houses are framed, and large. Few of them interiorly or exteriorly, have any pretensions to architectural taste, finish, or convenience of plan or arrangement."[52]

Aside from the church fronting the new plaza the most prominent building Hutton sketched was the two-story residence of Don José Antonio Carillo. This occupied a large site at the northwest corner of the plaza. Leading past it to the southwest (to the right on Figure 4.13) one can see the *Calle principal*, soon to be renamed Main Street. Roughly parallel to it ran the *Calle de la Zanja*, or Canal Street, later to be given the name of Los Angeles Street. The city's growth toward the southwest—begun with the abandonment of the first plaza—was to continue in this direction as businesses followed the Main Street axis. This development and the subsequent planning and growth of the city will be traced in a later chapter.[53]

Spain made one other attempt to create a civil settlement in California. A controversy with England in the 1780s over Nootka Sound on the British Columbia coast resulted in a treaty by which Spain yielded its claim to exclusive sovereignty of the northwest coast. British ships

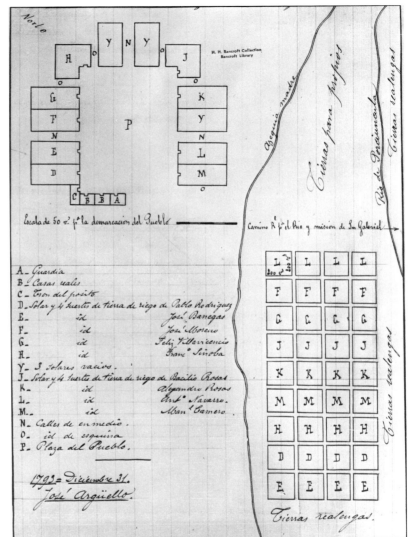

Figure 4.11 Plan of Los Angeles, California: 1793

Part of Los Angeles.

Figure 4.12 View of Los Angeles, California: 1847

Figure 4.13 View of Los Angeles, California: 1847

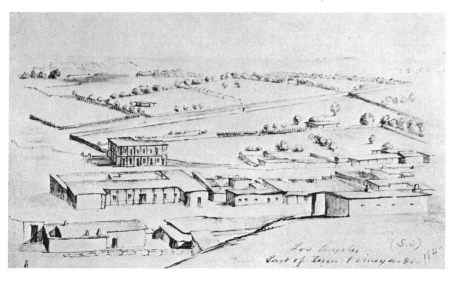

engaged in the sea otter fur trade made their appearance along the California coast, and there were continuing reports that Russia had plans to establish bases in the area. Captain Vancouver's visits to the Spanish settlements in California provided ample opportunity for Spain's old enemy to learn how undermanned and ill-equipped were the *presidios* that offered the only protection against possible foreign incursions.[54]

An expedition to occupy Bodega Bay north of San Francisco in 1793 withdrew after it was found the harbor was not satisfactory. As a partial substitute and as a measure to increase the population of California, the Marqués de Branciforte, Viceroy of New Spain, determined to found a fortified civil settlement at the north end of Monterey Bay. Its special status was indicated by the title of *villa*, and it was to bear the name of the viceroy himself.

Governor Diego de Borica and Engineer Alberto de Córdoba selected the site in 1796, and Córdoba prepared the plan reproduced in Figure 4.14. His design provided a great plaza 190 *varas* (527 feet) square with two 10-*vara* (28 feet) streets leading from each of its four corners. House lots 16 by 28 *varas* (44½ by 77¾ feet) were to face the plaza and four of the streets. Because Córdoba's design showed only the site for a church and omitted locations for government buildings and a town hall, Branciforte rejected this proposal.[55]

What changes were made in the town's design are not known, for no other plat or survey exists showing its details. In the spring of 1797 work was under way, presumably following a revised layout, and by August Córdoba could report that he had completed his surveys of the site and that several houses had been built.[56] Unlike other civil settlements, the houses for the settlers at Branciforte were constructed at government expense. The viceroy ordered them to be "houses of adobe, roofed with tile, and with shuttered windows . . . not to exceed 200 pesos."[57]

The location of the new town can be seen on Figure 4.15, which also shows the sites of Monterey and Mission Carmel. Branciforte's founding so close to the previously established Mission of Santa Cruz provoked an immediate protest from mission authorities, who cited various provisions of the Laws of the Indies in support of their case.[58] Three years later the matter was resolved in favor of the town, but in the meantime work was brought to a virtual standstill. In 1803 the town contained only 25 houses with a population of just over 100. The best agricultural lands remained under the control of the mission, government funds for building houses could not be found, and the settlers began to drift away to other and more attractive locations.

With the secularization of the mission in 1834 the two settlements were legally joined under the name Pueblo de Figueroa, but this was soon replaced with the more familiar Santa Cruz. By the mid-1840s the development of lumbering as the chief commercial activity in the area attracted many settlers, and at the end of the Mexican era its population was nearly 500. Most of them lived in the lower land along the cove west of the old *villa* or on the former mission lands. The lands originally surveyed for what was intended as the major civil community in Spanish California lay largely abandoned.[59]

Elsewhere in California the secularization of the missions with the expectation that each would become a civil *pueblo* produced mixed results. Governor Neve had insisted during his administration that the Indians of each mission should elect officials, but it is clear that this practice was merely symbolic and all real authority over the mission and its activities remained with the padres. Serra bitterly opposed this policy, nevertheless, and his successors over the years consistently fought every proposal or order that might give the Indians any degree of self-government.[60]

Several officials advanced various suggestions over the years aimed at changing the status of the Indian neophytes. Governor Pablo Vicente de Sola advocated organizing two new towns for the Indians or distributing them among the existing civil or military settlements.[61] An 1831 decree by Governor José María de Echeandía provided for the Indians of each mission to receive one or more farm tracts and a house lot, the latter to be laid out four to a block and so arranged as to create "beautiful and capacious streets and plazas."[62]

Following the suspension of this order a new governor, José Figueroa, instituted a different policy in 1833. His first plan was to create a new Indian *pueblo* somewhere on the coast and move to it those natives who seemed ready for an independent existence but placing them under the political jurisdiction of the nearest municipality.[63] On further reflection he decided to have lands surveyed at or near the mission buildings and convey them to the Indians. It was this system that was followed during the next few years, but very little seems to be known about the patterns of house lots, streets, and other elements of community design that were used.

Towns of some kind were developed near the missions of San Diego, San Luis Rey, Dolores, San Juan Capistrano, San Luis Obispo, and perhaps at others. San Luis Obispo seems to have been the most successful. At least it survived as a recognized community until the American occupation, when it was newly surveyed and entered a new era of existence. On the other hand, at San Luis Rey the new Indian pueblo of

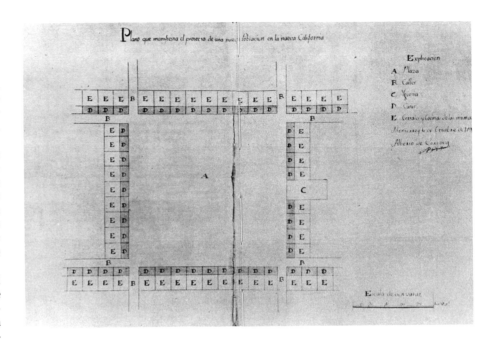

Figure 4.14 Plan of Branciforte, California: 1796

Las Flores had a short life. Pio Pico, a former governor, secured a grant of land there and increased his holdings by fraudulent methods until he gained almost complete control over the Indian village, which he proceeded to convert into a dependency of his *rancho*. Educated Spaniards and Mexicans systematically dispossessed the Indians of their newly acquired lands, and what may have been left of their holdings by 1846 soon fell to the equally land-hungry Yankees pouring into California.

One town—the only true civil settlement founded under Mexican rule—did grow up adjacent to a mission. This was Sonoma, founded in 1835. The town and the mission it incorporated within its boundaries, San Francisco Solano, dating from 1823, both represented a reaction to a foreign presence on California soil. For years the Spanish had worried about Russia; after 1812 they had good reason. In that year some 60 miles north of the Golden Gate the Russian American Company began the construction of Fort Ross, shown in Figure 4.16 as it appeared 16 years later. It took the form of a rectangle 300 by 280 feet surrounded by

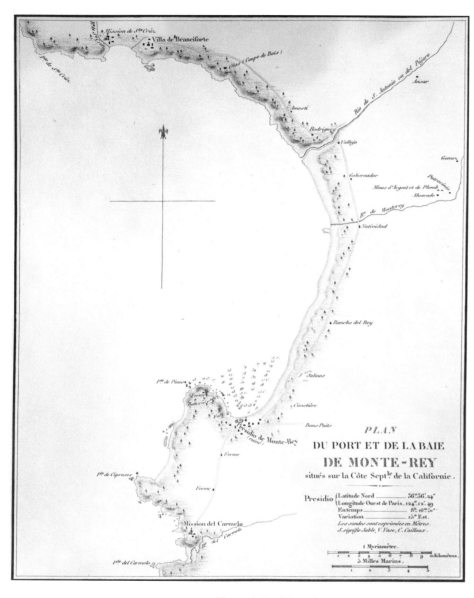

Figure 4.15 Map of Monterey Bay, California: 1844

a 12-foot-high stockade with two octagonal bastions at opposite corners. A visitor in 1836 found inside the fort a "chapel, commandant's house, office, warehouse, barracks, and some dwellings for distinguished guests." The population at that time consisted of "one hundred and fifty-four males and one hundred and six females and in all two hundred and sixty persons, of which one hundred and twenty are Russians, fifty-one creoles, fifty Kodiak Aleuts and thirty-nine baptized Indians."[64] Outside the walls was a series of buildings housing a blacksmith shop, tannery, barrel shop, bakery, carpentry shop, flour mill, and a variety of agricultural structures.[65]

Although the Russians proved friendly, their fortified settlement, at least as strong and probably better organized than any of the Spanish *presidios*, posed a threat if not of military action than at least to territorial claims north of San Francisco Bay. The first response by Spain was to plant the mission of San Rafael Arcángel near the bay's northern point in 1817. The founding of Mission San Francisco Solano in 1823 indicated that Mexican officials recognized the potential challenge by the Russians. Orders to establish a *presidio* in 1827 and attempts in 1834 to settle at what is now Sonoma and Santa Rosa failed to achieve results, but the following year Governor Figueroa directed Mariano G. Vallejo to lay out a town and bring settlers to the Sonoma Valley.[66]

Vallejo's plan for the *pueblo* of Sonoma as resurveyed and possibly extended in 1850 appears in Figure 4.17. Four decades after the event Vallejo described his work: "I undertook the task of planning the new town, tracing first a great plaza of two hundred and twelve *varas* [688 feet] square, leaving the small building which had been constructed as a church on the east side of the plaza; I built a barracks about one hundred *varas* [277½ feet] to the west of the church, and then traced the streets and divided the houselots as prescribed by the law."[67]

If Vallejo was referring to the Laws of the Indies, he was incorrect, for not only did he plan a square rather than an oblong plaza but he provided only one street leading to the midpoint of the south side of the plaza rather than the four such thoroughfares specified by the laws. It was nonetheless a notable achievement, marking the first time that in California a complete town, rather than a mere plaza surrounded by building lots, had been planned generally following the pattern prescribed by the Laws of the Indies.

Very little is known of the initial period of town growth, but the water color view reproduced in Figure 4.18 shows the Sonoma plaza in July, 1846, or shortly thereafter. The tower in the center was part of Vallejo's house, which stood just west of the army barracks. From its win-

Figure 4.16 View of Fort Ross, California: 1828

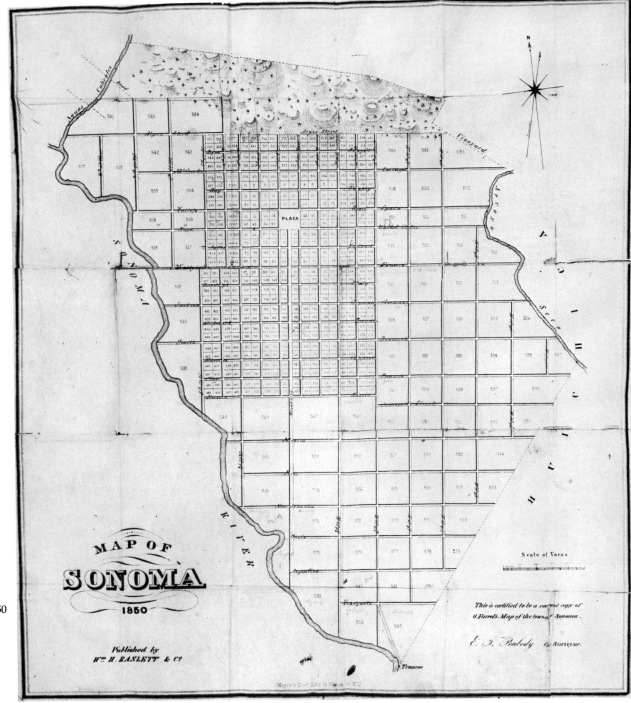

Figure 4.17   Plan of Sonoma, California: 1850

Figure 4.18 View of Sonoma, California: 1846

dows Vallejo could look down the broad street leading southward from the axis of the plaza toward San Pablo Bay. The mission church stood just off the northeast corner of the plaza at the intersection of the two streets entering it at that point. If the view is accurate, the other sides of the plaza were almost completely built up, giving at least the central portion of the town an impressive appearance.

Whether or not Vallejo followed the Laws of the Indies in reserving sites for public buildings is uncertain. In the pleasant, modern community that Sonoma has become, the city hall and courthouse occupy the center of the plaza, the result of an unfortunate decision made in the early years of the present century. While this has destroyed much of the original character of Vallejo's great open square, the restored mission and army barracks and a number of other buildings of the Mexican and early American period still stand as memorials to the last settlement founded in California under the ancient Laws of the Indies and to the distinguished citizen of the two republics who was responsible for their implementation.

The most important towns in Spanish and Mexican California were neither the secularized mission settlements nor the municipalities founded as civil communities. Instead, the *presidios*—especially Monterey—held this position. We have already mentioned briefly how development occurred in the vicinity of the *presidio* of Santa Barbara. The growth of the three other presidial towns is somewhat better documented.

The Royal Regulations of 1772 governing *presidio* administration in the Spanish borderlands authorized land grants to soldiers near the military posts. Twenty years later Governor José de Arrillaga issued a similar order to the California presidial commanders. This specified that all such grants should be located within an area around the fort defined as extending 2 leagues from the plaza, measured north, south, east, and west.[68]

While some land grants of this type were doubtless made in the eighteenth century, it was in the 1820s that significant expansion took place beyond the old *presidio* walls. José Bandini observed in 1828 that the *presidios* were no longer needed for protection against the Indians and recommended that they be demolished because "the cramped living quarters" they provided "can only discommode" their residents. He noted that "outside the presidios, private individuals have constructed adequate houses, and as more building of this kind may be seen every day it is certain that substantial towns will soon appear in California."[69]

At San Diego this process was under way by 1823 when Duhaut-Cilly found that below the *presidio* hill "on a sandy plain, are scattered thirty to forty houses of poor appearance, and some badly cultivated gardens."[70] Growth of this incipient town may have been stimulated during the years from 1825 to 1831 when Governor José María de Echeandía lived in San Diego although Monterey remained the official capital.

The population of San Diego at that time, as at other coastal settlements, included a number of Americans who had come to California to trade and had remained as settlers. One such foreigner was William Heath Davis who stated later that in 1831 "what is now called Old Town [San Diego] was at that date laid out, but it was not built for some time thereafter."[71]

The transition of the military post to the status of a *pueblo* took place in 1834 when Governor Figueroa authorized the election of a municipal council or *ayuntamiento*.[72] A few months later when Richard Henry Dana saw San Diego, he looked out from the "old ruinous presidio" to "the small settlement . . . directly below the fort, composed of about forty dark brown-looking huts, or houses, and three or four larger ones white-washed."[73]

What he observed must have been similar to the somewhat later view from the same vantage point reproduced in Figure 4.19.[74] Whether as the result of an informal agreement by the landowners or in conformity to an official survey of some kind (perhaps in 1831 as Davis states), the houses had been grouped around a rectangular plaza, and there is a suggestion of additional streets that provided a measure of order in the growing settlement.

Monterey passed through much the same process, although the results were somewhat more impressive. There, too, the *presidio* was allowed to deteriorate, was partially rebuilt, then abandoned altogether. West of the military post, however, a larger but more loosely organized community began to develop. In March of 1827, when the population was approaching 500, Duhaut-Cilly described the appearance of the community as seen from the bay: "To the right of the Presidio, on a little green field, are then seen, scattered here and there, about forty quite agreeably appearing houses, also roofed with tiles and painted white on the outside. These, with as many thatched huts, compose the whole of the capital of Upper California."[75]

By that time the town had achieved municipal or *pueblo* status, and a series of ordinances passed in 1828 and 1833 indicates concern over public order and sanitation.[76] Although the council may have concerned itself as well with regulations governing street planning, Dana

Figure 4.19 View of San Diego, California: ca. 1857

saw little evidence of such efforts. He thought the town made "a very pretty appearance" with its houses of "white-washed adobe" and roofs of red tiles, but the dwellings "about a hundred in number" apparently were casually located, being "dotted about, here and there, irregularly." He further noted that "there are in this place, and in every other town which I saw in California, no streets nor fences . . . so that the houses are placed at random upon the green." Other visitors in the 1830s recorded almost identical impressions.[77]

By 1842, when the view reproduced in Figure 4.20 was drawn, Monterey had assumed a more orderly pattern. This may have come about through some municipal effort or partly as the result of further growth and in-filling of lots that had previously been vacant. A young French visitor in the previous year described the town as "composed today of two parallel streets and of several groups of houses dispersed on the plain. . . . All the houses have their main facade turned towards the south-east in order to avoid the damages of the north-west wind which blows for half the year. Seen from the sea, the situation of Monterey is truly admirable; there is no position more picturesque and more favorable for the establishment of a great city."[78]

At the left one can see the church, formerly the chapel of the *presidio*, which was then in ruins and replaced by the fort on the hill at the far right. The Calle Principal led inland from the customhouse at the waterfront and was lined on its west side by a row of houses and commercial buildings. Other streets were less well defined.

Figure 4.21 shows Monterey in the same year but looking to the bay with the main street at the left. The most imposing building, a two-story structure facing the adobe garden walls on the opposite site, belonged to Thomas O. Larkin, the American consul and one of the many foreign residents of the town. There is no suggestion of a plaza in either of these views, and the first comprehensive attempt to plan a street system was not to occur until after the American occupation of California.

One other settlement originated toward the end of the Mexican era—a community that soon was to eclipse in size and importance all the others that had been founded by Spanish and Mexican authorities. It began as an off-shoot of the San Francisco *presidio*, which in 1834 was reorganized as a municipality. The boundaries of the new *pueblo* included the shoreline of the San Francisco peninsula and Yerba Buena cove at the foot of what is now Clay Street in the modern city. For some years ships engaged in the hide and tallow trade had anchored here. William Richardson, an English sailor who had settled in California in 1822 and married the daughter of a Mexican officer, had sought several

times to obtain land at the cove for his warehouse. In the spring of 1835 Richardson presented his proposal to Governor Figueroa, who asked "if there was any spot sufficient to lay off a small village or town."[79] Richardson prepared a map of the area, obtained a tract of land 100 *varas* (278 feet) square, and in September surveyed for the governor a single street in front of his lot as the Calle de Fundación. This ran approximately north and south, about on the alignment of the present Grant Avenue, and was intended as the base line for future streets that could be laid out as needed. Richardson's survey as redrawn a few years later is reproduced in Figure 4.22.[80]

One month after Richardson planned his street, Francisco de Haro, the first *alcalde* or mayor of the San Francisco *pueblo* of which the nascent Yerba Buena was a part, laid out a second thoroughfare. For some reason he planned this so it diverged at an acute angle from the first street at a point in front of Richardson's lot. On this peculiar pattern the village began to develop, and by 1838 five merchants and possibly a few other persons had built houses and stores on the slope overlooking the cove.

A year later Governor Juan B. Alvarado ordered the remapping and enlargement of the town to accommodate others who wished to settle there. A Swiss sailor, tavernkeeper, and surveyor, Jean Jacques Vioget, then prepared the plan reproduced in Figure 4.23 incorporating the two existing streets and adding the rectangular blocks between them and the waterfront. For some reason, possibly to fit the new streets to existing structures, Vioget laid out the streets and blocks at slight angles. His own lot was at the intersection of what later were to be named Clay and Kearny Streets. Diagonally across from this, Vioget provided a 50-by-50 *vara* (139 by 139 feet) open square or plaza. Later this was to be enlarged by the addition of adjacent lots to become Portsmouth Square.

It was apparently the Vioget survey or a copy of it that saloonkeeper Robert T. Ridley displayed in his bar and billiard parlor. One resident of the time recalled that "all persons wishing to purchase lots would apply to Ridley." He added to the map "the names of those who had lots granted." Soon it became "so soiled and torn from the rough usuage it received, that Captain Hinckley volunteered to make a new one." Hinckley was no draftsman, for "being very nervous he could not succeed in making the lines straight." John Henry Brown finally made a suitable copy, whereupon "the original map was put away for safe keeping," presumably at the old *presidio* with other public records.[81]

This easy and informal system of keeping land records in Yerba

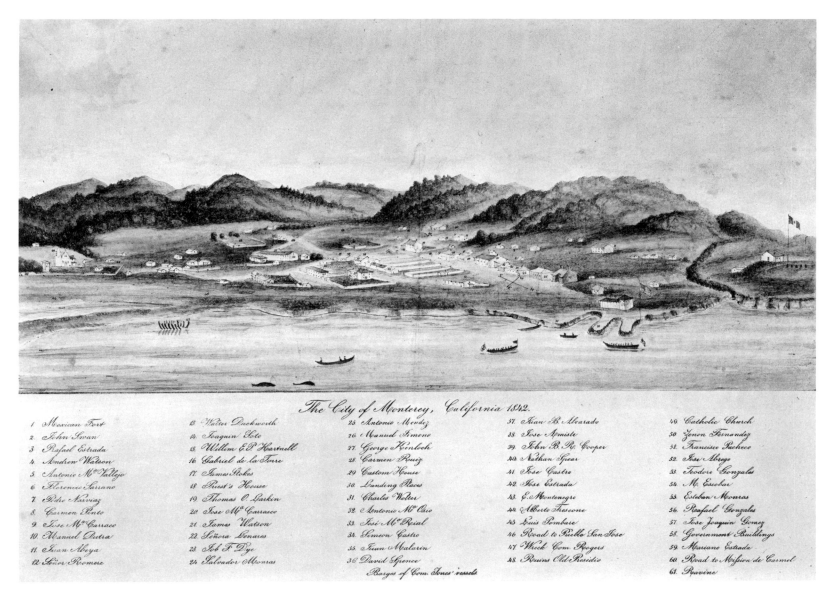

The City of Monterey, California 1842.

1. Mexican Fort
2. John Swan
3. Rafael Estrada
4. Andrew Watson
5. Antonio M.ª Vallejo
6. Florencio Serrano
7. Pedro Narvaez
8. Carmen Pinto
9. Jose M.ª Carraco
10. Manuel Dutra
11. Juan Abeya
12. Señor Reomere

13. Walter Duckworth
14. Joaquin Soto
15. William E.P. Hartnell
16. Gabriel de la Torre
17. James Stokes
18. Priest's House
19. Thomas O. Larkin
20. Jose M.ª Carrasco
21. James Watson
22. Señora Lenares
23. Job F. Dye
24. Salvador Msonras

25. Antonio Mendez
26. Manuel Simeno
27. George Kinloch
28. Carmen Ruiz
29. Custom House
30. Landing Places
31. Charles Wolter
32. Antonio M.ª Osio
33. Josi M.ª Rejial
34. Simeon Castro
35. Juan Malarin
36. David Spence
   Barges of Com. Jones' vessels

37. Juan B. Alvarado
38. Jose Armiste
39. John B.R. Cooper
40. Nathan Spear
41. Jose Castro
42. Jose Estrada
43. E. Montenegro
44. Alberto Trescone
45. Luis Pombare
46. Road to Puello San Jose
47. Wreck Com. Rogers
48. Ruins Old Residio

49. Catholic Church
50. Zenon Fernandez
51. Francisco Pacheco
52. Jose Abrego
53. Teodoro Gonzales
54. M. Escobar
55. Esteban Monras
56. Rafael Gonzales
57. Jose Joaquin Gomez
58. Government Buildings
59. Mariano Estrada
60. Road to Mission de Carmel
61. Ravine

Figure 4.20 View of Monterey, California: 1842

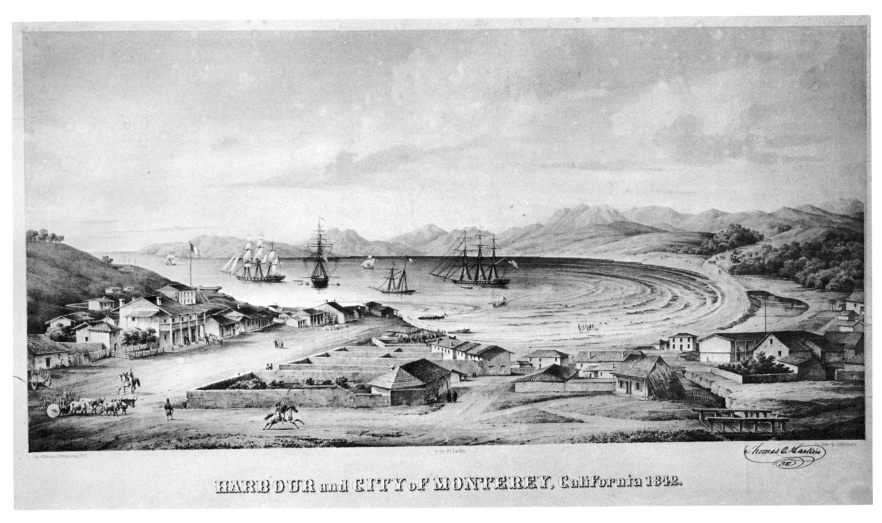

HARBOUR and CITY of MONTEREY, California 1842.

Figure 4.21 View of Monterey, California: 1842

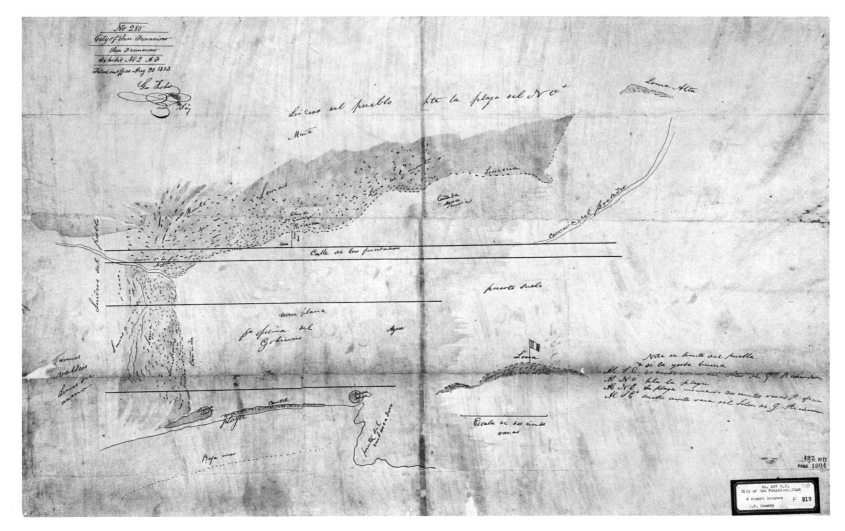

Figure 4.22　Plan of Yerba Buena (San Francisco), California: 1835

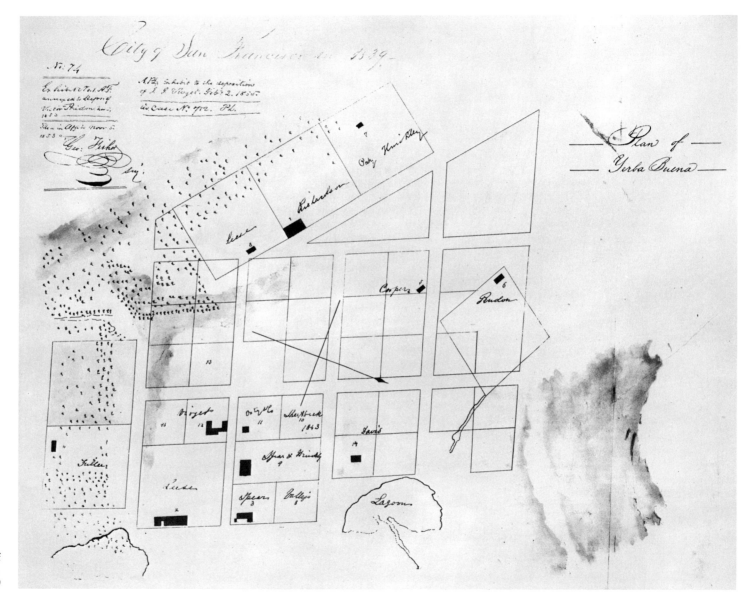

Figure 4.23 Plan of
Yerba Buena (San Francisco),
California: 1839

Buena was probably typical of all the widely dispersed municipalities that came under American jurisdiction following the Mexican War. Soldiers and civilians entering California at that time almost immediately began to modify the character of the towns. One culture overwhelmed another as the long period of Hispanic town planning came to an end. In the subsequent urban growth of California the pace of development would be enormously accelerated, and the orderly system of town layout prescribed by the Laws of the Indies would be supplanted. Instead of a single pattern to which all towns were theoretically to conform, a variety of urban designs would be introduced, and decisions on town planning would shift from a central authority to municipal officials or to individual entrepreneurs.

V

Towns in Transition: The Southwest During the Periods
of Mexican Control, Texas Independence, and
the Early Years of American Settlement

To land-hungry Americans moving relentlessly westward in the early years of the nineteenth-century, sparsely populated and ineffectively controlled Texas beckoned enticingly beyond the ill-defined and casually regarded Louisiana border. Illegal immigrants and squatters began to occupy the borderlands, joining many Spaniards who had moved to Texas following the Louisiana Purchase in 1803. Army deserters and fugitive slaves added to the numbers of those seeking land in Texas.[1]

Spanish officials, suspicious as always of foreigners and disturbed about boundary disputes with the United States following the transfer of Louisiana from French to American control, attempted to police the boundary but with little success. In 1819 a filibustering expedition commanded by Dr. James Long captured Nacogdoches. Forced to withdraw after proclaiming East Texas an independent country, Long returned in 1821 to seize La Bahía for a time before being taken prisoner.[2] The movement for Mexican independence was then already well under way, and it now appeared that a military invasion from the east posed an added threat to Spain's position.

Initial mass settlement of Texas by Americans was not to be carried out by force of arms, however, but under an elaborate set of laws providing for organized colonization by large groups receiving huge tracts of land to be surveyed into farms, ranches, and towns. During the short period between Mexican independence and the creation of the Republic of Texas, many new towns were to be planned in this manner and the foundations laid for an urban society.

This episode in Texas settlement began in the twilight of Spain's empire in North America when Moses Austin on January 17, 1821, received approval for his proposal to bring 300 families to settle in Texas. Although Austin died before he could undertake this project, his son, Stephen, resolved to carry it out. When he arrived in San Antonio in March, 1822, however, he learned that the new Mexican government refused to honor the agreement made with his father and that he would have to secure new authorization to proceed.

When Stephen Austin reached Mexico City, he found himself but one of many who sought colonization grants. Early in 1823 he succeeded in obtaining a new confirmation of his father's contract. In the following year the Mexican congress passed a general colonization law that set forth basic requirements and authorized each state to adopt more detailed legislation. Under this enabling act the newly organized state of Coahuila and Texas adopted its colonization statute on March 24, 1825. While Austin's contract thus had a somewhat different legisla-

tive base, its provisions were similar to those established by general law. Included were a number of specifications for the manner by which towns were to be founded and planned.[3]

The colonization law of Coahuila and Texas provided for settlement under contracts with *empresarios* who were to bring to Texas at their expense at least 100 families. The *empresario* was to receive 886 acres of farmland and 22,142 acres of grazing land for every 100 families brought to the colony. Each family was entitled to purchase at low prices and over a six-year period about one-fifth of this amount if it both farmed and raised livestock. No colony's border was to be within 50 miles of the United States boundary nor within 10 leagues (25 miles) of the coast except by special permission of federal authorities.

Commissioners appointed by the government were to supervise the founding of towns "on such sites . . . most appropriate" for that purpose. The area specified for the town was to consist of four square leagues, or 17,714 acres. Town lots were to be given to the *empresario* and to craftsmen for their shops. Other settlers were required to purchase lots at auction, and all owners became obligated to pay one dollar per lot annually for the buildings of churches.

The section dealing with town planning was brief: "The towns shall consist, as nearly as possible, of natives and foreigners; and in laying off the same, care shall be taken to have the streets well laid out and straight, running parallel north and south, and east and west, as nearly as the land shall permit."[4] This provision was supplemented in September, 1827, by a law setting forth instructions for the commissioners appointed to supervise each colony. After repeating the requirement for streets running east-west and north-south, the regulations added that they shall "be laid off straight" and 20 *varas* (55½ feet) wide. This new enactment also specified that the commissioner "shall designate a square measuring one hundred and twenty varas [330 feet] on each side, exclusive of the streets, to be called the *Principal* or *Constitutional square*. This shall be the central point from which the streets shall run for forming squares or blocks."

Sites for religious and public uses were also to be provided: "The block fronting the principal square, upon the east side, shall be destined for a church, curate's dwelling and other ecclesiastical edifices; and that on the west for municipal building or town halls. In another suitable place . . . [the commissioner] shall point out a block for a market square, one for a jail and house of correction, one for a school and other buildings for public instruction, and another without the limits of the town for a burial ground."[5]

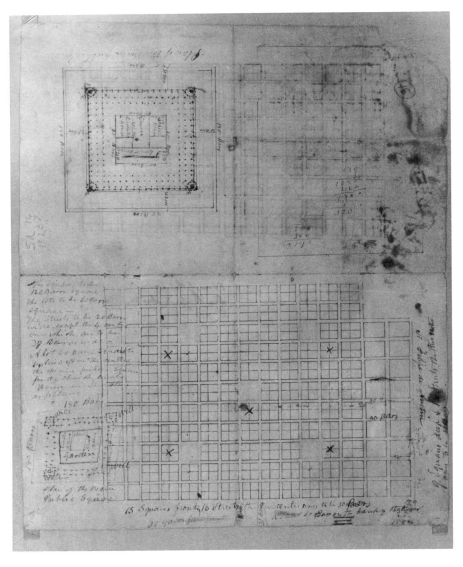

Figure 5.1 Plan of San Felipe de Austin, Texas: ca. 1824

While many of the provisions of this legislation may have had their origins in the Laws of the Indies, they allowed far more latitude to the commissioners in determining the form of towns, decisions that doubtless were influenced by the desires of the *empresarios* as well. It is worth noting that the *empresario* system itself had been incorporated in the Laws of the Indies as one method by which towns might be created, but this system was little used if at all in the northern borderlands of New Spain and, until now, had not been a technique of town founding in Texas, New Mexico, Arizona, or California.[6] Although this general legislation and the unique Austin contract did not produce major cities, the results were impressive when compared to the largely ineffective efforts by Spain to create an urban base in Texas.

Austin's colony lying between the San Jacinto and Lavaca rivers was the location for the first *empresario* town—San Felipe de Austin. Its site lay on the Brazos River about 80 miles from the coast. Two drawings of the proposed town prepared by Stephen Austin apparently predate the time of its official survey in July, 1824. One of these appears in Figure 5.1, which shows a gridiron of streets with five squares or plazas—one in the center of the plat and each of the others located two blocks from the edges of the town. Marginal notes indicate that the four streets passing by the central square were to be 30 *varas* (83¼ feet) wide, with all others 20 *varas* (55½ feet) in width. All blocks were to be platted 120 *varas* (333¼ feet) square and divided into four lots.

At the upper left corner of the drawing Austin sketched in more detail the projected division of the central plaza. On it he proposed to locate the courthouse, church, curate's dwelling, and the school. The X's in the blocks adjoining the five squares show where these open spaces were to be located according to a revised plan. That second drawing differs from the first also in having a detail of a typical block showing how the four square lots could each be divided into four smaller parcels.[7]

San Felipe actually took a different form. Whether this resulted from a change initiated by Austin or by Felipe Neri, the Baron de Bastrop, who served as the government commissioner, is not known. The revised design is reproduced in Figure 5.2. The main plaza of the town opens to the Brazos River and occupies a space larger than the standard block. Two blocks away from the river is the market plaza, two blocks beyond that is the military plaza, and two blocks further and just outside the town is the cemetery site. At the lower or eastern end of the town Bastrop and Austin set aside a four-block site designated the "Solar del Hospium," a tract of land for a hospital. To the west the town included surveyed plots of this size or larger as the agricultural lands of the settlers.[8]

Bastrop's election to the Coahuila and Texas legislature late in 1824 provided that body with a person of practical experience in town planning. He helped write the state colonization law and, perhaps, aided in drafting the instructions to the commissioners already described. Both proved helpful, for dozens of persons seeking to follow Austin's lead quickly filed petitions for *empresario* grants. Their locations and names can be seen on the map of Texas in 1836 reproduced in Figure 5.3. This map is also a useful guide to other place names and locations of towns that will be referred to presently.

The most successful of the *empresarios*, after Austin, was Green De-Witt, and his town of Gonzales was the most elaborately planned of all. DeWitt's grant centered on the Guadalupe River, and at a point almost directly east of San Antonio he had his surveyor, James Kerr, lay out the town of Gonzales in August or September, 1825. Although the first colonists temporarily abandoned this location after an Indian raid and settled illegally on the coast at the mouth of the Lavaca River, Gonzales was reoccupied by 1827 and surveyed officially in the 1831 under commissioner José Antonio Navarro by Byrd Lockhart.[9]

The plan in Figure 5.4 shows the town's design as drawn in 1903 by an old settler. It consisted of 49 blocks occupying a square tract divided by streets 20 *varas* (55½ feet) wide except for the four streets crossing at the center, which were made 30 *varas* (83¼ feet) in width. Each block was 120 *varas* (333¼ feet) square, divided into six lots 40 by 60 *varas* (111 by 166½ feet). Five open squares in the center of the town formed a cruciform pattern and were reserved for the principal plaza, the jail, the public buildings, the church, and parade ground. Two other squares were set aside for the cemetery and market.

The modern town of Gonzales has made good use of this remarkably tidy plan with its generous public reservations. While some of the uses occupy slightly different locations than those contemplated in the original design, the town still focuses its civic life around these sites planned a century and a half ago in accordance with the colonization laws and commissioners' instructions of the Mexican State of Coahuila and Texas.[10]

Other *empresarios* established many additional towns. The Mexican *empresario*, Martín de León, received permission in April, 1824—before the passage of the state colonization law—to settle in what was later found to be within the boundaries of DeWitt's colony. De León's town of Guadalupe Victoria on the east bank of the Guadalupe River was

Figure 5.2 Plan of San Felipe de Austin, Texas: 1824

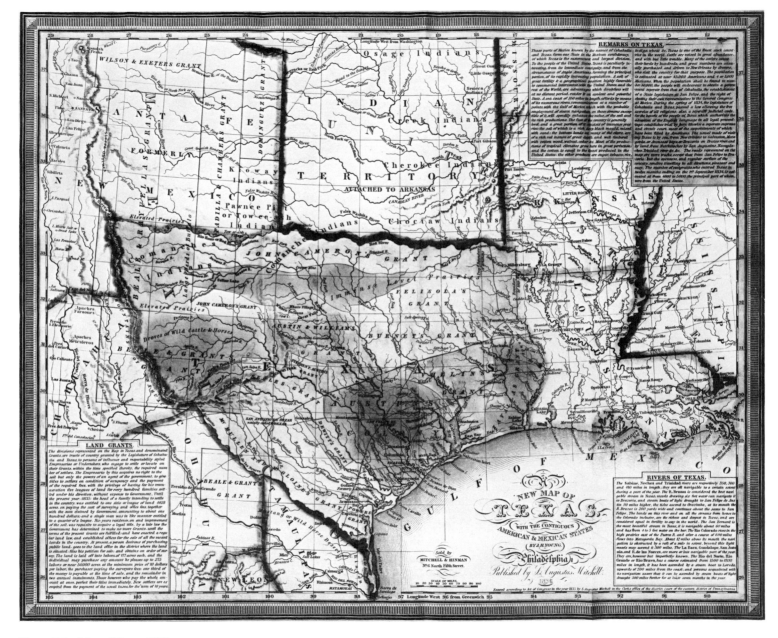

Figure 5.3　Map of Texas: 1836

thus flourishing before DeWitt arrived. The conflicting claims to this land were eventually resolved, and Victoria developed into a town populated chiefly by Mexicans.[11]

Two *empresario* contracts called for colonization by Irish Catholic families. James Powers and James Hewetson obtained approval in 1828 for settlement between the Guadalupe and Lavaca rivers within the 10-league strip along the Gulf Coast. A year later the western boundary was extended to the Nueces River. At the site occupied by the former Refugio mission, commissioner Jesús Vidáurri supervised the survey of the four-league townsite and the planning of the town of Refugio. Figure 5.5 shows the plan of the new community with its square plaza and grid streets laid out 30 *varas* wide rather than the 20 *varas* specified in the instructions to commissioners. The two lots facing the plaza on the east were first intended for church purposes, but the old mission church in the southwestern portion of the town was found to be suitable for religious use and the two lots were then made available for the school. Two lots facing the plaza on the west were reserved for municipal use.[12]

The second Irish colony centered on the town of San Patricio de Hibernia on the east bank of the Nueces River where commissioner José Antonio Saucedo directed the surveys for *empresarios* James McGloin and John McMullen in 1831. The usual gridiron plan with reservations for a square plaza, church, market, municipal buildings, and graveyard was laid out within the standard four-league tract.[13] Other *empresario* towns included Bastrop, Milam, and Liberty.[14]

Adding to the number of new settlements were several port towns on the Gulf of Mexico. Some kind of settlement apparently existed at the mouth of the Brazos as early as 1821, for the first of Austin's colonists passed through the place in that year even before his *empresario* contract had received final approval. In the next 14 years more than 25,000 settlers entered Texas through this town, named Velasco, or its sister community, Quintana, across the river.

The town plan of Velasco in 1837 is reproduced in Figure 5.6. By that time Texas, and indeed the entire nation, was engaged in an orgy of town planning and urban real estate promotion, and the illustration shown here may represent as much wishful thinking as hard fact. Nevertheless, Velasco must have been considered a community of some importance, since after the Battle of San Jacinto it served briefly as the temporary capital of the Republic of Texas. In 1875 a tropical hurricane devastated the area, and eventually the site was virtually abandoned.[15]

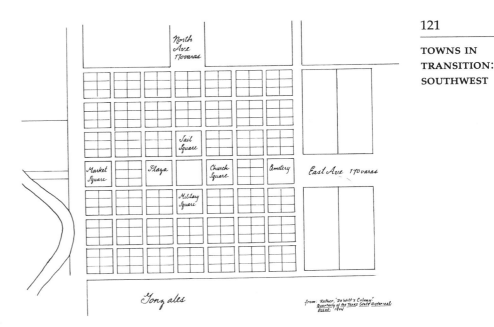

Figure 5.4 Plan of Gonzales, Texas: 1836

Matagorda, at the mouth of the Colorado River, was planned shortly after Austin secured approval in 1827 for his request to locate a town on the coast within the 10-league restricted zone. Its proprietors successfully promoted development of the town by donations of lots to certain settlers as well as through display of its plat in prominent locations. A damaged but legible copy of one of these lithographed plans is reproduced in Figure 5.7. Seth Ingram's name appears as the surveyor, and it was probably he or Austin who determined how the town was designed. The public square is of particular interest. Whether by accident or intent, its pattern conforms almost exactly to that prescribed by the Laws of the Indies, with streets entering its corners as well as the midpoints of its sides. By 1832 the town could boast of a population of 1,400 with another 250 persons residing nearby.

In 1860 when the view reproduced in Figure 5.8 was published, Matagorda presented a rather imposing appearance from the bay. Doubtless its residents and property owners hoped, as Col. Edward

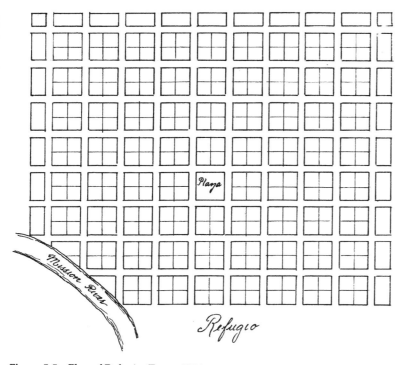

Figure 5.5 Plan of Refugio, Texas: 1834

Stiff had predicted in 1840, that their town "is probably destined to become the emporium of Texas at some distant day." Unfortunately, like so many of the exposed locations along the Gulf, Matagorda's site was continually battered by hurricanes. That of 1894 caused so much destruction that the county moved its seat of government to the newly planned town of Bay City, and Matagorda never fully recovered fom this natural disaster and its resulting fall from political glory.[16]

While only a few of the *empresarios* fulfilled all or most of their contract agreements, their efforts of colonize Texas drastically altered the population composition in the region. A decade after Texas was opened to foreign settlement there were five times as many Anglo-Americans in Texas as Spanish-speaking Mexicans. Not all of the new settlers resided in *empresario* colonies; many simply moved into Texas from the United States and occupied the land as squatters.[17] Attempts by Mexi-

cans to induce their own citizens to move to Texas proved largely futile, and officials began to realize that a province peopled mainly by persons with different cultural backgrounds might slip from their political control. Revocation of the colonization laws in 1830 slowed the stream of migration somewhat, but when the laws were reenacted in 1834 a new flood of settlers surged into Texas. By 1835 the population was estimated at 30,000, there were more than a dozen towns in various stages of development, and the movement for an independent Texas was well under way.[18]

Elsewhere in the Southwest the old Spanish settlements in Arizona and New Mexico were also experiencing a period of transition. In Arizona there were only two civil communities of Spanish origins. Tubac, the older, received a severe setback when the Spanish moved their military base to a site near the mission of San Xavier del Bac following the adoption of the Royal Regulations for *presidios* in 1772. While its remaining population warranted its formal elevation to *pueblo* status in 1838 under Mexican laws, Tubac remained a small, dusty community of adobe buildings at the foot of the Santa Rita Mountains.[19]

Near the new location designated for the *presidio* were several Indian settlements where mission fathers carried on their work. At one of them Hugo O'Conor, commander-inspector of the borderlands fortifications laid out the *presidio* of San Augustín del Tucson in August, 1775.[20]

By 1781 this had taken the form of an enclosure about 750 feet square surrounded by an adobe wall 10 to 12 feet high. Around the interior of the wall were located barracks, stables, a church, and houses for the families of soldiers and other civil settlers who made up the community. The interior of the large rectangle was divided by a line of buildings facing a street that led to the single gate placed midway along the western wall. The Plaza Militar on the north and the Plaza de las Armas to the south thus formed two elongated open spaces.[21]

No known surveys of this community, which combined the functions of a *presidio* and a *pueblo*, date from the Spanish or Mexican periods. The first detailed plan of Tucson was drawn in 1862, a few years after the Mexican garrison had departed following the Gadsden Purchase, which incorporated the southern part of Arizona into the United States. This is reproduced in Figure 5.9.[22] Either at an earlier period or after 1856, when American settlers began to move into the area in substantial numbers, many new streets and plazas were laid out south of the Calle del Arroya (now Pennington Street) and west of the Calle Real (the present Main Street), the intersection of which marked the southwestern corner of the old walled town.

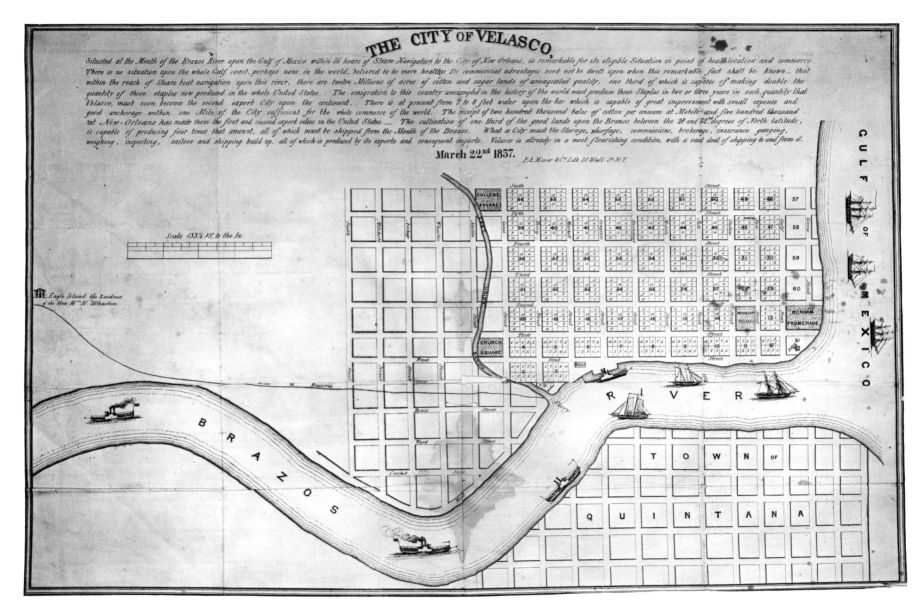

Figure 5.6 Plan of Velasco, Texas: 1837

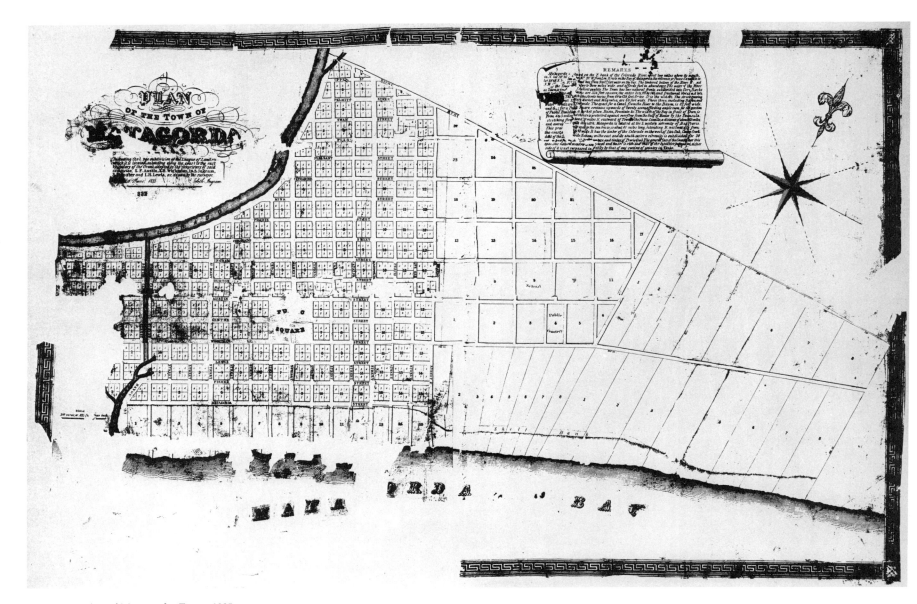

Figure 5.7   Plan of Matagorda, Texas: 1835

Figure 5.8 View of Matagorda, Texas: 1860

The impression of straight streets and rectangular plazas that this military survey conveys may be somwhat misleading. To a contemporary eye Tucson was scarcely so orderly. One visitor in 1858 described it as giving "the impression that it had originally been a hill, which, owing to an unexpected but just visitation of Providence, had been struck with lightning; and the dilapidated mud walls . . . that served as a shelter for the festering mass of corruption that breathed upon the site, were the residuum left in the shape of mud deposits, for not a white wall nor a green tree was to be seen there."[23]

As we have already seen in Chapter II, the first Americans to visit Santa Fe in neighboring New Mexico following the outbreak of war with Mexico were equally unimpressed by the appearance of the oldest of the Spanish towns now under American control. This community at the end of the Santa Fe Trail was a far more cosmopolitan place than distant Tucson and had successfully resisted most Anglo influences. In both towns, however, military occupation opened the door to permanent settlement from the north. While Tucson and Santa Fe retained much of their outward Hispanic character for many years, ultimately they, too, would be gradually transformed as a new culture penetrated and then superseded another.

In Texas the process moved at a far swifter pace. The tides of immigration sweeping into the region under Mexican rule swelled during the period of Texas independence and reached flood stage in the early years of statehood. It was an era of massive change in the pattern of

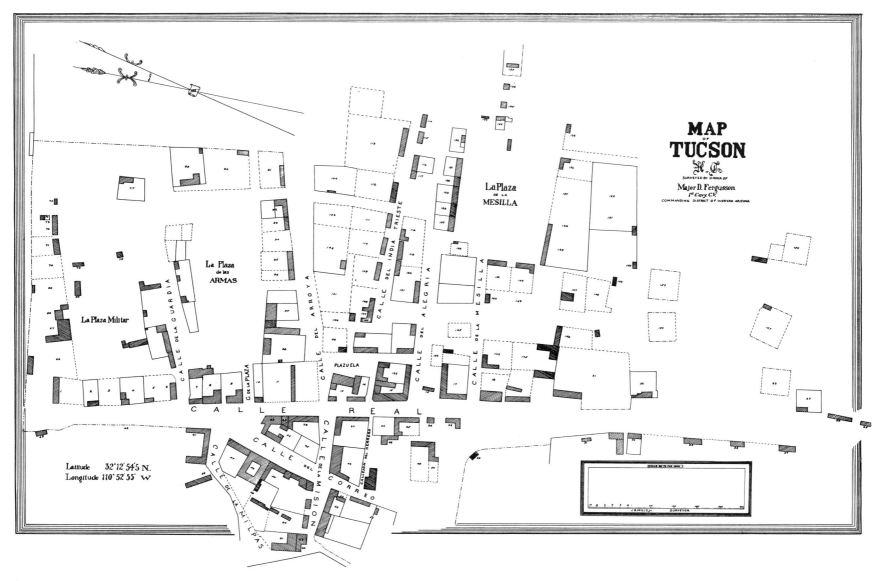

Figure 5.9   Plan of Tucson, Arizona: 1862

town location, planning, and development. Uniform laws governing town design were eliminated; individual townsite promoters now decided these matters. Some of the older towns, badly damaged during the Texas revolution, either vanished or lost their initial impetus for growth.

New cities rose to positions of importance and succeeded in capturing trade and manufacturing activity from older communities. San Antonio, the center of Spanish culture in Texas, underwent a slow but steady change in character while retaining much of its original Spanish and Mexican atmosphere. A new capital city, planned under governmental supervision, helped to stimulate settlement in the interior of the new nation. Within a few years after Texas was admitted to the Union in 1845 a major portion of its urban pattern had already emerged; further development in the later nineteenth century would be based, with some exceptions, on the network of settlements then in existence.

The Gulf Coast and the valleys of the Trinity and Brazos rivers attracted many persons seeking wealth through townsite promotion. Liberal policies of granting land in the seemingly limitless public domain of the new republic stimulated migration from the South and the East, and it was obvious that port towns and market centers would be needed to serve the rapidly increasing population.[24] Texas quickly became a major focus for land speculators eager to make their fortunes through the sales of town lots.

One of the earliest of the post-independence towns to be planned, and ultimately the most successful if measured by eventual size and population, began its existence when Augustus C. and John K. Allen purchased a plot of land at the tidal head of Buffalo Bayou a few miles north of its mouth at Galveston Bay. The deed was dated August 26, 1836, and only four days later the brothers announced that lot sales had begun in their new town of Houston. The plan of the embryo city, reproduced in Figure 5.10, suggests that the Allen Brothers possessed Texas-size ambitions, for in addition to reservations for a school and churches, they included a full block each for a courthouse and the state capitol, the latter identified as Congress Square. Indeed, their initial advertisement after describing in glowing terms the natural advantages of the site, the healthy climate, and its proximity to other settlements included the statement that "nature appears to have designated this place for the future seat of Government."[25]

Nature received some help from John Allen, who had been elected to the legislature that would decide where the capital was to be located. It was doubtless an advantage as well to have the town named for the popular war hero who became the first president of the republic. The Allens' campaign proved successful, and over the objections of representatives from more than fifteen other towns the legislature designated Houston as the seat of government on November 30, 1836.

It was a far from impressive sight during its early months of existence. One party visited Houston shortly after it was surveyed and found only "one dug out canoe, a bottle . . . of whiskey, a surveyors chain and compass and a grove inhabited by four men camping in tents."[26] Despite the Allens' boast that their town was on navigable water, it took three days for one boat to make the 12-mile trip from Harrisburg.[27] Francis Lubbock, later governor of Texas, was a passenger on board and described how he and his companions had to help the crew remove snags from the log-choked bayou by means of an improvised windlass on shore "to heave the logs and snags out of the way . . . and draw from the track of the steamer the obstructions." This was early in January, 1837, and the Lubbock party found that the town consisted only of a few tents and several houses under construction. So little had been accomplished that their boat had passed the site without anyone on board realizing that this was their destination.[28]

Another visitor who arrived in Houston at the end of March found "several rough log cabins, two of which were occupied as taverns, a few linen tents which were used for groceries, together with three or four shanties made of poles set in the ground and covered and weather boarded with rough split shingles." The most impressive structure was a "one story frame [building] two hundred feet or more in length . . . intended by the enterprising proprietors for stores and public offices."

Houston's initial construction boom had just started. "All . . . was bustle and animation. Hammers and axes were sounding in all directions, and I heard the trees falling around and saw some men engaged in laying the foundations of houses, others raising, and a number busily at work marking out the ground." Buildings could not be erected fast enough to accommodate all of the new residents. "Quite a large number of linen tents were pitched in every direction over the prairie, which gave to the city the appearance of a Methodist campground."[29]

A month later when President Sam Houston arrived at Houston he recorded that "now there are upwards of 100 houses finished, and going up rapidly (some of them fine frame buildings) and 1500 people, all actively engaged in their respective pursuits."[30] Among the buildings was a large one-story structure for the offices and meeting rooms of the government. This did not occupy the block designated for that

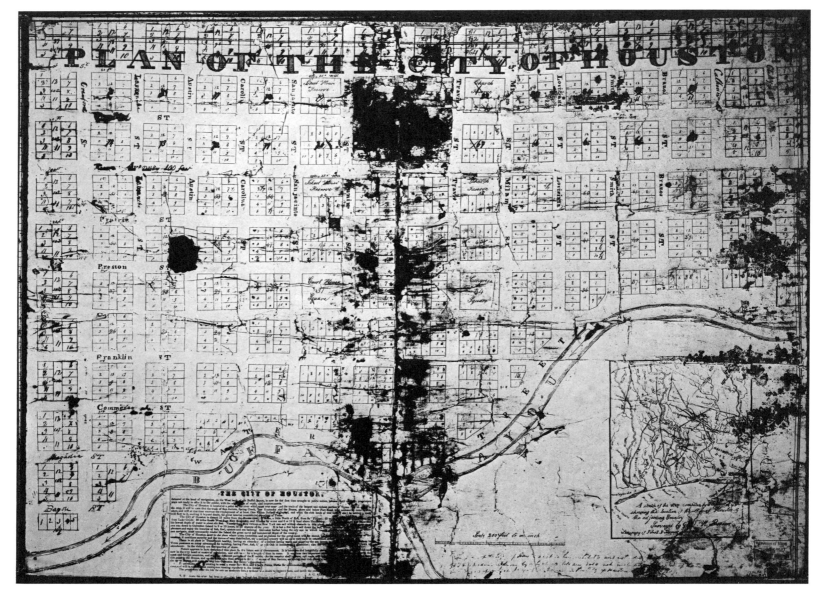

Figure 5.10   Plan of Houston, Texas: ca. 1836

purpose in the Allen plan, nor did its replacement, a two-story structure whose location at the northwest corner of Main and Texas Streets is indicated on the plan of Houston in 1839 reproduced in Figure 5.11.[31] Obviously, the town's prospects appeared bright, for the Allens had already laid off lots across Buffalo Bayou to the north and had planned an even larger extension to the original city tract on the south and east.

Houston was probably the most populous community in Texas at that time except for San Antonio; a census in 1839 indicated a population of 2,073, and the place had two theaters, several hotels, a number of boardinghouses, and a growing business district.[32] Unhappily for Houston and the Allens, the government in 1839 decided to move the seat of government from the growing city and to lay out a new town for this purpose far inland on the upper reaches of the Colorado River. This decision caused the citizens of Houston much anxiety, but the initial period of depression soon passed, and growth of the town resumed as cotton growing became an important activity in the vicinity. In 1840 about 1,000 bales were shipped from the docks at the foot of Main Street. Five years later, 14,000 bales moved down the channel, and by 1854 this had increased to nearly 39,000 bales. Hides and lumber were the other main items of export.[33]

Houston's great rival for the cotton trade occupied a seemingly more advantageous site to the south on the island commanding the entrance to Galveston Bay. The vulnerability of the site to frequent and devastating tropical storms was its major drawback, but the obvious need for a coastal port somewhere in the vicinity and its strategic location virtually guaranteed that a town would be established on this spot.

In 1837 the Galveston City Company issued an elaborate announcement describing the bright future of their projected city. The plan reproduced in Figure 5.12 accompanied this publication. The new town, according to its promoters, would shortly rival Havana and New Orleans in size and prosperity and would surely become the largest city in Texas. The eight-page prospectus ended with this promise to investors: "No new city or town of the present day, offers anything like the inducements for profitable investment to this. It is like commencing to build another New York, or another New Orleans; and all who embark in it are as certain of realizing great profits, as though they had early engaged in the projection of either of the other places. Now is the time to buy stock in this splendid city. Either stock or lots bought in it, must soon advance one hundred percent."[34]

Michael B. Menard, the leading figure in the Galveston City Company, doubtless either drew or supervised the preparation of the town's design. It provided for a town of enormous dimensions stretching nearly five miles in an elongated gridiron from a point near the eastern tip of the island. Broadway was designed to serve as the principal artery, and at the point where its axis changed direction slightly Menard placed a site for a college in the middle of a great square and facing "College Park" to the north.

Halfway to this point from the east, Bath Avenue crossed Broadway at "Houston Circle," terminating on the south at a beach resort and at the north in a proposed civic center composed of the customhouse, post office, exchange, and city hall grouped around a central square. Two other large squares with formal parks in the centers were also provided for, along with sites for churches, markets, and cemeteries. The little peninsula at the northeast was set aside for a park.

This elaborate scheme underwent some modification and simplification when the site was surveyed, and apparently other changes were made from time to time. There are several early maps of Galveston prior to 1900, and they all differ somewhat in the location and size of open squares and public reservations. All of them show, however, that Broadway was finally platted in a straight line and that the western portion of the original plan was eliminated.

Figure 5.13 is a reproduction of one of these maps, published in 1845 and showing at the lower right an inset of the ship channel leading from the Gulf of Mexico to the protected wharves and docks along Galveston Bay.[35] By that time the city was enjoying a land and building boom that must have satisfied its proprietors. A Texas guide published in 1840 stated that the new town "now contains five or six hundred houses, and about three thousand inhabitants" and was "rapidly increasing in wealth and population."[36] Another account written that same year, however, was less complimentary. Francis Sheridan, a member of the British diplomatic corps, found Galveston "very irregularly built" of wooden houses, some of which had brick foundations. He added that "the rapidity with which these houses are run up is inconceivable, & I will not trust my imagination to guess at the number built during my stay."[37]

More elaborate wooden houses soon appeared as well as some of brick, and both brick and cast iron commerical and warehouse buildings lined the waterfront in the decade of the 1850s when Galveston prospered from the Texas cotton trade.[38] The city also served as the principal port of entry for thousands of immigrants streaming into Texas from Europe and from other parts of the United States. By 1850 the population reached 5,000, a figure that was to double before the Civil War halted for a time the city's mushrooming growth.

Figure 5.14 purports to show the city's appearance in 1856. While

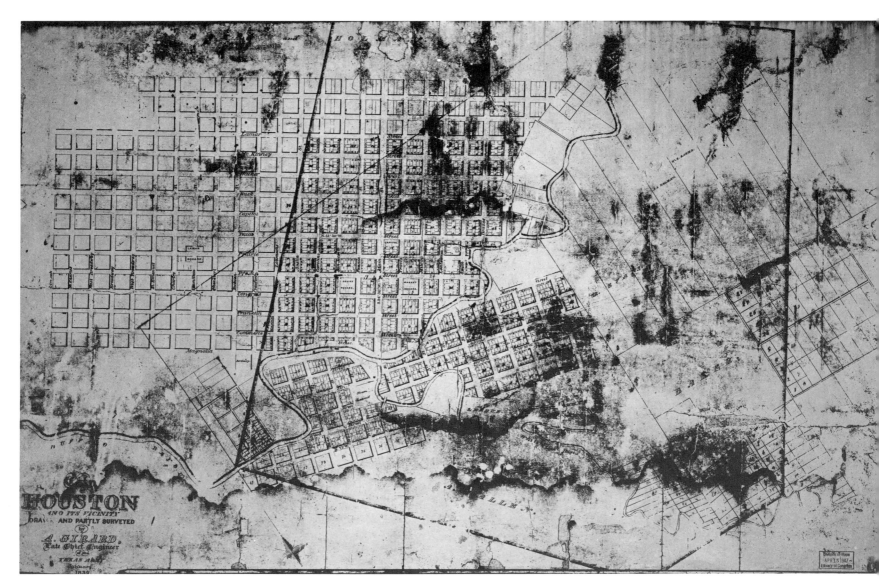

Figure 5.11 Plan of Houston, Texas: 1839

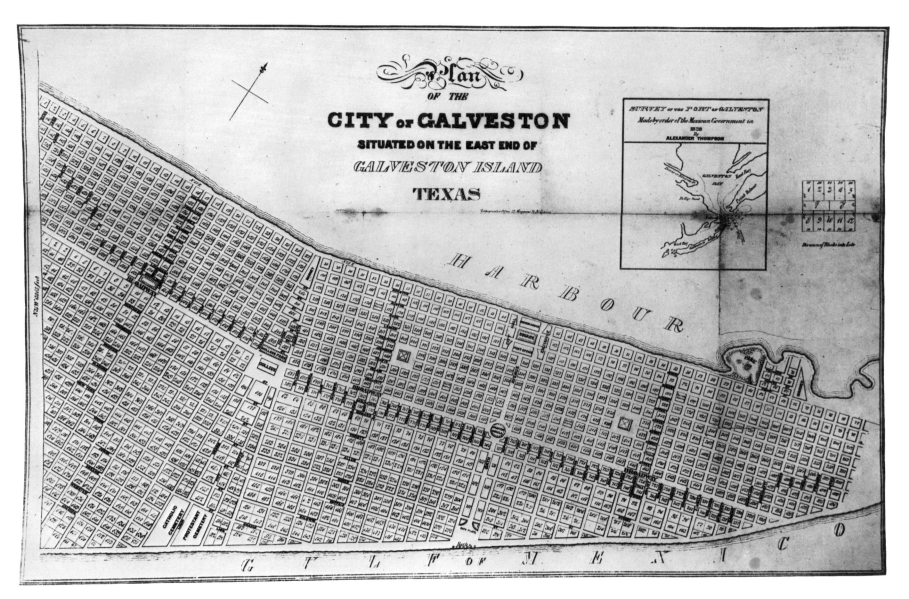

Figure 5.12 Plan of Galveston, Texas: 1837

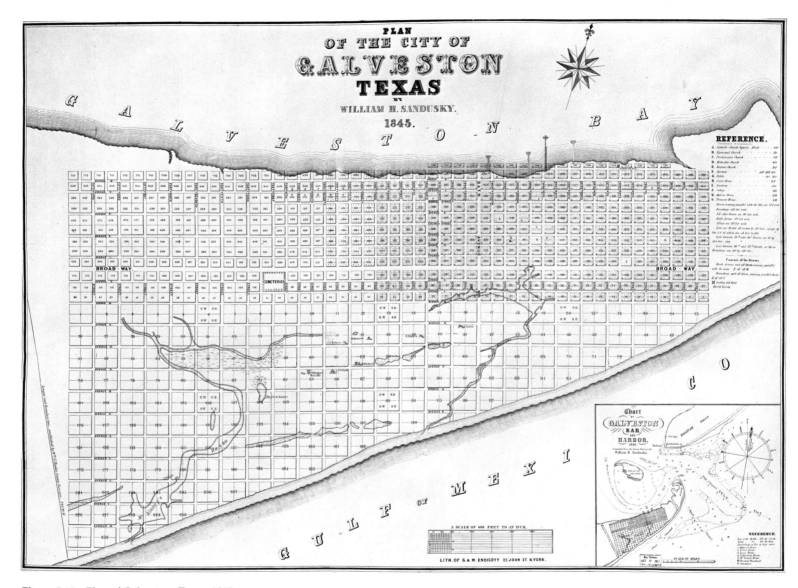

Figure 5.13 Plan of Galveston, Texas: 1845

Figure 5.14 View of Galveston, Texas: ca. 1855

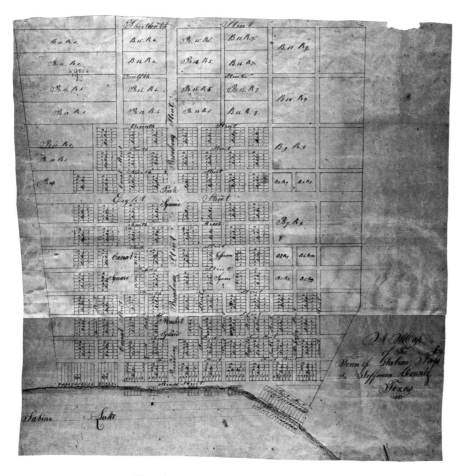

Figure 5.15 Plan of Sabine Pass, Texas: 1851

practically none of the details is correct, the general character of the city is probably depicted with some accuracy. The view looks west along the north shore of Galveston Island, where the docks and wharves were located. Little of the ordered geometry of the city's gridiron plan is reflected in this urban portrait, and the town seems to taper off sud-

denly beyond the tight cluster of buildings at the left, which doubtless is intended to represent the business district.

Although Galveston was never to realize the vision of its founders as another New York or New Orleans, its initial vigorous growth and profitable development must have stimulated many other town founding enterprises during the years of the Texas Republic. As one observer in 1837 noted, "a mania for towns is characteristic of all new countries and is especially so here. Many enterprising men have gone to Texas to seize upon the advantages which a new country affords to acquire wealth, and many of these have some city in prospect as the speediest means to effect their object. Should they all succeed, they will no doubt at some day make Texas as famous for her cities as Thebes was for her hundred gates."[39]

Even Sam Houston joined the ranks of speculators in what he called "town or city making" in 1839 after his first term as president of Texas.[40] With six men Houston formed the Sabine City Company and laid out a town at the mouth of the Sabine River near the Louisiana border. The notice by the proprietors that shares in the enterprise were on sale included a phrase that could have been borrowed from earlier advertisements for Houston and Galveston: "Nature seems to have intended this point for a great commercial mart."[41]

Houston and his companions certainly did their best to help nature, for the plan of Sabine City, reproduced in Figure 5.15, was an elegantly ordered design. Two wide streets, Broadway and Eighth, intersected at Park Square, an open space created by omitting three lots at each of the four corners of the intersection. Market Square near the shore of Sabine Lake took a slightly different form, while still a third variation of plaza design appears in the two larger open spaces on either side of Broadway—Canal Square and Jefferson Square. Very little seems to be known about the town's development. It was said to have achieved a population of some 6,000 later in the century, but it was overshadowed by Port Arthur and Beaumont and failed to fulfill its early promise.[42]

Sam Houston's successor as president of Texas, Mirabeau B. Lamar, also busied himself in 1839 with the founding and planning of a town—not as a private speculation but as a public project to establish a new capital city for the republic. Before Houston had been designated for this purpose, the provisional government of Texas had met at San Felipe, Washington (planned on the Brazos River in 1835), Harrisburg, Galveston Island, the military camp at San Jacinto, Velasco, and Columbia, where the first Texas congress met. Accommodations at Columbia were grossly unsatisfactory, and a joint committee was created to select still another site. Columbia, Washington, Fort Bend, Nacogdoches, Velasco, Hidalgo, Refugio, Goliad, Brazoria, San Jacinto, San Antonio—in all, fifteen places—attempted to secure the coveted designation before Houston won the honor.[43] The decision satisfied few people except the Allens and their fellow Houstonians, and it was almost inevitable that further attempts to move the seat of government would be made.

Houston's primitive conditions aided those favoring a further move. In 1837 and 1838 two joint congressional commissions were created to consider the issue and submit appropriate recommendations. President Houston vetoed one bill that would have transferred the capital to a place known as Eblin's League on the east side of the Colorado River about 100 miles from its mouth.[44]

In the election of 1838 the location of the capital became an issue. Voters from central and western Texas strongly supported the successful presidential candidate, Mirabeau Buonoparte Lamar, known to be an advocate of a more westerly site for the center of government. After Lamar's inauguration the congress passed an act providing for a third capital commission with final power of decision over the location, specifying only that the capital should be established between the Trinity and Colorado rivers and north of the San Antonio–Nacogdoches road, running roughly parallel to the Gulf Coast about 125 miles inland. The act directed the commissioners to purchase or, if necessary, take by eminent domain not less than one league nor more than four leagues of land and to survey 640 acres of this enormous tract as a city to be known as Austin.[45]

Lamar approved this act on January 14, 1839. Two days later the two houses of congress elected the members of the commission—two senators and three representatives. By the middle of February they had left Houston to visit the specified region and select the site. They completed their work in April and submitted a report to the president stating that they had acquired a 7,735-acre tract on the Colorado River for the sum of $21,000, with one portion yet to be surveyed. The report indicates that most existing owners sold their land to the commissioners, but at least one portion of the site had to be taken by eminent domain.[46]

On part of the site, the town of Waterloo had been platted on the east bank of the Colorado about 35 miles northwest of Bastrop, but only four families were then residing in this distant outpost of the Texas frontier. The map of Texas in 1844 reproduced in Figure 5.16 shows the location of Austin far to the northwest of the many other towns that had been founded up to that time.[47] It seems a bold, almost foolhardy, decision to place the capital city in such an isolated and undeveloped area, but despite almost unanimous opposition from the East Texas settlements, President Lamar's determination to use the capital city as an instrument for promoting settlement of the frontier was ultimately to prevail.[48]

The law under which the commissioners acted provided that, after receiving their report, the president was to "appoint an agent, whose duty it shall be to employ a surveyor . . . and have surveyed six hundred and forty acres of land . . . into town lots, under the direction of the President." Half of the lots were to be put up for auction after being advertised for 90 days prior to the sale. One-fourth of the purchase price was to be paid at the time of sale, with the balance payable in three equal installments over the following 18 months. The act directed the agent to reserve sites "for a Capitol, Arsenal, Magazine, University, Academy, Churches, Common Schools, Hospital, Penitentiary, and for all other necessary public buildings and purposes."[49]

President Lamar appointed Edwin Waller, a resident of Brazoria County, as agent. Toward the end of April, Waller advertised that lots would be put up for sale about August 1, and by May 20 he had reached the site of Austin, where L. J. Pilie and Charles Schoolfield began the town surveys under his direction. Waller probably took with him a proposed city plan that he and Lamar had prepared, for on May 23 Waller wrote the president that "the nature of the ground being such has rendered necessary in order to place the capitol and public buildings upon the high ground, a slight change in the plan of the city, placing the public square in the rear of the centre instead of the centre of the city."[50]

Although there is no record that Lamar had ever planned a town, he must have been familiar with the designs of the many Texas settlements that had been surveyed during the Mexican period and the early years of independence. Moreover, he had lived in two rather elaborately planned communities in his native Georgia, both created by the state government rather than by private interests, and he had been born near still a third town created by the state of Georgia. Two of them—Louisville, near his plantation home, and Milledgeville, where he attended school—were both founded as capital cities of the state. Lamar later moved to Columbus, Georgia, in 1828, the year it was planned by a public commission as a trading and market community to help stimulate settlement on Georgia's western domain.[51]

Waller played an important role in the planning and early development of the city of Austin. It was he who selected the precise location for the town within the much larger tract acquired by the commission-

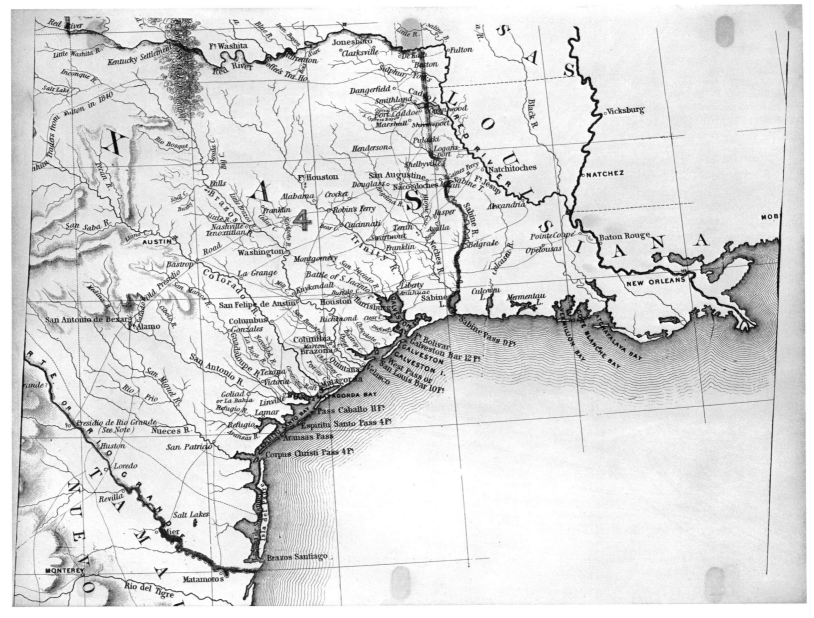

Figure 5.16 Map of Texas: 1844

ers. The town lay between two creeks and sloped upward away from the Colorado River to a commanding elevation, which Waller chose as the spot for the Capitol Square.[52] This reservation, 800 feet square and with 80-foot wide streets on all four sides, is the most prominent feature of the city plan reproduced to Figure 5.17. Entering the mid-points of Capitol Square were the two principal thoroughfares, College and Congress Avenues, each 120 feet wide. The former terminated on the west at two blocks reserved for the university and academy. Congress Avenue led up the slope from the river past flanking tiers of blocks divided so that the lots fronted this major street.

Facing Capitol Square Waller reserved half- and quarter-blocks for public buildings. Four other public squares, a market site, two half-blocks designated for churches, a block for the courthouse and jail, another block for the armory, and one for the hospital, and one large tract equal in size to four city blocks for the penitentiary completed the generous allocation of space for public and civic uses. The 80-foot streets parallel to Congress Avenue named for Texas rivers and those of identical dimensions parallel to College Avenue taking their names from trees divided the town into rectangular blocks through which 25-foot alleys were surveyed to divide one tier of lots from another.[53]

The energetic Waller somehow managed to get under construction in an incredibly short time the necessary buildings for the state offices. By the end of July one newspaper reported that "twenty or thirty buildings have already been completed, and . . . they are better buildings than were built during the first year in Houston."[54] Waller located most of them along Congress Avenue on what were intended as temporary locations. Waller placed the residence of the president in the center of block 85 south of Brazos Street at the brow of a hill looking over the lower part of the city. The building for the temporary capital stood on block 98 between Colorado and Congress.

These are the two most prominent structures appearing in Figure 5.18, a view of the infant city in January, 1840, with the presidential "mansion" at the right and the capitol at the left on the other side of Congress Avenue. The view is inaccurate in at least one respect, for Waller spaced the first buildings along Congress Avenue to leave a number of vacant lots between the structures.[55] He almost certainly adopted this policy to enhance the value of the intervening lots with an eye to the first land auction scheduled for August 1. That event proved a resounding success. Two hundred and seventeen lots sold at prices ranging from $120 to $2,700, and total sales came to about $300,000 before Sheriff Charles King of Bastrop County, who served as auctioneer, pounded his gavel for the last time.[56]

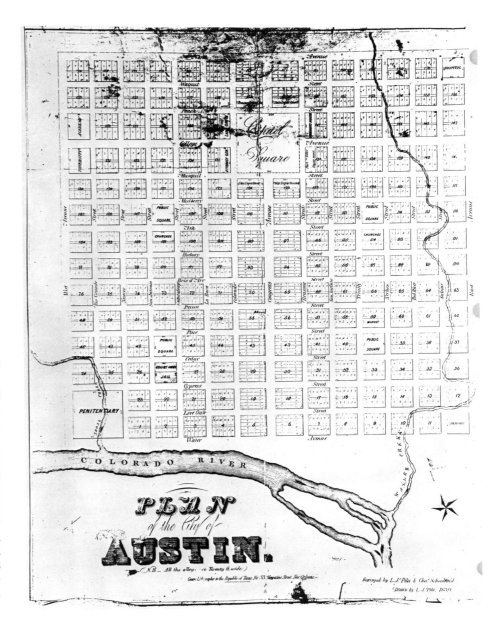

Figure 5.17   Plan of Austin, Texas: 1839

Figure 5.18   View of Austin, Texas: 1840

In late summer "between forty and fifty wagons freighted with the archives of the government, and books, papers, and furniture of the different Departments" left Houston for the new city. As the newspaper of the former capital bitterly remarked, "we have no consolation left, and that is, that we have done everything we could to prevent it, but it was to no avail."[57] President Lamar and members of his cabinet arrived on October 17 to be welcomed by Waller, a salute of 21 guns, and a 5-hour dinner that included no fewer than 39 toasts.[58]

Efforts to move the capital from Austin began with the first session of congress in the new city. These ultimately proved fruitless, although when Sam Houston resumed the presidency he called the congress into session at Washington and then at Houston when the Mexican army reoccupied San Antonio because Austin seemed a dangerously exposed location for the government. Houston's attempt in 1842 to spirit away the public archives in the dead of night was a less orthodox manner of trying to resolve the issue, but this, too, failed when an alert woman innkeeper fired a cannon to warn the citizens of the plot. The public documents were recovered when Houston's agents beat a hasty retreat.[59] A statewide referendum in 1850 as called for in the state constitution of 1845 resulted in a bare majority of the votes for Austin. Another referendum on the question in 1872 produced the same result, and the constitution of 1876 seemingly closed the issue by declaring simply that "the legislature shall hold its sessions at the city of Austin which is hereby declared to be the seat of government."[60]

Austin's population grew slowly and sporadically during its early years. In 1840 nearly 900 persons resided in the new town, but the invasion of Texas by Mexican forces in 1842 and the temporary transfer of government activities to Washington and Houston brought development to a virtual standstill. W. H. Emory's map of Texas in 1844 gives the population of the city as only 200, and the census of 1850 reported the number of residents as 629.[61]

Austin's first substantial boom took place during the 1850s, when its population grew to 3,500. Frederick Law Olmsted recorded his impressions of the town as he saw it early in 1856: "Austin has a fine situation upon the left bank of the Colorado. Had it not been the capital of the state, and a sort of bourne to which we had looked forward for a temporary rest, it would still have struck us as the pleasantest place we had seen in Texas. It reminds one somewhat of Washington [D.C.]; Washington, *en petit*, seen through a reversed glass. The Capitol—a really imposing building of soft cream limestone, nearly completed at the time of our visit, and already occupied—stands prominent upon a hill, towards which, nearly all the town rises. From it a broad avenue stretches to the river, lined by the principal buildings and stores. . . . Off the avenue, are scattered cottages and one or two pretty dwellings. They are altogether smaller in number and meaner in appearance than a stranger would anticipate."[62]

During the period of Austin's founding other towns were being established in the Republic. Not all of these proved capable of withstanding the competition for urban survival. Swartwout, on the Trinity River in southwestern Polk County, is one example. The plan of the town as laid out in 1838 by its promoters, James Morgan, Arthur Garner, and Thomas Bradley, is reproduced in Figure 5.19. Its orderly design and its streets named for states and U.S. and Texas heroes may have attracted the attention of Sam Houston, for he was a shareholder in the enterprise. For a time Swartwout seemed to have achieved a modest degree of success as a trading community and river port. Several stores, a church, school, hotel, warehouse, and a number of dwellings lined its

streets in the years before the Civil War. As river traffic dwindled, so did the town; the closing of its post office in 1875 symbolized its failure. Today an historical marker is the most substantial element of the scattered hamlet.[63]

By contrast, Marshall, 40 miles west of Shreveport and located not far from the southwestern corner of Arkansas, developed into an important community following its settlement in 1839. Named for Chief Justice John Marshall, the town was symmetrically laid out with an elongated public square at its center. As the plan in Figure 5.20 shows, two small blocks on its north and south sides created an unusual pattern. The main east-west thoroughfare entered the square at the mid-points of its shorter sides, while three streets led north and south.

Peter Whetstone donated this site for the courthouse square, along with a plot for a church, 10 acres of land for the school, and 190 other lots when the town was selected as the seat of Harrison County in 1842. Marshall quickly developed as one of the largest and most prosperous towns of the state prior to secession. During the Civil War, it produced clothing, leather goods, and ammunition for the Confederate forces and for a time served as the headquarters of the Confederate government of Missouri, which had been forced to flee that state when Union forces made its position untenable. From here the Texas and Pacific Railroad began its often-interrupted push across Texas in the 1870s that was to bring prosperity to such raw frontier towns as Dallas and Fort Worth at the expense of the older and far more sophisticated community designated as the nominal terminus of the line.[64]

Early in the 1840s the Republic of Texas reinstituted for a short time the old Mexican *empresario* system. One reason was to stimulate population growth beyond the existing frontier of settlement. The other was to raise revenues through sale of alternate 640-acre sections of land reserved by the republic within the *empresario* colonies.[65] Several foreign colonization groups came to Texas during this period to establish towns and take up agricultural lands nearby.

The leader of one such group was Henri Castro, who had come to America after the fall of Napoleon. Returning to France in 1838, he attempted to negotiate a loan for the Republic of Texas and was appointed consul general at Paris by President Sam Houston. Four years later he received a colonization contract for two tracts of land—one 25 miles west of San Antonio, the other on the Rio Grande. In 1844 Castro led a party of 35 settlers from San Antonio to the first of the two tracts, where Henry James surveyed the town of Castroville. Quihi in 1845, Vandenburg in 1846, and D'Hanis in 1847 were established in the same vicinity

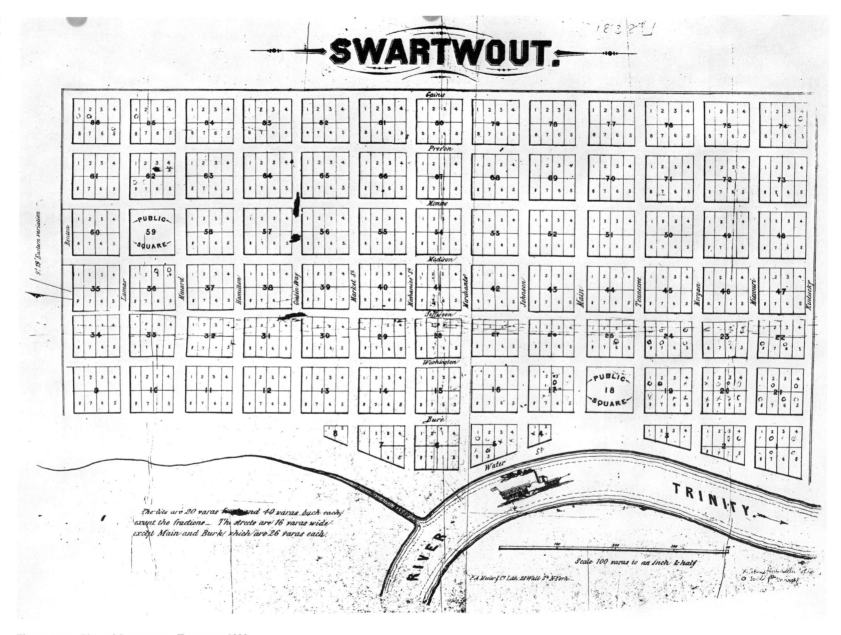

Figure 5.19   Plan of Swartwout, Texas: ca. 1838

to accommodate the more than 2,000 settlers Castro succeeded in bringing to Texas, most of them recruited from Alsace.

A survey of Castroville not quite 40 years after its founding is reproduced in Figure 5.21. Its street names recall many of the principal foreign cities of the world along with a few domestic heroes. Castro and James fitted their gridiron design into a bend of the Medina River with two diagonal streets added to provide better access to the water lots. Three contiguous blocks bounded by London, Petersburg, Angelo, and Amelia Streets were reserved for the Catholic Church and two schools. Across Angelo Street from the church a fourth block was designated as a public square named for Sam Houston. In the other direction and one block removed from the church, Castro and James provided a market square. Castro also donated a site for the courthouse facing Main Street in the block bounded by London and Paris Streets, the latter thoroughfare leading to the Medina River beyond the juncture of the two diagonals.

After an initial period of drought, famine, and an epidemic of cholera, Castroville enjoyed a peaceful and prosperous existence as the frugal Alsatians began to cultivate the surrounding farm lands to which they received title. They clung to the European custom of building their houses only in town and going to and from their fields at morning and night. Frugality may have been carried to a fault. In 1880 the residents refused to meet the demands of the Southern Pacific Railroad for a subsidy to insure rail service to the town. The line was built south of the settlement, Hondo became the county seat in 1892, and population of Castroville began to decline. A few old buildings in the modern community of less than 2,000 inhabitants are the only reminders of Henri Castro's dream of a city that would match the greatness of its street names.[66]

The achievements of a German colonization society formed in 1842 by a group of Prussian nobles, the Adelsverein, were more impressive. In 1844 Prince Carl of Solms-Braunfels arrived in Texas to direct their activities. He originally intended to settle his followers on an abandoned *empressario* grant in the upper Guadalupe River valley. When title to this land proved to be faulty Prince Carl arranged to purchase a substitute tract some 30 miles northeast of San Antonio. The location he chose appears on the map reproduced as Figure 5.22 showing also the sites of Castroville, Gonzales, Seguin, Bastrop, and Austin.[67]

The Prince, aided by his surveyor, Nicolaus Zink, planned the town of New Braunfels in 1845 near these older settlements, and his successor, John Meusebach founded Fredericksburg 80 miles to the northwest in 1846 on the trail to the old *presidio* of San Sabá. Prince Carl also laid

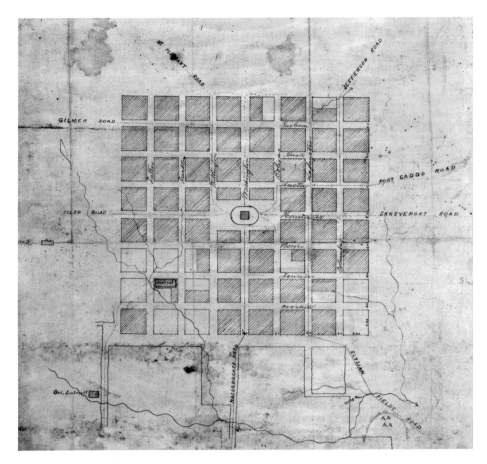

Figure 5.20 Plan of Marshall, Texas: ca. 1860

out a port town on Matagorda Bay to serve as the principal supply center for the colony. First named Carlshafen and then Indianola, its location and plan is shown in Figure 5.23 along with the plans of New Braunfels and Fredericksburg and their adjacent agricultural lands.

Under Prince Carl's direction Zink surveyed the streets of New Braunfels in a grid pattern with the two principal thoroughfares entering the midpoints of the sides of an elongated central square. A short

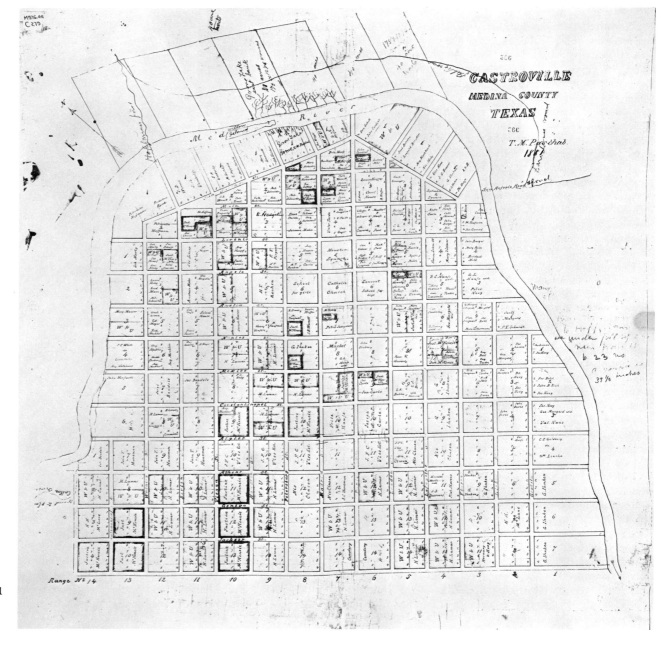

Figure 5.21 Plan of Castroville, Texas: 1881

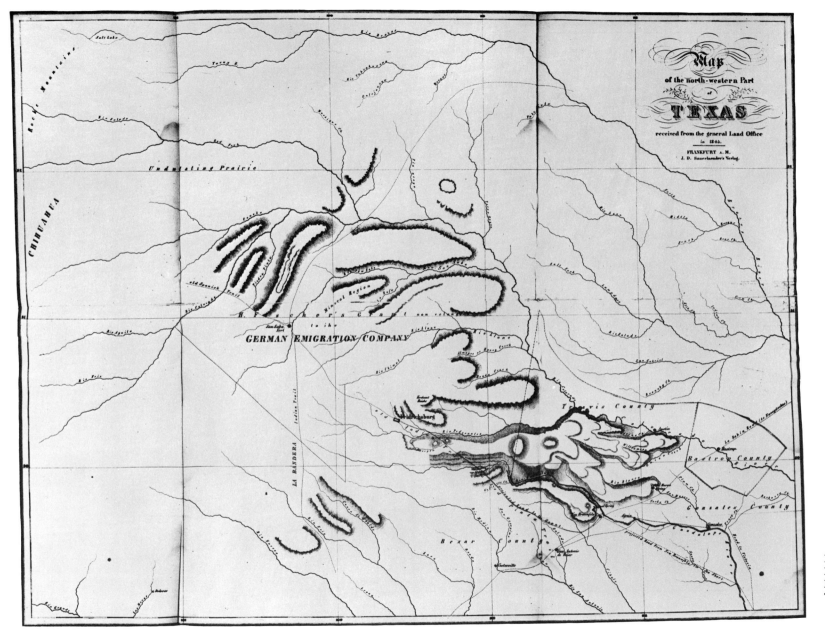

Figure 5.22
Map of
Northwestern
Texas: 1845

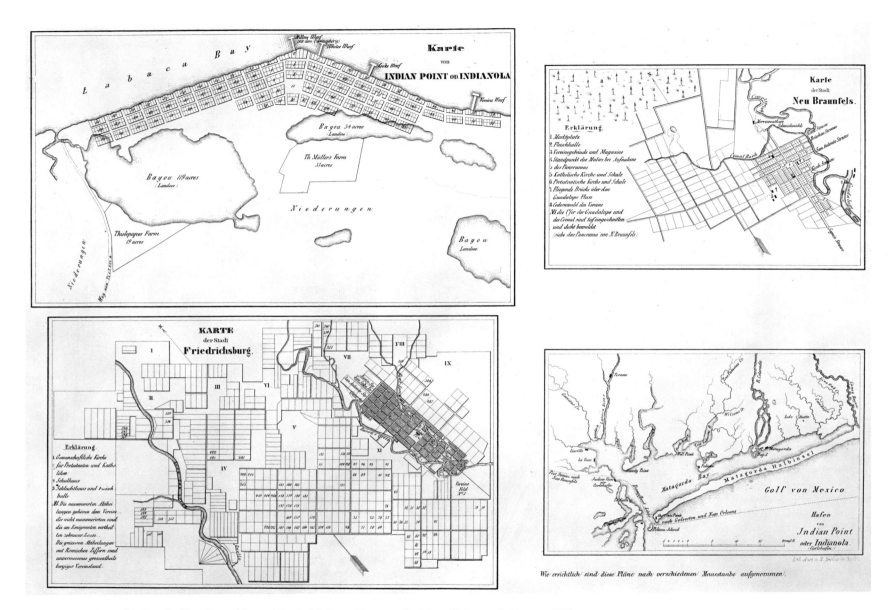

Figure 5.23 Plans of Indianola, New Braunfels, and Fredericksburg, Texas, and a Map of Matagorda Bay: ca. 1850

distance away they reserved a narrower strip of land for a marketplace, and also set aside sites for a school, churches, mills, and a town hall. The prince then supervised a drawing for town lots, and the settlers began to erect tents and cabins on the 226 locations selected in this manner.

Fredericksburg's design, as determined by John Meusebach the following year, took a somewhat different form. Its linear grid, six blocks wide by twelve blocks long, centered on a main street leading to a rectangular central square. The distant location of this settlement, exposed as it was to Indian raids, caused many hardships for the colonists. Nevertheless, by 1847 it contained a hotel, 18 stores, and according to Dr. Ferdinand Roemer, "many neat houses, enclosed carefully with a fence."

Roemer found New Braunfels even more impressive when he returned there on April 16, 1847, after an absence of several months: "Much had . . . been accomplished. . . . Numerous new houses had been built and the whole place looked much more like a city. The straight streets which formerly were only indicated on the ground plan of the city, now began to appear in reality." Roemer noted that the town had new neighbors: "A speculative American had laid out a new city between the fork of the Comal and the Guadalupe within view of the city of New Braunfels, called Comaltown. Another city called Hortontown, had been laid out on the other bank of the Guadalupe and several families had settled here."[68] A few years later Jacob de Cordova planned the settlement of Neighborville nearby, and in 1868 Braunfels was founded, adjoining Comal Town on the southeast. The plans or locations of these satellite communities and a more detailed drawing of New Braunfels as it existed in 1868 can be seen in Figure 5.24.

So rapid was the growth of New Braunfels that by 1850 it was the fourth most populous settlement in Texas with a population of 1,298. To that could be added Comal Town's 286 and the 139 persons residing in Hortontown. The community was exceeded in population only by Galveston with 4,177 inhabitants, San Antonio with 3,488, and Houston with 2,396. Marshall's population of 1,189 earned its rank as fifth in size. Then came Victoria with 806, Fredericksburg with 754, and Austin with 629 persons. The only other urban places listed in the census of 1850 were Bonham (211), Corpus Christi (533), Crockett (150), Eagle Pass (353), Lavaca (315), McKinney (192), Nacogdoches (468), Palestine (212), Richmond (323), Rusk (355), Zodiac (160), and the earliest of Prince Carl's towns—Indianola—with a population of 379.

Several pictorial representations of the towns founded by Prince Carl

and his group exist. Figure 5.25 shows Indianola as it appeared in 1860 from the bay. It publication in Hamburg indicates the continuing German interest in the circumstances of their former countrymen. The two sturdy wharves are rather more impressive than the town itself, which at that time consisted of a long string of houses, stores, hotels, saloons, and warehouses facing the waterfront.

New Braunfels was clearly the most successful of the Adelsverein settlements. As depicted in 1881 by Augustus Koch, the town is shown in Figure 5.26. By that time its first primitive structures had been replaced by far more substantial dwellings, stores, churches, and factories, many of them built of stone. Although many of the original blocks were only partially occupied, its two principal thoroughfares leading to the public square—Seguin and San Antonio Streets—were then almost solidly built up. The elongated marketplace to the right of the central square evidently still served its intended purpose, although most of the business activity of the town took place then as it does today in the main square. In the modern community one can find only here and there buildings that recall the time more than a century ago when New Braunfels ranked with the most important towns in Texas in size and culture.[69]

To many other groups, both American and foreign, Texas seemed to offer a promising future. Lyman Wight led a party of Mormons to Texas in 1845. Settling for a time in Austin, Wight and his followers moved in 1847 to within four miles of Fredericksburg and founded the community of Zodiac. Wight's break with the main body of the church over certain matters of doctrine, damaging floods, and the failures to convert the Indians of the vicinity led to a series of moves from place to place. Ultimately the Mormon colony fell apart, many of the members eventually re-joining their brethren in Utah.[70]

Other utopian groups—religious and sectarian alike—flocked to Texas. They included the followers of the French social reformer, Etienne Cabet, whose 1840 utopian proposal, *Voyage en Icarie*, included a long description of a model metropolitan center.[71] Robert Owen urged Cabet to seek a location in Texas to try out novel ideas of social reform. The Frenchman agreed to purchase one million acres from one of the Texas *empresarios* then in London and dispatched a small group of his countrymen to Texas via New Orleans. Everything quickly went wrong. The tract turned out to contain only 100,000 acres, and alternate sections belonged to the government. After a short time the group returned to New Orleans, where they met Cabet who had arrived with some 500 followers. Half of them defected when they learned of the

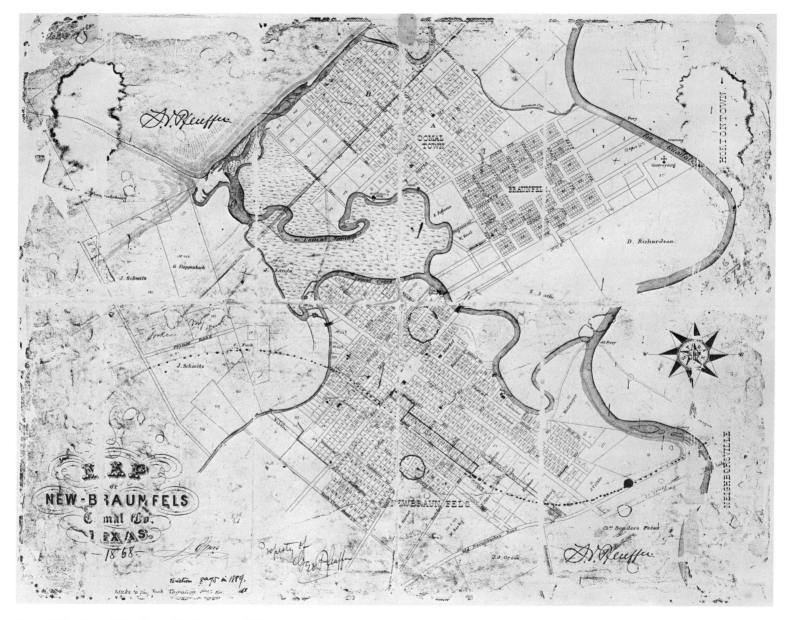

Figure 5.24 Plan of New Braunfels, Texas: ca. 1868

Figure 5.25 View of Indianola, Texas: 1860

Figure 5.26 View of New Braunfels, Texas: 1881

land swindle, and Cabet and the others relinquished further thoughts of Texas settlement and ultimately proceeded up the Mississippi to occupy the former Mormon town of Nauvoo, Illinois.[72]

The path to utopia is strewn with the wreckage of hundreds of failures, of which Texas witnessed its share. One of these involved a group dedicated to achieving the ideal society as prescribed by the well-known French socialist and reformer, Charles Fourier. Victor Considerant led them in 1855 to a site in northeastern Texas that he had selected on an earlier visit to America. It lay on the west fork of the Trinity River about three miles west of a little settlement growing up near the cabin of John Neely Bryan.[73]

Considerant's party consisted mainly of skilled craftsmen and professionals. In addition to carpenters, millwrights, blacksmiths, and shoemakers, the group included several architects, two engineers, a lithographer, a winemaker, physicians, a geologist, a painter, a botanist, a writer, two musicians, three bankers, and two caterers![74]

Near the center of the 2,080-acre tract, Considerant decided to locate the town. Figure 5.27 shows the intricate design for this community—La Réunion—which may have been the work of architects John Louckx and Rudolph Vreidag. The elaborate pattern of great radial boulevards combined with the more conventional gridiron streets and including a number of open spaces of odd shapes and sizes represented the first attempt to establish sophisticated European baroque planning principles on the western frontier. It was, however, more of a catalog of baroque design elements than an effectively integrated plan. The boulevards seem to lead nowhere, and except for the two open spaces near the center there seems to have been little thought given to how such civic squares should be laid out as monumental or formal features around which major buildings could be erected.

The governor's mansion facing the square at the left center and identified with the number "1" on the drawing was the most imposing structure erected. Considerant lived here, and it also served as a meeting room, fort, and place of worship. Apparently, the only other buildings existing when the plat was filed for record in June, 1858, are shown in black. Those facing the other central square appear to have been located without any regard for the orientation of what must have been intended as an important feature of civic design.

La Réunion proved a wildly impractical venture. The colonists possessed few of the skills necessary for frontier life; floods or drought destroyed their crops; and their attempts to organize life on a communal basis as Fourier had prescribed proved futile. By 1858 the experiment

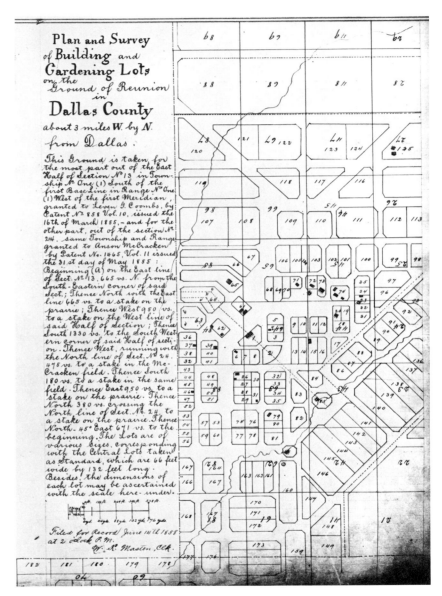

Figure 5.27 Plan of La Réunion (Dallas), Texas: 1858

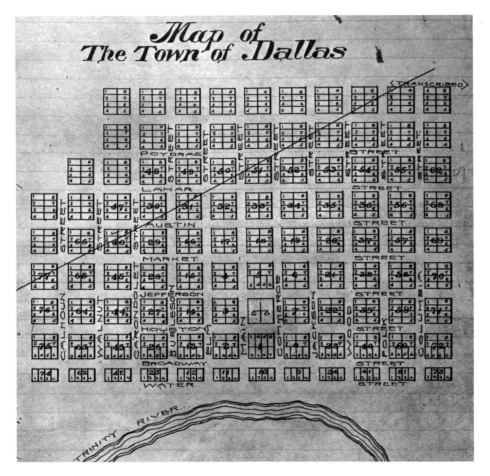

Figure 5.28 Plan of Dallas, Texas: 1855

ended. His followers repudiated Considerant; the company began to liquidate its assets; and most of the colonists moved to John Bryan's settlement three miles away. One more utopia had given way before the harsh realities of the American frontier.[75]

Three years before this occurred, John Bryan had filed the town plat reproduced in Figure 5.28 with the officials of newly created Dallas County. This paper community occupied Bryan's 640-acre headright claim granted him in 1841. Probably he had surveyed all or part of the tract as a town and sold some lots there as early as 1845, but he had failed to record his survey for fear that his title to the site would be contested.

Bryan either deliberately or unwittingly had squatted on a portion of one of the Texas *empresario* colonies. Complicating matters was another tract in the same area claimed by John Grigsby, who had received a one-league (4,605 acre) grant for his military service in the war of Texas independence. The diagonal line cutting across Bryan's town plat represents the boundary between the two claims.

While Bryan boldly extended his 80-foot streets and 200-foot blocks into a part of the Grigsby tract, only the larger section of Dallas nearer the river was ultimately developed on this pattern. As was to occur so often throughout the West and over and over again in Dallas, other and later landowners at the edges of the growing city surveyed their properties as they saw fit rather than following the original pattern of the first town planner. Bryan's own cabin stood in the middle of half-block number 10. A short distance away, identified by the rude representation of the scales of justice, he reserved a block for the courthouse.[76]

Around this nucleus Dallas began to develop. Growth took place at a leisurely pace despite Bryan's strenuous efforts to publicize his town. The census of 1850 did not list the place, and Bryan sold his interest two years later. Apparently he believed his community offered little economic promise. Bryan appeared to be correct, for at the outbreak of the Civil War its population was less than 800.

Thirty-five miles to the west of the embryonic town of Dallas, on what was then known as the West Fork of the Trinity River, another settlement was beginning to take form. This was Fort Worth, a former army post established in 1849. Major Ripley A. Arnold had first located his troops in the valley but soon moved them to a fine site at the top of a bluff overlooking the river. There he directed the construction of barracks, hospital, commissary storerooms, officers' quarters, guardhouse, and other buildings in a large rectangle facing an open parade ground.[77]

For four years this military post served to protect the thin line of settlers pushing westward from Indian raids. After it was abandoned by the army in the fall of 1853, it was occupied by a few persons who found it easier to modify the former military buildings than to construct their own houses and stores elsewhere. Some of its former army occupants returned to the area when their enlistments were up, and at an election held in November, 1856, Fort Worth mustered enough votes to capture the county seat from Birdville, nine miles to the east.[78] The first courthouse was erected on a portion of the old parade ground, which was evidently retained in whole or in part as the public square of the little settlement. Apparently the first streets followed the rectilinear pattern of the military post, and on them or fronting the courthouse square, stores, houses, a school, and other buildings were constructed to join those surviving from the brief period when Fort Worth served as a frontier garrison.

Roughly half-way between Dallas and Austin, another new city made its appearance on the Texas scene at midcentury. This was Waco on the Brazos River, where a few settlers had built their cabins and engaged in farming and trading with the Indians of a nearby village as early as 1844. On March 1, 1849, George Erath and Jacob de Cordova planned a town for a group of landowners who had finally acquired clear title to the area.

The gridiron street pattern extended outward from a central square. The main street led from the river to the midpoint of one of the square's sides and continued from the other side in the same manner. Two other streets formed the other sides of the square. Town lots fronting the square sold for ten dollars; others were half this price. Around the town the surveyors laid off rectangular farming tracts, which brought two to three dollars an acre.

The place proved attractive to settlers, and stores and a hotel were soon erected. In 1850 Waco succeeded in being designated the county seat for McLennan County in exchange for an offer of land for public purposes and a 10 per cent share of proceeds from the sale of all remaining lots. Waco Female College, established by the Methodists in 1857, and Waco University, founded in 1861 and renamed Baylor University 25 years later, made the new town an educational center.[79]

Such new and thriving cities as Galveston, Houston, and New Braunfels, soon eclipsed the older centers of La Bahía (now Goliad) and Nacogdoches. It must have seemed for a time that San Antonio, battered by the Texas revolution and then reoccupied by Mexican troops in 1842, would suffer a similar fate. The plan of the town in 1836 reproduced in Figure 5.29 indicates that it had undergone few changes under Mexican administration. The mission of San Antonio de Valero—The Alamo—had been virtually destroyed during the siege of the town, and damage elsewhere had been extensive. A major influx of German immigrants in the 1840s introduced new styles of buildings, but for the most part San Antonio consisted of one-story adobe structures clus-

tered around or near the two plazas separated by the parish church.

In 1844, a visitor from the nearby new town of Castroville estimated the town's population at "about 1,000 . . . nine-tenths of whom were Mexicans, and the Spanish language was generally spoke." Commerce Street, then called El Potrero ("the Horse Pasture"), was lined with flat-roofed houses of mortar and gravel. Most of the buildings on other streets and not fronting on the plazas were of "mesquite sticks . . . more or less chinked with clay, with roofs of tules, a kind of rush that grew very abundantly."[80]

Two views painted in 1849 show the character of the plaza that had been planned more than a century earlier as the center of the civil community. The first—Figure 5.30—shows the east side with Commerce and Market Streets leading to the loop in the San Antonio River. Figure 5.31 reveals the appearance of the opposite side with the church near the center flanked by two short streets connecting this civic open space with the old military plaza of the former *presidio* beyond.

The town expanded with the continued influx of Germans and the arrival of a substantial American population following the admission of Texas into the Union and the Mexican War. In the process its appearance was somewhat modified. Frederick Law Olmsted described the mixture of architectural styles he encountered on his visit in 1856:

"The singular composite character of the town is palpable at the entrance. For five minutes the houses were evidently German, of fresh square-cut blocks of creamy-white limestone, mostly of a single story and humble proportions, but neat, and thoroughly roofed and finished." A third plaza had developed around the Alamo. "This," Olmsted noted, "is all Mexican" with "windowless cabins of stakes, plastered with mud and roofed with river grass." In Commerce Street he found "American houses," set back somewhat from the street, "with galleries and jalousies and a garden picket-fence against the walk," or, in some cases, rising "in three-story brick to respectable city fronts."

Many of the Mexican buildings near and fronting the plazas had by that time been "put to all sorts of new uses. . . . Windows have been knocked in their blank walls, letting the sun into their dismal vaults, and most of them are stored with dry goods and groceries, which overflow around the door." Side by side with these structures Olmsted found around the plaza "American hotels, and new glass-fronted stores, alternating with sturdy battlemented Spanish walls, and confronted by the dirty, grim, old stuccoed stone cathedral."[81]

It is the town in this period of transition that the German artist Herman Lungkwitz depicted in 1852. Neither Spanish, German, or Ameri-

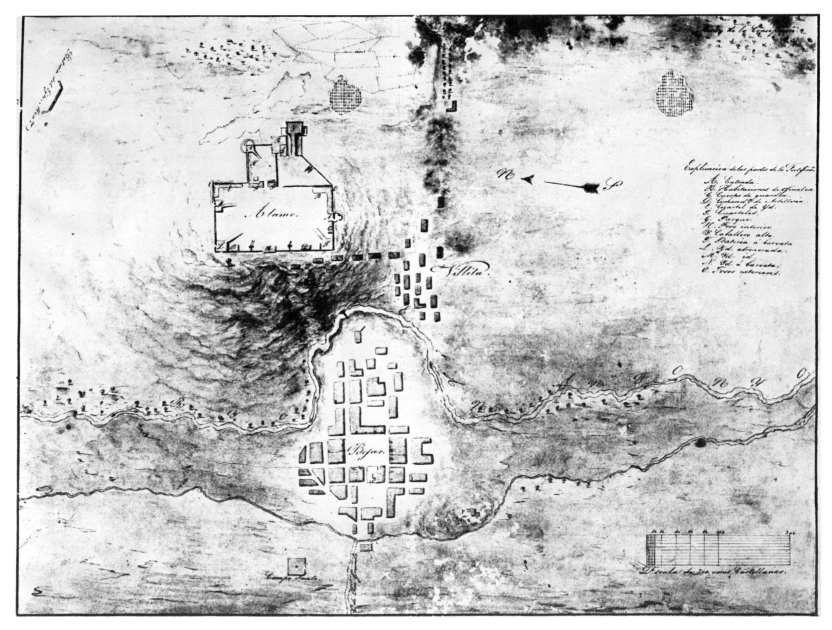

Figure 5.29 Plan of San Antonio, Texas: 1836

Figure 5.30 View of the East Side of the Main Plaza in San Antonio, Texas: 1849

Figure 5.31   View of the West Side of the Main Plaza in San Antonio, Texas: 1849

can, San Antonio as seen from the outskirts in Plate 5 was a fascinating combination of several cultures. Its population was about 3,500. During the next decade it more than doubled in size to exceed 8,000. The character of San Antonio—and indeed of all of Texas—had thus undergone a marked change in the brief period since independence. Scores of new towns now dotted the landscape, and although ranching and farming still retained an influential place in the economy of the region, urban life was gaining in importance. In the process, the remnants of the Hispanic tradition of town planning and architecture would be all but forgotten.

VI

Northern California: Urban Planning and Development
in the Post-Hispanic Years

To the military officials responsible for government in American California as well as to the land-hungry Yankee settlers who arrived soon after hostilities ceased between the United States and Mexico, nothing must have seemed stranger and less business-like than the system of land titles under which prewar residents claimed ownership of property. At best, local land records were imprecise; at worst, they were chaotic or nonexistent. Under Spain and Mexico, land had been transferred through verbal grants or the most informal of records and surveys. Since land existed in abundance and the population remained limited in numbers, exact boundary surveys and official records of such matters seemed of little importance.

In any event, everyone knew where one town lot, farm field, or *rancho* ended and another began because ownership patterns changed slowly and often had persisted through two or more generations of the same family. Where surveys had been carried out, they provided at most only an approximation of distances and compass bearings. The rawhide cords used by the Spanish instead of the normal surveyor's chain of relatively stable dimensions stretched or shrank depending on temperature and humidity. Rocks, trees, and streambeds were used to identify points of beginning and corners of tract boundaries. Description of such marks may have given the illusion of some precision; to find these points on the ground ten or fifty years later was quite another thing.[1]

Until 1850, when California gained admission to the union as a state, it was technically under military government. Municipalities continued to function but with officials appointed or approved by the commanders and their advisers.[2] These officials were directed to prepare adequate surveys to record existing town boundaries, the location of streets, and the dimensions of lots. These surveys provided an opportunity as well to plan and lay out additional areas for future urban expansion.

In 1846, Lt. Washington A. Bartlett, the *alcalde* appointed to administer the affairs of Yerba Buena, commissioned Jasper O'Farrell to resurvey and extend the town. O'Farrell was an Irish engineer who had lived for a time at Valparaiso, Chile, and then came to California as a surveyor. On February 22, 1847, O'Farrell completed the plan reproduced in Figure 6.1. It bore the new name of San Francisco, the result of a proclamation Bartlett issued three weeks earlier officially replacing the earlier name of Yerba Buena.[3]

O'Farrell rectified the 2½° deviations from right angles of the Vioget street system. This action, known as "O'Farrell's Swing," was accepted by all property owners except one, although it required a few buildings to be demolished or moved from their original locations when it was found they stood in the right-of-way of the new street lines. All the blocks except those interrupted by the waterline and the one containing the enlarged Portsmouth Square contained six lots, each 50 *varas* (138¾ feet) square.

Immediately prior to O'Farrell's survey San Francisco according to one account had a population of "between one and two hundred . . . composed almost exclusively of foreigners."[4] The view reproduced in Plate 6, although published 30 years later, shows the city's appearance with reasonable accuracy during the winter of 1846-47.[5] Montgomery Street then ran along the shore of Yerba Buena Cove as the eastern boundary. Kearney Street followed the contour of the slope a few hundred feet to the west. Clay and Washington led up the hill. Between them and facing the open ground of what was to become Portsmouth Square stood the customhouse and jail.

O'Farrell's survey provided the basis for San Francisco's first land boom, which transformed this placid village into a bustling town and, after the California Gold Rush, into a throbbing metropolis. The 50-*vara* lots were put up for sale at $12.00 each plus a recording fee of $3.62½. As the *California Star* reported on August 28, 1847, "there was originally a municipal regulation . . . which prohibited any man from purchasing more than one lot." Land speculators quickly found they could circumvent this by purchasing property in the name of others, thus acquiring "quite a number of lots . . . with the avowed intention of holding them at such prices as would enable them to reap a fortune."[6]

Municipal officials set O'Farrell to work again, surveying additional streets, blocks, and lots. Their motives were mixed. Many—perhaps all—were themselves involved in land speculation. They probably believed as well that the city was destined to grow and required an expansion plan. Further, sale of land provided a quick and easy method of raising municipal revenues. O'Farrell ran his street lines some distance into Yerba Buena Cove, and the blocks thus created on paper but still under water were cut up into lots 16½ by 50 *varas* (46 by 138¾ feet).

To the north, west, and south the gridiron streets of O'Farrell's first survey were extended for several blocks. Beyond this area to the south O'Farrell laid out a second gridiron section tilted 45° from the first. Here he planned blocks 200-by-300 *varas* (555 by 832½ feet) divided into 6 lots each 100 *varas* (277½ feet) square. The streets in this new grid were 75 and 80 feet wide, while those of his original survey and its extension were only 60 feet in width.

Figure 6.1
Plan of San Francisco,
California: 1847

Between the two grids O'Farrell planned Market Street with a width of 110 feet. This major thoroughfare ran from the cove toward the southwest in the direction of Mission Dolores. O'Farrell may have had this in mind when he determined its axis but a more likely explanation is that this alignment allowed him to follow a relatively level stretch of ground at the base of the steep hill whose southern slope terminated at this point.

O'Farrell's design as further extended in 1849 by William M. Eddy, then city surveyor, appears in Figure 6.2.[7] Aside from Portsmouth Square, which already existed, and the small square south of Market Street that Eddy provided, in the vast gridiron with which O'Farrell branded the steep hills of San Francisco he provided only two other civic open spaces. Both lay between Powell and Stockton Streets. That to the north is the modern Washington Square. The one on the south is Union Square. The latter gradually developed as the heart of the business district and is one of America's finest urban squares.

O'Farrell's handling of the transition between one gridiron section and the other betrays his limited understanding of even the most elementary aspects of town planning. The Y- and T-shaped intersections along Market Street have plagued the city from his day to ours. They have proved to be dangerous to traffic, awkward for construction, and a visual distraction. The spacing of the streets leading southeast from Market almost seems to have been deliberately intended to stifle the free flow of traffic.

A person looking only at this map and not knowing the location would never guess the nature of the site's topography. As a critic of San Francisco's design observed in 1869, it was "as rugged and irregular as that to which Romulus and Remus applied themselves on the banks of the Tiber." To Vioget and O'Farrell "it made but very little difference that some of the streets . . . followed the lines of a dromedary's back, or that others described semi-circles—some up, some down—up Telegraph Hill from the eastern front of the city—up a grade, which a goat could not travel—then down on the other side—then up Russian Hill, and then down sloping toward the Presidio."

The planners of San Francisco "little knew, when . . . at work . . . with . . . compasses and rulers, that every line . . . would entail a useless expenditure of millions." It was a "gage of battle . . . flung down to Nature on this peninsula" in "such a light and careless manner" that "provoked a struggle which cannot be ended probably in the life-time of the present generation. The work of grading, cutting down, and filling up, will have to be continued till the logical result of the contest has been reached." This observer regarded the Vioget plan as modified and extended by O'Farrell as a "first error" from which "there is, of course, no escape."[8]

If the drawing reproduced in Figure 6.3 is correct, only a small portion of the enormous grid plan for the city had been built on by the fall of 1848. The town then consisted of less than 70 buildings, some of which were still oriented to Vioget's irregular grid and with a few encroaching on the streets surveyed by O'Farrell to bring their intersections at right angles. Perhaps a few other structures existed elsewhere, scattered here and there along what at that time were still paper streets of the 1847 O'Farrell extensions.

Not even the most enthusiastic boosters of the town's future could have foreseen the spectacular growth that would soon occur following the electrifying news that gold had been discovered in the Sierras. Perhaps the principal virtue of the O'Farrell plan was that it provided a basic framework for accommodating the thousands of new residents that settled in San Francisco in so short a time. The results of the gold rush were chaotic enough; without a prior plan for streets, blocks, and lots of such generous proportions, conditions might have been much worse.

Bayard Taylor arrived in San Francisco in mid-August, 1849, to find "hundreds of tents and houses . . . scattered all over the heights, and along the shore for more than a mile." Near the waterfront where he landed, "on every side stood buildings of all kinds, begun or half-finished, and the greater part of them mere canvas sheds, open in front, and covered with all kinds of signs, in all languages. Great quantities of goods were piled up in the open air, for want of a place to store them."[9]

The view reproduced in Figure 6.4 was published six weeks after Taylor first saw the city. Dozens of ships, many of them deserted by their crews, who scrambled off in search of gold, crowded the harbor. On the left one can see the beginning of construction on the steep slopes of Telegraph Hill. Rincon Point to the right apparently had not yet been occupied, but the earliest streets of the town in the center of the view were jammed with buildings. Some filling of the shallows beyond Montgomery Street in the area O'Farrell had platted as water lots provided additional sites for warehouses, stores, and hotels.

So swift was the pace of development that when Taylor returned from his travels at the end of December he could scarcely believe it was the same town he had described less than five months earlier. He estimated that in the intervening period "more than four thousand

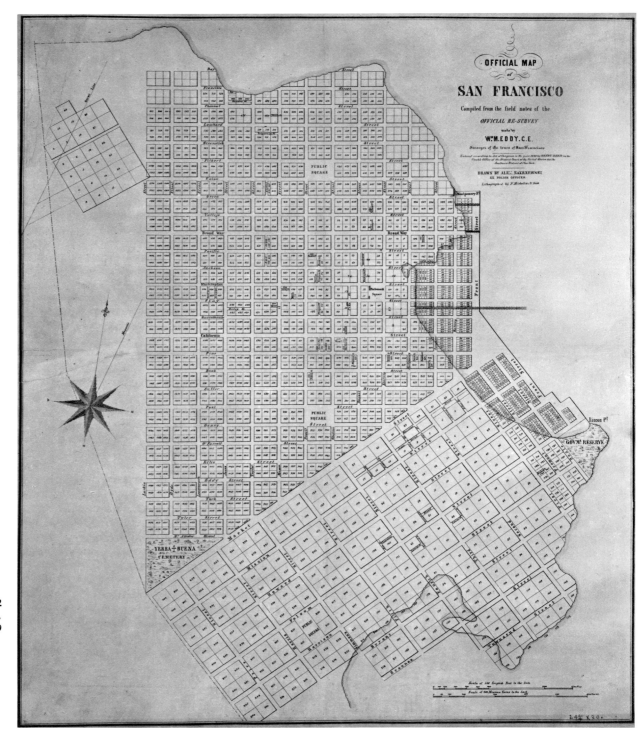

Figure 6.2
Plan of San Francisco,
California: 1849

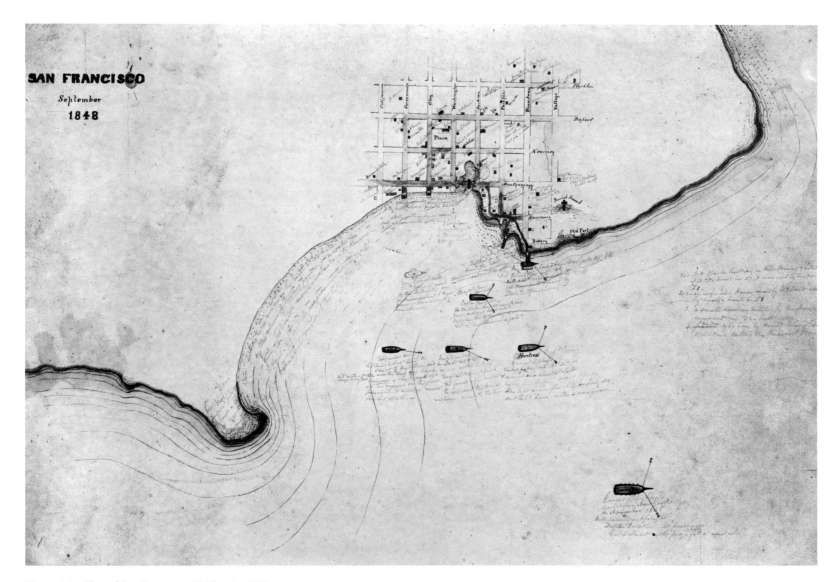

Figure 6.3   Plan of San Francisco, California: 1848

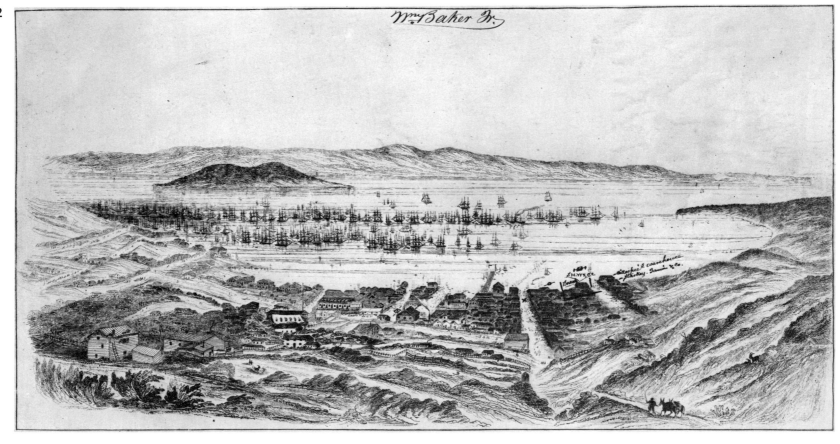

Figure 6.4 View of San Francisco, California: 1849

emigrants by sea had landed in San Francisco.'' Most of them immediately bolted for the mining districts, but enough remained or returned to swell the population and to contribute to the city's physical growth.

Taylor noted that now there were ''many . . . large three-story warehouses'' at the foot of Telegraph Hill. Looking northward from the same vantage point as the view in Figure 6.5 published in 1849, Taylor could see that ''the beautiful crescent of the harbor, stretching from the Rincon . . . a distance of more than a mile, was lined with boats, tents, and warehouses, and . . . several piers jutted into the water. Montgomery Street, fronting the bay, had undergone a marvellous change. All the open spaces were built up, the canvas houses replaced by ample three-story buildings, an exchange with lofty skylight fronted the water, and for the space of half a mile the throng of men of all classes, characters, and nations, with carts and animals, equaled Wall Street be-

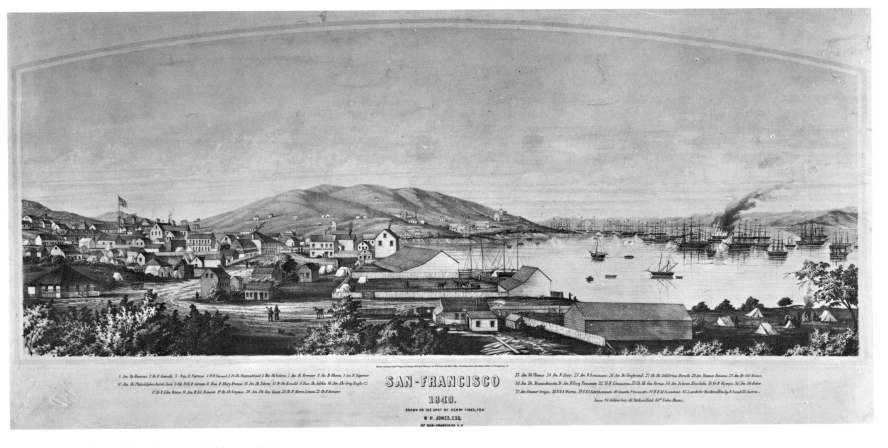

Figure 6.5 View of San Francisco, California: 1849

fore three o'clock." Equally dramatic changes had taken place elsewhere: "tents and canvas houses had given place to large and handsome edifices, blanks had been filled up, new hotels opened, market houses in operation and all the characteristics of a great commercial city fairly established." San Francisco, Taylor concluded, "seemed to have accomplished in a day the growth of half a century."[10]

The little village of Yerba Buena in July of 1846 had a population of

perhaps 200. Two years later it probably reached 1,000. In July, 1849, there were an estimated 5,000 residents; six months later, with the closing down of many mines for the winter, the city's population reached 20,000. By the end of 1852 this had more than doubled to 42,000.[11] Land prices followed the trend in population. E. Gould Buffum wrote in May, 1849, that the 50-*vara* lots sold for a few dollars by municipal authorities in 1847 brought $500 a year later, but "had now risen in value to from three to five thousand." Seven months later Buffum reported that "a lot on Portsmouth Square, which was purchased some three years ago for fifteen dollars, and sold last May for six thousand, was purchased a few days since for forty thousand dollars!"[12]

Land prices may have soared, and the tents and shacks of the first residents replaced by more substantial structures, but the town wore the unmistakable look of a raw and unfinished community. The view of the commercial heart of the town in 1851, reproduced as Plate 7, was drawn by an English visitor at about the time a fellow countryman recorded these impressions of San Francisco:

"Everything bore evidence of newness, and the greater part of the city presented a makeshift and temporary appearance, being composed of the most motley collection of edifices, in the way of houses, which can well be conceived. Some were mere tents, with perhaps a wooden front . . . some were composed of sheets of zinc on a wooden framework; there were numbers of corrugated iron houses, the most unsightly things possible, and generally painted brown; there were many important American houses, all, of course, painted white, with green shutters; also dingy-looking Chinese houses, and occasionally some substantial brick buildings; but the great majority were nondescript, shapeless, patchwork concerns, in the fabrication of which, sheet-iron, wood, zinc and canvass, seemed to have been employed indiscriminately; while here and there, in the middle of a row of such houses, appeared the hulk of a ship, which had been hauled up, and now served as a warehouse, the cabins being fitted up as offices, or sometimes converted into a boarding-house."[13]

Even O'Farrell's enormous grid could not accommodate the growing population, or at least those residents who found land speculation a fascinating and, on paper at least, a profitable pastime. Four years after the city received its charter from the new state legislature in 1851 Mayor James Van Ness proposed that the city survey and sell the lands within its boundaries lying beyond the limits of O'Farrell's plat. Three ordinances passed in 1856 asserted municipal ownership of all land not previously granted and occupied in this area, reserved several sites for public use, and approved the street plan reproduced in Figure 6.6.[14]

In what was called the Western Addition the city thus extended the rigid grid street pattern westward from Larkin to Divisadero Streets and, south of Market Street, platted the land in the vicinity of Mission Dolores. Municipal authorities reserved a number of squares or parks in the Western Addition. Perhaps this was in response to complaints the previous year published in the *Annals of San Francisco*. The authors

criticized the lack of open space in the O'Farrell plat as a "strange mistake" that could "only be attributed to the jealous avarice of the city projectors in turning every square vara of the site, to an available building lot." The unimaginative grid street system used by city officials drew a stinging rebuke: "The eye is wearied, and the imagination quite stupefied, in looking over the numberless square—all square—building blocks, and mathematically straight lines of streets, miles long and every one crossing a host of others at right angles, stretching over sandy hill, chasm and plain, without the least regard to the natural inequalities of the ground. Not only is there no public park or garden, but there is not even a circus, oval, open terrace, broad avenue or any ornamental line of street or building."[15] The several squares and small parks of the Western Addition provided a partial answer to this plea for civic beauty and recreation space, but the development of a major recreation area was not to be realized until a later date.

The new extension plan ignored topography as casually as before. The "natural inequalities of the ground" over which the new streets were to run can be seen in Figure 6.7, a view of the city from the northeast published in 1868. From the waterfront in the foreground, by then pushed several blocks eastward beyond Montgomery Street, to the far edge of the city in the direction of the Pacific Coast, the streets of the vastly extended grid rose and fell precipitously as they crossed the steep hills and ridges of the peninsula. Only a part of Telegraph Hill at the right had escaped the brand of the ubiquitous gridiron.

O'Farrell's and Eddy's design for the portion of the city south of Market Street suited the topography somewhat better, although the slopes of Rincon Hill, seen at the left foreground in the view, were as formidable as any encountered elsewhere. While many of the mansions of San Francisco's early elite were built here, Nob Hill, soaring above the business district on the original Yerba Buena site, developed as the fashionable residential area in the late 1860s. During the following decade San Francisco's distinctive cable cars came into general use, and the clanking of the cars and the slapping of the underground cables signaled the arrival of a partial solution to the problems created by the unwise adoption of the gridiron street system.

The New England editor and publisher Samuel Bowles visited San Francisco in 1865 and wrote amusingly of the steep and wind-blown sandy streets. He found his friend, the Reverend Horatio Stebbins, minister of the Unitarian Church, "holding on by main strength to a side hill that runs up at an angle of something like thirty degrees." Some of the streets were being re-graded, leaving "the early houses,—

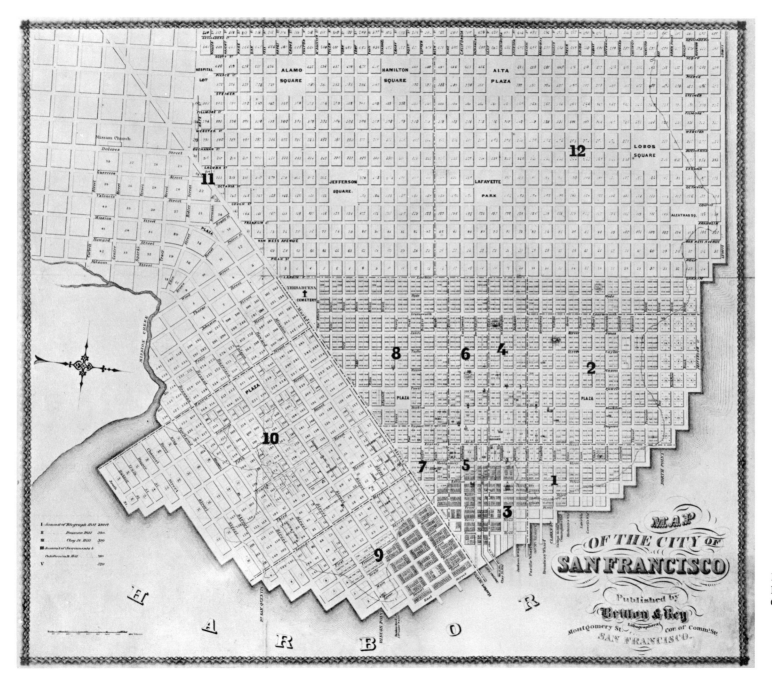

Figure 6.6
Plan of San Francisco,
California: ca. 1856

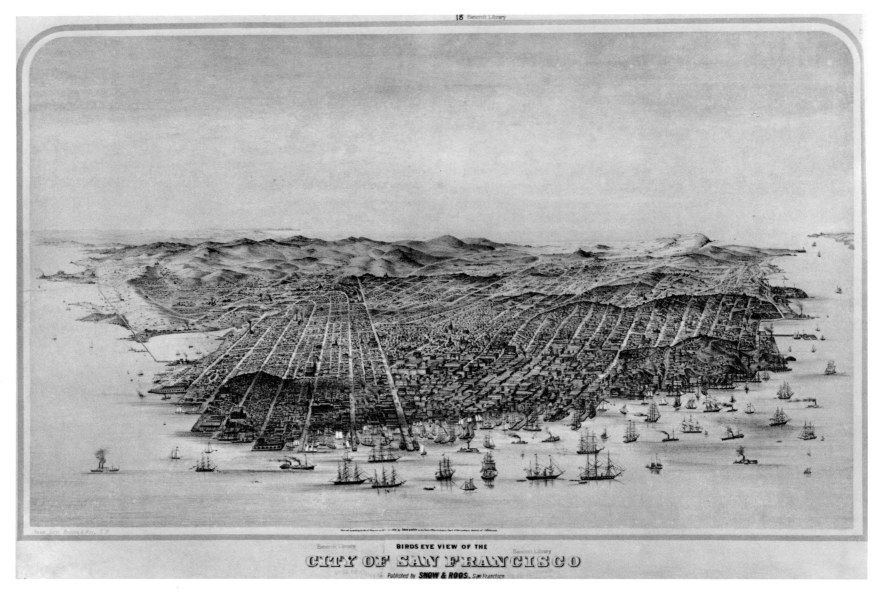

BIRDS EYE VIEW OF THE
CITY OF SAN FRANCISCO
Published by **SNOW & ROOS**, San Francisco

Figure 6.7   View of San Francisco, California: 1868

that is those built four or five years ago,—away up one hundred feet or more in the air, and reached by long flights of steep steps." The sandy soil and the strong winds created additional problems: "Wherever the hillsides and tops are fastened with houses or pavements, or twice daily seduced with water, there the foundations are measurably secure; and the deed of the purchaser means something; but all elsewhere, all the open lots and unpaved paths are still undergoing the changing and creative process. The daily winds swoop up the soil in one place and deposit it in another in great masses, like drifts of snow. You will often find a suburban street blocked up with fresh sand; and the owner of vacant lots needs certainly to pay them daily visit in order to swear to title; and the chance is anyway that, between one noon and another, he and his neighbor will have changed properties to an indefinite depth."[16]

While the other California towns of Spanish origin experienced a more leisurely growth rate, the influx of American settlers also required the preparation of expansion plans. At Monterey two new streets were surveyed as early as March 1847 under the first American *alcalde*, Walter Colton. An Englishman, William Robert Garner, who helped with this project observed that their work was handicapped because "each person has built his house on the spot and in the form he thought proper, without any attention to regularity." Sites for a jail, marketplace, cemetery, and public square were also mapped at this time.[17]

A more ambitious extension dates from 1849, when the council ordered a comprehensive plan prepared for the town, provided for compensation to persons whose property was found to lie within proposed streets, and specified that no one was allowed to build without a permit.[18] The faint lines on the faded manuscript plat reproduced in Figure 6.8 reveal the results of the survey prepared by Don Pedro Narvaez. The capital of California in the few months remaining when it would enjoy that status thus at last had an official town plan.

At its center, the surveyor had obviously been at pains to fit his streets to the existing pattern of land ownership and building occupancy. What resulted was a hodge-podge of short streets of various widths, angled intersections, and irregular blocks, one of which was designated as the plaza. Beyond this portion of the town the blocks took a more regular form created by generally straight streets spaced at greater distances to provide for deeper lots.

This design was no more unimaginative than that established to guide the development of San Francisco, and it may have been some-

Figure 6.8 Plan of Monterey, California: 1849

what more intelligently adapted to existing conditions. In any event, it proved adequate to accommodate most of Monterey's growth for the next several decades. When San José became the capital city in 1850, much of the potential for Monterey's expansion was lost. One happy outcome was that many of the older buildings from the Mexican period managed to survive until programs of preservation and conservation in the modern era could guarantee their continued existence.[19]

At the oldest of the California civil settlements, San José, surveyors set to work soon after the American occupation in an effort to provide adequate land records and to provide for the expansion that seemed inevitable. The *ayuntamiento* and *alcalde* engaged William Campbell and his brother, Thomas, to lay out streets and building sites in May of 1847. They proceeded to survey the land now bounded by Market, Julian, 8th, and Reed Streets in the heart of the modern city. How much of the old Spanish and Mexican town was incorporated in their plan does not seem to be known, and it is quite possible that the municipal authorities decided to subdivide what was essentially an open and undeveloped tract of land near or adjacent to the existing settlement. The Campbells did provide for a public square four times the size of the surrounding rectangular blocks, but it is unlikely that this occupied any part of whatever plaza may have been laid out in Spanish San José.[20]

Several persons claimed ownership of portions of the land within the townsite and challenged the right of officials to convey the lots that had been laid out. Charles M. Weber, the founder of Stockton, succeeded in gaining title to four of the city lots in recognition of the possible validity of his claim, but at least one other claim was denied. For some reason a second survey of the town was ordered later in 1847, and it is this plan by C. S. Lyman, later a professor at Yale, that appears in Figure 6.9.[21] It was Lyman's design that provided the basis for the initial growth of the city and its subsequent extensions.

Lyman enlarged and named Washington Square, adding the equivalent of two city blocks to its area. Now incorporated into the campus of San José State University, the square's original generous dimensions were 1,160 by 1,005 feet. Lyman also designated St. James Square, now a city park, 610 by 550 feet and the Market Place, 259 by 1,160 feet. The latter he skillfully arranged so that San Antonio Street would serve as an axis between it and Washington Square.

Market, Santa Clara, and Main (now 5th Street) Streets were made 100 feet wide. San José Street was only 60 feet in width, but all others were given a width of 80 feet. Except for the range of lots between San Fernando and Santa Clara Streets and in a few places at the edges of the tract, blocks were 550 feet long and divided into eight lots, each with a frontage of 137½ feet. Lyman for some reason platted the lots with a depth somewhat less than the frontage. He also seemed to have overlooked the need for access to the lots in the center of the blocks northwest of Market Place.

Beyond the limits of Lyman's town plat, J. D. Hutton in July and August of 1847 surveyed a large portion of the *pueblo* lands into 500-acre parcels. American newcomers proposed this division of the public lands for free distribution to all heads of families and were successful in persuading municipal officials to adopt such a policy. Figure 6.10 shows this division of land and the names of the new owners, who drew lots to decide the order of priority each person would have in selecting his tract. Although these so-called Five-Hundred-Acre titles were later de-

clared invalid by the California Supreme Court, several of the tracts near the city were previously subdivided as extensions of the town. The title to lots sold in these areas were confirmed by later conveyances from the city to their occupants.[22]

San José was near enough to the Sierra Mother Lode to profit by the California gold rush. Bayard Taylor, arriving in late August, 1849, called it "one of the most flourishing inland towns in California." Conditions remained somewhat primitive, for Taylor observed that the town "was mainly a collection of adobe houses, with tents and a few clapboard dwellings, of the season's growth, scattered over a square half-mile." Land prices had so risen that the price of lots was exceeded only in San Francisco.

A few weeks later Taylor returned from a visit to Monterey, where the legislature had just designated San José as the new capital. He observed "a wonderful change" in the town. "What with tents and houses of wood and canvas, in hot haste thrown up," it "seemed to have doubled in size. The Dusty streets were thronged with people; goods, for lack of storage room, stood in large piles beside the doors; the sound of saw and hammer, and the rattling of laden carts, were incessant." The action of the legislature had a marked effect on the price of lots, which "had nearly doubled in consequence of this change" in the status of the town.[23]

Enlargement of San José seemed essential, and by 1850, as shown in Figure 6.11, its boundaries had been considerably extended. To the south and the east owners of the 500-acre farm tracts laid off new streets following Lyman's grid system. Except for Reed's Reservation, later platted into blocks and lots, the proprietors did not set aside any land for squares or parks. To the north, on land that had not previously been laid out in farm plots, municipal authorities were more generous in reserving several squares for public uses. Only one of these spaces—East Square—was retained as a park, however, the others apparently being sold to provide additional sites for buildings.

San José did not enjoy its new status for long. The legislators met in a hastily erected adobe capitol erected on the east side of Market Square. The town had lacked funds to build this structure, and 19 citizens signed a note on which money was borrowed to pay for its erection.[24] Its unfinished state, the crowded conditions in the hotels, and the rivalry of other towns caused the legislators to choose Vallejo as the next seat of government.[25]

Helping to ease the inevitable slump that followed the transfer of

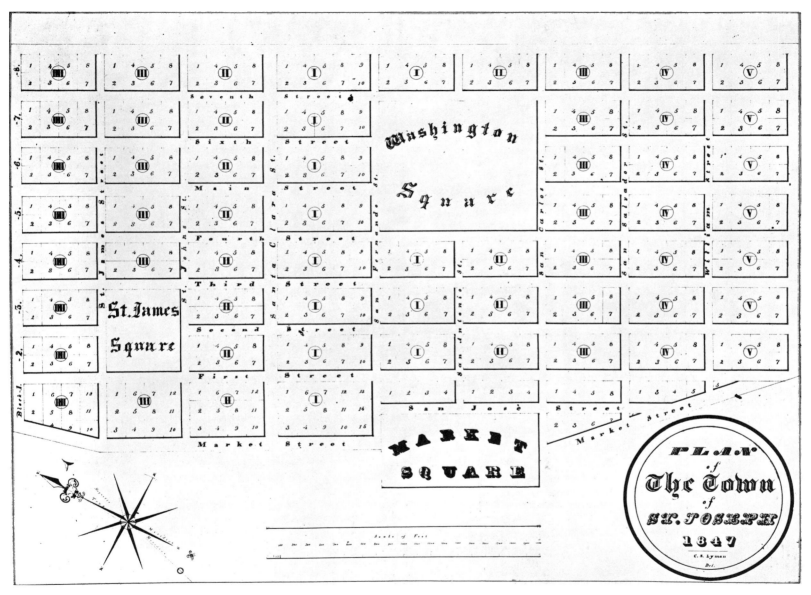

Figure 6.9 Plan of San José, California: 1847

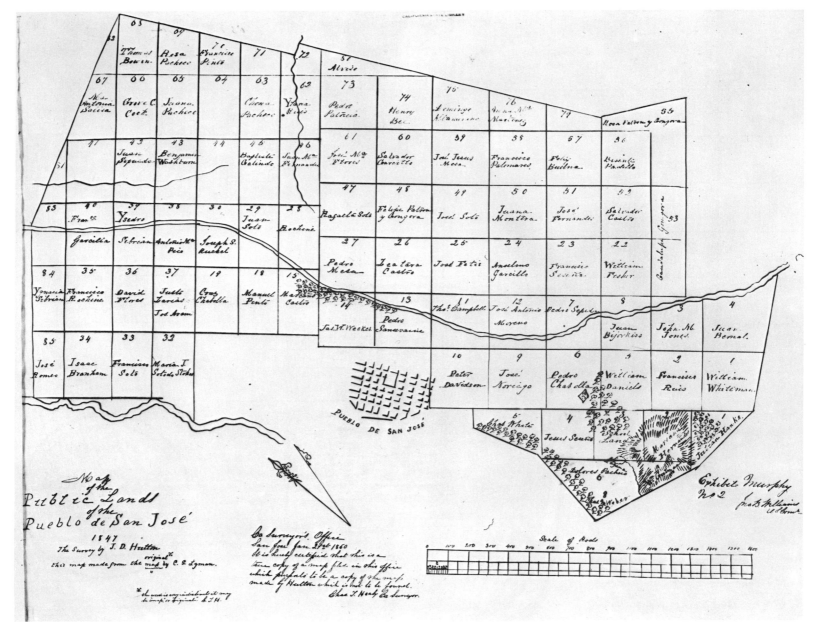

Figure 6.10
Map of San José,
California and
Vicinity: 1850

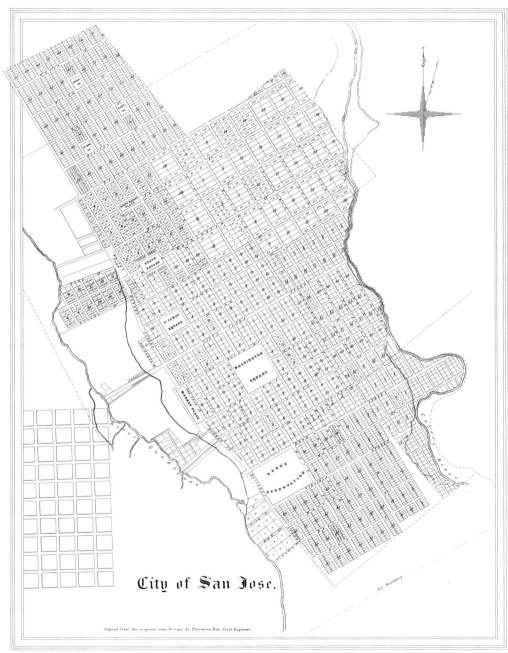

City of San Jose.

Figure 6.11
Plan of San José, California: 1850

governmental activities elsewhere was the development of the New Almaden quicksilver mine 13 miles south of town. During the 1850s and 1860s, production of mercury to meet the demands for gold refining provided a source of employment and wealth.[26] In 1853 about 100 houses were built in the city, and rumors of the construction of a railroad from San Francisco helped to revive the sagging market for real estate. The city council in a burst of unwise generosity voted to give away St. James Square for a depot site, an offer that happily never had to be consummated. In a more intelligent move, the city built a new city hall on Market Street north of Santa Clara Street.[27]

Levi Goodrich served as architect for this project, and in 1858, three years after its completion, he looked southward from its castellated roof to sketch the view reproduced in Figure 6.12. Market Street with its covered board sidewalks was obviously a prosperous business district. Market Square in the distance was not far from the southern limit of development at that time. The intersection of Santa Clara Street in the foreground was the center of activity. Washington Square, beyond the buildings in the left center of the view, marked the eastern extent of concentrated building. The town was still relatively compact, and its population did not exceed 3,000 in 1860.[28]

The long-planned and fervently hoped-for railroad finally made its first run to San Francisco on January 18, 1864. The San José *Mercury* two months earlier had boasted of the city's 77 stores, 18 hotels and restaurants, billiard parlors and bowling alleys, livery stables, and—perhaps rather sheepishly—of the 44 bars and saloons. The paper was quick to add that there were also six churches, so the "it will be seen that the Lord has one church to the devil's seven and one-third."[29] The railroad link up the peninsula to the California metropolis quickly stimulated further development—not only additional bars and a few more churches but stores, flour, lumber and woolen mills, breweries, and banks. During the decade of the 1860s the population of the city more than doubled to 7,000, and there must have been hundreds more living on nearby grain, fruit, and dairy farms that shipped their products to San Francisco via the railroad.[30]

San José at the end of that eventful period is shown in Figure 6.13 as seen from the northwest. The main elements of Lyman's original plan can be identified, with the still open expanse of Washington Square in the center as the most prominent. Opposite St. James Square on the west side of 1st Street stands the domed courthouse completed in 1868. The form of Market Square had been slightly modified by rounding its corners two years earlier, but its plan remained essentially unaltered.

Less orderly was the growth of that portion of the city west of the Guadalupe River along the right side of the view. This land had not been part of the Spanish *pueblo*, and the American municipality thus did not own the land. Its several proprietors were free to cut it into streets and lots in an irregular and disconnected pattern. Remaining in public ownership, however, were immense but disconnected tracts of land within the still larger *pueblo* boundaries confirmed to the city by federal authorities following years of adjudication. Their locations are shown on the map in Figure 6.14, the shaded portions of which represent municipally owned land in 1866. All other tracts lying within the the ancient *pueblo* boundaries had been validly granted or sold, most of them consisting of large *ranchos* conveyed to individuals during the Spanish or Mexican eras.

This map culminated years of litigation involving the claim submitted by the municipality of San José for ownership of the *pueblo* lands. The other municipalities with Spanish or Mexican origins went through the same process, as did all individuals claiming ownership under Spanish or Mexican law who wished to secure clear title that would be upheld in American courts.

Hearing these claims and counter-claims was the United States Board of Land Commissioners created by Congress in 1851.[31] Many owners of *ranchos* were unable to produce the required proof of ownership because they had received their land by verbal conveyance or they had lost the original written documents or surveys. Land-hungry Yankees insisted that the burden of proof lay with the claimant. If he could not prove ownership conclusively his land became part of the federal public domain and was subject to preemption.

On the whole the municipalities emerged from this long, complicated, and expensive process better than might have been expected. San José succeeded in having its *pueblo* claim confirmed for slightly more than 101 square miles, far in excess of the standard four square leagues, or about 28 square miles, prescribed by Spanish law.[32] San Diego's claim for 11 square leagues (roughly 50,000 acres or 78 square miles) was also upheld.[33] Los Angeles claimed 16 square leagues but ultimately had to be content with the standard 4 square leagues.[34]

In San Francisco the claims and counter-claims occupied lawyers, government officials, and judges for years. The stakes were enormously high, and a number of patently fraudulent claims were entered in the hope that somehow the commission and the courts would up-

Figure 6.12 View of San José, California: 1858

hold them. The city's jurisdiction over 17,754 acres (not quite four leagues) was finally established. However, by the time this decision was reached, only some 4,000 acres remained in municipal ownership. The federal government retained title to the land in the vicinity of the *presidio*. Other tracts along the southern portion of the city claim were held to have been validly transferred to private owners as ranchos. Part of the lands belonged to the mission. And the city itself had sold blocks and lots in its relentless expansion westward from the shores of the bay.[35]

The bulk of the remaining municipally owned lands occupied the

Figure 6.13 View of San José, California: 1869

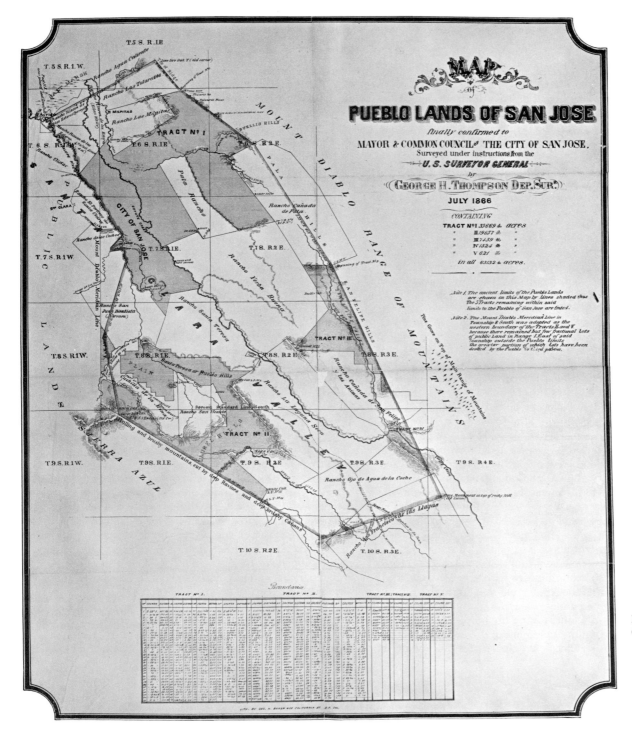

Figure 6.14 Map of San José,
California and Vicinity: 1866

hills and barren sandy slopes extending from the middle of the peninsula westward to the Pacific. Their desolate condition can be seen in Plate 8, a view showing the peninsula and bay as seen from the west in 1868. The most prominent feature in the foreground is the Cliff House, a restaurant and fashionable recreation spot constructed 5 years earlier. A road connected this rocky point to the city, but otherwise most of the land had not yet been developed.

Public authorities thus had a splendid opportunity to plan the remaining 4,000 acres in municipal ownership with greater care and skill than had been employed during the previous two decades of rapid growth. Instead, they continued the senseless grid street pattern over most of the area. They did, however, use part of these remaining *pueblo* lands to create one of America's finest parks.

Agitation for such a project began in the mid-1860s. Frederick Law Olmsted carried out some preliminary studies for a park system. He had earlier achieved a national reputation for his work with Calvert Vaux in designing Central Park in New York and had come to California to manage the Mariposa Mining Estates. While Olmsted's suggestions were not followed, an even larger tract than he proposed was designated for park purposes in 1868. The failure of the city to reserve sufficient land for this purpose at an earlier date required payment of more than $800,000 to extinguish private titles to some of the needed property. Under Park Superintendents William Hammond Hall from 1870 to 1887 and the talented John McLaren from 1887 to 1943, the tract of more than 1,000 sandy and largely barren acres was gradually transformed into Golden Gate Park.[36]

Stretching from the middle of the peninsula westward to the Pacific Ocean, the park is shown in Figure 6.15 as it existed toward the end of the century. Its superbly landscaped grounds, winding carriageways, and pedestrian paths made it a major attraction almost immediately for residents of the city as well as to the increasing number of visitors who journeyed west to see the great new city by the Golden Gate. It was an impressive achievement, rivaled only by Balboa Park in San Diego, the origins of which are discussed in a later chapter. Yet both projects represented the attainment of only a small part of the potential benefits that wise management of the *pueblo* lands from which they were created might have yielded for all of the communities with Spanish and Mexican origins. These two parks and the smaller but still important Elysian Park in Los Angeles were created almost by accident and not as the result of any far-sighted policy in administering the public land trust.

If there was any consistency in the treatment of the urban public domain, it was in the readiness of officials to dispose of it quickly and at almost any price. The historian of the San Diego lands, writing in 1929, vigorously criticized the trustees for their land policies: "Today the City can not show one dollar for more than 40,000 acres of its once most valuable estate, and efforts are stronger now than ever before to get these lands from the City."[37] Almost three decades earlier a Los Angeles historian reflected on the lost opportunities in that city: "All the great expanse, where lie now ten thousand homes, and many blocks of business buildings was once city property, and was sold for trifling amounts, and much of it actually given away in large tracts— and this outrage was committed not during the administration of the careless Californians, but after the occupation by thrifty Americans."

No "great foresight" was required to have achieved other and better results. "All that was needed was a small fraction of intelligence in the sale of it,—the withholding of pieces here and there, of every other lot in favorable tracts, and of occasional ten-acre divisions for parks. Had this policy been pursued, Los Angeles might be today the richest municipality of its size in the Union. That such folly could have been committed as to save practically nothing out of the whole area is almost incredible, but it is true."[38]

Henry George, even then a critic of land speculation, offered a different view in 1868 on how the municipal lands of San Francisco could have been used to benefit the public. He "regretted that the princely domain which San Francisco inherited as the successor of the pueblo was not appropriated to furnishing free, or almost free, homesteads to actual settlers, instead of being allowed to pass into the hands of a few, to make more millionaires."[39]

Nor was public ownership of land by the older communities of California used to assure its development on patterns other than the most routine and boring of street gridirons. Straight streets crossing at right angles were particularly inappropriate for nearly all of the rugged San Francisco site and much of San Diego. Only the stunningly beautiful locations of both cities with their superb views to mountains, bays, and ocean manage to overcome the basic deficiencies of their street systems. While it is true that the dramatic views one has down the precipitous hill streets of San Francisco can be overwhelming, this same effect could have been retained by skillful planning, while the continued dangers and original costly grading and construction costs could have been reduced.

Most private real estate developers were content to follow the city's lead and cut up land under their control into rectangular blocks. One such area prior to intensive development can be seen at the left of the view reproduced in Figure 6.16. This fine depiction of San Francisco is-

Figure 6.15 View of Golden Gate Park, San Francisco, California: 1892

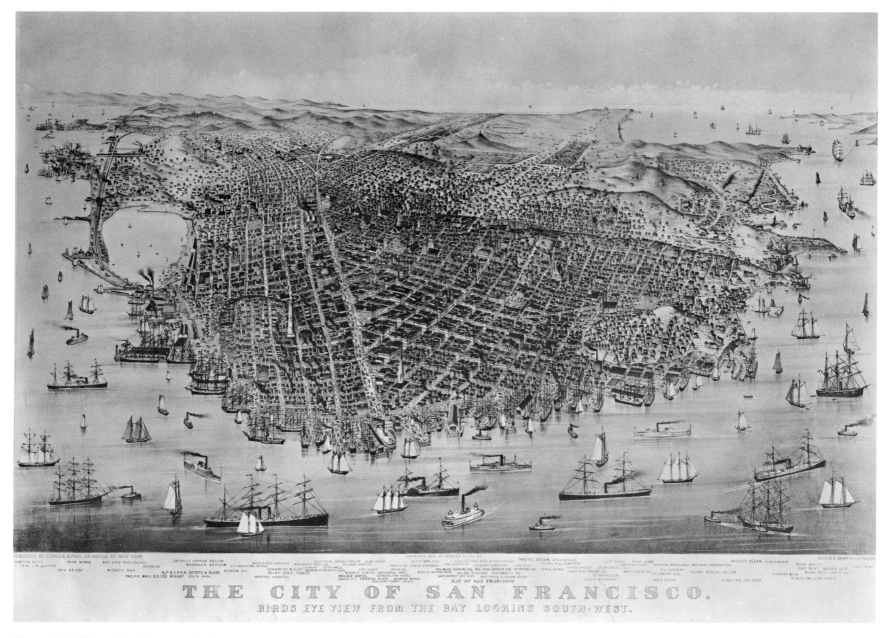

Figure 6.16 View of San Francisco, California: 1878

sued by the firm of Currier and Ives in 1878 shows the enclosure of Mission Bay by railroad tracks extending southward down the peninsula toward San José. An early attempt to develop this area under the name of Potrero Nuevo failed because of its distance from the city.[40] With the further expansion of the city, this land became ripe for development.

Figure 6.17 reveals the rigid gridiron imposed on this section of San Francisco, the portion on the right having been created by filling most of Mission Bay and a strip of land along the western shore of San Francisco Bay. While the two parks provided some relief from the otherwise unbroken grid of streets, the Potrero district represents another of the many lost opportunities for good planning so characteristic of San Francisco's history.

It is interesting, although perhaps fruitless, to speculate on how San Francisco might have developed if all or major portions of the city had been planned by that towering genius of nineteenth-century design, Frederick Law Olmsted. Persons skilled in urban planning were few in number anywhere in America, and they were rarer still on the western frontier. Olmsted's presence in California during the city's formative years of urban growth presented an almost unique opportunity for the employment of his skills and insights. It was an opportunity that was to be lost.

Olmsted's services were requested for quite a different kind of planning problem. In 1866 he produced a preliminary design for a residential community integrated with the campus plan for what was to become the University of California at Berkeley. For a site adjoining the little grid settlement that had already been laid out by Samuel H. Willey to help finance the infant College of California, Olmsted sketched a contrasting design.

Figure 6.18 shows his work. The Willey blocks on the hillside sloping westward to the bay are identified by the letter "F." Above appears the Olmsted plan with the college buildings to be located on a central mall (A), flanked by land reserved for campus expansion (D). The remaining sections Olmsted designated for residential purposes, to be "subdivided by simple lines into lots, each of one to five acres in extent, of suitable shape and favorably situated in all respects for a family home." Integrated into the design were extensive public grounds and "lanes bordered . . . on each side by continuous thick groves, and access to each private lot from these lanes is arranged by short approaches branching from them." Pointing out the advantages of the curvilinear street system following the natural contours of the land, Olmsted argued that this pattern would discourage through traffic:

"It will be observed, that . . . while the roads are so laid out as to afford moderately direct routes of communication between the different parts of the neighborhood, they would be inconvenient to be followed for any purpose of business beyond the mere supplying of the wants of the neighborhood itself,—that is to say, it would be easier for any man wishing to convey merchandise from any point a short distance on one side of your neighborhood to a point a short distance on the other side, to go around it rather than go through it."[41]

The Olmsted plan was not carried out, and the town of Berkeley grew from the little nucleus of Willey's grid to cover virtually the entire area from the University to the bay. The view shown in Figure 6.19 shows the town in 1891 as seen from a point above the campus looking west to San Francisco and the Golden Gate.

A few miles south of Berkeley another vast gridiron community was spreading its geometric pattern across the landscape. This was Oakland, with its neighbor towns of the east Bay area a region that attracted the attention of many land speculators hoping to duplicate the success of San Francisco on the opposite shore of the bay.

Julius Kellersberger, a Swiss surveyor who had received his training in Vienna, prepared the first plan for Oakland in 1852. Edson Adams, Horace Carpentier, and Andrew Moon had engaged him to lay out a town on land they well knew was owned by the sons of Luis Peralta. They counted on the confusion arising over Spanish land titles to enable them to support their squatters' rights. It was a bold land grab that ultimately succeeded.

Kellersberger's plan is reproduced in Figure 6.20. Five blocks designated by names and two others unidentified but not platted in lots were set aside as public reservations. Dividing the two latter blocks was Broadway, 110 feet wide. All other streets were surveyed 80 feet in width to create blocks 200 by 300 feet. Carpentier engineered a bill to incorporate the city, the new government promptly conferred on him ownership of some 10,000 acres of tidal lands and the exclusive rights to construct wharves, piers, and docks for a 37-year period. In return Carpentier undertook to build a school, three wharves, and to pay the town 2 percent of his dock receipts. Oakland was a reality, a town as one modern historian of urban planning in the area put it, "conceived in iniquity and nurtured on corruption."[42]

Nearby, Colonel Henry S. Fitch, a real estate promoter and auctioneer, laid out the town of Alameda for an Ohio lawyer and a Pennsylvania carpenter, W. W. Chipman and Gideon Aughinbaugh. Fitch had tried to purchase the site from one of the Peraltas, but Chipman

Figure 6.17   View of San Francisco, California: 1892

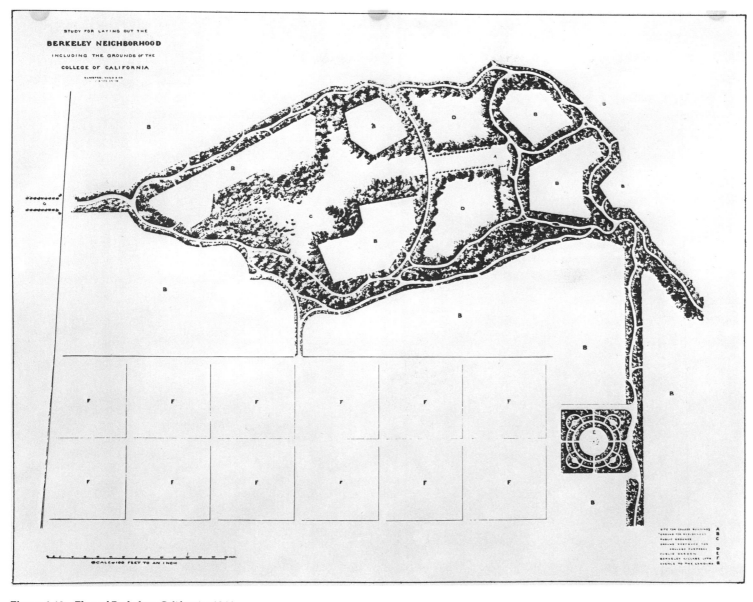

Figure 6.18 Plan of Berkeley, California: 1866

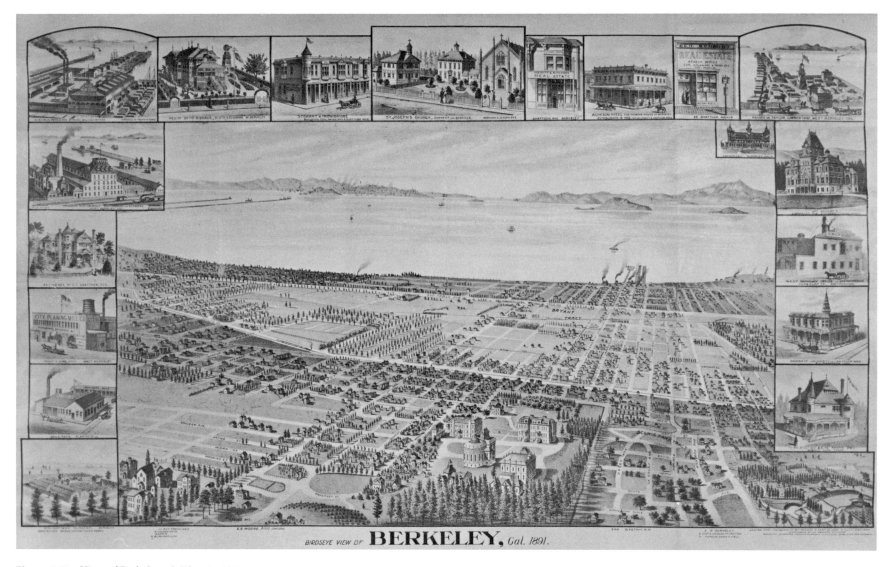

Figure 6.19 View of Berkeley, California: 1891

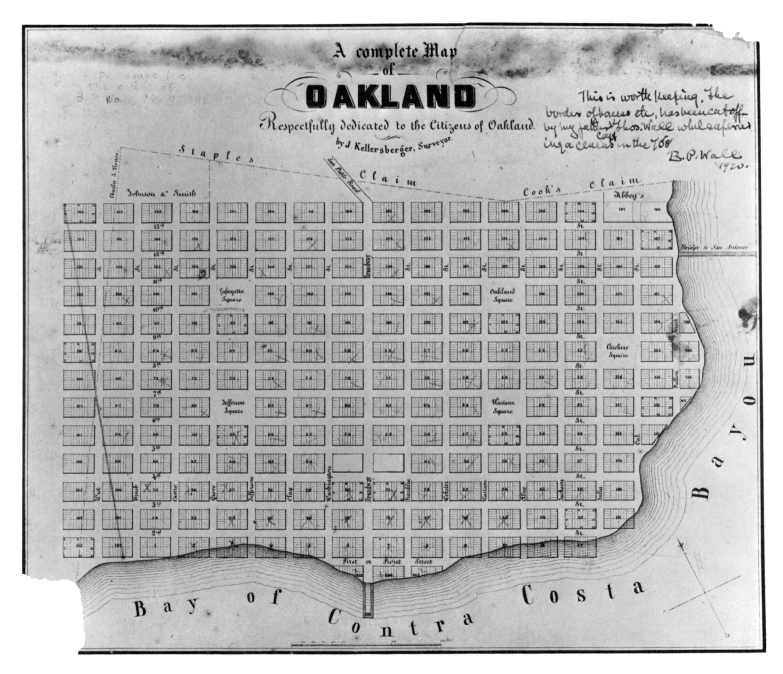

Figure 6.20
Plan of Oakland,
California: 1852

and Aughinbaugh outbid him. Fitch nevertheless made money from the transaction as a land huckster for the project and helped give birth to still another town of surpassing dullness. Alameda's location and the much larger Oakland as it extended over the years can be seen in Figure 6.21 showing the area as developed or proposed in 1868.[43]

By that time California was swarming with real estate promoters busy developing new towns. South of San Francisco between the bay and the ocean a series of suburban communities were founded: Burlingame, Menlo Park, Redwood City, San Mateo, and South San Francisco, among them. When Leland Stanford established a university as a memorial to his son, he had a portion of his ranch laid out adjacent to the campus as the town of University Park, later renamed Palo Alto.[44]

North of San Francisco other towns were beginning to grow. In Sonoma County a few miles northwest of Sonoma, the community of Santa Rosa had been surveyed in 1854. Its original design consisted of 24 rectangular blocks centering on what the original plat identified as a plaza.[45] By 1876, when the view reproduced in Figure 6.22 was published, its population exceeded 3,000, and it and its nearby rival, Petaluma, provided a market for the products of the rich agricultural lands in the Sonoma valley. Its business life focused on the plaza, and a number of industrial plants occupied sites along the San Francisco and North Pacific Railroad, whose tracks formed the western border of the town.

Halfway between Santa Rosa and Petaluma a less conventional design resulted from the planning efforts of Dr. Thomas S. Page, the owner of the Cotati Rancho. Around 1890 he produced the unusual plan for his town of Cotati reproduced in Figure 6.23. At the center he surveyed a hexagonal plaza and extended six streets outward from its corners. Page named the six boundary streets separating the town lots from the larger farming parcels beyond for his six sons. This spider web design may have attracted flies, but few settlers came to reside in Page's odd little town. Page's plaza was little more than a patch of weeds. Not until recent years, with the establishment of a state college, has the town had more than a handful of residents. Now it is a bustling and growing college town extending well beyond the original hexagon of its first eccentric plan.

The construction of the Central Pacific Railroad through the San Joaquin Valley in the 1870s resulted in the creation of several new towns as well as in the demise of others. Two of the most important of the new communities—Modesto and Fresno—were among the several planned by the railroad itself. In carrying out such activities, the railroad was following the precedents established during the construction of the first transcontinental line, whose effects on urban development will be treated in later chapters.

Modesto began in 1870 when railroad engineers selected a townsite on the bank of the Tuolumne River some 80 miles east of San Francisco. Earlier the citizens of the existing settlement of Paradise had refused to provide a suitable right-of-way through their town and rejected a proposal by the railroad to help finance the cost of a bridge across the river at that point. This decision proved disastrous for Paradise; when the first trains began service to the new railroad-sponsored town in October a mass migration began from Paradise and the other by-passed settlements of the area to the newly surveyed community a few miles distant.

The original town plan of Modesto consisted of a rectangle platted in a gridiron of streets running parallel and perpendicular to the railroad line slicing diagonally through the site on a northwest-southeast alignment. Officials of the line intended to name the town Ralston to honor W. C. Ralston, a San Francisco banker and wheat dealer. When at a public meeting Ralston declined to be memorialized in this fashion, a spokesman for the company declared "The parent of the infant is 'Modesty'—then the baby's name must be Modesto."[46]

By the end of November, only a few months after the town had been surveyed, a local newspaper could report that it was growing "with a rapidity unparalleled in California. Three or four buildings are added to the town daily. The addition of 25 houses makes a change. The town fronts on both sides of the track for three or four blocks and is compact with business buildings."[47] A month later the population reached nearly 300, and the town consisted of more than 70 buildings, many of which had been moved from Paradise and other, now rapidly declining settlements in the valley.

In 1871 Modesto became the county seat of Stanislaus County. County offices were moved to a building at the corner of 8th and I Streets, but by 1873 a new courthouse was completed on a block donated for that purpose by the railroad and located not far from the depot. With this added impetus to growth and the further development of wheat farming in the region, Modesto continued to attract settlers. In 1880 its population was nearly 1,700, and a decade later it exceeded 2,000.[48]

The view reproduced in Figure 6.24 shows Modesto in 1888, four years after its incorporation as a city. While the original site had not been fully developed, private landowners of adjoining tracts had al-

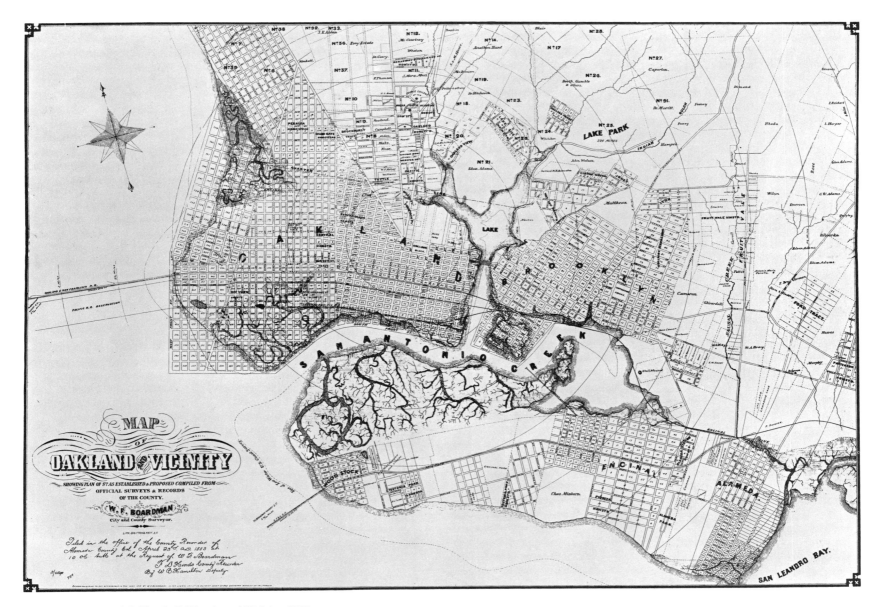

Figure 6.21 Map of Oakland, California and Vicinity: 1868

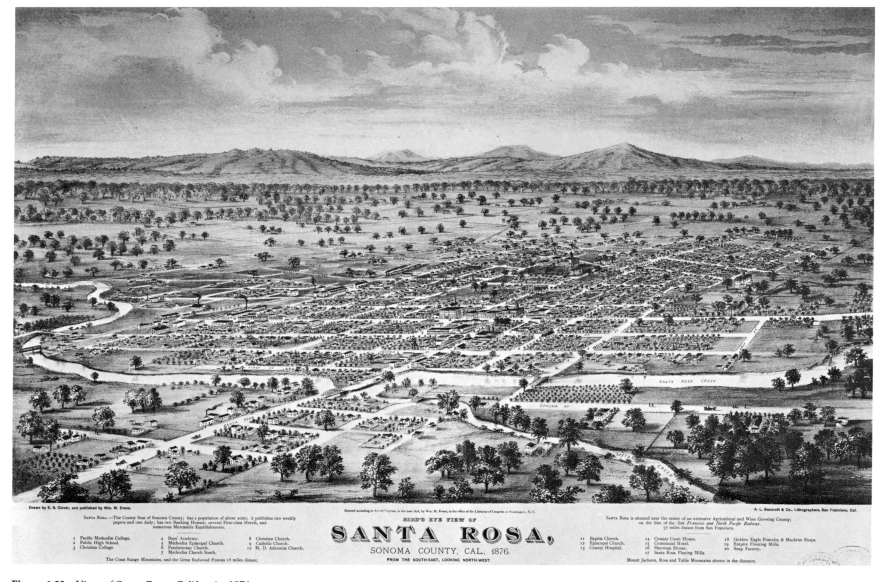

Drawn by E. S. Glover, and published by Wm. M. Evans.

Entered according to Act of Congress, in the year 1876, by Wm. M. Evans, in the office of the Librarian of Congress at Washington, D. C.

A. L. Bancroft & Co., Lithographers, San Francisco, Cal.

SANTA ROSA.—The County Seat of Sonoma County; has a population of about 4000; it publishes two weekly papers and one daily; has two Banking Houses; several First-class Hotels, and numerous Mercantile Establishments.

SANTA ROSA is situated near the center of an extensive Agricultural and Wine Growing County; on the line of the *San Francisco and North Pacific Railway*. 57 miles distant from San Francisco.

BIRD'S EYE VIEW OF

SANTA ROSA,

SONOMA COUNTY, CAL., 1876.

FROM THE SOUTH-EAST, LOOKING NORTH-WEST.

1 Pacific Methodist College.
2 Public High School.
3 Christian College.

4 Boys' Academy.
5 Methodist Episcopal Church.
6 Presbyterian Church.
7 Methodist Church South.

8 Christian Church.
9 Catholic Church.
10 S. D. Adventist Church.

11 Baptist Church.
12 Episcopal Church.
13 County Hospital.

14 County Court House.
15 Centennial Hotel.
16 Sherman House.
17 Santa Rosa Planing Mills.

18 Golden Eagle Foundry & Machine Shops.
19 Empire Flouring Mills.
20 Soap Factory.

The Coast Range Mountains, and the Great Redwood Forests 18 miles distant.

Mount Jackson, Ross and Table Mountains shown in the distance.

Figure 6.22   View of Santa Rosa, California: 1876

ready begun to survey their property in additional streets and blocks. Their plans followed the orientation of the north-south and east-west government land surveys. Little care seems to have been taken in providing adequate connections between the two gridiron systems, and dozens of dangerous and awkward intersections resulted—defects in the basic street pattern that continue to plague the modern city.

Much the same thing occurred at Fresno, which the Contract and Finance Company, a railroad subsidiary, laid out in 1872. The rigid gridiron design, shown in Figure 6.25 as filed the following year, is broken only by the courthouse square and the swath of land reserved for tracks, depot, and yards. The plan took its orientation from the northwest-southeast alignment of the railroad, which cut diagonally through the townsite. Railroad engineers made all the blocks 320 by 400 feet, pierced by 20-foot alleys, divided into lots 25 by 150 feet, and fronting on 80-foot streets.

Fresno's location seemed uninviting; barren sand plains stretched outward in all directions, and the nearest substantial supply of water was the San Joaquin River, ten miles away. A few hardy optimists settled in the new town that summer and fall. By the end of the year, however, the town had four hotels, three saloons, and two stores. Most of the inhabitants were railroad employees who lived in tents or in a few hastily erected shacks. A year and a half later there were still only 55 buildings in Fresno, 29 of which were stores, hotels, saloons, and some other business establishments. The other communities of Fresno County must have been no more imposing, for in March, 1874, the voters decided to make Fresno the county seat.[49]

The four-block site for the courthouse in the original plat of 1872 was thought to be located too far from the depot, and in 1876 the Contract and Finance Company deeded a site of similar size to the county three blocks closer to the tracks as can be seen in Figure 6.26. The public school block, one of the four in the first courthouse location, was apparently set aside for educational purposes at that time, and the block for the county hospital was also made available as the only other interruption to the now vastly expanded grid settlement.[50]

In its early years Fresno was little more than a dusty, straggling village, loosely clustered about the railroad depot. A new resident in 1878, R. W. Riggs, described the place as "not much of a town, a handful of houses in a desert of sand."[51] Mariposa Street between the depot and the courthouse served as the principal business street, but not all of the lots were occupied by buildings, and most of these were one- or two-story wooden structures. The census of 1880 reported that Fresno's population was only 800.

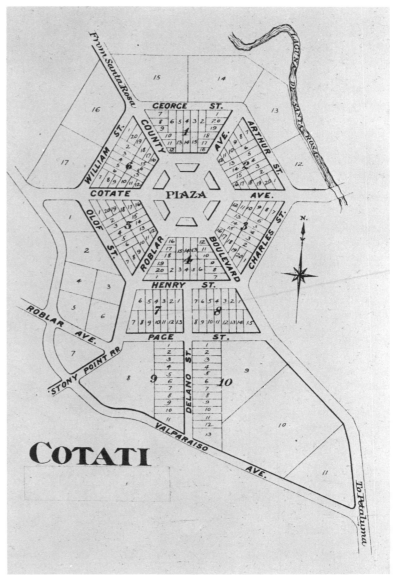

Figure 6.23 Plan of Cotati, California: 1898

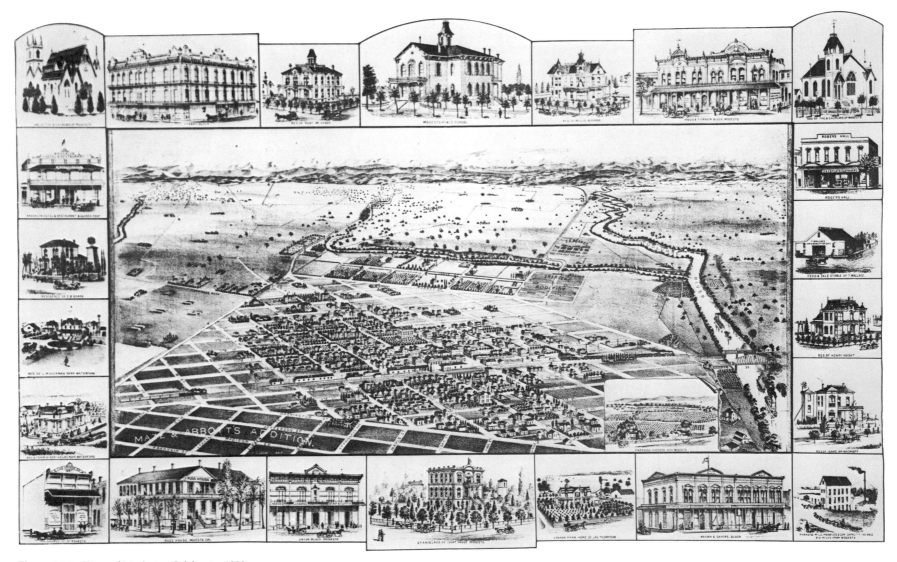

Figure 6.24 View of Modesto, California: 1888

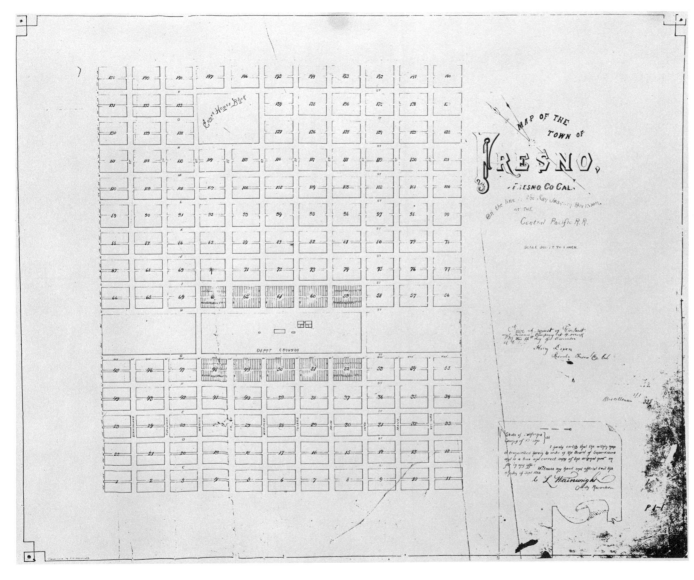

Figure 6.25 Plan of Fresno, California: 1873

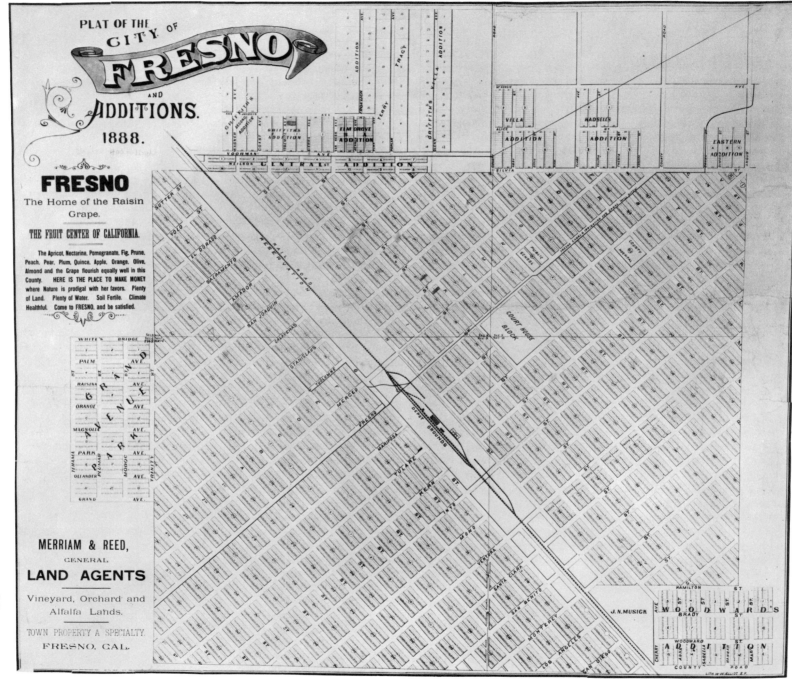

Figure 6.26
Plan of Fresno,
California: 1888

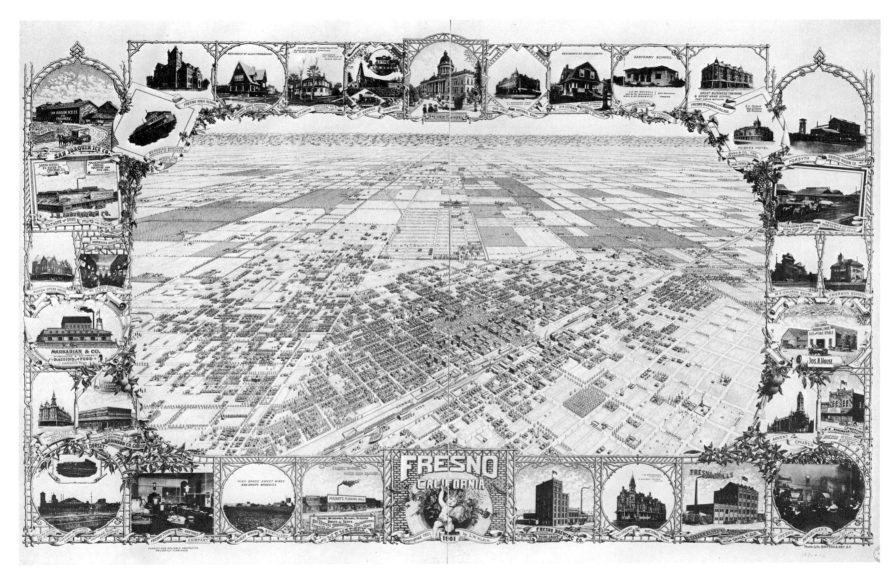

Figure 6.27 View of Fresno, California: 1901

The 1880s, however, proved to be prosperous years. Irrigation of the surrounding farms turned what had seemed to be a desert into highly productive agricultural land. The real estate boom that had affected virtually all cities in California attracted new residents to the San Joaquin Valley communities, and Fresno experienced a substantial growth. By 1890 the city's population exceeded 10,000, land outside the original townsite was subdivided into streets and lots, and in 1887 the county recorder had to hire two additional deputies to help him accept and record plats and to maintain records showing transfers of ownership.[52]

In November, 1887, no fewer than 1,100 deeds were filed at the county courthouse. It was in that month that the last lots owned by the railroad passed into private ownership. The plan of Fresno may have been no innovation in urban design, but as a land speculation it must have brought the railroad handsome financial rewards.

Fresno's prosperity was based on more than real estate speculation. It served as the principal packing center for the raisin grape industry. Fourteen packing houses were located in the city, and there were many others in the vicinity. Other crops, including cotton and figs, helped to diversify the agricultural economy, and Fresno developed as the chief market town for a large portion of the San Joaquin Valley.

When the view reproduced in Figure 6.27 was published in 1901 the city's population was more than 12,000. Its handsome courthouse standing on the large site reserved for that purpose, the many substantial business buildings between it and the railroad, and the elongated manufacturing district along the tracks indicate that, whatever the shortcomings of the town plan, its location had proved a wise choice.

While these older cities of Hispanic origin, the newer towns near the Pacific coast, and the railroad communities of the central valley were growing and changing, dozens of new urban centers were being created overnight in the Sierra mining region following the discovery of gold. Still other towns grew up as supply centers on sites located between the mining camps and shipping points on the coast. Some enjoyed a brief existence; others survived but remained small; and two—Sacramento and Stockton—developed as major urban centers.

It was the California gold rush that caused San Francisco's rapid growth and, by enormously speeding the pace of immigration to California, brought prosperity to other new or established towns as well. It is to this episode in town development of California and adjoining Nevada that we now turn before examining the pattern of urban development in the southern half of the state.

THE CITY OF ST. LOUIS.

Plate 1. View of St. Louis, Missouri: 1874

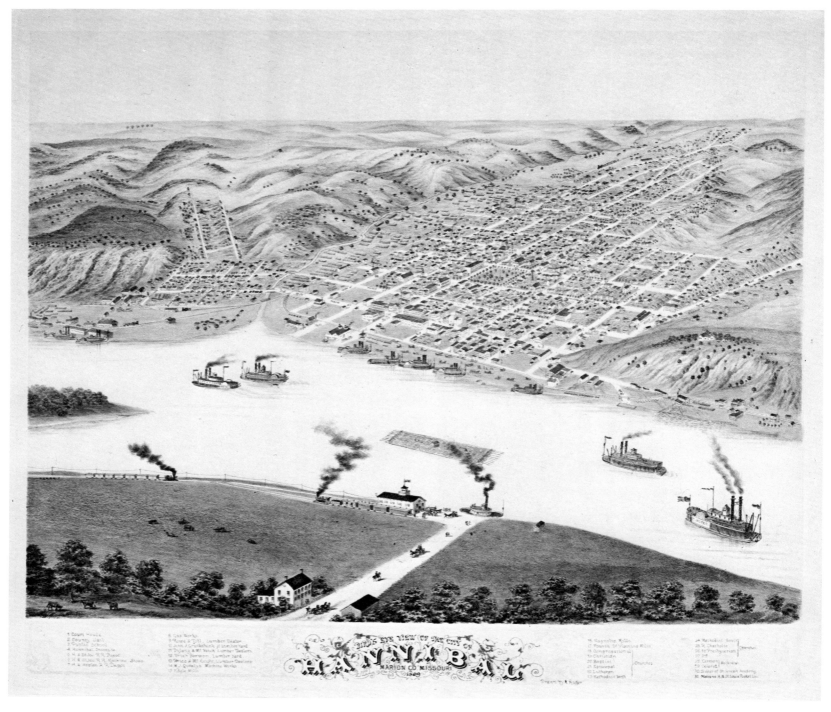

Plate 2. View of Hannibal, Missouri: 1869

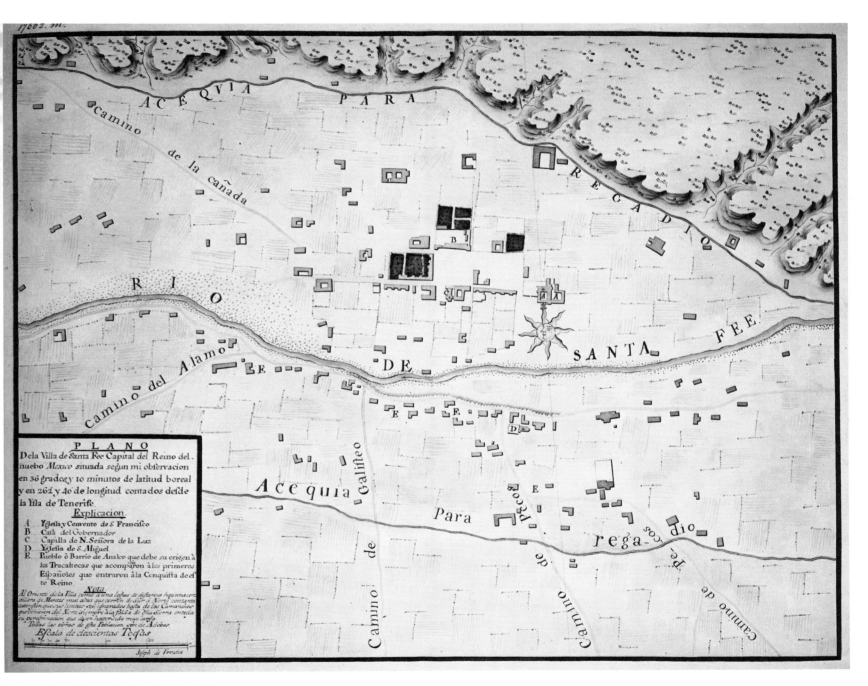

Plate 3. Plan of Santa Fe, New Mexico: 1766

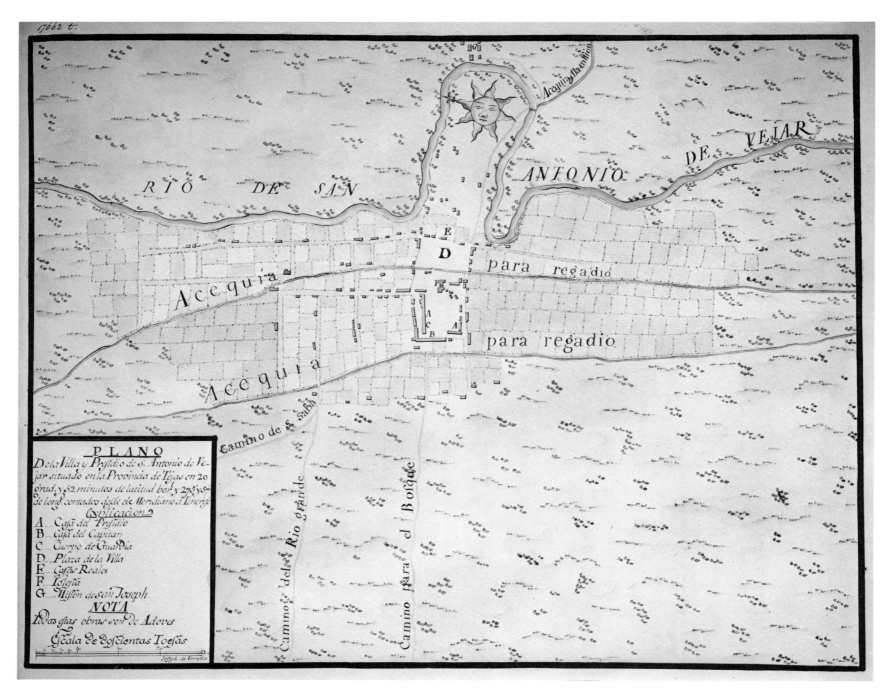

Plate 4. Plan of San Antonio, Texas: 1767

Main Plaza.

Alameda.

Alamo (1850.)

Mission de la Concepcion

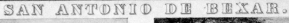

SAN ANTONIO DE BEXAR.

Mission San José

The New Bridge.

San Pedro Spring

Mission San Juan

Plate 5. View of San Antonio, Texas: 1852

VIEW OF SAN FRANCISCO, FORMERLY YERBA BUENA, IN 1846-7

BEFORE THE DISCOVERY OF GOLD

Plate 6. View of San Francisco, California: 1847

SAN FRANCISCO

LONDON PUBLISHED BY JOHN MC LEAN, DUNNE & CO.

Plate 7. View of San Francisco, California: 1851

Plate 8. View of San Francisco, California: 1868

SACRAMENTO CITY CA.

FROM THE FOOT OF J. STREET,

SHOWING I. J. & K. STS WITH THE SIERRA NEVADA IN THE DISTANCE.

NEW YORK PUBLISHED BY STRINGER & TOWNSEND 222 BROADWAY

Entered according to Act of Congress in the year 1850 by A.B. Townsend in the Clerks Office of the District Court of the Southern Dist N.Y.

Plate 9. View of Sacramento, California: 1849

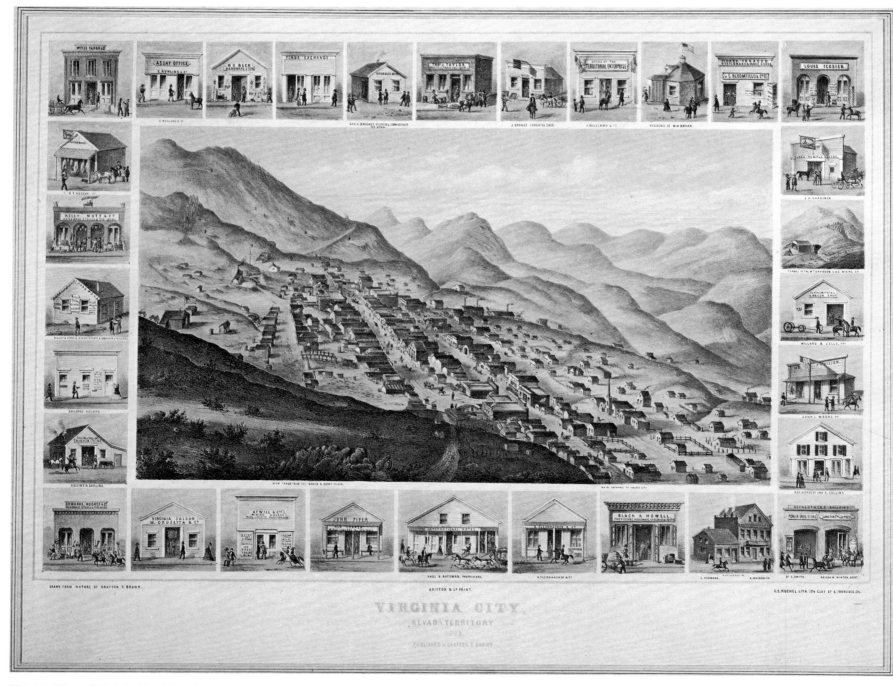

Plate 10. View of Virginia City, Nevada: 1875

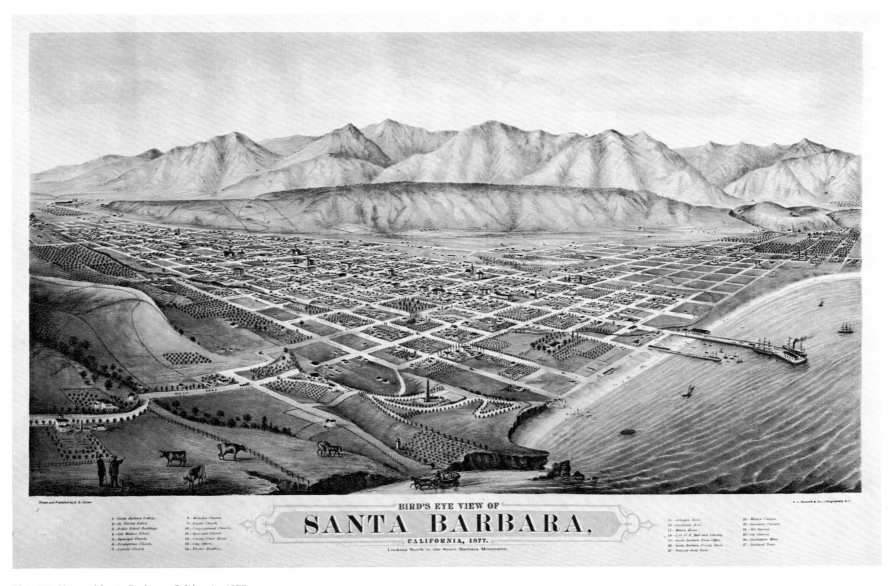

Plate 11. View of Santa Barbara, California: 1877

Plate 12. View of Los Angeles, California: 1857

Plate 13. View of Salt Lake City, Utah: 1870

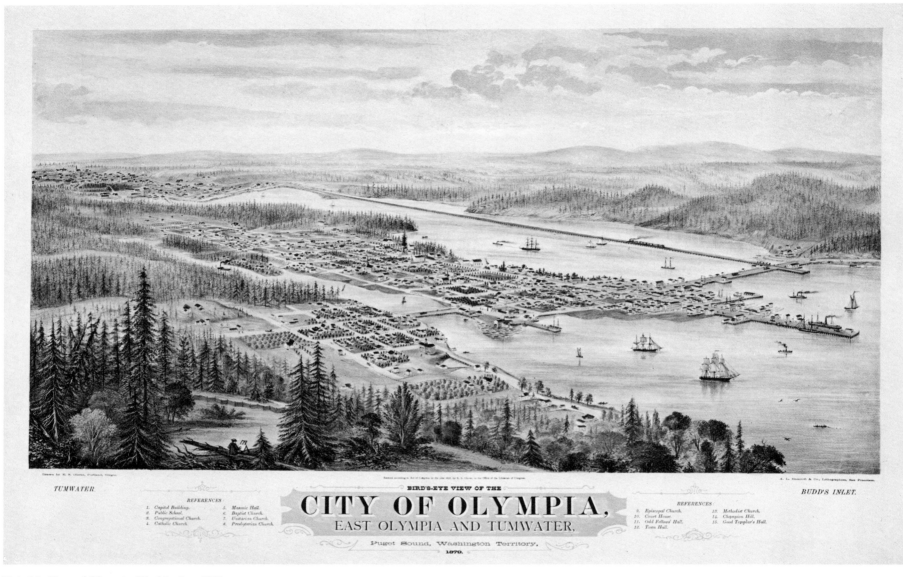

TUMWATER.

BUDD'S INLET.

BIRD'S-EYE VIEW OF THE
CITY OF OLYMPIA,
EAST OLYMPIA AND TUMWATER,
Puget Sound, Washington Territory,
1879.

REFERENCES
1. Capitol Building.
2. Public School.
3. Congregational Church.
4. Catholic Church.
5. Masonic Hall.
6. Baptist Church.
7. Unitarian Church.
8. Presbyterian Church.

REFERENCES
9. Episcopal Church.
10. Court House.
11. Odd Fellows' Hall.
12. Town Hall.
13. Methodist Church.
14. Champion Hill.
15. Good Templar's Hall.

Plate 14. View of Olympia, Washington: 1879

Scetched by H. LAMBACH.

Copy-right secured

Gast, Moeller & Co. Lith. St. Louis.

OMAHA

NEBRASKA

1867

Looking North from Forest Hill.

Plate 15. View of Omaha, Nebraska: 1867

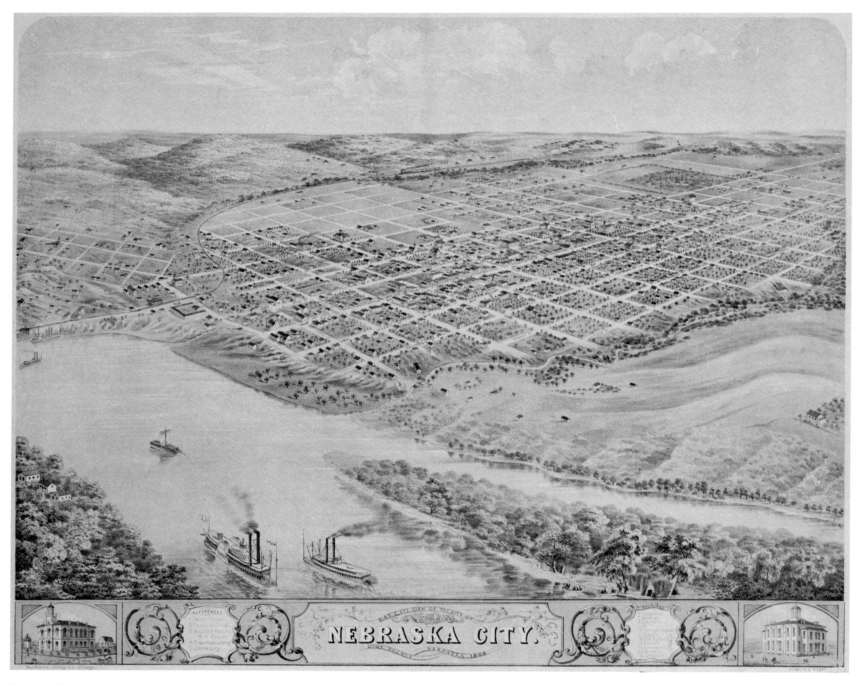

Plate 16. View of Nebraska City, Nebraska: 1868

Mining Camps and Towns of California and Nevada

THE conquest of California by American forces in 1846 focused the attention of the nation on that remote region. Although the pattern was soon to change, urban settlement at that time was concentrated along the coast. One exception was the community founded by John A. Sutter, a German Swiss who had immigrated to the United States in 1834, found his way to California five years later, took Mexican citizenship in 1840, and succeeded in obtaining from Governor Juan Alvarado an enormous grant of 48,000 acres in the Sacramento River valley. On a knoll near the mouth of the American River where it entered the Sacramento Sutter erected a massive adobe fort.

Sutter's fort was the center of a highly organized farming and trading enterprise presided over by its energetic and cultivated owner. As depicted by an artist some years later, the fort is shown in Figure 7.1 as it appeared in 1847 when it quartered a detachment of American troops. To young Joseph Warren, a naval officer who served in California during the Mexican War, it was an impressive sight: "The fort consists of a parallelogram enclosed by adobe walls, fifteen feet high and two feet thick, with bastions or towers at the angles, the walls of which are four feet thick. . . . A good house occupies the centre of the interior area, serving for officers' quarters, armory, guard and state rooms, and also for a kind of citadel. There is a second wall on the inner face, the space between it and the outer wall being roofed and divided into workshops, quarters, &c., and the usual offices are provided, and also a well of good water. Corrals for the cattle and horses of the garrison are conveniently placed where they can be under the eye of the guard. Cannon frown . . . from the various embrasures, and the *ensemble* presents the very ideal of a border fortress."[1]

This structure served as the center for a tightly organized trading, farming, and manufacturing enterprise. As Sutter recalled many years later, the little community included "workshops and dwellings, a bakery, a mill, and a blanket factory."[2] On the bank of the nearby American River, Sutter constructed a tannery and a dairy, and there were other outbuildings of various kinds. By 1847 Sam Brannan and George Smith had opened a store in one of these structures, a building that can be seen at the right of Figure 7.1.[3] The workshops mentioned by Sutter included shops for a blacksmith, a cooper, a shoemaker, and a gunsmith. There were also a candle shop, a brewery and distillery, a granary, and rooms for storing other foodstuffs.[4]

The fort, however, was not intended by Sutter to serve as a civil settlement for New Helvetia, as the Swiss proprietor called his domain. For this purpose he had selected a site on high ground three miles below the fort on the Sacramento River, where he planned the town of Sutterville. The plan of this town is reproduced in Figure 7.2 as it appeared in a German publication to attract settlers.[5] Sutter's European background is reflected not only in the German street names but in the elaborate formality of the design. From the market place at the waterfront, the 60-foot-wide Markt Strasse led to a large square, on the south side of which the city hall was to stand. Two blocks distant on either side of this main street were sites for two churches. Sutter planned other streets 40 and 50 feet wide and alleys 12 feet in width to provide access to tiers of lots either 60 or 100 feet deep. Lots in the blocks nearest the river were doubtless intended as sites for warehouses and industries.

Early in 1847 Sutter sent one of his employees, James Marshall, up the south fork of the American River to locate a site for a sawmill. Marshall returned to report favorably on a location in the Cullomah Valley, and in August of that year Sutter and Marshall entered into a partnership for the purpose of building and operating the mill. The two partners employed a number of other men, and by fall work was under way.[6] When the mill was first tried, the mill wheel would not turn properly because the raceway—the channel needed to return the water to the river—had not been excavated to the proper depth. Marshall directed the Indian laborers to remove more earth from the tailrace and, to flush out the loosened rocks and soil, he opened the floodgate each night to allow the water to carry off the material. On the morning of January 24, 1848, Marshall came to inspect the ditch, noticed some small, dull, yellow particles at the bottom of the ditch and, after hammering them to determine that they were malleable, realized that his earlier judgment of the character of the quartz rock in the vicinity had been confirmed. It was gold, and its discovery was to change the history of California and the nation.[7]

Marshall hurried to show Sutter his discovery. The two men tested the particles in every way they knew, and Sutter confirmed Marshall's opinion. Both decided to keep the discovery secret as long as possible, although Marshall had already announced his find to the employees at the sawmill, and it should have been obvious that it would not long remain private knowledge. When Sutter visited the mill to see for himself where the gold had been discovered he asked the workers to remain on the job until the mill was finished and meanwhile to keep the information about the discovery to themselves. This they agreed to do. Sutter then negotiated with the Indians of the area for a 20-year lease on a large area centered on the mill. However, when he sought to have

Figure 7.1 View of Sutter's Fort, Sacramento, California: 1847

this approved by the military governor in Monterey he was informed that the government could not sanction any transfer of land by Indians to individuals.[8]

Sutter entrusted one of the mill workers, Charles Bennett, to carry his request to the governor. Like the others at the mill, Bennett used his free time to dig for gold in the millrace and other streams. On his trip to Monterey he carried with him a buckskin pouch with six ounces of the particles he had found. At Benicia, San Francisco, and Monterey he proudly but indiscreetly displayed his treasure. Sutter himself was

scarcely more cautious, writing to General Mariano G. Vallejo at Sonoma on February 10 that he had discovered "a gold mine, which, according to experiments we have made, is extraordinarily rich."[9]

Information about the discovery began to leak out from other sources. Henry Bigler, a Mormon employed at the mill, wrote to several of his fellow Saints about the find. The Monterey *Californian* on March 15 and the San Francisco *California Star* three days later carried brief announcements reporting the discovery of gold.[10] Residents of the coastal towns greeted this news skeptically, but already most of Sutter's employees at the fort had seen gold with their own eyes and had abandoned their jobs to seek sudden wealth in the mountains. It was Sam Brannan, merchant, promoter, and publisher of the *California Star*, who convinced San Franciscans that the rumors were true when he returned to the city on May 8, 1848, after a quick inspection tour of Sutter's mill. Waving a bottle of gold dust and particles in one hand and his hat in the other, he rushed down Montgomery Street booming the news: "Gold! Gold! Gold from the American River!"[11]

The rush began almost immediately. Within a few days San Francisco was almost deserted. The *Californian* four months later described for its new readers how San Francisco reacted to the news spread by Sam Brannan, publisher of its rival newspaper: "Then commenced the grand rush. The inhabitants throughout the Territory were in a commotion. Large companies of men, women, and children could be seen on every road leading to the mines; their wagons loaded down with tools for digging, provisions, etc. Launch after launch left the wharves of our city . . . crowded with passengers and freight, for the Sacramento. Mechanical operations of every kind ceased. Whole streets, that were but a week before alive with a busy population, were entirely deserted, and the place wore the appearance of a city that had been suddenly visited by a devastating plague. To cap the climax, the newspapers were obliged to stop printing, for want of readers."[12] A letter sent from San Francisco on May 27 and published the following January in the New York *Herald* stated that of the 800 persons normally living in the town there were no more than 20 remaining.[13] Ships arriving at the port in normal trading calls were unable to leave; their crews deserted to join the rush to the gold fields. When the news reached Sonoma, San Jose, Monterey, Santa Barbara, Los Angeles, and San Diego, their residents reacted in much the same way, and these communities also for a time became ghost towns.

Coloma, as the location of Sutter's Mill came to be called, was naturally the destination of the hoards of persons who had abandoned their jobs in the coastal towns. Up the valley of the Sacramento and American rivers they came by boat, wagons, horeseback, or on foot. Sutter's Fort bustled with activity, and Governor Mason accompanied by Lt. William T. Sherman stopped there to dine with Sutter on July 2 on their official inspection tour to make an accurate report of the situation to Washington. When they arrived at Coloma they found some 4,000 miners busily digging and panning gold in the valley, including to Mason's dismay a number of deserters from his command.[14]

The site of this activity, as the view in Figure 7.3 shows, was strikingly beautiful. No one, however, had eyes for anything but the tell-

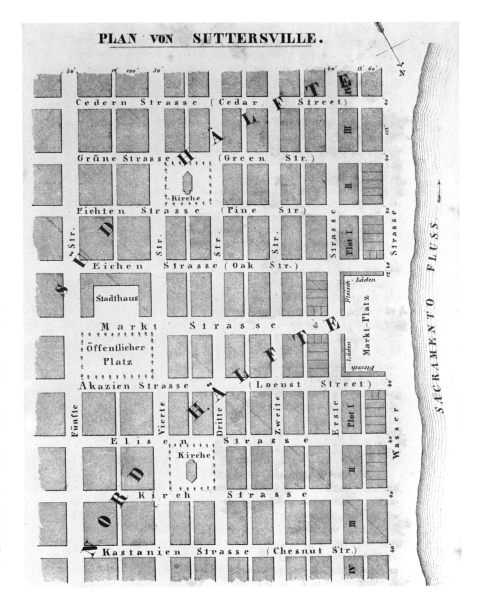

Figure 7.2 Plan of Suttersville, California: 1849

Figure 7.3 View of Sutter's Mill and Coloma, California: ca. 1850

tale glitter of gold in the river and its tributary streams. Hastily erected tents, shacks, and cabins provided shelter for the miners, who immediately began to fan out through the region in search of additional deposits. Soon discoveries in other areas were reported, and in a short time it became obvious that for a hundred miles or so along the river valleys running down the westward slopes of the Sierra there was gold to be had for all those willing to seek it out. Marshall himself found additional deposits at Old Dry Diggings, later Hangtown, and still later named Placerville. Others reported strikes in other places, located like Coloma, in the valleys of the Sierra foothills.[15]

Coloma began to take on the appearance of a town, the first of hundreds of mining camps that within a few years would dot the Sierra foothills. The enterprising Sam Brannan had already located a site for his store there before returning to San Francisco in May to spread the electrifying news up and down Montgomery Street. By August there were eight such establishments in the booming community. The sawmill was busily at work, supplying lumber for dozens of new structures. In the spring of 1849 the expanding town could boast a hospital, a bowling alley, hotels, saloons, and additional stores. By that fall many other businesses had been established: a gunsmith shop, an apothecary, the inevitable gambling halls, and several new hotels.[16]

Official reports filed by Governor Mason and Commodore Thomas Jones, commander of naval forces in California, reached Washington in the fall of 1848. Accompanying their written accounts were samples of gold, some of which were put on public exhibit. Even earlier reports through private channels had arrived in the East, but apparently had not excited a great amount of interest. The nation's attention was aroused, however, by a passage in President James Polk's annual message to Congress on December 5, 1848, confirming officially an "abundance of gold" in California. Polk attached to his message a copy of Governor Mason's report stating that a man could earn in one day's work mining gold twice the monthly pay of a private soldier.[17]

The stampede to the mines by Californians in 1848 was dwarfed by the mass migration that took place in 1849, when gold fever gripped the eastern half of the country. The exact number of the "forty-niners" will never be known, but it probably approached 80,000.[18] Swelling this throng of immigrants were thousands of persons from Mexico, the Pacific Islands, and, indeed, from all over the world. The movement continued unabated in 1850 and 1851. The population of California in 1848 was about 14,000; by the latter months of 1852 it reached 223,000.[19]

While many prospectors worked individually or in small groups, the overwhelming number gathered in clusters of tents, cabins, and other crude shelters near the richest strikes. What is remarkable is that these mining camps, which sprang up overnight in a region without civil government, populated by persons who were utter strangers, and whose inhabitants were motivated solely by the desire to enrich themselves soon evolved their own effective system of local government. A crude but workable form of community law and administration provided the basis for adjudicating conflicting mining claims, raising funds for supplying public services, dealing with criminals, and providing other functions necessary for community existence. The popular view of western mining camps as lawless, brawling, rough and disorderly, while not entirely incorrect, ignores important achievements in self-government.[20]

That perceptive observer, Bayard Taylor, noted these efforts at community organization and government during his visit to California in 1849: "At all these . . . settlements, however small, an alcalde is chosen and regulations established, as near as possible in accordance with the existing laws of the country. Although the authority exercised by the alcalde is sometimes nearly absolute, the miners invariably respect and uphold it. Thus, at whatever cost, order and security are preserved; and when the State organization shall have been completed, the mining communities . . . will, by a quiet and easy process, pass into regularly constituted towns, and enjoy as good government and protection as any other part of the State. Nothing in California seemed more miraculous to me than this spontaneous evolution of social order from the worst elements of anarchy. It was a lesson worth even more than the gold."[21]

The activities performed by mining camp governments included surveys of streets and lots. Some of these plats have survived; others are known to have been made. They were primitive attempts at town planning, providing a degree of order in the physical arrangement of the infant communities that at least a majority of their residents thought necessary. One such survey is reproduced in Figure 7.4, that of Coloma prepared in 1857. While this plat mainly reflects conditions as they had developed almost spontaneously during the first months of rapid settlement, it includes some obvious efforts at more orderly development. The precisely straight lines of the wide Main Street, the equally regular alignment of Back Street, and the right-angle intersections of High Street and three minor streets with these parallel primary thoroughfares are evidence that the survey went beyond merely recording what existed. Doubtless the property boundaries as drawn on this plat infringed in places on some of the buildings and lot claims of the first occupants.

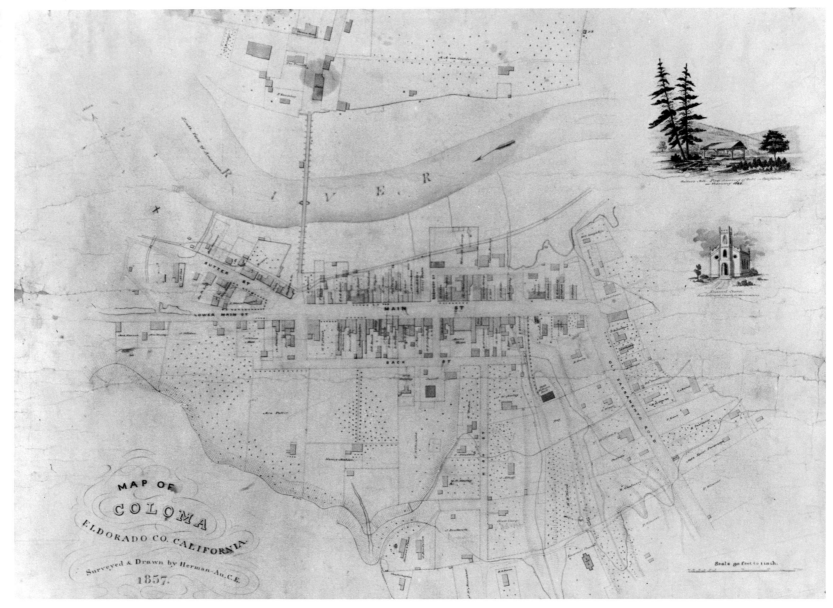

Figure 7.4 Plan of Coloma, California: 1857

At Sonora in Tuolumne County, the provisional town council took steps to bring some kind of order to the camp as early as February, 1850. It contracted with William Cooper to survey the community into 500 lots, and Cooper and T. W. Gulledge soon produced two copies of a plat for which they were to be paid the sum of five dollars for each lot. The council used the survey in settling disputes over land ownership in the town.[22]

The Cooper and Gulledge survey also did more than merely confirm existing town lot claims. Early records indicate that several buildings were found to encroach on the new street lines that the surveyors established.[23]

The view of Sonora in Figure 7.5 shows the town about two years later. It took a linear form with its major buildings lining Washington Street as it curved gently down to the valley from the slope in the background. Later that year, however, the community seized an opportunity to provide a more regular design for the growing town. A fire destroyed much of the town in June, 1852. Following that disaster a mass meeting of the residents approved a committee recommendation for widening streets and laying them out at right angles. At that time Washington Street was replatted to its full width of eighty feet, and there were doubtless other changes and improvements as well.[24]

The town survey brought additional benefits. Lot owners were able to sell property by reference to the official map and thereby avoid uncertainties over land titles.[25] Of more importance to the community was an action taken by the common council after the city received its charter from the new state of California in 1851. Sonora had been designated as the county seat of Tuolumne County, and one enterprising speculator advised a friend, Joshua Holden, to buy up as many vacant lots as he could. Holden reported this to the council, which promptly passed a resolution "that nobody should henceforth take up and locate vacant lots but they should be sold for the behoof and benefit of the town, as its property, to the highest bidder at auction." The proceeds derived from these sales were used to pay Cooper for his survey and to retire a debt incurred previously in building and equipping a hospital.[26]

A few miles north of Sonora lay Columbia, where a rich strike was made by Thaddeus Hildreth in the spring of 1850. As the news spread, miners flocked to the area, and within a month the population reached 5,000. The Rev. Daniel Woods described the community that same spring: "The houses are of every possible variety. . . . Most of these, even in winter, are tents. Some throw up logs a few feet high, filling up with clay between the lots. The tent is then stretched above, forming a

roof. When a large company are to be accommodated with room, or a trading depot is to be erected, a large frame is made, and canvas is spread over this. Those who have more regard to their own comfort or health, erect log or stone houses, covering them with thatch or shingles. . . . Some comfortable wigwams are made of pine boughs thrown up in a conical form, and are quite dry. Many only spread a piece of canvas, or a blanket, over some stakes above them, while not a few make holes in the ground, where they burrow like foxes."[27]

The Columbia of January 1852 as depicted in Figure 7.6 had emerged from this primitive phase. The uniform width of Main Street seen curving away from the cabins in the foreground suggests that early regulations of some kind may have been established governing building lines. The straight line of Washington Street leading from Main Street to the left side of the view is another indication that the location of buildings was not entirely a matter for individual decision.

By the end of 1852 Columbia had no fewer than 150 business places, of which one-fifth were saloons. There miners could wash the dust of the diggings from their throats and either boast of their day's discoveries or drown their sorrows if their luck had been bad. Fires in 1854 and 1857 resulted in the destruction of most of the frame buildings and the rebuilding of the town in brick. Many of the structures of this period remain, and Columbia, now a State Historic Park, exists as perhaps the best preserved of all the California gold towns. Among the buildings is the fine Wells Fargo and Company Express office built after the fire of 1857. On its scales were weighed more than $55,000,000 of gold taken from the rich deposits in the vicinity.[28]

Near the northern end of the Mother Lode region, another mining town rivaled Columbia in the value of gold extracted in its vicinity. This was Grass Valley, depicted in Figure 7.7 as it appeared to the artist on August 6, 1852. Gold was found here in August of 1849, but real development began a year later when George Knight tapped rich veins of gold-bearing quartz in Gold Hill. Extraction of gold from quartz veins was far more difficult than recovering placer deposits from creek beds by panning and the use of trough-like rockers, or the hydraulic methods employed to wash away gravel in so-called dry diggings deposited by ancient streams. But once stamping mills were developed to grind the quartz into fine gravel so that it could be washed, the yields proved dramatic. By 1857 the Gold Hill mine alone produced $4,000,000 worth of gold.

Its location can be found on the plan of the town reproduced in Figure 7.8, an undated lithograph but probably published in the same year

Figure 7.5   View of Sonora, California: 1852

Figure 7.6 View of Columbia, California: 1852

Figure 7.7 View of Grass Valley, California: 1852

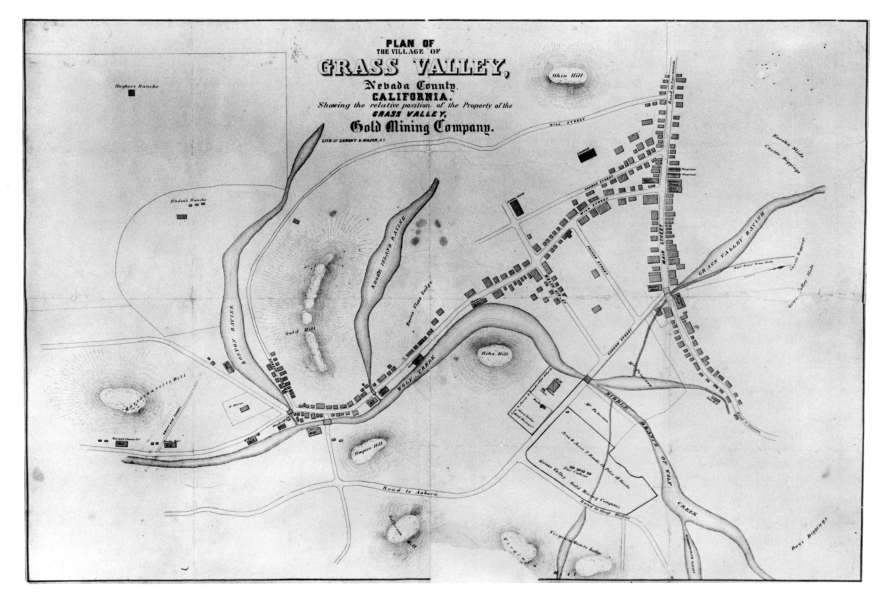

Figure 7.8 Plan of Grass Valley, California: ca. 1852

as the view. Like the survey of Coloma it shows evidence of an attempt to achieve some degree of uniformity in width of thoroughfares, building placement, and the alignment of what were then evidently new streets laid out on straight lines. A church and schoolhouse are prominently identified, as is the Masonic Hall, four hotels, and two express offices, along with the several stamping mills located on the stream banks.

No theater appears, although Grass Valley was the home of two famous female dancers and entertainers who performed before appreciative audiences in the California mining towns. Lola Montez lived in retirement in Grass Valley in a house believed to have been located at the corner of Walsh and Mill Streets. Lotta Crabtree lived nearby on Mill Street and learned to dance and act under the older woman's tutelage.

The speed with which many of the towns grew seems astounding. Four miles north of Grass Valley placer deposits attracted miners in September, 1849. A year later 400 buildings crowded the site, and the population reached 2,000. In 1851 the new charter for Nevada City provided for a mayor, a city council of nine aldermen, a marshal, a clerk, and a recorder. These officials managed to run up a debt of $8,000 purchasing a city hall and building a jail and a hospital. Irate taxpayers forced the suspension of most of the town's employees, and some of those who had lent funds to the city government in exchange for scrip found themselves with uncollectable claims on the municipal treasury.[29]

Nevada City unlike Sonora had no lots to sell to meet early expenses for municipal development, but its ambitious mayor and council were ultimately vindicated in their belief that the community would grow. Figure 7.9 shows the town in 1856. Surrounding the central panel are smaller views depicting an impressive array of the city's important buildings. Virtually all of them were built after 1851, when half of the town was ravaged by fire. Nevada City is perhaps the best preserved of the mining towns in northern California, and many of the structures shown in the view have fortunately survived to the present day.[30]

Even the apparently inexhaustible deposits of gold in California did not last forever. By the end of the 1850s hundreds of once-flourishing communities were deserted ghost towns or remained inhabited only by a few residents. Mark Twain recalled how in the 1860s he joined an old miner in the hills of Tuolumne County. They occupied one of only five cabins still standing. Yet as Twain observed, "a flourishing city of two or three thousand population had occupied this grassy dead solitude during the flush times of twelve or fifteen years before, and where our

cabin stood had once been the heart of the teeming hive, the centre of the city. When the mines gave out the town fell into decay, and in a few years wholly disappeared—streets, dwellings, shops, everything—and left no sign. The grassy slopes were as green and smooth and desolate of life as if they had never been disturbed. The mere handful of miners still remaining, had seen the town spring up, spread, grow and flourish in its pride; and they had seen it sicken and die, and pass away like a dream."[31]

The mining towns that managed to cling to life had to find a new basis for existence. California's favorable climate and its rapidly growing population combined to stimulate the development of agriculture, and a great many of the new immigrants began to cultivate the soil. So, while tens of thousands of miners returned to the East or went off in pursuit of mineral wealth in Nevada, Colorado, Montana, and elsewhere in the West, probably a majority of those who came in the gold rush remained in California. Many drifted to the coastal cities. Others resumed the trades and occupations they had abandoned in search of gold and settled in those mining communities that seemed to offer some promise as industrial or trading centers.

A few communities found that their locations, selected originally because of gold strikes, had other and more permanent advantages. Placerville, not far from Coloma, was one of these. First known as Old Dry Diggings, it later took the grim name of Hangtown after several persons suspected of robbery were strung up by irate citizens without benfit of trial.[32] Its location on the principal route overland to California through the Sierra passes promoted early commerical development. When the great silver strike of 1859 occurred in Nevada's Comstock Lode, Placerville became one of the major supply points. Through the pass formed by the south fork of the American River and into Placerville came the Pony Express and several stage lines. Three captains of American industry began their careers in this enterprising town. Mark Hopkins sold groceries from door to door. Young John Studebaker built wheelbarrows for sale to California miners and, after the discovery of silver in Nevada, wagons to haul supplies through the Sierra passes. Philip Armour could be found behind the counter in a Placerville butcher shop.

Placerville as it appeared in 1888, long after the mining days were gone, is shown in Figure 7.10. A small vignette at the bottom center recalls how the town looked shortly after it sprang into existence like so many others destined for a much briefer life. Relics of the past can still be seen in the modern town. At the lower end of Main Street, where

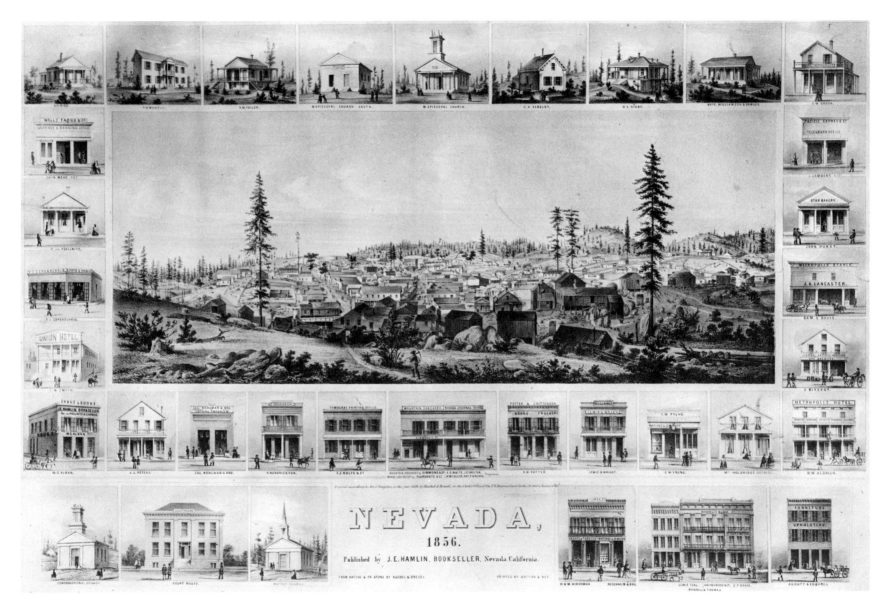

Figure 7.9 View of Nevada, California: 1856

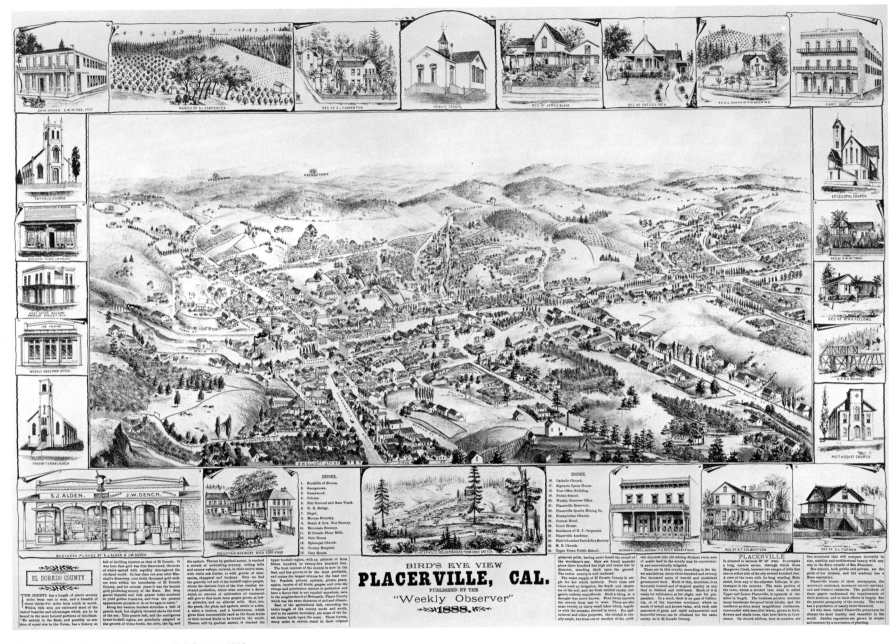

Figure 7.10 View of Placerville, California: 1888

the view shows a curious tower, stands the Old Hangtown bell tower, which once sounded fire alarms or was rung to summon vigilantes at times of real or fancied peril.

As important as Placerville once was as a local supply center for mining towns in the vicinity and a decade later for the booming silver cities in Nevada, it was dwarfed in this respect by three other cities more favorably situated to intercept persons and merchandise funneled through the port of San Francisco. Marysville, Stockton, and, above all, Sacramento, played a unique role during the days of the California gold rush. In all three communities city planning received far more attention than was possible in the mining communities so far examined.

Sacramento grew with furious speed on the land between Sutter's Fort and the American and Sacramento Rivers. John Sutter should have become the richest man in California, possessing as he did an established trading post and its surrounding lands favorably located to serve the first gold mining region. As it turned out the gold rush ruined rather than enriched Sutter. The thousands of miners pushing northeast from San Francisco squatted on his land, trampled his crops, and slaughtered his cattle. Although business at the fort boomed, Sutter had difficulty finding employees. Some of his workers evidently proved dishonest, helping themselves to merchandise or part of the gold taken in payment for goods sold to miners.

Sutter contributed to his own downfall. He was an extravagant man; when he entertained Governor Mason's party on their inspection tour to Coloma, Lt. Sherman estimated that the elaborate dinner, wines, and brandy must have cost at least $1,500.[33] This was an expenditure Sutter could scarely afford, for he was heavily in debt. In 1841 Sutter had purchased Fort Ross from its Russian owners, making a downpayment of only $2,000 and promising to pay the balance of $30,000 in cash and crops over the next four years.[34] Although Sutter dismantled Fort Ross and moved its building and equipment to his own outpost, most of his debt went unpaid. He had other debts as well, and at the very time his creditors began to press him for payment in 1848, he began drinking heavily.

When Sutter came to America he had left his family behind in Switzerland. His eldest son, John Augustus, Jr., had thus not seen his father for 14 years when he arrived at Sutter's Fort in the summer of 1848. The elder Sutter doubtless informed his son that an action was pending in the San Francisco courts that, if successful, would result in the attachment of all of his various properties to satisfy the remaining debt of $19,000 owed to the Russians. By October the two worked out an arrangement by which Sutter transferred all title to lands and much of his personal property to his son.[35]

The younger Sutter proceeded immediately to lay out the land in the vicinity of the fort and between it and the river as a town on an immense scale. He hired Capt. William H. Warner, an army topographical engineer, to survey the tract, and these two men evidently worked out the basic plan. Peter H. Burnett, whom young Sutter retained as his legal adviser and put in charge of lot sales may have suggested some modifications of its details based on his experience with townsite promotion in Oregon. Other ideas may have been put forward by Morton McCarver, who had been associated with Burnett in Oregon and who had approached Sutter with a proposal to aid him in developing the new community.[36]

Warner's plat for the city of Sacramento in 1848 as extended and resurveyed the following year by Clement W. Coote is reproduced in Figure 7.11. Sutter's Fort can be seen near the middle of the upper portion of the town. It and a few of the river blocks were the only elements not conforming to the vast, rectangular network of straight 80-foot streets and 20-foot alleys. M Street alone deviated from this policy of uniform street dimensions, being platted 100 feet in width. The younger Sutter set aside twelve squares for public use—reservations that were to prove exceedingly valuable to the city over the years as sites for parks and public buildings. Although in contrast to the nearby site of Sutterville much of the area embraced by the plan was subject to flooding—a disadvantage that its promoters doubtless took pains to conceal—this new and much larger city proved far more attractive to lot purchasers than did the elder Sutter's townsite in which he maintained an interest for a time.[37]

At the first auction of town lots on January 8, 1849, building sites near the fort proved most attractive. However, demand soon shifted for locations near the embarcadero at the foot of J Street. There tents, cabins, stores, and warehouses were hastily erected along the river bank where sailing boats and steamships could tie up to discharge their passengers and cargo. By June lots that had sold for $250 a few months earlier now brought $3,000. Not all of the merchants who set up business at Sacramento had to pay such prices; the younger Sutter distributed many sites as gifts in order to promote commercial development in the city and assure its ascendancy over rival Sutterville.[38]

The city a year after its founding is shown in Plate 9. It was a place, as John Letts observed a few months earlier, where in summer "all was confusion and dust, each generating the other. This is the point from

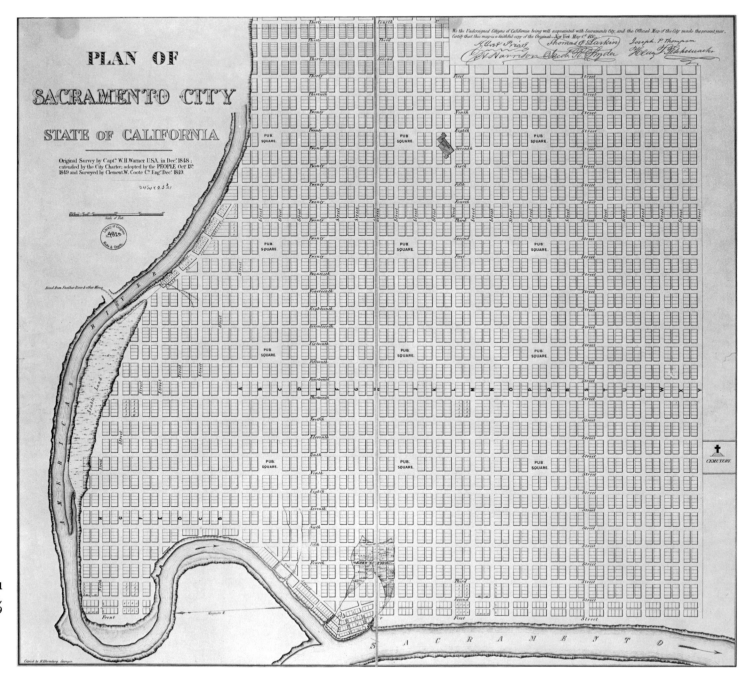

Figure 7.11
Plan of Sacramento,
California: 1849

which the first move is made, by land, for the mines, and every man was on the run; mule-teams were moving in every direction, some loading, others preparing to load, each surrounded by a halo of dust which rendered mules and driver invisible." Bustle, noise, and confusion remained, but, in November, Letts noted that "the town . . . was submerged in mud, the streets almost impassable. Flour, pork, bread, &c., were piled up along the sides of the streets without protection. There were many surmises as to the probability of the city being flooded."[39]

Surmise soon became fact. Rain through much of November and December caused flooding around the embarcadero district. A storm on January 8, 1850, left four-fifths of the city covered with water, and boats had to be used for transportation. The inhabitants voted funds for the construction of a levee nine miles long from a point above Sacramento to Sutterville. Only three feet high for most of its length, this early public works project proved inadequate and eventually had to be reconstructed on a more massive scale.[40]

The city did not escape a more commonplace form of disaster that regularly plagued the mining camps depending on Sacramento for supplies. Nearly two-thirds of the town went up in smoke on November 2, 1852, and the oldest buildings of the city—of which far too many have thoughtlessly been demolished in our own era—date from after that time. Much of the rebuilding was in brick, and, later, in cast iron.[41] Reconstruction took place at an astonishing rate. The rebuilt and extended city as it appeared in 1857 is shown in Figure 7.12. By that year the commerical and industrial economy of Sacramento was firmly established. In addition to its role as a supply center for the mining towns, the city served also as the trading center of a developing agricultural region. In addition, the city in 1854 succeeded in its efforts to become the state capital. The courthouse became the capitol and provided accommodations for state officials until 1869. River transportation continued to be important, although California's first railroad connected the city with Folsom as early as 1856, and it was from Sacramento that the western portion of the transcontinental route was built in 1860s.

The decline of mining in California slowed Sacramento's growth, but by 1870 its population exceeded 16,000. Figure 7.13 shows the city in that year, a few months after the new and still unfinished capitol had been occupied by government officials. This building was located on the site near the center of the original plat on four blocks facing 10th Street between L and N. It was a wisely chosen location, for the extra width of M Street as surveyed by Warner in 1849 provided a strong axial vista to the capitol portico and the dome towering above it.

In recent years M Street has been made much wider and is now known as Capitol Mall. Buildings along its sides have reinforced this central axis, and the extension of the original capitol grounds to include a large, landscaped area on the other side of the now enlarged building has provided Sacramento with an imposing central composition of public buildings. Extensive renewal and expressway projects in the past two decades have also changed materially the pattern of the old business district as shown in the 1870 view. A small portion of the nineteenth-century city facing the Sacramento River between L and I Streets has now been restored. This will present to modern visitors some vision of what Sacramento was like when it served as the principal inland city of California.

Two other cities of the interior almost equidistant from Sacramento to the north and south and also located on navigable rivers provided similar functions and services for the mining communities in the mountains. North of Sacramento on the Feather River, a tributary of the Sacramento, Marysville had by 1852 attained a population of 4,500.

The town had its beginning in December, 1849, when a group of landowners whose property lay where the Yuba River enters the Feather River employed a surveyor to lay out a town. Practically nothing is known of this planner except that he was French, his name was Auguste LePlongeon, and he was last heard of engaged in archaeological studies in the Yucatan.[42] Whatever his background, LePlongeon had notions of urban design a little more imaginative than most of his fellow planners of the period in California.

His plan as printed in 1852 is reproduced in Figure 7.14. It featured two octagonal "squares," named for Washington and Lafayette, each measuring about 650 feet from one side to the other. Seven other squares occupying spaces 300 by 350 feet appear, along with Yuba Square, a triangular open space with its apex at the intersection of Yuba and X Streets. The latter street and E and J Streets, all leading to the great octagonal spaces, scale about 125 feet in width, while the other streets seem to measure 100 feet wide.

It was certainly an unusual plan—too unusual, apparently, for the citizens of Marysville. The octagonal spaces have disappeared from the modern city, and quite possibly they were casualties at a very early date. Cortes and Napolean Squares still remain as does Miners Square and, in slightly modified form, Yuba Square. A baseball field occupies the site of Sacramento Square; of the others a modern map of the city shows no trace.

Figure 7.12 View of Sacramento, California: 1857

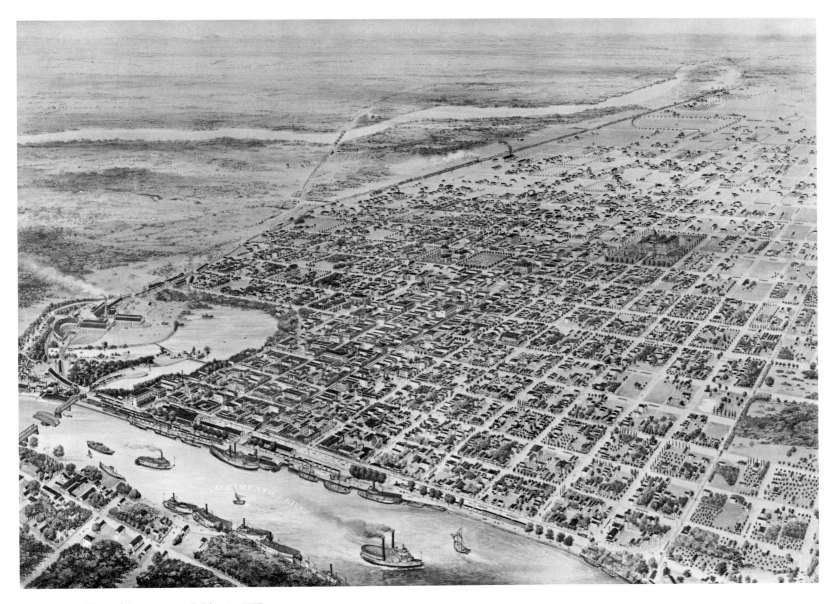

Figure 7.13   View of Sacramento, California: 1870

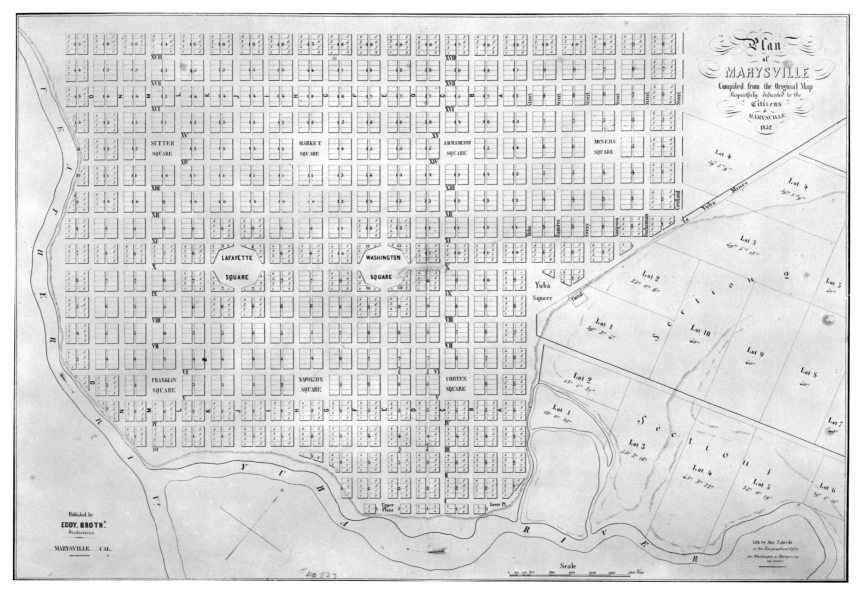

Figure 7.14   Plan of Marysville, California: 1852

Surpassing Marysville and rivaling Sacramento was the other principal transportation and supply center for the gold mines—Stockton, on the San Joaquin River. Its site lay within a 50,000-acre tract that Captain Charles M. Weber and his partner, William Gulnac, had acquired from the Mexican government in 1844. Three years later Weber founded the town of Tuleberg, but after the discovery of gold he engaged Major Richard P. Hammond to resurvey the site. Probably at that time the original design was extended to cover a much larger area, and it may have been altered in other respects as well. Weber renamed the town Stockton after his friend, Commodore Robert F. Stockton, commander of American naval forces in California waters during the Mexican War. Figure 7.15 is the Hammond survey of 1849 showing the ambitious plan for the city at the right and a map indicating its location on the left.

Two arms of the San Joaquin River penetrated the site, and along their banks Weber and Hammond skillfully platted a series of wide levees with ample locations for stores and warehouses. During the early years of growth, and throughout most of the nineteenth century, extensive port development took place to the north around the larger of the two channels, while Weber's Levee and Main Street served as the principal commercial thoroughfares.

When Bayard Taylor arrived in Stockton late in the summer of 1849 he "found a canvas town of a thousand inhabitants, and a port with twenty-five vessels at anchor." The community already had assumed a commanding role as the outfitting point for the southern mines and was alive with activity and noise as Taylor noted: "The mingled noises of labor abound—the click of hammers and the grating of saws—the shouts of mule-drivers—the jingling of spurs—the jar and jostle of wares in the tents." A few days later when he returned for a second visit, Taylor "found Stockton more bustling and prosperous than ever. The limits of its canvas streets had greatly enlarged during my . . . absence. . . . Launches were arriving and departing daily for and from San Francisco, and the number of mule-trains, wagons, etc., on their way to the various mines with freight and supplies kept up a life of activity truly amazing." Although Taylor commented that in the wet season "a great disadvantage of the location is the sloughs . . . which . . . render the roads next to impassable," he accurately foresaw that because "there seems . . . to be no other central point so well adapted for supplying the rich district between the Mokelumne and Tuolumne," Stockton's future growth was assured.[43]

Early in 1850 Stockton received the coveted designation as county seat for San Joaquin County, and a few months later obtained its first city charter. In 1851 the state insane asylum was located in Stockton, an institution that towns in the pioneer West ranked just behind the state capitol and the state university as desirable additions to a community and as symbols that the town was destined for permanency.

The location of the asylum can be seen in Figure 7.16, which shows Stockton in 1861 as its original gridiron plan was extended. Weber was generous in his reservations for public squares, churches, schools, and cemeteries. He could well afford such gestures. Taylor reported that Weber had "displayed a great deal of shrewd business tact, the sale of lots having brought him upwards of $500,000." And E. Gould Buffum observed in 1850 that in Stockton "real estate has risen greatly in value within the past six months—lots, which could have been purchased at that time for $300, being now worth from $3000 to $6000."[44]

Weber deserved his fortune. He proved to be a far more skillful manager of his Mexican land grant than did Sutter, and his plan for Stockton provided a sound basis on which the town could grow. By 1853 the city probably had a population of 5,000, a great many of whom were engaged in shipping and freighting. In some weeks, incoming cargo on boats from San Francisco amounted to as much as 2,800 tons of merchandise and supplies. Although the mining trade eventually dwindled, the rich San Joaquin Valley soon developed as a major wheat-growing region. Grain and hides began to move through the port of Stockton balancing the flow of shipping from the coast. The broad levees along the Stockton Channel provided attractive facilities for loading, unloading, and storing cargo.

The sites reserved by Weber for public purposes also proved useful. The public square on Main Street between Hunter and San Joaquin Streets provided a location for the courthouse in 1854. The two church sites in the block bounded by Lindsay, Hunter, and Eldorado Streets and Miners Avenue were occupied by the First Baptist and Episcopal Churches. Several of the school sites were similarly used for their intended purposes. These appear in the view of Stockton in 1870 reproduced as Figure 7.17. The city then had a population of about 10,000, but the railroad, which had arrived the year before, brought hopes of a much greater future. This indeed was to come as the city began its industrial expansion, much of it concentrating on the manufacture of farming implements and machinery to supply the wheat farmers of the region. Their annual golden crop was eventually to prove more important to the city than the mineral wealth whose discovery had been responsible for its early ascendancy.

Not all the riches of California came from the mines or from the fertile soil. Weber and other townsite promoters made far more out of the California gold rush than did all but a handful of the more fortunate

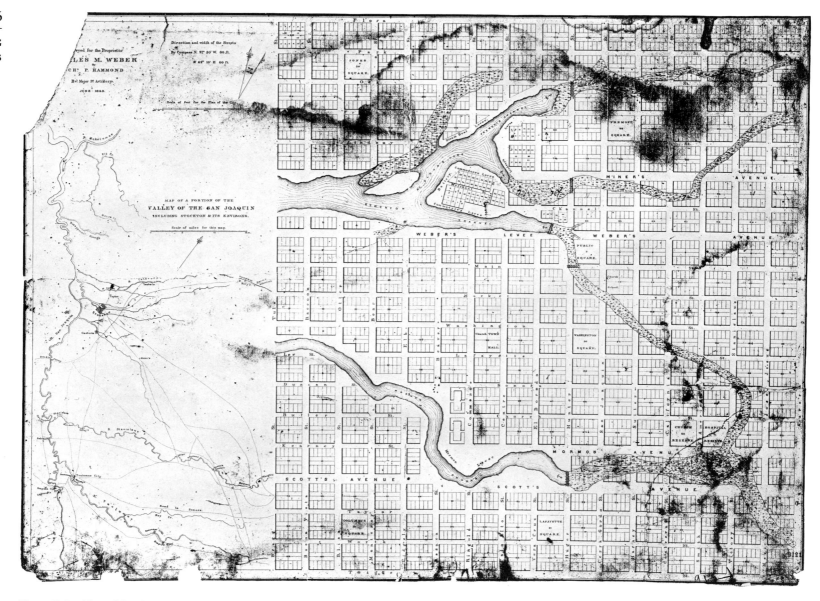

Figure 7.15 Plan of Stockton, California: 1849

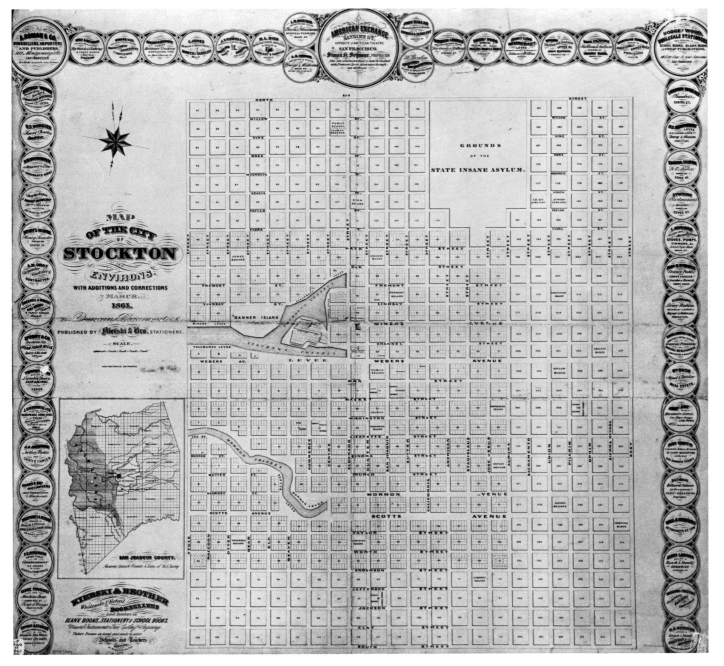

Figure 7.16 Plan of Stockton, California: 1861

Figure 7.17 View of Stockton, California: 1870

miners. Speculators were quick to seize the opportunity to dabble in the founding of cities. The costs of such ventures were slight: vacant land was abundant, surveying expenses were modest, and to advertise one needed only to pay for notices in the newspapers and for printed plats to be hung in hotel lobbies, real estate offices, and boat landings.

Success, of course, was not guaranteed. For every Weber there were dozens who failed in their attempts to duplicate his achievement at Stockton. Toualome City, the plan of which is reproduced in Figure 7.18, was the promotion of Messrs. McPherson and Nicholson of Stockton. Located on the north bank of the Tuolumne River near its mouth on the San Joaquin in 1850, this town appeared so promising that the editor of the *Stockton Times* changed the name of his paper to the *Stockton Times and Tuolumne City Intelligencer*. But the usual dry summer caused the river to drop to such a level that even the most shallow draft steamers could not reach the site, and the town quickly faded away.[45] The town of Boston on the northern bank of the American River across from Sacramento met a similar fate despite one observer's confident prediction in 1850 that "before many months the city of Boston . . . will rival its New England namesake in business and importance."[46]

The name of another great eastern city was borrowed by the promoters of a town on the south bank of the San Joaquin River near its mouth at Suisun Bay. Captain Hammond surveyed the site in June, 1849—the same month in which he worked on the plan of Stockton—for four ambitious promoters.[47] The lithograph reproduced in Figure 7.19 was published later that year in New York, the city whose name Col. J. D. Stevenson and his colleagues borrowed for their own. Those easterners bound for the gold country who saw this plat before their departure must have believed that a thriving metropolis awaited them. Possibly they had read a long letter from California printed on page one of the New York *Tribune* describing the site and containing the prediction that the new city "will become a large place in a short time, when it will take a great deal of trade from San Francisco."[48]

The proprietors advertised their City of New York of the Pacific in the newspaper *Alta California* on May 17, 1849. It was, they boasted, "laid out in the most beautiful and convenient manner." Center Street was described as 100 feet wide, all others being 75 feet in width, and lots were platted 50 by 100 feet, not one being "unfit for building purposes." The three public squares were to be donated for public use and "proceeds of the sales of all the lots fronting on the squares will be appropriated to the erection of public buildings." Those purchasing lots,

it was said, "will be required to make improvements within a specified time."[49] There were a few land sales, a hotel was built, and Stevenson energetically trumpeted the virtues of the town to every group of newcomers he could find along the San Francisco wharves. He also submitted proposals to the legislature on two occasions in vain attempts to have the town designated as the capital city.

No amount of promotional effort, however skillful, could overcome the disadvantage of the site. As Bayard Taylor observed in the fall of 1849, "There never will be a large town there, for the simple reason that there is no possible cause why there *should* be one."[50] The "city" remained essentially a paper town and became the butt of joking descriptions. John Letts referred to New York of the Pacific as a town of "newspaper notoriety," noting that he had been "informed that it now contains *one house*." Letts dryly observed that "there were not so many" when he saw the town toward the end of July, 1849, and finally commented: "it is said there has never been a death in the city."[51]

Stevenson probably profited from his townsite promotion although he failed to create a lasting community. The founders of Vallejo and Benicia enjoyed somewhat greater success even though their full expectations were not realized. Benicia was the oldest. Its site on the north side of Carquinez Strait, the channel connecting San Pablo and Suisun Bays, belonged to General Mariano Vallejo. In 1847 Vallejo, Robert Semple, and Thomas Larkin engaged Jasper O'Farrell, famous for his surveys of San Francisco, to help lay out the town as shown in Figure 7.20. It was an ambitious plan on a lavish scale and with generous provision for four public squares, Pacific Park, a city hall lot, and twenty others for municipal purposes.[52] Later the proprietors deeded blocks 114 and 115 as a cemetery. This site lay to the east of Pacific Park, separated only by the two half blocks on its eastern edge.[53]

Already in existence when gold was discovered, and lying directly on the water route to the northern mines, Benicia enjoyed a substantial boom in its early years. An army post and arsenal established on a site adjoining the town to the east in 1849 helped development.[54] The Pacific Mail Steamship Company constructed shops and wharves in 1850, the year in which the city received its charter; its population reached one thousand; and the proprietors spent $40,000 in various public improvements.[55]

For a time it appeared that ships bound from New York and other eastern cities might make Benicia rather than San Francisco their first port of call in California, and nearly every visitor to gold rush California who wrote of his experiences had a favorable word for Benicia.[56] Its fu-

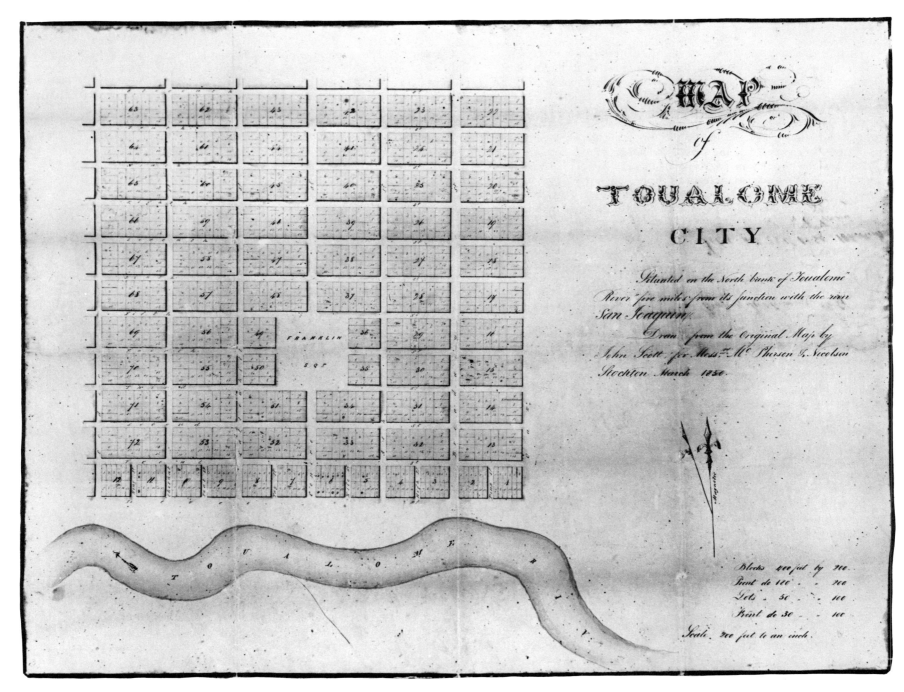

Figure 7.18 Plan of Toualome City, California: 1850

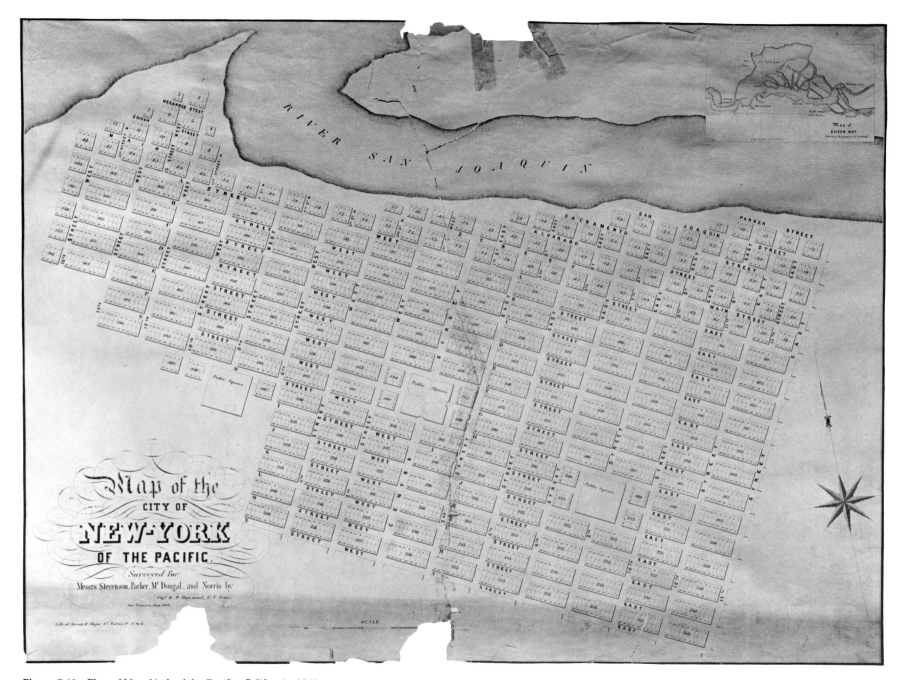

Figure 7.19 Plan of New York of the Pacific, California: 1849

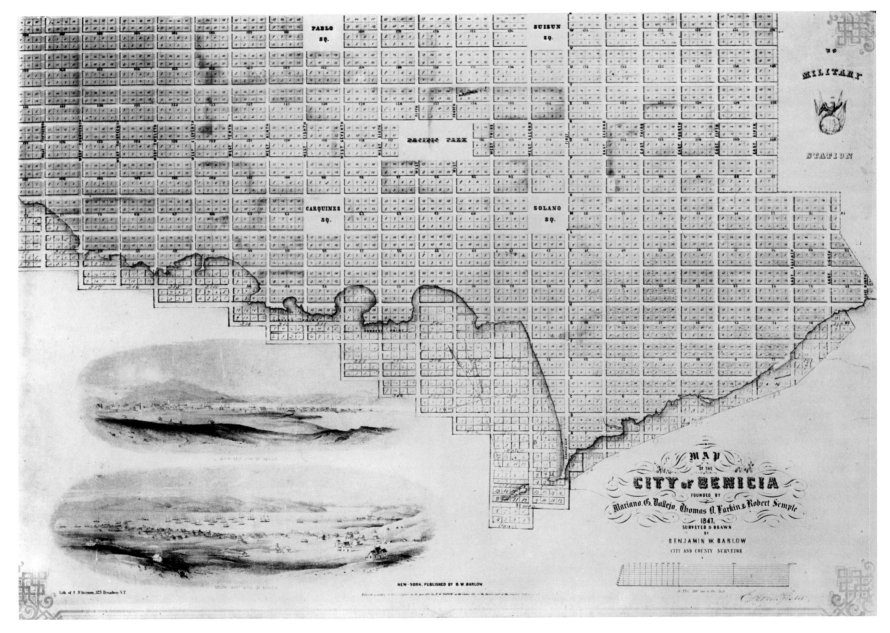

Figure 7.20 Plan of Benicia, California: 1851

ture seemed assured when the state legislature by an act passed May 18, 1853, declared the city the seat of government. Three years earlier lots had been selling for from $500 to $3,000, and the bright prospect of the community as the capital city must have encouraged sales and fanned the fires of speculation.

However, in 1854, disappointed in the inadequate accommodations offered at the still primitive Benicia, the legislature accepted an attractive offer from Sacramento and voted to move the government to that larger and more rapidly growing city. A proposed railroad to link Benicia with Marysville in 1853 failed to materialize, in 1858 Solano County designated Fairfield as the county seat after meeting for eight years in Benicia, and the steamship company moved to San Francisco.

Benicia's decline may have resulted from the greed of its proprietors. Several visitors commented about the inflated prices of town lots.[57] The inability of its proprietors to secure its designation as a customs port of entry, and Larkin's lack of energy in promoting the town, also contributed to its decline.[58] Benicia did not become a ghost town, but its hope of developing as the principal port of the San Francisco Bay area was forever lost. The view reproduced in Figure 7.21 shows the city in 1885 occupying only a small portion of its original vast grid of streets, squares, and blocks. In the lower left corner is a small view of the city hall, once the Solano County courthouse and for a brief time the state capitol. As preserved and restored in recent years, this building stands at the northwest corner of First and G Streets as a reminder to the residents of the modern industrial community of the different and more impressive role that the city might have played.[59]

Competition from a newly planned town on an adjacent site added to Benicia's problems. The sponsor of this rival city was none other than one of the original proprietors of the earlier community—General Vallejo. In 1850 the general entered the struggle to win the state capital for his town. He submitted a proposal to the legislature to lay out the town of Eureka at the mouth of Napa Creek and provide 156 acres of land immediately and $370,000 in cash within two years for public sites and buildings. This handsome offer exceeded all others, and the legislature accepted it by an act of February 4, 1851. While waiting for this decision, Vallejo and his surveyor, Charles Whiting, planned the town whose name was changed to that of its sponsor.

Figure 7.22 shows the plan of Vallejo, an enormous grid even larger than Benicia's interrupted only by a great circle on the axis of Capitol Street. While Vallejo obviously intended this to be the location for the main public building, the legislature convened on January 5, 1852, in a modest building located elsewhere. Vallejo provided in its basement a saloon and skittle-alley (known familiarly as the "third house"), possibly intended by him to distract the legislators from his failure to construct the promised public structures and to meet his other financial obligations.

After a week in Vallejo the disgusted lawmakers left to meet in Sacramento. They returned for their 1853 session, but when Vallejo asked to be released from his agreement, the legislature transferred the seat of government to Benicia.[60] John Russell Bartlett visited the town during this period, referring to it as "the great projected city of Vallejo, the once intended capital of the State." He observed that "it now stands naked and alone, its large houses tenantless. As the capital of California it might have become a place of importance; but without such factitious aid there is nothing to build it."[61]

Bartlett's appraisal of the city's prospects turned out to be erroneous, but it was good fortune and the accident of geography more than anything else that brought a measure of prosperity to the city. The view reproduced in Figure 7.23 depicting the city from the south in 1871 shows a portion of the large Mare Island naval shipyard complex that developed on a long, 900-acre spit of land purchased by the government in 1853. This important installation furnished employment for several hundred men, and Vallejo's economy (and pride) revived from the blow suffered when the legislature made its final departure. At the time the view was drawn, the population probably exceeded 3,000, a figure that gradually increased with the continued expansion of Mare Island shipbuilding and related facilities.[62]

The gold that drew tens of thousands to California and that created hundreds of mining camps, towns, supply centers, and speculative cities continued to be mined in great quantity throughout the decades of the 1850s and 1860s. Nevertheless, production declined from a peak in 1852 of $81,294,700 to little more than half that value in 1857.[63] Most of the rich placer and dry gravel deposits that could be easily worked with simple implements soon were nearly exhausted. Quartz mining in shafts required much more capital and machinery than men, and some prospectors began to turn elsewhere in their search for sudden wealth.

Some gold had been found on the eastern slope of the Sierra by Mormon settlers at Genoa in 1849. Others on their way to California had done some prospecting in the region with only modest success. A little silver had also been discovered. However, this region east of Lake Tahoe lay largely neglected for a decade after the rich California strikes.[64]

Figure 7.21 View of Benicia, California: 1885

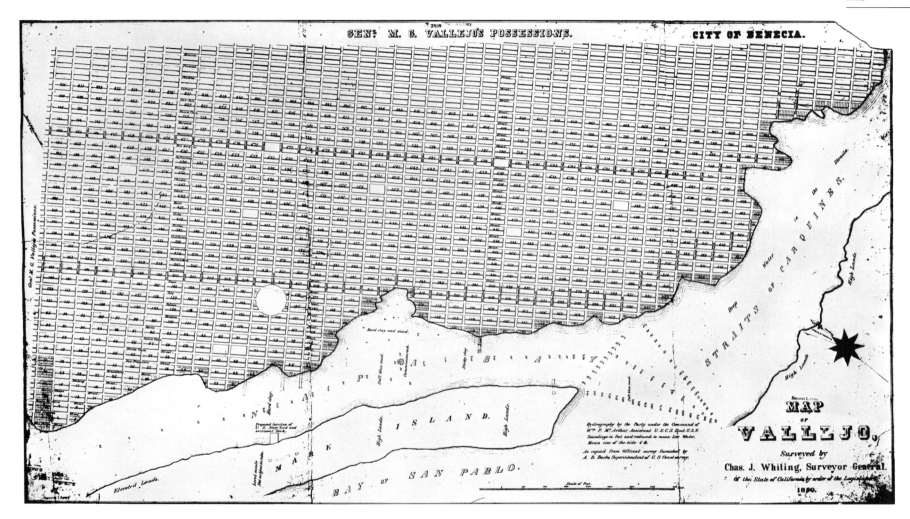

Figure 7.22 Plan of Vallejo, California: 1850

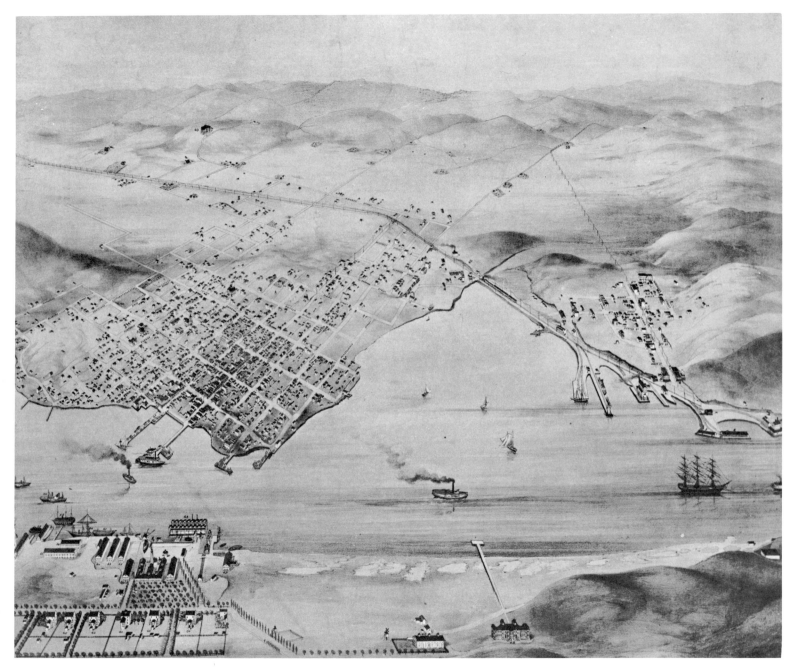

Figure 7.23
View of Vallejo,
California: 1871

Early in 1859 four prospectors found gold in impressive quantity in Gold Canyon, one of several steep ravines leading from Mount Davidson to the Carson River. The news attracted many others, including Henry Comstock who did little mining but busied himself staking out both mining and grazing claims. At one of the latter where his title was at best dubious he bullied two miners into sharing ownership of a deposit of decomposed ore—the fabulous Ophir mine of what was to become known as the Comstock Lode.[65]

The gold in the region was mixed with a puzzling blue or grey substance that was at first discarded. When samples finally were taken to Nevada City and Grass Valley for analysis, this mineral was identified as silver. The *Nevada Journal* announced the news in its July 1 issue and, eight days later, followed with a firsthand account by two respected and experienced miners of Nevada City who had visited the slopes of Mount Davidson, the rush began.[66] By the fall of 1859 thousands of persons were preparing to leave California, streaming through the mountain pass via Placerville, crowding the limited accommodations of Carson City, which had been platted in the fall of 1858, or pitching their tents and erecting cabins at Ophir on the steep slopes of Mount Davidson.

At a meeting in September the assembled miners voted to change the name of the camp to Virginia City. A month later Herman Camp and Henry de Groot surveyed the first street, later designated as A Street, running nearly north and south across the steep hillside following the supposed line of the Comstock ledge. A few miners whose cabins stood in the right-of-way of this thoroughfare refused to move, and the surveyors simply dodged these structures as best they could.[67] This first attempt to bring some order out of the usual mining camp chaos was only partially successful if we are to believe J. Ross Browne's description of Virginia City the following spring. Browne set out from Placerville in March, 1860, arriving at Virginia City in the vanguard of the vast hoard of would-be miners racing to this new source of instant wealth.

Browne's own view, reproduced in Figure 7.24, appeared in an issue of *Harper's Monthly Magazine* accompanied by these humorously accurate first impressions: "Frame shanties, pitched together as if by accident; tents of canvas, of blankets, of brush, of potato-sacks and old shirts, with empty whisky-barrels for chimneys; smoky hovels of mud and stone; coyote holes in the mountain side forcibly seized and held by men; pits and shafts with smoke issuing from every crevice; piles of goods and rubbish on craggy points, in the hollows, on the rocks, in the mud, in the snow, every where, scattered broadcast in pell-mell confu-

Figure 7.24 View of Virginia City, Nevada: 1860

sion, as if the clouds had suddenly burst overhead and rained down the dregs of all the flimsy, rickety, filthy little hovels and rubbish of merchandise that had ever undergone the process of evaporation from the earth since the days of Noah. The intervals of space, which may or may not have been streets, were dotted over with human beings of such sort, variety, and numbers, that the famous ant-hills of Africa were as nothing in the comparison."[68]

This busy, wildly confusing, ramshackle settlement grew with amazing speed. By October, 1860, several thousand persons and one hundred or so stores, shops, saloons, restaurants, boarding houses, and offices could be found on the mountainside.[69] New streets parallel to A Street were soon surveyed to accommodate the rapidly increasing population. The first business houses were located on B Street, a short distance down the slope, but C Street below it eventually developed as the principal location of the larger shops, saloons, hotels, and gambling houses. These streets were roughly graded and filled with crushed quartz waste from the mines. Apparently no cross streets were provided at first, and persons made their way as best they could up the steep hillside through informal lanes and passageways.[70]

The earliest detailed view of this booming mining metropolis was published in 1861 in San Francisco, where shares in Nevada mining companies were being bought and sold with frantic intensity, as they were in Virginia City itself. Reproduced in Figure 7.25, the view shows the city from the south looking down the several parallel streets that had been laid out roughly following the contours of Mount Davidson. The small views around the center panel show many of the principal buildings, including the office of the *Territorial Enterprise* where young Mark Twain began his career as a journalist. Twain came to Nevada with his brother, Orion, who had been appointed secretary of the Territory of Nevada when it was created early in 1861. He described the Virginia City of this period as a community that "claimed a population of fifteen . . . to eighteen thousand, and all day long half of this little army swarmed the streets like bees and the other half swarmed among the drifts and tunnels of the 'Comstock' hundreds of feet down in the earth." The town "had a slant to it like a roof. Each street was a terrace, and from each to the next street below the descent was forty or fifty feet." Standing "at a rear first floor window of a C Street house" a man could "look down the chimneys of the row of houses below him facing D Street." From one street to another was "a laborious climb . . . and you were panting and out of breath when you got there; but you could turn around and go down again like a house a-fire."[71]

Government under a city charter replaced the informal camp organization.[72] One of its functions was laying out new streets. The most important ran along the slope parallel to A, B, and C Streets. Cross-streets were staked off to replace the informal paths used during the first year or so to go up and down the steep hill.

In 1865 the town government proudly produced the first official plan of the town. It was printed in San Francisco on an heroic scale measuring within the borders 2½ by nearly 6 feet. This is reproduced in Figure 7.26. The plan was as simple as it was practical, given the conditions of topography. The main streets running with the contours of Mount Davidson were closely spaced so that the elevations of these terraced thoroughfares differed as little as possible. Even so, the short, precipitous cross streets were treacherous during the icy winters, and even in summers runaway wagons were commonplace.[73]

Land prices soared. Town lots in March, 1860, sold for $200 to $1,000. By 1864 choice locations with 40- or 50-foot frontage on major streets were priced at $10,000, $12,000, and as high as $20,000.[74] A view of C Street in 1868, reproduced in Figure 7.27, shows this solidly built-up business thoroughfare from the north after many of the first one- and two-story wooden structures had been replaced by more imposing buildings of stone and brick. Wooden sidewalks under projecting canopies connected the stores and shops and echoed pleasantly then, as they do today, with every footstep.

A different kind of commercial activity was located well down the slope where Virginia City's red light district could be found along a street lined with small, white, gaudily-furnished houses. As in all the western mining towns, prostitution flourished. Whores walked the streets and frequented the saloons. They were of all races and nationalities, as was the city's population.[75]

It was a community of enormous contrasts. Of gambling, vice, and crime there was certainly enough. Yet in 1865 Albert Richardson wrote of "a city of great brick blocks, costly churches, tasteful schoolhouses, imposing hotels, telegraph wires, five daily stages, two theatres [and] three daily newspapers—one nearly as large as the eight-page journals of New York!"[76] Down the hillside near the red light district, Chinese laborers huddled in miserable shacks and found release from their troubles in smoky opium dens. Above A Street, looking out over the great valley, wealthy mine superintendents and merchants lived in elaborate and opulent mansions.

The city at the height of its glory in 1875 can be seen in Plate 10. The artist depicted Virginia City viewed from the east against the soaring background of Mount Davidson. Along E, F, and G Streets one can see the mine entrances and smelters at the points where tunnels and shafts provided access to the rich deposits of silver lying beneath the city. Later that year the city received a devastating blow from which it never fully recovered. Fire broke out in a rooming house on the morning of October 26 and quickly spread from building to building. Pressure in

Figure 7.25   View of Virginia City, Nevada: 1861

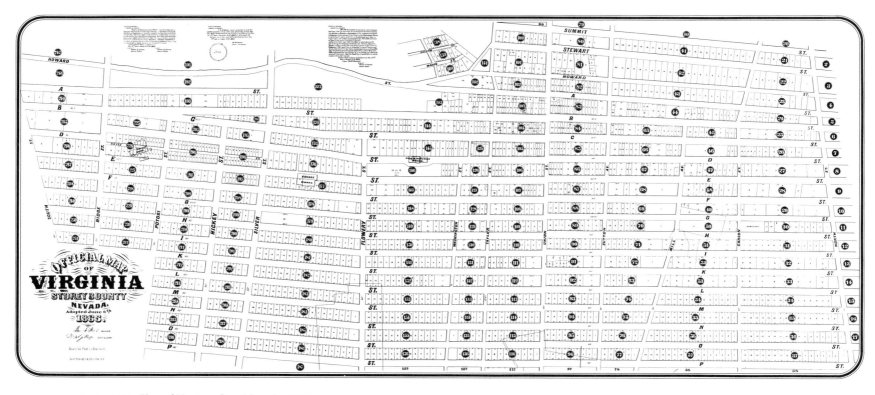

Figure 7.26　Plan of Virginia City, Nevada: 1865

the city's water mains proved inadequate, and despite heroic efforts by firemen and residents virtually the entire town was destroyed.

Although rebuilding began almost immediately, Virginia City's bonanza days were over. Mining continued for many years, but gradually diminished in importance, and the city began its decline in population and activity. The modern community lives principally on the tourist trade. Enough of the post-1875 city remains to provide the visitor with some appreciation of what Virginia City once was like when it throbbed with life as the queen city of the Comstock.

Discovery of gold and silver in the Virginia City region stimulated a flurry of prospecting elsewhere in the Nevada mountains, and other

mining towns soon grew up in the vicinity of gold and silver deposits found in these locations. The Esmeralda mines, discovered in the summer of 1860, were among the richest strikes. They were located in a remote part of the Sierras north of Mono Lake just across the California boundary.[77] Two towns, Aurora and Esmeralda, were surveyed that year, both of them laid out in the gridiron patterns shown in Figure 7.28. By May, 1861, nearly 2,000 miners, merchants, gamblers and speculators crowded Aurora's streets. Two years later the population reached nearly 10,000, and the Aurora business district consisted of 20 stores, 12 hotels, and 21 saloons. It was from here that young Mark Twain in 1862, disillusioned with mining, sent a few examples of his

Figure 7.27 View of C Street, Virginia City, Nevada: 1868

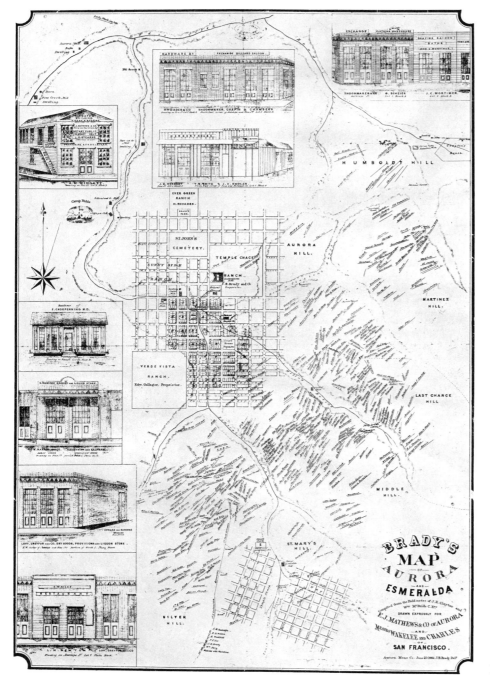

writing to the editor of the Virginia City *Territorial Enterprise* and was soon on his way to that city to begin his writing career as a cub reporter.[78]

Austin was another Nevada mining community where circumstances permitted the survey of the site into streets, blocks, and lots before miners occupied the location. In 1862 William Talcott found rich silver veins near a Pony Express station at a pass through the Toiyabe Range in central Nevada. When the ore was sent to Virginia City to be assayed, it was reported to be worth up to $7,000 a ton. The rush began early in 1863 and those miners who were not combing the hills to establish claims settled near the Reese River at what was called Jacobsville. Somewhat closer to the mountains at the mouth of a canyon another camp sprang up called Clifton.

In November of that year a townsite was surveyed farther up the canyon and named Austin. The new town, the official plat of which is reproduced as Figure 7.29, displaced Clifton. The design of this community is of no more than routine interest. Topography probably influenced surveyor G. F. Allardt to modify the gridiron plan so that Main Street would follow natural contours of the mountain terrain. Probably no one bothered to object to the clumsy intersections of the thoroughfares leading to and from Virginia Street or the awkward shape of the "Court Block." Indeed, its residents may have ignored the plan altogether, and certainly the "four thousand people" Albert Richardson estimated as the population in 1865 occupied land well beyond the boundaries of the official townsite. Richardson described Austin as a town that "straggles for three miles down a deep, crooked cañon" amidst "hundreds of shafts and ditches." It was, he remarked, "a city lying around loose."[79]

While additional discoveries continued to be made throughout much of Nevada, most of the population of the new territory could be found within a 25-mile radius of Virginia City. Not far away from what was then the growing metropolis of the Comstock Lode lay American City. Finding that its location for mining was less favorable than its first settlers had supposed in 1860, the residents determined to ensure the future of the community in another manner. In 1864 they attempted to lure away the Nevada territorial government from Carson City by offering $50,000 if the legislature would agree to move. Evidently included in the offer was the tract of land shown in Figure 7.30 identified as "Capital Park." The recorded town plat was deceptively neat and, as it turned out, wildly optimistic. The legislators declined American City's offer, and by 1867 the site had been abandoned.[80]

Figure 7.28   Map of Aurora and Esmeralda, Nevada and Vicinity: 1862

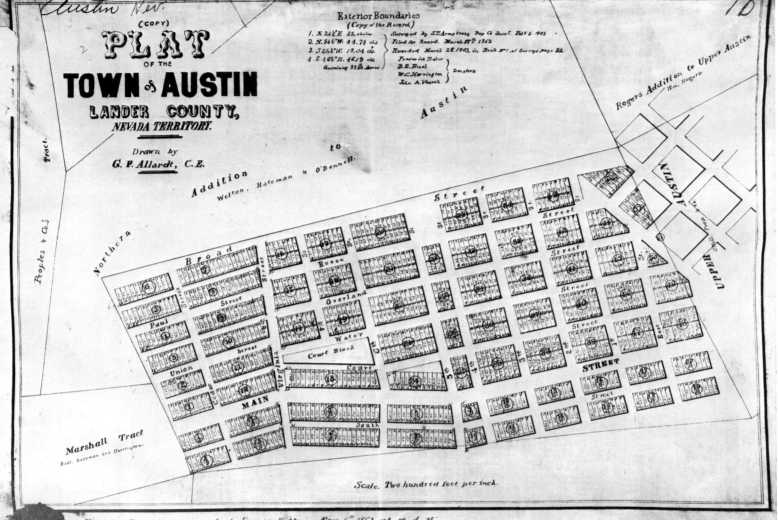

Figure 7.29
Plan of Austin,
Nevada: 1863

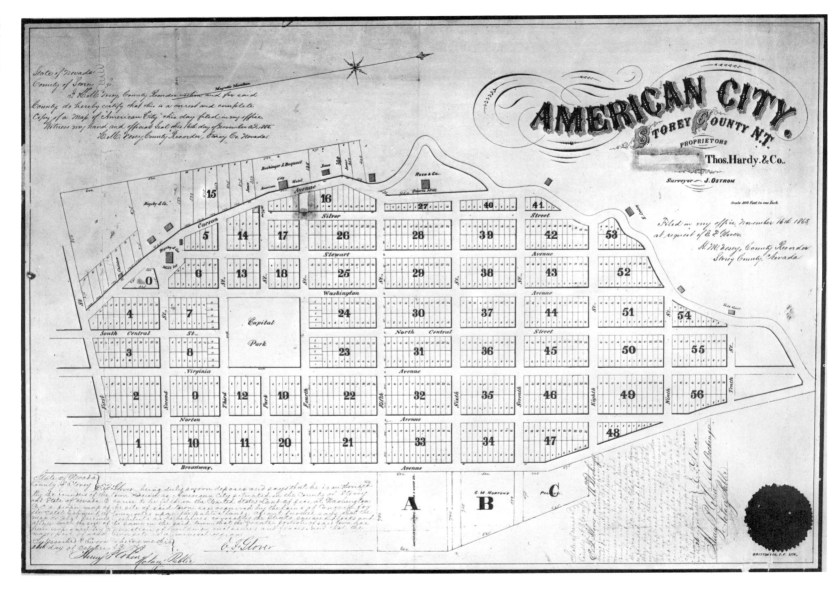

Figure 7.30 Plan of American City, Nevada: 1865

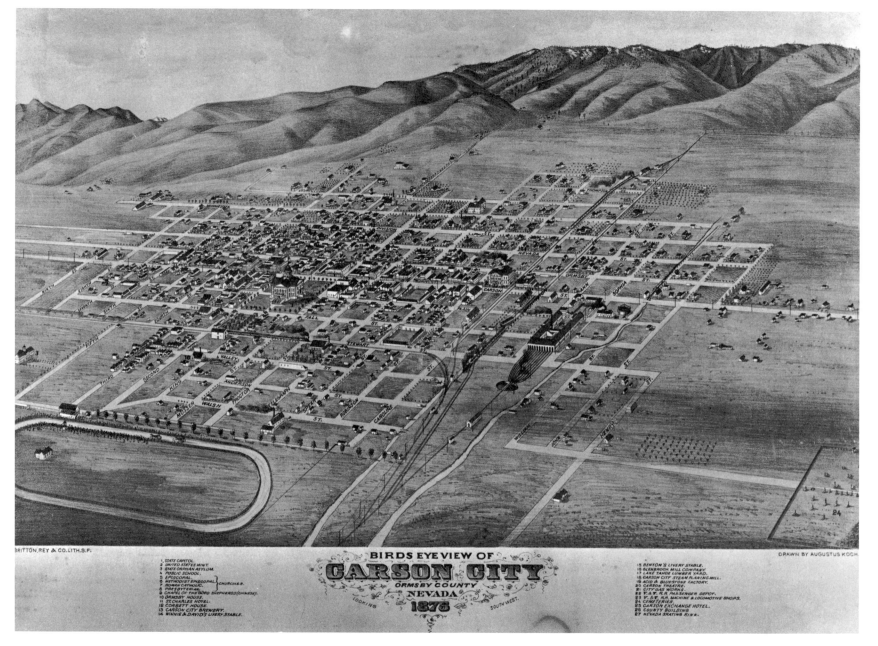

1. STATE CAPITOL.
2. UNITED STATES MINT.
3. STATE ORPHAN ASYLUM.
4. PUBLIC SCHOOL.
5. EPISCOPAL.
6. METHODIST EPISCOPAL.
7. ROMAN CATHOLIC.
8. PRESBYTERIAN.
9. CHAPEL OF THE GOOD SHEPHERDS (CHINESE).
10. ORMSBY HOUSE.
11. ST. CHARLES HOTEL.
12. CORBETT HOUSE.
13. CARSON CITY BREWERY.
14. WINNIE & DAVID'S LIVERY STABLE.

CHURCHES.

BIRDS EYE VIEW OF
CARSON CITY
ORMSBY COUNTY
NEVADA
1876
LOOKING   SOUTH WEST.

DRAWN BY AUGUSTUS KOCH.

15. BENTON'S LIVERY STABLE.
16. GLENBROOK MILL COMPANY.
17. LAKE TAHOE LUMBER YARD.
18. CARSON CITY STEAM PLANING MILL.
19. ACID & BLUESTONE FACTORY.
20. CARSON THEATRE.
21. CITY GAS WORKS.
22. V. & T. R.R. PASSENGER DEPOT.
23. V. & T. R.R. MACHINE & LOCOMOTIVE SHOPS.
24. CEMETERIES.
25. CARSON EXCHANGE HOTEL.
26. COUNTY BUILDING.
27. NEVADA SKATING RINK.

Figure 7.31   View of Carson City, Nevada: 1876

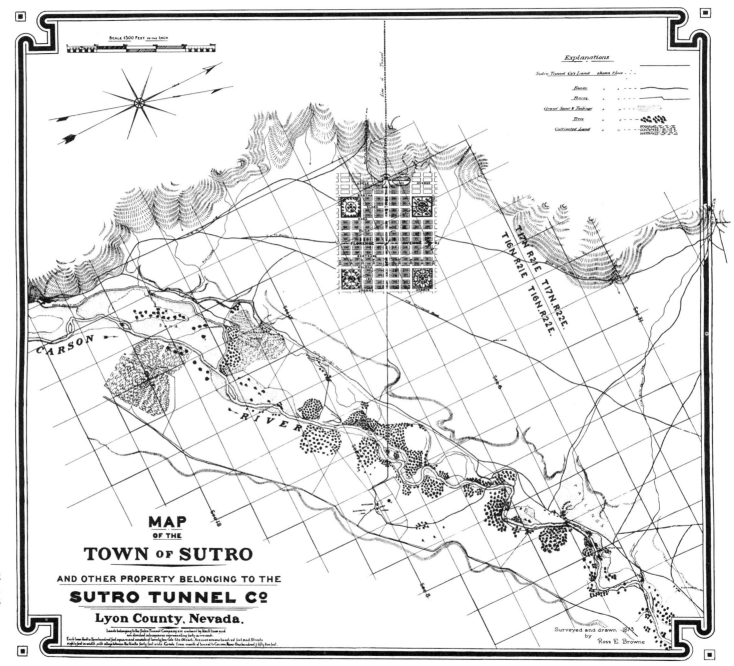

SCALE 1500 FEET TO THE INCH

Explanations

Sutro Tunnel Co's Land   shown thus

Roads
Fences
Gravel Sand & Tailings
Trees
Cultivated Land

CARSON   RIVER

MAP
OF THE
TOWN OF SUTRO
AND OTHER PROPERTY BELONGING TO THE
SUTRO TUNNEL CO
Lyon County, Nevada.

Surveyed and drawn 1873
by
Ross E. Browne

Figure 7.32
Plan of Sutro,
Nevada: 1873

The target of American City's promotional efforts—Carson City— was surveyed as a town in 1858 by Abraham Curry near an Overland Stage station and trading post of the route through the Carson River valley to California. Curry and William Ormsby began to publicize the town, booming it as the future seat of a separate territorial government as early as August 1859.[81] In 1860 the town population reached 700, a figure that was to double in the next twelve months as the new town became a supply point for the mining communities and capital of the territory.

The original plat of Carson City has apparently not survived, but its plan was the simple gridiron revealed by the view of the city in 1875 reproduced in Figure 7.31. Included in Curry's design was a plaza or public square, and it was on this square plot, equal in size to four of the normal city blocks, that the state capitol was begun in 1870. Five blocks to the north on the other side of Carson Street the view shows a somewhat older building—the U.S. Mint, which opened in 1866 and is now the Nevada State Museum. Diagonally across Carson Street to the northeast one can see the passenger station of the Virginia and Truckee Railroad, which in 1872 was completed between Carson City and Virginia City.

The most unusual town proposed during the early mining period of Nevada was the product of the fertile mind of Adolph Sutro. In 1860 as a resident of Virginia City he advanced the idea of constructing a long tunnel from Eagle Valley, four miles away, to hit the Comstock Lode more than 1,500 feet below the surface. The tunnel was to serve several purposes: to supply ventilation, to provide drainage, to afford emergency exits in case of fire or cave-ins, and to permit ore to be removed more efficiently and cheaply. After many years and countless objections and difficulties the tunnel was finally completed in 1878.[82]

As part of this enterprise Sutro envisaged a town at the mouth of the tunnel where workers employed at his smelters would live. The smelters were never built, Sutro sold out his interests in 1880 and moved to San Francisco to engage in various real estate and development projects, and the town at the tunnel's mouth never took the form he planned. That design as drawn in 1873 appears in Figure 7.32. A note beneath the legend provides the following description: "each town block is three hundred feet square and consists of twenty four lots 25 by 130' each. Avenues are one hundred feet and Streets eighty feet in width, with alleys between the blocks forty feet wide." Not mentioned is the most arresting feature of the proposed town: the four 4-block parks, one at each corner, laid out with diagonal walks and neatly geometrical planted areas. It was virtually the only attempt—and unsuccessful at that—to introduce some measure of elegance, beauty, and landscape embellishment in the Sierra mining frontier.

VIII

Urban Growth and Expansion in Southern California During the Post-Hispanic Era

THE gold rush affected the towns of southern California far less than their sister communities in the northern part of the state. The land boom that San Francisco and other cities of the Bay Area were enjoying by 1849 had little impact on Los Angeles and other southern settlements, except to slow and, in some cases, temporarily reverse their rates of growth as existing and potential residents were lured to the mining camps or supply centers in search of sudden wealth.

Initial town planning activities during the first years of American rule focused on established towns and concentrated on efforts to settle land claims and to provide areas for a modest amount of expansion. Preparation of adequate surveys showing existing streets and property lines were combined with the planning of new thoroughfares and the subdivision of portions of *pueblo* lands for sale to raise badly needed municipal revenues.

At the presidial town of Santa Barbara, incorporated as a city in the spring of 1850, surveyor Salisbury Haley set to work in 1851 mapping existing features of the community and planning new streets 60 and 80 feet wide. Haley based his grid pattern on the earlier orientation of the *presidio* and the ill-defined streets and blocks of the Mexican *pueblo* that had developed on adjacent land.

An ordinance adopted the next year specified that anyone "who has the intention of building a house on unoccupied land must obtain from the *Comisionado* a certificate which indicates that the house will not obstruct the lands and thoroughfares of the city."[1] This proved more difficult to administer than anticipated, since Haley's rawhide surveyor's "chain" stretched or shrank depending on the weather, and the distances indicated on his plat turned out to be far from precise.[2]

Litigation over property boundaries kept the lawyers of Santa Barbara busy for years, but these uncertainties did not prevent the city's expansion on the elongated grid of streets stretching from the Pacific shore along the coastal valley toward the mission. By 1877 when the view in Plate 11 was published, State Street, one of the two 80-foot thoroughfares, was lined with business buildings for several blocks. A new courthouse and an even newer city hall provided focal points for public affairs, and two piers at the foot of State and Chapala Streets welcomed coastal steamers and smaller craft.

The civil settlement of San Diego on the flat land south of the old *presidio* also was surveyed and extended by order of the *ayuntamiento* or council. Lt. Cave J. Couts of the American army submitted the drawings reproduced in Figure 8.1 to municipal officials in 1849. That on the left was his plan for the existing town (now known as "Old Town").

The plaza of the mid-1830s was given precise form, and Couts added a series of grid streets in all directions. The fact that these fit the existing building lines so well is added evidence that some kind of plan had been prepared for the settlement at an earlier date.[3]

The drawing at the right represented a new proposal for the layout of a port community several miles to the south along the west shore of the jutting peninsula dividing San Diego harbor from the shallow waters of False Bay (now Mission Bay). The location of this town—La Playa—can be seen on the map of the entire area reproduced in Figure 8.2. This official map of the *pueblo* lands of San Diego was prepared in 1856, when the municipality was pressing its claims for the lands of its original Spanish grant. As has been described, the other California towns of Hispanic origin were also engaged in efforts to have their public urban domains similarly confirmed by the American authorities.

Also to be seen on the map are other strips of coastal land platted into streets and lots, the first signs of the speculative mania for urban land and townsite promotion that would afflict most of the residents of the area for decades. The most important of these new areas was New San Diego, whose plan appears in Figure 8.3 and whose location can be noted in the previous illustration.

William Heath Davis, who had married into the prominent Estudillo family of old San Diego, persuaded the *alcalde* in 1850 to sell to him and three partners for $2,304, 160 acres of land at a location bordering deep water. Andrew F. Gray, chief surveyor for the U.S. Boundary Commission who had suggested the project to Davis, prepared the town design for New San Diego and received a share in the enterprise. Another share went to Lt. Thomas D. Johns, quartermaster and commissary of an army unit that was to establish its depot at La Playa. Instead, Johns obligingly ordered his supply ships to sail down the harbor and anchor at New San Diego, where a wharf and warehouse were under construction. Between Davis's New San Diego and Old Town another tract of 687 acres was purchased from the municipality and platted under the appropriate name of Middletown.[4]

Gray's design for New San Diego took the form of a gridiron of blocks each measuring 200 by 300 feet except for blocks 18, 19, and 20, down the center of which slips were to extend with wharfs on either side. He platted all streets 75 feet wide except for Atlantic Street (now Pacific Highway), Commercial Street (now Market), and an unnamed street to the north (the present Broadway), which he made 100 feet in width. Between India and Columbia Streets and Fourth and Fifth (now G and F) Streets he reserved an entire block as Pantoja Plaza. Davis do-

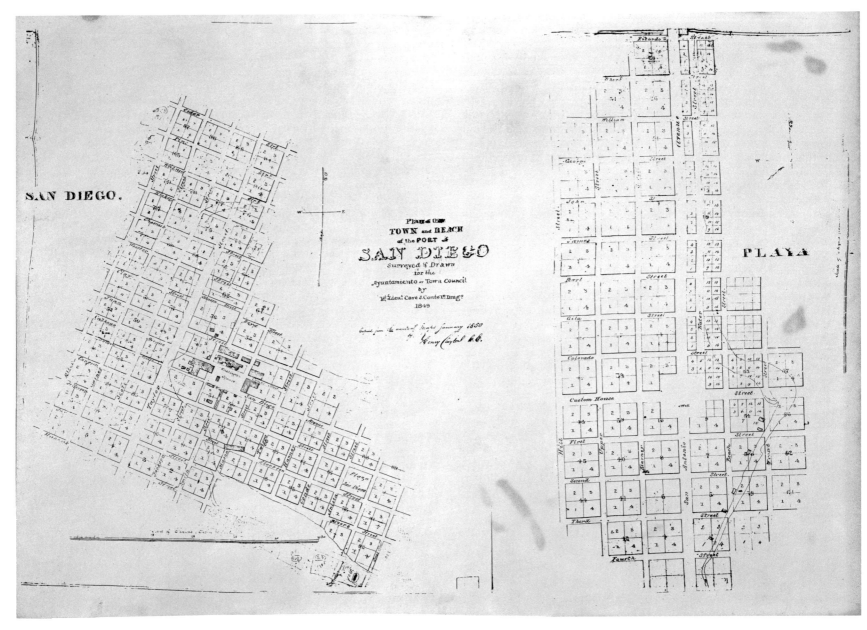

Figure 8.1 Plan of San Diego, California: 1849

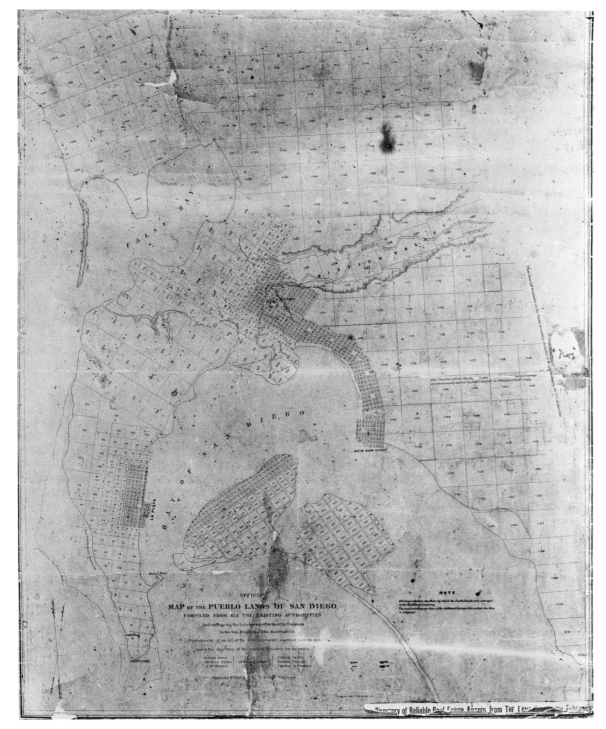

Figure 8.2 Map of San Diego, California and Vicinity: 1856

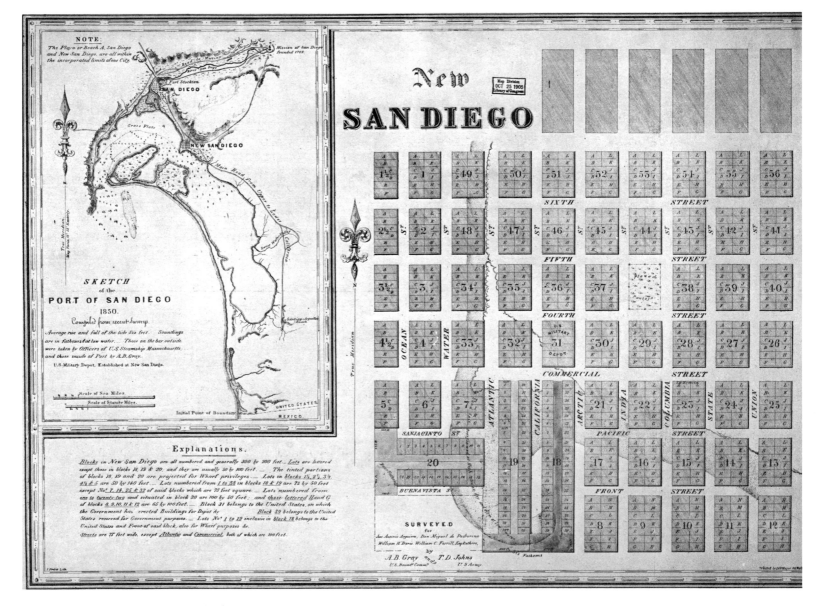

Figure 8.3 Plan of New San Diego, California: 1850

nated Block 31 to the government for the military depot that Lt. Johns had been bribed to relocate from its intended site at La Playa.

When John Russell Bartlett, U.S. boundary commissioner, saw the town in 1852 he observed that while "it consists of a few substantial frame houses, and . . . a large and fine wharf . . . there is no business to bring vessels here, except an occasional one with government stores." He noted a further disadvantage: "There is no water nearer than the San Diego river, three miles distant." Because of its fine natural harbor the bay in Bartlett's opinion would be "an important stopping place for shipping," but he cautiously concluded that "whether the Playa . . . , the old town of San Diego, or . . . New San Diego . . . will have the ascendancy remains to be seen:—each has its advantages and disadvantages."[5]

Davis made strenuous efforts to promote the town, building the wharf, several houses, and helping to establish a newspaper, two hotels, and a few stores. Gray went east to advertise the new community, to seek government approval for a post office, and to convince shiplines to make San Diego a regular port of call. He had only limited success, and Davis was forced to curtail his investments in the town because of serious financial problems in San Francisco when a fire in 1851 destroyed his business at a loss of $700,000. The lack of water and the partial destruction of the wharf with a resulting decline in shipping added to the proprietor's difficulties. By 1853 many of the buildings were taken down and reassembled in Old Town, and while the army depot remained until 1866 the townsite soon lay virtually abandoned.[6]

On April 15, 1867, the man who would be responsible for much of San Diego's development arrived on the steamboat *Pacific* from San Francisco. Alonzo Erastus Horton had found his way to California in 1851 after dabbling in real estate, shipping, cattle and a variety of other occupations in Oswego, New York; Milwaukee; and St. Louis. He had planned at least one town—Hortonville, Wisconsin—selling his interests there for $7,000 before coming to California to work as an express rider, gold trader, and storekeeper. After a period of time in the East he returned to open a furniture store in San Francisco. Early in 1867 he heard a lecture on the ports of the West Coast at which the speaker extolled San Diego as having one of the best harbors in the world as well as a marvelously healthy climate. Three days later Horton sold his business and boarded the *Pacific* for southern California.

Landing at the old Davis townsite, Horton immediately perceived the beauty of the area and the potential for town development. Inquiries at Old Town revealed that land could be acquired only by auction under the regulations adopted for disposing of city-owned real estate in the old *pueblo* grant. Because there was no demand for land, the terms of office of the trustees in charge of sales had lapsed, but at his request a new election was held, an auction took place, and Horton soon became the owner of 960 acres located east of New San Diego and Middletown. For this enormous tract he paid the trifling sum of $265, or about 27½ cents an acre.[7]

Horton followed the street orientation that Davis had used for New San Diego, platting the entire site in blocks 200 by 300 feet, each divided into 12 lots measuring 50 by 100 feet and fronting on 80-foot streets. Only D and H Streets were wider; they were extensions of Broadway and Market Streets from the Davis plat and were continued 100 feet wide through the Horton tract.

As finally surveyed and displayed to promote land sales, the Horton Addition plat is reproduced in Figure 8.4. This includes a location map on the right-hand side showing later surveys to the south. A large tract in this area from the municipal domain had been conveyed in 1872 as a subsidy to a projected transcontinental railroad. Below that can be seen the outline of National City that Frank and Warren Kimball laid out in 1868 as still another vast gridiron of rectangular blocks but with a slightly different orientation.[8]

Horton began an intensive publicity and sales campaign to promote his new town. Copies of his plat were displayed everywhere, and he carried with him a tin case containing maps of his property. On the steamers from San Francisco Horton ceaselessly talked to passengers about the great future of San Diego, showed them the plat, and arranged for them to be shown choice lots in the developing community. His enthusiasm proved contagious, and houses, hotels, and business buildings soon were under construction.

Despite the hostility of many Old Town residents Horton succeeded in 1871 in having the new courthouse built on a site where his tract adjoined Middletown. Earlier he had lured the San Diego *Union* from Old Town. Late in 1868 the newspaper, still in its former location, virtually conceded that the future of the area belonged to Horton's town, reporting that "the evidences of improvement, progress and prosperity are visible on every side. Buildings are in the process of erection in all directions. Lots are being cleared rapidly in Horton's Addition. Mr. Horton is selling $600 to $1,000 worth of lots every day. Restaurants, bakeries, livery stables, furniture stores, blacksmith shops, hotels, doctors' offices, wholesale and retail stores, saloons and residences are going up."[9]

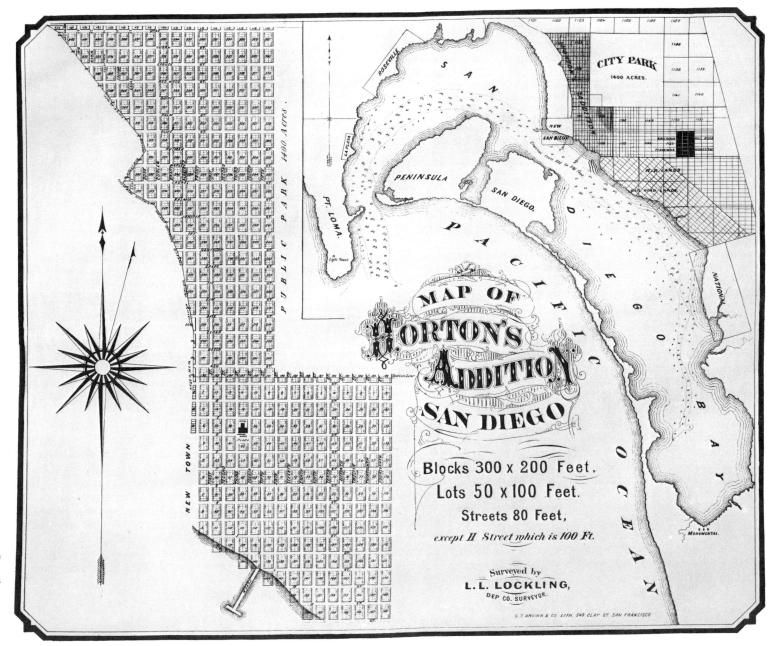

Figure 8.4
Plan of San Diego,
California: ca. 1868

Two views of San Diego in the 1870s reveal the rapid growth of the community under Horton's energetic leadership. Figure 8.5 shows the town as seen from the bay in 1873. By that time construction had also taken place on the streets that Davis had laid out in his abortive attempt to promote New San Diego.

More impressive is the view in Figure 8.6, published only three years later, revealing the appearance of the town from the hills rising steeply from the flat land along the bay. Two wharfs extending into the harbor offered landing facilities for passenger and cargo ships and provided the most convenient way by which supplies and new residents arrived at the town. Many of the new arrivals came from the East seeking the healthy climate that Horton and other land promoters of the area held out as one of the inducements to live and work in San Diego.

While the only open space on Horton's original grid plan was a small plaza on what is now the south side of Broadway between 3rd and 4th Avenues, this far-sighted developer was to be responsible for one of America's greatest and largest urban parks. Its location can be seen on the map reproduced in Figure 8.7 showing the entire urban area as platted in 1885. East of that portion of the Horton Addition behind Middletown, a nearly square tract of 1,400 acres was set aside as a park by the trustees administering the *pueblo* lands. Horton suggested this in 1867, recommending first that 320 acres should be so reserved and then proposing that 1,440 acres should be withheld from further land sales.[10] Forty acres at the southwest corner had already been sold before the Board of Trustees passed an ordinance creating the park reserve on May 26, 1868. The state legislature confirmed this action 20 months later. The bulk of this huge tract of land is now Balboa Park, a magnificent urban recreation area rivaled in San Diego only by the equally impressive but quite different water-oriented Mission Bay Park created out of the shallows and marshes of old False Bay.

In disposing of its extensive holdings of *pueblo* real estate, the municipality chose not to exercise any controls over the design of the lands it sold so quickly and so cheaply in the early years of the city's American period. Balboa Park, however, exists today as an indirect legacy of the Spanish land system and a tribute to the vision of Horton and those officials whom he persuaded to act with such boldness in providing for the future of what was then little more than a paper city.

At Los Angeles public officials followed a different policy from that of San Diego in disposing of the municipal domain. The occupation of the city by American military forces may have been viewed with alarm by its older residents of Spanish or Mexican extraction, but it at least brought to the town persons capable of making the surveys of streets and properties that had been badly needed for so long. The military governor of California, General Bennett Riley, directed the council of Los Angeles to undertake such a survey. At the council's request in June, 1849, Riley sent Lt. Edward Otho Cresap Ord to carry out the work with the understanding that its cost should be a municipal charge. Ord and a committee ultimately agreed that he should be paid $3,000 for the work. He was to locate the midpoints of the sides of the *pueblo* lands, which the city then claimed as consisting of 16 square leagues, as well as to record the developed area as it then existed, "including streets, roads, zanjas [ditches] outside of the fenced land, hills, plazas and crossings." In addition, within a defined area of substantial size Ord was "to lay out streets and blocks, where there are no buildings."[11]

With William Rich Hutton as his assistant, Ord completed his survey of existing features and the proposed new streets and lots by the end of August. Figure 8.8 shows the results of his work. North-south and east-west lines lead from the door of the church. Extended two leagues in each direction, they intersected at their midpoints the four sides of the 16-league square claimed by Los Angeles as its *pueblo* lands. The main elements of the old town—the plaza and the streets leading to the south and west—are recorded as Ord found them.

Ord's contribution to the future of the city are the two gridiron extensions on either side of the old town. The larger of the two was based on the line of Main Street extended in a southwesterly direction. Parallel streets 75 feet wide and 330 feet apart were intersected at right angles every 600 feet by streets with a width of 60 feet. Ord laid out a smaller but similarly designed extension to the north, tilting the grid slightly to follow the existing line of Main Street in that direction. Ord's map gives both English and Spanish names for the new streets, but the plat lacked more essential information such as exact bearings, street widths, and dimensions of blocks and lots. Their absence on the drawing, the loss of field notes or Ord's failure to provide them, and the use of wooden stakes instead of more permanent surveyor's marks caused almost endless confusion in future years about the exact location of property lines and the width and alignment of streets.[12]

The first land sales held in November, 1849, proved a disappointment to the council. They did not yield enough even to pay Ord's fee; 54 lots put up for auction brought from $25 to $50 each for total receipts of $2,490.[13] Although Los Angeles, with 1,200 residents, had been the most populous California community in 1840, ten years later just after

Figure 8.5 View of San Diego, California: 1873

Showing the central portion of the city, with the *actual* improvements; San Diego Bay and Peninsula, the Entrance
to the Harbor, Point Loma, and the Los Coronados Islands, twenty miles distant
in the Pacific Ocean.

BIRD'S EYE VIEW OF
SAN DIEGO, CALIFORNIA
~1876.~
FROM THE NORTH-EAST, LOOKING SOUTH-WEST.

The County Seat of San Diego County and the proposed Terminus of the Texas Pacific Railroad. Present Population,
about 3,000.   A commercial town; publishes two newspapers, "San Diego Union"
and "World," weekly and daily editions.

1. Presbyterian Church.
2. Baptist Church.
3. Methodist Church.
4. Episcopal Church.
5. Catholic Church.
6. Public Schools.
7. Point Loma Seminary.
8. San Diego Academy.
9. Bank of San Diego.
10. Commercial Bank.
11. City Hall.
12. Central Market Building.
13. Horton's Hall.
14. Telegraph Offices.
15. Horton House.
16. San Diego County Court House.
17. Lyon House.
18. Bay View Hotel.
19. Government Barracks.
20. San Diego Flouring Mill.
21. Book Store of Schneider & Kueppers.
22. San Diego Foundry.
23. San Diego Planing Mill.
24. City Brewery.

Figure 8.6   View of San Diego, California: 1876

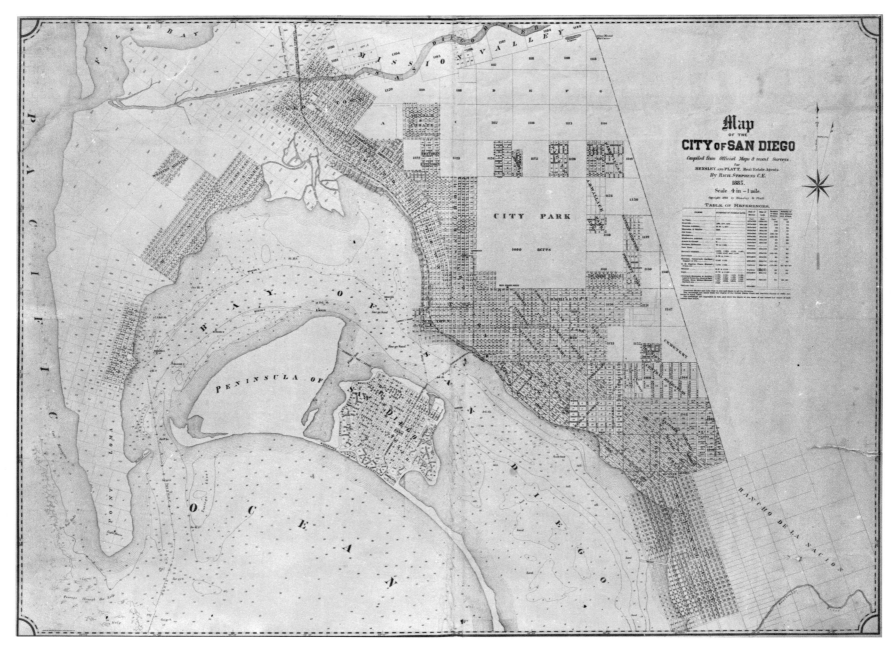

Figure 8.7 Plan of San Diego, California: 1886

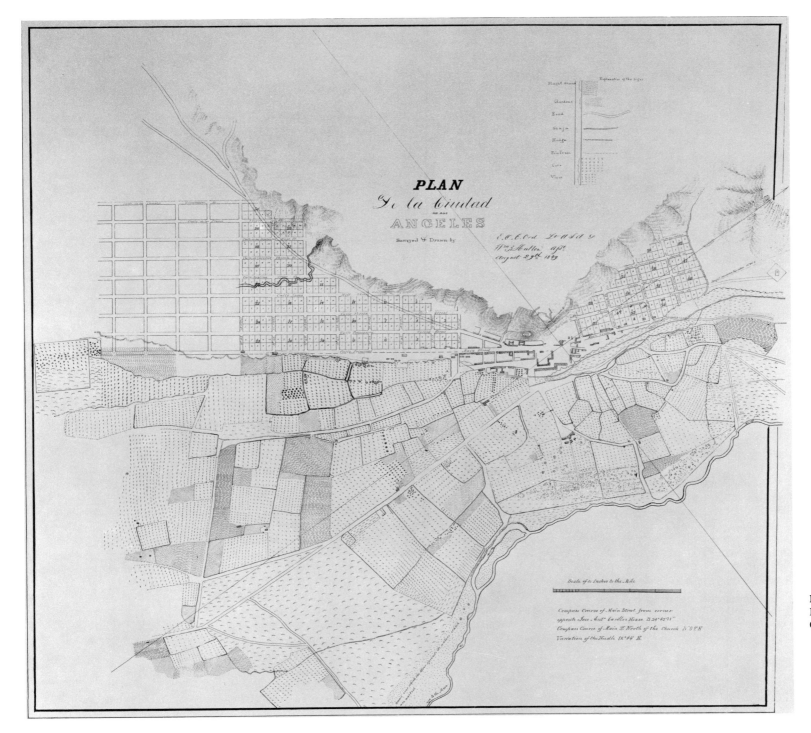

Figure 8.8
Plan of Los Angeles,
California: 1849

completion of Ord's survey it had grown to only 1,610. San Francisco, on the other hand, had mushroomed from a few dozen persons to nearly 35,000. The gold rush scarcely affected southern California except to lure away from its settlements the more adventuresome residents who scurried north to seek sudden wealth.[14] Under these circumstances, land sales by the financially hard-pressed council could not be expected to produce significant municipal revenues.

Nevertheless, the municipality in 1853 employed surveyor Henry Hancock to lay out the balance of the claimed *pueblo* lands in 35-acre parcels. The result of his work appears in Figure 8.9.[15] Hancock imposed a super-grid on the undeveloped and previously unsurveyed portions of the 17,714 acre *pueblo* tract. Complete numbered blocks consisted of six, eight, or ten 35-acre lots, each of which was just over 1,235 feet square. Five-rod (82½-feet) streets separated the blocks. Those running north-west and south-east were thus about 2,470 apart, while the others were spaced at intervals of approximately 3,700, 4,940, and 6,180 feet, depending on the number of lots in each block.

Some of these lots were sold, while others were given away by the municipality as an inducement to attract settlers. From this policy came the name of "Donation Lots" used to designate the Hancock survey. In the later development of the city this gigantic grid on a module much larger than used by Ord provided virtually the only control over the pattern of growth. As individual farm tracts were subdivided into smaller building lots, their owners laid out new streets as they wished, but with some exceptions and modifications, the Hancock grid survived as a form-giving and space-organizing element during the city's gradual and then, in the 1880s, almost explosive expansion.

At the end of its first decade under American administration, however, Los Angeles retained much of its original Spanish and Mexican character. The view in Plate 12 shows the town in 1857 as seen from the southwest looking toward the church and plaza. Main Street on the left and Los Angeles Street on the right were lined with one-story adobe structures, with here and there a more imposing two-story building breaking the horizontal skyline. The walled patios, the outdoor ovens, the corral to the rear of one of the houses, and the numerous horses in the streets suggest that old Hispanic traditions continued to dominate the community.

In 1860 the population of Los Angeles reached 4,385, and, while during the next decade the city would grow by less than 1,400 persons, its physical character underwent a marked change. The small views along the lower border of Figure 8.10 indicate that adobe-style architecture had given way to the latest fashions in eclectic Yankee design. The rec-

tangular blocks of the Ord survey on either side of the old *pueblo* began to fill up. Chuffing up Alameda Street from the lower left corner of the view can be seen a train on the railroad that from 1869 provided connections with the port town of Wilmington on the ocean.

While there was no lack of open space around the town, municipal officials had the foresight to reserve one block in the Ord grid for a civic park—the modern Pershing Square bounded by Olive, Hill, 5th, and 6th Streets. This can be seen in the view's upper left portion. Some years later the city would create a much larger recreation place when it set aside in 1886 500 acres of land still unsold from the Hancock survey and located beyond the steep hills rising to the right of the view. Although the city would later purchase additional land for recreation purposes and receive as gifts other extensive tracts for park use, these two sites were apparently the only public reservations made from the vast extent of the original *pueblo* grant.

The first Los Angeles real estate boom received its principal stimulus from railroad construction. In 1876 the Southern Pacific reached the city from the north, thus providing a link through San Francisco with a transcontinental line. The city was forced to offer a substantial subsidy to obtain rail service, but it proved vital to the future development of the region.[16] Even before the arrival of the railroad, landowners in the region began to subdivide their property in anticipation of industrial, commercial, and population growth that improved transportation would inevitably stimulate.

Steady expansion of the city continued toward the southwest during the decade of the 1870s. Figure 8.11, published in 1877, provides a view to the south. The plaza appears as the small circle at left center. Main Street and the rectangular blocks of the Ord grid extend to the right, but some development can be seen even beyond this area on a few of the original 35-acre farm tracts. At the far left, the newly subdivided portion of East Los Angeles can be seen on either side of Downey Avenue leading to the railroad depot.

A plan of this rather crudely designed addition to the city is reproduced in Figure 8.12. It was one of the early subdivisions laid out in the city by private speculators in anticipation of a transcontinental railroad connection. Because this portion of the city was already in private ownership at the time of the Hancock survey, his rectilinear street lines lay beyond its boundaries. Landowners were thus completely free to cut up their property in any manner they wished.[17]

South of this tract, the subdividers of Brooklyn Heights produced a more interesting and less routine pattern for their development. The view reproduced in Figure 8.13 shows the curving streets laid out in

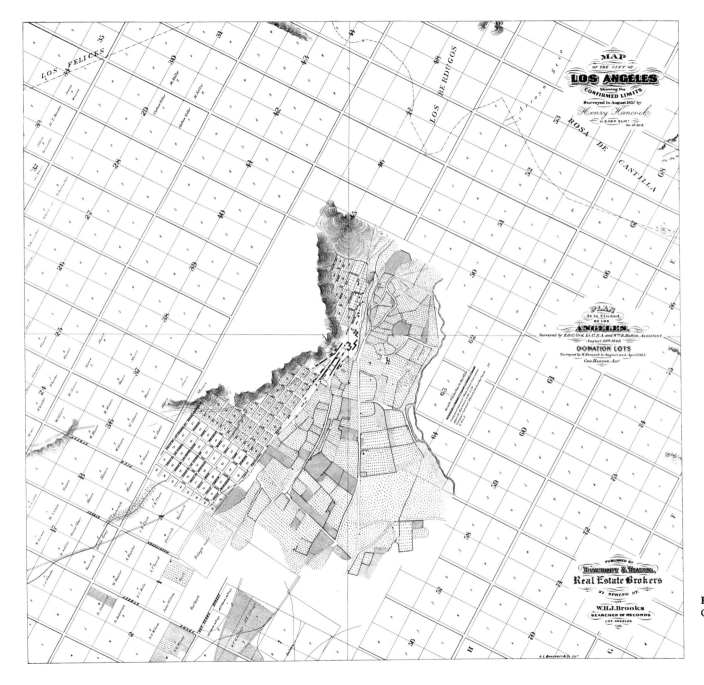

Figure 8.9 Plan of Los Angeles, California: 1857

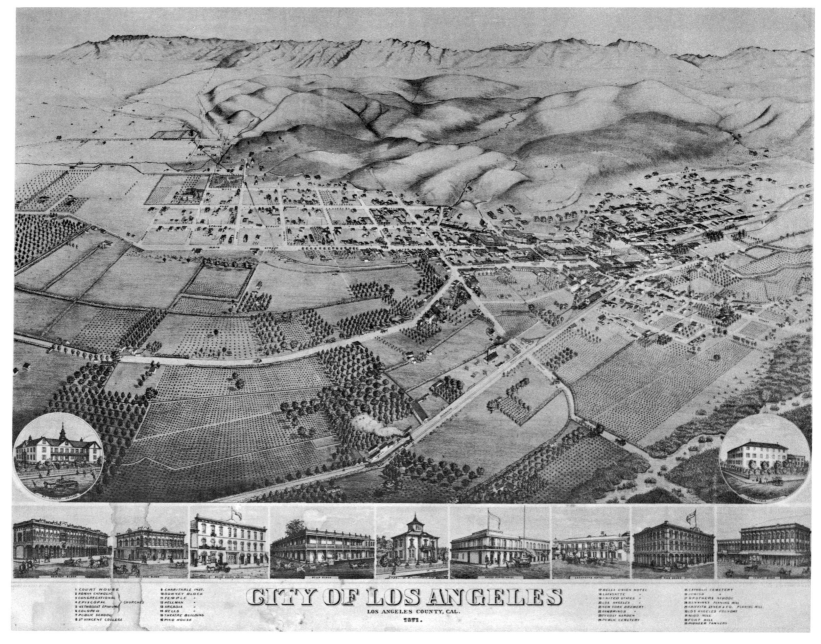

Figúre 8.10 View of Los Angeles, California: 1871

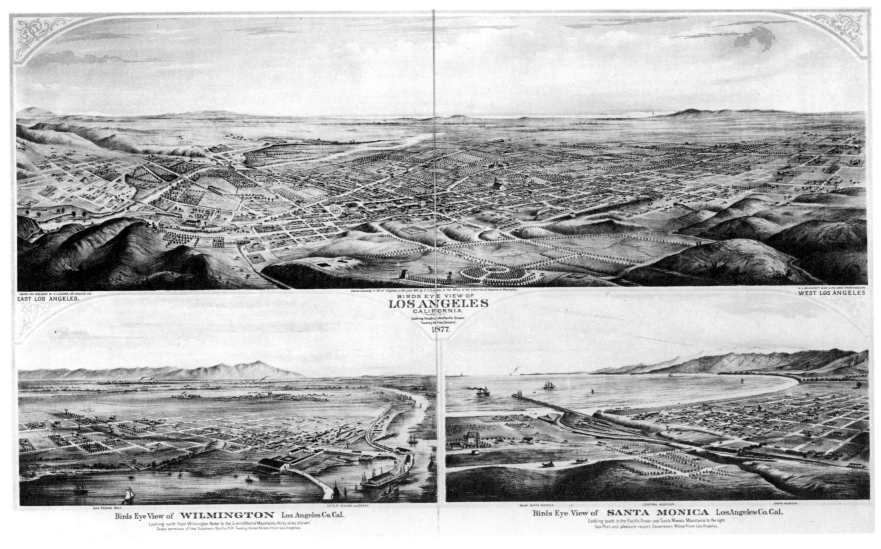

EAST LOS ANGELES.

WEST LOS ANGELES

BIRDS EYE VIEW OF
LOS ANGELES
CALIFORNIA.
Looking South to the Pacific Ocean
Twenty Miles Distant.
1877.

Birds Eye View of **WILMINGTON** Los Angeles Co. Cal.
Looking north from Wilmington Harbor to the SierraMadre Mountains, thirty miles distant.
Ocean terminus of the Southern Pacific R.R. Twenty three Miles from Los Angeles.

Birds Eye View of **SANTA MONICA** LosAngeles Co.Cal.
Looking south to the Pacific Ocean and Santa Monica Mountains to the right.
Sea Port and pleasure resort. Seventeen Miles From Los Angeles.

Figure 8.11 View of Los Angeles, Wilmington, and Santa Monica, California: 1877

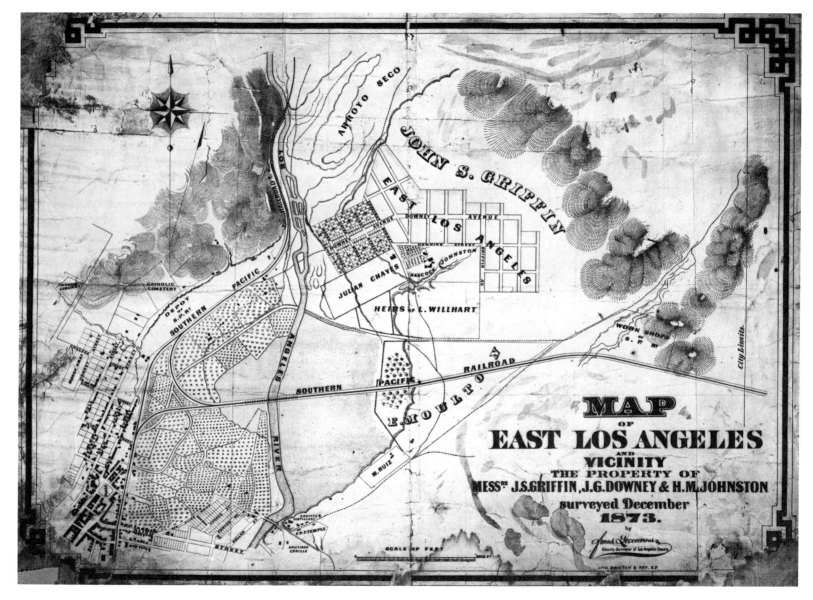

Figure 8.12   Plan of East Los Angeles, California: 1873

VIEW OF **LOS ANGELES** FROM THE EAST.

BROOKLYN HIGHTS

IN THE FOREGROUND.

PACIFIC OCEAN AND SANTA MONICA MOUNTAINS IN THE BACKGROUND.

REFERENCES

No. 1. Los Angeles and Independent R. R. Depot.
"   2. St Vincent College.
"   3. Catholic Cathedral.
"   4. M. E. Church.
"   5. Jewish Church.

No. 6. M. E. Church, South.
"   7. County Court House.
"   8. High School Building.
"   9. Episcopal Church.
"   10. Congregational Church.

No. 11. Alden Fruit Dryer.
"   12. Distillery.
"   13. City Gas Works.
"   14. Public School.
"   15. Sisters School.

No. 16. French Hospital.
"   17. Sisters Hospital.
"   18. Southern Pacific R. R. Depot.
"   19. Temple Block.
"   20. Pico House.

Figure 8.13 View of Los Angeles, California: 1877

what was then the latest suburban fashion. Prospect Park was reserved as an open space for the benefit of the residents. This and a few of the sinuous streets can still be found on modern maps of the city, fitted rather skillfully into two of the great blocks of the Hancock supergrid.

The development of port facilities preceded the arrival of the railroad and provided Los Angeles its principal links with northern California and the east via the transcontinental line. The smaller view in the lower left corner of Figure 8.13 shows Wilmington, which, with San Pedro three miles to the southwest, provided docks, wharfs, and warehouses for port activities.

Wilmington began its existence as New San Pedro, founded in 1858 by Phineas Banning to rival the older San Pedro a short distance away.

A crudely drawn plat of its commonplace gridiron design appears in Figure 8.14. Banning ran his wagons and coaches from the new port over a dusty road to Los Angeles, but in 1869, aided by a subsidy from Los Angeles, he succeeded in constructing a railroad to link the inland city with the harbor.[18]

For a time the new port town eclipsed its older rival, but eventually the Southern Pacific extended its line to San Pedro, shown in Figure 8.15, which soon regained its former position. With the continued growth of Los Angeles, both ports proved necessary, and over the years extensive harbor improvements were carried out to improve shipping facilities. Both towns prospered during the great southern California land boom of the 1880s.

A much more elaborate plan was provided for Santa Monica, the town established by Senator John P. Jones of Nevada in 1875 and shown in the lower right portion of Figure 13. Jones intended it as the ocean terminus of the Los Angeles and Independence Railroad built to tap the rich silver mines of Inyo County. The original plat, reproduced in Figure 8.16, shows the blocks Jones reserved for hotels, public buildings, parks, a university, a lumber and coal yard, and a proposed "Young Ladies Seminary." The initial auction of lots in mid-July brought its promoter more than $80,000, although the only building on the site at that time was a hotel erected at the pierhead where Ocean Avenue terminated at Railroad Avenue. By fall more than one hundred buildings had been constructed, including a second hotel, several saloons, stores, two livery stables, and that authentic symbol of a western town's bid for permanency—a newspaper.[19]

Land sales continued through the summer and early fall, and on December 1, more than 1,200 citizens of Los Angeles journeyed to Santa Monica on the first excursion train to run on the recently completed railroad line. Lots previously sold in July for up to $600 brought three and four times that amount in the early months of 1876. The Southern Pacific promptly began a rate war to protect its San Pedro interests and ultimately forced Senator Jones to sell out. The value of Santa Monica real estate fell drastically, and the census of 1880 recorded a population of only 417. The land boom later in that decade brought some life back to Santa Monica, but this bubble also burst. Not until well into the next century would Santa Monica be discovered by midwesterners moving to California and by residents of other nearby communities and eventually grow into the impressive residential community that one finds today.[20]

While most of the new towns springing up in Los Angeles County and the adjoining region in southern California originated as specula-tive ventures in townsite promotion, not all began in this manner. Several communities developed on former mission lands, incorporating what remained of the major mission buildings. San Gabriel, shown in Figure 8.17 as it appeared in the 1890s, was among them. On the fertile valley lands northeast of Los Angeles a number of settlers built houses on the old mission lands, locating their dwellings much as they pleased. In 1880 the place was described as still a mere village, "a scattering collection of Mexican adobes, interspersed here and there with a few frame buildings. A small hotel ekes out a precarious existence and waits for the 'boom,' that forlorn hope of every western town and village."[21] The boom eventually arrived, and San Gabriel, like so many other towns lying far from the outskirts of nineteenth-century Los Angeles, was finally swallowed up in the relentless expansion of the modern, sprawling metropolis.

Contrasting with San Gabriel's informal pattern were the precisely rectangular streets in San Luis Obispo and San Buenaventura (now Ventura). At both of these former mission sites, prosperous little towns had been developed by the mid-1870s. San Luis Obispo, halfway between Los Angeles and San Francisco and a few miles inland, is shown in Figure 8.18 as it appeared in 1877. The orientation of the old mission building occupying a block near the center of the town evidently provided the starting point for William Rich Hutton's survey of streets and blocks in 1850. Directed to lay out a main street 20 yards wide and other streets 15 yards in width, Hutton produced the usual gridiron plan of rectangular blocks.

The town's claim to four square leagues of land was not approved, and town officials were forced to file a townsite claim in 1868 with the General Land Office to provide clear title for the residents. As approved in 1871, the townsite contained slightly more than 552 acres of land. Probably by this time most of this was in private ownership, but a portion remained in public ownership to be disposed of in later years.[22]

Although in 1868 the population of San Luis Obispo was estimated at only 600, by 1883 it had grown to about 3,000 and could be described as "an orderly and prosperous city" whose "present condition is that of steady progress." Sidewalks had been built and its streets planted with trees, "gas and water-works have been constructed, a fire department organized, a military company equipped, a fine brick city hall erected," and the Pacific Coast Railway had made San Luis Obispo "the commercial center of the region."[23]

Ventura occupied a more strategic site, on the coast below Santa Barbara at the mouth of the San Buenaventura River. As the view in Figure 8.19 indicates, it, too, was a thriving town in 1877. Its growth had al-

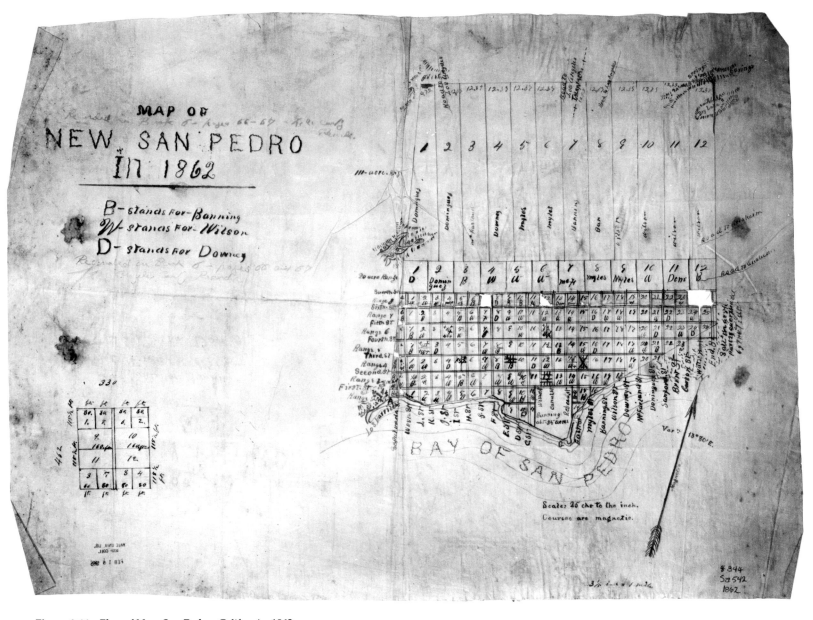

Figure 8.14 Plan of New San Pedro, California: 1862

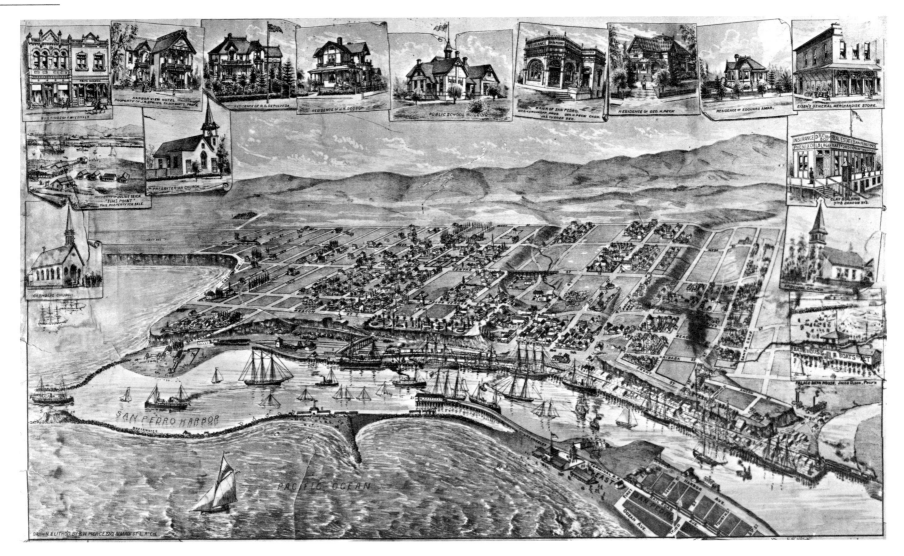

Figure 8.15 View of San Pedro, California: 1893

ready been stimulated by the discovery of oil in the vicinity, and the town could boast of two refineries. Expansion was then taking place up the long axis of Ventura Avenue leading from its intersection with Main Street in the direction of the newly opened oil fields to the east. Here, too, the mission buildings facing Main Street obviously suggested the orientation of the town's streets. Either by intent or through some happy accident, Figueroa Street, seen at the left extending from the coast, terminated at Main Street on the axis of the old mission church.[24]

Several other communities in southern California originated as towns planned for groups of settlers banded together in colonizing organizations. Riverside, Colton, Pomona, Pasadena, and Lompoc were among the cities founded in this manner.[25] Even earlier was Anaheim, whose successful development served as a model for the others,

One of the leading figures in the Anaheim colony was George Hansen, an Austrian who had come to California during the gold rush and who as a surveyor had helped Henry Hancock lay out the 35-acre donation lots of Los Angeles in 1853. In San Francisco with a number of other German-speaking immigrants he organized the Los Angeles Vineyard Society in 1857, and as their superintendent purchased 1,165 acres of the Rancho San Juan Cajón de Santa Ana from Juan Pacifico Ontiveras, whose estate located 25 miles southeast of Los Angeles Hansen had surveyed two years earlier.[26]

Hansen divided the land into 50 rectangular vineyard plots, each of 20 acres and separated by straight roads forming a grid of large blocks 20 and 40 acres in area. In the center of the tract he laid out 64 town lots, each 140 by 181½ feet. The Society reserved 14 of these for school and other public purposes and distributed the remaining 50 town lots with the larger vineyard parcels. Members obtained their land by drawing numbers, paying into the treasury the amount by which the value of their land exceeded $1,400, or being compensated for the difference between that average value and any lesser amount if they happened to draw the number of a less desirable parcel.

Before the drawing in January, 1858, the Society arranged for eight acres of each vineyard parcel to be planted with grapes. The organization also constructed an extensive network of irrigation ditches and planted willow saplings interwoven with horizontal bars around the entire tract. This living fence was interrupted only by four gates at the points where Los Angeles and Center Streets reached the boundaries of the tract.

Although few of the shareholder-settlers knew anything about wine making, production grew from 75,000 gallons in 1861 to 1,250,000 gal-

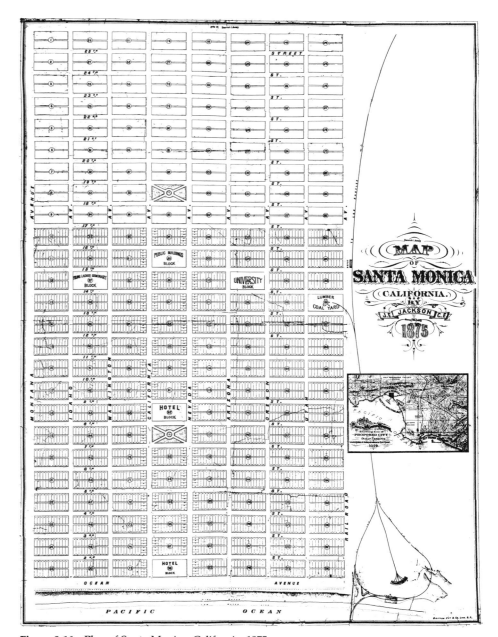

Figure 8.16 Plan of Santa Monica, California: 1875

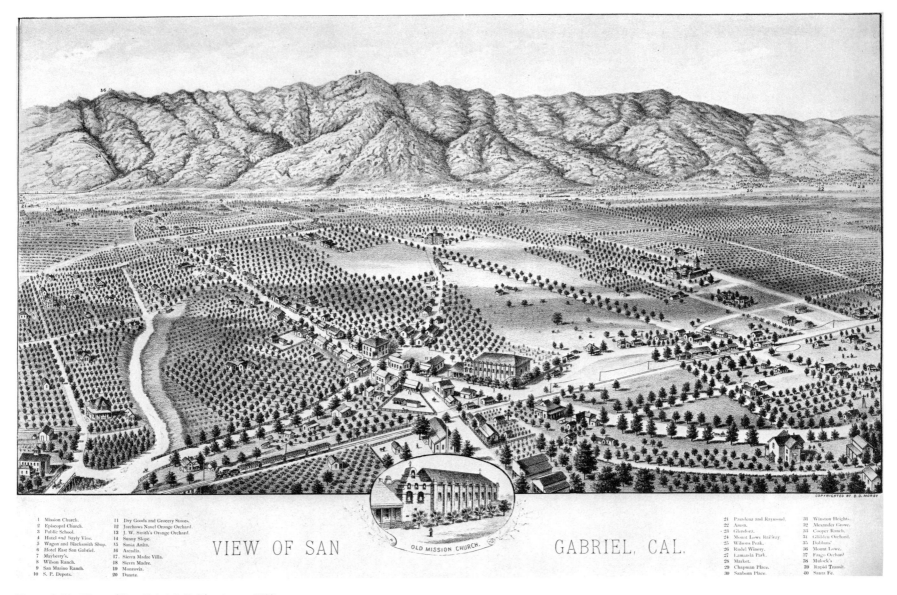

1	Mission Church.	11	Dry Goods and Grocery Stores.		21	Pasadena and Raymond.	31	Winston Heights.
2	Episcopal Church.	12	Jarchows Navel Orange Orchard.		22	Arosa.	32	Alexander Grove.
3	Public School.	13	J. W. Smith's Orange Orchard.		23	Glendora.	33	Cooper Ranch.
4	Hotel and Bayly Vine.	14	Sunny Slope.		24	Mount Lowe Railway.	34	Glidden Orchard.
5	Wagon and Blacksmith Shop.	15	Santa Anita.		25	Wilsons Peak.	35	Dobbins'
6	Hotel East San Gabriel.	16	Arcadia.		26	Rudel Winery.	36	Mount Lowe.
7	Mayberry's.	17	Sierra Madre Villa.		27	Lamanda Park.	37	Fargo Orchard
8	Wilson Ranch.	18	Sierra Madre.		28	Market.	38	Mahek's
9	San Marino Ranch.	19	Monrovia.		29	Chapman Place.	39	Rapid Transit.
10	S. P. Depots.	20	Duarte.		30	Sanborn Place.	40	Santa Fe.

VIEW OF SAN   OLD MISSION CHURCH.   GABRIEL, CAL.

COPYRIGHTED BY D. D. MORSE

Figure 8.17 View of San Gabriel, California: ca. 1892

Figure 8.18   View of San Luis Obispo, California: 1877

lons by 1884. Prospects appeared so encouraging that, at the end of the first decade of settlement, the boundaries were enlarged and the land under cultivation nearly trebled in size to 3,200 acres. It was then that several of the original vineyard parcels adjoining the first town lots were subdivided to provide an additional supply of building sites for the growing community. This addition can be seen in Figure 8.20 to the left of the single tier of blocks identified as "Anaheim Original Town."

This subdivision proved to be premature, for the view of Anaheim in the late 1870s reproduced in Figure 8.21 shows that at that time only one-fourth of the addition had been divided into smaller blocks. In the view, the intersection of Center and Palm Streets, where the earlier plat shows a projected "plaza," is near the lower left corner. This civic

Drawn and Published by E. S. Glover.

A. L. Bancroft & Co. Lith., San Francisco.

BIRDS EYE VIEW OF

SAN BUENAVENTURA, CAL. 1877.

FROM THE BAY, LOOKING NORTH.

REFERENCES.

A—Mission Buildings.
B—Methodist Church.
C—Presbyterian Church.
D—Congregational Church.
E—Public School.
F—Court House.
G—Post Office.
H—Santa Ana Water Co. Reservoir.

REFERENCES.

I—"Star" Oil Refinery.
J—"S. P." Oil Works.
K—Devil's Cañon.
L—Ojai Valley.
M—Oil District.
N—Location of Old Wells.
O—Hot Springs.
P—Oil and Sulphur Springs.

Figure 8.19 View of Ventura, California: 1877

square had not been developed, and the land beyond remained planted in grapes.

In 1884 a mysterious disease wiped out the hundreds of acres of vines, and Anaheim almost literally overnight lost its principal economic base. Many persons left the colony, and for a time the town appeared doomed. By 1890, however, some farmers had replanted their land with Valencia oranges, and within a decade Anaheim became the center of production for this variety in southern California. For many years the town existed as a small, quiet, but prosperous agricultural community before its recent mushroom growth following the establishment of Disneyland, a major-league baseball stadium, and the inevitable boom in motels and restaurants to serve tourist trade. There is almost nothing in the modern city to suggest its unusual beginnings as a colony of frugal, hard-working Germans who hoped to make it the capital of California wine-making.

The last three years of the decade of the 1870s proved a lean period for southern California. The land boom of 1874 to 1876 ended with a series of bank and business failures, and a period of protracted drought brought many wheat farmers and owners of cattle or sheep ranches to the verge or over the edge of bankruptcy. Soon, however, the discovery of artesian wells for irrigation, the rapid development of citrus fruit growing, and the beginning of an advertising campaign extolling the virtues of the region in the East and Midwest all helped to bring new residents to the region and to re-establish a healthy economy. By 1881 southern California had recovered from the recession and was ready for a new period of growth.

When the Santa Fe Railroad entered the region in 1885 to compete with the monopolistic Southern Pacific line, the rate of development sharply accelerated. A rate war between the two lines began in 1886. This followed a major promotional campaign by the newly organized Los Angeles Board of Trade, which had flooded the rest of the country with advertisements, tracts, posters, brochures, and books aimed at attracting new residents to the area. When rail fares from Kansas City to Los Angeles fell to $15, then to $5, and —for one day—to only $1, the lure of southern California proved irresistible.

Thousands and then tens of thousands of persons jammed the trains on the way west. Among them were many skilled land developers, speculators, and promoters who saw in the gathering interest in California an opportunity to profit. J. M. Guinn, an observer of the scene who analyzed its causes and effects a short time later, noted that ''these professionals . . . were adepts in the tricks of real estate boom-

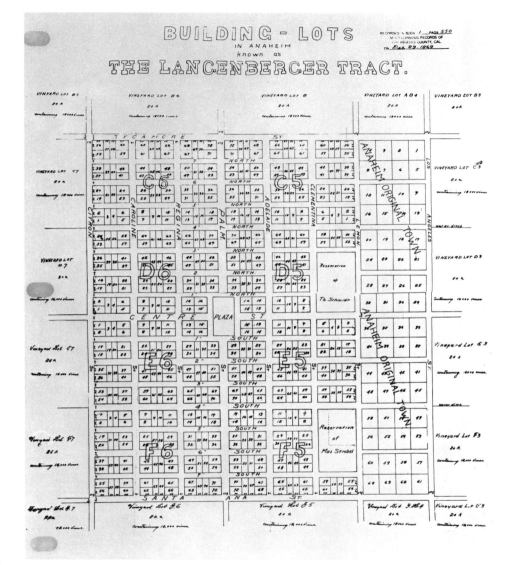

Figure 8.20 Plan of Anaheim, California: 1869

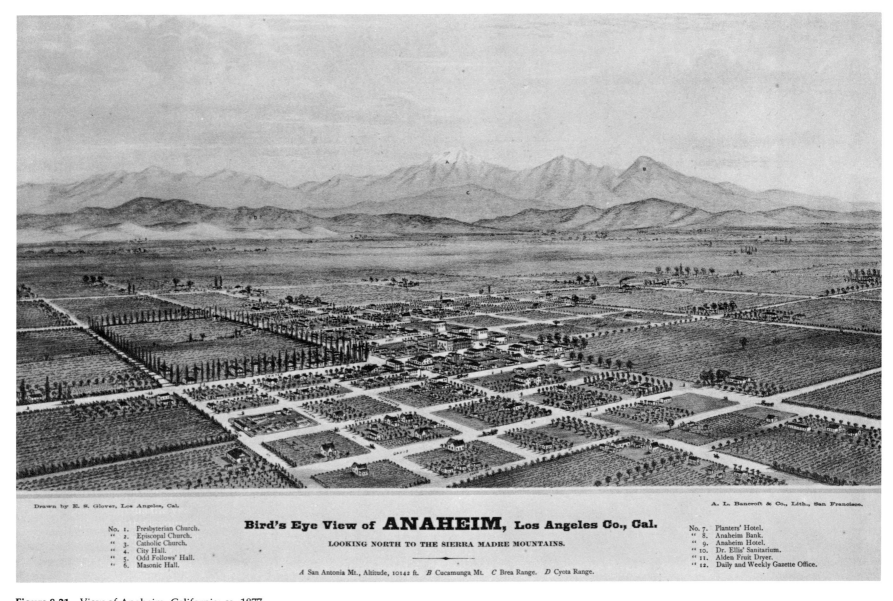

Drawn by E. S. Glover, Los Angeles, Cal.

A. L. Bancroft & Co., Lith., San Francisco.

Bird's Eye View of **ANAHEIM**, Los Angeles Co., Cal.

LOOKING NORTH TO THE SIERRA MADRE MOUNTAINS.

No. 1. Presbyterian Church.
" 2. Episcopal Church.
" 3. Catholic Church.
" 4. City Hall.
" 5. Odd Follows' Hall.
" 6. Masonic Hall.

No. 7. Planters' Hotel.
" 8. Anaheim Bank.
" 9. Anaheim Hotel.
" 10. Dr. Ellis' Sanitarium.
" 11. Alden Fruit Dryer.
" 12. Daily and Weekly Gazette Office.

A San Antonia Mt., Altitude, 10142 ft.   *B* Cucamunga Mt.   *C* Brea Range.   *D* Cyota Range.

Figure 8.21   View of Anaheim, California: ca. 1877

ing. They came here, not to build up the country, but to make money, honestly if they could not make it any other way. It is needless to say they made it the other way."[27]

The sudden influx of promoters, tourists, immigrants, and curiosity-seekers dramatically increased the demand for hotels, houses, and stores and sent the prices and rents of buildings soaring. Although not all of the land subdivided during the prosperous years of the 1870s had been occupied, the value of house lots soared dramatically. In January, 1886, recorded real estate sales in Los Angeles topped $1,000,000. By the end of that year monthly sales were averaging three times that amount. In 1887 even these figures seemed small; sales in July were nearly $12,000,000, and the value of all real estate sold in the three summer months totaled an astounding $38,000,000.[28]

Developers quickly began to subdivide vacant land in and around the city. A survey of Los Angeles at the end of 1887 showing all the older portions and the newly subdivided land within the boundaries of the old *pueblo* grant is reproduced in Figure 8.22. Aside from the general rectilinearity of most of the new developments, the only order imposed on the now sprawling community came from Henry Hancock's great grid of 1853, within which he had platted his 35-acre tracts.

Beyond the city borders landowners also began to subdivide property. H. H. Wilcox and Ivar Weid, who between them controlled much of the southern foothills of the Santa Monica mountains and adjacent tracts of more level valley land, planned Hollywood in February, 1887. Figure 8.23 shows a combination plan and view of the town that the promoters issued to advertise their new community. In the modern city the intersection of Sunset Boulevard and Vine Street marks the approximate location of the southwest corner of Hollywood's first streets as platted by Wilcox and Weid.

Hollywood remained for many years a mere hamlet of scattered houses, and real growth did not take place until well into the present century with the establishment there of the film industry. As it expanded, it swallowed up the site of one of the many unsuccessful boom communities of the late 1880s. Reproduced in Figure 8.24 is a promotional view of this would-be residential town—Cahuenga, an elaborately planned combination of grid, circular, and winding streets staked off on a tract of land bordering Sunset Boulevard. Apparently few lots were sold, for in a later period the streets were re-aligned to fit the generally rectangular pattern of the adjoining subdivisions, and the vision of Cahuenga's promoters vanished in the process.[29]

In the Los Angeles area, the most intensive efforts to create new towns could be found extending in a broad band east of the city

through the San Gabriel Valley. Here, as Guinn described events in his paper read to the local historical society in the year following the collapse of the boom, "very few new townsites had been laid off previous to 1887. As the last links of the Santa Fe Railway system approached completion the creation of new towns began, and the rapidity with which they were created was truly astonishing. During the months of March, April and May, 1887, no less than thirteen townsites were platted on the line. . . . Before the close of 1887 between the eastern limits of Los Angeles city and the San Bernardino County line, a distance of thirty-six miles . . . there were twenty-five cities and towns, an average of one to each mile and a half of the road."

The Southern Pacific line ran roughly parallel to and south of the Santa Fe tracks. Along its route, so Guinn tells us, "eight more towns claimed the attention of lot buyers, with three more thrown in between the roads, making a grand total of thirty-six cities and towns in the San Gabriel Valley."[30] Pasadena, located at the western entrance to the valley, rivaled Los Angeles in speculative activity. During 1886 and 1887, no fewer than 433 separate subdivisions or additions were recorded for Pasadena tracts—only one-fifth fewer than for Los Angeles itself. The peaceful little settlement established some years earlier through the efforts of a colonizing group from Indiana suddenly found itself in the wildest kind of speculative frenzy.[31]

Immediately north of Pasadena, the owners of a large tract of rolling foothill land organized the Pasadena Improvement Company in 1887 and subdivided that portion shown in Figure 8.25 to begin the new community of Altadena. The quality of their plan did not match the richness of their lyrical description of the site and its bright future—a brief passage occupying a portion of the lithograph beneath the illustration of a projected hotel. Its superlatives were characteristic of the promotional prose issued at the time by virtually all land developers:

"Altadena, lying on a sunny slope 500 feet higher, and three miles north of Pasadena, with the grand panorama of San Gabriel Valley at her feet stretching southward to the sea, and eastward to the beautiful San Jacinto; sheltered from frost on the north by the Sierra Madre Range with their ever changing shadows, and with hill and vale on the west, affords the choicest spot for the artist, the poet, invalid or business man to make his home, that can be found in all Southern California. Here the flowers bloom with brighter tint and sweeter perfume, the fruits have a richer hue and finer flavor, the air is pure and dry, the water free from lime and other impurities, and a more than abundant supply insures ample irrigation, which with the rich soil . . . needs only the taste and skill of man to make a veritable Eden of this favored spot."

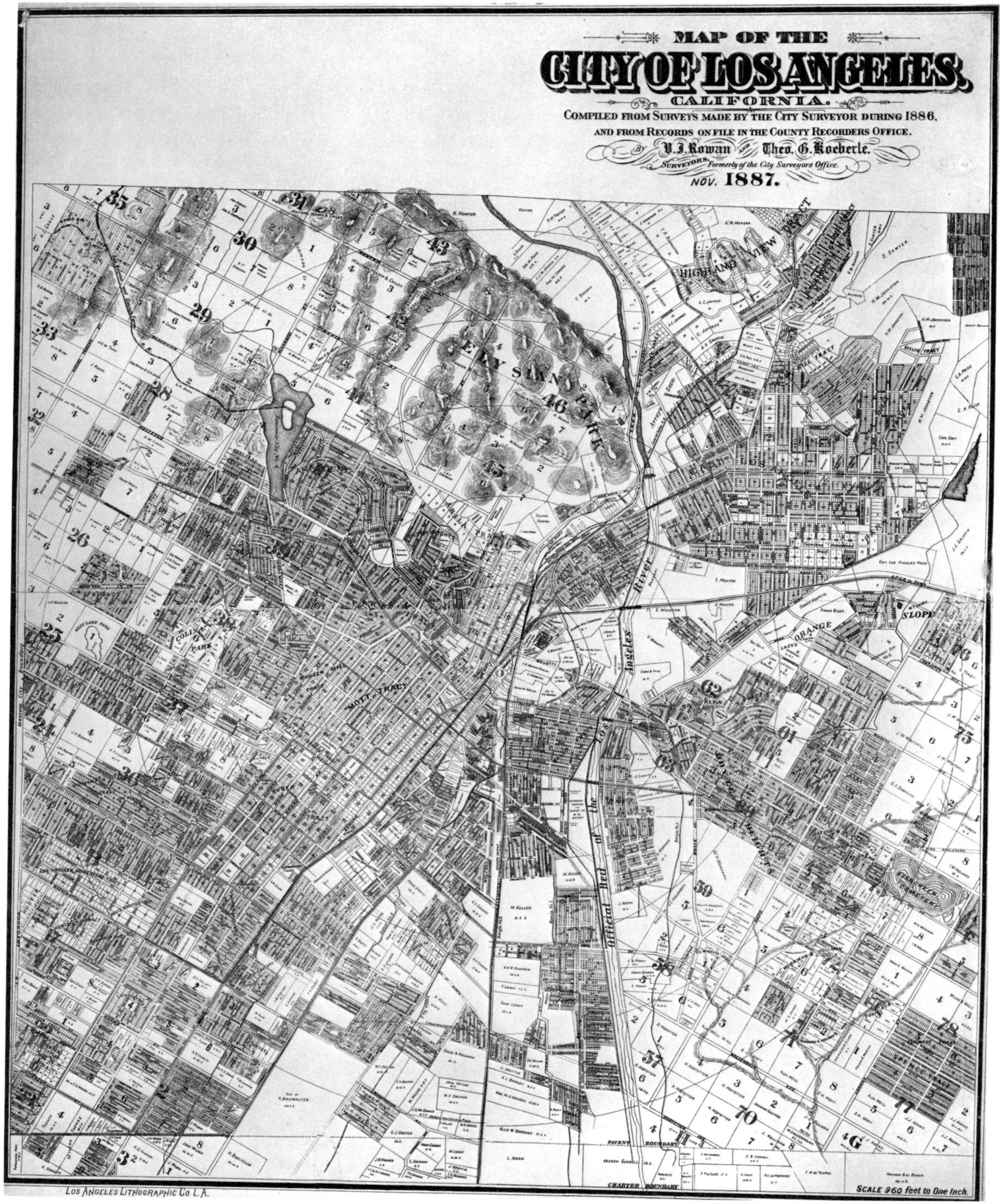

Figure 8.22 Plan of Los Angeles, California: 1887

Figure 8.23 Plan of Hollywood, California: ca. 1887

Figure 8.24 View of Cahuenga, California: 1887

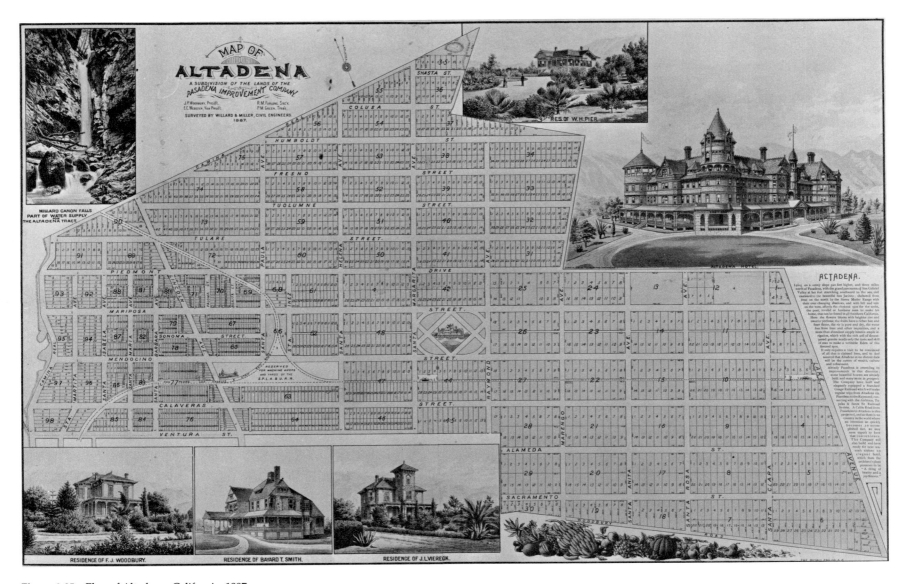

Figure 8.25 Plan of Altadena, California: 1887

Fifty miles east of Pasadena and Altadena, at the other end of the band of new towns Guinn described, lay San Bernardino. Bypassed by the Southern Pacific Railroad in the 1870s because its residents refused to pay the subsidy demanded by the line, it finally succeeded in obtaining rail service in 1883. At the beginning of the boom San Bernardino was already a firmly established town slowly expanding on the grid pattern fixed earlier by its Mormon founders.

The view in Figure 8.26 shows the city at the outset of its more rapid period of development during the boom years. In the foreground one can see numerous "additions" platted on former orange groves in anticipation of future sales. New arrivals, lured by vigorous advertising campaigns and promotional techniques, soon vied with one another to purchase choice lots. In a single week in May, 1887, $200,000 of real estate was sold. Assessed value of city property in that year was double what it had been two years earlier. Hundreds of acres of additional valley land was platted into streets and lots in the expectation that this kind of prosperity would continue indefinitely. When the boom subsided, San Bernardino was left with a surplus of subdivided land, but it survived the inevitable slump and after a period of relative stagnation continued to grow.[32]

South and west of San Bernardino another established but smaller community profited from the boom and grew substantially in size. This was Riverside, started as a planned agricultural colony in 1870 centering on a townsite one mile square intended to serve as a market and service center for the surrounding farm tracts. Land auctions were well attended. In April, 1887, one owner sold all of the lots in his subdivision. He received a total of $26,000, or an average price per lot of $300. Land in the vicinity had sold earlier at only $3.00 an acre.[33]

Southwest of Riverside near the Santa Ana Mountains, a completely new town with an unusual pattern was laid out in 1886. First known as South Riverside and, after its incorporation in 1896, as Corona, the entire settlement occupied some 12,000 acres purchased by one R. B. Taylor of Iowa. Taylor divided most of this enormous tract into rectangular farm parcels served by an irregular grid of roads, but near its northeastern edge he set aside a circle exactly one mile in diameter for a town.

Figure 8.27 shows Taylor's peculiar design, with the town proper located within circular Grand Boulevard and a wide Main Street neatly dividing the urban settlement in half and extending southward to the edge of the agricultural lands. Corona prospered; by May, 1887, more than one hundred buildings had been erected, and one enormously profitable auction of lots brought Taylor $50,000. Land sales were stimulated by plans for the Pomona and Elsinore Railroad to extend northwest and southeast from Corona and by the construction of a water pipe line from Temescal Canyon twelve miles to the east.

Although the water line was built and helped to provide irrigation to the farms in the vicinity, the railroad venture came to an end after the construction of only a few miles of line. Corona nonetheless managed to grow after the land boom came to an end elsewhere when tin mining in the nearby San Jacinto hills was carried on for a few years by an English concern. When this proved to be uneconomical, Corona's dreams of metropolitan status faded. The town briefly flickered into national prominence in 1913 when some local promoter conceived of turning Grand Boulevard into a racetrack. Barney Oldfield, Ralph De Palma, and Earl Cooper whirled around and around the circular course before a cheering crowd of residents and visitors who finally learned that Cooper had won the 300-mile race with an electrifying average speed of 75 miles an hour.[34]

Most of the new towns were located closer to Los Angeles along the two main railroad lines. Dozens of these speculative ventures were planned in the area east of Pasadena, including Huntington, Monrovia, Duarte, Azusa, Alosta, Chicago Park, Glendora, Altamont, and Gladstone.[35] Monrovia was a typical product of the time, a development promoted by a railroad construction engineer, William N. Monroe, and three other prominent men from Los Angeles. They divided an eight-square-mile tract into farms and orchards in the spring of 1886. The four associates retained engineer T. J. Flanagan to survey 60 acres of the area as a town. Figure 8.28 shows his routine gridiron design as it was extended somewhat by the time this view was published to aid in promoting land sales.[36]

At the first sales in May, 1886, town lots measuring 50 by 160 feet sold for a modest $100 to $150, and the five-acre parcels beyond the settlement were disposed of for $1,250. The full impact of the boom had obviously not yet been felt. By the end of that year, lot prices had soared to from $5,000 to $8,000. The next May when E. F. Spencer auctioned lots in his addition to the town, more than one thousand persons arrived on two trains. Before the day ended he had sold 160 lots for a tidy profit. Monrovia proved to be more than a paper town, and when it was incorporated in November, 1887, it had a population of 500, two hotels provided accommodations for guests, a number of business establishments had been started, and work was begun on a street railway.[37]

Figure 8.26 View of San Bernardino, California: ca. 1886

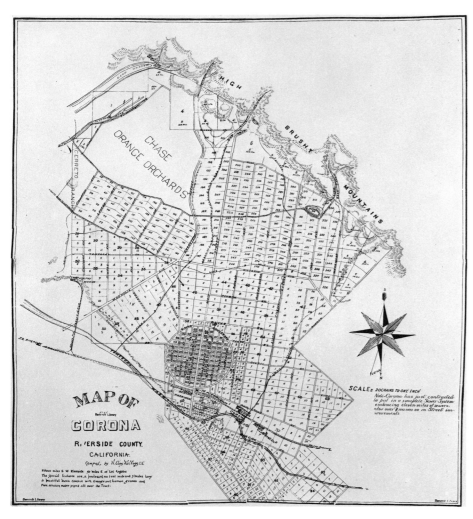

Figure 8.27 Plan of Corona, California: ca. 1900

A group of land speculators who observed Monrovia's success se-cured a parcel of land just to the south and quickly surveyed Chicago Park as a grid of streets forming a rectangular town five blocks long by

two and one-half blocks wide. The site lay on one side of the San Gabriel River, which at that point was a nearly dry gulch through which a bare trickle of water flowed except for rare occasions when heavy rains temporarily increased the depth to a few feet. The pro-moters nevertheless issued an alluring poster depicting steamboats ply-ing the river and discharging freight and passengers at nonexistent docks. Since three additions were subsequently platted adjoining the original townsite, dozens and perhaps hundreds of persons must have been duped into investing in this outright swindle.[38]

The site chosen by Jonathan S. Slauson for Azusa, a few miles to the west, was scarcely more attractive, consisting mainly of boulder wash and sand. Its sole advantage seemed to be that it straddled the line of the Santa Fe Railroad and still remained vacant and unplatted. Cer-tainly there was little in its design, shown in Figure 8.29, that could rea-sonably be expected to attract the interest of either speculators or would-be residents. Skillful promotion overcame for a time the limita-tions of its site and its plan. Guinn described the opening of land sales in April, 1887:

"Through the long hours of the night previous, and until nine o'clock of the day of sale, a line of hungry and weary lot buyers stood in front of the office where the lots were to be sold. Number two was offered a thousand dollars for his place in the line, number five claimed to have sold out for five hundred dollars, number one was deaf to all offers, and through the weary hours of the night clung to the 'handle of the big front door,' securing at last the coveted prize—the first choice. Two hundred and eighty thousand dollars worth of lots were sold the first day."[39] After two more days of sales, nearly half of the entire townsite was sold. At the end of two months Slauson and his associates could gleefully count $1,175,000 in gross receipts. Most of the this must have been profit, for few improvements were made to the town by its devel-opers aside from the construction of a hotel and brick business build-ing. Other than their initial costs for the land, their only other expenses would have been for advertising and promotion.[40]

South of Los Angeles near the lower end of Santa Monica Bay, the Redondo Beach Company directed its consulting engineer, William H. Hall, to plan a much larger and more intricate design for its projected port city. At the site the company constructed a large hotel and a $100,000 iron pier. The plan, reproduced in Figure 8.30, shows other proposed facilities: a Chautauqua Assembly hall, a railroad station, a lake with boat house and swimming area, parks and reservoirs, several church sites, and a great esplanade along the ocean shore. Redondo Beach proved attractive as a resort town, and most of the streets as orig-

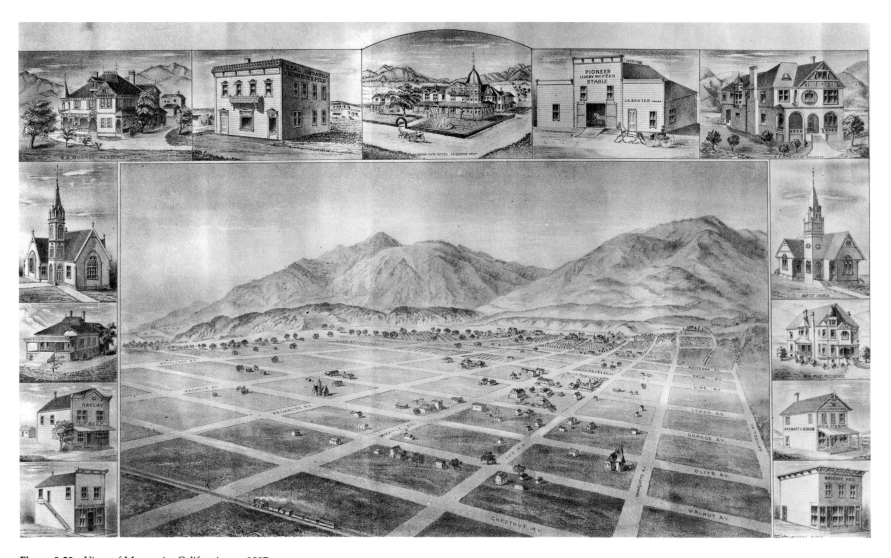

Figure 8.28 View of Monrovia, California: ca. 1887

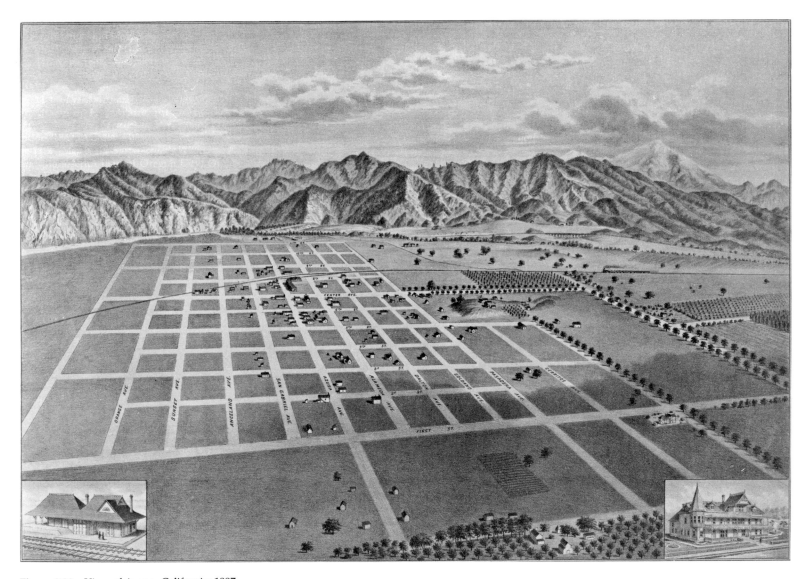

Figure 8.29 View of Azusa, California: 1887

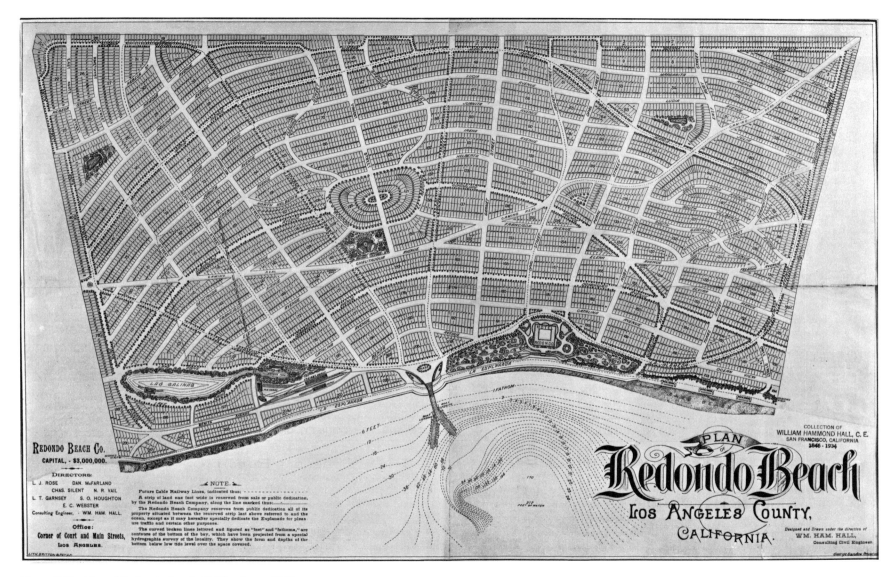

Figure 8.30   Plan of Redondo Beach, California: ca. 1887

inally surveyed by Hall have been retained in the modern city. Many of those active in promoting Redondo Beach were also associated with the development of Inglewood to the north and inland, a community that also weathered the cloud of recession following the bursting of the boom in the last year of the decade.[41]

As the enthusiasm for land speculation spread, towns on and near the coast north of Los Angeles began to feel the full force of promotional activities. In and around Ventura dozens of farm tracts and portions of ranches were cut up into streets, blocks, and lots. As the plan of the town reproduced in Figure 8.31 reveals, the rigid grid street system centering on the plaza was extended northward into the more rugged hill terrain north of the original community along the shore. Other additions were laid out in the northeast and northwest sectors of the town. During the three years of the boom, Ventura's population nearly doubled, and land prices were almost as high as in Los Angeles.[42]

Along the line of the Southern Pacific Railroad leading north and east to Bakersfield, a string of boom communities were hastily platted; some survived, others did not. North of this transportation corridor in the lovely but more isolated Ojai Valley there was also a flurry of speculation. Here the town of Nordhoff had been founded as early as 1874. It took its name from Charles Nordhoff, the traveler and writer who had been the author of an early book promoting settlement in California. It was soon surpassed by neighboring Ojai, a portion of which Edward T. Hare designed in the intricately geometric pattern shown in Figure 8.32. The twin communities were later to become a vacation resort, an art colony, and a center for various mystical religious sects.[43]

Distant San Luis Obispo did not escape the effects of the land boom, although agricultural land rather than town lots seemed to be most in demand. One noteworthy development in the county was the substantial expansion of the little health resort of El Paso de Robles (the Pass of the Oaks). Its site lay between the old mission town and Mission San Miguel Arcángel to the north. Here, in the upper reaches of the Salinas River, Indians, mission fathers, early travelers, and pioneer settlers had long enjoyed the supposedly curative baths afforded by natural sulphur springs. Before the beginning of the southern California land boom, Daniel Blackburn and his brother, James, had constructed a hotel, bathhouses, a physician's office, and a little village near the springs and had begun to advertise their development as a health resort.[44]

In the promotional literature produced to lure easterners to southern California, its healthful climate became a major point of emphasis.

Hospitals, sanitariums, and rest homes were built to accommodate visitors hoping to recuperate from some real or fancied disease.[45]

The proprietors of Paso Robles determined to take full advantage of the unique springs by developing their rather primitive little village into a major health center. The plan reproduced in Figure 8.33 shows the results. The town proper centered on the cottages and hotel facing a park extending eastward along the north side of the principal spring and bathhouse. Larger lots and farm tracts occupied the land to the north between the rising ground and the valley of the Salinas River. To the west the proprietors divided the remaining portion of the site into large "villa lots" served by streets extending irregularly outward from the checkerboard pattern of the town.

The oldest California settlement—San Diego—also became a center of land speculation and development. Like the other towns in southern California, the city had suffered a setback in its growth during the depression years of the mid-1870s. Its fine natural harbor—far better than that at Los Angeles—was of little advantage without railroad connections to the north and east. Construction of the California Southern line to Colton in 1882 did little to improve transportation facilities, and it was not until late in 1885 that the Santa Fe trains finally reached the city.[46]

The land boom that Los Angeles had been enjoying struck San Diego with full force. Noting that in 1885 the population of the area was "probably about five thousand people," the author of one promotional tract of the period claimed that "at the close of 1887, the time of writing this sketch, it has fully thirty thousand with a more rapid rate of increase than ever. New stores, hotels and dwellings are arising on every hand from the center to the farthest outskirts in more bewildering numbers than before, and people are pouring in at double the rate they did but six months ago. It is now impossible to keep track of its progress. No one seems any longer to know or care who is putting up the big buildings, and it is becoming difficult to find a familiar face in the crowd or at the hotels."[47]

The vast and largely unoccupied gridiron blocks that had previously been platted around the shores of the bay and up its surrounding hills offered building sites in abundance. Nevertheless, land prices shot up alarmingly. Business lots that had changed hands at $25 a front-foot soon brought $2,500. The assessed value of real estate in the county rose one-third between 1886 and 1887. There were the usual optimistic predictions of future population. One real estate firm in an advertisement published in the fall of 1887 maintained that "San Diego has a

Figure 8.31 Plan of Ventura, California: 1888

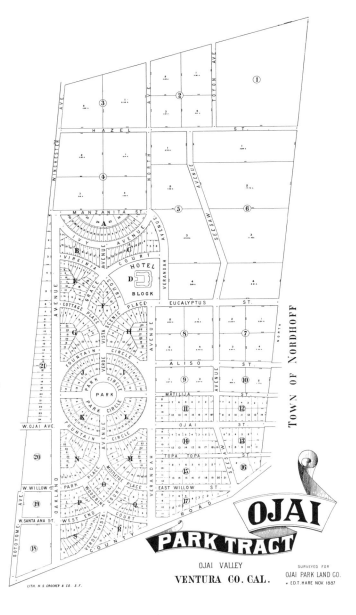

Figure 8.32 Plan of Ojai, California: 1887

population of 150,000 people," but then added more realistically, "only they are not all here yet."[48]

The large supply of already platted lots in San Diego and its adjoining communities did not discourage land developers from beginning entirely new towns. A Santa Fe Railroad subsidary, the San Diego Land and Town Company, laid out Chula Vista just south of National City. Otay, still further south, also began its existence during the great boom. More successful was Oceanside, forty miles to the north, which was platted in 1884. In between Oceanside and San Diego several other coastal communities were spawned during the boom: Encinitas, Sorrento, La Jolla, Pacific Beach, and Ocean Beach.[49] Dozens of other inland towns were also quickly platted, extravagantly advertised, and energetically promoted: Escondido, Lakeside, and La Mesa among them. The speculative fever spread across the Mexican border to infect Tía Juana, and there were several abortive proposals for founding new towns in Lower California as well.[50]

Nearly 100 miles northeast of San Diego, in what was then San Diego County but is now in Riverside County, a desert site between the San Jacinto and Little San Bernardino Mountains attracted the attention of one group of land speculators. Their plan for Palmdale is shown in Figure 8.34 as it was displayed in a large, brightly colored, and elaborately embellished lithograph. Their design took the form of a series of horseshoe-shaped avenues embracing a central grid of streets. One of these curving thoroughfares was hopefully named Good Luck Avenue. The lucky horseshoe evidently failed to work its magic, for there is no trace now of the whimsical pattern of this projected community in the modern town of Palm Springs that later developed as a luxury resort community on the site.

By far the most interesting of the San Diego land promotion schemes—because of the character of its plan and its relative success—was Elisha S. Babcock's town of Coronado. Babcock came to San Diego in 1884 from his home in Evansville, Indiana, seeking to regain his health. He noted that the narrow peninsula jutting northward to form San Diego Bay lay virtually vacant, and he conceived the idea of building an enormous hotel looking out to the Pacific near the point where the neck of the peninsula widened to form a large, flat area, then overgrown with tall brush and dune grass. Beyond the hotel he intended to develop a new city, the profits from which would finance the hotel project, whose cost he estimated at one million dollars.[51] The location of the Coronado peninsula can be seen in the center of Figure 8.35, a panorama of the San Diego Bay area in 1887. The old town of San

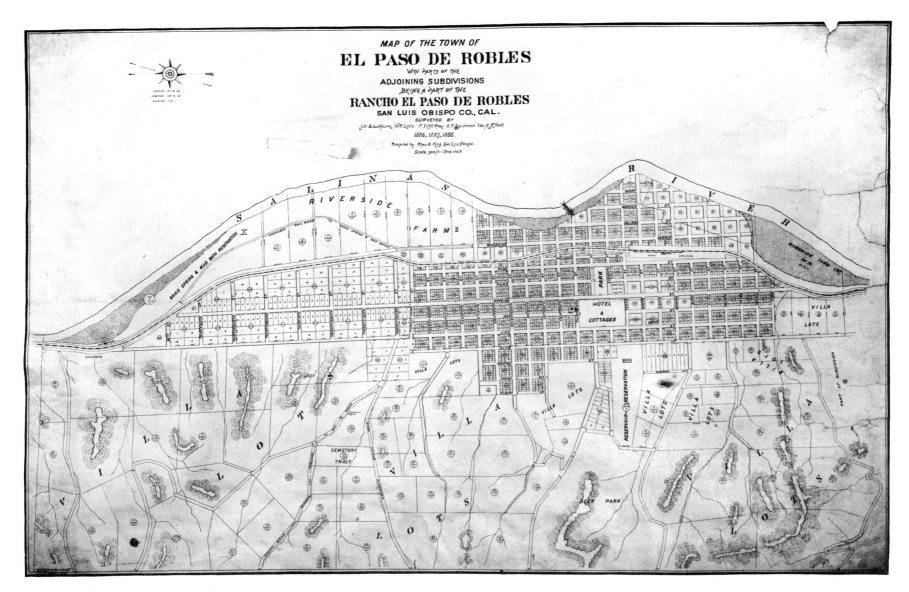

Figure 8.33 Plan of Paso Robles, California: 1888

280

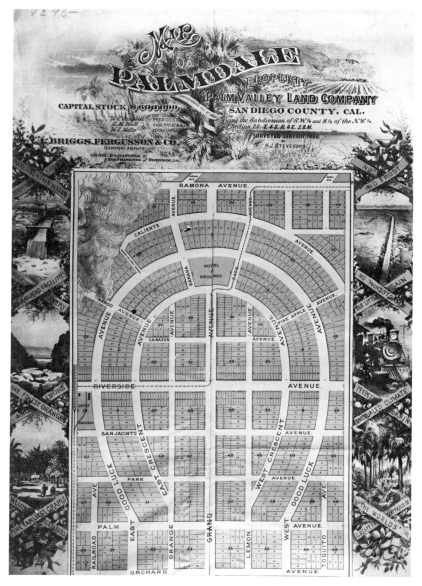

Figure 8.34 Plan of Palmdale (now Palm Springs), California: 1888

Diego appears at the far left, with the newer town and National City extending farther down the bay across the channel from Babcock's project.

After buying the entire peninsula for $110,000, Babcock began planning the development for the more than 4,000 acres that his Coronado Beach Company controlled. Joining him in the venture were three friends from Indiana, and, as architects, two Evansville brothers, James W. and Merritt Reid. The Reid brothers designed the hotel in a great quadrangle, the corners of which were embellished with imposing towers. Inside were 399 luxurious guest rooms, a theater, ballroom, dining rooms, and extensive facilities for recreation.

The Hotel Coronado, which still remains as one of America's great hotels, can be seen in the lower right corner of Figure 8.36. Complementing the main structure were a number of subsidiary buildings, of which the boathouse in the small cove at the neck of the peninsula was and is the most elaborate.[52] Matching the hotel in interest and complexity is the design for the town itself, which may also have been prepared by James and Merritt Reid.

The plan represents a unique combination of the three principal types of street systems—a basic grid, an overlay of two major radial streets leading to a central park, and a fringe on two sides of sinuous, curving thoroughfares in the naturalistic style made popular in the East by Frederick Law Olmsted. The radial streets focusing on the public open space at the center may well have been inspired by the plan of Indianapolis, with which Babcock and the Reids were doubtless familiar. Coronado's design, however, was no mere imitation of an existing plan, and except for the awkward angles created where the diagonals sliced across the grid streets, the contact lines between the three systems were handled with considerable skill.

Babcock managed the promotion of this vast enterprise with equal mastery. He spent thousands of dollars advertising the new town and hotel. Notices in railroad timetables throughout the country called attention to the project, and Babcock saw to it that brochures, posters, views, and other promotional literature were widely distributed. Unlike most of the boom towns, the services and facilities claimed to exist were actually constructed. Babcock built a trolley line to connect the hotel and town to San Diego by land, and he provided ferry service to the older city across the bay for those preferring to travel by water.

The company also constructed a water and sewer system and offered free water for one year and 120 single-trip tickets on either the trolley or the ferry to any lot purchaser spending $1,000 for improvements on his

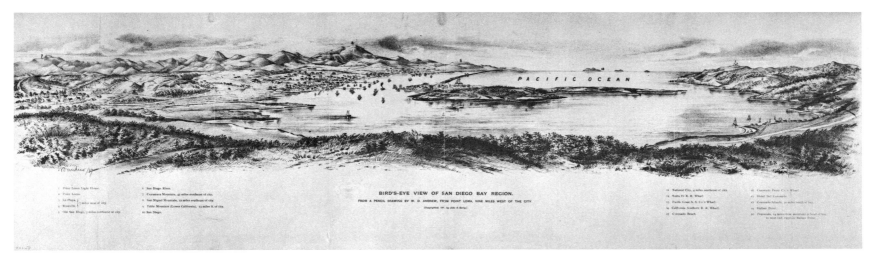

Figure 8.35   View of San Diego, California: 1887

property. Expenditures in excess of this amount were rewarded with additional tickets and free water for a longer period. These inducements and a constant barrage of high-pressure salesmanship produced tremendous financial returns. At the first auction in mid-November, 1886, the company sold 300 lots for a total of $110,000, exactly the cost of the entire site. The following March marked the high point; Babcock and his associates received $438,000 in that single month. Before the boom finally tapered off the company had taken in over $2,000,000.

By 1888 the southern California land boom was nearing its end. Even its most eager participants were aware that it could not last forever, and there were at least some who recognized the more humorous side of its excessively inflated promotional aspects. A Los Angeles real estate agent found his own way of poking fun at his colleagues by issuing this satiric circular:

"BOOM! BOOM! BOOM!
"The newest town out! Balderdash! Watch for it! Wait for it!
Catch on to it!

To meet the great demand for another new townsite we have secured 10,000 acres of that beautiful land lying on the top of Old Baldy, and will lay out an elegant town with the above very significant and appropriate name. The land is away up and has attracted more attention than any other spot in Southern California. Nine thousand acres will be at once divided into fine business lots 14 x 33 feet. All lots will front on grand avenues 17 feet wide and run back to 18 inch alleys. For the present one-tenth of the entire tract will be reserved for residences in case anyone should want to build. . . . To accommodate the inquisitive who are afraid to invest without inspecting the property a fast balloon line will be started in the near future. Parties will be permitted to return on the superb toboggan slide to be built in the sweet bye and bye. All lots will be sold at a uniform price of $/100 each. . . . All offers for lots will be refused previous to day of sale, and in order that all may have a chance no person will be permitted to buy more than 500 lots."[53]

Satire did not stop the boom, but lack of demand did. By the end of 1888 it was all over. Many speculators and unwise investors suffered financially, but not one bank failed because of their almost uniform policy of lending money only on agricultural land values for outlying subdivisions and by gradually reducing the ratio of loans outstanding to deposits on hand during 1887 and 1888.[54]

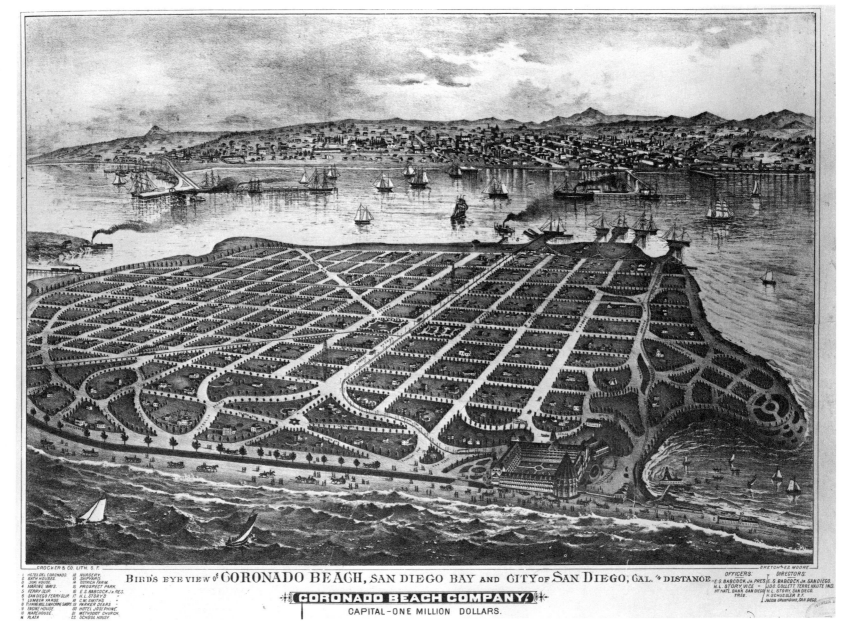

BIRD'S EYE VIEW of CORONADO BEACH, SAN DIEGO BAY AND CITY OF SAN DIEGO, CAL. ½ DISTANCE

SKETCH by E.S. MOORE

1 HOTEL DEL CORONADO.
2 BATH HOUSES.
3 JOB. HOUSE.
4 MARINE WAYS.
5 FERRY SLIP.
6 SAN DIEGO FERRY SLIP.
7 LUMBER YARDS.
8 PLANING MILL & MACHINE SHOPS.
9 ENGINE HOUSE.
10 WAREHOUSE.
11 PLAZA.
12 NURSERY.
13 SHIPYARD.
14 OSTRICH FARM.
15 PROSPECT PARK.
16 E.S. BABCOCK Jr. RES.
17 H.L. STORY'S
18 C.W. SMITH'S
19 PARKER DEARS.
20 HOTEL JOSEPHINE.
21 METHODIST CHURCH.
22 SCHOOL HOUSE

OFFICERS:
E.S. BABCOCK Jr. PRES.
H.L. STORY VICE "
1st NAT'L. BANK SAN DIEGO
TREAS.

DIRECTORS:
E.S. BABCOCK Jr. SAN DIEGO.
JOS. COLLETT, TERRE HAUTE IND.
H.L. STORY, SAN DIEGO.
H. SCHUSLER, S.F.
JACOB GRUENDIKE, SAN DIEGO.

CORONADO BEACH COMPANY.

CAPITAL—ONE MILLION DOLLARS.

Figure 8.36 View of Coronado, California: ca. 1887

Figure 8.37 View of Los Angeles, California: 1891

The boom did not consist solely of hot air, paper towns, and surveyor's stakes. Thousands of new residences, business buildings, hotels, and other structures were erected, and a vast public improvements had been constructed. True, dozens of newly platted towns remained virtually unoccupied. One survey revealed that, in Los Angeles County alone, in 60 towns with a total of 79,350 lots there were only 2,351 inhabitants.[55] Guinn, who witnessed the beginning and the end of the boom, summed up the consequences in these words:

"When the boom had become a thing of the past, those who had kept aloof from wild speculation, pursued the even tenor of their ways, building up the real cities and improving the country. Those who had invested recklessly in paper cities plowed up the sites of prospective palace hotels and massive business blocks, and sewed them in grain, or planted them with trees. . . . On the whole, with all its faults and failures, and all its reckless waste and wild extravagance, our boom was more productive of good than of evil to Southern California."[56]

Los Angeles itself had been transformed from a small city to the beginning of a modern metropolis. The view reproduced in Figure 8.37 shows the community in 1891 as it stood on the threshold of a new period of expansion. The small illustrations of individual structures surrounding the central panorama of the city from the northwest demonstrate the validity of Guinn's assessment. Pasadena, San Diego, and many other cities also owed much of their development or their founding to the impetus provided by the frenzied speculation mixed with solid achievement that characterized the penultimate decade of the nineteenth century in southern California.

IX

Cities of Zion: Origins of the Mormon West

IN the settlement of the American West the Mormon Church and its dedicated members played an enormously important role. In addition to creating one of the region's largest and most impressive communities—Salt Lake City—the Mormons during their first half-century of existence established a dozen or so smaller cities of more than local significance and well over 500 other towns located throughout the great central basin from the western Rockies to the eastern slopes of the Sierras. All of these communities were carefully planned under the direction of the church, many of them incorporating distinctive features originally specified by its founder, the remarkable Joseph Smith, and carried out under the personal supervision of his equally notable successor, Brigham Young.

It all began with a vision. On September 21, 1823, according to Smith's account, the Angel Moroni appeared before the 17-year-old boy and told him that buried in a hill near his home not far from Palmyra, New York, were tablets of gold inscribed with the text of the *Book of Mormon*. While Moroni showed young Joseph the plates of gold on that occasion and appeared before him several times during the next four years, it was not until 1827 that they were given to him to transcribe.

As translated by Smith during the next two years and published in 1830, the *Book of Mormon* told how two of the lost tribes of Israel, the Nephites and the Lamanites, came to America. Mormon, a prophet and leader of the Nephites, described how the virtuous Nephites were overcome by the Lamanites (the American Indians). This account was completed by Mormon's son, Moroni. The *Book of Mormon* revealed that the Garden of Eden had been located in America and that the continent would be "the gathering place in the last days" of the temporal world, an event that could be expected momentarily. The City of Zion was to be built to prepare a suitable place for Christ to rule on earth for a thousand years in a "land of promise; yea, even a land . . . prepared for you; yea, a land which is choice above all other lands."[1]

Joseph Smith's charismatic personality, impressive physical appearance, and persuasive speaking ability helped to convince a small group of disciples that a new religion should be formed to spread word of the teachings incorporated in the *Book of Mormon* as well as more direct wishes and instructions from the Lord, which Smith received through Divine Revelation. At Fayette, New York, Smith and five others met on April 6, 1830, to organize the Church of Christ, later to be renamed the Church of Jesus Christ of Latter-Day Saints. Within a month the congregation numbered 40 persons.

In October Smith sent missionaries westward to preach to the Indians. On their way they passed through Mentor, Ohio, where they succeeded in converting the Rev. Sidney Rigdon to Mormonism along with most of his followers. Rigdon journeyed to New York to meet Smith and not long thereafter the Mormon leader revealed that the Lord had directed the members of the church to settle in Ohio. It was the first of many moves by the faithful followers of the prophet on what was to be a long and painful westward migration. Smith led the New York Mormons to Kirtland, Ohio, where they found Rigdon's congregation. The combined group early in 1831 numbered some 225 persons who looked to Smith not only for spiritual leadership but also as a steward of many of their worldly possessions.

On March 7 Smith announced another important revelation from the Lord: "Gather ye out from the eastern lands, assemble yourselves together . . . ; go ye forth into the western countries."[2] Three months later Smith left Kirtland for Independence, Missouri, a small town on the western border of that state, which his missionaries had visited and described to him on their return. There, in July, the Lord revealed his wishes: "This is the land of promise, and the place for the city of Zion. . . . Behold, the place which is now called Independence is the center place; and the spot for the temple is lying westward, upon a lot which is not far from the court-house."[3] Soon a group of Mormons, most of them from New York, began to settle in and around Independence. Not quite a year later, when Smith made a second journey to Independence, the Mormon population had reached 300, a figure that doubled in the next twelve months.[4] The Kirtland congregation, however, remained the most important branch of the church, and it was in this Ohio town that the first Mormon temple was constructed.

Work on this structure began in the spring of 1833. It is not entirely clear if its location had been chosen as part of a complete city plan or if the design of the city was prepared later to fit the temple site. We do know that on March 23 the prophet and his advisers discussed purchasing land in Kirtland "upon which the Saints might build a Stake of Zion." Before the day ended they agreed to buy three farms which emissaries reported could be acquired for a total of $11,000.[5]

While the earliest graphic record showing Kirtland's intended design probably dates from 1835, Smith may have begun work on the town's plan two years earlier or perhaps even before. Certainly in the spring and summer of 1833 the Mormon leader was deeply preoccupied with the subject of urban form, for in July of that year he revealed detailed proposals for a new community near Independence, Missouri. Although circumstances prevented its realization, this proposed layout later served as a model for scores of Mormon towns elsewhere in the West. Its significance can best be understood through an exploration of possible sources of inspiration on which Smith may have drawn.

The Bible certainly exerted a powerful influence on Smith's concept of cities. In the description of the cities of the Levites and the proposals by Ezekiel for building Jerusalem, the Old Testament mentions cities planned "foursquare" and located in the center of surrounding agricultural lands. The Record of Ether in the Book of Mormon contains similar specifications. An early treatise on Mormon theology, Parley P. Pratt's *A Voice of Warning*, published in 1837, contains a long and revealing discussion of Biblical descriptions of cities that doubtless reflects Smith's thinking.[6]

Smith's first visit to New York City in October, 1832, may have provided a more concrete vision of a temporal urban paradise. Writing to his wife, the Mormon poured out his impressions: "This day I have been walking through the most splendid part of the city of New York. The buildings are truly great and wonderful to the astonishing of every beholder, and the language of my heart is like this. Can the great God of all the earth maker of all things magnificent and splendid be displeased with man for all these great inventions sought out by them. My answer is no it can not be, seeing these great works are calculated to make men comfortable wise and happy, therefore not for these works can the Lord be displeased."[7]

While Smith's visit to New York may have opened his eyes to the possibility of creating an equally impressive city for the Mormons, the idea of town planning would scarcely have been new to him. Kirtland occupied a site near the center of the former Connecticut Western Reserve in northeastern Ohio. The state of Connecticut sold this large tract to a syndicate known as the Connecticut Land Company, which in 1796 planned Cleveland as the central city of the territory and then disposed of the remainder of the land in whole or fractional five-mile-square townships. During the early years of the nineteenth century most of the new owners planned one or more towns or villages on their lands to promote settlement.

At least one of these planned new towns—Tallmadge, adjoining the modern city of Akron—had been developed as a religious community by the Rev. David Bacon. Although the design of this town was quite different from those Smith was to found, its existence as a nearby planned settlement for the new home of a religious sect may have suggested a similar policy to the Mormon prophet.[8]

Another religious group, the Shakers, had built one of their communities on the outskirts of Cleveland. It consisted of a carefully arranged complex of buildings similar in character to the Shaker settlements at Sodus Point in New York, not far from Palmyra. Smith probably visited both of these Shaker towns, and he doubtless knew that others existed in eastern New York at Mount Lebanon, in New Hampshire at Canterbury, and in southwestern Ohio a few miles north of Cincinnati, among other places founded by this energetic and dedicated sect.[9]

Smith's studies of other religious societies may have made him aware of additional planned towns established elsewhere in the Northeast. In western Pennsylvania, for example, there were two towns founded by a group of German Protestants led by Father George Rapp—Harmony, laid out in 1803, and Economy, planned in the mid-1820s. Smith might have known also of the Moravian settlements in eastern Pennsylvania—Bethlehem, Nazareth, and Lititz, established in the middle of the eighteenth century. South of the Western Reserve in eastern Ohio the town of Zoar had been planned in 1817 by another German religious sect under the leadership of Joseph Bimeler.

To the west, in Indiana, could be found New Harmony, the second of Father Rapp's planned towns, which he founded in 1814 after selling his earlier settlement at Harmony, Pennsylvania. Rapp eventually disposed of New Harmony as well. The purchaser was Robert Owen, whose plans for a secular utopia were well publicized throughout the United States in the 1820s and whose prescriptions for a communal society contained many points closely resembling those Smith was to advocate and partially implement at Kirtland and in the later Mormon towns in Missouri.[10]

Far outnumbering these towns founded for spiritual or utopian purposes were those planned by townsite speculators. The decade of the 1830s in the Midwest was a period of intense activity in town founding and urban real estate promotion. Printed plats of newly planned communities were displayed in hotel lobbies, saloons, on lake and canal boats, and in real estate offices. Newspaper articles, advertisements, and promotional brochures called attention to these ventures in urban planning.

In the mania for town planning, few sites were overlooked. As one observer of the period recalled, "the prairies of Illinois, the forests of Wisconsin, and the sandhills of Michigan, presented a chain almost unbroken of supposititious villages and cities. The whole land seemed staked out and peopled on paper."[11] Hundreds of towns thus came into existence, at least on paper, and no one living at that time could have remained unaware of how widespread this movement for town founding and urban development had become.

Thus when Smith turned his attention in 1833 to designing the town that the Lord had revealed to him would be the center of Zion on Missouri's western frontier, he had ample precedents on which to draw. The Mormon prophet, however, had created no ordinary religion, and he determined to plan a city that would be equally unusual.

Figure 9.1 shows the drawing Smith dispatched to his brethren in Missouri on June 25, 1833. Less than four weeks later—perhaps even before it arrived in Independence—a mob of "old settlers" in Jackson County began repeated and brutal assaults on the Mormons of the area. Joseph Smith and some of his followers had already felt the violent hands of those opposed to Mormon doctrines. The prophet himself had been tarred and feathered in Kirtland the previous year, and there had been occasional incidents of violence in Missouri. Nothing had matched the fury of the Independence mob, however, and from the end of July until their forced exodus northward across the Missouri River four months later the members of the western church could only fight desperately to protect their lives and property.

While in later years the Mormons would look on the City of Zion plan as a prototype to be followed wherever possible, Smith's original intentions were probably much more modest. He expected this plan to be used only for a town or towns at the "center stake" of Zion in Jackson County, Missouri, near Independence. Smith's own writings make it clear that only the location and not the design had been divinely revealed, and he thus felt free to depart from its specifications when he planned communities elsewhere. At Nauvoo, Illinois, for example, his last recorded effort at urban planning, the prophet did not use many of the distinctive features found in his earlier design.

The drawing itself, written specifications around it, and a long explanation prepared by Smith to accompany the plat all provide valuable information about his proposal.[12] The town's gridiron pattern was to be formed by streets each 8 rods or 132 feet wide. These formed square blocks of 10 acres measuring 40 rods or 660 feet on each side. A wider tier of blocks extending through the city from north to south was to be platted with dimensions of 660 by 990 feet. Individual lots were to contain half an acre of land, measuring 4 by 20 rods, or 66 by 330 feet. Smith specified regulations that were to govern the buildings erected on these parcels: "No one lot . . . is to contain more than one house, and that to be built twenty-five feet back from the street, leaving a small

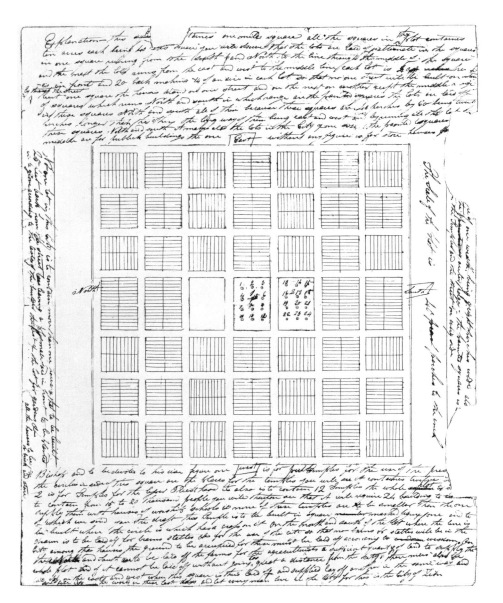

Figure 9.1 Plan of the City of Zion, Missouri: 1833

yard in front, to be planted in a grove, according to the taste of the builder; the rest of the lot for gardens; all the houses are to be built of brick and stone."

The three blocks in the center of the wider tier were to be set aside for special purposes. Smith's explanation described their intended use: "The one without any figures is for store-houses for the Bishop, and to be devoted to his use. Figure first is for temples . . .; the circles inside of the squares are the places for the temples. You will see it contains twelve figures." The other block was also to have 12 temples for "the lesser Priesthood." Smith designated precisely the purpose of each temple: "numbers 10, 11, and 12, are to be called, House of the Lord, for the Presidency of the High and most Holy Priesthood after the order of Melchizadek. . . . Numbers 7, 8, and 9, the Sacred Apostolic Repository, for the use of the Bishop. Numbers 4, 5, and 6, the Holy Evangelical House, for the High Priesthood of the Holy Order of God," and so on.

While Smith stated that "the plat contains one mile square," this is incorrect, for the measurements work out as 5,676 feet north and south by 5,742 feet east and west. This tract was only for the town proper, for, as Smith directed: "South of the plot . . . [land] is to be laid off for barns, stables, etc., for the use of the city; so that no barns or stables will be in the city among the houses; the ground to be occupied for these must be laid off according to wisdom. On the north and south are to be laid off the farms for the agriculturist, and sufficient quantity of land to supply the whole plot; and if it cannot be laid off without going too great a distance from the city, there must also be some laid off on the east and west." Apparently all farmers, as well as craftsmen and tradesmen, were to live in the city and go out daily to work the surrounding agricultural lands, for Smith admonished: "Let every man live in the city, for this is the city of Zion."

Perhaps the most distinctive feature of the proposed city, aside from the three large blocks for church use, was the peculiar orientation of the lots. Smith called attention to this in his instructions accompanying the plat: "You will observe that the lots are laid off alternately in the squares; in one square running from the south and north to the line through the center of the square; and in the next, the lots run from the east and west to the center line . . . so that no one street will be built on entirely through the street; but on one square the houses will stand on one street, and on the next one, another, except the middle range of squares. . . . The lots are laid off in these squares, north and south, all of them; because these squares are forty perches [rods] by sixty, being

twenty perches longer than the others . . . and by running all these squares, north and south, it makes all the lots in the city of one size."[13]

The intended City of Zion was "supposed to contain from fifteen to twenty thousand people." With 960 lots, each occupied by one family and with a total population of 15,000, the average family size would be just over 15. Or, if the upper population figure is used, the average number of persons per family would be slightly more than 20. In the normal 10-acre block, therefore, between 300 and 400 persons would be expected to live—a net residential density (excluding streets) of 30 to 40 persons per acre. This was certainly far greater than the densities of towns in the Midwest at the time, and it must then have been approached or exceeded only in the largest cities of the Atlantic seaboard.

It is doubtful if Smith considered the family size and density implications of his proposed city plan, but he did express confidence not only that the city would reach its intended population but that other urban centers would be required: "When this square is thus laid off and supplied, lay off another in the same way, and so fill up the world in these last days."

The City of Zion plat combined a number of traditional features of American town planning with other urban design elements far less common or unknown altogether. The gridiron street pattern, of course, was routine, but it is doubtful if any town had been planned or proposed with all of its streets 132 feet wide. Nor was there anything startling about a town where every house would stand on its own lot. There was, however, no precedent for the peculiar change in axis of the lots from block to block with the resulting alternating pattern of frontage that Smith employed. Nor is there any ready explanation for why he viewed this system as important or advantageous. With variations, this alternating frontage scheme was to be used over and over in scores of Mormon towns, although never precisely as Smith first proposed.

A number of the earlier planned communities founded by religious groups gave special prominence to church buildings located in central squares. This was also a familiar pattern in New England and upstate New York, where Joseph Smith spent his youth. In none of these settlements, however, can one find anything approaching so elaborate a complex as Smith's proposed three large squares, two of which were each to be occupied by twelve temples.

One other feature advanced by Smith, if not completely novel, was certainly uncommon. This was his specification that all houses were to be built 25 feet from the street line. A few such regulations had been adopted in a handful of colonial towns, but such restrictions must have been rare at the time Smith worked out the details of his proposed new community.

The concept of a community of limited population would also have been strange to the American western frontier where bigness was equated with success. The notion of a town with a predetermined finite size did have some precedents in colonial New England, but whether this idea may have come to Smith through his boyhood knowledge of Vermont or was devised by him independently can only be a matter of conjecture.

Perhaps the least unusual feature of the City of Zion was the proposed surrounding belt of agricultural lands that would be cultivated by farmers residing in the town. There were still remnants of this older New England practice in the little Western Reserve communities that had been planned and settled by persons from Connecticut and other parts of the Northeast. In many town plans it found expression in the system of "out-lots," farm fields surveyed at the edge of such towns as Buffalo, Cleveland, and numerous smaller communities throughout the region with which Smith was most familiar. In many later Mormon towns, including Salt Lake City, the term "out-lot" was commonly employed. This agricultural village pattern was also used by nearly all of the religious and utopian groups discussed earlier, and Smith's incorporation of this feature in his proposed community is not difficult to understand.

Although this plan could not be employed at Independence, Smith soon used a variation of it in the enlargement of Kirtland, where the growing Mormon population required some kind of town design. Reproduced in Figure 9.2 is a survey that probably dates from some time after October 29, 1835, a day on which Smith recorded that he "returned to our writing room . . . [and] made some observations to my scribe concerning the plan of the city, which is to be built up hereafter on this ground consecrated for a Stake of Zion."[14]

The intended city was much larger than that proposed earlier for Zion in Missouri, being 11,022 feet east-west and 10,956 feet north and south. The 225 blocks were all 40 rods, or 660 feet, square except for the center tier extending from north to the south, which was 43 rods east and west, and the adjoining tier of blocks to the east, which was 41 rods east and west. It seems likely that some of these blocks had already been laid out slightly wider than the standard 40 rods used elsewhere in the plan and previously advocated as the desirable size for the City of Zion.

The lot size, 4 by 20 rods, also corresponded to Smith's earlier specifications. And, as can be seen on the plat, the Kirtland design incorporated the peculiar alternating orientation of lot frontage as Smith had prescribed, although in a somewhat different and more consistent manner than appeared on his City of Zion drawing. The streets, however, were platted only 4 rods (66 feet) in width rather than the 8-rod (132 feet) width of the 1833 proposal. An equally significant departure from the City of Zion prototype was the treatment of the temple site. Instead of three large blocks as previously advocated, the temple plot occupied only a portion of the central block on a site measuring 15 by 40 rods, or 247½ by 660 feet.[15]

Some two thousand Mormons gathered at Kirtland for the dedication of the temple in March, 1836. Their numbers seemed to indicate that the prosperity of the town and its permanence as a religious center was assured. However, the temple and other improvements required money. Few Mormons possessed extensive wealth, and most had only modest means. Smith succeeded in borrowing some funds, but still more were needed. In November he organized the Kirtland Safety Society Bank Company, apparently believing that he could solve his financial problems simply by issuing bank notes. He chose a poor time to begin this enterprise. In the panic of 1837, the Mormon bank failed to meet its obligations, and it, like hundreds of others throughout the country, was forced to close.

This financial disaster aggravated religious dissension in the Mormon ranks. A number of church leaders denounced Smith as a false prophet and left the church. During the prophet's absence from Kirtland while preaching in Canada during July and August, 1837, and on a two-month visit to Missouri later in 1837, the Kirtland church split into rival factions. Smith made a final attempt to reassert his authority but failed. Learning that a warrant had been issued for his arrest on charges of banking fraud, Smith fled Kirtland for Missouri early in January, 1838. A number of the Mormons remaining faithful to him had previously moved to Missouri, and those at Kirtland who still believed in his teachings followed as soon as possible.[16]

Smith and the Ohio Mormons were re-united with their Missouri brethren at the new town of Far West in Caldwell County, north of the Missouri River. There in the summer of 1836 John Whitmer and W. W. Phelps had selected a site near the mouth of Shoal Creek on the Grand River. It was here that the Missouri Mormons, driven out of Independence late in 1833 and forced to move from temporary quarters in Clay County again in 1836, had planned a town for what they hoped might be a permanent home.

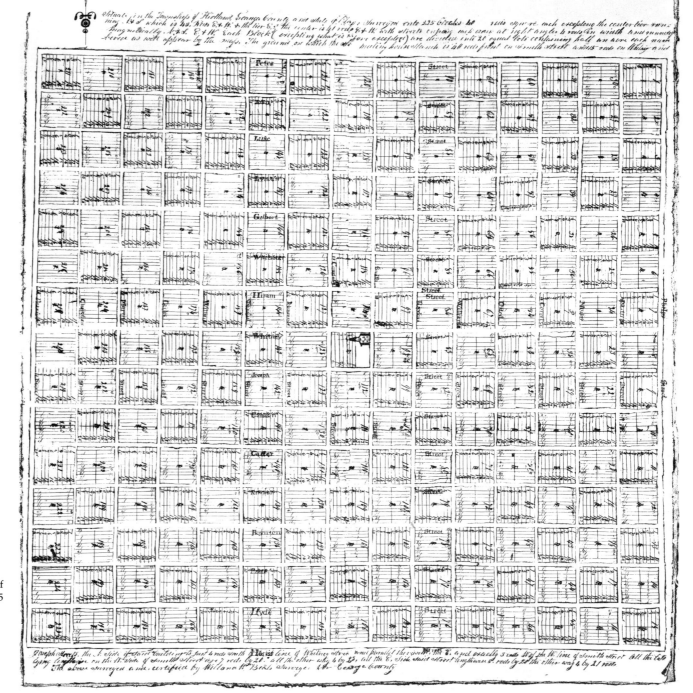

Figure 9.2 Plan of
Kirtland, Ohio: ca. 1835

The only surviving survey showing the details of Far West is reproduced in Figure 9.3. It is unclear if this represents the original design, the plan as modified in November, 1837, or a proposed layout that was never used. The drawing has no scale, but from notations on it of street widths it appears that the blocks were 40 rods square and contained 20 lots, each 4 by 20 rods. These dimensions and the peculiar alternating lot frontage pattern, somewhat modified, conform to the City of Zion pattern devised by Smith in 1833.

The streets, however, are only four rods wide except for the one running north and south on which front the three buildings located in the central block. This street appears to be eight rods in width, made up of what may have been the original planned width of six rods, plus an additional strip along the western edge measuring two rods wide. The entire site of 49 blocks with the boundary streets measures just under one mile square, being 5,148 by 5,181 feet.

Church historians state that Far West was originally planned with streets five rods wide except for four avenues that were each eight rods in width and ran north-south and east-west from a temple block. It has also been stated that the blocks were platted only 24 rods square.[17] All this is rather puzzling, and it is not made any clearer by the information that on November 6, 1837, at a meeting of church officials a number of changes in the town plan were recommended. They are described by Smith who was present on a visit: "Several topics were discussed, when it was unanimously voted . . . to alter the streets or lessen them so as to make each block contain four acres of ground, and each block to be divided into four lots."[18] This represented a significant change in lot size and—assuming square blocks—in the shape of lots. It was a pattern that Smith himself was to employ when he planned the great Mormon city of Nauvoo, Illinois.

Four days later at a meeting of all church members, the group voted to enlarge the town by making its boundaries two miles on a side, or four square miles in area. At that same meeting the church members adopted an important policy that generally was to govern Mormon town planning during the decades to follow. As Smith relates, "President Sidney Rigdon . . . laid before the meeting the subject of laying off cities, of consecrating lands for public purposes, and for remunerating those who lay them off. It was unanimously voted that all city plats hereafter laid off, after remunerating those for their labor who may be engaged in appointing and laying off the same shall be consecrated for the public benefit of the Church, for building houses for public worship, or such other purposes as the Church shall say."[19]

While Smith did not design the city of Far West, he was responsible for founding a second community in the Mormon domain of northern Missouri. This was Adam-ondi-Ahman, some 25 miles north of Far West in Daviess County. Smith's history of the church records that on May 19, 1838, he "went up the river about half a mile to Wight's Ferry, accompanied by President Rigdon, and my clerk, George W. Robinson, for the purpose of selecting and laying claim to a city plat." The location was on an elevation called Spring Hill by some of the Mormons who were farming in that vicinity, but according to Smith, "by the mouth of the Lord it was named Adam-ondi-Ahman, because, said He, it is the place where Adam shall come to visit his people."[20]

Heber C. Kimball recalled that after the temple block had been dedicated the prophet called him and Brigham Young to accompany him. "He led us a short distance to a place where were the ruins of three altars built of stone, one above the other, and one standing a little back of the other, like unto the pulpits in the Kirtland Temple. . . . 'There,' said Joseph, 'is the place where Adam offered up sacrifice after he was cast out of the garden.' "[21]

The plan of Adam-ondi-Ahman reproduced in Figure 9.4 states that the blocks measure 36 rods (594 feet) north and south and 32 rods (528 feet) east and west. Each block was divided into six lots 1 1/5 acre in area. Because the blocks were not square and the pattern of lots followed the peculiar system of alternating frontage, lots were of two dimensions. Those facing north or south fronting on the east-west streets measured 176 by 297 feet. Those lots fronting in the other directions were 198 by 264 feet.

Street widths are not specified on the plat. They appear to scale approximately 100 feet and were most probably six rods or 99 feet wide. If this is correct, the public square—doubtless intended as the temple block—would measure 594 by 1155 feet, or slightly less than 16 acres in area. Like Far West, Adam-ondi-Ahman was expected to become a large city. The entire tract included over four square miles, measuring nearly 2 1/8 miles by more than 2 1/4 miles and containing about 1900 lots.

Both of these towns grew quickly. By the spring of 1838 nearly 5,000 Mormons were living in Caldwell County, and Far West could boast of 150 houses, 2 hotels, 4 dry goods shops, 3 groceries, a printing plant, and 6 blacksmith establishments. A large school building constructed in 1836 also housed the church and courthouse. During the summer of 1838 thousands of new arrivals settled in the two towns and on farms in the surrounding countryside. One group from Canada arrived in 200 wagons. Another party of more than 500 persons came from Kirtland

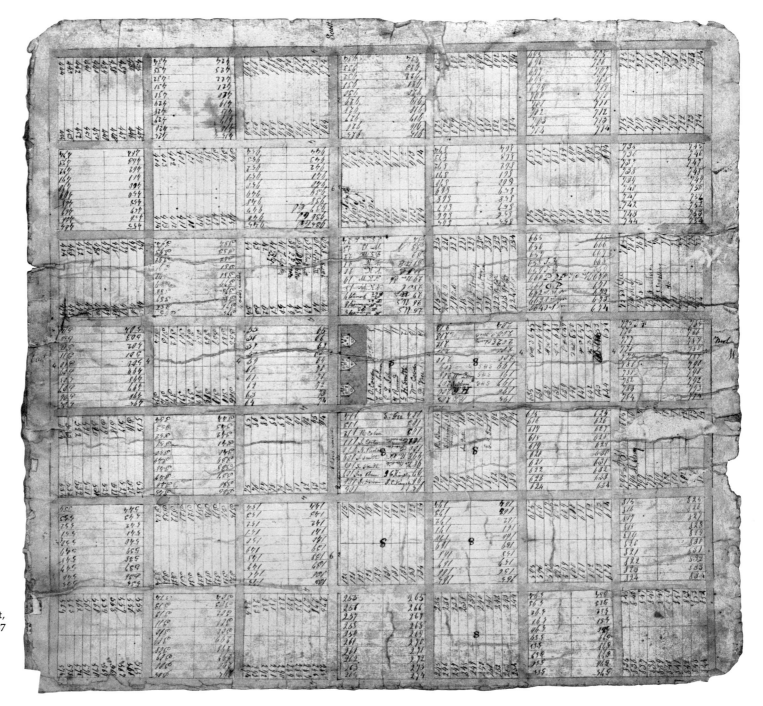

Figure 9.3 Plan of Far West,
Missouri: ca. 1837

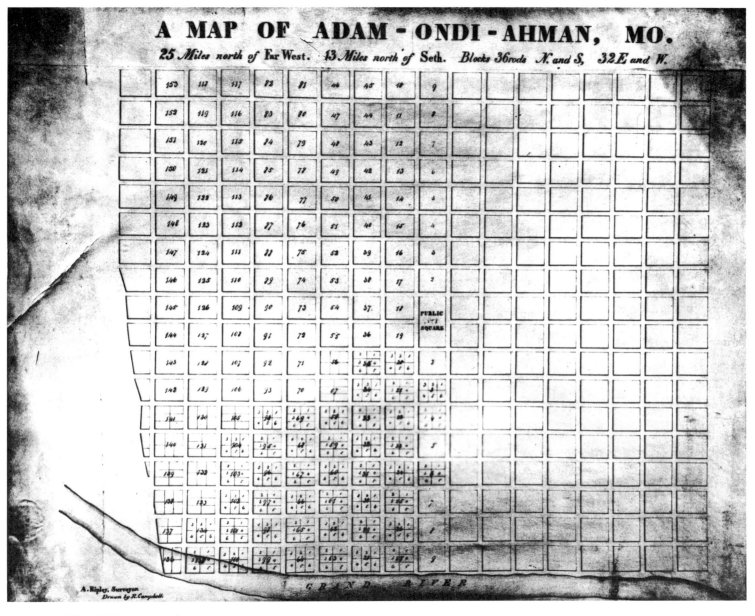

Figure 9.4 Plan of Adam-Ondi-Ahman, Missouri: ca. 1838

and was welcomed a few miles outside of "Di-Ahman" by the prophet himself, who escorted them to a temporary campsite on the public square adjoining the temple site.[22]

Preparations were soon under way for a third Mormon town. On September 1, 1838, Smith, accompanied by his brother, Hyrum, Sidney Rigdon, and a surveyor, selected a site 15 miles north of Far West and located about halfway between it and Adam-ondi-Ahman. There, according to the prophet, "the brethren were instructed to gather immediately into it, and soon they should be organized according to the laws of God." He then added: "A more particular history of this city may be expected hereafter, perhaps at its organization and dedication."[23]

While some settlement at this third site may have taken place, it and the established communities at Far West and Adam-ondi-Ahman were soon to be abandoned as the clouds of conflict once again gathered over the heads of the unfortunate Mormons. A violent incident at a polling place in Daviess County on August 6, 1838, began when a group of old settlers attempted to deny a party of Mormons the right to vote. Serious enough in itself, this event was greatly magnified by rumors on both sides. Bands of old settlers began to arm and terrorize the Mormons; the members of the church on their part retaliated by mobilizing themselves into para-military groups. Once again open warfare broke out, the Missouri militia was ordered into action, Smith and his fellow leaders were seized and clapped into jail, Far West was occupied, and the Mormons were orderd to leave the state.[24]

Once again the Mormons, hounded and persecuted by their relentless oppressors, were forced to flee and to abandon their lands and many of their possessions. With most of their leaders in the hands of the enemy facing charges of treason, murder, arson, and robbery, among others, their future appeared bleak.

One of the few senior church officials remaining at liberty was Brigham Young, a Mormon convert in 1832 who had been named one of the Twelve Apostles three years later. Smith managed to get word to Young that he should lead the Mormons out of Missouri, and it was he who organized the shattered community for their new exodus during the months between November, 1838, and April of the following year. Young proved to be an able and inspiring leader in this time of trial, gaining not only the confidence of his flock but acquiring experience in transportation logistics that he would later employ in the final and even more arduous pilgrimage of the Mormons during their eventual migration to the basin of the Great Salt Lake of Utah.

By the end of April, 1839, some twelve to fifteen thousand Mormons had managed to leave Missouri. Some found shelter in Iowa; most of them crossed the Mississippi River to Quincy, Illinois, and sought accommodations there and in farms and villages in the vicinity. As Young and other church leaders began to reorganize affairs of the scattered and demoralized community, they began to discuss the wisdom of attempting to found another town or towns. One possibility considered was the purchase of a 20,000-acre tract on the Iowa side of the Mississippi some 50 miles north of Quincy.[25] But in the absence of their prophet and leader, Joseph Smith, no action was taken. Unexpectedly, on April 22, 1839, Smith arrived in Quincy after being allowed to escape by his jailers.

Shortly thereafter the prophet entered into a series of land purchases. This resulted in the acquisition of many hundreds of acres of land in Lee County, Iowa, and more importantly, across the Mississippi in Hancock County, Illinois, in and around two small and largely vacant towns platted in 1834 and 1837 as Commerce and Commerce City.[26] On May 1, Smith and his advisers bought two parcels totaling 182 acres near Commerce. Subsequent purchases in the months and years to follow brought into church ownership most of that site on a point of land formed by a great bend in the Mississippi River.

Here Smith began to plan and develop the most important community to take shape under his direction—Nauvoo, for a short time the largest city in Illinois, the scene of still another Mormon persecution, and the point of departure for the final Mormon exodus. When Smith moved to the site there was little to suggest its future size and importance.

"When I made the purchase . . . there were one stone house, three frame houses, and two block houses, which constituted the whole city of Commerce. . . . The land was mostly covered with trees and brushes, and much of it so wet that it was with the utmost difficulty a footman could get through, and totally impossible for teams. Commerce was so unhealthful, very few could live there; but believing that it might become a healthful place by the blessing of heaven to the Saints, and no more eligible place presenting itself, I considered it wisdom to make an attempt to build up a city."[27]

To build up a city one needed land, money, and a plan. Smith lacked substantial funds, but he acquired most of the land for the city by borrowing, in the name of the church, $114,500. This added 500 acres of land adjoining his previous purchase. Adjacent properties would later be acquired, and they, too, were expensive. For better or for worse, Nauvoo began burdened by extensive debt. Smith expected to pay off this heavy financial obligation with the proceeds realized through sales of town lots.[28]

Possibly because of these circumstances Smith abandoned at Nauvoo attempts to carry out the features of his earlier City of Zion design. The streets of Nauvoo did follow the gridiron pattern of the earlier Mormon communities, but in this respect the town plan merely conformed to standard practice on the western frontier. Instead of the wide avenues provided in other Mormon communities, the streets of Nauvoo, with two exceptions, were only three rods (49½ feet) wide. Main Street, running north-south roughly midway through the original plat, was to be 87 feet wide to allow for a canal down its center. Water Street, crossing Main near its southern end, was to be given a width of 64 feet.

The only known plan of the city during its period of Mormon occupancy is that reproduced in Figure 9.5. It is undated but apparently was published in 1842. This shows the city after it had been enlarged. When Smith began his work only the 11 tiers of blocks extending eastward from the tip of the peninsula were within the area under church ownership. The temple site was not included in the original plat because the most commanding location for this important structure was not yet in Mormon ownership. This was at the edge of the steep bluff high above the river and overlooking the townsite located on the river terrace below.

The size of the blocks and their division into lots also failed to conform to the City of Zion prototype. Most of the blocks measure 24 rods (396 feet) east-west and 22 rods (363 feet) north and south, with an area of 3⅓ acres. The blocks were divided into only four lots having frontages of 198 feet on the east-west streets and 181½ feet on those running north and south.[29] Each lot, therefore, had an area of slightly more than eight-tenths of an acre. The pattern of lots with alternating frontage, a characteristic feature of earlier Mormon towns, was thus not to be repeated at Nauvoo. Perhaps Smith felt that a more conventional system of lot division might make it easier to dispose of house sites, or he may have decided to abandon his original idea because he or others had found it unsatisfactory or of no special value.[30]

Smith laid plans for other towns in the vicinity. On the Iowa side of the river he proposed a town to serve the newly organized Stake of Zarahemla.[31] In 1840 another Mormon community was surveyed near the eastern boundary of Hancock County, called Ramus.[32] Nashville, a second settlement on the Iowa side of the Mississippi, and Warren, an addition to Warsaw south of Nauvoo in Hancock County, were additional centers of Mormon activity.

It was Nauvoo, however, that received the prophet's greatest attention and investment of church funds. In July, 1839, Smith circulated a statement to church members everywhere urging them to gather at Nauvoo.[33] While many responded and came to the new town to purchase lots at the fixed price of $500 a lot, Smith was apparently not satisfied with the rate of migration. On January 15, 1841, he issued a proclamation stating that it was the word of the Lord that all Saints come to Nauvoo, take up a new life, and assist with the building of the temple, a project announced six months earlier. In May, 1841, he took the more drastic step of announcing that all Mormon stakes except for that of Zarahemla were to be discontinued, and all Saints were to gather at Nauvoo.[34] These directives, combined with the stunning success of missionary activities in England under the leadership of Brigham Young, produced a steady flow of new settlers to the Mormon town. Soon the newly surveyed site began to bustle with activity. By June, 1840, Smith stated that there were 250 houses, mostly of log construction, already occupied. In August he claimed that the population had reached nearly 3,000. On April 1, 1842, the Mormon publication, *Times and Seasons*, put the population at 7,000.[35]

In the summer of 1843 an English emigrant described the city in these words: ''From rising ground in Nauvoo we have a splendid sight of the country on the other side of the river, which is very pleasant. The extent of the city is four miles, laid out in lots and streets in nice order; I mean that each house has a piece of land attached to it, either a quarter, half, or whole acre of land, and some more, which makes the houses appear scattered. For two miles square the city is covered in that way, but in the center, near the temple they are quite close like other towns. . . . Two or three places in the city have a very business-like appearance with having different kinds of shops. We have many good brick houses, and others are frame, wood and log houses. Some of the houses appear strange to a person who has been accustomed to live in a fine-built place, but a great many are quite smart large brick houses, which would look well in any city. I was quite surprised to find as many good brick houses. Brick houses, stone, and others, are building as fast as they can.''[36]

Additional land acquired by the church or individual Mormons adjacent to the original Nauvoo tract was surveyed and laid out as exten-

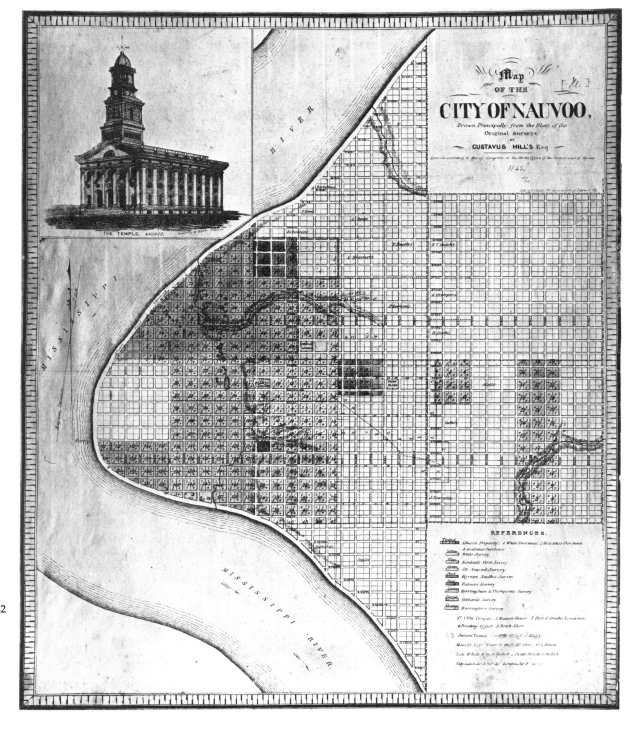

Figure 9.5   Plan of Nauvoo, Illinois: ca. 1842

sions of Smith's first design. Figure 9.6 shows the city in 1874, long after the Mormons departed, but it is a useful record of town growth of an earlier period. It also shows the location of the paper towns of Commerce and Commerce City. After the city of Nauvoo received its charter the city council, in March, 1841, vacated these plats so that the land they occupied might be made to conform to the city's layout.

The temple block also appears on this plan, and it was here that the Mormons concentrated their construction efforts. An early depiction of that huge structure appears as an inset on the published plan of the city in 1842 (Figure 9.5). The temple measured 128 feet long, 88 feet wide, and it rose 165 feet from its base to the top of the tower. The view in Figure 9.7 omits the temple tower, but it reveals how this mighty symbol of the Mormon faith dominated the town and the urban skyline. The view also shows close to the river at the righthand side the impressive Nauvoo House. This intended hotel was never completed, but the two stories that were built occupied an L-shaped site, each wing being 120 feet long by 40 feet deep facing Main Street between Water Street and the Mississippi.[37]

The years at Nauvoo witnessed the development of church ritual, the organization of its missionary ventures, and a growing prosperity as prairie land in the vicinity was broken for farming and as trade and industry developed in the town. The Nauvoo Legion, a military force organized and commanded by Smith, seemed to guarantee freedom from any attacks similar to those responsible for the exodus from Missouri. State politicians, conscious of the growing numbers of voters in the Mormon community, courted Smith's favor. Gentiles in the region might well be hostile to these people with their strange religion, they might envy their orderly town, they might be apprehensive about their growing political power, but, so it appeared, they could never again threaten seriously Mormon rights to exist.

It was at this moment in 1842 that Smith, perhaps overconfident of his position of unrivaled leadership and unquestioned authority, chose to reveal to his closest confidants the doctrine of plural marriage. All were shocked, many to the point where they apostatized. Some so bitterly opposed the new revelation that they openly attacked the prophet on this issue and in doing so wildly exaggerated what Smith really advocated. All the latent hostility of the neighboring population was aroused by this new evidence that the Mormons posed a threat to established order and morals. Smith's enemies soon began to plot his downfall.

An attempted assassination of the governor of Missouri, a person deeply involved in the previous Mormon persecutions in that state, was blamed on one of Joseph Smith's bodyguards. Smith was arrested, stood trial in Springfield, Illinois, and was acquitted. Arrested a second time on new charges, he was rescued by his Nauvoo Legion, tried before a Nauvoo court, and acquitted again. Where legal means failed mob action succeeded. Threats of violence brought Governor Thomas Ford to the scene, and he prevailed on Smith to surrender himself at Carthage, the county seat, for still another trial on charges of inciting to riot and treason. It was at Carthage jail that a mob killed Joseph and his brother, Hyrum, on June 27, 1844.

Smith's martyrdom set off a struggle for succession to church leadership, an issue ultimately resolved in favor of Brigham Young.[38] For a time, work continued on the city, and in 1845 the temple was completed and dedicated. The enemies of the Mormons soon realized that Smith's death had not altered the determination of these people to remain at Nauvoo, and in the late summer and fall of 1845 mobs again gathered to attack Mormon settlers outside of the city and to destroy their property.

Sometime in 1845 Brigham Young reached the momentous decision to abandon the community and to lead his people to the Far West well beyond the frontier of settlement. The population of the city of Nauvoo then exceeded 11,000, and there were several thousand Mormons at other communities in the vicinity or living on farms in the surrounding countryside. A wholesale migration of the entire Mormon community would obviously be a vast undertaking under the most favorable of circumstances, and it would be immensely more difficult if the Mormons were to be harassed and set upon by their enemies in Illinois.

The notion of large-scale colonization in the West did not originate with Young. Smith and other leaders had considered this possibility a few years earlier. Texas, Oregon, and California were among the locations discussed.[39] The eventual selection of Utah as the place of settlement was undoubtedly (and understandably) because of its isolated location and its unpopulated condition. The description of the Great Basin contained in the report of the exploring expedition headed by John Charles Frémont was thoroughly digested by Mormon leaders, and portions of it were published in Mormon journals.

The winter of 1845-46 saw Nauvoo virtually converted to a base camp for the great migration. Where a few years earlier nearly everyone was engaged in building houses, the temple, and other structures, now ef-

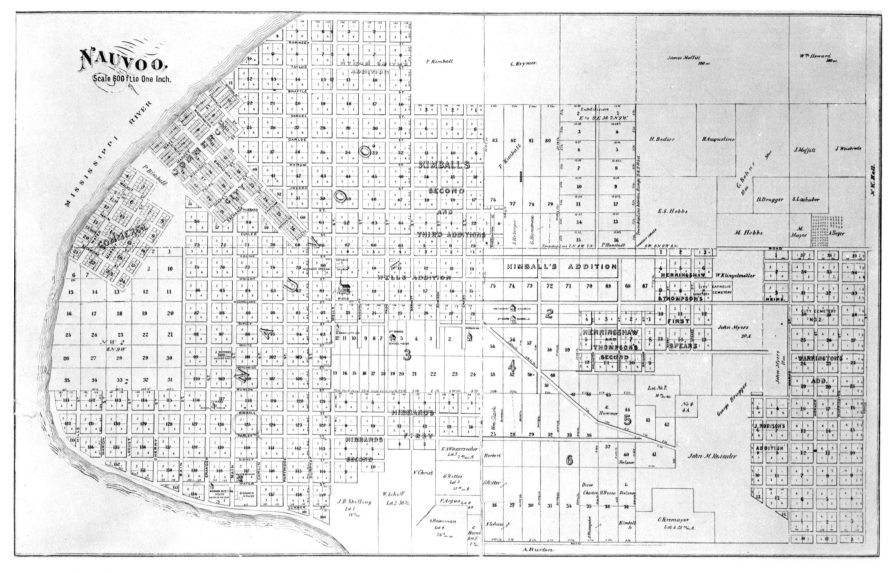

Figure 9.6 Plan of Nauvoo, Illinois: 1874

Figure 9.7   View of Nauvoo, Illinois: 1853

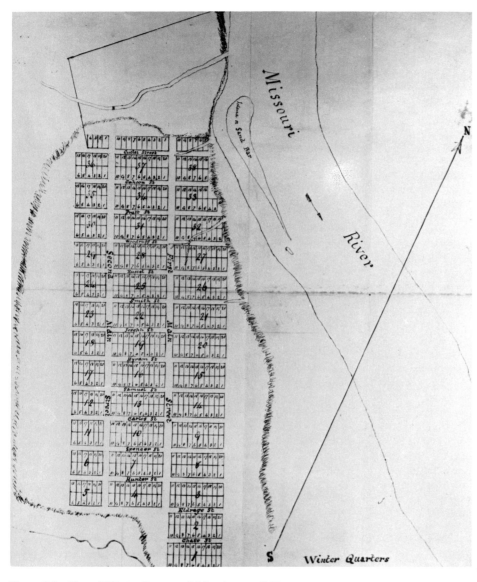

Figure 9.8 Plan of Winter Quarters, Nebraska: ca. 1847

forts were directed to the construction of wagons and in other preparations for yet another exodus. Farming implements were gathered, foods prepared, and household goods packed. All the while it was necessary to maintain an armed guard about the city to protect the inhabitants from attack.[40]

The migration began early in 1846, when several hundred Mormons crossed the Mississippi River to the Iowa side. A Missouri newspaper published that February summarized the Mormon situation and the plans for mass migration: "From ten to twelve hundred have already crossed the river from Nauvoo and are encamped on Sugar Creek, Iowa, seven miles distant. Among them were the *Twelve*, the High Council, all the principal men of the church, and about one hundred females. They were several days and nights in getting across the river. It is said to be the plan of the leaders to send this company forward as a *pioneer corps*. They are to proceed about five hundred miles westward, where they are to halt, build a village, and put in a spring crop. They are to remain there until those who follow in the spring reach them—when another pioneer company will start for a point five hundred miles still farther west, where they will stop, build a village, and put in a fall crop. The company remaining behind will, in the spring, move on to this second station; and in this manner they hope to accomplish the long journey which is in contemplation."[41]

The "villages" mentioned above were camps rather than settlements pretending to any permanence, and the distances between them were much shorter than 500 miles, but otherwise the newspaper was correct in outlining the method worked out by Brigham Young to transport the Saints from Nauvoo to a new place of refuge. Sugar Creek was the first camp. Garden Grove, Iowa, 150 miles west of Nauvoo was the second. Mt. Pisgah, 100 miles beyond was the third, and Miller's Hollow (later named Kanesville and still later, after the Mormon departure, Council Bluffs) was the final Iowa stopping and supply point.[42]

Across the Missouri River from Council Bluffs on the site now within the city of Omaha, Nebraska, Young established a more elaborate base where the bulk of the Saints—now numbering some 16,000—spent the winter of 1846-47.[43] Young gave the name Winter Quarters to this settlement. Its plan is reproduced in Figure 9.8. Here was no City of Zion but a simple, quick, and practical layout for a winter encampment that was expected to be abandoned after the last group of Saints had passed through on their way west. Brigham Young described the "town" in February, 1847:

"Winter Quarters is platted in 41 blocks, numbering 20 lots to a block, 4 rods by 10 covered by about 700 houses divided into 22 wards, with 22 bishops and counsellors over whom preside a municipal High Council of 12 High Priests."[44] Thomas Kane, who saw the unusual "city" that winter, recalled that it was "neatly laid out with highways and byways, and fortified with breast-work, stockade, and block-houses. It had, too, its place of worship, 'Tabernacle of the Congregation,' and various large workshops, and mills and factories, provided with water power."[45]

Dwellings were of two types: dugouts and log huts, the latter being the more numerous. Each of these primitive dwellings probably housed several families during the winter months. The meetinghouse measured only 32 feet square, and it, like the settlement itself, must have been excessively crowded when used for church or social purposes. A water-powered grist mill was completed in the spring of 1847 in time to grind the first crop of wheat.[46]

At Winter Quarters, Brigham Young organized the pioneer party to push ahead to the valley of the Great Salt Lake. Traveling with supplies in 72 wagons, this group consisted of 143 men and boys, 2 children, and 3 women. For much of the way their route paralleled the Oregon Trail along the valleys of the Platte and North Platte rivers. Young led his party along the north bank, however, to avoid possible trouble with Gentiles who might be following the established trail on the south side of the two streams.

From Fort Laramie, the trail wound through the mountains to South Pass. Some miles beyond, on the banks of the Green River in southwestern Wyoming the party met Samuel Brannan, a Mormon leader from New York who, on Young's advice, had led his flock to California by ship around Cape Horn. Brannan urged Young to come to California, reporting that his group had settled there and that the land was fertile. He also informed Young that the Mormon Battalion, a group of 500 younger Mormons recruited by the army for service in the Mexican War, was then in Los Angeles.

Young rejected Brannan's advice and announced his determination to settle in the Great Basin, now only a little more than a hundred miles away beyond the Wasatch Range. As they neared their destination Young dispatched a vanguard group of 42 men and 25 wagons to move ahead and seek out the most advantageous route. Erastus Snow and Orson Pratt on July 21, 1847, emerged from the western mouth of Emigration Canyon and saw for the first time the future home of the Saints.

Young, ill with fever, followed with the main party of the pioneer company three days later. Wilford Woodruff describes this moving episode:

"I drove my carriage, with President Young lying on a bed in it, into the open valley . . . [and] turned the side of my carriage around, open to the west, and President Young arose from his bed and took a survey of the country.

"While gazing on the scene before us he was enwrapped in vision for several minutes. He had seen the valley before in vision, and upon that occasion he saw the future glory of Zion and Israel, as they would be, planted in the valleys of the mountains. When the vision had passed, he said, 'It is enough. This is the right place. Drive on.' So I drove to the encampment already formed by those who had come along in advance of us."[47]

In all their previous locations the Mormons had concentrated on creating cities and towns. Utah was to be no exception. During the long march from Winter Quarters, Brigham Young and his companions must have discussed how the first community should be designed. They all knew the details of Joseph Smith's City of Zion plat, its variations as applied at Kirtland and in Missouri, and the much more conventional town plan used for Nauvoo. Previous theory and practice were to be combined and modified in the Great Basin.

Speed was essential, for thousands of Saints were on their way to the new Mormon kingdom. Explorations for some miles around their first camp convinced Young that no more satisfactory site for a city would be found. On the afternoon of July 28 Young convened a meeting of the eight Apostles then present. One of them, Wilford Woodruff, has left a detailed account of what then transpired:

We walked from the north camp to about the centre between the two creeks, when President Young waved his hand and said: 'Here is the forty acres for the Temple. The city can be laid out perfectly square, north and south, east and west.' It was then moved and carried that the Temple lot contain forty acres on the ground where we stood. It was also moved and carried that the city be laid out into lots of ten rods by twenty each, exclusive of the streets, and into blocks of eight lots, being ten acres in each block, and one and a quarter in each lot.

It was further moved and carried that each street be laid out eight rods wide, and that there be a side-walk on each side, twenty feet wide, and that each house be built in the centre of the lot twenty feet from the front, that there might be uniformity throughout the city.

It was also moved that there be four public squares of ten acres each, to be laid out in various parts of the city for public grounds.[48]

Orson Pratt, one of the Apostles, records that the group decided to incorporate the lot system of alternating frontages as first prescribed by Smith: "Upon each alternate block four houses were to be built on the east, and four on the west sides of the square, but none on the north and south sides. But the blocks intervening were to have four houses on the north and four on the south. . . . In this plan there will be no houses fronting each other on the opposite side of the streets, while those on the same sides will be about eight rods apart, having gardens running back twenty rods to the center of the block."[49] That evening the entire pioneer party gathered to learn these details and to give unanimous approval.

When surveyors began to run the street lines of the new city and stake out the blocks and lots, it became apparent that the 40-acre area agreed on for the temple block was excessively large. On August 2 a conference was held to discuss this matter, but the issue was not resolved. Two days later, however, it was decided to reduce the temple site to ten acres, making it uniform in size with the other blocks of the city.[50]

The city as surveyed in the summer of 1847 is shown in Figure 9.9. This was but the first of several parts of the city, others being surveyed as additional town lots became necessary to accommodate newcomers. It seems strange that the temple block was given so little prominence in the city plan. Joseph's City of Zion design, it will be recalled, incorporated a tier of large blocks running through the town, with the three in the center set aside for temples and other church purposes. At the City of the Great Salt Lake—as the members present voted to name it—no such feature was allowed to interfere with the mathematical regularity of the prevailing checkerboard design.

The other major change from Smith's earlier design was the reduced number of larger lots in each block, Salt Lake City having eight lots to the block, each measuring ten by twenty rods rather than twenty lots each four by twenty rods. The reversed lot frontage, the very wide streets, and the building set-backs obviously came from the City of Zion plat.

The Salt Lake City land policy adopted by the Mormon leaders differed substantially from that followed by Smith at Nauvoo. Brigham Young, on the first Sabbath celebrated in the valley, proclaimed the general principle: "No man will be suffered to cut up his lot and sell a part to speculate out of his brethren. Each man must keep his lot whole, for the Lord has given it to us without price. . . . Every man should have his land measured off to him for city and farming purposes, what he could till. He might till as he pleased, but he should be industrious and take care of it."[51] While that policy was ultimately to be modified, it was generally followed in the earliest years at Salt Lake City and at many of the other Mormon communities established subsequently. Young also specified that all streams would be held in common ownership as would all timber lands. Because of the scarcity of trees in the arid site, restrictions were placed on their use for fuel.[52]

Church leaders were allowed first selection of blocks and lots for themselves and their friends. Apparently this procedure was determined by the Quorum of the Twelve without submitting the matter to a general meeting. There is, however, no record of any person objecting to this decision. Brigham Young chose the block lying immediately to the east of Temple Square. Later he was to receive much additional land adjacent to this first parcel.[53]

No other town lot grants were made at this time. Instead, all settlers were grouped inside an adobe enclosure or fort located on the public square four blocks south and three blocks west of the temple site. In September, after the arrival of a party of more than 1,500 emigrants, the fort was enlarged to enclose the blocks immediately to the north and south. In this restricted area about 450 cabins were built, the rear walls of which backed against the adobe wall.[54]

Crops had been planted by the vanguard group that had preceded Young's arrival by a few days. Other farming areas were put under cultivation to provide food for those remaining in the city and in anticipation of the needs of emigrants. The general allocation of farm lands was not carried out until the following year. Brigham Young outlined the plan that was to be followed: "It is our intention to have the five acre lots next to the city accommodate the mechanics and artisans, the ten acres next, then the twenty acres, followed by the forty and eighty acre lots, where farmers can build and reside. All these lots will be enclosed in one common fence, which will be seventeen miles and fifty-three rods long, eight feet high; and to the end that every man will be satisfied with his lot and prevent any hardness that might occur by any other method of dividing the land, we have proposed that it shall all be

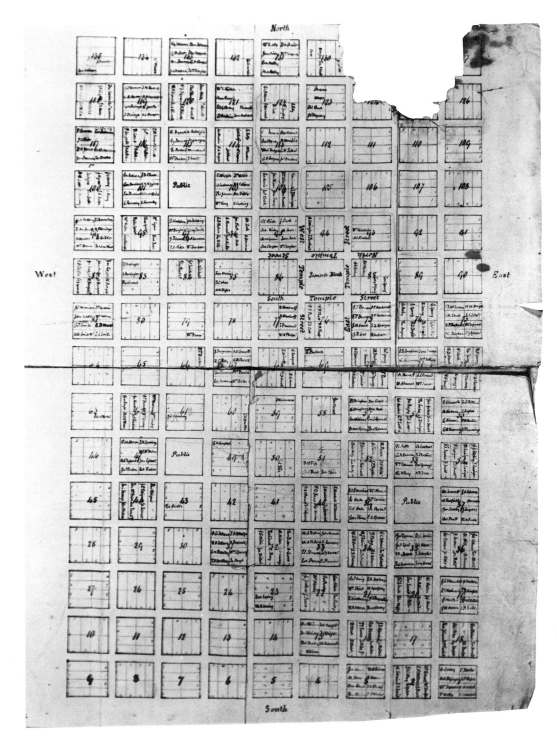

Figure 9.9 Plan of Salt Lake City, Utah: 1847

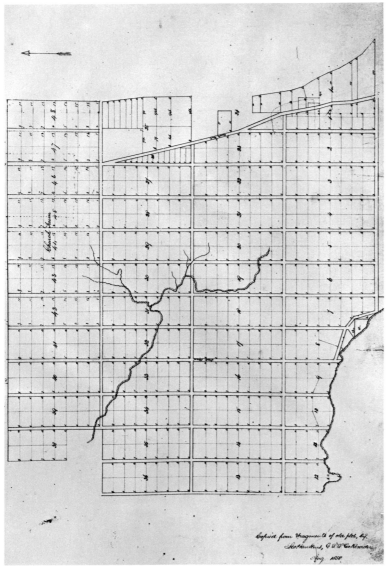

Figure 9.10 Map of Farm Tracts at Salt Lake City, Utah: 1858

done by ballot, or casting lots, as Israel did in the days of old."[55] Copies of several of these farm tract surveys have survived. Figure 9.10 shows the ten-acre plots in the so-called Big Field, which lay to the south of the city.

By October 10, 1847, all of the Mormon companies on the march to Utah from Winter Quarters had arrived in the new city—a total of slightly more than 2,000 persons.[56] While some of the emigrants began to plow, irrigate, and sow crops in the Big Field, which then consisted of some 5,000 acres, others helped construct cabins within the three blocks occupied by the fort and its extensions. These shelters were small and crowded. Eliza Snow described her accommodations as "a log-house about eighteen feet square, which constituted a portion of the east side of the fort. . . . This hut, like most of the those built the first year, was roofed with willows and earth, the roof having but a little pitch."[57] It was fortunate for these pioneers that the first winter they spent in the valley was comparatively mild. The major discomfort came in the spring when the roofs leaked, and the contents of most of the cabins were soaked.

That winter Bringham Young was in Winter Quarters to organize the migration for the spring and summer of 1848. On his journey eastward the previous September he wrote to Salt Lake City of his plans to arrange for the distribution of each Saint's "inheritance" of city lots and farming tracts. He instructed the members of the church to concentrate on completing the fort and to cultivate the farm fields in common for "should you spend the coming year in fencing individual lots, and building your home thereon, it will be impossible for you to furnish your families with bread and supply the demands of the emigration."[58]

The promised distribution of the inheritances took place in the fall of 1848. The blocks assigned to the elders of the church had already been allocated. Other members of the church now received their city lots by drawing numbers, a procedure supervised by Young and Heber C. Kimball. The only cost was a surveying and recording fee of $1.50. Farm parcels were allotted in the same manner. Regardless of the location of his five or ten-acre tract, each person was obligated to help construct the fence or wall around the Big Field in proportion to the size of his holding.[59]

With the influx of thousands of new settlers and the dismantling of the old forts it became necessary to survey additional city streets, blocks, and lots adjacent to the area planned in 1847. The older section was known as "plot A." It contained 135 blocks. In 1848 Plot B, with 63 blocks, and in 1849 Plot C, with 84 blocks, were laid out east and west of the original development on land that had been reserved for that

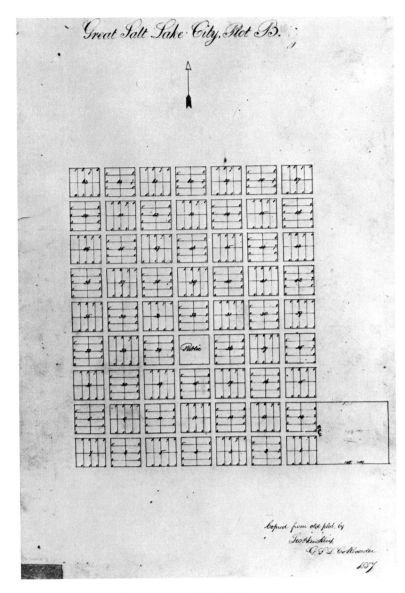

Figure 9.11 Plan of Salt Lake City, Utah: 1857

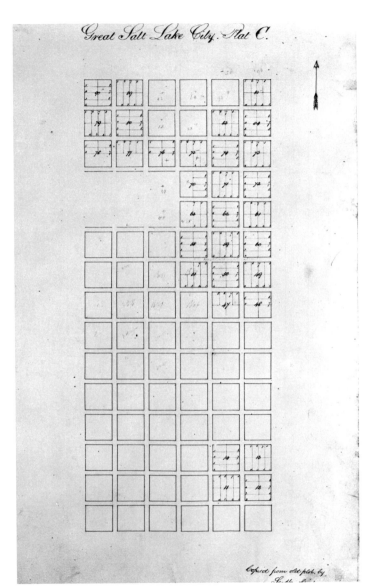

Figure 9.12 Plan of Salt Lake City, Utah: 1857

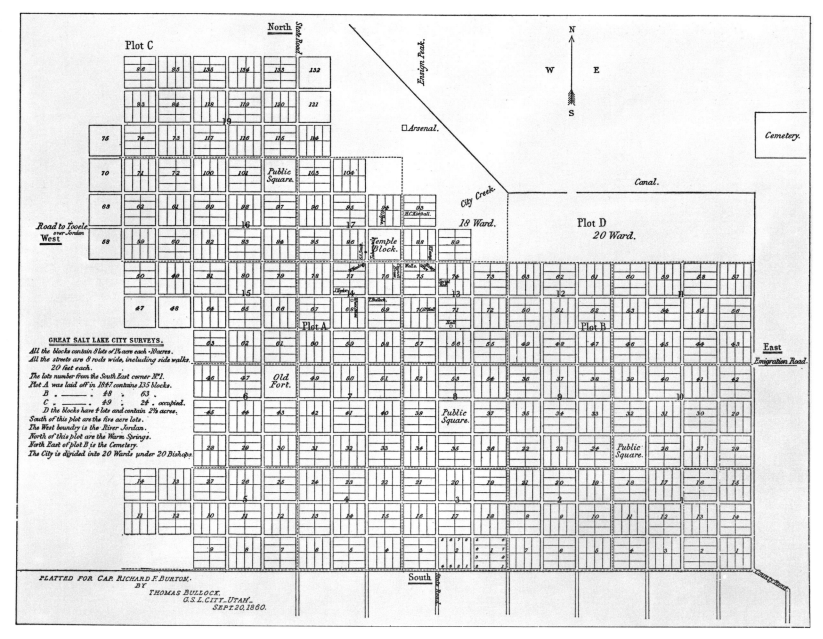

Figure 9.13 Plan of Salt Lake City, Utah: 1860

purpose. As can be seen in Figures 9.11 and 9.12, these new streets, blocks, and lots were uniform in dimensions to those surveyed at the time of initial settlement.

The overall plan of the city published to illustrate Richard Burton's *The City of the Saints* is reproduced in Figure 9.13, and depicts Salt Lake City as surveyed and extended through 1849.[60] South of the last street shown at the bottom of this plan lay the Big Field. Increased population made this, too, inadequate in size, and new farm tracts were laid out to the west of the city, beyond the Jordon River running north and south and connecting Utah Lake with the Great Salt Lake.

An early survey of this tract is reproduced in Figure 9.14. The lower and smaller portion of this plat shows the so-called Jordan Plot of farm parcels beyond the western addition to the city surveyed in 1849. The larger area identified as the Brighton Farming Plot lay to the south and west of the Jordan Plot. Here, too, farm parcels were allocated by lot. Since Mormon policy was to maintain all residences together rather than on individual farmsteads and because the Brighton farming tract was located some distance from Salt Lake City proper, a small portion of this parcel was laid out as an agricultural village. This is the section shown surveyed into 64 blocks and divided into smaller lots. This planned suburb was but one of many other new communities that occupied the attention of Brigham Young almost from the beginning of the settlement in Utah.

When Howard Stansbury arrived in Salt Lake City in August, 1849, to begin official government surveys, he was deeply impressed with what the Mormons had accomplished. It was, he said, "a city . . . . laid out upon a magnificent scale, being nearly four miles in length and three in breadth." He reported that it was "estimated to contain about eight thousand inhabitants and was divided into numerous wards, each at the time of our visit, enclosed by a substantial fence." Stansbury described the houses of the settlers as "principally, of adobe or sun-dried brick, which, when well covered with a tight projecting roof, make a warm, comfortable dwelling [and] present a very neat appearance." On the temple block he noted the construction of "an immense shed . . . which was capable of containing three thousand persons. It was called '*The Bowery*,' and served as a temporary place of worship, until the construction of the Great Temple."[61]

Four years later Frederick Hawkins Piercy sketched the infant city as it then appeared looking south from a point several hundred yards north of the temple block. Engraved and published in 1855 and reproduced here as Figure 9.15, it is a valuable record of early Salt Lake City,

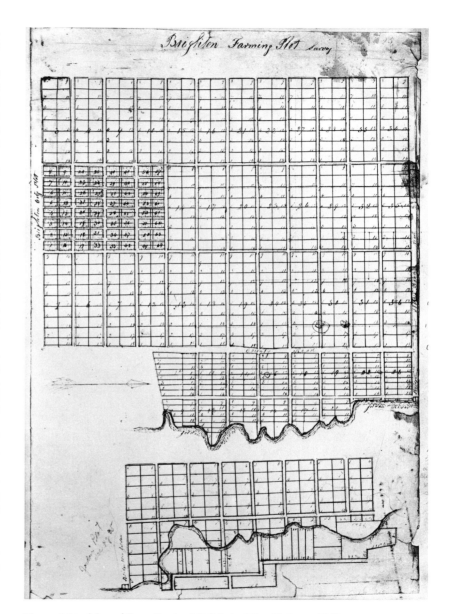

Figure 9.14 Map of Farm Tracts at Salt Lake City, Utah: ca. 1849

Figure 9.15 View of Salt Lake City, Utah: 1853

made all the more useful by these accompanying notes written by James Linforth: "The cluster of white buildings in the left . . . belonged to President B. Young until recently, when he donated them . . . to the P. E. [Perpetual Emigration] Fund. . . . The dark looking building to the right . . . and in the foreground, is President H. C. Kimball's. It was then unfinished. The street crossing the centre of the engraving, lies N. and S., and is called East Temple Street, proceeding down it, or south-ward, the largest building on the left is the Tithing Office and Church Store. A little lower down on the right, is the Council House. . . . Im-mediately in front of the Council House, and running to the extreme right of the engraving is Temple Block, on which are seen the Public Works to the left and the Tabernacle to the right."[62]

The "Public Works" referred to by Linforth consisted of a group of buildings on the northeast corner of the temple block. These housed shops for carpenters, masons, painters, and blacksmiths, all under the direction of a church-organized public works department established in 1850. Later, a machine shop, a foundry, and a nail factory were also constructed. This was all part of an intricate program designed to provide an industrial base for Salt Lake City and Utah, to furnish em-ployment for the thousands of emigrants attracted to the Mormon commonwealth from America and abroad, and, of course, to organize resources of men and materials for developing the city. In addition to construction of dozens of important church and civil buildings, the public works department also was responsible for building a high wall around the temple block and for completing nearly ten miles of a projected 20-mile, 12-foot-high wall that would have enclosed the entire city. The latter was essentially a "make-work" project, but it was also intended to furnish an example for settlers in other and smaller communities that were then being founded or were contemplated for the future.[63]

The days of trial, hostility, and persecution were not at an end, but the Mormons at last had found a region where their remarkable abilities in colonization and urban planning could be freely exercised. In Utah and in adjacent lands, the church would in the next few decades found scores of towns and bring under cultivation thousands of acres of semidesert land. The vision of Joseph Smith, the martyred prophet of the Mormons, was at last to become reality under the inspired leadership of his successor, Brigham Young.

X

Cities of the Saints: Mormon Town Planning in
the Great Basin Kingdom

BRIGHAM YOUNG's vision of the future extent of Mormon settlement and influence had almost continental dimensions. In March, 1849, he and his fellow Utah pioneers organized the provisional state of Deseret. Its proposed boundaries embraced the western half of Colorado, the southwestern quarter of Wyoming, the southern portion of Idaho, the southeastern corner of Oregon, the northwestern part of New Mexico, most of Arizona, all of Utah and Nevada, and the bulk of southern California from a point below Los Angeles to the Mexican border.

The map reproduced in Figure 10.1 shows a substantial portion of this area in 1855. Virtually all of the towns identified were established by the Mormons along with many smaller settlements that are not shown. With a very few exceptions, they came into existence as a result of a carefully planned and executed colonization program largely conceived by Brigham Young and administered by him and his subordinates. Young acted in a dual capacity. He was head of the church and also the elected governor of the provisional state of Deseret, which he sought to have admitted to the Union.

While waiting for this to occur, the Mormons elected members of the Deseret legislature, which proceeded to grant a charter to Salt Lake City and established other provisions for civil administration.[1] Legislative enactments and the officials selected to administer them supplemented church rules and officers, and Smith's position as head of both the religious and civil communities gave him enormous power. In founding more than 350 new communities during the three decades he lived in Utah, the Mormon leader used the resources of both church and state with remarkable wisdom and efficiency.[2]

Young employed systematic town founding as a method for expanding Mormon influence over an enormous region radiating outward from Salt Lake City. While he located most of the earliest communities in northern Utah, he established or planned others near the perimeter of the claimed borders of the state of Deseret and along the "Mormon Corridor," a chain of settlements extending south from Salt Lake City to the southern border of Utah and then leading southwest to the California coast via San Bernardino to San Diego.[3]

In the first ten years of colonization alone the Mormons created nearly one hundred new towns. By the end of the nineteenth century Mormon settlement in the Great Basin extended 1,000 miles north and south, 800 miles east and west, embraced an area of almost one-sixth of the United States, and consisted of at least 500 planned towns.[4]

This unprecedented achievement was made possible only through detailed planning of every aspect of settlement and the willing acceptance by colonists of the necessary discipline imposed by their civil and religious officials. The sequence of events that occurred and the planforms used at Salt Lake City served as a model for nearly all these ventures.

It may be useful to summarize the Mormon colonization process, in which town planning figured so prominently. It involved several steps. First, the general location of proposed settlement was determined. Then an exploring party was dispatched to determine the feasibility of settlement and the most advantageous sites. Colonists were then "called," as the selection process was known. Young chose persons with a variety of trades and skills that would be needed. He then provided the group with tools, implements, and supplies and dispatched them to the chosen site.[5]

When the cadre of settlers reached the selected location they began cultivating farm fields and constructing a fortified enclosure to protect the temporary cabin homes erected within. The following year surveyors would lay out the streets and lots for the town, generally following the pattern established at Salt Lake City. Colonists would receive their house lots and farm fields, and the new community would gradually take form. There were variations in this procedure. In some cases separate reconnaissance expeditions were not necessary because earlier explorations had furnished sufficient information about settlement sites. Nor were forts required at all new communities. And, as will be seen, not all the towns duplicated or followed closely the design of Salt Lake City.

It took a few years for this planned settlement policy to develop, and the first communities were established in a less systematic manner. In the fall of 1847 and the spring of the following year a few persons drove their cattle north of Salt Lake City in search of range land. Other persons joined them and sought permission to settle permanently in this area between the shore of Great Salt Lake and the Wasatch Range where mountain streams flowed across the plain to the lake. Farmington, Bountiful, Kaysville, and Centerville thus began their existence. At Bountiful the settlers grouped their cabins in a fort-like compound similar to that at Salt Lake City. The Kaysville settlers, on the other hand, elected to occupy rather widely scattered tracts in the vicinity of several springs.[6]

The plat of one of these early towns has survived, although it was drawn almost 20 years after initial colonization. As submitted to the General Land Office in 1868, the survey of Farmington appears in Figure 10.2. Possibly as extended before that time, the town was then laid out in blocks 495 feet square containing 6 lots, each slightly less than

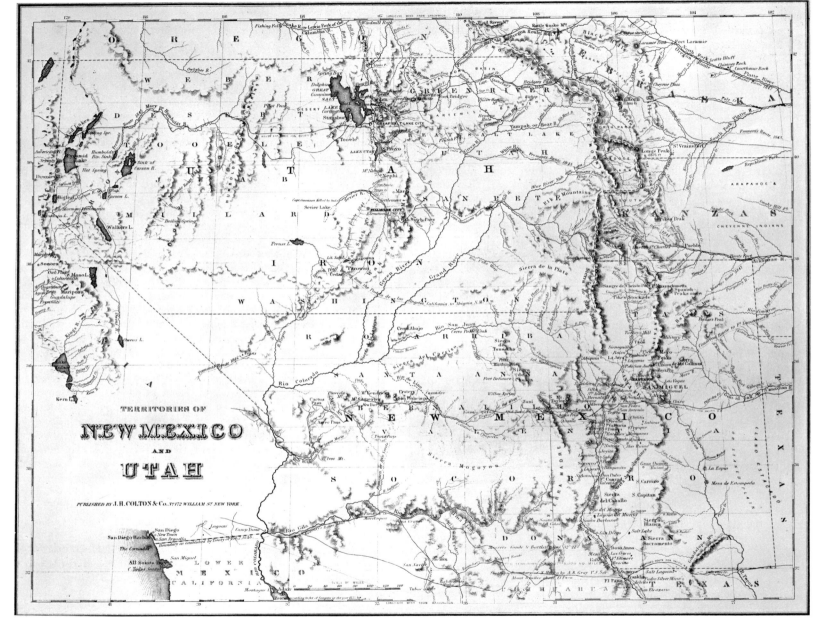

Figure 10.1 Map of New Mexico and Utah: 1855

one acre in area and bounded by streets uniformly 99 feet wide. No public square or church site is shown, and a further peculiarity is the pattern of reversed lot frontage. Instead of being arranged in alternate blocks, those blocks with lots fronting east or west occupy an area in the southwestern portion of the town.

A more important town was founded north of these settlements in the vicinity of the Ogden and Weber rivers. There Miles Goodyear had established a fur trading post as early as 1845. A few Mormons drifted northward to the site in 1847, and Captain James Brown of the Mormon Battalion bought the Goodyear tract, which included a fort.[7]

In 1849 the general conference of the church voted that a city should be created following an inspection of the site by Brigham Young, who recommended that the new town "should be laid out on the south side of Ogden River, at the point of bench land so that water from Weber and Ogden rivers might be taken out for irrigation and other purposes."[8] In 1850 Young established the basic plan for the city, advising the settlers "not to settle in the country but to move on to the city lots, build good houses, school houses, meeting houses, and other public buildings, fence their gardens and plant out fruit trees, that Ogden might be a permanent city and suitable headquarters for the northern country."[9]

After the city received its charter and the name of Ogden from the Deseret legislature early in 1851, Henry Sherwood surveyed the streets, blocks, and lots as planned by Brigham Young. The undated and fragmentary plat reproduced in Figure 10.3 shows Plots A and B as divided into square blocks of ten acres by 99-foot streets arranged in the familiar grid pattern. Each block was evidently intended to contain ten lots, and from the few that are so shown on the plat it is obvious that Joseph Smith's alternating system of reversed frontage was employed.

Portions of the surrounding land were also surveyed into farming tracts. Doubtless the most desirable were those located between the two rivers, where irrigation was easy. The five-acre farm parcels of Ogden are shown in Figure 10.4 as they existed in 1869. The seven larger squares at the right are the blocks at the western edge of the city. Two blocks to the east of Block 48 lay the square set aside for the Mormon Tabernacle. Three other blocks were reserved for public squares and the Tithing Yard of the Mormon Church. The street dividing the city from the five-acre farm parcels is Wall Avenue, so named from the eight-foot wall that was to have enclosed the town.[10]

Ogden's prosperity was aided by the construction of a road through the mountains from the east in the 1850s. This provided easier access to the Great Basin and became the principal route of Mormon immigrants

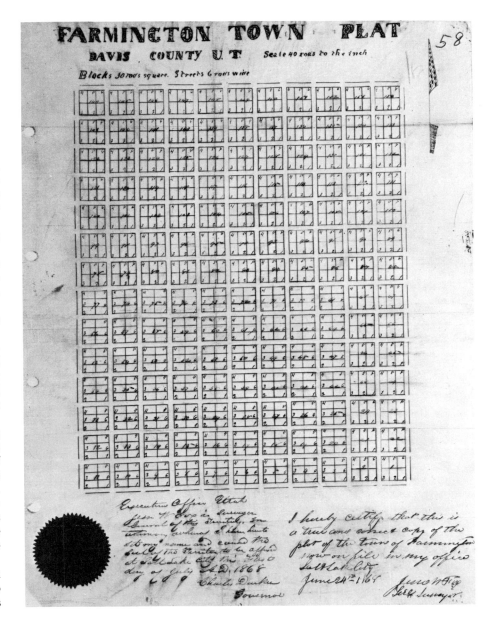

Figure 10.2 Plan of Farmington, Utah: 1868

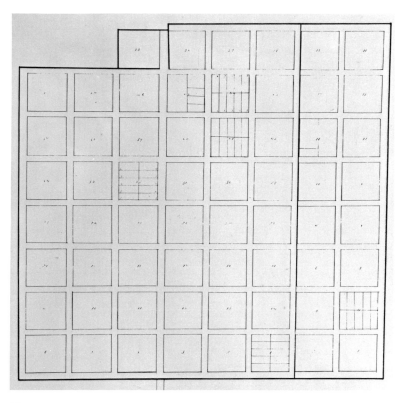

Figure 10.3 Plan of Ogden, Utah: ca. 1851

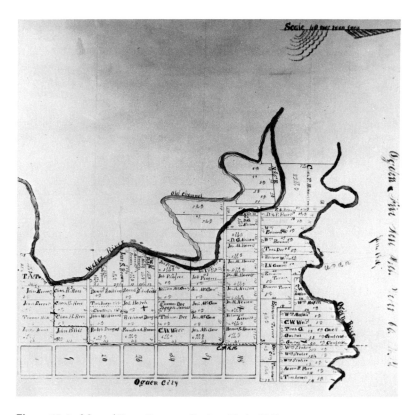

Figure 10.4 Map of Farm Tracts at Ogden, Utah: 1869

and, later, the Union Pacific Railroad. The arrival of the first locomotive on March 3, 1869, was a day of triumphant celebration.

Salt Lake City, bypassed by the transcontinental road, needed a connection, and in May Brigham Young began construction of the Utah Central line from the chief Mormon city to its now rapidly growing sister town 39 miles to the north. Completed in 1870 as the Utah Central Railroad, it continued northward under the name of the Utah Northern Railroad, reaching Logan in 1873 and Silver Bow, Montana, in 1880.

In its role as the transportation center of Utah, Ogden enjoyed rapid growth. By 1860 the town had nearly 1,500 persons. This doubled in the next ten years, and by 1880 reached 6,000. In 1890 there were more than 12,000 residents. The view of Ogden reproduced in Figure 10.5 shows the city from the southwest in 1875, when the original city tract was almost fully occupied. Ogden was a bustling town with its three railroads and its woolen, lumber, and flour mills, and other industries. The view also identifies two breweries—manufacturers of a product forbidden to Mormons. Ogden's railroads and its favorable commerical location attracted a substantial Gentile population, and the relations between the Mormon settlers and the newcomers of other faiths—or none—was not always the most cordial.[11] In this respect Ogden was to

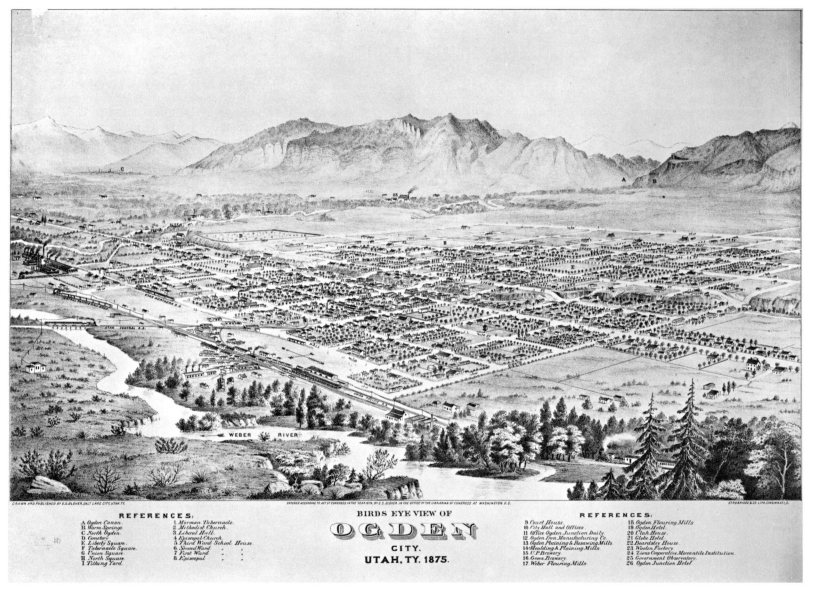

BIRDS EYE VIEW OF

OGDEN

CITY.

UTAH, TY. 1875.

REFERENCES:

A Ogden Canon.
B Warm Springs.
C North Ogden.
D Cemetery
E Liberty Square.
F Tabernacle Square.
G Union Square.
H North Square.
I Tithing Yard.

1 Mormon Tabernacle.
2 Methodist Church.
3 Liberal Hall.
4 Episcopal Church.
5 Third Ward School House.
6 Second Ward " "
7 First Ward " "
8 Episcopal " "

REFERENCES:

9 Court House.
10 City Hall and Offices.
11 Office Ogden Junction Daily.
12 Ogden Iron Manufacturing Co.
13 Ogden Plaining & Resawing Mills.
14 Moulding & Plaining Mills.
15 U.P.Brewery.
16 Grove Brewery.
17 Weber Flouring Mills.

18 Ogden Flouring Mills.
19 Ogden Hotel.
20 Utah House.
21 Globe Hotel.
22 Beardsley House.
23 Woolen Factory.
24 Zions Cooperative Mercantile Institution.
25 Government Observatory.
26 Ogden Junction Hotel.

Figure 10.5   View of Ogden, Utah: 1875

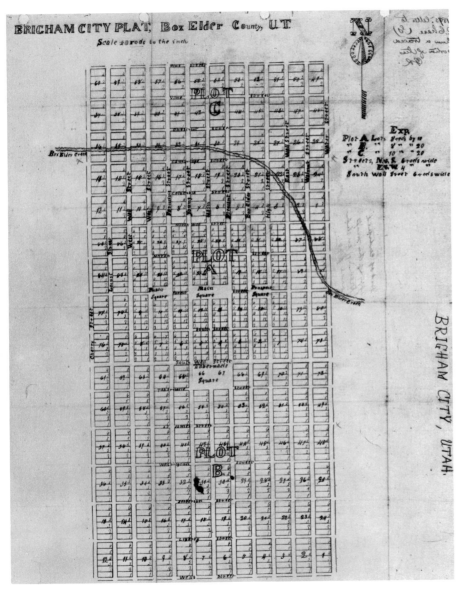

Figure 10.6 Plan of Brigham City, Utah: 1868

foreshadow developments at other Mormon settlements in Utah as Gentile population gradually penetrated what was at first the exclusive province of the Saints.[12]

Twenty miles north of Ogden several Mormon families settled on Box Elder Creek in 1850. Others joined them and helped to construct a fort as protection against possible Indian attack. This little community of some 200 persons began to farm on the nearby lands and in the spring of 1852 demolished the fort. Renewed fears of Indian raids caused Brigham Young to order a new fort built the next year, and then, in the fall of 1854 he dispatched Apostle Lorenzo Snow to lead 50 additional families to this area and organize the community more efficiently.[13]

Snow directed surveyor Jesse W. Fox to run new surveys. The former farm tracts of 40 and 80 acres were revised in keeping with the emerging Mormon policy to limit farms to small tracts of five to 10 acres. Fox surveyed a Big Field into small parcels and, doubtless under Snow's supervision, laid out the town site, which received the name of Brigham City. The initial plan for Brigham City occupies the middle part of the plat reproduced in Figure 10.6 and identified on that drawing as "Plot A."

Snow and Fox made no attempt to duplicate the design of Salt Lake City. All lots in the first section of the city as well as in the two later additions shown on the plan face east or west. In Plot A, lots were laid out 8 by 10 rods, and, except for the outermost two tiers of blocks on the east and west, were arranged in double tiers in each block. Plots B and C were surveyed in blocks with all lots running through from one street to the next and thus having double frontage. In Plot B lots measured 8 by 20 rods, and in Plot C the dimensions were 10 by 20 rods.

Unlike those in most Mormons towns, streets were not of identical width. All north-south streets were made 6 rods or 99 feet wide, as was South Wall Street running along the north side of Tabernacle Square. All other east-west streets were given a width of 4 rods or 66 feet. In another departure from standardized Mormon town planning, the design of Brigham City included an element of axial arrangement of streets and public squares. In most Utah towns with public squares, streets form the four borders, the square being simply a city block not divided into building lots. Here, on the other hand, the Main Square at the center and Prospect Square and Public Square each one block away on the east and west were arranged to be entered at the midpoints of their east and west sides. The effect was to interrupt Forest Street—the central east-west thoroughfare in Plot A—by a series of three open spaces. This provided an opportunity to locate public buildings on the axis of Forest Street and, if Main Square and Tabernacle Square had been retained as consolidated open spaces, on the north-south axis of Main Street running through the city from north to south.

Unfortunately, this opportunity for a more formal placement of important buildings was lost except on the east side of Main Square. This square itself was soon divided into two blocks with the extension of Main Street through its center. On the eastern block thus created, the Box Elder County courthouse was erected on the axis of Forest Street. The Tabernacle, eventually built on the square set aside for this purpose, might have been placed in the center of its assigned site. Instead, it, too, was built on the eastern half of the square rather than placed to terminate the view up and down Main Street. Formal axial design was either deliberately avoided by Mormon planners and builders or, more likely, was simply not understood as a device to provide greater visual interest and variety to the physical fabric of the city.

These buildings and the other structures of the thriving city appear in the view of 1875 reproduced in Figure 10.7. Served by the Union Pacific and the Utah Northern railways, Brigham City found itself advantageously located for trade, commerce, and industry. But the city owed its prosperity mainly to the energy and remarkable administrative abilities of Lorenzo Snow. In 1864 he organized a cooperative enterprise in which many citizens of Brigham City bought shares. This organization quickly broadened its activities from retail sales to include a wide variety of manufacturing. Virtually the entire economy of the city came under its jurisdiction, and most of the citizens were both stockholders and employees. Dividends were paid only in goods rather than cash, the stockholders receiving scrip redeemable for merchandise and supplies. The legend below the view in Figure 10.7 lists some of the principal manufacturing plants of the Brigham City Cooperative Mercantile and Manufacturing Company, which are shown occupying an industrial compound near the lower left-hand corner.[14]

Ogden and Brigham City clearly dominated the region north of Salt Lake City in trade, transportation, and industry. As religious centers, however, they were overshadowed by another planned city still further to the north about 20 miles below the Idaho border. This was Logan, the site of a Mormon Temple—one of only four in Utah, the others being at Salt Lake City, Manti, and St. George.

Logan was but one of several Mormon towns located in the Cache Valley of northern Utah in the late 1850s and 1860s. They included Wellsville, founded in 1856 by Peter Maughan, who had been selected for this task by Brigham Young; Mendon in 1857; and Smithfield and Providence in 1859.[15] At each location the settlers followed the instructions sent by Young: "Each settlement should by all means make a good strong fort to include all the inhabitants thereof, and large enough to store all their grain therein, with strong corrals adjoining, to secure all the stock in case of trouble with the Indians."[16]

The settlement at Logan in 1859 took this same form. On June 21 the Mormon pioneers drew lots for their farm tracts, and five weeks later received their lots in the fort in the same manner. The following spring Bishop William Preston and Surveyor Jesse Fox planned the city.[17] Figure 10.8 shows the design of the town as it had been extended from time to time during the first 60 years of its existence. With a few exceptions, these additions continued the traditional pattern of square blocks, gridiron streets, and alternating lot frontages that Preston and Fox used for their original surveys.

In 1859 thoughts of a temple would have been premature. Doubtless the tabernacle block was reserved at that time, but more mundane tasks than temple building occupied the settlers: building houses, digging irrigation ditches, and planting and harvesting crops. As the Cache Valley rapidly attracted additional settlers, Logan grew more rapidly than its older sister communities and the many other new towns that were established elsewhere in the region. In 1866 it received its charter as a city.

Three years earlier at a great meeting of church authorities, Apostle Wilford Woodruff predicted that the community would be selected as the site of a temple. Brigham Young, following Woodruff to the platform in the Bowery, announced "All that Brother Woodruff has said is revelation and will be fulfilled."[18] In 1877 the aging Brigham Young, in one of his last official acts, visited Logan to designate the temple site on a commanding elevation 90 feet higher than the nearby Tabernacle Square.

This limestone building with ornamented mouldings of sandstone is shown in Figure 10.9 shortly after its completion in 1884. Its two end towers soar 170 feet above the ground and provide a distinctive landmark that can be seen for miles. From its towers the masons engaged in its construction could gaze across the valley at the other Mormon towns now outstripped by Logan in both size and religious significance: Providence, Millville, Hyrum, Wellsville, Mendon, Paradise, Bensen, Hyde Park, Smithfield, and Weston.[19]

While these towns near the northern limits of the Mormon domain were being planned and developed, Brigham Young was busily engaged in creating even more settlements to the south of the Great Salt

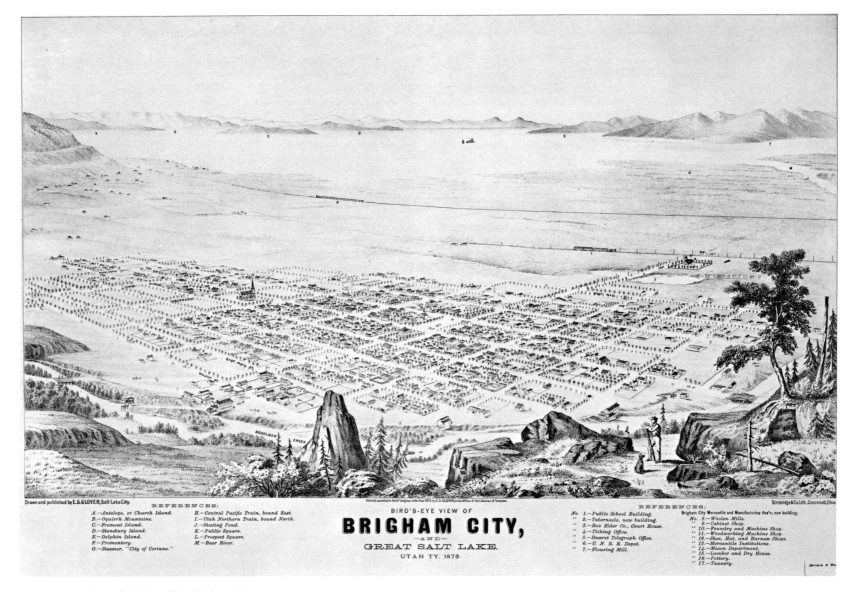

BIRD'S-EYE VIEW OF

BRIGHAM CITY,

—AND—

GREAT SALT LAKE.

UTAH TY. 1875.

REFERENCES:

A.—*Antelope, or Church Island.*
B.—*Oquirrh Mountains.*
C.—*Fremont Island.*
D.—*Stansbury Island.*
E.—*Dolphin Island.*
F.—*Promontory.*
G.—*Steamer, "City of Corinne."*

H.—*Central Pacific Train, bound East.*
I.—*Utah Northern Train, bound North.*
J.—*Skating Pond.*
K.—*Public Square.*
L.—*Prospect Square.*
M.—*Bear River.*

No. 1.—*Public School Building.*
" 2.—*Tabernacle, now building.*
" 3.—*Box Elder Co., Court House.*
" 4.—*Tithing Office.*
" 5.—*Deseret Telegraph Office.*
" 6.—*U. N. R. R. Depot.*
" 7.—*Flouring Mill.*

REFERENCES:

Brigham City Mercantile and Manufacturing Ass'n, now building.

No. 8.—*Woolen Mills.*
" 9.—*Cabinet Shop.*
" 10.—*Foundry and Machine Shop.*
" 11.—*Woodworking Machine Shop.*
" 12.—*Shoe, Hat, and Harness Shops.*
" 13.—*Mercantile Institutions.*
" 14.—*Mason Department.*
" 15.—*Lumber and Dry House.*
" 16.—*Pottery.*
" 17.—*Tannery.*

Figure 10.7 View of Brigham City, Utah: 1875

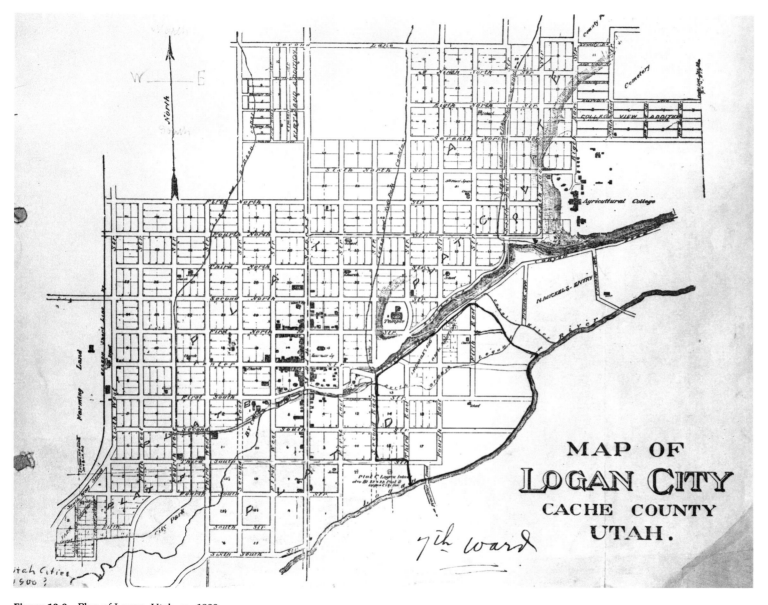

Figure 10.8 Plan of Logan, Utah: ca. 1900

Figure 10.9 View of the Mormon Temple at Logan, Utah: 1889

there only a few days after his arrival in Utah as leader of the Pioneer Company. Several families braved the terrible winter of 1849-50, and others joined this vanguard in the spring. They constructed a fort for protection against Indian raids, and in the autumn of 1853 Young sent Jesse Fox to survey the townsite of Tooele City near the mouth of Settlement Creek Canyon.[20]

Figure 10.10 shows Fox's plan for Tooele. It was designed on a generous scale, measuring about a mile and a half by a mile and a quarter. Fox provided lots of two sizes: 5 by 20 rods (82½ by 330 feet), and 10 by 20 rods. The larger lots containing one and a quarter acres predominated. While Fox employed the usual grid street pattern, streets were not of uniform width, and there was considerable variation in block size as a result of differences in distances between some of the east-west streets. Main Street, platted 7½ rods (123¾ feet), was curiously off-center, there being one more tier of blocks to the west than on the east side of town. Vine Street, 6 rods wide, was the principal east-west street. All other streets parallel to Vine were 4 rods in width. Fox laid out other north-south streets 5 and 6 rods wide and in addition provided a system of alleys running north and south, all of which were about 2 rods in width.

This city was partly walled in the spring of 1854 when the Ute Indians began their attacks on the southern settlements. The wall was intended to enclose the four southerly blocks platted in smaller lots, but the northwest portion was never completed.[21] Tooele's population was increased in 1853 when Brigham Young directed two of the Apostles to assemble 50 families and move them to the new city. Earlier, in January, the legislature granted Tooele its charter, and some years later designated it as the county seat, succeeding Richville. Growth was relatively slow despite these efforts to promote settlement in the area. In 1863 there were only 602 persons living in the town, and 25 years later the population was no more than 1,200.[22] Its residents engaged primarily in farming some 1,500 acres of small irrigated agricultural plots laid out by Fox at the time the city and its surrounding lands were platted.

Many other communities in the Tooele Valley and in Rush Valley to the south were developed in similar fashion, although in the absence of early plats it is impossible to say whether or not they resembled Tooele City in its design or followed more closely the pattern of Salt Lake City. These included Lake View, Batesville, E. T. City, Clover, Lake Point, Saint John, and Vernon.

More attractive for settlement was the potentially fertile crescent between the eastern shore of Utah Lake and the Wasatch. By 1851 a series

Lake and in the many valleys along the western slopes of the Wasatch Range. West of Salt Lake Valley and separated from it by the Oquirrh Mountains, the Tooele Valley attracted the attention of the Mormons almost from the beginning. Brigham Young led an exploring party

of new towns created under the supervision of the church stretched southward from Lehi and American Fork at the north end of the lake: Pleasant Grove, Provo, Springville, Spanish Fork, Payson, and Alpine.[23] Settlement began in the spring of 1849 when a group of 30 families led by John Higbee, who had explored the valley with Parley Pratt the previous year, built Fort Utah on the Timpanogas or Provo River. Stansbury's view of Fort Utah is shown in Figure 10.11, its appearance doubtless resembling the other forts built by Mormon settlers at many other locations. A log wall 14 feet high enclosed a quadrangle about 20 rods wide east and west and 40 rods north and south. The cabins were located close to the stockade, leaving an open space where the settlers erected a raised platform for their cannon.[24]

In September Brigham Young arrived at Provo to inspect the progress of settlement. On that visit he chose a site for the town two miles southeast of the fort. There a second fort was constructed, and in 1850 surveyor William Lemon began to stake out the streets, blocks, and town lots. The plan that he followed, reproduced in Figure 10.12, was a version of one announced by President Young the year before but now slightly modified in its dimensions.[25]

In its uniformity and symmetry the Provo plan recalled that of Salt Lake City. The dimensions, however, differed from its prototype. Eleven blocks square, the town occupied just over one square mile. All streets were to be five rods (82½ feet) wide, all lots 4 by 12 rods (66 by 198 feet, or three-tenths of an acre), and each block 24 rods square divided into 12 lots. Although the lines on the now faded and time-stained drawing are very faint, it can be seen that the orientation of the lots follow the system of alternating frontages that go back to Smith's City of Zion design. Five blocks were set aside for special purposes. That in the center, of course, was for the church. Blocks 25, 31, 91, and 97 were reserved for schools, each located conveniently in the center of the four quadrants of the city.

When Jules Remy visited Provo in 1855 only five years after its birth he found that it "was already a tolerably large town, well built, and one of the most important in the Territory, containing three thousand inhabitants." Its progress from a raw, frontier post to a more civilized state had been swift: "There is a public library, a musical society, a company of amateur actors, a town-hall, a church with its *bowery*, a building used as a tithe-warehouse, a seminary, five schools, and two hotels."[26]

Seventy miles south of Provo and 130 miles from Salt Lake City near the center of the Sanpete Valley Brigham Young laid the foundations

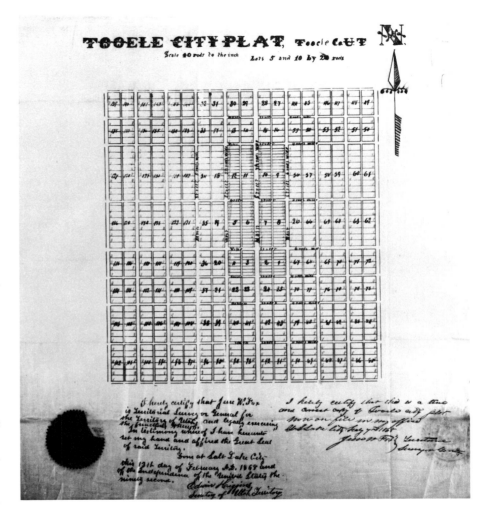

Figure 10.10   Plan of Tooele, Utah: 1868

Figure 10.11 View of Fort Utah near Provo, Utah: 1849

for another city in 1850. The year before, as was his custom, Young dispatched Isaac Morley and 30 men to begin the process of settlement. Leaving Salt Lake City in October, Morley's party was augmented along the way by other Mormons seeking new homes, and it was a group of 124 men and 100 women who finally arrived to spend the severe winter of 1849-50 huddled in dugouts, cabins, tents, and wagons. Less than half the livestock survived, but by May the colonists had managed to plant their first crops.[27]

Young arrived on August 4, 1850, selected the town site, and set William Lemon to work running the necessary surveys. Named for an ancient Nephite City mentioned in the *Book of Mormon*, Manti was designated by Brigham Young as the site of a temple, and the drawing dat-

ing from that year reproduced in Figure 10.13 shows the temple block as then reserved. It was one of 110 city blocks each 26 rods square divided into 8 lots each and bounded by streets uniformly platted 6 rods wide.[28] Here, too, the lot pattern echoed the Salt Lake City system with its alternating frontage pattern.

Manti, like so many other Mormon towns of the period, had a fortified enclosure. As described in the *Deseret News* for June 27, 1852, the Manti fort "has a gate on the west side in the center of the wall, and round bastions at the northwest and southwest corners. The wall is eight feet [high] and two feet thick and is set upon a foundation of stone three feet wide. The fort cost 610 days labor for men and boys over sixteen, 85 for boys under sixteen, and 125 days' team work."[29]

Other towns in the Sanpete Valley soon followed: Spring City, Mount Pleasant, and Ephraim, among them.[30] Although distant from the main Mormon base of Salt Lake City, these towns represented only the beginning of Brigham Young's ambitious colonization movement to the southwest. His plans were already taking form for a string of settlements extending from Salt Lake City all the way to the California coast. Along this corridor Mormon emigrants were to make their way to the new homeland. Towns in the southwest valleys of Utah would be needed for this purpose. Settlement in the area was hastened when Young received the welcome news that Parley Pratt's exploring party had discovered a deposit of iron ore near Little Salt Lake, which occupied a valley 250 miles south of Salt Lake City.

Young "called" Apostle George A. Smith to lead a group of settlers. Young and Smith then selected several members of the new colony and asked for volunteers to fill the remaining ranks. The party gathered at Provo in December, 1850. Equipment and supplies were carefully selected to provide the essentials needed until the new community could become self-sustaining.[31] Reaching the vicinity of the iron deposit in the middle of January, the settlers immediately set about the many tasks necessary to create their new community, which received the name of Parowan. Matthew Carruthers, one of the group, recalled the sequence of activities two years later:

"We formed our wagons into two parallel lines, some seventy paces apart. We then took our boxes from the wheels, and planted them a couple of paces from each other, so securing ourselves that we could not easily be taken advantage of by any unknown foe. This done, we next cut a road up the kanyon. . . . We next built a large meeting house . . . two stories high. . . . We next built a large square fort, with commodious cattle corral inside the enclosure. The houses were built some of hewn logs, and some of adobes, all neat comfortable and convenient. We next inclosed a field some five by three miles square, with a good ditch and pole fence. We dug canals and water ditches to the distance of some thirty or forty miles. One canal to turn the water of another creek upon the field for irrigating purposes, was seven miles long. We built a saw and a grist mill in the spring."[32]

The five-acre farming plots were distributed by drawing lots. John D. Lee described the procedure used at Parowan, doubtless similar to methods employed at many other settlements: "Each lot having been numbered previous on the stakes . . . each man's name applying for a lot formed a ticket which tickets was thrown together in a hat and shook up together then drawn out one by one . . . the first name drawn

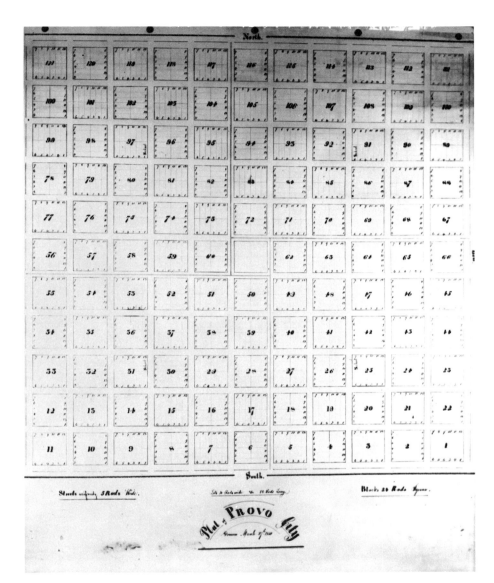

Figure 10.12 Plan of Provo, Utah: 1850

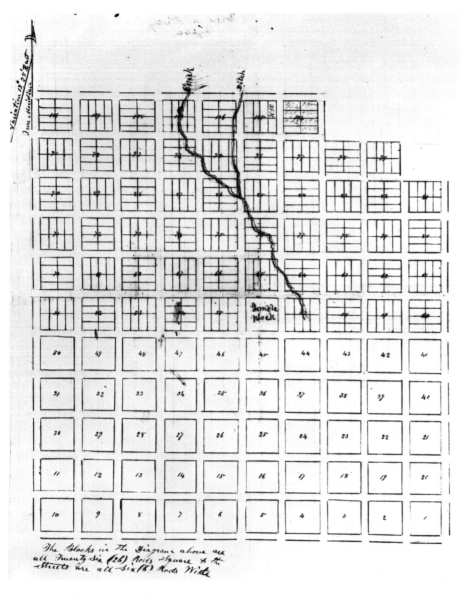

The blocks in the diagram above are all Twenty six (26) Rods Square & the streets are all Six (6) Rods Wide

Figure 10.13   Plan of Manti, Utah: 1850

took the first lot . . . which was number 2, Pres. Smith having taken number 1."[33]

Parowan thus began its existence, and in the fall of 1851 a second settlement was made 19 miles to the southwest. This was Cedar City, whose town plat was surveyed on November 4 by William H. Dame. It was shortly populated by a group of miners and iron workers from England, Scotland, and Wales who had recently arrived in the Great Basin.[34]

Mining and manufacturing of iron proved far more difficult than anticipated. Eventually the entire operation had to be abandoned, and the dream of a great industrial center in southern Utah evaporated.[35] Cedar City was eventually re-located a mile from its original site, and on this new location achieved some success as a farming and stock-raising center. Parowan, although incorporated as one of the five cities of the state of Deseret in 1851, dwindled in importance. When Remy visited the community in 1855 he could describe it only as "nothing more than a poor straggling village. . . . Its growth does not appear to have realized the expectations entertained of it."[36]

During the first five years of Mormon settlement in the Great Basin, the great majority of new towns was founded to the south and west of Salt Lake City. Recognizing that this first Mormon stronghold thus no longer occupied a position at the center of population, Brigham Young in 1851 resolved to locate the capital of the territory in the Pauvan Valley about half the distance from Salt Lake City to the present southern border of Utah. In October, Governor Young signed a joint resolution authorizing him to appoint a committee to select a site and to provide for the erection of public buildings for governmental purposes. A separate act of the legislature established Millard County and specified that the seat of government should be located there and called Fillmore City.[37]

Bishop Anson Call received instructions to recruit a group of 50 families to settle the place, but Brigham Young himself with a party of church officials and the members of the site selection committee traveled to the location to pick the exact location. On October 28 Young and the committee chose a spot on Chalk Creek at the foot of the Pavant Range 150 miles south of Salt Lake City. That same day Jesse Fox set to work surveying the city as an exact duplicate of Salt Lake City using streets 132 feet wide intersecting at right angles to form square blocks 10 acres in area, each with lots one and a quarter acres in size.[38]

Fillmore at first showed every sign of becoming a major town. Young encouraged church officials to acquire lots in the new community, and he "called" selected families from other settlements to move there. Anson Call soon completed a sawmill and a school, but because of the dry and rocky ground, it proved impossible to erect a stockaded fort as Young had advised. Instead, the settlers built their houses close together to enclose a central space and omitted doors or windows on the exterior walls. Work also began on the Capitol, and by December, 1855, its south wing was completed.

This building was intended as only the first part of an elaborate structure to take the form of a Greek cross with a 60-foot rotunda at the center. Figure 10.14 shows the Capitol at the right of the town, then surrounded by a wall 10 feet high and a quarter of a mile on each side. This was the Fillmore that welcomed Governor Young and the territorial legislature when they assembled on December 7, 1855, for their first meeting in the new capital city. It was also the only such occasion, for a year later the seat of government was returned to Salt Lake City. Fillmore, thus deprived of its principal reason for existence, settled into the usual role of a Mormon agricultural community.[39]

Cedar City and Parowan served as way stations on the Mormon Corridor. From Cedar City this took a southwesterly direction across the southeastern tip of what is now the state of Nevada. There Young determined in 1855 to establish a post that could also serve as a mission where Mormon doctrine might be introduced to the Indians of the area. Young called William Bringhurst for this task, and in June a party of 30 arrived at the Las Vegas springs. Construction of a fort was the first order of business, and by the end of the year an adobe and log structure enclosed an area 150 feet square, near which quarter-acre garden lots and 15-acre farming tracts were surveyed. Apparently no town lots were laid out, the settlement being intended merely as a mission and garrison community.[40]

A larger and far more important community began to take form much farther to the west. This was San Bernardino, California, founded in 1851 at the western end of Cajon Pass providing access to southern California between the San Gabriel and the San Bernardino Mountains. Amasa M. Lyman and Charles C. Rich led a party of nearly 500 Saints to this area that Mormon explorers earlier had noted as a possible town site. For $77,500 they acquired a Spanish *rancho* of more than 35,000 acres, constructed a fort 720 feet by 300 feet, and surveyed 1300 acres of land for sowing grain, another tract of 300 acres for vegetables, and began planting a vineyard.[41]

Surveying for the town began in 1852, but not until the fall of the following year did surveyor Henry G. Sherwood complete his work.[42]

Sherwood's town plat followed the design of Salt Lake City, as Figure 10.15 reveals. Dimensions of streets, blocks, and lots in San Bernardino, however, were not quite so generous. Streets were 5 rods wide, all blocks 36 rods square, and each was divided into 8 lots measuring 9 by 18 rods. A temple block was reserved in anticipation that San Bernardino would become the religious center for the California Mormon communities.[43] Development of agriculture and industry was rapid, the city was incorporated in 1854, and one observer in that year noted that "at least one hundred new buildings have been put up within the last four months." He estimated the population then at 1,200, noting that "a large immigration is now on the way from Salt Lake."[44]

San Bernardino, although by far the largest, was but one of several Mormon settlements that Brigham Young established around the distant borders of the Great Basin. In 1853 Young sent Orson Hyde and a settlement party to establish a base at or near James Bridger's fort in the southwestern corner of Wyoming. They eventually acquired the fort, founded a town known as Fort Supply 12 miles to the southwest, and, in 1857, surveyed a second town between these two locations called City Supply.[45]

Another settlement along the northern boundary of the Mormon domain lay well to the northwest in Idaho on the south fork of the Salmon River. Here, some 380 miles from Salt Lake City, a small group of pioneers established Fort Lemhi in June, 1855. When Brigham Young visited the location 11 months later, he found a small stockade near which 22 five-acre farming lots had been surveyed. On his advice the missionaries constructed a nine-foot high wall enclosing a space 16 rods square adjacent to the first fortification. By the fall new settlers brought the population to about 100 persons.[46]

Even more distant from the Utah settlements were the Mormon communities in western Nevada. Some of their residents had served in the Mormon Battalion and had passed through the Carson Valley on their travels to Salt Lake City from California, where they had been released from service. Most of them could be found at Mormon Station—a place established in 1849 and also known as Reese's Station. Organized colonization directed by the church began in 1856, when Orson Hyde laid out streets and blocks at Mormon Station and named the town Genoa. He also planned a second town in the Washoe Valley called Franktown.[47]

Five years after the Mormons arrived in the Great Basin, the church announced in public what had long been practiced by a small minority of Mormons—the doctrine of plural marriage. This aggravated tensions

Figure 10.14 View of Fillmore, Utah: 1855

that already were building between the church and the federal government. When Congress created the territory of Utah in 1850, its boundaries, while generous, were much smaller than the area claimed by the state of Deseret.[48] President Fillmore appointed Brigham Young territorial governor and named three other Mormons to positions of importance, but he also appointed three non-Mormons to major posts. Conflicts over administrative policy inevitably occurred between the Gentile appointees and those Mormons occupying governmental positions who viewed federal power as a threat to the combined spiritual and secular authority exercised by the church.

Associate Justice Perry Brocchus, invited to address a general conference of the church in 1851, alluded to the still covert practice of polygamy in a manner many considered highly offensive, and Brigham Young rebuked him publicly with heated words. Shortly thereafter the territorial secretary, supported by Brocchus and Chief Justice Lemuel Brandenbury, objected to the method used to apportion representation for the territorial legislature, records were impounded to be taken to Washington, and Secretary Broughton Harris and the two judges left their offices for the national capital.

More serious were later disagreements culminating in the destruction by a group of militant Mormons of the personal library and papers of Judge George P. Stiles, and the scandalous behaviour of Judge W. W. Drummond who arrived in Utah with one Ada Carroll, a woman not his wife whose occasional presence on the bench beside the judge infuriated the Mormons. Public outcry in the East over the polygamy issue continued to mount. The Republican convention in 1856 adopted a resolution condemning polygamy and slavery as twin evils. President Buchanan the following year announced Young's removal as territorial governor and directed an army of federal troops to escort the new governor, Alfred Cumming, to Salt Lake City.

Memories of persecutions at the hands of civil and military authorities during their wanderings from Ohio to Missouri and Illinois were rekindled by these events. Young acted to mobilize his people. He sent orders to all the outlying Mormon colonies directing their residents to return promptly to Utah from such distant places as San Bernardino, Nevada, and the Salmon River. Hundreds of the faithful obeyed, selling their lands for what they could or abandoning them altogether, never to return. Meanwhile, when government troops neared Utah, Lot Smith led a band of guerrilla fighters to burn off forage lands between South Pass and Fort Bridger and to destroy government supply wagons. Colonel Albert S. Johnston's troops were forced to spend the

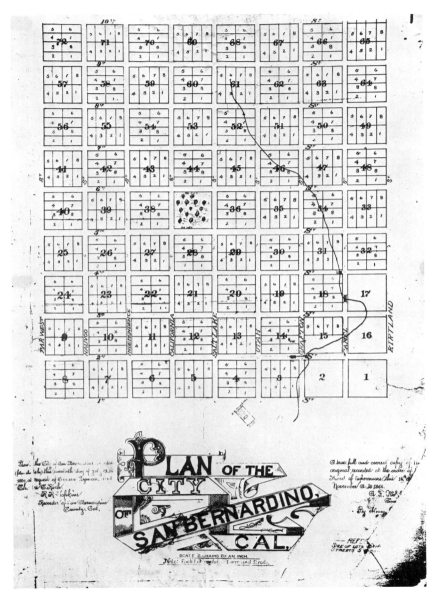

Figure 10.15 Plan of San Bernardino, California: 1854

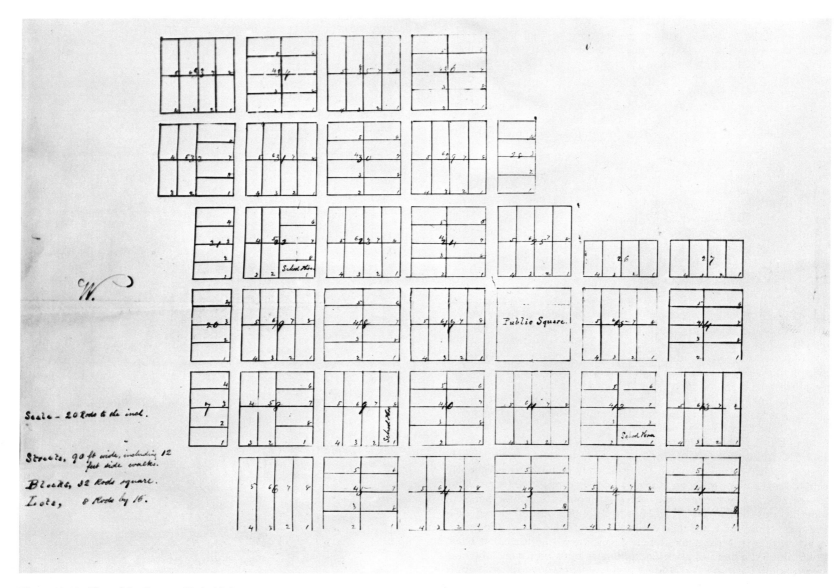

Figure 10.16 Plan of St. George, Utah: 1862

winter of 1857-58 near Fort Bridger, and Johnston and Cumming faced the prospect that, if they attempted to force their way to Salt Lake City the next spring, Brigham Young would make good his threat to institute a scorched earth policy, destroying all that had been built up over the past decade and lead his people in search of still another homeland.

In April and May Young ordered the abandonment of all of the Mormon settlements north of the Utah Valley. Salt Lake City was deserted as were all the towns to the north except for a few Mormons left with instructions to fire the buildings rather than submit to a military occupation. This tragedy was not to be played to its final act. Cumming aranged to visit Young, and the Mormons' old friend from Philadelphia, Thomas L. Kane, arrived to help work out a compromise. In the East, critics of Buchanan made their voices heard. In the end peace commissioners arrived from Washington with a presidential pardon for Young, an agreement was reached that the army would be allowed to enter the territory and establish a camp some distance from any settlement, and that no Mormon would be molested. Cumming was to be accepted as governor, and all Mormons would be directed to return to their homes.

By July of 1858 most of the 30,000 or so who had fled from Salt Lake City and the northern towns were on their way back to their homes. The Utah War was over, and while disagreements between Mormons and the federal government were not to end, resumption of colonization was once again possible.[49] New communities were badly needed to accommodate the Mormons recalled from the outlying settlements in Idaho, Nevada, and California and to take care of the two to four thousand immigrants who arrived each year following the termination of hostilities. In the decade following the Utah War about 150 new towns were founded. While most of these were established within previously settled areas, others were in regions largely unoccupied or very sparsely populated.

The most southerly part of Utah in the Virgin River region was settled in this period. A few Mormons at an Indian mission on the Santa Clara River had succeeded in growing cotton in 1855, and three years later Brigham Young sent another small group to establish a cotton farm nearby. In the winter of 1861-62 Young organized the first of several groups of colonists that in the next few years were responsible for creating new towns and opening the region for cotton cultivation and other semi-tropical crops.[50]

This venture was one of the most carefully organized colonization projects of Young's career. In addition to devoting his usual attention in choosing leaders and key members of the party, Young drafted detailed instructions concerning desirable characteristics of the site to be selected for the principal city.[51] Reaching the Virgin River in December, 1861, the settlers proceeded to survey a town site at the mouth of the Santa Clara. No fort was thought necessary because the Paiute Indians lacked the force to threaten the security of the colony. The design of the town—St. George—incorporated the familiar elements used in so many earlier Mormon communities as illustrated in Figure 10.16 and described by a member of the group: "Saint George site was surveyed and the city was laid out in Blocks, 32 rods square, each containing 8 lots. The streets 90 feet wide including 12 foot side walks. Thirty-six blocks were in this Plot of which one was set apart as a Public Square. In all two hunderd and fifty-six lots 8 by 16 rods. Three of these lots were reserved for school purposes."[52] Many years later the decision was made to erect a temple at St. George. Begun in 1871, it was completed in 1877, the first of the four Utah temples to be finished.[53]

Apostle Orson Pratt led a smaller group eastward from St. George up the Virgin River to lay out Rockville. This tiny village of 20 lots took the form of a single street, on each side of which fronted 10 lots, 8 by 12 rods in size. As Figure 10.17 shows, the canyon walls formed a narrow, irregular valley, and the five-acre farming plots could not take the neat, geometric form used at most of the other Mormon settlements.

The plans of two other Virgin River towns of this period have survived. These communities were located on opposite sides of the stream a few miles down river from Rockville. Virgin City, shown in Figure 10.18, occupied the north bank, and Grafton City, whose plan is reproduced in Figure 10.19, the south. Neither town bore the slightest resemblance to the other Mormon settlements we have examined. Only in their combination of town lots and surrounding agricultural lands did they seem to belong to the Mormon tradition.[54]

The recall of Mormons from San Bernardino meant the abandonment of the Mormon Corridor concept of a string of settlements from San Diego or Los Angeles to the Mormon domain in Utah. Brigham Young advanced as a substitute the notion of using the lower Colorado River for steamship transportation up to a point in southeastern Nevada and then freighting goods and persons overland via St. George to the more thickly populated part of Utah.[55] In November, 1864, Young instructed Bishop Anson Call to "take a suitable company, locate a road to the Colorado, explore the river, find a suitable place for a warehouse, build it, and form a settlement at or near the landing."[56]

Callville (also known as Call's Landing or Call's Fort) was the result. Its utilitarian plan appears in Figure 10.20, which also shows three warehouses built by the Deseret Mercantile Association, a group of Salt

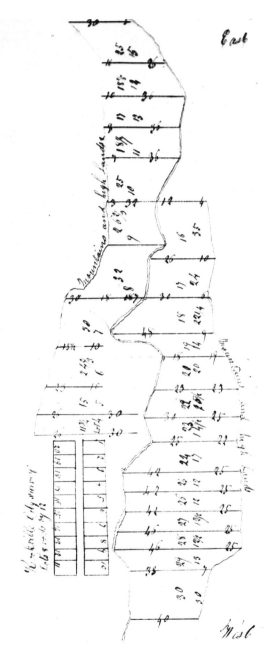

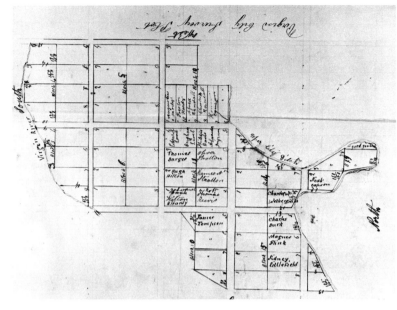

Figure 10.18 Plan of Virgin City, Utah: 1862

Figure 10.17 Plan of Rockville City, Utah: ca. 1862

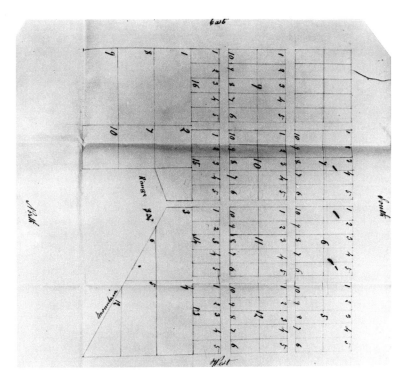

Figure 10.19 Plan of Grafton City, Utah: 1861

Figure 10.20 Plan of Callville, Arizona: ca. 1865

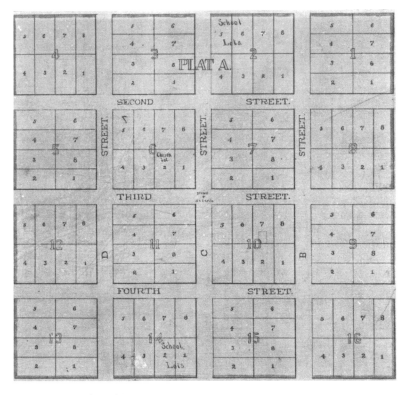

Figure 10.21   Plan of Mesa, Arizona: 1882

mons became interested in Arizona in 1851, when a group of them passing on their way to California occupied for one year the site of Tubac, then part of Mexico and virtually unoccupied. Permanent settlement resumed at about the same time as the founding of Callville when several other small towns and agricultural villages were established on the lower Virgin River near the mouth of the Muddy River in what was then Arizona but is now part of Nevada.[58] When this area was designated as part of Nevada and taxes were levied retroactively on the Mormon property, most of the settlers abandoned their homes and returned to Utah.

Planned colonization in other parts of Arizona proved more successful. Most of these settlements were made during the 1870s along the Little Colorado River, which flows northwesterly from a point about midway along the eastern boundary of Arizona. They included Sunset, Brigham City, St. Joseph, Obed, Woodruff, and St. Johns.[59] These were among the last of the Mormon towns founded in the lifetime of Brigham Young, who died in 1877. His interest in urban planning and development continued to the end, for in that year no fewer than twenty new communities were established under the jurisdiction of the church whose activities he had so ably directed.

More than 100 miles southwest of the Little Colorado River towns, the Mormons also planned a series of settlements in the Salt River Valley in the vicinity of Phoenix. Mesa, whose plan is reproduced in Figure 10.21, was surveyed in 1878 with streets 132 feet wide forming square blocks divided into eight lots arranged in the alternating frontage pattern.[60] Mesa is now a temple city, but this is a modern development marked by the completion of an imposing structure in 1927. In the original survey only a single lot was set aside for church purposes. Alma, laid out in 1880, and Tempe, planned in 1882 joined Mesa as additional Mormon towns in this region. A third concentration of Mormon communities developed in the upper Gila and San Pedro River valleys in southeastern Arizona.[61]

Many of the Arizona Mormon towns experimented at least briefly with a form of organization known as the United Order. This was an attempt vigorously promoted by the church during the 1870s to apply the early precepts announced in 1831 by Joseph Smith as Divine revelation and known then as the Order of Enoch or the Law of Consecration and Stewardship. According to these teachings, Mormons were supposed to give over all their property to the church and then receive a "stewardship," or such property and possessions as were deemed necessary for the person or family.[62] At Kirtland and the Missouri set-

Lake City merchants who joined with the church in financing this venture. The site of the town was in the modern state of Nevada on the right bank of the Colorado about 15 miles upstream from the eventual location of Hoover Dam. It is now under the waters of Lake Mead. Although some efforts were made to develop river trade to Callville, this proved impractical, and the coming of the railroad through northern Utah in 1869 brought to an end further attempts to develop an access route to Utah through the Southwest.[57]

Settlement by Mormons south of the Utah border in northern Arizona was, however, promoted vigorously by the church. The Mor-

tlements, some redistribution of property was carried out in this manner, but it existed more as an article of faith and rhetoric than a practical and generally applied economic system. At Salt Lake City and elsewhere from the early days of Utah colonization, tithing, or donating to the church one-tenth of all income or labor, served as a substitute. Various kinds of co-operative business enterprise also acted as a method of marshaling community resources for the common good. The remarkable co-operative manufacturing, farming, retailing, and service organization flourishing at Brigham City under the direction of the energetic Apostle and later church president, Lorenzo Snow, provided a model of its kind.

Convinced that a more genuinely communal system should not be universally adopted, and influenced as well by economic reversals during the business depression in the early 1870s, Brigham Young began a vigorous campaign to convert Mormon communities to the United Order, particularly the smaller and less prosperous settlements on the frontier of development.[63] Despite its place in Mormon theology, the United Order as a practical method of organizing human enterprise failed to gain wide acceptance even with the backing of the respected leader of the church.[64] However, several established communities went through the formality of accepting the doctrine, and a few new centers were founded with this as the basis for organization. Among the latter were Lehi, Arizona, and Orderville, Utah.

Lehi, the plan of which appears in Figure 10.22, was located a short distance east of Phoenix and was founded in the summer of 1877 by a group of 80 persons led by Dan W. Jones. The unique design of the community reflected its organization under the United Order with all property held in common ownership. A correspondent to the Prescott *Miner* described the community as follows: "The work done . . . is simply astounding, and the alacrity and vim with which they go at it is decidedly in favor of cooperation of communism. Irrespective of capital invested, all share equally in the returns. The main canal is two and a half miles long, eight feet deep, and eight feet wide. Two miles of small ditch are completed and four more are required. Their diagram of the settlement, as it is to be, represents a mile square enclosed by an adobe wall about seven feet high. In the center is a square, or plaza, around which are buildings fronting outward. The middle of the plaza represents the back yards, in which eleven families, or eighty-five persons are to comingle."[65]

Lehi's experiment with frontier communism did not last long, and most of the families associated with its founding moved to other loca-

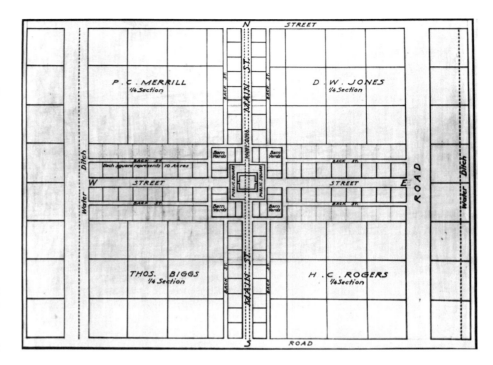

Figure 10.22 Plan of Lehi, Arizona: 1880

tions. The abandonment of the United Order led to the replanning of the site, for in 1880 Henry Rogers surveyed the townsite into a little grid of six blocks, each 26 rods square, formed by straight streets four rods wide.[66] The unusual and untypical original town design was thus replaced by a more conventional layout.

One of the best documented of the United Order settlements is Orderville, located in Long Valley near the southern border of Utah. One childhood resident of the community recalled that before beginning the community "all property was turned in and appraised; each family was given credit for the amount. . . . Those who contributed became stockholders. . . . All individual accounts were balanced at the end of the year. To each man a like credit was given for work . . . and at the end of each year those whose debts exceeded their credits . . . had their debts cancelled; and those whose credits exceeded their debts turned their surplus credit to the company. . . . If a man became dissatisfied and wanted to withdraw, he was paid up to his invested capital and his accumulations up to the time he quit work."[67]

The design of the community, like that of Lehi, Arizona, reflected the economic organization. The town occupied a square site 495 feet on each side. Dwellings took the form of row houses around the four sides of the square facing "shorter rows a few feet in front, with one or two openings in each row to serve as streets for the passage of teams and pedestrians." The southeastern corner of the square was occupied by a two and one-half story house "for most of the official families." Outside but nearby this residential compound could be found "livestock corrals, and chicken coops . . . the commissary and work shops," and "the store with an office room." Beyond lay the gardens, orchards, and farm fields.[68]

Orderville enjoyed a measure of prosperity for a time, but its curious mixture of stockholder capitalism with religious communisn did not last beyond the first generation of settlers. As children grew up they discovered that not having contributed property when the United Order was established they had no voice in the enterprise. Wages were higher elsewhere than those fixed for internal purposes at Orderville, and younger residents were inevitably attracted to other, more conventionally organized communities. The passage of the federal law making polygamy unlawful forced many of the elder members of the community into hiding. By 1885 the order was disbanded and the experiment ended.[69]

By 1877, the year of Brigham Young's death, the basic settlement structure of Utah had been established. In a long strip following the western slopes of the mountains, desert plains and upland meadows had been converted to productive farming and grazing. Cities and towns dotted this now fertile region, occupying sites chosen by or under the direction of the church president. Most of these had been planned by him personally or by others who followed his directions and worked according to his instructions. The map of Utah reproduced in Figure 10.23 shows the more important communities that had thus been established by the early years of the 1870s. The total at the time of Young's death, including a great many of the smaller Utah settlements not shown on this map and those in Arizona, Idaho, Nevada, and California, reached the astonishing number of 358.

Despite Young's efforts to promote even distribution of settlement and population throughout the habitable portions of the Mormon domain, the bulk of the Saints lived in valleys between Provo on the south and Logan on the north, a distance of approximately one hundred miles. Dominating this heartland of Utah as its spiritual, governmental, and economic center, Salt Lake City had continued its growth and development during the 30 years between its founding and it founder's death.

When Samuel Bowles, the Massachusetts journalist, editor, and publisher, saw Salt Lake City in 1865 he was captivated by the beauty of the site, the fertility of the irrigated farm fields in the valley, and the ditches along the streets of the city brimming with mountain water "keeping the shade trees alive and growing, supplying drink for animals and water for household purposes, and delightfully cooling the summer air."[70] The city as it existed at the time of Bowles' visit is shown in Figure 10.24. The vantage point is virtually identical with that from which Frederick Piercy sketched the city in 1853.

On Temple Square, to the right, is the Tabernacle, begun in 1864, not yet completed at the time the view was drawn, but by October, 1867, ready to accommodate 5,000 worshippers under its gigantic oval, wooden roof spanning 150 feet and arching 70 feet high above the foundations of its 44 sandstone piers. An even more prominent building was rising nearby. This was the great Mormon Temple begun on February 14, 1853, but not completed and dedicated until exactly 40 years later. The artist of our view thus anticipated this great event by a quarter of a century, but his depiction of the building is accurate and doubtless followed the drawings for its design prepared by Truman O. Angell, the church architect. Its six spires soar above the city, that in the center of the east facade rising 210 feet and topped by a gilded statue of the angel Moroni.

East Temple Street (later Main Street), 132 feet wide and flanked by irrigation ditches, stretches off to the south. Beyond Temple Square this thoroughfare developed as the principal business street. Here, as in many other parts of the expanding city, the pattern of alternating lot frontages proved an impractical nuisance. Lots originally laid out to front on streets of lesser commercial importance were soon replatted to face East Temple Street. At the same time many of the original lots already fronting this artery were divided into two or more parcels of more convenient size for mercantile purposes. Similar adjustments in the lot pattern continued over the years, and in most of Salt Lake City this peculiar feature, once so characteristic of Mormon town planning, no longer exists.[71]

Across East Temple Street from the walled Temple Square lay a block occupied by the Tithing Office and Yard, the Church office, the Lion

House built in 1855-56 as the residence for some of Brigham Young's wives, Brigham Young's office built in 1852, and the Beehive House constructed as his official residence. These buildings and others in the central part of the city in 1870 can be seen more clearly in a detail from a more extensive depiction of the city reproduced in Plate 13.

The view is to the northeast. In the block east of Young's office and residences one can see a complex of buildings also belonging to the church leader. These included a school for his 56 children. Between these two blocks ran First East Street, which as the modern State Street is on the axis of the Capitol, begun in 1912 on a superb site overlooking the city from the hill to the north of the Young blocks. At the time of the view the street passed under an imposing arch surmounted by an enormous eagle. It then continued to City Creek Canyon, where the water supply of the city and mills were located and placed under Young's control.

Several civic buildings also appear in this view. At the lower left, identified by the number 8, is the first county courthouse under construction as early as 1853. This building was also used by the territorial legislature, as was the first city hall two blocks south of Brigham Young's school and identified on the view as number 7. This structure in 1962 was moved to the grounds of the new capitol. Near the city hall on the block to the northwest and identified as number 6, the view shows the imposing Salt Lake Theatre, completed by 1862 to enrich the cultural life of the growing city.

Occupying the upper right portion of the view can be seen an addition to the city surveyed sometime prior to 1857 on sloping bench land north of South Temple Street and known locally as "The Avenues." Here a different module of land division was used, creating much smaller square blocks divided into four square lots and with narrower streets that are off-set from the lines of those leading northward from the older portion of the city to the south.[72] In this section and especially fronting South Temple Street, a number of large homes were built. Those occupying lots opposite the northern ends of the older north-south streets enjoy unusually favorable views over the city and in turn provide attractive terminations of vistas from the south. It was an unconscious but effective bit of urban design.

The city by 1875 had grown to the point where it occupied virtually all of the area originally reserved for urban purposes. Reproduced in Figure 10.25 is a view published that year showing the city as seen from the northwest. Its population probably exceeded 16,000, for census takers five years earlier reported a population of 12,854, a substantial in-

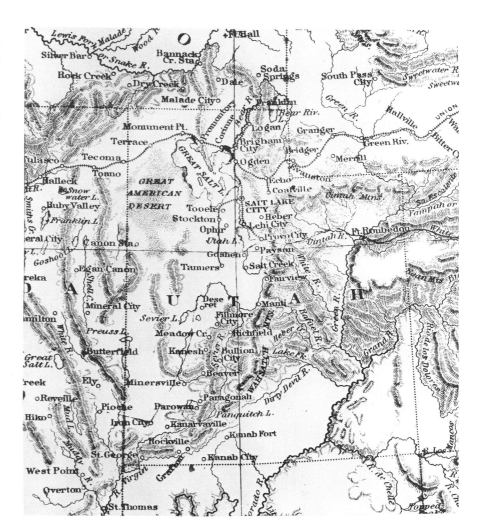

Figure 10.23 Map of Southern Utah and Northern Arizona: 1874

Figure 10.24 View of Salt Lake City, Utah: 1867

crease from the 1860 figure of 8,236, and by 1880 Salt Lake City had 20,768 residents.[73] It was a community primarily of single-family homes located on spacious lots and fronting on broad streets.

Its economy began to flourish as the nation and the region recovered from the Panic of 1873. The railroads aided local industry, and the payroll of Fort Douglas, just visible in the view at the upper left, helped to stimulate local trade.[74] Mining in the mountain ranges provided an additional impetus to growth and had a more lasting effect than the temporary but welcome trade of the California forty-niners who had passed through Salt Lake City a quarter of a century earlier.

The effect on the city was noted by an English traveler, Charles Marshall, in 1871: "For a year past Main Street has been growing constantly more bustling and animated. . . . Already miners, by scores, by hundreds, and even by thousands, have poured into the Territory, and commenced operations. . . . The town feels the change. Business has grown active. . . . Every second shop in Main Street has heaps of

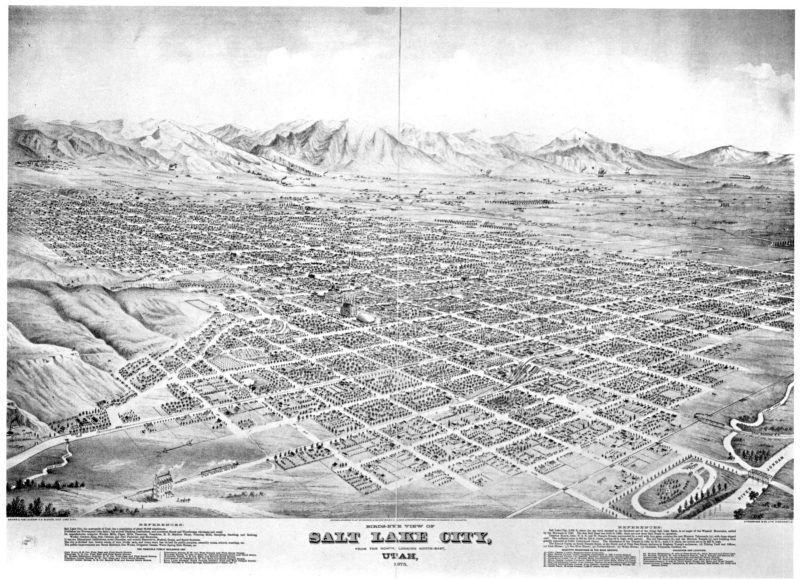

Figure 10.25 View of Salt Lake City, Utah: 1875

Figure 10.26 View of Salt Lake City, Utah: 1887

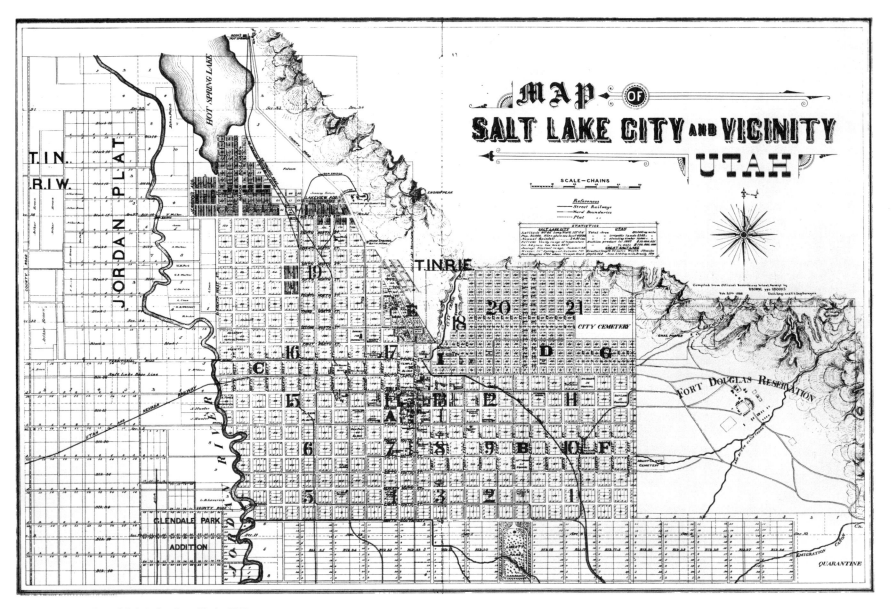

Figure 10.27 Plan of Salt Lake City, Utah: 1888

specimen ores on shelves within, or deposited in the windows."[75]

A decade and a half later, Main Street was solidly built up with three- and four-story buildings along a three-block stretch extending southward from the corner of Temple Square. The view in Figure 10.26 shows this thoroughfare in 1887 as seen from the south. At the northern end of this busy business district, along its east side, could be found the several structures occupied by Zion's Cooperative Mercantile Institution, which had been organized in 1868. In the modern city the Z.C.M.I. store still stands as an architectural landmark, its three tiers of magnificently wide windows separated by narrow columns masking its remodeled modern interior.[76]

Almost from the beginning of settlement a few non-Mormons lived in Salt Lake City. They became more numerous in the early territorial days, increased substantially after the Utah War, and continued to grow more rapidly with the coming of the railroads and the development of mining in Utah. Main Street eventually reflected this dual nature of the population. Business activities at its northern end were predominantly owned and operated by Saints. Clustered at the south end of the concentrated business area—four blocks away from South Temple Street—were enterprises mainly financed by Gentile capital.[77]

At the beginning of the fifth decade of its existence Salt Lake City had expanded somewhat beyond the area originally envisioned by Brigham Young as necessary for potential expansion. The plan reproduced in Figure 10.27 shows the division of land in and around the enlarged city in 1888. On the south in the former Big Field and to the west in the Jordan Plat most of the five-acre farm parcels were then still in agricultural use. One exception can be noted: in 1880 the city acquired a farm once owned by Brigham Young below Ninth South Street and opened it to the public two years later as Liberty Park.

The "Avenues" north of South Temple Street had been extended northward to the steep hills, as this portion of the city was divided into blocks much smaller in size than in the first town plots. North of Temple Square some in-filling of streets and lots had taken place in a curiously awkward pattern that represented the only deviation from the otherwise geometric orientation on the grid system. And, to the northwest on the land near Hot Spring Lake, a triangular area had been platted into small lots arranged in a tight grid centering on Marion Boulevard.

Virtually all visitors to the city came away impressed by what they saw. Typical was a correspondent for *Harper's Weekly* who described the Mormon center to his readers in these words: "It is one of the most beautiful of all modernly built cities. . . . Residences of the rich have been built alike in the Mormon and in the Gentile section, large mercantile establishments have taken the place of adobe huts; but the wisdom with which the city was laid out has become plainer with every improvement. . . . There is nothing lacking in site or plan to make the city a religious capital. And all that appeals to the religious zeal of the Mormons has appealed to the appreciation of the Gentiles. It appeals to the admiration also of all visitors. . . . There is not yet a single narrow street, not a house wherein the sunlight cannot find its way, nor one whereby a stream does not run, and from which perpetual snow is not visible."[78]

Forty years after Brigham Young led his weary, persecuted, but faithful followers to the Great Basin, Salt Lake City had become one of the most important communities in the West and one of the handsomest. Joseph Smith's vision of a great City of Zion had at last become reality under the wise and effective leadership of the Prophet's successor.

XI

Urban Planning and Development in the Pacific Northwest

WHEN Brigham Young led the Mormons up the valley of the Platte River from Winter Quarters toward Utah, he followed a route that others bound for new homes in the West had already traveled. Young chose to march along the north bank of the Platte to avoid Gentle settlers plodding westward on its other side along the Oregon Trail. The trail's dusty tracks terminated at The Dalles, 175 miles east of the mouth of the Columbia River. At that point wagons were taken apart, put on rafts, and floated downstream to the mouth of the Willamette River, which drained a narrow but fertile valley on the western slope of the Cascade Mountains.[1]

It was along the Willamette that in the 1840s pioneer residents of Oregon planned dozens of cities—some to remain only paper towns, others to become communities of modest size, and one to attain true metropolitan stature. Although these early communities provided far more business and residential lots than even the increasing numbers of immigrants to the Pacific Northwest required, later townsite speculators vied with one another in creating still more urban settlements. Nearly all of these developers regarded water power and water transportation as essential, and they sought locations with advantages similar to those of the Willamette: along the valley of the Columbia, on the rugged and uninviting Pacific Coast, and around the shores of Washington's Puget Sound. Only in later years did urban settlement spread to the interior following the construction of good wagon roads, and, eventually, the extension of rail service to the region.

While in 1840 the region was largely a wilderness, it was neither uncharted nor completely uninhabited by whites. Lewis and Clark and later explorers had mapped much of the area, and the Hudson's Bay Company maintained a string of fortified trading posts stretching through western Canada and then dipping southward to the Columbia River. At the river's mouth stood Fort George, so renamed in 1813 when the English North West Company acquired John Jacob Astor's trading post of Astoria founded two years earlier.[2] One hundred miles upstream, Fort Vancouver occupied a site on the north bank of the Columbia opposite the mouth of the Willamette. Presiding over its affairs since he founded the post in 1824 was the remarkable John McLoughlin, a Scot who held the position of Chief Factor for the Hudson's Bay Company and was virtually governor of the Oregon territory.[3]

Despite British claims to the region south of the Columbia, McLoughlin aided several groups of American missionaries to establish their little settlements among the Indians. The earliest of these missions dates from 1834, and while they achieved practically no success in converting the natives to Christianity, their existence in distant Oregon created much interest in the region among residents of the East. Some highly exaggerated accounts of the wealth, fertility, and favorable climate in Oregon sent back by missionaries and travelers did much to stimulate immigration to the area.[4]

Even earlier, in 1829, the imaginative but impractical Hall J. Kelley had put forward a detailed proposal for the settlement of the Oregon country. This included plans for two towns: one on the Pacific Coast north of the Columbia's mouth intended to occupy a site of no less than five square miles, the other an inland trading town that Kelley suggested be built near the mouth of the Williamette.[5] While Kelley's settlement expedition met with complete failure, the publicity it received helped to stir early interest in the Northwest.

Conflicting British and American claims to the region resulted in an agreement in 1818 that settlers from both countries would be allowed entry. The promotion of American colonization thus became a matter of some importance, for it seemed inevitable that the issue of ultimate political jurisdiction would be resolved mainly on the basis of the nationality of the majority of its residents. McLoughlin's strategy was to keep American settlement confined to the area south of the Columbia in the hope that a final territorial division would follow that river and that Britain would retain what is now the state of Washington.

Geography aided McLoughlin, for the fertile valley of the Willamette River offered better opportunities for farming than any other spot. From the very beginning of Oregon colonization, however, town founding and promotion as well as the development of agriculture occupied the energies of a great many persons. During the first half-dozen years of the immigration to Oregon, a score or more of towns were hastily platted on sites that seemed to offer favorable prospects.

McLoughlin did not depend on geography alone to promote settlement south of the Columbia. At the falls of the Willamette a few miles from its mouth he ordered a town laid out on land that had been claimed by the Hudson's Bay Company as early as 1828. McLoughlin retained Lansford Hastings to survey its streets in the winter of 1842-43, and he offered lots free to all settlers who agreed to build on them, charging only for the cost of the legal conveyances. By that fall according to Hastings the new town of Oregon City consisted of "fifty-three buildings . . . among which, were four stores, four mills, two of which were flouring-mills, one public-house, one black-smith's shop and various other mechanics' shops; a church was also in contemplation, and in fact commenced." The donation lots "which were obtained gratuitously, only the spring previous, were then worth at least one thousand dollars each, and their value was daily increasing with the improvements of the town."[6]

In Oregon City the provisional government organized by American settlers conducted its business, and from 1848 to 1851 the town was the formal capital of Oregon Territory created after the boundary controversy was settled in 1846. In that year Captain Warre sat on the opposite bank of the Willamette to draw his sketch of the town from which the lithograph in Figure 11.1 was prepared.[7] The view shows the steep bluff rising in back of the town, which then consisted of two streets running parallel to the river crossed by several shorter streets leading from the foot of the bluff to the water's edge.

One visitor a year later referred to Oregon City as a "bustling little village . . . with its neatly-painted white houses, and its six or seven hundred inhabitants."[8] By that time Jesse Applegate had been directed to lay out additional streets and lots to accommodate the expected influx of population. The plan reproduced in Figure 11.2 shows the result of his work and the extent of the community by 1849. The two tiers of blocks fronting Main Street, which Hastings had surveyed, occupied most of the lower land along the river. Applegate's new streets assumed a more rigid pattern but were located with some respect for topography. At the right what appears as a wide avenue between the Hastings survey and Applegate's addition marks the approximate line of the bluff dividing the town into upper and lower sections. As a link between the two parts of the settlement Applegate provided a public square overlooking the lower town.

Although Hastings confidently predicted that Oregon City would become "a place of very considerable manufacturing and commerical importance," he added more cautiously that "other towns are already springing into existence, as additional evidence of the unbounded energy and enterprise of American citizens."[9] These rival communities diverted population from Oregon City and slowed its growth. The view of the town in 1858 reproduced in Figure 11.3 indicates that a decade and a half after founding, the original area as laid out by Hastings still contained virtually all of the town's buildings, although the first crude structures had been replaced by more substantial stores, mills, and houses.

Numerous competitors threatened Oregon City's position. In the twenty miles or so from the mouth of the Willamette to the falls, townsite speculators founded several communities. Opposite Oregon City on the west bank of the river, Robert Moore laid out Linn City in 1843, and a year later Hugh Burns planned Multnomah City nearby.[10] On a tract adjoining Oregon City above the falls, Absalom F. Hedges surveyed Falls City in 1845.[11] Green Point and Clackamas City were laid out between the falls and the mouth of the Clackamas River, and by 1849 their population with that of Oregon City totaled 1,200.[12] Downstream, Lot Whitcomb founded Milwaukie in 1847 at a spot he claimed to be the head of navigation on the Willamette and surveyed the site in a gridiron street pattern. Three years later its newspaper boasted that Milwaukie had a population of "more than 500" and that the town contained "a good school, post office, tin shop, cabinet manufactory, shoe shop, blacksmith shop, three stores, printing office, warehouse, three taverns, two sawmills, [and] a sawmill and grist mill being built."[13]

Three or four miles up the Willamette from its mouth, Peter Burnett, later to be the first governor of California, planned the town of Linnton with General Morton M. McCarver in 1844. McCarver selected the site at what he thought was the head of navigation, but this proved not to be the case. As Burnett later recalled, the "town speculation was a small loss to us, the receipts from the sale of lots not being equal to the expenses."[14]

Their experience might have been far different if they had chosen another site roughly halfway from the mouth of the Willamette to Oregon City, although this tract—eventually to become the Oregon metropolis of Portland—changed hands with such bewildering frequency that the early owners obviously did not realize its potential value. William Overton first claimed the 640 plot in 1844, immediately selling a half-interest to Asa Lovejoy for the twenty-five-cent filing fee and the legal work required to prepare the necessary papers. Shortly thereafter Overton sold his remaining interest to Francis Pettygrove, an Oregon City merchant, for $50 in merchandise.

Lovejoy and Pettygrove cleared a portion of the land, decided to lay out a town, and tossed a coin to determine which man would have the right to chose the name. Pettygrove , a native of Calais, Maine, selected that of the largest town in his home state, and Portland it became. In the summer of 1845 they hired Thomas Brown to survey an elongated grid of streets extending eight blocks along the river and two blocks deep. Brown divided each block into eight lots measuring 50 by 100 feet fronting on streets 60 feet wide. This established a basic pattern that was to be extended many times over the years.[15]

Figure 11.4 shows the earliest surviving plat of the town as enlarged later in 1845 to include a third tier of blocks along the inland side,

Figure 11.1 View of Oregon City, Oregon: 1846

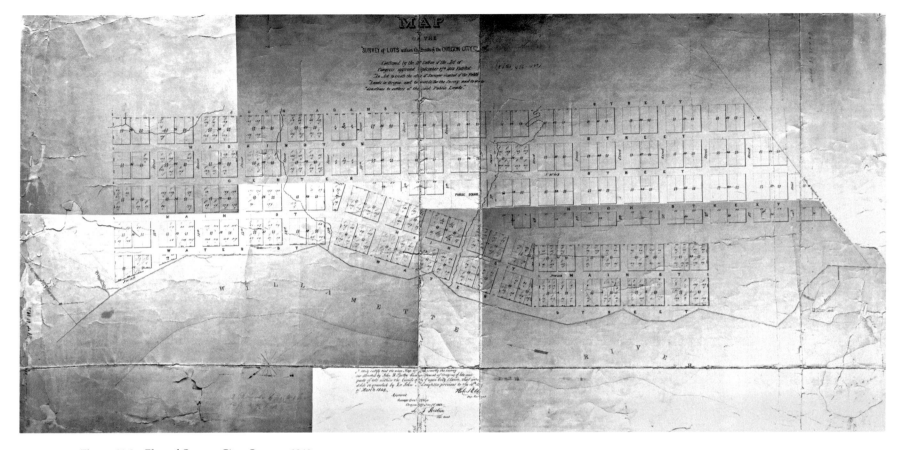

Figure 11.2   Plan of Oregon City, Oregon: 1849

eleven other blocks on the down-river side of Brown's survey, and two larger parcels of land reserved by Pettygrove and Benjamin Stark, who in November, 1845, bought Lovejoy's interest in the townsite for less than $400. Stark was the cargomaster of the American bark *Toulon*, the first ship to discharge freight at Pettygrove's warehouse in Portland. His duties on shipboard left the active promotion of Portland in Pettygrove's hands.

The energetic Yankee built a wharf in front of his warehouse at the foot of Washington Street running along the side of his reserved tract. He also vigorously promoted the sale of town lots, and by the early fall of 1846 according to one observer there were "twelve or 15 new homes . . . already occupied, and others building."[16] This was only the begin-

Opposite: **Figure 11.3**   View of Oregon City, Oregon: 1858

FROM NATURE BY KUCHEL & DRESEL.

KUCHEL & DRESEL, LITHOGRAPHERS, 176 CLAY ST. S.F.

OREGON CITY,

CLACKAMAS COUNTY, OREGON.

1858.

Published by CHARMAN & WARNER, Oregon City.

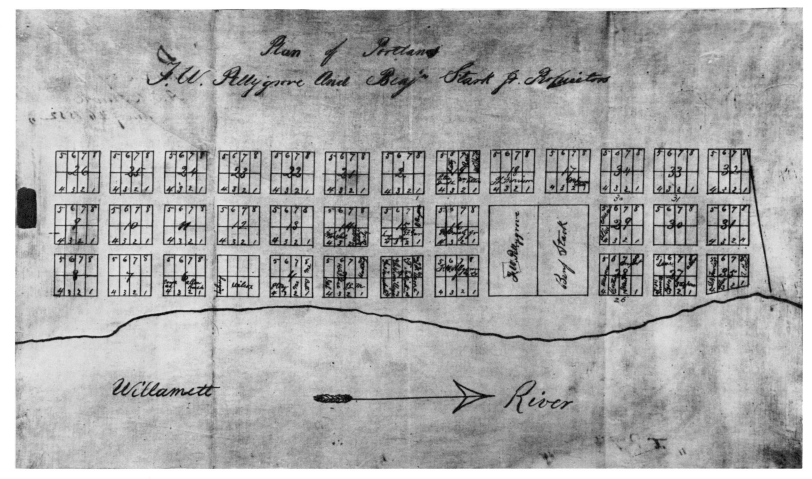

Figure 11.4   Plan of Portland, Oregon: 1845

ning of Portland's ascendancy, for in November, 1850, another visitor found "under way not less than 150 new houses." noting that "there have been built over 100 dwellings during the last summer and fall, eighteen stores, six public boarding houses, [and] two large churches."[17]

Slightly more than a year later the Rev. Ezra Fisher characterized Portland as "the principal port in Oregon." He counted "thirty-five wholesale and retail stores," several steam-powered flour and saw mills, "six or eight drinking shops and billiard tables," many shops belonging to mechanics, and noted that "from eight to fifteen merchant vessels are always seen lying at anchor in the river or at the wharves."[18]

By this time Pettygrove had sold his interest for $5,000 and left Oregon temporarily to try his luck in California. The purchaser, Daniel Lownsdale, now controlled the destiny of Portland, and in 1848 he had new surveys made to enlarge the community still further, as shown in Figure 11.5. To the consternation of many of the residents who contested the action unsuccessfully in the courts, Lownsdale subdivided the previously open area along the river for business and warehouse purposes. He did, however, provide a great many new sites for public use elsewhere.

Lownsdale dedicated two blocks near the center of the expanded city for public squares. These were bounded by Salmon and Madison and 3rd and 4th Streets. He also reserved other locations for schools, churches and such fraternal organizations as the Masons, Odd Fellows, and the Sons and Daughters of Temperance. Blocks 132 and 172 were set aside for public markets.

It was apparently Lownsdale who also created the most unusual feature of Portland's plan. Along the western edge of the town he laid out a strip of eleven narrow blocks for public parks. In subsequent additions to the town this unique physical element was extended to run almost the entire length of the community. While in later years public officials unfortunately disposed of a number of these park blocks for building purposes, many of them still remain to provide an attractively landscaped greenbelt in the heart of the modern city.[19]

As Portland's population increased, Lownsdale formed a town company with Stephen Coffin and William Chapman, and the three men continued to enlarge the city.[20] In 1850 they engaged John Brady to lay out additional streets to the south and, beyond the park strip, to the west. Two years later the city council adopted this as the town's first official map.[21] North of the original townsite John H. Couch began to subdivide the land on his claim as well. As Figure 11.6 shows, he used a slightly different axis for his streets to provide better access from the curving river bank. With a clumsiness that seems almost wilful Couch platted his streets without any regard for proper connections to those already in existence. However, Couch did recognize the importance of the strip park, and in subsequent extensions of his addition he provided for its continuation through his land.

This vast gridiron far exceeded in size the amount of land actually occupied by buildings. The view in Figure 11.7 shows Portland in 1858 as seen from the opposite bank of the Willamette. Virtually all the built up area appears to be located along the river or within a block or two of its banks. Nevertheless, the border views of individual structures indicate that Portland's development had been astonishingly swift and that its future propects appeared bright.

The town retained much of its frontier atmosphere. Tree stumps remained in the few streets that had been officially opened. Someone had the idea of whitewashing them so they would present less of a hazard to travel after dark. Residents of rival towns promptly dubbed the place "Stumptown," a derisive name that Portlanders grew to loathe. While Portland surpassed Oregon City in population by 1850, it was still quite small. In 1855 its population was just over 1,200, and although it more than doubled in size during the next five years, it still had less than 2,900 inhabitants by 1860.

In June, 1851, the owners of the Milwaukie *Western Star* announced that henceforth they would publish their newspaper in Portland under the name of the *Oregon Weekly Times*. The departure from Portland's rival town of its only newspaper symbolized the defeat of Lot Whitcomb's upriver community in the brief battle to determine the location of the major port for the region. Shallow draft vessels still called at Milwaukie as they cautiously ventured up the Willamette to Oregon City, but ocean-going ships and the larger boats plying the Columbia tied up at Portland to discharge and load cargo and passengers.[22]

Portland's proprietors and merchants profited from Milwaukie's decline, but their position seemed to be threatened in 1850 when Henry M. Knighton hired William H. Tappan to design a town on a mile-square tract of land Knighton had purchased four years earlier. Knighton's land lay on the left bank of the Columbia about two-thirds of the distance from the river's mouth to Portland and just below the point where a small branch of the Willamette entered the river.

The proprietor of this new entry in the contest for urban supremacy came from St. Helens in Lancashire, England, and he gave this name to his town whose elaborate plan is reproduced in Figure 11.8. Knighton may have been an Englishman, but except for St. Helen's Square he used appropriately American patriotic names for the other four civic open spaces. The four subsidiary squares were simply open blocks, but Washington Square at the center was given a less conventional pattern with four main streets leading to the midpoints of its sides and two other streets entering its corners at the north and south.

Knighton began to construct a wharf for the Pacific Mail Steamship Company, maintaining that St. Helens was the true head of deep-water navigation on the Columbia. When Ezra Meeker arrived there in 1852 its residents were full of optimism. Meeker recalled that everyone felt that "here was to be the terminus of the steamship line from San Francisco." Snatches of conversation he overheard seemed reassuring:

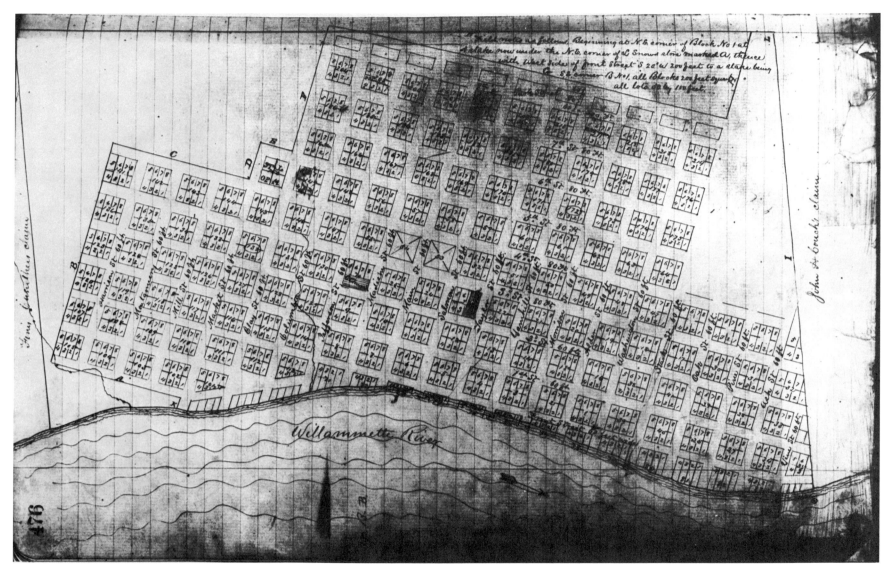

Figure 11.5 Plan of Portland, Oregon: 1848

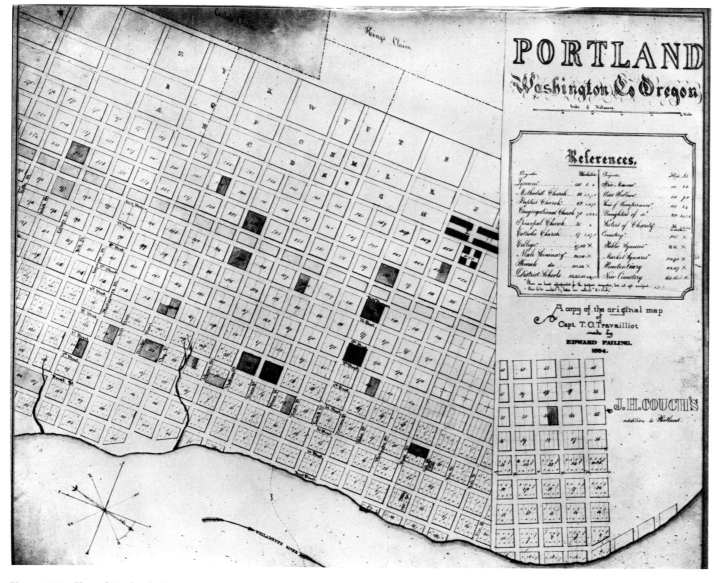

Figure 11.6 Plan of Portland, Oregon: 1853

Figure 11.7 View of Portland, Oregon: 1858

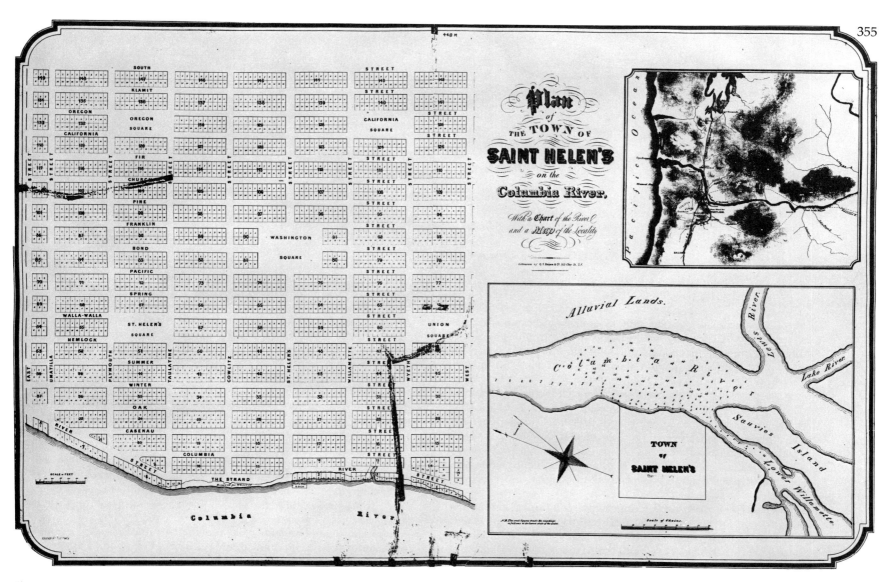

Figure 11.8 Plan of St. Helens, Oregon: ca. 1875

" 'Wasn't the company building this wharf?' 'They wouldn't set sixty men to work on the dock without they meant business.' 'Ships can't get up that creek.' (meaning the Willamette), 'the big city is going to be here.' " A few weeks later Meeker noticed that work on the dock had ceased. "We soon learned . . . why, as the steamship company had given up the fight against Portland, and would thenceforward run their steamers to that port."[23] Although St. Helens managed to survive, Knighton's dreams of a great port city were clearly never to be realized.[24]

Unusual town designs like that for St. Helens could not overcome inherent disadvantages of location. In 1844 John M. Shively claimed the land formerly occupied by the fur trading post of Astoria at the mouth of the Columbia. There he planned a new town while retaining the old name. As can be seen in Figure 11.9, Shively provided a number of public sites: three squares to be used for churches, two circular parcels for schools, a customhouse, a cemetery, and a fishmarket at the water end of Broadway, a street 120 feet wide between the two portions of the town laid out in streets 60 feet in width.[25]

Evidently this plan was widely circulated in an attempt to attract settlers. Judge William Strong, arriving in the summer of 1850 referred to the "avenues and streets, squares and public parks, wharves and warehouses, churches, schools and theaters," adding ruefully, that they were only "upon the map." Instead of this thriving metropolis, Strong found instead "a straggling hamlet consisting of a dozen or so small houses, irregularly planted along the river bank, shut in by the dense forest."[26]

Two decades later Astoria presented a more impressive appearance, but it remained a rather primitive community. The view in Figure 11.10 shows the town from the Columbia about 1870. By that time a salmon cannery provided a basis for more intensive economic development, and although the treacherous mouth of the Columbia prevented the growth of Astoria as a port of much importance, fishing and salmon processing attracted enough persons to allow Astoria's slow growth to continue.

In the process Shively's plan underwent substantial modification. Broadway was eliminated, and the grid section to the east was replatted so that the orientation of its streets would follow more closely the axes of those on the west. This was carried out so thoughtlessly that many of these thoroughfares did not connect and simply ended abruptly at the former line of division between the two parts of the town.[27]

The towns located above the falls of the Willamette could not hope to surpass Portland in size and importance, and their growth helped to stimulate development of that Oregon port as their major link with the rest of the nation. The most important upriver town beyond Oregon City was Salem, which began its existence in 1846 when a group of settlers in the vicinity of the Methodist mission pooled some of their adjoining land, had it surveyed in town lots, and agreed to use a portion of the proceeds from sales to provide funds for the Oregon Institute, which in 1851 became Willamette University.[28]

William H. Willson, one of the property owners, acted as the agent for the group, and his town plan is reproduced in Figure 11.11. Wilson and his fellow residents of Salem were doubtless already thinking of their community as the future capital of the territory. The name of Capitol Street at the eastern edge of the town leading past Willson's house hints of this. A more obvious indication is the one-block-wide strip of land identified as Willson Avenue south of Court Street. A note accompanying the plat states that Block 6 at the western end of Willson Avenue was intended as a public square and that the unnumbered blocks at the avenue's other end were reserved by Willson for unspecified purposes. Not shown on the plat but located south of Willson Avenue were the grounds of the Oregon Institute. Willson thus provided in his design for a generous expanse of open land that might be used for public buildings.

Salem succeeded in obtaining the designation as the seat of government at the meeting of the first territorial legislature in Oregon City convened by Governor Joseph Lane in 1849. A claim that the capital location law had not been properly drawn caused the governor and some members of the legislature and the supreme court to refuse to move to Salem, but the U.S. Congress in 1852 confirmed the validity of the enactment. Despite this, in January, 1855, the legislators voted to establish the government in Corvallis; six months later they returned to Salem, this time to stay although the issue continued to occupy the time of the lawmakers until 1864. Corvallis eventually received a consolation prize when in 1868 Corvallis College, begun a decade earlier, was made the land-grant college. In 1885 the state took over full control of the institution, and work began on a campus site to the west of the town whose undeviating gridiron street pattern had preempted other possible locations along the Willamette.[29]

Land speculators and townsite promoters founded a host of other towns prior to 1860 in the central and upper Willamette Valley: McMinnville, Amity, Oswego, Independence, Monmouth, Albany, Buena Vista, Sublimity, and many others.[30] Among them was a little settlement established in the upper part of the valley in 1846 by Eugene Skinner. The year following the creation of Lane County in 1851, Skin-

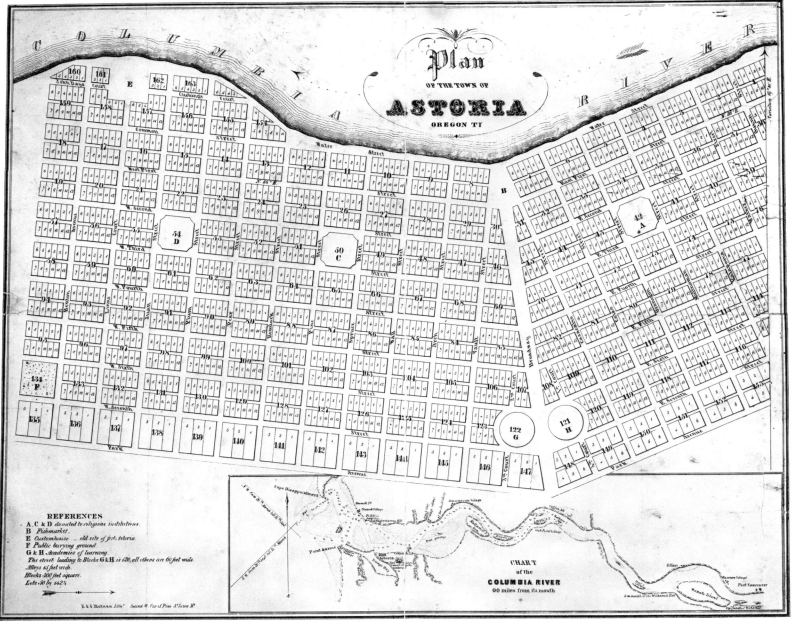

Figure 11.9   Plan of Astoria, Oregon: ca. 1850

Figure 11.10 View of Astoria, Oregon: ca. 1870

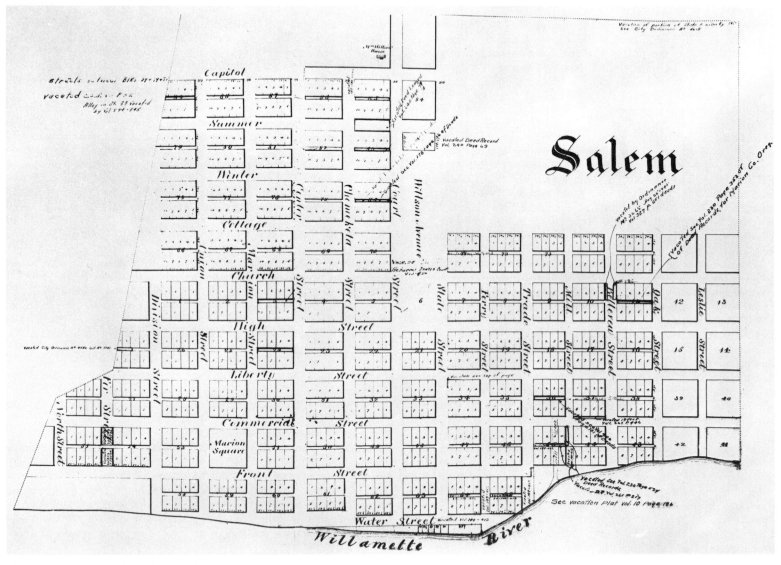

Figure 11.11 Plan of Salem, Oregon: 1850

ner and Judge D. M. Risdon surveyed a town in the traditional grid pattern and succeeded in having it named the county seat. In February, 1854, Skinner reported to former governor Joseph Lane, then serving as the territorial delegate to the U.S. Congress, about progress of settlement: "Eugene City is fast improving. There are now three stores, two blacksmith shops, and numerous small buildings going up."[31]

Two years later another new building appeared. It can be seen in the middle view at the top above the 1859 general depiction of the town reproduced in Figure 11.12. This was Columbia College, the first institution of higher learning in the town. Although its life was brief, it helped to establish Eugene as an educational center, and in 1872 it was selected as the site of the state university. The town itself in 1859 presented anything but an imposing sight, and the periodic floods that covered the low-lying portions of the town justified the nick-name of the community as "Skinner's Mudhole." A more fitting memorial to the founder is Skinner Butte Park occupying a hilltop location from which one can view the modern city on both sides of the river and extending far up and down the Willamette Valley.

While these and other early Oregon towns passed through their frontier years, a few pioneer town founders pushed northward into what is now Washington. They did so despite the efforts of the Hudson's Bay Company to deter settlement beyond the Columbia River. One of these men, Michael Simmons, in 1845 led a small group to the falls of the Des Chutes River at the southern end of Puget Sound to establish the first town in that region. At New Market, later changed to Tumwater, the settlers built a flour mill and a saw mill and cleared land for farming. Soon a number of other new arrivals in the Oregon country came to claim land in the vicinity.[32]

Following the agreement with Britain in 1846 establishing American authority over the territory on both sides of the Columbia, additional settlers followed this vanguard. Some of them joined Edmund Sylvester, who earlier that year with Levi L. Smith occupied a claim on a peninsula to the north of Tumwater. Sylvester was later to recall that the site attracted his attention because of its "advantages of trade with the shipping and with the improvements these Falls would bring in here in time." Ships "could not go above" this point, and Sylvester felt his "market would be with the shipping that came . . . for lumber."[33]

In 1850 Sylvester engaged William L. Frazer to lay out a town whose gridiron streets extended down the peninsula formed by the river on one side and a creek on the other. As resurveyed in 1870, Frazer's linear plan for what was to become the capital of Washington is reproduced in

Figure 11.13. Following established custom Sylvester offered several free lots to merchants who would built stores at this new town of Olympia. Among them was Michael Simmons, who sold out his interest in Tumwater and built the first commercial building in Olympia at the corner of First and Main Streets. There he displayed merchandise brought from San Francisco by the *Orbit*, a brig that the enterprising Simmons purchased to begin American maritime trade between Puget Sound and California.[34]

The early years of the 1850s saw the beginning of a number of other settlements in Washington. Several persons claimed land on the western shore of Puget Sound where Admiralty Inlet connects the northern part of that body of water with the Strait of Juan de Fuca. They joined together to plan Fort Townsend in 1851. One member of the group was Francis Pettygrove, who after laying out Portland had unwisely speculated in town lots at Benicia, California. It may have been this experienced but then impoverished town promoter who planned Port Townsend's little grid of streets in a final effort to make his fortune in urban real estate.[35]

North of Olympia and a few miles south of where Tacoma would later be located, Lafayette Balch selected a site in 1851 for his town of Port Steilacoom. Two miles above this spot William Bolton established a shipyard where he constructed several sloops for the Puget Sound trade. Their cargoes soon were to include products manufactured or processed at Steilacoom, where Nicholas De Lin built a barrel factory, brewery, sawmill, and salmon-packing plant, and M. F. Guess in 1858 began the first brickyard on Puget Sound. The town thus had a promising start and in 1853 became the earliest chartered city in Washington Territory.[36]

The view of Steilacoom in 1862 reproduced in Figure 11.14 indicates, however, that this town—like the other early communities of Washington—consisted of only a few dozen houses facing four or five unpaved streets leading from the edge of the forest to the wharves thrust out into the waters of Puget Sound. Ten years later when Mrs. Frances Victor recorded her impressions of the Northwest she noted that Steilacoom had "only three hundred inhabitants," and the most impressive building in the place was the jail, "built of brick, and very substantial."[37]

Dozens of other groups of settlers cleared the forests, erected houses, and built docks on the shores of Puget Sound in efforts to create

Opposite: **Figure 11.12** View of Eugene, Oregon: 1859

A.J. WELCH.

H. SHAW.

COLUMBIA COLLEGE.

E. F. SKINNER.

J.L. BRUMLEY.

T. CHASE.

ABRAM M. PEEK.

A. RENFREW.

FROM NATURE BY KUCHEL & DRESEL, 176 CLAY ST. SAN FRANCISCO.

L. DANFORTH & BRO.

A.A. SMITH.

J. TEAL.

MULHOLLAN & LOCKE.

KUCHEL & DRESEL, LITH.

EUGENE CITY,

LANE COUNTY, OREGON.
1859.
PUBLISHED BY DANFORTH & BRO.

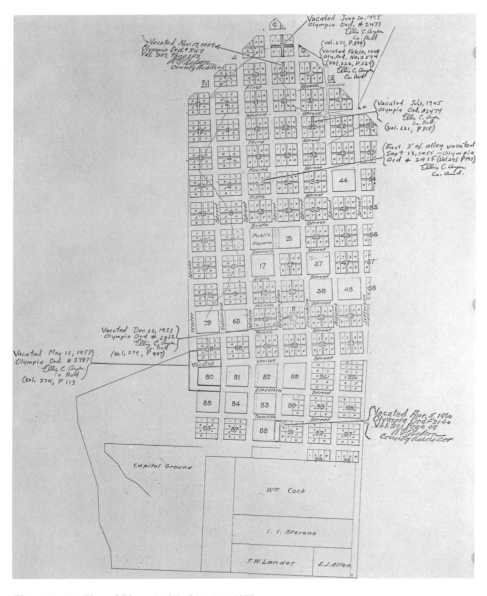

On the map (handwritten annotations):

Vacated June 26, 1945
Olympia Ord. # 2473
Ellis C. Ayer
Co. Aud.
(Vol. 271, P. 510)

Vacated Nov. 17, 1959
Olympia Ord. # 547
Vol. 357, Page 153
W. Chilson
County Auditor

Vacated Feb. 10, 1948
Olympia Ord. No. 2574
(Vol. 226, P. 569)
Ellis C. Ayer
Co. Aud.

Vacated July, 1945
Olympia Ord. # 2474
Ellis C. Ayer
Co. Aud.
(Vol. 221, P. 315)

East 3' of alley vacated
Sept. 13, 1955 — Olympia
Ord # 2915 (Vol 295 P143)
Ellis C. Ayer
Co. Aud.

Vacated Dec. 22, 1953
Olympia Ord # 2812
Ellis C. Ayer
Co. Aud.
(Vol. 279, P. 447)

Vacated May 12, 1953
Olympia Ord. # 2757
Ellis C. Ayer
Co Aud
(Vol. 274, P 113)

Vacated Apr. 5, 1960
Olympia Ord # 3140
Vol. 367, Page 69
W. Chilson
County Auditor

Capitol Ground

Wᵐ Cock

I. I. Stevens

F. W. Lander   E. J. Allen

Figure 11.13 Plan of Olympia, Washington: 1870

towns.[38] Among them were John Low and Charles Terry, who staked out a claim to a point of land extending into Elliott Bay along the eastern shore of the sound and approximately midway to Admiralty Inlet. Returning to Portland for their families, they recruited additional settlers, and late in the autumn of 1851 the group disembarked from the schooner *Exact* at Alki Point. The name came from the Chinook jargon meaning "future." The women in the party were more impressed with its present dismal appearance and promptly collapsed in tears.[39]

They had reason to weep. Low and Terry platted the land as the town of New York, but although a few stores and houses were erected here, its harbor proved unsuitable because of dangerous winds that wrecked several vessels. In 1852 most of the settlers packed their belongings and moved four miles away to the east side of Elliott Bay, where another primitive town had been laid out on the land claimed by Dr. David S. Maynard of Olympia. Maynard and his neighboring property owners had formed a townsite company, sounded the waters of the bay, and selected the most promising location for their community, to which they gave the name of Seattle.[40]

Its site and the location of Seattle's first streets and buildings can be seen in Figure 11.15. A single street followed the shore of Elliott Bay and was crossed by five others at right angles. Two of them were casually surveyed across a tidal marsh, which at high water made the town almost an island. The largest building was located in the middle of Yesler Way. This was the sawmill erected by Henry Yesler, who came to Seattle in 1852 and, when he agreed to construct his mill in the nascent town, was promptly given a share of the townsite. This industry and Maynard's fish-packing plant furnished the principal sources of employment. The heavy forest cover and the rugged topography of the land in the vicinity made farming almost impossible, and from the beginning the residents of Seattle depended on exports of lumber and fish for their economic survival.[41]

Yesler was later to recall how after his mill "was commenced in '52, the town grew rapidly. . . . The saw dust we filled swamps with, and the slabs we built a wharf with." Seattle had few buildings, and Yesler's cookhouse "was used for all kind of public purposes—for preaching, for holding court, lawyer's office, hotel," and for entertaining "all the strangers who travelled up and down the Sound."[42]

In December, 1853, the new minister, the Rev. David E. Blaine, described the tiny settlement in a letter to a friend: "Our village contains about thirty houses," Blaine wrote, "and I think twenty-six of these

Figure 11.14   View of Steilacoom, Washington: 1862

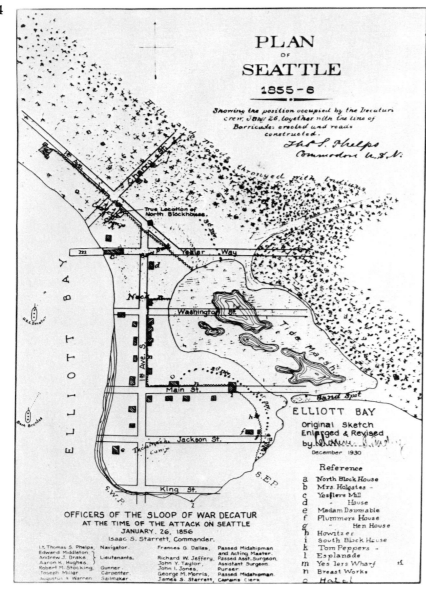

Figure 11.15 Plan of Seattle, Washington: 1856

have been put up during the last six months, but as yet [Seattle] . . . is mostly in the woods." In August of the following year Mrs. Blaine added a postscript to her husband's letter to his mother: "What would you think to go through a town which has but one street built on, and that but thinly, with nothing to mark the different lots, the sides and middle of the street all alike, stumpy, with miserable Indian shanties scattered all about and Indians meeting you at every step?"[43]

By the summer of 1855, however, Seattle had three stores, a school, a hotel, perhaps 45 houses, and a post office.[44] Despite an Indian attack the next January, which was beaten off only by marines from the *USS Decatur*, Seattle continued to grow. The editor of an Olympia newspaper in the autumn of 1857 reported that the town then had four stores, two taverns, "five mechanic shops," a tannery, and that Yesler's steam sawmill was "running night and day" with a work force of "from twenty to twenty-five hands."[45]

Although Seattle's original plat provided ample room for its handful of residents, the townsite proprietors extended its streets to provide additional blocks and lots. Figure 11.16 shows the design of the enlarged community, now dignified with a public square at the north end of Sixth Street whose boundaries splayed outward at its intersection with Washington Street to create a triangular open space in front of the square. The discovery of gold on the Fraser River in Canada in 1858 attracted a few more residents to Seattle to help supply the hordes of men bound for the mines. A saloon, a dance hall, a hardware store, and a blacksmith shop joined the existing stores in the little business district, but Yesler's sawmill continued to be the chief reason for the community's existence, and for many years Seattle's fortunes depended almost solely on the timber resources of the area.[46]

As these Puget Sound communities were passing through their initial years, other towns were begun elsewhere. Among them were three settlements laid out adjacent to trading posts or forts, including Fort Vancouver. The elaborate complex of buildings at that Hudson's Bay Company post already had a "village" west of the main stockade, where many of the employees and tradesmen lived.[47] West of this village Henry Williamson built a house in 1845 only to have it removed by John McLoughlin. Williamson promptly rebuilt his cabin, filed a claim for the land at Oregon City, and in 1848 after the U.S. Army had established Columbia Barracks north of the trading post, surveyed his land as the town of Vancouver. Two years later while Williamson was in California, Amos Short claimed the same site and prepared a new survey. Short's plan can be seen in Figure 11.17, which also shows the Hudson's Bay Company land and the adjoining army post.[48]

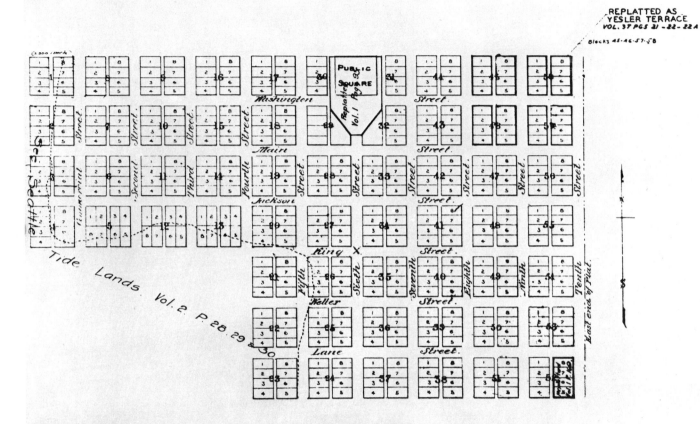

Plat of the

Town of Seattle

King County, Washington Territory.

Explanation.
Blocks 240 by 256 feet including an alley running North & South of 16 feet wide. Lots 60ft. by 120 varying according to Plat. Streets running due East and West & North & South 66 ft. wide.

This day personally appeared D.S. Maynard, and acknowledged the within to be a true copy of the Plat of the Town of Seattle, in King County, Washington Territory and that the same is in accordance with hiss free will, wishes and desire of which he is proprietor
Seattle May 23d 1853
H.L. Yesler

Recorded in the Records of King County Washington Territory in Vol. "D" Page 6. Transcribed Vol 1. of Deeds. Page 10. Re-recorded (year order Councils Com's at the King Term of Court 1873) in this Plat Book. March 10th 1873
J.C. Harris
Draughtsman.

Figure 11.16 Plan of Seattle, Washington: 1853

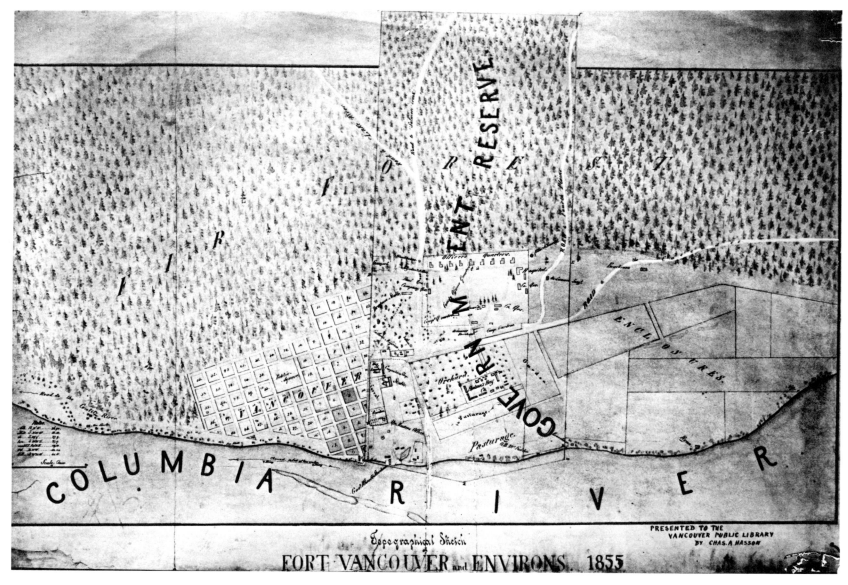

Figure 11.17 Map of Fort Vancouver and Vancouver, Washington and Vicinity: 1855

Short doubtless followed the rectangular boundaries of his property when he planned the grid of streets running awkwardly at angles to the bank of the Columbia River. He did have the foresight to reserve for public use a strip of land at the foot of what is now Daniels Street as well as a public square a few blocks to the north. This latter feature survived still another re-survey of the town by R. H. Landsdale and now, as the Esther Short Park, provides an attractive landscape area in the heart of Vancouver's business district.[49]

Further up the Columbia at The Dalles, the army built Fort Lee in 1849 near the site of the abandoned Methodist, Catholic, and Presbyterian missions. By 1852 a little town had grown up in the vicinity of the fort, and three years later officials of newly created Wasco County had it formally laid out as the county seat in a grid of 24 blocks fitted into an irregular site where Mill Creek entered the Columbia River.[50]

By 1858, as the view in Figure 11.18 reveals, The Dalles had achieved a modest degree of success. In the following year, the county built the first courthouse at Union and Third Streets to join the smaller structures depicted in the border views already lining its business thoroughfares. In the early 1860s the discovery of gold in eastern Oregon and adjoining Idaho brought boom times to the little city, and in later years the town developed as a center for the wheat and wool trade in the region.[51]

Far to the east of The Dalles and just north of the Oregon border, the U.S. army established a military post in the Walla Walla Valley during the Indian wars of 1855-58. When the area became available for white settlement in the fall of 1858, a village began to develop, but it was not until 1865 that it was formally surveyed into the grid pattern of streets, blocks, and lots shown in Figure 11.19. By that time the gold mining boom across the border in Orofino, Idaho, was in full swing, and Walla Walla, with Lewiston, served as one of the chief supply centers for the mining towns. More than 50 new buildings were completed before October, and 30 more were under construction.[52]

By the 1870s these communities of the Pacific Northwest entered a new phase of development. The pioneer years had passed, and many of the towns and small cities of the region had become almost indistinguishable from eastern urban centers with far earlier origins. Travel accounts and the work of artists specializing in town views during the decades of the 1870s and 1880s provide revealing glimpses of the progress of urbanization in an area that only a few years previously had been a forest wilderness populated by Indians and the occupants of scattered fur-trading posts.

When Mrs. Frances Fuller Victor made her extensive tour of Oregon and Washington in 1871, she set out by steamer from Astoria, which she referred to as "neatly built, and containing four or five hundred inhabitants," although she shrewdly commented that it would "require time and capital to develop," because it was "cut off from the interior by the rugged . . . Coast Range."[53] St. Helens she thought "has an air of cheerfulness not common to embryo towns," and felt that either here or at nearby Columbia City "an important town" might develop.[54] Mrs. Victor also admired the "beautifully situated" location of Vancouver but noted that a sand-bar that had formed in the river was "rapidly ruining her prospects of becoming an important river-port."[55]

The Dalles impressed her as a community with a greater future. It was then "a town of about twelve hundred inhabitants," and the original "hastily erected board-houses" had been replaced by "real homes." Mrs. Victor noted that "gardens blossom with exquisite flowers; shade-trees shelter and adorn the promenades; churches and school-houses abound; and the place is one of the pleasantest in Oregon."[56] A dozen years later Henry Wellge drew the view reproduced in Figure 11.20. A branch of the Union Pacific then served the city, its lines running down Front Street from the crossing of Mill Creek. It was otherwise a handsome little town with its numerous churches, schools, and public buildings, and its compact business district extended for three blocks along Second Street.

More than a hundred miles beyond The Dalles Mrs. Victor entered the Umatilla River. After traveling some 35 miles, she came to "the small, new town of Pendleton—the county-seat, beautifully located, and situated on the main lines of travel."[57] It was indeed a new town; G. W. Bailey and Moses Goodwin had laid out a portion of the latter's farm only a year earlier, after they had engineered the transfer of the county seat from Umatilla to this new location.

As the roundup point for cattle drives and the center of a wheat-growing region of increasing importance, Pendleton began to grow. When the view shown in Figure 11.21 was published in 1884, buildings occupied most of the original townsite. A special act of Congress made available an adjoining 640 acres from the Umatilla Indian Reservation, and this land was platted to extend the grid street pattern of the town westward along the river terrace. As the view shows, the railroad was built several blocks from the river, and the town was not cut off from one of its most attractive features.

Northeast of Pendleton and across the boundary between Oregon and Washington lay Walla Walla. Travelers found it necessary to dis-

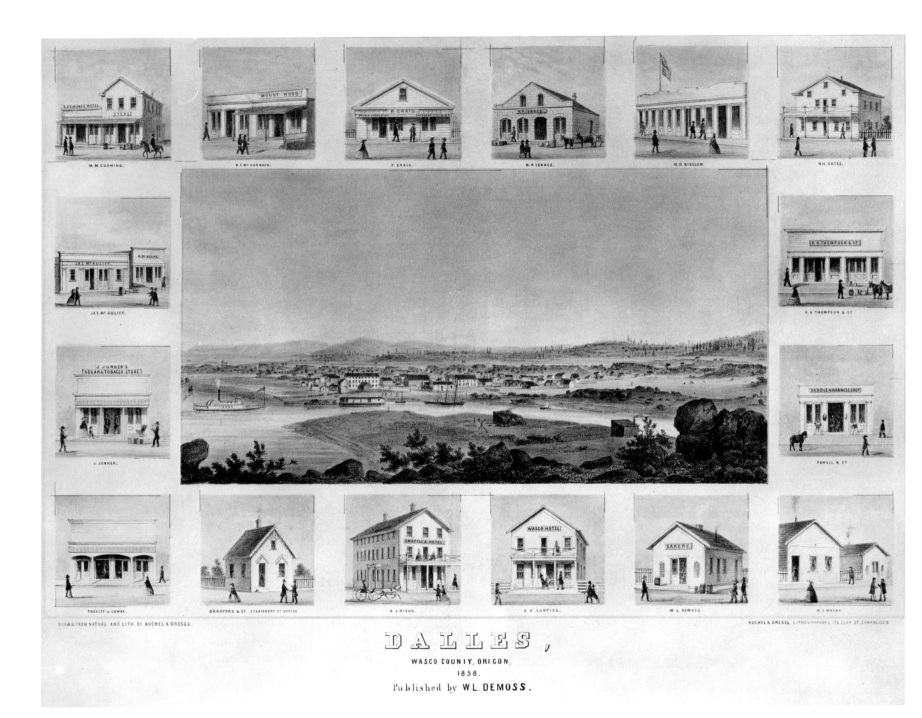

Figure 11.18 View of The Dalles, Oregon: 1858

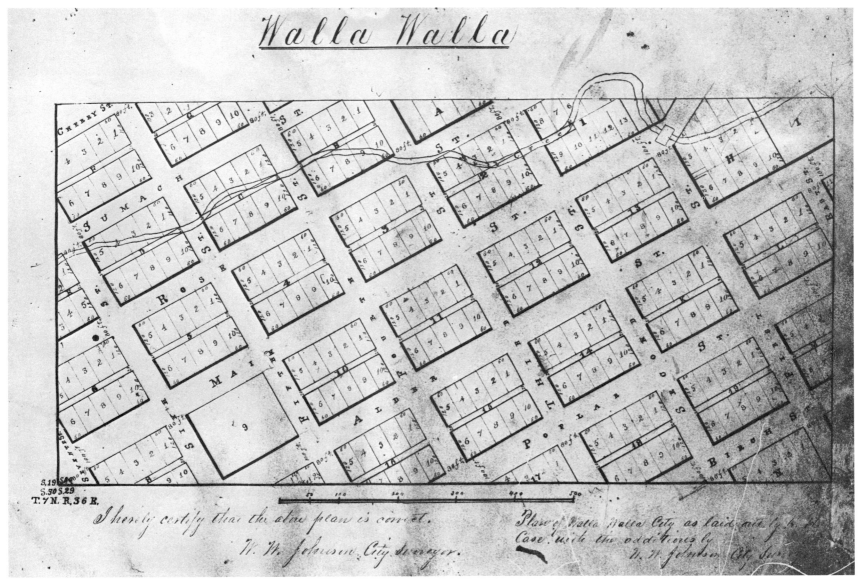

Figure 11.19 Plan of Walla Walla, Washington: 1865

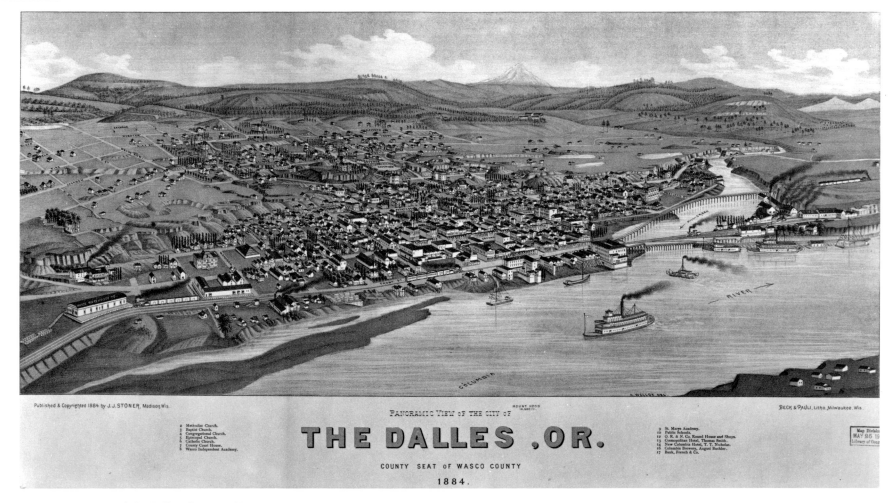

Figure 11.20   View of The Dalles, Oregon: 1884

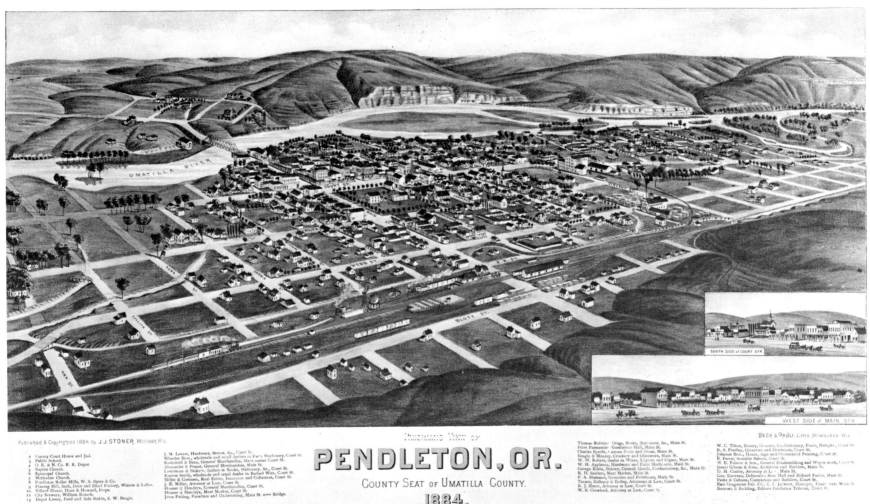

Figure 11.21 View of Pendleton, Oregon: 1884

embark from river steamers at the mouth of the Wallula River and go the remaining miles by stagecoach. Mrs. Victor found it a hot, dusty journey and was cheered by her "first glimpse of this lovely valley." She was surprised to find at this distant location a town with "neat residences and embowering trees, and the general air of comfort and stability which it presents." The liquid sound of the town's peculiar name was echoed by the pleasant noise of sparkling water diverted from a stream into "a hundred tiny rivulets which course through [Walla Walla] . . . laughing, and glinting in and out every body's garden, carrying coolness, fertility, and music to each well-kept homestead."[58]

The view of 1876 reproduced in Figure 11.22 reveals how the spacious community had developed from the little grid of streets illustrated earlier in this chapter. Not yet reached by a major railroad, the town relied for rail service to Wallula on Dr. D. S. Baker's local line, which began operation in 1875 to bring passengers and goods from the steamers landing at the mouth of the Walla Walla River. Merchants of the business district along Main Street did "a profitable business" according to Mrs. Victor, who commented on "the thronged appearance of the streets." But Walla Walla served as more than a market center for wheat farmers. Near the left side of the view one can just make out the first building of Whitman College, Washington's oldest institution of higher learning, which received its charter from the territorial legislature in 1859.[59]

Mrs. Victor continued her journey with visits to some of the villages and hamlets then beginning their existence in eastern Oregon: La Grande with 640 residents; Baker with 312; and Canyon City—all county seats in this sparsely populated area. Later she toured the Umpqua Valley in southwestern Oregon, where she passed through Oakland and Wilbur, both with academies operated by the Methodist Church. Roseburg, a county seat, she found "a pretty little town of five hundred inhabitants, charmingly located in one of the oak parks bordering the Umpqua River."[60]

In the next valley south formed by the Rogue River, she entered the area where a gold rush had occurred in the winter of 1851-52 on Jackson Creek. At the time of her visit, the chief town and county seat was Jacksonville, shown in Figure 11.23 as it appeared slightly more than a decade later. Mrs. Victor described it as a "thriving business place, being the point of exchange between the mining and the agricultural population." Jacksonville presented a surprisingly neat appearance for a former mining camp, the result perhaps of the early creation there of a provisional municipal government whose *alcaldes*, patterned after those

of California, adjusted land claims, surveyed streets, and arranged for essential public services until the legislature provided a more conventional form of local government.[61]

In the year this view appeared, Jacksonville received a serious blow. The Oregon and California Railroad, later to become part of the Southern Pacific, designated its station site a short distance to the east, and its engineers planned their own town of Medford there. Lacking rail service and with its mines no longer profitable to operate, Jacksonville began a long decline. Eventually county officials moved the county seat to Medford, leaving the mining community with more than 60 old buildings of varied architecture to depend on the tourist trade for much of its livelihood.[62]

During her journey Mrs. Victor found urban development in the Willamette Valley the most impressive of all. Eugene, with a population of "about nine hundred," and Corvallis, larger by one or two hundred, both caught her eye because of their beautiful locations. Three miles above Eugene she noted that "the new town of Springfield [is] already a thriving place, with flouring and saw-mills, and several manufactories."[63] Albany, whose plan in 1878 is reproduced in Figure 11.24, was substantially larger with a population of around 2,000. In addition to what Mrs. Victor called "the best court-house" outside of Portland, Albany could point to its college begun by the Presbyterian Church as Albany Academy in 1858, four churches, an open square on which the courthouse faced, and a number of mills and wharfs along the river. The Oregon and California Railroad by 1872 provided rail connections through Albany between Portland and Roseburg only 85 miles from the California border, and urban development in the valley was further stimulated by this improvement in transportation.[64]

Salem in 1871 still lacked its state capitol, for while under construction this building was destroyed by fire, and officials of the government occupied rented quarters on Commercial Street. The year following Mrs. Victor's visit, the legislature appropriated funds for a new building, and a state commission wisely selected a site between Capitol and Summer Streets at the east end of the mall Willson had provided in his original plan. By 1876 this was completed, and, as the view in Figure 11.25 shows, the Marion County courthouse was constructed at the other end of the mall to create, with Willamette University on the south, an imposing little civic center.

The mall itself was "inclosed with a neat and substantial fence, and the grounds laid off in drives and walks," according to the city directory issued in 1874. Its editor boasted that "in a few years this Avenue will

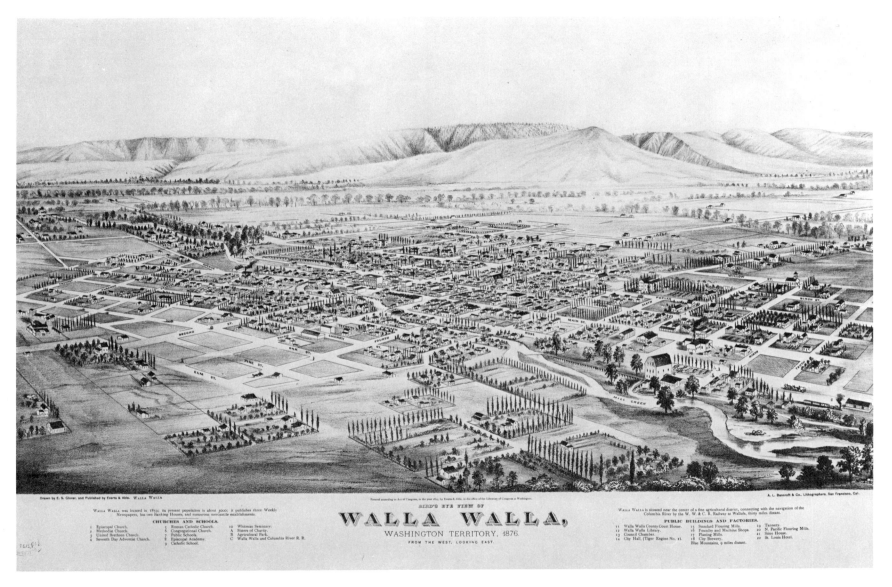

Drawn by E. S. Glover, and Published by Everts & Able.   WALLA WALLA

Entered according to Act of Congress, in the year 1875, by Everts & Able, in the office of the Librarian of Congress at Washington.

A. L. Bancroft & Co. Lithographers, San Francisco, Cal.

WALLA WALLA was located in 1859; its present population is about 3000; it publishes three Weekly
Newspapers, has two Banking Houses, and numerous mercantile establishments.

BIRD'S EYE VIEW OF

WALLA WALLA,

WASHINGTON TERRITORY, 1876.

FROM THE WEST, LOOKING EAST.

WALLA WALLA is situated near the center of a fine agricultural district, connecting with the navigation of the
Columbia River by the W. W. & C. R. Railway at Wallula, thirty miles distant.

CHURCHES AND SCHOOLS.

1 Episcopal Church.
2 Methodist Church.
3 United Brethren Church.
4 Seventh Day Adventist Church.
5 Roman Catholic Church.
6 Congregational Church.
7 Public Schools.
8 Episcopal Academy.
9 Catholic School.
10 Whitman Seminary.
A Sisters of Charity.
B Agricultural Park.
C Walla Walla and Columbia River R. R.

PUBLIC BUILDINGS AND FACTORIES.

11 Walla Walla County Court House.
12 Walla Walla Library.
13 Council Chamber.
14 City Hall, (Tiger Engine No. 1).
15 Standard Flouring Mills.
16 Foundry and Machine Shops.
17 Planing Mills.
18 City Brewery,
    Blue Mountains, 9 miles distant.
19 Tannery.
20 N. Pacific Flouring Mills.
21 Stine House.
22 St. Louis Hotel.

Figure 11.22   View of Walla Walla, Washington: 1876

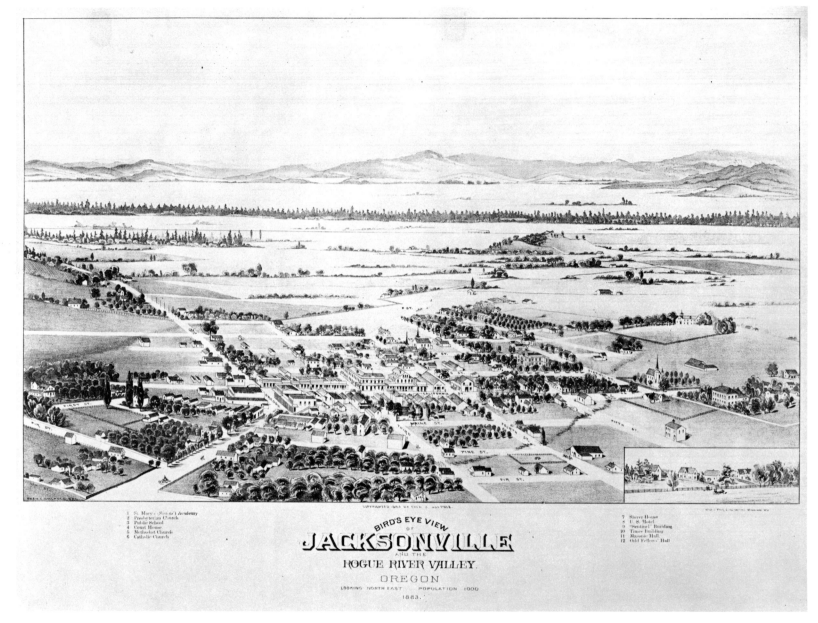

Figure 11.23 View of Jacksonville, Oregon: 1883

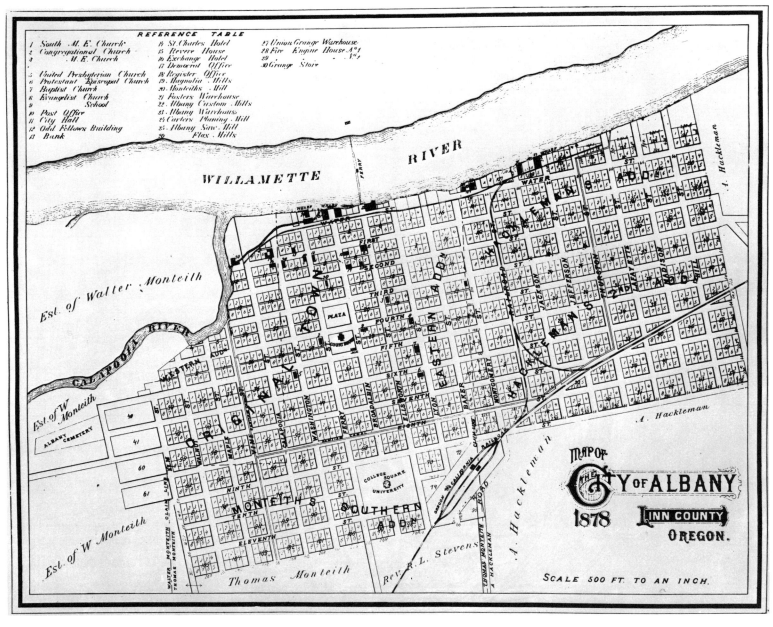

MAP OF
THE CITY OF ALBANY
1878 LINN COUNTY
OREGON.

SCALE 500 FT. TO AN INCH.

Figure 11.24   Plan of Albany, Oregon: 1878

PUBLIC BUILDINGS AND FACTORIES.

Oregon State Capitol Building .... at A.
Marion County Court House Building " B.
Willamette University Building " C.
Academy of the Sacred Heart " F.
Salem Public Schools " G.
Water Works at G. Gas Works " H.
State School for the Blind " I.
Oregon Home for the Sick.
State Penitentiary two miles distant.
County Fair Grounds " " "

THE MANUFACTURING INTERESTS COMPRISE :
Flouring Mills, Saw Mills, Wagon Factory,
Pump Factory, Woolen Mills, Oil Mills,
Machine Shops and Foundries,
Sash and Door Factories, Chair Factory,
Agricultural Implement Works,
Planing Factory, Bag Factory, &c.
Mount Hood, sixty miles distant.

Entered according to Act of Congress, in the year 1876, by F. A. Smith, in the Office of the Librarian of Congress, at Washington, D. C.

BIRD'S EYE VIEW OF
SALEM, OREGON
FROM THE WEST, LOOKING EAST.
1876.

A. L. Bancroft & Company, Lithographers, San Francisco, California.

CHURCHES AND SOCIETIES.

M. E. Church, cor. State and Church Sts.
Trinity M. E. Church, cor. Liberty and Court Sts.
First Baptist Church, cor. Liberty and Marion Sts.
First Presbyterian Church, bet. Chemeketa and Center.
Congregational Church, S. E. cor. Liberty and Center.
Evangelical Church, N. E. cor. Liberty and Center.
St. John's Catholic Church, cor. Cottage and Chemeketa Sts.
Christian Church, cor. High and Center Sts.
St. Paul's Episcopal Church, cor. Church and Chemeketa Sts.
Cumberland Presbyterian Church, High Street, near Union.

SOCIETIES :—Masonic, Odd Fellows, Good Templars,
Natural History and Turn Verein,
Opera House,
Three Newspapers, (Two Daily,)
Several First-class Hotels,
Banks and numerous Mercantile Institutions.

Situated on the Willamette River, Forty Miles above
Portland, on the Oregon and California Railway.

Drawn by E. S. Glover from F. A. Smith's Photograph, and Published by F. A. Smith, Commercial Street, Salem, Oregon.

Figure 11.25 View of Salem, Oregon: 1876

be one of the noted parks on the coast." The public square in the business district had been similarly enclosed and planted, and offered itself as "a favorite resort for celebrations and pic-nic parties."[65] The railroad line fortunately had been located to the east of the capital, and a long strip of open space along the banks of the Willamette provided a fine view of the river and the steamboats that still plied its waters.

Salem was indeed, as Mrs. Victor put it, "a comfortably built town with an air of stability and propriety about it." She approved enthusiastically of the town's wide streets, large lots, and its neat dwellings with their well-kept gardens. She referred to the many locust and maple trees lining the streets and in the public grounds as " 'lungs' to the city, should it grow large enough to need this breathing-space in its midst." Summing up her impressions, she concluded that "Salem is probably the pleasantest town in Oregon."[66]

Not only was Salem pleasant but it was prospering. A large woolen mill, two flour mills, two tanneries, a foundry, four wagon shops, three breweries, three saddle and harness shops, and a wide variety of other manufacturing plants and retail stores provided a firm economic base to supplement employment in government offices and the state penitentiary. The fair grounds of the Agricultural Society of Oregon also annually attracted thousands of visitors and helped to maintain Salem's position as a trading center for the rich farming country in the surrounding area.

Oregon City had likewise undergone a period of expansion and transformation. The plan reproduced in Figure 11.26 shows the location of a number of mills that occupied sites below the falls of the Willamette on either side of the river and which had earned for the town the title of "The Lowell of the Pacific Coast." Lumber, paper, wool, and flour were all processed or manufactured in the growing city, whose original plan was now almost lost in the center of a series of speculative subdivisions thrusting out their streets in all directions according to the whim of the developer or his surveyor.

Portland continued to dominate the region with a population in 1870 of over 8,000, which would more than double before the end of the decade. Mrs. Victor characterized it as "a cheerful-looking town . . . well paved, with handsome public buildings, and comfortable, home-like dwellings." She found it well supplied with hotels, churches, shops of every kind, many fine schools, a public library, a skating rink, four banks, and a theater under construction. Strangely, she did not comment on the unique strip of parks that the view reproduced in Figure 11.27 shows near the edge of the built-up portion of the city as extended to the south and also northward through the Couch addition.

The courthouse on 4th Street faced one of the two adjacent public squares. There, according to Mrs. Victor, "brass bands are in the habit of discoursing sweet sounds . . . one or two afternoons in a week, when all the youth, beauty, and fashion of Portland come out for a promenade." On the higher ground beyond the courthouse and the parks, only a few houses were then built, but Mrs. Victor accurately forecast that this area would become "very desirable for residences from its superior healthfulness, and the fine views to be obtained."[67]

Owners of land across the Willamette from Portland also subdivided their property to take advantage of the building boom. A reporter for a San Francisco newspaper who climbed to the top of the courthouse in 1865 when it was still under construction described East Portland from this vantage point as a "suburban village . . . yet half town and country."[68] Its several gridiron sections can be seen in the view of the city reproduced in Figure 11.28. In the years to come, much of Portland's growth would take place in this direction following the construction of the first bridge across the Willamette in 1887 and the annexation of East Portland and adjoining Albina in 1891.[69]

The wooded hillside appearing at the lower left corner of this view was included in a city park whose site had been acquired shortly before Mrs. Victor's visit but had not yet been developed. Here President Theodore Roosevelt in 1903 laid the first stone for the base of the 34-foot shaft of granite erected as a memorial to Lewis and Clark, whose expedition a century earlier marked the opening of the Northwest for American exploration and eventual settlement.[70]

Railroads aided Portland's industrial expansion. Two lines provided freight and passenger service to southern Oregon and California, the first transcontinental train on the Northern Pacific system arrived in Portland in the fall of 1883, and the following year the Union Pacific reached the city. As the editor of *The West Shore* asserted, "in the extent and convenience of her railroad facilities Portland has no rival in the northwest."[71] Water transportation continued to play an important role in Portland's development, for as the river steamers were gradually replaced by road and rail for local shipping, ocean-going vessels found their way to the city's docks and wharves in increasing numbers.

Nothing to compare with Portland's rapid growth and substantial improvements could then be found in Washington. Nor did the capital city of Olympia offer anything to rival Salem's fine civic complex. Mrs. Victor observed of Olympia that "like all towns hewn out of the forest, it has a certain roughness of aspect, caused by stumps, fallen timber, and burnt, unfallen trees." She estimated the town's population as "about thirteen hundred," and the view of the city reproduced in Plate

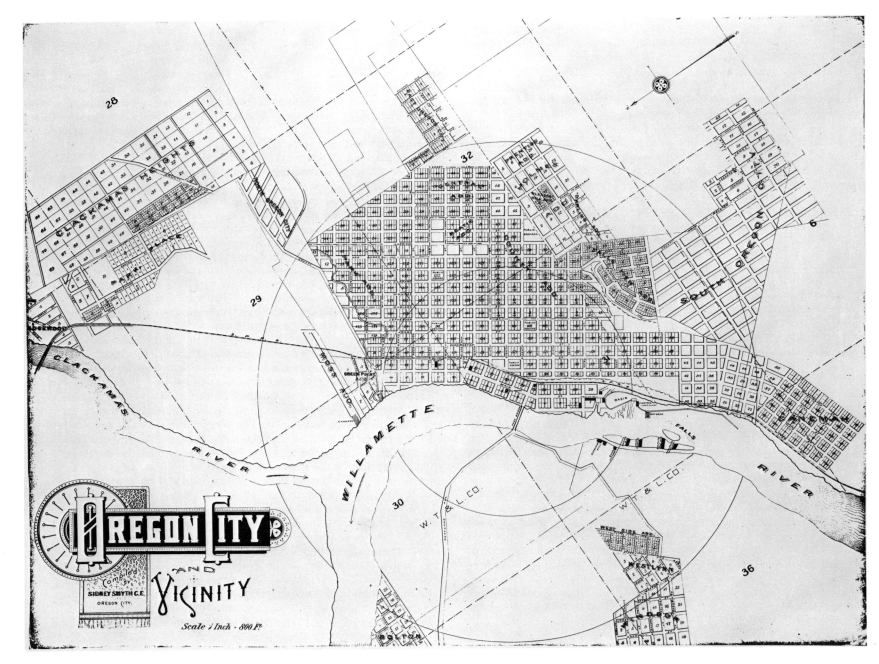

Figure 11.26 Plan of Oregon City, Oregon: date unknown

CITY OF PORTLAND, OREGON.

PUBLISHED BY P.P. CASTLEMAN 1870.

Figure 11.27 View of Portland, Oregon: 1870

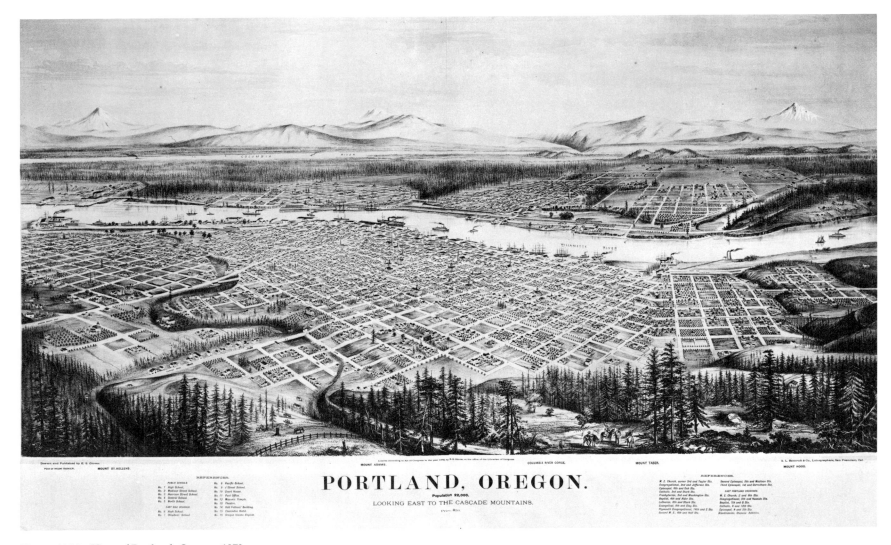

Figure 11.28 View of Portland, Oregon: 1879

14 showing it eight years after her visit suggests that it had grown little if any during the intervening period.[72]

Olympia's development was hampered by a long and bitter controversy over the location of the seat of government for Washington Territory that began as soon as Oregon and Washington were separated in 1853. Governor Isaac Stevens called the first legislature to meet in Olympia, but the act creating the new territory provided that its legislative body should determine the location of the seat of government.[73] Vancouver, Steilacoom, and Port Townsend representatives advanced claims for their towns, and while Olympia eventually won this legislative battle, funds to construct an adequate capitol were withheld.

Meeting first in a store on Main Street, then in the Masonic Hall, the legislators continued to debate the capital city issue. In 1861 they voted in favor of Vancouver, but the Supreme Court invalidated this enactment on a technicality. A previous referendum indicated an overwhelming preference for Olympia, and although capital removal bills were introduced in many subsequent sessions of the legislature up to the year of statehood in 1889, Olympia succeeded in beating back all contending cities.[74]

Thus it was not until 1863 that a building was built to house government offices on the 10-acre site donated by Edmund Sylvester far from the center of town on 13th Street. In the view, one can see this structure standing at the edge of Olympia's built-up area slightly above and to the left of center of the lithograph. It served its purpose until 1903, and it was on this site, as then enlarged, that the present complex of state buildings began to take form after a New York firm won a competition for their design in 1911.

At Olympia Mrs. Victor boarded the Puget Sound steamer bearing the town's name. After calling at Steilacoom, the vessel passed through the narrow strait where Point Defiance juts into the south. In Commencement Bay to the north, she noted briefly that here "the town of Tacoma is situated."[75] General Morton McCarver, unsuccessful at Linnton in Oregon, planned this town in 1868 and shortly thereafter began his campaign to have it designated as the Pacific terminus of the Northern Pacific Railroad. Because Tacoma's growth was so intimately connected with the railroad, its fascinating planning history is treated in Chapter XVII with other towns created by the western rail companies.

Port Townsend, shown in Figure 11.29 seven years after Mrs. Victor's visit, was then little changed from the town she described as consisting of two parts: "the business portion . . . located on low ground, only fairly above the reach of the tide, while the residences are nearly all upon the bluff." Only the location of the capital here could have stimulated much development, for while Port Townsend had a large and deep harbor, Mrs. Victor noted that "it is too much exposed to winds from all points of the compass to be a good one, or to compare favorably with very many others on the Sound."[76]

What was soon to become the dominant city of the region was then scarcely more impressive, although as Mrs. Victor steamed up to Seattle she immediately noticed the "fine structure" of the territorial university, "so situated that it can be seen for a long distance up and down the Sound." She was also struck by the town's "great extent of wharfage" and its harbor swarming "with every description of watercraft; from the handsome steamer . . . and the tall three-masted lumber ships, to the little, wheezy tug and graceful 'plunger.' "[77]

There was no question that Seattle was growing: with a population of just over 1,100 in 1870, it increased to 3,500 by the end of the decade. Seattle also expanded its network of streets far beyond the little gridiron on the point of land where the town had its beginnings. In the view reproduced in Figure 11.30, that area appears at the bottom right corner. Now the town extended for some distance along the water and had begun to thrust its streets up the steep hills separating its harbor from Lake Washington in the background. The largest building in town was the university, which Arthur A. Denny, at the urging of the Rev. Daniel Bagley, persuaded the legislature to erect in Seattle once the city's hopes for obtaining the capital had been dashed. Denny's donation of 10 acres of his property north of the business district fixed its site until a new and much larger location was planned beginning in 1891 on the other side of the hills along the western shore of Lake Washington.[78]

In the 1880s Seattle passed through an explosive period of growth. By 1890 its population reached 43,000, more than twelve times the number of inhabitants only ten years earlier. Figure 11.31 shows the rapidly expanding city not quite midway through that boom decade. Seattle had by then probably pulled even with Tacoma, which, to Seattle's consternation and bitter disappointment, had been selected as the Northern Pacific's terminal and port town.

A branch line to Seattle provided a connection with the Northern Pacific in 1883, although Tacoma businessmen succeeded in suspending operations on this line for a time. Under the leadership of Judge Thomas Burke, Seattle interests continued to press for better rail serv-

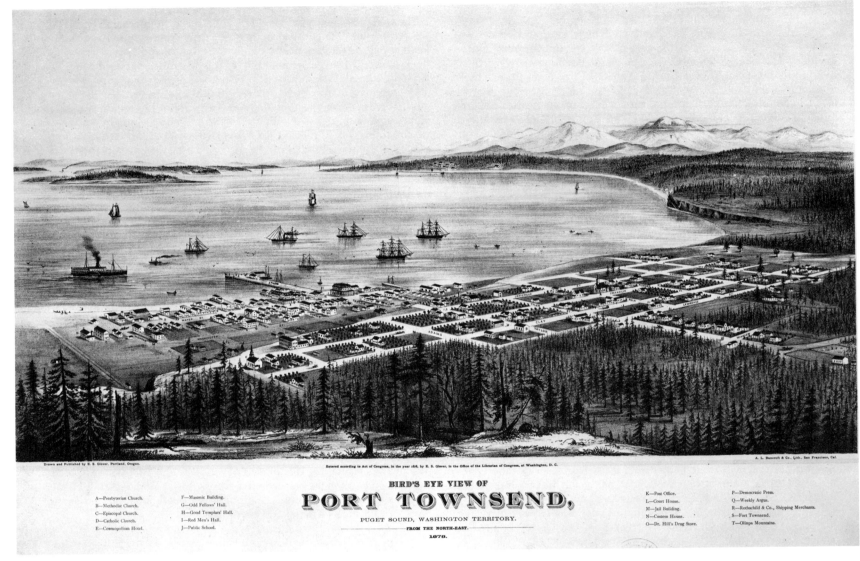

Entered according to Act of Congress, in the year 1878, by E. S. Glover, in the Office of the Librarian of Congress, at Washington, D. C.

BIRD'S EYE VIEW OF

PORT TOWNSEND,

PUGET SOUND, WASHINGTON TERRITORY.

FROM THE NORTH-EAST.

1878.

A—Presbyterian Church.
B—Methodist Church.
C—Episcopal Church.
D—Catholic Church.
E—Cosmopolitan Hotel.

F—Masonic Building.
G—Odd Fellows' Hall.
H—Good Templars' Hall.
I—Red Men's Hall.
J—Public School.

K—Post Office.
L—Court House.
M—Jail Building.
N—Custom House.
O—Dr. Hill's Drug Store.

P—Democratic Press.
Q—Weekly Argus.
R—Rothschild & Co., Shipping Merchants.
S—Fort Townsend.
T—Olimpa Mountains.

Figure 11.29   View of Port Townsend, Washington: 1878

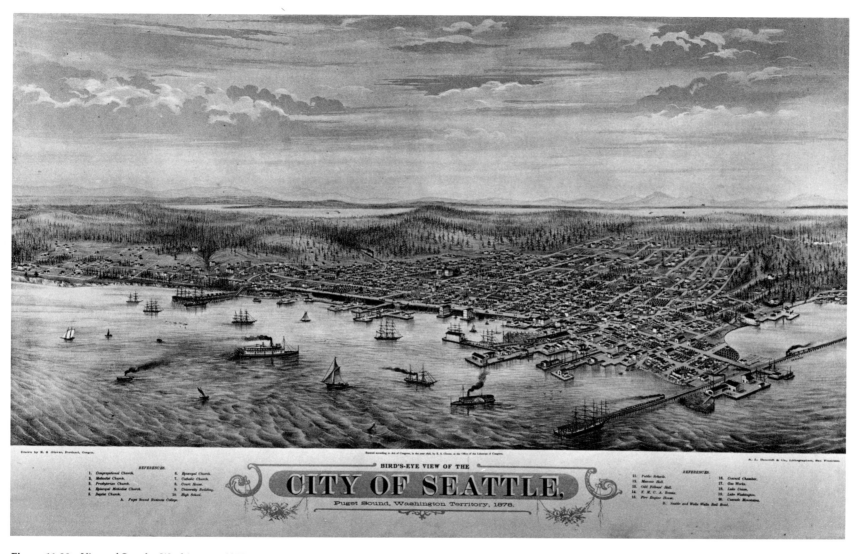

Figure 11.30 View of Seattle, Washington: 1878

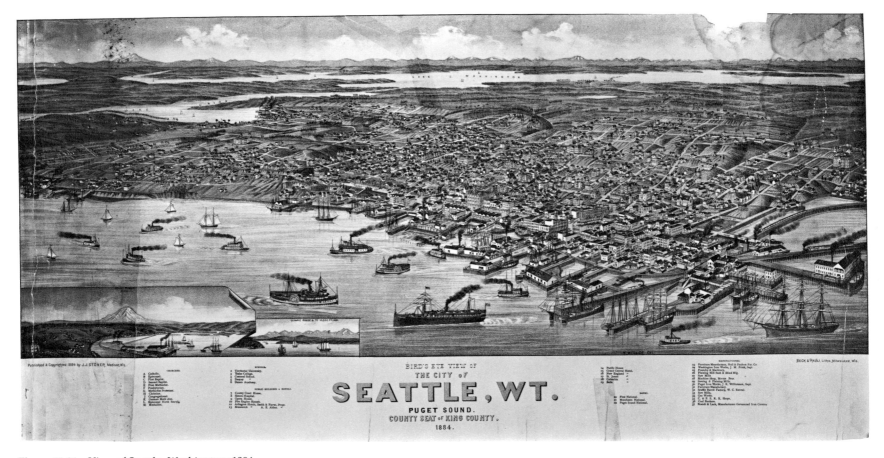

Figure 11.31 View of Seattle, Washington: 1884

ice. A line to Walla Walla was begun in 1874, the Great Northern made Seattle its terminal point in 1891, and eventually the Northern Pacific moved its main operations from Tacoma in final recognition that Seattle had won the fight as the dominant metropolis of the Puget Sound region.[79]

One historian of the city in 1890, reviewing the events of the previous ten years, recalled how Seattle capital had "built warehouses, graded streets, planned the erection of a big hotel, and a pretentious opera house." It was a time when "Seattle was in the midst of its transition from a frontier town to a great commercial city." The transition was not quite complete, for, as he recalled, "in the very midst of this business activity, three murderers were lynched in the public square."[80]

Seattle's physical fabric, if not its social conscience, was transformed in these years. The editor of the Seattle *Weekly Chronicle* pointed with pride to improvements in the community: "Four years ago the chief business of the city was confined to a street macadamized with sawdust and chiefly confined to small wooden buildings. You now glide over substantial streets and become dazzled with the display of costly and useful goods in large and commodious mercantile establishments."[81] The attractive shoreline of Lake Washington caught the eye of speculative real estate developers, and other additions to the city were laid out between the two bodies of water on higher elevations, where people of wealth and position erected imposing mansions from which they could look down on Seattle's bustling docks, warehouses, railroads, and industrial plants.

Seattle's hinterland in central and eastern Washington was also passing through a period of urbanization. Beyond the Snoqualmie Pass through the Cascades lay Ellensburg in the upper reaches of the Yakima River. Until the Northern Pacific reached this place in 1886, the town consisted of nothing more than a crossroads village with a general store, saloon, a post office, and a blacksmith shop surrounded by a few scattered houses. Only three years after the first train drew up by the depot the local newspaper described the changes that had taken place:

The Northern Pacific Railroad Company, when they constructed the depot building and round house, thought they anticipated the future, but they didn't. These buildings will be enlarged this season. The Ellensburg post office was enlarged last summer, and now it is too small by half. Another and greater enlargement is absolutely necessary. The court house was thought to be big enough to meet the demands of a growing city and county, but it now is an insignificant building utterly inadequate for the county business. The public school house was good enough for the village days of Ellensburg but now it is so small that only one fourth the children of the city are accommodated.[82]

If much of this smacks of frontier boosterism, it also contained more than a grain of truth. The town's population grew from a few hundred to perhaps 4,000 in three years. This upstart community promptly entered the ranks of contenders for the capital, whose location, as statehood approached, once again became an issue in 1889. A few ambitious real estate men offered to donate "a magnificent park site . . . surrounded by a 100 foot drive nearly 4000 feet in length" for the capitol site.[83] In the first referendum held to decide the location of the capital, Ellensburg ran third, behind only Olympia and Yakima. However, Ellensburg's boom days ended by 1891 when it became obvious that speculative real estate subdivision had far outstripped any reasonable requirements for building sites.

South of Ellensburg the Northern Pacific followed its more common practice of planning its own towns rather than enriching landowners in existing communities. Four miles north of the little settlement of Yakima City, the railroad in February, 1885, platted 3,000 acres of land in a pattern of 100- and 120-foot streets parallel and perpendicular to its tracks with only a single block in the huge grid left open for a public square. Soon thereafter the company advertised its determination "to build here at this central spot in Washington, the State Capital City, [and] attract colleges [and] manufactories."[84] Within a year most of the hundred or so buildings of old Yakima City were moved to the new town, it received its charter, became the county seat, and by 1892 with a population of 5,000 was well on its way to becoming the second largest city in Washington east of the Cascades.[85]

Two towns near the Idaho border contended for commerical and industrial supremacy in eastern Washington. The older of the two was Spokane Falls, formally laid out as a town in 1878 by L. W. Rima for James N. Glover on the latter's land south of the great falls of the Spokane River. This gridiron plat of 20 blocks established the basic orientation of streets that all subsequent subdividers would follow. Later that year Glover sold half of his interest in the townsite to A. M. Cannon and J. J. Browne of Portland, and the three men began a campaign to promote settlement and industrial development based on the water power that the falls could produce.[86]

Immediate success eluded them. In 1880 Spokane was still a mere hamlet of some 50 houses clustered near the falls on the south bank of the river. These first settlers shared their town with older residents, for as one eye-witness recalled, "Indian tepees dotted the hillsides and pleasant places along the river, and blanketed braves loafed and stalked majestically in the shade of the silent pines, and their ponies browsed at will over the grounds of the future city." A primitive rope ferry provided the only means of crossing the swiftly flowing river, and transportation was by horse or wagon along rough, winding roads.[87]

The approach of the Northern Pacific Railroad being built eastward from Ainsworth near the mouth of the Snake River touched off a vigorous campaign in several little settlements of the region of promote their

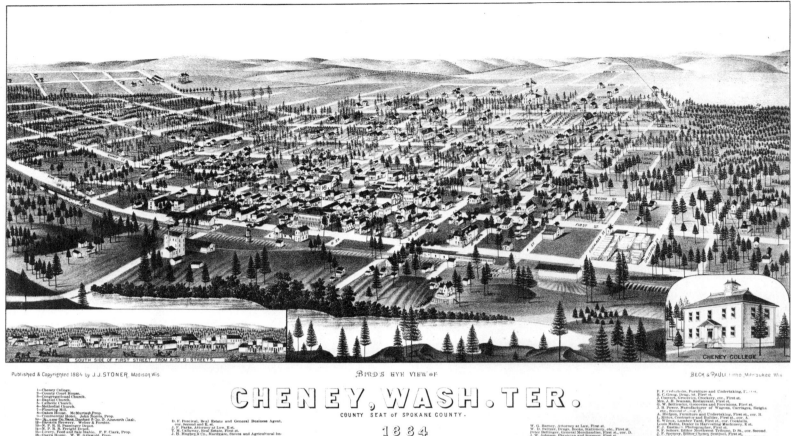

Figure 11.32 View of Cheney, Washington: 1884

future prosperity. Southeast of Spokane the newspaper of tiny Spangle claimed that its ''star shines brighter and brighter every day,'' and boasted that ''if Spangle had not been built Spokane Falls might have made a fair country village, but now this is destined to be the city of the upper country.''[88] Sprague, southwest of Spokane, was selected by the Northern Pacific for its division point and shops. This was a blow to

Spokane's hopes, and the town suffered another setback in 1880 when Cheney won the election to determine the location of the county seat.[89]

Cheney had been laid out by the railroad only that year a few miles to the south of Spokane. The view of the town in 1884, reproduced in Figure 11.32, shows the typical design of straight streets with intersections at right angles characterizing so many of the communities in the

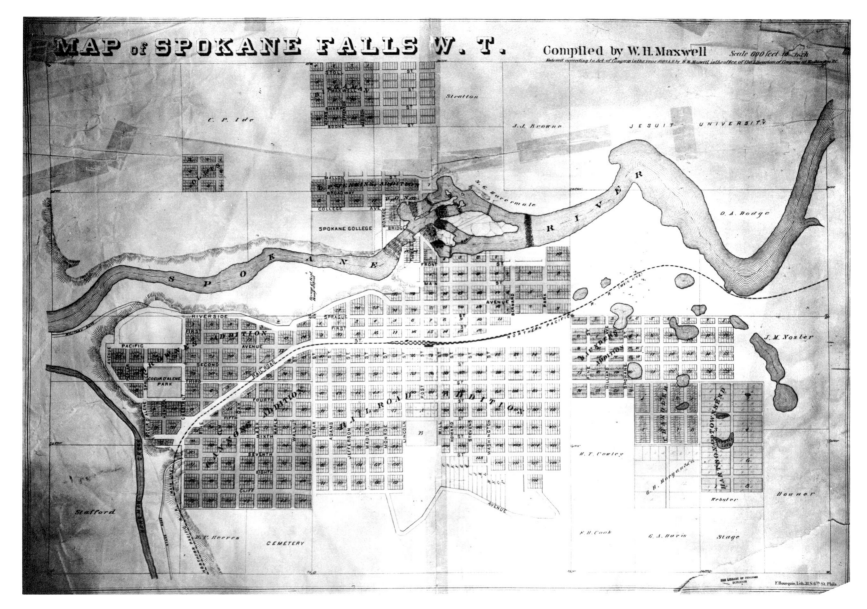

Figure 11.33 Plan of Spokane, Washington: 1883

Figure 11.34 View of Spokane, Washington: ca. 1890

Northwest. With its new courthouse bounded by Fourth, Fifth, D, and E Streets, Cheney College two blocks beyond, its "opera house" on First Street, and its thriving business district, Cheney appeared to have won not only the county seat but the more important contest for the chief business center of the eastern Columbia plain.

Such outward signs of early prosperity proved deceiving. Although the railroad reached Cheney earlier, Spokane welcomed its first train shortly thereafter when, on June 25, 1881, "hundreds of citizens . . . came to witness the last strokes uniting our fair city to the marts of commerce," a ceremony followed by the arrival of a locomotive pulling

six boxcars loaded with excursionists from the county seat.[90] A group of Spokane civic leaders promptly wired General John Sprague, head of the western division of the railroad, a message of congratulations, which included a boast that with its resources of water power the town would soon be "another Minneapolis." Sprague relied with a message ending in a word of encouragement: "May your prosperity exceed your most sanguine anticipations."[91]

Railroad service was all Spokane needed, and Sprague's well-wishes, possibly to his surprise, were to be realized. The town almost immediately entered a dizzy period of booming development that saw its 1880 population of 350 expand to nearly 20,000 in the decade and reach almost 37,000 before the century's end. Everyone seemed to be in the land business. The plan reproduced in Figure 11.33 shows the many additions to Glover's first streets platted by 1883. The largest lay south of the depot, which stood near the southern end of the original townsite. At the western end of town and north of the tracks was the addition laid out by J. J. Browne, one of Glover's partners. In 1883 this subdivision "existed in name only, there being no houses on it." Five years later a horse-drawn trolley connected this flourishing neighborhood with the city's then rapidly developing business and industrial center.[92]

The park that Browne laid out appropriately bore the name of Coeur d'Alene for the mining area just over the Idaho border where the discovery of gold in 1883 had set off a mad rush and made Spokane its main supply center. Prospectors jammed the city's streets, hotels, saloons, bawdy-houses, and shops. Enterprising industrialists erected flour and lumber mills to supply the miners. Many of those who struck it rich returned to settle, and they and the city's merchants, bankers, and mill-owners began to erect elaborate houses on higher ground overlooking the lively city and the tumbling falls that by the end of the decade had been tapped to provide electric power to light the city's streets and homes.[93]

Spokane inevitably recaptured the county seat from Cheney. Officials decided to build the courthouse on the north side of the falls where Col. D. P. Jenkins donated block 5 of his addition as a site.[94] Bridges across the river replaced the picturesque but inefficient rope ferry, and the north side of the city began to grow. Even the terrible fire of 1889, which wiped out the entire center of the city from the tracks to the river in a 5-block-wide swath, did not stop Spokane's development. A tent city sprang up in the devastated area, rebuilding commenced immediately, and larger and better business blocks were soon ready for trade on Riverside Avenue to replace those that had lined Front Street, formerly the chief commercial artery.[95]

The Spokane of this period is depicted in the view reproduced in Figure 11.34.[96] The city was soon to feel the full force of the depression of 1893, and for years it would fight about what civic leaders felt were unfair freight rates established by the railroads that had brought it from a crude village to a throbbing little metropolis. But Spokane weathered these crises and continued to attract new business, industry, and residents who heeded the invitation extended by its newspaper in 1883: "if you want lands, health, labor, business, wealth, and to grow up with most favored conditions in the country, come to Spokane."[97]

In the American settlement of California, the Pacific Northwest, and Utah, the western frontier had leaped over the Great Plains, and by the middle of the nineteenth century there were in reality two frontier lines. One was pushing slowly eastward from the Pacific Coast, while the other extended along the western borders of Minnesota, Iowa, Missouri, and Arkansas. Shortly after midcentury this older frontier line would once again begin to advance. In the settlement of Kansas and Nebraska, to which we now turn out attention, town founding and urban planning would play an important role as new residents poured into the central plains with even greater speed than during the initial settlement of the region we have just explored.

XII

Urban Planning on the Central Plains:
The Settlement of Nebraska

IN 1854 an enormous new area of the country was opened to settlement and urbanization by the Kansas and Nebraska Act signed by President Pierce on May 30. The law created two new territories occupying the land between the Missouri River and Minnesota Territory to the Continental Divide and extending from the 37th to the 49th parallels of latitude.[1]

A long and bitter debate preceded the adoption of this legislation. It set in motion events that culminated in the Civil War, for the act repealed the Missouri Compromise, under which Missouri and Maine were admitted as states with the proviso that except for Missouri slavery would be prohibited in the territory of the Louisiana Purchase north of the latitude of Missouri's southern boundary. The new act incorporated the doctrine of "popular sovereignty" by which the decision on slavery would be left to the new settlers. Senator Stephen A. Douglas, chairman of the committee on territories, promoted the measure as a device to secure southern support for the creation of the new territories—a necessary first step in the development of a transcontinental railroad, which he had long advocated.

The South was eager for the railroad, but championed a route through Texas, New Mexico Territory, and the Gadsden Purchase area, which had been added to the nation in 1853. Southern leaders opposed the creation of new territories north of this region to block a central or northern route for the proposed railroad. Southerners were equally adamant in their hostility to additional free states because it would upset the balance of political power on the slavery issue. The price for their reluctant support of the Kansas-Nebraska Act was elimination of any antislavery provision.

Residents of such border states as Missouri and Iowa supported the notion of a transcontinental railroad. By that time also it had become obvious that much of Nebraska and Kansas was suitable for agriculture under proper farming methods. Land speculators began to look eagerly at the lands beyond the Missouri River. In the region itself at least one Indian tribe—the Wyandots, who had been removed from Ohio to an area near the mouth of the Kansas River—began to agitate for territorial status in the belief that somehow they would benefit from such a development. Douglas was able to secure the support of President Pierce, efforts to obtain cession of Indian lands in much of the territories were successful, and at the beginning of the summer of 1854 the stage was set for a new wave of internal colonization.[2]

At the time the Kansas-Nebraska Act became effective, the only settlement of whites with any claim to the status of a true community was Bellevue, on the west bank of the Missouri some ten miles north of the mouth of the Platte River. Here a small group of buildings was occupied by missionaries and used for residential, school, and religious purposes; the office of the Indian Agent; and the trading post of the American Fur Company, directed since 1824 by Peter A. Sarpy. This settlement as sketched in 1833 by Karl Bodmer appears in Figure 12.1.

Sarpy and his fellow residents, numbering perhaps 50 in all, had watched with interest the progress of the legislation that created the new territories of Kansas and Nebraska. They realized that opening of the region to settlement would lead to the creation of towns. They were determined not only that Bellevue would be among the first of these new communities but that it should be the capital of Nebraska Territory.

Even before the passage of the necessary federal legislation Sarpy and his colleagues on February 9, 1854, organized the Bellevue Town Company. Six months later the newly established newspaper, the *Nebraska Palladium*, announced that "within the last month a large city upon a grand scale has been laid out, with a view of the location of the capital of Nebraska, at this point, and with a view to making it the center of commerce, and the half-way house between the Atlantic and Pacific Oceans."[3]

The original plat of Bellevue in 1854 with a few minor additions of a slightly later period appears in Figure 12.2. For a proposed seat of government it seems curious that no location was designated for the Capitol itself. The most prominent site, occupying a space equal to four normal city blocks, was the cemetery. Three other open squares appear, each one block in size and bearing patriotic names—Jefferson, Washington, and Union. The street pattern followed the gridiron system so widely employed in the West, but the northern third of the town closest to the Missouri River was tilted slightly from the alignment of the southern portion. Where these two sections met, Sarpy and his associates introduced a wedge-shaped park named Bellevue Common. Streets were platted in widths of 80 and 100 feet, with two—Mission and Main Streets—being given a width of 120 feet. Most blocks had 12 lots, each 46 by 130 feet, divided into two tiers by 16-foot alleys. With 4,440 lots in the original plat and 200 or so added almost immediately, the new town could have accommodated a population of some twenty thousand or more.[4]

As the oldest settlement in Nebraska, Bellevue seemed a likely spot for the territorial capital. This prize went to Omaha, however, and the residents had to be content with the town's designation as the seat of

Figure 12.1 View of Bellevue, Nebraska: 1833

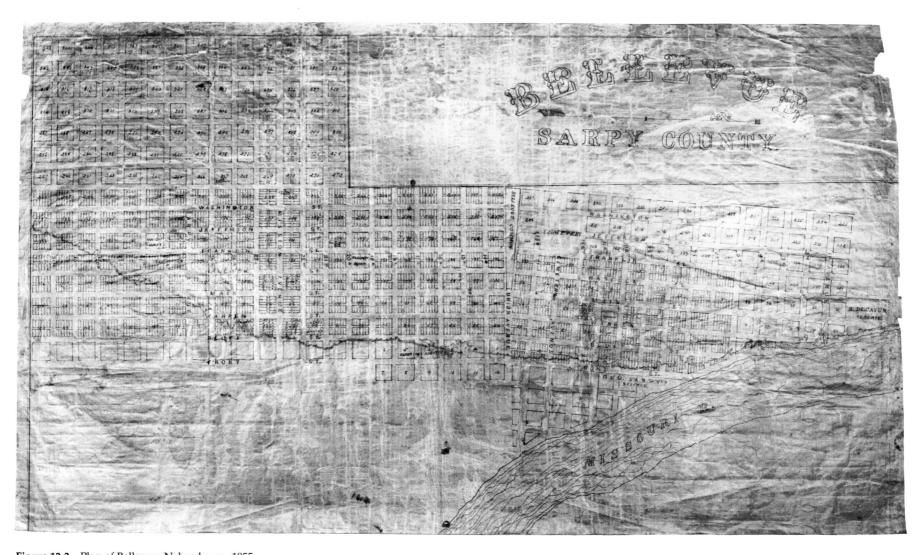

Figure 12.2 Plan of Bellevue, Nebraska: ca. 1855

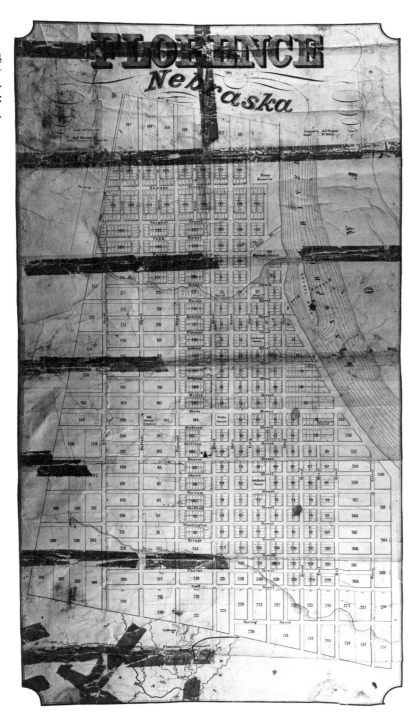

Figure 12.3 Plan of Florence, Nebraska: ca. 1855

Sarpy County in 1857. Bellevue's hope to become the terminus of the Union Pacific Railway met a similar fate some years later, and the town began to decline. The removal of the county seat to Papillion in 1875 reflected and hastened its dwindling importance. Bellevue College, which began instruction in 1884, offered renewed expectations of growth, and when it became the University of Omaha, Bellevue seemed destined to become an educational center. This prospect, too, eventually faded when the institution was forced to close for lack of funds after its final commencement exercises in 1919.[5] While the town still exists as the oldest, continuously occupied settlement in Nebraska, it has been dwarfed by its old rival to the north, Omaha. The cemetery and the two open squares of the original plan can still be found, but the triangular Bellevue Common disappeared long ago with the dreams of the founders of the town.

Bellevue was but one of many locations where towns were hastily platted in the summer and fall of 1854 along the Missouri River. The site of the former Mormon camp and temporary town of Winter Quarters across the river and six miles upstream from Council Bluffs, Iowa, was reoccupied early in the summer and replatted as the town of Florence. Soon copies of the town plat, reproduced in Figure 12.3, were prominently displayed in Iowa and the other infant Nebraska towns, and newspapers of the region carried the following announcement in September:

Sale of Lots!! In the town of Florence, formerly Winter Quarters, Nebraska Territory. One hundred choice Lots in said Town have been selected by the proprietors thereof, which will be offered at Public Sale on the fifteenth of October, next, to the highest and best bidder for ready money. . . .

The town is situated on a beautiful bluff . . . with a good permanent steamboat landing for at least a mile in length. There are two fine streams running through the town on both sides of which are excellent mill privileges. . . . There are extensive lime stone quarries, excellent clay for brick making and other purposes, plenty of first rate sand, gravel and an abundance of good timber.[6]

The plan of Florence followed the orientation of its predecessor Mormon camp, but it was substantially larger, reflecting the expectations of its founders that it would become a major city. The new town incorporated the old Mormon cemetery, and the town company voted funds to enclose and improve this plot. This was not pure sentiment, for two months later, in November, 1854, the company tendered stock in the town company to "Elder John Taylor one of the twelve Apostles of the Mormon Church for the purpose of securing his influence in favor of Florence."[7] The company wished to secure approval by the Church of Jesus Christ of Latter-Day Saints of the use of Florence as an outfitting point for emigrants bound for Utah. In this they were successful, and several of the handcart expeditions during the period 1856 to 1860 departed from Florence on the long and arduous trip west.

Florence's prosperity, like so many of the other newly created towns in the region, was temporary. By 1856 the population was 357. This increased to 1,158 in 1860, but four years later Mormons shifted their assembly point to Wyoming located on the Missouri River several miles below the mouth of the Platte.[8] The resulting loss of local trade caused a drastic decline in Florence's population, and in 1870 the town had less than 400 inhabitants. Other factors were at work. The dynamic development of Omaha as the territorial capital and then as the railroad center of the region after the completion of the first transcontinental route overshadowed its nearby rivals such as Florence. Eventually Florence itself was engulfed by the growing metropolis to the south and today forms a small part of Omaha.

While Bellevue and Florence occupied sites previously used for settlement, other Nebraska towns sprang up on virgin locations. The promoters of each community saw it as the future dominant city of Nebraska. They published elaborate maps, advertised sales of lots, occasionally constructed a hotel or some other structure to indicate the prosperity that was to come, and freely criticized the location and prospects of rival towns.

Most of the early towns, like Bellevue and Florence, were located along the banks of the Missouri River since water transportation by steamboat was far more convenient than the primitive roads and trails to the interior. The shallow Platte River was unusable for navigation except by the smallest craft, and the first towns were therefore clustered along the eastern boundary of the territory.

None exhibited much skill in town design. Knowledge of sophisticated town planning techniques was rare anywhere on the various American frontiers, and the layout of Nebraska communities testifies to its absence during the period of mass town founding in the middle of the nineteenth century. Speed and speculative advantage were the two principal criteria in the design of towns of this region and period—not beauty or monumentality.

We can sample the plans of the Missouri River towns in Nebraska by moving from south to north—omitting for the moment Omaha, which was destined for a more important role in the development of the territory and state than the other river towns that today are of minor importance or that have disappeared altogether—victims of a process of urban Darwinism by which only the fittest survived.

Figure 12.4 is the unimaginative plat of St. Deroin, one of five towns platted along the Missouri in Nemaha County near the Kansas boundary. Its name came from Joseph Deroin, an Otoe Indian chief who joined with Robert Hawke in 1854 to establish a community for the sale of goods to the Otoe Indians nearby. As at Florence, the founders used the cardinal points of the compass as their basic orientation for the gridiron street pattern rather than making the streets run parallel and perpendicular to the river bank. The place was not destined for prosperity. In 1882 it was described by a local historian as containing "but one store . . . two blacksmith shops, one hotel and one flouring-mill."[9]

Three miles north of St. Deroin lay Aspinwall, whose elaborately lithographed plan, printed in New York about 1857, is reproduced in Figure 12.5. The town's design, surveyed and drawn by W. E. Harvey, is rather impressive with its orientation to the river, the space reserved as a levee, and the large square prominently reserved for the courthouse. The variation in the size of the lots suggests also that the founders of the town had some notion of segregating business from residential uses—a concept lacking in many of the towns of the period. Despite its attractiveness as a two-dimensional design and the large and handsome colored lithograph depiction that was doubtless prominently displayed throughout the territory, Aspinwall did not achieve the success its proprietors sought. The designation as county seat, a guarantee on the frontier of at least a measure of prosperity, eluded Aspinwall. Eight hundred lots remained unsold by 1882, the same year in which a state history described it as a "village," and before the end of the century no more than a half-dozen structures remained on the site.

A few miles to the north Dr. Jerome Hoover laid out Nemaha City in 1855 on a completely regular grid pattern, each street being precisely 66 feet wide, each block containing eight lots 66 by 132 feet divided into groups of two by alleys passing north-south and east-west through the blocks. Block 65 represented the only bow to civic amenities, a notation on the plat stating that it was set aside as a public square. Hoover's original plat appears in Figure 12.6 in all its overwhelmingly monotonous regularity. Nemaha managed to survive, although today it has less than 300 inhabitants. The unreliable Missouri River gradually shifted its course, and the town now stands some distance away from the stream that was expected to bring it prosperity as a port community.

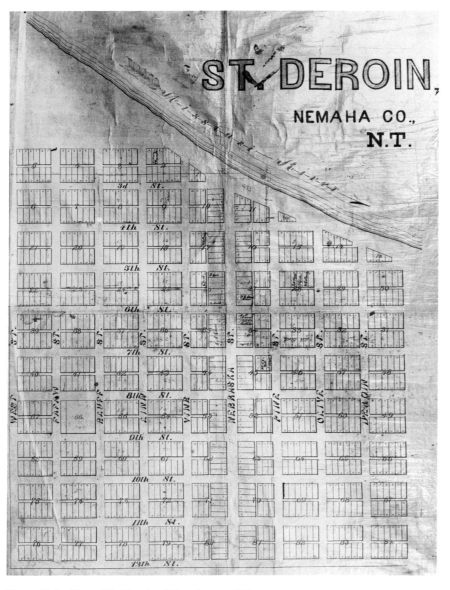

Figure 12.4 Plan of St. Deroin, Nebraska: ca. 1855

Brownville achieved greater success for a time, but it, too, lost out to other, more favored towns in the competition for trade, transportation, and as the seat of county government. Richard Brown founded the town in 1854, and in the following year he had his plan of streets, blocks, lots, public square, and levee printed in St. Louis for display to prospective settlers. Brown added to the published plat a rhapsodic description of the site, a glowing account of the progress of settlement, and a prophecy of the great future that lay ahead. The inflated prose is so typical of the promotional efforts of town founders in the Kansas and Nebraska region during this period that it deserves extended quotation:

Brownville is one of the most flourishing towns in Nebraska, of the most rapid growth & flattering prospects, as it enjoys a situation perhaps surpassed by none & equalled by few in America. . . . It is already a large & prosperous town. . . . The River is crossed by a splendid Ferry. The position of the town is in the centre of Nemaha County & is the seat of Justice. The surrounding country has been settled with great rapidity & the town is laid out with much taste & presents a fine appearance, several broad streets meet from different points at a public Green situated on a gentle elevation which commands a pretty view of the River & where the new Court House is to be completed. The place is one of the best for Commercial purposes on the Upper Missouri, having a good landing place, naturally formed by flat Rock. The navigable waters which are accessory to it form a market & an outlet for the products of the country to the Commercial World, which will not fail to secure to Brownville a rapid, solid & permanent increase of population & wealth. The Smoke of Steam Mills & Furnaces & the crowded Streets from Morning till night are sufficient indications of the superior importance of the place & the extent of business already carried on in several branches. . . . It has a Military Company, contains two First Class Hotels & some Boarding Houses, the Nemaha Valley Bank, a Land Officer, a Printing Establishment, a Church, a Literary Institution & the largest Steam Mill in Nebraska. It is the nearest & most convenient place for Shippers to land Freight for the Forts & Annuities for the Indians. Also best crossing, nearest & best Route for Emigrants on their way over the Plains and therefore bids fair to become the principal Town of Nebraska."

Brown's plat with the accompanying triumph of town "puffing," as such descriptions became known, is shown in Figure 12.7. The new

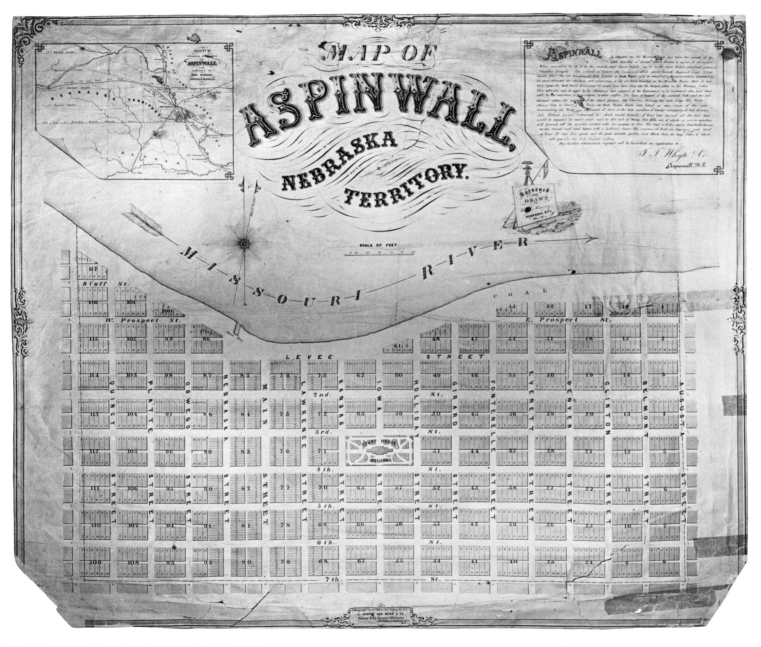

Figure 12.5   Plan of Aspinwall, Nebraska: ca. 1857

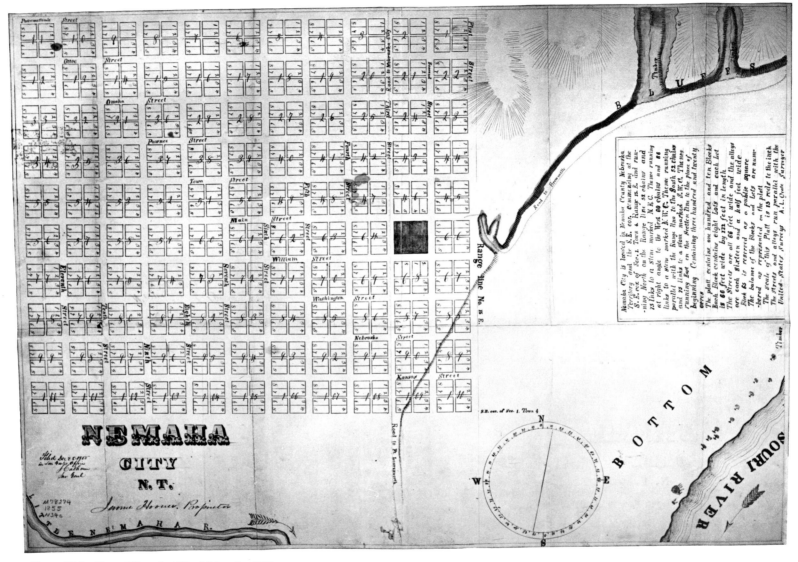

Figure 12.6 Plan of Nemaha City, Nebraska: 1855

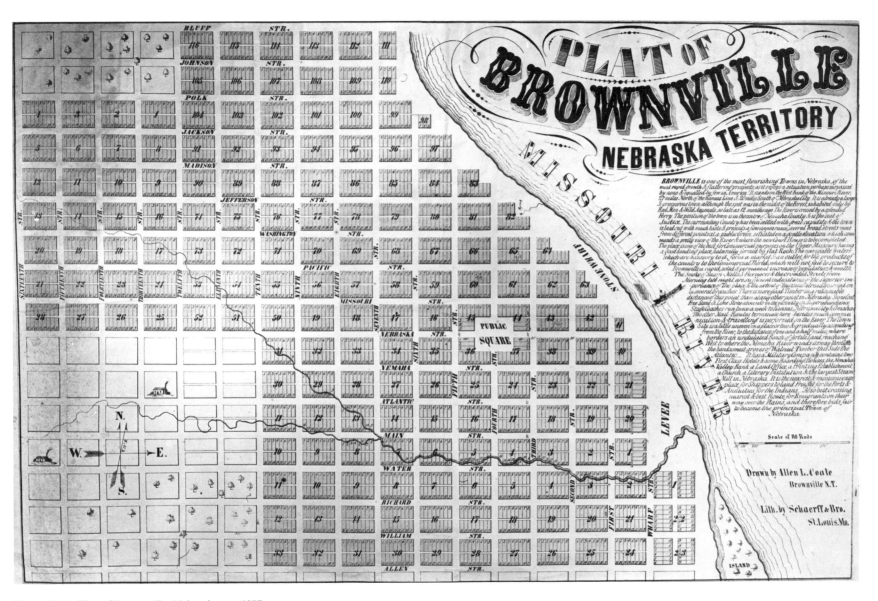

Figure 12.7   Plan of Brownville, Nebraska: ca. 1855

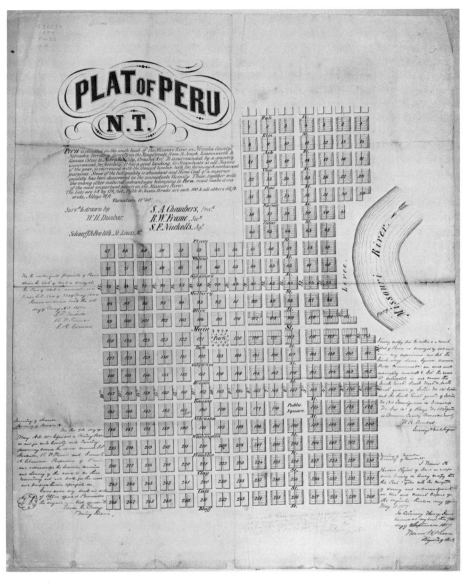

Figure 12.8   Plan of Peru, Nebraska: ca. 1857

town did attract a substantial volume of trade, and at the high point of steamboat travel on the Missouri it was a regular port of call for the 44 packets that served the river towns as early as 1857. In July of that year the Brownville's *Nebraska Advertiser* boasted that "There have been one hundred and thirty steamboat arrivals at the Brownville wharf since the opening of navigation this Spring, and at every arrival, without a single exception, there were passengers of freight or both landed here."[10] The financial panic of 1857, the failure of the town to attract a major railroad, and the movement of the county seat to Auburn in 1885 all contributed to the town's swift decline from its initial temporary success. Today it is a tiny community but with a wealth of old buildings standing as reminders that it was once a busy river port.

Six miles above Brownville, near the northern border of Nemaha County, lay Peru, created early in the boom year of 1857. It, too, had its handsome, large, colored lithograph plat printed in St. Louis for advertising purposes. Its conventional checkerboard pattern can be seen in Figure 12.8, complete with park, public square, and two principal streets—Main and Fifth—intersecting at a point near the area set aside for the levee, which its promoters expected to be the center of trade and commerce. This town, too, prospered for a time, and then diminished in size as other cities more favorably located on major transportation routes gained in favor. The Nebraska State Normal School, which opened in the fall of 1867, provided a more lasting economic base for the community, and the town was saved from the fate of many of its contemporaries.[11]

Two counties lay between Nemaha County and the Platte River—Otoe and Cass—and nowhere in Nebraska was there greater activity in town founding during the years from 1854 to 1857. In Cass County alone, 27 new communities sprang into existence during the boom year of 1857.[12] Most of these are among the 64 ghost towns of Cass County. In Otoe County the names and locations of 16 defunct towns have been determined, most of which were established during the same period.[13]

The two most important towns in this area were Nebraska City in Otoe County, which will be described later, and Plattsmouth in Cass County. The site of Plattsmouth, just south of the mouth of the Platte River, had previously been occupied by Samuel Martin, who had established an Indian trading post there in 1853 under government license. Even before the Indians relinquished their titles to land in the area in the spring of 1854, a number of settlers crossed from the Iowa side of the Missouri and marked claims to lands in the vicinity. Martin and several associates organized the Plattsmouth Town Company in October of 1854 and prepared their survey for filing the following month. They persuaded the legislature to designate the new town as the county seat, a ferry across the Missouri provided easy access for settlers, and river steamers were soon making regular calls at the town.

The proprietors had greater prospects in mind. As the two large reservations in Figure 12.9 designated as "Depot Grounds" suggest, they regarded the town as a likely candidate for the Missouri river terminus of the transcontinental railroad whose contemplated construction had been such an important factor in the establishment of Nebraska Territory. The Platte River trail had played a major role in the exploration of the West, and it seemed highly probable that those responsible for locating the new railroad would give it serious consideration in selecting the transcontinental route.

In this, the citizens of Plattsmouth were eventually disappointed despite intensive efforts to establish their town as a railroad center. Bonds in the amount of $50,000, depot grounds, and additional city lots were offered to the Burlington and Missouri line in 1869 on condition that the railroad locate its Nebraska headquarters in the city. Construction started, and the town began to have visions of a bright future. The offices of the railroad were, however, built in Omaha, and Plattsmouth had to satisfy itself with a locomotive repair shop of a railroad that entered Plattsmouth over a bridge from Iowa only to run north to Omaha, where it reinforced that town's growing dominance as the rail center of Nebraska and doomed Plattsmouth to remain a small and unimportant locality.[14]

North of Omaha, to which we shall return shortly, the number of new towns diminished somewhat, but there were far more than could ever be supported by the population. Two that have survived had somewhat more elaborate plans than those that have been described, although both followed the typical grid system. Tekamah, the county seat of Burt County, and Dakota, the seat of a county of the same name opposite Sioux City, Iowa, where the Missouri begins to bend toward the west, both were begun in 1855. Tekamah's plan featured a large "Central Park." As can be seen in Figure 12.10, this took the form of a circle set in a space the size of four normal city blocks. Evidently this park was to be landscaped in a naturalistic manner with free-form planting beds and curving walks. The same style, on a much larger scale, was to be employed in New York City two years later by the young Frederick Law Olmsted in his design for a more famous and widely imitated Central Park.

As we shall see, several Kansas towns of this period also incorpo-

401

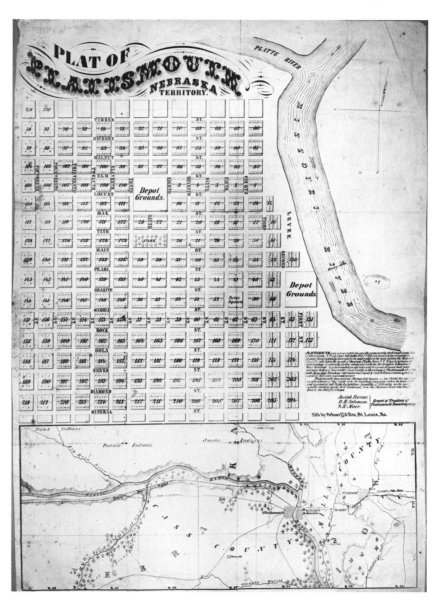

Figure 12.9 Plan of Plattsmouth, Nebraska: 1855

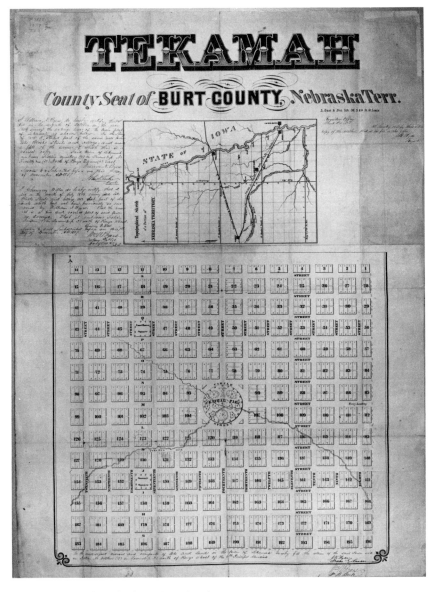

Figure 12.10   Plan of Tekamah, Nebraska: 1855

rated in their plans parks or public squares designed—on paper at least—in this manner. Whether William N. Byers, the surveyor of Tekamah, or the planners of the Kansas towns with similar features, were influenced by the same sources as Olmsted will probably never be known. It seems likely, however, that they, like Olmsted, knew that this naturalistic pattern was being used in the layout of eastern private estates and also in the design of the so-called "rural cemeteries," which by the 1850s were so highly regarded as beauty spots in such cities as Boston, New York, Philadelphia, and Cincinnati.[15] Tekamah's primitive little park was a brave effort to provide an element of urban amenity on the raw frontier of mid-nineteenth-century Nebraska.

The possible influence of an eastern plan can also be seen in the design of Dakota, or Dakota City.[16] The original plat is reproduced in Figure 12.11 and shows a central public square on the north side of Broadway which had the generous width of 150 feet. Four other public sites can be seen symmetrically located nearby. The two on the east were designated as market squares, the one in the northwest as a site for a college, and the remaining one as Seminary Square. The general pattern resembles, although not in exact details, the design of Philadelphia, with its grid streets and five public squares. Like Philadelphia, too, the east-west streets, with the exception of Broadway, bear the names of trees.

Not only did the town plan provide an unusually generous number of public sites, but the founders attempted to give them additional prominence by planning the streets passing them on their north and south sides with greater width. Vine, Locust, Hickory, and Elm Streets were thus platted 100 feet wide, while all other streets in the town except for Broadway were made 80 feet in width.

Dakota became a thriving place when the United States Land Office opened in 1857, and it also was designated as county seat and a place where the United States District Court convened twice a year. An imposing three-story hotel, the Bates House, soon added an air of affluence, and the town's future as the metropolis of northern Nebraska seemed assured. This proved an illusion. After statehood, the district court moved elsewhere, and in 1875 the Land Office joined the exodus. The decline in importance of river traffic made its influence felt as well, and well before the end of the century the citizens of Dakota must have realized that their greatest problem was not in coping with growth but in fighting decline and decay.

More remarkable for its street names than for any unusual feature of its plan was St. John's City in the northern part of Dakota County. Figure 12.12 shows the plat of the town founded in 1856 by a colony of Roman Catholics from Iowa. Doubtless it was Father Jeremiah Trecy who decided on the plan and the street names. The north-south streets bore the conventional numbers, but those running east-west constituted a partial hagiology of the canonized: St. Margaret, St. Elizabeth, St. Monica, St. Anastasia, etc.

In frontier towns where the public squares were normally merely undivided blocks of the regular grid, St. John's and St. Mary's Parks took a more sophisticated pattern. Streets leading to them entered at their midpoints, and the surrounding blocks were notched at the corners to provide the necessary space. Two other public sites, one for a public square—possibly to contain a courthouse or other civic building—and the other designated as St. Terrance's Park, were given the more conventional configuration. Despite its interesting layout and the support of the church, St. John's City failed to attain a population of more than 200. After the panic of 1857 a slow depopulation began, and within two decades of its founding the town had dwindled to no more than a handful of houses.

Scores, probably hundreds, of other minor towns were platted along the banks of the Missouri in Nebraska in the first three years of the territory's existence. Some existed only on paper. Other enjoyed a brief existence and then faded away. It is no exaggeration to state that only a minority survived in some fashion to the present time.[17] The frontier proved as competitive for towns as it did for individuals. Nowhere was the battle for urban supremacy more fiercely contested than in Nebraska, and it is to the town that eventually emerged as the dominant metropolis that we now turn.

The site that Omaha was to occupy lay across the river from Council Bluffs, Iowa, a city of perhaps 2,000, which had prospered from the Mormon emigration and the California gold rush. The leaders of this community aspired to attract the transcontinental railway. They reasoned that if the Nebraska territorial capital could be located immediately opposite the town on the west bank of the river, Council Bluffs would prosper and that prospects of obtaining the railroad would be vastly enhanced. Even if this scheme did not succeed, the possibility of speculative gain from town promotion was too tempting an opportunity to pass by.

As early as 1853 William Brown, who operated a ferry across the Missouri at that point, staked out an illegal claim for a townsite on land still in Indian possession. Brown's enterprise attracted a number of other citizens from Council Bluffs, and in June of that year they made an in-

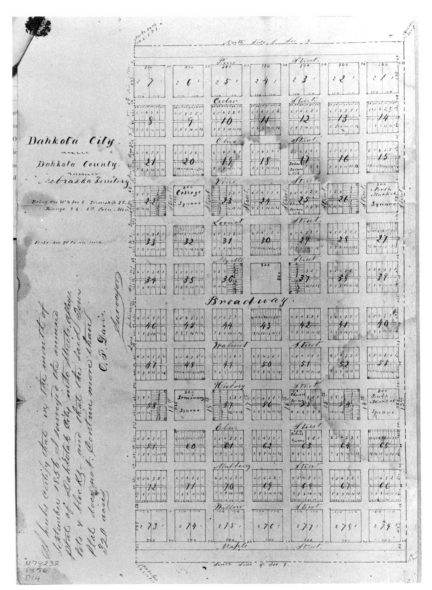

Figure 12.11   Plan of Dakota, Nebraska: 1856

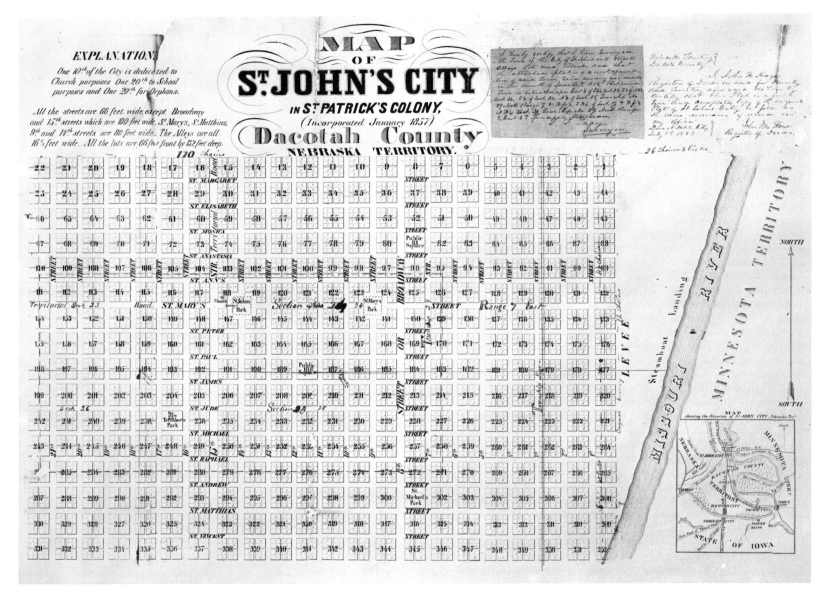

Figure 12.12 Plan of St. John's, Nebraska: 1856

spection of the area. Anticipating that the Indian title would soon be voided, they carried out some preliminary surveys, and later in 1853 a group headed by Dr. Enos Lowe bought out Brown, purchased a steam ferry, and organized the Council Bluffs and Nebraska Ferry Company. They succeeded also in securing the appointment of a post-master for Omaha City even before the approval of the territorial bill.[18] A. D. Jones, a surveyor, received the appointment and following the opening of the territory completed the final town plan under the direction of Dr. Lowe.

Soon a published version of the plat was available from printers in St. Louis, and in the form reproduced in Figure 12.13 could be seen in hotels, real estate offices, stores, and at ferry landings.[19] In the first issue of the *Omaha Arrow*, printed on July 28, 1854, in Council Bluffs, this description appeared:

> The lots are sixty-five feet front and one hundred and thirty-two in length, every lot running back to an alley twenty feet wide; and, instead of laying off the entire tracts into small lots for speculation, our lots have been laid off around the business part on a liberal scale, including an ample number of commanding and beautiful points for private residences and gardens. All the streets are one hundred feet wide, except two avenues which lead to Capitol Square, which are one hundred and twenty feet wide. All the alleys are twenty feet wide. Squares have been reserved and set apart for all the leading and principal denominations, and for Masonic and Odd Fellows halls.[20]

It seems strange that the proprietors of the town under whose sponsorship the *Arrow* began publication did not stress the one feature of the town plan that set Omaha apart from the other frontier settlements then quickly being surveyed up and down the river. This was the elongated park occupying the space of seven city blocks between Jackson and Davenport Streets. Perhaps it was just as well, since three years after its designation as a park the city council with Mayor Lowe's approval donated a portion of the tract to a hotel company, and the remainder of the strip was divided into uniform blocks and lots and put on the market for further building development. The resulting Herndon House, an imposing four-story brick structure erected at a reputed cost of $75,000, furnished badly needed transient accommodations in the infant city, but the opportunity to create a green heart in the very center of the community was thus irretrievably lost.[21] Washington Square, one of the two open spaces two blocks north and south of Capitol Avenue, was also vacated in that same year. The first county courthouse soon occupied the southwest corner after the remainder of the block had been divided into lots and sold to help finance the new building.[22]

A more important structure was soon under construction on Capitol Square. That building represented Omaha's victory in the bitter fight to secure the territorial capital—a prize eagerly sought by every new town along the river. The struggle left deep scars, created political rivalries, and was ultimately to lead to the transfer of the seat of government away from Omaha when the territory became a state.

The details of this controversy need not detain us, but it should be noted that in virtually every western state the same issue arose and was strongly contested in the knowledge that the locality securing the designation of capital city had an assured future. In Nebraska Bellevue seemed to have this guarantee. Francis Burt, whom President Pierce appointed as territorial governor, evidently intended to call the first meeting of the legislature at that place where he arrived in October, 1854. He was ill on arrival, his condition worsened, the oath of office was administered at his bedside, and by October 18 he was dead.

Territorial Secretary Thomas B. Cuming succeeded Burt, becoming acting governor. A young man of twenty-five who had edited a Keokuk, Iowa, newspaper, he was naturally inclined to favor Iowa interests, and on December 20 he revealed that the first legislative session would be held at Omaha. Moreover, despite a census that revealed that the area south of the Platte River contained twice as many persons as the portion of the territory to the north, Cuming apportioned 14 seats in the legislature to the North Platte counties and only 12 to those of the south.[23]

Mass meetings, indignant editorials, charging Cuming with accepting bribes, attempts to detach the South Platte counties from the territory in favor of annexation to Kansas, and other expressions of outrage and opposition failed to deter Cuming and his supporters. On January 16, 1855, the legislature convened in Omaha's only brick building, a two-story structure built by the Council Bluffs and Nebraska Ferry Company facing the park strip on the eastern side of Ninth Street. By the end of the month Cuming was able to sign one of the first laws enacted—an act designating Omaha as the territorial capital.[24]

Three weeks later Mark Izard arrived in Omaha to assume the office of governor. Under his administration construction began on the Capitol located on the commanding site set aside for this purpose by the founders of the town. Congress appropriated $50,000 for this build-

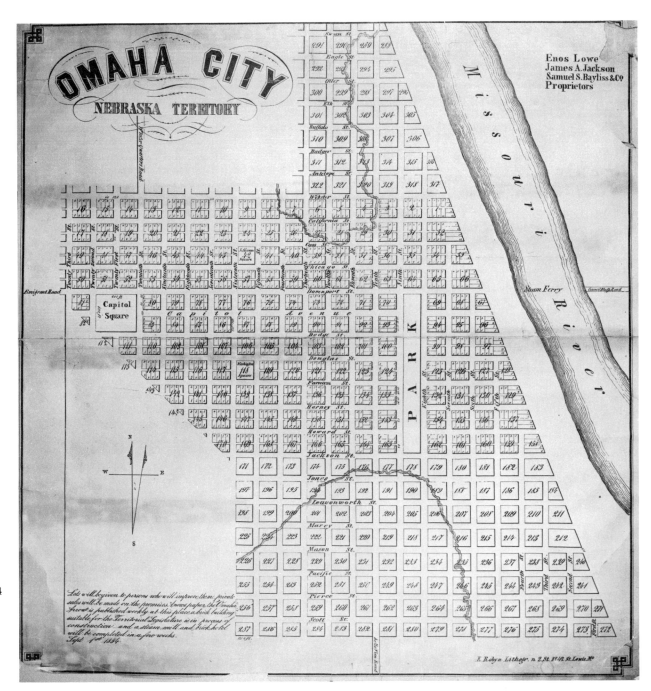

Figure 12.13
Plan of Omaha, Nebraska: 1854

ing, and the city of Omaha added $60,000. Opponents of Omaha charged that the project was tainted with graft and that the city and those holding the construction contract would receive far more benefits than the territory. Work proceeded, nevertheless, and at the session of 1857 the legislators were able to meet in the new building although it was not yet finished.[25]

The Capitol as it appeared to an artist slightly more than a decade later is the most prominent feature of the 1869 view of Omaha reproduced in Figure 12.14. The building dominated the skyline, and from its eastern windows one could see the entire city stretching out below.

By 1857 Omaha throbbed with activity. Its population increased daily as new settlers arrived on river steamers or by ferries from Iowa. The infant settlement by April, 1857, had a population of about 2,000. Two months later this had grown to 3,000. Even its enemies conceded that progress in the capital was impressive. The editor of the Nebraska City newspaper admitted that Omaha's "buildings are fine, large, elegant, and commodious and generally built with neatness and good taste. . . . The site of the town, too, is a beautiful one, while the view from the Capitol is really magnificent."[26]

The rapid increase in population set off a construction boom and unprecedented speculation in town lots. Persons who had filed early land claims to property adjoining the original town or who had purchased tracts from the first claimants soon began to subdivide their land into streets, blocks and lots. Figure 12.15 shows the expanded area of the city as platted in 1857. The vast majority of lots were unoccupied, but everyone was confident that they would soon all be built on and that even further expansion of the city would be needed. Lots which in 1855 had sold for $100 and in 1856 for $600 brought as much as $4,000 during the summer of 1857.[27]

The mania for town lot speculation gripped not only Omaha but all of the towns already founded and those hastily created during the boom year of 1857. J. Sterling Morton, frontier Nebraska editor, politician, historian, and first-hand witness described the atmosphere that prevailed during the speculative years of 1856 and 1857:

"The greater portion of the summer of 1856 was consumed in talking and meditating upon the prospective value of city property. Young Chicagos, increascent New Yorks, precocious Philadelphias and infant Londons were duly staked out, lithographed, divided into shares, and puffed with becoming unction and complaisance. The mere mention of using such valuable lands for the purpose of agriculture was considered an evidence of verdancy wholly unpardonable, and entirely sufficient to convict a person of old-fogyism in the first degree."[28]

In the next chapter on the towns of Kansas we shall look further at the causes, techniques, and consequences of the urban land boom of the 1850s. In Nebraska's sister territory, speculation was even more intensive during this period if only because Kansas contained a substantially greater population. In both territories the bubble burst in the fall of 1857 with the failure of several New York and Ohio financial institutions. Virtually every bank in Nebraska, which, since July, 1856, had been issuing almost unlimited quantities of bank notes, collapsed.

The resulting depression was severe, nearly all construction came to a halt, and at least for a time town lot speculators were discouraged from the creation of further new towns or the extension of those that existed. Indeed, in Omaha at least, whole sections of newly subdivided additions to the city were vacated and reverted to farms. The plan of Omaha reproduced in Figure 12.16 shows the street system in 1866 on the same scale as the preceding illustration. Even at that date, with the city designated as the eastern terminus of the Union Pacific Railroad and its economic future assured, land developers had not ventured much beyond the original bounds of the first town survey of 1854. Not until the completion of the transcontinental line and the further settlement of the Great Plains was Omaha to begin its growth into the modern manufacturing and food processing center that the present metropolis has become.

The character of the city at this time can best be appreciated by an inspection of two views of Omaha in 1867 and 1868 reproduced as Plate 15 and Figure 12.17. Much of the river frontage had been pre-empted by railroad yards, lines, and spurs serving the levees where steamers were still active. On Farnham and Douglas Streets most of the stores, hotels, and other places of business could be found. Elsewhere the scale was primarily domestic with the skyline broken here and there by church steeples and, of course, by the Capitol on its elevated site, which marked the western edge of the town. In 1867, however, the government of the new state of Nebraska abandoned this building when it moved the seat of government to a new town founded for that purpose many miles to the southwest. We shall return to this episode and the handsome town that resulted from this decision after an examination of Nebraska City.

Nebraska City in Otoe County was the one town in early Nebraska that threatened Omaha's supremacy. Its leading citizens had been among the most prominent of those residents of the South Platte region who attempted to deny Omaha the designation of territorial capital. And, for a few years after 1858, it rivaled Omaha as a center of transportation and commerce.

Figure 12.14 View of Omaha, Nebraska: 1869

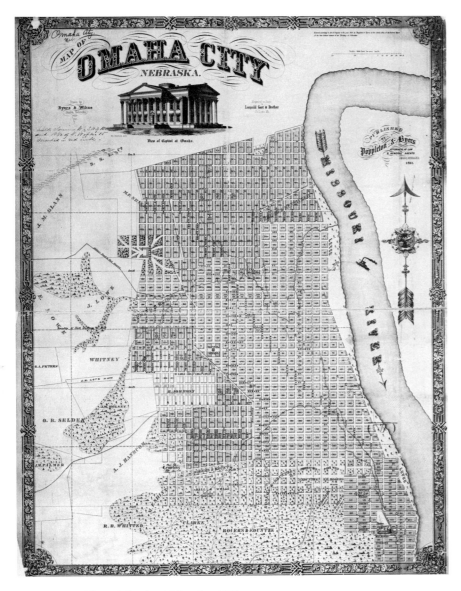

Figure 12.15 Plan of Omaha, Nebraska: 1857

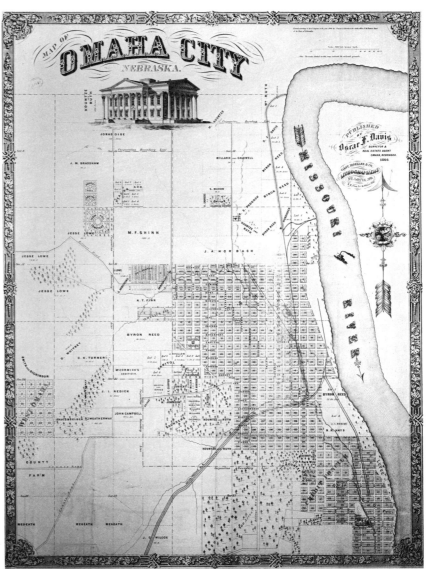

Figure 12.16 Plan of Omaha, Nebraska: 1866

Figure 12.17   View of Omaha, Nebraska: 1868

Nothing in its plan distinguished Nebraska City from the dozens of other river towns of early territorial days. The Nebraska City Town Site Company under the leadership of S. F. Nuckolls began its surveys on May 10, 1854, in anticipation of the passage of the territorial act and soon produced a standard gridiron plat. The site had previously been occupied by the first Fort Kearny, established in 1847 and moved in the following year to a location 160 miles west on the Platte River. The first public sale of lots took place a year later with J. Sterling Morton, newly arrived as editor of the *Nebraska News*, as auctioneer. His amusing account of that event reveals some of the difficulties encountered by town promoters of the period as well as the great expectations they held out for future development:

"There must have been a multitude in attendance, which numbered at least seventeen or eighteen, and about five of them were not members of the town company, and against them every patriotic resident of this hopeful neighborhood . . . bid with great and vehement vigor. That was a proud period in the babyhood of this settlement. It demonstrated the fact that there was some exchangeable value to lots. Everybody began to feel wealthy, and put on the comfortable airs of proprietary and pecuniary plethora. We had lots to sell; the whole world wanted to buy lots, and we could make supply equal to demand, until the plains from the Missouri River to the Rocky Mountains had been chopped up into lots."[29]

Nebraska City grew at a leisurely pace despite these promotional efforts. One part of the town clustered near the river around the site of the abandoned fort. The other occupied higher ground some distance west of the river. When the perceptive Mollie Sanford arrived in the spring of 1857 she observed that Nebraska City was not yet "much of a city. The town proper is situated on the hill or bluffs back from the river. But few houses are built yet. We are stopping where the town was first settled, down near the river in Kearney City. This place is three years old. I hear there are churches and stores up in the other town. Here, there are nothing but rude cabins and board shanties not even plastered."[30]

The depression of 1857 halted Nebraska City's modest growth for a time, but by the spring of 1858 it learned the encouraging news that it had been selected as the base for the overland freighting firm of Russell, Majors, and Waddell. This company, previously headquartered in Leavenworth, Kansas, held a War Department contract to transport supplies to military forts and camps as far west as Utah and New Mexico. At the western edge of Nebraska City the firm constructed its complex of warehouses, barns, blacksmith shops, wagon repair shops,

boardinghouses, and other buildings necessary for such a major enterprise. Sturdy Murphy wagons from St. Louis and Studebakers from South Bend, Indiana, lined the riverbank, thousands of oxen grazed in the pastures around the town, and hundreds of new residents arrived seeking accommodations, supplies, and entertainment.[31]

Other overland freighting firms joined Russell, Majors, and Waddell in Nebraska City. Between 1858 and the time the railroad brought an end to long distance commerical wagon transportation 64 companies based in Nebraska City were involved in freighting.[32] While many of these were small, others were of considerable size. All this brought instant prosperity to Nebraska City, although other cities of the territory, chiefly Omaha, also shared in the overland freighting business.

The streets of Nebraska City bustled with activity. Mollie Sanford lived above the Russell, Majors, and Waddell office and recorded the view from her window in May, 1858: "Today the streets are full of ox teams loading up to start on a trip to Utah. All is commotion, the hallowing of the drivers, the clanking of chains and wagon-masters giving orders."[33]

The next year saw even more movement and excitement as those bound for the gold camps of Colorado joined the wagon trains of the commercial freighters streaming through the town and on to the westward plains. In 1865 Alfred Mathews stood on the Iowa side of the Missouri River and drew the sketch from which the lithographed view in Figure 12.18 was prepared. Wagon trains can be seen leading from the levee into town, while others are shown on Main Street plodding up the long ascent from the river terrace. The city at that time had only recently completed rebuilding from a disastrous fire which in March, 1860, destroyed 46 business buildings including the elaborate four-story Nuckolls House, perhaps the most elegant hotel in Nebraska.[34]

Railroad transportation to the West brought a sudden end to the overland freighting business from Nebraska City, which had failed in its attempts to secure the route of the transcontinental line. Nebraska City investors did organize the Midland Pacific Railway Company in 1866, but not until 1871 did the line begin service to Lincoln, 58 miles to the west.[35] By that time it was too late for the city to recapture its once dominant position as a freighting terminus, and the view of Nebraska City in 1868 reproduced in Plate 16 shows the town at the end of its period of rapid expansion. Many of the buildings lining Main Street recall the glorious days of the city's prosperous past when most of the goods and many of the settlers bound for the West passed through this pioneer river port.

Figure 12.18 View of Nebraska City, Nebraska: 1865

While these infant cities along the Missouri River were contending for trade, speculating in town lots, bickering over the location of the capital, and attempting to attract railroads from the East, additional communities were springing up in the interior. Many of these, like those lining the Missouri, existed only on paper, but others succeeded in their fight for survival. By 1857 an astonishing number of town names appeared on maps of Nebraska. Reproduced in Figure 12.19 is a portion of the map of Kansas and Nebraska published in an edition of Colton's atlas in that year. While the settled area of Nebraska was plainly concentrated in a relatively narrow zone following the Missouri River, a number of new towns can be seen strung out along the now well-traveled route to Colorado along the north bank of the Platte River.

The most westerly of these towns was Columbus, near the mouth of the Loup River. Here in 1856 two rival townsite companies, the Elkhorn and Loup Fork Bridge and Ferry Company and the Columbus Town Company merged under the latter's name to develop a town and a ferry at the difficult crossing of the Loup.[36] The directors of the company took steps to attract settlers and to stimulate economic growth. They donated 18 shares of stock to one John Rickly on the condition that he establish a sawmill. Gifts of city lots were made to no fewer than 12 newspapers in Nebraska, Ohio, and Missouri, doubtless with the understanding that favorable publicity would be forthcoming. Other donations followed: two lots to anyone who would build a house worth at least $200; three lots for every twenty thousand bricks produced by a local brickyard; and one share of stock to the first white woman taking up residence in the city!

In 1857 stockholders were assessed $25 for each share held to raise funds for the construction of a hotel, that symbol on the frontier that a town was truly in being. Churches of any denomination were offered three lots to aid in the construction of houses of worship; a house built by the company was donated as a school in 1859; and in 1867 the city council, in a burst of promotional generosity, offered Columbus Square as a ten-acre site for state buildings if the Nebraska legislature designated the city as the state capital. In this the city was unsuccessful, but Columbus did secure the county seat by offering the same site to Platte County for the construction of a courthouse.

The view of Columbus in Figure 12.20 shows the town as it appeared eight years after that great day of June 1, 1866, when the line of the Union Pacific Railroad arrived. That fascinating visionary, railroad and urban promoter, eccentric publicist, and politician—George Francis Train—had once boomed Columbus not only as the Nebraska seat of the government but as the capital of the United States. The little town of the view with its scattered development on a gridiron pattern interrupted diagonally by a steep escarpment scarcely suggests that it once cherished the hope of becoming a major metropolis. George F. Train's connection with Columbus as well as his other activities in railroad and town promotion will be examined in a later chapter dealing with the influence of railroads on western town development. At that time we will take up the founding and growth of other communities in the valley of the Platte as well as those elsewhere in Nebraska closely linked to the development of rail transportation.

Towns not located on the Missouri River or on the early rail lines were slow to develop despite vigorous promotion efforts by their founders. Pawnee City, the county seat of Pawnee County, which adjoins the Kansas border and is among the second tier of counties west of those along the Missouri River, is an excellent example. Surveyed early in 1857, this little town was unable to secure a rail connection until 1881 when a branch of the Burlington line finally provided improved transportation. The view in Figure 12.21 shows the settlement two years earlier when it served as a local trading center for the farmers in the vicinity and as the seat of county government. Its population was then under 800, but with its newly constructed courthouse on the square facing Washington Street, its impressive school two blocks away at the edge of town, the two-story brick Woods Hotel (now the Hotel Pawnee), four churches, a race track, and several local industries, it was the largest and most imposing town of the county.

Today Pawnee City retains a few of the structures built before a disastrous fire in 1881 and many of those that were constructed immediately afterward as replacements for destroyed buildings. Several buildings of historic interest had been moved to an outdoor museum, and others are scheduled to be preserved in this fashion. Among them is the dwelling built in 1864 by David Butler, the first governor of the state of Nebraska and a leader in Pawnee City civic affairs.[37] In 1867 Butler found himself involved in the founding and planning of the much larger and greater city of Lincoln, designed to serve as the permanent capital of the new state.

The initial controversy over the location of the territorial capital in Omaha had never really died. Legislators raised the issue at almost every session. In 1857 only Governor Izard's veto, which failed by a single vote to be overruled, prevented the capital from being moved to the almost nonexistent "town" of Douglas in Lincoln County more

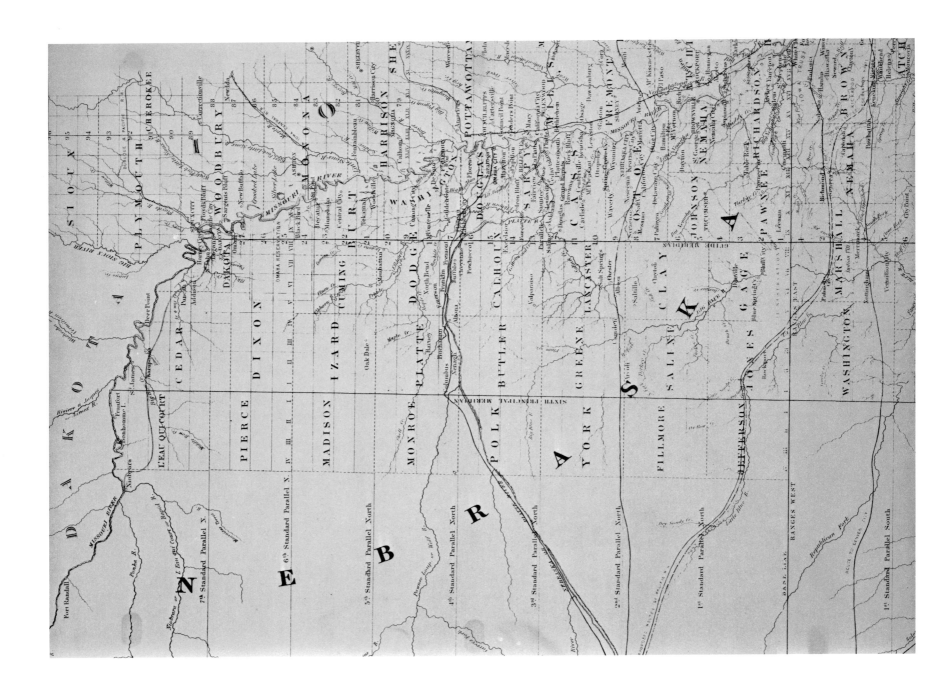

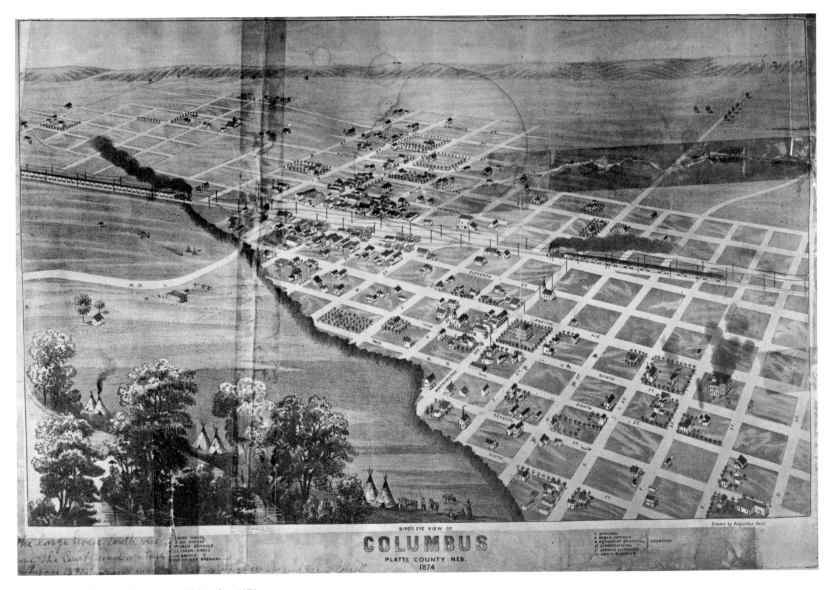

BIRD'S EYE VIEW OF

COLUMBUS

PLATTE COUNTY NEB.
1874

Drawn by Augustus Koch.

Figure 12.20   View of Columbus, Nebraska: 1874

Opposite: **Figure 12.19**   Map of Nebraska: 1857

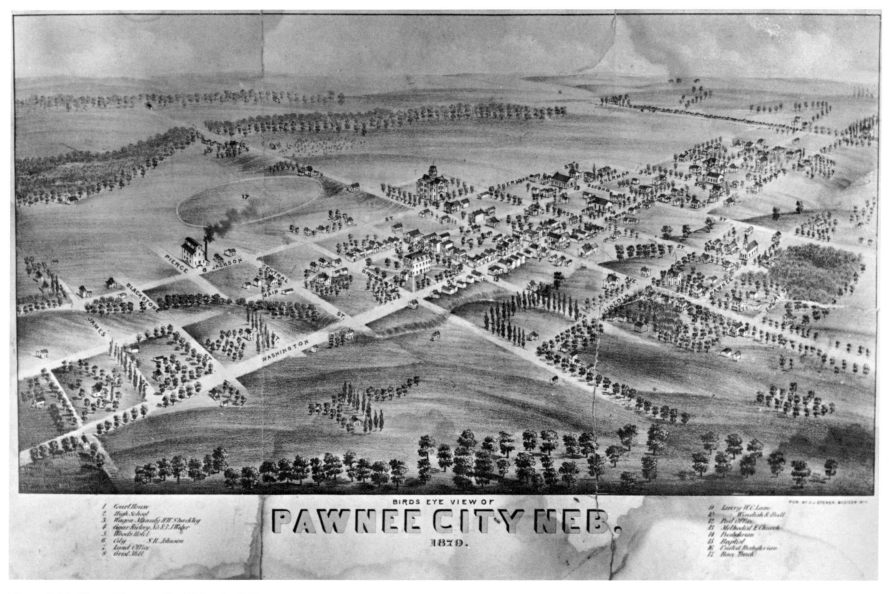

Figure 12.21 View of Pawnee City, Nebraska: 1879

than 50 miles southwest of Omaha.[38] Other attempts by opponents of Omaha in the years that followed were beaten back by a majority of the members of the legislature from the counties north of the Platte River who outnumbered their adversaries through a system of apportionment that unfairly gave them a numerical advantage.

When President Andrew Johnson, on March 1, 1867, proclaimed the admission of Nebraska Territory as a state, a new opportunity arose to resolve the conflict. Governor David Butler called the previously elected state legislators to a special session to organize the new government. This time the South Platte representatives were not to be denied, and after bitter debate the new state legislature passed a measure which the governor signed on June 14 marking the end of Omaha as a capital city.[39]

The act directed a three-man commission consisting of the governor, the secretary of state, and the auditor to locate a capital site on a one-square-mile tract of land, have it surveyed and laid out as a town, sell lots in alternate blocks at public auction, and use the proceeds for the construction of public buildings. The new capital was to be located somewhere within an area comprising Seward County, the southern portion of Saunders and Butler Counties, and the northern two-thirds of Lancaster County.[40] The act named the new city Lincoln and further specified that the state university and the state penitentiary were both to be located within its boundaries.

Governor Butler, Secretary of State Thomas Kennard, and Auditor John Gillespie set out from Nebraska City on July 18 to tour the designated region. Accompanying them was Augustus F. Harvey, who numbered among his accomplishments skills as a surveyor, lawyer, editor, and politician. The four men visited a number of possible sites, finally reaching the little settlement of Lancaster on Salt Creek, a tributary of the Platte. Nearby lay extensive salt deposits, which had attracted the first settlers some years earlier. A small grid town had been platted and a handful of buildings erected in the area of what is now O and Tenth Streets.[41]

While much of the land surrounding Lancaster remained in the public domain, most of the property regarded as suitable for development had already been claimed. The owners, nevertheless, offered to assemble enough private land to make up the necessary 640 acres specified in the act and to donate it to the state if the commissioners selected the site for the capital city. On July 29 the commissioners, doubtless with the advice of Harvey, met at Lancaster to discuss the merits of the various locations they had inspected. The first vote favored Lancaster by two

votes to one, and a second vote made the matter unanimous. The commissioners directed Harvey to survey the site and lay out the town while the legal details of land transfer to the state were being worked out. Harvey completed his work by August 12, the commissioners met again in Lancaster the following day, and on August 14 issued the formal proclamation designating Lincoln as the new seat of government.[42]

Harvey's plan is shown in Figure 12.22. It is an interesting design, by all odds the most successful of any adopted for a Nebraska community. In its generous provision of public sites and open spaces; its recognition that major public buildings could be so located as to provide vistas down major streets; its differentiation of lot sizes between those intended for business and those to be used for residential purposes; and its variation of street widths depending on proposed functions, this plan ranks high among those of western America. Moreover, and more important, the three-dimensional city that developed on this two-dimensional plan became one of the most impressive and pleasant communities of the country. The details of Harvey's design and the early years of the city's growth thus deserve extended examination.

Three major sites stand out clearly. Each occupied an area of four normal 300-foot square blocks, or, with the land that would have been used for cross streets, about 12 acres each. The one to the north Harvey set aside for the university, the one on the east for the Capitol, and the one toward the southwest corner of the town for a park. While most of the city streets were platted with a width of 100 feet, the streets on the north-south axis of each of these major sites were made 20 feet wider. Streets on the east-west axis of the university and the Capitol also were given this additional width as was D Street, running along the south side of the park, and O Street, which was the main route through the city and intended for the principal business thoroughfare. Fronting this street, around the market square, and along a portion of Ninth Street to the south Harvey laid out the business lots 25 feet wide. All other blocks contained 12 lots 50 feet wide and divided into two tiers by alleys.

Five sites of one block each for "common" or elementary schools were distributed through the city, with one site reserved for a high school. Harvey located the courthouse square near the center of town, bounded by Ninth, Tenth, J, and K Streets. Completing the list of public sites were those for the market on the north side of O Street, and, two blocks to the north, a block reserved for the "State Historical & Library Association." One other detail indicates Harvey's skill as a planner. The blocks on the east and west side of the Capitol square, Univer-

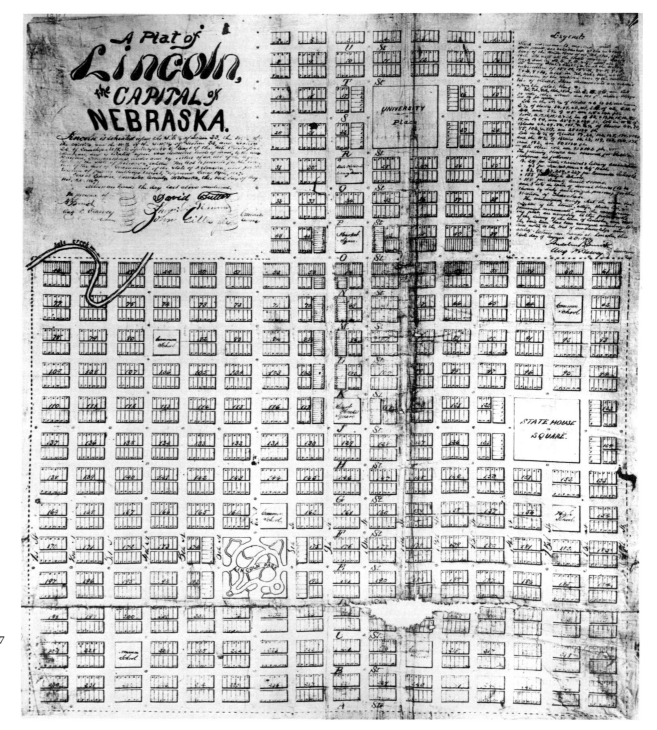

Figure 12.22 Plan of Lincoln, Nebraska: 1867

sity Place, and Lincoln Park, and the block east of the courthouse square were all designed so that the lots would front these important sites.

Not evident on the plan but described in Harvey's notes were reservations of three contiguous lots each for ten churches and for three adjacent lots facing Ninth Street north of the courthouse square for the fraternal orders of the Odd Fellows, the Masons, and the Templars. All these features of Lincoln's design mark its superiority to the typical speculative town of the western frontier, where the desire to pinch out of the site the last available lot resulted in hundreds of dull, graceless communities lacking most of the qualities that can enrich the physical fabric of city life.

By 1874, as revealed in the view reproduced in Figure 12.23, Lincoln had made a successful start toward its development, which for many years was to be guided by Harvey's remarkably far-sighted plan. The commissioners found their work far from easy, however. The first public auction of lots on September 17, 1867, resulted in so few bids and at such low prices that the project seemed doomed at the outset. It was vital that sufficient funds be raised to build the Capitol, for if that could not be accomplished there was the danger that the legislature could be persuaded to designate another site or retain Omaha as the seat of government.

The commissioners resorted to an old trick of private town speculators: rigging the bidding to make it appear that Lincoln town lots were in substantial demand. They approached a group of Nebraska City supporters and arranged with them to bid on lots at the appraised value up to a total of $10,000. The commissioners agreed that unless an additional $15,000 was realized the Nebraska City group would be released from their agreement.[43] The second day of the auction proved successful, and after five days of sales the commissioners realized nearly $35,000. Auctions at Omaha and Nebraska City during the following two weeks added nearly $20,000 more. Eventually the state obtained about $300,000 from the sale of real estate in Lincoln.[44]

Although of questionable legality, this action probably assured the city of its future. The commissioners were soon involved in other irregularities. The capital removal law specified that funds derived from land sales were to be deposited with the state treasurer, Augustus Kountze. Kountze was from Omaha and had naturally opposed moving the capital from that city. The commissioners feared, probably with some justification, that if they turned over the funds to him they would have difficulty getting the money released for construction of the public buildings. Instead, they deposited the proceeds in their own account.

The commissioners were also charged with extravagance in the capitol construction project and in exceeding authorized budget figures for the university building and the insane asylum. A joint committee of the legislature began investigations of these and more serious allegations that the commissioners had personally profited from land sales and that the governor had lent school funds to friends instead of investing them in federal or state bonds. In 1871 Governor Butler was impeached, convicted of misappropriating state funds, and removed from office.[45]

Despite these events Lincoln's growth continued. By 1874, as Figure 12.24 shows, additional lands adjacent to the original plat had been surveyed and laid off in streets, blocks, and lots. Apparently these areas were in private ownership, and while street lines of the original town were generally extended, the additions were not planned with the same care exercised by the commissioners. Several changes appear, the most obvious being along the western side of town where adjustments in the street and block pattern were made to accommodate the railroad lines, which by that date had reached the city.

The original market square had earlier been made available for the post office. What appears on Figure 12.22 as the "Historical Block" near the university became the market square after the supreme court ruled that the intended grant of land for its original purpose had lapsed through non-use. The post office later became the city hall, and in modern times the State Historical Society building was erected on the north axis of the Capitol where Fifteenth Street now terminates at R Street, the southern boundary of the now greatly expanded university campus.

By 1885, the date of the view appearing in Figure 12.25, Lincoln was approaching 20,000 population, but the university buildings, the Capitol, the elaborate post office, the imposing depot of the Burlington and Missouri River Railroad, a number of the fine churches, and its substantial business district must have given it a more cosmopolitan air than suggested by the number of its inhabitants.[46] The view records one important feature representing a modification in the original plan. This is the municipal water works at the site of a large well dug in Lincoln Park following passage of bond issues in 1881 and 1885. Fortunately, not all of the 12-acre park was needed for the pumping station and 75-foot stand-pipe, and the southern half was landscaped and devoted to recreation purposes as intended.

The view anticipates the completion of the second Capitol in Lincoln, dating from 1888, which on the same site replaced the hastily erected and poorly constructed building planned by the commissioners. Im-

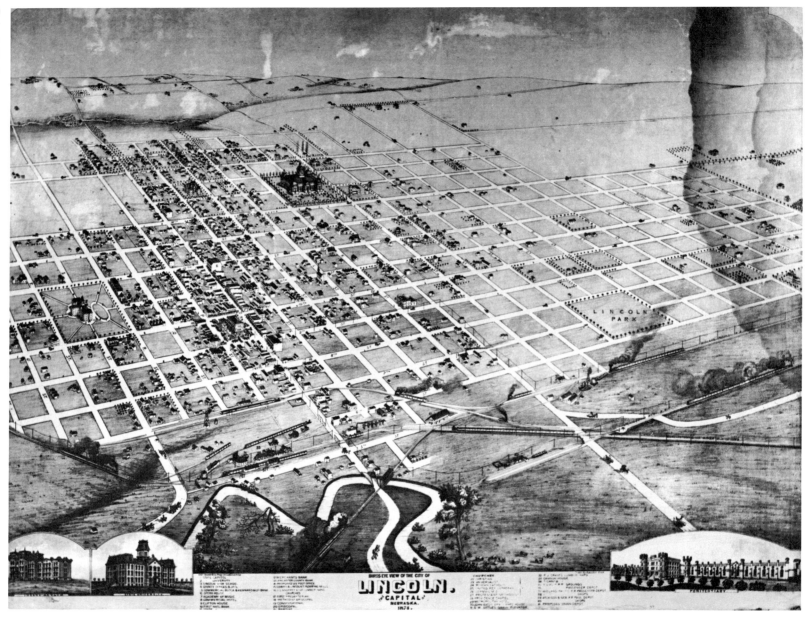

Figure 12.23   View of Lincoln, Nebraska: 1874

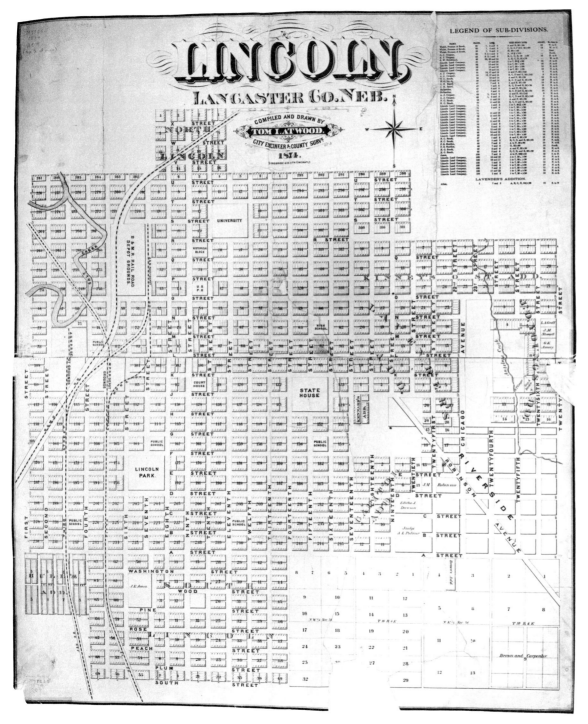

Figure 12.24 Plan of Lincoln, Nebraska: 1874

Figure 12.25 View of Lincoln, Nebraska: 1885

mediately to the south of the Capitol can be seen one of the schools built on the location reserved for that purpose in the original plan. Another appears just to the north of the water works.

On the view of 1885 one can just make out a large residence located in the block southeast of Capitol Square. Thomas P. Kennard, one of the three commissioners who helped to create Lincoln, erected this man-sion as a symbol of his faith in the future of the city. The Kennard Man-sion is now maintained by the Nebraska Historical Society as the Nebraska Statehood Memorial—a fitting reminder of the early period in what has become one of the most visually pleasing cities of the American West.

XIII

The Central Plains: Towns of Kansas

URBAN settlement in Kansas resembled that of Nebraska in many respects. There was the same emphasis on land speculation, excessive planning of cities resulting in many paper communities and ghost towns, widespread use of the gridiron pattern, conflicts over the location of the territorial and, later, the state capital, early concentration of new towns along the Missouri River, and promotion of railroads as the key to urban prosperity. There were, however, important differences in both the speed and the character of urban growth. The tempo of development in Kansas exceeded that in Nebraska during the formative period. In 1860 the population of Kansas exceeded 100,000, over three times that of its neighboring territory. By 1870 the population reached 364,000, while that of Nebraska was only 123,000. In 1880 Kansas could boast of nearly one million, while Nebraska could claim less than half that number.

Because the Kansas River was deeper than the shallow Platte and was navigable at least part of the year, more towns sprang up in the interior of Kansas during the early settlement period than in Nebraska. Perhaps because of this greater dispersion and its less favorable position with respect to the transcontinental railroad no single town in Kansas achieved the dominance enjoyed in Nebraska by Omaha. While the eventual capital city of Kansas—Topeka—had a plan of some interest, its design did not approach the quality of Lincoln's. With a greater number of towns and a larger urban population, Kansas exhibited a wider variety of town layout than did its sister territory, particularly in the designs and distribution of open spaces and public building sites.

Finally, unlike Nebraska, urban origins and growth in Kansas were closely linked to the great national ideological conflict over the issue of slavery. The organization of settlement companies professing abolitionist or pro-slavery goals heightened the normal commercial competition of rival townsite speculators. Probably a minority of immigrants to Kansas came because of their support for or opposition to slavery in the territory and the nation, but many of the important towns in Kansas originated from the efforts of such organized militant settlement groups. Their leaders promised not only speculative profits from townsite promotion but opportunities to spread or stamp out the "peculiar institution" of slavery. As a result, the urbanization of Kansas took place in an atmosphere of bitter partisanship and, at times, of armed conflict.

Twelve days after presidential approval of the territorial legislation in 1854 a group of pro-slavery and speculatively inclined men from the Missouri town of Weston occupied a 320-acre tract belonging to the De-

laware Indians three miles south of Fort Leavenworth. Protests by Delaware chiefs resulted in an order by the commander of the fort directing the settlers to leave, but after the town company agreed to pay for the land the Indians withdrew their objections. Soon the site was surveyed into rectangular blocks and lots arranged in a typical grid pattern.

Leavenworth's plan as filed in the surveyor general's office appears in Figure 13.1. Seven shallow blocks along the river were intended for warehouses and fronted on the levee, which widened to become the elegantly named Esplanade. Lots on the eastern or river side of the next tier of blocks also faced north or south along streets that, like those which intersected them at right angles, were all 60 feet wide with the exception of Delaware, which was 10 feet wider. Lots measured 24 by 125 feet except for the eight lots of double width on each side of the single public square and those near the stream on the south where industry was expected to develop. Alleys 14 feet in width provided rear access to virtually all properties. Such were the beginnings of the largest center of pro-slavery sentiment in Kansas.

The proximity of Fort Leavenworth, which had been established in 1827 and already had played an important role in westward migration, helped the early growth of the town. Soldiers enjoyed the diversions, harmless or otherwise, which the new town afforded, and in 1855, when the fort was being enlarged and reconstructed, civilian workmen employed on the project provided an additional market for the small body of merchants and tradesmen who had taken up residence in the new community.[1] River steamers made regular calls at the levee, farmers and residents of smaller settlements in the interior depended on Leavenworth for supplies, and by 1856 it claimed a population of 3,000, although it probably had no more than half that number of permanent residents. In 1860, however, the census listed nearly 7,500 persons.

A view of the infant city published in 1857 is reproduced in Figure 13.2. From the water, the Planters Hotel dominated the skyline. Many of its clients were associated with the inland freighting company of Majors, Russell, and Company, which had established itself in Leavenworth to handle military business. This same firm, expanded and with an additional partner, was to bring prosperity to Nebraska City to the north and performed much the same function in Leavenworth during the latter part of the 1850s.

An English observer in the spring and summer of 1856 described the town as it appeared to him and to the artist of our view in these words:

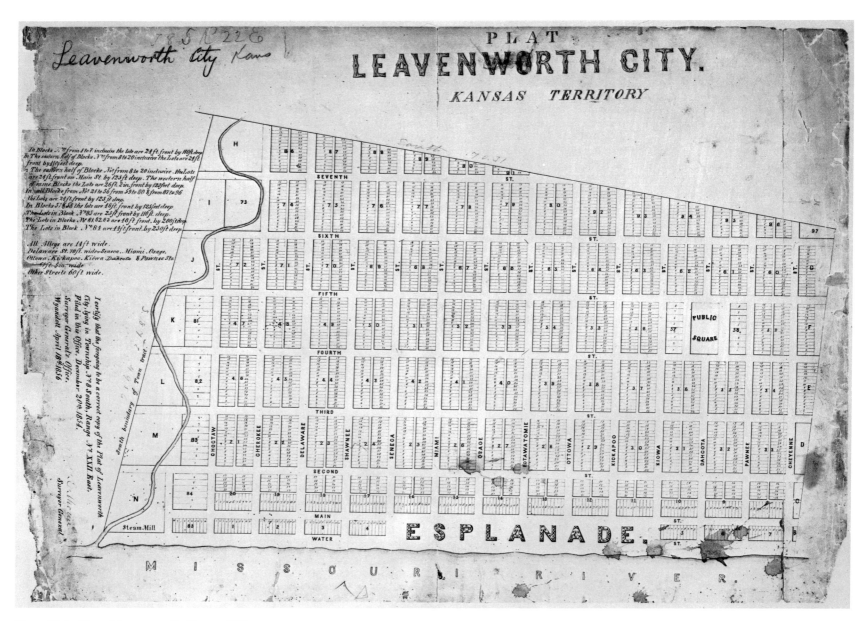

Figure 13.1 Plan of Leavenworth, Kansas: 1854

LEAVENWORTH CITY, KANSAS TER!

SETTLED FALL OF 1854.

3000 Pop 1856

Figure 13.2 View of Leavenworth, Kansas: 1857

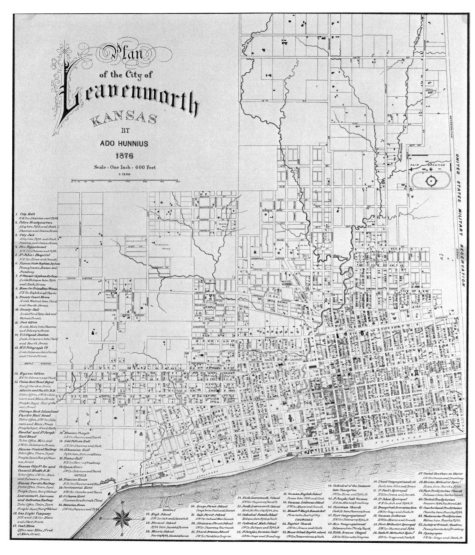

Figure 13.3   Plan of Leavenworth, Kansas: 1876

"At the time of my visit, goods of every kind lay in piles upon the quay, while the road was further blocked up with long wagons, each with six or more yoke of oxen, preparing to cross the plains. The stores fronting the *levée* presented an irregular line of erections, for the most part built of wood; some of one story, some of two, but in all cases covered almost from top to bottom with signboards, inscribed in characters more remarkable for size than beauty."

This visitor noted the primitive nature of the streets: "Passing back from the front street, other streets parallel and rectangular are reached, very regular as to their latitude and longitude, but very irregular in their grading . . . the surface of the ground being exceedingly uneven and occupied with buildings before it has received the needed levelling."

Not only were the streets irregular in their elevation but they were not yet free of obstructions: "Could the plan of the city be carried in mental vision, the houses would be found to be very regularly built upon broad avenues, which, upon paper, make Leavenworth an imposing city. But as the trees of the primeval forest are not wholly removed, and their stumps continue to interrupt the intended thoroughfares, it is impossible at times to keep to the authorized avenue or street. . . . The pedestrian finds himself following a track which conducts him now along the line of a future avenue, now diagonally intersecting it, again branching off through a projected 'improvement,' and then crossing what is one day probably to be a garden, between some log-hut and its yet humbler out-house."[2]

The great land boom of 1857 affected Leavenworth as it did all other Kansas towns. Albert D. Richardson, perhaps the most reliable of all observers of Kansas during its formative years, described land prices in the Leavenworth of 1857: "Building lots . . . upon the river landing, were valued at ten thousand dollars. Three or four blocks back, they sold for two thousand, and on the hills half a mile away, for twelve hundred. Prices were fast rising, money plentiful, and everybody speculating. . . . Suburban lands three miles from the river, bought during the previous winter for one hundred dollars per acre, were now divided into building lots which commanded from one hundred to two hundred dollars each. Hotels were crowded with strangers, eager to invest. Almost any one could borrow gold without security or even a written promise to pay; and the faith was universal that tomorrow should be as this day and yet more abundant."[3]

The city required many decades before exhausting the extensions platted during the 1857 boom. The plan reproduced in Figure 13.3 dates from 1876. Many of the blocks laid out to the south and west during the

1850s still lay unoccupied or only sparsely settled twenty years later. The older portion of the city, however, was almost fully occupied. Grounds of Fort Leavenworth blocked expansion to the north, but south of Three-Mile Creek, the earlier limit of the city, many new streets appear running generally parallel and perpendicular to the river. The plan also shows that Delaware Street, the town's widest thoroughfare, had become the principal commercial center. By that time, also, the railroad had reached the city. The price paid for this symbol of progress was the preemption of the waterfront by the railroad lines, thus shutting off the majestic Missouri River from the town. This misfortune, which would have been difficult to avoid because of topography, Leavenworth shared with many other river communities in Kansas and Nebraska.

Our final glimpse of Leavenworth dates from a slightly earlier year. In Plate 17 the city is shown in 1869 toward the end of the steamboat era. Nine years previously Horace Greeley speculated on the possibility that Leavenworth, with the New York and St. Louis, would be one of "the three great cities of America."[4] And only two years before the date of the view, Bayard Taylor called Leavenworth "the liveliest and most thriving place west of the Mississippi River." It was an open question in his mind whether Kansas City or Leavenworth would become the major metropolis of the Missouri Valley.[5]

Leavenworth's rival among the pro-slavery towns of Kansas and a formidable contender for the overland freighting trade was Atchison, 25 miles to the north. It was named for Senator David Atchison of Missouri, an advocate of slavery in the new territory who had proposed to a group of associates in Weston, Missouri, that a town be formed to tap the western trade along the Missouri River. By September, 1854, surveyor Henry Kuhn produced a standard grid plan, stockholders were assessed $25 each to build a hotel, and the town company donated $400 toward the cost of a press for a town newspaper, which began publication early the next year as the *Squatter Sovereign*. In 1857 North Atchison was laid out as an addition to the then thriving community.[6]

The plan reproduced in Figure 13.4 shows this enlarged town. Probably the wide K Street and Second Street, the latter running past Court House Square and serving the narrow business lots, were expected to become the principal mercantile thoroughfares. Instead, C Street, near the southern edge of the original community, assumed this role. Later extensions of the town to the south gave it a central location, and it was soon lined with shops, hotels, saloons, and offices for five or six blocks from its end at the river bank and steamboat landing.

The favorable location of Atchison at a point where the Missouri

Figure 13.4   Plan of Atchison, Kansas: ca. 1858

River bends to the west attracted several firms in the overland freighting business. In 1858, 24 wagon trains started west from Atchison carrying nearly 3,000 tons of supplies and merchandise loaded on 775 wagons. The Colorado gold rush doubled this traffic in the latter part of 1859 and early 1860, with 33 wagon trains departing Atchison bound for Denver alone. One of these was made up of 125 wagons drawn by more than 1,500 oxen and carrying 750,000 pounds of merchandise. When the last wagon left the levee, the lead wagon was almost out of sight beyond the western limits of the city.[7]

A portion of Commerical Street in the modern city has been converted to an attractively designed pedestrian mall in an effort to keep pace with contemporary suburban shopping centers. In 1866, as revealed in the view of Figure 13.5, it had quite a different character. Wagons, horses, elegantly dressed townspeople, and rough frontiersmen crowded its dusty surface or stepped carefully along its board sidewalks. The Butterfield Stage still rumbled westward past timber or brick business houses. A year earlier no fewer than 5,000 wagons hauled over 10,000 tons of freight to the mining communities of Colorado, Idaho, and Montana and to the growing Mormon markets in Utah.[8] This seemingly endless prosperity, however, was not to last.

Atchison and Nebraska City had much in common: a favorable location with respect to wagon routes west, an initial prosperity depending almost exclusively on the overland freighting business, a single business running from the waterfront toward the west, a utilitarian grid plan with few if any frills, ambitious town promoters, and wildly optimistic predictions of a glorious future. Yet by 1880 the seemingly prosperous city shown in Figure 13.6 had already lost some of its momentum despite its financial support of railroad lines, a donation by the town company of a site for the county courthouse and 64 lots to be sold to raise funds for the building's construction, and the usual frontier town promotional advertising. Omaha to the north and Kansas City to the south succeeded in capturing the major railways, river traffic dwindled, and Atchison, like Nebraska City and Leavenworth, was left as a small city serving mainly the manufacturing and trading needs of the immediate vicinity.

Pro-slavery settlers from Missouri found it relatively easy to establish new towns in Kansas. They knew the region better than those who came from east of the Mississippi, and their sources of supply and political support lay near at hand. Abolitionists, for the most part, came from the Northeast, they were not familiar with frontier life, and they were forced to bring supplies from considerable distances or to outfit themselves at inflated prices in such places as Kansas City. To overcome these problems facing immigrants who were determined that slavery would be barred from Kansas, colonization and settlement companies were formed to provide a greater degree of organization and financial support. The most important was the New England Emigrant Aid Company, which was responsible for the founding of Lawrence, the center in Kansas of Abolitionist activity.[9]

Eli Thayer, a Worcester educator and politician, organized the company in the spring of 1854 and became its president. Amos Lawrence, the Massachusetts industrialist, served as treasurer. The officers of the company selected three agents, Samuel Pomeroy, Charles Robinson, and Charles Branscomb, to direct actual settlement activities in Kansas. By August 1 the first party of 29 colonists from Massachusetts reached the site of their intended city some 40 miles up the Kansas River. Much of the site had already been claimed, and it was necessary later to offer the original owners shares of stock in the town company to secure the most suitable land. Apparently some preliminary surveys were carried out almost immediately, for when a second and larger group of settlers arrived early in September the main street of the town had already been laid out by A. D. Searle. An immediate conflict between the two groups over land claims was resolved, a town association was established, and the settlers agreed to name the new community in honor of Amos Lawrence. Soon Searle was at work surveying streets, blocks, and lots in the central portion of the town tract, which extended two and a half miles east and west along the Kansas River and one and a half miles to the south.[10]

The plan that Searle produced, doubtless in consultation with agents Pomeroy and Robinson, who had accompanied the second party of settlers, appears in Figure 13.7. Searle platted all the gridiron streets a generous 80 feet wide with three exceptions, which he made 100 feet in width. One was Massachusetts Street, running south from the levee and through the group of four parks to the east of Mount Oread. Hancock Street, bisecting the "College Grounds" and crossing Massachusetts Street in the center of the four parks was another. The third was Pinkney Street, which ran westward from the levee at the end of Massachusetts Street and divided two other park reservations.

Searle also provided a number of other park or public building sites in addition to those already mentioned: Roger Williams Park in the northwestern sector, the "Public Grounds" near the city's western edge, an elongated site rather indecisively labeled "Capitol Hill County Buildings," one block each for a church and school at the spur of Mount

Figure 13.5   View of Street in Atchison, Kansas: 1866

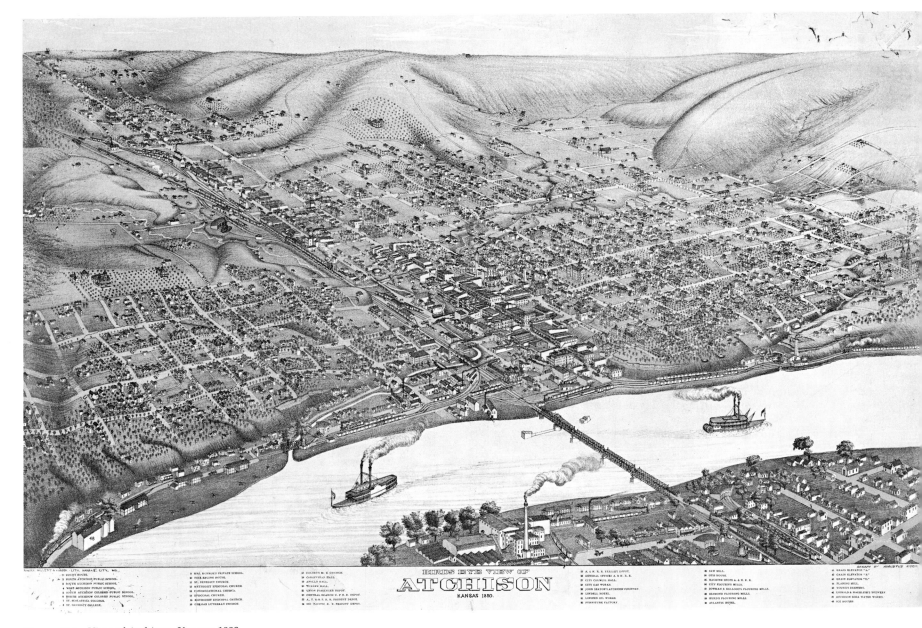

Figure 13.6 View of Atchison, Kansas: 1880

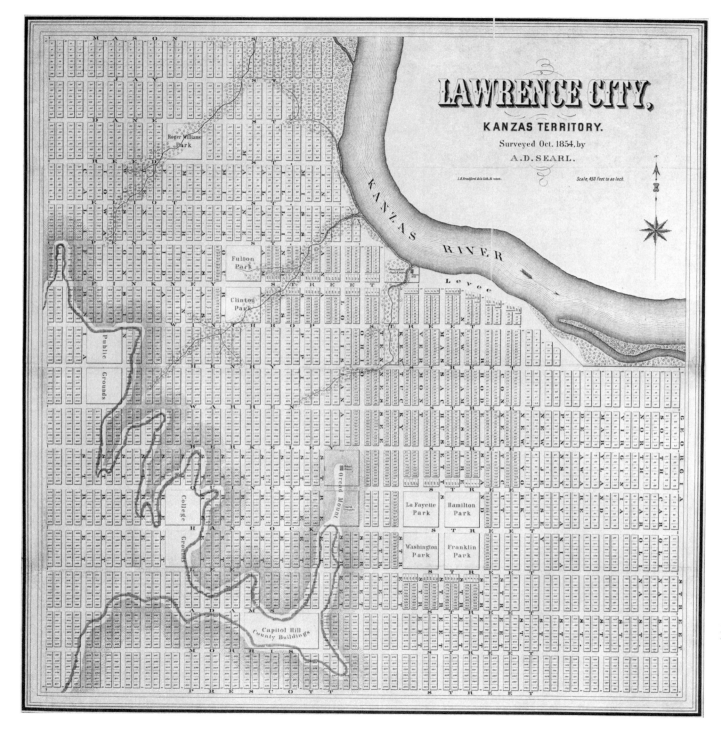

Figure 13.7 Plan of Lawrence, Kansas: 1854

Oread, a reservation for "shops & mills" at the west edge of the levee, and two blocks immediately south of this embryonic industrial district undesignated as to intended use. Except for the last mentioned these sites were two blocks wide (four in the case of the "Capitol Hill" tract) so that, in addition to streets bounding them on their eastern and western sides, a street terminated at their northern and southern ends. This broke some of the monotony of the gridiron street pattern and provided opportunities for the creation of attractive vistas.

Searle obviously gave some thought to how the blocks should be divided into lots. Smaller lots facing the streets in the central portion of the plat may have been intended for business purposes, although the number seems excessive. More likely, this pattern resulted from Searle's attempts to provide a greater number of lots so that the distribution of them to settlers would cause less contention.[11] It should be noted as well that Searle varied the otherwise consistent orientation of the lots along the north and south sides of the cluster of four parks flanking Massachusetts Street. For some reason, he did not provide a similar modification in the lot pattern around the other park and public building sites.

An early view of Lawrence in May, 1858, looking southwest is reproduced in Figure 13.8. The horseshoe-shaped ridge of Mount Oread acted as a barrier to urban growth to the west, and most of the buildings were concentrated along Massachusetts Street near the river. Growth had obviously been far slower than expected; indeed, the view, printed in Cincinnati for promotional purposes, probably exaggerated the extent of development.

The first settlers found life hard in the infant prairie town. Most of the good timber lands in the vicinity had already been claimed by pro-slavery Missourians. It was not until November that the Emigrant Company sawmill began operations. Most of the early residents lived in tents or in crude board shelters. E. D. Ladd described the appearance of Lawrence and the methods of house construction in November of 1854: "Our city presents quite a gothic appearance in the style of its residences. Besides the tents, there are a number of houses of the same form . . . covered with . . . shingles, three to three and a half feet long, unshaved; then we have others of the same tent form, made of poles set in the ground, the tops meeting overhead and ribs nailed on horizontally . . . and then thatched with prairie grass. . . . There are some log houses roofed with cotton cloth, tarred and sprinkled with sand."[12]

While a friendly visitor in the spring of 1856 could describe Lawrence as consisting of "about 150 houses, a few of them very comfortable,

several good stores, three churches begun or provided for, two weekly papers, a very fine Hotel nearly finished, &c," he felt obliged to point out that "Lawrence has no livery stable, furniture store, machine shop, foundry, and but very few stone masons."[13]

Only the central portion of Searle's ambitious plat was needed to accommodate new residents in the early years of growth and development. A plat published in the late 1850s and reproduced in Figure 13.9 reveals the more modest dimensions of Lawrence in this period. It also shows a few deviations from the plan prepared by Searle, of which the changed form of the park area on the axis of Massachusetts Street is the most significant. One can observe that the four park sections of the original design had been consolidated into one open space, and that a single tier of lots had been laid out around its edge on what previously had been part of the recreational lands. Why this was done is unclear. Apparently, it was the work of Samuel Pomeroy, agent for the Emigrant Company, seeking additional lots to distribute to the prior landowners on the townsite who had raised questions about ownership rights.[14] Eventually, Massachusetts Street was to continue southward, cutting the new and smaller park area in two, and new streets serving the lots fronting the park were built around its edges.

Despite the hardships of a harsh environment, severe financial difficulties of the Emigrant Aid Company and what appears to have been mismanagement of its affairs, the difficulties of transportation on the Kansas River, and the bitter struggles between the pro-slavery and abolitionist forces that diverted to the political arena energies that might otherwise have been spent on community building, Lawrence continued to grow as additional settlers arrived from the East. Housing conditions improved with the importation of prefabricated buildings constructed in sections by the Cincinnati firm of Hinkle, Guild, & Company.[15] The Aid Company sawmill, in full operation by the spring of 1855, made possible additional buildings of more conventional construction.

Not even the burning of the hotel in Lawrence and the offices of two abolitionist newspapers, the *Herald of Freedom* and the *Kansas Free State*, by a mob of pro-slavery men in the spring of 1856 could stop the town's growth. Indeed, the tragic development of open warfare that year following John Brown's massacre of five pro-slavery men at Pottawatomie Creek in retaliation for the raid on Lawrence served to strengthen that town's position as the center of free-state activities.

Lawrence a few years after the Civil War is depicted in Figure 13.10. Searle's plan had served well as a guide for initial development, and

Figure 13.8 View of Lawrence, Kansas: 1858

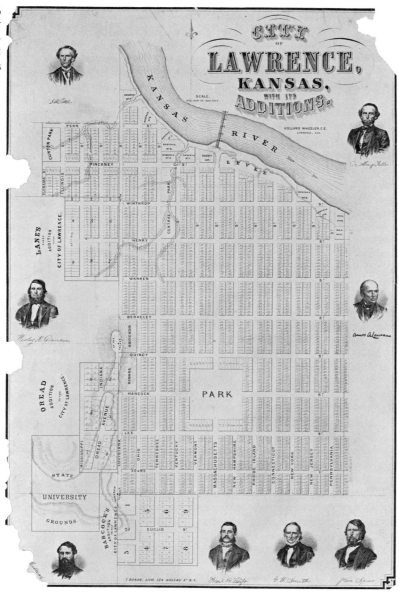

Figure 13.9 Plan of Lawrence, Kansas: ca. 1858

with the coming of the railroads the city continued its growth. More important to the town than the railroad-oriented industries, however, was the state university. Its first building appears in the view slightly to the left and below the center. The location was on the block designated on Searle's plan as "School House," rather than the two blocks set aside for the college grounds. Gradually Kansas University was to expand along the curving ridge of Mount Oread and, together with fraternity and sorority houses, to occupy virtually the entire elevation as well as the bowl-shaped depression almost enclosed by the ridge. The modern city, while only of modest size, is an attractive community dominated visually by the university buildings on its commanding site overlooking the park to the east and the business buildings stretching from the river southward along Massachusetts Street.

Lawrence was but one, albeit the most important, of the towns sponsored by the Emigrant Aid Company and other settlement groups from New England. The policy of the company was, as expressed by its secretary, to "dot Kansas with New England settlements," so that "New England principles and New England influences should pervade the whole Territory."[16] Shortly after the planning of Lawrence the company's agent, Dr. Charles Robinson, assisted in founding another town, many of whose settlers had been brought to Kansas through the company's efforts. The motives of those most deeply involved in this enterprise, however, were not so much to assure that "New England principles and New England influences" should be established as to obtain a handsome return on a speculative investment.

Cyrus K. Holliday arrived in Kansas with $20,000, the proceeds from the sale of a small railroad line he had promoted in his native Pennsylvania. Only twenty-eight but already comparatively wealthy by frontier standards, Holliday came west seeking new worlds to conquer. In the fall of 1854 he and a group of associates inspected several possible sites for a new town. After making their selection, they returned to Lawrence, and with Robinson's help recruited several persons recently arrived from the East. During the first week in December they began laying out the new town, which was given the name of Topeka.

Apparently Holliday himself prepared the plan in his capacity as president of the Topeka Association. Two weeks later A. D. Searle arrived from Lawrence to run exact surveys and make more precise the original design, which had been crudely platted and staked out by Holliday with compass and cord.[17] Searle's survey of Holliday's plan was soon printed for promotional purposes and is reproduced in Figure 13.11.

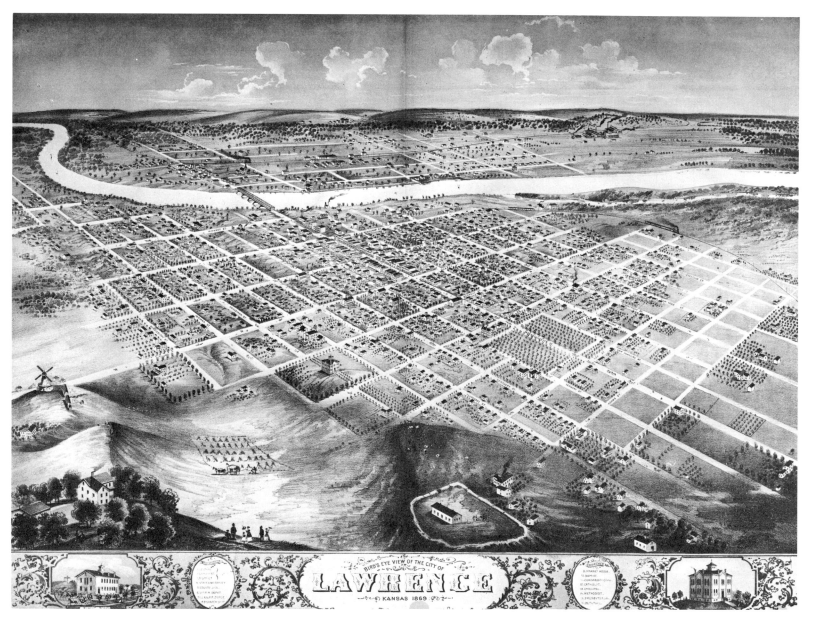

Figure 13.10   View of Lawrence, Kansas: 1869

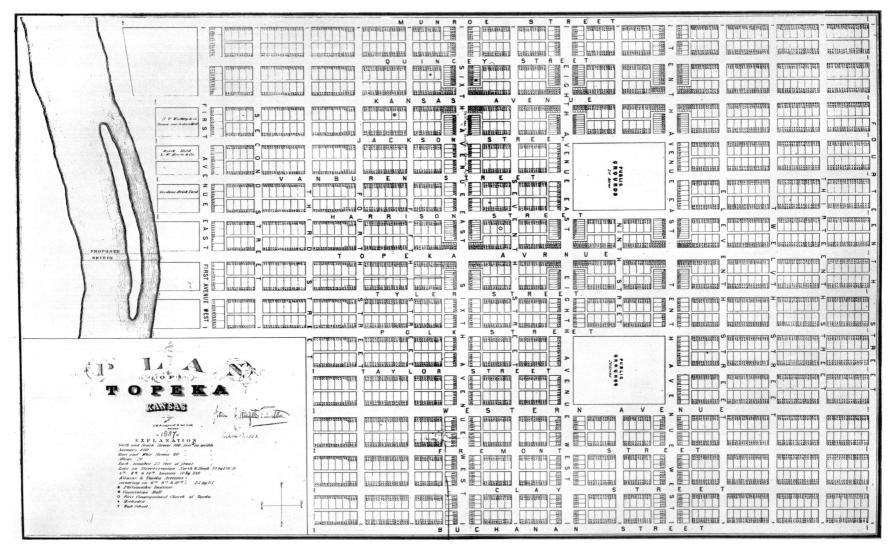

Figure 13.11 Plan of Topeka, Kansas: ca. 1856

The design is more curious than successful, but it is certainly not without merit. The longitudinal axis followed the gradual slope upward from the south bank of the Kansas River. The compass bearing of the streets running up and down this slope deviated eastward from true north by nearly 19°. Holliday obviously considered topography more important than trying to fit the town plat into the system of neat rectangular township surveys prescribed by the General Land Office of the federal government. This axis for the streets running the length of the town also allowed Holliday to lay out a cross-street generally parallel to the river and to provide streets parallel with this that were nearly level as they crossed the slope line at right angles.[18]

Most of the streets running east-west were made 80 feet wide except for First, Sixth, Eighth, and Tenth Avenues, which Holliday platted 130 feet in width. Of the north-south streets, Kansas, Topeka, and Western Avenues were also 130 feet wide, while all others were 100 feet. Alleys were planned to afford rear access to all lots, most of which fronted the north-south streets except for those along the four wider avenues crossing the town in its shorter dimension.

Holliday designated two 20-acre sites between Eighth and Tenth Avenues as "Public Grounds." Probably he intended them to be used as parks, and he may well have been influenced by the park blocks at Lawrence. Eventually, as we will see, these large and strategically located plots were devoted to other uses. In the early years of the town they lay vacant, as did most of the blocks neatly laid off in several thousand building lots.

A liberal policy of donating lots to persons who would erect needed buildings or carry on important trades helped to attract some new settlers. The first articles of agreement of the Topeka Association reserved one-sixth of all the lots for this purpose, with another one-sixth being offered to the Emigrant Aid Company if it would erect "a mill, a school house, receiving house, etc."[19] Despite these and other promotional efforts and the political importance that Topeka began to assume in the antislavery movement, the population three years after its settlement probably did not exceed three or four hundred.

Far more successful in attracting settlers at the beginning of territorial days were the towns along the Missouri River. Like Atchison and Leavenworth they enjoyed the advantages of reliable water transportation. By 1857, as the map of Kansas in Figure 13.12 shows, no fewer than seventeen towns lined the western bank of the Missouri. While perhaps one or two appearing on the map were towns in name only, several others in addition to the two pro-slavery communities we have already examined became flourishing settlements.[20]

Sumner, located a few miles south of Atchison, attracted early attention. John P. Wheeler, a surveyor and violent abolitionist from Massachusetts, platted the town in 1856. With the help of a beautifully executed lithograph view that he had printed in Cincinnati the following year Wheeler succeeded in luring hundreds of settlers from New England who had been warned to avoid the pro-slave towns of Leavenworth and Atchison. Sumner's design resembled the stereotyped gridiron layouts of Nebraska rather than the more imaginative plans of some of its sister towns in Kansas. Two streets, each 100 feet wide, crossed at the center of the town. One of the blocks at that point was reserved as a public square. Another block near the river bore the title, "College Park." Two church sites and one for a school, each consisting of two blocks, were also designated. Otherwise, it was a no-nonsense grid plan of streets 60 and 80 feet wide.[21]

Albert Richardson was among the early settlers. In 1857 he "found the town with few houses completed, but many in progress. Its aspect was promising, and its shares sold for one hundred dollars. Six weeks later they had doubled in value."[22] Many persons came to Sumner from Massachusetts, perhaps attracted by the name in the belief that the ardent abolitionist senator from Massachusetts, Charles Sumner, had an interest in the town. In fact, the name came from the senator's brother, George, who had invested in the project.

Among the settlers arriving in 1858 was young John James Ingalls, later to serve as senator from Kansas. He, like many others, had seen the view of Sumner reproduced in Plate 18 and, while he "was not surprised at not finding a Boston or New York," he was shocked at how the primitive conditions of the town differed from the thriving community depicted in the view. Only the Sumner House, a handsome hotel, resembled "its representation in the lithographic fiction," which had lured him to Kansas. From there, a building "whose floors are as destitute of carpets as its walls are of paper or its table of decency," he wrote these impressions of the town in a letter to his father the day following his arrival.

The hotel "is situated at the summit of the 'bluff' on which the 'city' is located, and is reached by a rude street of the most preposterous grade imaginable. It is immensely steep; more like the roof of a house than anything else I can compare it to, and so gullied with rains, so interspersed with rocks and the stumps of trees, in many cases several feet high, that a New Hampshire teamster of ordinary temerity would shun the task of traversing it." Ingalls described the other streets as "merely footpaths leading up and down the wild ravines to the few log huts and miserable cabins which compose the city." Of the college

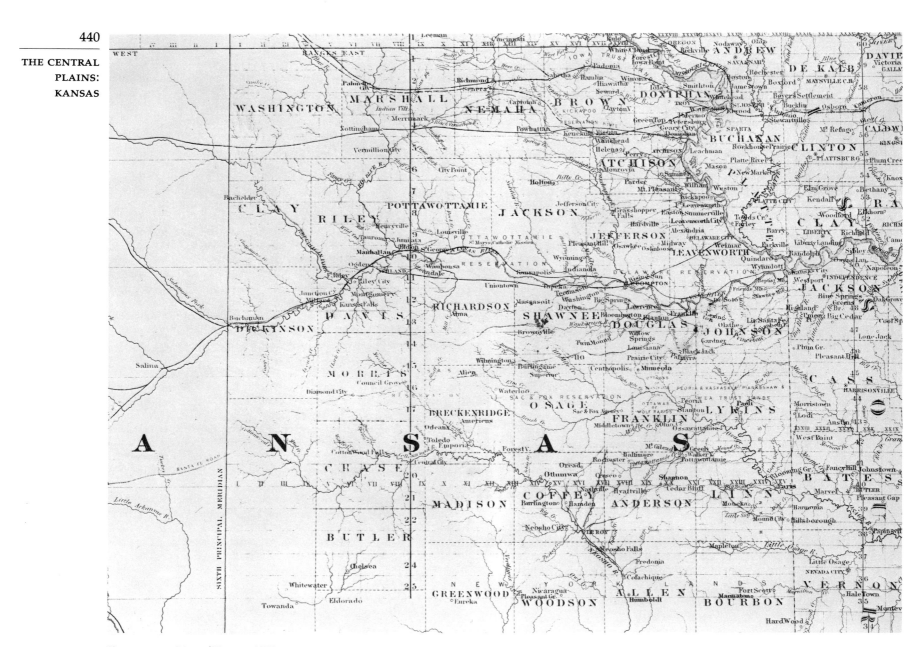

Figure 13.12 Map of Kansas: 1857

shown on the hill in the right-hand side of the view, Ingalls observed that "no person here of whom I have inquired has even so much as heard the idea advanced."

The population may have been as much as 2,000, but Ingalls estimated that there were not more than 200 houses, only "twenty or thirty of which are visible from any one point, some without windows and doors, some without chimneys, some without shingles or clapboards, nearly all without cellars, and situated on heaps of stones or stumps of old trees, and distributed without any regard to order or regularity." The view shows four churches; Ingalls found none. What appears near the center of the view as a substantial manufacturing plant was actually "a rickety old blacksmith's shop." In his initial despair he wrote his father "I am quite unable to convey to you any definite idea of the disappointment, not unmingled with anger and mortification, with which I contemplate the state of affairs here. . . . It is so unlike anything I ever saw or dreamed of that I am not yet prepared to say whether I shall like it or not."[23]

Like it or not, Ingalls remained in Sumner for some time. In December he wrote that he was involved in drafting the city charter, and the following month he reported that he was helping as a lobbyist to secure its passage by the legislature. By February, 1859, his attitude had changed from that of an eastern critic to a frontier town boomer: "Improvements are going on in Sumner to a considerable extent. It compares very favorably with any of the towns in the territory which I have visited, and I believe I have seen all except Topeka and Manhattan."[24]

Sumner's life was brief. A severe drought in the fall of 1859 and the following spring and summer brought ruin to the farmers of the vicinity. A greater disaster struck in June when a tornado destroyed or severely damaged nearly every building in the town. This was followed in September by a plague of grasshoppers.[25] Sumner never recovered from these calamities. Many of the remaining buildings were pulled down and their materials used by former residents who moved to Atchison, Leavenworth, or other Kansas localities. In 1866 Albert Richardson passed by the site of the town where he had lived for two years and observed that there were no more than "five or six" buildings then standing along the deserted streets by then choked with "young oaks and cottonwoods."[26]

Many other towns met a similar fate or languished as sleepy hamlets. One of these was Quindaro, whose plan is shown in Figure 13.13 as laid out in 1856 on the Missouri a few miles above the mouth of the Kansas River. It took its name from the Indian princess whose portrait

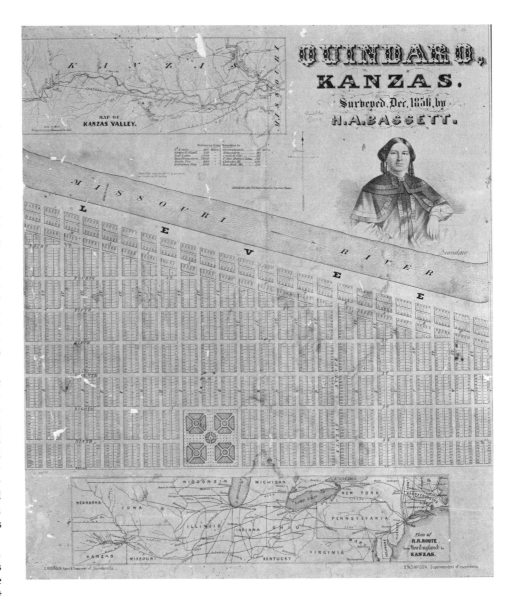

Figure 13.13 Plan of Quindaro, Kansas: 1856

appears on the lithographed plan printed in Boston to attract settlers. She was the wife of Abelard Guthrie, who lived nearby, served as vice-president of the town company, and had been active in aiding escaped slaves find their way to freedom. Many New England settlers soon arrived, and during the land boom of 1857 Quindaro was the scene of much buying and selling of property. There was talk of railroads, a ferry provided connections with the east bank of the Missouri, a large hotel and even larger sawmill were erected, and steamboats discharged passengers and cargo at the levee that stretched along the river the full length of the town. The town company purchased a shallow draft steamboat at Cincinnati and established regular service to Lawrence.[27]

The neat regularity of the plan scarcely suggests the nature of the site, which Richardson described in 1857 as "in dense woods, among great ledges, sharp hills, and yawning ravines—the roughest site for a town which it hath entered into the heart of man to conceive." Despite this unfavorable topography Richardson observed that its promoters confidently expected that "here was absolutely certain to spring up the St. Louis of the Missouri River. The proprietors proved this to me incontestably by maps and statistics; by geography that never blunders and figures which can not lie. . . . Quindaro would have five thousand people within two years; and—as I was a newspaper correspondent . . . and as I could serve them by writing the truth, the simple uncolored truth—a few choice lots could be secured for me at very low figures!"[28]

But vigorous promotion and advertising of Quindaro's supposed advantages could not alter the hard facts of nature. Attempts to cut the main street, Kansas Avenue, through a formidable bluff ultimately failed, and the street ended at a rocky ledge halfway up the hill. The elaborately designed formal park at the southern edge of town remained a paper dream, and settlers soon began to drift away to more favorable locations. While in May, 1859, Horace Greeley observed that Quindaro "insists that it is still alive" among the "bleaching bones of several dead cities" along that part of the Missouri River, it did not survive for long, and in 1871 the town plat was officially vacated.[29]

Far more successful in its early years, and ultimately as part of Kansas City, Kansas, expanding north and west to embrace the old site of Quindaro, was Wyandotte located strategically at the mouth of the Kansas River. The land in this area belonged to the Wyandot Indians, a highly civilized tribe that had been moved to Kansas from Ohio and whose land was distributed to individual members of the tribe instead of being held in common after its members attained citizenship by a

treaty in 1855. The earlier Indian town was replaced in 1857 when the Indian land titles were confirmed. Four settlers from the East and three of the Wyandots joined as stockholders in organizing the town company. Under their direction surveyor John H. Millar staked out the plan reproduced in Figure 13.14.

Through the center of the town Millar laid out four major streets each 100 feet wide: Washington, Nebraska, Kansas, and Minnesota Avenues, running from the levee to the western limits. Other streets appear to be 80 and 66 feet in width, of which Wyandotte Avenue and those near the levee apparently were intended to be most important among the thoroughfares oriented north and south. Breaking the otherwise relentless rhythm of the grid were Oakland Park and Huron Place, each occupying the space of two normal elongated city blocks. The latter site was designated as the location of a seminary and four churches, one at each corner.

When Richardson visited Wyandotte in 1857 the embryonic city was only four months old but already its population had reached 400. The town had been laid out just in time to take advantage of the widespread interest in Kansas migration and land speculation. While at that early date there were only "a few pleasant white warehouses and residences" among the "unpainted plank shanties . . . many more were going up; and meanwhile waiting settlers dwelt under heaven's canopy or in snowy tents. Everywhere busy workmen were plying ax, hammer, and saw."[30]

By the end of 1857 Wyandotte enjoyed the facilities deemed essential by townsite promoters: warehouses, a stagecoach line, ferries across both rivers and soon a bridge crossing the Kansas or Kaw River, assorted shops, and a variety of local industries including sawmills and blacksmith shops. Horace Greeley received a favorable impression when he visited the community in the spring of 1859: "Wyandot [sic], though hemmed in and impeded . . . by an Indian reserve back of it, is alive, and is becoming, what it ought fully to be, the outlet and inlet between Southern Kansas and the Missouri River. It has a beautiful location, and decided natural advantages."[31]

Despite this initial auspicious beginning, ten years after Greeley's inspection the town had hardly become a major metropolis. The view in Figure 13.15 clearly shows nothing more than a town of modest size although of a pleasant enough character. The business district occupied two blocks on Minnesota Avenue, which passed by Huron Place with its cupola-topped school. The churches of the town, however, had not been built on the corners of this square (and indeed it lacked its south-

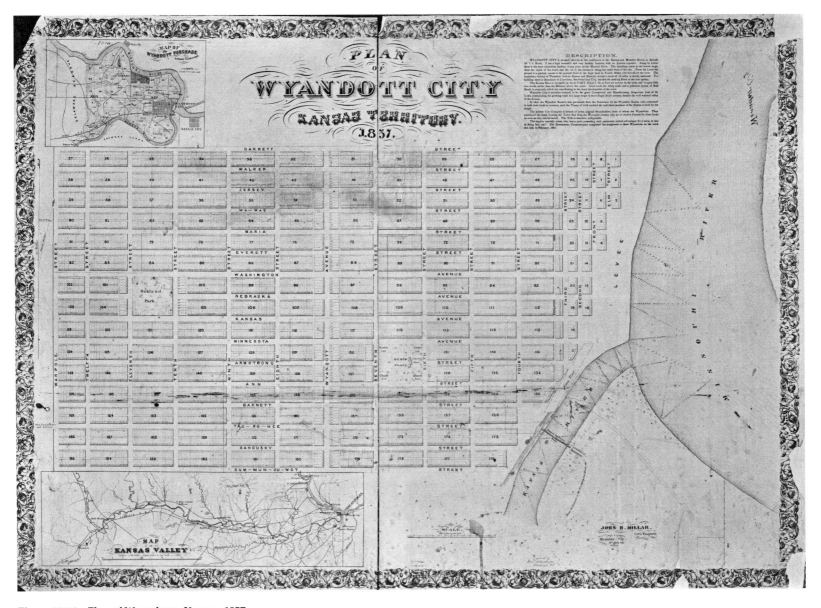

Figure 13.14   Plan of Wyandotte, Kansas: 1857

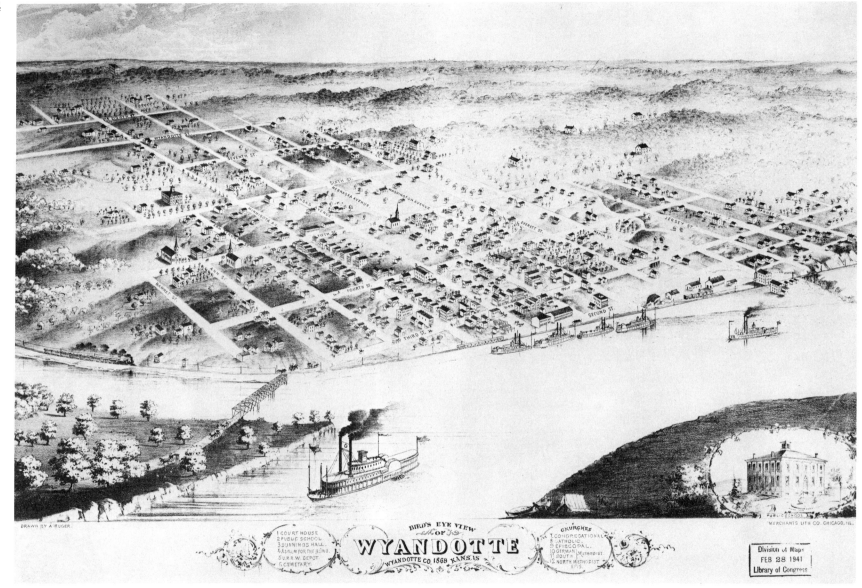

Figure 13.15 View of Wyandotte, Kansas: 1869

western corner altogether) but on scattered sites, three of which fronted Fifth Street.

Quindaro, its upstream rival, had faded nearly into oblivion by that year, but Wyandotte faced new competition from Kansas City, Kansas, which had been planned close by on the south bank of the Kansas River in 1868. In later years other towns pushed their way into existence in this vicinity: Armstrong in 1871 and Armourdale in 1880. Under authority of a statute enacted by the legislature, Governor Martin in 1886 issued a proclamation consolidating the three cities into a single municipality under the name of Kansas City, Kansas, and the modern industrial growth and vast expansion of the state's second largest city properly dates from that time.

The relative merits of the plans of Wyandotte and Quindaro clearly had little to do with the former's survival and the latter's demise. The geographic factors of location and site conditions played a dominant role here as they did elsewhere. In retrospect it seems that one might easily have predicted which community would have succeeded and which failed. Albert Richardson at the time saw that Quindaro had little chance of maintaining its existence. Yet that same Richardson invested in Sumner town lots and chose that short-lived town as his residence. Under the influence of speculative promotion, promises, rumors, soaring prices for town lots, and increased immigration to the new territory, it was much more difficult for those living through this period to predict or even guess which of the dozens of new towns had an assured future.

As Richardson observed, "on paper, *all* these towns were magnificent. Their superbly lithographed maps adorned the walls of every place of resort. The stranger studying one of these," which Richardson illustrated with the plan reproduced in Figure 13.16, "fancied the New Babylon surpassed only by its namesake of old. Its great parks, opera-houses, churches, universities, railway depots and steamboat landings made New York and St. Louis insignificant in comparison." Then, using the view in Figure 13.17, Richardson continued: "but if the new-comer had the unusual wisdom to visit the prophetic city before purchasing lots, he learned the difference between fact and fancy. The town might be composed of twenty buildings; or it might not contain a single human habitation. In most cases, however, he would find one or two rough cabins, with perhaps a tent and an Indian canoe on the river in front of the 'levee.' Any thing was marketable. Shares in interior towns of one or two shanties, sold readily for a hundred dollars. Wags proposed an act of Congress reserving some land for farming purposes before the whole Territory should be divided into city lots. Towns enough were started for a State containing four millions of people."[32]

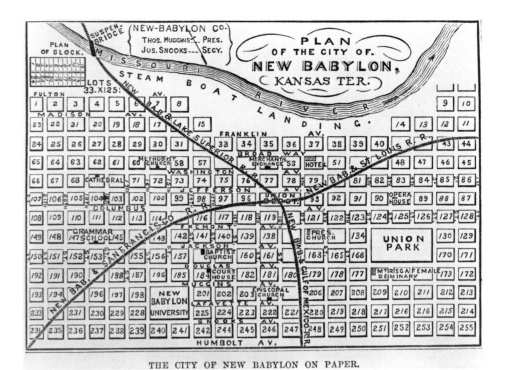

THE CITY OF NEW BABYLON ON PAPER.

Figure 13.16 Plan of New Babylon, Kansas: 1857

One of Lawrence's early settlers recalled the casual way in which some towns were created: "In 1857 a convivial party of gentlemen had gathered at the Eldridge House, Lawrence, when the suggestion was made that before they separate they lay out a town. In the party were several surveyors, who at once proceeded to make the proper drawings; a fine lithograph was procured and the blank space filled in, which completed the certificate of the birth of Oread."[33] Later that year the group found a suitable site about ten miles northeast of Burlington and had B. L. Kingsbury stake it out. Not a single house was ever constructed, and the project may have been intended more as a joke than as an outright fraud.

Both whimsey and hoax were involved in the projected town of the

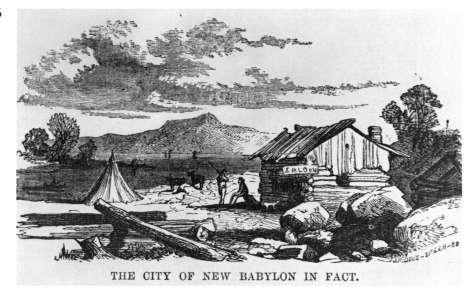

THE CITY OF NEW BABYLON IN FACT.

Figure 13.17   View of New Babylon, Kansas: 1857

Figure 13.18   Plan of Octagon City, Kansas: 1856

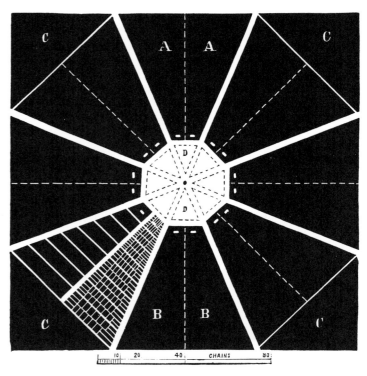

Vegetarian Settlement Company, an organization founded by Henry Stephen Clubb in 1856 to create a town in Kansas peopled by those who shared Clubb's aversion to fowl, fish, and flesh. Clubb's prospectus included the usual town plan shown in Figure 13.18 along with the following summary of his ambitious settlement project: "The plan contemplated by the company embraces an area of four of these octagon villages, forming a city of sixteen square miles, with a square in the centre of 584 acres, to be appropriated to an agricultural college and model-farm, to be cultivated by the students, who will pay for their education by their labor."[34]

Clubb held out to potential settlers the promise of speculative profits through the eventual subdivision into town lots of the 16 farms whose houses would be grouped near the center of the tract facing an octag-

onal street. His diagram shows for two of the farms how this might be accomplished through the creation of streets connecting the radial thoroughfares of the original plan and the division of the blocks thus created into urban building sites. Clubb also assured those interested that much had already been accomplished on the site and that those arriving would find comfortable accommodations and substantial improvements.[35]

A few hardy but gullible settlers completed the long and tiresome journey to the designated location in southeastern Kansas only to discover that the "improvements" consisted of a single crude cabin 16 feet square standing alone in a stretch of otherwise unoccupied prairie. The vision of an urban complex composed of octagonal towns was never to be realized.[36]

The most elaborate plan for any of these paper cities was produced by the surveying party sent out by the American Settlement Company, organized in New York City in the fall of 1854. Their design for the intended community of Council City appears in Figure 13.19 as published in New York and proudly displayed along with the company's prospectus at its Broadway office.[37] The company soberly stated that "there are now within and adjacent to the city upwards of six hundred inhabitants, a steam saw mill, a grist mill, shops, stores, schools, &c.," but, despite its claimed location along the Santa Fe Trail, Council City's site was so isolated on a minor tributary of the Osage River that it never attracted more than a handful of residents and disappeared completely within a few months.[38]

Council City's failure was a minor tragedy, for its plan incorporated many interesting features. Most arresting was the pattern of half-block public squares arranged diagonally outward from the corners of the two large parks. Broadway and New York and Pennsylvania Avenues were given the generous width of 180 feet, while all other streets were intended to be 100 feet wide. Excellence of plan, however, proved no substitute for wise site selection, and Council City joined the growing list of paper towns dotting the map of Kansas.[39]

As the Kansas map of 1857 in Figure 13.12 shows, within three years after the opening of the territory, town companies had penetrated well westward along the valley of the Kansas River. Fort Riley at the fork of the Republican River lay near the edge of the settlement. Manhattan, several miles downstream at the mouth of the Big Blue River, was one of several towns then in existence. It had developed from two earlier settlements of 1854, which, with the arrival of another party from the East, were consolidated, enlarged, and replatted in the spring of 1855 as Boston. Then, a few weeks later, another group from Cincinnati appeared by steamboat carrying with them ten Cincinnati prefabricated houses and bound for a location still further upstream. On seeing signs of settlement, the leaders of the new arrivals decided to merge their interests with the first group, half of the town was turned over to them, and the name was changed to the present Manhattan.[40]

Adjacent to Fort Riley stood the town of Pawnee, created in 1854 by the Pawnee Town Association, in which Andrew H. Reeder, the first territorial governor, had a financial interest. Reeder, apparently not a man who allowed thoughts of conflict of interest to weigh heavily on his mind, also owned shares in Tecumseh, located a few miles downstream from Topeka. In that enterprise he was associated with a number of southerners who confidently expected their colleague to des-

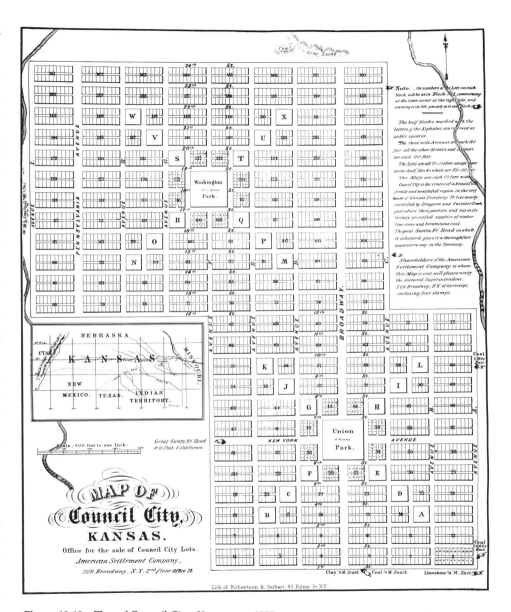

Figure 13.19 Plan of Council City, Kansas: ca. 1855

ignate it as the meeting place for the first territorial legislature. The same printers who produced the view of Sumner prepared the equally attractive representation of Tecumseh reproduced in Figure 13.20. It was another "triumph of chromatic mendacity," showing a number of nonexistent buildings, the most prominent being the imaginary Capitol dominating the skyline on the crest of the hill above the town.[41]

Reeder, angered over the temporary invasion of Missourians who had illegally helped to elect a predominantly pro-slavery legislature on March 30, 1855, surprised his colleagues by designating Pawnee as site where the first territorial legislature would meet.[42] On July 2 the governor opened his office at Pawnee, moving there from the Shawnee Methodist Episcopal Indian mission, where he had administered the affairs of the territory for all but his first two months of office, which he spent at Fort Leavenworth. In a hastily constructed stone building in Pawnee, Governor Reeder convened the overwhelmingly pro-slavery legislators.

They promptly voted to move back to the Shawnee mission, designated it as the temporary capital, and directed the governor to establish his office there until a permanent capital had been selected. Reeder's veto was overruled, and by July 6 the legislature stood adjourned until ten days later when they were to reassemble at the mission complex.[43]

The free-state supporters, meanwhile, had convened at Lawrence to denounce the results of the election and the adoption by the Pawnee legislators of the laws of Missouri as the statutes of Kansas because they legalized slavery. In the fall of that year at Topeka they drew up an antislavery constitution, held elections, and sought admission to the union as a state. Border warfare soon broke out, and the news of "bleeding Kansas" captured the attention of the entire country.[44]

Early in August, 1855, the "official" legislature designated Lecompton, midway between Lawrence and Topeka, as the permanent capital of Kansas. The proprietors of the town, who included Samuel D. Lecompte, the chief justice of Kansas Territory, hastily revised its original plat to provide a site for the Capitol and the courthouse.[45] The plan, reproduced in Figure 13.21, contained little else to suggest that the town was to be the seat of government of a large territory. The view of the town below the title grossly exaggerated the appearance of the community at this time, but soon the town began to grow. During 1855-59 five hotels were built, a land office was opened, work began on the Capitol, and Lecompton town lots soared in price as the population reached nearly 1,000.[46]

It was here that a constitutional convention assembled in the fall of 1857 to adopt a pro-slavery document. The political complexion of Kan-

sas was changing, however. Increasing immigration to the territory from the Midwest and East permitted the free-state party to win a majority in the territorial legislature. This body arranged for a special referendum on January 4, 1858, to test the acceptance of the constitution that had been approved in another referendum two weeks earlier. This time the constitution was rejected. President Buchanan nevertheless submitted the pro-slavery constitution to Congress with a recommendation that it be accepted and Kansas admitted as a state. A third referendum called for by an act of Congress resulted in a decisive defeat for the Lecompton constitution. Statehood was deferred, but the slavery issue had been settled.[47]

Lecompton's days were numbered by these events. The legislature now controlled by free-staters, adjourned to meet in Lawrence. There on February 10, 1858, they voted to move the capital to Minneola, a projected town some 20 miles south of Lawrence in Franklin County. Its plan is shown in Figure 13.22 with an inset view of an elaborate building for the Capitol and a map showing half a dozen proposed railroads leading to the "city" from all points of the compass. Thirty-five of the 52 legislators were said to have had a financial interest in the town. Aside from its rather interesting pattern of streets, blocks, and public grounds around the proposed Capitol site, however, the town plan was otherwise without much merit.

Governor James W. Denver vetoed the capital removal bill, but nevertheless the legislature called a meeting of a new constitutional convention at Minneola. The delegates evidently were not impressed and after a session lasting only one day voted to move their meeting to Leavenworth. Eventually, the United States attorney general held that the capital removal bill was invalid, and Minneola soon all but vanished.[48]

The constitutional convention meeting in Leavenworth broke up in disagreement, but in July, 1859, a new body assembled at Wyandotte to prepare the document that would guide Kansas to statehood. After prolonged and bitter debate, punctuated with charges of bribery, the convention selected Topeka as the temporary capital with the proviso that the question would be submitted to the voters after the first legislature convened in that city.[49]

Although Topeka had in effect served as the capital of the free-state movement during the years when representatives of antislavery forces met regularly as though they had official status, its facilities were strained by its new status. When the first state legislature convened on March 26, 1861, not quite two months after Congress had approved statehood, the Senate had to meet in rented chambers on the third

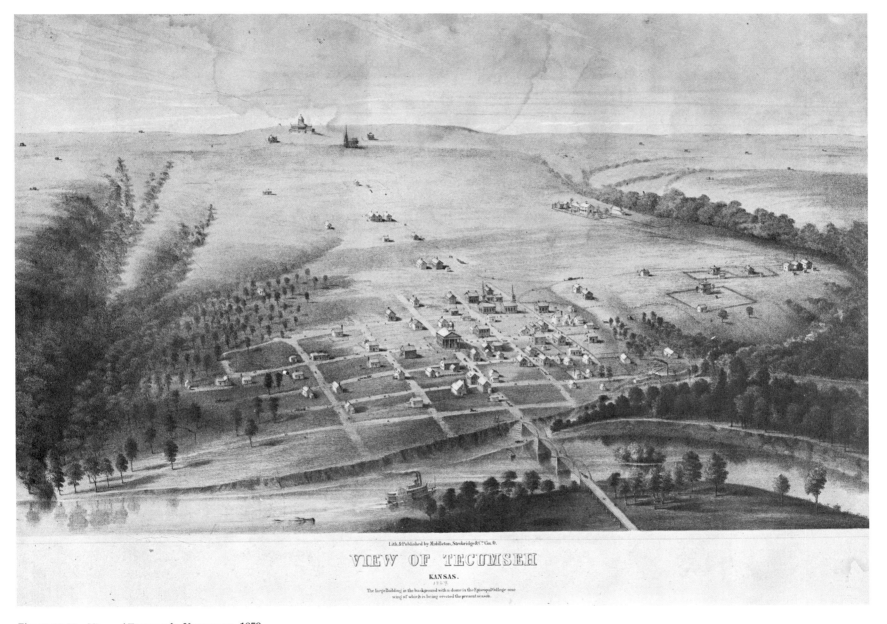

VIEW OF TECUMSEH

KANSAS.

1859.

The large Building in the background with a dome is the Episcopal College one
wing of which is being erected the present season.

Figure 13.20 View of Tecumseh, Kansas: ca. 1859

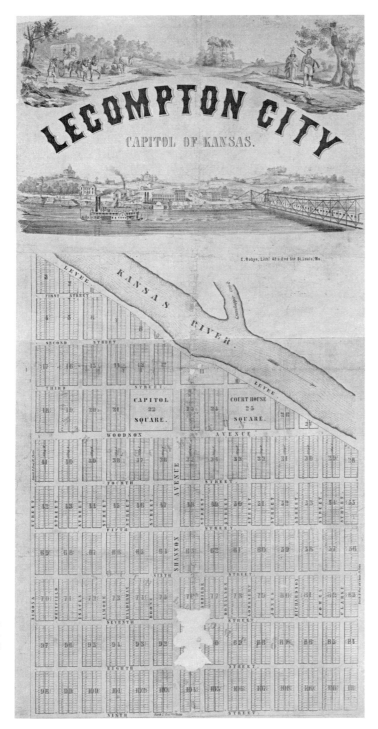

Figure 13.21
Plan of Lecompton,
Kansas: ca. 1855

story of an office building at the southeast corner of Sixth and Kansas Avenues. Governor Charles Robinson, formerly the Emigrant Aid Company agent, had offices in the same building. The House met first in another building and then, when its roof developed a leak, in the Congregational Church at Seventh and Harrison Streets. Various other makeshift arrangements were necessary for the frontier town of less than one thousand to accommodate the functions of the state government.[50]

On November, 1861, the voters of the state approved Topeka as the permanent capital, and the legislature a few months later accepted from the city a gift of the easterly of the two 20-acre public reservations that had been set aside in the original plan. Not until 1866, however, did construction get under way for the Capitol on this site and after three years only the east wing of the building was available for occupancy. The city in that year is shown in Figure 13.23 with the still unfinished Capitol depicted as though completed .

It was far from an impressive community. Beyond the Capitol stretched the rolling plains whose horizontality the city shared. Only an occasional church spire, factory smokestack, or business block on Kansas Avenue provided vertical accent marks for the scattered one- and two-story dwellings, stores, and domestic out-buildings.

Yet the railroad had arrived—and not just a single line but two, one resulting from the efforts of Topeka's founder, Cyrus Holliday. To the right in the view, following the Kansas River, the tracks of the Kansas Pacific (later the Union Pacific) can be seen. The line had arrived in Topeka amidst great excitement on January 1, 1866, and by 1871 it provided service through Topeka from Kansas City to Denver. Running along the eastern edge of the city were the tracks of the Atchison, Topeka & Santa Fe line, which, as the St. Joseph & Topeka Railroad, had been started at Topeka in 1868. Cyrus Holliday served as the first president and as a director until his death in 1900 and, it is said, was determined that the smoke and noise of the train should not smudge the sky or shatter the peace of the city he had so carefully, if not skillfully, laid out. The tracks therefore did not slice through the city or along its waterfront as was to be the case in so many of the railroad towns of the West. Holliday saw to it that the shops of the railroad were located at the northeast corner of the town, both downwind and downstream from the community as it then existed.[51] These can be seen in our last glimpse of Topeka, the view of the city in 1880 reproduced in Figure 13.24.

By that year the city attained a population of 15,000. Much of the un-built upon portions of the original plat had been filled in, the other 20-

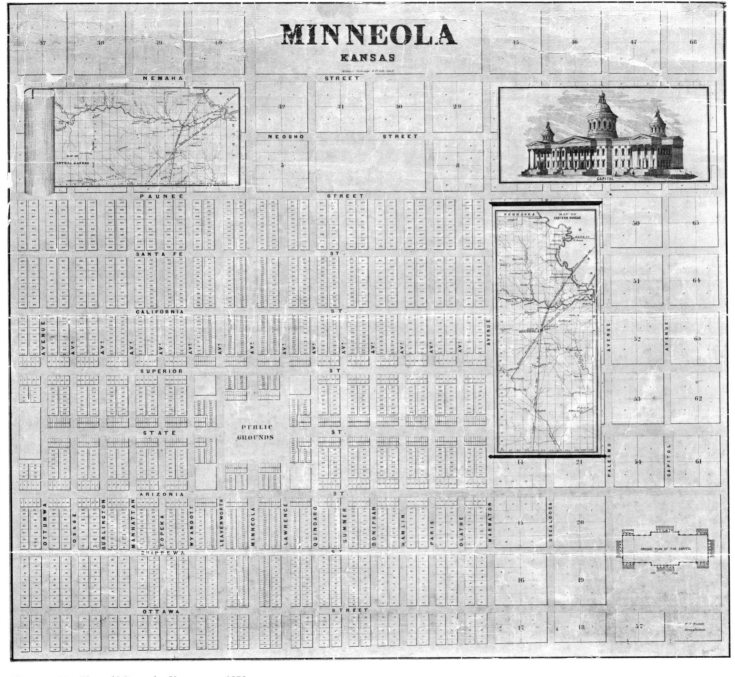

Figure 13.22 Plan of Minneola, Kansas: ca. 1858

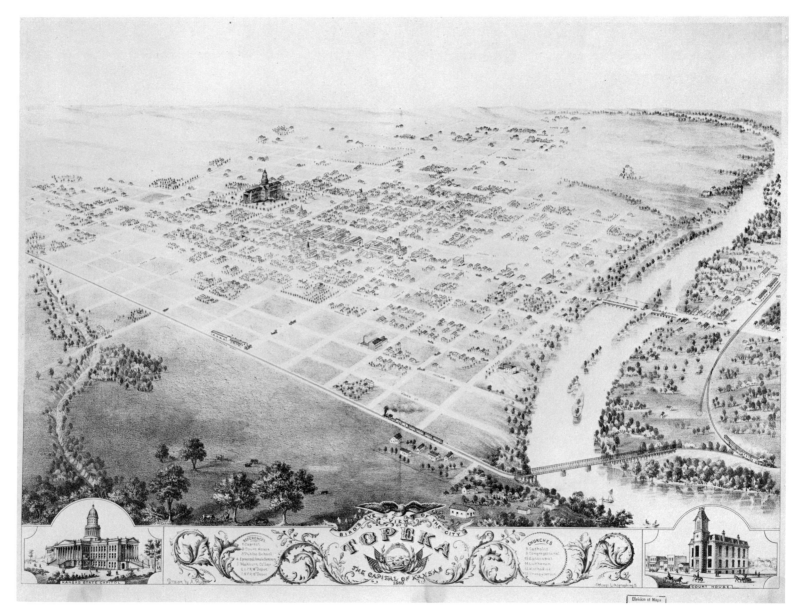

Figure 13.23 View of Topeka, Kansas: 1869

BIRDS EYE VIEW OF
TOPEKA
KANSAS

1 STATE CAPITOL.
2 COLLEGE OF THE SISTERS OF BETHANY.
3 WASHBURN COLLEGE.
4 INSANE ASYLUM.
5 COURT HOUSE.
6 U. S. CUSTOM HOUSE AND POSTOFFICE.
7 LINCOLN PUBLIC SCHOOL.
8 WASHBURN PUBLIC SCHOOL.

9 HARRISON STREET PUBLIC SCHOOL.
10 CLAY STREET PUBLIC SCHOOL.
11 NORTH TOPEKA PUBLIC SCHOOL.
12 PRESBYTERIAN CHURCH.
13 BAPTIST CHURCH.
14 EPISCOPAL CHURCH.
15 M. E. CHURCH.
16 CHURCH OF THE ASSUMPTION.

17 UNION PRESBYTERIAN CHURCH.
18 CONGREGATIONAL CHURCH.
19 AMERICAN LUTHERAN CHURCH.
20 EVANGELICAL CHURCH.
21 COLORED BAPTIST CHURCH.
22 COLORED SECOND BAPTIST CHURCH.
23 COLORED M. E. CHURCH.
24 MISSION CHURCH.

25 NORTH TOPEKA PRESBYTERIAN CHURCH.
26 N. TOPEKA CONGREGATIONAL CHURCH.
27 NORTH TOPEKA BAPTIST CHURCH.
28 ROLLING MILLS.
29 MACHINE SHOPS OF A. T. & S. F. R. R.
30 DEPOT A. T. & S. F. R. R.
31 SHAWNEE MILLS.
32 CAPITAL IRON WORKS.

33 TOPEKA CARRIAGE FACTORY.
34 PASSENGER DEPOT K. P. R. R.
35 FREIGHT DEPOT K. P. R. R.
36 FARMERS MILLS.
37 INTER-OCEANIC MILLS.
38 DISTILLERY.
39 FIFTH AVENUE HOTEL.
40 TEFFT HOUSE.

41 PAPENDICK'S HOTEL.
42 TOPEKA HOUSE.
43 PLANTERS HOUSE.
44 CITY BUILDING.
45 JNO. D. KNOX'S CONTEMPLATED HOME
46 KNOX'S PEAK.
47 OPERA HOUSE.
48 TURNER HALL.

Figure 13.24 View of Topeka, Kansas: 1880

acre square had been occupied by the College of the Sisters of Bethany, Washburn College had been started on a site well to the south of the city and is just visible in the view at the upper left corner, and the west wing of the Capitol had been built.[52] The city was to experience almost a decade of rapid growth and prosperity. By 1889 the population had more than doubled to 35,000. When the first part of the Indian Territory in Oklahoma was opened for settlement in that year, several thousand residents of Topeka joined in the disorderly scramble for land in that new frontier, and it was not until nearly the turn of the century that Topeka reached its earlier peak and began a slower period of growth at a less hectic pace.

We shall return to Kansas in a later chapter that deals in more detail with the influence of railroads on urban planning and growth in the cities of the Great Plains. It is a region that has still to realize the potential foreseen by Bayard Taylor on his return from Colorado in 1867. Taylor saw more than the rough beginnings of a frontier culture in Kansas and Nebraska. "No one of us," he observed to his contemporaries, "will live to see the beauty and prosperity which these States, even in their rude, embryonic condition, already suggest. The American of to-day must find his enjoyment in anticipating the future. He must look beyond the unsightly beginnings of civilization and prefigure the state of things a century hence, when the Republic will count a population of two hundred millions, and there shall be leisure for Taste and Art. We have now so much ground to occupy, and we make such haste to cover it, that our growth is—and must be—accompanied by very few durable landmarks. All is slight, shabby, and imperfect. Not until the greater part of our vacant territory is taken up, and there is a broad belt of settlement reaching from ocean to ocean, will our Western people begin to take root, consolidate their enterprise, and truly develop their unparalleled inheritance."[53]

Taylor's century was passed some years ago at which time the nation had indeed reached his amazingly accurate population forecast of two hundred million. Many of the communities that, during Taylor's day, seemed destined for growth and, in time, beauty, have stagnated, dwindled, or disappeared altogether. Others, like Omaha and Kansas City, have achieved a substantial measure of industrial prosperity. A few, like Topeka and, above all, Lincoln, grew with an eye to beauty in the consciousness that the quality of the physical environment is as important an element of greatness as size or industrial wealth. Taylor's belief that leisure for the cultivation of "Taste and Art" would transform the conditions of the raw frontier he observed from a Butterfield Stage has not yet been realized, nor is it inevitable that mere time alone will bring this about. The tradition of speculation that played such an important role in the planning of these cities persists as perhaps the dominant force in modern city growth. If that can be replaced by an attitude that places community goals above that of any individual the cities of the plains may finally vindicate Taylor's large vision of a distant future.

XIV

Rush to the Rockies: Denver and
the Mining Towns of Colorado

In the summer of 1858 the news that two groups prospecting for gold in the valley of the South Platte River had struck it rich set off a new mining rush rivaling California's a decade earlier. The accounts reaching Kansas and Missouri contained more rumor than truth, for the two parties had panned only limited amounts of gold. The mere sight of these samples displayed in the frontier settlements along the Missouri River, however, was enough to excite the residents of that region, which had been hard-hit by the panic of 1857. Farmers lacked markets for their products, the orgy of townsite speculation that had swept Kansas and Nebraska had left many persons hopelessly in debt, business remained bad, and unemployment was widespread. Little wonder that tens of thousands in the border settlements responded to the electrifying news that sudden wealth lay across the plains at the base of the Rocky Mountains.

In the tradition of the frontier, the amount of gold that had been found or was rumored to exist became greater as the word spread eastward. Newspapers of such economically depressed communities as Omaha and Leavenworth helped exaggerate these stories in hopes of capturing for their towns the outfitting, supply, and freighting business that would be generated by a new gold rush. In this they succeeded. Many persons left for the mountains in the late summer and early fall of 1858. Thousands more from eastern states joined the stream of migrants in the following spring.[1]

In Leavenworth a young Vermonter, Libeus Barney, observed that "the emigration is really a godsend to this . . . town . . . and Leavenworth is realizing glorious profits out of the general excitement." The town throbbed with activity and was prospering beyond its wildest hopes. Barney described the scene in a letter dispatched to a Vermont newspaper: "This being the terminus for laying in supplies, everything in the way of provisions and implements for digging, find ready sale at a handsome advance. Thousands are leaving here daily and in every variety of way the mind can conjecture. Now a party with guns, pistols and picks, their blankets thrown over their shoulders, and with provisions scarcely sufficient to last a week, off they start for the mines. . . . Here another party, with hand-carts loaded down with all the necessaries for a comfortable journey— . . . burden enough for a yoke of oxen. . . . And still again a company of 8 or 10 appear with six yoke of oxen and a monster wagon attached, loaded to excess with the necessaries and a keg or two of luxuries, and off they move."[2]

Most persons headed for the spot where the first strikes had been reported—the mouth of Cherry Creek on the South Platte River.[3] Here a bewildering number of townsites were hastily platted by at least five groups claiming large tracts of land in the vicinity of what was to become the City of Denver.

First in the area was a party from Lawrence, Kansas, organized by John Easter. On their way via the Santa Fe Trail and then northward along the eastern slope of the Rocky Mountains, they paused to lay out a town they called El Paso.[4] Moving on to Cherry Creek, where they arrived in August, 1858, they camped in several places while panning for gold with only limited success. The group divided when it came time to establish a winter settlement. Some wished to settle at the mouth of Cherry Creek, but most of those who remained in Colorado that winter formed a town company and had William Hartley lay off the "city" of Montana on the east bank of the South Platte River six miles to the south. A dozen cabins were erected in September and October, and the population early the next month after a few new settlers arrived consisted of 57 men and 2 women.[5]

Seven members of the Lawrence party joined two Indian traders who occupied claims on the east side of Cherry Creek to form a second town company. It was to be an ambitious undertaking, embracing, as the articles of agreement read, "six hundred and forty acres of land" laid out "into streets, lots, blocks, etc.," each member being entitled to an equal share "except such lots as the company shall see proper to donate to settlers, or for other purposes."[6]

William Hartley, who had planned Montana, was a member of this group, and on September 25 he surveyed the boundaries and streets of the new town of St. Charles. The proprietors decided to build a cabin on each quarter-section of the mile-square site to establish their claim, leave the two Indian traders, John S. Smith and William McGaa, to occupy them during the winter, and return to Kansas to attract settlers and obtain a city charter from the legislature of Kansas Territory, which was presumed to have jurisdiction over the region.[7]

Four cabins and two men were insufficient to hold this townsite claim against an invasion that came in November. Two Kansas groups, one from Lecompton and the other from Leavenworth, arrived on the site and decided to plan their own town on the land previously surveyed by the St. Charles Company. In this bald incident of claim-jumping they appear to have had the consent—willing or forced—of Smith and McGaa who became directors of the new town company.[8] The November arrivals could and did maintain that they were acting on behalf of the territorial government of Kansas. Before they left home they had secured appointments for some of their members as officials of

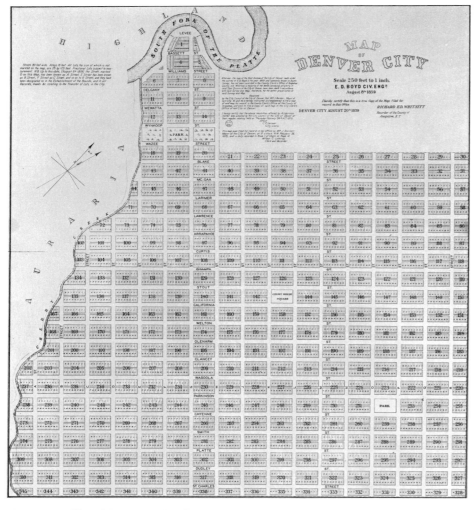

Figure 14.1 Plan of Denver, Colorado: 1859

Arapahoe County, Kansas, from Governor James W. Denver.[9] This scarcely gave them the authority to occupy another company's land, but they were able to continue possession by a combination of superior numbers, threats, and by passing out shares of stock in their company to a few members of the St. Charles group when they returned in the spring of 1859 to find their site taken over by the newcomers.

Samuel Curtis and James S. Lowry quickly laid out the substitute town, which for obvious political reasons was named Denver. Although the group was not then aware of the fact, the governor whose name the town bore had resigned his post in October. The officers of the Denver Town Company, as it turned out, did not need his anticipated support to uphold their questionable actions.

Denver's plan as established late in 1858 and resurveyed nine months later is reproduced in Figure 14.1. Except for the levee at the bend of the South Platte and a few lots and alleys there, the city did not deviate from its gigantic gridiron pattern even along the meandering course of Cherry Creek that formed its western boundary. The surveyors laid out all streets to a uniform width of 80 feet providing blocks 266 by 400 feet bisected by 16 foot alleys. Each standard block contained 32 lots, 25 by 125 feet, and with no fewer than 328 full and fractional blocks the plan provided enough building sites for a city of many thousand persons. The planners named the streets running northeast-southwest, including at the foot of the plan a street called St. Charles, a reminder of the original claimants. Some of the other streets took the names of leaders of the town company, including Larimer, named for General William Larimer, Jr., who soon emerged as the most energetic promoter of the new town and one of Denver's most prominent civic leaders.

Cross-streets in the original survey were designated only by letters. A note on the plat states that D Street was first known as A Street, suggesting that in November, 1858, that may have marked the first town boundary on that side of the community. Later, numbers replaced the letters. F Street became 15th, G Street 16th, and so on.[10] This area now comprises the downtown section of Denver, although a portion of the eastern part of this original plan was later to be replatted on a grid system with streets running north-south and east-west, creating a series of awkward intersections where the two street systems join.

Five blocks of the Denver City plan were intended for public use: a park square in the eastern part of the plat, a courthouse square near the center, and three contiguous blocks between Wynkoop and Wazee Streets shown as some kind of landscaped park. None was ever used for these purposes, and the three park blocks near the river were soon replatted into alleys and lots on the standard pattern used throughout the rest of the city.[11] The lots in the remaining blocks were distributed to the 41 members of the town company, the holder of each share being entitled to 146 lots. Each shareholder was required to erect a cabin within 90 days or lose title to his lots.

The Denver Town Company faced competition from a slightly earlier rival on the opposite side of Cherry Creek. There the Auraria Town Company held its organizational meeting on November 6, 1858, to formalize a settlement that had begun at the end of August on a 1200-acre site.[12] Surveyor Henry Allen, an Iowan, assisted by William Foster, surveyed the tract into blocks 280 by 396 feet, 80-foot streets, and 66 by 132-foot lots arranged in two tiers of 6 lots separated by 16-foot alleys. As shown in the upper left portion of Figure 14.2, Auraria's streets followed a slightly different orientation from those of the Denver Town Company's, and filled in with a second grid the area between Cherry Creek and the South Platte River.

On the northwest bank of the South Platte River still another town began its existence in 1858. This was Highland, staked out on December 14 by D. C. Collier and General Larimer, the latter's boundless real estate ambitions apparently not completely satisfied by the platting of Denver. As Henry Villard noted, this last of the Cherry Creek settlements had "a very picturesque and advantageous site," but it suffered because of inaccessibility until bridges were built across the river. Although Villard claimed that at the end of 1859 "a large number of buildings are completed and in process of erection," the townsite remained sparsely settled for many years.[13]

The "fifty-niners" began to arrive in great numbers some months after the establishment of these communities. These newcomers found more town lots than gold nuggets. The initial small deposits along the streams in the vicinity were soon exhausted. Indeed, many persons who had flocked to the area in 1858 gave up in disgust and returned home before the end of that first year of the Colorado rush. Despite the flow of exaggerated stories about instant wealth that inundated the East, no one was rich and many persons began to think that they had been hoaxed.[14] Nevertheless, by midsummer of 1859, 300 cabins and a few more substantial structures could be found scattered here and there in Auraria and Denver. Albert Richardson described the community as "a most forlorn and desolate-looking metropolis. Of the two or three hundred rough log cabins which composed it, more than half were unfinished and tenantless." He and his companion, Horace Greeley, "took lodgings at the first-class hotel—an enormous wooden structure

with walls of logs, a floor of mother earth, and windows and roof of cotton cloth." Finding this unsatisfactory, the two journalists "selected the best empty . . . [cabin] . . . we could find" and moved in. Their temporary home, Richardson records, was "twelve feet square, of hewn pine logs . . . the cracks within chinked with wood, and outside plastered with mud."[15] Richardson's book, *Beyond the Mississippi*, included the series of views of Denver in 1859 shown in Figure 14.3.

Richardson and Greeley found the settlements almost empty of "permanent" residents because in May the news that everyone had hoped for reached the Cherry Creek towns. John H. Gregory, prospecting in the mountains on one of the forks of Clear Creek less than 30 miles to the west had struck a rich deposit of gold-bearing quartz. One of his companions displayed samples of the ore in Denver on May 8, 1859, when he came to town for supplies. As Henry Villard reported, "on the following day an universal exodus took place. . . . Whoever could raise enough provisions for a protracted stay in the mountains, sallied out without delay. Traders locked up their stores; bar-keepers disappeared with their bottles of whiskey, the few mechanics that were busy building houses, abandoned their work, the county judge and sheriff, lawyers, and doctors, and even the editor of the *Rocky Mountain News*, joined in the general rush."[16]

When Villard reached the scene a few days later, he found "hundreds of men busily engaged in ripping open the very bowels of the mountains with pick and shovel. Pine huts had already been erected and tents pitched in large numbers. Sluices, long toms and rockers were in full operation; ditches crossed the gulch in every direction; slides checkered the mountain sides."[17]

A series of mining camps extending for several miles up and down Gregory Gulch sprang suddenly into life, and several of them developed as permanent towns.

Denver and Auraria profited from the bonanza even after it became evident that to extract gold from the stubborn quartz would require shaft mining, stamping mills, and other elaborate mining equipment beyond the resources of individual miners. As one exuberant resident of Denver wrote to a friend in the East, "to tell the truth . . . we didn't any of us realize how anxious we had grown . . . till this great and inspiring news suddenly dropped down on us like a denizen from Heaven. But the trouble has passed from us like a cloud from the face of the sun. Henceforth Denver City has nothing to do but sit down and grow. . . . Now is the time to buy lots. . . . This is only the beginning. Parties have gone into the mountains in all directions and last night's

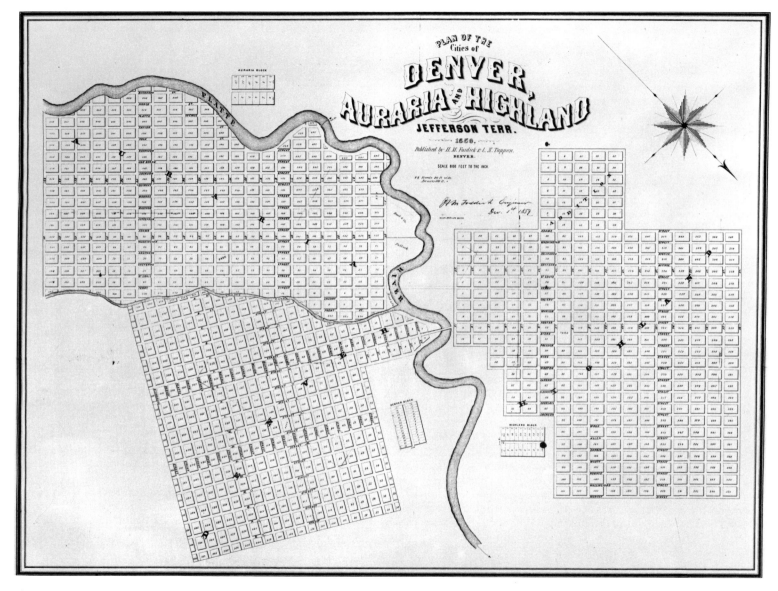

Figure 14.2 Plan of Denver, Colorado: 1859

news may be repeated at any hour from any quarter. The Rocky Mountains is full of gold and there are fortunes for all in this country."[18]

Sales of Denver and Auraria town lots increased after the news of Gregory's strike reached the communities. Libeus Barney reported in mid-July that lots selling for $20 only six weeks earlier now brought $300.[19] Barney himself started construction that month on Apollo Hall on the north side of Larimer Street near Cherry Creek. A restaurant, saloon, and gambling hall occupied the first floor. On the second floor a large room provided a community meeting place. The space also served as Denver's first theater, but the performers had to shout their lines to make themselves heard over the nightly tumult in the saloon below.[20]

In the fall Auraria and Denver enjoyed a building boom when many miners returned from the mountains for the winter and as immigrants continued to arrive from the East. Toward the end of November Barney wrote that "every man who possesses sufficient knowledge of mechanics to beat a mortise and shove a plane, turn an auger and drive a nail . . . is employed upon one structure or another." Not all buildings were of timber: "even respectable brick buildings are in course of construction, isolated and in blocks." The largest structure was 50 by 60 feet and 3 stories high, the top floor above these used for merchandising being fitted out as the Masonic Hall.[21]

The first city directory appeared in the winter of 1859-60. It proudly announced that the following businesses and professional offices then flourished in Denver and Auraria: "twelve wholesale and retail, and twenty-seven retail houses, dealing in groceries, provisions, clothing, hardware, crockery, liquors, drugs, etc., etc., three commission and forwarding houses, eight hotels, nine boarding houses, eleven restaurants, twenty-three saloons, four billiard saloons, four ten-pin alleys, two livery stables, one U.S. post office, two express offices, one newspaper, one union school, four lumber yards, one news depot, two theatres, fourteen lawyers, fourteen physicians, seven surveyors and architects, four contractors for building, nine real estate and mining claim agencies, and a considerable number of representatives of various trades, such as butchers, cabinet-makers, carpenters, watchmakers, blacksmiths, masons, barbers, etc., etc."[22]

The view of the two communities in Figure 14.4 shows their appearance in 1860. Auraria can be seen on the left occupying the low-lying land west of Cherry Creek and, on the right, appears that portion of Denver located on high ground sloping upward from the creek and the South Platte River.[23] The vast gridirons platted by the two town companies were still largely vacant, but a substantial start had been made in

Figure 14.3 Views of Denver, Colorado: 1859

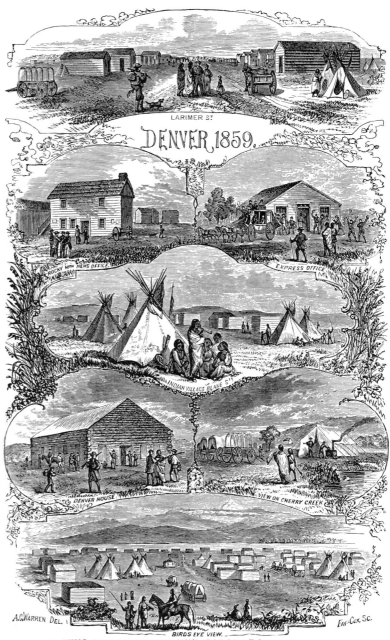

SEVEN VIEWS IN DENVER, COLORADO 1859.

Figure 14.4 View of Denver, Colorado: 1860

the development of what was eventually to become the dominant city of the Rocky Mountain states.

More than Cherry Creek divided the two settlements, for Denver and Auraria became intense rivals. Residents of each praised their own town while condemning the other harshly. A Denver booster referred to those living in Auraria as "them contumacious villains" who were living in "huts and hovels and shanties that you would't drive a cow into for shelter, while ours are to be called palaces by comparison."[24] The proprietor of the *Rocky Mountain News* diplomatically erected his building on stilts in the bed of Cherry Creek. There he published this pioneer newspaper containing news of both communities until a disastrous flood in 1864 forced its relocation to a safer site.[25]

Some of the ill-feeling between Auraria and Denver stemmed from the geographic and social backgrounds of their founders. Auraria was created largely by Georgians who naturally were supporters of slavery. Many of those active in the Denver Town Company came from Lawrence, the center of the free-state movement in Kansas Territory. Although Auraria had the earlier start and for a time was the more populous of the two communities, Denver gradually forged ahead. A major impetus to its growth was the location in Denver of the Central Overland California & Pike's Peak Express Company offices and station. The developer of this stage line, W. H. Russell, was a friend of General Larimer, and Larimer saw to it that Russell was given a share in the Denver Town Company in exchange for his agreement to locate the express company offices in Larimer's town.[26]

Despite ill-feeling that occasionally erupted into actual conflict, cooperation between the two rival groups soon developed. In June, 1859, a mass meeting resulted in a declaration creating the Territory of Jefferson.[27] While this decision never received congressional recognition, the new provisional government provided a measure of law and order for the growing towns on Cherry Creek and the mining camps in the mountains until Colorado Territory was officially organized in early 1861. The first meeting of the Jefferson Territory legislature in December, 1859, saw the approval of an act uniting the communities under the cumbersome title, "City of Denver, Auraria and Highlands."[28] The details finally were worked out over the next few months, and on April 6, 1860, Auraria and Denver were consolidated under the name of the latter town. Appropriately enough, the ceremony took place on the Larimer Street bridge over Cherry Creek, a structure completed just a month earlier.[29]

Construction in the now united Denver boomed that summer. Libeus

Barney recorded the scene: "Building in Denver is progressing very rapidly. Dwellings, stores, banking-houses and hotels, mushroom like, spring into existence all over the city." One of the new buildings was "an assay office and mint." Another addition to the urban scene was the "hospital . . . now ready for the reception of patients, whether mangled, bruised, pistoled or knifed."[30]

The hospital did not suffer for want of patients. Denver was, as Barney noted, "a fast town, in a wicked way." Villard wrote that "shooting affrays . . . occurred frequently," while Richardson observed that "almost every day was enlivened by its little shooting match. While the great gaming saloon was crowded with people, drunken ruffians sometimes fired five or six shots from their revolvers, frightening everybody pell-mell out of the room."[31]

Denver retained for many years some elements of this raw, brawling, and lawless frontier atmosphere. But the city wore another face—one of the settled respectability and permance as noted by Bayard Taylor during his visit in the summer of 1866. In that year Alfred E. Mathews published a series of lithograph views of Denver and the mining towns of Colorado. His view of the city from the plains to the east, reproduced in Figure 14.5, is exactly what Taylor saw when he "perceived, through the dust, a stately square Gothic tower, and rubbed my eyes with a sense of incredulity. It was really true; there was the tower, built of brick, well-proportioned and picturesque. Dwellings and cottages rose over the dip of the ridge, on either side; brick blocks began to appear, and presently we were rolling through gay, animated streets, down the vistas of which the snowy ranges in the west were shining fairly in the setting sun."[32]

When the French mining engineer, Louis L. Simonin, passed through the city a year later he too was struck by the attractive houses, "the churches, whose number already exceeds the half dozen," and the "wide streets, quite open, watered, [and] planted with trees." In Denver, Simonin commented, "the movement of life is everywhere. One would hardly believe himself at the end of the prairies, 2,000 miles from New York." His account appeared in a series of articles in *Le Tour du Monde* accompanied by many illustrations, including that in Figure 14.6. This view on F (now 15th) Street might have inspired his observation that "rapid carriages pass and repass everywhere, or heavy wagons laden with the commodities of the East, ready to leave for the mining towns."[33] In less than a decade the crude, scattered log or plank shelters of Denver's pioneer residents and merchants had been replaced by solid rows of brick and stone warehouses, stores, and offices.

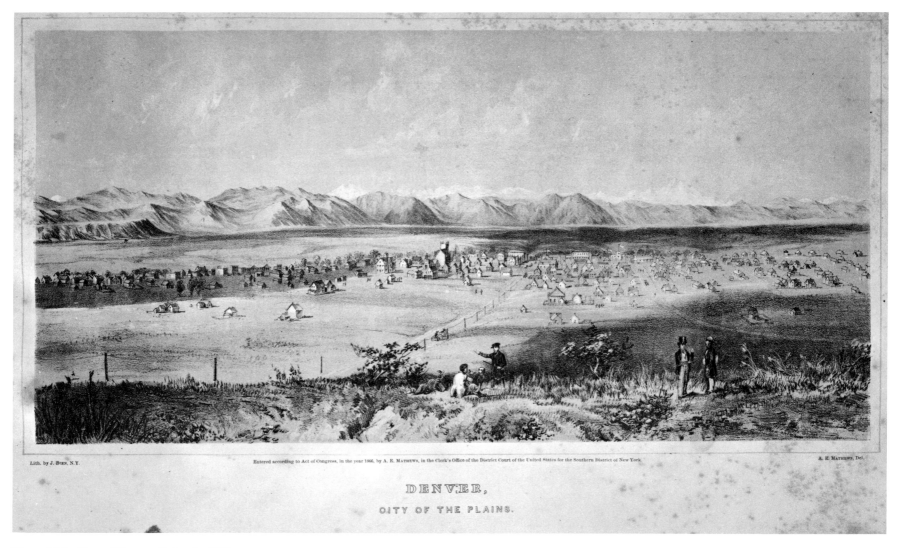

Entered according to Act of Congress, in the year 1866, by A. E. Mathews, in the Clerk's Office of the District Court of the United States for the Southern District of New York.

DENVER,

CITY OF THE PLAINS.

Figure 14.5 View of Denver, Colorado: 1866

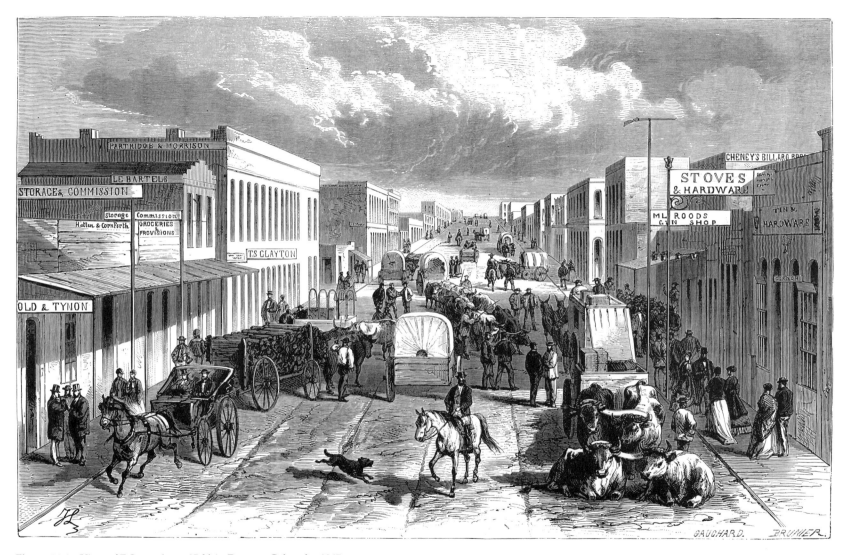

Figure 14.6 View of F Street (now 15th) in Denver, Colorado: 1867

Denver was Colorado's Sacramento, serving as the principal source of supplies needed in the mines. While at the time of Simonin's visit a great many additional strikes had been made elsewhere, the mining communities in and near John Gregory's first discovery of gold-bearing quartz remained the most important. Simonin's map showing the location of these mountain towns and the hundreds of separate mining claims of the region is reproduced in Figure 14.7.

As in California and Nevada the miners in mining areas of Colorado formed mining districts and adopted rules and regulations governing various kinds of claims. Those in effect at Gregory Gulch as early as the summer of 1859 specified how claims could be made, recorded, and enforced, and limited the area that could be claimed by any one person. They also contained one reference to town lots indicating clearly that mining and not town design held first priority: "Any person may take up, by recording, forty feet front and one hundred deep, for a building lot; but shall not secure the same against being used for mining, if found rich. Should any person work out the ground on which a house stands, he shall secure the house against damage."[34]

Nevertheless, an early plan provided some degree of direction for urban growth in Central City, the chief town of this area. The earliest known survey of the community is reproduced in Figure 14.8. It bears the date March, 1863, and a later annotation in 1921 by Hal Sayre stating: "I made the survey of Central City and this map in 1863, being the first survey and map of the place made." It is possible that some kind of informal plat may have been prepared as early as 1860 and that the Sayre survey three years later was an effort to provide more precise street and property lines.[35]

The plan reflected the rugged topography of the site. Lawrence, Eureka, Gregory, Spring, Nevada, and Main Streets followed the creek at the bottom of the steep gulch that led up from the right-hand side of the plat and branched into two forks. Other streets laid out parallel to these roughly followed the contours of the valley walls. Short, steep cross-streets provided access up and down the slopes. The view of Central City in 1866 reproduced in Figure 14.9 shows the settlement viewed up the valley of Gregory and Eureka Gulches. By that time Lawrence Street had become almost solidly built up with business blocks, hotels, gambling halls, saloons, warehouses, and the other familiar structures of frontier mining communities.

Below Central City lay Black Hawk where Gregory Gulch emptied into the north fork of Clear Creek. This town developed on a similar pattern with its streets running on either side of the creek banks and others carved out of the hillsides above. The view in Figure 14.10 shows Black Hawk in 1862 as seen looking up Gregory Gulch from across Clear Creek. From this point Gregory Street wound up the valley to Central City. From Central City, Nevada Street led still farther up the narrow valley of Nevada Gulch to Nevada City. At the height of mining activity in the region there was an almost continuous line of buildings, mines, and cabins crowded together and forming an irregular, linear community.

Bayard Taylor described conditions as he saw them in the summer of 1866: "Commencing at Black Hawk,—where the sole pleasant object is the Presbyterian Church, white, tasteful, and charmingly placed on the last step of Bates Hill, above the chimneys and mills in the uniting ravines,—we mount Gregory Gulch by a rough, winding, dusty road, lined with crowded wooden buildings: hotels, with pompous names and limited accommodations; drinking saloons,—'lager beer' being a frequent sign; bakeries, log and frame dwelling-houses, idle mills, piles of rusty and useless machinery tumbled by the wayside, and now and then a cottage in the calico style, with all sorts of brackets and carved drop-cornices."

Central City, Taylor noted, "consists mainly of one street, on the right-hand side of the gulch; the houses on your left, as you ascend, resting on high posts or scaffolding, over the deep bed of the stream." The intersection of Main Street marked the center of the business district "where the principal stores are jammed together in an incredibly small space." As a younger man observing the California mining camps, Taylor had been less critical of their appearance. Now he found "the whole string" of towns extending up Gregory and Nevada Gulches had "a curious rickety, temporary air, with their buildings standing as if on one leg, their big signs and little accommodations, the irregular, wandering, uneven street, and the bald, scarred, and pitted mountains on either side." It was a place, he concluded, where "everything is odd, grotesque, unusual; but no feature can be called attractive."[36]

Taylor saw Central City and its sister towns at a time when their fortunes were at a low ebb. The first, easily mined gold deposits soon were worked out, and in the mid-1860s many mines closed. However, by the end of that decade engineers introduced new methods for treating refractory ores, and a new boom began.[37] Smelters and mills blackened Black Hawk's skies, as did the locomotives of the narrow gauge Colorado Central Railway, which reached the town from Golden in 1872. The less accessible Central City did not enjoy rail service for another 6

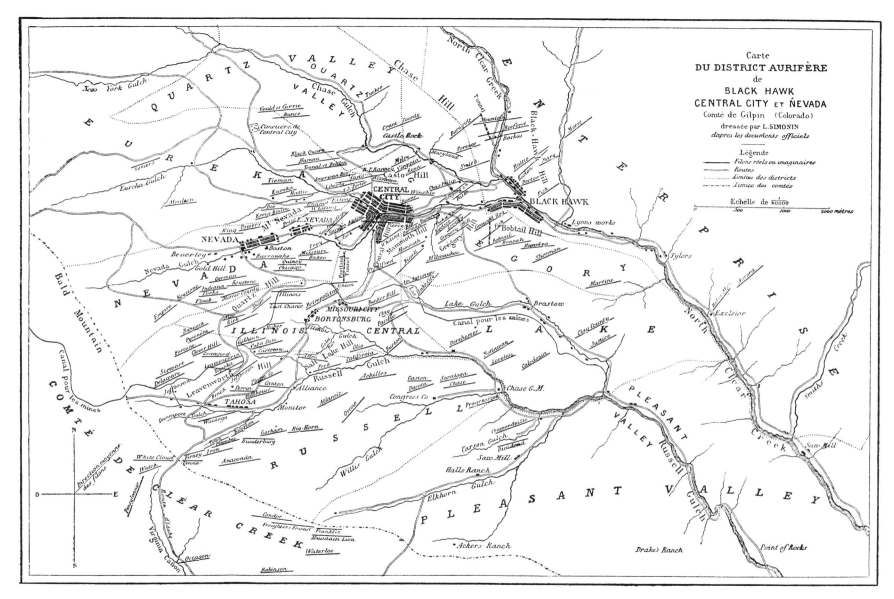

Figure 14.7 Map of Central City, Colorado and Vicinity: 1867

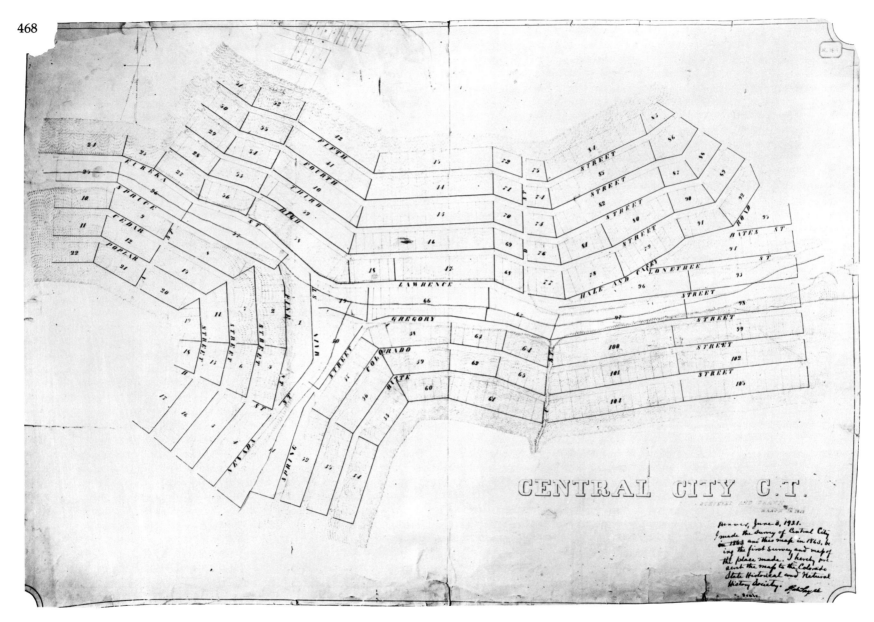

Figure 14.8 Plan of Central City, Colorado: 1863

CENTRAL CITY;

FROM THE SIDE OF MAMMOTH HILL LOOKING UP GREGORY AND EUREKA GULCHES.

Figure 14.9 View of Central City, Colorado: 1866

Figure 14.10 View of Black Hawk, Colorado: 1862

years, but its mines once again produced incredible amounts of gold, and the town prospered as never before.

The view in Figure 14.11 depicts the two communities in 1873. While many new buildings had been built in Black Hawk since its earliest years, it was Central City that had grown and expanded most rapidly. The platted but largely unoccupied streets of the previous decade now were graded to provide access to new and occasionally impressive homes overlooking the valley. The largest building in the town was the 90-room Teller House, fronting Eureka Street at Pine opposite the Gilpin County courthouse and the Central City *Register* Building. Completed in 1872, its most famous visitor of the period was President Ulysses S. Grant, who was escorted to its door over a pavement of silver bricks worth $13,000 laid down for the occasion.[38]

Central City did not escape destruction from fire, for on the morning of May 21, 1874, the town was almost totally destroyed by flames originating in a Chinese laundry. Only the Teller House and a few other structures remained; all the rest lay in ruins. Before reconstruction began, the city council specified that certain streets in the town should be widened. This legislative directive provides some indication of how narrow the original thoroughfares must have been: "Eureka and Lawrence Sts., from Pine to the eastern limit should be 45 feet; Main St., 50 feet the entire length; Gregory St., 40 feet; Spring St., 40 feet; High St., 30 feet."[39] Central City rebuilt, and the town once again flourished. Distinguished actors and entertainers appeared at the city's Opera House and were entertained by Central City society at the refurbished Teller House. But as other and newer mining areas proved more rewarding, many of the city's wealthy residents moved to Denver, and the town began a long period of decline. Tourism has brought a measure of prosperity to the modern town, many of whose buildings have been preserved and restored. During the summer months the Opera House once again comes alive, and Central City, never completely a ghost town, has found a new basis for existence.[40]

Many other mining towns and supply centers began their existence at the same time as Central City and Black Hawk or were founded in the years to follow near newly discovered gold and silver deposits. The location of most of them can be seen on the map of Colorado in 1874 reproduced in Figure 14.12.

One of these was Idaho Springs near the site of George Jackson's gold strike early in 1859. Jackson returned to Denver and Auraria, quietly informed some of his friends of his discovery, and with them organized the Chicago Mining Company. This group surveyed a site for a camp along the south fork of Clear Creek. The community went through a series of names—Sacramento City, Jackson Diggings, Idaho Bar, and Payne's Bar—before becoming known as Idaho City or Idaho. The date of the plat reproduced in Figure 14.13 is not known, but it may well have been prepared as early as 1859 or at least copied from a survey made at the time the camp was first settled or shortly thereafter. Colorado and Canon Streets were laid out 60 feet wide, other streets being 40 feet wide and the alleys 20 feet in width. The surveyor, whoever he may have been, plainly expected Colorado Street to be the principal thoroughfare. Instead, the business district developed around the intersection of Second Avenue and Miners Street squarely in the center of the eastern half of the town plat.[41]

When the territorial legislature created Clear Creek County, Idaho gained the coveted designation of county seat. The town also attracted attention because of the nearby hot springs, whose waters were believed to possess curative properties. When the mining boom waned, the town, now named Idaho Springs, developed as a small health resort, and the spring waters were bottled and sold throughout the country.

Southwest of Idaho Springs was another important mining town that eventually was to become the county seat. This was Georgetown, one of the best preserved of all the Colorado mining communities. George Griffith and his brother found gold here in 1859 and helped to organize a mining district the next summer. At that time some kind of town was staked out, but the plat was lost.[42] It is doubtful if this caused anyone much worry, for in less than three years nearly all the miners left for other areas where gold could be extracted more easily than from the peculiarly stubborn ores of this high mountain valley.

The ore, however, turned out to be rich in silver, and the miners returned in the mid-1860s. In 1867, as the view of the town in Figure 14.14 reveals, little distinguished the settlement from scores of other mining villages and hamlets scattered throughout the Colorado Rockies. That year, however, the residents employed Charles Hoyt to survey the site as a town, named it Georgetown in honor of the original prospector, and succeeded in capturing the county seat from Idaho Springs. Early the next year the territorial legislature granted a city charter to the now thriving community.[43]

Hoyt surveyed an area of nearly one square mile in an elongated gridiron pattern of streets extending a mile and one-half from the foot of Burrell Hill down the half-mile wide Clear Creek valley. It seems likely that he incorporated whatever may have survived of the earlier

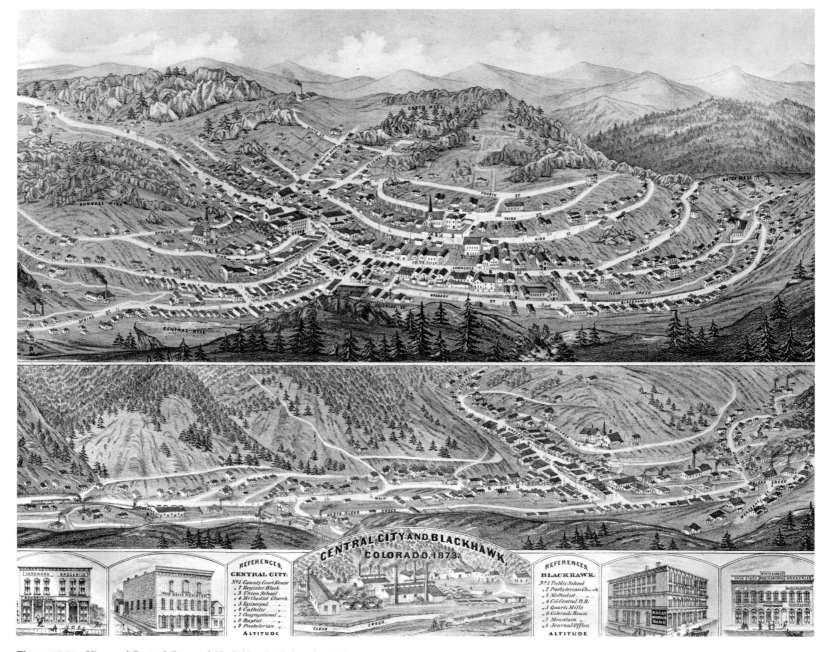

Figure 14.11 Views of Central City and Black Hawk, Colorado: 1873

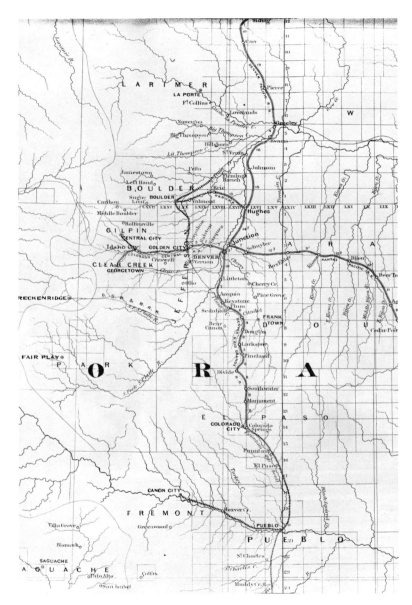

Figure 14.12 Map of Colorado: 1874

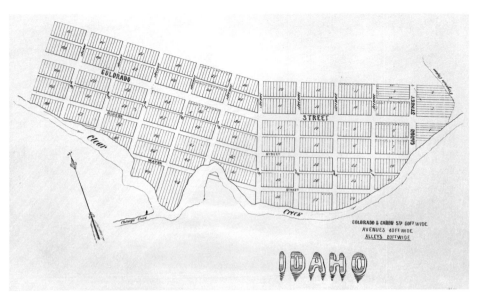

Figure 14.13 Plan of Idaho Springs, Colorado: date unknown

streets laid out in 1860. The results of his efforts can be seen in Plate 19 showing Georgetown in 1874 as viewed from one of the towering peaks enclosing the valley on three sides.

As a local historian commented six years after the date of this view, "compared with those of other mountain towns, the streets of Georgetown are quite regular," a marked contrast to the wildly rugged character of the mountain environment. The early buildings of the town, we are told, were not particularly impressive. Most were of frame construction, brick being used "to some extent, and stone, the most abundant material, still less." Even the town hall and courthouse were of timber, "utility and convenience" not being "sacrificed to elegance in either instance." Cushman's Opera House, one of the few brick structures, was in the 1880 "nothing but a massive monument of inefficient workmanship, the building having been condemned by the city authorities as unsafe."[44]

Yet less than five years later Georgetown could be described as a city containing "some very good business blocks, and stores and shops of

Figure 14.14   View of Georgetown, Colorado: 1867

all kinds." There were "two banks, eight stamp mills, ore sampling and reduction works, five churches, good schools . . . and quite a number of hotels." The town had gas lights and "water, the finest in the world, is conducted in pipes from a mammoth reservoir, 500 feet above the city."[45] Among the hotels referred to was the Hotel de Paris on Alpine Street opened in 1876 by Louis du Puy. This eccentric Frenchman served the finest of food and wine in a lavishly embellished setting that would have done credit to Paris itself. The building still stands and is once again open as a museum—a reminder of the days when Georgetown was the silver capital of Colorado.[46]

On the 1874 map of Colorado in Figure 14.12, Breckenridge appears as an isolated but major settlement southwest of Georgetown. The cartographer was more than a decade behind the times, for while the town in 1860 had a combined permanent and transient population of 5,000 it had dwindled to no more than 500 in 1866 when Bayard Taylor described it as "a flag-staff, with something white at half-mast; canvas covered wagons in the shade; a long street of log-houses; signs of 'Boarding,' 'Miner's Home,' and 'Saloon,' and a motley group of rough individuals." Nearby Montgomery, which according to Taylor had once reached "a population of three thousand," was then a village one-tenth that size. It was neatly destroying itself, Taylor noted, since "as the cabins of those who left speedily became the firewood of those who remained, there are no apparent signs of decay."[47]

Dozens of other mining towns suddenly sprouted and as quickly withered when the easily worked placer deposits or those of decomposed quartz became exhausted or when richer strikes elsewhere beckoned. Not far from Breckenridge lay Hamilton, once dizzy with prosperity but in 1868 only a huddle of "desolated cabins, doorless, windowless," as Samuel Bowles described the scene. Across the stream Bowles found Tarryall, "where thousands dug and washed sands for gold three and four years ago" now "only two or three . . . mud-patched" cabins. In the same South Park region of Colorado Bowles visited Montgomery, where once "there was an opera house, and saloons and stores by the dozens." In the summer of 1868 there were still "a hundred or two houses standing, but only one now occupied."[48]

It was not only the camps, towns, and cities of the mountain mining areas that failed to prosper or even survive but many of those that had been hastily laid out on the plains at the base of the Rockies. Not all of the Fifty-Niners expected to make their fortunes exclusively from gold mining. As Henry Villard observed in 1860, "the West . . . abounds with masters of the popular Anglo-American art of town-making.

Three or four years ago, it was fairly overrun by these magicians that understood to perfection how to turn little or nothing into real or supposed fortunes." He went on to observe that while the depression of the past few years had "knocked the enchanting wand out of their palsied hands," the mining rush "filled them with hopes of retrieving their fallen fortunes." These speculators did not think of "pleading with the pick and shovel for a smile of fortune. They desired not to pitch into, but on to the ground. They cared less for good placers than promising places. They proposed to realize their expectations of speedily accumulating wealth, not by mining, but out of mining."[49]

The town of El Paso, platted in 1858 by the Lawrence, Kansas, group that eventually settled in the Denver area, was abandoned with the first news of gold at Gregory Gulch. Arapaho City, also founded in 1858, seems to have come to an end at the same time and for the same reason.[50] Mount Vernon, whose plan is reproduced in Figure 14.15, did not die so quickly. The Mount Vernon Town Company was organized in 1860, and its officers began settlement a few miles south of Golden. When in 1867 they submitted the plat shown here to the General Land Office, they added this note to the drawing: "The improvements in Said Town consist of Seven dwelling houses, a Blacksmith Shop, a store & 2 Hotels Several Barns, Stables and the usual outbuildings." A small army of structures would have been needed to occupy the gigantic gridiron the ambitious proprietors provided, and the townsite eventually surrendered to the invading sagebrush.[51]

Colorado City at the base of the foothills leading up to Pikes Peak began its existence in 1859. Henry Villard thought its prospects excellent because of its location "at the head of the Southern or Arkansas route" from the border settlements of Kansas to the mining region. He claimed that by the end of 1859 "nearly two hundred buildings" had been completed, including branches of "nearly all the principal business houses of Denver."[52] Libeus Barney was likewise impressed by what he had heard of Colorado City and wrote to his Vermont newspaper that "it is considered by many as the most available location for a large city of any of the numerous sites yet built upon. . . . It is but a few weeks since the first house was built there; now, so say reports fifty are completed, and many more are in course of erection."[53]

Neither Villard nor Barney actually saw the new town, and they relied on reports from others. Albert Richardson, however, visited the infant community at the end of October. Riding in from the south he describes that he "reached a little sign-board labeled in bold capitals 'COLORADO AVENUE.' I had not seen a human being since morning,

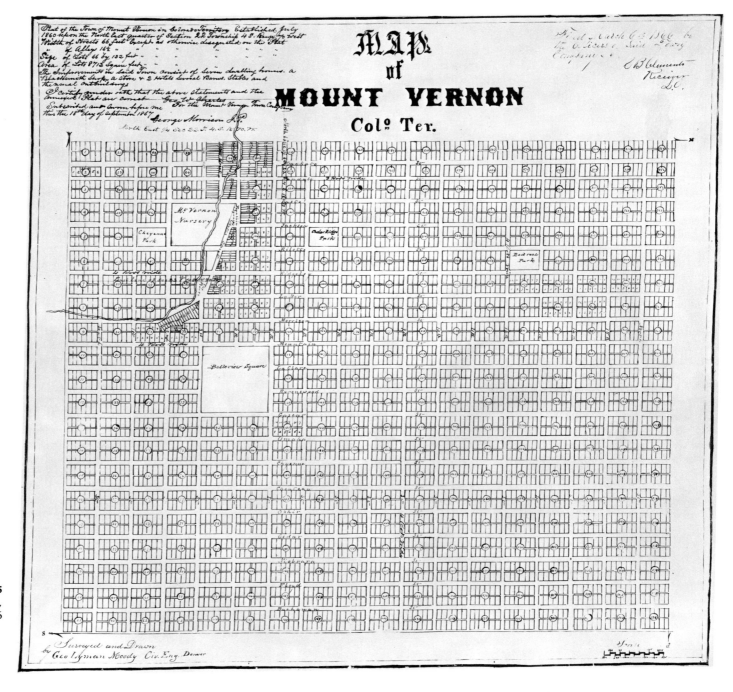

Figure 14.15
Plan of Mount Vernon,
Colorado: 1866

and the idea of a city in these solitudes savored of the ludicrous; but there it stood, unmistakable evidence of civilization and speculation." A mile beyond the sign he "reached Colorado City . . . containing fifteen or twenty log-cabins."[54]

When Alfred E. Mathews prepared his lithograph view of Colorado City in 1866 he found the town not much advanced from the condition described by Richardson seven years earlier. The Mathews view is reproduced in Figure 14.16 and shows the settlement consisting only of a single street on which fronted perhaps two dozen structures. It was this community that the first legislature designated as the capital of Colorado Territory, apparently in the belief that a location roughly midway along the north-south mountain barrier would be desirable. A three-man commission was appointed to choose the location for public buildings within the limits of the townsite. One meeting at the primitive town was enough, however, and the second session of the legislature promptly adjourned to meet temporarily in Denver after its members decided that the seat of government should be moved to Golden.[55]

Golden became Denver's principal rival. Barney described it as "next to Denver and Auraria in population and business significance," adding that "there are some who think she will outstrip this place [Denver] ere another year."[56] Henry Villard pointed out the advantages of its location between the Cherry Creek settlements and the rich Clear Creek mining area, as well as the "excellent water-power and pasturage" and "an abundance of timber" available in the immediate vicinity. By the beginning of 1860 the town contained "over two hundred well built houses, a population of several hundred, a number of stores, hotels, saloons, and mechanical establishments."[57]

A group calling itself the Boston Company had founded Golden at the mouth of Clear Creek Canyon in the summer of 1859. Claiming two square miles for the entire townsite, they proceeded to survey one-fourth of the area immediately and laid out the balance of the tract into streets and blocks the next year.[58] The town could not have been more than a few weeks old when Richardson caught a glimpse of the place and was moved to comment amusingly on its name and the ambitions of its promoters: "Of course its founders regarded it as an embryo Babylon. Golden City! How smoothly fell the unctuous syllables from the lips. How suggestive of merchant princes and pockets full of rocks. The El Dorado which Pizarro sought was studded with golden palaces and paved with precious stones—'the City of the Gilded King'; but our democratic El Dorado must be the city of the golden people."[59]

A bird's-eye view of Golden in 1873, reproduced as Figure 14.17, reveals the typical gridiron plan used by the planners of the city. By this time, a railroad served the town, several mills and smelters were in operation, and it was the site of the Colorado School of Mines established as a church-supported institution on 1869 but financed by the territory from 1870 and the state after 1876. The decision of the legislature in 1862 to make Golden the capital of the territory proved an empty honor. While Golden was technically the capital, most of the governmental business was transacted at Denver. A formal transfer of the territorial capital to Denver took place in 1867. When Colorado was admitted as a state in 1876 the constitution provided that Denver was to serve as the capital city for five years, after which the permanent location was to be determined by a referendum. Denver easily won, and Golden remained as the political capital only of Jefferson County.

The depression of 1873 hit Colorado at a time when mining activities had declined from the feverish pitch of the bonanza days. The mineral resources of the Colorado Rockies were, however, not exhausted, and the region was soon booming again with a new rush. Beyond Breckenridge in an area known as California Gulch near the headwaters of the Arkansas River Will Stevens in 1874 began reworking some of the former gold diggings. He and his partner, Alvinus Wood, had some success, but they encountered some difficulties with heavy black sands that clogged their sluices. Wood was a geologist, and one day his curiosity led him to examine the sand more closely. It proved to be carbonate of lead that assayed 40 ounces of silver to the ton. The secret could not be kept long, and in 1876 a new rush began rivaling that of 1859.[60]

New and even richer strikes were made in the region as miners swarmed over the hills. Even Governor John Routt joined the search to work a claim he had purchased, returning to Denver only for brief visits to perform his executive duties. When his term expired, he came back to his Morning Star mine and soon was a millionaire.[61] Horace A. W. Tabor, who had opened a store in the area after a decade and a half of unsuccessful prospecting, grubstaked two miners in return for a one-third interest in any claim they might file. His total investment was $50. The resulting Little Pittsburgh mine proved incredibly rich, and less than a year after the find in May, 1878, Tabor sold out for $1,000,000.[62]

That year saw 5,000 people jammed into Leadville, the principal settlement of the area. It was only the beginning. By May 1, 1879, the population jumped to 8,000; two months later, 10,000; and by the end of the year it was between 15,000 and 18,000.[63]

Helen Hunt, writing in the spring of 1879, described conditions at Leadville as she had observed them several months earlier: "In six months a tract of dense, spruce forest had been converted into a bus-

PIKE'S PEAK AND COLORADO CITY.

Figure 14.16   View of Colorado City, Colorado: 1866

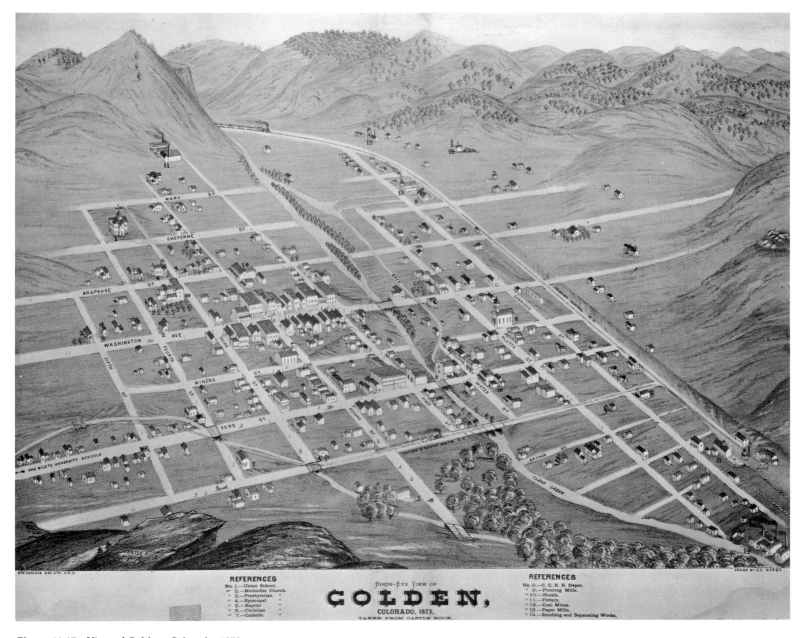

Figure 14.17 View of Golden, Colorado: 1873

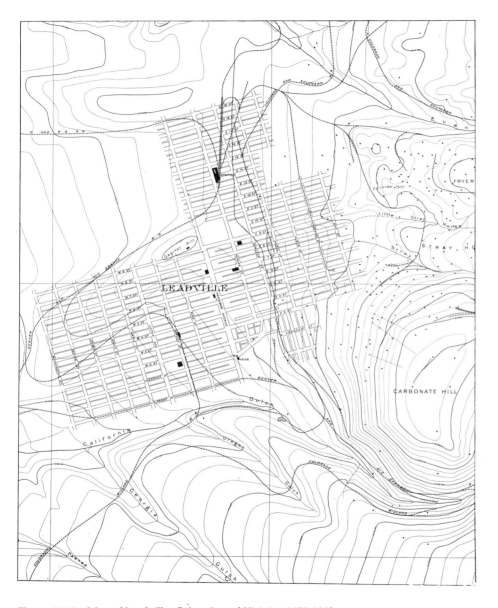

Figure 14.18 Map of Leadville, Colorado and Vicinity: 1879-1910

tling village. To be sure, the upturned roots and the freshly hacked stumps of many of the spruce trees are still in the streets. . . . Some of the cabins seem to burrow in the ground; others are set up on posts, like roofed bedsteads. Tents; wigwams of boughs . . . cabins wedged in between stumps; cabins built on stumps; cabins with chimneys made of flower-pots or bits of stove pipe . . . cabins half roofed; cabins with sail cloth roofs, cabins with no roofs at all,—this represents the architecture of the Leadville homes. . . . Everybody was talking, nearly everybody jesticulating. All faces looked restless, eager, fierce. It was a Monaco gambling room emptied into a Colorado spruce clearing."[64]

A town government organized in 1878 did much to relieve the inevitable chaos and confusion. Tabor was elected mayor, and he and his successor the next year, William H. James, ordered streets to be surveyed. In 1879 city council passed an order directing the removal within 10 days of all buildings encroaching on these official street lines. Mayor James was one of those who complied, tearing down a stable he had previously erected not knowing where the streets would be.[65]

The official plan was a utilitarian grid occupying the sloping land leading up to Evans, Stray Horse, and California Gulches. The federal government survey of the town and the adjacent mining area made in 1879 and reproduced in Figure 14.18 shows the pattern of streets then established. Many of these had been added that year to accommodate the rapidly increasing population.[66] Real estate prices soared. On Chestnut Street lots in 1877 sold for $10 to $40; at the end of the 1879 they brought from $500 to $5,000. Thirty-one real estate firms were in business in 1880, and at these prices they must have profited more than many mine owners. The demand for lumber was so great that at one time 30 sawmills operated day and night. Even so, lumber remained scarce, and many persons who could have afforded better accommodations built houses and other structures of logs.[67]

Development proceeded at an amazing pace. One historian writing in 1879 described Leadville as "a well and substantially built city, having brick blocks, well-laid-out streets, water-works, gas-works, opera-houses, daily newspapers, banks, and all the adjuncts that make up great and prosperous cities."[68] The town nonetheless wore the appearance of a frontier community. The view in Figure 14.19 shows Chestnut Street in 1878 looking west from its intersection with Harrison Avenue. These were the principal business thoroughfares, while West State (designated as Second Street in Figure 14.18) seems to have been the entertainment center of the town. No less than 21 saloons lined the sides of the first block on State Street west of Harrison.[69] Between West

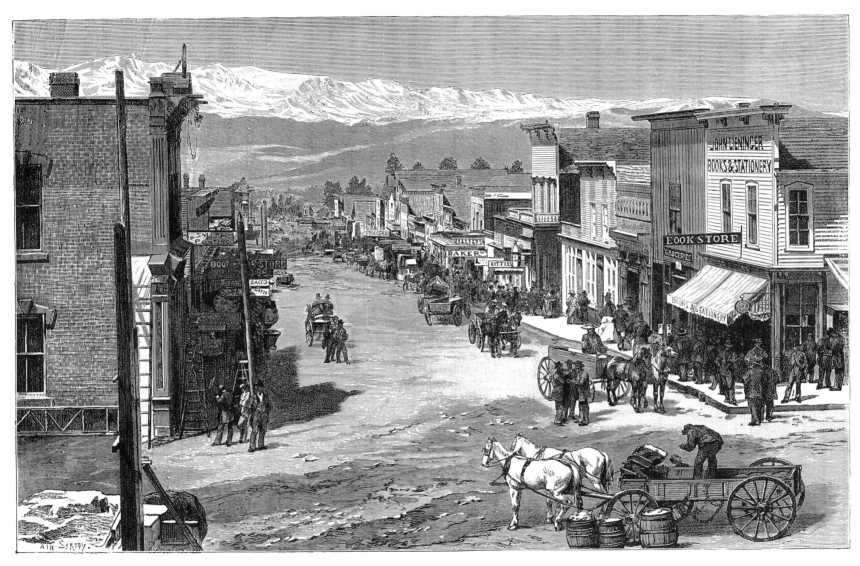

Figure 14.19 View of Chestnut Street in Leadville, Colorado: 1878

State and Chestnut was "Stillborn Avenue," one of several red-light districts that flourished in the booming city.

The arrival of the Denver and Rio Grande Railway on July 23, 1880, had been delayed by the famous battle of that line with the Santa Fe for exclusive rights to the Royal Gorge on the Arkansas River, but rail transportation became a reality at last and further stimulated growth and industrial development.[70] The station was located in the north end of town, but dozens of spurs looped through other parts of the town following natural contours of the land and interrupting the tidy gridiron street pattern with dozens of level crossings. These lines can be seen on the map in Figure 14.18 and the view of Leadville in 1882 reproduced in Figure 14.20.

That view reveals the astonishing growth of the city in its first five years. Its gigantic grid spread over the floor of the 10,000-foot high valley and up the slopes of the surrounding hills honeycombed with mines. At the mouth of most of them, smelters belched forth smoke produced in the refining process that clouded the skies for miles. The seemingly prosperous city of this period was, however, already on the verge of decline. By 1880 a labor surplus led to a cut in wage rates, and the miners went on strike. Although the conflict was eventually settled after much bitterness and violence, the boom days were over. Some of the mines closed as the silver deposits were exhausted; manipulation of mining stocks resulted in bankruptcy for others. The repeal in 1893 of the Sherman Silver Purchase Act and a second violent strike in 1896 hastened the decline in production. The town never died, but the Leadville of today is but a faint shadow of the lusty, tumultuous city that grew so quickly at the foot of the silver mountains.

During the 1880s further strikes of gold or silver or both occurred in such places as Gunnison, Aspen, and Creede, but the greatest mineral discovery in Colorado was yet to come. Southwest of Pike's Peak in 1878 Bob Womack noticed some peculiar rocks in the valley of a small stream called Cripple Creek. Although they indicated ore deposits worth $200 a ton when he took them to Colorado Springs to be assayed, few persons showed any interest because an earlier announcement of a find near the same area had turned out to be a hoax. Not until a German nobleman and well-known resident of Colorado Springs, Count James Pourtales, announced in 1891 that he had invested $80,000 in a mine did the rush begin.[71] Before it was over, and Cripple Creek and its sister mining towns eventually and inevitably declined, $400,000,000 in gold would be removed from an ancient volcanic deposit roughly circular in shape and having a radius of just over two miles.

The new mining region is shown on the map in Figure 14.21, a por-

tion of a U.S. Geological Survey made in 1894. Around the golden circle can be seen a number of towns whose names flashed into headlines as the true nature of the discovery came to be known: Victor, Goldfield, Altman, Independence, and Cameron. The largest and most important was Cripple Creek itself, laid out by a Denver real estate concern on ranch land its two partners, Horace Bennett and Julius Myers, had purchased in 1885. They quickly surveyed a grid of streets on 80 acres of this hilly land into 30 blocks and 766 lots. This was in 1891, Bennett and Myers had not yet realized that this was a major strike, and they priced their lots at $25 each with corner lots at just twice that price. Adjoining this first townsite another was laid off on a placer claim in February, 1892, comprising 140 acres divided into grid streets and 1320 lots. This second settlement was given the name Cripple Creek, a name that soon was applied as well to the earlier Bennett and Myers town of Fremont.[72]

As the boom got under way, additional streets were added, extending or running parallel to those of the earlier surveys. This was rugged country, and the streets rose and dipped steeply as they crossed the broken slopes of the mountainside. Bennett Avenue running east and west became the principal business thoroughfare, its western termination being the hillside rising above Poverty Gulch. Between Fourth and Fifth Streets, Bennett Avenue sloped so steeply from side to side that it had to be divided into two terraced lanes, one 15 feet above the other and supported by a stone wall.[73]

One block south of Bennett Avenue, Myers Street developed as a rowdy and raucous red-light district. When Julian Street visited Cripple Creek in 1914 on a trip to the West gathering material for a series of articles in *Collier's Weekly*, he apparently saw little of the then decaying city except for this section. His article, at least, dealt almost entirely with a prostitute he had interviewed. The mayor of Cripple Creek demanded that *Collier's* publish a more balanced account of the town. When editor Mark Sullivan rejected a substitute article, the city fathers retaliated by renaming Myers Street for the author who had caused them such distress—and Julian Street it became.[74]

In its early years Cripple Creek grew as rapidly as Leadville. The first crude and temporary shelters soon gave way to more substantial buildings, and electricity and piped water became available by 1893. The lots that Bennett and Myers sold for $25 and $50 brought $3,000 to $5,000 only two years later. The two men made $500,000 from lot sales in their first 80-acre townsite alone and an equal amount from land platted on their other ranch lands as later additions to the town.[75]

Their success encouraged others. Frank and Harry Woods bought

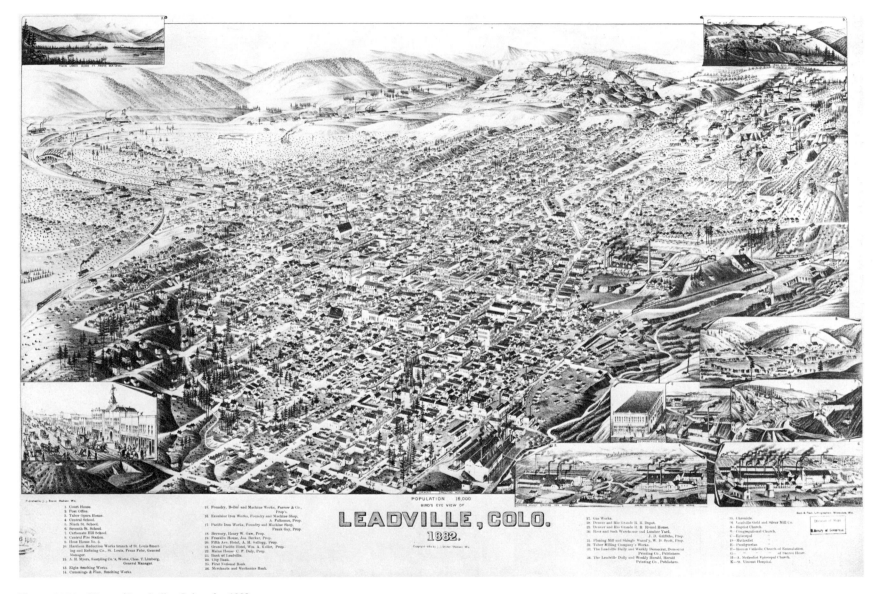

Figure 14.20 View of Leadville, Colorado: 1882

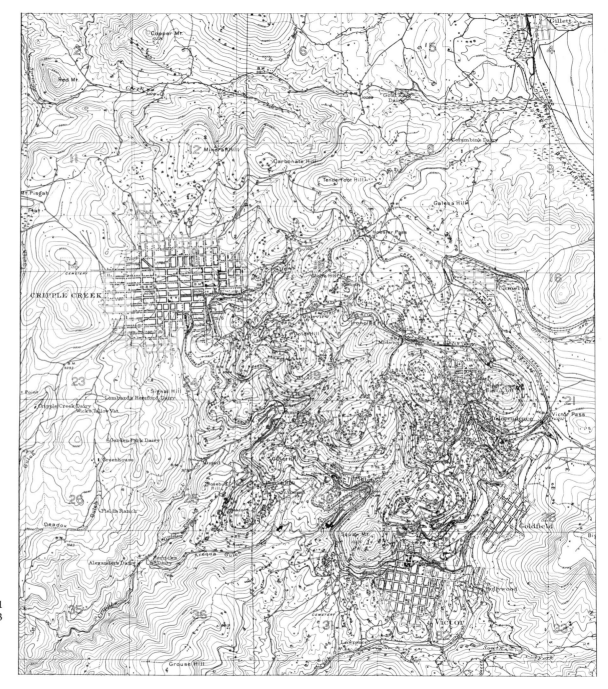

Figure 14.21
Map of Cripple Creek, Colorado and Vicinity: 1894-1903

136 acres of land in 1893 and surveyed it into the townsite of Victor. While excavating for the foundation of a hotel Frank hit a 20-inch vein of gold. Within a few months the mine was producing net earnings of $50,000 a month. The news seemed to bear out their assertion that all Victor lots were gold mines—and so they were for the Woods boys, who had paid only $1,000 for the entire tract and made an additional tidy profit out of land sales.[76]

Figure 14.22 shows Cripple Creek and Victor as they appeared in 1896. Bennett Avenue in the larger of the two towns was then solidly built up with two-, three-, and four-story buildings almost to the foot of the mountain. Parallel and cross-streets in the business district were almost equally developed. The view also gives some impression of the roller-coaster topography of the city that Bennett and Myers had platted on that portion of their ranch too steep to be of much value. Yet Cripple Creek, like all the other mining towns, entered a period of long decline from which it never recovered. In 1900 its population was 25,000 and that of the entire mining district 50,111. Only 20 years later the district population shrunk to one-tenth this figure.[77]

Each successive gold or silver strike in the Colorado mountains both threatened and reinforced Denver's position as the chief city of the region. Typically, news of these discoveries resulted in at least a temporary drain of population as residents of the city rushed to the new mining camp. Yet the city benefited at the same time, since it served as the entrepôt and supply point for persons coming from the East to try their hands at mining, to speculate in townsite promotion, or to establish stores, shops, or professional offices. With the inevitable decline in mining activity at each mountain town, many persons drifted back to Denver to take up permanent residence.

One of the city's early historians could describe the effect of the great Leadville rush in 1879 in these words: "The year opened with a great rush of travel through Denver to Leadville. Every train came in loaded down with pilgrims for the new Mecca, many of them, as usual in such cases, no more fitted to succeed in that great lottery than so many children. . . . Denver, too, was contributing largely to the immigration in that direction, but, despite this fact, the city seemed to grow every day, and houses to live in, and stores to do business in, were in greater demand than supply. Building operations commenced early in the year, if, indeed, they ever ceased throughout the winter, and new structures multiplied on every hand. By May, the streets of Denver were almost impassible, being blockaded with building material in almost every direction."[78]

Already the city had expanded well beyond the confines of the original Auraria and Denver City townsites, as the plan of 1871 in Figure 14.23 reveals. Landowners beyond the original platted area had begun to have their tracts surveyed into streets to take advantage of the increasing demand for building sites. Several major additions lay to the northeast and were cut up in blocks and lots following the orientation used by Larimer and his associates of the Denver Town Company. Others, however, shifted to the north-south and east-west bearings of the township and section line surveys giving little attention to proper linkages of the resulting new streets with those first platted in 1858. Along Colfax Avenue, marking the southern boundary of the Auraria and Denver surveys, and Broadway, the western boundary of a new tract notched into the old Denver Town Company area, a series of awkward triangular intersections and building plots resulted.

One of these new additions was created in 1868 by Henry Brown, a carpenter and building contractor. It was he who platted Broadway as the western boundary of his elongated 16-acre homestead, laying out three narrower streets parallel to Broadway and extending 5 blocks south of Colfax. At the southeastern intersection of the two major thoroughfares, Brown reserved and donated to the territory a tract for the capitol. This action enabled the city to comply with a legislative stipulation in 1867 that a site of at least 10 acres be provided as a condition for moving the seat of government from Golden to Denver.[79]

On the view of Denver in 1874 reproduced in Plate 20, Brown's Bluff, as he called the addition, can be seen extending diagonally from the upper right-hand corner. On this elevated land, some of the city's finest mansions were erected in the vicinity of the capitol site. By this time the city had a population approaching 15,000 and, despite the panic of 1873, was continuing to grow. While it still had some of the aspects of a frontier town, many of the gambling houses had been closed, and the saloons along Blake Street were brought under municipal regulation.[80]

Growth of the city had been stimulated in the summer of 1870 by the completion of the Denver Pacific Railway connecting the city with Cheyenne. A few years earlier the citizens of the city had been horrified to learn that the Union Pacific would bypass Denver far to the north because of the difficulty of continuing a line westward through the tortuous high mountain passes. That colorful promoter of western railroads and speculator in town development, George Francis Train, came to Denver in 1867 to offer his advice to civic leaders: "Colorado is a great gold mine! Denver is a great fact! Make it a railway center!"[81] A few

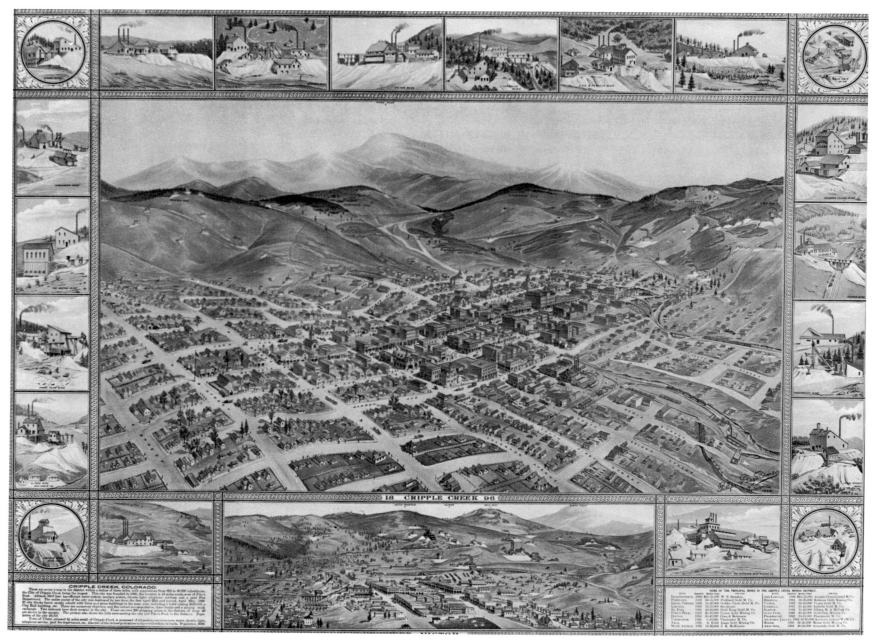

Figure 14.22 Views of Cripple Creek and Victor, Colorado: 1896

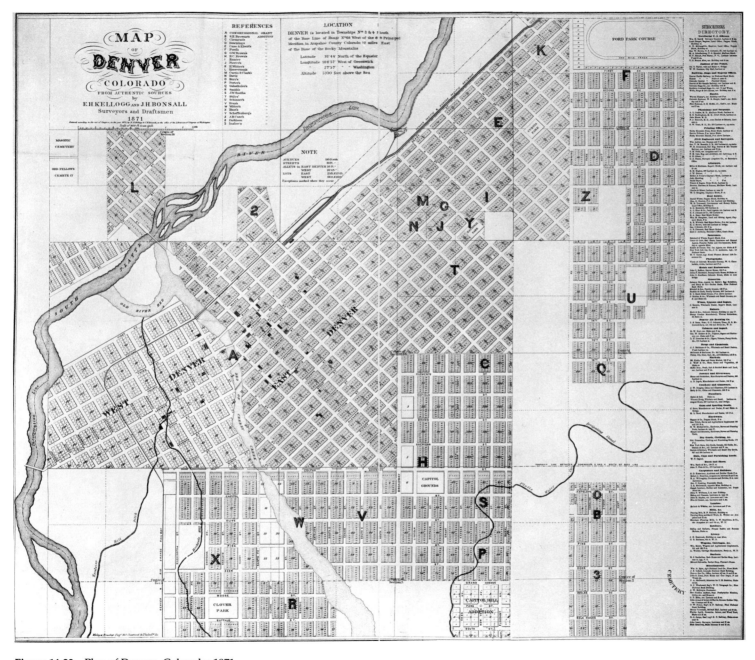

Figure 14.23 Plan of Denver, Colorado: 1871

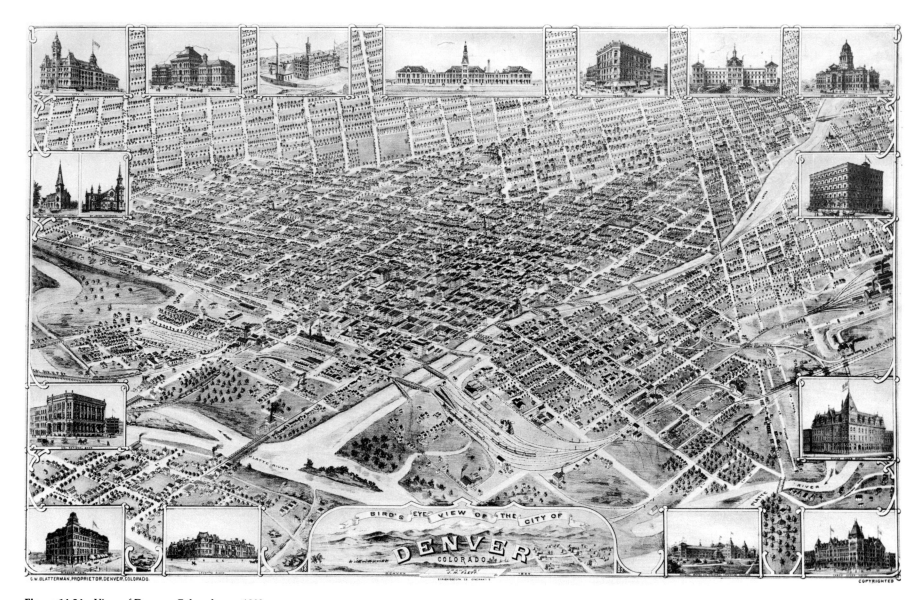

Figure 14.24 View of Denver, Colorado: ca. 1882

months later the city passed a bond issue to help finance the 100-mile line to Cheyenne, ground was broken on May 18, 1868, and the first locomotive steamed into the station grounds between 19th and 20th Streets near the South Platte River on June 22, 1870. Not quite two months later the first train arrived on the Kansas Pacific line from the east over the Kansas and Colorado plains, and Denver at last had its railroads. Soon the Denver and Rio Grande would provide connections from the city to the south, and in the years to follow other lines were constructed to complete the transportation network.[82]

The census of 1880 reflected what the railroads had done for Denver, listing the population at nearly 36,000. By 1885, three years after the view in Figure 14.24 was published, the city's population was estimated to have almost doubled. Many of Denver's principal buildings shown in the small views around the borders of this lithograph were listed in a guide to Colorado published in 1885: "the Tabor Opera House, Windsor Hotel, City Hall, Court House, Cathedral, Tabor Block, Barclay Block, and Union Depot." A fire ordinance in 1886 restricted further construction to masonry buildings, but already, according to the guide, it was a city "built principally of brick and stone; the streets are broad with a natural hard gravel and clay pavement; the sidewalks are mostly laid with large flagging stone, beside which are rows of trees . . . nourished by the rippling streams of water coursing along the gutters at nearly all seasons of the year."

The industrial base of the city included smelters, "nine foundries and machine works; five flouring mills . . . six large breweries; and any number of small manufactories." A street railway system "comprising forty-six cars, and 230 horses" provided local transportation to nearly all sections of the now extensive community.[83] In a scant quarter of a century, the crude and disorderly camps at the mouth of Cherry Creek had become a city of impressive size and appearance.

.XV.

The Expanding Mining Frontier: Camps and Towns of Idaho,
Montana, and South Dakota

DURING the years that mining towns and supply centers were springing up in Colorado, other new communities of the same character were being established in the territories to the north and west and, somewhat later, in the Black Hills of South Dakota. Exploitation of mineral resources, swift population growth, and wholesale town founding characterized this region as they had earlier in California and Nevada.

The earliest Idaho gold strikes occurred in the Snake River area. Here Captain Elias Davidson Pierce found traces of gold early in 1860. At Walla Walla, in western Washington, Pierce assembled a small group that prospected the mountains up the tributaries of the Clearwater River. In the spring of 1861, 1,000 miners were clustered in Pierce City and Orofino; by the end of that summer the population had soared to perhaps, 7,500.[1]

Lewiston, at the confluence of the Clearwater and Snake rivers, began its development as the principal supply center for the northern Idaho mines. A young Nez Percé Indian named Reuben started the settlement in February, 1861, with the construction of a warehouse. Joining Reuben at this site, William Craig began the operation of a ferry and was soon collecting $4,000 a week in tolls from the hordes of miners arriving at what was then largely a city of tents.[2]

The Idaho mining camps resembled those in California and Nevada. John T. Outhouse described Orofino in June, 1861: "At a meeting of miners, this town was named Oro Fino; it is on the creek of that name; thirty-five miles from its mouth. The town is building up very fast; about sixty buildings are set up or in course of erection—11 stores, 2 smith shops, 2 hotels, 2 markets, 1 doctor and 1 bakery."[3] By the middle of August substantial growth had taken place. John Phillips wrote that "Oro Fino City has about four hunderd houses and tents at this time, and is improving very fast. There are about fifteen hundred inhabitants in and around Oro Fino, but no Chinamen. There are sixteen stores, eighteen saloons, six bakeries, four hotels, three restaurants, two smith shops, two shoe shops, one tin shop, four meat markets, two express offices, five laundries, two bankers, and four doctors. Fortunately there are no lawyers yet."[4]

The growth of Pierce City was equally rapid. Joaquin Miller, the poet who had participated in the California gold rush, arrived in the spring of 1861 and found the place "a brisk town, neatly laid out, built of hewn logs, brooks through the streets, pine trees here and there on the gently-sloping hillside to the sun, with white tents all around and up and down the mountain of dark woods to the east." All around him

Miller observed "red-shirted men, mules, long lines of laden, braying mules, half-tame Indians with pack paniers, a few soldiers off duty, crowds of eager people coming and going—action, motion everywhere."[5]

South of Pierce and Orofino, additional gold discoveries in the Salmon River valley led to the creation of new mining camps, among them Elk City and Florence. Henry Miller, who had left his job as editor of the Portland *Oregonian* to join the throng of treasure hunters, reported on August 17, 1861, that "Elk City has increased in size from three brush shanties to twenty substantial log houses in the space of two weeks."[6] Another reporter for a Sacramento paper a week and a half later mentioned that the town consisted "of one street, on which are about twenty finished and about an equal number of unfinished buildings" built of logs. He added: "It is just three weeks since the first log of the first building was laid down. So if a question should arise as to the comparative antiquity of Elk City and other venerable cities of the world, it is very likely that at least Damascus, if not several other oldish places, would bear away the palm."[7]

Florence early in 1862 was a community of "five log houses, three stores and two whiskey mills." But, an observer pointed out, "some hundred or more lots are claimed and fenced or rather poled in and held at one to four hundred dollars. It is sure to be a town in course of human events as it will be supported by near two thousand miners with their pockets lined with the needful."[8]

Augustus Knapp recorded the rush to the Idaho mining regions that spring: "every road leading out of Oregon into Washington Territory is one solid, moving mass of human beings and animals—a perfect column, moving forward, all coming one way—as many as 600 to 1,000 daily passing between Lewiston and Florence." When Knapp reached Florence on June 3 he estimated that "there are now about 9,000 men here—some 6,000 who are at work in every ravine and gulch near by, while the balance are out prospecting in every direction."[9]

The discovery of new gold desposits along the Boise River valley in the summer of 1862 resulted in a shift of population to this southern area of Idaho. New mining camps sprang up, among them Placerville, Centerville, Pioneer, and Bannack—the latter town later renamed Idaho City. By the end of 1864 the population of this new gold field reached 16,000. Idaho City alone was said to have had some 6,000 residents.[10]

Plans and views of these settlements cannot now be located, but the historian, Hubert Howe Bancroft, writing in 1890 evidently had access

Figure 15.1 View of Atlanta, Idaho: date unknown

to such material. He described the plan of Idaho City in some detail: "Main and Wall streets were compactly built for a quarter of a mile, crossed by but one avenue of any importance. Main street extended for a quarter of a mile farther. Running parallel with Elk Creek were two streets—Marion and Montgomery—half a mile in length. The remainder of the town was scattered over the rising ground back from Elk and Moore creeks. There were 250 places of business, well-filled stores, highly decorated and resplendent gambling-saloons, a hospital for sick and indigent miners, protestant and catholic churches, a theatre, . . . three newspapers, and a fire department." Bancroft also mentioned that Placerville "was built like a Spanish town, with the business houses around a plaza in the centre."[11]

Many of the Idaho mining camps, like those elsewhere in the West, developed on or near rich placer deposits. Although these were easily worked, they were soon exhausted, miners moved on to new locations, and the camps declined or disappeared altogether. Recovery of gold from quartz veins, on the other hand, often led to more permanent settlements, where stamping mills and refineries replaced the less costly and elaborate devices used in the recovery of gold from stream deposits.

Such a community was Atlanta at the foot of the Sawtooth Range up the middle fork of the Boise River. An undated view of this settlement published not long after its founding appears in Figure 15.1. The town had been surveyed in 1865 in an effort to establish a more traditional community in an area where gold had been found two years earlier and where a number of smaller camps had rapidly developed.[12]

The discovery of silver in 1863 along the Snake River near the southwest corner of the modern state of Idaho produced another cluster of mining camps and towns: Silver City, Ruby City, Boonville, and many others. Albert Richardson visited what had come to be called the Owyhee District in 1865. He described the "metropolis" of the region as "a straggling strip of town far up among the mountains, at one end called Boonville, at the other Silver City, and in the middle Ruby City." Boonville consisted "of a dozen deserted frame and log buildings, the gulch between them torn and gashed with ditches."

Richardson used a small view of Ruby City, reproduced in Figure 15.2, to illustrate his book. He found it "a disorderly collection of buildings, on a wooded hill-side sloping down to Jordan creek." Nearby, "hidden in the winding valley," Richardson observed the "many quartz mills—the cause, the support, the very life of the settlement."[13]

The early Idaho mining camps and towns, like others in the American West, were frequent victims of fire. These tent and timber com-

Figure 15.2 View of Ruby City, Idaho: 1865

munities could be almost completely destroyed in a matter of hours even if their citizens had provided some kind of firefighting equipment and organization. On the night of May 18, 1865, the first of several fires in Idaho City virtually consumed the entire town in two hours. A pioneer merchant of the settlement described the results in a letter to his sister: "That portion of Idaho City, lying upon the South side of Wallula St., was saved. This, with the exception of a few houses around the edge of the town, was all that was left that night when the clock struck twelve, of one of the largest, and most flourishing mining towns, ever built up west of the Rocky Mountains. About four fifths of the city was destroyed. Out of about three hundred business houses of all kinds, only about twenty or thirty were saved."

Reconstruction could be rapid. The letter telling of this disaster was written two months after it occurred. By that time, however, its author could assure the reader that the town had been "nearly rebuilt once more, and everything looks gay. Drinking Saloons, Billiard Saloons, Gambling Houses, Dry Goods establishments, Barber Shops, and every thing else have opened in grander style, and upon a larger scale than before. Two theaters give nightly entertainments, to large audiences."[14] Orofino was not so fortunate. It was completely destroyed by a fire in 1867 and never recovered.[15]

Idaho's largest city and its capital—Boise—dates from this period, but the town owed its initial prosperity to its role as a supply center rather than as a mining community. Like Sacramento, it developed in the shadow of a fort and, also like the California capital, it was planned by its founders rather than first growing spontaneously as a mining camp.

After repeated recommendations to Washington, military officials in the West finally secured approval for the construction of a fort in the Boise Basin to protect miners from Indian attacks. They directed Major Pinkney Lugenbeel to select a site and establish an army post on the Boise River in 1863. Lugenbeel on July 4 chose a location where the primitive road to the mining district met the Oregon Trail.

Three days later eight settlers of the region met to organize a town adjacent to the fort, and one of their members, Henry C. Riggs, surveyed the first plat, reproduced in Figure 15.3.[16] A town company of 17, including Lugenbeel and several other soldiers, divided the 120 lots among them. Three weeks later Lugenbeel wrote to his daughter: "They have laid off a town in this valley and called it Boise City. I believe they have given me some three or four lots. If the town is ever worth anything, I will give the lots to you children. There will be a town somewhere in this valley which will be of a good size, but where it is to be remains to be determined."[17]

The major need not have worried. From this modest and uninspired beginning Boise grew rapidly. The town company donated lots to businessmen as an inducement to locate in the new community. They also began a vigorous campaign to obtain the coveted designation of the spot as capital of Idaho Territory, which had received congressional approval in March, 1863. By the end of the first month of its existence the original plat had evidently been extended, for a traveler at that time described the town as having "a principal street one mile and a quarter in length by ninety feet wide and from one end to the other is a continual line of frame buildings. The town has become a perfect pandemonium."[18]

At the end of the summer, 1864, Boise's population was nearly 1,700, and by the end of the year it succeeded in wresting the seat of government from Lewiston, where the territory had first been organized. Further expansion of the town became necessary as well as the selection of a site for the capitol. Figure 15.4 shows the enlarged community as platted in 1867 with two city blocks consolidated near the center as Capitol Square. This element in the plan and the diagonal street bordering the Fort Boise tract were the only deviations from the vast grid of uniformly rectangular blocks.[19]

The town had a raw, unfinished appearance. Albert Richardson included in one of his travel accounts of the West the view of the new capital as it appeared in 1865 reproduced in Figure 15.5. Noting that it was "a trading, not a mining city," he observed that "its broad, level, treeless avenues, with their low, white-verandahed warehouses, log cabins, new, neat cottages and ever-shifting panorama of wagons and coaches, Indians, miners, farmers, and speculators remind one of a prairie-town in Kansas or Iowa."[20]

Efforts to improve the appearance of the city included large-scale tree planting as early as 1864, the erection of many brick buildings, and the construction of a few even more imposing structures of sandstone. Seventeen years after its founding, Bancroft in his history of the region could describe Boise "as the most important as well as the most beautiful town in the territory." Perhaps it had little competition for this position, but as the view in Figure 15.6 shows, it must have been an impressive community nonetheless. Bancroft observed that "the streets are wide and well shaded, the residences neat and tasteful, standing in flowery enclosures kept green by streams of living water flowing down the streets. The squares devoted to public buildings are well kept, and the edifices of brown stone. Up and down the river are many charming drives, and altogether the place is an attractive one."[21]

Shortly after the Idaho mining rush began, important discoveries of gold farther to the east set off still another episode of rapid settlement and town founding in what would eventually become the state of Montana. For this region of the upper Rocky Mountains, both written and graphic documentation of the mining camps and towns exists in rich abundance.[22]

The first important gold discovery in Montana occurred in July, 1862, on Grasshopper Creek near what is now the boundary between Idaho and Montana. By October the mining camp of Bannack was enjoying its brief period of growth. The population that fall was only some 400, but by spring this had more than doubled and reached an estimated 2,000 in midsummer of its first full year of existence.[23] Following the creation

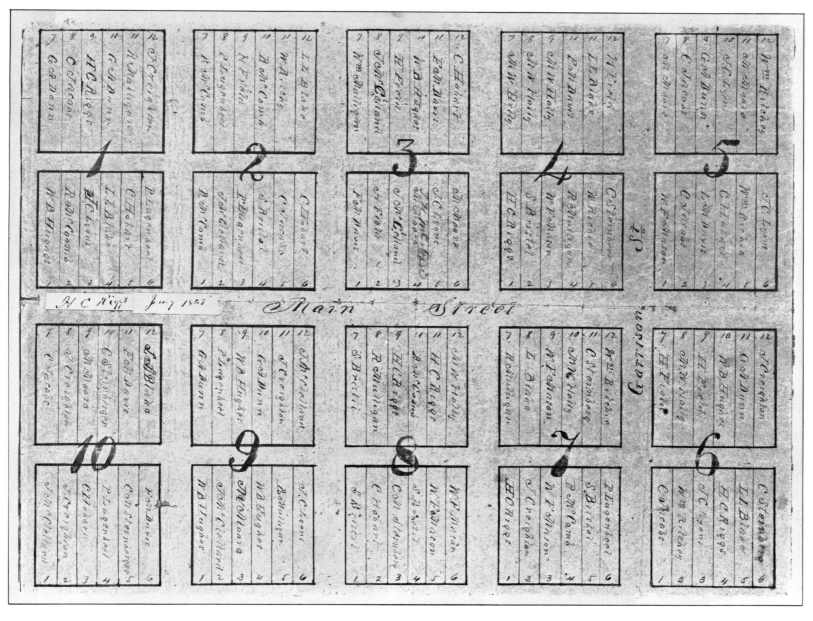

Figure 15.3 Plan of Boise, Idaho: 1863

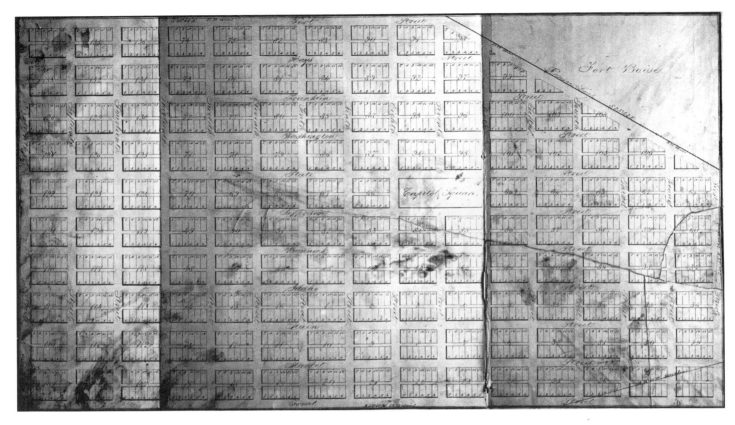

Figure 15.4 Plan of Boise, Idaho: 1867

of Montana Territory in May, 1864, the town became the temporary territorial capital, but Bannack's fortunes began to decline as the placer deposits were worked out and prospectors made richer strikes elsewhere.[24]

An early settler of Bannack, Granville Stuart, noted in his diary at the end of July, 1863, that a "new discovery" of gold at Alder Gulch fifty miles to the east "is now attracting attention from everywhere. The mines are turning out big. People passing here every day on their way over. All the miners here are abandoning their diggings and going over and we have about decided to move also."[25]

Stuart reached the new mining region toward the end of August. Its development had been extremely rapid since the first gold discovery

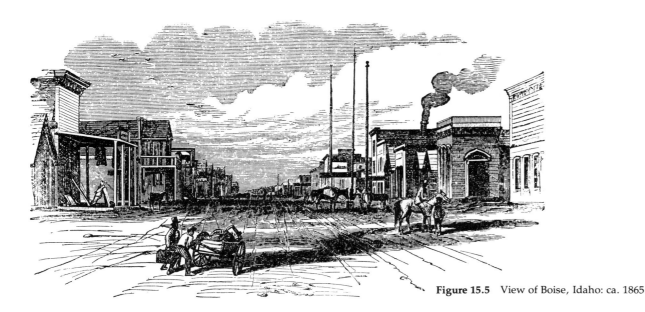

Figure 15.5 View of Boise, Idaho: ca. 1865

three months earlier, and the stampede to stake out claims that followed the news. On June 16 several of the new arrivals organized a townsite company, filed a claim for 320 acres of land, and had the site surveyed as the town of Varina, a name chosen to honor Mrs. Jefferson Davis. Settlers from the northern states felt this inappropriate, and the name of the new community was soon changed to Virginia City.

Stuart recorded the activity and appearance of the town in its first months of existence: "People flocked to the new camp from every direction. . . . There were no houses to live in and not much in the way of material to construct houses. Every sort of shelter was resorted to, some constructed brush wakiups; some made dug-outs, some utilized a convenient sheltering rock, and by placing brush and blankets around it constructed a living place; others spread their blankets under a pine tree and had no shelter other than that furnished by the green boughs overhead. . . . The first building was erected by T. L. Luce, on Cover Street and was occupied by a baker, but Henry Morier was soon in the

field and had his building up and a saloon started. I think this is about the first time in the history of founding a mining camp where the bakery got ahead of the saloon."[26]

Other mining camps sprang up along the narrow confines of Alder Gulch. Downstream were Laurin, Alder, Ruby, Junction City, Adobetown, Nevada City, and Central City. Farther up the gulch were Pine Grove, Highland, and Summit. One contemporary observer described the elongated mining complex as consisting of "housing and stores . . . mostly on one street and . . . built of loggs, mud, & stones with dirt roofs. The street runs along 'Virginia Gulch' where, for a width of 500 to 1000 feet, shovelled, uplifted, and piled, it looks as if an enormous Hog had uprooted the soil."[27]

Stuart recalled that one day a report circulated that gold had been found within the townsite itself. By morning "claims were being staked off the main streets and on the rear of all of our lots." Above Stuart's store "one enthusiastic man began to sink a hole in the street . . . and it

Figure 15.6 View of Boise, Idaho: date unknown

began to look like we would be dug up and washed out without cere-mony."[28] The report proved to be false, and the miners moved out of town to more profitable locations.

Early in 1864 Virginia City was incorporated under the laws of Idaho Territory, and at the end of the year its status as a city was confirmed by the new territorial legislature of Montana. In February of the following year the territorial capital was moved from Bannack to Virginia City. This event and the continued success of miners in the vicinity brought both prosperity and a degree of order to the raw mining community. In the summer of 1864 an estimated 10,000 persons lived in the Alder Gulch communities, of which a third resided in Virginia City.[29]

The town's main street consisted of business buildings in two com-pact rows nearly a mile long. In addition to general retail stores, there were eight hotels, and the usual mining town places of diversion: sa-loons, dance halls, gambling halls, billiard parlors, and whorehouses.[30] Money to support these commercial activities was plentiful; during the first five years of mining in the Alder Gulch region, more than $30,000,000 of gold was produced from its mines and placer deposits.[31]

The original survey of the old Varina Townsite Company had to be extended to accommodate the enlarged population. Figure 15.7 shows what apparently is the first official survey of the town as carried out by order of its city council in May, 1868. It embraced an area just under 580

streets had a width of 50 feet as did every north-south street except Broadway, which was laid out 60 feet wide. Clearly the center of the town was expected to focus where Wallace and Broadway crossed; in fact, the principal business buildings were built closer to Alder Gulch along Wallace Street between Main and Broadway and on Jackson between Wallace and Idaho.[32]

Corbett provided a site for the proposed capitol between what is named North Park and the New Cemetery. A second park, Vista Ramble, was to occupy four blocks at the foot of Fairweather Street, while a third open space, Terrace Park, was allotted a six-block site near the southeast corner of the town. The capitol never materialized despite the creation of a commission in February, 1865, empowered to secure a site for the building providing the price for the land did not exceed $200.[33]

A view of Virginia City five years after its founding is reproduced in Figure 15.8. The artist, Alfred E. Mathews, depicted the town from the northwest. The street leading diagonally from the lower left to center right toward Alder Gulch is Jackson. Near the center of the view is the intersection of this business thoroughfare with Wallace Street. Parallel with Wallace and rather vaguely defined in the view is Cover Street following the winding course of Daylight Creek. The precise lines of the survey of 1868 apparently included a number of buildings within its right-of-way, but a tolerant city council had earlier ordered that "houses not in the middle of the street will not be disturbed."[34] There were obvious limits to how far local officials would go to provide geometric order in the face of established property rights.

Virginia City, like Bannack, soon experienced a decline in mining activity with the exhaustion of the rich and easily worked placer deposits. Prospectors moved to other areas in Montana as news spread of new discoveries. James W. Taylor in his report to the secretary of the treasury on the mineral resources of the eastern Rockies summarized the situation as he saw it in 1867:

> No permanent prosperity and no fixed centres of population are possible until such time as the superficial placers have ceased to yield a prolific booty of easy extraction. The long rows of deserted habitations, once teeming with the busy life of a flourishing mining town, bear melancholy testimony to the inefficiency of the placers alone to lay the foundations of permanent towns and cities. The real prosperity of a mining country may be dated from the time when the majority of the gulches, bars, &c., are worked out, since, at such time, the people are compelled to turn their attention to the

acres, far more land, as it turned out, than the city would ever require.

J. L. Corbett, the civil engineer responsible for this survey, doubtless followed the instructions of the city fathers in attempting to plan a city with some of the amenities and embellishments expected of a capital. He also may have incorporated some of the features of the earlier Varina townsite design that might have included one or more of the open spaces shown in the plat of 1868. That earlier plan certainly provided the basic orientation of the gridiron streets that Corbett extended eastward.

Wallace Street is shown with a width of 75 feet, with Idaho Street parallel and one block south being 59 feet wide. All other east-west

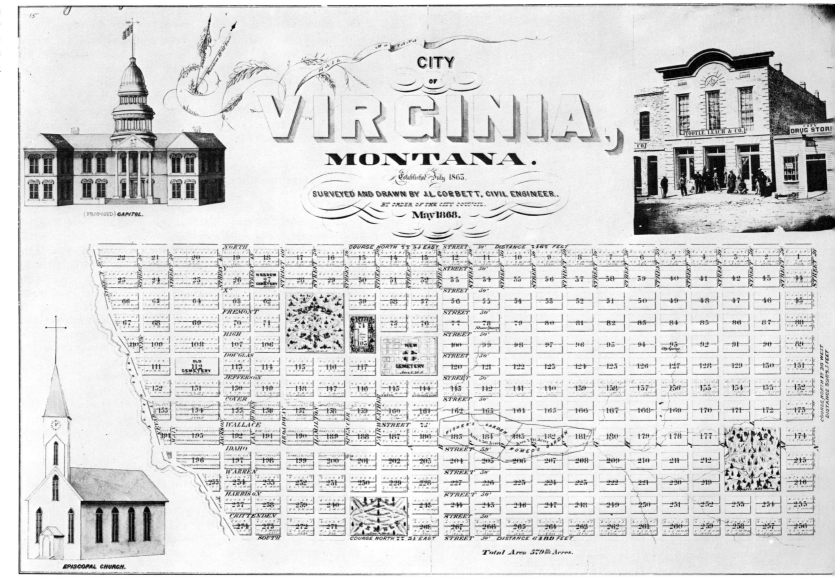

Figure 15.7 Plan of Virginia City, Montana: 1868

A.E.MATHEWS DEL.& LITH.,N.Y.

Entered according to act of Congress in the year 1868 by A.E.Mathews in the Clerks Office of the District Court of the Southern District of New York.

VIRGINIA CITY.

Plate III.

Figure 15.8 View of Virginia City, Montana: 1868

quartz veins, which alone promise permanency and a lasting source of revenue to well-directed enterprise.[35]

By 1875 Virginia City's hope to become a major metropolis was at an end. A view of the city in that year, reproduced in Figure 15.9, shows the community from approximately the same vantage point as the Mathews view seven years earlier. Cover Street had at last been freed of encroachments, but the parks, the capitol square, the new cemetery, and the vast gridiron of streets so confidently surveyed in 1868 are nowhere to be seen. The city's chance to survive as the administrative and legislative center of Montana had been lost as well, for in the year this view was published the territorial legislature moved the seat of government to Helena. Only in recent years has there been a revival of the once-prosperous community with its restoration as a tourist center where visitors can recapture some of the flavor of its past glories.

Ninety miles north of Virginia City, a small, group of discouraged prospectors in July, 1864, decided to try their luck one more time at a place they named Last Chance Gulch. Panning the stream, they found fine gold and small nuggets and decided to stake a claim. Two members of the party returned for supplies to Virginia City, where their preparations aroused the curiosity of others. Soon the news was out, and a new rush began. District mining laws had been drafted by those who remained at the site of the discovery, and these were adopted at a meeting of the first arrivals at the end of July.[36]

Hundreds of miners and the usual camp population of gamblers, merchants, saloon-keepers, prostitutes, and loafers crowded into the area and began the process of community building that had been repeated so often on the mining frontier. Some of its new residents felt that the town needed some form of organization to guide its destiny. On October 30 they convened a meeting of citizens, who agreed to a series of propositions as recorded in the following minutes:

At a meeting of the citizens of Last Chance Gulch for the purpose of naming the town and electing commissioners, etc., on motion, G. J. Wood was elected chairman and T. E. Cooper, secretary. After several motions and balloting, the name of Helena was given to the town, and G. J. Wood, H. Bruce, and C. L. Cutler were elected town commissioners, and ordered to lay out the town and get their pay for the work by recording the lots at two dollars each, the proceeds to go to the commissioners for their labor and trouble. They were further authorized to make such laws and regulations as may be deemed necessary, to regulate the location and size of lots,

streets, alleys, etc. At a meeting of the commissioners it was decided that the lots should be thirty feet front by sixty feet deep, and that any person might pre-empt a lot by laying a foundation on the lot, which foundation should hold the lot ten days, and if a person record his lot at the time of laying the foundation, then the foundation should hold good for twenty days. And it was decided that if there were no improvements made on the lots at the expiration of the ten or twenty days, the lots should be jumpable; but all persons should record their lots. G. J. Wood was elected recorder of the town. All disputes to be settled by the commissioners or an arbitration, until civil law is established."[37]

The earliest plat of Helena, reproduced in Figure 15.10, dates from 1868 as surveyed by A. C. Wheaton for entry at the U.S. Land Office. Its central portion, however, probably represents the attempts at town planning under the leadership of George P. Wood four years earlier following the citizens' meeting.[38] Wood and his colleagues obviously had to fit their new streets to a pattern of occupancy already established by those who had poured into the camp prior to its organization under a provisional government.

The sinuous lines of Main and Clure Streets flanked the curving course of the gulch. Below Broadway, Jackson Street narrowed to little more than a lane running parallel to Main. The early planners of Helena could do little more than run their street lines between existing buildings in this portion of town. Other streets laid out on land not yet occupied could be wider and straighter.

Just below the inner corner of the legend on the upper right-hand portion of the plat one can see Helena's early attempt at some kind of civic focus. Here Wood and his associates created a public square where the courthouse and jail were to stand. These buildings had not yet been erected when the first view of Helena was published in 1865. This appears in Plate 21 showing the town as seen from the northwest. The street running across the view is Main Street. The intersection at the right center marks the crossing of Main and Bridge Streets, while the other street extending toward the mountains is Wood Street.

When Andrew Fisk arrived in Helena in October, 1866, he noted that while "it is not so large a place as I thought it was . . . it is the busiest place I ever saw." He was impressed by the "many fine buildings," but mentioned that only one was of stone and this was "in course of construction."[39] A year later James Miller thought it a more imposing community: "Helena I found to be the finest city in Montana. It has, I

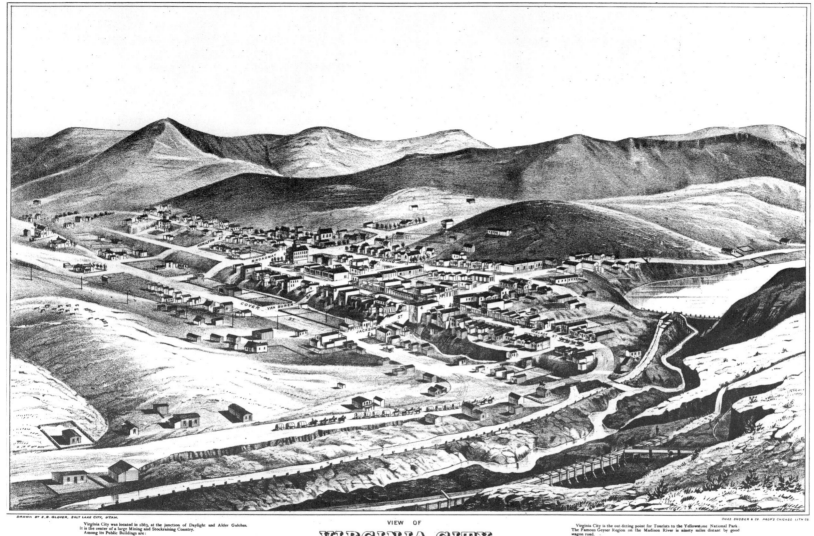

Figure 15.9 View of Virginia City, Montana: 1875

Figure 15.10 Plan of Helena, Montana: 1868

should judge, about 5000 inhabitants . . . & is well built, as is usually the case, in a ravine or gulch. The stores along the chief business street are usually built very respectably in style and size, two or three stories high, with plate glass doors, windows, etc."[40]

Rich quartz deposits in the vicinity provided a more stable mining base than in most of the other mining areas, and Helena survived the working out of the placer deposits in Last Chance Gulch. A view of the city in 1875, reproduced in Figure 15.11, reveals how the city had developed on the system of streets platted a few years earlier. Notes on this lithograph mention that the city had three newspapers, "several Banking Houses, and numerous blocks of Brick and Stone Stores and Warehouses." In addition to mining, industrial activities included "Planing Mills, Sash, Door and Blind Factories, Foundries and Machine Shops, Flouring Mills, Sampling and Smelting Works, Breweries, Distillery, &c." A hospital, a public school, and four churches provided important civic services for the growing community. The federal government recognized the importance of Helena by locating its Assay Office there in the year this view was published. It stood at the corner of Warren and Broadway in one of the blocks bordering the public square, in the center of which the courthouse had by then been erected.

Many of the buildings appearing in this view had been built to replace those destroyed in major fires of 1869, 1871, 1872, and 1874. An earlier fire led to the organization of a fire company, but the conflagration in 1869 destroyed $500,000 worth of property before the firefighting equipment that had been ordered arrived in the town. The fire of 1874 was an even greater disaster with total damage estimated at $850,000, including the loss of the library of the Historical Society of Montana, which had been formed by ambitious and far-sighted citizens as early as 1864.[41]

Although Helena could boast of its accomplishments and its new status as territorial capital after 1875, it still had the unmistakable appearance of a frontier community only a few years removed from its days as a town of tents and cabins. A *Harper's Weekly* artist in 1878 recorded his impressions of what is doubtless Main Street in the view shown in Figure 15.12. The plank sidewalks, the wagon trains, the prospector leading his pack horse, the visiting Indians, the Chinese coolie, the false-fronted stores—all illustrate elements of the urban mining frontier in transition, a change symbolized by the town clock and the telegraph wires strung overhead.

An equally dramatic example of rapid urbanization took place on Silver Bow Creek, midway between Helena and Bannack, where G. O.

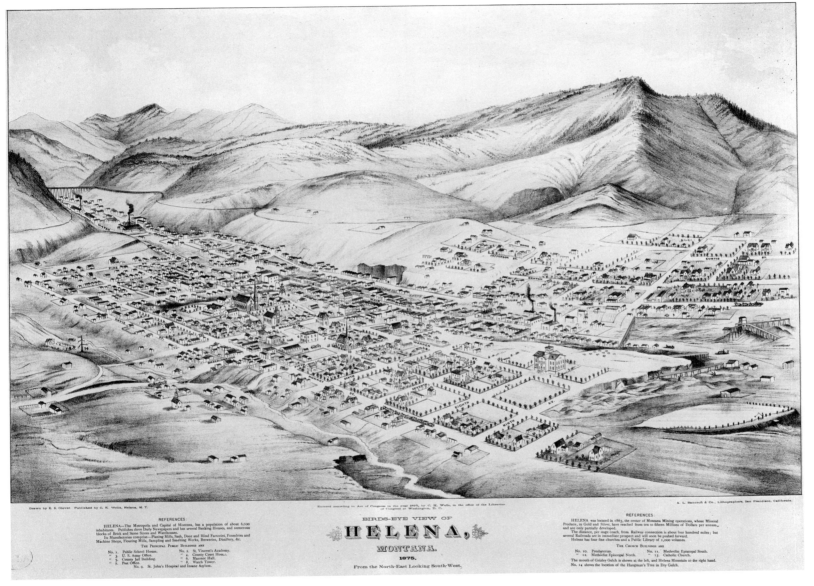

Figure 15.11 View of Helena, Montana: 1875

Figure 15.12 View of Street in Helena, Montana: 1878

Humphrey and William Allison found gold in 1864. Apparently the deposits did not prove exceptionally rich, for the population of the tiny camp numbered less than 50 in the first two years, reaching less than 500 by 1867. The placer deposits were soon nearly worked out, water was scarce, and three years later the population had dwindled to some 200 persons. The townsite that had been platted during its year of peak prosperity seemed destined to join so many others of the mining West as a ghost town.

In 1874 one of its early residents, William Farlin, returned to the region to stake out several claims. Soon the news leaked out that the black rock ledges passed over by previous miners contained a rich concentration of silver. A new, larger, and more prolonged boom began. It was intensified when Marcus Daly, digging for silver, found a vein of copper 50 feet wide. In 1876, a townsite patent was issued for the town of Butte, laid out in a sloping gridiron up the mountain rising to the south of Silver Bow Creek.

The familiar process of town building created the city seen in Figure 15.13 showing the city in 1884 three years after the Utah and Northern Railroad linked the city to the main line of the Union Pacific at Ogden. Five years later the Great Northern line provided additional transportation facilities, bringing people and supplies to the booming city and hauling eastward ore and refined copper and silver from Butte's smoky smelters.

Its population was then 10,000, enough to support three banks, seven churches, four hospitals, two newspapers, an opera house, and several schools. With a piped water system, electric lights, and a gas works, Butte could claim that in two decades it had achieved a level of urban services equal to most of the long-settled communities of the East.[42] As the seat of Silver Bow County, Butte also gained some prominence as a center of government. But despite its growing population, it failed in its initial efforts to be designated the capital, the fight for which occupied much of Montana's political life for years. Finally, in 1894, Helena won a closely contested referendum held to decide the capital location issue. Its opponent was Anaconda, another copper mining town laid out by Marcus Daly in 1883.[43]

The mining towns of Montana could not have existed without supply and transportation centers. Corresponding to Sacramento, Stockton, Denver, and Lewiston in earlier mining regions, such Montana towns as Benton, Bozeman, and Missoula served as transfer points between one means of transportation and another, as outfitting stations for prospectors bound for the mines, and as continuing sources of supplies required for the camps and their occupants.

Benton's location gave it an early advantage, situated as it was at the head of steamer navigation on the Missouri River and adjoining Fort Benton, a long-established fur-trading post. Richardson estimated that in 1865 three-fifths of all supplies entering Montana came by river from such places at St. Louis or Sioux City to be landed at Benton and then carried by wagon to Helena, 140 miles away or to Virginia City, nearly twice that distance.[44] It was a long and expensive trip from St. Louis; passengers paid $150 for the 60-day voyage from St. Louis, and freight rates averaged about 12¢ a pound on side-wheel steamers carrying around 500 tons of freight.[45]

The plan of Benton reproduced in Figure 15.14 is undated, but it probably was surveyed on this ambitious scale sometime prior to 1870, possibly being enlarged from the settlement of more modest size that had been laid out in 1859 adjacent to the fort. Its appearance in the 1870s scarcely reflected the enormous grid of streets appearing in this survey. John Barrows, viewing the settlement from the deck of the *Key West*, on which he had just arrived, did refer to the place as a "lively little town." The emphasis must have been on the first adjective, for Barrows tells us that Benton "was less than a town of one street," being "a town of one side of one street. This street was parallel to the cut bank of the river and not far from it. On the land side of the road there were a string of low buildings extending from the old adobe fort of the fur traders to a point perhaps a quarter of a mile upstream." A later exploration of the settlement revealed to Barrows that it contained "three general stores . . . two hotels, a number of blacksmith shops and innumerable saloons and gambling halls."[46]

While Benton became the county seat of Chouteau County, its population in 1880 was only 1,618, and it continued to decline in importance as the railroads took the place of steamboat traffic. Its streets—100 feet and 80 feet in width—have proved of ample width to handle all traffic requirements. Now known by the name of the fort, Fort Benton today bears little resemblance to the bustling river port of a century ago when it served as the principal shipping point for the mining regions located to the southwest.

Far more successful was the town founded in the summer of 1864 by W. J. Beall and Daniel E. Rouse along the trail John M. Bozeman had opened from Wyoming to the Montana mines. The Gallatin Valley site proved favorable for wheat, and Bozeman induced two men to set up a flour mill in the vicinity. Soon the farmers had established a lively trade with grocers and bakers in Virginia City and Helena.[47]

The official plat for the town of Bozeman, filed with the Gallatin County recorder in 1870, is reproduced in Figure 15.15. Streets are of

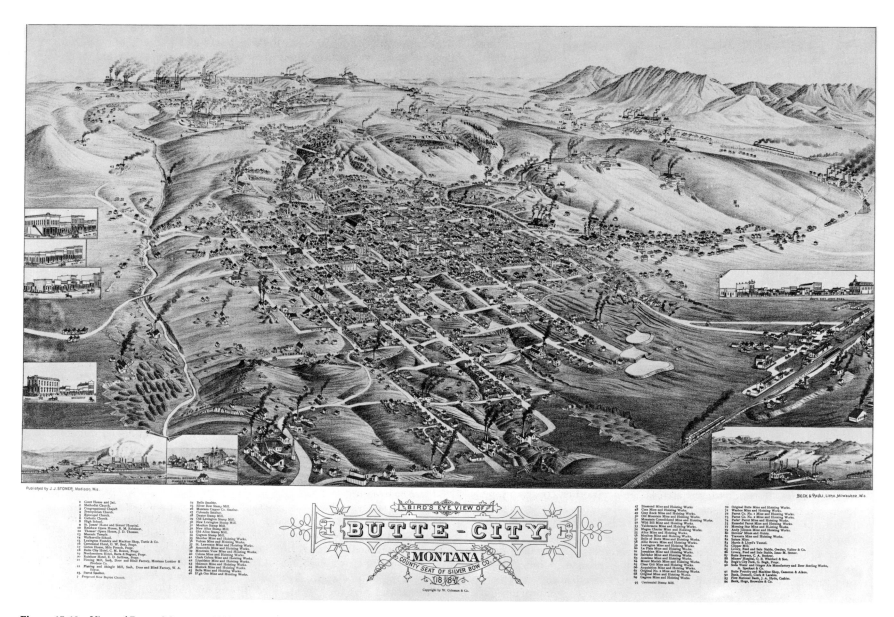

Figure 15.13 View of Butte, Montana: 1884

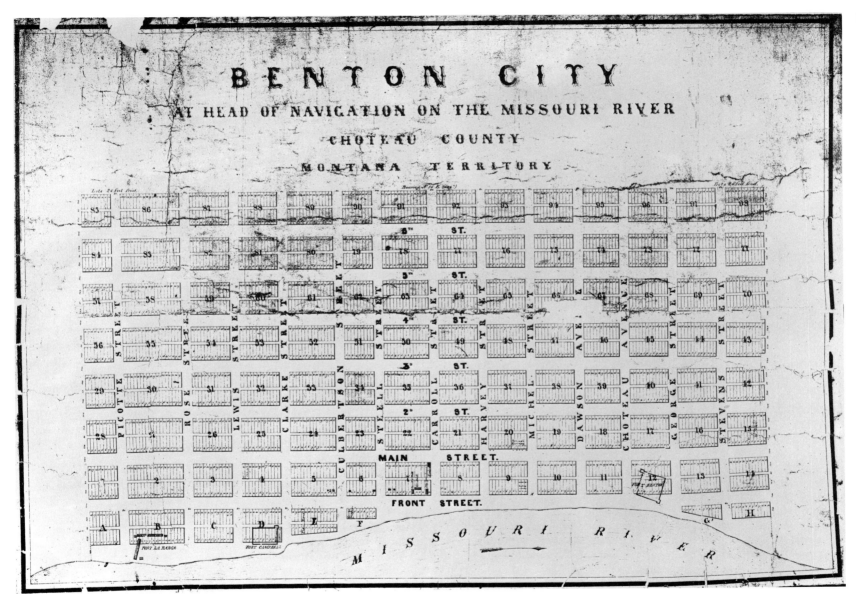

Figure 15.14 Plan of Benton, Montana: ca. 1870

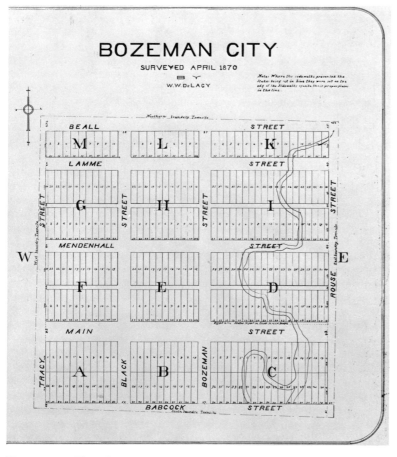

Figure 15.15 Plan of Bozeman, Montana: 1870

odd widths: 58, 67, and 93 feet, suggesting that this survey had to be adjusted to the actual pattern of occupancy under an older and less formal design. The surveyor found it necessary to note that along the north line of Main Street between Rouse and Bozeman Streets he had set his "stakes 10 feet in street to avoid houses."

This utilitarian little grid was extended to accommodate additional settlers. The arrival of the Northern Pacific Railroad in the spring of

1883 set off a minor boom and reinforced Bozeman's position as seat of Gallatin County, a position it had achieved three years after its founding. Commerical coal mining in Rocky Canyon, not far from the new town, further stimulated its growth.

A view of Bozeman drawn in 1883 and published on January 2, 1884, appears in Figure 15.16 and shows the city as seen from the southwest. Several blocks of Main Street were by then solidly developed with two- and three-story mercantile buildings, the courthouse stood proudly on a rise of ground at the lower end of Main Street, and two school-houses—depicted in inset views at the bottom of the lithograph—provided for the educational needs of the thriving settlement. A more important educational addition to the city dates from 1893, when the legislature designated the community as the site for what was to become Montana State College. Bozeman had joined the ranks of cities contending in 1892 for the honor and certain prosperity of becoming the state capital, and the state college was awarded to the town as a kind of consolation prize when it failed to achieve its primary goal.

The principal educational center of Montana, Missoula, passed through a similar stage of development. Its founder, C. P. Higgins, built a trading post with Frank Worden a few miles west of the present city in 1860. Five years later the two men opened a flour mill, a saw mill, and a store on a new site to begin the development of the town. Its location near the Idaho border on the Clark fork of the Columbia River and along the Mullan military road brought a constant flow of wagon trains through the valley, and the town enjoyed a modest but steady growth in population and buildings.

As in Bozeman, however, it was the railroad and later the main branch of the public university system that assured Missoula's permanency. The arrival of the Northern Pacific in 1883 was recognized by its citizens as an important event, and its designation by the railroad as a division point where shops would be constructed resulted in a sharp jump in industrial employment.

Fortunately for the town, the right-of-way of the railroad was surveyed several blocks away from the river, with the depot being located at the north end of Harris Street and the shops farther to the east. Missoula as it appeared in 1884 can be seen in Figure 15.17. The town then took the form of an elongated grid stretching east and west between the river and the railroad.

When Missoula succeeded in obtaining the state university in 1895 another period of growth began. This event also brought the expansion of the town across the river to the south where the university was located. The modern city has expanded in all directions beyond the origi-

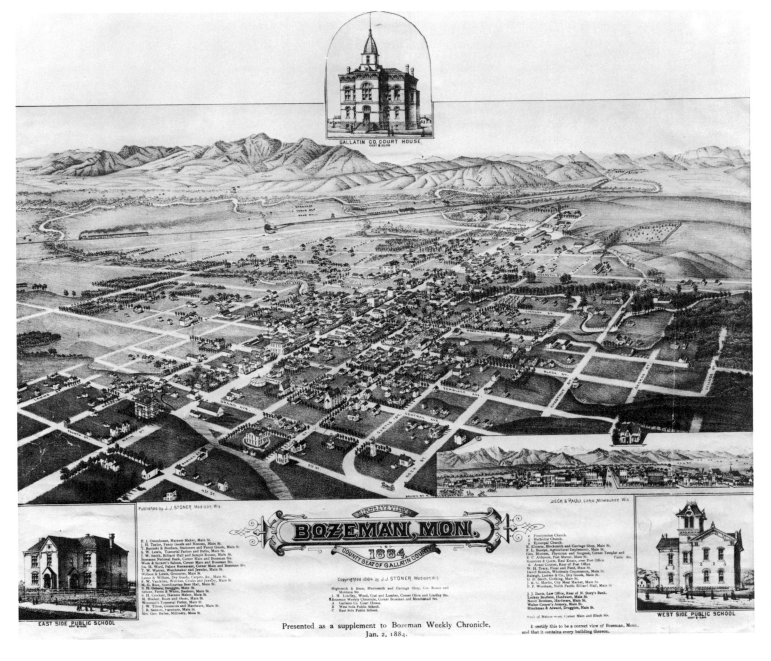

Figure 15.16
View of Bozeman, Montana: 1883

Figure 15.17 View of Missoula, Montana: 1884

nal modest beginnings. Successive additions have followed the whims of private landowners and, in common with many other towns of the mountain West, there is no evidence until recent years that the city attempted to guide its growth according to some comprehensive development plan.[48]

Many other towns were founded in Montana as a result of the mining rush. Real estate speculators soon saw that they might gain as much through townsite promotion as in working placer claims. At least two efforts were made to divert the burgeoning trade of Fort Benton to new river ports laid out for that purpose. The earliest was Kercheval City, planned in 1866 by the Rocky Mountain Wagon Road Company on the south bank of Musselshell River. The promoters expected this town to serve as a port of entry for freight shipped overland along the road the company was building to Helena. However, steamer captains refused to stop at the town, and even before the site was swept away in a flood the enterprise had failed.[49]

Two years after this attempt at town founding, the Montana Hide and Fur Company surveyed another townsite on the Musselshell, this time at its mouth and taking its name from the river. Although it enjoyed some initial success with a population of perhaps fifty persons, only one steamboat called at the port to discharge its cargo of some eighty tons of supplies. Indian raids and the abandonment of the venture by the company in 1870 brought an end to the tiny settlement.[50]

An earlier effort to undercut the position of Fort Benton began in 1865 at the mouth of the Marias River 30 miles downstream. Captain Jim Moore of the steamer *Cutler* had been forced to land his passengers and cargo at this point the previous year because of low water. At Virginia City he organized a group of 20 men to accompany him to the site and construct a cabin. In the spring they engaged William Foster to survey their projected town of Ophir. The *Montana Post* championed this project, referring to it in one dispatch as "a natural site for a city, with its wharves and warehouses." Two weeks later the paper again called the attention of its readers to the new town:

> While some say the building of a large city is quite out of the question, we think it is a necessity and will soon be demonstrated to be a certainty. The American Fur Company steamer will go up to Fort Benton, but no man in his senses will ride forty miles of difficult shallow water to get to a place where there is no fuel or feed, while both are to be had in abundance at Ophir. The climate is excellent. There is little snow. Blacksmiths, bakers, merchants, and

mechanics are already there. Lumber is being hauled and a group of men from St. Paul will erect a hotel in the fall, which will be a good inducement to the business men wintering there. A solid and substantial fortune awaits any man of energy who plants his stake at Ophir and no more important service can be rendered to the community that the erection of a town at a point whither heavy goods can be brought by water, thus avoiding the weary journey and the many disadvantages of a pilgrimage across the plains.[51]

How many persons believed this editorial nonsense is not known, but no "solid and substantial fortune" was ever made in Ophir with the possible exception of Captain Moore's and his associates'. By the end of 1865 the project was dead, and the *Montana Post*, whose publisher may well have invested in Ophir town lots, turned its attention to other matters.

There were dozens, perhaps hundreds, of other camps and towns in the mining regions of Montana whose history is similar to those we have examined. The map in Figure 15.18 shows the pattern of settlement that had emerged by 1874 in southwestern Montana and the adjacent portion of northern Idaho. As in California and Nevada, the mining rush had brought almost instant urbanization to an area previously occupied by Indians, hunters, and trappers, and a few military garrisons. Not all of these communities would survive; many had already declined or disappeared by the time this map was published. Others had never achieved the fleeting distinction of even being noted by cartographers.[52]

In the quarter of a century since the discovery of gold in California prospectors had ranged throughout the mountain West in their relentless search for new bonanzas. By 1874 only one region—the Black Hills of South Dakota—remained for exploitation. This rugged and wildly beautiful area some 60 miles wide and extending approximately 125 miles north and south lay in the middle of the plains occupied by the Sioux Indians. Although a few early explorers and, later, miners bound for California or Montana had temporarily penetrated the area and found promising traces of gold, the Black Hills and their surrounding plains were barred to settlers by the government and by the vigilant resistance of the Indians.

Several parties of would-be prospectors from the settled parts of eastern Dakota had been turned back in the 1860s by military commanders under orders to maintain the frontier between whites and Indians.[53] In 1868 the Laramie Treaty established the Great Sioux Reser-

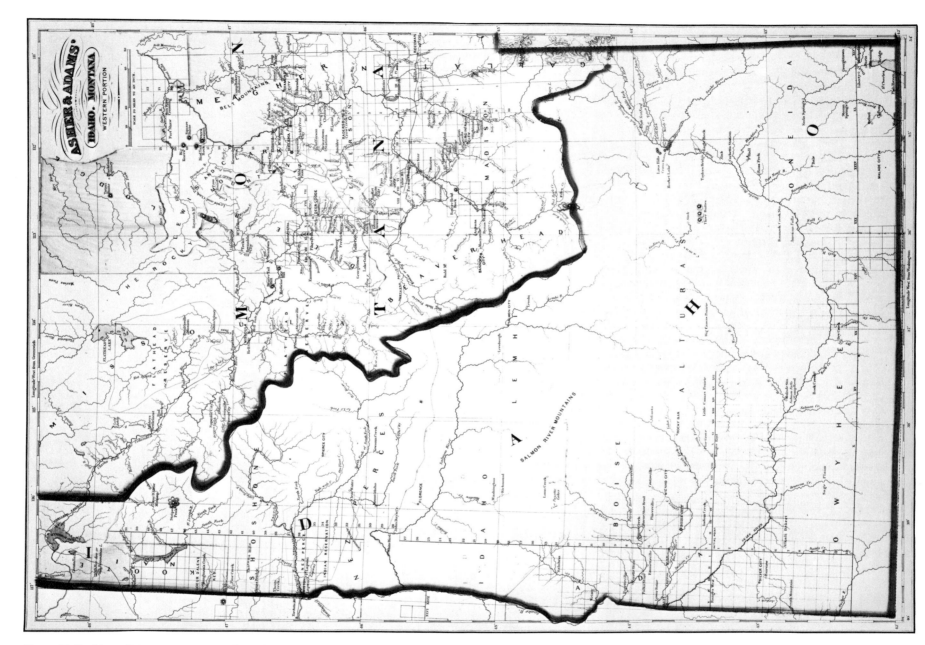

Figure 15.18 Map of Western Montana and Northern Idaho: 1874

vation in Dakota Territory stretching from the Nebraska line to the 46th parallel and extending from the Missouri River westward to the 104th meridian. Under its terms, the Indians agreed to allow the construction of the Union Pacific line and to permit emigrant wagon trains to proceed unmolested through ceded border territories. In return, the federal government abandoned certain military posts, closed the Bozeman Road to the Montana mining region, and guaranteed Indian hunting rights in a large area south of the reservation.[54]

Not all the Sioux tribes agreed to these provisions, and when surveyors of the Northern Pacific line began their work along the Yellowstone River in 1871 the Indians attacked. This resulted in military retaliation. Federal troops were active in the following two years, but the Indians continued their raids. General Philip Sheridan believed that the establishment of a major post in the Black Hills would be desirable, and in the summer of 1874 General George Custer received orders to carry out a reconnaissance of the area.[55]

Custer set out from Fort Lincoln across from Bismarck on the west bank of the Missouri with an expedition of more than 1,000 men. Whatever else he may have accomplished, Custer verified the earlier reports of gold in the Black Hills. On July 30 at French Creek two members of his party found traces of the mineral in the sand, and for a few days soldiers, scouts, and teamsters, and scientists busily panned the streams of the area. When Custer returned to Fort Lincoln after two months of exploration, the news of this discovery spread quickly. Prospectors disregarded orders against civilian trespass of the reservation, slipped by army patrols, and began mining operations at the French Creek location. One group from Sioux City constructed a stockade that winter, and the next spring surveyed a nearby plot as Harney City. Although soldiers ejected this pioneer party from the area, at least 800 other miners entered the region during the summer of 1875. A new gold rush was on, and the army found itself unable to stop it. As soon as patrols rounded up one group of miners and escorted them out of the area another would appear.[56]

Custer City was the first community to be established near the original strike on French Creek. The usual mining district was formed with regulations governing claims, and a commission was appointed to survey streets and lots for the town.[57] In the spring of 1876 one of its residents recorded this impression of the infant settlement: "There were but few houses completed, but many under construction. The people were camped all around, up and down French Creek, in wagons, tents, and temporary brush houses or wickiups. The principal business

houses were saloons, gambling houses and dance halls, two or three so-called stores with very small stocks of general merchandise and little provisions. Most of the business was being done in tents."[58]

North of Custer another camp, Hill City, was laid out on the banks of Spring Creek in 1876. It was soon joined by Rockerville 12 miles to the east on the same stream. Between the two was Sheridan, first named Golden City, which had sprung up the previous year.[59] By March, 1876, an estimated 10,000 persons had swarmed into the region and were beginning to fan out in all directions in search of instant wealth.

In May of that year news of rich strikes at Deadwood Gulch 50 miles north of Custer brought a stampede of miners from the older settlements that left many of them nearly unoccupied. Nearly 6,000 persons lived in Custer before this occurred. Within a few weeks less than 100 residents remained, and its 1,400 log cabins were dismantled and the timbers hauled away or used for fuel. Although its population grew to perhaps 400 in 1877, a census of 1878 revealed that only 57 persons then resided in this pioneer mining community.[60]

Hill City suffered the same fate. When Richard Hughes arrived there on May 11, 1876, he found it "mainly a town of abandoned cabins. From the number of the cabins it was evident that there had been quite a population a short time previous, but the majority of the people had moved north in search of better prospects than Spring Creek offered."[61] Hughes followed the migration to the Deadwood Gulch area, which he reached a few days later. There he found the town of Deadwood, "laid out twenty days previous to our arrival in a dense forest of pine and spruce timber; Main Street ran north and south, parallel with Whitewood Gulch, and two or three other streets crossed at right angles. Only Main Street was taking form at this time, as a number of log cabins had been built and others were under way; while for some two or three blocks in length, the trees had been cut."[62]

This city, which for a time was the largest of the northern Black Hills mining communities, had been platted on April 26, 1876, by Craven Lee, Isaac Brown, and J. J. Williams where Deadwood and Whitewood creeks joined to form a Y-shaped site bounded by the steep hillsides of the stream valleys.[63] While it was easy enough to draw street and block lines on a map and put lots up for sale, it was another thing to provide clear title to such town property. Hughes describes the conflicts that already had arisen in Deadwood between town and mining claims:

"The question of title to lots already was causing trouble. The miners who had located the ground claimed the right to the entire area from surface to bedrock for the whole width of the gulch; while many of those intent on putting up buildings contended that the miners were entitled to no more ground than they found necessary to use in their mining operations." Such clashes of property interests, Hughes tells us, were resolved in a crude but effective way: "The claim owners had the better of the argument, as they had the undoubted right to enter upon any part of their claims, and a statement that it was intended to sink a shaft in the center of a house being erected by a squatter usually brought the latter to terms."[64]

An early view of Deadwood appears in Figure 15.19 as published in an Eastern magazine in the fall of 1876. In fact, Deadwood proper was but one of several communities straggling up and down the narrow, winding valley of the gulch where miners were finding increasingly rich placer deposits. Central City, Gayville, North and South Deadwood, Fountain City, Chinatown, and Cleveland were among these camps that lined the stream banks and rose up the precipitous slopes. By the fall of 1877 the population of this area was said to be "about 12,000, a good deal less than in midsummer." Deadwood's population was then estimated at 4,000, Central City 1,500, and Gayville 1,200.[65]

Deadwood soon outgrew the original main street running parallel to Deadwood Creek. Other streets led off along the banks of Whitewood Creek in an irregular mosaic of little grid subdivisions. While the most important streets followed the contours of the hills, others pitched steeply down the slopes to provide intersections of cross-streets approximately at right angles.

A new resident in 1880 described his impressions of the town as it appeared in the view reproduced in Figure 15.20. "Main Street," a small portion of which is shown in the inset view at the upper right, "is the chief business street. All times of the day, Sundays and all, business is red-hot. Hacks 'to all parts of the city.' 'Here you are for Central.' 'All aboard for Lead.' Large heavy freight wagons, each with twelve yoke of oxen, fruit stands, bootblacks, newsboys, loafers and gamblers elbow and jostle each other; large brick blocks in process of erection, piles of bricks, heaps of mortar, stacks of lumber; all indicating the most intense business activity."

The town already had distinct neighborhoods. "At the parting of the creeks to the left is South Deadwood. Still farther on up Whitewood creek is Ingleside, mostly occupied by neat and tasty residences. It is one of the best parts of town. Cleveland lies the farthest up the gulch. Here stands the hospital of the Sisters of Charity. The city is steadily growing in this direction. On the right of Deadwood creek is City Creek, a very pleasant part of town; and still farther to the right, up

above Main street and somewhat back of it, is Frost Hill, a fine elevation and fast being covered with fine residences."[66]

Three miles away lay Lead, platted on July 14, 1876, the site of the Black Hills' richest gold mine, the Homestake. Possibly because the townsite was surveyed before the true value of its gold deposits was known, the town has a more regular plan than Deadwood. The view in Figure 15.21 shows the community in 1884 as viewed from the north. In the foreground one can see some of the mills where stamping machines crushed the quartz and allowed the gold to be recovered. From the various properties of the Homestake Mining Company alone, nearly $60,000,000 of gold was extracted by the end of the nineteenth century.[67]

The largest town of the Black Hills was less important for its deposits of gold than for its role as a supply center. This was Rapid City, founded in February, 1876, by a company led by John R. Brennan. Samuel Scott surveyed the site on Rapid Creek, where that stream issued from Rapid Canyon. This point marked the division between the mountains and the prairie stretching eastward to the Missouri River nearly 200 miles away. It also lay midway between the northern and southern sections of the Black Hills.

Scott's basic plan, as resurveyed and possibly extended some years later, appears in Figure 15.22. Although Scott was a surveyor and civil engineer, the only instruments available to him were a pocket compass and a tape. Magnetic deviation from true north doubtless explains why the checkerboard of streets fits so uneasily within the larger grid of the later official surveys of government township and sections lines appearing on the map.[68]

The town founders drew lots to determine ownership of property in the central portion of the new community. They began a vigorous campaign to attract additional settlers. One man from Bismarck seeking a location for his sawmill was induced to set up business in Rapid City. Brennan met a party of 100 prospectors coming west and guided them to the town to join another group of similar size that had been persuaded to make the town their base of operations. A third party of immigrants, however, refused to settle in the town unless they were given every other city block, and they moved farther up the creek to establish their own community of Upper Rapid.[69]

The town survived Indian raids in the vicinity and by the end of 1876 had a population of some 300 in addition to many miners prospecting the creek in the foothills beyond. In 1878 Rapid City succeeded in capturing the title of county seat of Pennington County from Sheridan. A

Figure 15.19   View of Deadwood, South Dakota: 1876

DEADWOOD, BLACK HILLS, DAKOTA.

Figure 15.20 View of Deadwood, South Dakota: 1884

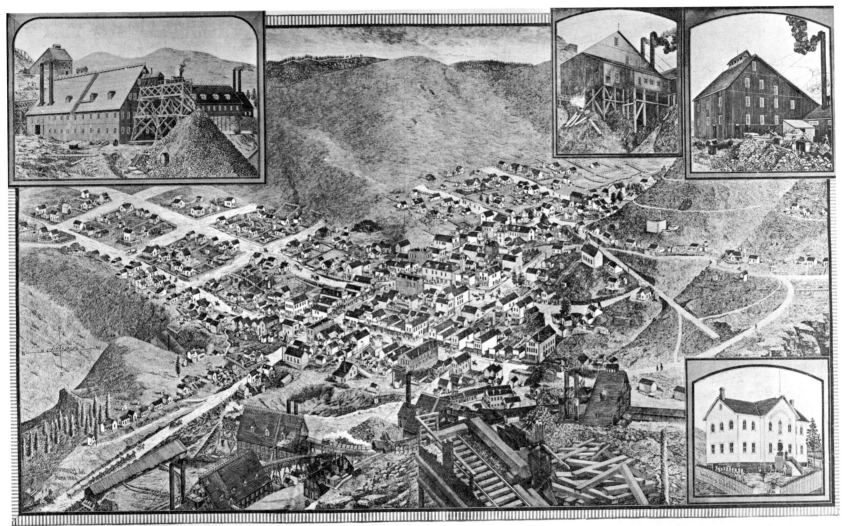

LEAD CITY, BLACK HILLS, DAKOTA.

Figure 15.21   View of Lead, South Dakota: 1884

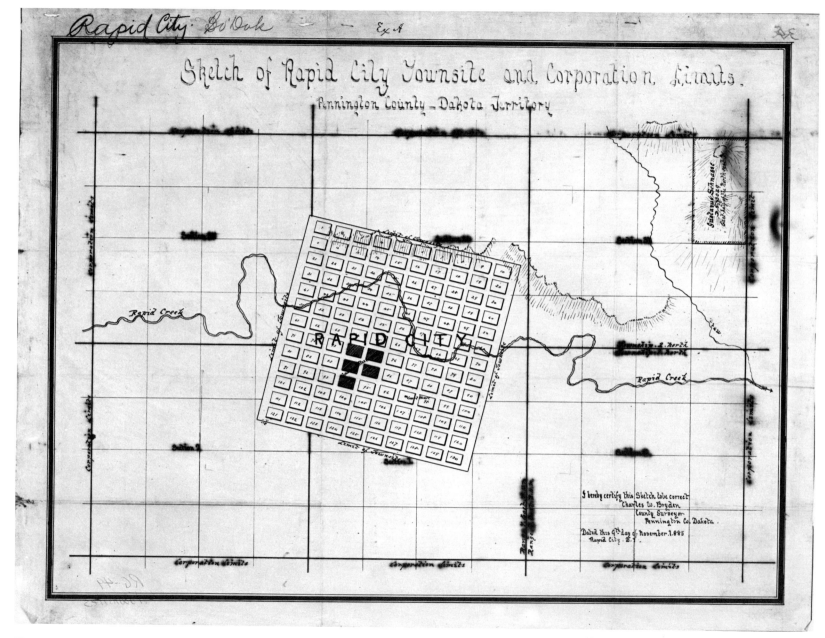

Figure 15.22 Map of Rapid City, South Dakota and Vicinity: 1885

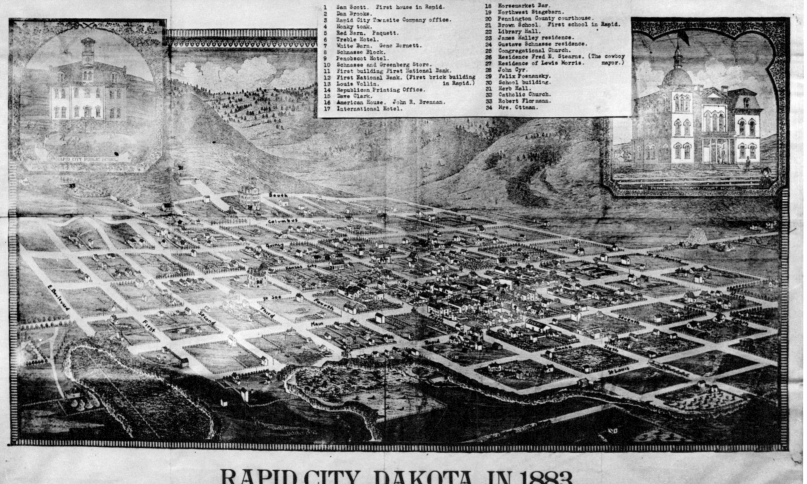

COMPLIMENTS OF KELLOGG & BAILEY,
The RAPID CITY REAL ESTATE DEALERS.

1 Sam Scott. First house in Rapid.
2 Dan Brooks.
3 Rapid City Townsite Company office.
4 Honky tonk.
5 Red Barn. Paquett.
6 Treble Hotel.
7 White Barn. Gene Barnett.
8 Schnasse Block.
9 Penobscot Hotel.
10 Schnasse and Greenberg Store.
11 First building First National Bank.
12 First National Bank. (First brick building in Rapid.)
13 Louis Vollin.
14 Republican Printing Office.
15 Dave Clark.
16 American House. John R. Brennan.
17 International Hotel.
18 Horsemarket Bar.
19 Northwest Stagebarn.
20 Pennington County courthouse.
21 Brown School. First school in Rapid.
22 Library Hall.
23 James Halley residence.
24 Gustave Schnasse residence.
25 Congregational Church.
26 Residence Fred E. Stearns. (The cowboy mayor.)
27 Residence of Lewis Morris.
28 John Cyr.
29 Felix Posnansky.
30 School building.
31 Herb Hall.
32 Catholic Church.
33 Robert Flormann.
34 Mrs. Ottman.

RAPID CITY, DAKOTA, IN 1883.

For Reliable Information or Bargains in RAPID CITY REAL ESTATE call on or address KELLOGG & BAILEY, Flormann Block, Sixth Street.

Figure 15.23 View of Rapid City, South Dakota: 1883

year earlier regular stage lines began operation from Sidney, Nebraska, and Rapid City began to assume a permanent role as the gateway to the Black Hills.

The town as it appeared to a frontier artist in 1883 is shown in Figure 15.23. The two most important buildings, the school and the court-house, are illustrated in the upper corners. Another educational institution, the South Dakota School of Mines, was established in Rapid City in 1885. A year later the town achieved another triumph with the completion of the Fremont, Elkhorn & Missouri River Railway, linking the town with Gordon, Nebraska, on July 4. Eventually, in 1907, two major railways—the Chicago & North Western and the Chicago, Milwaukee, St. Paul & Pacific—reached Rapid City to reinforce its position as a transportation and supply center for both the Black Hills and the rich farming region of the western Dakota prairies.[70]

The rush to the Black Hills marked the end of the period of mass town founding of western mining communities that had begun with the discovery of gold in California. It was a remarkable epoch in the nation's urban history. Without the successive discoveries of vast mineral wealth in each of the mining regions, the pace of settlement, the creation of new territories and states, and the development of cities would certainly have been more leisurely and, doubtless, somewhat more orderly. Nevertheless, despite conditions that scarcely favored efforts to organize rationally the physical form of mining communities, town planning played an important role.

In California, this appears to have been limited to attempts to provide some kind of order for mining camps that had been established almost spontaneously. In Nevada and Colorado, on the other hand, there were examples of planning before a basic form had fully emerged. Finally, in the later phases of the bonanza West and with occasional earlier examples, mining towns were often planned and surveyed immediately after the discovery of gold or silver and before the arrival of most of their eventual residents.

In his pioneering study of 1885, *Mining Camps: A Study in American Frontier Government*, Charles Shinn overlooked the significance of this aspect of western mining towns.[71] Shinn described how groups of miners thrown together in regions lacking civil government organized mining districts, adopted laws governing mineral claims, created provisional towns, and provided for the administration of justice. This impressive response to the need men felt for formal, institutional constraints on human conduct was all the more remarkable because circumstances offered maximum rewards for individual initiative and enterprise.

As have other and later scholars, Shinn failed to note attempts at community planning in some of the earliest mining towns and in most of the later ones. Documentary records of the period, early cartographic and pictorial material, and the remnants of the towns themselves support the conclusion that urban planning was far from unknown on the western mining frontier. Such evidence would have strengthened Shinn's thesis that all of the essential elements of Eastern culture quickly found expression in these new towns and camps located hundreds of miles from the edge of established society.

XVI

Railroads to the Rockies and the Urban Settlement of
the Central and Northern Great Plains

THE possibility of a railroad line to span the continent and link the Atlantic and Pacific coasts of the United States began to be discussed only a few years after the first eastern railways began operation. Asa Whitney, the most persistent advocate of a transcontinental line, presented to Congress in 1845 his proposal for a route from Lake Michigan to the Northwest. A New York merchant involved in the China trade, Whitney offered to purchase a strip of land 60 miles wide at 10¢ an acre with the proviso that title to the land would pass to him only with the completion of the tracks through each successive 10-mile long section. Other persons suggested that the project should be carried out by the federal government or with the participation of the states involved. With the rapid settlement of California after 1848, the need to provide better transportation connections to this new and growing part of the country became obvious.

Virtually every proponent of a transcontinental railroad believed that only one line would be possible. The leaders of established towns on what was then the frontier of settlement realized that growth and prosperity would surely be theirs if they could secure the eastern terminus of the line. In older cities in the Midwest and along the Atlantic Coast nearly everyone realized the importance of arranging connections between the railroads already providing them passenger and freight service and any new railway to the Pacific.

During the decade of the 1850s the location of the Pacific Railroad emerged as a major national issue. In 1853 the federal government ordered elaborate surveys of possible routes to be carried out under the direction of Jefferson Davis, secretary of war. When Davis made his final report to Congress in 1855, he, as might be expected, recommended a southern route. His recommendation proved unacceptable to the North, and Congress found itself unable to reach an agreement. The secession of the southern states helped to resolve the conflict, and after prolonged debate Congress decided in favor of a central route.

Under the terms of the federal charter granted on July 1, 1862, the western portion of the line was to be constructed by the Central Pacific, a company formed a year earlier by four prominent merchants in Sacramento: Leland Stanford, Collis P. Huntington, Mark Hopkins, and Charles Crocker. The eastern part was to be built by a new company, the Union Pacific. In an effort to satisfy the cities contending for the route, Congress provided for five branches at the eastern end to serve Kansas City, Leavenworth, St. Joseph, Sioux City, and a place to be designated by the president on the western boundary of Iowa. President Lincoln later designated Council Bluffs as this point, but the practical effect of his proclamation was to award the prize to Omaha on the

western side of the Missouri River opposite Council Bluffs. The Omaha branch was to be constructed by the Union Pacific, while existing railroads were to provide the other four connections. It was, eventually, the "branch" to Omaha that became the main line.

Congress provided generous subsidies to the two companies. Across lands in the public domain they received a right-of-way 400 feet wide plus "all necessary grounds for stations, buildings, workshops, and depots, machine shops, switches, side tracks, turntables, and water stations." Far more important, the act granted "every alternate section of public land, designated by odd numbers, to the amount of five alternate sections per mile on each side of said railroad . . . and within the limits of ten miles on each side." These alternate one-mile square sections could be disposed of as the railroads wished. Any lands so granted remaining unsold three years after completion of the entire line were to become open for pre-emption at $1.25 an acre, but settlers were required to pay the amount due to the railroads, and not to the government.

The law also extended government loans in the form of 30-year treasury bonds secured by a first mortgage on the railroad property. The companies could borrow in this manner $16,000 per mile of track for most of the route, $48,000 a mile for the portions of the line in the Sierras and Rockies, and $32,000 a mile in the region between these two mountain ranges.[1] Two years later Congress doubled the amount of land granted in alternate sections, reduced the security on the government bonds issued as loans to a second mortgage, and authorized the companies to issue their own bonds to raise additional funds. At that time Congress also liberalized the provisions governing the sale of stock to individuals and eliminated an earlier restriction on the amount of stock that could be held by a single person or corporation.[2]

Land grants to railroads as a form of subsidy were not new. The Illinois Central line had been an early beneficiary of this policy, and although its charter prohibited it from laying out towns, the directors of the line circumvented this restriction by forming a separate company for this purpose.[3] No such prohibition appeared in the transcontinental railroad act of 1862, and both the Central Pacific and the Union Pacific were to use their granted lands as townsites laid out by them or by associated enterprises. Sales of town lots were regarded as a profitable activity by these roads as it was by the other western lines, which received similar land grant subsidies in subsequent years.

These new railroads were not long in being organized. The Burlington extended its line from Chicago across Iowa, through Lincoln and by 1879 had reached a point halfway across Nebraska to connect with the Union Pacific. Later it was to reach Cheyenne and Denver in the decade of the 1880s and Billings before 1900. The Kansas Pacific, expanded from its original status as one of the five branches of the Union Pacific, reached Denver from Kansas City in 1870 by a route through Topeka. Paralleling this line to the south was the Atchison, Topeka, and Santa Fé, which followed the Arkansas River valley to southeastern Colorado. The Santa Fé line was built as far as Granada, Colorado, by 1873.

The major line across the northern plains was the Northern Pacific chartered by Congress in 1864. Construction was delayed until 1870, when Jay Cooke had become its financial agent. With leased lines from Duluth and St. Paul providing connections to the East, this road was projected through the southern parts of North Dakota and Montana to Puget Sound. The panic of 1873 found the track only as far west as Bismarck, North Dakota, but by 1883 the line provided connections between its eastern terminals and the Pacific Coast.

As each of these lines pushed westward, new towns sprang up at the temporary terminal points. Some of these communities enjoyed only a brief existence, other managed to survive as hamlets or villages, while a few grew to substantial size. The nucleus of these end-of-track communities was the colorful collection of dormitory cars supplied by the railroad to house some of its large crew of workers. One of these cars is shown in Figure 16.1 as used on the Northern Pacific line in 1883. This was rolled into place where the railroad had previously claimed the land as part of its land grant. Usually this site was surveyed into streets and blocks, since normally the railroad would plan on locating at least a station and water tower at such a spot. No lots could be sold until such time as the section of track had been inspected and approved by government officials and the patents to the land claimed by the railroad had been issued.[4]

Tents, shacks, and temporary buildings of all kinds were quickly occupied by gamblers, prostitutes, saloon keepers, merchants, and others attracted by the opportunity to separate the railroad employees from their weekly payrolls as quickly as possible.[5] The young Englishman, William A. Bell, who had come to America to observe and record the process of railroad construction as a photographer, described one of these towns—Salina, Kansas—on the Kansas Pacific line in 1867:

> On the open grass land . . . several broad streets could be seen, marked out with stakes, and crossing each other like a chessboard. The central one was deeply cut up with cart-rucks, and

strewn with rubbish. There had been heavy rains, and the mud was so deep that it was almost impossible to move about. On each side of this main street were wooden houses, of all sizes and in all shapes of embryonic existence. Not a garden fence or tree was anywhere to be seen. Still paddling about in the mud, we came to the most advanced part of the 'city,' and here we found three billiard saloons, each with two tables, and the everlasting bar. Then came an ice-cream saloon; then a refreshment saloon. . . . All these 'institutions,' as well as a temporary school-house, and several small well-stocked shops made of wood unpainted, evidently represented first principles—the actual necessities, in fact, of Western life. Opposite was a row of substantial 'stores' having their fronts painted. . . . Trying to escape up a side street we discovered the Methodist Chapel, the Land Agency Office, labelled 'Desirable town lot for sale,' the Masonic Hall (temporary building), and the more pretentious foundations of the Free School, Baptist Chapel, and Episcopal Church. The suburbs consisted of tents of all shapes and forms, with wooden doors; shanties, half canvas, half wood. These were owned by squatters upon unsold lots.[6]

While Salina managed to survive after the railroad moved its temporary terminus, many of the other end-of-track towns disappeared altogether. In 1878 Garland, Colorado, served for a brief time as the terminus of the Denver and Rio Grande Railroad. When the track had been constructed another 45 miles westward and a new terminal designated, Garland, according to one witness, began "to move forward, and on every hand we see men tearing down the frail wooden structures with which it is built, and starting westward with them. Soon Garland will be a thing of the past and only battered oyster cans, cast-off clothing, old shoes, and debris generally will mark the site of where once stood a flourishing city, with its hotels, its stores, its theatre comique, etc. The citizens appear to take it as a matter of course, and are getting ready to vacate the premises. Even the postoffice is getting ready to move out."[7]

The remains of a similar town in Kansas are depicted in Figure 16.2 as sketched by an artist for *Harper's Weekly* in 1874. The western plains were dotted with dozens of such communities, which in numbers are probably exceeded only by the ghost towns of the mining regions in the Sierra and Rocky Mountains. As soon as one town died, however, another sprang to life. Bell mentions that when Cheyenne was the terminal of the Union Pacific, it reached a population of 5,000 almost over

Figure 16.1 View of Railroad Construction Train on the Northern Pacific Railroad: 1883

night. An acquaintance from Denver told him "that while he was standing on the railway platform, a long freight train arrived, laden with frame houses, boards, furniture, palings, old tents, and all the rubbish which makes up one of these mushroom 'cities.' The guard jumped off his van, and seeing some friends on the platform, called out with a flourish, 'Gentlemen, here's Julesburg.' The next train probably brought some other 'city' to lose for ever its identity in the great Cheyenne."[8]

On the Burlington line through Nebraska, the townsites were selected by a group of railroad officials and their friends who organized themselves as the Eastern Land Association. Because the eastern part of the state by 1870 had been settled by homesteaders, it was necessary in some cases for the group to purchase land. They bought 120 acres adjoining Beatrice in 1872, laying off the tract as South Beatrice. Other

methods of land acquisition were also employed. At Lowell four agents of the Association built a single house where four quarter-sections of land joined. Each "occupied" one corner of the house, plowed a few acres of land, and then entered a claim under the pre-emption laws as *bona fide* settlers. With ownership confirmed, the agents transferred their title to the Association, which promptly cut it up into lots 22 by 140 feet.[9]

Thomas Doane, one of the founders of the Association, located many of the railroad's townsites on land grant sections. Because he feared that later settlers might disregard the railroad's claims, he erected four two-story frame houses in the vicinity of ten of the stations on the line between Lincoln and Kearney. The names were chosen in alphabetical sequence: Crete, Dorchester, Exeter, Fairmont, Grafton, Harvard, Inland, Juniata, Kenesaw, and Lowell.[10] As mechanical as the system of

Figure 16.2   View of a Deserted Railroad Town in Kansas: 1873

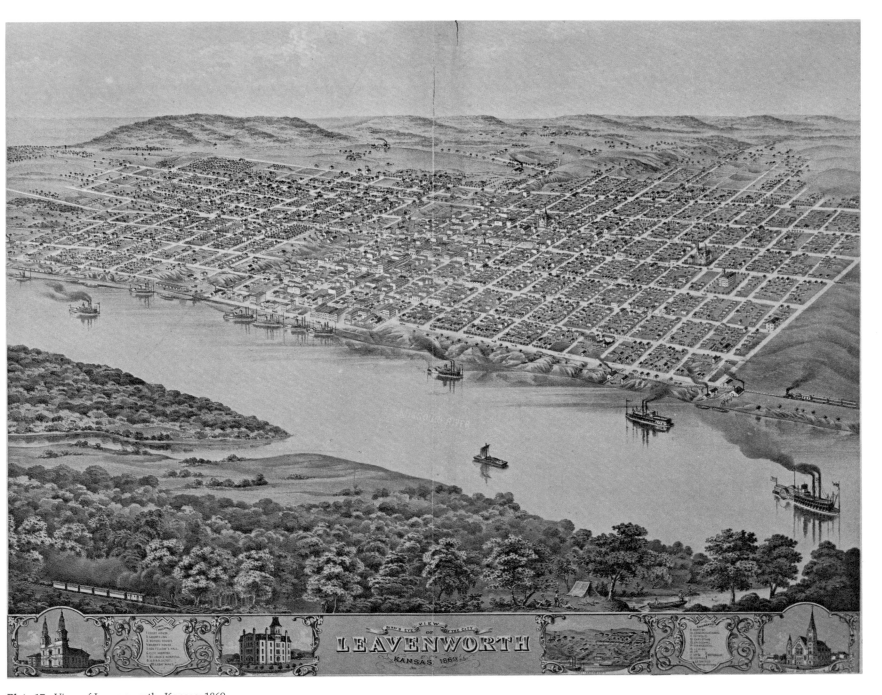

Plate 17. View of Leavenworth, Kansas: 1869

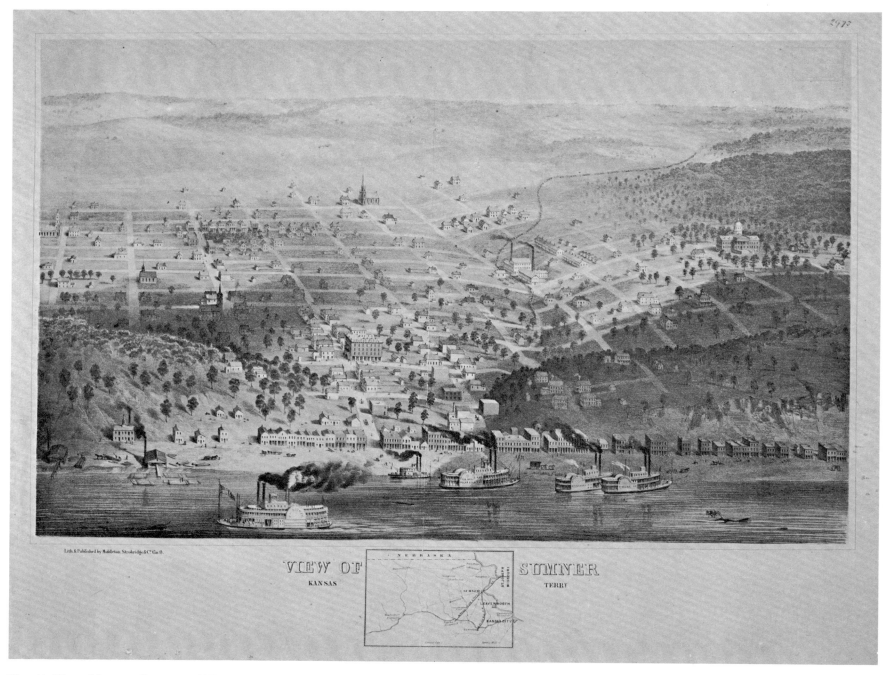

Plate 18. View of Sumner, Kansas: ca. 1857

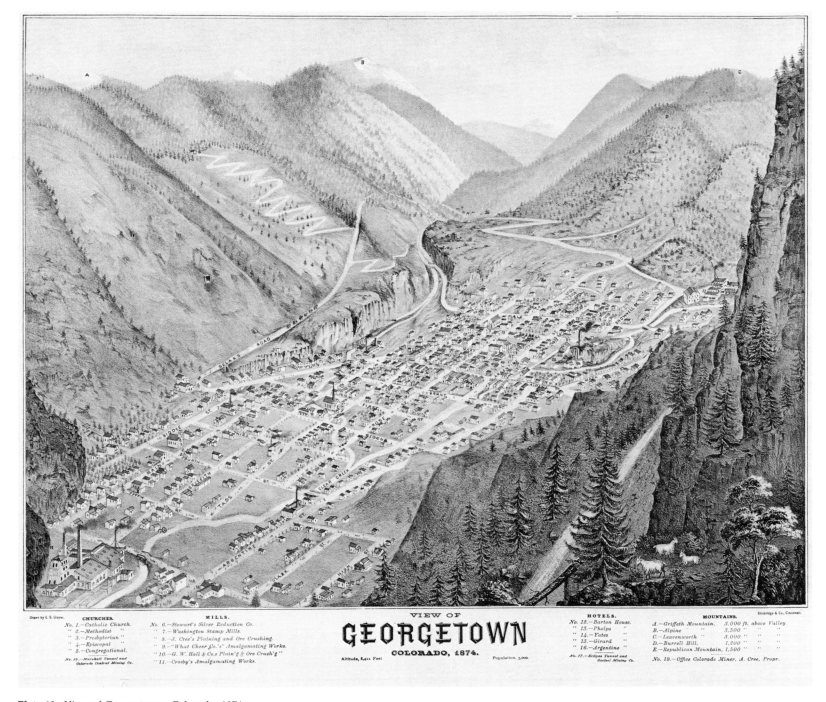

VIEW OF

GEORGETOWN

COLORADO, 1874.

Altitude, 8,412 Feet.   Population, 3,000

Drawn by L. S. Gover.

Strobridge & Co., Cincinnati.

CHURCHES.
No. 1.—Catholic Church.
" 2.—Methodist "
" 3.—Presbyterian "
" 4.—Episcopal "
" 5.—Congregational.

No. 18.—Marshall Tunnel and
Colorado Central Mining Co.

MILLS.
No. 6.—Stewart's Silver Reduction Co.
" 7.—Washington Stamp Mills.
" 8.—J. Cree's Plaining and Ore Crushing.
" 9.—"What Cheer Co.'s" Amalgamating Works.
" 10.—G. W. Hall & Co.s Plain'g & Ore Crush'g "
" 11.—Crosby's Amalgamating Works.

HOTELS.
No. 12.—Barton House.
" 13.—Phelps "
" 14.—Yates "
" 15.—Girard "
" 16.—Argentine "

No. 17.—Eclipse Tunnel and
Goshel Mining Co.

MOUNTAINS.
A.—Griffeth Mountain.   3,000 ft. above Valley.
B.—Alpine   3,500 "   "   "
C.—Leavenworth "   3,000 "   "   "
D.—Burrell Hill.   1,200 "   "   "
E.—Republican Mountain. 1,500 "   "   "

No. 19.—Office Colorado Miner. A. Cree, Propr.

Plate 19. View of Georgetown, Colorado: 1874

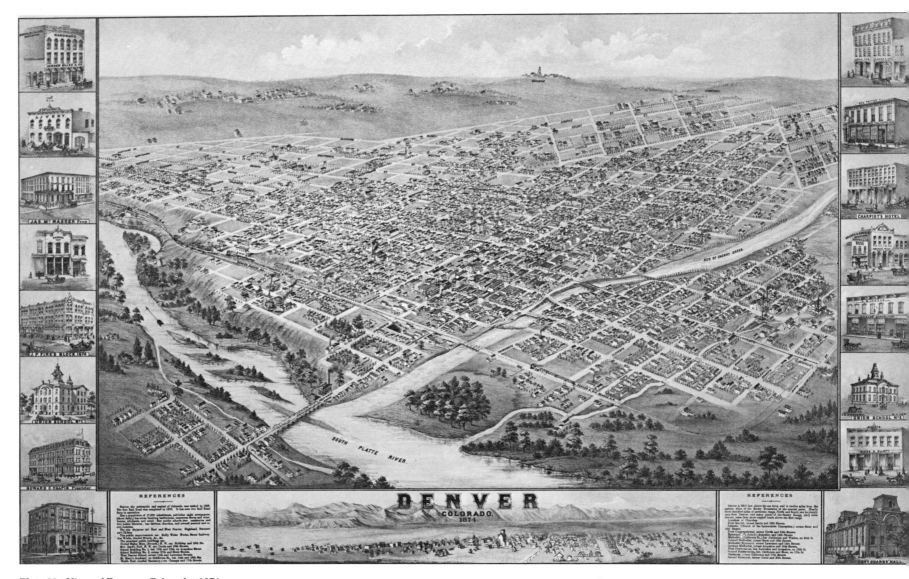

Plate 20. View of Denver, Colorado: 1874

HELENA.

(in 1865.)

[Montana Territory.]

Entered according to Act of Congress in the year 1866 by J. J. Bechler in the Clerks Office of the District Court of the Eastern District of Pennsylvania.

Plate 21. View of Helena, Montana: 1865

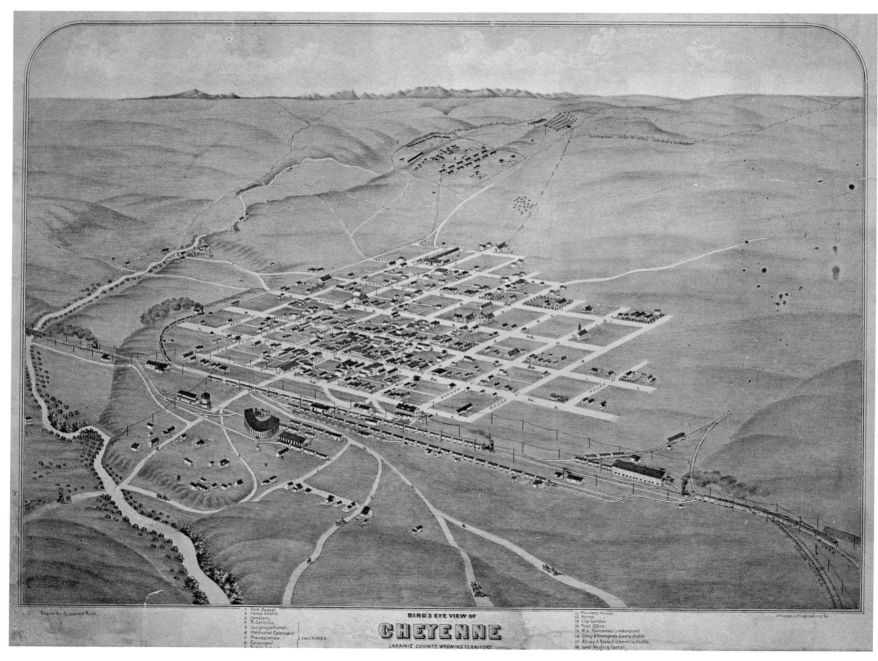

BIRD'S EYE VIEW OF

CHEYENNE

LARAMIE COUNTY, WYOMING TERRITORY.

1 Fort Russel.
2 Camp Carlin.
3 Cemetery.
4 R. Catholic.
5 Congregational.
6 Methodist Episcopal.
7 Presbyterian.
8 Episcopal.
CHURCHES.

11 Planters House.
12 Korns.
13 City Garden.
14 Post Office.
15 W.L. Thomsons Lumberyard.
16 Glrey & Vontajmes Livery Stable.
17 Ab sey & Reels Elkhorn Liv.Stable.
18 Great Western Corral.

Plate 22. View of Cheyenne, Wyoming: 1870

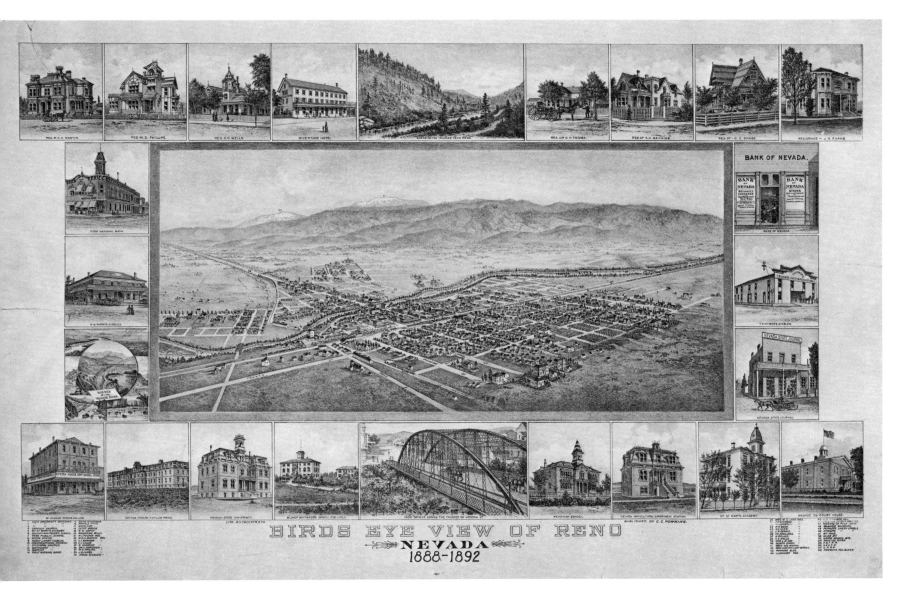

BIRDS EYE VIEW OF RENO
NEVADA
1888-1892

Plate 23. View of Reno, Nevada: 1890

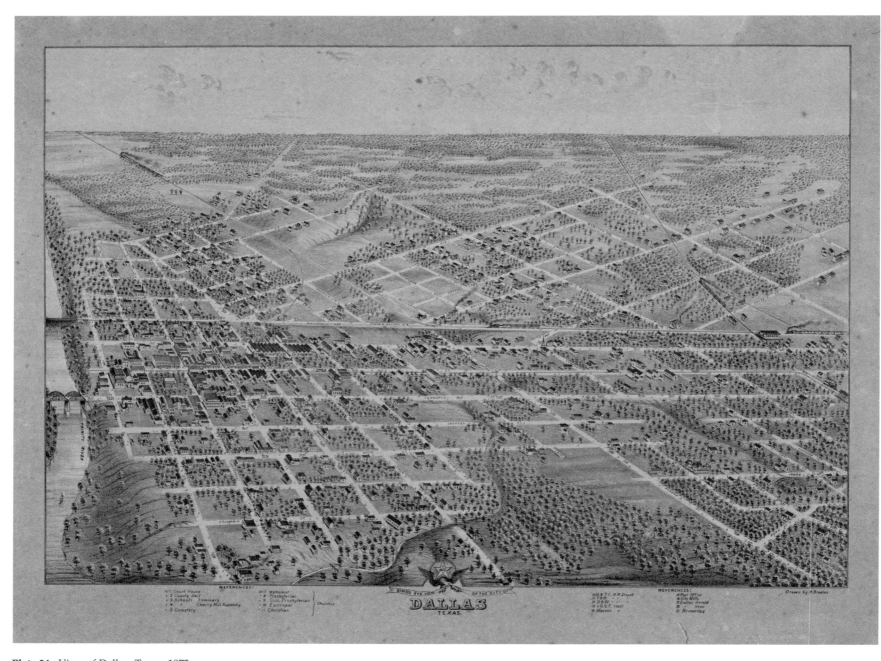

Plate 24. View of Dallas, Texas: 1872

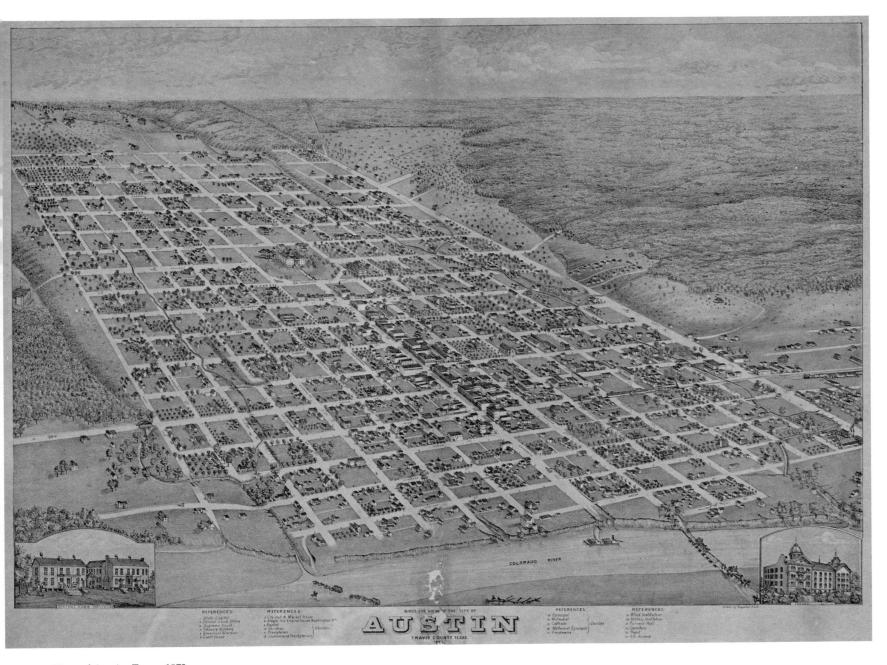

REFERENCES:

1 State Capitol
2 General Land Office
3 Supreme Court
4 Treasury Building
5 Governors Mansion
6 Court House

REFERENCES:
7 City Hall & Market House
8 Steam Fire Engine House Washington N°1
9 Baptist
10 Christian
11 Presbyterian
12 Cumberland Presbyterian

Churches

BIRDS EYE VIEW OF THE CITY OF

AUSTIN

TRAVIS COUNTY TEXAS.

REFERENCES
13 Episcopal
14 Methodist
15 Catholic
16 Methodist Episcopal
17 Freedmans

Churches

REFERENCES
18 Blind Institution
19 Military Institution
20 Turners Hall
21 Cemetery
22 Depot
23 U.S. Arsenal

COLORADO RIVER

Plate 25. View of Austin, Texas: 1873

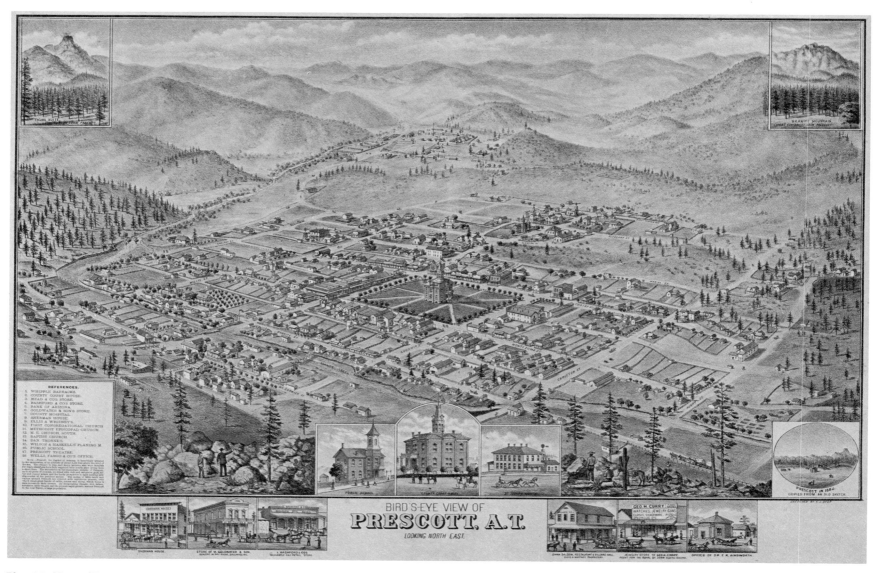

Plate 26. View of Prescott, Arizona: ca. 1885

PERSPECTIVE MAP OF

FORT WORTH, TEX.

1891

Plate 27. View of Fort Worth, Texas: 1891

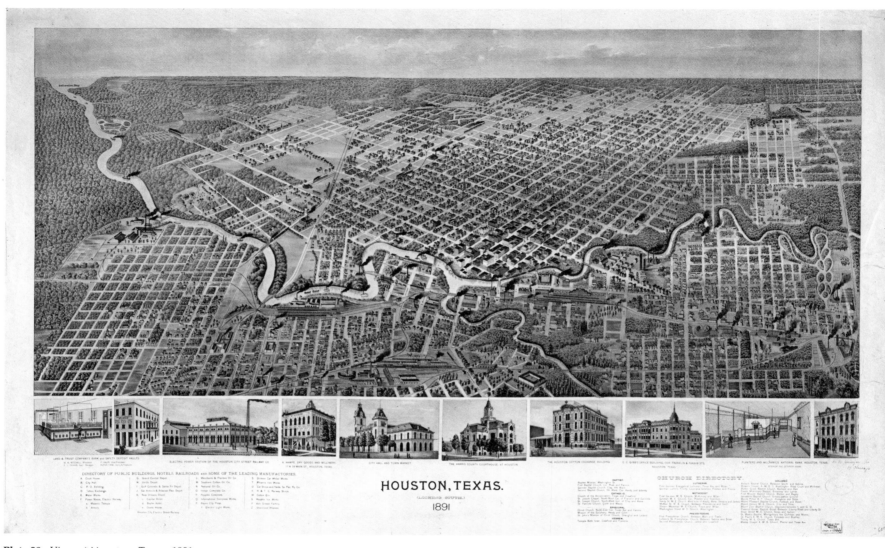

Plate 28. View of Houston, Texas: 1891

Plate 29. View of San Antonio, Texas: 1886

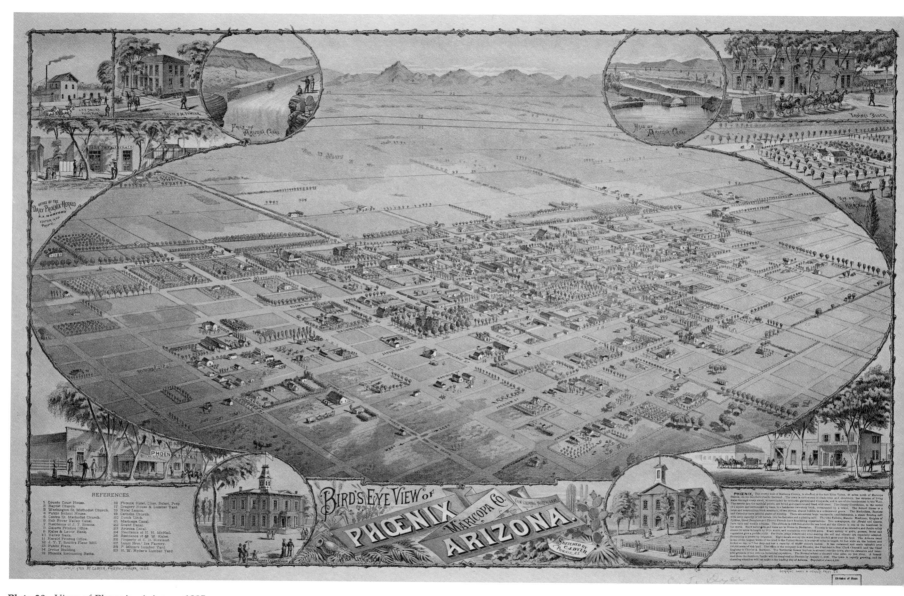

Plate 30. View of Phoenix, Arizona: 1885

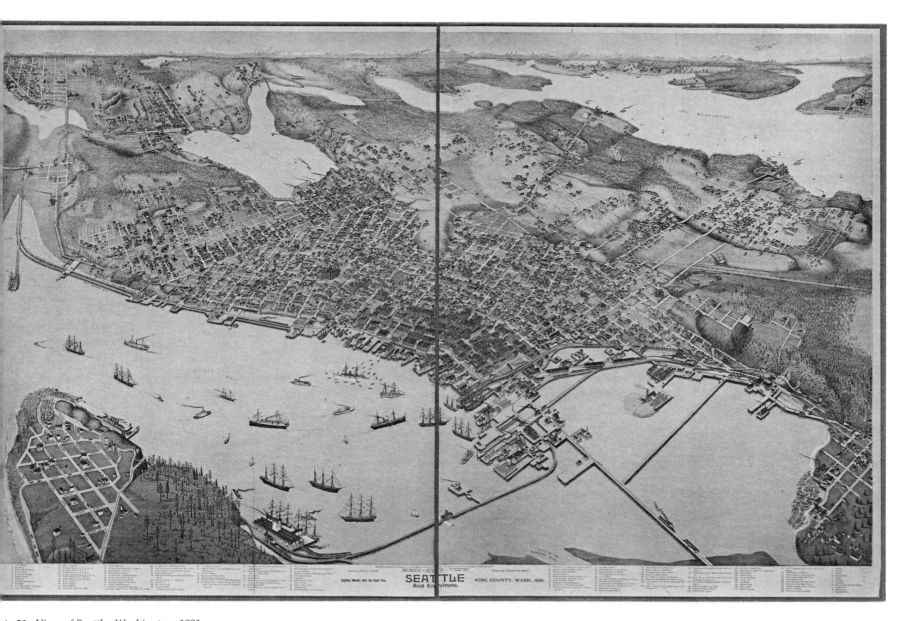

Plate 31. View of Seattle, Washington: 1891

Plate 32. View of Los Angeles, California: 1894

nomenclature was the pattern of land planning adopted for these towns. Harvard as it appeared a few years after its founding is shown in Figure 16.3. The Burlington tracks split the town into two parts, and streets parallel with the tracks and crossing at right angles made up the gridiron framework on which the town slowly took form.

More important than towns such as Harvard were the railroad division points. Here were the shops, roundhouses, yards and sidings, warehouses and other buildings needed at these regional centers of railroad activity. Their plans, although somewhat larger, scarcely differed from those used for the smaller station towns. North Platte was the farthest west of the Union Pacific division towns in Nebraska. Grenville M. Dodge, chief engineer of the railroad, laid out the town in November, 1866, to serve first as an end-of-track construction base. Within a few weeks the population reached 5,000 and remained at that level until spring, when the terminal moved to Julesburg. The number of residents then dropped to some 300, but the completion of the railroad shops and roundhouse provided a stable economic base for the community. The railroad work force of slightly more than 100 men in 1867 increased to nearly 500 by the early 1880s, a government land office added to the importance of the place, and it was made the county seat of Lincoln County.[11]

The prosperous community as it existed in 1888 is depicted in Figure 16.4. Dodge planned the town in the usual checkerboard pattern with the 400-foot Union Pacific right-of-way providing the axis for the streets. He had the foresight to set aside two blocks near the center for a courthouse and school. Dividing these two blocks was the principal business street, which led to the station located opposite the locomotive roundhouse.

Dodge selected the location for a more important city in the spring of 1867. By that time his survey parties had reached the base of the Rockies at a point just north of the Colorado boundary. There he was joined by General C. C. Augur, who had instructions to establish a military post at the new railroad division point so that railroad surveyors and construction workers could be protected against Indian attack. Despite the presence of some troops, an Indian raiding party killed two men, and their graveyard marked the beginning of Cheyenne, later to become the capital of Wyoming.[12]

Figure 16.5 shows Dodge's plan for Cheyenne as approved by the city council of the new community on February 1, 1868. Dodge designed Cheyenne on an immense scale, making up in size what his plan lacked in imagination. His townsite measured two miles on each side,

divided into uniform blocks 264 by 280 feet. All of the streets were 80 feet wide. Alleys 16 feet in width divided the blocks into two parts and provided rear access to the lots, most of which measured 66 by 132 feet. In the two tiers of blocks facing the Union Pacific grounds, smaller lots, 24 by 132 feet, were obviously intended for mercantile purposes.

By the middle of July the company's agent began selling lots, and the city began its period of mushroom growth. When the French mining engineer, Louis Simonin, visited the new community later that year, he recorded these impressions of the boom town:

"Everywhere I hear the sound of the saw and the hammer; everywhere wooden houses are going up; everywhere streets are being laid out, cut on the square, and not at oblique angles as in Europe. There is no time to hunt for names for these streets. They are street number 1, 2, 3, 4, or A, B, C, D, etc. . . .

Already stores are eveywhere, especially of ready-made clothing, restaurants, hotels, saloons. To clothe oneself, eat, drink, and sleep, says the American, such are the four necessities which must be provided for in all newborn settlements. Already there are two printing shops, two newspapers, book shops, banks, stagecoaches, then the post office and the telegraph. . . .

Houses arrive by the hundreds from Chicago, already made, I was about to say, all furnished, in the style, dimensions, and arrangements you might wish. Houses are made to order in Chicago, as in Paris clothes are made to order at the Belle Jardiniere. Enter. Do you want a palace, a cottage, a city or country home; do you want it in Doric, Tuscan, or Corinthian; of one or two stories, an attic, Mansard gables? Here you are! At your service![13]

Simonin estimated that Cheyenne's population at that time when the end of the track was still 20 miles to the east exceeded 3,000. Shortly after the first train arrived on November 13, the city had reached 6,000. It was a predominantly male population; only about 400 women and 200 children lived in the new city. By February, 1868, however, a school was in operation, enrolling 114.[14]

Like the other end-of-track railroad towns, Cheyenne presented a rough face to the world with its saloons, gambling halls, and brothels. Tents and crude shacks mixed with more substantial structures, and its unpaved streets were either dusty or muddy depending on the state of the weather. Respectable settlers in the early months of the town's existence must have found certain aspects of frontier life strange and distasteful as indicated by this announcement inserted in one of the news-

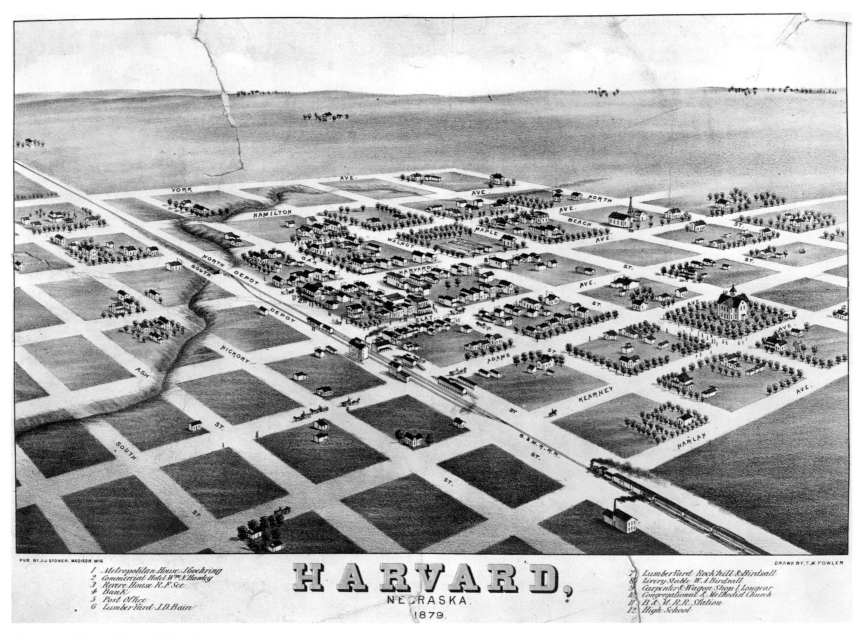

Figure 16.3 View of Harvard, Nebraska: 1879

Figure 16.4 View of North Platte, Nebraska: 1888

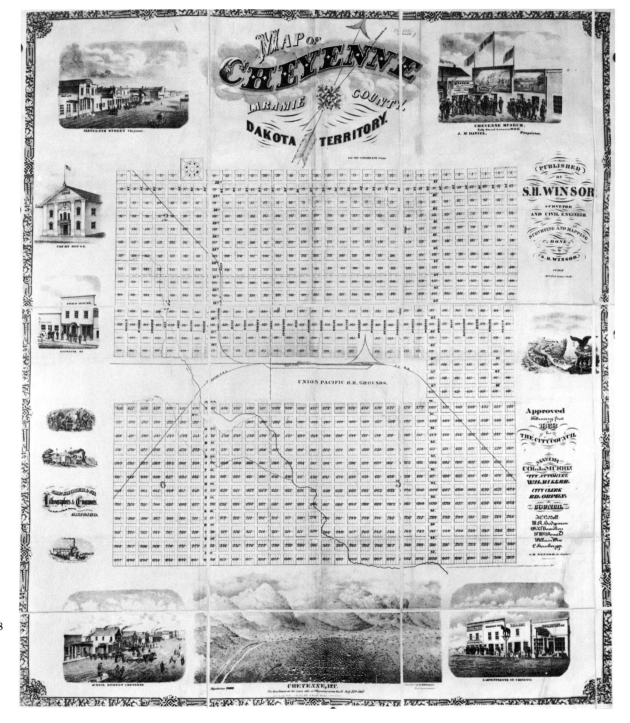

Figure 16.5 Plan of Cheyenne, Wyoming: 1868

papers by a minister: "Tomorrow I shall celebrate the divine service in the saloon which Mr. A. has so kindly put at my disposal. We have as yet no church, but that will come before long. In the meantime, those who come tomorrow and who have prayer books will do well to bring them."[15]

As the Union Pacific tracks were extended westward, most of the gamblers, prostitutes, and other undesirables moved to the next terminal town, and Cheyenne settled into a more stable existence. The town as it appeared in 1870 is shown in Plate 22. Only a small portion of the gigantic grid that Dodge had surveyed was then occupied. Although the Union Pacific agents had to call upon the army to evict squatters on its town lots in October, 1867, three years later the demand had obviously slackened. The residents of Cheyenne feared that their town, like so many of the others that had been created by the railroad on its march from the East, would be replaced by newer settlements to the west, but even with its reduced population, the town could boast of many substantial houses and at least five churches. While the latter were still outnumbered by saloons, they at least provided more appropriate settings for Sunday worship.

Cheyenne's hopes for the future brightened when the Union Pacific decided to erect shops and a roundhouse as well as a railroad hotel, on which construction began in the summer of 1868. That summer, too, saw the beginning of the Denver Pacific Railroad from Denver to connect with the Union Pacific at Cheyenne. Financed by Denver interests, this line was later to merge with the Kansas Pacific, which was building west from Kansas City, and was to provide the Colorado city with rail connections to the East via two routes. The Denver Pacific route can be seen at the lower right-hand corner of the view of 1870, a connection that brought some benefit to Cheyenne but far more to its rival to the south, which soon outstripped Cheyenne in the race for supremacy as the major city on the eastern slope of the Rockies.

With the organization of the territory of Wyoming in 1869 Governor John Campbell designated Cheyenne as the provisional capital. Eventually, as in the other western territories, other cities attempted to secure this prize. Laramie became Cheyenne's chief competitor. In 1873 the House passed a capital removal bill, which it sent to the Council the upper chamber of territorial government. Fearing they would be defeated, the Cheyenne numbers failed to appear and thus deprived the Council of a quorum. A rump session of the Council passed the measure anyway, but it was vetoed by the governor.[16] The issue was finally settled in 1886, when the legislature approved the construction of the

capitol in Cheyenne, the state university at Laramie, and an insane asylum at Evanston. The other contender for recognition, Rawlins, obtained its share of the pork barrel two years later when the legislature passed an appropriation to erect the penitentiary at that city.

The Cheyenne of 1882, shown in Figure 16.6, was therefore a capital without a capitol. It could, however, boast of a city park seven blocks north of the railroad on the axis of Ransom Street whose southern end terminated at the railroad hotel. North and west of the park, fronting on Twenty-Fourth Street, the capitol was erected on two blocks consolidated as one. Hill Street provided a vista from the Capitol toward the business district, which occupied the area immediately to the west of Hill Street and extended three or four blocks northward from the railroad.

From Cheyenne, the Union Pacific built across the southern edge of Wyoming to Laramie, which Dodge's surveyors laid out on the usual grid system. It, too, enjoyed a boom and then watched much of its population depart for the next terminal town. Benton, planned by railroad agents, yielded a reported $17,000 in town lot revenues.[17] The total profits realized from townsite development by the Union Pacific have apparently never been calculated. They were, of course, enormous when one remembers that the land cost nothing, surveying costs were kept to a minimum, and land sales were handled by agents who also performed other duties. In these early years of construction, revenues from land sales, in which town lots bulked large, must have exceeded those derived from freight charges.

Profits of this magnitude naturally attracted numerous speculators. Some were not connected with any railroad but seized opportunities where they could to create new towns along or near the western railroads. Others worked with the railroads in various ways but did not hesitate to engage in purely private speculation on their own account.

Among the latter was the colorful eccentric, George Francis Train. Writing his autobiography in 1902 at the age of 74, Train claimed much of the credit for the development of the Union Pacific and stated that he had been responsible for the selection of Tacoma as the terminus of the Northern Pacifc line, but commented that these activities were only the beginning of "a hundred other projects, which . . . would have transformed the West in a few years." One of his plans "was the creation of a chain of great towns across the continent, connecting Boston with San Francisco by a magnificent highway of cities."[18]

In 1866 Train concentrated his operations in Omaha. Albert Richardson described him as "the head of a great company called the Credit

Figure 16.6 View of Cheyenne, Wyoming: 1882

Foncier, organized for dealing in lands and stocks—for building cities along the railway from the Missouri to Salt Lake. This corporation had been clothed by the Nebraska legislature with nearly every power imaginable, save that of reconstructing the late rebel States."[19] In Omaha, Train purchased 500 acres of land at the outskirts of the city, platted a portion of it into lots, erected a number of prefabricated dwellings shipped from Chicago, and also invested in hotel property.[20]

Train also purchased 800 acres of land adjoining Columbus, Nebraska, which he began promoting as the future capital of the state and the most desirable place for the seat of government for the entire country. At his Hammond House hotel he set aside suites for the president of the United States and the chief executive of the Union Pacific.[21] He projected another great hotel in Cheyenne where he arrived in November, 1867, in the company of Thomas C. Durant, the vice president of the railroad. According to one observer, Train "had not been in town six hours" before he organized a company to build a three-story structure 132 feet square. This building, like virtually all of the projects conceived in the fertile brain of this frontier promoter, was never completed.[22]

The linking of the Union Pacific and the Central Pacific at Promontory Point, Utah, on May 10, 1869, gave to the new towns along the transcontinental line substantial advantages over rival communities not so favorably served by rail transportation or lacking rail connections altogether. Railroad and townsite promoters in other parts of the Great Plains were soon busy with their own projects for additional transcontinental lines.

The Northern Pacific, chartered in 1864 but not active until 1870, began its movement westward when it entered Dakota Territory from Minnesota to reach Fargo on the west bank of the Red River early in 1872. From Fargo, the railroad was projected in an almost straight line westward across what is now North Dakota. Thomas P. Canfield, president of the Lake Superior and Puget Sound Company, a railroad subsidiary established to plan townsites along the route, followed the survey line to the Missouri River to select sites for towns.

On the James River, halfway between the Minnesota line and the Missouri, Canfield founded Jamestown, shown in Figure 16.7 as it existed in 1883. It was then enjoying the fruits of a great land boom made possible by the development of rail transportation that brought thousands of homesteaders to the Dakotas. Towns grew as agricultural lands were brought under cultivation, and there was lively speculation in town lots. In 1882 the James River National Bank purchased a lot for

its new building, which appears on the view as the largest structure fronting Main Street at the corner of Fifth Avenue. They paid $2,700 for the lot; four years earlier it had sold for $25. It was reported that a dozen speculators in Jamestown had each made from $75,000 to $150,000 during three years prior to 1882. So widespread was townsite speculation that the Minneapolis *Morning Call* proposed that the coat of arms of the territory should consist of "a real estate agent rampant supporting a corner lot, a la Atlas, on a field verdant dotted with railroad spikes and champagne bottles, alternately, a drove of railroad stock being watered in the distance."[23]

The routine grid plan of Jamestown was repeated at Bismarck on the east bank of the Missouri River. The townsite plat appears in Figure 16.8 and shows the blocks on either side of the railroad, which the company retained. The usual group of speculators, gamblers, loafers and other types familiar to the end-of-track communities had already gathered at what they believed would be the location of the town according to the preliminary railroad surveys. Immediately before the line was extended to the area in 1873, however, company officials shrewdly shifted the right-of-way about a mile north and were able to plat their town on a site under control of the line. At first named Edwinton for Edwin F. Johnson, the railroad's chief engineer, Bismarck was renamed later in 1873 to flatter the German Chancellor and to attract German capital to the line, which was experiencing severe financial difficulties with the collapse of Jay Cooke's empire in the panic of 1873.

Bismarck remained the western terminus of the Northern Pacific for the next six years. During that period the city prospered, especially after the discovery of gold in the Black Hills in 1874, when Bismarck served as the base for supplies destined for Deadwood and the other mining towns. The Dakota land boom of the early 1880s aided Bismarck's growth after the railroad had resumed its march toward the Pacific. A further impetus to development came in 1883. Following considerable maneuvering, Bismarck secured the designation as capital of Dakota Territory after a commission selected for this purpose had toured the territory and examined proposals from eleven communities.[24]

The statute required that any city selected must provide at least $100,000 and 160 acres of land. Bismarck offered double this amount of land, and this area laid out into lots added to the vast amount of subdivided land that then surrounded the original townsite. The extent of these surveys can be seen in Figure 16.9. This map was published in 1883, a momentous year for the city. It had achieved its ambition to be-

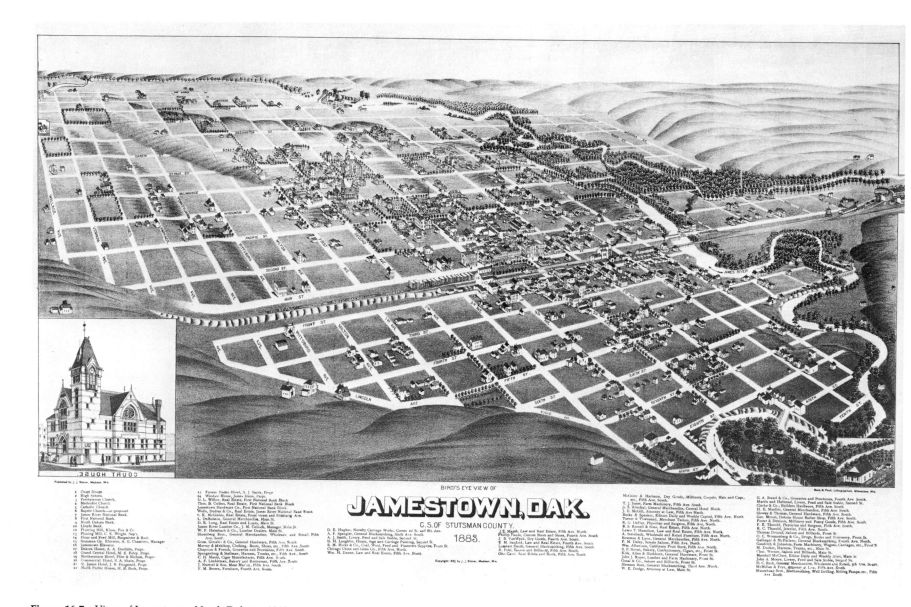

Figure 16.7 View of Jamestown, North Dakota: 1883

come the territorial capital, and the railroad that had been responsible for its founding had finally connected with other lines in the West to provide a link with the Pacific Coast.

Henry Villard, then president of the Northern Pacific, brought ex-President Grant to Bismarck on their way west to duplicate the golden spike ceremony that had marked the completion of the Union Pacific a decade and a half earlier. The city celebrated their visit with an elaborate ceremony at which citizens of the town proudly joined territorial officials in laying the capitol's cornerstone. Mingling with eastern and foreign guests was no less a personage than Sitting Bull, who evidently had been forgiven for his part in the killing of General Custer, formerly a familiar figure in Bismarck on his frequent visits from nearby Fort Lincoln.

Even at the height of its boom, Bismarck did not begin to fill the nearly endless grid that speculators had surveyed in hopes of seeing a great metropolis rise on the upper Missouri. The city in 1883, shown in Figure 16.10, occupied only a modest portion of the gigantic network of straight streets that would-be real estate developers had so mechanically traced up and down the hills east of the river. When the boom had run its course by the mid 1880s, Bismarck scarcely exceeded 3,000. By 1890 it had lost one-third of its population despite the fact that Bismarck was retained as the capital of the new state of North Dakota.

Construction on the Northern Pacific finally resumed, and by 1881 surveys had been extended to the Rocky Mountains along the Yellowstone River in southern Montana. Midway across the modern state, a townsite company organized by the railroad, the Minnesota and Montana Land and Improvement Company, began the promotion of another typical railroad town. At a point where topography required a crossing of the river and where a division point would be needed, officials of the line began seeking a suitable site. Examining maps of the sections granted the railroad, they noticed that the government base line passed through the Yellowstone Valley. They observed that along this line the alternate odd-numbered sections to which they were entitled did not join at the corners but had a common boundary along the survey base. They were thus able to claim two complete sections or twice the normal 640 acres for townsite purposes.[25]

At the nearby settlement of Coulson, land speculators and others attracted to potential terminal towns had already begun to gather. The new town sponsored by the railroad, however, soon eclipsed the earlier community, and business and speculative activity concentrated on Billings, named for Frederick Billings, the president of the Northern Pacific from 1879 to 1881.

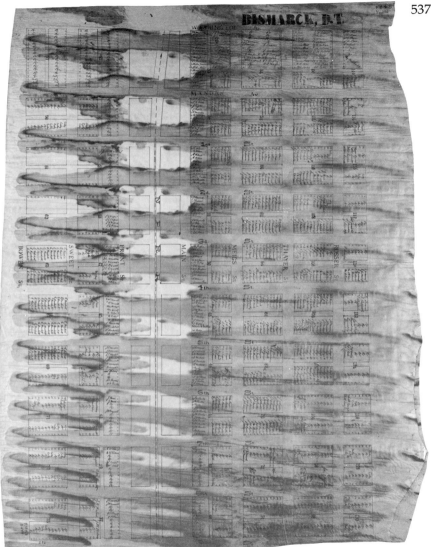

Figure 16.8   Plan of Bismarck, North Dakota: ca. 1873

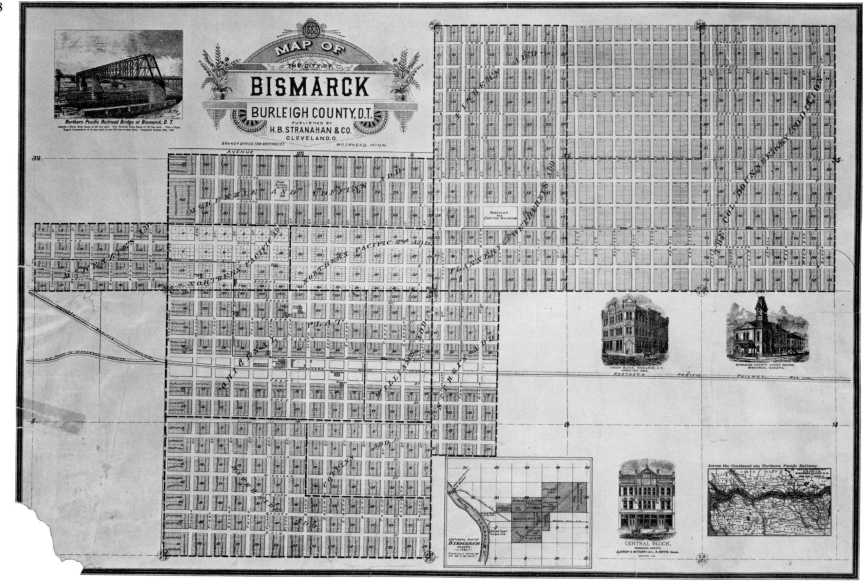

Figure 16.9 Plan of Bismarck, North Dakota: 1883

Figure 16.10 View of Bismarck, North Dakota: 1883

Herman Clark, head of construction for the line, laid out the town, and the survey reproduced in Figure 16.11 was completed by April, 1882. It was designed to accommodate 20,000 residents, and Clark announced plans to build saw mills, a bank, a huge hotel, a brick foundry, and shipping facilities for cattle. The new town was widely advertised in such cities as St. Paul, Chicago, and New York, and within a few months the company had sold nearly all of its lots. By the spring of 1882 tents and shacks dotted the townsite, and more substantial structures were being erected on the streets near the railroad where business lots had sold originally for $500 but soon were changing hands at much higher prices.

In a rare burst of candor a publicist for the Northern Pacific described the promotional efforts that had created this community in so short a time: "Billings . . . is a good example of a town made by the boom process. A few months ago it had no existence save in the brains of its inventors. The bare prairie was staked out in streets, avenues and parks. . . . A map was engraved, and within a few weeks after the place got its name, the 'Billings boom' began to be talked of. . . . Billings lots were advertized in every town from St. Paul to Miles City, and whole blocks were sold in Chicago and New York. The purchasers knew no more about the valley of the Yellowstone than about that of the Congo. . . . Within sixty days from the time when Billings got a local habitation and a name, lots to the value of $202,000 were sold within its limits, and before thirty more days had elapsed the purchasers had advanced the imaginary value of their holdings from one hundred to three hundred per cent."[26]

Much of the land in the town was held by absentee speculators. Local newspapers estimated in June, 1882, that 2,000 persons owned town lots but that the resident population did not exceed 500. The future, however, seemed bright enough for a street railway company to be organized in that year, and its promoters were able to sell 900 shares of stock. The first horse-drawn cars went in service the following spring. When the first trains reached Billings on August 22, 1882, traveling across the Yellowstone River bridge, the pace of development increased, and the designation of Billings as the seat of Yellowstone County helped to attract additional settlers. Stockyards stimulated the development of cattle shipping. In 1883 nearly 20,000 cattle and more than 600,000 pounds of wool were shipped to eastern markets over the Northern Pacific from Billings. Cattle shipments doubled the following year.

Like earlier railway towns, Billings experienced a declining rate of growth once the initial excitement attending the founding subsided and the railroad turned its attention to other townsite promotions. A disastrous fire in 1885 and a series of droughts that depressed the cattle business resulted in a loss of population during the end of the city's first decade. Better years followed, however, and the view in Figure 16.12 shows the thriving city as it appeared in 1904.

By that year the Burlington Railroad also served the city. Its line (in the foreground of Figure 16.12) skirted the edge of North Park, one of the two large public reservations set aside in the original plan. The Yellowstone County Fairgrounds had been constructed on this site, while South Park, diagonally across the city, served less specialized recreational needs of the expanding community. The foundation of Billings may have been based largely on promises and promotional exaggerations, but in the competition for urban survival on the western railroad frontier, Billings succeeded in living up to the expectations of its planners.

The region lying between the Union Pacific route and that of the Northern Pacific was not neglected, although construction of railroads across South Dakota lagged somewhat behind other areas. The earliest settlement in Dakota Territory followed the pattern established in Kansas and Missouri slightly earlier. Beginning in 1856 townsite companies from Iowa and Minnesota began to plat typical frontier grid settlements along the Missouri and the Big Sioux rivers in the extreme southeastern corner of the territory. The Western Town Company in May, 1857, claimed 320 acres some 60 miles up the Big Sioux and named the community Sioux Falls. The Dakota Land Company that same year began to stake out claims to several townsites: Sioux Falls City near the other town of nearly the same name; Flandreau, farther down the river; and Medary, between the two. In 1858 and 1859 the Dakota Company surveyed six other townsites in the Big Sioux Valley, the lower portions of which forms the border between northwestern Iowa and southeastern South Dakota.

Another town company, the Upper Missouri Land Company, founded by Captain John Blair Todd and Colonel Daniel Frost, began operations in the spring of 1858. These two traders hoped to claim townsites in the region between the Big Sioux and Missouri rivers as soon as a treaty of cession was included between the federal government and the Yankton Sioux Indians. As licensed traders they could enter the Indian lands legally, and as they went about their normal business affairs they also built small posts at sites likely to prove attractive as towns. Three of their eight locations were to constitute the principal early communities on the Missouri: Vermillion, Yankton, and Bon Homme.[27]

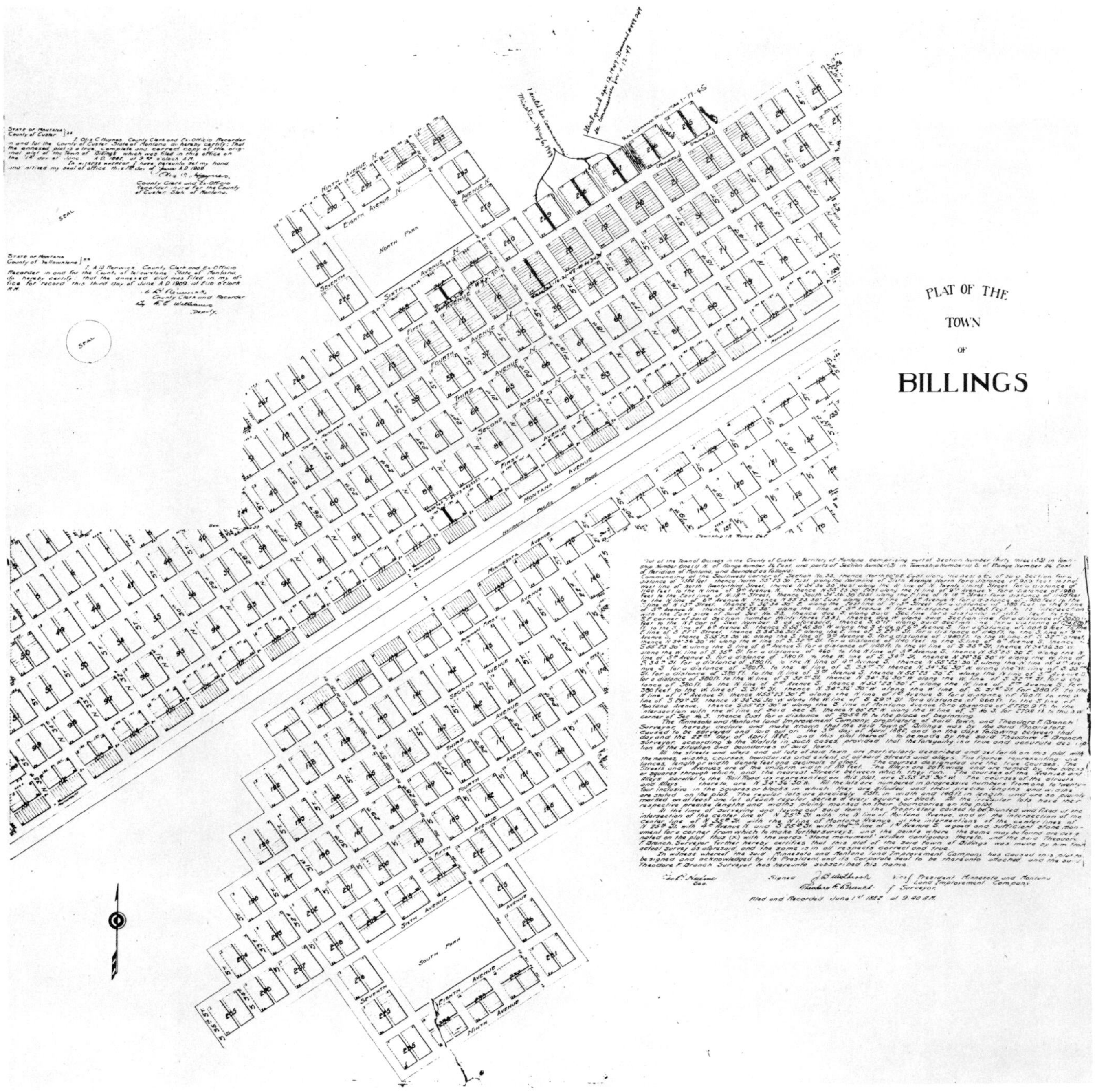

Figure 16.11
Plan of Billings, Montana: 1882

Figure 16.12   View of Billings, Montana: 1904

These settlements were apparently not nearly so elaborate as those laid out in Kansas and Nebraska in the boom years of 1854-57. The plan of Yankton in 1859 as re-surveyed in 1866 appears in Figure 16.13. It had been formally platted in the former year as soon as the Indian territory became available for settlement, although it had been occupied by squatters prior to that time. The simple little gridiron design running back from the river, with its market square occupying the block in the northeast corner, probably was typical of the other Dakota communities that had their beginnings at this time.

Todd and others lobbied for the establishment of a territorial government, and when Congress finally responded in 1861 Todd succeeded in persuading Governor William Jayne to make Yankton the provisional seat of government. In the tradition of frontier politics, the location of the territorial capital became a major issue. One early Yankton settler who was to become a prominent politician and historian stated that, during the legislative debates that ultimatley confirmed Yankton's position, "Excitement ran to a high pitch during a few days on the last stages of the bill. . . . A little blood was shed, much whiskey drank, a few eyes blacked, revolvers drawn, and some running done."[28]

Yankton and the other settlements of the first Dakota frontier found it difficult to adjust to the new era of the railroad. The Dakota Southern Railroad was promoted by local interests, connecting Sioux City, Iowa, with Vermillion in 1872 and reaching Yankton the following year. This and other local lines lacked the resources to push westward, and Congress refused to approve land grants similar to those that subsidized the construction of the Union Pacific and the Northern Pacific. Local bond issues by municipalities and counties proved insufficient.[29] The panic in 1873 put a temporary stop to further railroad activities for several years.

Two major lines began construction toward the end of the decade. The Chicago and North Western crossed the Minnesota border in the summer of 1878 and began to push west toward the Missouri River, following an alignment roughly through the middle of what was to become the state of South Dakota. One mile west of the James River in 1880, the railroad's subsidiary, the Western Town and Lot Company, created the town of Huron on a site selected two years earlier by its manager, Marvin Hughitt. Railroad depots, shops, offices, and round-houses provided a firm economic base, settlers were attracted to the town, it became an important marketing center, and—a few years later—a major but ultimately unsuccessful contender for the honor and profit of becoming the state capital.[30]

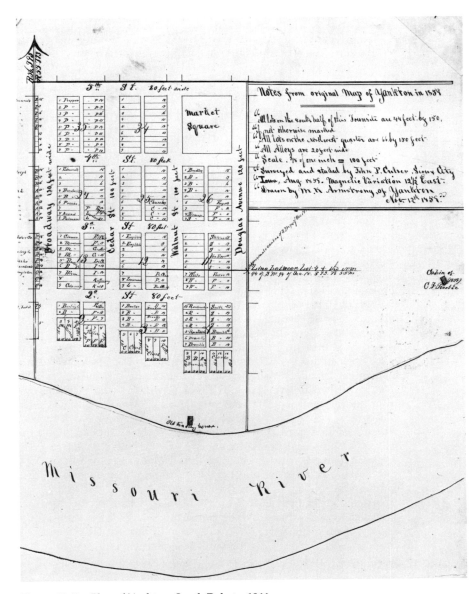

Figure 16.13   Plan of Yankton, South Dakota: 1866

Meanwhile at a site on the east side of the Missouri opposite Fort Pierre, company agents posing as prospective cattle ranchers quietly bought out claims of squatters at that location. There they laid out Pierre in the pattern shown in Figure 16.14 as the modest beginnings of the town that was ultimately selected as the capital of South Dakota.[31] Pierre owed much of its early growth to the Black Hills trade, for it served as a freighting center from which goods and supplies proceeded by wagon from the railroad terminus.

Along the northern segment of South Dakota, the Chicago, Milwaukee, and St. Paul line was responsible for the creation of many new towns during the prosperous years of the late 1870s and the first part of the next decade. Entering the territory from Ortonville, Minnesota, in the spring of 1880, the line was speedily graded and constructed westward. In January, 1881, Aberdeen, shown in Figure 16.15 as it existed two years later, was laid out under the direction of Charles H. Prior, immigration agent for the railroad, to accommodate the expected rush of settlers and speculators. Its spacious courthouse square, city park, and church and school sites provided an attractive framework for settlement. Within a year it had 500 permanent residents, and its growth thereafter was steady, as other railroads arrived to make the new town the hub of transportation in the northeastern part of the state and an important center of wholesaling and distributing.

A second line of the Chicago, Milwaukee, and St. Paul extended across the southern part of the territory. Its goal was to reach the Missouri River to tap the wagon freighting trade to the Black Hills. After the company planned the town of Mitchell on the James River early in 1880, it pushed down American Creek to the Missouri. On the east bank the railroad townsite company laid out Chamberlain. The plan was curiously irregular, as shown in the plat of the town ten years later reproduced in Figure 16.16. The original townsite appears along the railroad with its edge bordering the river. By the time this drawing was prepared, several disconnected additions had been made as land speculators vied with one another for town lots at the new end-of-track community.[32]

Virtually all of the railroad towns planned either by the rail companies or by individuals owning property along their routes used the orderly, if unimaginative, gridiron system of straight streets and rectangular blocks. Even Chamberlain's irregularities represented only a slight departure from this type of design and doubtless resulted from prior ownership of portions of the site by a few individuals who were unwilling to have their lands replatted.

Figure 16.14 Plan of Pierre, South Dakota: 1880

Figure 16.17 shows one intentional departure from the grid system—the plan of Elliott, North Dakota—as laid out by Thomas M. Elliott at the junction of the Fargo and Southwestern line with the Dakota and Great Southern Railway. A promotional guide published in 1884 states that "in platting the town site Mr. Elliott executed the counterpart of the plan of his home town in the Dominion of Canada." Mr. Elliott doubtless came to the Dakota prairies from either Guelf or Gooderich, Ontario, both of which have radial street patterns nearly identical to the town Elliott named after himself.

The intention of the developer, we are told, was "to have the business portion of the town . . . built up on one side of the . . . railway and

Figure 16.15 View of Aberdeen, South Dakota: 1883

the residence portion on the other side." The plat, the guide continues, "presents a pretty picture, and has the merit of being unlike any other town on the line." The author felt certain that this "novel plan . . . will attract visitors and secure investors." The reader was asked to "fill, in your imagination, every block forming the circle around the Parks with good substantial business houses and neat, attractive residences, and people the town with three to five thousand . . . ; dot thickly the streets and thoroughfares with teams drawing into town heavy laden vehicles

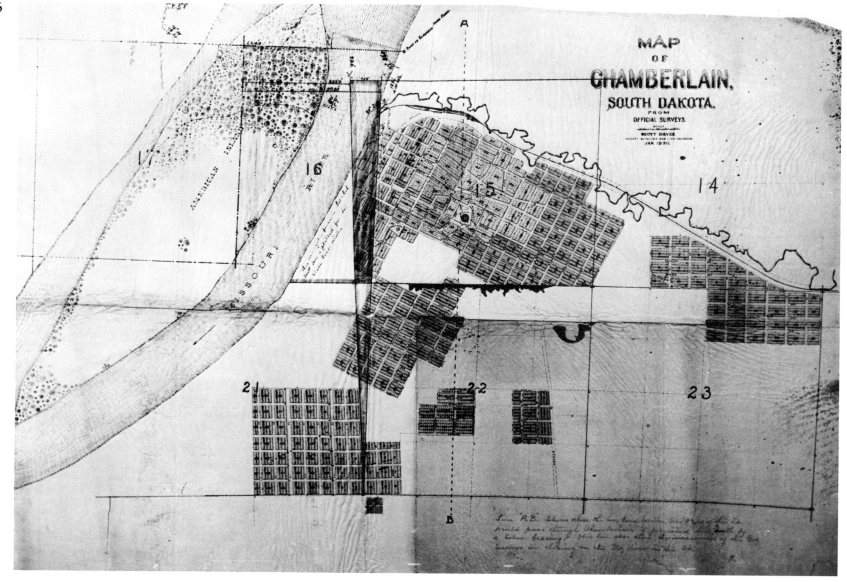

Figure 16.16   Plan of Chamberlain, South Dakota: 1890

burdened with the liberal products of the thousands of fertile acres of well improved farms tributary to the town . . . and you have the outline and shadow of the picture, that will in reality ornament Tom Elliott's town site in the near future."[33]

While imagination might thus produce a vision of the future town, reality proved less fortunate. Perhaps the whimsical pinwheel pattern struck potential settlers as more novel than attractive. Or, with what amounted to two towns in which to select a lot, the choice seemed too difficult. More likely, the location of Elliott may not have been a favorable place for farmers to shop or market their crops. Whatever the reason, Elliott never developed as planned. One half of the town was abandoned altogether, and the 100 or so modern inhabitants can barely trace the original odd street system in the remnants of the other half that has survived to the present day.

In that portion of the Great Plains served by the Union Pacific and its rival lines to the north, virtually every important community owed its origins to a railroad townsite company. The railroads regarded the creation of towns and their promotion as an essential element of business enterprise. Not only did their creation afford splendid opportunities for quick profits from land sales, but their continued existence was vital in the development of passenger and freight traffic. Wherever possible, therefore, the railroad companies created their own communities.

In much of Kansas, settlement preceded the coming of the railroad, and there were fewer opportunities for the development of entirely new towns. But here, as elsewhere, it was the railroads that brought prosperity to existing communities or, if the lines bypassed established settlements, left them ruined. In central and southern Kansas a unique category of towns flourished for a time because of a combination of circumstances prevailing for a period of two decades or so beginning in the late 1860s. These were the cattle towns—the shipping points that sprang up at the points where cattle trails from Texas met the Kansas Pacific and the Atchison, Topeka, and Santa Fe lines as they built west. More colorful and rowdy than beautiful or well planned, these towns nonetheless possessed a distinctive character that set them apart from other communities of western America.

Well before the Civil War, cattle raising in Texas had become a major industry. The Texas longhorn was a hardy animal, and he needed to be, for if the Texas range was a good area for production it lay a long distance from markets. While cattlemen shipped some of their steers to New Orleans and other cities by steamboat, most of the animals reached the market on foot. The first trail drive to New Orleans took

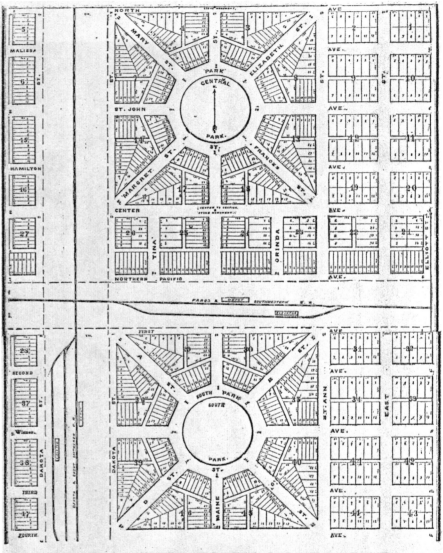

Figure 16.17 Plan of Elliott, North Dakota: 1884

place in 1842. One herd of Texas cattle reached Ohio four years later, and after the Gold Rush to California enterprising Texas drovers regularly coaxed their herds over the long journey west to fill the demand for beef that had so suddenly developed in the San Francisco and Mother Lode regions. In 1856 some herds were driven all the way to Chicago.[34]

The Civil War interrupted the cattle trade, but in 1866 several Texas cattlemen sent their herds northward along the Shawnee Trail by way of Fort Smith, Arkansas, to Sedalia, Missouri, served by the newly constructed Missouri Pacific Railroad. While a good part of western Missouri remained open at that time, many areas through which the herds passed had been settled and fenced. Even experienced trail drivers could not prevent their steers from damaging fences and crops. Moreover, local cattle breeders correctly realized that a vastly increased supply of cattle from other producing areas would depress prices. More important was the fear that local stock of beef or dairy cattle would be infected by the dreaded splenic fever to which hardy Texas longhorns were virtually immune but to which northern breeds were susceptible.[35]

Outraged farmers in western Missouri and eastern Kansas succeeded in securing the passage of quarantine laws to prohibit entirely invasion of their region by Texas cattle. Where law enforcement lagged, vigilantes did not hesitate to act. Cattlemen, both producers and buyers, turned elsewhere in their search for suitable shipping points. It was the beginning of the conflict between settled farmers and those who relied on the open range for their living. As the plains frontier receded westward during the next 20 years, the cattle trails leading north from Texas had to move also, usually resulting in the establishment of a new terminal point along the advancing rail lines from which shipments could be made to eastern and northern meat packing centers.

The first of the major Kansas cattle towns was Abilene, 100 miles up the Kansas River from Topeka and, in the spring of 1867, for a few months the end of the line of the Kansas Pacific Railroad. It was here that Joseph G. McCoy decided to build a stockyard, pens, and loading chutes to ship cattle east by rail. He also constructed Drover's Cottage, a hotel to accommodate cattle buyers from eastern cities and the Texans in charge of the herds.

Abilene had been laid out in 1861 by Charles Thompson on the extremely simple and unprepossessing design shown in Figure 16.18. Although Thompson succeeded in getting the town designated as the county seat of Dickinson County, his other promotional efforts failed to

attract many settlers. McCoy initially had inspected the vicinity of Junction City, some miles east, and had also ventured further west to look at Salina, which was on the route of the Kansas Pacific. High land prices at Junction City led McCoy to Abilene, which, in his words "was a very small dead place, consisting of about one dozen log huts—low, small, rude affairs, four-fifths of which were covered with dirt for roofing; indeed, but one shingle roof could be seen in the whole city. The business of the burg was conducted in two small rooms, mere log huts, and of course the inevitable saloon, also in a log hut, was to be found."[36]

McCoy's enterprise changed Abilene from a sleepy hamlet to a busy, raucous, prosperous, and vice-ridden town almost overnight. East of the original townsite on his 250-acre tract McCoy laid out an almost identical gridiron addition oriented to the railroad and the adjoining stockyard, and soon this was the scene of much construction of cattle shipping and transient living accommodations. The largest building was Drover's Cottage with nearly 100 rooms in its three-story frame structure.[37] This building with its long veranda facing the railroad can be seen in Figure 16.19. Nearby at the edge of town lay McCoy's stockyards and loading chutes.

McCoy sent agents to Texas to advertise the new facilities, and although it was too late in the year to divert much trade to Abilene, some 35,000 head of Texas longhorns were shipped to the packinghouses of Kansas City and Chicago or to farms in Kansas, Nebraska, or Illinois for fattening. Business in 1868 increased enormously, and in the four-year period beginning that spring, more than a million head of cattle passed through McCoy's yards.[38]

The physical fabric of the town expanded with the cattle business. By 1871 the resident population approached 1,000, and the town contained a brick courthouse and a school house of stone, a jail, three hotels in addition to the Drover's Cottage, two banks, several boarding hotels, at least three restaurants, a number of clothing stores where the cowboys could refit themselves after the long ride from Texas, two lumber yards, a blacksmith shop, a variety of other mercantile establishments, and two churches. Abilene's fame obviously depended less on places of worship than locations where spirits of other kinds might be invoked. Estimates of the number of saloons vary, but no cowboy whose throat was parched from the dust of the trail had to walk far to satisfy his thirst. Gambling and drinking facilities could also be enjoyed in a group of 20 or so frame dance halls and brothels north of and some distance removed from the railroad tracks.[39]

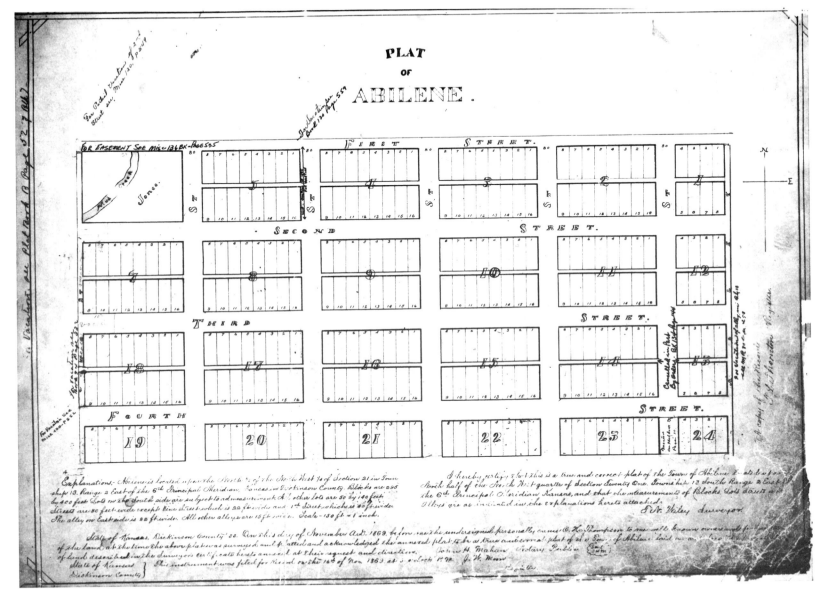

Figure 16.18 Plan of Abilene, Kansas: 1869

Figure 16.19   View of Drovers Cottage in Abilene, Kansas: ca. 1870

Abilene was the first of the Kansas "cow towns," but it established a pattern to which they all conformed. Rough, noisy, crude, lively, and at times dangerous, each, like Abilene, flourished as a cattle shipping point only for the period when it enjoyed the momentary advantage of being located at the end of the railway and beyond the rapidly advancing farming frontier.

Ellsworth, 60 miles west, succeeded Abilene as the principal shipping point on the Kansas Pacific after 1871. By the middle of June in the following year, with several stock shipments already made, 100,000 head of cattle could be found in the immediate vicinity awaiting cattle trains to take them to market. Here the Kansas Pacific Railway installed a siding and purchased, repaired, and enlarged a stockyard built earlier by a St. Louis cattle dealer. Many of the tradesmen of Abilene and, doubtless, most of the "soiled doves" who inhabited the brothels there transferred their operations to the new trade center.[40]

Ellsworth soon had a formidable rival in Wichita 85 miles directly south of Abilene. The Santa Fe line had been building southwest from Topeka and, by the spring of 1871, had reached a point near Newton, a rival of Wichita in the northeast corner of Sedgwick County, of which Wichita was the county seat. Wichita was farther south, a location that would result in a shorter overland drive from Texas, but the engineers of the railroad, after making a preliminary survey of a route through Wichita, decided to bypass the town and run the line west from Newton.

Citizens of Wichita eventually succeeded in obtaining county approval of $200,000 in bonds to finance the Wichita and South Western Rail Road Company which, with help from the Santa Fe, was built north to connect with the main line at Newton. Completed in May, 1872, the railroad transported over 70,000 head of cattle in that year from its immense and newly constructed stockyard.[41]

Two rival landowners were responsible for Wichita's original layout. Each attempted to gain the upper hand in diverting urban growth to his own portion of the city, and the city for many years reflected in its physical pattern the competition between these men and their associates. The site had first been settled by the Wichita Indians in 1864, and their presence attracted several traders. Among them was Jesse Chisholm, who opened a trail southward through Indian Territory in what is now Oklahoma. It was the Chisholm Trail, over which the Texas cattle were later to be driven to Abilene. The Wichitas departed in 1867, but systematic white settlement was delayed until the issue of Indian ownership was resolved by treaty two years later.

While the treaty commissioners were still negotiating with the Indians, a group of speculators in April, 1868, formed the Wichita Town and Land Company at Emporia with the intention of laying out a huge city on 640 acres of land at the confluence of the Arkansas and Little Arkansas rivers and with an adjoining 320 acres surveyed into five-acre plots. The group sent David Munger to establish a store and hotel and arrange for the town plan to be prepared. The town company abandoned this ambitious scheme when they found that the terms of the treaty provided that land in the area would be made available only to persons already living on the site and in tracts no larger than 120 acres.

Munger promptly filed a pre-emption claim and began selling town lots according to a plan that he recorded on March 25, 1870, as soon as his title was confirmed. Munger's plat is reproduced in Figure 16.20, a conventional gridiron design with Central Avenue as its southern boundary and with two blocks set aside for a courthouse and a park. A few hours earlier, however, another town plan had been recorded by

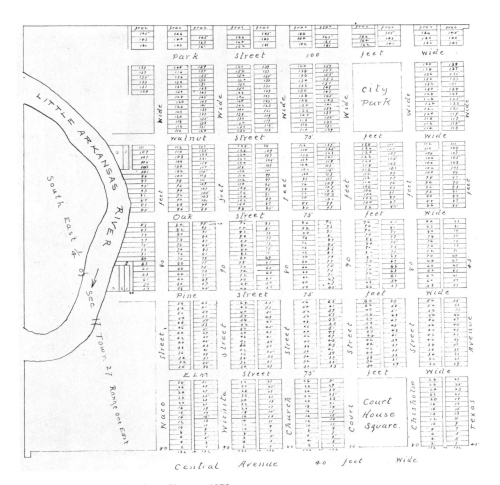

Figure 16.20　Plan of Wichita, Kansas: 1870

William Greiffenstein, who had arrived in the area the previous year, purchased the eastern half of a quarter-section of land adjoining Munger's claim to the south from the first squatter to have his title confirmed, and decided to enter the business of town promotion.

Greiffenstein's plan as copied from his drawing on a piece of brown paper torn from a sack in his store is shown in Figure 16.21.[42] The

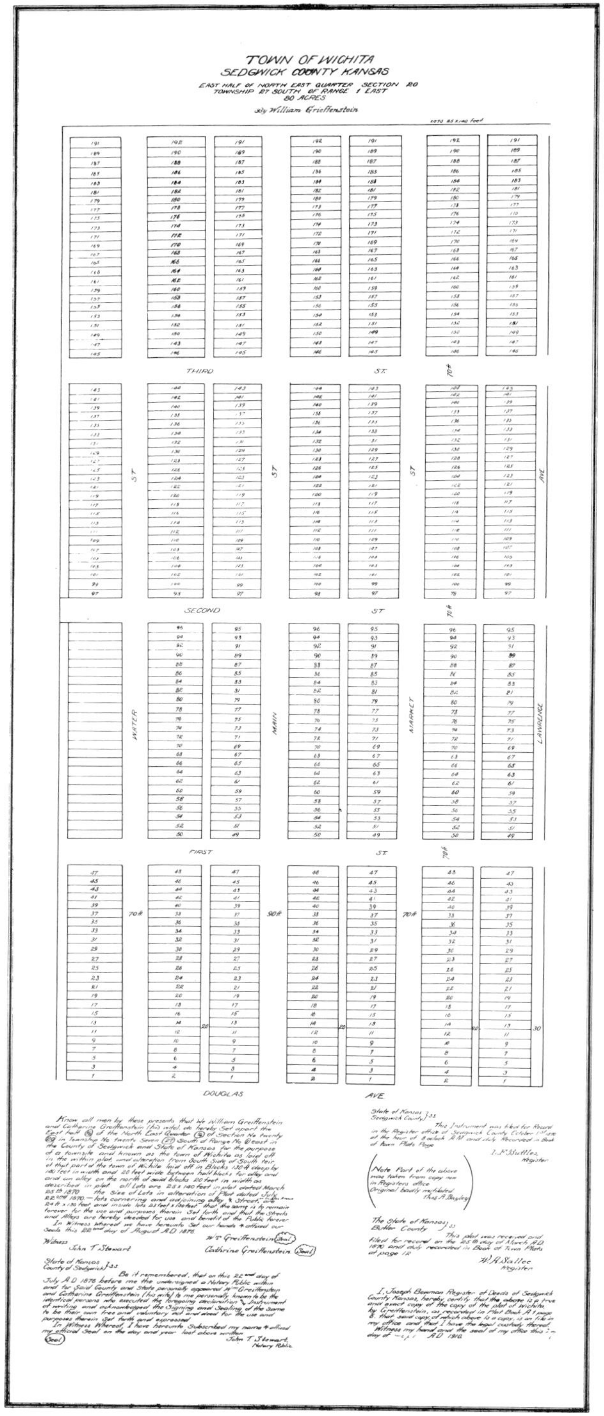

Figure 16.21
Plan of Wichita, Kansas: 1870

northern boundary lay along Munger's Central Avenue. At the other end the blocks terminated at Douglas Avenue. This was given a width of 114 feet when Greiffenstein extended his town in February, 1871, by recording a second plat on his own newly confirmed pre-emption claim. This added three blocks to the south between Water Street and Lawrence Avenue. The Main Street of Greiffenstein's plats was a continuation of Munger's Church Street, a name that was soon dropped in favor of North Main.

Greiffenstein obviously possessed no skills as a town planner, but he proved to be a shrewd promoter in attracting development to his section of Wichita at the expense of Munger and his backers. Where his two plats joined, at the intersection of Main Street and Douglas Avenue, Greiffenstein gave away several choice lots to businessmen who agreed to build on them at once. He himself constructed a brick office building, the Eagle Block, on one of the corners. Munger also followed the practice of donating lots, but although he was able to attract two banks and several other businesses to locate along North Main Street, his portion of Wichita lagged behind despite its earlier start. Most of the important commercial buildings along Main Street could be found south of Central Avenue rather than on the portion of Main under Munger's ownership.

The new property owners in the Douglas Avenue area joined with Greiffenstein in promoting the construction of a toll bridge extending the street across the Arkansas River. Opened in July, 1872, the bridge produced revenues of nearly $10,000 by the end of the year—a sum equal to about one-third of its cost. It was not only the revenue that proved attractive but the trade that its traffic brought to Douglas Avenue and to that portion of Main Street within the original Greiffenstein tract.

The Wichita of that period is shown in Figure 16.22. The view is to the southeast with the Douglas Avenue bridge prominently visible in the foreground. The main business corner can be seen exactly where Greiffenstein wished it, and the principal commercial buildings of the town extended for three blocks north on Main and toward the river on Douglas Avenue. Already landowners other than Munger and Greiffenstein had platted their property into rectangular blocks to extend the city up and down the river as well as eastward toward the tracks of the new railroad.

The population at the time the view was published approached 2,000. Like the other Kansas cattle towns, Wichita was at first inhabited predominantly by men, but the city in 1875 had an almost even balance

This panorama of Wichita was drawn in 1873

Figure 16.22 View of Wichita, Kansas: 1873

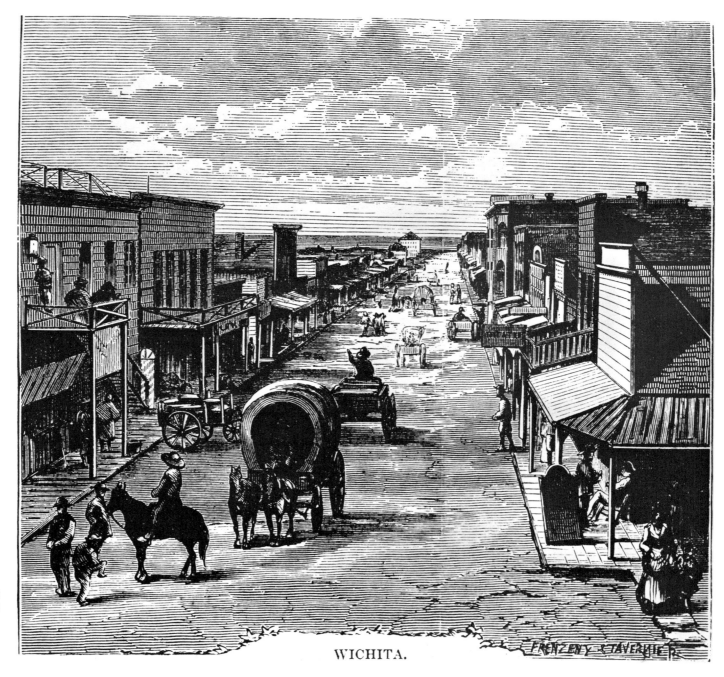

Figure 16.23
View of Wichita, Kansas: 1873

WICHITA.

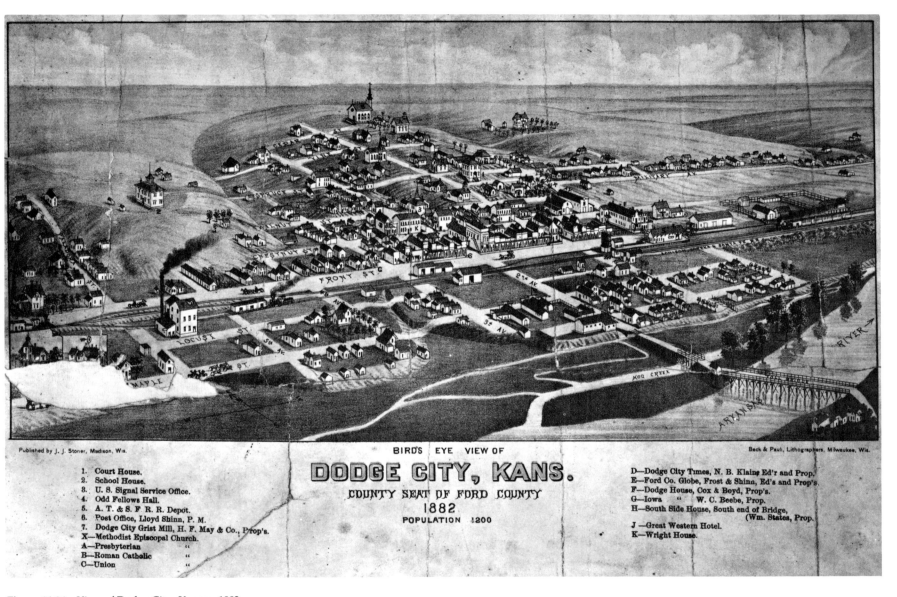

BIRD'S EYE VIEW OF

DODGE CITY, KANS.

COUNTY SEAT OF FORD COUNTY
1882
POPULATION 1200

1. Court House.
2. School House.
3. U. S. Signal Service Office.
4. Odd Fellows Hall.
5. A. T. & S. F. R. R. Depot.
6. Post Office, Lloyd Shinn, P. M.
7. Dodge City Grist Mill, H. F. May & Co., Prop's.
X—Methodist Episcopal Church.
A—Presbyterian "
B—Roman Catholic "
C—Union "

D—Dodge City Times, N. B. Klaine Ed'r and Prop.
E—Ford Co. Globe, Frost & Shinn, Ed's and Prop's.
F—Dodge House, Cox & Boyd, Prop's.
G—Iowa " W. C. Beebe, Prop.
H—South Side House, South end of Bridge,
(Wm. States, Prop.
J —Great Western Hotel.
K—Wright House.

Figure 16.24 View of Dodge City, Kansas: 1882

between the sexes in every age group.[43] The cattle trade attracted not only land speculators, merchants, suppliers, and commission agents but the less desirable elements of the frontier. Wichita had its problems, as did Abilene and the other railroad and cattle towns, with rowdy saloons, dance halls, whorehouses, and gambling dens. Efforts by local reformers to ban gambling, prostitution, and drinking met with only modest and sporadic success.[44] The inevitable decline in the cattle trade did more to domesticate Wichita than did all the activities of those engaged in the antivice movement.

By 1875 Texas cattle drovers began to seek other shipping points where they could avoid the growing opposition by Sedgwick County farmers who had begun to fence the plains and break the soil for wheat growing. The boom in land prices and building came to a halt, and Wichita declined somewhat in population until grain milling, local agricultural trading, and industry provided a further impetus for growth. Main Street today bears no resemblance to its appearance in 1873 shown in Figure 16.23. The old battles for supremacy between the "Douglas Avenue Crowd" and the "North-Enders" have been forgotten. Douglas and Main is still an important business corner, but it is but one of many in the heart of the largest city in Kansas. The old days are recalled, in a completely synthetic setting, by "Cowtown Wichita" on Slim Park Drive. There nearly 40 replicas of buildings of the cattle era can be inspected—as can "Old Abilene," a similar area in the first of the Kansas cattle towns—by those who hope to recapture some of the atmosphere of the days of the cowboys and the long, dusty trail drives from Texas.

Two months after Greiffenstein opened his toll bridge in 1872, the Santa Fé railroad reached Dodge City a few miles west of Fort Dodge on the Arkansas River. Enterprising officers of the fort had already formed a town company, entered a claim for 87 acres of land, and laid out a little town on the usual rectangular pattern. Many buffalo hides and a few cattle were shipped from there, but the cattle trade began in earnest when the railroad in 1877 constructed a stockyard exceeded in capacity only by the line's installation at Wichita. In that year a new cattle trail was opened from Texas—the Texas or Western Trail—and over it great herds began their slow movement to the Dodge City yards.[45] For several years Dodge City flourished as the most important cattle shipment center in Kansas before the farming frontier once again moved westward, bringing the fences and the tilled fields so hated by cattlemen.

Dodge City in 1882, at the height of its prosperity, appears in Figure 16.24. The legend below identifies the principal buildings of the town, which had a resident population three years later of just under 1,500

persons. Transient cattle buyers and cowboys who arrived during the summer brought this figure much higher and filled the streets, hotels, saloons, shops, and cafes. High cattle prices in 1882 brought wealth to everyone, and a bright future seemed assured.

Nevertheless, Dodge City succumbed to the same forces that had caused the decline of earlier cattle towns. Enclosure of range land by farmers made cattle driving difficult and eventually impossible. Legislation designed to prevent infection of local livestock by splenic fever caused the cattle trade to diminish, as did a drastic decrease in prices paid for livestock after 1882. Even without these factors, however, the days of the Kansas cattle towns were numbered. Railways constructed southwest to Texas in the 1880s at last made it possible for cattlemen to ship their steers directly to eastern and northern markets without the necessity of long drives to Kansas shipping points.

Samuel Prouty, editor of the Dodge City *Kansas Cowboy*, who earlier had vigorously fought the encroachment of farmers on trail and range land, conceded in 1885 that an era had passed: "Dodge City has been for the past ten years an exclusive cattle town. The cattle traffic made money for its citizens but it did not make a town. It was a question whether the country would ever warrant the making of a respectable town here. The rains of the past three years, the assurance that the soil of the country is susceptible of successful cultivation, the recent absorption of the public domain by settlers, the removal of the cattle trail and the rapidly disappearing cowboy, have now thoroughly convinced our people that a permanent commerical metropolis at this point is demanded by the needs of the country."[46]

Dodge City never achieved the metropolitan status envisaged by Prouty, but the modern little community has an atmosphere quite different from the old days when Bat Masterson and Wyatt Earp strode its streets and called at such lively frontier recreation centers as the Dodge House or the nearby Long Branch Saloon in their efforts to maintain law and order. Only a two-block reproduction of old Front Street, operated as a tourist attraction, recalls the days when Dodge City was the cowboy capital of the West.

During the years that the major transcontinental railroads filled the middle and northern great plains with hundreds of new towns, they were also engaged in similar land development projects in the mountain regions beyond. These lines and others built to provide north-south connections with the major routes were responsible for creating many of new communities in this more difficult terrain. It is to the railroad-created towns of this region that we now turn our attention.

XVII

Railroad Towns of the Mountain States and
the Southern Plains

SHORTLY before the Union Pacific laid its first track at Omaha, the Central Pacific line began construction of its portion of the great transcontinental route. On January 8, 1863, ground was broken at the foot of K Street in Sacramento. The "big four"—Stanford, Crocker, Huntington, and Hopkins—placed the work under the supervision of Theodore D. Judah, who had surveyed and developed the earlier Sacramento Valley Railroad to Folsom which opened in 1856.

The route eastward following the valleys of the Sacramento and American rivers posed no difficulties for the initial phase of construction. The Sierras, however, proved a formidable barrier, and the right-of-way from Auburn through the Donner Pass to Truckee required elaborate grading, tunneling, bridging, and the construction of shed-like structures over the tracks in many places to protect the track from avalanches. It was not until the end of 1867 that the line emerged from the most difficult mountain terrain.

In the previous year Congress modified the original legislation that had specified that the Central Pacific was to build only to the Nevada boundary. Now the company received authorization to extend its tracks until it met the Union Pacific. For the western line, this amendment provided an opportunity to gain additional land grants for every mile built, and early in 1868 the railroad began its race to the east. That spring notices appeared throughout California announcing an auction of lots at a new town in what by then had become the State of Nevada:

This sale will afford a grand opportunity for favorable investments in town lots suitable for all kinds of business and trades. The depot being permanently located at this point will give the town of RENO a commanding position of vast importance to secure the trade of Nevada and that portion of California lying east of the Sierras, and will be the natural market for the produce of the rich agricultural valleys north.

Situated on the Truckee River, affording water-power unsurpassed in the United States . . . it is unnecessary to enumerate the many advantages this town will possess as the center of immense milling and manufacturing operations.

The sale will take place on the ground, where, prior thereto, a plot of the same can be seen and information in relation to terms obtained.[1]

The "plot" displayed for the benefit of those interested is reproduced in Figure 17.1. It had been prepared by or under the direction of Charles Crocker, who was in charge of construction contracts for the Central Pacific. Crocker had been forced to acquire the 40-acre site from Myron Lake, who, since 1863, had operated a toll bridge at a crossing of the Truckee River which had first been developed by C. W. Fuller a few years earlier to capitalize on the mining rush to the Comstock Lode at nearby Virginia City.

On the restricted site Crocker's surveyor produced a gridiron plan oriented to the depot, warehouses, platforms, and other structures erected along the railroad a few hundred feet north of the river. This pattern extended to the banks of the Truckee, and its curving alignment and the irregular boundaries of the tract resulted in many blocks of odd shapes and sizes. Lake also reserved two substantial plots of land at the bridgehead, which added further variety to the size of the lots.

Crocker plainly hoped that the commerical section of town would develop facing the railroad, and on what is still called Commercial Row along the south side of the tracks, the first business houses were erected. Two fires in 1873 and 1879 virtually wiped out the frame buildings that were built for commerical purposes, but beginning in the early 1880s brick buildings began to take their place. Eventually the center of retail trade shifted to the two blocks on Virginia Street between the river and the railroad. It is in this area that the casinos were built when the legislature in 1931 legalized gambling and also reduced the legal residence period for divorces to six weeks.

The Reno of 1890 can be seen in Plate 23. The view is from the northeast and shows the expansion of the town north of the tracks where the bulk of the residential area was then located. At the northern end of Lake Street, one can see the first buildings of the University of Nevada, which opened its doors in 1886 after being moved from Elko. South of the Truckee on the west side of South Virginia Street, the courthouse can also be seen on its one-acre site donated in 1871 by Myron Lake when Reno became the seat of Washoe County. Its location and the knowledge that frequently in the past the bridge over the Truckee had been washed out by floods caused one observer to comment that "Reno is on the north side of the river; the [Central Pacific] is on the north side; nineteen-twentieths of the commerce of the county is on the north side. If the bridge goes, it's 8 miles by way of Glendale and 10 miles by way of Hunters' to get to the courthouse."[2]

At the left, the view shows the Virginia & Truckee Railroad, which by 1872 provided rail service to Virginia City and the Comstock Lode mines of that rich silver district. In 1900 and 1902 the new mines at Tonopah and Goldfield depended on rail transportation from Reno, the nearest point to this discovery of mineral wealth. A town of 3,200 in

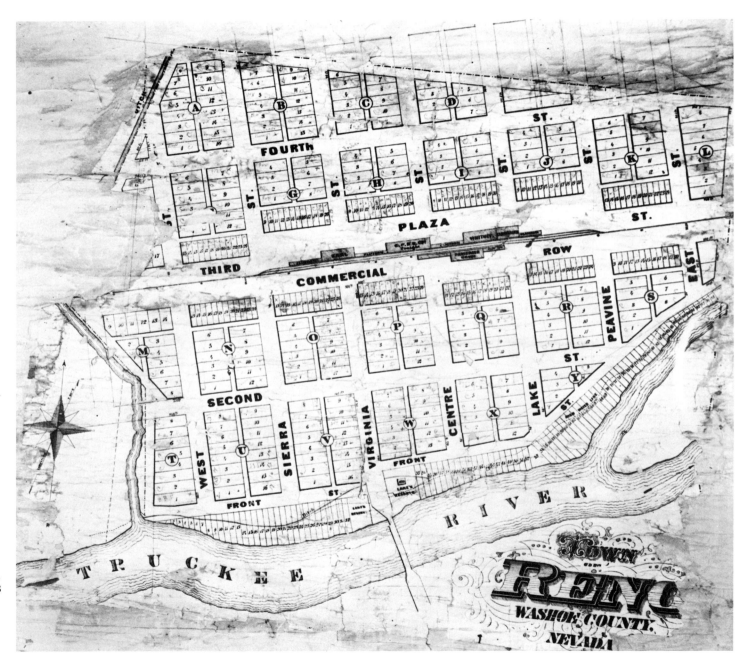

Figure 17.1 Plan of Reno, Nevada: ca. 1868

1890, Reno grew to 4,500 in 1900. The town then took the form shown in Figure 17.2, an interrupted, irregular grid created by the uncontrolled subdivision of land at the outskirts of the original town. In the next ten years as the population doubled, the southern portion of the city expanded to rival in size the older part of the town north of the tracks.

Reno was the principal town created by the Central Pacific line on its route east. Central and eastern Nevada and western Utah was forbidding territory—arid and broken and with sparse vegetation. Such settlements as Lovelock and Winnemucca, created only because the railroad needed occasional points for stations, water towers, and supply points, remained small and unimportant stops along the transcontinental route.[3]

While the promoters of the Central Pacific were busy with their new town of Reno, Union Pacific engineers were similarly involved with the planning and development of Laramie, Wyoming, on the western slope of the first range of the Rocky Mountains. In February, 1868, agents of the line located and laid out the town, and in April held the first sale of town lots. In anticipation of this event a tent city had already taken form, and land speculators quickly purchased 400 lots at prices ranging from $25 to $260. On May 4, five days before the first train arrived at the new end-of-track community, the land agent at Laramie could report to the company that he had sold lots worth $34,400, taking in $7,315 in cash and extending credit for the balance due.[4]

The editor of the *Frontier Index* wrote a few days later: "The first train of railroad cars reached Laramie City and there was great rejoicing. Real estate went up and the fluid extract of corn went down. To purchase a lot within sixteen blocks of the *Index* office was a financial impossibility."[5] That first train brought all the usual paraphernalia required for a terminal town: lumber, shacks, portable shanties, tents, and other materials needed for quick shelter. Gamblers and prostitutes mingled with shopkeepers and settlers, many of whom moved from Cheyenne in anticipation of better times at the newest of the railroad communities. An observer reported these conditions to the Cheyenne *Daily Leader* while at the same time indicating his doubts about the permanence of the prosperity that Laramie then enjoyed: "There are at Laramie City a goodly number of respectable shops and new buildings are being erected. Almost every branch of trade is represented. Many of the dwellers live in tents at present, but the town will soon be built up of logs, boards, and shingles and will be filled with goods and tradesmen. As to what will come of it three months hence? Ask some of the towns along the Union Pacific for an answer."[6]

Laramie did, of course, decline in population when the railroad extended its tracks westward, but the town continued to grow nonetheless. The cattle trade and shops of the railroad provided an initial economic base, and from a city of 800 in 1870 Laramie grew to just under 2,700 ten years later. By 1890 nearly 6,400 persons lived in the town, which by that time had been designated as the site of the state university.

The city as it existed in 1894 appears in Figure 17.3. As one might expect, the railroad surveyors provided the usual checkerboard plan of streets intersecting at right angles and oriented parallel and perpendicular to the tracks. All blocks measured 264 by 280 feet. Business lots were 24 feet wide and residential lots 66 feet, both types having a depth of 132 feet from their frontage on streets uniformly 80 feet wide. Sixteen-foot wide alleys divided the blocks in half. Later additions followed this general pattern, but in the 1890s development was confined mainly to the area of the original railroad plat.

From Laramie the Union Pacific moved its next base of construction operations to Benton, and then to Green River, near the western boundary of the state of Wyoming. At Green River, some 2,000 squatters occupied the site before the railroad townsite surveyors had a chance to plan the town. The squatters, led by H. M. Hook, formerly mayor of Cheyenne at the time the Union Pacific called in federal troops to evict illegal occupants of that earlier railroad townsite, argued that they held title from an earlier land grant to the Overland Mail Company. The Union Pacific negotiated for a time with Hook and his followers and then simply built the line twelve miles west to Bryan, a new townsite over which they exercised unquestionable control.

The settlement at Green River is shown in Figure 17.4, dominated by Castle Rock towering a thousand feet above the river from which the town took its name. By the end of October, 1868, Green River's short-lived boom had ended. As the editor of the Cheyenne *Daily Leader* observed, "The history of the rise and fall of Green River is ready to be written. Shooting and violence have characterized the short existence of the place, which has been both brief and unpoetic, and is played out. By Monday next there will not be twenty-five persons in the once famous city. The business portion of the community now consists of one house, one whiskey mill, one billiard hall and an outfitting store which is already packing up to leave. Bryan is a little better, but has seen its best days and the rush is now for Bear River, alias Gilmer. The end of the track is now beyond Granger, sixty-five miles west of here and going at a lively rate."[7]

By the middle of December, 1868, Union Pacific trains ran as far as

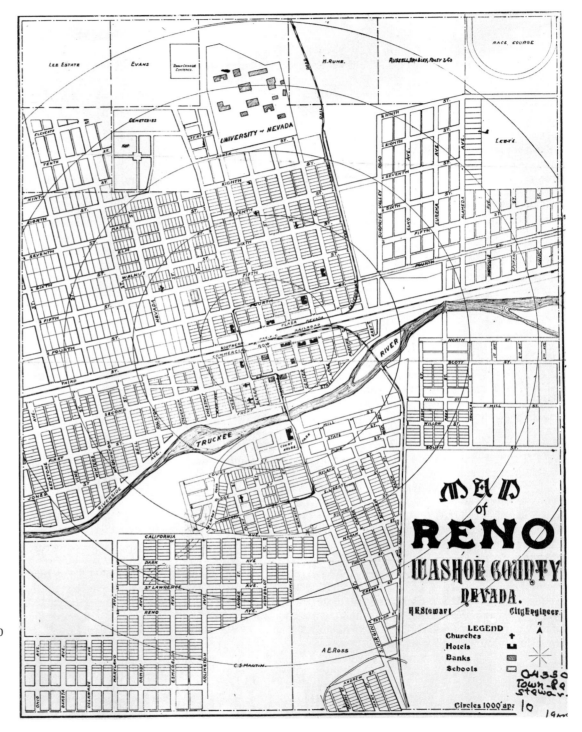

Figure 17.2 Plan of Reno, Nevada: 1900

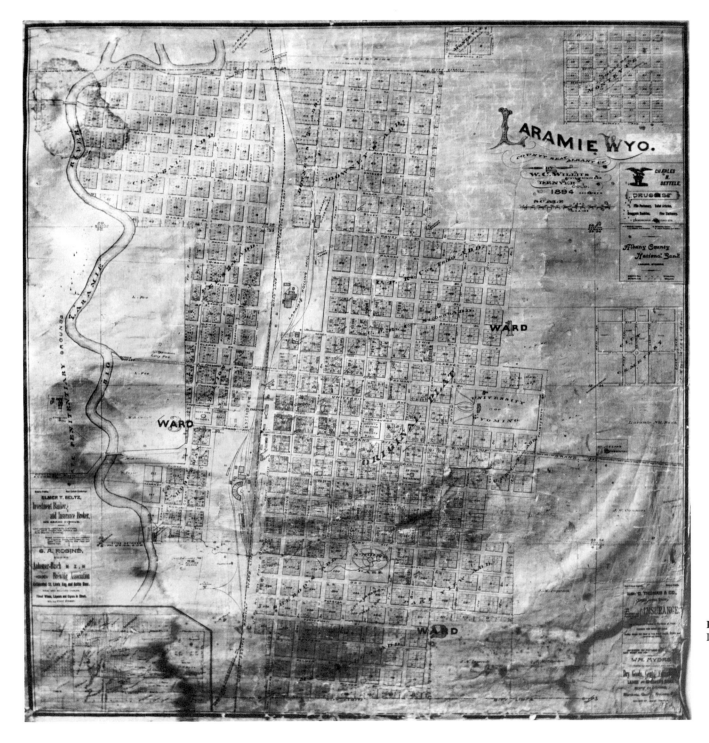

Figure 17.3
Plan of Laramie, Wyoming: 1894

Figure 17.4 View of Green River, Wyoming: date unknown

Evanston, only a few miles from the Utah boundary, by March of the following year the tracks reached Ogden, and on May 10, 1869 the last spike was driven at Promontory Point north of Great Salt Lake to link the Central Pacific and the Union Pacific. President Leland Stanford of the Central Pacific and Vice President Thomas C. Durant of the Union Pacific sent the following telegram to President Ulysses S. Grant in Washington: "Sir: We have the honor to report the last rail laid and the last spike driven. The Pacific railroad is finished."[8]

Both north and south of the first Pacific railroad other lines were soon under construction through the great mountain barrier to link the East with the West. Additional railroads were also built to provide north-south connections between the major transcontinental routes. On all of these later railroads townsite promotion and community development played an important role in company policy or were carried out by private speculators who depended heavily on the coming of rail service to crown their efforts.

In the previous chapter we examined the town development activities of the Northern Pacific line in the plains of North Dakota and southeastern Montana. Before the crash of 1873 that railroad reached the Missouri River at Bismarck. Work also began on its Pacific Division, and, just before the depression halted further progress, tracks had been laid from Tacoma southward to Kalama on the Columbia River about 75 miles south of Puget Sound.

Tacoma owed its origin to Morton M. McCarver, a land speculator and townsite promoter with experience in Iowa and California. McCarver was impressed by the potential of a site on the east shore of Puget Sound halfway between Olympia and Seattle, and in 1868 laid out a little grid settlement, which he called Commencement City. Later that year he changed the name to Tacoma, the plan of which appears in Figure 17.5.[9] Railroad construction was then being enthusiastically discussed by leaders of the young cities in the Northwest, and McCarver soon began to promote his new town as a possible Pacific terminus for a transcontinental line.

In October, 1872, a committee of high officials of the Northern Pacific journeyed to Puget Sound to examine possible locations for the line's western terminal. Olympia, the capital of Washington Territory, was eliminated because of shallow water at low tide. Seattle, then a tiny lumber village of perhaps 20 houses, appeared to lack enough level land along the water for rail sidings, warehouses, and yards. Steilacoom also was rejected because of its inadequate harbor. The committee recommended Tacoma as its first choice but also included the names of Mukilteo and Seattle in its report to the board of directors in New York. After further deliberations the board dispatched two commissioners to the scene for additional investigations. On June 30, 1873, they telegraphed the board their recommendation that the Tacoma site be selected, adding that they had purchased or had options on several thousand acres of land. On July 3, they received a coded wire from General George W. Cass, the line's president, that its executive committee had approved the Tacoma area as the site for its Pacific terminal and new town.[10]

The tracts that the railroad acquired lay at the head of Commencement Bay about one mile east and south of McCarver's earlier settlement. Although McCarver had been the most vigorous booster of the area as the railroad terminus and had been informed by the company's commissioners in July that the company had approved the Commencement Bay location, in the end he did not make the fortune he anticipated. Company officials doubtless reasoned that since it was the railroad alone that would be responsible for the success of the new community the company required no help from McCarver and did not need to share its profits with any outside party. The Lake Superior and Puget Sound Land Company, later retitled the Tacoma Land Company, took title to the site and under the general directions of its parent corporation assumed responsibility for the town's development.

In 1873 the vice president of the railroad was Charles B. Wright, who, as a director, had also served as a member of the committee that had investigated sites in Puget Sound the year before. Wright took a personal interest in the planning of the town and secured the services of Frederick Law Olmsted, the great American landscape architect who had planned New York's Central Park and many other large urban recreation areas in the naturalistic style of which he was the acknowledged master. Olmsted also had planned several suburban communities, the most notable of which was Riverside, Illinois, which he designed near Chicago in 1869.[11]

The published plan for Tacoma, reproduced in Figure 17.6, bears the date of October, 1873. It seems unlikely that Olmsted visited the site; probably he worked only from topographic surveys furnished by the railroad engineers.[12] It is a curious design for what was obviously destined to be a transportation, shipping, and industrial center. A single railroad line leading to a small wharf is the only hint that Olmsted's Tacoma might be something more than a residential community similar to those he designed elsewhere.

The curvilinear streets reflected the steep topography of the hillside

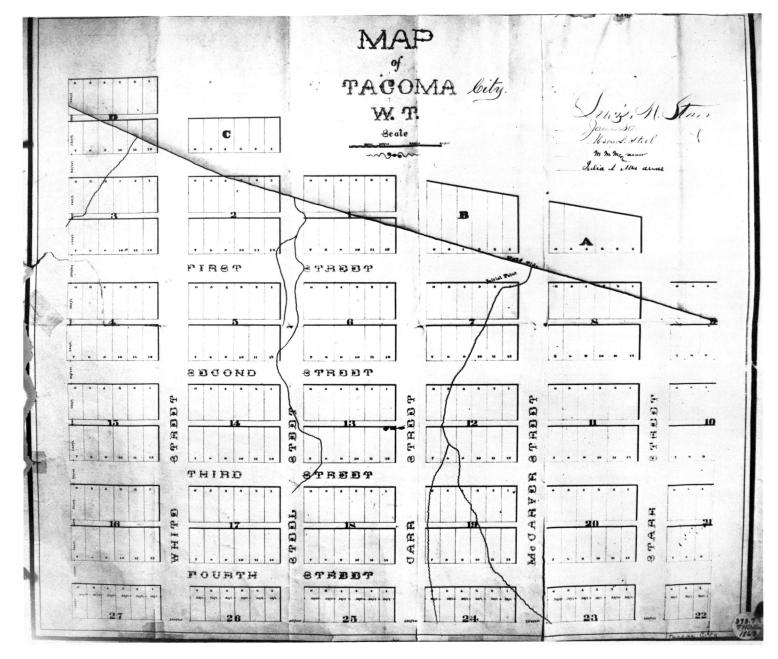

Figure 17.5 Plan of Tacoma, Washington: 1869

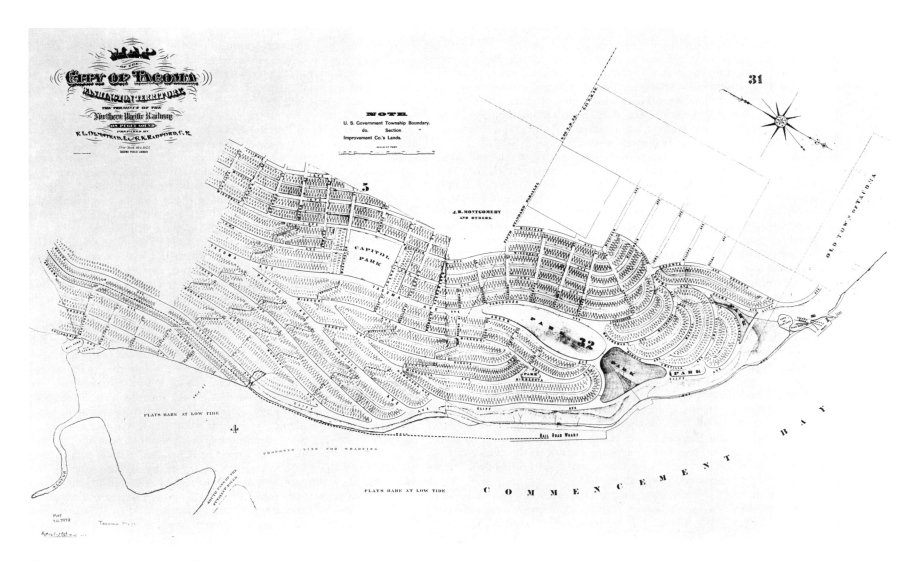

Figure 17.6 Plan for Tacoma, Washington: 1873

location, and this aspect of the plan demonstrates Olmsted's ability to work with and enhance the natural conditions of the landscape rather than to subjugate them to a preconceived layout. But one looks in vain for any feature that might have served as a community focal point. If Olmsted had some notion where the business district should be located the plan offers no clue. Several park sites appear, but none designated for schools. One might have expected this from a railroad engineer, but from one who was the nearest to a professional city planner America could then offer, these shortcomings seem incomprehensible.

Objections of quite a different kind were voiced at Tacoma when Olmsted's plan was displayed. It was, observed one horrified critic "the most fantastic plat of a town that was ever seen. There wasn't a straight line, a right angle or a corner lot. The blocks were shaped like melons, pears and sweet potatoes. One block, shaped like a banana, was 3,000 feet in length and had 250 lots. It was a pretty fair park plan but condemned itself for a town."[13] Westerners conditioned to hundreds of settlements beyond the Mississippi were simply unable to conceive of a town not composed of the simplest of rectilinear elements.

The Tacoma Land Company reconsidered the Olmsted plan, summarily rejected its *avant garde* contour planning concept, and commissioned railroad engineer Isaac Smith to prepare another plan. This, reproduced in Figure 17.7, was said to resemble that of Melbourne, Australia. However close the similarity between Smith's design and that of the city halfway around the globe, the new plan was as dull and utilitarian as Olmsted's was exotic and impractical. At least the railroad received ample land for its facilities. One and three-eighths miles of wharfs extended northward along the shore from the terminal near the foot of Division Avenue. Unfortunately, the numbered streets at right angles to the shoreline led directly up the steep slopes. At their intersections with those parallel to the water, extensive grading became necessary, and the present stair-step appearance of the center of the modern city is a direct result of Smith's casual disregard of the site's topographic problems and possibilities.

The panic of 1873 limited the pace of Tacoma's early growth. The view of the town five years later in Figure 17.8 shows a community of some 600 persons concentrated around the intersection of Ninth Street and Pacific Avenue. Old Tacoma, off the view to the left beyond the wharf depot, could boast only half that number of inhabitants. By 1884, however, the town had entered a period of substantial growth in anticipation of the completion of the Northern Pacific line from the East. In that year, the two towns of Tacoma consolidated as a single munici-

pality in time to celebrate the opening of the elaborate Tacoma Hotel designed by the well-known eastern architectural firm, McKim, Mead and White. On the view reproduced as Figure 17.9, this imposing structure can be seen atop the bluff midway between the first of the great wharfs and the trestle carrying the Cascade Division tracks across the end of Commencement Bay.

On June 1, 1887, the last spike was driven on the transcontinental line of the Northern Pacific, which for the previous three years had been forced to follow circuitous routes over other railroads for its Pacific Coast traffic. Tacoma was then experiencing a dizzy period of land speculation. Rudyard Kipling visited the city at this time and reported that "Tacoma was literally staggering under a boom of the boomiest. . . . The rude boarded pavements of the main streets rumbled under the wheels of hundreds of furious men all actively engaged in hunting drinks and eligible corner-lots. They sought the drinks first. . . .

"The hotel walls bore a flaming panorama of Tacoma in which by the eye of faith I saw a faint resemblance to the real town. The hotel stationery advertised that Tacoma bore on its face all the advantages of the highest civilization and the newspapers sang the same tune in a louder key. The real-estate agents were selling house-lots on unmade streets miles away for thousands of dollars."

Kipling found Tacoma unimpressive. On its streets "five-story business blocks of the later and more abominable forms of architecture [alternated with] board shanties. Overhead the drunken telegraph, telephone, and electric-light wires tangled on the tottering posts whose butts were half-whittled through by the knife of the loafer. . . . We passed down ungraded streets that ended abruptly in a fifteen-foot drop and a nest of brambles; along pavements that beginning in pine-plank ended in the living tree; by hotels with Turkish mosque trinketry on their shameless tops, and the pine stumps at their very doors."[14]

Leaders of Tacoma, on the other hand, shared visions of a city on Puget Sound to rival New York or Chicago in size and importance. The Tacoma Land Company's steady flow of booster literature was joined by similar material from individual real estate promoters and the powerful Chamber of Commerce, which was organized in 1884 and soon moved to its new building on Pacific Avenue and Twelfth Street. Smelters, grain elevators, flour and lumber mills, warehouses, and factories producing a variety of products fought for sites along the busy port. The ubiquitous George Francis Train turned up, claiming that he had first recommended the site to the Northern Pacific, offered to go around the world trumpeting Tacoma's greatness and was promptly

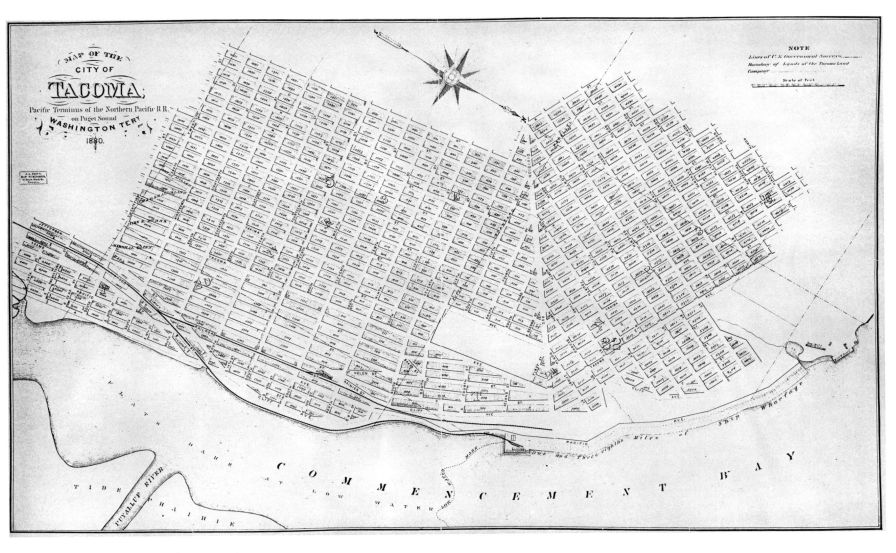

Figure 17.7 Plan of Tacoma, Washington: 1880

VIEW OF

NEW TACOMA AND MOUNT RAINIER,

Puget Sound, Washington Territory.

TERMINUS OF THE NORTHERN PACIFIC RAILROAD.

Figure 17.8   View of Tacoma, Washington: 1878

Figure 17.9 View of Tacoma, Washington: 1884

dispatched by the Tacoma *Ledger* in March, 1891, to return exactly sixty-seven days, thirteen hours, three minutes, and three seconds later. Train's feat beat Nelly Bly's record of 1890 by five days.[15]

The Northern Pacific's rival for freight and passenger traffic in the Northwest was the Great Northern Railroad. Under the guiding hand of James J. Hill this most northerly of the transcontinental lines extended its track westward after 1879 and eventually reached Seattle in 1893.[16] Hill, a Canadian by birth, came to St. Paul in 1876. There he knew Paris Gibson, a prominent civic leader and industrialist who founded the first important flour mill in Minneapolis and was also a partner in a woolen mill located at the falls of the Mississippi.

When Gibson moved to Montana in 1879 after business reverses, it was only natural that he would investigate the water power resources at the falls of the Missouri River. He and three associates roughed out a preliminary plan for an industrial city above the falls and opposite the mouth of the Sun River. Gibson realized that railroad connections would be necessary for the success of his project and began a correspondence with Hill. The two met in St. Paul late in November, 1882, and Gibson succeeded in obtaining Hill's financial support.

Within two years Gibson had acquired the necessary land. The Black Eagle Dam, built in 1884, provided a source of controlled water power for industry. Three years later the Great Falls Water Power and Townsite Company received its corporate charter, and by mid-October, 1887, Hill's railroad began regular service to the new town over more than 500 miles of track that the company laid that year from Minot, North Dakota. Another railroad financed by Hill, the Montana Central, provided a connection between Great Falls and Helena and, two years later, to Butte.[17]

The plan of Great Falls in Figure 17.10 and a view of the city in 1891 reproduced in Figure 17.11 reveal an urban design of surpassing dullness, which carried geometric utilitarianism to an extent rarely duplicated even in the American West. Except for the 90-foot width given to Central Avenue, which began at the passenger depot and terminated somewhere short of the eastern horizon, all streets were 80-feet wide. Three sites, each a miserly three lots each, were set aside for school purposes. The potential beauty of "Cascade Park" stretching northeasterly along the river from the depot seemed doomed by the bisecting tracks of the railroad leading to the mines and smelter. The extensive railroad yards on the west side of the town promised a noisy and sooty welcome for anyone unfortunate enough to take up residence in the immediate vicinity.

Great Falls may not have received a generous planning legacy, but the combination of abundant water power and railroad transportation brought quick mercantile and industrial success. The poet, Joaquin Miller, writing his history of Montana in 1894, observed that since the coming of the railroad "Great Falls has made marvelous progress, and is now a city of 12,000 people. With the exception of the Niagara Falls, it has the greatest water power in the United States. It has already large smelters, refineries and flouring mills, and the day seems near at hand when it will be the leading industrial city of the Northwest."[18] Miller's prophecy contained more poetry than truth, since the major industrial cities of the Northwest do not seem worried that Great Falls will outstrip them in this century. The city is, however, the largest in the state; if it is far from the loveliest it has at least retained the industrial character imposed on it when Gibson and Hill created a city by mixing water with iron rails.

Extensions to the basic railroad network in the Northwest added to the number of towns already created by railroad companies along the major east-west routes. The Mormon Church began work on the Utah Northern in 1872 to connect northern Utah with Montana. The Union Pacific acquired the railroad in 1878 and extended its tracks to Butte by 1881. In that same year the Union Pacific began construction of the Oregon Short Line Railway to connect its main line with Oregon. With the consent of Congress the railroad purchased 40 acres of land from the Indians of the Fort Hall Reservation at a point where the two lines crossed. On this restricted site, the company platted a small community in 1882 and the next year constructed the Pacific Hotel as virtually the only substantial building in a town then composed mainly of tents, remodeled box cars, and the usual end-of-track sheds and shanties.

Pocatello, named for the Indian leader who aided the railroad in securing the transfer of tribal lands, quickly became an important shipping center, but persons attracted to the town for commercial reasons found it difficult to build stores and dwellings without encroaching on Indian lands. An additional 39 acres of land were obtained, but when railroad shops were established in 1887 even this enlarged site proved too confining. Petitions to the Secretary of the Interior finally resulted in the passage by Congress in 1888 of the Pocatello Townsite Bill, and in the summer of 1889 an enormous tract of over 1,800 acres was platted, as shown in Figure 17.12.

In typical fashion the surveyor laid off the 60- and 80-foot streets parallel and perpendicular to the Oregon Short Line tracks. Early business buildings, mostly one-story, frame structures, located east of the tracks on Front Street a block or two north and south of Center Street. The west side of town took form as the residential district following the construction by the railroad of two rows of houses adjacent to the tracks. Other residences, mostly temporary, were built nearby and around the Pacific Hotel. Not until after July, 1891, when town lots were put up for auction, did Pocatello begin to assume the air of a permanent settlement as residents gradually built more substantial buildings on their newly acquired property. By 1890 the town contained nearly 2,500 inhabitants, the railroad shops employed several hundred men, and in 1892 some 200 buildings were erected including "a dozen expensive brick and stone blocks."[19] Another new railroad-initiated town was well on its way to become the second largest city of Idaho.[20]

Along another branch line in neighboring Wyoming, the Chicago and North Western's Wyoming Central Railway platted a town in 1888 between its tracks and the North Platte River. The railroad's Pioneer Townsite Company held its first sale of lots that November to begin the

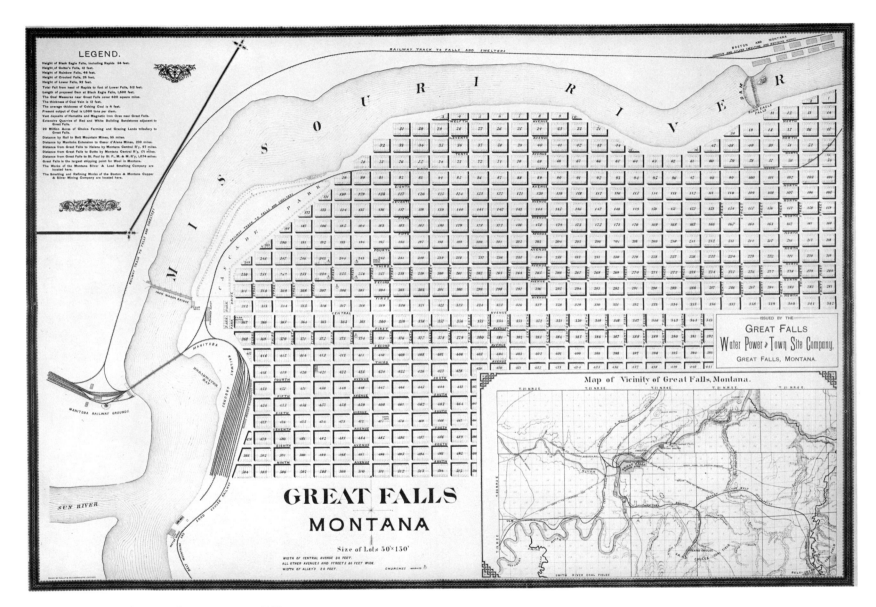

Figure 17.10 Plan of Great Falls, Montana: ca. 1887

PERSPECTIVE MAP OF

GREAT FALLS, MONT.

1891.

ADDITIONAL INFORMATION MAY BE OBTAINED BY WRITING TO

J. BOOKWALTER,

General Agent,

GREAT FALLS WATER POWER AND TOWN SITE COMPANY,

GREAT FALLS, - - MONTANA.

Figure 17.11 View of Great Falls, Montana: 1891

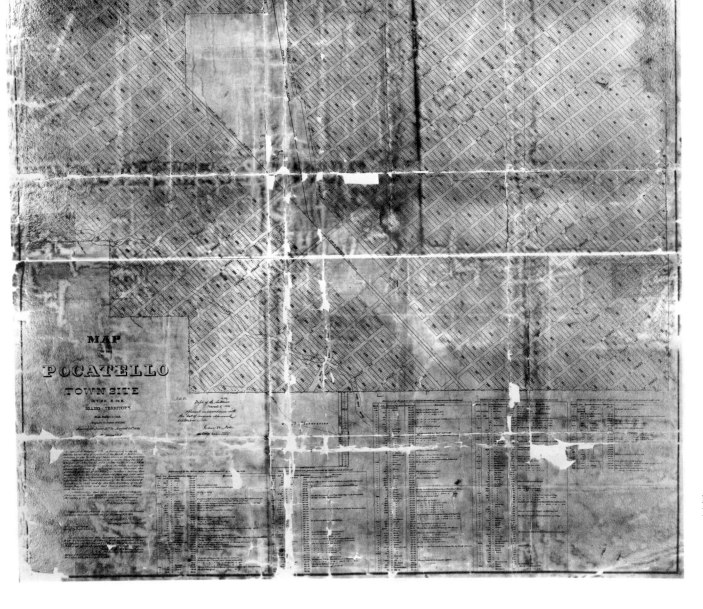

Figure 17.12 Plan of Pocatello,
Idaho: 1889

existence of Casper, whose plat is reproduced in Figure 17.13. The railroad had been forced to enter into an agreement with Joseph M. Carey to secure a portion of his ranch lands for the townsite. The J. M. Carey Company took title to alternate lots in the newly platted town as its price for making the site available to the railroad.[21] Casper's plan suggests that its surveyor could not decide whether the railroad right-of-way or the cardinal points of the compass should determine the orientation of the streets. The result was an awkward compromise producing a number of clumsy, acute-angled intersections where First Street slashed diagonally across the ends of the other thoroughfares.

In the 1870s one of the smaller railroads of the West aggressively pursued a policy of town founding and development as it built south and west through Kansas and Oklahoma into the southern plains of Texas. This was the Missouri, Kansas, and Texas, or "Katy" Railroad, whose General Manager, Robert S. Stevens, was responsible for the creation of a number of new communities.[22] The line began at Junction City, Kansas, near Fort Riley on the Kansas River and served by the Kansas Pacific Railroad. Its initial route led southeasterly through Emporia to Humboldt. Later, what became the main line started at Sedalia, Missouri, and followed a southwesterly route to intersect the first below Humboldt at what became Parsons, Kansas, a town surveyed and laid out by the Parsons Town Company, which Stevens organized in October, 1870. When the first lots were put up for auction in February of the following year, nearly $18,000 was collected in the first three days. A week later, more than $30,000 had been realized.

Stevens built the line almost directly south through the eastern edge of what is now Oklahoma and was then Indian Territory. Where the Katy tracks crossed the surveyed route of the Atlantic and Pacific, Stevens encouraged Elias C. Boudinot, a Cherokee who had helped promote the railroad, to fence in a tract nearly two miles square for the townsite of Vinita. The Atlantic and Pacific retaliated by changing its point of crossing three miles north, reaching its own agreement with Boudinot by giving him one-third of the new townsite, and it was there that Vinita was finally laid out and developed.

The Katy bridged the Verdigris and Arkansas rivers, and five miles south of the latter stream Stevens established an end-of-track settlement, which he named Muskogee. This town was to be extended at the end of the period of tribal government, and it developed into a pleasant community. For the first 20 years of its existence, however, it was a wide open, brawling frontier town whose early character was established on its first day when "before breakfast, one man was dead and the murderer was being chased over the prairies by a lot of men."[23]

South of Indian Territory beyond the Red River lay Texas, where the laws confining Stevens to land within 200 feet of the right-of-way within tribal boundaries no longer applied. Citizens of Sherman, Texas, an established town a few miles south of the Arkansas, confidently expected the Katy to build a major terminal and divisional point at their city. Stevens, however, saw no reason to enrich others when he could benefit his own line by developing a new town elsewhere for that purpose. Unfortunately, every foot of land had already been pre-empted. With the aid of William Munson, a young civil engineer who had recently settled in Sherman, Stevens was able to purchase several contiguous farms on the first high land south of the Red River.[24]

Following plans prepared and filed on September 20, 1872, by his engineer, George Walker, Stevens proceeded to develop the new town of Denison, named for the vice president of the line. As president of the Denison Town Company, Stevens directed the first sales of lots in the new town while Shermanites looked sadly on. A rival railroad, the Houston and Texas Central, maintained its terminal a few miles away at Red River City, but eventually an agreement between the two lines provided for an interchange point at Denison, and the town boomed. Lot sales averaged $1,000 a day for the first three months. Houses were moved from Sherman and Red River City. Within a matter of months Denison took on the appearance of a finished city, although, as the view of the town in 1875 reproduced as Figure 17.14 indicates, it was far from the most beautiful of communities.

Its growth continued at a rapid and reasonably steady pace. The Denison Town Company attempted to restrict business enterprises on Main Street to those of more respectable character. Brothels and lower-class saloons and dance halls were relegated to Skiddy (now Chestnut) Street paralleling the main thoroughfare to the south. Soon the city fathers developed a handsome park south of the business district and near the shops of the Katy. By 1891, the date of the view reproduced in Figure 17.15, Denison had plainly passed through its frontier period and had become a prosperous residential, industrial, and transportation center for northeast Texas.[25]

So extensive was town building by the western railroads that one would have thought someone directly connected with such activities might have drawn on his experience and prepared suggestions for future railroad town planners. Such a work did appear in 1872, bearing the following laboriously explicit title: *How to Build a City, Designed for the Consideration of Founders of Towns, Architects, Civil Engineers, Sanitary*

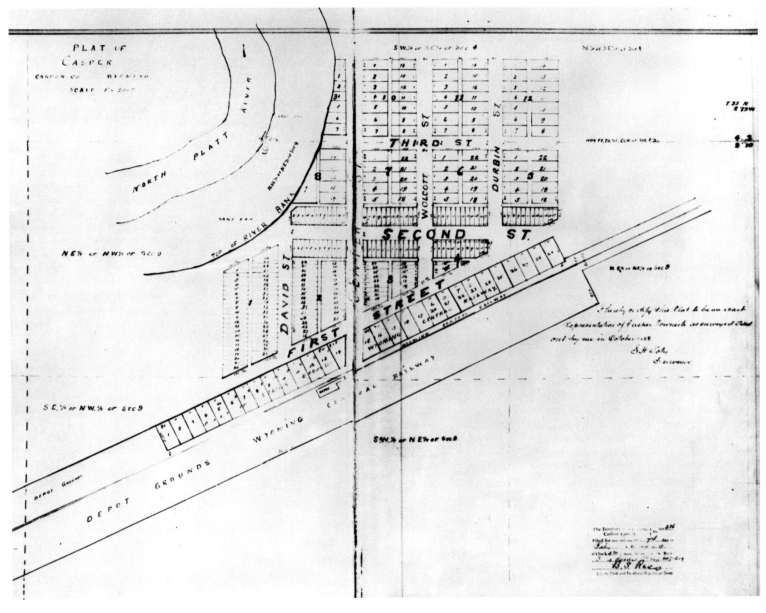

Figure 17.13 Plan of Casper, Wyoming: 1888

Figure 17.14   View of Street in Denison, Texas: 1875

Figure 17.15   View of Denison, Texas: 1891

Organizations, Municipal Authorities, Builders, and Especially the Managers of the Various Railroads to the Pacific.[26] Its author, one P. Gerard, apparently had no connection with any railroad nor, so far as can be determined, any actual experience with town planning. Nevertheless, some of his suggestions had considerable merit.

Gerard's plan for a portion of model railroad town is reproduced in Figure 17.16. It is a gridiron that would have dwarfed any of the actual railroad-built towns if it had ever been developed. Gerard proposed that the rail lines be depressed and pass through the city in open cuts bridged by the great avenues marked "B" on his plan. He also suggested that the town include three trenched passages for livestock so that cattle could be driven from one part of the town to another without interfering with normal surface traffic movement. Five tiers of small blocks extending through the city from north to south, marked "A" on the plan, were intended as sites for public buildings and parks. Supplementing this system of small parks was the large recreation area near the northwestern corner of the city shown with diagonal and circular drives and paths. Gerard planned every third street exclusively for residential purposes, and he proposed that the business district be compactly built, located near the center of the town, and bordered by broad avenues. Every feature of the community from the public toilets in the parks to the design of lampposts in the streets was described in meticulous detail by this railroad utopian whose proposals evidently drew little attention and, if his book was ever read by those responsible for the planning of the railroad towns in the West, it certainly was not regarded as a model to be followed in actual city development.

The town developers of the western railroads were far more interested in obtaining quick profits from land sales than in planning beautiful or functionally efficient communities. Where towns already existed along their proposed rights-of-way, they used the threat of creating rival towns as a device to obtain substantial subsidies in exchange for building to and through established cities. In 1874, as one example among dozens, the Denver and Rio Grande forced little Canon City, Colorado, to deliver $50,000 in bonds and titles to town lots later sold for about $25,000 as its price for extending its tracks from the railroad town of Labran.[27]

Existing towns that did not comply with railroad demands of this sort may have preserved their honor, but they usually lost almost everything else. San Bernardino, California, refused to provide a subsidy to the Southern Pacific Railroad, which promptly laid out its own town of Colton a few miles south. San Bernardino stagnated until the Santa Fe

line eventually provided it with rail service some years later in 1885.[28] In order to secure a Southern Pacific connection, Los Angeles in 1872 paid a subsidy in cash, stocks of the Los Angeles and San Pedro Railroad, and 60 acres of land for depot grounds worth more than $600,000. It was a heavy burden for a city and county with only 15,000 residents, but in the long run it proved an investment that paid handsome dividends in population growth and rising land values.[29]

Railroads could make or break a town, and they naturally preferred the latter where it had been established by a rival line. In 1878 Santa Fé engineers laid out the town of Cleora in Colorado near the confluence of the South Arkansas River with the Arkansas. When the Denver and Rio Grande secured the exclusive right to build through the Grand Canyon of the Arkansas, they could not avoid Cleora but planned their own community of Salida as a division point a few miles away. Cleora was dead and knew it, and soon the buildings of the town and all its inhabitants moved to Salida, where the Denver and Rio Grande made a tidy profit by selling lots to the distressed citizens of the older town.[30]

Under the direction of General William Jackson Palmer, the Denver and Rio Grande specialized in building its own towns and destroying or undermining those that already existed. Palmer had been in charge of building much of the Kansas Pacific line to Denver. After he completed that undertaking in 1870, he resigned to organize his own railroad with the goal of connecting Denver to Mexico City by a north-south route along the eastern base of the Rockies. In this region he determined to create a series of towns, profiting by the rise of land values inevitably associated with the coming of rail transportation and, as the towns filled up with settlers, deriving revenues from carrying passengers and freight along the main line and the spurs he intended to build westward through mountain passes to mining communities. Palmer also invested in mineral lands, whose value would rise as his railroad opened up transportation corridors through the rugged mountain region.

Palmer's outstanding engineering and financial abilities were matched only by his lack of ethics in achieving success. It should be added that what from the perspective of our own time appears to be the most blatant lack of corporate and personal integrity was in his own age accepted as ordinary sharp American business practice. Moreover, the Denver and Rio Grande did not receive federal land grant subsidies, and Palmer was forced to finance its development from other sources. The continuing need for local subsidies and the profits to be made from townsite promotion may have led him into activities that under different circumstances he might have shunned. Palmer would probably have risen to the top in any era and within the confines of any level of established commerical morality; all that we know for certain, however, is that the man and his times proved a perfect match.

Salida was only one of several towns that Palmer founded with the twin goals of destroying an existing community and creating a new one nearby where he could exercise complete control and realize all the profits from land sales. His chief agent in these activities was A. C. Hunt, a former governor of Colorado Territory and an investor in the Denver and Rio Grande. It was Hunt who informed the residents of Pueblo, Colorado, that the main line of the railroad would by-pass the town unless the company received funds for the construction of 25 miles of track. In fact, Palmer intended to run the main line to and through Pueblo since it was in 1870 an incorporated municipality of 700 persons whose passenger and freight traffic the railroad badly needed.

The plan of Pueblo as it then existed appears in Figure 17.17. Settlement began on the site where Fountain Creek joined the Arkansas River as early as 1842 when James Beckwourth established a trading post at an adobe fort. Four years later a group of Mormons built cabins for a temporary camp not far away on the south side of the Arkansas River, but their community was soon abandoned.[31] A Ute Indian massacre in 1854 put an end to the trading post, and the place was not resettled until four years later when a part of Pueblo was occupied and given the name Fountain City. Then, in 1860 a group of Denver promoters had the site surveyed into streets and town lots as shown in the illustration.

On June 20, 1871, the voters of Pueblo County approved a bond issue of $100,000, to be made available to the railroad on condition that the line's depot be located within one mile of the courthouse. Hunt and Palmer, not content with this sum, asked for and obtained an additional bond issue of $50,000 to help finance a spur line from Pueblo westward to Canyon City. Residents of Pueblo had every reason to believe that their property values would soon soar as a result of their generous subsidy and that the established town would quickly become a thriving railroad center.

They were horrified and angered when they learned that Palmer had directed his engineers to bridge the Arkansas and locate the depot south of the river at the edge of a huge tract of nearly 50,000 acres of land owned by his Central Colorado Improvement Company. By the time the railroad arrived in 1872, Palmer had platted the new town of South Pueblo adjoining and south of the Denver and Rio Grande tracks

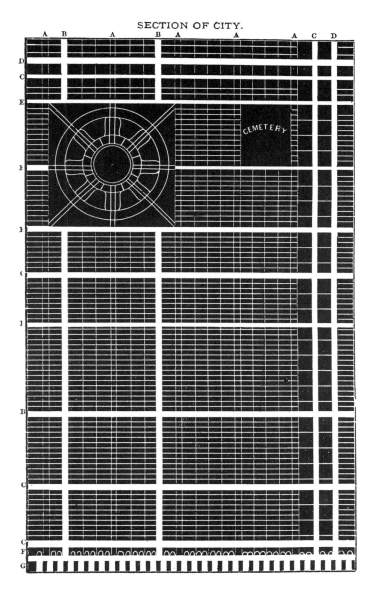

Figure 17.16 Plan for a Model Town: 1872

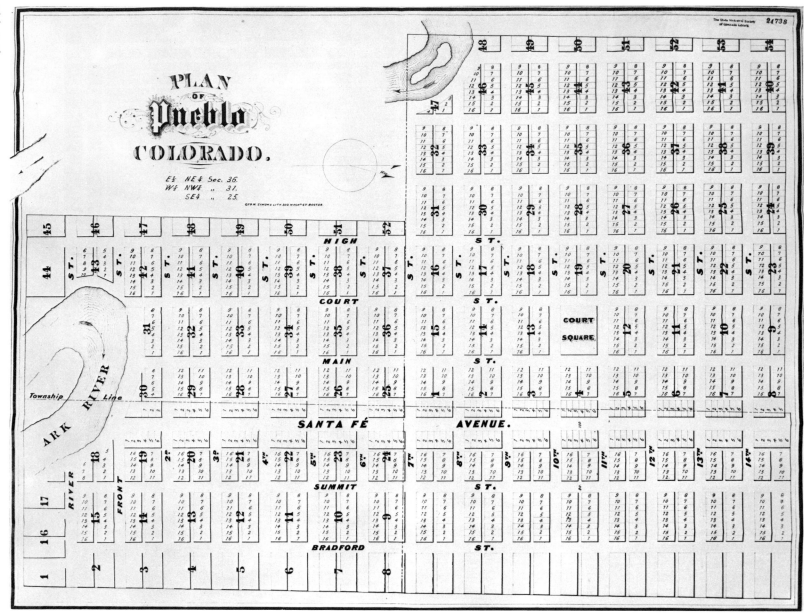

Figure 17.17   Plan of Pueblo, Colorado: ca. 1870

and yards. Much of the remainder of his lands was surveyed into farming plots, provided with irrigation ditches, and sold to settlers on easy terms.

The two Pueblos can be seen in Figure 17.18 as viewed from the north looking over the old town to Palmer's new community. Much of South Pueblo followed the usual gridiron plan, but Palmer's town designers had the good sense to introduce curving streets in the steeply sloping area leading up from the river to the level land beyond.

Palmer's plan to draw development to his town was only partially successful. When the Santa Fe Railway reached the area in 1876, its tracks entered the town on the north side, and most of the extensions to the city as it quickly developed into a major industrial community were to that side of the city. By 1890, as the view in Figure 17.19 shows, the two cities had blended, and South Pueblo no longer existed as a separate municipality. Development had been exceedingly rapid. From a population of slightly more than 3,000 in 1870 the city grew to 25,000 in 1880. Coal from the mines at Trinidad furnished fuel for the smelters of Leadville ore and the steel plants occupying sites adjacent to the railroads. Colorado's second largest city was clearly a creature of the railroads although only its southern portion owed its plan directly to rail interests.

The wily Palmer achieved a more complete victory at Durango, Colorado, near the southwestern corner of the state. Animas City on the Animas River, with the population of more than 2,000 was the logical town for the Denver and Rio Grande to serve. Palmer decreed otherwise, and in 1880 his surveyors laid off a new town only one and a half miles below Animas City. The editor of that community's newspaper commented as follows when he heard the first rumors of a rival-to-be: "The Bank of San Juan has issued a circular in which it is stated that a branch office will be opened at 'the new town of Durango on the Rio Animas.' Where the 'new town of Durango' is to be or not to be God and the D. and R. G. Railroad only know. If they are in 'cahoots' we ask for a special dispensation."[32] Seven months later, after the greater part of Animas City had relocated in Durango, the new town's *Daily Record* taunted: "All of Animas City is coming to Durango as fast as accommodations can be secured. Even the *Southwest* is coming, despite its small opinions of our dimensions. It will move down some time next week."[33]

Durango was a commerical but hardly an artistic success. Its original plat shows a rigid grid pattern with the streets running north-south given numbers and those crossing at right angles designated by letters.

All were platted of uniform width except for a wider thoroughfare in a north-south orientation bearing the imaginative name, "Boulevard." The view of the city in 1889 reproduced in Figure 17.20 shows a rather dreary frontier settlement whose chief glory was its splendid mountain setting formed by the ranges enclosing its narrow valley site.[34]

The policy of the Denver and Rio Grande in promoting its own interests through determining where stations would be located was clearly stated by its president in 1874. In an open letter to the commissioners of Douglas County explaining his refusal to construct a station at their new county seat of Castle Rock, he pointed out that stockholders understood they had "an interest in some 15,000 acres of land to be bought at selected points along the line at which the company agreed to locate its stations." This land, purchased "at high average prices," also required additional capital for improvements. Profits from land development would "compensate for the smallness of the then existing population and traffic."[35]

Only at one location did this policy that Palmer applied so consistently result in the creation of a community that became something more than a commerical success. This was Colorado Springs, Palmer's first venture in town founding along the Denver and Rio Grande. Its history demonstrated that skillful planning, substantial investments in community facilities, and honesty in promotion of settlement and land sales were not incompatible with realization of both immediate and long-term profits of substantial magnitude. Unfortunately, Palmer did not follow this precedent, nor did the other developers of railroad towns elsewhere in the country seem to realize that good planning did not necessarily result in reduced revenues. The history of the founding and development of Colorado Springs, then, is an investigation of what a good part of the American urban West might have been. The opportunities lost in the planning of towns along the western railroads loom large when compared with such occasional modest urban truimphs as Colorado Springs.

The venture began when Palmer asked his agent in 1870 to purchase 320 acres of land some 70 miles south of Denver for the first major townsite along the projected railroad. A. C. Hunt, then beginning his association with the line and having previously expressed his high opinion of a site not far from Pikes Peak, contracted for an enormous tract of nearly 10,000 acres. Included in this domain were the mineral springs at Manitou in the foothills of the Rockies and a large area of level and gently rolling land below. In between lay Colorado City, a small settlement serving as the seat of El Paso County and taking the

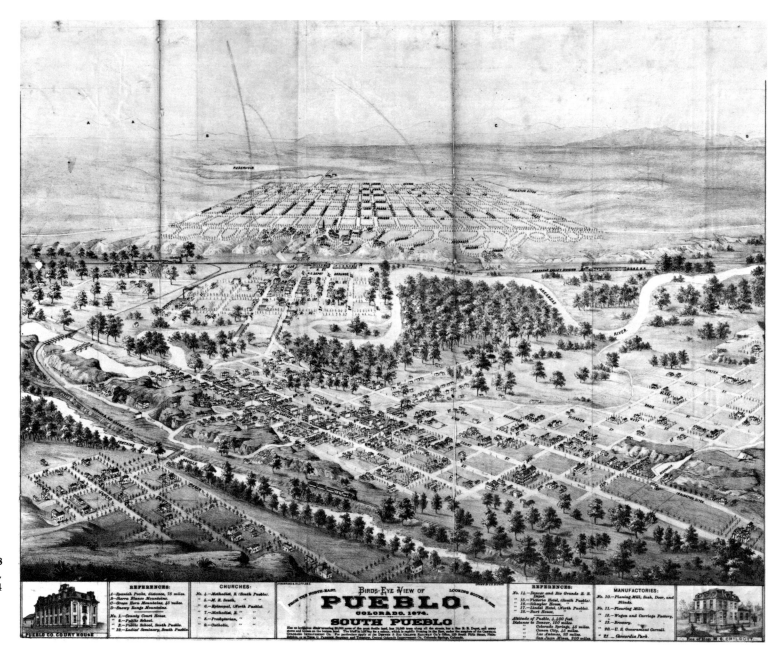

Figure 17.18
View of Pueblo,
Colorado, 1874

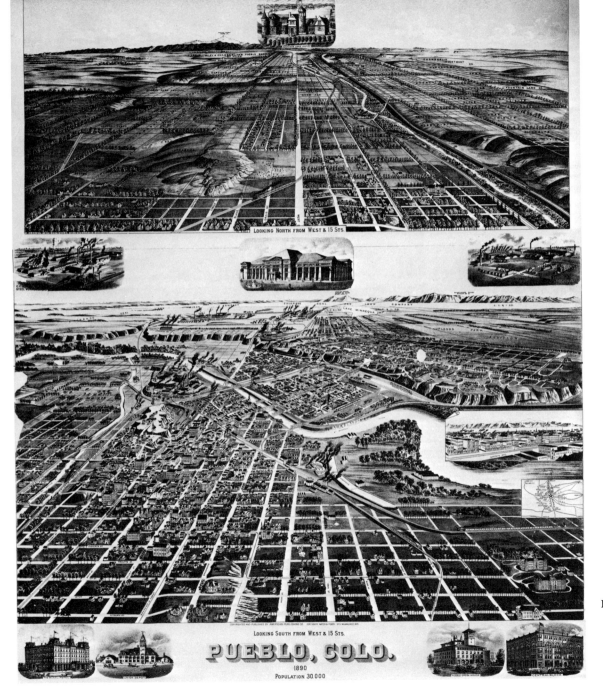

Figure 17.19 View of Pueblo, Colorado: 1890

Figure 17.20 View of Durango, Colorado: 1889

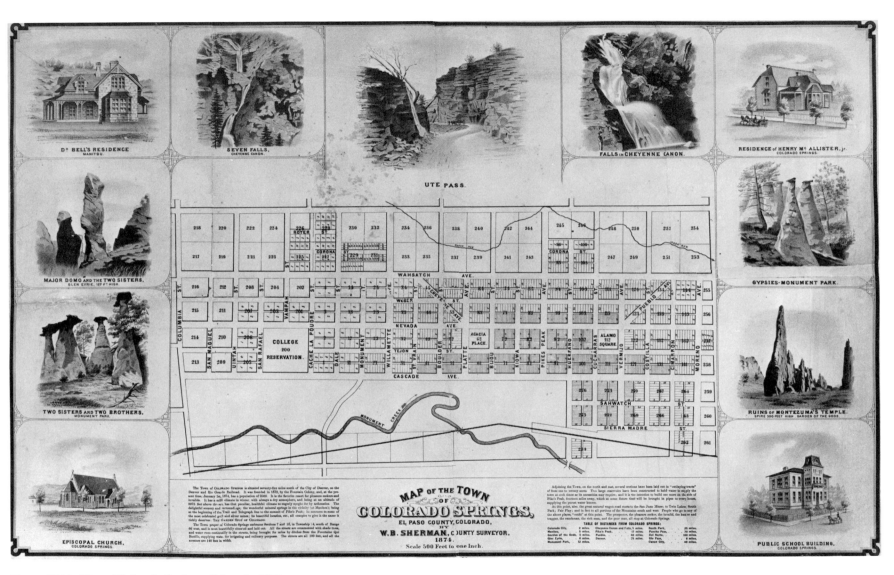

Figure 17.21 Plan of Colorado Springs, Colorado: 1874

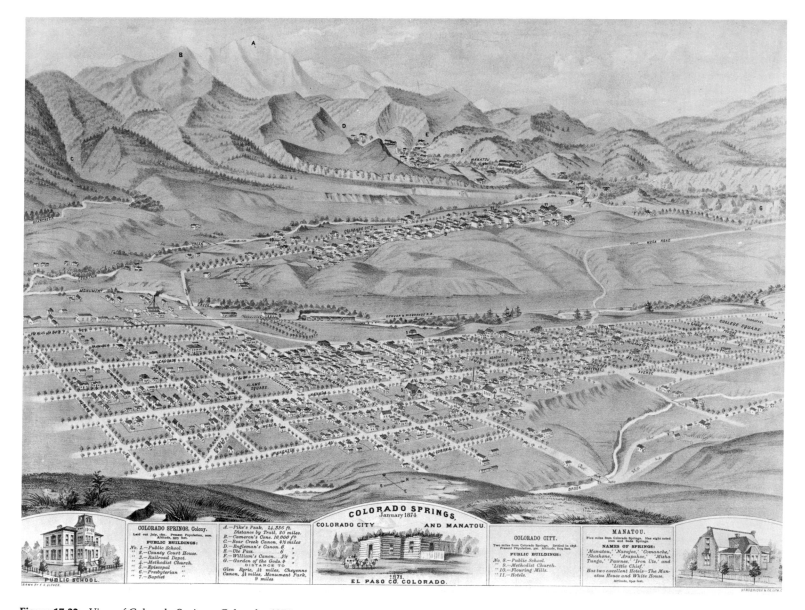

Figure 17.22 View of Colorado Springs, Colorado: 1874

form of a linear community along the road leading to Ute Pass. On the level area west of where this road crossed Monument Creek, Palmer determined to develop a residential and resort community of outstanding quality.

In June, 1871, the Colorado Springs Company held its organization meeting in Denver, and on the 27th of the month its officers left for the site of the new town, where Colonel Greenwood, the chief engineer of the railroad, shortly began to lay out the town. On July 31, three months before the railroad tracks to the infant town were completed, the first surveyor's stake was driven at the southeast corner of Pikes Peak and Cascade Avenues, and the plan shown in Figure 17.21 soon was extended over the empty plains.

Greenwood, doubtless with Palmer directing his hand, introduced a touch of the baroque into the otherwise standard gridiron. Pikes Peak Avenue, as its name suggests, was surveyed so that the tip of the great mountain 20 miles away terminated the vista down this thoroughfare from its eastern end. Two diagonal streets, Pueblo Avenue on the south and Cheyenne Avenue to the north, led inward from Wahsatch Avenue to end at Alamo Square and Acacia Place, two parks each occupying the space of one city block. The center lines of the two diagonal streets, if prolonged, intersect the extended axis of Pikes Peak Avenue slightly west of where the elaborate Antlers Hotel provided a vigorous element in the townscape after 1882. Land reserved for a college was not vacant for long. Colorado College held its first classes in 1874 in temporary quarters on Tejon Street, but shortly thereafter moved to the site set aside originally for that purpose.

The town company put up for sale two-thirds of the town lots and outlying farm plots to purchasers who agreed to make substantial improvements within one year. The remaining properties, interspersed among those offered for immediate sale, were held off the market in anticipation of higher prices in the future. Intial lot prices were deliberately kept low to attract settlement: residential lots sold for $100, business lots for $175, and farming tracts for $30 an acre.

Growth was rapid, speeded by the arrival of the railroad. By the end of 1871, 159 structures had been completed, foundations were laid for the Colorado Springs Hotel, cottonwood trees were planted along the streets, and irrigation ditches were dug to bring water into the townsite. Palmer appointed General Robert A. Cameron manager of the town company, and his advertising and promotional efforts brought thousands of visitors to look and hundreds to stay and make their homes in the new city.

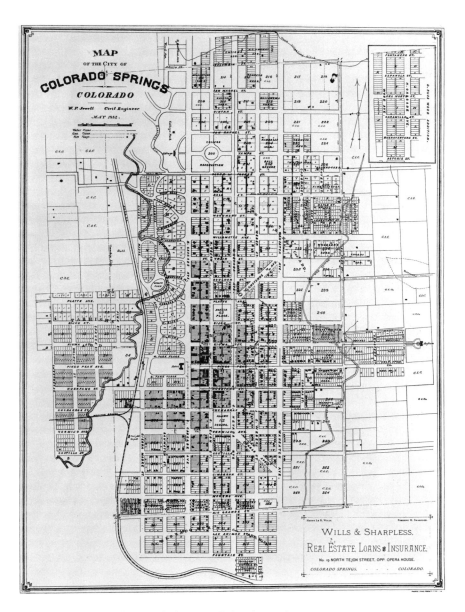

Figure 17.23   Plan of Colorado Springs, Colorado: 1882

Figure 17.24 View of Colorado Springs, Colorado: 1882

By 1874 the town had assumed a settled air. The view in Figure 17.22 shows the extent to which Colorado Springs had developed. The new town had captured the county seat of El Paso County from the older settlement of Colorado City, and the courthouse was built facing Cascade Avenue. Farther south on that thoroughfare at the intersection of Pikes Peak Avenue was the steadily expanding business district, with the first public school at its northern edge. Four churches, three of them closely grouped on Weber Street near its intersection with Pikes Peak Avenue, indicated to the increasing number of visitors that this community was to be no rowdy railroad town of the usual type. Cameron and Palmer reinforced this image by including restrictions in all deeds prohibiting the manufacture or sale of intoxicating liquors on the premises. An opera house, a museum, several resort hotels, and other improvements added to the appeal of the city. The restaurant in the Denver and Rio Grande depot offered elaborate menus beginning with oyster stew or mock turtle soup and continuing with such dishes as ham in champagne sauce or lobster salad.

Cameron tirelessly advertised and promoted the advantages of Colorado Springs as a residential and recreation center. The nearby Garden of the Gods, with its picturesque wind-sculptured rock formations, proved to be one of the principal scenic attractions of the West, and Cameron did not miss an opportunity to bring distinguished visitors to witness this and other natural wonders of the Rockies. Newspaper accounts of their visits proved excellent publicity for the resort city.

Palmer entertained many American and foreign dignitaries at his Glen Eyrie estate, where he lived in baronial fashion in a towered castle near the Garden of the Gods. When visitors were not being feted, Palmer rode daily into Colorado Springs to observe progress in his city to which he lavishly donated land and money for parks and boulevards and to countless charities. He also provided the land for Cragmor Sanatorium on the outskirts of the town, which soon became

one of the leading centers for the treatment of tubercular patients.[36]

Extensions to the thriving city soon were needed. The plan reproduced in Figure 17.23 shows Colorado Springs in 1882 with the additions made by that date. Of greatest interest are the curving streets west of Cascade Avenue between the Antlers Hotel and the campus of Colorado College. The beauty of this residential district was enhanced by the winding creek valley running through the area, which soon became a neighborhood of fine homes. Seven years after this plan was published the Chicago, Rock Island & Pacific Railroad selected Colorado Springs as its western terminal. This added transportation facility coupled with the gold strike at Cripple Creek in 1891 brought industrial development to the older community of Colorado City.

Figure 17.24 shows the city in 1882 as viewed from the east. The building in the lower right corner is the first structure erected at the Colorado School for the Deaf and Blind, founded in 1874. In the middle distance is Colorado City with its new gold smelters. In Colorado Springs itself the two-block-square parks and the diagonal streets leading to them identify the central portion of the city's original plat. Near the northeastern corner of one of them—Acacia Place, or North Park—now stands an equestrian statue of Palmer at the intersection of East Platte and North Nevada Avenues. Unveiled in 1929, it commemorates the achievements of the person who created Colorado Springs.

Palmer's deep and personal attachment to Colorado Springs and his successful efforts to establish there a city of beauty and grace contrast strangely with his lack of care in the planning of his later towns. In those activities he differed little if at all from the other railroad town builders whose work in the West was characterized by a lack of attention to any but the most routine and unimaginative aspects of urban design. Palmer's Colorado Springs stands as a reminder of the quality that might have been handed down to our generation and those to come by the builders of the western railroads.

XVIII

Tracks and Towns: Railroads and Urban Growth in
Texas and the Southwest

TEXAS and the territories to the west suffered little of the devastation that the Civil War brought to the South. Within a short time following the end of strife, the region was ready to resume the development of its urban base even more rapidly than during the three decades prior to 1860. In this period the further extension of the railroad network through the area was to play a decisive role. Along the routes of the transcontinental lines and the connecting links between them, new towns sprang up. Others, by-passed by the railroads, declined or disappeared altogether despite their advantages of earlier origins.

As a state with its own public domain, Texas was able to supplement federal land grants for railroads with land subsidies of its own. One line receiving such assistance was the Texas and Pacific, whose charter authorized it to build westward from Marshall, near the northeast corner of the state, to the Yuma crossing of the Colorado River, and on to San Diego.[1] Construction of this line proved enormously beneficial to the towns it served.

Dallas lay directly west of Marshall. At the end of the Civil War, it was still not much more than a village slowly filling up portions of John Bryan's little grid of blocks along the Trinity River. By 1872, when the view in Plate 24 was drawn, the town was booming, for in that year the Houston and Texas Central Railroad ran its first train to Dallas, and the Texas and Pacific tracks—shown here incorrectly as already open—were nearing the city. The completion of the Texas and Pacific line to Dallas the following year accelerated the city's expansion. Farmers and ranchers brought wagons of wheat, wool, cotton, and hides to be shipped south and east, and wholesalers, merchants, and tradesmen flocked to the town to take advantage of this new market.

As the view shows, the Grigsby tract to the north of Bryan's townsite had finally been laid off in streets, blocks, and lots. The old, diagonal dividing line between the two claims provided one axis for a new gridiron system. This can be seen more clearly in Figure 18.1, the official map of Dallas prepared in 1875 when the city boundaries were extended to embrace an area of nearly three square miles.

This survey records many other substantial extensions of the street pattern made by that time. While several of Bryan's thoroughfares leading from the Trinity had been extended eastward with their original 80-foot width, others had been platted much narrower. At the Grigsby line several of the streets do not meet those laid out by Bryan; others are slightly offset, which created dangerous and unattractive jogs. Elsewhere, the parquet-like design of many separate gridiron additions testifies to the lack of public controls over city growth and the willfulness of individual landowners who failed to realize or simply ignored the problems they were creating for future generations as they separately determined the confused and tortuous thoroughfare system of downtown Dallas.

It would not be until well into the present century that a comprehensive city plan would be prepared that would eventually result in a program of street widening, park development, railroad grade intersection elimination, and other major improvements. Before that occurred, however, Dallas would continue expanding virtually without guidance in all directions. As a prospering market and manufacturing center that dominated its region economically and culturally Dallas was a success; as an example of frontier urban planning it remained an all-too-typical failure.[2]

West of Dallas, on the projected line of the Texas and Pacific, little Fort Worth was just emerging from a period of decline caused by the Civil War. Most able-bodied males had enlisted in the Confederate cause, and others moved away seeking opportunities elsewhere. The entire population of the county at the beginning of the conflict had numbered only 6,000. During the war it dwindled to one-sixth this figure. Not until the end of that decade of turmoil did the town regain its former position as a minor trading center and stopping point on the way west.

The cattle trade did much to revive Fort Worth. By 1870, 300,000 head of cattle were being driven through Fort Worth and across Indian territory. The last major point for provisioning, Fort Worth began to prosper as trail hands and bosses purchased food and clothing for the long, hot drive northward. When the Missouri, Kansas, and Texas line reached Denison in 1873, the distance was shortened, but most of the drives continued to pass through Fort Worth.[3]

It seemed clearly only a question of time before one of the western railroads would reach Fort Worth, and the announcement that the Texas and Pacific had started construction from Marshall was received with wild enthusiasm in the frontier town. Residents had every right to be confident that the line would soon reach them, for in charge of construction was General Grenville M. Dodge, whose reputation as the man who built the Union Pacific was both well-earned and widely known.

Fort Worth entered a dizzy period of boom construction and expansion. Dozens of businessmen opened shops in anticipation of the profits to be made. Construction of permanent buildings lagged behind the demand for shelter, and a tent city blossomed at the edge of town.

Figure 18.1 Plan of Dallas, Texas: 1875

Banks and newspapers were organized, an ice cream parlor opened, hotels were built, restaurants and saloons flourished, and real estate offices thrived as land prices soared.[4]

At the height of the boom, Fort Worth was stunned by the news that the great financial house of Jay Cooke and Company had failed. It was but the first of many such announcements as the cloud of depression spread across the country in 1873. Dependent on loans from eastern bankers, the Texas and Pacific suspended construction with its tracks ending at Eagle Ford, a tantalizing 26 miles east of Fort Worth.

Fort Worth as it appeared in the few dismal years to follow can be seen in Figure 18.2, a view published in 1876 showing the town from a point over the Trinity River. Most prominent is the courthouse standing in the center of the former military quadrangle. Main Street leads from it southeasterly off to the prairie, where D. D. Morse, the artist, stubbornly but inaccurately depicted the railroad that remained only a hope and not a reality.

Three sides of the courthouse square appear to be almost solidly built up as do the first three blocks of Main Street. Scattered rather forlornly about the boom-expanded gridiron of streets can be seen the one- and two-story houses of those who chose to remain in Fort Worth during the depression years. Here and there appear somewhat larger structures—a church, a few more substantial residences, and two factories, each bravely spouting a plume of smoke.

Perhaps the most exciting event of those otherwise gloomy years was the opening of a telegraph line to Dallas in 1874. Over its wires the mayor of that city, which already was enjoying rail transportation, dispatched this rather smug reply in response to an earlier message from Mayor W. P. Burts of Fort Worth: "Dallas responds to your greetings most heartily and extends to her sister city . . . its congratulations in at last being able to tell of her glories in electric words, and trusts that the near future will bind us with iron bands as well as by the great electric tongue of thought."[5]

Not all residents of Dallas were as outwardly polite. A former Fort Worth lawyer, Robert Cowart, who had abandoned the town in favor of its larger rival, wrote an article in the Dallas *Herald* claiming that his former home was such a dead community that a panther had been discovered asleep in the main street.[6]

No panther or any other animal could have drowsed in the streets of Fort Worth in 1876 when almost the entire town turned out to build the remaining 26 miles of railroad before the Texas and Pacific could be forced to surrender its Texas land grants for non-compliance with the original subsidy agreement. Fort Worth capital rallied to the task, and employees of local shops and factories rolled up their sleeves and fell to work grading the right-of-way, tamping ballast, laying ties, and spiking track in a race with the clock and calendar. It was a glorious day in Fort Worth when locomotive No. 20 noisily chuffed into the town on July 19, 1876, shortly before noon. Pistol shots from enthusiastic onlookers added to the noise of the rapid clanging of the engine bell and its shrill whistle whose cord had been tied down while a local newspaper editor threw logs into the firebox to maintain sufficient pressure in the steam boiler.[7]

As General Dodge extended the Texas and Pacific line west of Fort Worth he reverted to the practice he had followed on the Union Pacific of planning new towns as profitable real estate ventures to help finance construction and generate freight and passenger traffic. One hundred and sixty miles beyond Fort Worth, his townsite agent concluded an arrangement with a group of ranchers east of Catclaw Creek. The railroad agreed to run its line through the tract and locate a station near its center. The landowners contracted to furnish all the land needed for the depot, yards, and cattle pens at a nominal price. In exchange for a 50 percent interest in the remaining portion of the 2,000-acre site the railroad company was to lay out the town, advertise it, and put up lots at auction.[8]

On Tuesday, March 15, 1881, the first lots were sold in Abilene, a name selected for the former Kansas railhead to which the ranchers had once driven their longhorns. Like its northern namesake, Abilene's plan followed the utilitarian grid pattern so widely used by the engineers and surveyors employed by the railroads for their townsite designs. One lot must have seemed very much like all the others, but at the end of two days of sales 317 pieces of property had been conveyed to some 200 new owners at an aggregate price of over $50,000. Another new town was born, a process to be repeated farther to the west as the Texas and Pacific line gradually moved westward through Sweetwater, Big Spring, Midland, and Odessa.[9]

In its westward march across the state, the Texas and Pacific had as its goal the strategic crossing of the Rio Grande at the historic pass through which Oñate had made his way to New Mexico nearly three centuries earlier. The principal town in this area was El Paso del Norte (now Ciudad Juárez) on the Mexican side of the great river. The American settlement on the left bank consisted of a series of ranchos and scattered farms grouped around several hamlets, including El Paso itself, founded in 1849 by Benjamin Franklin Coons and later known as

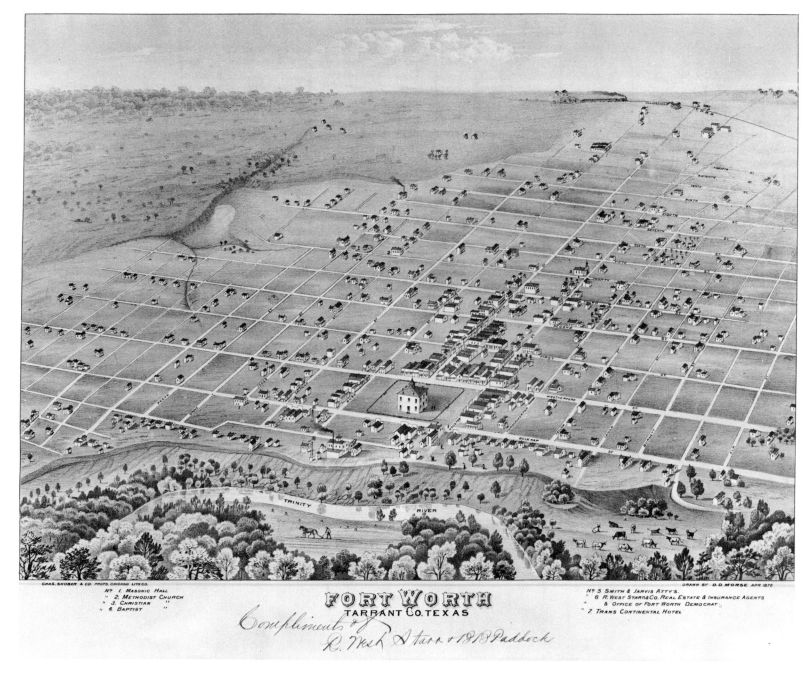

CHAS. SHOBER & CO. PROPS. CHICAGO LITH CO.

DRAWN BY D.D.MORSE APR.1876

Nº 1. MASONIC HALL
" 2. METHODIST CHURCH
" 3. CHRISTIAN "
" 4. BAPTIST "

Nº 5 SMITH & JARVIS ATTY'S.
" 6 R. WEST STARR & CO. REAL ESTATE & INSURANCE AGENTS
    & OFFICE OF FORT WORTH DEMOCRAT
" 7. TRANS CONTINENTAL HOTEL

FORT WORTH
TARRANT CO. TEXAS

TRINITY   RIVER

Figure 18.2   View of Fort Worth, Texas: 1876

Smithville, and Frontera, Hart's Mill, Magoffinsville, Concordia, the old mission settlements at Ysleta and Socorro, and the county seat of San Elizario.[10]

During the years of the California gold rush, thousands of persons passed through the area, and in 1858 El Paso became a stop on the Butterfield Overland Stage Company route between St. Louis and San Francisco. The town began to develop, survived the conflict between the Union and Confederate forces over nearby Fort Bliss, and obtained a city charter in 1873.

The arrival of four major railroads almost simultaneously in the early years of the following decade transformed little El Paso from a sleepy adobe village into a busy, booming, and expanding city. The Southern Pacific won the race, reaching El Paso on May 19, 1881. Three weeks later the first trains of the Santa Fé line entered the town. On January 1 of the next year the Texas and Pacific connected with the Southern Pacific line at Sierra Blanca, 92 miles east of El Paso, from which point its trains had access to the West Coast over the Southern Pacific tracks. During this same period, the Mexican Central Railroad opened service between Mexico City and El Paso del Norte across the Rio Grande.[11]

The principal graphic record of El Paso at this time is the plan reproduced in Figure 18.3. It was published in the fall of 1884 by J. Fisher Satterthwaite of New York to promote the large extension of the town he had begun two years before, northwest of the original community that had grown up around the point where El Paso and San Francisco Streets intersected to form an irregular plaza.[12] To the right of the old plaza a rectangular public square probably indicates an attempt to bring a greater degree of order to El Paso's structure following the city's incorporation and the influx of Anglo population into what had previously been a largely Mexican community.

Satterthwaite's huge tract, whose boundaries are indicated on the drawing, occupied a large portion of what is now downtown El Paso. The easterly part of this he planned in rectangular blocks bounded by straight streets, thus continuing the module established by the public square (now known as San Jacinto Plaza). For the remaining and larger part of his land he used a confusing, almost aimless series of radial thoroughfares that seem to have no functional basis for their alignment and which, in their numerous angled intersections, would have created an aesthetically disastrous, inefficient, and dangerous pattern. Fortunately for the city, a few of these streets were not constructed, and others have been somewhat modified in later years.

Well planned or not, Satterthwaite's addition attracted a population. The developer claimed in 1884 that more than 80 houses had been built

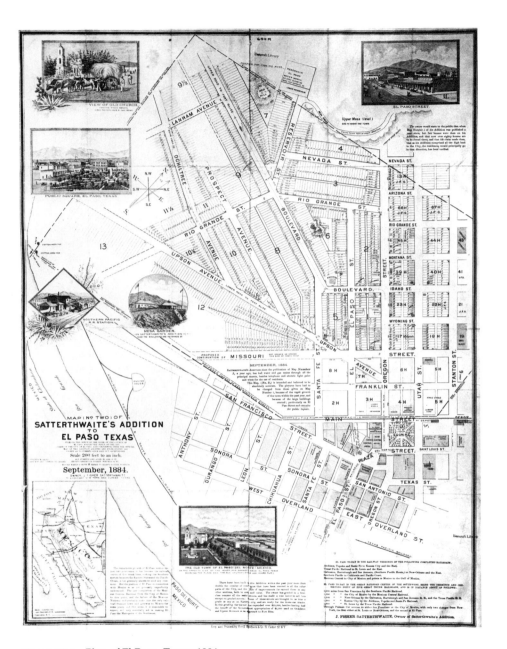

Figure 18.3 Plan of El Paso, Texas: 1884

in his tract during the previous year, and land developers elsewhere were doubtless encountering similar success and financial rewards. As the principal rail connection with Mexico, the center of a mining area of growing importance, and well located to tap the trade of the expanding ranching and farming activities in the Rio Grande Valley, El Paso thus entered an era of growth and economic development that has been buttressed over the years by the expansion of Fort Bliss, increased tourist travel, and the growth of the University of Texas at El Paso from its origins in 1917 as the Texas College of Mines and Metallurgy.

The coming of the railroads to the Texas panhandle fostered the growth of towns in that hot and arid region. As the Fort Worth and Denver line entered this area in 1887, James T. Berry, who had been active in the development of Abilene, and knew of the profits to be made in townsite speculation, filed an application with the General Land Office for a section of land along the projected right-of-way. Several other persons claimed adjoining land, but Berry offered the railroad $25,000 if it would locate its passenger and freight station on his townsite. This served as a guarantee that Berry would deed to the railroad the necessary land for the tracks and station and an undivided one-fourth interest in the remainder of the square-mile section when his title was perfected.[13]

Berry's town—first called Oneida and then changed to Amarillo— won the designation as county seat of newly organized Potter County. The vote was close, but Berry won by promising each cowhand of the nearby enormous RX Ranch two lots in the town if it was selected for the honor. Amarillo's plan as staked out by Henry H. Luckett was a no-nonsense gridiron relieved only by Block 40 reserved for the courthouse. Amarillo's unimaginative pattern together with portions of the adjacent townsites laid out by Berry's competitors are reproduced in Figure 18.4. Berry and Luckett platted their blocks 250 by 300 feet, divided into 10 or 24 lots and served by streets uniformly 80 feet wide.

The town attracted merchants and residents, and there was every reason to believe that Amarillo's development would continue. Then in the fall of 1888 H. B. Sanborn, the proprietor of one of the unsuccessful townsites in the county seat election, platted section 169 adjacent to Amarillo on the east. Sanborn managed to undermine Berry's town through an aggressive campaign of lot sales and promotion in Houston and by offering to trade lots in his new development for property in the older town. He paid the cost of moving buildings and in some cases arranged for the owners to retain title to their original property as well. Heavy rains in the spring of 1889 caused some flooding in the lower

portions of old Amarillo, and this misfortune hastened the exodus. Within two years there was little left of the original town of Amarillo. Its center simply moved one mile to the east where it remains today in the heart of the trading and manufacturing metropolis of the panhandle.

South of Amarillo, approximately halfway to Midland, a similar conflict between rival townsites took place but with a different resolution. In 1890 two groups of real estate speculators, each hoping to capture the county seat of Lubbock County, platted the towns of Lubbock and Monterey not far from one another. Residents of each were offered lots in the other town if they would move, and other inducements were extended in efforts to capture population and potential county seat votes.

In December the two factions concluded a truce and agreed to abandon both townsites in favor of a third that would be jointly owned. An intricate arrangement of ownership was worked out so that each company received alternate blocks or lots in the new town, thus equalizing the potential value of the property that would be shared.[14]

Figure 18.5 shows the design for the new Lubbock laid out near the center of the county early in 1891. Fifteen streets running north and south intersect an equal number of cross-streets to form 210 rectangular blocks and 30 half-blocks along two sides of the town. All streets were made a generous 75 feet wide, and the proprietors platted three north-south and two east-west thoroughfares 100 feet in width. These met at the courthouse square, which occupied an elongated site twice the size of the normal city blocks plus an additional 100-foot strip of land where the central north-south thoroughfare was interrupted to terminate at the center of the square's longer sides.

Development of Lubbock was slow. One difficulty stemmed from the peculiar system of alternating lot ownership. W. E. Rayner, who had been the proprietor of Monterey, believed that the town would grow but decided to hold on to his property until he could realize higher prices than prevailed during the first decade and a half of the town's existence. Businessmen who wished to expand found that Rayner owned the adjoining lots and was unwilling to put them on the market. Finally, in 1906 a company was formed to purchase all of Rayner's property. After he agreed to the company's offer the lots were quickly snapped up, and the company was liquidated in 1909.[15]

Lack of rail service proved an equally serious problem. A series of proposals for connections to one of the major lines in the region came to nothing. The city and its impatient residents were forced to wait until the fall of 1909, when a branch of the Pecos and Northern Texas line

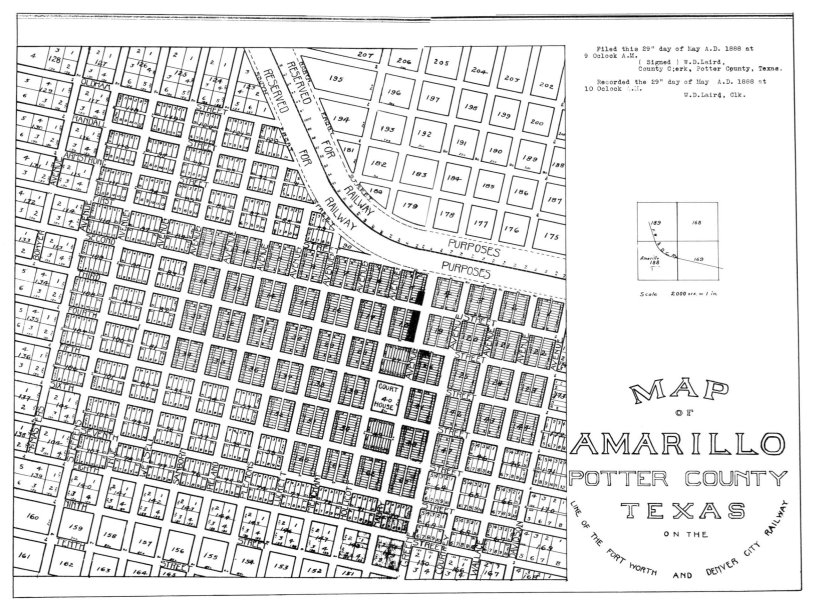

Filed this 29" day of May A.D. 1888 at
9 Oclock A.M.
(Signed) W.D.Laird,
County Clerk, Potter County, Texas.

Recorded the 29" day of May A.D. 1888 at
10 Oclock A.M.
W.D.Laird, Clk.

Scale   2000 vrs. = 1 in.

MAP
OF
AMARILLO
POTTER COUNTY
TEXAS
ON THE
LINE OF THE FORT WORTH AND DENVER CITY RAILWAY

Figure 18.4 Plan of Amarillo, Texas: 1888

Figure 18.5 View of Wichita Falls, Texas: 1890

connected Lubbock to Plainview and the outside world. One more crude prairie town of perhaps 1,800 persons was on its way to becoming the city in fact that its charter of that same year promised on paper.

Amarillo and Lubbock were not the only towns in northern Texas that shifted locations from their original sites. At the falls of the Wichita River some miles above its mouth, M. W. Seeley laid out Wichita Falls in 1876 on the north bank. His plat included a public square imbedded in a grid of straight streets. More imaginatively but quite inaccurately, he showed a series of wharves along the river covered with bales of cotton. A steamer in the river waited to take on this imaginary cargo for shipment down the Red River to the Mississippi.

River travel proved impossible except for noncommercial craft of very shallow draft, and a projected railroad to Dallas failed to materialize. Until 1882, with the coming of the Fort Worth and Denver Railroad, the residents of Wichita Falls relied for transportation on what was called locally the T. B. & W.—Two Bulls and a Wagon! The city had to offer the Fort Worth and Denver line a substantial subsidy to obtain rail service, but it proved a worthwhile investment.

A public sale of town lots scheduled to coincide with the arrival of the first train was eagerly attended. A heavy rainfall and flood intervened, however, to change the focus of interest to the south side of the river when it was found that many of the lots marked for sale lay temporarily under water. Most of the subsequent growth of Wichita Falls thus took place south of the intended focal point around the first public square. When Wichita Falls became the county seat the following year, a new location had to be found for the building that housed governmental offices.

The view reproduced in Figure 18.6 shows the city in 1890 when completion of the Wichita Valley railroad added a further stimulus to growth. The business district then occupied a compact area between the river and the new courthouse, but elsewhere houses, churches, mills, and the school were scattered throughout the extensive grid of streets, many of which had been surveyed by the owners of land adjoining the original plat. A third rail line in 1895 brought a new boom, and by the early years of the present century Wichita Falls had more than 100 places of business. They included no fewer than 21 saloons, an attraction to nearby ranchers and thirsty cowhands and responsible for the origin of the town's nickname of Whiskeytaw Falls.[16]

Throughout Texas as the nineteenth century drew to a close, towns such as Wichita Falls were thriving, including a line of settlements stretching westward from the Arkansas border to the Wichita River. One of these towns was Honey Grove, shown in Figure 18.7 as it appeared in 1886 in an attractive view issued by a Milwaukee publishing company. Although its population was then only 1,200, the business directory printed below the title of the view suggests the diversity of activities even such a modest size community could offer.

The large public square that B. S. Walcott doubtless provided when he planned the town in 1852 suggests that he had in mind obtaining the designation of county seat. Although nearby Bonham achieved this honor, Honey Grove grew nonetheless. The artist's drawing shows a busy market scene with the square filled with horses and wagons. The solid enclosure of this central open space by banks, hardware stores, furniture shops, dry goods establishments, a drug, book, and stationery store, and several emporiums of "general merchandise and fancy goods" indicates that Honey Grove's rail connections via the Texas and Pacific line shown at the bottom of the view provided a sufficient basis for economic development.[17]

A few miles eastward the traveler would have encountered a larger town with a less sweet but more impressive name. This , too, was an old settlement— founded by George W. Wright in 1839 and originally called Pinhook. Becoming the seat of Lamar County in 1844, the town under its new name of Paris profited from its location on the Central National Road, which the Republic of Texas opened to connect San Antonio with a crossing of the Red River.

The arrival of the Texas and Pacific line triggered the usual boom in town lots and business growth. By 1885 when the view reproduced in Figure 18.8 was published, Paris had obviously become a community of substantial size and wealth. Its handsome courthouse stood on its own block one street removed from the public square on which the most important business buildings could be found. Just off the square to the southeast and fronting the horse-drawn trolley plying between the depot and the business district stood the imposing Opera House. Here Miss Frances Willard in 1882, failing to obtain a church for the purpose, held a mass meeting of stern-jawed puritans to organize the Texas branch of the Woman's Christian Temperance Union. She must have encountered some stiff opposition in Paris. The little city, like its French namesake, abounded with bars and saloons. One could be found in the lofty Lamar Hotel diagonally across South Main Street from Miss Willard's meeting place, while the swinging doors of Clark and Hatten's Opera Saloon beckoned invitingly from its location opposite the theater's portal.[18]

Other flourishing little communities along the Oklahoma border also included Sherman, Gainesville, and Greenville, all considered important enough by T. M. Fowler in 1891 for him to depict them in the early

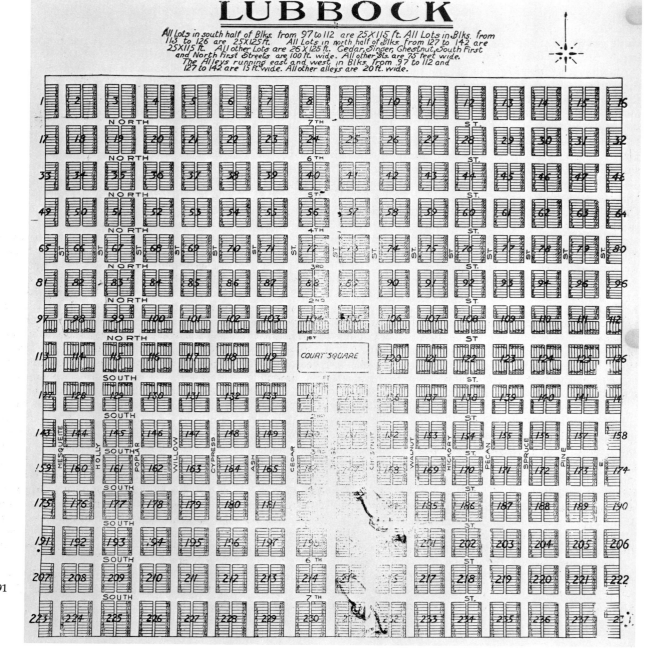

Figure 18.6 Plan of Lubbock, Texas: ca. 1891

HONEY GROVE, TEX.

FANNIN COUNTY.

1886.

1 High School.
2 Walcott Institute
3 Methodist Episcopal Church.
4 Baptist   "
5 Presbyterian   "
6 Cumberland Presbyt'n "
7 Episcopal   "
8 Christian   "
9 Colored Churches.
10 Dramatic Hall.
12 Rail Road Depot.
13 Post Office, T. D Bloys, P. M.

14 First National Bank, T. U. Cole, Cashier.
15 W. Underwood, General Merchandise and Fancy Goods.
16 J. L. Ware, General Merchandise, Fancy Goods & Notions
17 J. H. Robnett, General Merchandise and Fancy Goods.
18 J. B. McKee & Co.,   "
19 { W. D. Wilkins,
   { W. D. Wilkins & Co., Bankers.
20 J. B. Ryan, Drugs, Jewelry, Books and Stationery.
21 S. L. Erwin & Co., Hardware, Farm & Mill Machinery.
22 Burgher & Stephens,   "

34 H. S. Williams, Wagon and Carriage Repair Shops.
35 A. N. Kinsworthy, Gen'l Blacksmithing and Repair Shops
36 R. B. Smith, Traveling Salesman.
37 C. H. Walcott, { Real Estate
   { The Walcott Residence, oldest in the City
38 The Stobaugh Residence.

39 B. O. Walcott's Cotton, Gin and Flour Mills.
40 J. H. Johnson's   "   "
24 Weekly Herald, J. M. Terry, Publisher In Pierce Block.
41 Dr. S. J. Harrison, Physician and Surgeon.
42 Gin Mills.
43 Planing Mills.

23 T. B. Yarbrough, Dry Goods, Clothing, Hats and Caps.
24 Pierce, Wood & Co., Wholesale and Retail Groceries.
25 Scott Bros., Staple and Fancy Groceries.
26 F C. Fisher & Sons, Hardware, and Manufacturers of Tinware, Walcott's Block
27 B. F. Barnum, Furniture Dealers, Walcott's Block.
28 W. R. Burnett, Painter and Paper Hanger.
29 Yeager House, W. D. Yeager, Prop'r.
30 Smith Hotel, T. M. Coulter, Prop'r.
31 A. H. Smith's Livery, Feed and Sale Stables.
32 J. D. Burgher & Co., Lumber Yard and Grain House. Dealers in Grain, Lumber, Sash, Doors, &c.
33 T. H. Seaton's Lumber Yard and Residence.

Figure 18.7   View of Honey Grove, Texas: 1886

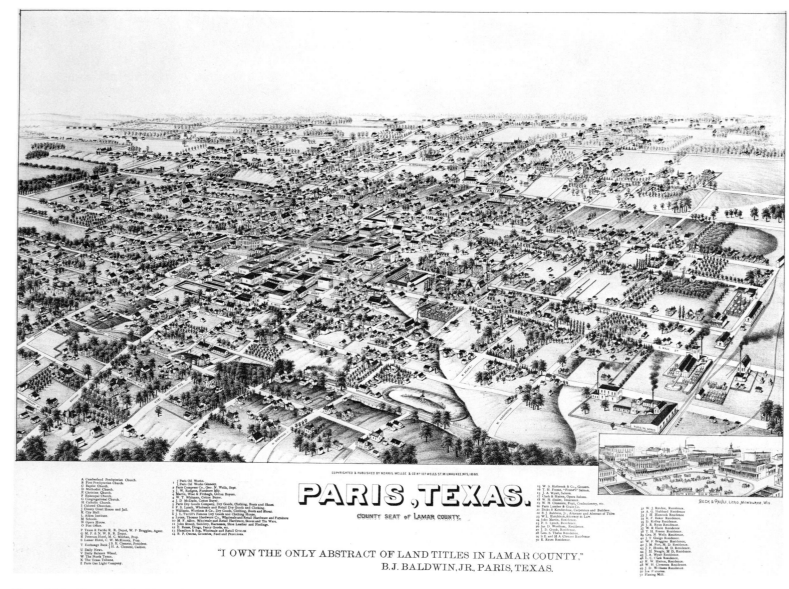

Figure 18.8   View of Paris, Texas: 1885

years of his long career as an artist and publisher of urban bird's-eye views.[19] Sherman had been snubbed by the Katy railroad when Robert Stevens in 1872 decided to promote his own town of Denison to the north, but now with railroads of its own, it had surpassed its newer rival. Gainesville, the seat of Cooke County, west of Sherman, began its existence in 1850. For nearly 20 years it suffered from Indian raids, but eventually began to grow as a center of cattle raising, and, after the depression of 1893, developed as a market town for the cotton farmers of the region.[20] Cotton growing, pressing, and related manufacturing also provided Greenville a firm economic base, one supported strongly by the four railroads that eventually were built to serve its once isolated location in Hunt County southeast of Sherman.[21]

In eastern Texas, two towns of more striking character resulted from the efforts of enterprising corporate leaders, each of whom founded new communities with elaborate designs of more than passing interest. One—New Birmingham—proved unsuccessful and ultimately vanished; the other—Port Arthur—while encountering early economic difficulties, finally grew to become a major city.

New Birmingham was the brainchild of A. B. Blevins, a sewing machine salesman from Birmingham, Alabama. Noticing some outcrops of iron ore in Cherokee County in central east Texas, Blevins conceived the idea of creating a new center for iron and steel production. In 1888 he organized the New Birmingham Iron and Land Company with the aid of capital raised in St. Louis and New York. On a portion of the 20,000-acre tract of land purchased by the company Blevins began to develop a new industrial community.

The plan for this development is reproduced in Figure 18.9. One of the names appearing on the drawing is that of N. F. Barrett, identified as a landscape engineer. Eight years earlier Nathan Barrett and an architect, Solon S. Behman, collaborated on the plan for Pullman, Illinois, perhaps America's most skillfully planned company town of the period.[22] The rather prosaic design for New Birmingham leads one to believe that it was Behman who was responsible for the innovative and imaginative plan of Pullman. Barrett's rather meaningless curvilinear parks in New Birmingham indicate little understanding of urban planning techniques, and both their location and layout appear mechanical and arbitrary. The absence of some kind of open space buffer between the proposed manufacturing district at the bottom and the rest of the town certainly stands out as a more serious deficiency.

The initial period of development saw the construction of two steel furnaces, a brick plant, a school, and the imposing Southern Hotel, a small view of which appears above the title of the published plan of the town. Overnight guests entertained here by Blevins included such personages as Jay Gould, Grover Cleveland, and representatives of the firm of Robert A. Van Wyck, financiers of the project.[23] Their presence seemed to confirm Blevins's vision of a future great industrial metropolis.

In the fall of 1891 the company summarized its accomplishments: "On Nov. 12, 1888 New Birmingham had not a single house completed. It was entirely in the woods. Today, with nearly 400 buildings completed and occupied, she claims and justly so, a population of 1,500. The streets are graded, and houses and streets lighted with electricity; the business houses are the best class of brick buildings; it boasts a street railway and a magnificent hotel, the Southern, with all modern improvements. The industries represented today are two blast furnaces, a pipe foundry, planning mill, sash and door factory, steam laundry, and steam bakery and other industries being negotiated for."[24] A year later the population was estimated at 3,000, and the new town seemed to have secured a firm footing.

More capital was needed than could be found in the East, and company officials went to England seeking financial backing. English investors were interested enough in the project to send representatives to New Birmingham, but this promising source of financing was cut off by the passage in 1891 of the Texas Alien Land Laws restricting foreign investment within the state. The panic of 1893, a drop in the price of pig iron, and the destruction by fire in 1896 of one of the blast furnaces combined with the lack of capital to doom the project. The company went into receivership, and within a few years the site lay virtually abandoned. By the mid-1940s only memories of the name remained of what had once been a thriving industrial community.[25]

More remarkable in its plan and the circumstances of its founding, Port Arthur succeeded where New Birmingham failed. Both its site and design were determined by a colorful business tycoon, Arthur Edward Stilwell. Born and educated in Rochester, Stilwell moved to Kansas City as a young man of 27 after establishing himself as a successful insurance salesman. There he dabbled in real estate and construction before joining with a former mayor, E. L. Martin, in building the Kansas City Suburban Belt Railroad.

The success of this venture led Stilwell to conceive of developing a rail line from Kansas City to the Gulf Coast. With the aid of Philadelphia capital later supplemented by funds raised in Holland, he pushed his Kansas City, Pittsburg and Gulf Railroad Company line southward

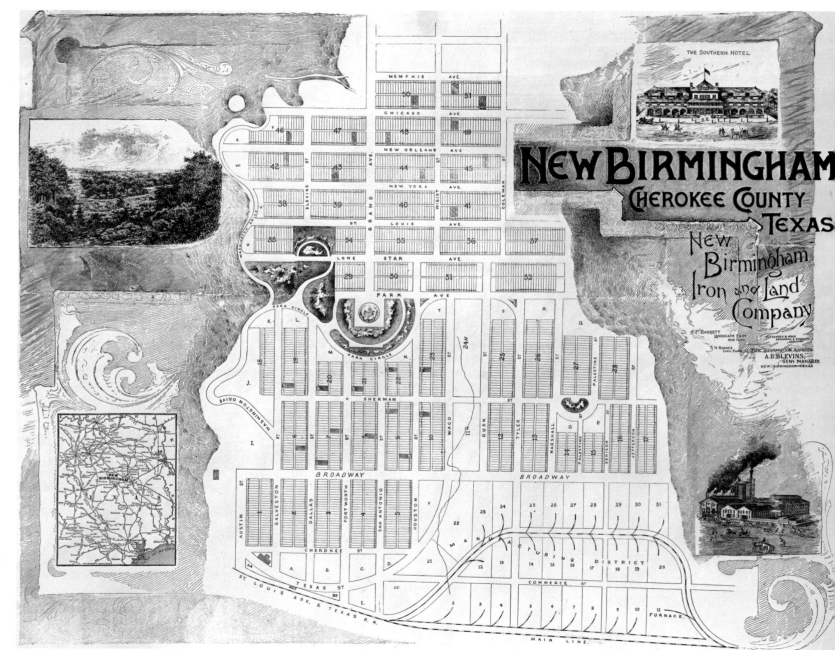

Figure 18.9
Plan for New
Birmingham,
Texas: ca.
1888

through Missouri, Arkansas, Louisiana, and into Texas. Along the route he created dozens of new towns, some named for his Philadelphia backers and others, like Amsterdam, Zwolle, and DeRidder, for Dutch towns or business associates. In 1895 with his engineer, Robert Gilham, and his townsite agent, Frank Henderson, Stilwell selected and acquired more than 45,000 acres of land on the western shore of Sabine Lake near the Gulf of Mexico, not far above the site where President Lamar had located his town of Sabine Pass half a century earlier.

On 4,000 acres of this huge tract Stilwell's Port Arthur Townsite and Land Company began developing the town that its promoter claimed had been planned with the help of friendly spirits. Throughout his career, Stilwell was later to maintain, he had been helped by spirits or "Brownies" and he once wrote that Port Arthur was the only city "ever located and built under directions from the spirit world . . . so recognized and acknowledged."[26]

What is apparently the first published plat of the town, reproduced in Figure 18.10, would seem to have more worldly origins with its routine gridiron street system, extensive area for railroad yards, and large industrial and wharf section to the southwest along the shore of Sabine Lake. Unusual, however, especially for a railroad-sponsored town, was the spacious Lake Shore Park bordered on its north side by a winding drive separating the recreation area from a range of very large lots fronting the park and the lake. Equally arresting is the oval park reached from the lake by Stilwell Boulevard, 120 feet wide, and from the west edge of the town by the equally broad Thomas Boulevard.

This was only the first section of the new town contemplated by Stilwell and his spirit mentors. Figure 18.11 shows the complete design as published around 1897. To the east Stilwell added a second gridiron section as large as the first. Here, too, he provided another broad thoroughfare—De Queen Boulevard—running north and south, and two park blocks midway between the shore and Thomas Boulevard like the public square of the first section. It is the northern sector, however, that departed from the usual pattern of towns of the period. Here Stilwell, perhaps inspired by spiritual guidance, planned an intricate series of radial streets leading off Gilhan Circle, each becoming the axis of a little grid of square blocks pierced, like those elsewhere in the town, by alleys serving the rear of the lots. Two five-sided parks and two smaller triangular spaces at intersections of the radials added further embellishment to the design.

Stilwell began a forceful advertising and promotional campaign, flooding newspapers with editorial copy, advertising widely, publish-

ing a series of pamphlets boasting of the advantages of the new town and its port facilities, and escorting visitors and potential investors around the site. He had much to show: a railroad station, the 70-room Sabine Hotel, a natatorium and pier with restaurant and dance pavilion designed to lure tourists to the town, and several commercial buildings as well as scores of houses completed and under construction. By the end of 1897 the population approached one thousand, and banks, churches, and a school added to the urban fabric.

The success of the project depended on deep-water access to the Gulf of Mexico. Sabine Lake with an average depth of only six feet could not serve unless a channel could be dredged across it to Sabine Pass, the entry to the lake from the waters of the Gulf. When Stilwell attempted to do this, rival property owners at the lake's outlet obtained an injunction stopping work on the grounds that this operation would cause their own harbor to fill with silt. Stilwell eventually found it necessary to build a canal parallel to the west shore of the lake. Although this was completed in 1899, its cost far exceeded original estimates. Coupled with finacial problems of the parent railroad company, this additional burden proved too much for Stilwell, and he was forced to relinquish control of his corporate empire.[27]

The railroad, reorganized as the Kansas City Southern under the direction of John Warne ("Bet-a Million") Gates, took over the townsite company. Its prospects seemed dim because of the heavy expense of operating and maintaining the canal with only a moderate amount of freight moving to and from the port. It was then, early in 1901, that oil was discovered in vast quantities only a few miles north of the city in the famous Spindletop Oil Field.

Beaumont, platted in 1835, was the town nearest to the discovery, and it became a boom town overnight. While eventually a canal was built to connect Beaumont with the Gulf, Port Arthur became the chief shipping point for crude oil and also a major refining center.[28] The construction of a pipeline from the Spindletop area to the port facilities Stilwell had first developed reinforced its advantageous location. By 1908 Port Arthur ranked thirteenth among American ports as measured by the value of the products moving by ships from its harbors and docks. Under its new owners the town grew swiftly, but with several changes.

Stilwell's intricate network of fan-shaped radial boulevards and avenues north of Gilham Circle (now Blue Bonnet Park) underwent the most drastic modification. Only the southernmost pair—Wilhelmina (now Blue Bonnet) Avenue on the east and Nederland Avenue to the

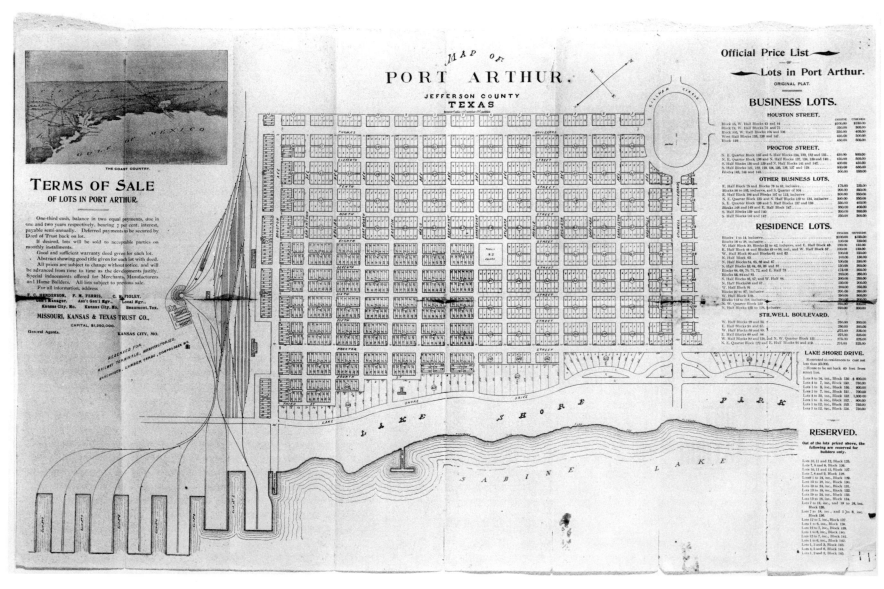

Figure 18.10 Plan of Port Arthur, Texas: 1896

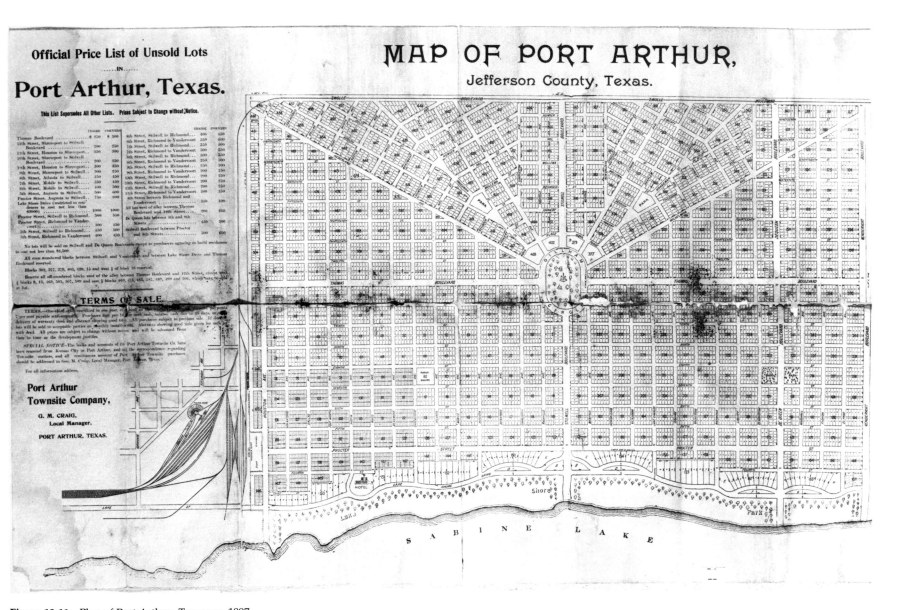

Figure 18.11 Plan of Port Arthur, Texas: ca. 1897

west—were retained. The company replatted the entire area north of these two thoroughfares into a more conventional gridiron pattern. The two parks in this portion of the original plan were retained but were changed in shape from their five-sided configuration to occupy square blocks in the replatted district. The two park blocks flanking De Queen Boulevard between 7th and 8th Streets also survived, although a school later was built to occupy that on the east side.

Along the waterfront Stilwell's park and the irregularly curving Lake Shore Drive were allowed to remain. To this pleasant feature of the town has been added the even larger Pleasure Island—a large recreation development on reclaimed land separated from the original town by the Sabine-Neches Ship Channel. Thus, while not all of what his spirit mentors revealed to Stilwell was carried out, enough was accomplished and remains to set Port Arthur apart from towns of less exotic origins.

Well before Stilwell founded Port Arthur, the principal Texas port of Galveston had entered a rapid period of development. In 1870 the city had 14,000 inhabitants. A decade later it could boast of an additional 8,000 residents. A view of the city as it appeared shortly thereafter is reproduced in Figure 18.12. The crossing of the two principal streets—Broadway and Bath (now Rosenberg) Avenue—can be clearly seen dividing the city into four quadrants. That to the northeast (lower left in the view) contained the principal business district, wharves, warehouses, and docks. By that time railroad connections to the mainland provided additional transportation facilities by which cotton, hides, wheat, and other Texas products reached the city to be shipped to foreign ports or to the eastern United States. Then the most populous city in Texas, the continued preeminence of Galveston seemed assured.

Fifteen years later disaster struck when a hurricane on September 8, 1900, drove the Gulf waters over the city, drowning at least 6,000 persons and virtually leveling the town. Galveston rebuilt; a seawall 17 feet above mean low tide and 7½ miles long was erected, and the entire city site was filled to this level on the Gulf side and graded gradually to the natural elevation of the land along Galveston Bay. It was an enormous undertaking, and during the long years of reconstruction other cities surpassed Galveston in size and commercial importance.[29]

Galveston's inland rival, Houston, still had not fully overcome its difficulties with steamboat travel up the winding channel of Buffalo Bayou, but major dredging and widening projects were begun in 1869 by the Buffalo Bayou Ship Channel Company, to which eager citizens subscribed the sum of $100,000. Several railroad lines radiating out-

ward from the city tapped the hinterland, and as the badly damaged but still legible plan reproduced in Figure 18.13 reveals, the central part of the city had begun to fill up. The publishers of this lithograph claimed a population in 1869 of 15,000—a wildly inflated figure—but plainly Houston was at last beginning to fulfill the destiny foreseen for it by the Allen brothers three decades earlier. The spirit of land speculation still pervaded the town, and the many additions laid out by owners of outlying property followed no planned pattern. Rugged individualism in urban development was to characterize the city for generations and has not altogether been overcome even in our own era.

Galveston and Houston faced competition from Indianola, the port established on Matagorda Bay through which German colonists bound for New Braunfels had passed to their new homes in Comal County. From 1850 to 1861 it had served as a military depot, supplying Army posts in Texas. It became the county seat and starting point for one of the first railroads in the state. Tanneries and food processing plants provided a nucleus for future industrial growth, and the population in 1860 was 1,150.

It was apparently after the Civil War that a town company prepared the enormous expansion plan reproduced in Figure 18.14. Its ambitious design provided a system of major thoroughfares 150 feet wide forming sections of the community served by other grid streets 60 and 70 feet in width. In addition to the courthouse square on the waterfront at the foot of Houston Street, the plan provided for several other open spaces. One of these—Military Square—took the unusual form of a cross occupying the space of five of the normal city blocks. The only Texas precedent for this pattern was Gonzales, from which it may have been copied.

By 1875 Indianola had a population of 6,000. In that year a tropical hurricane devastated the town, a disaster that was repeated in 1886. The second storm was scarcely necessary to kill the hopes of Indianola's promoters. Completion of the railroad from Galveston to San Antonio in 1877 diverted much of the shipping to Galveston and with it the basis for Indianola's existence. Following the hurricane of 1886 the town's residents abandoned the site, many of them moving to Port Lavaca, which was designated as the new county seat.[30]

Far down the coast of the Gulf of Mexico, Corpus Christi was also enjoying a brisk period of growth and improvement in the latter years of the century. The town had originated as a trading post established in 1840 by Henry Lawrence Kinney. Five years later General Zachary Taylor and his troops encamped there and brought some life and trade

Figure 18.12 View of Galveston, Texas: 1885

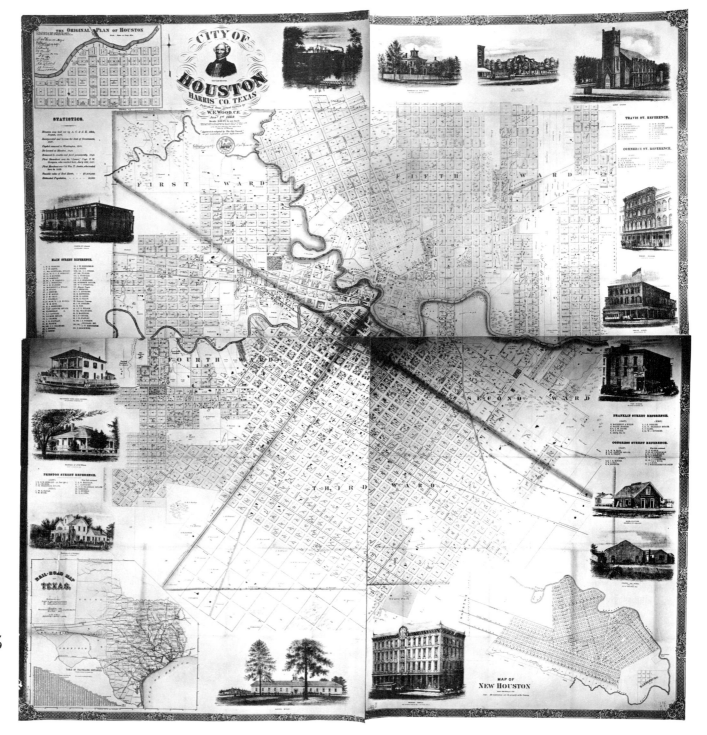

Figure 18.13   Plan of Houston,
Texas: 1869

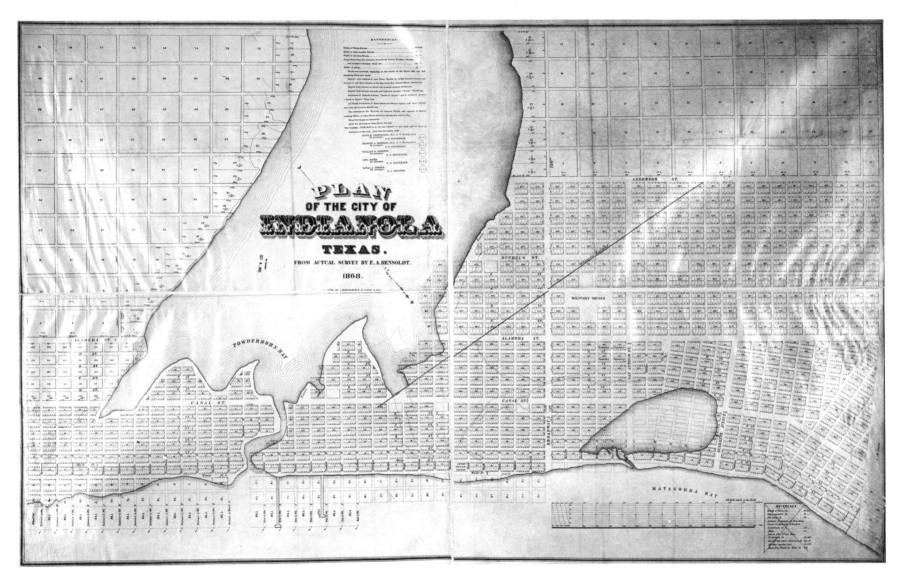

Figure 18.14 Plan of Indianola, Texas: 1868

to the little town, which in 1846 was designated the county seat of Nueces County. With the beginning of rail service in 1873, the extension of the line to Laredo eight years later, and the deepening of the shallow channel connecting Corpus Christi Bay to the Gulf, Corpus Christi assumed an important role as a market and shipping point for hides, cattle, wool, and cotton.[31]

Directly west of Corpus Christi, once-somnolent Laredo on the Rio Grande had awakened to the quickening step of urbanization. The view reproduced in Figure 18.15 shows the city about 1890, greatly expanded from the tiny plaza settlement of the eighteenth century. If one is to judge from the gigantic net of projected streets extending to the horizon, its residents and land developers anticipated an even greater period of growth in the years ahead.

Laredo consisted of more than empty streets and hopes, however. Railroad service beginning in 1882 and extended in subsequent years provided Laredo many of the advantages with respect to trade with Mexico enjoyed by El Paso. By the time this view was published, a new bridge had replaced the more picturesque but less efficient ferry across the river to the Mexican town bearing the same name. Tanneries, brick manufacturing plants, lumber yards and furniture shops, a woolen mill, Fort McIntosh, and the complex of activities associated with railroad maintenance and repair, all provided employment for Laredo's increasing population, which had jumped from 3,521 in 1880 to 11,319 a decade later. Extensive irrigation of the surrounding arid but fertile valley lands provided additional jobs, and in 1898 many farmers turned to the production of onions, for which the area has become well known.

As a sign of municipal progress, Laredo city fathers set aside a large tract of land for a park lying on the axis of the principal thoroughfare leading northward from the bridge through the closely built-up business district. While this typically American feature proved a welcome addition to the town, Martin Plaza near the river continued to serve as a more intimate recreational space. Here the old Mexican custom of the evening promenade of young men and women took place. Passing in different directions around the bandstand in the center of the plaza, couples would gradually pair off under the watchful eyes of their elders. Laredo thus combined features of two cultures.[32]

Austin had likewise undergone substantial changes and development. The Capitol that Frederick Law Olmsted admired and described as a "really imposing building" can be seen in the 1873 view of the city reproduced in Plate 25. While several minor changes had been made in the original allocation of other public building sites, the city's development clearly had followed the Lamar-Waller design in all important re-

spects. Two years before the view was published, the Houston and Texas Central Railroad reached the city, and the half-block first designated as a market became the site of its passenger depot. Perhaps in anticipation of the further growth of the city that the railroad might stimulate, four additional tiers of blocks had been surveyed on hitherto vacant land beyond the Capitol.

As important to Austin's future as the railroad was the state university. Although authorized by the legislature in 1858, not until 1883 did the institution open its doors to instruction with a faculty of eight. The block set aside in the original plan was clearly too small, and the university was located north of the original town. Its site as designated a decade prior to its construction can be seen on Figure 18.16, a survey including the entire tract acquired by the Republic of Texas within which Waller had planned the first portion of the city.

For reasons that are not entirely clear, officials in charge of disposing of the remaining land adopted a rather confusing parquet-like pattern of several separate grid systems, each following different orientations. Linking them together, however, was a system of major roads that established a basic module of land division. Until comparatively recent times this super-grid, much like Hancock's surveys of the Los Angeles pueblo tract in 1857, provided the principal control over the form and location of urban growth.

North of Austin, roughly midway to Dallas, the upper Brazos River town of Waco also experienced substantial growth following the Civil War. The completion of an impressive suspension bridge over the river in 1870 opened a new trading area for the town's merchants, and the arrival of a branch railroad a few years later further stimulated urban expansion.

By 1886, when the view reproduced in Figure 18.17 appeared, the population of the city was nearing 15,000, and the prosperous community could boast of a diversified manufacturing base and a thriving business district. Two railroad bridges provided additional connections to the east bank of the Brazos, and Waco's rapid expansion to the north, west, and south was well under way. The first buildings of Baylor University, the oldest such institution in the state, can be seen facing Fifth Street near the center of the left half of the view. In less than four decades another major Texas settlement had thus passed through its infancy as a crude pioneer village to an age of lusty urban adolescence.[33]

The same forces that had brought change to established towns and provided new patterns for those founded during this period also were at work in the oldest of the Texas municipalities. In 1870 San Antonio's population was more than 12,000. Three years later Augustus Koch

Figure 18.15 View of Laredo, Texas: ca. 1890

Figure 18.16 Plan of Austin, Texas: 1872

Figure 18.17   View of Waco, Texas: 1886

prepared the view illustrated in Figure 18.18. While no over-all plan guided the town's growth, the Spanish and Mexican tradition of the plaza evidently proved too strong to be overlooked even by the land speculators who vied with one another in promoting new real estate ventures at the outskirts of the city. In addition to the irregularly shaped Alamo Plaza to the left of the river's loop and the older rectangular main and military plazas near the center of the view, several new open spaces can be seen.

The arrival of the first railroad in 1877 brought further growth. At the end of the decade, population exceeded 20,000, and the census of 1890 revealed that San Antonio had almost doubled in size to become a community of 38,000 people. By then more modern and conventional structures had been erected in place of many of the older Mexican and German buildings in the center, and the historic core of the city had been dwarfed by suburban expansion spreading in all directions.

Beyond the western border of Texas in the territory of New Mexico, the long-awaited railroads provided the necessary impetus to urban development and growth. East of Santa Fe, not far below the point where the shorter but more dangerous Cimarron Cut-Off rejoined the old Santa Fe Trail, the little town of Las Vegas served as the trading center for the Gallinas and Pecos River valleys. When it became evident that the Santa Fé line would pass that way the town experienced a major boom.[34]

Across the Gallinas River a major addition was laid out to accommodate the tracks, depot, and shops of the railroad, and when the first train rolled into Las Vegas on July 4, 1879, the future of the now rapidly expanding community was firmly established.[35] The town's prosperity was aided by indecision in Santa Fe concerning whether to subsidize the railroad bearing its name to assure its entry into the ancient capital city or to build its own line south to Albuquerque to connect with the railroad at that point. For many months Las Vegas was the terminus of the railroad and thus functioned as a transshipping point. During this period a number of large mercantile firms located their warehouses and stores in the city.[36]

Old and New Las Vegas appear in Figure 18.19 as depicted in 1882. In the background one can see the older Hispanic town tightly clustered around its plaza, while in the foreground the artist shows the newer American town oriented to the railroad. In both settlements the hotels, saloons, gambling halls, and bawdy houses that marked the end-of-track towns on the transcontinental railroads carried out a lively trade.

To some of the less savory frequenters of such places, respectable citizens addressed an announcement and warning one early spring day in 1882: "Notice to thieves, thugs, fakirs and bunko-steerers among whom are J. J. Harlin, alias 'Off Wheeler,' Saw Dust Charlie, Wm. Hedges, Billy the Kid, Billy Mullin, Little Jack the Cutter, Pock-marked Kid and about twenty others: if found within the limits of this city after ten o'clock p.m. this night you will be invited to attend a grand necktie party, the expense of which will be borne by 100 substantial citizens."[37]

Whether this particular "necktie party" ever took place is not known, but other public hangings from a windmill in the plaza were so numerous that the owner of the windmill dismantled it because these unhappy events interfered with his business. When the railroad moved on, many of the gamblers, thieves, and con-artists followed it west, leaving Las Vegas a quieter but less colorful community serving as a marketing and service center for the large ranches and irrigated farms of the surrounding region.

From Las Vegas the Santa Fé line continued along the base of the Sangre de Cristo range, but the railroad engineers followed the old Santa Fe Trail up the western side of the mountains only to Galisteo Creek and then struck directly west to Albuquerque. Exactly where the tracks would be laid and the station located remained uncertain. One group led by Father D. M. Gasparri opposed the construction of the line over the valuable irrigated farms around the town unless the wealthier merchants of the community agreed to purchase the land from the poorer farmers at a favorable price and donate or sell the land to the railroad. Others began to buy up tracts of land in the vicinity hoping to profit if their land became necessary for the railroad project.

It was the Santa Fé Railroad itself, through its subsidiary New Mexico Town Company, that made the ultimate choice. Two miles east of the existing town three comparative newcomers, Elias S. Stover—formerly governor of Kansas—Judge William Hazledine, and Franz Huning, bought several large parcels of land in the spring of 1880 and deeded them to the railroad for $1.00. They had been informed of the site chosen for the depot and yards and acted on behalf of the railroad. In return, the three men were to receive one-half of the net profits from land sales in what was then called New Albuquerque.

On April 5 the first freight train arrived with supplies for its construction crew, but the elaborate welcoming ceremony did not take place until the 22nd when Franz Huning presided over festivities attended by company officials, townspeople, and invited guests from other towns in the territory. Judge Hazledine delivered a flowery oration, which was followed by an excursion to Bernalillo and, after all had returned,

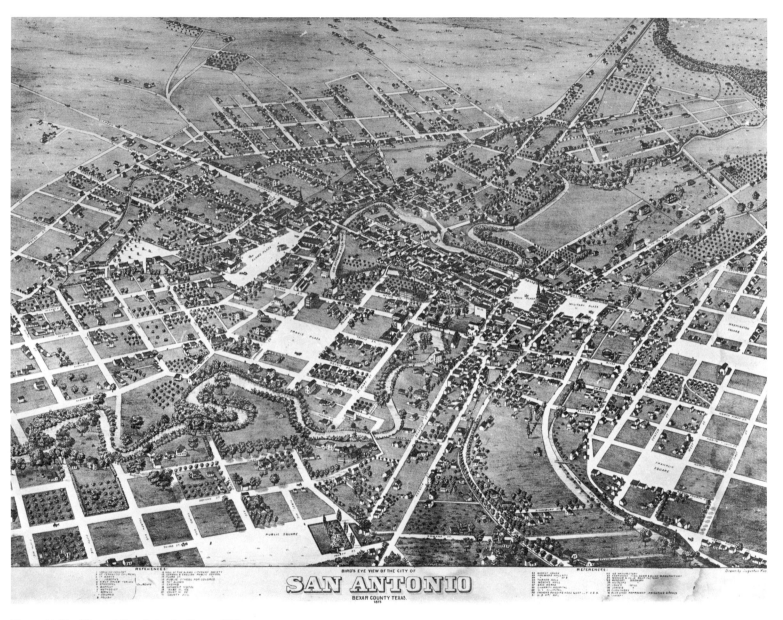

Figure 18.18 View of San Antonio, Texas: 1873

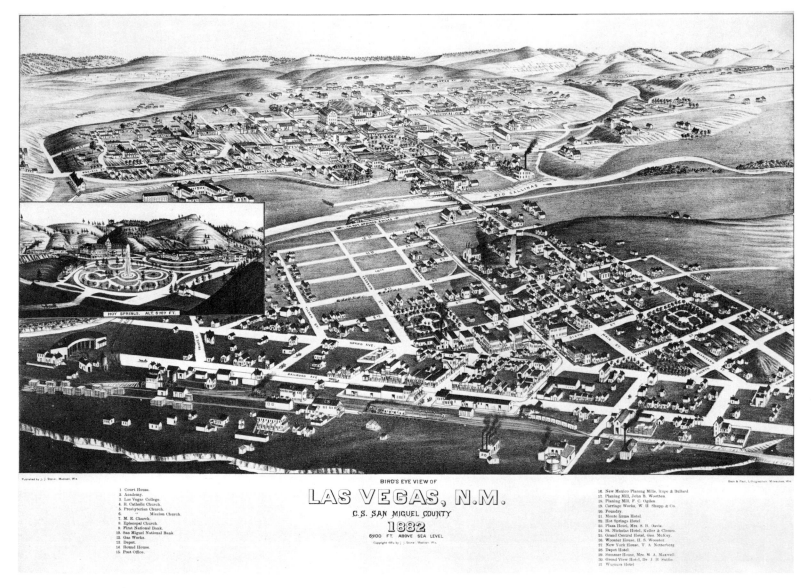

Figure 18.19 View of Las Vegas, New Mexico: 1882

by a celebration at the Old Town plaza, the historic center of the community whose virtual death had been signaled earlier in the day by the steady tolling of the engine bell.[38]

The first hastily erected frame shacks at the new town were soon replaced by more imposing structures, and by 1886, as the view in Figure 18.20 reveals, the community by the tracks had far outstripped its older neighbor near the Rio Grande to the west. The railroad shops, yards, and depot grounds provided the major axis for New Albuquerque, whose promoters had laid it out in the checkerboard pattern so widely used in other railroad communities. Railroad Avenue (now Central Avenue), running at right angles from the tracks, joined an older wagon road near the western boundary of the new town and led to a corner of the plaza in old Albuquerque. It was from this nucleus rather than the older settlement that the city expanded as it quickly grew to become the largest city of the territory.

While Santa Fe jealously retained its status as political capital, its failure to obtain more than branch lines of the Santa Fé and the Denver and Rio Grande doomed its prospects for substantial industrialization and continued domination as a marketing center. Even so, Santa Fe underwent a gradual transition from a sleepy, provincial Mexican settlement to a town with more American characteristics.

The view reproduced in Figure 18.21 shows the community in 1882. The elaborately Victorian Palace Hotel on Washington Avenue was built across from the then-extensive complex of buildings constituting the military post and occupying a great quadrangle north of the plaza. Other hotels, churches, the railroad depot, a few factories, and a gas works testify to the changes that improved transportation in the region and Anglo immigration had brought.

One observer in 1884 accurately summarized the city's future role: "The mining districts are all at a distance. No stock country is tributary. Agriculture is limited to the possibilities of irrigation in a small valley. Santa Fé is destined to be renewed as a picture of the past—a peaceful seat of learning, a quiet health resort, and a Mecca for the antiquarian."[39]

Elsewhere in New Mexico the railroad resulted in the creation of new towns or the expansion of existing communities. Raton, Springer, and Gallup on the Santa Fé and Las Cruces and Deming on the Southern Pacific, all trace their growth from this period. In the neighboring territory of Arizona the expanding rail network made a similar impact on the patterns of urbanization and settlement.[40] Towns served by the railroad prospered, while others, like Prescott, despite its promising start, lost out in the race to urban supremacy if they failed to achieve rail service at an early date.

Before the Southern Pacific arrived in 1880, Tucson presented the uninspiring appearance shown in Figure 18.22. Nevertheless, despite the handicap of unreliable and slow wagon and stagecoach transportation, the town had taken on a more permanent atmosphere than scornful visitors described in earlier years. More than a dozen stores, a brewery, a hotel, four restaurants, numerous saloons and gambling houses, and a barbershop and bathhouse lined the streets or fronted the old plazas. Tucson flourished because of its position from 1867 to 1877 as seat of government for Arizona Territory and as a shipping and supply point for the mounting number of mining towns that had sprung up with the discovery of Arizona's mineral wealth. It also served as a popular entertainment center for the miners, whose gold and silver were welcomed but whose rowdy and often lawless behaviour distressed its more genteel citizens.[41]

Improved transportation facilities after 1880 helped Tucson survive the economic shock and the blow to civic pride caused by the transfer of the capital. So did the establishment there of the University of Arizona in 1890 on a desert site donated by a few of the town's leading gamblers after town fathers ignored for five years the opportunity to acquire this institution through the donation of a 40-acre tract specified by the legislature in 1885 as a condition to its founding.[42]

The orderly design for Tucson's rival, the planned capital city of Prescott, reflects its American origins. The town dates from 1864, the year after President Lincoln signed the bill creating Arizona Territory. Governor John N. Goodwin decided to lay out a completely new town for governmental purposes on Granite Creek near the center of mining activity in the region.[43]

A novel and, as it turned out, illegal, procedure was used in establishing the new capital. Richard C. McCormick, the territorial secretary, suggested pre-empting a 320-acre site under a Congressional Act approved on March 3, 1863. This authorized the president "to reserve from the public lands . . . town sites on the shores of harbors, at the junction of rivers, important portages, or any natural or prospective centres of population." The secretary of the interior was to have such sites surveyed, fix the price of lots, and offer them at auction.[44]

Territorial officials and the few land owners of the vicinity decided to invoke this statute, and "on account of the great delay which must attend communication with the Secretary of the Interior" to appoint three commissioners "to represent the interests of the government, and

Figure 18.20   View of Albuquerque, New Mexico: 1886

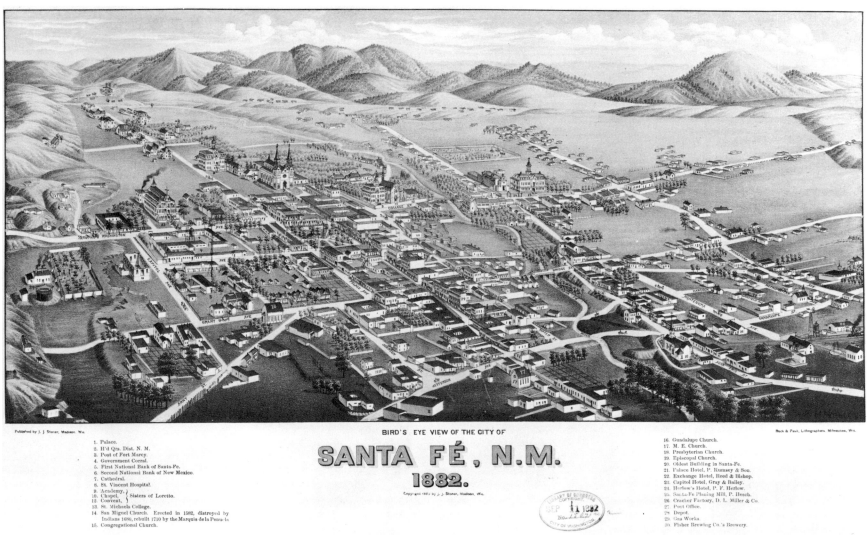

BIRD'S EYE VIEW OF THE CITY OF

SANTA FÉ, N.M.
1882.

Copyright 1882 by J. J. Stoner, Madison, Wis.

1. Palace.
2. H'd Qrs. Dist. N. M.
3. Post of Fort Marcy.
4. Government Corral.
5. First National Bank of Santa-Fe.
6. Second National Bank of New Mexico.
7. Cathedral.
8. St. Vincent Hospital.
9. Academy, } Sisters of Loretto.
10. Chapel, }
11. Convent, }
12. Convent, }
13. St. Michaels College.
14. San Miguel Church. Erected in 1582, distroyed by Indians 1680, rebuilt 1710 by the Marquis de la Penuela
15. Congregational Church.

16. Guadalupe Church.
17. M. E. Church.
18. Presbyterian Church.
19. Episcopal Church.
20. Oldest Building in Santa-Fe.
21. Palace Hotel, P. Rumsey & Son.
22. Exchange Hotel, Reed & Bishop.
23. Capitol Hotel, Gray & Bailey.
24. Herlow's Hotel, P. F. Herlow.
25. Santa-Fe Planing Mill, P. Hesch.
26. Cracker Factory, D. L. Miller & Co.
27. Post Office.
28. Depot.
29. Gas Works.
30. Fisher Brewing Co.'s Brewery.

Figure 18.21   View of Santa Fe, New Mexico: 1882

Figure 18.22 View of Tucson, Arizona: ca. 1878

those of the citizens of the Territory." A tax on each lot sold was to be levied to meet the expenses of the survey, which Robert W. Groom, one of the commissioners, carried out in June, 1864.[45] While this may have seemed an expedient procedure to follow, title to town lots in Prescott remained uncertain until a new survey was completed in 1871 and approved the next year under the proper townsite statute.[46]

No one seemed to be bothered by this legal issue when the first lots were auctioned on June 4, 5, and 6. Sales on the first day brought almost $4,000, more than four times the appraised value of the lots. The lot purchased by the *Arizona Miner* was the most expensive; its publisher paid $245 for this site where his newspaper would be printed. It appeared to be a small sum for a share in what the paper described in its June 22 issue as "destined, we think, to be the chief town of this part of the Territory." That edition of the paper described in detail the town plan reproduced in Figure 18.23:

"The streets all run with the cardinal points of the compass, and are an hundred feet wide." All blocks were 325 by 600 feet "including an alley of 25 feet running lengthwise. The lots, saving those facing the plaza, are 50 × 150 feet. Those upon the plaza, which is composed of an entire square, are 25 × 125 feet on the north and south and 25 × 150 feet on the east and west sides."

The two open spaces and the streets leading to them received special attention: "The land reserved for the public buildings . . . is an entire square, situated on the highest point, from which a grand view of the surrounding country can be had. This square is directly connected with the plaza by a street called Union Street. . . . From the public park a street called Liberty Street . . . runs . . . in the opposite direction, thus opening the public grounds to access and view from every quarter."[47]

It was the scholarly but overly ingenious McCormick who proposed the name Prescott in honor of the American historian. The names of Cortes and Montezuma Streets continued this theme, as did that of Alarcon, so-called to commemorate Hernando de Alarcon, who had ascended the Colorado River as far as Arizona in the sixteenth century. McCormick may also have suggested some of the details of the town plan to Surveyor and Commissioner Robert Groom.

Not all Arizonians were satisfied with the designation of Prescott as the capital. At the first meeting of the newly elected legislature in the fall of 1864, representatives from other areas began an insistent effort to have the seat of government removed to other locations. In 1867 Tucson succeeded in being named the capital city, and despite the mining

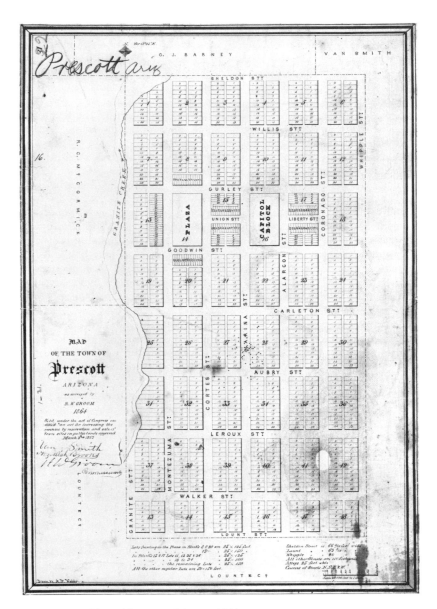

Figure 18.23 Plan of Prescott, Arizona: 1864

activity in its vicinity Prescott experienced a severe economic slump. Gambling and drinking occupied most of its 500 or so residents during the lean years of the late 1860s.

A revival of mining during the next decade was made possible by the introduction of more modern machinery, and cattle raising provided an additional and welcome element in the economic life of the region. More important to Prescott's growth was the return of the territorial government in 1877, although, in every subsequent session, debates over the location of the capital took place.

When the view in Plate 26 was published, about 1885, Prescott was well on its way to becoming an established community. It had, said a history of the territory, "the appearance of a home-like, Eastern town. Its buildings are of wood, brick, and stone. It contains the handsomest mercantile establishments in the Territory, many of which would be a credit to older and more pretentious communities." The courthouse standing in the middle of the plaza was the most imposing building, but its two banks of brick, its "fine theater and . . . large public hall," school, and hospital were also regarded with pride. The population was then "about 2,000" and was said to be "rapidly increasing, for aside from its importance as a business point, Prescott has special home attractions."[48]

Prescott may have been attractive for home builders; to railroad engineers its difficult terrain and isolated location proved quite the opposite. Prescott waited with increasing impatience for rail service, and it was not until 1893 that a branch line linked the town with the Santa Fé at Ash Fork to the north. It was too late by four years; in 1889 the legislature transferred the capital to Phoenix, which, while not on one of the main railroads, had built the Maricopa and Phoenix Railroad to connect the city with the Southern Pacific. With the final loss of the capital, Prescott was forced to abandon its hopes for significant growth.

In addition to Tucson, Prescott, and a number of mining camps and towns of more temporary character, other communities were established as settlers moved into the territory. On the east bank of the Colorado River across from Fort Yuma in California, Charles Poston and Hermann Ehrenberg surveyed the town of Colorado City in 1854. Its strategic location at the ferry across the river on the principal southern wagon route to California can be seen in the foreground of Figure 18.24. A short distance upstream, Arizona City made its appearance. By 1870 more than 1,100 persons resided in the area, the two settlements had grown together, the name was changed to Yuma, and the enlarged community captured the county seat from the mining town of La Paz.[49]

Less successful was Gila City, 20 miles upstream from Yuma on the Gila River. A gold strike in 1858 produced the usual mining camp with its artificial prosperity and inflated land prices. By 1864 the boom collapsed when the first rich and easily worked deposits had been exhausted, and one observer commented that this "promising Metropolis of Arizona consisted of three chimneys and a coyote."[50] Sharing a similar fate was Ehrenberg, two miles north of the modern town of the same name and 140 miles above Yuma on the Colorado. It served as a shipping point for central Arizona after its founding in 1863, but when the Southern Pacific Railroad bridge was constructed to cross the Colorado at Yuma, Ehrenberg suffered a rapid decline and by the turn of the century was virtually deserted.[51]

The most important town of northern Arizona, Flagstaff, began its existence in 1876 when a group from the East looking for a place to settle in Arizona celebrated the Fourth of July at F. F. McMillan's ranch. They stripped the branches from a lofty pine to serve as a flagpole and later surveyed a townsite at the location. Six years later the construction crew of the Santa Fé line established its camp and temporary terminus half a mile to the east, where they laid out a new town. A fire in the original settlement and the advantages of rail service caused most of the older residents to move to the newer town. By 1892, as the view in Figure 18.25 shows, the community was beginning to fill up the gridiron streets laid out parallel and perpendicular to the railway. The principal business buildings were erected along the street next to the railway and facing its depot and water tower.

Cattle raising and lumbering in the vicinity provided the chief source of income for Flagstaff's residents, its status as county seat added to the economic base, and the establishment of a state college in 1899 provided a further impetus for development. In later years the tourist and resort business also became important, and its population of 1,271 in 1900 grew to over 3,000 in the next two decades.[52]

A far more elaborate town plan was prepared for a site below Tubac near the southern boundary of Arizona. Its design as published in 1878 by the Calabasas Land and Mining Company is reproduced in Figure 18.26, a gigantic checkerboard of straight streets and square blocks occupying more than a square mile of land in the Santa Cruz River valley. Two 100-foot-wide streets—Sonoita and Santa Cruz Avenues—were intended as the principal thoroughfares, and at their intersection Colonel Charles P. Sykes, the promoter of this speculative development, erected in 1882 the elaborate Santa Rita Hotel.[53]

Sykes and his colleagues hoped to make Calabasas the chief place of

FORT YUMA COLORADO RIV! CAL!

1850

Lith. Geo H. Baker, San Francisco.

Figure 18.24 View of Fort Yuma, California: ca. 1868

FLAGSTAFF, ARIZ. AND THE SAN FRANCISCO PEAKS, ON THE ATLANTIC & PACIFIC R.R.
GATEWAY TO THE GRAND CAÑON OF THE COLORADO.

Figure 18.25 View of Flagstaff, Arizona: 1892

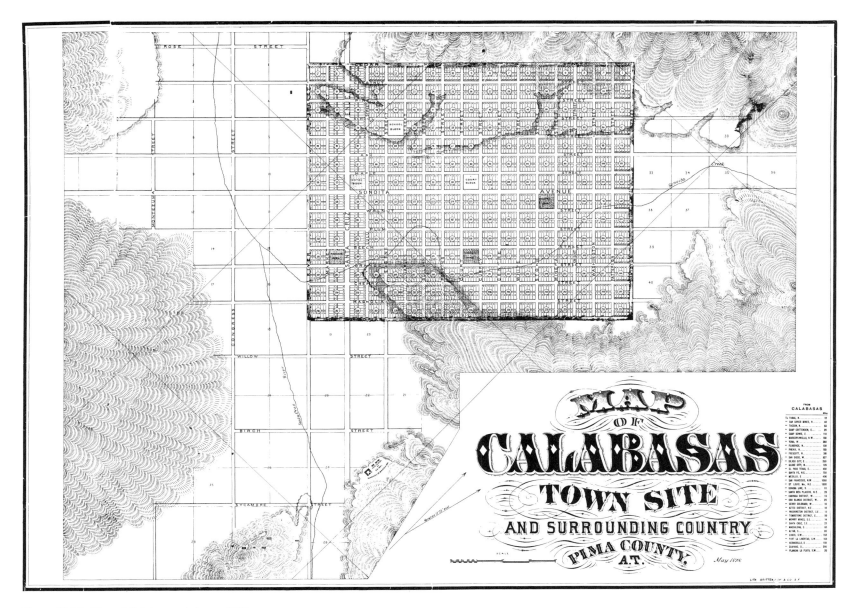

Figure 18.26 Plan of Calabasas, Arizona: 1878

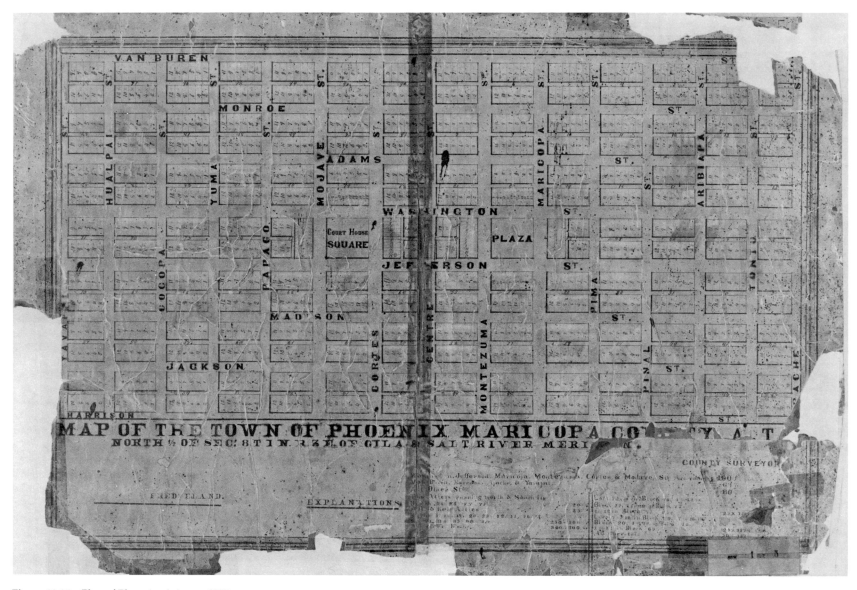

Figure 18.27 Plan of Phoenix, Arizona: 1887

entry for trade with Mexico, and for a time it enjoyed a period of rapid development and land speculation. Sykes advertised his town widely. Apparently some of his claims for the future were overdone; his enemies maintained that he represented the town as lying at the head of navigation on the Santa Cruz River. So it was, according to a contemporary historian—"by small fish and tadpoles; but even for them it was the head of navigation." By 1884 when this scornful observation appeared, the speculation had begun to fail, and our commentator remarked that "from present indications, the city of Calabasas will have to wait half a dozen centuries for its greatness."[54] Nogales, half in Arizona and half in the adjoining Mexican state of Sonora, became the point of entry in that region after the Sonora Railroad was connected to the New Mexico and Arizona line in 1882. The few buildings of Calabasas barely survived into the twentieth century, and its site is now vacant and all but forgotten.[55]

What ultimately was to become the largest city in Arizona and its permanent capital has less flamboyant origins. In the valley of the Salt River, roughly halfway between Tucson and Prescott, some 50 settlers in 1867 began to improve the prehistoric Indian irrigation ditches in the area. They built their houses together in a cluster to which they gave the name Phoenix.

By the summer of 1870 the residents decided to claim land for a townsite and have it formally surveyed. Several locations were examined and discussed, and it was not until a mass meeting of citizens was held in October that a way was found to resolve the issue. A committee was appointed to recommend a site. After its report was considered, the matter was put to a vote. The committee's proposal to move the village some 3½ miles west of its location was approved, and Captain William A. Hancock was set to work laying out the town under the direction of three townsite commissioners elected by the Salt River Valley Town Association.[56]

Some lots were put up for sale in December, 1870, but it was not until the following spring that Hancock completed the town plan illustrated in Figure 18.27. Its 98 blocks, 300-feet square, filled the standard 320-acre townsite specified in the federal statutes. Hancock made the four border streets 63 feet wide and all others 80 feet in width except for six 100-foot streets running past the Plaza and the Court House Square. The placement of these two open spaces may have been inspired by the similar location of the two public squares at Prescott. Hancock, however, neglected to link those at Phoenix by a short cross-street, instead cutting the two intervening blocks into small business lots served by T-shaped alleys.

Sales of town lots were encouraging. A letter to the Prescott *Arizona Miner* written a few days after the first auction claimed that that town already numbered "between 500 and 600 souls, and . . . more than fifty people have arrived here within the last two weeks." This correspondent reported that the sale of lots on December 23 and 24, 1870, resulted in 61 sales at an average price of $43.50.[57]

Newspapers in the fiercely competitive towns of the West did not often boost rival communities, but in the summer of 1871 a Tucson editor called its readers' attention to opportunities in the new town that had just been designated the county seat of Maricopa County: "Phoenix town lots, selected with care at this time, must prove good investments. A year or two ago the land there was vacant; now it is a county seat. . . . The great overland railroad may hit it, and cannot miss it many miles."[58]

In fact, the Southern Pacific built across the territory 30 miles to the south of Phoenix. Stagecoaches and wagon trains provided the only freight and passenger service to the town until 1887, when enterprising investors provided a spur connection leading south to Maricopa Station. Two years later, as the result of energetic promotion and skillful lobbying, Phoenix secured the coveted honor of becoming the third territorial capital. Rail transportation thus helped to place in contention still another competitor in the race for urban survival, growth, and greatness that characterized the American West in the last decades of the nineteenth century.

.XIX.

Rushing for Land: Oklahoma's Overnight Cities

As the nineteenth century drew to an end, virtually all of the American West had been settled. Only one large area remained technically closed to white occupancy—the region between Texas and Kansas that had been set aside for the surviving Indians who had been removed from their traditional homelands as the frontier advanced. Solemn and supposedly irrevocable treaties between the tribes and the federal government guaranteed the Indians perpetual use of these lands. Beginning in 1889, this territory was thrown open under a settlement policy that abrogated Indian rights and violated every principle of rational town planning.

Popular belief holds that, prior to this date, Oklahoma was a wild, little-known land, inhabited by uncivilized savages who warred with one another and whose only contact with the white man was to buy his liquor or lift his scalp. Many white Americans cling to this myth because only by accepting it as true can they justify the kind of cultural genocide authorized and encouraged by public officials and eagerly participated in by tens of thousands of private citizens. Facts refute this legend.

Reproduced in Figure 19.1 is a General Land Office map of 1876 showing the tribal boundaries as they then existed in Indian territory.[1] Occupying the eastern and southern portions of Indian Territory were the "Five Civilized Tribes," Cherokees, Creeks, Choctaws, Chickasaws, and Seminoles, who had early been dispossessed of their lands in the southeastern United States during a period from 1817 to 1842. When these tribes re-established themselves in Indian Territory, their numbers were diminished by thousands who had died during the long journey from their homelands under the close watch of federal troops. Those who survived attempted to re-create on the strange, new tribal lands the advanced native cultures that had evolved over countless years in their former homelands.

Many of these Indians and others who were moved to the adjoining reservations had been educated by whites in the Southeast. Some received such training from missionaries who joined the Indians in their new territories. It is questionable which culture—white or Indian— was superior. The Cherokees possessed a written language and had adopted a constitution to govern their affairs. Seminole chiefs such as Osceola exhibited skills in statecraft rivaling those of any white. The Creeks had developed a highly sophisticated community pattern with three types of enclosed meeting or ceremonial places as the focus of their towns.[2] The Choctaws were skilled farmers, and their leaders displayed great diplomatic skill in negotiations with the whites. The Chickasaws shared many of these same characteristics. These five tribes, then, deserved the name "civilized," and indeed many of their members had lived and traded with whites in their native regions and had adopted many of the ways of the whites, regrettably including slavery.

In what is now Oklahoma many Indians took up farming, but others could be found in Indian towns, living in the vicinity of the missions operated by the major Christian churches, or clustered near the office of the government Indian agents assigned to administer the programs of the Bureau of Indian Affairs, which had been created in 1832. With the coming of the railroads additional towns sprang up at the stations established by the lines.

At the time the map in Figure 19.1 was published, the Missouri, Kansas, and Texas (the "Katy") Railroad cut diagonally through the eastern part of Indian Territory to Denison, Texas, which it reached late in 1872. The Atlantic and Pacific line (later the St. Louis and San Francisco or "Frisco") reached Vinita in 1871 and was later to build to the center of Indian Territory at what is now Oklahoma City. Other lines soon followed, the most important of which was the Santa Fé, which entered Oklahoma from Arkansas City, Kansas, and ran almost directly south toward Texas.[3] At the successive terminal points on each of these railways during their construction, temporary towns quickly mushroomed and, often, as quickly vanished in the same sequence of events and results already described on the transcontinental lines through the middle and northern plains. Settlements developed around some of the permanent stations, which were generally located about ten miles apart. At the Santa Fé's Oklahoma Station (later to become Oklahoma City) the station agent described the embryonic community as consisting of "the depot, railway agent's cottage, section house, post office . . . , quartermaster's agent's house, George Gibson's boarding house, and a stockade belonging to G. B. Brickford, a contract government freighter."[4] The following year the Santa Fe constructed a stockyard, enlarged its depot, and built a new freight house to accommodate the increase in trade and in anticipation of the opening of this part of Oklahoma to homesteaders.

In addition to these railroad hamlets and the Indian towns at which lived a number of white traders, government agents, and others, many

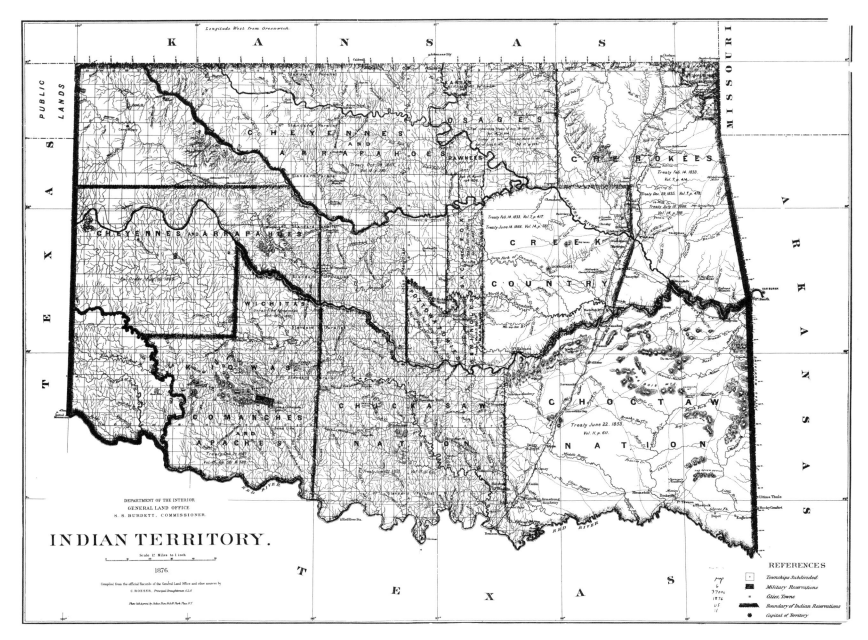

Figure 19.1 Map of the Indian Territory in Oklahoma: 1876

whites could be found in the Cherokee Outlet south of the Kansas border and west of the Arkansas River. In 1883 the Cherokee Strip Live Stock Association succeeded in obtaining a lease from the Cherokees for grazing rights in the Outlet. The association divided the area into some 100 holdings, and within each tract Texas cattlemen erected housing for their employees, built corrals, and used the land for fattening cattle driven north from Texas ranges before they were moved to shipping points on the railroads of southern and central Kansas.[5]

Pressures from two directions soon ended this arrangement: the formal opening of Oklahoma to white settlement and the creation of many new towns and cities. John W. Noble, secretary of the interior, questioned the validity of the lease. He maintained that Cherokee ownership of the Outlet was open to question and that in any event the Indians had no authority to enter into leases of this nature. This was but the latest in a series of moves by the federal government to limit tribal rights and put back in the public domain much or all of the land originally set aside in perpetuity for Indian use. The new policy began in earnest immediately after the Civil War when the government declared that by their support of the Confederacy the Indians of the Five Civilized Tribes had forfeited many of the rights conferred by earlier treaties. In 1866 a new series of treaties was imposed on the eastern Indians, by which the government gained authority to settle additional Indians from other parts of the country on portions of the original reservations. In exchange for modest sums that did not reflect the true value of the land, the tribes were forced to cede to the government large tracts of their reservations for this purpose.[6]

The government's action in moving Indians from Kansas and Nebraska and elsewhere in the West to reservations in Oklahoma reflected the desire of white settlers to occupy the vacated areas. By 1879 the Indian lands in Oklahoma became the target for land-hungry farmers and speculators. Advocates of a policy of opening Oklahoma for settlement maintained that parts of the region had never been assigned to specific tribes and that properly this could be regarded as land in the public domain available for homestead and townsite claims under the laws and regulations prevailing elsewhere in the West. They urged also that tribal ownership in common be terminated and that separate allotments should be made to individual Indians with the remaining land in the established tribal areas subject to claim and entry in the normal manner.

Heading this movement was the fanatic and tireless David L. Payne, who for five years led groups of Oklahoma "Boomers" into Indian terri-

tory only to be evicted by federal troops. Payne simply refused to wait until the area might be opened to legal settlement and announced on various dates that he and his followers would enter the region, establish a town, and begin farming in the vicinity. One of his posters is reproduced in Figure 19.2. This includes the statement that "The Colony had laid off a city on the North Fork of the Canadian River, which will be the Capital of the State."

Early in 1880 Payne mounted his first invasion. A great mass meeting in Kansas City sponsored by the Kansas City *Times* heard Elias C. Boudinot, a prominent Cherokee and virtually the only Indian of note to advocate the opening of Oklahoma to white settlement, argue that the "Unassigned Lands"—an area near the center of the region not reserved for any specific tribe—were part of the public domain and available for homesteading.[7] U. S. Marshal C. C. Allen refuted this position by reading a presidential proclamation stating that these lands were not open for settlement. While this announcement dampened the enthusiasm of Payne's followers and led many to abandon attempted settlement, a small group accompanied Payne on April 26, 1880, when he crossed the Kansas border south of Arkansas City.

Six days later the party reached a site now in Oklahoma City about a mile west of the Santa Fe railroad. This group quickly staked out a town and surveyed homesteads nearby. On May 16, however, a detachment of troops from Fort Reno arrested the members of Payne's band, escorted them to the post, and three weeks later released them at the Kansas border. Before leaving the site, however, Payne showed Lieutenant George Gale around the "town," which the officer later described in an article in a Wellington, Kansas, newspaper. According to Gale, Payne had laid out an enormous community of 720 blocks, each 300 by 600 feet in size and separated by 80-foot streets. From a public square occupying a knoll at the center, eight main streets, each terminating at a small park, extended outward. Trees and brush had been cut so that the lines of these principal avenues were plainly visible.[8]

A second invasion in July of the same year and another in the fall of 1881, the latter expedition having started from Texas, resulted in a similar sequence of events. Six other abortive attempts at settlement, the last occurring in the summer of 1884, kept federal troops busy patrolling the Kansas or Texas borders. It was Payne's death later that year rather than the effectiveness of federal intervention that finally stilled his efforts.

Payne's ceaseless activities focused the attention of the nation on the Oklahoma land issue. The claim by the "Boomers," as they were known, that they had a legal right to homestead on the Unassigned Lands was regarded as serious enough to warrant presidential attention, and Chester Arthur in 1884 issued a proclamation reaffirming the government position previously stated by President Garfield that these lands were closed to settlement. Proclamations proved easier to issue than to enforce, and by the mid 1880s small groups of Boomers slipped into Oklahoma in ever-increasing numbers. William Couch, who succeeded Payne as the leader of the movement, led two final, large-scale invasions of the area but then transferred his energies to the legislative arena. He traveled to Washington to press his case with officials of President Cleveland's new administration shortly after the inauguration ceremonies in March, 1885. Although Secretary of the Interior L. Q. C. Lamar was hostile, many members of Congress listened to Couch sympathetically. Already, in fact, the legislators had passed an act authorizing the president to appoint a body to begin negotiations with some of the tribes over land titles. A Senate subcommittee held hearings in Kansas on the Oklahoma land question in the summer of 1885.

Three and a half years of legislative maneuvering culminated in the passage by both houses in 1889 and the approval by President Cleveland as he left office of laws compensating the Creeks and Seminoles for their remaining rights in the Unassigned Lands. The legislation further provided that the president by proclamation could open these lands to homestead settlement. On March 23 President Benjamin Harrison in one of his first executive acts announced that the lands in question would be open to settlement at noon on April 22. The usual homestead and townsite laws governing disposition of the public domain were to apply, with the additional provision that no person entering the area before the appointed time would be allowed to acquire a homestead. This proviso originated with Senator Henry Dawes as a rider to the Senate bill.[9] Dawes believed his measure would insure a fair chance for anyone seeking land. His intentions were laudable, but the provision proved impossible to enforce. Thousands of persons slipped across the border of the Unassigned Lands before the April 22 date and concealed themselves in woods, ravines, or other hiding places near choice sites.

The claims of these "Sooners," as they came to be called, created almost endless confusion, bitterness, and litigation over land ownership. In addition to these persons whose entry into the area was patently illegal, there were thousands of occupants engaged in a variety of occupations as surveyors, railroad employees, soldiers, U.S. deputy marshals, land office clerks and others. John Pickler and Cornelius Mac-

Figure 19.2 Broadside Promoting Settlement in Oklahoma: 1880

CAPT. PAYNE'S
OKLAHOMA COLONY

Will move to and settle the Public Lands in the Indian Territory before the first day of December, 1880. Arrangements have been made with Railroads for

LOW RATES.

14,000,000 acres of the finest Agricultural and Grazing Lands in the world open for

 FREE HOMES

For the people—these are the last desirable public lands remaining for settlement. Situated between the 34th and 38th degrees of latitude, at the foot of Washita Mountains, we have the finest climate in the world, an abundance of water, timber and stone. Springs gush from every hill. The grass is green the year round. No flies or mosquitoes.

The Best Stock Country on Earth.

The Government purchased these lands from the Indians in 1866. Hon. J. O. Broadhead, Judges Jno. M. Krum and J. W. Phillips were appointed a committee by the citizens of St. Louis, and their legal opinion asked regarding the right of settlement, and they, after a thorough research, report the lands subject under the existing laws to Homestead and Pre-emption settlement.

Some three thousand have already joined the colony and will soon move in a body to Oklahoma, taking with them Saw Mills, Printing Presses, and all things required to build up a prosperous community. Schools and churches will be at once established. The Colony has laid off a city on the North Fork of the Canadian River, which will be the Capital of the State. In less than twelve months the railroads that are now built to the Territory line will reach Oklahoma City. Other towns and cities will spring up, and there was never such an opportunity offered to enterprising men.

MINERALS!

Copper and Lead are known to exist in large quantities—the same vein that is worked at Joplin Mines runs through the Territory to the Washita Mountains, and it will be found to be the richest lead and copper district in the Union. The Washita Mountains are known to contain Gold and Silver. The Indians have brought in fine specimens to the Forts, but they have never allowed the white men to prospect them. Parties that have attempted it have never returned.

In the early spring a prospecting party will organize to go into these Mountains, and it is believed they will be found rich in GOLD AND SILVER, Lead and Copper.

The winters are short and never severe, and will not interfere with the operations of the Colony. Farm work commences here early in February, and it is best that we should get on the grounds as early as possible, as the winter can be spent in building, opening lands and preparing for spring.

For full information and circulars and the time of starting, rates, &c., address,

T. D. CRADDOCK,
General Manager,
Wichita, Kan.

GEO. M. JACKSON,
General Agent,
508 Chestnut St., St. Louis.

October 23d, 1880.

Bride, inspectors for the government land surveys, reported that at Guthrie before noon on April 22, 300 persons were present, a majority of whom were legally entitled to be on the site but were not technically entitled to file land claims.[10]

Many, perhaps a majority, of the "Legal Sooners" saw no conflict of interest or violation of law in claiming land as soon as the designated opening hour had arrived. Indeed, a number of them had doubtless sought employment in the territory solely to give them an advantage over the vast majority who were massed at the borders in compliance with the regulations. A great many lawyers were also among the early settlers, and they found their skills in considerable demand by claimants contending for title to the same parcels of land.

The Unassigned Lands comprised 1,887,796 acres of flat to gently rolling plains in the heart of modern Oklahoma. The location of this area is shown on the map in Figure 19.3. Less than twelve thousand 160-acre homesteads were available; five times that many persons joined in the land rush—speculators, would-be settlers, spectators, and officials who poured into the Unassigned Lands on or shortly after April 22.

Although apparently the entire area had been surveyed into the standard six-mile square townships and divided into quarter-sections of 160 acres, neither the boundaries nor the street, block, and lot layout of towns had been determined. The townsite legislation of the public domain first enacted in 1844 and amended and amplified in 1867 applied generally to the lands opened in 1889, although the size of an individual town was limited to 320 acres.[11] Such a tract could be claimed anywhere if not already subject to a homestead claim. By its failure to specify that townsites should be designated and laid out in advance, Congress set the stage for the most disorderly episode of urban settlement this country, and perhaps the world, has ever witnessed.

Congress also failed to provide any form of civil government structure for the area, an incredible oversight that was not to be remedied for more than a year. This negligence added to the confusion accompanying the founding of towns. Under federal townsite legislation, officials of an incorporated town or the judge of a county in which an unincorporated town was established were to "enter" (file a claim for) the townsite at the nearest government land office. Following payment for the townsite at the minimum price, the title to the site would be transferred to these officials as trustees who would then dispose of lots to the occupants according to their respective interests. However, since no

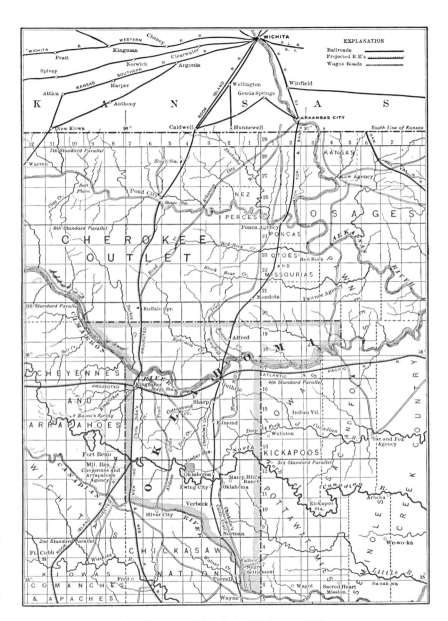

Figure 19.3 Map of the Unassigned Lands in Oklahoma: 1889

territorial government existed, towns could not be incorporated. Nor, since counties had not been established, could a county judge serve as trustee.

Towns, therefore, did not exist as legal entities, and persons claiming and occupying town lots surveyed by private townsite companies held no valid title.[12] What appeared to be deeds to town lots were nothing more than claims to property that might or might not be validated at some unknown future date if the company issuing the certificates succeeded in having its townsite entry approved. Under these circumstances it is a wonder that towns were created at all, but they help to explain both the chaos attending their establishment and the unremarkable character of their plans.[13]

The beginning of the rush set the stage for the wild confusion that was to follow. Those taking part had been admitted to the Indian territory bordering the Unassigned Lands three days prior to April 22. Probably the largest number gathered along the northern border in the Cherokee Outlet preparing to make the rush on foot, on horseback, in wagons, buggies, racing sulkies, carriages, and even bicycles. Fifteen Santa Fé trains from Kansas and six from Texas waited at the north and south borders. Passengers jammed the coaches, crowded on the steps and roofs of the cars, and hung precariously from the locomotives.[14] Some had in mind specific parcels of land that they had previously inspected, while others were complete strangers to the region and hoped to find a choice site by chance. Troops assigned to prevent entry to the lands before the legal hour patrolled the borders and with some exceptions succeeded in restraining the tense, impatient, and land-hungry mass of humanity.

A typical scene immediately after bugle call and gunshot signals announced the hour of noon is shown in Figure 19.4. A reporter for *Harper's Weekly* recorded his impressions in these words: "The last barrier of savagery in the United States was broken down. Moved by the same impulse, each driver lashed his horses furiously; each rider dug his spurs into his willing steed, and each man on foot caught his breath hard and darted forward. A cloud of dust rose where the home-seekers had stood in line, and when it had drifted away before the gentle breeze, the horses and wagons and men were tearing across the open country like fiends. The horsemen had the best of it from the start. It was a fine race for a few minutes, but soon the riders began to spread out like a fan, and by the time they had reached the horizon they were scattered about as far as eye could see."[15]

The first two stations on the Santa Fé south of the Cherokee Strip were Orlando and Alfred, and while a number of the would-be settlers who chose to come by rail scrambled off at these points, most passengers continued on to Guthrie or to Oklahoma Station, which were more centrally located.[16] As the train began to slow at Guthrie "the impatient boomers began to leap from the cars and run up the slope. Men jumped from the roofs of the moving cars at the risk of their lives. . . . The coaches were so crowded that many men were compelled to squeeze through the windows in order to get a fair start at the head of the crowd. Almost before the train had come to a standstill the cars were emptied. In their haste and eagerness, men fell over each other in heaps, others stumbled and fell headlong, while many ran forward so blindly and impetuously that it was not until they had passed the best of the town lots that they came to a realization of their actions."[17]

The first train to reach Guthrie included a number of persons who had intended to lay out a town on what they had expected to be an unoccupied site. Instead, "the slope east of the railway . . . was dotted white with tents and sprinkled thick with men running about in all directions." The *Harper's* correspondent recorded their reaction: " 'We're done for,' said a town-site speculator, in dismay. 'Some one has gone in ahead of us and laid out the town.'

" 'Never mind that,' shouted another town-site speculator, 'but make a rush and get what you can.' "[18]

This advice proved easier to give than follow. Hamilton S. Wicks described the confusing situation at Guthrie for a national magazine a few months after his own opening day experience: "There were several thousand people converging on the same plot of ground, each eager for a town lot which was to be acquired without cost or without price. . . .

"The situation was so peculiar that it is difficult to convey correct impressions of the situation. It reminded me of playing blind-man's-bluff. One did not know how far to go before stopping; it was hard to tell when it was best to stop, and it was a puzzle whether to turn to the right hand or the left. Every one appeared dazed, and all for the most part acted like a flock of stray sheep."[19]

The "stray sheep" did not include at least two groups of shrewd and thoroughly dishonest men who had taken possession of the lands adjacent to and east of Guthrie station at noon of that day and quickly platted the area in two adjacent 320-acre towns. The town of Guthrie occupied the eastern half of Section 8 of the six-mile square surveyed township. That had been claimed as a townsite by two U.S. Marshals, about 50 of their deputies, and, according to rumor, a Santa Fé railroad representative, a federal attorney, one or more federal land officials, and other prominent persons.[20] The *Harper's Weekly* correspondent describes how he saw a man standing beside a tent who, when ques-

Figure 19.4 View of the Oklahoma Land Rush: 1889

tioned how he had managed to stake his claim so early, admitted that he was a deputy marshal. When the legality of his occupancy of a town lot was challenged on the grounds that the law prohibited anyone in government service within the territory from claiming land, he coolly responded, " 'That may all be, stranger; but I've got two lots here, just the same; and about fifty other deputies have got lots in the same way. In fact, the deputy-marshals laid out the town.' "[21]

The plan of Guthrie, along with three other towns laid out that day adjoining it—two to the east and one to the west—is reproduced in Figure 19.5. Only the railroad and the previously established government land office site break the monotony of Guthrie's rigid grid pattern stamped on the site by the deputy marshals and their equally unscrupulous and unskilled associates.

That pattern was extended on either side of the initial townsite, the land to the east being regarded as more favorable. Another group of illegal Sooners planned East Guthrie on the west half of Section 9 of the government township. They came from Winfield, Kansas, and had engaged N. A. Haight to prepare the survey. Haight attempted to visit the site ten days before the opening, but the military guard did not allow him to leave his railway car. Relying on his memory of the area, which he had visited some years earlier as a government surveyor, he nevertheless drew what purported to be a surveyed plat. The members of the townsite company doubtless had this in hand when, precisely at noon on April 22, 200 of them emerged from a hiding place "about a mile east of the west half of section nine" and proceeded to occupy the area, stake it off, and, the following day, elect a mayor and other city officials.[22]

Finding the land near the railroad already laid out and claimed by these Sooners, most of the legal settlers pushed eastward along the right-of-way of Oklahoma Avenue, which led from the station past the land office. As a correspondent described the scene, after they reached "the spot where the deputy-marshals had ceased laying out lots, they seized the line of the embryo street and ran it eastward as far as their numbers would permit. The second train load of people took it where the first left off, and ran it entirely out of sight behind a swell of ground at least two miles from the station. The following car loads of homeseekers went north and south, so that by the time that all were in for the day a city large enough in area to hold 100,000 inhabitants had been staked off, with more or less geometrical accuracy."[23]

Figure 19.6 shows the first train load of settlers laying out town lots. Probably this is in the portion of Figure 19.5 identified as Capitol Hill, whose plan indicates that some thought was given to providing a few of the amenities of urban life rather than the maximum number of lots. The large park, however, may have been added later when the excitement of the land rush had subsided and municipal institutions had begun to take form. The prominent location of "Capitol Square" on the axis of Oklahoma Avenue was an indication that the settlers of Capitol Hill anticipated the establishment of a territorial and ultimately of a state government and that the Guthrie area would be a contender for designation as the seat of its administration.

Figure 19.7 shows the plan adopted for West Guthrie on the other side of the first townsite. If the citizens of Capitol Hill, as the eastern limit of the community, aspired to the capitol, those in West Guthrie were determined to secure the territorial or state university. Accordingly, they reserved a four-block tract for this purpose facing Oklahoma Avenue. To the south they set aside a large parcel of land along Cottonwood Creek for a park. Except for these plots of land, a mill site, and one block for a school, West Guthrie represented simply an extension of the other Guthries to the east.

Somehow in all the confusion, a rough kind of frontier democracy prevailed. Although no provision had been made for municipal government, the occupants of the separate "cities" realized that some form of local government was absolutely essential. Looming large in every occupant's mind was the need for a set of officials to make proper, legal "entry" of the townsites at the land office so that eventually land titles could be secured. Other forms of municipal regulation and services would be needed.

On April 25, only three days after the opening run, Guthrie elected a mayor and council.[24] By July 23 a commission had prepared a charter, which was passed by referendum and provided the basis for city government until the following year when Congress belatedly passed an act providing for the establishment of municipalities. In the meantime the Guthrie council simply assumed that it had power to act. As early as April 27 it had passed an ordinance regulating gambling, and the city treasurer's records reveal that fines had been collected from 27 persons violating its provisions prohibiting gambling in the streets. The experience at Guthrie in creating municipal institutions was duplicated with only minor variations in procedure in the adjoining towns and at Oklahoma City, El Reno, Norman, Stillwater, and Kingfisher, the other principal towns that were created overnight elsewhere in the territory.[25]

The character of Guthrie in its infancy is revealed by the photograph

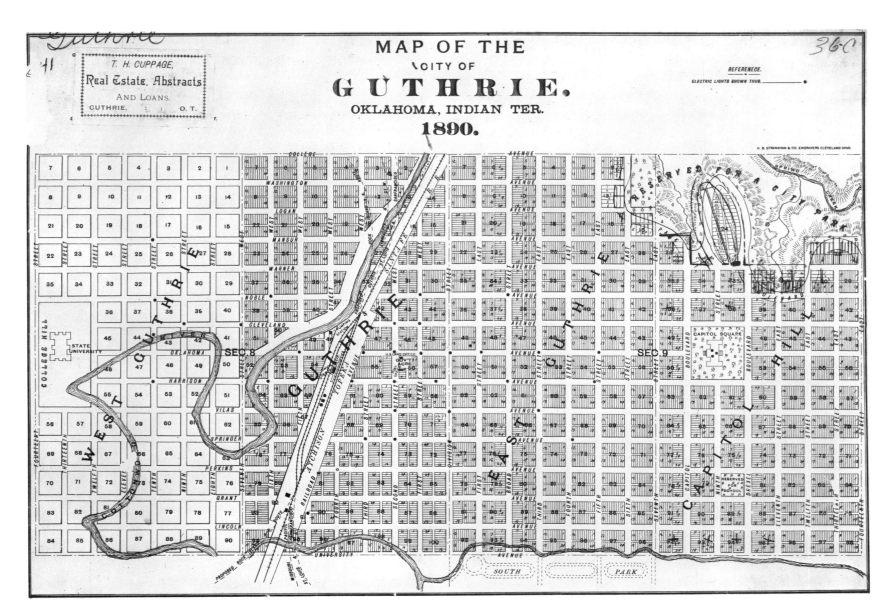

Figure 19.5 Plan of Guthrie, Oklahoma: 1890

LAYING OUT TOWN LOTS IN GUTHRIE, TWENTY MINUTES AFTER THE ARRIVAL OF THE FIRST TRAIN.

Figure 19.6   View of Guthrie, Oklahoma: 1889

taken on April 27, 1889, reproduced in Figure 19.8. This was probably made from the roof of the government land office at Oklahoma and Second Street looking southwest toward the Santa Fé tracks and to West Guthrie. Although still a city of tents, even at that early date permanent structures were being erected. Part of the area shown in the photograph, the southern half of the West Guthrie townsite (technically the southwest quarter section of Section 8) had been claimed as a homestead immediately after noon on April 22 by an employee of the railroad. What followed was typical of the land title controversies that plagued Oklahoma for many years.

The occupants of the area, as already indicated, had organized a city government, which had filed a claim for the land as a townsite. Two other persons subsequently filed homestead claims, arguing that the first claimant was a "sooner" who could not receive a valid title. The register and receiver of the Guthrie government land office held hearings and recorded no fewer than a thousand pages of testimony and evidence. Eventually the case reached the commissioner of the General Land Office and the secretary of the interior. A further appeal was taken to the secretary by one of the parties who later pursued his claim in an action brought before the federal district court. This case dragged on for several years, during which time no one could be certain of possessing a valid title to the land in question despite continued occupancy and extensive improvements.[26] This procedure was by no means untypical of the hundreds of conflicts arising over town lot titles under the chaotic conditions that federal land policy had created.

At Guthrie the elected city council assumed the power to settle disputes over town lot land titles, and it appointed boards of arbitration to hear and decide claims. These boards, one of which sat sternly for the group portrait shown in Figure 19.9, issued "title certificates" to the successful claimant, but their decisions were often disputed, and the "titles" they awarded were of questionable legal status. Three months after the towns at Guthrie Station were laid out, a reporter observed that "these boards of arbitration . . . have caused as much kick and dissatisfaction among the people as any other three movements made. The members were paid $10 a day each and there were five on each board. They pretended to adjust matters for weeks, and cost the people small fortunes. They did, it is claimed, adjust admirably for themselves and those who stood in with the rings. After the first boards came others. Cases were resubmitted, and in cases, how many it is impossible to determine, two parties hold certificates to the same lot. These certificates are issued by the mayor, and are supposed to give title to the

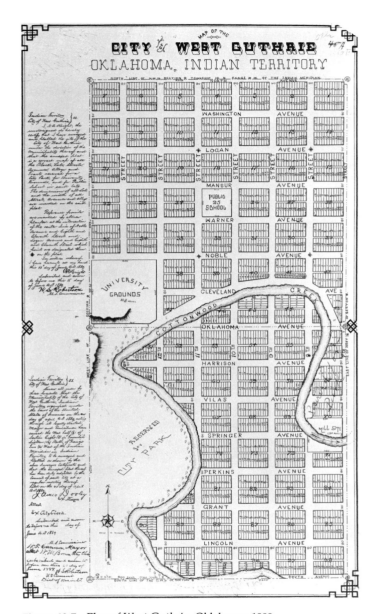

Figure 19.7 Plan of West Guthrie, Oklahoma: 1889

Figure 19.8   View of Guthrie, Oklahoma: 1889

lot, for no lot can be sold unless the supposed owner has a certificate. This duplication of certificates will no doubt work many innocent parties great injustice and loss. Another thing, in issuing certificates the city is supposed to guarantee the lot. But it offers little protection, and lot jumping is of almost daily occurrence."[27]

Adding to the confusion and discontent of many were the results of more leisurely and accurate surveys of street, block, and lot lines that had been so hastily laid out in the first hectic hours of the opening. A number of persons found themselves occupying what turned out to be alleys, a portion of another owner's lot, or a parcel of land lying entirely within a street right-of-way.

Many left Guthrie and other towns in disgust over the seemingly

Figure 19.9 The Guthrie, Oklahoma Arbitration Board: 1889

hopeless title situation, jumped claims, or because they could not endure the hardships and uncertainties of frontier existence. Yet most of the estimated 10,000 persons who descended on Guthrie on April 22 remained to try and build a city. In three weeks Oklahoma Avenue, shown on May 14, 1889, in Figure 19.10, had assumed unmistakable signs of permanence. Some of the commercial buildings appearing in this photograph as well as many frame houses in Guthrie arrived from Kansas or Texas in sections, although probably a majority were of conventional construction. Tents continued to be used by a large number of residents and places of business, and the temperature inside these canvas dwellings unsheltered from the burning Oklahoma sun must have been almost unbearable.

Dust contributed to the general discomfort. As the *Harper's Weekly* observer noted, "the red dust was ankle-deep in the main street. . . . It rose in clouds and hovered above the feverish city until the air was like fog at sunrise; it sifted through the provision boxes in the tents, it crept into blankets and clothing, and it stuck like wax to the faces and beards of the unhappy citizens."[28]

The municipal government shortly took action to improve conditions, and by July 22 a newspaper reporter observed with some surprise how Guthrie had progressed: "It is amazing what ninety days have accomplished. All the main streets are graded, there are miles of sidewalks, cross walks are being put in and everything looks as neat as a pin. Sprinkling carts are run upon the main streets and keep down the dust. . . . Guthrie has its waterworks, hydrants being available on all the principal streets. The poles for a system of electric lighting are now being placed. The ties for a street railway are piled here and there on Oklahoma Avenue but the gentleman who has an unlimited franchise will doubtless use his pleasure about putting them down."[29]

Guthrie's growth continued at a rapid pace, aided by the city's success in gaining the designation of territorial capital. By the end of 1891 most of the lots in the several townsite claims were occupied, and the business district near the depot consisted of two and three-story brick and stone structures. Figure 19.11 shows the city at that time as viewed from the southeast when its population was slightly over 10,000 and it was enjoying the height of its prosperity. Less than two decades later, however, Guthrie's status was reduced to that of a provincial trading town when voters in the newly formed state of Oklahoma approved a measure moving the seat of government to Oklahoma City.

This action brought further expansion to a halt, and the basic urban pattern so rapidly surveyed at the time of the land rush still accommo-

dates most of the city. Standing in front of the old Land Office site in Guthrie one can still imagine what it must have been like in the first exciting days of the rush. The buildings that now stand where tents and false-fronted wooden stores were once so hastily thrown up are somewhat larger but still in frontier scale. Fine examples of late nineteenth century commercial structures, they seem frozen in time as mute witnesses to a remarkable period of almost overnight urbanization.

Oklahoma City in this respect contrasts sharply with its old, but non-vanquished opponent. The modern visitor to the original townsite is dwarfed by the skyscrapers of a thriving metropolis and finds it difficult to reconstruct mentally the conditions of the city at the time of its birth. Yet the same street plan laid out then serves today, including the jogs and off-sets of the north-south streets resulting from the attempts by two land companies to settle the same site. They are a curse to modern traffic, and, as we shall see, caused oaths of quite a different kind in 1889.

What was then called Oklahoma Station on the Santa Fé Railroad was the scene of another mad scramble for land. The station agent has left us a vivid description: "On that memorable day, so far as the eye could see, people seemed to spring up as though by magic. On they came from every direction; some on horseback, some in vehicles; some had spades, some stakes, some hand bags, some pots and pans, other cooking utensils of varying degrees, and so forth. Words are inadequate to describe the scene. History was in the making.

"The first train from the south came in about two o'clock in the afternoon. It was crowded—people clambered together from the platform, on the car roofs, everywhere. There must have been two thousand persons aboard that train. The rush was on in full. Train load of humanity, followed train load, and a city was made in a day."[30]

As at Guthrie, those who entered the territory legally at noon found that a townsite company had already staked out streets and blocks at Oklahoma Station. Its members occupied the choice lots on Main Street leading at a right angle from the Santa Fe tracks, and they were offering other lots for sale under the name of the Seminole Town and Improvement Company. One of the five directors named in its Kansas charter was William Couch, the successor as leader of the Boomers to David Payne, and undoubtedly the moving force within the company.[31] Its members had somehow eluded border guards, concealed themselves near the station, and emerged at noon with a previously prepared town plat, which their surveyor, Charles Chamberlain, immediately began to stake out on the ground. They proceeded with military precision. One

Figure 19.10   View of East Oklahoma Avenue in Guthrie, Oklahoma: 1889

witness noted that "as early as 12:45 p.m. the town of Oklahoma City was surveyed and all valuable lots taken."[32] At 3:15 that afternoon Louis O. Dick appeared at the Guthrie land office to file a townsite application for Oklahoma City stating that he did so as trustee for the occupants and that a plat would be submitted as soon as it could be prepared. Four days later Dick mailed the plat to Guthrie, together with what purported to be minutes of a meeting of the occupants of the town on April 22, which recorded that he had been elected their trustee and directed to file the application and plat on their behalf.[33]

The "occupants" constituted only a small portion of what probably

numbered 10,000 persons. They included officials of another townsite company whose members arrived in the vanguard of those rushing from the southern border. Finding the Seminole Company occupying the west side of the tracks, the Oklahoma Town Company proceeded to lay out a town east of the station only to discover that this tract had been set aside as a military reservation. Withdrawing to the western side of the tracks they erected a large tent south of the area the Seminole Company occupied and went through the motions of electing city officers.[34]

The following day the Oklahoma Town Company evidently attempted to survey a portion of the area south of Main Street, but it soon became obvious that the claims of the two town companies conflicted. Angelo Scott and others finally succeeded in organizing a mass meeting that lasted for three tumultuous hours that afternoon. As Scott recalls the results, "it was finally decided to elect a committee of 14 men with power to divide the townsite into streets, alleys, lots, and blocks, beginning at a certain designated spot, and to name the streets."[35] This committee apparently did not include any of the leaders of the Seminole Company, which by that time had probably completed its own surveys for the area north of Main Street.[36]

The citizens group began its work at the township line, which ran east from the Santa Fé tracks. This became the centerline of Reno Avenue, which was laid out 100 feet wide. Subsequent events can best be followed by reference to the first printed plan of Oklahoma City published later that year and reproduced in Figure 19.12. The citizens' committee decided to claim the maximum townsite of 320 acres, which would include all of the area shown on Figure 11 from Reno Avenue to the north. This claim was entered at the Guthrie land office early on April 24.

California and Grand Avenues were also platted with a width of 100 feet parallel to the township line and connected by 80-foot cross-streets running exactly north and south. The survey proceeded slowly because it was necessary to settle land claims at the same time. Five members of the committee of fourteen acted as an arbitration board "passing from lot to lot, hearing the evidence of the parties and summarily deciding the cases on the spot. An immense crowd attended the committee, and the press of the throng soon became so great that it was found necessary to nail three long boards together, thus forming a triangle within which the committee could be protected from the crowd."[37]

By Friday, April 26, the citizens' survey reached Grant Avenue. Then it became obvious that the earlier plat of the Seminole Company and

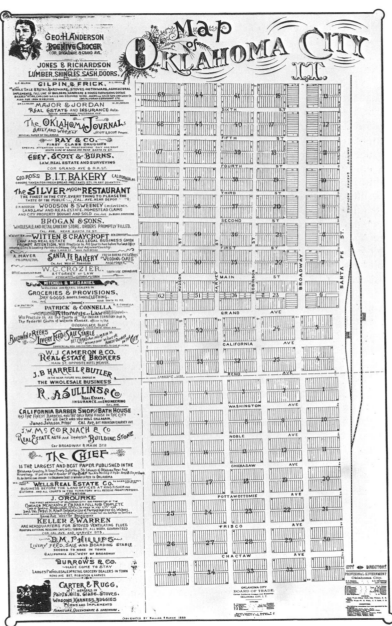

Figure 19.12   Plan of Oklahoma City, Oklahoma: 1889

that of the citizens' group did not match. The Seminole Company had planned its streets parallel and perpendicular to the railway, which was not on an exact north-south alignment. Moreover, the Seminole Company had platted its north-south streets only 60 feet wide with the exception of Broadway, which had a width of 100 feet.

When a telegram to the secretary of the interior brought the reply that the Seminole Company did not have exclusive rights to the townsite, the committee of fourteen decided to carry the citizens' survey beyond Main Street to the northern limits of the claim. On Saturday morning, however, as the surveyors prepared to begin, "a group of quiet men, some with Winchesters in their hands, appeared upon the scene and suggested that it would be just as well for the party to discontinue its work then and there."[38] The law of the rifle prevailed. The committee, informed of this confrontation, convened another mass meeting, and this time representatives of the Seminole interests were persuaded to participate. Five men from each group were selected to reconcile the two plans, surveyors were put to work, and by that evening the two plats were joined between Grant Avenue and Main by platting several irregular, gore lots in the five blocks affected. No agreement could be reached, however, on a method to overcome the off-sets on the north-south streets, and these inconvenient and dangerous jogs were allowed to remain.

On that compromise grid pattern, totally lacking in parks or even the usual courthouse square, Oklahoma City soon took form. The view reproduced in Figure 19.13 shows the town in its swaddling days looking from the Santa Fé watertower west along California Street. While, as at Guthrie, many persons still occupied tents, frame structures were quickly erected, and the real work of building a town commenced South of Reno Avenue a new townsite had been claimed, surveyed on April 23, and organized as the municipality of South Oklahoma. There were no conflicts about its plan, but unfortunately its north-south streets did not quite conform to those of the citizens plat to the north, and an additional set of jogs was created at Reno Avenue.

Municipal elections in Oklahoma City on May 1 resulted in a triumph for candidates from the north end, with William Couch emerging victorious as mayor and other members of the Seminole Company capturing a majority of the seats on the council. These men proceeded to enact and enforce a series of measures designed to give legal status to the certificates of "title" issued by the Seminole Company. One ordinance declared it a misdemeanor to claim adverse possession against the holder of a certificate issued by the company or by the city government. The jail was "crowded so full there was not room for another man," accord-

ing to one observer, who added that when juries "got to acquitting the fellows who were charged with being on lots without certificates," the judge—a Seminole Company man—dispensed with juries and summarily convicted and fined persons charged with violations.[39]

Federal troops were directed to intervene if necessary to prevent the overthrow of the mayor and council, and the town was bitterly divided into two factions. A referendum on a city charter had to be suspended because of the threat of violence, and the "municipality" of South Oklahoma soon became embroiled in political conflicts of its own. In the fall of 1889, acting under orders of the U.S. attorney general, the U.S. marshal of Kansas, R. A. Walker, suspended elections in Oklahoma City and placed the town under the control of several deputy marshals.[40]

The uncertainties over land titles and the political conflicts for control of the machinery of government did not prevent rapid development of the town. The view in Figure 19.14 shows the city from the northeast as it appeared on February 22, 1890, just ten months after it was founded. Lining the four main east-west streets were the principal business buildings, and elsewhere virtually all of the lots were occupied by houses, churches, and schools.

Conditions at two other Oklahoma towns founded in 1889 were less turbulent than at Guthrie and Oklahoma City. In the April rush by homesteaders, an 80-acre tract at the junction of the two branches of Stillwater Creek was somehow overlooked. There the Stillwater Townsite Company decided to plan its town almost a month after the opening of the territory. Three claimants of adjoining homesteads agreed to include their land, and the townsite was enlarged to 240 acres. The plan reproduced in Figure 19.15 was adopted as the design for the L-shaped parcel of land assembled in this manner. Early in June the residents elected a provisional town government and drew lots to determine ownership of the building sites.[41]

The following year the territorial legislature provided for the establishment of an agricultural college in Payne County but required that either the county or the town in which the institution would be located was to provide $10,000 in bonds and an 80-acre site. When the voters of the county rejected the bond issue in a referendum early in 1891 the residents of Stillwater voted to raise the required sum and approved the donation of 200 acres of land for the institution. The territorial government accepted this offer, and the Oklahoma Agricultural and Mechanical College thus began its existence, graduating its first class of six young men in 1896.[42]

South of Oklahoma City at Norman, a group of Santa Fé Railroad

Figure 19.13   View of Oklahoma City, Oklahoma: 1889

Figure 19.14 View of Oklahoma City, Oklahoma: 1890

civil engineers had already completed an illegal townsite survey when the first train of legal settlers arrived from the south. Apparently the "Sooners" realized that their claims might be voided, and they turned over their first hasty survey notes to a townsite company headed by D. L. Larsh, who had been employed by the railroad as its station agent at Purcell. The two parties then proceeded to complete the town survey, platting streets parallel and perpendicular to the railroad tracks. With only about 150 settlers on the spot, there was room for all, and the conflicts over land titles that marked the founding of Guthrie and Oklahoma City were not duplicated at Norman.

The town's design, however, shown in the official plat filed with the General Land Office the next year (Figure 19.16), showed no more imagination or skill than was employed elsewhere. The courthouse block was located inconveniently near one corner of the townsite, and only the large park at the northwest edge of town indicated any concern with civic amenities. The selection of Norman as the site for the university, however, changed the character of the dusty community. Its citizens in 1891, joined with those of Cleveland County in authorizing a bond issue of $15,000 and a donation of 40 acres of land to secure this prize. The university's first president, David Ross Boyd, led a campaign to plant thousands of saplings on the campus and along the town's streets, and within a few years Norman appeared prosperous and attractive.[43]

At other stations along the Santa Fé, smaller and less successful towns sprang into existence. Edmond, shown as it appeared in 1891 in Figure 19.17, was located approximately midway between Oklahoma City and Guthrie. Before the land rush, it consisted of the usual collection of buildings around the depot: a store or two, the water tower, a few houses, and miscellaneous out-buildings. Evidently this site was not as highly regarded as those to the north and south, for Edmond did not experience the same frenzied boom that occurred at Guthrie and Oklahoma City. Nevertheless, the site was regularly surveyed into a gridiron of streets and blocks and quickly was transformed from a sleepy stop on the railroad to a bustling little village whose new residents doubtless hoped and expected would one day become a major city.

Congress belatedly provided a basis for local government and the adjustment of land titles with the passage on May 2 and 14, 1890, of acts creating Oklahoma Territory and authorizing the entry of townsite claims by boards of trustees to be appointed by the secretary of the interior. The permissible size of a townsite was increased to 1280 acres, and

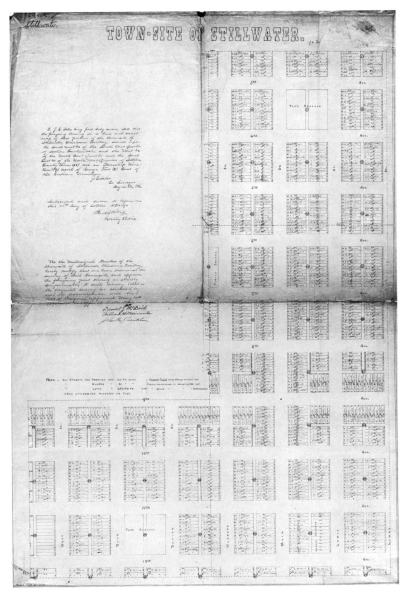

Figure 19.15 Plan of Stillwater, Oklahoma: 1890

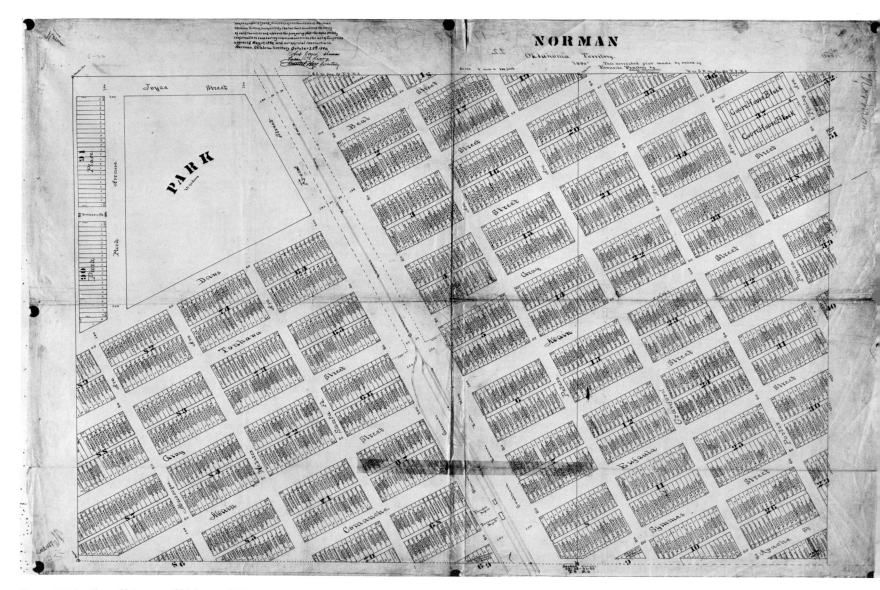

Figure 19.16 Plan of Norman, Oklahoma: 1890

Figure 19.17 View of Edmond, Oklahoma: 1891

any lots not disposed of to occupants were to be sold. The proceeds were to be given to the municipal government, or the unoccupied lots could be reserved as sites for public buildings or parks.[44]

Under this legislation the new towns proceeded to re-organize their governmental structure. The four townsites at Guthrie were consolidated late in the summer of 1890 and incorporated as a single municipality. Oklahoma City and South Oklahoma also merged, and the combined community held its first legal election on August 9. The boards of trustees appointed by the secretary of the interior as specified in the legislation set about their unenviable task of determining rightful ownership of town lots. In carrying out their duties, they followed Secretary Noble's suggestion that existing town plats be recognized as establishing the pattern of streets, blocks, and lots. Nevertheless, their decisions were not always agreed upon by rival claimants, and administrative appeals, and, in some cases, court action, prolonged for months or years final determination of town lot ownership.[45]

In the meantime the territorial legislature was convened by President Harrison's choice as first governor, George W. Steele. Instead of concentrating on the many pressing problems of organizing the new government, the legislature spent much of its time debating where to locate the capital. Congress had designated Guthrie for this purpose, but supporters of Oklahoma City and Kingfisher succeeded in obtaining the passage of bills designating their favorites as the capital. Governor Steele vetoed both measures, the Oklahoma City bill in October, and the Kingfisher legislation in November. Further attempts in later sessions failed, and Guthrie remained the territorial and first state capital until 1910 when, after much political maneuvering, the legislature voted to move the seat of government to Oklahoma City. A Capitol Commission was then authorized to acquire a 650-acre tract northeast of the original townsite, reserve land for the Capitol and executive mansion, and plat the remaining land.[46]

The rush of 1889 into the Unassigned Lands established a procedure for land disposal in Oklahoma that was repeated several times in the next few years although with some significant changes in the laws and administrative regulations affecting the location and design of towns. Lands opened for settlement were acquired from the various Indian tribes, whose members were given individual allotments when tribal ownership in common was terminated. The remaining lands thus added to the public domain were thrown open for settlement.

In September, 1891, 20,000 persons scrambled across the borders of the former Iowa, Sac and Fox and Pottawatomie-Shawnee reservation east of what was then the new Oklahoma Territory. In a departure from events of two years earlier, the townsites of Chandler and Tecumseh were surveyed in advance. A separate run for town lots in these two communities caused much disorder and confusion, and this experiment was not regarded as successful.

On April 19, 1892, the Cheyenne and Arapaho lands west of the territory of Oklahoma were opened by run. Although the area available for settlement comprised three and a half million acres, much of it was broken and arid, and only about 25,000 persons participated in the event. Here, as in the area opened in 1891, the government designated county boundaries in advance of the opening to provide a basic framework for local government, but much of the area was devoted to ranching, and few towns of any consequence developed.

The largest area to be made available by run was the Cherokee Outlet north of the Cheyenne and Arapaho reservation and the old Unassigned Lands. Potential settlers regarded this as choice land, and the government made extensive preparations for its opening, anticipating correctly that perhaps a 100,000 persons would stream across the borders on September 16, 1893, the date fixed by President Cleveland's proclamation four weeks earlier.[47]

Congress provided elaborate legislation governing the conditions by which settlement could take place, which the secretary of the interior, Hoke Smith, supplemented with rules and regulations intended to prevent the confusion that accompanied previous land rushes. Many of these were incorporated in the presidential proclamation; others took the form of instructions to federal officials in the field. All persons intending to make the rush into this vast six-and-a-half-million-acre domain were to register in advance at a number of booths provided at several points along the borders. Certificates entitling persons to claim either a homestead or a town lot were then to be issued.

Secretary Smith sent Alfred Swineford, inspector of surveys general, to the Outlet to locate sites for the land offices and to recommend sites for townsites to be planned by federal surveyors as county seats. Swineford apparently made no effort to conceal the location of the sites he favored, which, naturally enough, tended to be at stations already established on the Santa Fe or the Rock Island railways. Railroad officials, always alert for opportunities to turn speculative profits, induced a number of Cherokees to take up their authorized allotments of land at these spots with an understanding that the railroads would buy their land as soon as the territory was opened. Learning of this scheme to gain control of entire townsites, Secretary Smith directed that some of

Swineford's sites be moved a few miles away from their tenative locations. Among these were Pond Creek, Enid, Perry, Newkirk, and Alva.[48]

Government surveyors produced no masterpieces of civic design in laying out the official townsites, but their work represented a considerable improvement over what had resulted from the chaotic conditions prevailing during the opening of 1889. The plan of Enid, the largest city in the old Cherokee Outlet, is shown in Figure 19.18 as designed by surveyor Morris Bien. He provided east-west streets 100 or 110 feet wide. Eighty-foot north-south streets completed the conventional grid pattern. Streets 120 feet wide surrounded the courthouse and land office block. Midway along the south boundary of the townsite Bien introduced a public square of ten acres and reserved three other blocks for public purposes of just under three acres each. Unfortunately, he was compelled to observe the already established township and quarter-section lines, and the 320-acre site was thus divided by the Rock Island Railroad line slashing diagonally through the town from the northeast.

Woodward, located near the western end of the Cherokee Outlet, also occupied a site cut diagonally by the railroad. As the plan reproduced in Figure 19.19 reveals, this resulted in many small triangular parcels of land where the Santa Fé right-of-way divided the square blocks created by equally spaced streets following the cardinal points of the compass. Near the center, the surveyor placed the courthouse and land office site on two blocks consolidated as one, and between this reservation and the railroad he set aside two blocks as parks. At each of the four corners of the town he designated one block for school purposes.[49]

A. W. Barber was able to provide a more satisfactory relationship of the town of Alva to the Santa Fé Railroad right-of-way. His plan for what has become the trading center of Woods County along the Kansas border is reproduced in Figure 19.20. Around the five-acre courthouse square and land office site near the center of town Barber platted his business lots. The square itself is bordered by streets 110 feet wide on the north and south sides and two short streets nearly 180 feet in width on the east and west. Three public squares and a school site of slightly less than three acres each complete the deisgn.[50]

In addition to the townsites planned by government surveyors in the Cherokee Outlet, other towns were founded through the procedure used in the Unassigned Lands. The existence of government-appointed townsite boards of trustees eliminated much of the uncertainty over land titles and also improved somewhat the quality of the town designs that eventually gained land office approval.[51] In at least one case—at Ponca City—the 2,300 members of the townsite company agreed that they would accept certificates of ownership to lots assigned to them by chance. The names of the members were written on cards and placed in a box. Another box contained block and lot numbers. One card was drawn from each box simultaneously to determine the location of each participant's new home.[52]

Despite all the precautions, the opening of the Cherokee Outlet was accompanied by numerous instances of "soonerism" and fraud in claims for both homesteads and town lots. Both Silas Lamoreaux, commissioner of the General Land Office, and Secretary Smith concluded that rushing for land should be abandoned in favor of some kind of auction or lottery, and President Cleveland's annual message to Congress in December, 1893, recommended that future openings of public land be conducted on a different basis.[53]

Nevertheless, when the Indian tribal title to the tiny Kickapoo Reservation was extinguished and the area opened to settlement on May 23, 1895, after only five days' notice, another land rush took place for the 175,000 acres remaining after allotments had been made to individual members of the tribe. This, however, was to be the last time this disorderly and unsatisfactory method of parceling out the remains of Indian Territory was to be employed in Oklahoma.

Homesteads in the Kiowa-Comanche-Apache and the Wichita-Caddo lands in the southwestern portion of Oklahoma were disposed of by lottery on August 6, 1901. For the three new counties created at that time, government surveyors laid out three townsites as county seats. Here, at Anadarko (the plan of which is reproduced in Figure 19.21), Lawton, and Hobart, lots were put up for auction, and many of those unsuccessful at the lottery for homesteads crowded into the tent cities to bid for town lots. The design of these three communities followed the general patterns of the government-planned towns of the Cherokee Outlet, each having a courthouse square and one or more school or park sites fitted into a rectangular street system. Auction proceeds totaled nearly three-quarters of a million dollars, over half of which was contributed by sales of lots at Lawton. These funds were used for bridge and road construction, and the erection of the three courthouses.[54]

Remaining under tribal jurisdiction in Oklahoma were the extensive lands of the Cherokees, Creeks, Seminoles, Choctaws, and Chickasaws along the eastern and part of the southern border. Relentlessly the fed-

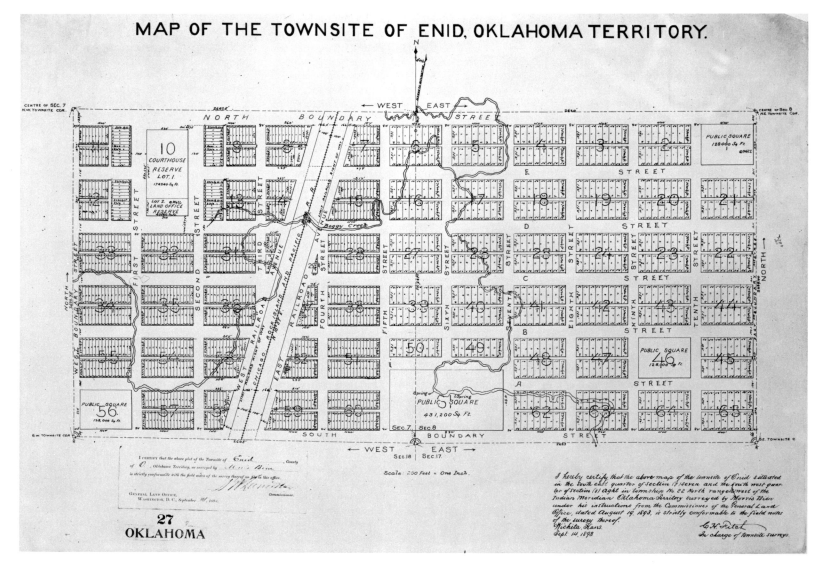

Figure 19.18 Plan of Enid, Oklahoma: 1893

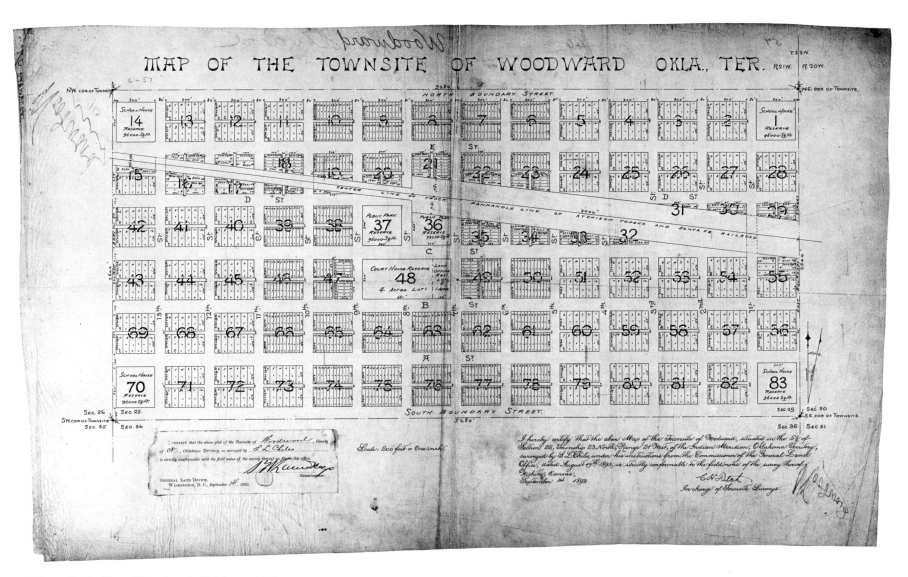

Figure 19.19 Plan of Woodward, Oklahoma: 1893

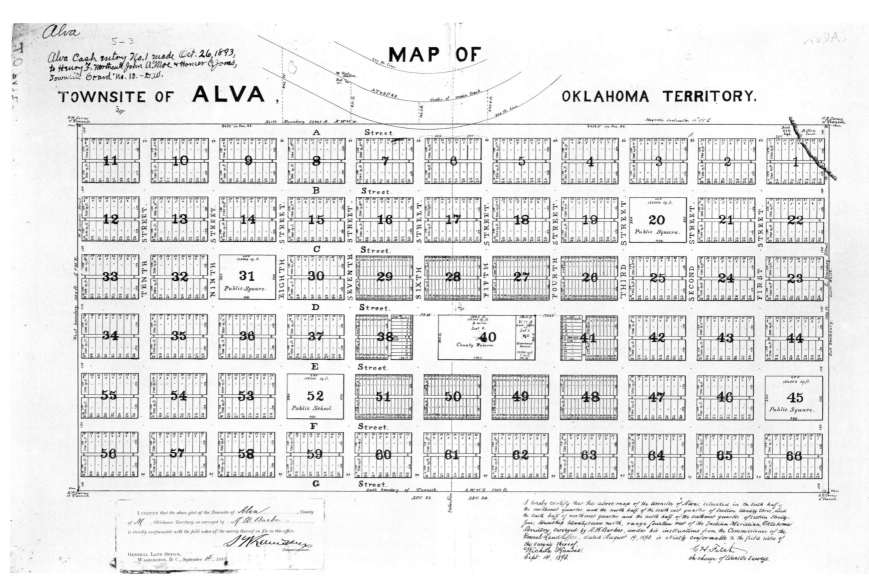

Figure 19.20 Plan of Alva, Oklahoma: 1893

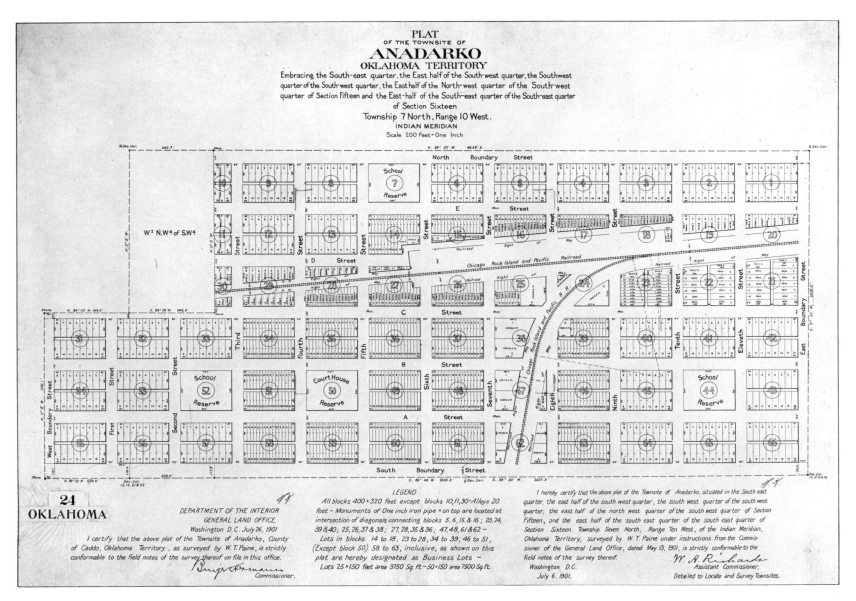

Figure 19.21   Plan of Anadarko, Oklahoma: 1901

Figure 19.22 Plan of Caddo, Oklahoma: 1901

eral government exerted pressure to end tribal ownership in common and to compel distribution of parts of these choice areas to individual Indians. Reluctantly the Indians capitulated after they had failed to secure support in Washington for a separate state and in the face of federal legislation that undercut much of their authority.

Congress created a commission on March 3, 1893, to negotiate the end of common ownership in the reservations of the Five Civilized Tribes. Under the chairmanship of Henry L. Dawes, but after 1897 with Tams Bixby as its driving force, the Dawes Commission attempted to reach agreements with the various tribes. All proposals were rejected.[55] Congress on June 28, 1898, seized the initiative with the passage of an act permitting citizens of towns in the Five Nations to petition a U.S. court for incorporation. The measure legalized the ownership of land in these towns by whites, many of whom had occupied lots in the Indian towns by purchasing from Indians guarantees that title would be transferred if ownership in severalty was eventually approved.[56] Tribal courts were abolished, and U.S. citizens were made eligible to vote in town elections along with tribal citizens. The act provided that towns be formally surveyed and platted by townsite commissions of three persons, one of whom was to be a tribal representative.[57]

By that time the majority of the population in the area of the Five Civilized Nations was no longer Indian. A steady influx of substantial numbers of whites into the region had begun at the time of the first railroad construction. White employees of Indians, licensed traders, and intruders added to the numbers of non-Indians. By 1890 the Indians were in a minority. In 1895 out of a total population of about 320,000 only 70,000 were Indians.[58] The act of 1898 thus gave both political power and the rights of land ownership to whites living in towns. Although the Five Nations continued to resist complete dissolution of tribal authority and land ownership, eventually they were forced to capitulate.

Government surveyors began their work of staking out the lines of streets, blocks, and lots in towns that had been settled over the years without much attention to property boundaries. In some cases the surveyors attempted to adjust their favored grid system to existing buildings. The plan of Caddo in the Choctaw Nation, reproduced in Figure 19.22, shows, however, that, even with several modifications in the width, location, and spacing of streets and with wide variations in the size and shape of lots, many houses and other buildings encroached on bordering lots or extended out into the street rights-of-way.[59] The quality of the plans established during this period was not very high, an unfortunate characteristic that may have been caused by the speed with which the surveys were carried out and the fact that existing patterns of occupancy prevented surveyors from introducing such elements as parks and public squares in all but a handful of their townsites.[60]

One town given precise form at this time occupied a site near the northern border of the Creek Nation just south of the dividing line between the Osage and Cherokee reservations. It was undistinguished in plan and indistinguishable from the many other townsites laid out by the various commissions. Its name commemorated Tallasi, an important Creek Indian town in Alabama. When the Creeks were moved westward from their original homeland, a small group of them settled on the north bank of the Arkansas River a few miles downstream from the mouth of the Cimarron. There they laid out their traditional square meeting and ceremonial place. The settlement was essentially agricultural, but shortly before 1880 a post office was established there to which the name Tulsa was assigned as a simplified spelling of the ancient name brought from Alabama. Early in 1882 contractors for the Frisco Railroad established a base at Tulsa in anticipation of the line's extension southwesterly from Vinita, which had been its terminus for some years.

The surveys for the railroad right-of-way provided for an alignment running diagonally through the upper portion of the eventual townsite. A stockyard, a station, and the usual collection of railway-oriented activities soon developed, to be joined by a hotel, several stores, a livery stable, a lumber yard, a schoolhouse, and a growing number of dwellings. Most of the business uses fronted Main Street, which the railway engineer had laid out at right angles to the track from a point near the station.[61]

As in many, perhaps most, of the "Indian" towns, white settlers played an increasingly important role. Nearby, white cattlemen either leased land from Indians or simply encroached on tribal grazing lands. Tulsa became an important cattle shipping point after the arrival of the railroad, and this activity attracted additional businesses as well as persons engaged in less respectable occupations who gravitated to frontier cattle towns. Churches and saloons, mission schools and gambling halls all found their place in the growing community.

In 1895 a federal judge ruled that towns in Indian Territory had a right to incorporate. Immediately a movement for a city charter got under way, but the Creeks refused to sell the land, and it was not until 1901 when the Dawes Commission concluded an agreement with the Creek Nation that the town was established as a corporate entity. Under the terms of the agreement, the townsite must first be platted.

Its lots were to be appraised and those holding occupancy titles under the former system of Indian tenure were to be offered their property at a price of from one-half to two-thirds of the appraised land value. The federal townsite commission engaged J. Gus Patton to lay out the town. Excitement generated by the news that oil had been discovered at nearby Red Fork heightened the speculative fever that had already swept the town when it became apparent that land titles would soon be confirmed.

Patton's survey as approved the following year by the Department of the Interior is reproduced in Figure 19.23. Using Main Street and the railroad right-of-way as coordinates, Patton stamped a vast and undeviating checkerboard plan across the tract. With two or three exceptions in the northwest corner of the town, all streets were made 80 feet wide. Most of the lots measured 100 by 140 feet, except for those near the railroad where the business district existed and in a few other locations. Alleys 20 feet wide divided nearly all of the blocks into two parts.

The appraised value of all of the lots in the entire townsite was established at the ridiculously low figure of $107,173.30. Under the law, land not occupied and improved was to be sold at auction with the proceeds to be turned over to the Creek Nation. By their approval of all kinds of fictitious claims of prior occupancy by actual settlers and dozens of speculators, the townsite commission disposed of virtually all of the lots to claimants. The sum of $659 was all that found its way to the Creek treasury.

On its overwhelmingly monotonous plan and with land titles achieved largely through deceit and trickery, the citizens of Tulsa proceeded to build what became a handsome town. The plan might be dull, but the leaders of the community possessed exceedingly sharp minds and an energetic spirit. They attracted additional railroad lines by underwriting part of the costs of construction. Three enterprising Tulsans constructed a toll bridge across the Arkansas River in 1904 to provide convenient access to the nearby oil fields which by then were being exploited. Other leaders saw to it that the Frisco railroad ran shuttle trains to the oil fields in the morning and back to Tulsa at night so that workers would live and spend their money in the city. Henry Kendall College, founded in Muskogee in 1894, was lured to Tulsa in 1907, and from this modest Presbyterian institution grew the modern University of Tulsa.

In the year of statehood for Oklahoma—1907—Tulsa's population was just over 7,000. During the next three years this more than doubled, and by 1920 it reached 72,000. Figure 19.24 shows the vibrant and

Figure 19.23 Plan of Tulsa,
Oklahoma: 1901

Figure 19.24   View of Tulsa, Oklahoma: 1918

thriving city of that period. The view is to the southwest and includes all of the original townsite plus the additions of subsequent years. Surveyors of these new streets laid them out exactly north-south and east-west, and the angular junctions of the two grid systems make it easy to trace the limits of Patton's original railroad-oriented survey two decades earlier.

The rapid settlement of Oklahoma completed the basic urban pattern of the American West. Few cities of major consequence would be established in the region after 1900; instead, the growth of city population would take place principally in those towns having origins in the nineteenth century or earlier. In the concluding chapter we shall look at a few of the towns that were founded toward the end of this period and return for a final glimpse of the region's most important urban places at the turn of the century.

The Urban West at the End of
the Frontier Era

Two years before the close of the nineteenth century the U.S. Census Office published an elaborate statistical atlas based on the census of 1890, a volume similar in scope and content to one issued a decade earlier. Its compiler, Henry Gannett, included a series of maps showing population density and the frontier of settlement at 10-year intervals beginning with the first census of 1790. In commenting on the final map Gannett observed:

> In 1890, which closes this series, the progress of settlement is seen to have been at least equally rapid with that of the decade before. Settlements in the Rocky Mountains had increased enormously, and had joined with those moving up the plains, forming a continuous body of settlement. Those of Montana, Washington, Oregon, California, and Utah had spread until throughout this region the settled area has become the rule and the unsettled area the exception. There is no longer any frontier line.[1]

It was an earlier and slightly different version of this statement that caught the attention of Frederick Jackson Turner in 1893 and which he used as the starting point for his famous essay on the western frontier and its effect on the American character. In formulating his hypothesis, as we noted in the Preface, Turner assumed that in the settlement of the West, towns and cities sprang up only after successive occupation of the region by Indian traders, ranchers, and farmers. Only near the end of his long career did he realize that no much neat sequence prevailed. In notes for a lecture written in 1925 he conceded that "often the economic stages represented by these waves of advancing population were blended or intermixed."[2]

Even this modification of his basic thesis did not go far enough, for, as we have seen, the founding of towns by such disparate groups as the Spanish, the Mormons, the Forty-Niners, the settlers of Kansas and Nebraska, and the Western railroad companies, among others, preceded rather than followed the development of ranching or farming. As Richard Wade, writing about the urbanization of an earlier "West" in the Ohio and middle Mississippi valleys, asserted, "The towns were the spearheads of the frontier. Planted far in advance of the line of settlement, they held the West for the approaching population. . . . Whether as part of the activity of the French and Spanish from New Orleans or of the English and Americans operating from the Atlantic seaboard, the establishment of towns preceded the breaking of soil in the transmontane west."[3] This generalization applies with equal validity to the trans-Mississippi West.

Both Gannett the geographer and Turner the historian, therefore, viewed the closing of the frontier period primarily in its agricultural context. Both men saw this as a turning point in the nation's history. While there still remained in the West vast areas yet to pass into private ownership, the absence of any meaningful line separating the settled from the unsettled portions of the region signaled to them the end of a long and eventful era. Further territorial expansion and internal colonization could no longer be regarded as an option open to Americans. In analyzing what he believed to have been the influence of the free land frontier of the rancher and the farmer on the country's history and in calling attention to the closing of these opportunities, Turner clearly implied that the direction and character of American life would be substantially affected.

What Turner and his followers failed to grasp is that by 1890 a significant part of the West's population resided in urban places and that it was these town and city dwellers who were largely responsible for whatever distinctive Western characteristics the region possessed. In trade and transportation, mining and manufacturing, art and architecture, printing and publishing, religion, recreation, education, administration, banking , politics, and virtually every other aspect of life, town and city residents and institutions dominated Western culture and civilization.

Moreover, Western cities by 1890 closely resembled older communities east of the Great Plains. In providing the basic public facilities and municipal services that distinguish urban from rural places, the towns and cities of 1890 that would become the region's major metropolitan centers of the future were already far advanced. With varying degrees of accomplishment, Western cities supplied water and gas, lighted streets, regulated the disposal of sewage, collected garbage, constructed and maintained streets and sidewalks, operated markets, fought crime, provided mass transportation, cared for the sick, buried the dead, extinguished fires, controlled nuisances, educated their youth, and offered opportunities for recreation.

Private companies supplied some of these services—as, indeed, they did in many Eastern cities. Public agencies were responsible for others, and not all of the young cities of the West offered this full range of urban activities. But plainly by 1890 the pioneering days had passed, and the larger communities of the Western states and territories ranked favorably in these aspects of municipal life with all but the most important older, and wealthier cities of the East.[4]

The editor of one western journal published in Portland openly invited such a comparison. Writing in 1886, he began a long description of his own city with these words: "One of the deepest rooted and most erroneous impressions the East entertains of the West is that the towns and cities are all new, illy constructed, poorly provided with the conveniences for health, comfort and the transaction of business, socially and morally below par, of a mushroom growth, and possessing those peculiar characteristics which have always been associated in the popular mind with the 'frontier.' "

He suggested that if "a resident of some Eastern city—one that is progressive and possessed of commercial vigor" could be suddenly "set . . . down in the streets of Portland . . . he would observe little difference between his new surroundings and those he beheld but a moment before in his native city." In Portland he would find "the rows of substantial brick blocks . . . , the well-paved and graded streets, the lines of street railway, the mass of telegraph and telephone wires, the numerous electric lights and street lamps, the fire-plugs and water hydrants, the beautiful private residences surrounded by lawns and shade trees suggesting years of careful culture, the long lines of wharves and warehouses on the river front, and the innumerable other features common to every prosperous Eastern city and commerical port."[5]

Not every western city possessed Portland's full range of urban services or the atmosphere of a long-settled community that this prosperous Oregon city had so quickly acquired. Nevertheless, the progress of urbanization in the American West was impressive not only in population growth and physical expansion but in improvements in public services, diversification of activities, widening of economic and social opportunities, and in attempts to introduce some of the amenities of urban living.

It was not only in the provision of utilities and public services that the major western communities in 1890 resembled those of the East. Their economic functions were those that cities in the East—and indeed elsewhere throughout history—have performed: processing of regional agricultural products, manufacturing goods for local consumption and importing others for wholesale and retail distribution, and providing for the cultural, educational, and recreational needs of their residents and those in their hinterlands. Moreover, the attitudes of their citizens and their political and social institutions differed little from those of urban areas settled earlier in the nation's development.[6]

There was good reason for these similarities. As Blake McKelvey has observed, "often it was a group of restless but vigorous men from an eastern city who planted the new towns of the West."[7] Eastern urban values, ideals, customs, methods, and institutions were thus transplanted on the western frontier with far fewer modifications than are generally assumed. Tradition proved far stronger than the forces of innovation. The creation of acting town governments in the mining camps of California in 1849 or in the instant tent and shack cities of Oklahoma four decades later are sharply etched examples of the persistence of familiar patterns of community life.

Even if one grants that in their earliest years the newly founded towns of Western America exhibited a raw and unfinished aspect that distinguished them from older prototypes in the East, by 1890 much of this "frontier" appearance had been substantially altered. Hitching posts, unpaved streets, plank sidewalks and backyard wells and privies were no monopoly of the urban West. They were American small-town phenomena that could be found from New England to the South and westward to and beyond the Mississippi.

Neither in their original plans nor in their patterns of expansion did western cities depart significantly from eastern models, illustrating again the persistence of habit, the strength of tradition, and the sources of capital and population. Clearly by 1890 the underlying physical framework on which these cities were later to grow had largely been determined. In some cases streets, blocks, and lots had been surveyed on such an extensive scale that it would be decades before actual development would catch up. San Diego is but one example of a Western community requiring few additions to its street network from the time of the boom of the 1880s until well after the first World War. In other cities the original plan, while needing to be extended and enlarged from time to time, fixed subsequent main axes of growth and strongly influenced directions of expansion. In virtually all of the cities the original gridiron street system was repeated almost endlessly in each subsequent addition to the urban fabric.

The western urban frontier could by 1890 be regarded as closed in still another and equally important sense. The basic locational pattern of western urban centers had been firmly fixed. Of the 31 western urbanized areas—cities and their surrounding suburbs—that in 1970 contained a population of over 200,000, all but Tulsa already existed in 1890. Only four cities—Lincoln, Topeka, Galveston, and Pueblo—that were among the 20 western communities in 1890 with a population of 20,000 or more would not grow sufficiently to be included in the list of major centers in 1970. While a number of towns were founded in the West after 1890 and suburban growth would increase in importance, the major western cities at the end of the nineteenth century continued to dominate the urban scene in the region.[8]

Table I shows the rank order and population of the western cities over 20,000 in 1890 and the corresponding data for western urbanized areas which in 1970 had populations exceeding 200,000.[9]

The decade of the 1890s is a convenient and appropriate time to stop our investigation of western urban planning and development—not

TABLE I · Rank Order and Population of Western Cities Over 20,000 in 1890 and Urbanized Areas Over 200,000 in 1970

Cities in 1890			
1. San Francisco	298,997	11. Dallas	38,067
2. Omaha	140,452	12. San Antonio	37,673
3. Denver	106,713	13. Tacoma	36,006
4. Lincoln	55,154	14. Topeka	31,007
5. Los Angeles	50,395	15. Galveston	29,084
6. Oakland	48,682	16. Houston	27,557
7. Portland	46,385	17. Sacramento	26,386
8. Salt Lake City	44,843	18. Pueblo	24,558
9. Seattle	42,837	19. Wichita	23,853
10. Kansas City, Kansas	38,316	20. Fort Worth	23,076

Urbanized Areas in 1970			
1. Los Angeles-Long Beach	8,351,266	7. Kansas City, Missouri and Kansas	1,101,787
2. San Francisco-Oakland	2,987,850	8. Denver	1,047,311
3. Houston	1,677,683	9. San Jose	1,025,273
4. Dallas	1,338,684	10. Phoenix	863,357
5. Seattle-Everett	1,238,107	11. Portland, Oregon & Washington	824,926
6. San Diego	1,198,323		

12. San Antonio	772,513	22. Wichita	302,334
13. Fort Worth	676,944	23. Albuquerque	297,451
14. Sacramento	633,732	24. Tucson	294,184
15. San Bernardino-Riverside	583,597	25. Austin	264,499
16. Oklahoma City	579,788	26. Fresno	262,908
17. Omaha, Nebraska & Iowa	491,776	27. Oxnard-Ventura-Thousand Oaks	244,653
18. Salt Lake City	479,342	28. Las Vegas, Nevada	236,681
19. Tulsa	371,499	29. Spokane	229,620
20. El Paso	337,471	30. Corpus Christi	212,820
21. Tacoma	332,521	31. Colorado Springs	204,766

because there was no longer any frontier line of agricultural settlement but because the more important frontier of wholesale town founding was by that time virtually at an end. Diminished opportunities for creating additional farms or ranches posed no threat to the existence or prosperity of these major urban centers or to most of the smaller communities elsewhere in the West. They had already developed beyond all expectations with hinterlands whose true agricultural potential had so far been but inefficiently exploited. As remaining arable and grazing lands were brought into production and older agricultural holdings were improved and made more efficient, existing towns and cities seemed likely to experience continued growth and consolidation of their positions of political, cultural, and economic leadership. Indeed, with the passing of time the cities of the West became far less dependent on their surrounding rural population for their own economic well-being, while farmers and ranchers could scarcely have existed without the towns and the services and facilities they provided.

While in Madison or Chicago, Turner might lecture with implied pessimism about what lay ahead for the nation now that the frontier era was closed, it is doubtful if anyone in Omaha, Dallas, Denver, Salt Lake City, Los Angeles, San Francisco, Portland, or Seattle would have understood or agreed with what he seemed to project as a mature America within finite boundaries and lacking the political and economic "safety-valve" of free land on the ever-advancing edge of western settlement. The cities of the West—many of them, like San Francisco, long before 1890—had become substantially independent of their immediate rural surroundings and were reaching out for broader state, regional, and national markets, sources of population, economic and political ties, and a style of life that linked them ever more closely to the rest of the country. By the end of the nineteenth century the gap between the urban and the rural West was far greater in every respect than whatever differences may have still distinguished a western city from its eastern counterpart.

A final look in the 1890s at western communities that were then or would become important will serve as both a summary of conditions that prevailed and an index of the accomplishments of some four centuries of urban growth in the western two-thirds of the nation. Beginning with some of the towns in the Great Plains (omitting those of Oklahoma that we have just examined), our journey will take us to Texas and the Southwest, the mountain states, the Pacific Northwest, and to California.

The capital cities of both Nebraska and Kansas had developed not only as governmental centers but as places with important trading and manufacturing functions. Both ranked among the 20 most populous cities of the West in 1890, Lincoln with a reported 55,154 and Topeka with 31,007 inhabitants. Figure 20.1 shows Lincoln as seen from the southwest at this time. In less than 25 years, the town planned by the state commissioners had become a flourishing city.

Served by several railroads, the location of the state university, with a thriving business district on O Street, and the site of several state institutions in addition to the state capital, Lincoln possessed a diversified economic base that other cities might envy. The many parks, squares, and sites for schools, churches, fraternal societies, and other civic purposes added to the city's attractiveness. And, as one contemporary observer noted, "the society of Lincoln is of an intelligence and culture unusual in towns so far west, and the wealth is considerable. The city is therefore well kept and handsome."[10]

The modern community has made the most of the opportunities provided by its founders in their well-designed plan. The present Capitol—the third on the same site—dominates the skyline with its great 400-foot tower rising from a massive, low, office base. Portions of 15th Street leading to the Historical Society building and the university campus have been converted to a handsome pedestrian mall. Along the western axis of the Capitol on J Street a number of new civic and cul-

tural buildings provide an additional focus of architectural interest.

Overshadowing Lincoln in industrial importance was Omaha, whose location as the gateway to the West on the Union Pacific Railway made it possible for the city to withstand the blow to its pride and economy when it lost its status as capital city. Dozens of land developers extended its original grid of streets north, south, and west as one can see in the view reproduced in Figure 20.2 showing the city from a point above the Iowa side of the Missouri River in 1905.

The railroads had been responsible for Omaha's growth to more than 140,000 in 1890, making it then the second most populous city in the West, exceeded only by San Francisco. The city obligingly had turned over the land along its waterfront to railroad purposes. Tracks and yards and the industries they served thus shut off the community from the great river that rolled almost unseen by its eastern boundary. At the turn of the century Omaha may have been a great rail and industrial center, but it yet had far to go in creating an urban environment with beauty and amenities to match its mercantile and transportation advantages.

The northern great plains then, as now, remained a region of widely spaced, small towns and cities. Sioux Falls, near the southeastern corner of South Dakota, was the largest urban center with a population of just over 10,000. Yankton and Aberdeen were each only one-third this size, while Deadwood, with its mining boom behind it, had declined to a town of slightly more than 2,000 persons. Bismarck and Watertown, in North Dakota, were no larger, and whatever dreams of urban growth the residents of these little settlements may once have entertained had surely begun to fade.

At the southern end of the great plains, however, the cities of Texas continued their vigorous expansion. Dallas, San Antonio, Galveston, Houston, and Fort Worth were all among the 20 largest western communities in 1890, although Dallas, the most populous, still had a population of less than 40,000. Its rate of growth had been enormous; a decade earlier its inhabitants had numbered only one-fourth this figure. Assessed property values had jumped even more, rising from slightly over $4,000,000 in 1880 to more than $30,000,000 a decade later.

Eight railroads provided the Dallas of 1890 with an almost unrivaled transportation system. Cotton, woolen, and flour mills, meat packing plants, wholesale agricultural implement warehouses, lumber and brick yards, and a variety of other businesses supplied products for shipment to eastern markets as well as serving the immediate region.

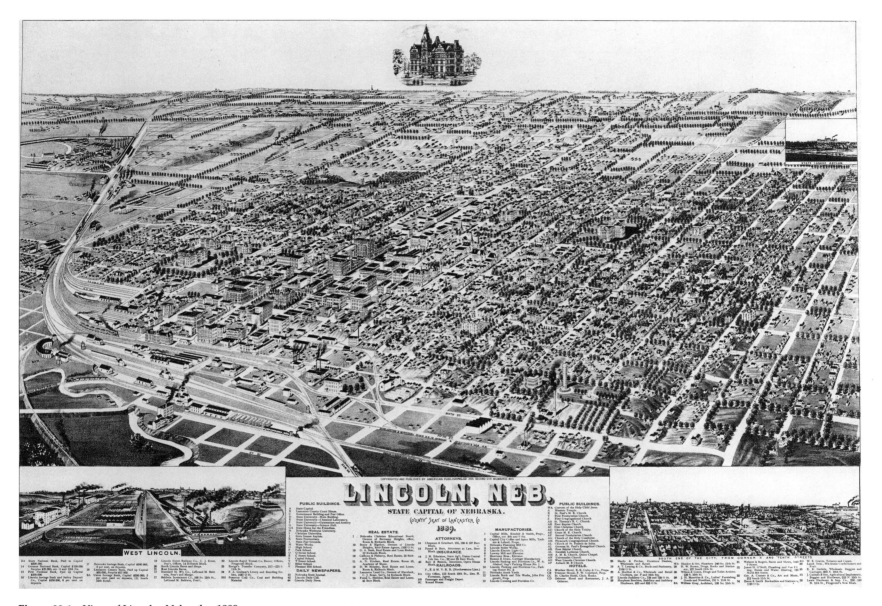

Figure 20.1 View of Lincoln, Nebraska: 1889

Published by THE OMAHA DAILY BEE—1906.

FROM THE ORIGINAL PAINTING BY E. J. AUSTEN

COPYRIGHT by the BEE PUBLISHING Co. 1906

Edw. J. Austen. 1905

PANORAMIC VIEW OF OMAHA

Figure 20.2 View of Omaha, Nebraska: 1905

Forty miles of paved streets, a water works, and a newly constructed sewer system with 22 miles of mains testified to the city's efforts to offer its many new residents the latest in municipal services. Three parks with a total area of nearly 300 acres indicated also that beauty and opportunities for recreation had not been forgotten. Forty-four churches raised their spires above the rooftops of the still largely horizontal community in 1890, although a seven-story hotel and a new county courthouse under construction that year would begin to change the urban profile.[11]

Fort Worth had undergone an equally dramatic transformation from a dusty cow town and trading center of 6,600 persons in 1880 into a thriving city of 23,000 ten years later. The view in Plate 27 shows how by 1891 the railroads that Fort Worth had worked so hard to obtain less than two decades before now provided access to the many industrial plants of the city. Their proud plumes of smoke must have seemed the authentic mark of progress in the days when atmospheric pollution and an economically healthy community were regarded as almost synonymous.

In the view one can see portions of the 15-mile-long system of street railways linking the outlying sections of the city to its compact business district stretching along Main Street for several blocks. Main Street led from the railroad station at the left to terminate at the handsome new Tarrant County courthouse, occupying the center of the square from which formerly one could overlook the valley of the Trinity River. Now the county jail and some smaller buildings partially blocked this view except through the opening leading to the new bridge crossing the river.

While most of the streets remained unpaved, the construction of 20 miles of water mains and 13 miles of sewers had doubtless done much to improve health conditions. Apparently Fort Worth had not yet recognized an obligation to provide public recreation facilities, for no parks appear in the view. Nor had the city fathers attempted to control the design of additions to the city as the owners of outlying farms divided their land into blocks and lots to profit from the real estate boom. The many gridiron subdivisions following separate axial alignments created a disjointed pattern that in a later era of automobile travel would cause serious problems. Fort Worth officials, in common with municipal legislators elsewhere, would surely have regarded such interference with the wishes of property owners as both unnecessary and grossly inappropriate.[12]

Houston's increase in population during the decade of the 1880s did not equal that experienced in the newer cities of Fort Worth and Dallas, but it was substantial nonetheless. In 1890 the census reported a population of 27,557, representing a growth of 11,000 residents in ten years.

Plate 28 shows the city in 1891 as viewed from a point over its northern borders looking south to the flat expanse of land stretching to the Gulf of Mexico. Buffalo Bayou winds its irregular way through the center of the city now crossed at several places by bridges connecting the northern industrial and transportation quarter with the business district and principal residential areas to the south. Ample subdivided land existed for the continued expansion that the future would bring. Evidently Houston always had real estate developers with unlimited faith in growth. Unfortunately, their expectations exceeded their skills in land planning, and even in 1890 the vast, interrupted grid of Houston's streets had become oppressively dull and monotonous.

Any considerations of land planning must have been muted in this era of rapid commerical and industrial expansion. Widening and dredging of Buffalo Bayou to permit larger ships to enter the channel during the 1890s spurred economic growth. By 1900 Houston overtook Dallas and Galveston in population, and with nearly 45,000 residents ranked a close second in Texas only to San Antonio, which it would also soon surpass.[13]

Galveston gamely hung on for a time in the race for urban supremacy with a population of 29,084 in 1890 and 37,789 at the turn of the century. But the terrible hurricane later that year reduced its numbers by 6,000 in a single day, and the city never recovered its earlier momentum.

San Antonio had also experienced a prolonged period of expansion far beyond the limits of the old Spanish and Mexican settlement clustered around the loop of the San Antonio River. Figure 20.3 shows the enlarged city in 1889 with its new subdivisions at the urban fringe. Developers of a few of these broke with the tradition of grid design and planned their land to incorporate curving streets and irregular blocks by way of contrast to the rectilinearity prevailing elsewhere in the city.

With admirable foresight, city officials had reserved land for parks in both the northern and southern quarters. The earliest of these appears on a map as a large rectangle north of the central district. Here city surveyor François Giraud in 1852 set aside a tract of land to preserve the San Pedro Springs—a distinctive feature that had attracted the original settlers to the location.[14]

Streets and open spaces in the older part of San Antonio still followed the early eighteenth-century pattern that the pioneering Canary

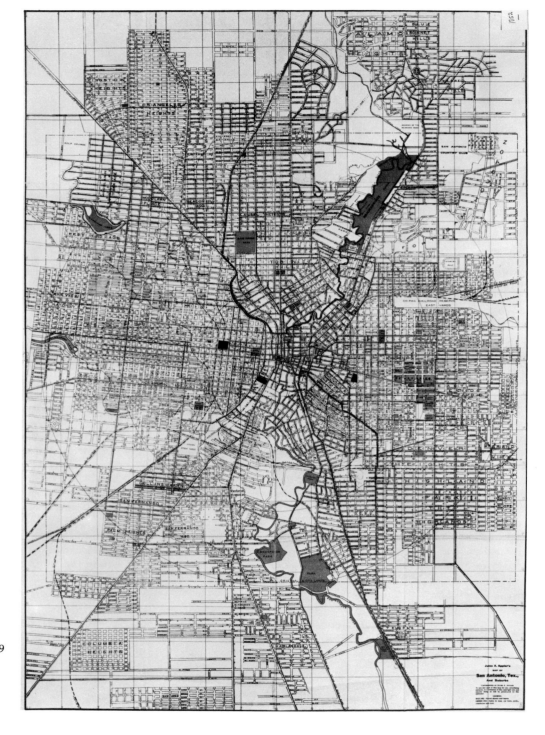

Figure 20.3 Plan of San Antonio, Texas: ca. 1889

Islanders had occupied after the town was planned. These can be seen in the center of Plate 29, a view of the city published in 1886. The twin plazas are prominent features, separated by San Fernando Cathedral on the spot once occupied by the parish church. To their right, beyond the loop in the river, one can see the remaining portion of the Alamo facing a new plaza around which offices and hotels had been constructed.

Old buildings in the center fared less well than the street plan as new and taller structures replaced the low adobes of an earlier generation. Despite many tragic and needless demolitions, not every building of the past was destroyed to pave the way for modern progress. La Villita, an area of humble dwellings south of the river loop survived and was restored in the 1930s as a center for artisans' shops and art galleries. The old Governor's Palace on the west side of Military Plaza and the restored remains of the Alamo are other important reminders of the Spanish period, as are the restored missions in the vicinity.[15]

The unique feature of central San Antonio, however, is the *Paseo del Rio*, an extended river walkway following the loop of the San Antonio River. This project began in 1939, and was extended and further improved in subsequent years. Twelve to fifteen feet below the level of the busy downtown streets, the pleasantly landscaped walks allow the pedestrian to stroll at leisure along the stream banks and to shop, drink, eat, or simply sit and reflect on the traditions of this ancient city whose original Spanish plan still forms the core of a modern metropolis.

Although smaller than its more commercially oriented sister cities of Texas, the capital of the state also had become a community of substantial size and importance. From just under 15,000 in 1890, Austin's census a decade later revealed that it had grown by more than one-third to reach 22,258. Figure 20.4 shows the city slightly before this period in 1887. Near the top appears the impressive building of the University of Texas set in the middle of a large square. This provided the orientation for gridiron additions to the city, surveyed on a slightly different axis from the Lamar-Waller town in 1839. On the horizon beyond, one can see the imposing buildings of the Texas State Hospital. To the right of East Avenue other extensions to the city appear, some of them unhappily at the awkward angles surveyed by the state when the remaining portions of the entire tract beyond the original city boundaries were put up for sale.

Congress Avenue was then solidly built up with major business buildings. The view up this impressive thoroughfare terminated at the new Capitol, completed in 1888 after a fire had destroyed the older

building seven years earlier. The concept in the original plan of a frame of state office buildings surrounding the Capitol had been only partly realized. Instead, the half-blocks facing Capitol Square on two of its sides remained open as an extension of the square.

In most other respects, however, the generous vision of President Lamar and Judge Waller for a city that combined beauty with functional utility had been realized. The two men deserve a place in the pantheon of western city planners who looked beyond their own era to create for future generations one of the country's notable urban plans. If the buildings of central Austin do not yet match in quality that of the base from which they rise, perhaps time will remedy this shortcoming.[16]

The principal cities in the Southwest, El Paso, Albuquerque, Santa Fe, Tucson, and Phoenix, also had undergone substantial change by the end of the century. During the decade from 1890 to 1900, El Paso grew by 50 percent, increasing its population from 10,338 to 15,906. It had ample room for expansion, for during the 1880s land speculators had continued to survey vast areas for future development. One visitor at that time observed that "the published plan of the town site . . . shows that its people have great expectations. The projected rectangular streets gridiron the desolate waste of foothills—at present a regular Sahara—occupying space enough for a second Chicago."[17]

El Paso's large, new customhouse reflected the increasing volume of exports from the United States passing through the city to Mexican markets. In 1887 and 1888 the declared value of such products exceeded $11,000,000. Smelting, food processing, cigar manufacturing, cattle shipping, and other industries bolstered its economy, and the city was thus launched on its steady growth that would bring its population in 1970 to well over 300,000.[18]

Albuquerque, while smaller than El Paso, grew even more rapidly, almost doubling in size from 1890 to 1900, when its population numbered 6,238. Its enormous grid pattern provided generous room for further growth, as Figure 20.5 reveals. By the time this plan was published in 1898, the new area served by the railroad had far outstripped the old Spanish town that can be seen in the upper portion of the drawing. The contrast between two modes of urban settlement could not be stronger—the old town with its tight cluster of adobe structures grouped around the plaza on which the parish church also faced; the sprawling American city of detached frame, brick, and stone buildings scattered throughout the grid of streets with a focus on the main business thoroughfare and the railroad that had created the beginnings of the modern community.[19]

Santa Fe represented a more close-grained combination of Spanish

Figure 20.4 View of Austin, Texas: 1887

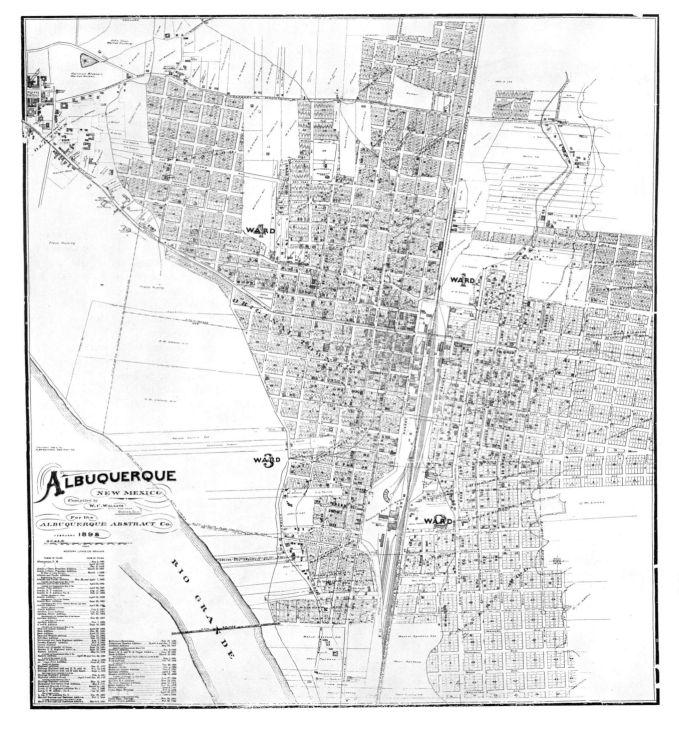

Figure 20.5
Plan of Albuquerque, New Mexico: 1898

and American influences. Most of its buildings were still of adobe but later structures in a variety of styles mingled with these remnants of the past. One of the most imposing edifices was the Victorian Territorial Capitol begun south of the river in 1884. Its location can be seen in Figure 20.6 showing the city about 1886. This capitol enjoyed only a brief life, burning in 1892 and being replaced eight years later by a building described as neo-English Renaissance in character.[20]

The basic street pattern and the old plaza testified to the Spanish origins of the central portion of the little city. A visitor in 1884 found this area "on the whole . . . sleepy and ancient looking; crooked streets, too narrow for but one sidewalk, find their ways like paths among the jutting, irregular fronts of adobe buildings." Around the plaza he encountered "most of the American business buildings, but Mexican adobe structures are inserted between them. The old, crooked walls of Jesus Ascencion Garcia's Broad Gauge Saloon are buttressed by a brand new brick bank building."

Traditional forms of transportation prevailed. "On the street a stylish dog-cart dashes past its original undeveloped type—a great, heavy structure resting on two oxen and two thick disks of wood, which creak on wooden axles. More primitive even than that, comes a drove of . . . burros, each bearing much more than his bulk of cord-wood or hay, and all driven by an Indian from the pueblo of Tesuque or by a darker looking Mexican."[21]

Left off the main line of the transcontinental railroad, Santa Fe declined in population during the decade of the 1890s, dropping from 6,185 to 5,603. Even so, many of the older buildings continued to be replaced by more modern and supposedly better structures. Not for many years, in a more enlightened era, would a new generation of citizens—painfully late—realize that preservation or restoration of their architectural heritage should be undertaken.

Modifications of the old Spanish presidial town of Tucson proved more drastic. By 1893, as shown in Figure 20.7, Tucson's irregular grid of streets leading outward from the walled plazas of the early nineteenth-century settlement had been extended in a more conventional pattern. The drawing shows that additions to the north, east, and south followed a rigid system of rectangular blocks broken only by the diagonal slash of the Southern Pacific Railway, which had reached the city 10 years earlier to set off a local land boom and stimulate growth of population and economic activity.

While several new public reservations had been set aside for various uses, the old military plaza in the block bounded by Alameda, Myers, Washington, and Main Streets had been cut up into building sites. The

much larger block identified as Military Plaza dates from 1863, when Union troops surveyed the tract as an army post. This, too, eventually disappeared when in later years the land was put up for sale to raise funds for the construction of a sewer system. Only the portion between 12th and 13th Streets remains, the western half occupied by the public library and the eastern part as Armory Park.[22]

The new streets and blocks exceeded the demand for building sites, for in 1900 the town's population was only 7,351. Tucson's development for many years proceeded modestly, and significant expansion did not occur until after the second World War. Then the city began an almost explosive period of growth that by 1970 brought the population of Tucson and its suburbs to nearly 300,000.

Tucson now spreads out for miles in all directions from the nineteenth-century community in a huge gridiron branded across the flat desert. Little is left of the buildings of its formative years, and only the broken grid and narrow streets of the older portion of the city recall its Spanish and Mexican beginnings. A recent evaluation of Tucson's record of preservation of historic buildings makes depressing reading: "A pitifully small number of important landmarks . . . [have been] preserved; and St. Augustine Church, the Orndorff Hotel, the Territorial Capitol, and nearly all the charming family homes of prominent territorial citizens are gone, sacrificed to questionable and shortsighted programs of economic progress and municipal improvement."[23]

Phoenix, which in 1970 had a population of 863,000 and was the Southwest's largest metropolis between Dallas and Los Angeles gave few indications 90 years earlier of its enormous potential. The editor of the Phoenix *Gazette* observed in 1882 that "no railroad trains rush into its midst, no machine shops give employment to large number of people, no factories support its populace," and no smelters processed the rich mineral ores of the Arizona mountains.[24]

Phoenix then had a population of less than 2,000, and it was not much larger when the view reproduced in Plate 30 was published in 1885. The most prominent building at that time was the courthouse, standing in the center of the block assigned for that purpose in the original town plan near the southwestern edge of the compactly built-up portion of the town. No smoky railroad locomotives yet defiled the clear desert air, but the completion of a branch line to the Southern Pacific in 1887 brought modest amounts of both pollution and prosperity to the young agricultural community and began to change its character.

The railroad helped Phoenix wrest the territorial capital from Prescott in 1889, and the city's more central location overcame larger Tucson's

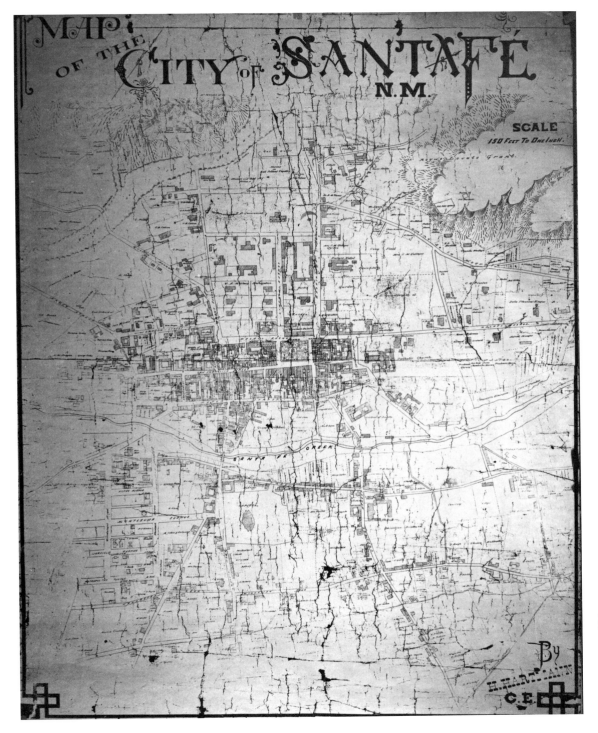

Figure 20.6   Plan of Santa Fe, New Mexico: ca. 1886

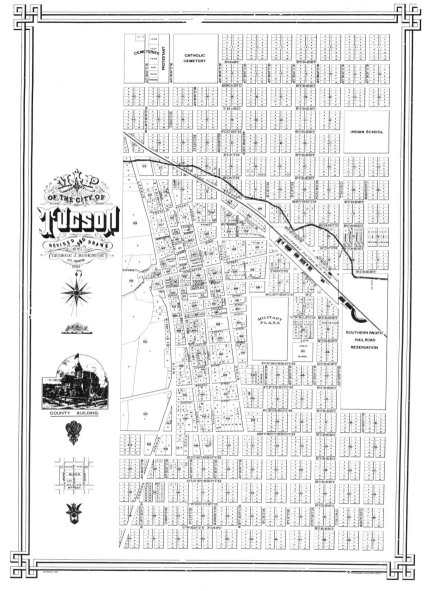

Figure 20.7 Plan of Tucson, Arizona: 1893

claim for the same prize. The growing town provided a 10-acre site for the capitol to the west of the already developed area. As had been done elsewhere in Phoenix, a great variety of trees was immediately planted to make the capitol grounds more attractive and provide welcome shade from the burning summer sun.

It was the Phoenix of that year, possessing the transportation facilities and governmental payroll that along with its superb winter climate would enable it to outstrip its original rivals, that one observer could describe in these admiring words: "Phenix [sic!] has all the improvements required in a modern town—a municipal organization, a chamber of commerce, police and fire departments, public water in pipes and by surface irrigation, gas and electricity for illumination, street cars, telephones, two daily newspapers, banks, and loan companies."[25] Almost overnight, then, Phoenix had transformed itself from a raw, new, and isolated farming town into a modern little city with most of the advantages and improvements of much older communities in the East.

Impressive as these achievements in urban development might be, they were overshadowed by those of the major metropolis of Denver. With its population of 106,713 in 1890, it ranked third behind Omaha and San Francisco in size and importance among western cities. Its growth rate had been enormous; in the ten years since the previous census, Denver tripled in population.

Eastern visitors and residents of the region crowded Denver's many fine hotels. By far the most imposing was the elaborate five-story Windsor House, which opened its doors in 1881 at the corner of Larimer and 18th Streets. Most persons arrived in the city by way of the equally impressive Union Depot, a great stone structure more than 500 feet long standing at the foot of 17th Street, which terminated at the railroad tracks leading into the city along the valley of the South Platte River.

A person stepping out of the majestic Windsor House could not fail to have been impressed by the scene before him on Larimer Street, which William Thayer ecstatically compared to New York's Broadway in "enterprise, stability, and rush." Here, he observed, "Eastern solidity, tact, and forethought seem to be mixed up with Western dash, in about equal parts. The result is a bustling, thriving inspiring scene."[26]

Denver continued to attract artists as well, among them Henry Wellge, who depicted the city in 1889 as reproduced in Figure 20.8. It was the year before the cornerstone was laid for the Colorado capitol on the land donated earlier by Henry Brown. The view incorrectly shows

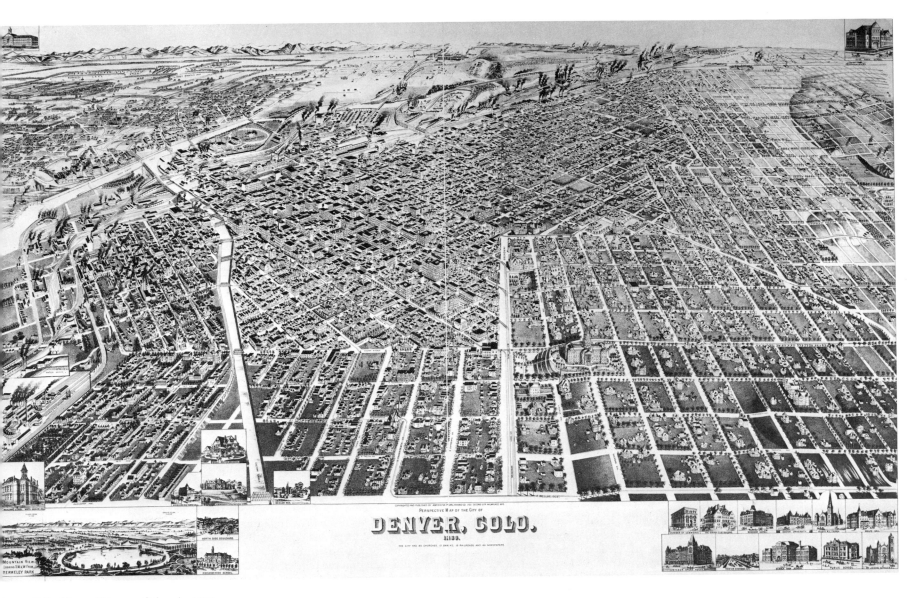

igure 20.8 View of Denver, Colorado: 1889

this great domed structure with its entrances facing north and south. When construction began, following designs by E. E. Myers, the axis was rotated 90 degrees so that the principal entrance faced Broadway and looked west to the majestic stretch of the Colorado Rockies, which provided the city an unrivaled natural backdrop. It was this building that established the nucleus for the later Denver Civic Center extending for several blocks westward with the City-County building closing the main axis at its other end.

The city now stretched far beyond even the generous area originally platted at the beginning of the Colorado gold rush only 30 short years earlier. Handsome mansions for the families that had grown rich on gold, real estate, manufacturing, banking, and the cattle trade filled the blocks laid out east of the capitol, and thousands of more modest dwellings lined the streets of the many other checkerboard additions extending off to the horizon.

A long complex of industrial buildings, each belching its smoky sign of progress, lined both sides of the railroads in the river valley. The densely built business district was solid with nascent skyscrapers along 17th and 18th Streets from their diagonal intersections with the wide slash of Broadway running along the base of the capitol hill. Denver did not neglect other aspects of civil development. The Tabor Grand Opera House was one of the wonders of the West, and city fathers had begun work on a park system to provide both facilities for recreation and visual contrasts with the man-made physical fabric of the city that had grown so swiftly at the western edge of the central Great Plains.[27]

South of Denver a western visitor in the 1890s would have encountered a much smaller and more placid community of quite different character but possessing a remarkable degree of beauty and sophistication. General Palmer's city of Colorado Springs had only 11,140 residents at the beginning of the last decade of the century, but it would more then double in the ten years ahead, and each summer tourists swelled its size well beyond the census figure.

The English editor of Karl Baedeker's guide to the United States, James Muirhead, spent nearly three years in the country gathering materials for that indispensable volume. Nowhere did he encounter a more pleasing spot than this well-planned resort town. In his own informal book on America he recorded his impressions of Colorado Springs "as an oasis of Eastern civilization and finish in an environment of Western rawness and enterprise." Muirhead noted that "its wide, tree-shaded streets are kept in excellent order," and that there were no manufacturing plants. "The inhabitants consist very largely of educated and refined people from the Eastern states and England . . . The tone of the place is a refreshing blend of the civilization of the East and the unconventionalism of the West." Another kind of blend was absent, for as Muirhead observed, "no 'saloons' are permitted."[28]

If a tourist could not drink whiskey in Colorado Springs unless he had the foresight to bring his own supply, at least he could intoxicate himself daily on the superb view of the Rockies looming over the town to the west. Figure 20.9 shows the city in its magnificent setting as it appeared about 1890. Beyond the pleasantly landscaped town and to the right one can see the picturesque red sandstone formations comprising the Garden of the Gods. Towering over all on the axis of the principal street terminating at the huge Palmer House is Pikes Peak, whose lofty summit could be reached by a cog-wheel railroad from Manitou, a smart spa nestled in a cleft in the mountains. This one urban legacy to the West bequeathed by General Palmer does much to absolve his sins in creating elsewhere so many shabby and routinely planned railroad towns.

A more adventuresome traveler in the 1890s might have made his way north to less sophisticated towns in Wyoming and Montana. There would have been little to attract his attention in Cheyenne or Laramie unless he possessed an abiding interest in railroad shops, stockyards, saddle-making, and wagon manufacturing; although at the former town he could have inspected the Wyoming capitol and at the latter the new building for the state university for which taxpapers had provided the princely sum of $75,000. Nevertheless, if he realized how young both towns were he might have been impressed by Laramie's population in 1890 of 6,388 and Cheyenne's 11,690.[29]

The largest city of the northern Rockies in 1890 was Helena, with a population of 13, 834. Rail service beginning in 1883 helped stimulate growth, and during the following year more than 300 buildings were erected. Many of these were mansions for what were said to be at least 50 millionaires then residing in the community. The fashionable suburbs of Kenwood and Lenox date from this time, an era that also saw vast speculative subdivision expansion elsewhere in the vicinity as Helena enjoyed its most vigorous period of growth.

The view of the city in Figure 20.10 shows the city in 1890. The business district on Main Street, Broadway, and nearby thoroughfares then consisted of impressive buildings of brick and stone, some of which are illustrated in the border views. At the lower left is an inset of Lenox. At its western edge, commanding a view of the city from the crown of a hill, the state capitol was soon to be started on a site bounded by 6th

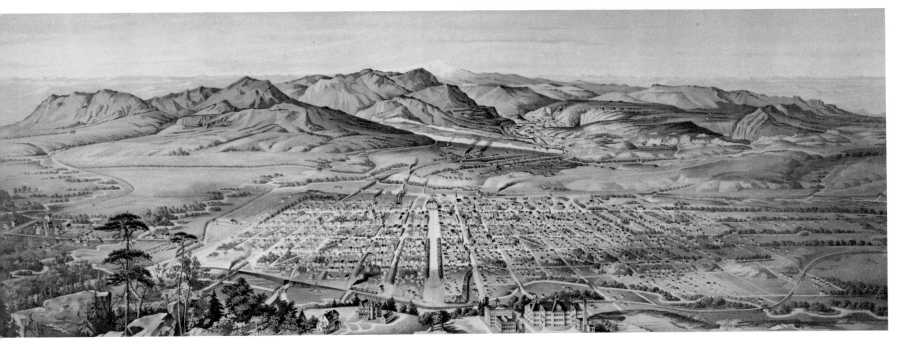

Figure 20.9 View of Colorado Springs, Colorado: ca. 1890

and Lockey Avenues and South Montana and Roberts Streets. This land was donated to the state by the developers of this exclusive residential neighborhood.

Here, as elsewhere beyond the bounds of the original townsite, land developers reverted to a rigid north-south and east-west orientation for their streets. The view reveals the rather confusing pattern that resulted where the older parts of town merged with these later additions. No one at the time could have worried a great deal about such matters; the most important goal was to cut up land as cheaply and easily as possible and place lots on the market before the boom ended.

This flurry of activity did not have long to last. The depression years of the 1890s proved cruel to Helena, its population declined, and by 1900 it had been far surpassed in size by Butte, whose deposits of copper offered greater long-term economic security that Helena's gold mines. In 1890, however, there was little indication of the troubles that lay ahead. As Hubert Bancroft observed at the end of his historical summary tracing Helena's remarkable rise from mining camp to capital city during a dynamic quarter of a century, the city exhibited "a general style of comfortable and even elegant living vividly in contrast with the cabins of its founders."[30]

Far more elaborate and substantially larger, with its 1890 population of 45,000, the Mormon capital of Salt Lake City had more than doubled in size during the previous decade. While most of its residents still lived within the boundaries of Brigham Young's original plat, newer houses

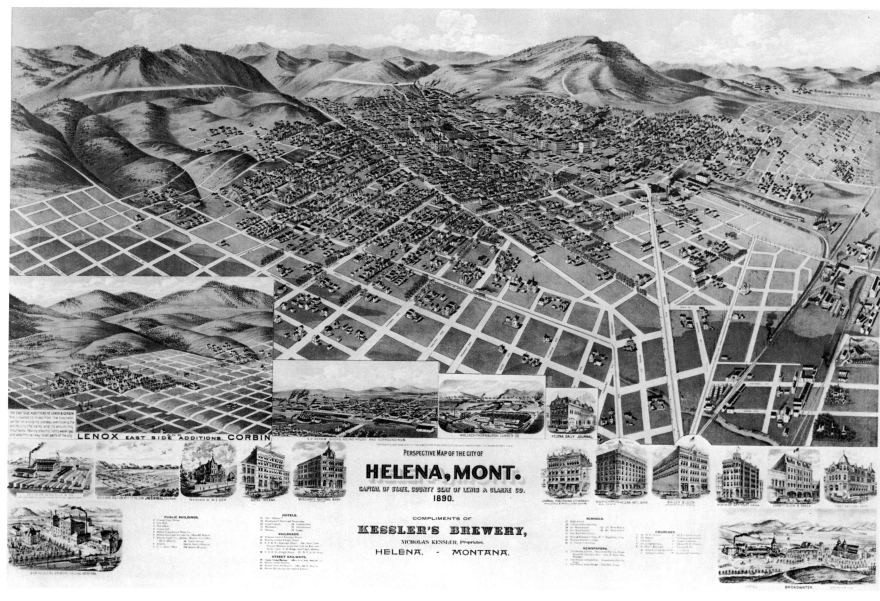

Figure 20.10   View of Helena, Montana: 1890

could now be found on the old lake terraces or bench land north and east of the first settlement area.

Salt Lake City enjoyed the latest in municipal services. Gas and electricity lighted its streets and houses, and a modern system provided water for drinking and fire-fighting, although streams still sparkled through the city in the open irrigation ditches along its broad streets. In 1888 the first electric street railway received its charter to begin competition with the horse-car lines whose 13 miles of routes provided slow but reliable service to the center of town from the neighborhoods at the outskirts.[31]

The city as it appeared from the south in 1891 is shown in Figure 20.11. In the foreground Liberty Park occupies the site once owned as a farm by the city's founder. Adjoining agricultural tracts in the Big Field farming area would soon be subdivided into house lots as the city continued to grow. In the center the Tabernacle and the nearly completed Temple with its spires soaring above the city stand as monuments to Mormon enterprise and religious piety. On the hill to the north, the view shows a large domed building looking down on the city below. This is the Utah capitol, its location correctly indicated although the artist anticipated its construction by more than 20 years.

Fort Douglas appears at the far right, just beyond the extensive site that in 1900 would be chosen for the University of Utah, which had previously held its classes in a variety of buildings elsewhere in the city. At the left, beyond the Jordan River, which for many years marked the western boundary of the town, one can see the Great Salt Lake, after which the city had taken its name.

A few other cities would be founded by the Mormons, and virtually all of the hundreds of others already established by them would continue to grow. Their orderly design and planned development are tributes to the industry and perseverance of those pariah pioneers who created an oasis kingdom from a nearly barren desert.

Salt Lake City stands out as by far the most impressive of these urban centers. Although its basic plan showed no great sophistication in civic design, Mormon builders provided in their Temple and Tabernacle exciting and contrasting architectural forms that brought to the city a unique three-dimensional character. The original wide streets have proved adequate for most modern traffic requirements, and the locations reserved for parks and schools have been of immense benefit to the community over the years. Towering over all these works of mere humans are the everlasting hills and mountains forming a superb backdrop to the daily drama of urban life and serving as a constant reminder of man's transient role on nature's stage.

In the Pacific Northwest during the closing years of the nineteenth century, Tacoma, Seattle, and Portland all contended for domination. In 1890 Tacoma's population was 36,000, a dramatic increase from the figure of just under 1,100 ten years earlier. Real estate transactions reached $16,000,000 annually, and there seemed no end in sight for its future development. Figure 20.12 shows the city of that period with its busy railroads and industries crowding the waterfront, the imposing business district on higher ground, and the spires of the city's numerous churches punctuating the skyline.

The railroad that made Tacoma, however, provided an even greater stimulus to growth elsewhere. The extension by the Northern Pacific of what was at first regarded as a branch line to Seattle made that younger city to the north a disturbing rival for the railroad's freight and passenger service. The Union Pacific, which had promised to build its line to Tacoma, changed its plans just as the city was recovering from the depression of 1893 when all 21 of its banks had been forced to close. Tacoma suffered another and more damaging blow when James J. Hill selected Seattle as the Pacific Coast terminus of his Great Northern line.

Tacoma never quite achieved the greatness it sought and expected. From 1890 to 1900 its population remained nearly stable, and while it did manage to grow at a moderate rate in subsequent years, both Seattle and Portland far surpassed Tacoma in commercial and cultural importance. Today Tacoma is an important city whose 1970 urbanized area population exceeded 300,000, but it is clearly not destined to attain the position as the major metropolis of the Pacific Northwest to which its founders and early leaders aspired.[32]

Even by 1890 Seattle's population exceeded that of Tacoma. The city's 43,000 inhabitants were concentrated near the business district adjacent to the wharfs and railroad terminals along Elliott Bay. But as the view in Plate 31 shows, many other detached clusters of development and small suburbs dotted the shores of Lake Washington and Lake Union, clung to the sides of the steep slopes between these bodies of water, or occupied hilltop locations with superb views in all directions.

Most of the business district had been destroyed two years earlier by a fire which gutted virtually every building in a 50-block area. Seattle rebuilt with amazing speed. A contemporary historian describing the process a year later claimed that the event was viewed as "a benefit rather than a calamity." Property owners and municipal officials "replatted the streets, changed the grades, and set to work to build a better city than that which had been destroyed."[33]

Nearly 500 new buildings, 60 wharfs and warehouses, newly paved

686

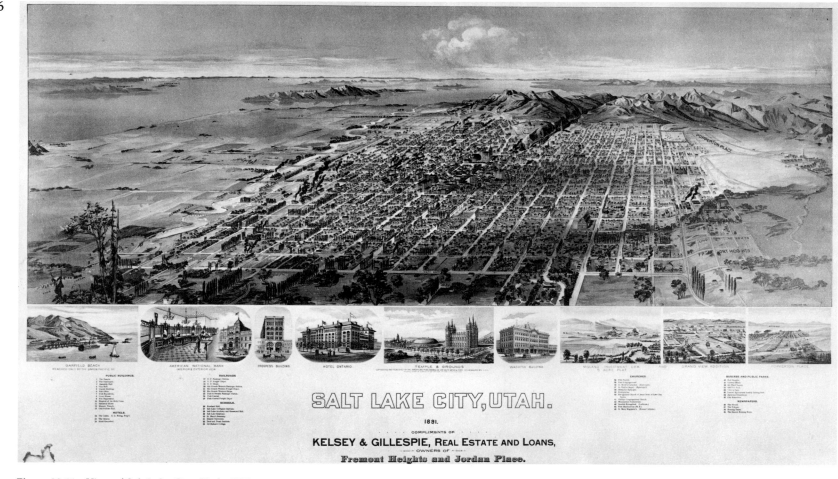

Figure 20.11 View of Salt Lake City, Utah: 1891

Figure 20.12 View of Tacoma, Washington: 1889

streets, and a sewer system were all constructed and in use by the time the view was published in 1891. Other improvements followed. To supplement the city's public recreation grounds, then consisting of two tracts donated by the Denny and Kinnear families, the city purchased land for the 188-acre Woodland Park in the northern part of the city. Its site adjoining Green Lake appears near the upper left corner of the view. The city organized a board of park commissioners, which in 1892 engaged E. O. Schwagerl, a landscape gardener and engineer, to prepare a plan for the development of Woodland Park and to study the needs for additional recreational grounds. As later revised and extended by the Olmsted Brothers' firm in 1903 Schwagerl's work provided the basis for the city's many subsequent park and recreation projects.[34]

By 1900 Seattle's population had nearly doubled, reaching 80,671 and making it the sixth largest city in the West. The discovery of gold in the Yukon in 1897 brought a major boom to the city when it became the principal outfitting point for persons rushing to this new source of mineral wealth. The prosperous community thus could afford to tax its residents for a long-deferred but badly needed reconstruction project—the wholesale regrading of the excessively steep streets that had been so carelessly platted up the broken hillsides of the rugged site.

Engineers and construction crews employing hydraulic methods borrowed from mining operations washed away entire hills and used the material to fill more than 1,400 acres of tidal flats. While the grades were modified and many streets widened in the process, the basic plan of the city remained essentially unchanged, and the central portion of the modern metropolis of more than 1,200,000 must still contend with the erratic street pattern established by its original founders and the many speculative developers who added to it without public guidance or direction.

The older, slightly larger, and somewhat slower growing city of Portland had by 1890 taken on a more settled appearance than the still rapidly changing Seattle. Figure 20.13 reveals the appearance of Oregon's metropolis when its population stood at 46,385. The border views of major buildings suggest that a visitor would have thought the city to be much more populous, and in the quality of their appearance and construction they would have struck him as the equal of any in the country.

The editor of the principal American travel guide of this period had only praise for Portland's accomplishments: "The streets . . . are wide, regularly laid out, well paved and well lighted. The buildings of the business thoroughfares would do credit to any city, and the same may be said of many of the churches, the post-office, the custom-house, and other public edifices, as well as private residences. The markets are good and spacious. There are public and other schools of various grades, a large library, well conducted newspapers, 16 banks, 3 public halls, a good theater, 12 lines of street-railway, with 76 miles of road, all cable or electric except two miles, water-works owned by the city, gas, manufacturing establishments, telegraphic communication with all parts, an immense wholesale and retail business, and, in fine, all the features of a flourishing modern city."[35]

Portland, like Seattle, doubled in size during the decade of the 1890s, although roughly 20,000 of its 1900 population of 90,426 could be accounted for by the annexation of its neighboring communities of Albina and East Portland. During the following ten years, however, Portland added 117,000 to its population and expanded in all directions during the giddy land boom accompanying this rapid influx.

At the southern end of the Pacific Coast the explosive growth of Los Angeles, halted during the depression years after 1888, soon resumed. In the decade of the land boom it had jumped from a sleepy town of 11,000 in 1880 to more than 50,000 by 1890; by the end of the century this population more than doubled. Plate 32 shows the city roughly midway through the decade. The embryonic metropolis now stretched in all directions from its original nucleus, and the artist was compelled to divide his lithograph into two parts—the upper portion showing the city as seen looking north and the lower depicting the view to the south with the Pacifc Ocean on the horizon.

Dredging and other improvements of the San Pedro harbor, a project begun in 1899 with federal funds, enabled Los Angeles to offer better port facilities and further stimulated expansion and growth. One historian of the city writing in the summer of 1901 noted that "the city is growing with greater rapidity than at any time in its history, if we except the one or two years of the boom . . . and the increase of business is on even a greater ratio than that of population."

This observer accurately forecast what the future would bring: "The southwestern region of the United States will support at least one great city, and all doubt as to where that city will be located is now at an end. The little pueblo that Governor De Neve founded 120 years ago, in order that grain for the army might be raised in California instead of imported from Mexico, has at last grown to be the active, prosperous city of his dreams. That it should someday become one of the great metropolitan centers of the nation is not a dream, but the natural outgrowth of existing conditions."[36]

Many other towns in the surrounding area either founded before the

Figure 20.13 View of Portland, Oregon: 1890

land boom or surviving its collapse shared the prosperity enjoyed by Los Angeles. Near the upper right corner of the view of Los Angeles to the north one can just make out the location of Pasadena, then still separated from the sprawling mass of Los Angeles that had not yet engulfed the intervening hills and valleys. Pasadena had profited by the land boom of the previous decade, as the view in Figure 20.14 showing the city in 1893 clearly reveals. It had swiftly developed as a modern town, which the editor of *Appletons' Guide* could describe admiringly: "The streets are lighted with gas; there are lines of horse-cars, three banks, two daily newspapers, and a public library; and the hotel, the *Raymond*, is large, well appointed, and beautifully situated."[37]

The Raymond Hotel can be seen at the lower right corner of the view overlooking the city from its lofty site. Almost as imposing are the many mansions of wealthy residents, some of which are shown in the border vignettes. These were to increase in number as Pasadena's advantages as a beautiful and healthy residential community became known, a reputation carefully cultivated by the city's real estate interests and public officials. In the decade of the 1890s Pasadena's population nearly doubled in numbers to reach over 12,000.

Not all cities in California were able to maintain such a rapid pace of growth. It took San Diego many years to recover from the ill effects of the land boom of the 1880s. In 1900 its population was only 17,700, barely 1,500 more residents than found at the previous census. San José, less affected by the excesses of the boom, also grew only moderately from 18,060 to 21,500 during this same period. Oakland, already a city of nearly 49,000 in 1890, grew more rapidly, but its population at the end of the decade was only one-third greater.

A visitor to the urban West in the 1890s wishing to save the best for last would wisely have scheduled his final stop in San Francisco. Then, as now, it stood out as the most attractive, diversified, and cosmopolitan of American western communities, and even then it was often mentioned as one of the great cities of the world. The sophisticated and experienced English travel writer, James Muirhead, found himself overwhelmed by the majesty of its location and appearance. Attempting to convey its beauty to his fellow countrymen, Muirhead described his impressions of the city as seen from a distance:

> The man who has stood . . . above Oakland and has watched the lights of San Francisco gleaming across its noble bay, or who had gazed down on the Golden Gate from the heights of the Presidio, must have an exceptionally rich gallery of memory if he does not

feel that he has added to its treasures one of most entrancing city views he has ever witnessed. The situation of San Francisco is indeed that of an empress among cities. Piled tier above tier on the hilly knob at the north end of a long peninsula, it looks down on the one side over the roomy waters of San Francisco Bay . . . while in the other direction it is reaching out across the peninsula . . . to the placid expanse of the Pacific Ocean.[38]

The city that Muirhead found so entrancing is shown in Figure 20.15 as seen from a point above the bay looking southwest. San Francisco was then a major metropolis of not quite 300,000. A half-century of growth had covered its steep hills with houses, filled Yerba Buena cove and pushed out its shoreline elsewhere, lined Market Street and adjoining business blocks with lofty stores, offices, and hotels, witnessed the reclamation of a stretch of barren dune sand into one of America's finest parks, bordered its bay waterfront with wharfs, docks, and warehouses, stamped a ubiquitous grid street pattern nearly everywhere and solved part of the resulting transportation problem on its precipitous thoroughfares by a system of cable cars that toiled up the slopes and braked cautiously down the other sides.

It was a city that had built museums, an opera house, theaters, churches, libraries, and an imposing city hall, and whose men of wealth had erected stately mansions on Nob Hill overlooking the business district. It was a city of breath-taking views up and down its steeply pitched streets and out to the water of the bay or ocean. It was a city whose leaders as early as 1904 recognized that a comprehensive plan for its future was desirable and retained Daniel H. Burnham to prepare it.[39]

It was a city whose energy and determination overcame the ravages of the earthquake and fire that in 1906 destroyed 30,000 buildings occupying nearly 500 blocks comprising its commercial, civic, and residential core.

Yet San Francisco was also a city that in rebuilding would virtually ignore the Burnham Plan and the opportunities it held out for reconstruction on an improved pattern. It was a city that not only tolerated the slums of Chinatown but exploited them as a tourist attraction. It was a city that relentlessly encroached on the waters of San Francisco Bay by filling hundreds of acres for industrial and commercial use. It was a city that dumped most of its industrial and human waste into the surrounding waters. It was a city that had squandered most of its treasure of municipally owned land.

Figure 20.14 View of Pasadena, California: 1893

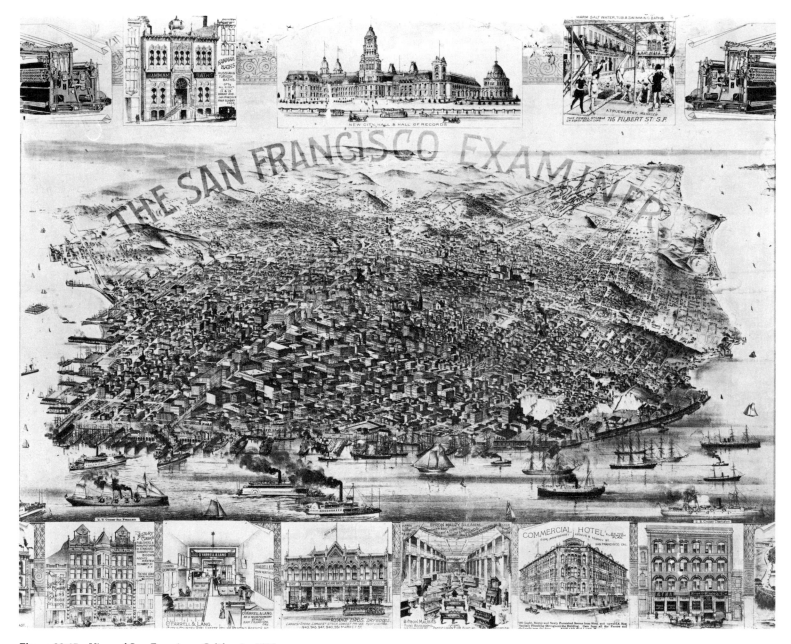

Figure 20.15   View of San Francisco, California: 1890

San Francisco was, in short, a vibrant, exciting, compact, and urbane community whose magnificent location overcame the deficiencies of its planning and whose promise for the future outweighed in the popular mind the squalor in which its poor and deprived were forced to exist or the manner in which it squandered its resources. Despite its shortcomings it was a city that every other community in the West envied in its wealth, size, services, and position. At the turn of the century San Francisco—comparatively young in years but mature and worldly-wise in character—thus symbolized the enormous change that had taken place beyond the Mississippi during the long years following the initial Spanish thrust into New Mexico to begin the urbanization of the American West.

To most Americans the settlement of the urban West, of which San Francisco represented the apotheosis, seemed a glorious accomplishment. William M. Thayer reflected this widely held attitude when in 1888 he rapturously described the region as "interlaced with railway track, peopled by the most adventurous and enterprising men and women from every quarter of the globe, dotted with populous and wealthy cities that have grown into power and beauty as if by magic, commerce appropriating every mountain and valley, lake and river to its mighty growth, and Christian civilization crowning the whole with the benediction of Almighty God."

Thayer looked ahead optimistically "when fifty and a hundred years more of progress have passed away." Then, he prophesied, "when all the public lands are appropriated to the growing industries; when the inventions and discoveries of art and science have enabled human enterprise to swell the harvest of precious metals to untold millions; when a teeming population dots the vast domain with towns and cities that surpass their sister municipalities of the East in wealth and enterprise, and when learning and religion have founded the finest schools and universities, and reared the costliest temples for the worship of God from the banks of the Missouri to the Pacific Slope, then will the dwellers in our land and other lands, behold here a national growth and consummation without a parallel in human history."[40]

A more thoughtful and perceptive observer writing in that same year found it more difficult to equate growth with progress. In his *The American Commonwealth*, that distinguished English scholar, politician, and diplomat, James Bryce, devoted a chapter to what he called "The Temper of the West." While the energy, courage, and skills of the trans-Mississippi frontiersman and settler impressed him on his travels through the region, he came away troubled by the mania for specula-

tion, the wasteful pace with which land had been cleared and cities built, the senseless exploitation of mineral and timber resources, and what he saw as an excessive preoccupation with material goods and economic power. This "passionate eagerness . . . towards the material development of the country . . . is so absorbing," he wrote, "that it almost ceases to be selfish . . . it takes from its very vastness a tinge of ideality."[41]

To Bryce it seemed both strange and self-deluding that residents of every hamlet, town, and small city appeared to be convinced that their community was destined to become a great metropolis. He attended the laying of the cornerstone of the capitol at Bismarck in 1883. What struck him most was the location of the building. "It was not in the city, nor even on the skirts of the city; it was nearly a mile off, on the top of a hill in the brown and dusty prairie. 'Why here?' we asked. 'Is it because you mean to enclose the building in a public park?' 'By no means; the Capitol is intended to be in the centre of the city; it is in this direction that the city is to grow.' It is the same everywhere from the Mississippi to the Pacific. Men seem to live in the future rather than in the present."[42]

Such unbounded confidence in the future Bryce regarded with some sympathy and understanding, but he felt that the westerner's determination to promote rapid growth at any cost had unfortunate consequences. He addressed a series of searching questions to his American friends: "Why sacrifice the present to the future, fancying that you will be happier when your fields teem with wealth and your cities with people? In Europe we have cities wealthier and more populous than yours, and we are not happy. . . . Why, then, seek to complete in a few decades what the other nations of the world took thousands of years over in the older continents? Why do things rudely and ill which need to be done well, seeing that the welfare of your descendants may turn upon them?"[43]

Bryce concluded his observations of the American West on a sombre note: "Politically, and perhaps socially also, this haste and excitement, this absorption in the development of the material resources of the country, are unfortunate. As a town built in a hurry is seldom well built, so a society will be the sounder in health for not having grown too swiftly. Doubtless much of the scum will be cleared away from the surface when the liquid settles and cools down. Lawlessness and lynch law will disappear; saloons and gambling-houses will not prosper in a well-conducted population; schools will improve and universities grow out of the raw colleges which one already finds even in the newer Territories. Nevertheless . . . the unrestfulness, the passion for speculation, the feverish eagerness for quick and showy results, may so soak into the texture of the popular mind as to colour it for centuries to come. These are the shadows which to the eye of the traveller seem to fall across the glowing landscape of the Great West."[44]

Those shadows were to lengthen in the years to come. While in the minds of a few thoughtful residents of western cities Bryce's comments may have struck a responsive chord, most persons in the burgeoning West—if they read his words at all—must have rejected his observations as the unjustified criticism of an effete and overly sensitive foreigner. As the twentieth century dawned, virtually all Americans and especially those living in the West remained convinced that to grow bigger was to become better. In the decades ahead it was this belief that shaped the policies of the region's cities. Order and beauty continued to be subordinated to wealth and size as the frontier era passed into history and a new stage of urban development began.

In three hundred years of town planning and city growth, western America had created a basic urban framework. What had scarcely been started in 1890—and which today remains unfinished—was the shaping of an urban civilization. In that sense elements of the western urban frontier still exist throughout the country—a new frontier in urban development whose challenge is not to found new towns in a wilderness but to replan those that exist in forms and patterns worthy of man as he approaches the twenty-first century.

This is a task that calls for all the energy and determination that frontier settlers brought to the West during those long decades of town founding and development we have explored. It will require infinitely greater skills and sensitivity than all but a handful of those pioneer planners possessed. It will demand even more. Bryce's warning that the "texture of the popular mind" may have been so colored by the "unrestfulness, the passion for speculation, [and] the feverish eagerness for quick and showy results" that the effects might persist for centuries has yet to be disproved. Somehow this, too, must change.

It is by no means certain that we have the abilities or—of equal importance—the will to transform our cities with their ugly, fetid ghettos, their decaying business districts, their drab central neighborhoods, or their sprawling, formless suburbs into safe, healthy, convenient, and beautiful communities. History has a heavy hand, and we still are held within its grasp. To loosen its tightened fingers we will need creative but realistic visions of an urban future as inspiring as those dreams of power, wealth, freedom, conquest, and opportunity that led men into the American West to people it with towns and cities.[45]

NOTES

Full bibliographical information is given in the Selected Bibliography at the end of the book. In addition to a section on general works about the American West, specific references are given for individual chapters.

PREFACE

1. Frederick Jackson Turner, "The Significance of the Frontier in American History," *Annual Report of the American Historical Association*, Washington, D.C., 1894, 199-227.

2. Ibid., 226-227.

3. Ibid., 227.

4. Ibid., 214. Turner identified this work as *Peck's New Guide to the West*, published in 1837. In a later version of his paper with additional material and notes, he lists elsewhere John M. Peck, *A New Guide to the West*, Cincinnati, 1848. See Everett E. Edwards (comp.), *The Early Writings of Frederick Jackson Turner With a List of All His Works*, 194. In both versions of the essay Turner cites several other studies where a similar analysis of sequential occupancy can be found.

5. One of the earliest studies dealing with Turner's hypothesis challenged the assertion that towns came only as an end-product of frontier settlement. This was limited to an investigation of the Northwest. See Edmond S. Meany, "The Towns of the Pacific Northwest Were Not Founded on the Fur Trade." In the flood of subsequent papers and books on Turner and his ideas this subject did not surface again until recent years. Two works suggest that an urban interpretation of the Western frontier experience may be in the making: Earl Pomeroy, "The Urban Frontier of the Far West," in John G. Clark (ed.), *The Frontier Challenge: Responses to the Trans-Mississippi West*, 7-29; and Richard A. Bartlett, *The New Country: A Social History of the American Frontier, 1776-1890*, Chapter VII, "The Urban Frontier," 401-440. Another recent history of the American West incorporates brief passages on the importance of urbanization in topical chapters. See Arrell Morgan Gibson, *The West in the Life of the Nation*. Gibson, however, is far from consistent. He manages to treat the Mormon settlement of the Great Basin without mentioning the central role town founding played in Mormon colonization policy.

6. The prevailing, but mistaken, opinion on this point is summarized in the following statement from a collection of readings on the West assembled by two well-known scholars: "Most of the towns and cities of the West grew haphazardly by accretions of individuals with little community planning or cohesion." Robert V. Hine and Edwin R. Bingham (eds.), *The Frontier Experience: Readings in the Trans-Mississippi West*, 338. The authors compound this error by stating that, except for New England and a few religious or utopian settlements elsewhere, American communities were not planned. Conventional historians have yet to discover or digest the growing literature on the history of city plan-

ning in the United States demonstrating that America is a nation of planned cities, although the results were not always, or even mainly, attractive or beneficial.

7. Turner, "Frontier in American History," 205.

I · CITIES ON THE WAY WEST: THE BEGINNING OF URBANIZATION IN THE OHIO AND MISSISSIPPI VALLEYS

1. In two major studies I have traced the planning and development of colonial towns in the United States. Several chapters of my general survey of American urban planning deal with the colonial period in the English, French, Dutch, and Swedish colonies. See John W. Reps, *The Making of Urban America*, 56-203. In a more recent volume I have explored in greater detail the town planning tradition in colonial Virginia and Maryland: John W. Reps, *Tidewater Towns*. Both books contain extensive bibliographies and are profusely illustrated.

2. For a series of drawings showing the development of Savannah's unique pattern and a small reproduction of the commissioners' plan of New York in 1811 see Reps, *Making of Urban America*, 201, 298. Early plans and views of Baltimore are reproduced in Reps. *Tidewater Towns*, 283-295.

3. Francis Baily, *Journal of a Tour in Unsettled Parts of North America in 1796 & 1797*, 27.

4. For a history of the planning of Washington and its later growth see Reps, *Monumental Washington: The Planning and Development of the Capital Center*.

5. Baily, *Journal*, 38.

6. Ibid., 51.

7. John Melish, *Travels Through the United States of America . . .*, I, 54. Melish gives the population of Pittsburgh in 1810 as 4,768.

8. In my treatment of these towns planned by the state of Pennsylvannia I have drawn on an unpublished seminar paper prepared under my direction in 1973 by Robert E. Miller, "State Planned Towns in Pennsylvania: Allegheny, Beaver, Franklin, Waterford, Warren and Erie." Published sources include Solon J. and Elizabeth Hawthorn Buck, *The Planting of Civilization in Western Pennsylvania*; Joseph H. Bausman, *History of Beaver County, Pennsylvania*; William J. McKnight, *Pioneer Outline History of Northwestern Pennsylvania*; Catharine Van Cortlandt Mathews, *Andrew Ellicott: His Life and Letters*; Charles A. Babcock, *Venango County Pennyslvania*; and S. B. Nelson, *Nelson's Biographical Dictionary and Historical Reference Book of Erie County, Pennsylvania*.

9. A helpful history of the founding and early development of Buffalo is Robert Warwick Bingham, *Cradle of the Queen City*.

10. For a summary of the provisions of the Act of 1785 see Roy M. Robbins, *Our Landed Heritage*, 7-11.

11. *U.S. Statutes at Large*, v, Chapter XVII, An Act for the Relief of the Citizens

of Towns upon the Lands of the United States, May 23, 1844. The limitation to 320 acres was modified in 1867 to permit townsite claims of up to 1,280 acres if the inhabitants numbered over 1,000. *U.S. Statutes at Large*, XIV, Chapter CLXXVII, "An Act for the Relief of the Inhabitants of Cities and Towns upon the Public Lands," March 2, 1867.

12. For a survey showing the earthworks more clearly as well as for reproductions of other plans and views of Marietta see Reps, *Making of Urban America*, 220-223.

13. Baily, *Journal*, 83.

14. Ibid., 88-89.

15. Ibid., 102.

16. Ibid., 111.

17. Ibid., 110.

18. I have traced in much more detail the complicated history of the planning of Detroit under Judge Woodward in Reps, *Making of Urban America*, 264-272.

19. For some of the background of the planning of Indianapolis see Donald F. Carmony, "Genesis and Early History of the Indianapolis Fund, 1816-1826," 17-30; and Nathaniel Bolton, *Early History of Indianapolis and Central Indiana*.

20. Sandusky's plan, believed to have been based on the Masonic emblem, is described and illustrated in Reps, *Making of Urban America*, 277-284.

21. Alfred J. Wright, "Joel Wright, City Planner," 287-294.

22. James Silk Buckingham, *The Eastern and Western States of America*, II, 502. Buckingham's work is a mine of information about the design of towns and their conditions in 1840.

23. Henry McRaven, *Nashville*, 15-16. The town developed from a frontier station called Nashborough, established by James Robertson in 1779. The log fort stood between the southeastern corner of the public square and what is now Church Street. A reproduction of a manuscript plan of the town in 1804 can be found in Jesse C. Burt, *Nashville: Its Life and Times*, opposite p. 17.

24. A drawing showing the street pattern and location of the principal buildings of Knoxville prior to 1800 can be found in Betsey Beeler Creekmore, *Knoxville*, 46.

25. A manuscript plan of Louisville attributed to Clark is reproduced in Reps, *Making of Urban America*, 213.

26. Jefferson to C.F.C. de Volney, February 8, 1805, in Liscomb and Bergh (eds.), *The Writings of Thomas Jefferson*, XI, 66.

27. For a more extended treatment of Jeffersonville's original plan and its redevelopment, see Reps, *Making of Urban America*, 314-321; and Reps, "Thomas Jefferson's Checkerboard Towns," 108-114.

28. For Jackson see Reps, *Making of Urban America*, 321-323; and "Jefferson's Checkerboard Towns." The unique plan of Circleville is described in *Making of Urban America*, 484-490 and Reps, "Urban Redevelopment in the Nineteenth Century: The Squaring of Circleville," 23-26. The original plan of Brawley is reproduced in *Making of Urban America*, 381.

29. Baily, *Journal*, 121.

30. The several plans for the Cairo site are reviewed in Reps, *Making of Urban America*, 382-389; and Reps, "Great Expectations and Hard Times: The Planning of Cairo, Illinois," 14-21.

31. New Madrid's plan and the unusual circumstances of its founding by Col. George Morgan are treated in Reps, *Making of Urban America*, 477-484; and Reps, "New Madrid on the Mississippi: American 18th Century Planning on the Spanish Frontier," 21-26. See also Max Savelle, *George Morgan, Colony Builder*.

32. A redrawn plan showing Memphis a few years after its founding appears in Gerald M. Capers, Jr., *The Biography of a River Town: Memphis: Its Heroic Age*, 32.

33. Baily, *Journal*, 147.

34. Ibid., 149.

35. Baily's complete description of the town, its fortifications, social life, and other aspects of New Orleans can be found in his *Journal*, 162-175. The estimate of 12,000 as the population in 1805 is from S. P. Hildreth, "History of an Early Voyage on the Ohio and Mississippi Rivers," 140.

36. Descriptions of the French towns in this region as observed in 1765 can be found in Philip Pittman, *The Present State of the European Settlements on the Mississippi*. Their appearance in 1811 is described in H. M. Brackenridge, *View of Louisiana; together with a Journal of a Voyage up the Missouri River, in 1811*. Views of these communities in 1846 and 1847, along with many others, appear in Henry Lewis, *Das Illustrirte Mississippithal* (1854), republished in a facsimile edition as *The Valley of the Mississippi Illustrated*. For slightly earlier views drawn in 1841 and 1842 of the towns in the central portion of the Mississippi Valley see John Casper Wild, *The Valley of the Mississippi; Illustrated in a Series of Views*. Originally published in several parts during the years 1841 and 1842 in St. Louis, they are now available in a facsimile edition with the same title.

37. A detailed account of the founding and early development of St. Louis is Charles E. Peterson, "Colonial Saint Louis," 94-111.

38. Timothy Flint, *Recollections of the Last Ten Years in the Valley of the Mississippi*, 136-137.

39. Ibid., 311, editor's note 15.

40. Buckingham, *Eastern and Western States*, III, 118, 144.

41. Chicago's planning and early growth is reviewed in a number of sources, including the following: A. T. Andreas, *History of Chicago*, Homer Hoyt, *One Hundred Years of Land Values in Chicago*; Bessie Louise Pierce, *A History of Chicago*; Joseph N. Balestier, *The Annals of Chicago*; and Joseph Kirkland, *The Story of Chicago*.

42. Kirkland, *Chicago*, 117. Kirkland states that, when the school section lots were sold, they brought only $38,619.47.

43. Buckingham, *Eastern and Western States*, III, 260-261.

44. Flint, *Recollections*, 30-31.

45. Buckingham, *Eastern and Western States*, III, 162, 200-201.

46. William Watts Folwell, *A History of Minnesota*, I, 223-226.

47. As quoted in ibid., I, 255.

48. Ibid., I, 362.

49. Doty planned several other towns during his career, including Astor (now part of Green Bay), Caramaunee, Menasha, Town of the Island, and Fond du Lac. His curious design for the latter community is reproduced in Reps, *Making of Urban America*, 367. There is a good biography of Doty: Alice Elizabeth Smith, *James Duane Doty, Frontier Promoter*.

50. For a more extended treatment of the planning of Madison see Reps, *Making of Urban America*, 275-277.

51. Brackenridge, *View of Louisiana*, 205.

52. Ibid., 211.

53. Edwin C. McReynolds, *Missouri: A History of the Crossroads State*, 52-53. See also Jonas Viles, ''Population and Extent of Settlement in Missouri before 1804,'' 189-213.

54. The development of trade between Santa Fe and these Missouri towns is summarized in McReynolds, *Missouri*, 92-107; and in Everett Dick, *Vanguards of the Frontier*, 187-204. A number of more extended studies of this topic exist, but perhaps the most interesting is the contemporary account by one of its chief participants: Josiah Gregg, *Commerce of the Prairies*.

55. Charles Joseph Latrobe, *The Rambler in North America*, I, 128.

56. Two other towns in western Missouri played important roles as early trading centers and as assembly points for wagon trains bound for Santa Fe, Oregon, or California. They were Weston and Saint Joseph, both located north of Kansas City.

57. As quoted in Darrell Garwood, *Crossroads of America: The Story of Kansas City*, 21. For a map showing the locations of Independence, Westport, and Kansas, see ibid., 25.

58. Charles N. Glaab, ''Business Patterns in the Growth of a Midwestern City: The Kansas City Business Community Before the Civil War,'' 156-174.

59. These precursors to true urbanization are the subjects of Dick's *Vanguards of the Frontier*. Such early settlements in the region from the western Rockies to the Pacific Coast are also described in Early Pomeroy, *The Pacific Slope*.

60. Flint, *Recollections*, 31, 33.

II · SPANISH SETTLEMENTS IN THE SOUTHWEST: EVOLUTION OF POLICY, ELEMENTS OF COLONIZATION, AND THE FIRST TOWNS OF NEW MEXICO

1. On his first voyage, in December, 1492, Columbus built the fort of La Navidad from the timbers of the *Santa Maria*, which had been wrecked off the same coast many miles to the west of what later would be Isabella. A crude woodcut view of La Navidad appeared in an illustrated edition of a letter from Columbus to Gabriel Sánchez, published in Basel in 1493. It was the first depiction of a European settlement in the New World. A reproduction of this view can be found in *The Journal of Christopher Columbus*, 127.

2. Reyes Católicos to Nicolás de Ovando, Granada, September 16, 1501, ''In-

strucción . . . al Fray Nicolás de Ovando . . . sobre lo que habia de facer en las Islas é Tierra Firme . . . come Governador dellas,'' *Colección de Documentos Inéditos Relatives al Descubrimiento, Conquista y Organización de las Antiquas Posesiones Españolas de América y Oceanía sacados de los Archives del Reino*, Madrid, 1879, XXXI, 13-25, as translated and quoted in Daniel Garr, ''Hispanic Colonial Settlement in California: Planning and Urban Development on the Frontier, 1769-1850,'' 58. Garr's study, done under my direction, has been of substantial help in bringing to my attention material that I otherwise might have overlooked. It is the most thorough investigation of Spanish urban policy in California available, but it also includes much useful material on events leading up to that episode of colonization. I am happy to acknowledge my debt to him, not only for his dissertation but for our discussions on these matters, which stimulated my own thinking.

3. The earliest printed view of Santo Domingo, of which the de Bry engraving in Figure 2.1 is a close copy, appeared in *Expeditio Francisci Draki Equitis Angli in Indias Occidentalis*, Leyden, 1588. Another version published nearly a century later is reproduced in Reps, *The Making of Urban America*, 27, from Arnoldus Montanus, *De Nieuwe en Onbekende Weerld . . .*, Amsterdam, 1671.

4. Gonzalo Fernández de Oviedo, *Natural History of the West Indies*, 11-13.

5. Woodbury Lowery, *The Spanish Settlements within the Present Limits of the United States*, 104. A map showing the location of the 15 towns that had received royal charters in 1508 appears in Carl O. Sauer, *The Early Spanish Main*, 152.

6. ''Ynstruction para el Governador de Tierra Firme,'' in Manuel Serrano y Sanz (ed.), *Orígenes de la dominación española en América*, Madrid, 1918, I, cclxxxi, as quoted in Richard M. Morse, ''Some Characteristics of Latin American Urban History,'' 319.

7. Real Cédula de Población otorgada á los que hicieron Descubrimiento en Tierra Firme,'' Burgos, 1512, *Colección de Documentos Inéditos . . .*, II, 558-667, as cited by Garr, ''Hispanic Colonial Settlement in California,'' 62, n 12.

8. Bartolomé de Celada, ''Testimonio de la Fundación de la Villa de la Frontera de Cáceres, en la Provincia de Honduras, y de la Posesion que en ella tomó, a nombre de Su Magestad, June 6, 1526,'' *Colección de Documentos Inéditos*, XIV, 57-64, as quoted in Garr, ''Hispanic Colonial Settlement in California'', 62-63. While Celada's words might have meant that he attempted to duplicate in some way the street and plaza pattern of Seville itself, a comparison of early plans of that city and Spanish colonial towns in the Western Hemisphere suggests he was referring instead to some kind of model or standardized town design prepared by officials of the Council of the Indies.

9. Fernando Chueca Goitia and Leopoldo Torres Balbas, *Planos de Ciudades Iberoamericanas y Filipinas Existentes en el Archivo de Indias*, I, xv. This volume is the most extensive published collection of reproductions of early Spanish town plans in the colonies. It includes 350 illustrations, the legends of which are printed in a companion volume.

10. Charles Wilson Hackett (ed.), *Historical Documents Relating to New Mexico, Nueva Viscaya, and Approaches Thereto to 1773*, 20.

11. O. Garfield Jones, ''Local Government in the Spanish Colonies as Pro-

vided by the Recopilación de Leyes de Los Reynos de Las Indias," 66-69. See also Garr, "Hispanic Colonial Settlement in California", Appendix A.

12. Real Ordenanzas para Nuevas Poblaciones, etc., MS 3017, Bulas y Cédulas para el Govierno de las Indias, Archives of the Indies, Seville. The Spanish text of the town planning sections and a preliminary translation can be found in Zelia Nuttall, "Royal Ordinances Concerning the Laying Out of New Towns." A revised translation was published under the same title in 1922. It is this latter translation that is quoted extensively in the following paragraphs. I have made one change in Nuttall's translation. She used "arcades" as equivalent to the Spanish *portales*. The Spanish word means a roofed passageway at ground level along the street facades of buildings. It might or might not be arched. For "arcades" I have therefore substituted "porticoes," which is neutral as to the form taken by the protective roof. In practice, most if not all of the limited number of *portales* constructed in the Spanish colonial towns of North America took the form of a post and beam structure supporting a continuous flat roof. The posts defined the boundary between what we would call the sidewalk and the roadway.

13. Jones, "Local Government," 66, n 4.

14. Vitruvius, *The Ten Books of Architecture*, 27. For a comparison of Vitruvian principles and sections of the Laws of the Indies, see Dan Stanislawski, "Early Spanish Town Planning in the New World," 94-105. A more extended treatment of the possible sources of the Laws of the Indies can be found in Reps, *Making of Urban America*, 4-15, 30-32; and Garr, "Hispanic Colonial Settlement in California," 60-61.

15. For a plan of Philippeville and its possible influence on the intended layout of Sir Walter Raleigh's proposed town on Roanoke Island in North Carolina, see Reps, *Tidewater Towns: City Planning in Colonial Virginia and Maryland*, 27-28.

16. An eighteenth-century plan of Santa Fe is reproduced in L. Torres Balbas, L. Cervera, F. Chueca, and P. Bidagor, *Resumen Historico del Urbanismo en España*, Plate XIII.

17. An examination of plans of some 200 cities in Chueca Goitia and Torres Balbas, *Planos de Ciudades Iberoamericanas*, in addition to drawings from other sources, leads me to the conclusion that cities meeting both of these specifications were very few in number.

18. Jones, "Local Government"; Herbert Ingram Priestly, "Spanish Colonial Municipalities," 397-416; and Marc Simmons, *Spanish Government in New Mexico* are among the sources of information about local government in the Spanish colonies.

19. A *villa* was considered to be a larger and more important municipality than a *pueblo*. Ranking above both was the designation of *ciudad*.

20. It may be useful here to introduce the Spanish terms for the elements of the *pueblo* land system. The house lot was a *solar*. Farming plots were *suertes*. Tracts reserved to the crown were known as *realengas*. The *ejidos* were the common lands. For definitions of words and measurements used in Spanish survey-

ing, see Katherine H. White, "Spanish and Mexican Surveying Terms and Systems," 24-27. The most commonly encountered unit of linear measurement is the *vara*, roughly equal to an English yard, but varying slightly from place to place. In Texas the *vara* has been defined as 33.33 inches, and I have used this in converting *varas* to feet in this and other chapters.

21. The classic analysis of the role of the mission in Spanish colonization is Herbert E. Bolton, "The Mission as a Frontier Institution in the Spanish American Colonies," 42-61.

22. Kino letter to the viceroy in Mexico, in Ernest J. Burrus (trans.), *Kino's Plan for the Development of Pimería Alta, Arizona & Upper California*, 27-28.

23. Report on the Texas Querétaran missions by Father Francisco Xavier Órtiz, as quoted in John Francis Bannon, *The Spanish Borderlands Frontier, 1513-1821*, 135.

24. The description of the mission and Duflot de Mofras's illustration of the exterior of the mission compound can be found in Reps, *Making of Urban America*, 46-47.

25. Views of Mission San Carlos Borromeo del Rio Carmelo at Carmel, California, in 1791 shortly after its founding can be found reproduced from the originals in the Bancroft Collection at the University of California, Berkeley in Donald C. Cutter, *Malaspina in California*.

26. The development of the concept of missions as towns, the difficulties encountered in carrying out this policy, and the results in California are explored in some detail in Garr, "Hispanic Colonial Settlement in California," 316-352. A useful investigation would be a comparative study of the mission towns in Texas, New Mexico, Arizona, and California.

27. The University of Santa Clara received its charter in 1855, a year before this view was published. The mission church became the chapel of this institution. Earthquakes in 1865 and 1868 so badly damaged the chapel that it had to be demolished and was replaced by a frame church. After this burned in 1926, a replica of the older building was erected in its place. U.S. Federal Writers' Program, *California: A Guide to the Golden State*, 380.

28. Benjamin Davis Wilson, *The Indians of Southern California in 1852*, 25.

29. For discussions of the *presidio* as a Spanish frontier institution see Odie B. Faulk, "The Presidio: Fortress or Farce?" 22-27; and Paige W. Christiansen, "The Presidio and the Borderlands: A Case Study," 29-37.

30. *Reglamento e Instruccion para los Presidios . . . 1772*, Title 11, as translated in Sidney B. Brinckerhoff and Odie B. Faulk, *Lancers for the King*, 35.

31. Contemporary accounts of several explorations in the region are in Herbert E. Bolton (ed.), *Spanish Exploration in the Southwest, 1542-1706*. A recent bibliography of the principal sources for this aspect of Spanish colonization as well as for other subjects appears in Bannon, *Borderlands Frontier*, 257-287. Bannon's own compact treatment of the topic can be found in Chapter Two, pp. 8-27.

32. "Articles of agreement which the viceroy, Don Luis de Velasco, made with Don Juan de Oñate, governor and captain-general of the provinces of New

Mexico . . . ," in Hackett, *Historical Documents Relating to New Mexico*, 265, 267.

33. Bannon, *Borderlands Frontier*, 36; George P. Hammond, *Don Juan de Oñate and the Founding of New Mexico*, 90-95.

34. Ibid., 98-99.

35. Gaspar Pérez de Villagrá, *A History of New Mexico*, Gilberto Espinosa (trans.), Chicago, 1962, 147.

36. Frederick Webb Hodge, George P. Hammond, and Agapito Rey, "Editorial Notes," in their *Fray Alonso de Benavides' Revised Memorial of 1634*, 233, quoting from a contemporary document not identified by the editors.

37. Ibid., 233. For a brief account of archeological investigations of the San Gabriel site see Marjorie F. Tichy, "New Mexico's First Capital," 140-144.

38. Testimony of Joseph Brondate, July 28, 1601 and Ginés de Herrera Horta, July 30, 1601 as reported in "Investigation Made by Don Francisco de Valverde . . . Regarding Conditions in the Province of New Mexico. July, 1601," Archivo General de Indias, *Audiencia de México*, legajo 26, as translated in George P. Hammond and Agapito Rey, *Don Juan de Oñate: Colonizer of New Mexico, 1595-1628*, Part II, 629, 652.

39. Bannon, *Borderlands Frontier*, 37-41. Many of the documents of the period relating to these events may be found in Hammond and Rey, *Don Juan de Oñate*, Part II.

40. "Instructions to Don Pedro de Peralta . . . March 30, 1609," from Luís de Velasco, Archivo General de Indias, *Audiencia de México*, legajo 27, as translated in Hammond and Rey, *Don Juan de Oñate*, Part II, 1087-1088.

41. In my investigation of the early settlement of Santa Fé I have found helpful a research paper prepared under my direction at Cornell University in 1970 be Steven Andrachek, "Towns of New Mexico: Santa Fe and Albuquerque."

42. "Marquis of Guadalcázar to the King, May 27, 1620," Archivo General de Indias, *Audiencia de México*, legajo 29, as translated in Hammond and Rey, *Don Juan de Oñate*, Part II, 1140.

43. Peter P. Forrestal (trans.), *Benavides' Memorial of 1630*, 23-24 and n 53. Benavides' expanded version of this account written in 1634 reads as follows: "Spaniards . . . may number up to two hundred and fifty. Most of them are married to Spanish or Indian women or to their descendants. With their servants they number almost one thousand persons." Hodge, Hammond, and Rey, *Benavides' Revised Memorial*, 68.

44. Ralph Emerson Twitchell, *Old Santa Fe*, 55-58 provides a detailed description of the town and its buildings as they may have existed at the end of the seventeenth century.

45. For the text of these rather confusing petitions, descriptions, and orders see Twitchell, *Old Santa Fe*, 51-57 and n 124.

46. Ibid., 137-138, 150-151. Vargas's description of the town at that time is of interest. On the day of his "fortunate conquest" it had "only one gate, its entrance built and constructed for the defense of its ravelin, a redout entrenched above in the form of a half tower with its trench and likewise on the said front to

the south two round towers and two others on the north side and its false flanks with two plazas and its dwellings three stories high and many of four and in truth most perfectly planned in its capacity and amplitude." Quoted by Twitchell, *Old Santa Fe*, 137, from Archive No. 94-a, *The Spanish Archives of New Mexico*, II, 117.

47. See Twitchell, *Old Santa Fe*, 58-60 for a detailed description of the building written in 1716. A useful guide to this and other historic buildings in Santa Fé is Sylvia Glidden Loomis (ed.), *Old Santa Fe Today*.

48. Eleanor B. Adams and Fray Angelico Chavez (eds. and trans.), *The Missions of New Mexico, 1776*, 13, n 3. This church underwent extensive repairs toward the end of the eighteenth century, and in 1869 it was replaced by the present Cathedral of St. Francis, a structure begun under Bishop Jean Baptiste Lamy. Loomis, *Santa Fe Today*, 39.

49. A. von Quthenau, "The Spanish Military Chapels in Santa Fé and the Reredos of Our Lady of Light," 175-194; Eleanor B. Adams, "The Chapel and Cofradia of Our Lady of Light in Santa Fe," 327-341.

50. Eleanor B. Adams (ed.), *Bishop Tamarón's Visitation of New Mexico, 1760*, 47. The bishop's uncomplimentary remarks may have been directed to the loosely strung out Indian *barrio* south of the river rather than to the more compactly built Spanish town centering on the plaza.

51. Adams and Chavez, *Missions of New Mexico*, 39-40.

52. Lawrence Kinnaird (ed.), *The Frontiers of New Spain: Nicolas de Lafora's Description, 1766-1768*, 91. Lafora added this comment about the map: "It also shows that its presidio is incapable of defense." He stated that "the population amounts to 2,324 persons, divided among the eighty families of soldiers, 274 Spanish settlers, and 89 families from various Indian nations."

53. Fray Juan Agustin de Morfi, "Geographical Description of New Mexico . . . Year of 1782," in Alfred Barnaby Thomas (ed. and trans.), *Forgotten Frontiers*, 92. Morfi's own description of Santa Fé seems more balanced than that of Dominguez. While he stated that the city was a "settlement in part regular and the most of it without order," he found the *plaza* "square and beautiful."

54. Teodoro de Croix, "General Report of 1781," in Alfred Barnaby Thomas (ed. and trans.), *Teodoro de Croix and the Northern Frontier of New Spain, 1776-1783*, 107.

55. Twitchell, *Old Santa Fe*, 139. Twitchell states that the site for Santa Cruz was on the south bank of the Santa Cruz River across from the modern town bearing the same name. The location was near the mouth of the river where it enters the Rio Grande.

56. Adams and Chavez, *Missions of New Mexico*, 82; Morfi, "Description of New Mexico," 94; Adams, *Tamarón's Visitation*, 63.

57. Hackett, *Historical Documents Relating to New Mexico*, III, 379. The text of the certificate with some explanatory material can also be found in Lansing B. Bloom, "Alburquerque and Galisteo: Certificate of their Founding, 1706," 48-51.

58. Adams and Chavez, *Missions of New Mexico*, 151.

59. Morfi, "Description of New Mexico," 101.

60. W.W.H. Davis, *El Gringo; or, New Mexico and Her People*, 353.

61. Marc Simmons, "Settlement Patterns and Village Plans in Colonial New Mexico," 13, Simmons' article is an excellent summary of settlement forms and how they developed in the region. An interesting and useful study would be a comparison of the efforts of Spain in New Mexico and England in Virginia and Maryland to stimulate the growth of settlements. There appear to be many parallels. Much of my *Tidewater Towns* deals with this aspect of English colonial policy.

62. Bainbridge Bunting and John P. Conron, "The Architecture of Northern New Mexico," *New Mexico Architecture*, VIII (1966), 16. Truchas was referred to by Dominguez as "not of ranchos, but around two plazas because Governor Velez Cachupin issued orders to this effect since they are almost on the borders of the Comanche tribe, whose people make incursions from that vicinity." Adams and Chavez, *Missions of New Mexico*, 83.

63. A modern plan of Madrid Plaza as it has survived, with a conjectural reconstruction of its original buildings and a history of its development can be found in Hugh and Evelyn Burnett, "Madrid Plaza," 224-237. See also Louis B. Sporleder, "La Plaza de Los Leones," 28-38.

64. Pedro Bautista Pino, *Exposicion sucinta y sencilla de la Provincia del Nuevo México, Cadiz, 1812*, in H. Bailey Carroll and J. Villasana Haggard, *Three New Mexico Chronicles*, 27.

65. A. Wislizenus, *Memoir of a Tour to Northern Mexico, Connected with Col. Doniphan's Expedition, in 1846 and 1847*, 19-20, 28.

III · SPANISH TOWNS OF THE TEXAS FRONTIER

1. Carlos E. Castañeda, *Our Catholic Heritage in Texas*, I, 248-267; Herbert E. Bolton, "The Spanish Occupation of Texas, 1519-1690," 1-26.

2. Herbert E. Bolton, "Defensive Spanish Expansion and the Significance of the Borderlands," in James F. Willard and Colin B. Goodykoontz (eds.), *The Trans-Mississippi West*, 1-42.

3. The La Salle expedition is summarized in John Francis Bannon, *The Spanish Borderlands Frontier, 1513-1821*, 94-97. For a more extended treatment see Henry Folder, *Franco-Spanish Rivalry in North America, 1524-1763*, Glendale, California, 1953, 155-188; William E. Dunn, *Spanish and French Rivalry in the Gulf Region of the United States, 1678-1702*; E. W. Cole, "La Salle in Texas," 473-500; and Herbert E. Bolton, "The Location of La Salle's Colony on the Gulf of Mexico," 165-182.

4. The search for La Salle's colony by the Spanish occupied many persons for several years, and the thoroughness with which this was conducted indicates the degree of concern it caused in New Spain. News of the colonization attempt reached Mexico in 1685 when the pirates who had taken one of La Salle's ships were in turn captured by the Spanish. Interrogation of the crew in Vera Cruz turned up the information about La Salle's intentions. For the details of the search, León's expeditions, and the founding of the first mission in east Texas see Castañeda, *Catholic Heritage*, I, 279-353.

5. Ibid., I, 356, 359-360.

6. Francisco Céliz, *Diary of the Alarcón Expedition into Texas, 1718-1719*, "Introduction" by the editor, 11.

7. Peter J. Hamilton, *Colonial Mobile*. For an account of these events by an eighteenth-century Spanish colonial historian see Juan Agustín Morfi, *History of Texas, 1673-1779*, I, 157-159. Mobile was moved in 1710 from its original site to the mouth of the Mobile River. Hamilton reproduces a manuscript plan of the settlement in 1711. This also is reproduced in Reps, *The Making of Urban America*, 79.

8. The puzzling role of St. Denis in the settlement of western Louisiana and east Texas is covered in Ross Phares, *Cavalier in the Wilderness: The Story of the Explorer and Trader Louis Juchereau de St. Denis*. See also Robert C. Clark, "Louis Juchereau de Saint-Denis and the Reestablishment of the Tejas Missions," 1-26. St. Denis wooed and married the grandaughter of Diego Ramón, captain of the *presidio* of San Juan Bautista. Although he had been dispatched on his mission to found Natchitoches by Antoine de la Mothe Cadillac, French governor of Louisiana, St. Denis offered his services to the Spanish. With his new wife's uncle, Domingo Ramón, in command, he guided the party of settlers and missionaries that re-established the East Texas settlements in 1716. It seems likely that he served as a double agent, since during a visit to Mexico City he sent two reports to Cadillac reporting on his activities. For a brief summary of the St. Denis affair see Bannon, *Borderlands Frontier*, 110-112.

9. The Franciscans were from one of the institutions for the training of missionaries in Mexico, the College of the Holy Cross of Querétaro. Others from the College of Our Lady of Guadalupe of Zacatecas caught up with and joined the party some weeks later. Bannon, *Borderlands Frontier*, 113-114; Morfi, *History*, I, 185.

10. See R. B. Blake, "Locations of the Early Spanish Missions and Presidio in Nacogdoches County," 212-224. Blake questions the correctness of some of the sites as identified by Herbert Bolton and Carlos Castañeda.

11. Morfi, *History*, I, 187; Robert S. Weddle, *The San Sabá Mission: Spanish Pivot in Texas*, 9, and map 4.; Castañeda, *Catholic Heritage*, II, 55-62, 66-67.

12. Céliz, *Alarcón Expedition*, 14-18; Castañeda, *Catholic Heritage*, II, 70-77.

13. *Testimonio del título de Governador y Instrucciones que se dió a Don Martín de Alarcón*, as summarized by Hoffman in Céliz, *Alarcón Expedition*, 22-23; Castañeda, *Catholic Heritage*, II, 88-91.

14. Céliz, *Alarcón Expedition*, 49. Morfi refers to the founding of the mission and the "presidio of Bexar." He described the mission as "scarcely more than two gunshots from the villa of San Fernando, founded later." Morfi, *History*, I, 190.

15. Bannon, *Borderlands Frontier*, 118.

16. Castañeda, *Catholic Heritage*, II, 115-119.

17. Bannon, *Borderlands Frontier*, 120.

18. Castañeda, *Catholic Heritage*, II, 130-136.

19. Ibid., II, 124-129. Sometime before 1727 the mission was moved to a second location on the west bank of the river, from which it probably was moved again to its present location. Its original location erroneously appears on Aguayo's map of 1730 reproduced in Figure 3.5. See Marion A. Habig, "Mission San José y San Miguel de Aguayo, 1720-1824," 500-502. For a more extended history of the mission see the same author's *San Antonio's Mission San José*.

20. Castañeda, *Catholic Heritage*, II, 135-140. For studies of the Aguayo expedition see also Charles W. Hackett, "The Marquis of San Miguel de Aguayo and His Recovery of Texas from the French, 1719-1723," 193-214; and Eleanor Claire Buckley, "The Aguayo Expedition into Texas and Louisiana, 1719-1722," 1-65. A contemporary account used by Castañeda, Hackett, and Buckley is Juan Antonio Peña, *Derrotero de la Expedición en la Provincia de los Texas*, Mexico City, 1722. It is from this work that the illustrations of the *presidios* founded by Aguayo are taken. A reproduction of a manuscript map prepared in 1722 showing the route followed by the expedition appears in Hackett, "Aguayo," opposite p. 206. In my review of Aguayo's accomplishments, the design of his *presidios*, and the founding and early development of San Antonio, I found helpful a study prepared under my direction by Robert M. Craig as a seminar paper at Cornell University: "Spanish Texas and the Development of San Antonio." Unpublished seminar paper, Department of City and Regional Planning, 1971.

21. Castañeda, *Catholic Heritage*, II, 142-143; Morfi, *History*, I, 208-215.

22. Ibid., I, 213.

23. Aguayo to the King, June 13, 1722, in archives of Santa Cruz de Querétaro, K, Legajo 4, N. 10, folio 3, as quoted in Hackett, "Aguayo," 208. While Morfi states that the *presidio* was re-established and dedicated on August 15, he adds later that on Aguayo's homeward march to San Antonio on November 29, 1721, "he outlined the fort" and then left three days later "leaving the execution of the plan to the experienced captain in command of the presidio." Morfi, *History*, I, 213, 222.

24. Ibid., I, 218.

25. Peña, *Derrotero*, as translated and quoted in Clark Wissler, Constance Lindsay Skinner, and William Wood, *The Pageant of America*, I, *Adventurers in the Wilderness*, 337.

26. Morfi, *History*, I, 218; Castañeda, *Catholic Heritage*, II, 144-145.

27. Morfi, *History*, I, 224.

28. Ibid., I, 227.

29. Mardith K. Schuetz, *Historic Background of the Mission San Antonio de Valero*, 4. Castañeda is apparently in error when he states that "the mission stayed at its first location." *Catholic Heritage*, II, 92. The frequent movement of these institutions in their early years suggests that most of their structures must have been of the most primitive character.

30. Castañeda, *Catholic Heritage*, II, 160-167. Its site was later to be occupied by Mission Concepción when it was moved from East Texas. See Castañeda's note in Morfi, *History*, I, 241, n 109.

31. Ibid., I, 226.

32. Report to the King by the Marquis of San Miguel de Aguayo, June 13, 1722, in archives of Santa Cruz de Querétaro, K, Legajo 4, N. 10, folios 5-6, as quoted in Hackett, "Aguayo," 212.

33. Morfi, *History*, I, 228, and Castañeda's note in ibid., 242, n 113.

34. Buckley states that this order included provisions for moving 10 or 12 families at a time from the Canary Islands. Buckley, "Aguayo Expedition," 62. It was such a group that was transported to San Antonio for settlement in 1731.

35. Kathryn Stoner O'Connor, *The Presidio La Bahía del Espíritu Santo de Zúñiga, 1721 to 1846*, 12-17; Castañeda, *Catholic Heritage*, II, 179-188.

36. Extensive quotations from Rivera's recommendations appear in Morfi, *History*, II, 244-258. See also Castañeda, *Catholic Heritage*, II, 211-231; and Charles W. Hackett, "Visitador Rivera's Criticisms of Aguayo's Work in Texas," 162-172.

37. Castañeda, *Catholic Heritage*, II, 231-241.

38. Rivera's report of 1728, as quoted in Morfi, *History*, II, 257-258.

39. A long summary of the numerous recommendations, reports, projects, and royal decrees aimed at producing settlers for the Texas frontier can be found in Castañeda, *Catholic Heritage*, II, 268-275.

40. Ibid., II, 274-280.

41. Ibid., II, 280-282.

42. Ibid., II, 283-288. There were originally ten families and five bachelors in the party, numbering 59 persons in all. Three others dropped out, but two young men previously arrived from the Canary Islands joined the party, marrying the daughters of Juan Curbelo. Three other marriages took place, and there were therefore fifteen families who were entitled to lands in the proposed new town.

43. "Order for the Establishment of San Antonio," November 30, 1730, manuscript in State Public Library of Guadalajara, as translated and quoted in Lota M. Spell, "The Grant and First Survey of the City of San Antonio," 75. Castañeda, in *Catholic Heritage*, II, 298-299 paraphrases from what is obviously an identical or very similar document that he identifies as being issued on November 28, 1730: "Para que el Governador de Texas; y en su ausencia el Capitán del Presidio de Sn. Antonio, Reconosca el Parage donde ha de fundarse la Poblazón a que han ido las quince familias, lo mida, deslinde, y Reparta . . . ," Archivo General de la Nación, Mexico, *História*, Vol. 84.

44. In computing these dimensions I have used the distance of 33.33 inches to the *vara*. The distances are as follows: church to town limits, 1,093 *varas*; town limit to outer boundary of commons, 1,093 *varas*; boundary of commons to outer limits of pasture lands, 2,186 *varas*; boundary of pasture lands to outer limits of farm tracts, 2,186 *varas*—a total of 6,558 *varas*, or roughly 18,200 English feet. This is approximately 3.45 miles for each side of the outer boundaries, giving an area of about 11.9 square miles. As will be noted in a later chapter, the town

grants for the Spanish *pueblos* in California were normally more than twice this size.

45. A conjectural diagram of this survey and a copy of an official city survey of 1852 on which some of these land divisions can be seen are reproduced in Spell, "Grant and First Survey," 80, 81.

46. *Ibid.*, 83-85. See also Castañeda, *Catholic Heritage*, II, 303-304 who cites the following manuscript in the State Public Library at Guadalajara: "Acta de Fundación de la Villa San Fernando," apparently the same document used by Spell.

47. Morfi, *History*, I, 92. Morfi served as chaplain to Teodoro de Croix, appointed in 1776 as Comandante General of the newly organized Provincias Internas. It was on a six-month tour of Texas and northern Mexico with Croix that Morfi determined to write his history of Texas. His detailed diary of the trip provided some information, but he also examined local records and archives in Texas and on his return began a systematic study of pertinent documents in Mexico. See the biographical introduction of Morfi by Castañeda in Morfi, *History*, I, 15-35. The report submitted by Croix himself in 1781 adds a little to our knowledge of conditions at the town: "The . . . presidio of Bejar and the Villa of San Fernando, capital of the province, are built, in spite of their long establishment, with huts and little wooden houses which a wind and rain storm largely destroyed last year. They have neither walls nor stockade to protect them from the attacks of the Indians." Alfred Barnaby Thomas (ed. and trans.), *Teodoro de Croix and the Northern Frontier of New Spain, 1776-1783*, 77.

48. Herbert E. Bolton, *Texas in the Middle Eighteenth Century*, 18, citing Fernández de Santa Ana, *Descripción de las Misiones del Colegio de la Santa Cruz en el Rio de San Antonio, Año de 1740*, manuscript in Francisco Figueroa (comp.), Memorias de Nueva España, Archivo General y Público, Mexico, XXVIII, 200-207.

49. Bolton, *Texas*, 27-32; Bannon, *Borderlands Frontier*, 167-172.

50. A complete treatment of the San Xavier mission episode can be found in Bolton, *Texas*, 135-278. While the *villa* or civil settlement advocated by the mission fathers did not receive approval, the *presidio* was intended to include some if its features. The decree of March 30, 1751, ordering its establishment included instructions to its commander for the recruitment of civilian settlers and for the granting of house lots and farm parcels to civilians and soldiers. Apparently twenty families of citizen settlers volunteered to move to the region. Bolton, *Texas*, 244-247. The San Xavier missions are also treated at length in Castañeda, *Catholic Heritage*, III, 241-338. The plan for the *presidio* was evidently prepared in Mexico, since the captain of the fort in a report to his superiors dated December 24, 1751, referred to "the plans or map, as . . . ordered me in the office of my commission." For the text of this document and the results of archeological investigations at the site see Kathleen Kirk Gilmore, *The San Xavier Missions: A Study in Historical Site Identification*, Austin, 1969.

51. For Escandón and his accomplishments I have relied on the following works: Lawrence F. Hill, *José de Escandón and the Founding of Nuevo Santander; Bol-*

ton, *Texas*, 281-302; Florence Johnson Scott, *Historical Heritage of the Lower Rio Grande*, and "Spanish Colonization of the Lower Rio Grande, 1747-1767," in Thomas E. Cotner and Carlos E. Castañeda (eds.), *Essays in Mexican History*, Austin, 1958, 3-20; Lillian J. Stambaugh, *The Lower Rio Grande Valley of Texas*, San Antonio, 1954; and Castañeda, *Catholic Heritage*, III, 130-196. While all of these works refer to the numerous towns founded by Escandón, almost all of which were on the Mexican side of the Rio Grande, not one deals primarily with his extraordinary record as a town planner. Reproductions of manuscript surveys of several of his Mexican towns appear in Fernando Chueca Goitia and Leopoldo Torres Balbas, *Planos de Ciudades Iberoamericanas y Filipinas Existentes en el Archivo de Indias*, I. A full-scale study of Escandón's career as an urban planner and the later development of his towns would be a useful undertaking. Abundant documentary and graphic materials relevant to such an inquiry are available.

52. In addition to that of Reynoso, plats of the following are reproduced in Chueca Goitia and Torres Balbas, *Planos de Ciudades*: Altamira, Burgos, Camargo, Dolores, Escandón, Horcasitas (designated a *ciudad*), Revilla, Padilla, San Fernando, Güemez, Santa Bárbara, Aguayo, Llera, and Soto la Marina.

53. These dimensions appear on the drawing, as they do on the other surveys of Escandón's towns. The plazas of Camargo and Horcasitas were 224 *varas* square; that of Soto la Marina measured 120 by 112 *varas*. In the two former towns the street and block layout differed in that all blocks were 200 *varas* square. The large block at the southwest corner of Soto la Marina was omitted along with the western half of the adjoining block fronting the plaza because of a bend in the river on which the town was located.

54. Herbert E. Bolton, "Tienda de Cuervo's *Ynspección* of Laredo, 1757," 187-203. The word "town" (doubtless "*pueblo*" in the original) is used on pp. 192, 193, 198, 199, and 201.

55. Scott, *Lower Rio Grande*, 65-66, 71-72. Laredo's growth was stimulated by its location on the route from Mexico to San Antonio. In 1794 it was reported to have a population of 636. David M. Vigness, "Nuevo Santander in 1795: A Provincial Inspection by Félix Calleja," 475, n 27.

56. Bolton, *Texas*, 316-317; O'Connor, *La Bahía*, 18-27; Castañeda, *Catholic Heritage*, III, 177-181.

57. Manuel Ramírez de la Piszina to the Viceroy, February 6, 18, and 20, 1750, as summarized in ibid., III, 179.

58. Report by Angel Martos y Navarrete in 1762, as summarized in O'Connor, *La Bahía*, 37.

59. Morfi, *History*, I, 102.

60. For the many proposals leading to the founding of this *presidio* and mission see Castañeda, *Catholic Heritage*, III, 339-400. Morfi, *History*, II, 353-370, should be consulted for the details of the offer by Pedro Romero de Terreros to pay the costs of the San Sabá venture. See also Bolton, *Texas*, 78-93.

61. Castañeda, *Catholic Heritage*, III, 401-409; Weddle, *San Sabá*, 61-89.

62. Ibid., 90-128; Bannon, *Borderlands Frontier*, 138-139; Castañeda, *Catholic*

Heritage, III, 99-136. The two missions on the Nueces River were named San Lorenzo del Cañón and Nuestra Señora de la Candelaria. Castañeda, *Catholic Heritage*, III, 163-167.

63. Ibid., III, 156-157.

64. Weddle, *San Sabá*, 169.

65. Even 80 years later, long after the Spanish abandoned the fort, it remained an impressive sight. The German scholar, Ferdinand Roemer, described it in 1847 as follows: "The fort lies close to the river on the left or north bank, which is here about twenty feet high. The ruins consist of remnants of masonry work five to six feet high (in some places from fifteen to twenty feet), and plainly show the design of the whole structure. The outer walls of masonry are an almost square rectangle whose shorter wall, lying near the river, measures 300 feet, while the longer wall measures 360. On to the inner side of this outer wall are built several casemates, or rooms, each eighteen feet deep and opening into the courtyard. The whole number of these surrounding the court is about fifty. In the northwest corner of the plot of ground is a main building with a courtyard and seven rooms, the walls of which are still partially preserved as high as the upper crossbeams. The main entrance to the fort lay on the west side, and besides this there was a little opening towards the water. On three corners of the fort there were projecting towers for defense and on the northwest corner a larger and round tower." Ferdinand Roemer, *Texas*, Bonn, 1849, as quoted in Adele B. Looscan, "The Old Fort on the San Saba River as Seen by Dr. Ferdinand Roemer in 1847," 138.

66. Weddle, *San Sabá*, 176-181, 210-212.

67. For a detailed report of archeological investigations of the site and translations of contemporary documents relating to its founding see Kathleen Gilmore, *A Documentary and Archeological Investigation of Presidio San Luis de las Amarillas and Mission Santa Cruz de San Sabá*.

68. The text of the decree of 1772 and much material dealing with its background and consequences can be found in Sidney B. Brinckerhoff and Odie B. Faulk, *Lancers for the King*. Included is a map showing the location of the *presidios* on the new defensive perimeter. See also Bolton, *Texas*, 377-386; the introduction by the editor in Lawrence Kinnaird (ed.), *The Frontiers of New Spain: Nicolas de Lafora's Description, 1766-1768*, 1-42; and Castañeda, *Catholic Heritage*, IV, 200-258.

69. In his *Dictamen*, or recommendations, of 1768 Rubí wrote: "How painful and assailable to many would be the proposal I would like to make now, the abandonment of the site of the villa and the five wealthy missions of San Antonio de Béjar. . . . Such a removal, which undoubtedly involves many difficulties, could be justified by repeated examples of what has been done with other larger colonies to promote their development or security. But I do not dare go so far, nor do I trust my own judgment sufficiently to propose so great an innovation," as quoted in Castañeda, *Catholic Heritage*, IV, 249.

70. Bolton, *Texas*, 378, 382.

71. For the circumstances leading up to the founding of Bucareli and such facts as are available concerning its plan I have relied on Bolton, *Texas*, 387-438; and Castañeda, *Catholic Heritage*, IV, 303-330.

72. Ibid., IV, 343. The text of Ybarbo's letter to Croix on May 13, 1779 describing the evacuation of Bucareli and asking permission to settle permanently at Nacogdoches is in Ernest Wallace and David M. Vigness (comps.), *Documents of Texas History*, 25-27.

73. Castañeda, *Catholic Heritage*, V, 32. The same census listed a total of 554 Indian neophytes at the five missions in the San Antonio area.

74. Francisco Xavier Fragoso, *Derrotero* . . . , Archivo General de la Nación, Mexico, *Historia*, Vol. 43, document 17, as cited in Castañeda, *Catholic Heritage*, V, 168.

75. Governor Juan Bautista Elguezábal to Commandant General Nemesio Salcedo, June 20, 1803, as cited in ibid., V, 288.

76. This and many other suggestions of a similar nature advanced during the years 1803-1805 are described in Castañeda, *Catholic Heritage*, V, 285-310.

77. Ibid., V, 311-317.

78. Ibid., V, 317-336.

79. Odie B. Faulk, *The Last Years of Spanish Texas, 1778-1821*, The Hague, 1964, 127.

80. This and other information concerning Palafox is drawn from Carmen Perry (ed. and trans.), *The Impossible Dream by the Rio Grande*. See pp. 27-28 and 90 for the population data referred to.

81. Jesse E. Reeves, *The Napoleonic Exiles in America*, 531-656.

82. The quotation is from an anonymous account that appeared in *Journal des Voyages, Découvertes et Navigations Modernes*, XVI (1822), 194-204, as edited and translated by Jack Autrey Dabbs, "Additional Notes on the Champ-d'Asile," 347-358. A longer description can be found in Frédéric Gaillardet, *Sketches of Early Texas and Louisiana*, 123-214. This is taken from Hartmann and Millard, *Le Texas, ou Notice historique sur le Champ d'Asile*, Paris, 1819.

83. A manuscript plan of Champ d'Asile was drawn in 1819 by José Echandia. It is entitled *Fortificación y obras hechas en la orilla izquierda del Rio Trinidad Provincia de Texas p^r. los aventueros al mando de los Generales Lallemand y Rigaut*. The original is in the Servicio Histórico Militar in Spain. A reproduction appears as plate 117, Vol. II of Servicios Geografico & Historico del Ejercigo Estado Mayor Central, *Cartografia de Ultramar*, Madrid (?), n.d. This plan shows the same elements appearing in the view herein reproduced but arranged in more rectangular fashion and with some of the major fortifications still incomplete.

84. The dissolution of the Texas missions and the transfer of land to the Indian residents is described in Castañeda, *Catholic Heritage*, V, 35-66; Paul H. Walters, "Secularization of the La Bahia Missions," 287-300; and Habig, *Mission San Jose*, 91-133.

IV · EXPANSION OF THE SPANISH BORDERLANDS:
URBAN SETTLEMENT OF ARIZONA AND
CALIFORNIA IN THE HISPANIC ERA

1. The life and work of the remarkable Kino is the subject of Herbert E. Bolton's *Rim of Christendom*.

2. Ray H. Mattison, "Early Spanish and Mexican Settlements in Arizona," 274-281. For references to other studies of Spanish settlement in Arizona see the bibliographical notes in John Francis Bannon, *The Spanish Borderlands Frontier, 1513-1821*, 272-274.

3. Bannon, *Borderlands Frontier*, 146-48 summarizes these activities. See also Peter Masten Dunne, *Black Robes in Lower California*; and Francis J. Weber, "Jesuit Missions in Baja California," 408-422, for a more extended treatment of the missions in that part of Mexico.

4. Hubert Howe Bancroft, *History of Arizona and New Mexico*, 382.

5. Records of Tubac are fragmentary. In 1838 Tubac became a *pueblo* under Mexican laws and received a land grant of 9 square leagues (61 square miles), somewhat over twice the territory normally designated for municipal purposes. General Land Office, Phoenix, Arizona, MS *Journal of Private Land Grants*, III, 35, as cited in Mattison, "Spanish and Mexican Settlements," 283.

6. The complete account of this expedition can be found in "Diary of Sebastián Vizcaíno," in Herbert E. Bolton, *Spanish Exploration in the Southwest, 1542-1706*, 52-103.

7. The full text of this document as translated by Emma Helen Blair appears as Appendix A, 503-513 in Irving Berdine Richman, *California under Spain and Mexico, 1535-1847*. Richman's study is perhaps the best single-volume treatment of settlement and development in California. Other useful works on which I have also relied include Charles E. Chapman, *The Founding of Spanish California*; and Hubert Howe Bancroft, *History of California*. Of special value because of its emphasis on the mission, *presidio*, and *pueblo* settlements is Daniel Garr, "Hispanic Colonial Settlement in California: Planning and Urban Development on the Frontier, 1769-1850." Garr's examination and analysis of relevant manuscript records, chiefly those at the Bancroft Collection in the library of the University of California, Berkeley, provided me with much information that would not have otherwise come to my attention. My debt to him is substantial. The bibliography for this chapter lists three of his articles drawn from his dissertation but incorporating additional research.

8. Miguel Costansó, "The Narrative of the Portolá Expedition of 1769-1770," 147-149.

9. The words are those of Father Juan Crespí, chaplain and historian of the expedition, as quoted in Bannon, *Borderlands Frontier*, 157. A slightly different version, identified as a letter written by Crespí from San Diego on February 8, 1770, is quoted in Theodore E. Treutlein, *San Francisco Bay: Discovery and Colonization, 1769-1776*, 30.

10. Richman, *California*, 83-89.

11. Several of the missions important for their role as future civil settlements will be mentioned later. The California missions have been the subject of an extensive literature. A contemporary account of them in their early years is by Father Francisco Palóu, *Noticias de la Nueva California*, completed in 1783, published in 1857, and translated and edited by Herbert E. Bolton as *Historical Memoirs of New California*. The most elaborate modern study is Zephyrin Engelhardt, *The Missions and Missionaries of California*. Helpful descriptions of the present state of the mission buildings together with brief historical notes can be found in Robert G. Ferris (ed.), *Explorers and Settlers: Historic Places Commemorating the Early Exploration and Settlement of the United States*, The National Survey of Historic Sites and Buildings, v. Early illustrations of the missions appear in various sources. One of the most important is Henry Chapman Ford, *Etchings of the Franciscan Missions of California*. I have examined the copy in the Detroit Institute of Arts. In the library of The Hispanic Society of America in New York City there is a magnificent 4-volume collection of mission photographs, each approximately 16" x 20" taken by C. E. Watkins of San Francisco. The title page reads *Franciscan Missions of California*. The photographs are undated, but appear to have been taken in the 1880s. The volumes were acquired by the Society in 1923 and have the accession number 41342.

12. Jeanne Van Nostrand, *A Pictorial and Narrative History of Monterey: Adobe Capital of California, 1770-1847*, 19. This splendid volume reproduces every known illustration of Monterey for the period indicated in its title. These are accompanied by an informative and lucid text as well as by notes on the artists and illustrators. It is a model of topographic art history.

13. George Vancouver, *Voyage of Discovery to the North Pacific Ocean . . . 1798*, as quoted in Van Nostrand, *Monterey*, 36.

14. These expeditions are discussed in Treutlein, *San Francisco Bay*, 39-51, 57-62. Contemporary accounts, diaries, and reports of these and other explorations of California are cited in Bannon, *Borderlands Frontier*, 276.

15. Font's *Complete Diary*, as quoted in Treutlein, *San Francisco Bay*, 82.

16. The words are those of Father Francisco Palóu, who accompanied the expedition. See George Ezra Dane (trans.), "The Founding of the Presidio and Mission of our Father Saint Francis, Being Chapter 45 of Fray Francisco Palóu's Life of the Venerable Padre Fray Junípero Serra, Written at the Mission of San Francisco de Asis, and Newly Translated from the Original Edition of 1787," 103.

17. Vancouver's description is from an extract from his *Voyage of Discovery*, "San Francisco in 1792," *California Historical Society Quarterly*, XIV (1935), 114. A plan of the *presidio* in 1792 showing only the three sides as Vancouver described it is in the manuscript *California Archives*, Bancroft Library, University of California, Berkeley, VI, 234.

18. A plan of this and a map showing the location of the two establishments in 1794 is reproduced in Richman, *California*, following p. 344. This is the modern Fort Point, occupied by Old Fort Scott, which was built after the American

occupation of California in the middle nineteenth century and named for General Winfield Scott in 1882. There are apparently no remains of Castillo San Joaquin, which it replaced. Herbert M. Hart, *Old Forts of the Far West*, 92-97.

19. The year was 1827, and the observer was the French explorer, A. Duhaut-Cilly. The California portions of his *Voyage Autour du Monde* (Paris, 1834) appear as translated by Charles Franklin Carter in "Duhaut-Cilly's Account of California in the Years 1827-28," 130-166, 214-250, 306-336. The quotations are from a passage on p. 140.

20. Palóu, "Founding of the Presidio and Mission of our Father Saint Francis," 105.

21. Vancouver, "San Francisco in 1792," 117.

22. Duhaut-Cilly, "Account of California," 142.

23. In the modern city the intersection of Santa Barbara and Canon Perdido Streets marks the approximate location of one corner of the *presidio* enclosure.

24. In addition to the missions mentioned in the text, the others founded prior to 1786 include San Juan Capistrano (1776), Santa Clara (1777), and San Buenaventura (1782). During the years 1789-91 Missions La Purisma Concepción, Santa Cruz, and La Soledad were established. Five more missions were created in 1797-98: San José, San Juan Bautista, San Miguel Arcángel, San Fernándo Rey de España, and San Luis Rey de Francia. Other and later missions were Santa Ynez (1804), San Rafael Arcángel (1817), and San Francisco Solano (1823). U.S. Federal Writers' Project, *California: A Guide to the Golden State*, 687-689.

25. Felipe de Goycoechea, Santa Barbara, December 3, 1785, California State Papers, Missions, I, 5-10, as cited in Garr, "California," 185.

26. Duhaut-Cilly, "Account of California," 157. Bancroft gives the population of Santa Barbara as 300 in 1800, 460 in 1810, and more than 700 in 1820. Bancroft, *California*, I, 672; II, 118, 361.

27. The full text of the regulations with an explanation of their background and consequences is in Sidney B. Brinckerhoff and Odie B. Faulk, *Lancers for the King*. Title 11 of the regulations, p. 35, contains the passage quoted.

28. The administrative hierarchy for the government of California is described in Edwin A. Beilharz, *Felipe de Neve: First Governor of California*, 20-33. This excellent study is the only full-length treatment of Neve.

29. Lindley Bynum, "Governor Don Felipe de Neve," 58-59.

30. Francisco Palóu, *Historical Memoirs of New California*, IV, 167-168.

31. The house lots surveyed by Moraga measured 20 by 40 *varas* (55½ by 111 feet). Beilharz, *Felipe de Neve*, 103. A recently discovered drawing, probably dating from before 1780, shows how Moraga arranged the lots in an extended quadrangle to form the town. This is reproduced in Daniel Garr, "A Frontier Agrarian Settlement: San José de Guadalupe, 1777-1850." The floods destroyed the dam built for irrigation in the spring of 1778. Oscar Osburn Winther, "The Story of San José, 1777-1869," 7. In August, 1778, Neve reported to Croix that he had found it necessary to relocate the farm lands to an area "more suitable and closer

to the population, changing the distribution which I have made." Neve to Croix, Monterey, August 11, 1778, *California Provincial Records*, I, 92, as quoted in Garr, "California," 227-228.

32. This process is described in Frederick Hall, *The History of San José and Surroundings*, 25-31. Moraga's map may not be complete, since the records used by Hall indicate that 36 *suertes* or farming tracts were distributed at that time. Three of the squares shown on Moraga's survey are designated as "Realengo" or farm lands reserved for later settlers. Only 18 are shown with the names of the new owners.

33. The details of this controversy based on how the Laws of the Indies should be interpreted is recorded in some detail in Garr, "California," 228-233. Neve and Serra disagreed on many matters, a situation not uncommon throughout the Spanish colonies where civil and religious authorities frequently pursued different policies. For some of the specific issues over which these two able men differed see Beilharz, *Felipe de Neve*, 45-66. Later disputes on the location of the boundary line between *pueblo* and mission are described in Hall, *San José*, 57-81.

34. *California State Papers, Missions and Colonization*, I, 249, as quoted in Garr, "California," 241.

35. San José City Planning Commission, *The Master Plan*, 4.

36. *Narrative of Nicholas "Cheyenne" Dawson (Overland to California in '41 & '49, and Texas in '51)*, San Francisco, 1933, 29-30, as quoted in Winther, "San José," 19.

37. Edwin Bryant, *What I Saw in California*, 315-316.

38. "Neve's Instructions to Fages, his Successor," September 7, 1782, in Beilharz, *Felipe de Neve*, 165.

39. *California State Papers, Missions*, I, 61-64; and *Provincial State Papers*, XI, 181-183, as cited by Garr, "California," 242.

40. Beilharz, *Felipe de Neve*, 86-88.

41. *Reglamento para el Gobierno de la Provincia de Californias*, Mexico City, 1784, as translated by Charles F. Lummis, "Regulations and Instructions for the Garrisons of the Peninsula of California . . . ," 180-181. The *reglamento* text may also be found in John Everett Johnson (trans.), *Regulations for Governing the Province of the Californias approved by His Majesty by Royal Order, dated October 24, 1781*.

42. Lummis, "Regulations and Instructions," 181-185.

43. Beilharz, *Felipe de Neve*, 104-109. Twelve families had arrived at Mission San Gabriel. One dropped out before leaving for the *pueblo* site. Of the remaining 11 heads of families, Beilharz states that "three were of Spanish blood, at least in part, two were negroes, two mulattoes, and four were Indians. Three of them . . . were dropped from the list by March 21, 1782. The remaining eight . . . with their families . . . gave Los Angeles a starting population of thirty-two," p. 109.

44. "Translation of Portion of Order of Governor Felipe de Neve for Founding of Los Angeles," in "Padron and Confirmation of Titles to Pueblo Lands," 154-

155. This is identified as from "a certified traced copy from Surveyor-General's office, filed as evidence in Los Angeles District Court Case No. 1344, March 11, 1869."

45. Census of Los Angeles, August 17, 1790, *California Provincial State Papers*, v, 154, as cited by Garr, "California," 261. A year earlier Felipe de Goycoechea stated that three new houses "were to be arranged in Streets." Goycoechea to Governor Pedro Fages, February 18, 1789, *California Provincial State Papers*, v, 120-121, as quoted in Garr, "California," 261. Also in 1790, Goycoechea reported that the town included 14 houses of adobe enclosed by a wall and 17 others outside the wall "separated from said square forming a street." Goycoechea, "Edad de Los Angeles," 1790, *California State Papers, Missions*, i, 69, as quoted in Garr, "California," 262.

46. J. M. Guinn, "The Story of a Plaza," 247-249. Of this change in the town plan Garr comments that "this sudden uprooting of Los Angeles' political, social and geographic nucleus underscores the ephemeral quality of frontier town planning in California," Garr, "California," 264.

47. Bancroft, *California*, i, 461; Duhaut-Cilly, "Account of California," 246.

48. J. M. Guinn, "From Pueblo to Ciudad: The Municipal and Territorial Expansion of Los Angeles," Historical Society of Southern California, *Publications*, vii (1908), 216.

49. Ibid., 218.

50. Ibid., 219.

51. *California Departmental State Papers, Los Angeles*, iii, 111-112, as cited and described in Garr, "California," 276.

52. Bryant, *What I Saw in California*, 405.

53. A detailed description of the buildings appearing in the Hutton views as seen and drawn in 1853 by Charles Koppel from an almost identical vantagepoint will be found in Ana Begue de Packman, "Landmarks and Pioneers of Los Angeles in 1853," 57-95. A useful location map accompanies this study, which includes reproductions of the Koppel view and a number of nineteenth-century photographs of individual buildings. Also helpful in identifying old landmarks and sites is W. W. Robinson, *Los Angeles from the Days of the Pueblo*.

54. Richman, *California*, 160-166.

55. Branciforte to Borica, January 25, 1797, *California State Papers, Missions and Colonization*, i, 79-83, as cited in Garr, "California," 298.

56. Córdoba to Borica, August 12, 1797, *California Provincial State Papers*, x, 150, as cited in Garr, "California," 306.

57. Berica to Cárdoba, May 15, 1797, *California Provincial State Papers, Indices*, 258-261, as quoted in Garr, "California," 305. By undertaking house construction as a royal charge, the viceroy hoped to relieve the soldier-citizens of some of the normal tasks of colonization and thus allow more attention to military duties. In 1795 Branciforte noted that a soldier in a new settlement had to be "a courier, cowhand, mason, shepherd, laborer, serving so that he barely has the time to get the necessary amount of sleep." "Informe del Real Tribunal y Au-

diencia de la Contaduría de Cuentas sobre Fundación de un Pueblo que llamará Branciforte," November 18, 1795, *California Provincial State Papers*, vii, 399, as quoted in Garr, "California," 305.

58. For this controversy and a comparison of the mission's argument with the earlier and similar situation at San José, see ibid., 301-304.

59. Garr, "California," 308-315 traces the nineteenth-century history of the town. The only full-length study of Branciforte is Lesley Byrd Simpson, *An Early Ghost Town of California, Branciforte*. Some additional material on the early status of the *villa* and its relations with the nearby mission of Santa Cruz can be found in H. A. van Coenen Torchiana, *Story of the Mission Santa Cruz*, especially pp. 217-232.

60. Mission secularization in California is treated clearly and concisely in Richman, *California*, 228-264, 282-285. The attempts to convert missions to civil settlements are described more specifically in Garr, "California," Chapter iv, "Mission Pueblos and Indian Towns," 316-352.

61. Engelhardt, *Missions and Missionaries*, iii, 112.

62. "Decreto de Secularizacion de Misiones," January 6, 1831, *California Departmental Records*, iv, 66-78, as quoted in Garr, "California," 334.

63. Engelhardt, *Missions and Missionaries*, iii, 473-476.

64. Manuscript travel journal of Father Ivan Veniaminov, Alaska State Library, as quoted in E. O. Essig, "The Russian Settlement at Ross," 196. For Duhaut-Cilly's similar description of Fort Ross see his "Account of California," 325.

65. Essig, "Russian Settlement at Ross," 192.

66. The colonization proposal of 1834 proceeded to the stage of surveying a town site a few miles north of Santa Rosa on what is now called Mark West Creek. For this project see Richman, *California*, 248-252 and Garr, "California," 201-207. The text of the order to Vallejo appears in Thomas Gregory, *History of Sonoma County*, 36. A portion is quoted in Reps, *The Making of Urban America*, 51-54. Figure 31 in that work is a reproduction of a plan of Sonoma in 1875. For other material on Sonoma see Lawrence Kinnaird, *History of the Greater San Francisco Bay Region*, i, 286-288, 434.

67. Mariano G. Vallejo, *Recuerdos Historicos y Personales tocante a la Alta California*, ms, Bancroft Library, 1875, iii, 19, as quoted in Garr, "California," 208.

68. The order was issued on October 22, 1791, approved by the viceroy in January, 1793, but became operative in June, 1792. Pedro de Nava to Arrillage, January 19, 1793, *California State Papers, Missions and Colonization*, i, 317-319, as cited in Garr, "California," 87.

69. José Bandini, *Descrision de l'Alta California en 1828*, Doris Marion Wright (trans.), Berkeley, 1951, 4, as quoted in Garr, "California," 91-92.

70. Duhaut-Cilly, "Account of California," 219.

71. William Heath Davis, *Seventy-Five Years in California*, 258.

72. Richard F. Pourade, *The History of San Diego*, iii, 14-15.

73. Richard Henry Dana, *Two Years Before the Mast*, 121.

74. This view is undated, and its source is unknown. It is from a photograph in the collection of the San Diego Title Insurance and Trust Company, where it has been given the date of ca. 1857. A number of other similar views exist. One is a lithograph in the Honeyman Collection of the Bancroft Library entitled *San Diego, 1850*, signed in the stone as drawn by C. G. Conts (probably Cave J. Couts), printed by Britton & Rey in San Francisco. This company was known by this title only during the years 1852-58 according to Harry T. Peters, *California on Stone*, 62. Another view can be found in W. H. Emory, *Notes of a Military Reconnoissance*. A fourth is the sketch drawn by M. T. Powell in the winter of 1849-50, now in the collection of the Henry E. Huntington Library and Art Gallery, San Marino, California. Duhaut-Cilly, "Account of California," 154-155.

75. Duhaut-Cilly, "Account of California," 154-155.

76. Monterey Ayuntamiento, December 6, 1828, *California Departmental State Papers*, I, 239-242; II, 159-161. Garr summarizes the 1833 ordinances as follows: "These were directed at environmental considerations. The owner of hogs caught running in the streets would be fined twelve reales for a first offense. Settlers must clean in front of their houses at least twice weekly and the garbage was to be used as landfill for holes caused by erosion and the manufacturing of adobes; further, bricks were to be made in restricted areas or on one's own property. Another article warned against cutting trees on public land for personal gain." Garr, "California," 130.

77. Dana, *Two Years Before the Mast*, 73. Other brief descriptions of Monterey in the 1830s can be found in Faxon Dean Atherton, *California Diary*; William S. W. Ruschenberger, *Narrative of a Voyage Round the World*, II, 400-404; Abel Aubert Du Petit-Thouars, *Voyage Autour du Monde*, II, 84, 110; Richard A. Pierce and John H. Winslow (eds.), *H. M. S. Sulphur at California, 1837 and 1839*, 28.

78. Eugène Duflot de Mofras, *Exploration du Territoire de l'Orégon, des Californies, et de la Mer Vermeille*, I, 403-404.

79. William Richardson, as quoted in "Alcalde Grants in the City of San Francisco," *Pioneer, or California Monthly Magazine*, I (1854), 196.

80. In writing these paragraphs on the origins of San Francisco I have had the benefit of a detailed study on the subject carried out by Stephen Morris under my direction in 1970. His seminar paper, "Urban Development and Planning in Early San Francisco," Department of City and Regional Planning, Cornell University, July, 1970, was an exhaustive analysis of available literature and early graphic documents. The more important sources of information about the planning and development of San Francisco in pre-Gold Rush days include the following: "Yerba Buena Biographies," 123-131; Jacob N. Bowman, "The Spanish Anchorage in San Francisco Bay," and "The Third Map of Yerba Buena," XXV (1946), 319-324 and XXVI (1947), 267-269; John W. Dwinelle, *Colonial History of San Francisco*; Neal Harlow, "The Maps of San Francisco Bay and the Town of Yerba Buena to 100 Years Ago," 365-378; and Zoeth S. Eldredge, *The Beginnings of San Francisco*.

81. John Henry Brown, *Reminiscences and Incidents of Early Days of San Francisco, 1845-1850*, 24-25.

V · TOWNS IN TRANSITION: THE SOUTHWEST DURING THE PERIODS OF MEXICAN CONTROL, TEXAS INDEPENDENCE, AND THE EARLY YEARS OF AMERICAN SETTLEMENT

707

NOTES TO PAGES 108-119

1. Odie B. Faulk, *The Last Years of Spanish Texas, 1778-1821*, 120.

2. Faulk, *Spanish Texas*, 125-140. Long's activities in Texas are described in Henry Stuart Foote, *Texas and the Texans*, 201-217. The background of the revolutionary movement and the intrusions into Texas by Americans and French settlers are treated at length in Carlos E. Castañeda, *Catholic Heritage*, VI, 1-175.

3. Ibid., 190-198. The details of Austin's negotiations, official communications relating to his project, and the relevant legislation may be found in Joseph M. White, *A New Collection of Laws . . . of Mexico and Texas*, I, 559-622. The colonization statutes and much additional material are also in John and Henry Sayles (comps.), *Early Laws of Texas*, I.

4. Decree No. 16, Colonization Law of Coahuila and Texas, March 24, 1825, Secs. 34-37, in ibid., I, 70-71.

5. Instructions to Commissioners, September 4, 1827, Laws and Decrees of Coahuila and Texas, in ibid., I, 74. In my treatment of the *empresario* towns of Texas I have been helped by research carried out under my direction at Cornell University by Deborah F. Pokinski, whose research paper of 1970, "Town Planning in Colonial Texas: The Mexican Empresario System, 1821-1836," analyzed materials available in Ithaca and offered a number of conclusions.

6. At least one precedent for this method of settlement existed within the Spanish colonial territory in what is now the United States. This was New Madrid, founded in 1789 by George Morgan in Missouri, then part of Spanish Louisiana. See Reps, "New Madrid on the Mississippi," 21-26. Max Savelle, *George Morgan, Colony Builder*, provides additional material on the background of this settlement and Morgan's negotiations for a land grant similar to the Texas *empresarios*. It should be noted as well that prior to Austin's application there were proposals for Texas colonization of a similar nature. Some of these are reviewed in Castañeda, *Catholic Heritage*, VI, 176-186.

7. The second drawing is among the manuscript maps in the Stephen F. Austin Collection, Eugene C. Barker Texas History Center, University of Texas, Austin. Like the first, it is undated. The sequence of their drawing is my hypothesis based on what appears to me to be the most plausible explanation of their differences. On the drawing reproduced in Figure 5.1 is a notation obviously added at a later time giving 1823 as a conjectural date.

8. The text of Bastrop's appointment as commissioner and the order naming the town San Felipe de Austin are in Sayles, *Early Laws of Texas*, I, 49-51. A brief description of the town by a resident who arrived in 1827 appears in Noah Smithwick, *The Evolution of a State*, Austin, 1900, as quoted in Ernest Wallace and David M. Vigness, *Documents of Texas History*, 63-64. Smithwick described the settlement in 1827 as consisting of not more than 200 persons living in "twenty-five or perhaps thirty log cabins strung along the west bank of the Brazos River."

A collection of materials on San Felipe de Austin is Corrie Pattison Haskew (comp.), *Historical Records of Austin and Waller Counties*.

9. Ethel Zivley Rather, "De Witt's Colony," 120-121.

10. A modern air view of Gonzales is reproduced in D. W. Meinig's short but extremely valuable study in historical geography, *Imperial Texas*, Figure 13. The town proper lay at one edge of a much larger tract surveyed into rectangular farming parcels. Near its southern edge ran East Avenue extending outward from the cometery block and platted no less than 170 *varas* (472 feet) wide. Another street of identical width, North Avenue, led northwards parallel to Water Street which was 50 *varas* (138¾ feet) wide. The extraordinary width of these thoroughfares serving the agricultural tracts on two sides of the town was without precedent, and it is difficult to understand why they were laid out with these overly generous dimensions. A reproduction of the design of the outer portions of the town may be found in Rather, "De Witt's Colony."

11. Castañeda, *Catholic Heritage*, VI, 203-205. I have not been able to locate an early plan of Victoria, but its modern central square and gridiron street pattern indicate that it must have been designed in a form similar to the other *empresario* towns of the period. Further information on Victoria and some of the other *empresario* settlements can be found in Mary Virginia Henderson, "Minor Empresario Contracts for the Colonization of Texas, 1825-1834," 295-324. *Empresario* colonies under the laws of the state of Tamaulipas are described in Leroy P. Graf, "Colonizing Projects in Texas South of the Nueces, 1820-1845," 431-448.

12. William H. Oberste, *Texas Irish Empresarios and Their Colonies*, 115-119. Another plan of Refugio, possibly earlier than the one illustrated here, is reproduced in Oberste, opposite p. 121.

13. Ibid., 58-63. Saucedo's report of the planning of the town is quoted at length by Oberste, who also reproduces a redrawing of an 1835 survey of the town opposite p. 62.

14. Bastrop was first named Mina. It was established in 1832 in the area of S. C. Robertson's colony after Austin became the *empresario*. Milam's initial name was Viesca. It also lay in the Robertson colony and was located at the falls of the Brazos River. Castañeda, *Catholic Heritage*, VI, 200; and Dermot H. Hardy and Ingham S. Roberts (eds.), *Historical Review of Southeast Texas*, 417-418. A manuscript plan of Liberty, probably drawn during the Civil War, is in the Records of the Chief of Engineers, Headquarters Map File Z-42, Cartographic Branch, National Archives. It shows a regular gridiron street pattern with what appears to be a town square or *plaza* occupying an area equal in size to two normal city blocks.

15. Walter Prescott Webb (ed.), *The Handbook of Texas*, 835-836. A brief note by J. P. Bryan on the obscure origins of Velasco and Quintana can be found in his edition of Mary Austin Holley, *The Texas Diary, 1835-1838*, notes on Figures 1 and 3, p. 73.

16. Edward Stiff, *The Texan Emigrant*, 32; Webb, *Handbook of Texas*, II, 157; Junann J. Stieghorst, *Bay City and Matagorda County: A History*, 30-35.

17. T. R. Fehrenbach, *Lone Star: A History of Texas and the Texans*, 150-151. Jonesborough, on the Red River just south of what is now the Oklahoma border, was one such squatter settlement that existed by 1820. Many others were apparently established in northeastern Texas.

18. Castañeda, *Catholic Heritage*, VI, 218-219; Fehrenbach, *Lone Star*, 187.

19. Ray H. Mattison, "Early Spanish and Mexican Settlements in Arizona," 283. A view of Tubac in 1878 appears in Richard J. Hinton, *The Hand-Book to Arizona*.

20. Sidney B. Brinckerhoff and Odie B. Faulk, *Lancers for the King*, 95; Cameron Greenleaf and Andrew Wallace, "Tucson: Pueblo, Presidio, and American City, A Synopsis of its History," 21.

21. Greenleaf and Wallace, "Tucson," 22. Contemporary descriptions of Tucson in the Spanish and Mexican period are strangely lacking. The town's appearance in 1847 as recalled in 1889 by a former American soldier can be found in "Tucson in 1847: Reminiscences of Judge F. Adams," 83-85.

22. For the circumstances leading to the preparation of this survey see Charles Byars, "Documents of Arizona History: The First Map of Tucson," 188-189. Byars speculates that it was drawn to facilitate land sales and to help in reconciling conflicting property claims.

23. Samuel Woodworth Cozzens, *The Marvellous Country; or, Three Years in Arizona and New Mexico, the Apaches' Home*, 153-154.

24. The Texas Constitution of 1836 guaranteed more than 4,000 acres of land to every resident head of a family. Families moving to Texas from March, 1836, to October, 1837, were entitled to 1,280 acres, later reduced to 640 acres. A preemption law authorized squatters to purchase up to 320 acres at 50 cents an acre. Special land grants to army veterans and their heirs were also provided for. Fehrenbach, *Lone Star*, 282-283.

25. Columbia, Texas, *Telegraph and Texas Register*, August 30, 1836, as quoted in David G. McComb, *Houston: The Bayou City*, 10-12. The advertisement is typical of the real estate promoter's language that was soon to appear throughout the region and which had already been widely employed in the United States during the great land boom of the middle 1830s.

26. From an account by Dr. Pleasant W. Rose, as quoted in B. H. Carroll (ed.), *Standard History of Houston, Texas*, 28.

27. Harrisburg, downstream on Buffalo Bayou, was another early Texas municipality, dating from 1826. Nearby were two other largely paper towns—Lynchburg and New Washington. Andrew Forest Muir, "The Municipality of Harrisburg, 1835-1836," 36-50. A plat of Harrisburg in 1839 showing a typical grid plan is among the Deed Records of Harris County, Texas, Vol. F, p. 11.

28. Francis R. Lubbock, *Six Decades in Texas*, 45-46. Water transportation to Houston remained slow and hazardous for many years. Not until much later would widening and dredging of the tortuous, shallow, and overgrown channel finally create an adequate ship canal and make possible the Allens' vision of their city as a major port. This development and other aspects of Houston's

growth are traced in Marilyn McAdams Sibley's fine study, *The Port of Houston: A History*. Reproduced in this work are also a number of early drawings and photographs of the city.

29. Anonymous account of Houston originally published in the *Hesperian* magazine in Columbus, Ohio, between September, 1838, and April, 1839. Reprinted as *Texas in 1837*, Andrew Forest Muir (ed.), 27-29.

30. Houston to Robert A. Irion, April 28, 1837, in Amelia W. Williams and Eugene C. Barker (eds.), *The Writings of Sam Houston, 1813-1863*, IV, 29.

31. The Allens built this building and rented it to the state for $5,000 a year beginning in the fall of 1837. Adele B. Looscan, "Harris County, 1822-1848, IV. The Beginnings of Houston," 41. A sketch of the second capitol in December, 1837, by Mary Holley is reproduced in her, *Texas Diary*, 37. According to Mary Holley, the capitol cost $30,000 to construct and measured 70 by 140 feet.

32. Looscan, "Harris County," 46.

33. McComb, *Houston*, 26; Kenneth W. Wheeler, *To Wear a City's Crown*, 69.

34. *City of Galveston, on Galveston Island, in Texas. . . Accompanied with a Plan of the City and Harbor*. The only copy of this promotional brochure and map that I have located is in the collection of the Historical Society of Pennsylvania.

35. The other maps referred to include the following: *Map of the City of Galveston*, copied from a survey by John D. Groesbeck in 1838 and printed by L. M. Bradford and Co. in 1854 (Map Room, Yale University Library); *Richardson's Map of Galveston City & Island*, surveyed by R. C. Trimble and William Lindsey, printed by Pessou and Simon, New Orleans, 1867 (Texas State Archives, Map Collection, No. 1686); *Map of the City of Galveston, Texas*, drawn by Jackson E. Labatt, printed by Strobridge and Company, Cincinnati, 1869 (Texas State Archives, Map Collection, No. 114a); and *John A. Caplen's Map of Galveston*, drawn by J. V. Smith, published by John A. Caplen, printed by Frey Stationery Co., St. Louis, 1890 (Division of Geography and Maps, Library of Congress).

36. Francis Moore, Jr., *Map and Description of Texas*. The volume contains several small views of missions in Texas and one of the town of Goliad, formerly La Bahía, in addition to H. S. Tanner's map of Texas in 1840.

37. W. W. Pratt (ed.), *The Journal of Francis Sheridan, 1839-1840*, Austin, 1954, 120.

38. The most important buildings surviving from this and later periods of growth are illustrated and described in Howard Barnstone, *The Galveston that Was*.

39. Muir, *Texas in 1837*, 12-13.

40. *Writings of Sam Houston*, II, 310, in a letter to Anna Raguet, February 8, 1839.

41. "Proprietor's Notice Concerning the City of Sabine, May 1, 1839," ibid., II, 312-313.

42. Lorecia East, *History and Progress of Jefferson County*, 69, 73; Webb, *Handbook of Texas*, II, 525. A reproduction of a Sabine City stock certificate appears in Sue Flanagan, *Sam Houston's Texas*, 53.

43. Ernest W. Winkler, "The Seat of Government of Texas: I. Temporary Location of the Seat of Government," 140-171. In writing this portion of the chapter on the founding of Austin, I have found helpful a research paper prepared under my direction at Cornell University by Steven E. Sher in 1970, "Austin, Texas and Lincoln, Nebraska."

44. Ernest W. Winkler, "The Seat of Government of Texas: II. The Permanent Location of the Seat of Government," 206.

45. Winkler, "Seat of Government, Permanent Location," gives the text of this interesting statute, 211-213, 225-227.

46. The text of the report appears in ibid., 217-220. The second paragraph states that title had been acquired "as per the Deed of the Sheriff of Bastrop County bearing date March 1839, and per the relinquishments of Logan Vandever, James Rogers, G. D. Hancock, J. W. Herrall, and Aaron Burleson by Edward Burleson all under date of 7th March 1839." Condemnation proceedings to acquire land were held April 3, 1839, at a court convened in Bastrop for that purpose before a jury of six persons. Police Court Records of Bastrop County, County Clerk's Office, Bastrop, A, 51-53, as cited by Sam A. Suhler, "Stephen F. Austin and the City of Austin: An Anomaly," 280.

47. For descriptions in 1836 of a number of the towns shown on this map see Mary Austin Holley, *Texas*. Several of the towns are also mentioned in John R. Bartlett, *Personal Narrative of Explorations*. Frederick Law Olmsted recorded his impressions of Texas settlements in 1855 and 1856 in his *A Journey Through Texas*.

48. A year or two earlier Lamar had camped at the site of Austin while on a buffalo hunt. According to tradition, he looked out from the hill on which the capitol was to be built and remarked that "this should be the seat of future empire." Alex. W. Terrell, "The City of Austin from 1839 to 1865," 114. Whether this statement is legend or not, Lamar evidently did instruct the commissioners to examine this location before they left for their exploration of the region. Two days after the commission was elected a reporter at Houston wrote the editor of the Matagorda newspaper that "it appears to be the general impression here, at present, that the Colorado will be the favored river whose banks will be honored by the metropolis of Texas." Matagorda *Bulletin*, January 24, 1839, as quoted in Winkler, "Seat of Government, Permanent Location," 215-216. Winkler also quotes several of the newspaper editorials opposing as well as supporting the chosen site, 221-224.

49. This portion of the act is quoted in ibid., 225-227.

50. Waller to Lamar, May 23, 1839, *Papers of Mirabeau Buonaparte Lamar*, Charles Adams Gulick, Jr., Winnie Allen, Katherine Elliott, and Harriet Smither (eds.), II, 588. While Waller's bond as agent is dated April 12, he had received a letter from Lamar's private secretary on March 2 informing him that the president would appoint him agent and wished to speak to him about his duties as soon as possible. Winkler, "Seat of Government, Permanent Location." Quoting a letter in Seat of Government Papers, manuscript in the Texas State Library.

Waller had applied for the position by a letter dated February 5, 1839. *Lamar Papers*, ii, 436.

51. The plans of Louisville and Milledgeville were first brought to my attention by Joan N. Sears in a research paper prepared in 1969 under my direction at Cornell University, "Brunswick, Milledgeville, Macon, Columbus—Four Towns Founded by the State of Georgia." Lamar's associations with these two towns are summarized in Webb, *Handbook of Texas*, ii, 13. The tradition of public initiative in the planning of capital cities in America has not been adequately explored. Chapter XII describes how Lincoln, Nebraska, was created under procedures similar to those used at Austin. Other state capitals planned under public sponsorship include Columbia, S.C.; Raleigh, N.C.; Jackson, Miss.; Tallahassee, Fla.; Columbus, Ohio; Indianapolis, Ind.; and Jefferson City, Mo., all prior to the founding of Austin. In the colonial era, Annapolis and Williamsburg were founded in the same manner as the capitals of Maryland and Virginia. The capital of Virginia was transferred to Richmond and the size of that existing town more than doubled with the planning under state supervision of an entirely new portion of the community. Iowa City, the territorial and first state capital of Iowa, was similarly founded under public sponsorship. The Texas legislation providing for the development of a new town as the seat of government on land acquired for that purpose was thus not a novel venture but one firmly rooted in American tradition.

52. In the Texas State Archives, Map 926B, *City of Austin and Vicinity*, shows the boundaries of the entire tract acquired by the commission. It also shows an outline plan of the city on its 640-acre plot. Capitol Square appears only four blocks from the river, with three tiers of blocks on either side, and only one tier of blocks separating it from the northern boundary. This plat is signed by W. H. Sandusky, identified as "Draughtsman," and is dated 1839. This drawing may represent a first attempt by Waller to carry out some version of the plan that I have suggested was prepared by him and Lamar before Waller left Houston.

53. Waller suggested naming the streets leading from the Colorado for the rivers of Texas. He proposed the name of Colorado Avenue for what became Congress Avenue. The cross-streets he proposed to identify by number, and it may have been Lamar who substituted the names of trees. Waller to Lamar, July 11, 1839, *Lamar Papers*, iii, 41. Eventually the names of trees were abandoned, and the streets were assigned numbers.

54. Columbia *Telegraph*, July 31, 1839, as quoted in Winkler, "Seat of Government, Permanent Location," 231.

55. Buildings built by Waller with block and lot numbers are listed in ibid., 231-232 from information in a report issued on November 28, 1840, by the acting secretary of the treasury.

56. Ibid., 229.

57. Houston *Morning Star*, August 13, 1839 and Houston *Intelligencer*, as quoted in the Colorado *Gazette*, September 28, the text of which appears in Winkler, "Seat of Government, Permanent Location," 234.

58. The full account of the ceremonies as printed in the Austin City *Gazette* for October 30 appears in ibid., 234-240. It must have been something of an understatement to say that after this marathon of dining, drinking, and speaking that began at 3 p.m. that "about 8 p.m. . . . the company . . . dispersed; all, apparently, highly pleased with the entertainment of the day."

59. Ibid., 240-245; Terrell, "City of Austin," 123-125.

60. The referenda of 1850 and 1872 and the constitutional provision of 1876 are reviewed in Ralph Wooster, "Texans Choose a Capital Site," 351-357.

61. Austin's gloomy prospects during these difficult years are described in Wheeler, *City's Crown*, 25-29.

62. Olmstead, *Journey Through Texas*, 110.

63. Aline Rothe, "Swartwout, Texas," in Webb, *Handbook of Texas*, ii, 694.

64. Sally M. Lentz, "Marshall, Texas," in ibid., 148.

65. Fehrenbach, *Lone Star*, 283-284.

66. The principal work on the Castro colony is Julia Nott Waugh, *Castro-Ville and Henri Castro, Empresario*. See also Amelia W. Williams, "Castro, Henri"; Curtis Bishop, "Castro's Colony"; and Ruth Curry Lawler, "Castroville, Texas," in Webb, *Handbook of Texas*, i, 308-390; and U.S. Writers' Program, *Texas*, 605-608.

67. In my treatment of this episode in the settlement of Texas I have relied chiefly on the following: Oscar Haas, *History of New Braunfels and Comal County, Texas, 1844-1946*, Austin, 1968; Rudolph L. Biesele, *History of the German Settlements in Texas, 1831-1861*, and "Early Times in New Braunfels and Comal County," 75-92; and Gilbert Giddings Benjamin, *The Germans in Texas: A Study in Immigration*. I have also found useful an unpublished research paper prepared under my direction at Cornell University by Deborah F. Pokinski in 1971, "The Development of the County Courthouse Town Plan: Town Planning on the Texas Frontier, 1836-1860."

68. Ferdinand Roemer, *Roemer's Texas, 1845 to 1847*, 291. Near Fredericksburg there were at least three other hamlets or villages in which German colonists settled: Sisterdale, Boerne, and Comfort. Fehrenbach, *Lone Star*, 294.

69. There are at least two other views of New Braunfels. One is a German lithograph panorama of the town in 1847, an impression of which is in the Prince Maximilian Archives of the University of Texas Library in Austin. The other is a small steel engraving, a copy of which is in the author's collection. This also was published in Germany, probably ca. 1855. It was the New Braunfels of this period that Frederick Law Olmsted described on his visit early in 1856. "The main street of the town, which we soon entered upon, was very wide—three times as wide, in effect, as Broadway in New York. The houses, with which it was thickly lined on each side for a mile, were small, low cottages, of no pretensions to elegance, yet generally looking neat and comfortable. Many were furnished with verandahs and gardens, and the greater part were either stuccoed or painted. There were many workshops of mechanics and small stores, with signs oftener in English than in German." Olmsted, *Journey Through Texas*, 142-143.

70. Davis Bitton, "Mormons in Texas: The Ill-Fated Lyman Wight Colony, 1844-1858," 5-26.

71. I have translated and quoted a portion of this description in John W. Reps, *The Making of Urban America*, Princeton, 1965, 465.

72. Odie B. Faulk, "The Icarian Colony in Texas, 1848: A Problem in Historiography," 132-140. The problem in historiography is that very few accounts of Cabet's venture exist, and they all seem to disagree on even the most elementary facts.

73. George H. Santerre, *White Cliffs of Dallas*, 27-33. Considerant had spent some time in 1853 with the leading American follower of Fourier, Arthur Brisbane, and lived for six weeks at the principal Fourier community, the North American Phalanx at Red Bank, New Jersey. Traveling to Texas, he met Bryan and noted the attractive site a few miles from his little community. On Considerant's return to France he published his *Au Texas*, organized the European American Society of Colonization, raised funds for his colony, and recruited his followers. He sent François Cantagrel to Texas in 1854 to purchase the necessary land.

74. Santerre, *White Cliffs*, 36-37, includes a full list of the colonists with the occupations of most of them. Several are listed as agriculturist, orchardist, agronomist, or gardener. Other occupations included lime manufacturer, bookkeeper, distiller, designer, realtor, jeweler, tailor, mason, butcher, grocer, cooper, barber, brewer, educator, naturalist, and scholar. For another study of this settlement project see William J. and Margaret F. Hammond, *La Réunion, a French Settlement in Texas*.

75. For a contemporary account of life at La Réunion written by a Polish visitor see Marion Moore Coleman (trans. and ed.), "New Light on La Réunion," 41-68, 137-154. Unfortunately, this extended report of activities in the colony provides no information about its highly unusual town plan, a feature it shares with the works of modern historians of the venture.

76. George H. Santerre, *Dallas' First Hundred Years, 1856-1956*.

77. A redrawn plan of the military post may be found in Oliver Knight, *Fort Worth: Outpost on the Trinity*, 25. See also Herbert M. Hart, *Old Forts of the Far West*, 14, for a similar drawing.

78. The background of this referendum and its sequel in 1860 confirming Fort Worth's position as the seat of government of Tarrant County is described in Knight, *Fort Worth*, 40-45.

79. Roger N. Conger, *A Pictorial History of Waco with a Reprint of Highlights of Waco History*, 5-12.

80. Memoir of Auguste Frétellière, as quoted in Charles Ramsdell, *San Antonio, a Historical and Pictorial Guide*, 34.

81. Olmsted, *Journey Through Texas*, 149-150.

VI · NORTHERN CALIFORNIA: URBAN PLANNING AND DEVELOPMENT IN THE POST-HISPANIC YEARS

1. The methods by which Spaniards and Mexicans acquired land titles and the procedures established after 1846 for processing these title claims are de-scribed in Hubert Howe Bancroft, *History of California*, VI, 529-548. The difficulties and uncertainties over land titles as seen by a contemporary observer can be found in Bayard Taylor, *Eldorado, or Adventures in the Path of Empire*, 139-143. For a broad view of the problem with California land titles and how they were resolved see Lawrence Kinnard, *History of the Greater San Francisco Bay Region*, I, 430-445. A more recent treatment is Paul Gates, "The California Land Act of 1851," 395-430.

2. Some aspects of local government during the interim period between military conquest and statehood are treated in Bancroft, *California*, V, 616-686.

3. The text of Bartlett's proclamation appears in Clarence M. Wooster, "Brief History of San Francisco Lands," 8. O'Farrell and his work are the subject of Helen Putnam Van Sicklen's "Jasper O'Farrell: His Survey of San Francisco," 85-100. Correspondence between Bartlett and O'Farrell relating to the surveys of San Francisco can be found in ibid., 98-99. O'Farrell also surveyed the town of Sonoma in 1848. Since the process of publication began on this book, two splendid studies have appeared with much important information and interpretive material dealing with the early years of San Francisco's growth. See Roger W. Lotchin, *San Francisco, 1845-1856: From Hamlet to City*; and Gunther Barth, *Instant Cities: Urbanization and the Rise of San Francisco and Denver*.

4. Edwin Bryant, *What I Saw in California*, 323-324.

5. The town in 1846-47 was little changed from its condition in 1843. See the reproduction of a manuscript view of San Francisco drawn in that year with an identification of its buildings in Bruno Fritzsche, "San Francisco in 1843: A Key to Dr. Sandels' Drawing," 3-13.

6. As quoted in Van Sicklen, "O'Farrell," 92. Conditions in the conveyances made by Bartlett also specified that the new owner was required to build a house and to fence the lot within one year. For this and other information concerning land titles in San Francisco see Alfred Wheeler, *Land Titles in San Francisco, and the Laws Affecting the Same*. The real estate boom in San Francisco during the early years of American administration is described in Bruno Fritzsche, "San Francisco, 1846-1848: The Coming of the Land Speculator," 17-34.

7. O'Farrell's survey of 1847 as copied in 1849 is reproduced in Mel Scott, *The San Francisco Bay Area: A Metropolis in Perspective*, 25.

8. M. G. Upton, "The Plan of San Francisco," 132-133, 137. Upton was under the impression that Vioget alone was responsible for the San Francisco grid street pattern and that O'Farrell had attempted to introduce a system better adapted to the site. I have found no evidence to indicate this was the case. Upton's article was one of the first serious critiques of a western city plan, but it contained some humorous passages as well. The author visualized Vioget "endeavoring to clamber up the rough sides of Telegraph Hill, on his way home . . . slowly making his way on all-fours, and fearful of broken bones and a cracked crown," arriving finally "at the corner of Montgomery and Vallejo Streets." In another part of the essay Upton observed that "for the topography with which . . . [Vioget] had to deal he manifested a contempt entirely proper in a person engaged in an engineering romance," 132-133.

9. Taylor, *Eldorado*, 42-43.

10. Ibid., 152-153, 226. Taylor observed that the city still retained some frontier character. December rains created certain problems: "The mud in the streets became little short of fathomless, and it was with difficulty that the mules could drag their empty wagons through. . . . The plank sidewalks, in the lower part of the city, ran along the brink of pools and quicksands, which the street inspector and his men vainly endeavored to fill by haulling cartloads of chaparral and throwing sand on the top; in a day or two the gulf was as deep as ever. . . . One could not walk any distance without getting at least ankle-deep." Ibid., 229.

11. Frank Soulé, John H. Givon, and James Nisbet, *The Annals of San Francisco*, 173, 226, 244, 413.

12. E. Gould Buffum, *Six Months in the Gold Mines*, 111, 121.

13. J. D. Borthwick, *Three Years in California*, Edinburgh, 1857, as quoted in Lula May Garrett, "San Francisco in 1851 as Described by Eyewitnesses," 255.

14. Scott, *San Francisco Bay Area*, 42-43.

15. Soulé, *Annals of San Francisco*, 160.

16. Samuel Bowles, *Across the Continent . . . in the Summer of 1865*, 289-290. Bowles commented that "if but the early San Franciscans had thought of Boston, and followed the cow-paths, what a unique, nice town they would have made of this!" (288-289).

17. The two streets were Alvarado and Castro (now Tyler) running roughly parallel to the old Calle Principal leading to the waterfront. William Robert Garner, *Letters from California, 1846-1847*, 193-194.

18. Ignacio Esquer and Ambrosio Gomez, August 27, 1849, California Archives, *Unbound Documents*, 181-182, as cited by Daniel Garr, "Hispanic Colonial Settlement in California," 142-143.

19. An early statement of the problems and possibilities of historic conservation in Monterey is Aubrey Neasham, "The Preservation of Historic Monterey," 215-224.

20. Some of the details of the Campbell survey are described in Frederic Hall, *The History of San José and Surroundings*, 176-178. Hall stated that this drawing was "on file in the office of the city authorities, but so worn that it is rather difficult to wholly trace the survey." I have not had an opportunity to examine this plat.

21. Hall was unaware that Lyman drew this plan in 1847. In *San José* he describes a second Lyman survey of 1848. This differs from the first only by the addition of three more tiers of blocks extending the grid northeast of 8th Street. I am indebted to Mr. Sanford Getreu, Planning Director of San José, for sending me a copy of this second Lyman survey for examination in 1972, together with several other copies of old maps and views of the city.

22. Hall, *San José*, 181-182, 185.

23. Taylor, *Eldorado*, 52-53, 149.

24. This transaction was to cause the city much trouble in 1852. Those signing the note claimed that in satisfaction for it they were entitled to ownership of all remaining *pueblo* lands. A full account of this appears in Hall, *San José*, 206,335-347, 474-479.

25. The conduct of what was known as "The Legislature of a Thousand Drinks" and its effect on conditions in San José is briefly described in Oscar Osborn Winther, "The Story of San José, 1777-1869," 152-154.

26. Winther, "Story of San José," 157-159; Hall, *San José*, 396-414.

27. Ibid., 258, 262.

28. Winther, "Story of San José," 165, citing Bayard Taylor's estimate of the population in 1860 as 2,500 and the San José *Mercury* census of 1861 showing a population of 3,340.

29. San José *Mercury*, November 5, 1863, as quoted in Winther, "Story of San José," 167.

30. Ibid., 167-169.

31. An Act to Ascertain and Settle the Private Land Claims in the State of California. 9 *U.S. Statutes at Large* 631. Chap. XLI, Public Acts of the 31st Congress, 2nd Sess. Section 14 of the statute dealt with what doubtless appeared to be the simple issue of municipal land claims. It provided that the existence of any city, town, or village on July 7, 1846 should be considered *prima facie* evidence of ownership of all land within its borders. Individuals who could prove they had received land from a municipality would, of course, be confirmed in their title, but all other land was assumed to be part of the municipal domain.

32. Hall, *San José*, 480-483, contains the text of the surveyor's field notes for the exterior boundaries as shown on Figure 6.14. The area is given as "one hundred and one and seventy-six one-hundredths" square miles.

33. H. C. Hopkins, *History of San Diego: Its Pueblo Lands & Water*, 227. The author at the time this book appeared was deputy city attorney in charge of land title litigation.

34. W. W. Robinson, *Maps of Los Angeles*, contains a reproduction of the official boundary survey as confirmed to the city. See Map 7, pp. 40-41.

35. For a reproduction of a map showing the boundaries of the San Francisco *pueblo* lands and the military reservations and *ranchos* contained within the municipality see Scott, *San Francisco Bay Area*, 42. An exhaustive study of the pueblo land issue in San Francisco containing the text or lengthy extracts from pertinent documents is John W. Dwinelle, *The Colonial History of the City of San Francisco*. Dwinelle represented the city in the case, and the first portion of the volume contains his brief.

36. Scott, *San Francisco Bay Area*, 51-53. McLaren served as superintendent until his death at the age of 96. He was a revered figure in San Francisco and steadfastly defended the park against attempted encroachments over the years. It was he who stabilized the sandy soil by the use of special beach grasses imported from Europe and shrubs brought from Australia. U.S. Writers' Program, *San Francisco: The Bay and Its Cities*, 330-331.

37. Hopkins, *San Diego*, 261.

38. Charles Dwight Willard, *The Herald's History of Los Angeles City*, 264. Willard echoed a similar lament by a Chicago historian writing in 1892 about the quick and casual sale of the 640-acre school tract in that city in 1832. This land in the heart of Chicago came into the hands of public officials as the school section reserved in each township of the federal domain. The land brought less than

$40,000 in 1832. It was estimated to have a value of $100,000,000 in 1892. See Joseph Kirkland, *The Story of Chicago*, 116. The full story of the disposal of urban public domains in the United States remains to be written.

39. Henry George, "What the Railroad Will Bring Us," 303.

40. Scott, *San Francisco Bay Area*, 29. Scott states that the land had been subdivided by Dr. John Townsend and Cornelius de Boom as early as 1849.

41. Olmsted, Vaux and Company, *Report upon a Projected Improvement of the Estate of the College of California, at Berkeley, near Oakland*, 19, 23-24.

42. Scott, *San Francisco Bay Area*, 35. For studies of Kellersberger's plan of Oakland see Jack J. Studer, "Julius Kellersberger, A Swiss as Surveyor and City Planner in California, 1851-1857," 3-14; and Studer, "The First Map of Oakland, California: An Historical Speculation as Solution to an Enigma," 59-71. For a more extended account of Oakland's founding and early development see Lois Rather, *Oakland's Image: A History of Oakland, California*.

43. Brief histories of Oakland, Brooklyn, and Alameda can be found in Bancroft, *California*, VI, 475-479. For a more detailed treatment consult Kinnard, *San Francisco Bay Region*, I, 482-502.

44. Palo Alto's plan was a rigid gridiron—the work of Timothy Hopkins, foster son of Stanford's associate in his railroad enterprises, Mark Hopkins. The campus plan by Frederick Law Olmstead was far more imaginative. A reproduction of the Olmsted firm's plan for the campus and adjoining residential district appears in Albert Fein, *Frederick Law Olmsted and the American Environmental Tradition*, Figure 5, following p. 69. The plan is discussed and illustrated with a map of the Palo Alto area in the mid-1890's in Scott, *San Francisco Bay Area*, 82-83.

45. The first plat of the town is in the land records of Sonoma County, Map Book 1, p. 1. The designation of the public square as a *plaza* indicated the lingering influence of Spanish terms in the early period of American development in California.

46. Solomon P. Elias, *Stories of Stanislaus*, 44. For other brief accounts of the founding of Modesto see Bancroft, *California*, VI, 514; and U.S. Writers' Program, *California: A Guide to the Golden State*, 443.

47. Elias, *Stories of Stanislaus*, 43, quoting the Tuolumne *City News* for November 25, 1870.

48. Elias, *Stories of Stanislaus*, 258-259, 58.

49. Paul E. Vandor, *History of Fresno County, California*, I, 152-153.

50. Ibid., I, 155.

51. Diary of R. W. Riggs, as quoted in ibid., I., 355.

52. Ibid., I, 361.

VII · MINING CAMPS AND TOWNS OF CALIFORNIA AND NEVADA

1. Joseph Warren Revere, *Naval Duty in California*, 59. There are many other similar descriptions. See, for example, Edwin Bryant, *What I Saw in California . . . in 1846, 1847*, 267.

2. Sutter's description is quoted in Erwin G. Gudde, *Sutter's Own Story*, 65-66. The modern reconstruction of Sutter's Fort on the original site is substan-

tially smaller than it was in Sutter's day. A detailed plan of the fort was published in Germany in 1848 as an illustration in Heinrich Künzel, *Obercalifornien*. An English translation by Anthony and Max Knight, with an introduction by Carroll D. Hall, is available: *Upper California*, San Francisco, 1967. The plan is reproduced on p. 18.

3. Oscar Lewis, *Sutter's Fort: Gateway to the Gold Fields*, 153.

4. Theressa Gay, *James W. Marshall: The Discoverer of California Gold: A Biography*, 1967.

5. The date of the founding of Sutterville or Suttersville is given by Lewis (*Sutter's Fort*, 162) as 1844. A more recent history of Sacramento states that it was founded in 1846. See Aubrey Neasham and James E. Henley, *The City of the Plain: Sacramento in the Nineteenth Century*, 11.

6. Gay, *Marshall*, 127-137.

7. The exact date of the discovery is a matter of controversy. I have followed Gay (*Marshall*, 148-152) in giving the date as January 24. Some years after the fact, Marshall stated that it was January 19.

8. See the text of the letter from Col. R. B. Mason to Sutter, March 5, 1848, in Lewis, *Sutter's Fort*, 151.

9. Bennett's trip to Monterey is described in ibid., 151-152, a passage also containing the quotation of Sutter's letter to Vallejo.

10. The texts of both news accounts are given in Gay, *Marshall*, 177.

11. Ibid., 184-185; Lewis, *Sutter's Fort*, 155-157.

12. San Francisco *Californian*, September 23, 1848, as quoted in *History of Amador County, California*, 55.

13. The text of the letter is quoted at length in Gay, *Marshall*, 185-186.

14. Ibid., 196-199.

15. For the location of some of these early strikes see Rodman W. Paul, *California Gold: The Beginning of Mining in the Far West*, 36-39.

16. For the early growth of Coloma see Gay, *Marshall*, 226-246.

17. William S. Greever, *The Bonanza West: The Story of the Western Mining Rushes, 1848-1900*, 10.

18. U. S. Department of the Interior, National Park Service, *Prospector, Cowhand, and Sodbuster*, 8-9. This source gives the total movement of persons in 1849 as 77,500. The largest number, 55,000, arrived by land, most of them via the Platte River route to South Pass and then across the Great Basin and through the Sierra passes. Ten thousand persons were estimated to have crossed the continent by southern trails, skirting the southern end of the Rockies. Another 7,500 went by boat to the Isthmus of Panama, crossed to Panama City on the Pacific Coast, and completed their trip by boat northward along the coast of Mexico and California to San Francisco.

19. Paul, *California Gold*, 24-25.

20. The pioneering study of this aspect of California's mining camps is Charles Howard Shinn's *Mining Camps: A Study in American Frontier Government*, published first in 1885. It is now available with a useful introduction by Joseph Henry Jackson, New York, 1948.

21. Bayard Taylor, *Eldorado, or Adventures in the Path of Empire*, 197. See also a

similar and earlier comment in the same work in which Taylor concluded with these words: "The capacity of a people for self-government was never so triumphantly illustrated. Never, perhaps, was there a community formed of more unpropitious elements; yet from all this seeming chaos grew a harmony beyond what the most sanguine apostle of Progress could have expected" (p. 78).

22. Note by Carlo M. De Ferrari, in Thomas Robertson Stoddart, *Annals of Tuolumne County*, 104; Edna Bryan Buckbee, *The Saga of Old Tuolumne*, 30.

23. Ibid., 181-182.

24. Ibid., 198-199.

25. For a copy of a deed transferring property by reference to the map see Stoddart, *Tuolumne County*, 110.

26. Ibid., 102.

27. Rev. Daniel B. Woods, *Sixteen Months at the Gold Diggings*, New York, 1851, 121, as quoted in Paul, *California Gold*, 73.

28. Elizabeth Gray Potter, "Columbia—'Gem of the Southern Mines,' " 267-270; California State Department of Parks and Recreation, *Columbia State Historical Park*, undated leaflet.

29. Shinn, *Mining Camps*, 201.

30. A superb pictorial record of Grass Valley and Nevada City is Jim Morley and Doris Foley, *Gold Cities*.

31. Mark Twain, *Roughing It*, 435.

32. The circumstances giving rise to the name of Hangtown are mentioned in one of the best of the many accounts of early mining days in California. It is particularly useful because of the large number of lithograph illustrations from drawings by G. V. Cooper, including a view of Hangtown when it consisted of only a few cabins. See John M. Letts, *A Pictorial View of California*, 108-109 and the illustration opposite p. 112.

33. Gay, *Marshall*, 197, citing a letter by William T. Sherman to a friend in Monterey, August 25, 1848, manuscript papers of William T. Sherman, Library of Congress, II.

34. Lewis, *Sutter's Fort*, 44-49.

35. Ibid., 166-167.

36. Ibid., 170-171. Burnett received one-fourth of the gross receipts derived from land sales at Sacramento in payment for handling all of John Jr.'s legal affairs and conducting land sales. See his own account of this transaction and other aspects of his role in promoting Sacramento in Peter H. Burnett, *An Old California Pioneer*. According to Burnett, "The prices for lots in the same locality were fixed and uniform; and I made it an inflexible rule not to lower the prices for speculators, thus preventing a monopoly of the lots. I discouraged the purchase of more than four lots by any one person." (p. 175). McCarver's career as a town planner and frontier promoter is reviewed in Michael B. Husband, "Morton M. McCarver: An Iowa Entrepreneur in the Far West," 241-254. According to Husband, the two Sutters had accepted McCarver's proposition to manage the townsite promotion but later engaged Burnett to serve in his place. McCarver had earlier participated in the planning of Burlington and McCar-

verstown, Iowa, and, with Burnett, the town of Linnton, Oregon. Many years later he was to plan the town of Commencement City in Washington, a settlement that was ultimately embraced by Tacoma. McCarver's role in securing this location as the western terminus of the Northern Pacific Railroad is described in Chapter VII.

37. The senior Sutter was outraged at his son's action in planning Sacramento rather than promoting Sutterville. Many years later Hubert Howe Bancroft interviewed Sutter at Lititz, Pennsylvania, where Sutter had retired. The old man stated, "Had I not been snowed in at Coloma Sacramento never, never, would have been built." Bancroft, *History of California*, VI, 447. Sutterville was humorously described by John Letts when he saw it in July, 1849: "We . . . walked a mile back from the *town* to view '*Capitol Hill*,' the *anticipated* site of the State House. Although we did not break ground for the cornerstone, we were among the first to know the *precise spot*. The *town* . . . contained three houses, visible to the *natural* eye, but to the eye of the worthy proprietor's imagination, it numbered many thousands." Letts, *Pictorial View of California*, 60. A view of the riverfront at Sutterville can be found opposite p. 59.

38. Bancroft, *California*, VI, 448; E. Gould Buffum, *Six Months in the Gold Mines*, 110-111.

39. Letts, *Pictorial View*, 6k, 132.

40. Bancroft, *California*, VI, 453-454; 457-458.

41. For a survey of architectural development in Sacramento see Joseph Armstrong Baird, Jr., "Architectural Legacy of Sacramento: A Study of 19th Century Style," 193-207.

42. Earl Ramey, "The Beginnings of Marysville," 213.

43. Taylor, *Eldorado*, 60, 76.

44. Ibid., 76; Buffum, *Six Months in the Gold Mines*, 155.

45. Note by Carlo De Ferrari in Stoddart, *Tuolumne County*, 111. The abortive settlement of Toualome City should not be confused with the community of Tuolumne in the Sierra mining area near Sonora.

46. Buffum, *Six Months in the Gold Mines*, 154.

47. Associated with Hammond were James Blair and William T. Sherman. Both were young army officers who, like Hammond, had been sent to California at the time of the Mexican War but whose peacetime military duties were not excessively burdensome. Sherman recalled that for running "the preliminary surveys of the city of 'New York of the Pacific,' " each of the three surveyors received "five hundred dollars and ten or fifteen lots." Sherman "sold enough lots to make up another five hundred dollars, and let the balance go; for the city . . . never came to anything. Indeed, cities at the time were being projected by speculators all round the bay and all over the country." William T. Sherman, *Memoirs*, II, 73-74.

48. New York *Tribune*, August 30, 1849.

49. The text of the advertisement appears in full in Ernest A. Wiltsee, "The City of New York of the Pacific," 26.

50. Taylor, *Eldorado*, 162.

51. Letts, *Pictorial View*, 57. Buffum, in his *Six Months in the Gold Mines*, 150-151, on the other hand, strongly praised the site and the city plan.

52. *History of Solano County*, 169.

53. A copy of a plan of Benicia showing this revised design is reproduced in Reps, *The Making of Urban America*, Figure 185. I am indebted to Margaretta Jean Darnall, whose unpublished paper, "Town Planning of the State Capitals of California During the American Period," prepared under my direction for a graduate seminar at Cornell University in 1969, brought to my attention the earlier plan of Benicia that I have reproduced here. Her paper has also been helpful to me in my treatment of the towns of Vallejo, Sacramento, and San José.

54. A manuscript survey of this installation in 1856 can be found in the Fortifications Map File, Records of the Office of the Chief of Engineers, Record Group 77, Cartographic Branch, National Archives.

55. Bancroft, *California*, VI, 473.

56. See, for example, Taylor, *Eldorado*, 161-162; and Buffum, *Six Months in the Gold Mines*, 28, 150. William Heath Davis, on the other hand, correctly foresaw that Benicia's prospects were limited. For his interesting account of how the promoters of Benicia attempted to lure Davis and his San Francisco business enterprises to the new city see William Heath Davis, *Seventy-Five Years in California*, 316. Davis came to California permanently in 1838 after two visits in 1822 and 1831. In 1845 he moved from Monterey to San Francisco, then called Yerba Buena, and became one of its business and civic leaders.

57. That irrepressible comic genius of early California, George Horatio Derby (writing under the pseudonym of John Phoenix), was one. He described how he inquired the price of "lot No. 97, block 16,496—situated as per map, in the very centre of the swamp." When he was informed that " 'it would be held at about three thousand dollars,' he shuddered—and retired." John Phoenix, *Phoenixiana*, 82.

58. Bancroft, *California*, VI, 473.

59. An earlier view of Benicia in 1853 showing the town from the west at water level is in U.S. War Department, *Reports of Explorations and Surveys, to Ascertain the Most Practicable and Economical Route for a Railroad . . .*, V, *California Geology*. It shows only 36 buildings clustered in two widely separated locations, and its appearance could scarcely have helped the efforts of the town's promoters to attract new residents.

60. Bancroft, *California*, VI, 475.

61. John Russell Bartlett, *Personal Narrative of Explorations . . .*, II, 14.

62. A plan of Vallejo in 1868 can be found among the maps in the California Section, California State Library, Sacramento. It shows two additions to the city, one on each side of the original plat. They are also gridiron plans laid out with streets roughly parallel and perpendicular to the water and are thus turned approximately 45° from the orientation of Vallejo's first streets. These additions were almost certainly speculative in nature and laid out well in advance of need. They do not appear on the view of the city in 1871, and a modern map of Vallejo indicates that only small portions of these areas were developed as planned.

63. The value of annual production from 1848 to 1873 is tabulated in Paul, *California Gold*, 118, 241.

64. Effie Mona Mack, *Nevada*, 193-204; Greever, *Bonanza West*, 87-90.

65. Ibid., 90-92. Comstock sold out early and in August received only $11,000 for his one-sixth share.

66. Extracts from the two news accounts are quoted in Mack, *Nevada*, 208-209.

67. Eliot Lord, *Comstock Mining and Miners*, 63-64. A conflicting date is given in Hubert Howe Bancroft, *History of Nevada, Colorado, and Wyoming, 1540-1888*. Citing the Carson *Tribune*, August, 1870, Bancroft states that "O. H. Pierson laid off the town in lots some time in July," 108, n 33. If this is true, Comstock and his associates arranged for the first town lot survey before they sold their interests.

68. J. Ross Browne, *A Peep at Washoe and Washoe Revisited*, 64-66.

69. The Virginia City correspondent for the San Francisco *Evening Bulletin*, October 17, 1860, as cited in Lord, *Comstock Mining*, 94, listed the following business, office, and industrial activities: "38 stores, general merchandise, 4 cigar and tobacco stores, 3 druggists' stores, 2 stationers' stores, 2 fruit stores, 25 saloons, 9 restaurants, 7 boarding houses, 1 hotel (the International), 4 butchers' shops, 9 bakers' shops, 7 blacksmiths' shops, 3 tinsmiths' shops, 1 gunsmith's shop, 7 shoemakers' and cobblers' shops, 1 saddler's shop, 2 carpenter shops, 1 paint shop, 1 tailor, 3 watchmakers, 2 barbers, 6 physicians' offices, 1 dentist, 8 law offices, 2 express offices, 2 assay offices, 1 surveyor's office, 5 brokers' offices (agents and brokers), 1 auction and commission house, 1 dressmaker's shop, 4 machine-sewers' rooms, 10 livery stables and feedstores, 10 laundries, 1 bathhouse, 1 theatre, 1 music hall, 1 school-house, 1 post office, 9 quartz mills, 5 lumber yards."

70. Greever, *Bonanza West*, 95.

71. Twain, *Roughing It*, 304-305.

72. Virginia City received its first charter from the legislature of Utah Territory in 1861. It was incorporated under an act of Nevada Territory late in 1862, a charter substantially modified in February, 1864. Lord, *Comstock Mining*, 198.

73. J. Ross Brown revisited Virginia City in 1863 before this survey was published and probably before earlier street lines had become well established. His amusing description at that time follows: "The city lies on a rugged slope, and is singularly diversified in its uprisings and downfallings. It is difficult to determine, by any system of observation or measurement, upon what principle it was laid out. My impression is that it never was laid out at all, but followed the dips, spurs, and angles of the immortal Comstock. Some of the streets run straight enough; others seem to dodge about at acute angles in search of an open space, as miners explore the subterranean regions in search of a lead. The cross streets must have been forgotten in the original plan—if ever there was a plan about the eccentric city. Sometimes they happen accidentally at the most unexpected points; and sometimes they don't happen at all where you are sure to require them. A man in a hurry to get from the upper slope of the town to any opposite point below must try it underground or over the roofs of the houses, or take the

715

NOTES TO
PAGES 219-228

customary circuit of half a mile. Every body seems to have built wherever he could secure a lot. The two main streets, it must be admitted, are so far regular as to follow pretty nearly the direction of the Comstock lode. On the lower slope, or plateau, the town, as viewed from any neighboring eminence, presents much the appearance of a vast number of shingle-roofs shaken down at random, like a jumbled pack of cards. All the streets are narrow, except where there are but few houses, and there they are wide enough at present." *Peep at Washoe*, 179-181.

74. Lord, *Comstock Mining*, 94, 198.

75. Ibid., 93, 199.

76. Albert D. Richardson, *Our New States and Territories*, 44.

77. Mack, *Nevada*, 213-214.

78. Stanley W. Paher, *Nevada Ghost Towns and Mining Camps*, 466. Paher's massive compilation of pictorial material on Nevada mining towns, accompanied by an informative text, is a valuable source of information and ranks as one of the best of the scores of works published on western mining communities.

79. Richardson, *New States and Territories*, 42-43. Another and similar description of Austin in 1865 is in Samuel Bowles, *Across the Continent . . . in the Summer of 1865*, 14-143. A view of Austin can be found in another work by Bowles: *Our New West*, Hartford, 1869, 272. This may be compared to a photograph of the town in the late 1860s in Paher, *Neveda Ghost Towns*, 167.

80. Ibid., 31.

81. Mack, *Nevada*, 229.

82. The complicated story of the Sutro Tunnel is summarized in Greever, *Bonanza West*, 116-120.

VIII · URBAN GROWTH AND EXPANSION IN SOUTHERN CALIFORNIA DURING THE POST-HISPANIC ERA

1. Santa Barbara Archivo, 87-88, as quoted in Daniel Garr, "Hispanic Colonial Settlement in California," 195.

2. Yda A. Storke, *A Memorial and Biographical History of the Counties of Santa Barbara, San Luis Obispo and Ventura, California*, 63.

3. A helpful guide to the buildings and streets of Old Town in San Diego with old photographs and a detailed location map is Orion M. Zink, "Places and People in Old Town, Part I—Places in Old Town," 3-21.

4. Andrew F. Rolle, "William Heath Davis and the Founding of American San Diego," 33-34. The Middletown tract was purchased by a number of residents of the area, including Cave J. Couts, Juan Bandini, and José María Estudillo, Davis's brother-in-law. They made no effort to develop the tract, and its design with the several plazas that can be seen in Figure 3 was later somewhat modified. Elizabeth C. MacPhail, *The Story of New San Diego and of its Founder, Alonzo E. Horton*, 16; H. C. Hopkins, *History of San Diego: Its Pueblo Lands and Water*, 189.

5. John Russell Bartlett, *Personal Narrative of Explorations*, II, 97.

6. Rolle, "Davis," 35-42; MacPhail, *New San Diego*, 10-12. For the history of the military depot in San Diego see George Ruhlen, "San Diego Barracks," 7-15. According to Ruhlen, the military lands included all of blocks 31 and 39 and half of block 18. The post was vacated in 1866, reoccupied during 1869-71, abandoned once again, and reactivated in 1876. The National Guard armory now occupies the old barracks site on block 31.

7. MacPhail, *New San Diego*, 7-9, 13-15; Ward T. Donley, "Vision of Greatness (Alonzo E. Horton)," 21-26.

8. MacPhail, *New San Diego*, 41, 45. Conveyance of 5,000 acres of pueblo land to the San Diego and Los Angeles Railway Company on April 2, 1870, is briefly described in Hopkins, *San Diego*, 253.

9. San Diego *Union*, November 21, 1868, as quoted in Donley, "Vision of Greatness," 40. The first issue of the paper printed in Horton's town was that of June 30, 1870. Donley reproduces the editorials of that and the previous issue announcing the paper's move on p. 36.

10. While MacPhail in *New San Diego* credits Horton with the idea for the park, the initiative may have come from others. See Hopkins, *San Diego*, 319-324, where the author notes that E. W. Morse presented the petition to the trustees having jurisdiction over the public lands of the city. Hopkins indicates that Morse may have acted at Horton's request. Joshua Sloane, secretary of the board of trustees also played a prominent role in the project, and it was he who secured the passage of the act by the state legislature confirming the reservation. Hopkins, *San Diego*, 254.

11. Ord's contract from which the quoted portions are taken, together with extracts from council records relating to the survey, can be found in W. W. Robinson, "Story of Ord's Survey as Disclosed by the Los Angeles Archives," 121-131. See also, J. Gregg Layne, "Edward Otho Cresap Ord: Soldier and Surveyor," 139-142.

12. For the Spanish and English names of streets on the Ord survey see J. M. Guinn, "The Plan of Old Los Angeles and the Story of its Highways and Byways," 46-48. Derogatory comments on Ord's work by later Los Angeles County surveyors can be found in Robinson, "Ord Survey," 127-131. Among them is the following by Franz Lecouvreur in 1870: "This so called official map, is as utterly useless to the surveyor as so much waste paper." Lecouvreur noted that perhaps the original drawing, then vanished but once consisting of "several small sheets of paper cut into shapes to fit each other and pasted together" may have contained essential surveying data on its margins, Lecouvreur observed that if these had been cut away and destroyed, such an act "would certainly crown the stupidity of a full grown baboon." W. W. Robinson's elaborate study of old maps of Los Angeles and vicinity, *Maps of Los Angeles From Ord's Survey of 1849 to the End of the Boom of the Eighties*, is a mine of useful information on the city's growth.

13. J. M. Guinn, "From Pueblo to Ciudad: The Municipal and Territorial Expansion of Los Angeles," 220; Robinson, "Ord Survey," 126-127. The lots were located close to the existing developed area in blocks 4, 5, 7, and 8 in the south-

western district and blocks 32 and 34 in the northern district.

14. Robert M. Fogelson, *The Fragmented Metropolis*, 20.

15. This map was published about 1875 to show Ord's plan and the Hancock survey of 1853 plus the official survey of the municipal boundary in 1857. Two other drawings of the 35-acre parcels may be noted. One is an untitled and unsigned manuscript drawing of ca. 1860 measuring 56 inches by 60 inches in the History Division, Los Angeles County Museum of Natural History. The other is a manuscript survey reproduced in Robinson, *Maps of Los Angeles*, Number 8, p. 42, copied from a drawing by George Hansen, and recorded November 23, 1868, in Book 1 of Miscellaneous Records of Los Angeles County, pp. 463-464. The Hansen survey shows all or portions of only blocks 56 to 77 of the so-called Donation Lots. I have used the dimensions of streets and lots shown on this survey in my description of Hancock's plan appearing in the text.

16. The struggles of the city for railroad connections are described in Remi A. Nadeau, *City-Makers*, 71-87; and Glenn Chesney Quiett, *They Built the West*, 256-283.

17. The early development of East Los Angeles is briefly dealt with in Charles Dwight Willard, *The Herald's History of Los Angeles City*, 318-319. Development in this portion of the city was stimulated by the construction of street railways that by the end of the 1870s provided service to major districts in the growing city.

18. *History of Los Angeles County, California*, 144.

19. Nadeau, *City-Makers*, 191-196.

20. Ibid., 197-198, 222, 249, 252.

21. *History of Los Angeles County, California*, 130.

22. *History of San Luis Obispo County, California*, 356-357.

23. Ibid., 361.

24. The facts concerning the survey of the town lands are obscure. They were summarized by a nineteenth-century historian: "As early as 1848 Don José Arnaz laid out a town site near the Mission, advertised the advantages of the place in the Eastern papers, and offered any one a lot who would make improvements thereon. There being no response, the subject was not agitated further until 1862, when Waterman, Vassault & Co., owning the lands of the ex-Mission, laid out a town. The survey was rejected by the Board of Trustees after the town was incorporated, and another substituted." *History of Santa Barbara and Ventura Counties California*, 351.

25. Oscar Osburn Winther, "The Colony System of Southern California," 94-103.

26. For the planning and development of Anaheim I have relied on the following: Mildred Yorba MacArthur, *Anaheim "The Mother Colony"*; Hallock F. Raup, "The German Colonization of Anaheim, California," 123-146; Hallock F. Raup, "Anaheim: A German Community of Frontier California," 7-11; Richard Dale Batman, " 'Anaheim Was an Oasis in a Wilderness'," 1-8; Lucile E. Dickson, "The Founding and Early History of Anaheim, California," 26-37; and *History of Los Angeles County California*, 155-159.

27. J. M. Guinn, "The Great Real Estate Boom of 1887," 15.

28. Glenn S. Dumke, *The Boom of the Eighties in Southern California*, 46-49. Dumke's study, on which I have relied heavily, is both authoritative and entertaining. For a briefer and earlier study of the same topic see his "The Real Estate Boom of 1887 in Southern California," 425-438.

29. Cahuenga is mentioned briefly in Dumke, *Boom of the Eighties*, 178, along with a number of other boom communities that became ghost towns.

30. Guinn, "Boom of 1887," 15.

31. The history of Pasadena with an amusing, anecdotal chapter on the land boom period, can be traced in J. W. Wood, *Pasadena, California Historical and Personal*. See also Dumke, *Boom of the Eighties*, 85-92.

32. Ibid., 119-120.

33. Wallace W. Elliott, *History of San Bernardino and San Diego Counties*, 130-135, contains material on the early history of the colony. A view of the town appears as the frontispiece illustration. See also Dumke, *Boom of the Eighties*, 124-126; and Merlin Stonehouse, "The Michigan Excursion for the Founding of Riverside, California," 193-209.

34. U. S. Writers' Program, *California: A Guide to the Golden State*, New York, 1942, 632; Dumke, *Boom of the Eighties*, 126-127; and Elmer W. Holmes, *History of Riverside County, California*, 255.

35. The land boom in the Glendora area, including the development of Alosta, is described in Donald Pflueger, *Glendora*.

36. A printed copy of the original plat entitled *Map of the Town of Monrovia* is in the History Division, Los Angeles County Museum of Natural History. It included only the land lying between Magnolia and Charlotte (now Canyon) Avenues and from a half-block south of Walnut Avenue to the rear of the lots fronting on Lime Avenue.

37. Dumke, *Boom of the Eighties*, 79-81; John L. Wiley, *History of Monrovia*, 42-54. For information on land prices in Monrovia see also Joseph Netz, "The Great Los Angeles Real Estate Boom of 1887," 65.

38. Dumke, *Boom of the Eighties*, 181-182; Wiley, *Monrovia*, 54-55.

39. Guinn, "Boom of 1887," 16.

40. Dumke, *Boom of the Eighties*, 83-84. For the elaborate promotional techniques used to boom the town of Gladstone, an eventual failure, see ibid., 182-187; and Netz, "Great Los Angeles Real Estate Boom," 65-66. The methods used by a Quaker group to promote their new town of Whittier are described in Harry W. Nerhood, "Whittier, California: The Life of a Boom Town of the 'Eighties as Reflected in its First Newspaper," 36-44. Whittier's boom-time birth and its recovery from the excesses of land speculation are also reviewed in Benjamin F. Arnold and Artilissa Dorland Clark, *History of Whittier*, 11-37.

41. Dumke, *Boom of the Eighties*, 61-63, 69.

42. Ibid., 168-169.

43. Ibid., 172, 198.

44. A short history of this project and biographical sketches of its promoters appears in *History of San Luis Obispo County California*, 369-376. A view of the village appears opposite p. 44.

45. John E. Baur, "Los Angeles County in the Health Rush, 1870-1900," 13-31.

46. Theodore Strong Van Dyke, *The City and County of San Diego*, 21-24; Quiett, *They Built the West*, 320-322.

47. Van Dyke, *City and County of San Diego*, 28.

48. Dumke, *Boom of the Eighties*, 138. The advertisement appeared in the October 1, 1887, issue of the San Diego *Union*.

49. Ibid., 148-150.

50. Ibid., 154-156.

51. In my treatment of Coronado I have drawn on ibid., 144-146; Hopkins, *San Diego*, 207-211; and J. Harold Peterson, *The Coronado Story*, 11-23.

52. A plan of the town issued by the Coronado Beach Company is reproduced in John W. Reps, *The Making of Urban America*, 407.

53. As quoted in Quiett, *They Built the West*, 280. Quiett's chapter on real estate promotion in Los Angeles (pp. 256-283) contains much useful material on the booms of the 1870s and 1880s.

54. Netz, "Great Los Angeles Real Estate Boom" 66-67.

55. Ibid., citing a study by V. J. Rowan in 1889.

56. Guinn, "Boom of 1887," 21.

IX · CITIES OF ZION: ORIGINS OF THE MORMON WEST

1. *The Book of Mormon*, 1 Nephi 2:20. Literature on the Mormons is extensive. Most of the sources on which I have drawn for my brief summary of the early years of Mormonism, as well as many others, are listed in Philip A. M. Taylor, "Recent Writing on Utah and the Mormons," 249-260; and Thomas G. Alexander and James B. Allen, "The Mormons in the Mountain West: A Selected Bibliography," 365-384.

2. Joseph Smith, *History of the Church of Jesus Christ of Latter-Day Saints*, I, 163.

3. Smith, *History*, I, 189.

4. Fawn M. Brodie, *No Man Knows My History*, 120-121.

5. Smith, *History*, I, 335.

6. The relevant passages can be found in the Liverpool edition of 1854, 132-175.

7. Joseph Smith to Emma Smith, October 13, 1832, MS in library of the Reorganized Church of Jesus Christ of Latter Day Saints, as quoted in Brodie, *No Man Knows My History*, 123.

8. Plans and views of Cleveland, Tallmadge, and other Western Reserve towns and an account of their planning appear in John W. Reps, *The Making of Urban America*, 227-239.

9. A useful summary of Shaker history with an annotated bibliography is Marguerite Fellows Melcher, *The Shaker Adventure*. For a study of the Shaker community of North Union near Cleveland see Caroline B. Piercy, *The Valley of God's Pleasure*.

10. Plans and views of these religious and utopian communities, together with an analysis of their designs can be found in Reps, *Making of Urban America*, 443-458; and *Town Planning in Frontier America*, 390-410. The Rappite town of Harmony should not be confused with the settlement of the same name in northeastern Pennsylvania where Smith met his wife, Emma, in 1825.

11. Joseph N. Balestier, *The Annals of Chicago*, 27.

12. The text of Smith's "Explanation of the plat of the city of Zion, sent to the brethren in Zion, the 25th of June, 1833" appears in Smith, *History*, I, 357-362.

13. There is a minor discrepancy between Smith's description and the plat itself. If the center blocks were 60 rods east and west and divided into lots with frontages each of 4 rods, each block would contain 30 lots in two rows of 15. The plat shows each of the blocks divided into 32 lots, arranged in two rows of 16.

14. Smith, *History*, II, 293.

15. There may have been a second plan for Kirtland, one corresponding more closely to the City of Zion scheme. Among the records of the historian of the church in Salt Lake City is an undated and untitled manuscript plat believed to be a survey of either Kirtland or Zion in Independence. It is signed at the lower right corner as "Drawn by F. G. Williams." Williams was active in the business affairs of the church at Kirtland and was deeply involved in the building of the Temple. He had been converted to Mormonism in Ohio late in 1830 and joined the Lamanite mission to Missouri led by Parley Pratt. According to one Mormon historian, Williams had a hand in preparing certain plans for the Temple (and possibly the city) at Independence following a revelation to Smith in August, 1832, regarding the Missouri temple: "It is evident . . . that certain drawings of the house or temple of the presidency, which was to be a pattern and a plot plan of the City of Zion, were prepared . . . and sent to the brethren in Zion from Kirtland. The first drawings it seems were prepared by Frederick G. Williams and the second, which corrected the first under the direction of Oliver Cowdery." Alvin R. Dyer, *The Refiner's Fire*, 101. The Williams town plat includes two central squares, each with twelve temples. If this indeed is a plan for Independence and not Kirtland, then Williams may deserve some of the credit for devising the basic plan form employed or attempted by Mormon town builders in Kirtland, in Missouri, and in the Far West.

16. For a treatment of these events in Kirtland see Brodie, *No Man Knows My History*, 194-207; and B. H. Roberts, *A Comprehensive History of the Church of Jesus Christ of Latter-Day Saints*, I, 396-407.

17. Ibid., I, 424. Another church history, quoting from *History of Caldwell and Livingston Counties, Missouri*, includes this description of Far West: "It was laid out in blocks 396 feet square, and the streets were alike on a grand scale. The four principal avenues were each 132 feet wide, and all the others 82½ feet wide." *History of the Church of Jesus Christ of Latter Day Saints 1836-1844*, 77.

18. Smith, *History*, II, 521.

19. Ibid., II, 524-525.

20. Ibid., III, 35.

21. As quoted in Orson F. Whitney, *Like of Heber C. Kimball, An Apostle*, 222.

22. Roberts, *Comprehensive History*, I, 425.

23. Smith, *History*, III, 68.

24. These tragic events are described in all histories of the Mormons. See, for example: Roberts, *Comprehensive History*, I, 438-493; Ray B. West, Jr., *Kingdom of the Saints*, 72-101; and Brodie, *No Man Knows My History*, 225-240. Smith's own account appears in his *History*, III, 149-199.

25. Robert Bruce Flanders, *Nauvoo: Kingdom on the Mississippi*, 25. Flanders's work is based on exhaustive research, and I have relied on it heavily for information on the religious, social, political, and business aspects of the Nauvoo community.

26. Thomas Gregg, *History of Hancock County, Illinois*, 955.

27. Smith, *History*, III, 375.

28. The details of this second purchase of land are described in Flanders, *Nauvoo*, 41-42.

29. These dimensions appear on a detailed town plat of Nauvoo in 1874 published by A. T. Andreas in his *Illustrated Historical Atlas of Hancock County, Illinois*, Chicago, 1874, 136-137.

30. It will be recalled that the alterations of the plan of Far West—changes Smith evidently approved—anticipated the block and lot system at Nauvoo.

31. An entry for July 2, 1839, in Smith's history of the church states that he "spent the forenoon of this day on the Iowa side of river. Went, in company with Elders Sidney Rigdon, Hyrum Smith, and Bishops Whitney and Knight, and others, to visit a purchase lately made by Bishop Knight as a location for a town, and advised that a town be built there, and called Zarahemla." Smith, *History*, III, 382.

32. Gregg, *Hancock County*, 819. The name was changed by state authorities to Macadeonia, and later the town was renamed Webster. A plan in 1874 can be found in Andreas, *Atlas of Hancock County*, 48. This shows the original plat consisting of 20 blocks and 5 half blocks. Street widths, block size, and lot dimensions conform to those of Nauvoo. The central block in the grid was reserved as a public square. For some reason the street intersections are not quite at right angles, the east-west streets being three degrees off a true east-west bearing. See also Flanders, *Nauvoo*, 138-139.

33. Smith, *History*, III, 362-363, 390-391.

34. Ibid., IV, 267-273, 362.

35. Ibid., IV, 133. The figure from *Times and Seasons* is cited in Flanders, *Nauvoo*, 51, n 64.

36. Letter from James Needham to Thomas Ward, July 7, 1843, published in the *Millennial Star*, IV (October 1843), 87-88, as quoted in Joel Edward Ricks, *Forms and Methods of Early Mormon Settlement in Utah and the Surrounding Region, 1847 to 1877*, 7.

37. Designs and construction of these two structures are discussed in detail in Flanders, *Nauvoo*, 179-210.

38. For the process by which Mormon leadership devolved on Brigham Young see ibid., 306-322.

39. For an analysis of how this idea developed see ibid., 287-299; Leonard J.

Arrington, *Great Basin Kingdom*, 39-42; and Milton R. Hunter, *Brigham Young The Colonizer*, 8-10.

40. A vivid and detailed account of the last months at Nauvoo can be found in the diary of Hosea Stout. See Juanita Brooks (ed.), *On the Mormon Frontier: The Diary of Hosea Stout, 1844-1861*, I, 41-117.

41. *Daily Missouri Republican*, February 13, 1846, as quoted in William Mulder and A. Russell Mortensen (eds.), *Among the Mormons: Historic Accounts by Contemporary Observers*, 166.

42. The rules of the camps and the arrangements made for supplying the march are summarized in Arrington, *Great Basin Kingdom*, 19-21.

43. The exact number of Mormons on the march during 1846 is not known. There may have been as many as 20,000. The figure of 16,000 comes from Thomas Kane, who identified 14 locations in the fall of that year where groups of Mormons could be found in numbers of from 50 to 11,250. The latter figure is for Winter Quarters. See Thomas Leiper Kane, *A Friend of the Mormons*, 31-32. This collection of Kane's papers is a valuable, first-hand source of much information about the Mormon migration. A non-Mormon, Kane was a helpful friend to the members of the church.

44. Letter from Brigham Young as quoted in West, *Kingdom of the Saints*, 172.

45. From a lecture by Thomas Kane in Philadelphia, 1850, as quoted in Mulder and Mortensen, *Among the Mormons*, 212-213.

46. Life in Winter Quarters is described in E. Widtsoe Shumway, "Winter Quarters, Nebraska, 1846-1848," 115-125. Estimates of the population of Winter Quarters vary. One contemporary Mormon source states that there were 538 log houses and 83 sod house dugouts for an initial population of 3,000, a figure that doubled by the beginning of spring. R. Don Oscarson and Stanley B. Kimball, *The Traveller's Guide to Historic Mormon America*, 73. As has already been noted, Kane put the population in 1846 at 11,250.

47. From a sermon by Wilford Woodruff, July 24, 1880, as quoted in Preston Nibley, *Exodus to Greatness*, 428. Woodruff, then a member of the Council of the Twelve Apostles, was later to become the fourth president of the church. His statue, with those of Brigham Young and Heber C. Kimball, stands atop the This is The Place Monument in Emigration Canyon. At the base of the monument are figures of Orson Pratt and Erastus Snow.

48. Wilford Woodruff, *Journal*, as quoted in Edward W. Tullidge, *History of Salt Lake City*, 46-47.

49. Orson Pratt, *Journal*, July 31, 1847, as quoted in Leland Hargrave Creer, *The Founding of an Empire*, 307.

50. Tullidge, *Salt Lake City*, 47-48.

51. William Clayton, *Journal*, July 28, 1847, as quoted in Arrington, *Great Basin Kingdom*, 46.

52. Roberts, *Comprehensive History*, III, 269.

53. Woodruff, *Journal*, as quoted in Tullidge, *Salt Lake City*, 48. Woodruff's journal contains two entries describing these allotments. The first records that each apostle present received one block. The second indicates that on August 13

further grants were made extending their holdings several blocks further. Woodruff himself was given 8 blocks, Orson Pratt 4, George Smith 8, and "President Young . . . the tiers of blocks south through the city." Woodruff adds that the amount of land varied "according to the companies organized with each." This refers to the system of organization worked out for the march from Nauvoo to Utah when each Apostle and other leaders were made responsible for one or more "companies" or groups of emigrants.

54. Arrington, *Great Basin Kingdom*, 47.

55. Letter from Brigham Young to Orson Hyde, October 9, 1848, as quoted in Hunter, *Brigham Young The Colonizer*, 137.

56. Roberts, *Comprehensive History*, III, 301.

57. Eliza Snow, *Journal*, as quoted in West, *Kingdom of the Saints*, 198. One of the original log cabins has been preserved and occupies a site at the southeastern corner of Temple Square.

58. As quoted in a lengthy extract from Young's letter in ibid., 192-195.

59. The procedure for allocating land is summarized in Hunter, *Brigham Young The Colonizer*, 136-138. Hunter states that the original plan for dividing the Big Field into 5-, 10-, 20-, 40-, and 80-acre plots was revised and that only 5- and 10-acre tracts were surveyed. In its first General Epistle issued by the then newly reconstituted First Presidency of the Church, this account was sent to Mormons throughout the world in the spring of 1849: "A field of about 8000 acres has been surveyed south of and bordering on the city, and plotted in five and ten acre lots, and a church farm of about 8000 acres. The five and ten acre lots were distributed to the brethren, by casting lots, and every man is to help build a pole, ditch, or a stone fence as shall be most convenient around the whole field, in proportion to the land he draws." As quoted in Tullidge, *Salt Lake City*, 54.

60. The manuscript plan on which the Burton engraving is based is in the office of the church historian in Salt Lake City. It is on a sheet measuring 18¾ inches by 23⅞ inches. Street lines are drawn in black, lot lines in red. While unsigned and undated, its legend is in the hand of Thomas Bullock whom Burton identifies as the cartographer on his printed version. It was not possible, because of rough and broken topography north of the Temple Block, to extend the streets of Plot A as first surveyed. This area was later laid out with several diagonal streets running northwest to southeast.

61. Howard Stansbury, *Exploration and Survey of the Valley of the Great Salt Lake of Utah*, 128, 130.

62. Frederick Hawkins Piercy, *Route from Liverpool to Great Salt Lake Valley*, 288.

63. For the organization of public works in Salt Lake City see Arrington, *Great Basin Kingdom*, 108-112.

X · CITIES OF THE SAINTS: MORMON TOWN PLANNING IN THE GREAT BASIN KINGDOM

1. The word "Deseret" is from the *Book of Mormon* and means "honey bee," a symbol of thrift and industry. B. H. Roberts, *A Comprehensive History of the Church of Jesus Christ of Latter-Day Saints*, III, 422, n 15. For the organization of the provisional state see Dale L. Morgan, "The State of Deseret," 65-239. Edward W. Tullidge, *History of Salt Lake City*, 58-59, gives the text of the petition to Congress for the admission of Deseret to the Union.

2. For the impact of church policies on local government see James B. Allen, "Ecclesiastical Influence on Local Government in the Territory of Utah," 35-48.

3. The development of the Mormon Corridor concept is traced in Milton R. Hunter, "The Mormon Corridor," 179-200.

4. Leonard J. Arrington, *Great Basin Kingdom*, 84-85, 88. Milton R. Hunter, in his *Brigham Young The Colonizer*, 361-367, provides a list and location maps of the 358 Mormon towns founded or planned during Young's years in Utah. They are conveniently arranged by date of founding.

5. Young's method of selecting leaders and other members of settlement groups by "calling" is described in Joel Edward Ricks, *Forms and Methods of Early Mormon Settlement in Utah and the Surrounding Region, 1847 to 1877*, 48-51.

6. Ricks, *Early Mormon Settlement*, 76-77; Hunter, *Brigham Young*, 196-197. By 1855 Bountiful occupied a town tract 1600 by 3300 feet, most of which was enclosed by an adobe wall 6 feet high. Thirty houses and two adobe schools provided living and educational accommodations for the 150 families living in this community. Letter from George A. Smith and Ezra T. Benson to the *Deseret News*, February 27, 1855, as quoted in Ricks, *Early Mormon Settlement*, 77.

7. Utah Historical Records Survey, *A History of Ogden*, Ogden, Utah, 1940, 16-19; Edward W. Tullidge, *Tullidge's Histories*, II, 9-14; Ricks, *Mormon Settlement*, 53-54. Stansbury described the settlement in August, 1849, as "an extensive assemblage of log buildings, picketed, stockaded, and surrounded by ·outbuildings and cattle yards." Howard Stansbury, *Exploration and Survey of the Valley of the Great Salt Lake of Utah*, 83. Early in 1850 the fort was re-located a quarter of a mile southeast on higher ground.

8. Brigham Young, *Journal*, 1849, 138, as quoted in Ricks, *Mormon Settlement*, 54.

9. *Deseret News*, I, 95, as quoted in Utah Historical Records Survey, *Ogden*, 21.

10. Only half of the wall was completed. After the need for this fortification had passed, the stones were used for buildings and for the construction of culverts. Utah Historical Records Survey, *Ogden*, 32. For additional information about the founding of Ogden and other early Utah settlements see Hubert Howe Bancroft, *History of Utah*, 305-320.

11. For some of the tensions generated by this transition from a community wholly occupied by persons of one religion to one with a more cosmopolitan mixture see Utah Historical Records Survey, *Ogden*, 51-55. Bernard De Voto treats the same theme and writes from personal recollections in "Ogden: The Underwriters of Salvation," in Duncan Aikman (ed.), *The Taming of the Frontier*, 27-60. A more elaborate study is Robert Joseph Dwyer, *The Gentile Comes to Utah*.

12. In addition to Gentile settlers at Mormon-founded communities there were, of course, towns in Utah established by non-Mormons. Several were built by the railroads. One was Corinne, surveyed by the Union Pacific in 1869 on the salt flats a few miles west of Brigham City. See Bernice Gibbs Anderson, "The Gentile City of Corinne," 140-154. Others include Stockton and Ophir in Tooele

County, southwest of Salt Lake City. The former dates from 1864, when it was planned as a base for mining and smelting operations. See Tullidge, *Tullidge's Histories*, II, 76-79. Ophir was a mountain mining town of the same period. Manuscript plats of both towns are among the Townsite Surveys, General Land Office Records, Record Group 49, Cartographic Branch, National Archives.

13. Information on the early history of Brigham City appears in Tullidge, *Tullidge's Histories*, II, 289-293; Hunter, *Brigham Young*, 271-275; and Hicks, *Mormon Settlement*, 63-64.

14. The legend identifies the buildings from 8 to 17 as follows: Woolen Mills, Cabinet Shop, Foundry and Machine Shop, Woodworking Machine Shop, Shoe, Hat, and Harness Shops, Mercantile Institutions, Mason Department, Lumber and Dry House, Pottery, and Tannery. In addition, the cooperative operated several farms with 5,000 sheep, 500 milk cows, and 100 hogs. At Mantua, not far away, it began a colony to raise flax. In southern Utah, near Wahington, another colony was engaged in producing cotton. See Arrington, *Great Basin Kingdom*, 324-325 for a brief summary of his more extensive treatment in "Cooperative Community in the North: Brigham City, Utah," 199-217.

15. Ricks, *Mormon Settlement*, 64-65, 94.

16. Letter from Brigham Young to Peter Maughan, January 23, 1859, as quoted in ibid., 65.

17. Tullidge, *Tullidge's Histories*, II, 351, 354.

18. Ibid., II, 451. Tullidge also gives the full text of the city charter, 397-406.

19. For a full account of town settlement in the Cache Valley see the two chapters written by the editor in Joel E. Ricks (ed.), *The History of a Valley*, 32-86. Unfortunately, Ricks includes only one town plan, that of Oxford as surveyed in 1864. Oxford is located at the northern end of the valley in Idaho. The bibliographical essay contributed to this volume by S. George Ellsworth, pp. 458-478, would be useful as a beginning point for further research on community plans and planning in this part of the Mormon region.

20. Hunter, *Brigham Young*, 238-239. According to Hunter, Fox had laid out the town of Grantsville, 11 miles northwest of Tooele, a year earlier. Tullidge's brief historical sketch of Grantsville dates that community's town lot survey as 1851. *Tullidge's Histories*, II, 99.

21. Ibid., II, 95. In December, 1854, Alexander Gee reported to the *Deseret News* that "the wall is now half finished around the city and unlike most places where the people have commenced to wall in their cities, we have not a patch here and there, but as far as it is built it is finished, and I am proud to say that it is as substantial and handsome as any I have seen in all the settlements I have every visited." *Deseret News*, December 11, 1854, as quoted in Hunter, *Brigham Young*, 239.

22. Hunter, *Brigham Young*, 239; Tullidge, *Tullidge's Histories*, II, 96.

23. Settlement and economic development of the Utah Valley is summarized in Leonard J. Arrington, "Economic History of a Mormon Valley," 97-107; and in Hunter, *Brigham Young*, 221-233.

24. J. Marinus Jensen, *History of Provo*, 33-35. The view of Fort Utah is from the frontispiece illustration in Stansbury, *Exploration and Survey*. Stansbury pro-

vides another view of the fort from the exterior opposite p. 142. The only original plat of a Mormon fort I have been able to find is that of Fort Herriman. This is an undated and unsigned manuscript drawing in the records of the Salt Lake County Recorder, *Pioneer Plat Book*, 43. It is approximately square, and while there is no scale and there are many discrepancies in the dimensions given for various lots, it would appear that it was 540 feet on each side. It is divided into 24 lots with a central open space about 180 feet square. A single street, 16 feet wide, leads from this space to the middle of the northern wall. Herriman is located in the southern part of Salt Lake County 2 miles north of the mouth of Rose Canyon. A redrawing of the fort erected in 1853 at American Fork can be found in Lowry Nelson, *The Mormon Village*, 181. Nelson also reproduces a modern plat of the city of American Fork, which at the time of his study was apparently little changed from the original layout. Blocks were square, approximately 10 acres in area. Lots contained 1¼ acres and were arranged in the alternating frontage pattern used at Salt Lake City. Streets varied in width. Three were 6 rods wide, three others 5 rods, and the other four were 4 rods in width.

25. On Young's visit in September, 1849, he announced that the city would be a mile square, "laid off in blocks of 4 acres each, divided into 8 lots of ½ acre each reserving the center block of 4 acres for a chapel and 4 [for] school houses—the streets to be five rods wide." Manuscript notes by Thomas Bullock, September 17, 1849, as quoted in Ricks, *Mormon Settlement*, 57. According to Jensen's *Provo*, 63-64, only the northwest quarter of the town was surveyed in 1850. Andrew J. Stewart completed the survey the following year. Jensen states that all streets were 5 rods wide except Main (later, Fifth West) and Center Streets, which were laid out 8 rods in width. This does not correspond with Figure 10.12 where, as a note on the plat reads, streets are "uniformly 5 rods wide." A manuscript plat of Provo in the Office of the Church Historian, Salt Lake City, dated April 20, 1864, does show two streets of greater width than all others. This change from the plat in Figure 10.12 may have been made at some time after 1850 or 1851. On the 1864 plat the blocks along the south side of Center Street are not square. My guess is that they were originally laid out square like all the rest and subsequently reduced 3 rods in their north-south dimension to allow the street to be made wider. The same applies to what was originally called Main Street. These streets crossed at the northeast corner of the open square shown on the plat of 1850 in Figure 10.12.

26. Jules Remy, *A Journey to Great Salt-Lake City*, II, 323-334. Two years earlier George Smith noted that the local industries included "three sawmills, one gristmill, one shingle machine propelled by water, one carding machine and fulling mill, and one manufactory of brown earthenware. There is also a turning lathe for turning wooden bowls, one thrashing machine, propelled by water power, and two cabinet shops." *Deseret News*, September 27, 1853, as quoted in Hunter, *Brigham Young*, 222.

27. Ricks, *Mormon Settlement*, 57-58; Hunter, *Brigham Young*, 243-247.

28. The Manti Temple, started in 1877 and completed in 1888, was not built on the site designated for this purpose in the plat of 1850. Instead, a site on an elevation at the edge of town was used for this imposing structure. See the aerial

photograph of Manti reproduced in Nelson, *Mormon Village*, Appendix, Plate H.

29. As quoted in Leland Hargrave Creer, *Mormon Towns in the Region of the Colorado*, 2.

30. A portion of a modern survey of Ephraim showing lots lines appears in Nelson, *Mormon Village*, 141. A vertical aerial photograph is reproduced in the Appendix of Nelson's study as Plate L.

31. For the Smith party in 1850-51 these included "two carriages, three hundred and sixty eight oxen, twelve mules, twenty beef cattle . . . one hundred and one wagons, one hundred horses, one hundred and forty six cows . . . one hundred twenty one chickens, 58,992 lbs. of flour, 3486 lbs. corn, 1267 lbs. barley, 1228 lbs. groceries, 35,370 lbs. wheat, 2163 lbs. oats, 3240 lbs. potatoes, 9¼ sets carpenter's tools, 1 set mill irons for saw mill, 3 sets whip saws, 110 spades and shovels, 72 scythes and cradles for grain, 45 grass scythes, 436 panes of glass, 190 pounds of nails, 3½ sets Blacksmith's tools, 57 plows, 137 axes, 98 hoes, 1 brass cannon 6 pounder, 129 guns, 9 swords, 1001 lbs. of ammunition, 44 saddles and 52 pistols." Henry Lunt, *Journal*, 4, as quoted in Ricks, *Mormon Settlement*, 52.

32. Letter from Matthew Carruthers, February, 1853, *Millennial Star*, XV, 458, as quoted in Ricks, *Mormon Settlement*, 59.

33. John D. Lee, *Journal*, 1850-1852, January 31, 1851, 192, as quoted in Ricks, *Mormon Settlement*, 60.

34. Hunter, *Brigham Young*, 184.

35. For details of this enterprise and the difficulties encountered, see Arrington, *Great Basin Kingdom*, 122-127.

36. Remy, *Journey*, 360-361.

37. Resolution Number II and Chapter XXXVIII, approved October 4, 1851, *Acts, Resolutions and Memorials . . . of the Legislative Assembly of the Territory of Utah*, 224, 388-389.

38. Hunter, *Brigham Young*, 265-267; Ricks, *Mormon Settlement*, 61-62. The members of the committee responsible for selecting the site were Orson Pratt, Albert Carrington, Jesse W. Fox, and William C. Staines. *History of Brigham Young, 1847-1867*, 110. This volume consists of the text of three manuscripts in the Bancroft Library, University of California, Berkeley. They were compiled by Mormon church officials in 1885 for Hubert Howe Bancroft and together comprise an abridged version of three extended manuscript historical records assembled under the direction of Brigham Young. The report of the site selection committee is quoted and commented on in Everett L. Cooley, "Report of an Expedition to Locate Utah's First Capitol," 329-338.

39. Hunter, *Brigham Young*, 267-270. The view of Fillmore in 1855 is from Remy who estimated the population then at "not . . . more than eight hundred inhabitants." Remy, *Journey*, II, 334.

40. Glenn S. Dumke, "Mission Station to Mining Town: Early Las Vegas," 257-270. Remy in 1855 commented that Las Vegas "will never become considerable, inasmuch as the soil capable of cultivation is extremely limited, and the surrounding desert extends to a considerable distance." Its "real utility" was as

a "halting-place, where the mail, and travellers in general may renew their stock of provisions." Remy noted that "all that is now to be seen in the fort is a house and a barn. There were thirty-three Mormons in it, almost all elders, and not a single woman." Remy, *Journey*, II, 412-413. The Las Vegas mission settlement is also described in Hunter, *Brigham Young*, 322-333.

41. John Henry Evans, *Charles Coulson Rich*, 203-213. George William Beattie and Helen Pruitt Beattie, *Heritage of the Valley*, 188. Two views of the Mormon fort at San Bernardino in 1852 are reproduced as the front end-papers of the Beattie's book. A plan of the fort as redrawn from L. A. Ingersoll, *Century Annals of San Bernardino County*, Los Angeles, 1904, is in Paul Bailey, *Sam Brannan and the California Mormons*, 152.

42. H. F. Raup, *San Bernardino, California*, 20-21.

43. What was intended as the temple block is now known as Pioneer Park.

44. Letter from Benjamin Hayes to the *Southern Californian*, October 19, 1854, as quoted in Beattie, *Heritage of the Valley*, 225. For additional material on the Mormon era of San Bernardino see Wallace W. Elliott, *History of San Bernardino and San Diego Counties California*, 84-87.

45. Hunter, *Brigham Young*, 282, 286.

46. Ibid., 335-337. For a more detailed treatment of Mormon activities in this area see John D. Nash, "The Salmon River Mission of 1855," 22-31; and W. W. Henderson (ed.), "The Salmon River Mission," 3-24. Apparently no town was ever planned here. The fort was abandoned in March, 1858.

47. Hunter, *Brigham Young*, 255-262 describes the process of settlement in Nevada. There is a manuscript town plan of Genoa among the Townsite Surveys, General Land Office Records, Record Group 49, Cartographic Branch, National Archives, dated 1865. I think it likely this represents the town as replatted after the Mormons departed in 1857.

48. Utah Territory included all of the present state of Utah, the western part of Colorado, the southwestern corner of Wyoming, and all but the southerly tip of Nevada. No part of present California, Arizona, New Mexico, Idaho, or Oregon fell within the limits of the new territory. Subsequent enactments in 1861, 1862, 1866, and 1868 reduced Utah to its present size. See the map showing these successive boundaries compared to those of the State of Deseret in Arrington, *Great Basin Kingdom*, 85.

49. A compact account of the Utah or Mormon War can be found in Howard Roberts Lamar, *The Far Southwest, 1846-1912*, 327-351. The definitive study is Norman F. Furniss, *The Mormon Conflict, 1850-1859*. See also Bancroft, *History of Utah*, 512-542.

50. Ricks, *Mormon Settlement*, 67-68. For a study emphasizing the economic aspects of Mormon settlement in this region see Leonard Arrington, "The Mormon Cotton Mission in Southern Utah," 221-238. A briefer treatment appears in his *Great Basin Kingdom*, 216-222.

51. "In selecting a location for a city there are a few requisites to which we desire to call your attention. First and most important is a good central position . . . and a local Head Quarters for all the settlements upon the San Clara, and Rio

Virgin . . . such a location we think may be found at or near the junction of these Rivers. Great care should be exercised in locating upon high ground, with dry gravelly soil a good distance from the river bottoms, and consequently free from the unpleasant and unhealthy miasma usually arising from bottom lands in warm climates. The next consideration will be the obtaining of a supply of good pure water for domestic purposes, this may be accomplished by conducting water from springs many of which you will probably find at no great distance, and by the digging of wells; but no reference should be had to the procuring of water sufficient for mills or manufacturing purposes, all such establishments should be located on the streams as convenient to the settlement as proper sites can be found. The above essential procured, you will next look around for building materials, good stone, and good timber, and when found open practicable roads to them, so that they may be easy of access to all." "Letter from Brigham Young to Elders Orson Pratt, Erastus Snow, and the Brethren of the Southern Mission," *Brigham Young Letter Book, 1861-1864*, 602, as quoted in Ricks, *Mormon Settlement*, 69-70.

52. Letter from Erastus Snow to Brigham Young, March 10, 1862, in J. G. Bleak, *Annals of the Southern Mission* Book A, 131, as quoted in Ricks, *Mormon Settlement*, 71.

53. A brief summary of Mormon temple construction can be found in Arrington, *Great Basin Kingdom*, 339-340. Arrington cites Juanita Brooks, "The St. George Temple," *Improvement Era*, XLIX (1946), 370ff as the best account of the construction of the St. George structure.

54. These communities in southern Utah and others in adjacent portions of Nevada were located in an area given the name "Dixie" because of their emphasis on cotton production. Their economy was precarious. Although fairly substantial quantities of cotton were produced in the early years, along with tobacco, grapes, and wine, by 1867 only 300 acres of cotton fields were in cultivation. Arrington, *Great Basin Kingdom*, 216-223, describes these settlements and their economic difficulties.

55. The *Deseret News* for March 2, 1864, quoted Brigham Young as follows: "We shall shortly want another path to bring home the Saints, and we want to prepare for it. . . . The Colorado is not far from our southern settlements, only one hundred twenty-five miles from Saint George." He added that if he were living in the area "he would soon have steamboats passing up the Colorado." Quoted in Hunter, *Brigham Young*, 82.

56. As quoted in ibid., 83.

57. The ill-conceived project to develop the Colorado River for navigation is covered in Leonard J. Arrington, "Inland to Zion: Mormon Trade on the Colorado River, 1864-1867," 239-250. Some additional material may be found on Callville in James H. McClintock, *Mormon Settlement in Arizona*, 113-116. McClintock states that Callville was abandoned in 1869.

58. McClintock, *Arizona* lists them as follows: Beaver Dams, St. Thomas, Overton, St. Joseph, West Point, Mill Point, and Simonsville. St. Thomas appears to have been the most important. McClintock describes it as consisting of 85 city lots, each one acre in area, and equal numbers of 2½-acre vineyard lots and 5-acre farm parcels.

59. A map showing the location of these and other Mormon communities is in McClintock, *Arizona*, 139. Some information about these early Mormon communities in Arizona appears in Hubert Howe Bancroft, *History of Arizona and New Mexico, 1530-1888*, 530-534.

60. Mesa's condition in 1884 was described by an anonymous historian as follows: "The town of Mesa City was laid out with wide streets, and into ten-acre blocks, which were sub-divided into lots of one and one-fourth acres each. Most of the residents own from two lots to a whole block, which have been improved by building comfortable houses, many of them more than ordinarily large and tasty for a new place. They are nearly all built of adobe, the soil have been first ground in a brick mill, and thus reduced to a state of homogeneity uncommon to this very common building material. The result is a smooth, solid surface, that when laid into a wall, looks as well as the ordinary plaster finish." *History of Arizona Territory*, 283.

61. For information on these settlements see McClintock, *Arizona*, 232-257.

62. For a summary of this doctrine see Arrington, *Great Basin Kingdom*, 7-9. A more elaborate treatment can be found in his "Early Mormon Communitarianism: The Law of Consecration and Stewardship," 341-369.

63. Mark A. Pendleton, "The Orderville United Order of Zion," 143-144.

64. The brief experience with the United Order in Utah is summarized in West, *Kingdom of the Saints*, 310-316. A much more detailed treatment can be found in Arrington, *Great Basin Kingdom*, 323-349.

65. As quoted from a newspaper account of unspecified date in McClintock, *Arizona*, 205.

66. Ibid., 209.

67. Emma Carroll Seegmiller, "Personal Memories of the United Order of Orderville, Utah," 164-165.

68. Seegmiller, "Orderville," 174. An English journalist who visited the community in 1882 left these observations: "The settlement itself is grieviously disappointing in appearance . . . [and] at first sight looks like a factory. The wooden shed-like buildings built in continuous rows, the adjacent mills, the bare, ugly patch of hillside behind it, gives the actual settlement an uninviting aspect. But once within the settlement, the scene changes wonderfully for the better. The houses are found, the most of them, built facing inwards upon an open square, with a broad side-walk, edged with tamarisk and mulberry, box-elder and maple-trees, in front of them. Outside the dwelling-house square are scattered about the school-house, meeting-house, black-smith and carpenters' shops, tannery, woolen-mill, and so forth, while a broad roadway separates the whole from the orchards, gardens, and farm-lands generally." Phil Robinson, "The Orderville Brethern," from the 1883 Boston edition of his *Sinners and Saints*, as quoted in William Mulder and A. Russell Mortensen (eds)., *Among the Mormons*, New York, 1958, 397. For some additional material on Orderville see Ricks, *Mormon Settlement*, 105-114.

69. For the establishment and abandonment of the United Order in another Utah community see Feramorz Y. Fox, "Experiment in Utopia," 355-380.

70. Samuel Bowles, *Across the Continent . . . in the Summer of 1865*, 90. The irrigation ditches within the city were noted by virtually every traveler who visited it. They were dug in the spring of 1849, and the bishop of each ward supervised their maintenance as well as the bridges needed to provide crossings at intersections and elsewhere. Dale L. Morgan, "The Changing Face of Salt Lake City." 216-217.

71. This is apparently true also in many parts of other Mormon towns of substantial size.

72. A plat of this addition is among the surveys in the Salt Lake County Recorder's *Pioneer Plat Book*. It is identified as Plat D and contains this notation: "Copied from old plot, by Leo Hawkins. G.S.L. Co. Recorder 1857."

73. *U.S. Census*, Population, 1860, 1870, and 1880.

74. For the development of Fort Douglas see Leonard J. Arrington and Thomas G. Alexander, "The U.S. Army Overlooks Salt Lake Valley: Fort Douglas, 1862-1965," 326-350. In 1900 the University of Utah began to occupy its present site between Fort Douglas and the eastern edge of the city.

75. Charles Marshall, "Salt Lake City and the Valley Settlements," *Fraser's Magazine*, July, 1871, as quoted in Mulder and Mortensen, *Among the Mormons*, 378.

76. An excellent photograph of the Z.C.M.I. building appears in A. R. Mortensen, "Main Street," *The Valley of the Great Salt Lake*, Salt Lake City, 3rd ed., 1967, 99. This volume is a reprint of the articles in the *Utah Historical Quarterly*, XXVII (July, 1959) without the footnotes. Mortensen's article contains a number of other photographs of Main Street from early to modern times. A fine view of Main Street from the roof of the Temple can be found in *Harper's Weekly*, October 30, 1886, 705.

77. D. W. Meinig, "The Mormon Culture Region: Strategies and Patterns in the Geography of The American West, 1847-1964," 212-213. Meinig reproduces an aerial photograph of the city from the west showing the Hotel Utah built in 1911 on the former Tithing Office site and the Hotel Newhouse erected in 1915 four blocks to the south, identifying them as symbols of cultural and social differences. The article is a splendid venture in historical geography and is a sophisticated and enlightening examination of many aspects of Mormon colonization and settlement.

78. "Salt Lake City," *Harper's Weekly*, XXX (October 30, 1886), 706.

XI · URBAN PLANNING AND DEVELOPMENT IN THE PACIFIC NORTHWEST

1. There are many works on the Oregon Trail. Two that have been helpful to me are W. J. Ghent, *The Road to Oregon*; and U.S. Writers' Program, *The Oregon Trail*.

2. The earliest comprehensive study of Astoria was written by Washington Irving in 1836. The most recent edition, with copious notes and an introduction by Edgeley W. Todd, is Irving, *Astoria*. A summary of Astoria's founding and early years with extracts from contemporary descriptions can be found in Grace P. Morris, "Development of Astoria, 1811-1850," 413-424. For a view of Fort George in 1846 see Captain H. Warre, *Sketches in North America and the Oregon Territory*. Warre's sketchbook, from which the lithographs in the published edition were prepared, is in the collection of the American Antiquarian Society. Most of the sketches and watercolors have been reproduced in facsimile with the brief text of the published work and under the same title, with an introduction by Archibald Hanna, Jr., Barre, Massachusetts, 1970. The Fort George sketch is Number 42.

3. For McLoughlin see Richard G. Montgomery, *The White-Headed Eagle: John McLoughlin*.

4. Charles H. Carey, *A General History of Oregon Prior to 1861*, I, 281-316, summarizes the missionary period in Oregon. One of the few mission stations remaining in 1844 was the Baptist establishment under the Rev. Jason Lee some 50 miles up the Willamette and a few miles east of the river. It was described by one observer as consisting of "dwelling-houses, barns, shops, store-houses, churches, school-houses and mills. In all, there are about fourteen buildings, belonging to this station, which are located at different points in this valley, varying from one to eight miles in distance, from each other." Lansford W. Hastings, *The Emigrant's Guide to Oregon and California*, 54.

5. Fred Wilbur Powell, "Hall Jackson Kelley—Prophet of Oregon," 1-54. Kelley's sketch of the proposed trading town can be found opposite p. 36. It was to consist of a grid of four streets running north and south and an equal number crossing at right angles. The blocks were to be divided into parcels of 40 and 160 acres. For another account of Kelley and his career and the text of his principal writings see Powell, *Hall J. Kelley on Oregon*.

6. Hastings, *Emigrant's Guide*, 56.

7. A reproduction of Warre's original watercolor can be found in the 1970 edition of his *Sketches in North America*, Number 59.

8. J. Quinn Thornton, *Oregon and California in 1848*, I, 287. Despite the date indicated in the title of this work, Thornton described the town as he saw it in 1847.

9. Hastings, *Emigrants' Guide*, 56.

10. Howard McKinley Corning, *Dictionary of Oregon History*, 148-149. Linn City was swept by fire in 1861 and, while its residents were in the process of rebuilding, a flood totally destroyed what was left of the town, and it was never rebuilt. Multnomah City is mentioned in a letter from Burns to Wyndham Robertson, October 29, 1844, quoted in Wyndham Robertson, Jr., *Oregon, Our Right and Title*, 31. Both towns are briefly described in Eugene E. Snyder's fine study, *Early Portland, Stump-Town Triumphant*, 27-28.

11. Corning, *Dictionary of Oregon History*, 111; Carey, *Oregon*, II, 649.

12. Ibid., II, 649-650.

13. Milwaukie *Western Star*, November 21, 1850, as quoted in ibid., ii, 651. A map of 1852 showing Milwaukie's grid layout is reproduced in the *Oregon Historical Society Quarterly*, lxviii (1967), 161.

14. Peter H. Burnett, *Recollections and Opinions of an Old Pioneer*, 138. Both men were to have somewhat greater success in townsite promotion elsewhere—Burnett at Sacramento and McCarver at Tacoma. For Burnett's contribution to Sacramento see Chapter vii. McCarver's role in helping to create Tacoma is described in Chapter xvii. His various town promotion activities are reviewed in Michael B. Husband, "Morton M. McCarver: An Iowa Entrepreneur in the Far West," 241-254.

15. For the founding and early development of Portland I have relied on a number of sources: Harvey Whitefield Scott, *History of Portland, Oregon*; Corning, *Dictionary of Oregon History*, 57, 152-153, 187, 200-201, 273, 495-496; Carey, *Oregon*, ii, 653-658; and Snyder, *Early Portland*, 30-46. I have also found helpful the study of Portland and the other pioneer towns of the Willamette Valley prepared as a seminar paper under my direction at Cornell University in 1973 by Howard John Iber: "Early Town Planning in Oregon's Willamette Valley."

16. From a description by Lt. Neil Howison, as quoted in Snyder, *Early Portland*, 37.

17. As quoted from an unidentified source in Carey, *Oregon*, ii, 655.

18. From an account written in January 3, 1852, as quoted in ibid., ii, 655.

19. The history of Portland's park blocks has apparently not been adequately documented. It is just possible that Lownsdale, a native of Kentucky, borrowed this idea from Louisville, where on two occasions similar strips of common land had been surveyed at the outer edge of that city. See John W. Reps, *The Making of Urban America*, 212-215.

20. In 1849 Lownsdale sold half of his half-interest to Coffin. A year later each sold one-third of their respective interests to Chapman. Benjamin Stark continued as a silent partner with his one-half interest. Snyder, *Early Portland*, 64-67.

21. The Brady survey is too badly damaged and faded to reproduce. A photocopy is in the collection of the Oregon Historical Society in Portland.

22. Milwaukie's decline and the reasons for it are reviewed in Snyder, *Early Portland*, 113-126.

23. Ezra Meeker, *The Busy Life of Eighty-Five Years of Ezra Meeker*, 61-62.

24. Corning, *Dictionary of Oregon History*, 135-137, 214; U.S. Writers' Program, *Oregon*, Portland, 1940, 278. In 1850 Knighton attempted to organize a railroad company to link St. Helens with Lafayette, a town founded in 1847 in the western Willamette Valley. The failure of this project ended St. Helens' chance to outstrip Portland. Carey, *Oregon*, ii, 734-735. See also Snyder, *Early Portland*, 130-142, for material on St. Helens and nearby Milton, which Captain Nathaniel Crosby, Jr., also attempted to promote as a major port. Crosby and his partner, Thomas H. Smith, offered "to give to every head of a family 2 town lots and to every single man one town lot, who will become an actual settler . . . within 6 months and build a house upon the same." They also agreed to sell building

materials on credit and to "give a mill site together with land sufficient for the purpose of a grist mill" to a person who would agree to build one. As quoted from an October, 1850, advertisement in the Portland *Spectator* in Snyder, *Early Portland*, 141.

25. In the Deed Records (Book D, Deeds, p. 84) of Clastrop County, Oregon there is a redrawing of a slightly different plat of Astoria dated 1844 but not recorded until 1847. It omits the three church blocks and the cemetery and does not include two tiers of blocks along the south edge of the plat. The circular school sites are also shown one tier of blocks closer to the river, and the custom house square is one tier of blocks closer to Broadway.

26. Address delivered in 1878 before the Oregon Pioneer Association, as quoted in Carey, *Oregon*, ii, 658.

27. Corning, *Dictionary of Oregon History*, 13, 223; U.S. Writers' Program, *Oregon*, 149-157.

28. Carey, *Oregon*, ii, 659-663; Corning, *Dictionary of Oregon History*, 215; U.S. Writers' Program, *Oregon*, 228-237. The peculiar manner in which the land was assembled for the town of Salem was later to cause almost endless legal battles over land titles. For a long recital of the facts up to 1874 see J. Quinn Thornton, "Salem Titles," in *The Salem Directory; Embracing a Resident and Business Directory, for 1874*, Salem, 1874, 1-48 (separately paged, following p. 108 of the directory).

29. Walter C. Winslow, "Contests over the Capital of Oregon," 173-178; Corning, *Dictionary of Oregon History*, 43-44. Corvallis was planned by Joseph C. Avery in 1848 and was first named Marysville. The existence of the California town by the same name prompted the legislature to change it in 1853. Carey, *Oregon*, ii, 665-666; U.S. Writers' Program, *Oregon*, 158-166.

30. Howard McKinley Corning, "Ghost Towns on the Willamette of the Riverboat Period," 55-67; Lloyd D. Black, "Middle Willamette Valley Population Growth," 40-55; Carey, *Oregon*, ii, 663-664.

31. As quoted in ibid., ii, 668.

32. Edmund S. Meany, "First American Settlement on the Puget Sound," 136-143; Hubert Howe Bancroft, *History of Washington, Idaho, and Montana, 1845-1889*, 1-10; Edgar I. Stewart, *Washington: Northwest Frontier*, i, 393-394; Cecil Dryden, *Dryden's History of Washington*, 114-115; Mary W. Avery, *Washington: A History of the Evergreen State*, 168.

33. "Edmund Sylvester's Narrative of the Founding of Olympia," *Pacific Northwest Quarterly*, xxxvi (1945), 335.

34. Bancroft, *Washington*, 15-17; "Sylvester's Narrative," 335, 337. In the spring of 1853 Ezra Meeker passed through Olympia. He estimated the population at "about 100," and described it as having "three stores, a hotel, a livery stable, and saloon, with one weekly newspaper." Meeker, *Busy Life*, 68.

35. Bancroft, *Washington*, 19-20, 366. Ezra Meeker was impressed with the beauty of the Port Townsend site when he approached it in 1853: "The nearer we approached the embryo city, the greater our admiration. The beautiful, pebbly beach in front, the clear, level spot adjoining, with the beautiful open and comparatively level plateau in the background, and with two or three vessels at an-

chor in the foreground, there seemed nothing lacking to complete the picture of a perfect city site.'' With the advantage of over a half-century of hindsight Meeker then added: ''Poor, innocent souls, we could not see beyond to discover that cities are not built upon pleasure grounds, and that there are causes beyond the ken of man to fathom the future destiny of the embryo towns of a new commonwealth.'' Meeker, *Busy Life*, 97-98.

36. Bancroft, *Washington*, 18, 366; U.S. Writers' Program, *Washington: A Guide to the Evergreen State*, 68, 484; Lucile McDonald and Werner Lenggenhager, *The Look of Old Time Washington*, 122.

37. Frances Fuller Victor, *All Over Oregon and Washington*, 244.

38. For brief accounts of these early settlements see Bancroft, *Washington*, 27-38. Another helpful source of information on the names and dates of founding of Washington's towns is James W. Phillips, *Washington State Place Names*.

39. Bancroft, *Washington*, 22, quoting a manuscript account by W. N. Bell, one of the early settlers of Seattle.

40. Ibid., 23-25; Clarence B. Bagley, *History of Seattle from the Earliest Settlement to the Present Time*, I, 19-23. The town was named for an Indian chief.

41. ''Henry Yesler and the Founding of Seattle,'' *Pacific Northwest Quarterly*, XLII (1951), 271-276; Stewart, *Washington*, I, 397.

42. ''Henry Yesler,'' 273.

43. As quoted in Bagley, *Seattle*, I, 33, 36.

44. Ibid., 37-38, 44-45.

45. As quoted in ibid., 46. The commander of the *Decatur*, Thomas Phelps, wrote an account of Seattle and the Indian attack seventeen years after the event. See Thomas Phelps, *Reminiscences of Seattle, Washington Territory, and of the U.S. Sloop-of-War Decatur during the Indian War of 1855-1856*. This edition contains a reproduction of Phelps's plan of the town. The end papers reproduce his view of the settlement from the harbor. Phelps described Seattle in October, 1855, as a town of ''about thirty houses, including a church, hotel, boarding-house, five or six stores, and a blacksmith and carpenter-shop'' (p. 5).

46. Frederic James Grant, ''Seattle: A Chapter from an Uncompleted History,'' 636-642.

47. The village is described in an elaborate study of Fort Vancouver: John A. Hussey, *The History of Fort Vancouver and its Physical Structure*. Hussey's exhaustive work includes many reproductions of manuscript and printed plans and maps showing the development of the fort.

48. Controversy over ownership of the land in this area continued for many years. See ibid., 99-114.

49. U.S. Writers' Program, *Washington*, 281, 283.

50. A plat of The Dalles as filed for record in 1861 is among the records of the Wasco County Clerk at The Dalles. The town was originally named Dalles City, but the U.S. Post Office restored the older name of the place, and it has retained its peculiar and rather awkward designation ever since.

51. Priscilla Knuth, '' 'Picturesque' Frontier: The Army's Fort Dalles,'' LXVIII (1966), 293-333, (1967), 5-52; Corning, *Dictionary of Oregon History*, 241; Carey, *Oregon*, II, 670.

52. U.S. Writers' Program, *Washington*, 290-291; D. W. Meinig, *The Great Columbia Plain*, 201-204; Martha J. Lamb, ''A Glimpse of the Valley of Many Waters: Its Settlement and Development,'' 193-210.

53. Victor, *Oregon and Washington*, 48, 50, 55. Mrs. Victor, the author of the previously published *River of the West*, lived on the Pacific Coast for five years, three of them in Oregon. Her new work was based on an extensive tour of the region made during the summer of 1871. Subsequently she wrote a substantial part of the text for the history of Oregon issued by Hubert Howe Bancroft under his name. Corning, *Dictionary of Oregon History*, 18.

54. Victor, *Oregon and Washington*, 71-72.

55. Ibid., 75-76.

56. Ibid., 91-92.

57. Ibid., 102.

58. Ibid., 107.

59. Ibid., 107; U.S. Writers' Program, *Washington*, 292-293.

60. Victor, *Oregon and Washington*, 214.

61. Ibid., 219; Carey, *Oregon*, II, 669-670. An early view of Jacksonville was issued ca. 1858 by Kuchel and Dresel of San Francisco. An impression is in the collection of the Amon Carter Museum of Western Art, Fort Worth, Texas. It is a lithograph bearing the title, *Jacksonville, O.T.* and was printed by Britton and Rey in San Francisco. While it is undated, its style and format are identical to many other views of western mining camps and towns published by the Kuchel and Dresel firm in 1858 and 1859.

62. U.S. Writers' Program, *Oregon*, 188-189, 327.

63. Victor, *Oregon and Washington*, 179-181.

64. Corning, *Dictionary of Oregon History*, 180-181; Carey, *Oregon*, II, 711.

65. *Salem Directory . . . for 1874*, 11.

66. Victor, *Oregon and Washington*, 169-170.

67. Ibid., 147-153.

68. Dispatch from the Portland correspondent of the San Francisco *Bulletin*, October 23, 1865, as quoted in *The Portland Directory for the Year Commencing January, 1867*, Portland, Oregon, 1867, 9. The directory also includes the text of the Portland city charter of 1864 and a number of city ordinances passed through the summer of 1866. A folding plan of Portland dated 1867 can be found in some copies of this directory, including that in the Cornell University Library. Another plan of this period was published in 1871 by Russell, Ferry, and Woodward of Portland. It was drawn by W. F. Brown and printed in San Francisco by the A. L. Bancroft company. An impression is in the collection of the Oregon Historical Society in Portland.

69. In 1881 J. K. Gill and Co. of Portland published an identical view with changes only in the imprint, subtitle, and legend. Impressions of this state of the lithograph can be found in the Honeyman Collection of the Bancroft Library at the University of California, Berkeley, and in the Oregon Historical Society, Portland.

70. In 1883 the editor of a Portland publication described the park for his readers as ''a beautiful tract,'' which ''with slight expense improvements can be

made that will give us one of the most lovely and attractive parks to be found in the Union." He also referred to the older strip park in the town below as having "driveways along its full length on either side, and many elegant residences facing it on both sides. With the improvements contemplated and the growth to larger proportions of the shade trees, these boulevards and parks will rival those of older cities." *The West Shore*, September, 1883, 201.

71. Ibid., September, 1883, 204. For the development of rail service to Portland see Glenn Chesney Quiett, *They Built The West*, 339-399. Brief summaries of the railroads serving Portland appear in Corning, *Dictionary of Oregon History*, 177-178, 180-181, 182, 252.

72. Victor, *Oregon and Washington*, 234, 237.

73. Section 13 of the congressional act establishing the Territory of Washington can be found in Arthur S. Beardsley, "Early Efforts to Locate the Capital of Washington Territory," 241, n. 5.

74. Beardsley's "Efforts to Locate the Capital" is the definitive study of the issue. These activities are also summarized in Steward, *Washington*, II, 130-132.

75. Victor, *Oregon and Washington*, 245.

76. Ibid., 249.

77. Ibid., 274.

78. Charles M. Gates, *The First Century at the University of Washington*, 8-10. I have also found helpful in my treatment of Seattle a research paper written under my direction at Cornell University by Barbara F. Dittrich in 1971, "A History of the Planning of Seattle, Washington, and the University of Washington Campus from 1851 to 1911."

79. Burke's remarkable career is the subject of Robert C. Nesbit, "*He Built Seattle*": *A Biography of Judge Thomas Burke*. See also Quiett, *They Built the West*, 439-495.

80. Grant, "Seattle," 641.

81. As quoted in Nesbit, "*He Built Seattle*," 41, from the issue of March 30, 1883.

82. Ellensburg *Capital*, April 25, 1889, as quoted in Samuel R. Mohler, "Boom Days in Ellensburg, 1888-1891," 290.

83. Ellensburg *Capital*, April 4, 1889, as quoted in Mohler, "Ellensburg," 296.

84. From an undated poster, a copy of which was furnished me by the Yakima County Planning Department along with a copy of a manuscript plat of North Yakima (now Yakima) in the records of the Recorder of Yakima County, Yakima, Washington. It shows 8 streets running north and south and 17 east-west streets on the east side of the railroad tracks and a smaller grid of 4 north-south and 9 east-west streets on the west side.

85. U.S. Writers' Program, *Washington*, 299-304; Dryden, *Dryden's History of Washington*, 318-320; Meinig, *Great Columbia Plain*, 236, 267-268.

86. N. W. Durham, *History of the City of Spokane*, I, 337-338.

87. From a description by E. A. Routhe, as quoted in Durham, *Spokane*, I, 361.

88. As quoted in Meinig, *Great Columbia Plain*, 322.

89. The capture of the county seat by Cheney is a fascinating story. The town received 14 more votes than Spokane, but when the ballots were recounted in the latter city—then serving as the temporary county seat—its representatives announced that because of "irregularities" Spokane had won by a vote or two. Five months later on the night of March 20, 1888, a band of Cheney citizens stole into the frame courthouse at Spokane where with the help of the friendly county auditor they constituted a recanvassing board, counted the ballots once again, announced that Cheney was truly the victor, and marched off with all of the county records to place them under armed guard at Cheney. E. E. Perry, "How Cheney Captured the County Seat," in Durham, *Spokane*, I, 395-398; Lucile F. Fargo, *Spokane Story*, 142-145.

90. As quoted from what was then the Spokan *Times*, in Fargo, *Spokane Story*, 146. Citizens of the town debated whether or not the town's name should include a terminal "e" as well as the word "Falls." Eventually the last letter was included and the second word dropped in the official name adopted for the city.

91. As quoted in Quiett, *They Built the West*, 505-506.

92. Recollections of Frank Dallam, as quoted in Durham, *Spokane*, I, 401; Fargo, *Spokane Story*, 199.

93. Spokane in the days of the Idaho gold rush is described in ibid., 150-163.

94. Durham, *Spokane*, I, 410.

95. For the fire and its aftermath see Fargo, *Spokane Story*, 164-167, 200-201; Durham, *Spokane*, I, 415-420, 429-436.

96. The view probably dates from 1890 when the first Spokane Industrial Exposition was held on the site shown in the view. Ibid., I, 435. The name of Spokane Falls became simply Spokane in 1891, when the city obtained a new charter. A view of the city in 1887 originally appearing in the *Northwest Magazine* is reproduced in Quiett, *They Built the West*, opposite p. 513.

97. As quoted in Durham, *Spokane*, I, 403, from an issue of the Spokane *Chronicle* in October, 1883.

XII · URBAN PLANNING ON THE CENTRAL PLAINS: THE SETTLEMENT OF NEBRASKA

1. The modern states of Kansas and Nebraska, while large, occupy about half of the combined area of the two territories as originally established. Nebraska Territory was by far the larger of the two, including all of the present state, two-thirds of Wyoming, virtually all of Montana, the northeastern corner of Colorado, and all of the Dakotas west of the Missouri River.

2. Writings on the Kansas-Nebraska Act are extensive. An excellent summary of its background and legislative history can be found in James C. Olson, *History of Nebraska*, 70-81. See also Roy F. Nichols, "The Kansas-Nebraska Act: A Century of Historiography," 187-212.

3. July 15, 1854, as quoted in Olson, *Nebraska*, 84.

4. Street, block, and lot dimensions and numbers, as well as other information on the plat, are given in William J. Shallcross, *Romance of a Village: Story of Bellevue*, 89-93. Another early plan of Bellevue is in the townsite records of the Bureau of Land Management, Department of the Interior, Silver Spring, Maryland. It is unsigned and undated, but was probably published ca. 1857. I have

been unable to relate its street pattern to the plan reproduced herein or to a street map of the modern city. It may have been intended as an extension of the town to the west. The only named street common to both plans is Sarpy.

5. Ibid., 141-173.

6. Omaha *Arrow*, September 29, 1854, as quoted in Donald F. Danker, "The Nebraska Winter Quarters Company and Florence," 30-31.

7. Nebraska Winter Quarters Company, *Minutes*, September 13, 1854, and November 4, 1854, manuscript in Library of the Nebraska Historical Society, as quoted in Danker, "Winter Quarters Company," 44.

8. Ibid., 46. Wyoming was platted in 1855. For its history and a copy of the original plat see Helen Roberta Williams, "Old Wyoming," 79-90. Descriptions of Wyoming during the Mormon period can be found in Andrew Jenson (comp.), "Latter-Day Saints Emigration from Wyoming, Nebraska—1864-1866," 113-127. With the decline in Mormon migration, Wyoming lost its principal economic base and swiftly declined in population.

9. A. T. Andreas, *History of the State of Nebraska*, III, 1174. This early history of the state contains a wealth of information, not all of it entirely reliable, on virtually all of the early towns of the state.

10. July 2, 1857, as quoted in Norman A. Graebner, "Nebraska's Missouri River Frontier, 1854-1860," 219-220.

11. A useful survey of the early years and historic buildings of Nemaha County and its three adjoining counties in southeastern Nebraska—Johnson, Pawnee, and Richardson—is John Q. Magie and Carl H. Jones, *A History and Historic Sites Survey of Johnson, Nemaha, Pawnee, and Richardson Counties in Southeastern Nebraska*.

12. G. H. Gilmore, "Ghost Towns in Cass County, Nebraska," 181. Gilmore lists the following: Avoca, Bluffdale, Bradford City, Brooklyn, Caladonia, Cedar Bluff, Cleveland, Eldorado, Elgin City, Factorville, Franklin, Glendale, Granada, Independence City, Independence North, Liberty, Marseilles, Montevalle, Oreopolis, Osage, Platteau, St. Charles, Smithland, Troy, Tysonville, Washington City, and Waterville.

13. John C. Miller, "Ghost Towns in Otoe County," 185-191. Miller lists them as follows: Brooklyn, California City, Cambridge, Condit, Delaware City, El Dorado, Erie, Groveland, Knoxville, Marietta, Nesuma, Saltfille, St. Charles, St. Peters, Summerville, and Woodville.

14. Andreas, *Nebraska*, II, 488-489.

15. For a brief summary of the evolution of rural cemetery and naturalistic park planning in the United States and its importance in city planning see John W. Reps, *The Making of Urban America*, 325-348, and the references cited, 556-557.

16. The addition of the word "city" to a more distinctive place name was a popular practice in western frontier town development. It was obviously intended to convey an air of permanence and importance—all the more important to the promoter if the town, as was common, was small and with dubious prospects. The device became known as "kiting" a town—by adding a tail to its body.

17. It would be impossible to list, describe, and reproduce plats of all of these communities. The most complete treatment can be found in Andreas, *Nebraska*. Many of the early manuscript or printed plats are in the map collection of the Nebraska Historical Society or can be found in county records. Occasional articles on Nebraska towns have appeared in *Nebraska History*, such as those cited and J. R. Johnson, "Covington: Nebraska's Sinful City," 269-281.

18. Congressman Bernhart Henn of western Iowa announced the appointment on May 6, 1854, in a letter to Dr. J. D. Test of Council Bluffs. Andreas, *Nebraska*, II, 681. See also Olson, *Nebraska*, 84-85, for a summary of these preliminary activities.

19. The promoters of Omaha must have circulated the lithographed plat widely. An October issue of the New York *Herald* included this item: "Omaha City, Nebraska Territory, promises to be a second edition of Chicago and other flourishing Western cities. . . . We have before us a plan of Omaha City, laid out in lots, numbered one up to three hundred and twenty-two. We have here Jefferson Square and Capital Square. . . . Altogether the prospects of Omaha City are good." Quoted in Alfred D. Jones, "Omaha's Early Days," 152-54.

20. As quoted in Consul Willshire Butterfield, "Omaha," 194-195.

21. Details of the transaction are described in Authur C. Wakely, *Omaha: The Gate City and Douglas County Nebraska*, I, 110-111. The donation of land for the hotel resulting in the abandonment of the park proved unnecessary, since the hotel was built on lots 7 and 8 of block 124 facing the park on the west. James W. Savage and John T. Bell, *History of the City of Omaha Nebraska*, 84-85.

22. Wakeley, *Omaha*, 130-132.

23. Olson, *Nebraska*, 88-89. For a long and somewhat partisan account of Cuming's activities in connection with apportionment of the legislature and his decision to designate Omaha as the site of its first meeting see J. Sterling Morton and Albert Watkins, *Illustrated History of Nebraska*, I, 164-193.

24. The measure passed the House by fourteen votes to eleven and the Council by seven votes to six. Savage and Bell, *Omaha*, 53-54.

25. For the details of its construction and financing as well as the controversies surrounding the building of the Capitol see Wakeley, *Omaha*, 129-130.

26. *Nebraska News*, December 19, 1857, as quoted in Graebner, "Missouri River Frontier," 221. No such praise of a rival town could appear in a frontier paper without compensating criticism, and the editor felt obliged to inform his readers that Omaha's growth had been artificially stimulated. "Remove the Capitol and Omaha is dead. She has no natural advantages aside from a beautiful *site*; her landing is a poor one; she is a good distance from the river; timber is sparse in the vicinity; she has no such country around and back of her as has Nebraska City."

27. Wakeley, *Omaha*, 108; Graebner, "Missouri River Frontier," 220-221.

28. Address by J. Sterling Morton at the first Nebraska Territorial Fair, Nebraska City, September 21, 1859, as quoted in Addison E. Sheldon, *Land Systems and Land Policies in Nebraska*, 39, n. 49.

29. Quoted from an unidentified source in Andreas, *Nebraska*, III, 1201.

30. Donald F. Danker (ed.), *Mollie: The Journal of Mollie Dorsey Sanford in*

Nebraska and Colorado Territories, 1857-1866, 12. This journal kept by an articulate and observing young settler in Nebraska and, later, Colorado, gives a fascinating glimpse of life on the Great Plains and Colorado mining frontiers.

31. In 1859 the company employed 1,100 men, operated 700 wagons, and owned nearly 6,000 yoke of Oxen. Andreas, *Nebraska*, III, 1203. The company spent more than $300,000 in developing its terminal complex in Nebraska City. Olson, *Nebraska*, 111.

32. Ibid., 110.

33. Danker, *Mollie*, 69.

34. Graebner, "Missouri River Frontier," 231.

35. Andreas, *Nebraska*, III, 1196-1197.

36. Donald F. Danker, "Columbus, a Territorial Town in the Platte Valley," 278. I have relied on Danker's article for much of my information about the development of Columbus.

37. A brief history and an inventory of buildings of historic importance in Pawnee City appears in Magie and Jones, *Historic Sites Survey*, 88-97.

38. For the details of the legislative maneuvering on the capital removal issue through 1857 see the following: Wakeley, *Omaha*, 67-69; Morton and Watkins, *Nebraska*, 275-278, 298-302; Savage and Bell, *Omaha*, 59-62; and Andreas, *Nebraska*, I, 115.

39. The legislative activities leading to the passage of the removal act are summarized in Addison E. Sheldon, *Nebraska: The Land and the People*, I, 388-394. A fuller account can be found in Morton and Watkins, *Nebraska*, III, 8-24.

40. Between 1857 and 1867 the names and boundaries of the counties in this area had changed from those shown in Figure 21. On that map the area can be traced as comprising the counties of Greene and Lancaster and the southern half of Butler and Calhoun Counties.

41. A conjectural redrawing of the Lancaster plat is reproduced in A. B. Hayes and Samuel D. Cox, *History of the City of Lincoln*, and also in N. C. Abbott, "Lincoln: Name and Place," Nebraska State Historical Society, *Publications*, XXI, Lincoln, 1930.

42. The text of the commissioners' report can be found in Hayes and Cox, *Lincoln*, 124-134. A seminar paper, "Austin, Texas, and Lincoln, Nebraska," prepared under my direction at Cornell University by Steven E. Sher in 1970 has been helpful to me in my research on the early development of the city of Lincoln.

43. Olson, *Nebraska*, 155; Morton and Watkins, *Nebraska*, III, 33.

44. Olson, *Nebraska*, 155; Andreas, *Nebraska*, III, 1042.

45. Olson, *Nebraska*, 156-160; Morton and Watkins, *Nebraska*, III, 62-90.

46. The actual population of the city at this time is a matter of some question. "By 1880 Lincoln . . . claimed a population of 13,003. We cannot be too sure how this figure was secured but we do know that on May 19, 1876, the city council in secret session resolved that inasmuch as the last census of Lincoln showed a decrease of 2,600 the committee on finance be authorized to employ a competent person to take a new census. And we do get an idea of the ingenuity of Lincoln citizens along this line when we observe that whereas the census of 1880 indi-

cated a population of 13,003 that of 1890 gave the figure 55,159, or an increase of over four hundred per cent in ten years' time. The council must have seen that a competent man indeed and in truth secured the job of census taker for Uncle Sam that year. Even with a healthy steady growth it was forty years before the United States census figures ever exceeded that of the padded census of 1890." Everett N. Dick, "Problems of the Post Frontier Prairie City as Portrayed by Lincoln, Nebraska, 1880-1890," 133. Dick adds that in 1890 the probable population was 29,000.

XIII · THE CENTRAL PLAINS: TOWNS OF KANSAS

1. E. T. Carr, "Reminiscences Concerning Fort Leavenworth in 1855-'56," 375-382.

2. T. H. Gladstone, *The Englishman in Kansas*, 141-143.

3. Albert D. Richardson, *Beyond the Mississippi*, 53-54. Richardson incorporated a great deal of sly humor in his reports of the West, a feature that makes his classic account of settlement in the region as entertaining as it is informative. In describing the use of cottonwood for lumber at Leavenworth, Richardson commented that "when put in green and left unpainted, it warps wonderfully, making the house twist about like a corkscrew." See also his account of the techniques of making fraudulent land claims and the accompanying amusing illustrations, pp. 137-141.

4. Horace Greeley, *An Overland Journey*, 48.

5. Bayard Taylor, *Colorado: A Summer Trip*, 4.

6. Frank W. Blackmar (ed.), *Kansas: A Cyclopedia of State History*, I, 108-109.

7. Sheffield Ingalls, *History of Atchison County Kansas*, 72.

8. Walker D. Wyman, "Atchison, A Great Frontier Depot," *Kansas Historical Quarterly*, XI (1942), 307.

9. Originally this organization was called the Massachusetts Emigrant Aid Society, but its name was changed to reflect its broader basis of support. For its activities see Samuel A. Johnson, *The Battle Cry of Freedom*; and Edgar Langsdorf, "S. C. Pomeroy and the New England Emigrant Aid Company, 1854-1858," 227-245, 379-398. The settlement efforts of another similar but smaller organization are described in Alberta Pantle, "The Connecticut Kansas Colony," 1-50.

10. James C. Malin, "Emergency Housing at Lawrence, 1854," 37.

11. The system of land sales, donations, and company retention of a portion of the Lawrence town lots is summarized in ibid., 39-40.

12. Letter from E. D. Ladd, November 11, 1854, as quoted in ibid., 44. On November 30 Ladd wrote: "The residences of our city, of which I gave you a partial description in my last, have, since that time, put on a new and strange appearance. Most of the tent-shaped buildings have a covering of turf, cut up in square pieces and laid on; the former condition not being considered a sufficient protection against the cold of winter" (44-45). Two contemporary sketches showing buildings in Lawrence of the type described by Ladd are reproduced with descriptive notes in Malin's useful article.

13. Letter from Charles B. Lines to the New Haven *Daily Palladium*, April 15, 1856, as quoted in Pantle, "Connecticut Kansas Colony," 14-15.

14. Langsdorf, "Pomeroy and Aid Company," 235.

15. James C. Malin, "Housing Experiments in the Lawrence Community, 1855," 112-113. These prefabricated cottages were sold in other Kansas towns and in Nebraska as well. Malin states that "Leavenworth imported many Hinkle cottages, so many that one section of the town was nicknamed Cincinnati."

16. Letter from Dr. Webb to S. C. Pomeroy, October 30, 1854, as quoted in Langsdorf, "Pomeroy and Aid Company," 233.

17. For several accounts of the site selection and town company organization, including Holliday's, see James L. King, *History of Shawnee County, Kansas*, 117-136.

18. This feature of Topeka's plan is discussed in Wallace S. Baldinger, "The Amateur Plans a City," 5. Baldinger also points out that, given the conditions of sun, temperature, and wind at Topeka, the lots of the town had an almost ideal orientation. He suggests, rightly I believe, that this was more accident than intent, since "such subtleties of orientation were probably unknown or merely guessed at in Holliday's time."

19. F. W. Giles, *Thirty Years in Topeka* (1886), 17. Giles was secretary of the Topeka Association and assisted Holliday with his compass survey of the town.

20. The cities shown on the map, beginning at the south, are as follows: Wyandotte, Quindaro, Weimar, Delaware City, Leavenworth, Kickapoo, Port William, Sumner, Atchison, Doniphan, Geary City, Petersburg, Palermo, Elwood, Whitehead, Iowa Point, and White Cloud. Brief histories of most of them can be found in Blackmar, *Kansas*.

21. A copy of a lithographed plat of Sumner in 1857 is in the collection of the Kansas Historical Society. It measures 29 inches by 46 inches and was doubtless intended for display purposes.

22. Richardson, *Beyond the Mississippi*, 56.

23. Ingalls' letter, October 5, 1858, Kansas State Historical Society, *Collections*, xiv (1915-18), 99-100. In a later letter Ingalls referred again to the deceptive view that had aroused his enthusiasm for Kansas as "That chromatic triumph of lithographed mendacity." Sheffield Ingalls, *Atchison County*, 93.

24. Ingalls' letter to his father, February 16, 1859, Kansas State Historical Soceity, *Collections*, xiv (1915-18), 111.

25. Sheffield Ingalls, *Atchison County*, 87.

26. Richardson, *Beyond the Mississippi*, 549.

27. *Wyandotte County and Kansas City, Kansas*, 337.

28. Richardson, *Beyond the Mississippi*, 33.

29. Greeley, *Overland Journey*, 25.

30. Richardson, *Beyond the Mississippi*, 29.

31. Greeley, *Overland Journey*, 25.

32. Richardson, *Beyond the Mississippi*, 58-59. Other observers commented in the same vein. A correspondent for the New York *Tribune*, writing from Tecumseh in 1857, reported that "the number of towns laid out in this territory is something extraordinary. Every man who owns a quarter section, well located, lays it out at once into a town, so that they dot the map like the block agencies of a checkerboard. Of course but one in three or four can succeed—the rest must revert into farms." The New York *Daily Tribune*, May 20, 1857, as quoted in Roy M. Robbins, *Our Landed Heritage*, Lincoln, 1964, 196-197. Horace Greeley observed in 1859 that "it takes three log houses to make a city in Kansas, but they begin *calling* it a city so soon as they have staked out the lots." Greeley, *Overland Journey*, 39.

33. Reminiscences of James G. Sands, November 8, 1902, as quoted in George Martin, "Some of the Lost Towns of Kansas," 432.

34. The full text of the prospectus appears in an appendix to Miriam Davis Colt, *Went to Kansas*.

35. Russell K. Hickman, "The Vegetarian and Octagon Settlement Companies," 377-385.

36. Some of Clubb's earlier vegetarian tracts had been published by the New York firm of Fowler and Wells. Orson Fowler, one of the partners, had written a book on house design advocating the octagonal plan as the most efficient. Clubb may have picked up the idea from Fowler and expanded the concept to the scale of an entire town.

37. The constitution and the proposals and plans of the company are printed in full in [C. W. Dana], *The Garden of the World, or the Great West . . . by an Old Settler*, 221-225.

38. A brief history of the American Settlement Company and its town appears in Blackmar, *Kansas*, ɪ, 67-68.

39. Among them was Whitfield City, enthusiastically and inaccurately described in a guidebook of the period as a budding metropolis whose "manual-labor college" was in the process of being established. At least one hardy pioneer made the long journey from the East to find only surveyor's stakes as an indication that the site had ever been visited by man. See Fannie Cole, "Pioneer Life in Kansas," 354-355; and, for an extract from *History of Kansas and Emigrants Guide* containing the promotional passage about Whitfield City, Everett Dick, *The Sod-House Frontier*, 53. Dick's chapters, "Town-Building Mania" and "The River Cities of the Fifties," summarize speculative townsite promotional techniques in Kansas, Nebraska, and the Dakotas during the early settlement period.

40. Julia Louisa Lovejoy, "Letters from Kansas," 29-44; Blackmar, *Kansas*, ɪɪ, 213-214. The plat of Manhattan is reproduced in F. P. Graham, *An Introduction to City Planning in Kansas*, 18. It shows a gridiron plat centered on a large public park occupying an area equal in size to nine of the standard blocks, six one-block public squares, and an irregularly shaped park at the confluence of the Big Blue and Kansas Rivers. In May, 1859, according to Horace Greeley, Manhattan was "an embryo city of perhaps one hundred houses." Greeley, *Overland Journey*, 58.

41. The plat of the town as laid out in 1854 is in the collection of the Kansas Historical Society. It shows a much more modest size community consisting of 27 blocks arranged in typical checkerboard fashion with a single public square

probably intended for the courthouse, the building shown in the view terminating the street leading from the bridge. That building never existed, and Tecumseh's efforts to be designated as the county seat of Shawnee County failed when the legislature authorized a referendum to decide the issue. In the ensuing election Topeka polled a majority of the votes. King, *Shawnee County*, 31.

42. The governor did advise his private secretary to "buy in Pawnee" prior to issuing his proclamation, an indication that Reeder may have had financial as well as political reasons for his unexpected choice of so western a location. See text of a letter from John A. Halderman, September 8, 1903, in Franklin G. Adams, "The Capitals of Kansas," 332.

43. Robert W. Richmond, "The First Capitol of Kansas," 321-325, contains an account of the brief legislative proceedings at Pawnee and the building in which the governor and members of the legislature met. It is now restored and serves as a museum under the administration of the Kansas Historical Society. Pawnee soon vanished. A new survey of the Fort Riley reservation in 1855 revealed that the town had been built on military property. Residents were evicted and all the buildings except the "Capitol" were razed. See also Adams, "Capitals of Kansas"; and Henry Shindler, "The First Capital of Kansas," 331-337.

44. The literature of Kansas during this tragic period is extensive. For a summary of these events see William Frank Zornow, *Kansas: A History of the Jayhawk State*, 69-79. The sources cited by Zornow may be consulted for a more detailed treatment of this period.

45. There are two undated printed plans of Lecompton in the collection of the Kansas Historical Society. What is almost certainly the earlier of the two is completely different from that reproduced in Figure 13.21. It bears the title, "Lecompton Kansas Territory," and, like the other plan, was printed in St. Louis by E. Robyn.

46. Ely Moore, "The Story of Lecompton," 473. Even in 1858 when the city was near the height of its prosperity Lecompton did not appear particularly impressive. A view of the town in that year, reproduced in Myle H. Miller, Edgar Langsdorf, and Robert W. Richmond, *Kansas: A Pictorial History*, shows a straggling village mainly of one-story houses stretching back a few hundred feet from the river.

47. The confusing series of elections and referenda are described in Zornow, *Kansas*, 75-79.

48. For Minneola see the following: Martin, "Lost Towns of Kansas," 433-434; and Adams, "Capitals of Kansas," 342-344.

49. Two votes were taken. At the first, delegates could vote for any city of their choice. Twenty-two places received at least one vote, with Topeka receiving a plurality of 15 out of the 50 cast. The second vote involved only the three cities receiving the highest number of votes on the first ballot: Topeka, Lawrence, and Atchison. In this vote Topeka was favored by 29, Lawrence by 14, and Atchison by 6. Adams, "Capitals of Kansas," 374.

50. Ibid., 347-348.

51. Baldinger, "The Amateur Plans a City," 10.

52. The view of 1880, as was often true for those of other cities, anticipated completion of the Capitol by a number of years. The central portion was not begun until 1883, and it was a full twenty years later before it and its dome were completed and turned over to the state by the contractor. King, *Shawnee County*, 145.

53. Taylor, *Colorado: A Summer Trip*, 184.

XIV · RUSH TO THE ROCKIES: DENVER AND THE MINING TOWNS OF COLORADO

1. For an account of the first prospectors and how the news of their discoveries reached the East, see Phyllis Flanders Dorset, *The New Eldorado*, 3-17.

2. Libeus Barney, *Letters of the Pike's Peak Gold Rush*. Barney's letter was published in the Bennington, Vermont *Banner*, May 11, 1859, one of many remarkably informative communications from this perceptive observer.

3. Knowledge of Colorado's geography was limited. Although Pikes Peak lay some 60 miles to the south, the legend on the canvas covers of many wagons bound for Cherry Creek read "Pikes Peak or Bust."

4. Nolie Mumey, *History of the Early Settlements of Denver (1599-1860)*, 45; Hubert Howe Bancroft, *History of Nevada, Colorado, and Wyoming, 1540-1888*, 366, 388.

5. Mumey, *Denver*, 47-48. The site is now bounded by West Evans Avenue, South Tremont Street, West Iliff Avenue, and the South Platte River.

6. See ibid., 54-58 for the full text of the articles of agreement and the constitution of the town company.

7. Ibid., 59-60; William McGaa, "A Statement Regarding the Formation of the St. Charles and Denver Town Companies," 126-127.

8. In a statement written many years after the fact and in an attempt to enforce his own claims to some 72 acres of land within the city of Denver, McGaa maintained that he was forced to abandon his position as a member of the St. Charles company and join the new one when its members threatened him with the destruction of his cabin and told him that he would be forced to leave the area. McGaa, "Statement," 127. Mumey, on the other hand, indicates that McGaa encouraged the new arrivals to jump the St. Charles claim. Mumey, *Denver*, 82.

9. The county boundaries had been established earlier by the first territorial legislature of Kansas to include the area around Cherry Creek. Because of the lack of settlement, no effective governmental jurisdiction had been exercised. According to Denver himself, as he recalled events in 1890, it was his idea to make the appointments. See the text of his letter to General William Larimer, November 14, 1890, in George C. Barns, *Denver, The Man*, 225-226.

10. [W. B. Vickers], *History of the City of Denver, Arapahoe County, and Colorado*, 194.

11. The single park block in the eastern corner was eliminated when this entire section was replatted sometime prior to 1871. The "Court House Square"

remained unoccupied for years. The view of Denver in 1874, reproduced in Plate 20, shows this as an open block. By 1882, as shown on the view in Figure 14.24, a major structure had been erected on the site. This later was demolished and the block used for the United States Customhouse and other federal offices in a building erected in 1930.

12. Mumey, *Denver*, 63, 66.

13. Henry Villard, *The Past and Present of the Pike's Peak Gold Regions* (1860), 134-135.

14. D. C. Oakes, the author of the first guidebook to the Colorado mining region was threatened with lynching in 1859 when on his return trip to Denver he met a party of disgruntled miners. Reading his enthusiastic descriptions, they had made their way to the diggings but had found nothing. Oakes saved his neck only by hiding in his wagon as it passed by the angry would-be miners. Near Julesburg Oakes came across a tombstone on which he read the following epitaph scrawled in charcoal and axle grease:

> Here lies the remains of D. C. Oakes
> Who was the starter of this D--- Hoax!

Mumey, *Denver*, 74-76. See Bancroft, *Nevada, Colorado, and Wyoming* for other and similar inscriptions dedicated to the "memory" of Oakes and his *Pike's Peak Guide and Journal*, published in the fall of 1858 in Pacific City, Iowa.

15. Albert D. Richardson, *Our New States and Territories*, 14-15. Richardson's drawing shows his cabin with a whiskey keg as the chimney. In another view he depicted St. Charles Street as two parallel rows of surveyor's stakes vanishing over the horizon. The land on either side is completely unoccupied except for half a dozen prairie dogs sitting on their mounds.

16. Villard, *Gold Regions*, 37. The circumstances of Gregory's discovery are described in Dorset, *New Eldorado*, 28-29, along with the nearly simultaneous strike by George Jackson on the nearby south fork of Clear Creek. For my treatment of the Colorado mining communities I have been helped by a research paper carried out under my direction at Cornell University by Ellen E. Lamb in 1970, "Colorado Mining Towns."

17. Villard, *Gold Regions*, 38.

18. Letter from R. E. Whitsitt to Daniel Witter, May 16, 1859, and postscript, June 17, *Colorado Magazine*, i (1893), 283-285. The text is also given in Mumey, *Denver*, 190-196.

19. Barney, letter, July 12, 1859, *Gold Rush Letters*, 41.

20. Mumey, *Denver*, 169-171.

21. Barney, letter, November 23, 1859, *Gold Rush Letters*, 53.

22. *Denver City and Auraria, the Commerical Emporium of the Pike's Peak Gold Regions in 1859*, 11-12. A facsimile of the entire directory accompanies Mumey, *Denver*. This directory provides some clues as to the differing character of the two communities. Of the 27 merchants, 18 were in Denver and 9 in Auraria. Denver also had 6 of the 9 real estate offices. The 8 physicians were evenly divided as to

location. Auraria led in industrial activities with 3 of the 5 lumber yards, both of the gunsmiths and the 2 tinsmiths, the only brewery, and 2 of the 3 blacksmiths.

23. Two other views of this period should be noted. One of Auraria appeared in the *New-York Illustrated News*, July 7, 1860. It is a wood engraving measuring approximately 6 inches by 9 inches. A view of Denver, similar in character, was published in *Frank Leslie's Illustrated Newspaper* for August 20, 1859.

24. Letter from R. E. Whitsitt to Daniel Witter, May 16, 1859, as quoted in Mumey, *Denver*, 192. Whitsitt added that in Auraria "they are making a great hullabaloo because they have got the first board roof, but every building in Denver City will have a fine board roof . . . before another winter sets in. . . . Meanwhile a good mud roof ain't a thing to be despised in a dry country like this. If they are well made, there is no particular danger of them washing down on a family, the way some folks complain of, unless it rains unusually hard, and a smart man will put a new coat of adobe on any ordinary roof in a single day. They are a warm thing in the winter and if you shoved the snow off when it falls particular heavy, they won't leak so very hard. 'Tisn't as if pioneers were sporting velvet carpets and satin upholstery that a little stream of muddy water running down here and there would spoil."

25. Mumey, *Denver*, 136.

26. Villard, *Gold Regions*, 133, n 81. According to one Denver historian in 1876, the company received 1,460 lots (ten shares) as an inducement to locate its office in Denver rather than Auraria. O. J. Goldrick, "Historical Sketch of Denver, Colorado, 1858-1876," in Nolie Mumey, *Prof. Oscar J. Goldrick and his Denver*, 24. An advertisement by the stage company in the first city directory announced that "coaches will start from St. Joseph, Leavenworth City and Atchison," making the run to Denver in 6 days. Stations were located "every twenty miles, where passengers will obtain their regular meals and comfortable beds." *Denver City and Auraria . . . in 1859*, outside back cover.

27. An earlier proposal was for a state constitution. Richardson was alluding to this when he wrote of Denver in June, 1859: "Making governments and building towns are the natural employments of the migratory Yankee. He takes to them as instinctively as a young duck to water. Congregate a hundred Americans any where beyond the settlements, and they immediately lay out a city, frame a State Constitution, and apply for admission into the Union, while twenty-five of them become candidates for the United States Senate." Richardson, *New States and Territories*, 14.

28. Mumey, *Denver*, 197.

29. Ibid., 197-198; Vickers, *Denver*, 196.

30. Barney, letter, July 9, 1860, *Gold Rush Letters*, 89.

31. Ibid., 90; Villard, *Gold Regions*, 129; Albert D. Richardson, *Beyond the Mississippi*, 186.

32. Bayard Taylor, *Colorado: A Summer Trip*, 36. For information about Mathews, as well as other western illustrators, see Robert Taft, *Artists and Illustrators of the Old West*.

33. Louis L. Simonin, *The Rocky Mountain West in 1867*, 32-33.

34. Villard, *Gold Regions*, 87. Villard gives the complete regulations of the mining district, 83-88.

35. One local historian states that "near the end of the summer in 1860 Nathaniel Albertson, John Armour, and Harrison G. Otis platted the townsite of Central City." Frank R. Hollenback, *Central City and Black Hawk Colorado Then and Now*, 9. Bancroft did not know of the Sayre plat of 1863 when he wrote that "Central City was not surveyed into lots until 1866, when George H. Hill laid it off." Bancroft, *Nevada, Colorado, and Wyoming*, 611, n 3. The 1866 survey was made to comply with the provisions of the federal townsite act so that lot titles might be confirmed to their owners who until that time had only squatter's rights.

36. Taylor, *Colorado*, 56-57.

37. Dorset, *New Eldorado*, 166-170.

38. Ibid., 179-180. Grant's reaction to the appearance of the Teller House is not recorded, but a Central City banker, Frank Young, commented sourly that the building "might easily be taken for a New England factory, and cut off a story or two and it might pass fairly well for a cavalry barracks."

39. As quoted from an unidentified source in Hollenback, *Central City*, 11.

40. A convenient guide to the town is ibid. It contains a series of photographs of the principal surviving buildings, a summary history of each, and a legible map showing their locations.

41. This can be seen on a view of Idaho Springs in 1882, published by J. J. Stoner, Madison, Wisconsin, a copy of which is in the collection of the Western History Department, Denver Public Library.

42. *History of Clear Creek and Boulder Valleys, Colorado*, 281.

43. Ibid., 283.

44. Ibid., 288.

45. George A. Crofutt, *Crofutt's Grip-Sack Guide of Colorado*, II, 95. A 1966 reprint published in Golden, Colorado, contains a pictorial supplement of nineteenth-century photographs of many of the towns mentioned in the guide. A view of Georgetown is among them. See p. 185.

46. For a summary of du Puyt's career and his Hotel de Paris see Dorset, *New Eldorado*, 199-202.

47. Taylor, *Colorado*, 112, 119.

48. Samuel Bowles, *Our New West*, 141, 149.

49. Villard, *Gold Regions*, 11-12.

50. Sara E. Robbins, *Jefferson County, Colorado: The Colorful Past of a Great Community*, 4-6.

51. Ibid., 27. *Crofutt's Guide*. 123, described Mount Vernon in 1885 as "a small town, postoffice, hotel and store."

52. Villard, *Gold Regions*, 137.

53. Barney, Letter, November 23, 1859, *Gold Rush Letters*, 57-58.

54. Richardson, *Beyond the Mississippi*, 275.

55. Bancroft, *Nevada, Colorado, and Wyoming*, 417. According to Bancroft, 390, in the summer of 1860 Colorado City had 300 houses. On the other hand, when Richardson passed through the town on a second trip that summer he noted that it then contained only "a hundred log houses," *Beyond the Mississippi*, 312.

56. Barney, Letter, November 23, 1859, *Gold Rush Letters*, 57.

57. Villard, *Gold Regions*, 135-136.

58. Bancroft, *Nevada, Colorado, and Wyoming*, 381.

59. Richardson, *Beyond the Mississippi*, 195-196.

60. Dorset, *New Eldorado*, 245-246.

61. Ibid., 247; William S. Greever, *The Bonanza West*, 183-184.

62. Ibid., 184.

63. Don L. Griswold and Jean Harvey Griswold, *The Carbonate Camp Called Leadville*, 96, 98-99.

64. Helen Hunt, "To Leadville," 547-575.

65. Greever, *Bonanza West*, 185; Griswold, *Leadville*, 133-134.

66. For the street system planned in 1878 and expanded the next year see ibid., 115-116.

67. Ibid., 131-133.

68. *History of Clear Creek*, 69.

69. Griswold, *Leadville*, caption on photograph, "West State Street, 100 Block (1879)," following p. 130. Preceding this photograph is another in 1879 looking north on Harrison from the same intersection shown in Figure 14.19. Two cabins appear in the center of the street. One probably belonged to C. E. Wyman, who found his supposedly corner lot squarely in the middle of Harrison Avenue when it was surveyed. He refused to move it, and eventually the city government was forced to take possession and tear it down. Griswold, *Leadville*, 133. Wyman operated one of the 118 gambling halls in Leadville at the corner of Harrison and State. A sign over the band pit read "Don't Shoot the Pianist—He's Doing his Damndest." Oscar Wilde, who visited Leadville and lectured to a crowd of bewildered miners on "Ethics in Art," was said to have remarked that the sign "was the most rational bit of art criticism he had ever read." Dorset, *New Eldorado*, 261, 274.

70. For the "Royal Gorge War" see Glenn Chesney Quiett, *They Built the West*, 55-60; and Griswold, *Leadville*, 134-150.

71. The story of Cripple Creek is amusingly told in Marshall Sprague, *Money Mountain: The Story of Cripple Creek Gold*. See pp. 3-84 for Womack's role and that of others leading up to the Cripple Creek rush.

72. Ibid., 89-90.

73. Robert Guilford Taylor, *Cripple Creek*, 51. Taylor's monograph is a valuable study tracing in detail the physical development of Cripple Creek and the neighboring towns from their founding to the present.

74. Sprague, *Money Mountain*, 278-284.

75. Ibid., 93-94.

76. Ibid., 165.

77. Ibid., Table III, Table IV, 300-301.

78. Vickers, *Denver*, 239.

79. Ibid., 216; Edith Eudora Kohl, *Denver's Historic Mansions*, 17-18. See Kohl, p. 20, for a map showing the Brown homestead boundary and its division into streets and the capitol site.

80. Vickers, *Denver*, 230. Vickers states that the census of January, 1874, showed the population to be 14,197. A reference on the view of Denver in Plate 20 gives the population as 17,000, doubtless somewhat exaggerated.

81. Ibid., 216. For an account of the mass meeting Train addressed on the evening of November 15, 1867, see Quiett, *They Built the West*, 157-159.

82. Vickers, *Denver*, 221-222.

83. Crofutt, *Crofutt's Guide*, 31-32.

XV · THE EXPANDING MINING FRONTIER: CAMPS AND TOWNS OF IDAHO, MONTANA, AND SOUTH DAKOTA

1. William S. Greever, *The Bonanza West*, 257-259; Harold E. Briggs, *Frontiers of the Northwest*, 8-9.

2. Merrill D. Beal and Merle W. Wells, *History of Idaho*, I, 287, 291.

3. Port Townsend, Washington *North West*, July 26, 1861, as quoted in " 'We're Off to the Mines': Elk City, Pierce, and the Clearwater Gold Rush," 10.

4. Steilacoom, Washington *Puget Sound Herald*, September 5, 1861, as quoted in ibid., 12.

5. Joaquin Miller, *An Illustrated History of the State of Montana*, 102.

6. Portland, *Oregonian*, September 3, 1861, as quoted in "Off to the Mines," 14.

7. Sacramento *Daily Union*, September 16, 1861, as quoted in ibid., 15, 18.

8. G. W. Hall to H. A. Judson, January 10, 1862, in the Olympia, Washington *Overland Press*, February 24, 1862, as quoted in "Fabulous Florence," 23.

9. Sacramento *Daily Union*, June 19, 1862, as quoted in ibid., 30.

10. Briggs, *Frontiers of the Northwest*, 11.

11. Hubert Howe Bancroft, *History of Washington, Idaho, and Montana, 1845-1889*, 420-421.

12. E. B. Smith, "Pioneer Background of Atlanta," undated MS in the Idaho Historical Society.

13. Albert D. Richardson, *Beyond the Mississippi*, 504-505.

14. Letter from Charles N. Teeter to his sister, Idaho City, July 16, 1865, "Letters from the Boise Basin, 1864-1865," 29-30.

15. "Those Were the Days: Idaho in 1860," 26, n 27.

16. For the site selection and early planning of Boise I have drawn on the following: Eugene B. Chaffee, "Boise: The Founding of a City," 2-7; Gertrude Illingworth Porter, "An Historical Study of the Establishment of Boise City and Fort Boise," 9-19; and "Boise, City of Trees: A Centennial History."

17. Letter from Major Lugenbeel, July 27, 1863, as quoted in "First Plat of Boise City," Idaho Historical Society, *Eleventh Biennial Report, 1927-1928*.

18. "Waifs of Travel by 'Chaos,' " as quoted in Porter, "Boise City," 18.

19. The fight over the capital location is described in Eugene B. Chaffee, "The Political Clash Between North and South Idaho over the Capital," 255-267; and Annie Laurie Bird, "A Footnote on the Capital Dispute in Idaho," 341-346.

20. Albert D. Richardson, *Our New States and Territories*, 78.

21. Bancroft, *Washington, Idaho, and Montana*, 542, n 4.

22. An unpublished seminar paper by Robert Michael Craig, "Montana Mining Towns," prepared under my direction at Cornell University in 1971, has been useful to me in writing the foregoing section of this chapter on the Montana mining frontier.

23. Merrill G. Burlingame and K. Ross Toole, *A History of Montana*, I, 124; II, 182.

24. James McClellan Hamilton, *From Wilderness to Statehood: A History of Montana, 1805-1900*, 279, 338-339.

25. Granville Stuart, *Forty Years on the Frontier*, I, 254.

26. Stuart, *Forty Years*, I, 263-264.

27. James Knox Polk Miller, *The Road to Virginia City*, 75.

28. Stuart, *Forty Years*, I, 271-272.

29. Burlingame and Toole, *Montana*, II, 177; Merrill G. Burlingame, *The Montana Frontier*, 88; Briggs, *Frontiers of the Northwest*, 19.

30. Briggs, *Frontiers of the Northwest*, 20, citing the Virginia City, *Montana Post*, September 18, 1864.

31. Burlingame, *Montana Frontier*, 88.

32. Larry Barsness, *Gold Camp: Alder Gulch and Virginia City, Montana*, 68-71.

33. Hamilton, *Wilderness to Statehood*, 338.

34. Virginia City *Montana Post*, March 25, 1865, as quoted in Barsness, *Gold Camp*, 69.

35. *Report of James W. Taylor, on the Mineral Resources of the United States East of the Rocky Mountains*, 45.

36. Burlingame, *Montana Frontier*, 90. Burlingame states that the rules were adopted on July 29, 1864. Joaquin Miller, *Montana*, 272, gives the date as July 20 and provides the following text of these brief regulations: "That the gulch be named Last Chance Gulch, and the district . . . Rattle Snake District . . . . That mining claims . . . extend for 200 feet up and down the gulch, and from summit to summit. That no person be allowed to hold more than one claim by premption, and one by purchase, except as regards the discovery claim. That the discovery party shall have the prior right to the use of the gulch water. That claims, when pre-empted, be staked and recorded. That any person, besides his own claim, be allowed to record one for his actual partner, and one only, and that he can represent both; but if a partner be so recorded for, it must be specified, and the name given in full."

37. Ibid., 273-274.

38. Citing the Helena *Republican* for September 20, 1866 as his authority, Hubert Bancroft stated that Wood "was the only one of the committee who ever attempted to discharge the duties of his office. . . . If Helena shows defects of

grade and narrowness of streets in the original plan, it could not be otherwise in a town hastily settled, without surveys, and necessarily conforming to the character of the ground." Bancroft, *Washington, Idaho, and Montana*, 721, n. 5.

39. Diary of Andrew J. Fisk for 1866, in Helen McCann White (ed.), *Ho! For the Gold Fields: Northern Overland Wagon Trains of the 1860's*, 214-215.

40. Miller, *Road to Virginia City*, 112.

41. Bancroft, *Washington, Idaho, and Montana*, 755, n. 1.

42. Ibid., 752, n 1.

43. For some details concerning Anaconda and Daly's role in its promotion as well as a summary of the capital site issue, see Burlingame and Toole, *Montana*, II, 199-202.

44. Richardson, *Beyond the Mississippi*, 482-483.

45. Greever, *Bonanza West*, 224; Alton B. Oviatt, "Fort Benton, River Capital," in Burlingame and Toole, *Montana*, I, 139-141.

46. John R. Barrows, *Ubet*, as quoted in Oviatt, "Fort Benton," 141.

47. Burlingame and Toole, *Montana*, II, 170-171.

48. In tracing the development of Missoula I have relied on information in U.S. Federal Writers' Project, *Montana*, 172-182; Burlingame and Toole, *Montana*, II, 230-234; and Bancroft, *Washington, Idaho, and Montana*, 784, n 5.

49. Oviatt, "Fort Benton," 147; James H. Bradley, "Account of the Attempts to Build a Town at the Mouth of the Musselshell River," 304-305.

50. Bradley, "Account," 305-313.

51. Virginia City *Montana Post*, April 8 and April 22, 1865, as quoted in Briggs, *Frontiers of the Northwest*, 478-479.

52. Two popular but useful studies of the mining towns of this region are Norman D. Weiss, *Ghost Towns of the Northwest*; and Muriel Sibell Wolle, *Montana Pay Dirt*. A similar treatment of Wyoming ghost towns is Mary Lou Pence and Lola M. Homsher, *The Ghost Towns of Wyoming*.

53. Briggs, *Frontiers of the Northwest*, 25-29; Greever, *Bonanza West*, 286-288; Watson Parker, *Gold in the Black Hills*, 3-23.

54. Herbert S. Schell, *History of South Dakota*, 88-89.

55. Schell, *South Dakota*, 126-127.

56. Ibid., 129-130.

57. Harold E. Briggs, "The Black Hills Gold Rush," 91.

58. The diary of George V. Ayers, in Agnes Wright Spring, *The Cheyenne and Black Hills Stage and Express Routes*, 363.

59. Hill City was platted in February, 1876, by Robert Florman, Thomas Harvey, John Miller, and Hugh McCullough. Sheridan was surveyed in the fall of 1875. Parker, *Gold in the Black Hills*, 80.

60. Briggs, "Black Hills Gold Rush," 96.

61. Richard B. Hughes, *Pioneer Years in the Black Hills*, 77-78.

62. Hughes, *Pioneer Years*, 108.

63. Parker, *Gold in the Black Hills*, 92.

64. Hughes, *Pioneer Years*, 108.

65. *Appleton's Annual Cyclopedia, 1877*, 245-246, as quoted in Briggs, "Black Hills Gold Rush," 97.

66. Letter from George S. Pelton in the Glyndon, Minnesota *Red River Valley News*, September 9, 1880, as quoted in Arthur J. Larsen (ed.), "A Journey to the Black Hills in 1880," 47.

67. Greever, *Bonanza West*, 308.

68. Hughes, *Pioneer Years*, 150-151, n. 32.

69. Parker, *Gold in the Black Hills*, 84.

70. U.S. Federal Writers' Project, *A South Dakota Guide*, 143-145.

71. Charles Shinn, *Mining Camps*.

XVI · RAILROADS TO THE ROCKIES AND
THE URBAN SETTLEMENT OF THE
CENTRAL AND NORTHERN GREAT PLAINS

1. Chapter 120, July 1, 1862, *U.S. Statutes at Large*, XII, 489-498.

2. For the background of the transcontinental railroad movement and the early legislation that was proposed and finally adopted see Robert Riegel, *The Story of the Western Railroads*, New York, 1926.

3. Paul Gates, *The Illinois Central Railroad and Its Colonization Work*, Chapter VII, "Town-Site Promotion." I have summarized the town planning activities of the Illinois Central line in *The Making of Urban America*, Princeton, 1965, 389-392, which contains a reproduction of the standard plat used by the Illinois Associates for 33 of the towns they founded.

4. Grenville M. Dodge, chief engineer for the Union Pacific, recalled many years later that in 1867 at Cheyenne "we had claimed, laid out, and leased the lots to the occupants, and organized the local government. There was then no title to be obtained to the town, but we treated this as all the towns, claiming it for the company, laying it out into town lots and not allowing anyone to locate there without taking an agreement from us allowing them to occupy it and agreeing to deed it to them when we got a title." Grenville M. Dodge, *How We Built the Union Pacific Railway*, 38. The land system used by the Union Pacific is also described, as it applied to Grand Island, Nebraska, in Othman A. Abbott, "Building a City in the Prairie Wilderness," 121-132. The author, once lt. governor of Nebraska, recalls that after the town had been surveyed into the usual grid pattern "a copy of the . . . plat was left with the Union Pacific station agent and from it he sold lots, giving the purchaser a contract for a deed at some unspecified time in the future. . . . Quit Claim Deeds were given when cash was paid and the purchaser trusted the railroad company to make good his title to the lots when the Government should ultimately survey the land. This was done on the petition of the residents to the board of county commissioners."

5. Samuel Bowles, observing conditions at the Union Pacific terminus of Benton in 1868 after traveling westward from Omaha, stated that "only a small proportion of . . . [the] population had aught to do with the road, or any legitimate occupation. Most were the hangers-on around the disbursements of such a

gigantic work, catching the drippings from the feast in any and every form that it was possible to reach them. Restaurant and saloon keepers, gamblers, desperadoes of every grade, the vilest of men and of women made up this 'Hell on wheels,' as it was most aptly termed." Samuel Bowles, *Our New West*, 56.

6. William A. Bell, *New Tracks in North America*, I, 19-20.

7. Letter from John Morgan, March 13, 1878, *The Colorado Magazine*, xxv (1948), 261.

8. Bell, *New Tracks*, 18.

9. Richard C. Overton, *Burlington West*, 287-288.

10. Thomas M. Davis, "Building the Burlington Through Nebraska—A Summary View," 322-323.

11. A. T. Andreas, *History of the State of Nebraska*, III, 1096-1098.

12. Dodge, *Union Pacific*, 23.

13. Louis L. Simonin, *The Rocky Mountain West in 1867*, 63-64.

14. T. A. Larson, *History of Wyoming*, 44.

15. Announcement in the Cheyenne *Argus* or *Leader*, as quoted in Simonin, *Rocky Mountain West*, 66.

16. Larson, *Wyoming*, 127.

17. Ibid., 57.

18. George Francis Train, *My Life in Many States and in Foreign Lands*, 293.

19. Albert D. Richardson, *Beyond the Mississippi*, 565.

20. James W. Savage and John T. Bell, *History of the City of Omaha Nebraska*, 101.

21. Andreas, *Nebraska*, III, 1268. Andreas quotes David Anderson's humorous description of Train's approach to the Columbus venture: "Train was seized with the one idea that the capital of the United States might, could, would and should be on the Transcontinental-International Highway and as nearly as possible in the geographical center of the Union. So he measured the maps in all directions of earth, heaven and hell. On the map of Uncle Sam he found Columbus within ten miles of the center; on the map of the world within one mile; and on the map of the universe exactly in the center. It was moreover, directly on the perpendicular line twixt the upper and the nether world, exactly under the zenith, and over the nadir—felicitous spot on which heavenly light could fall. . . . So he bargained for 800 acres of land and laid out the 'Capital Addition,' and began to locate the capstan, ropes and pulleys which would move the gubernatorial mansion of Nebraska and the executive mansion of the Union to Columbus. They did not move worth a cent and are not an inch yet advanced on their long journey; for . . . George set his machinery at least fifty years too soon."

22. J. H. Triggs, *History of Cheyenne and Northern Wyoming*, 23. This early history is essentially a promotional tract, but it contains useful material on the early development of Cheyenne.

23. The quotation and the information on land values are from Elwyn B. Robinson, *History of North Dakota*, 151.

24. The commission conducted its organizational meeting under unusual circumstances. The statute required it to convene for this purpose in Yankton, then the territorial capital. Citizens of that town contended that only the governor and legislature could legally fix the site of the capital and prepared to serve writs on the members of the commission to prevent them from acting. The commission chartered a special train, and while it moved slowly through Yankton at 6:00 a.m. the members passed the motions necessary for formal organization. Merle Potter, "The North Dakota Capital Fight," 25-53; and Howard Roberts Lamar, *Dakota Territory, 1861-1889*, 205.

25. "Memoirs of H. M. Rowley," MS edited by I. D. O'Donell in the Billings Public Library, as cited in Waldo O. Kliewer, "The Foundations of Billings, Montana," 258. Kliewer's valuable study is the source for much of the information on early Billings incorporated in this portion of the chapter.

26. This passage appears in E. V. Smalley, "The New North-West," 769-779. Smalley's *History of the Northern Pacific Railroad*, contains nothing of this sort.

27. Early settlement in this region of South Dakota is described in Harold E. Briggs, *Frontiers of the Northwest*, 348-358. See also Lamar, *Dakota Territory*, 36-41; and Herbert S. Schell, *History of South Dakota*, 72-76.

28. Moses K. Armstrong, *Early Empire Builders of the Great West*, 63-64.

29. Schell, *South Dakota*, 110-115.

30. Huron's plan included a large park occupying an area equal in size to four of the normal gridiron city blocks. A reproduction of a view of the town can be found in Mildred McEwen Jones, *Early Beadle County, 1879-1900*.

31. An exhaustive description of the capital location fight in South Dakota can be found in George W. Kingsbury, *History of Dakota Territory*, III, 163-218, a chapter that includes several photographs of early Pierre.

32. Schell, *South Dakota*, 155, 163.

33. J. E. Dyer, *Dakota: The Observations of a Tenderfoot*, Fargo, N.D., 1884, 89-91.

34. Ralph H. Brown, *Historical Geography of the United States*, 436. For a longer discussion of the Texas cattle trade before and after the Civil War see the introduction by Ralph P. Bieber to Joseph G. McCoy, *Historic Sketches of the Cattle Trade of the West and Southwest*. McCoy's book, first published in 1874, is the most valuable contemporary account of the cattle trade.

35. "Spanish" or "Texas" fever was carried by a tiny tick. Although the ticks died in the winter, during which time Texas cattle could safely come in contact with other breeds, weather conditions obviously favored drives in the spring, summer, and early fall. See T. R. Havins, "Texas Fever," 147-162.

36. McCoy, *Cattle Trade*, 116-117.

37. George L. Cushman, "Abilene, First of the Kansas Cow Towns," 244.

38. U.S. National Park Service, *Prospector, Cowhand, and Sodbuster*, 48.

39. The red light district had moved to this location following the incorporation of the town in 1870 and the passage of an ordinance prohibiting houses of ill-fame within the city limits. At the time of incorporation, all places selling liquor were licensed. There were thirty-two such establishments within the city, and there must have been more beyond the corporate boundary. Cushman, "Abilene," 249.

40. Robert R. Dykstra, *The Cattle Towns*, 37, 40-41. Dykstra's study of Abilene,

Ellsworth, Wichita, Caldwell, and Dodge City is a splendid piece of scholarship and represents a major contribution to American urban history.

41. Ibid., 55, 162. Dykstra describes in some detail Wichita's successful efforts to secure rail connections.

42. I have relied on ibid., 41-47, 228-237, for details of Munger's and Greiffenstein's initial ventures in town planning and, in the section to follow, on the effect the two rival plats had on town development.

43. See the graph showing changing age-sex compositions of the populations in Wichita, Dodge City, and Caldwell in Dykstra, ibid., 247.

44. Ibid., 254-256.

45. The Western Trail continued northward beyond Dodge City to Ogallala, Nebraska, on the Union Pacific railroad near the northeast corner of Colorado. That town's development and decline as a cattle shipping point closely resembled the experience in the Kansas communities. See Norbert R. Mahnken, "Ogallala—Nebraska's Cowboy Capital," 85-109.

46. Dodge City *Western Cowboy*, October 31, 1885, as quoted in Dykstra, *Cattle Towns*, 341-342.

XVII · RAILROAD TOWNS OF THE MOUNTAIN STATES AND THE SOUTHERN PLAINS

1. Lawrence G. Means, *Reno: A Criterion for Progress*, 2.

2. As quoted in ibid., 5.

3. Plans of these two towns are among those in the collection of the Nevada Historical Society, Reno. They both show routine grid plans of the most elementary kind.

4. T. A. Larson, *History of Wyoming*, 56.

5. As quoted in Harold E. Briggs, *Frontiers of the Northwest*, 396.

6. May 5, 1868, as quoted in ibid., 396.

7. October 31, 1868, as quoted in ibid., 397.

8. As quoted in J. R. Perkins, *Trails, Rails and War: The Life of General G. M. Dodge*, 241.

9. This plan is dated 1869. A reproduction of McCarver's earlier plat with the name "Commencement City" crossed out and the new name added appears as Figure 244 in John W. Reps, *The Making of Urban America*, where I erroneously dated it as ca. 1873. McCarver's town founding and promotional activities in the American West are described in Michael B. Husband, "Morton M. McCarver: An Iowa Entrepreneur in the Far West," 242-254.

10. Eugene V. Smalley, *History of the Northern Pacific Railroad*, 193-194; Glenn Chesney Quiett, *They Built the West*, 411-412. Formal ratification of the executive committee's decision by the board of directors was delayed until September 10, 1873. Tacoma Land Company, *Tacoma, the Western Terminus of the Northern Pacific Railroad*, 1.

11. Olmsted's plan for Riverside is reproduced as Figure 204 in Reps, *Urban America*. For Olmsted's work see Albert Fein, *Frederick Law Olmsted and the American Environmental Tradition*, New York, 1972.

12. Olmsted's name is spelled incorrectly on the lithograph, suggesting that the railroad or its town subsidiary was responsible for its final drafting and publication. Olmsted's usual practice was to submit a printed report to his clients. I have been unable to find any copy of such a report on Tacoma.

13. As quoted from an unidentified source in Quiett, *They Built the West*, 414.

14. Rudyard Kipling, *From Sea to Sea*, II, 43-44.

15. Quiett, *They Built the West*, 425-427.

16. Originally the St. Paul and Pacific, this railroad was intended as the St. Paul connection for the Northern Pacific. Reorganized in 1879 as the St. Paul, Minneapolis and Manitoba, it became the Great Northern in 1890 after its consolidation with other roads. Hill served as general manager from 1879 until he acquired control of the line in 1883 and became its president.

17. Much of the foregoing material on the founding of Great Falls is derived from Clifton B. Worthen and Oscar O. Mueller, "Central Montana."

18. Joaquin Miller, *An Illustrated History of the State of Montana*, 419.

19. Pocatello *Tribune*, February 10, 1893, as quoted in Robert L. Wrigley, Jr., "The Early History of Pocatello, Idaho," 363, from which most of the foregoing is drawn.

20. Pocatello was later the scene of a land rush when, on June 17, 1902, more than 400,000 acres of land withdrawn from the Indian reservation were thrown open to settlement in a manner similar to that employed earlier in Oklahoma. Wrigley, "Pocatello," 364-365.

21. Larson, *Wyoming*, 160.

22. The construction and colonization activities of the Katy are described in one of the best railroad histories: V. V. Masterson, *The Katy Railroad and the Last Frontier*, on which I have relied for my information in this section of the chapter.

23. Letter, February 16, 1908, from F. O. Marvin, who located the site of the railroad's depot at Muskogee, as quoted in ibid., 144.

24. Helping Munson on one occasion was Augustus A. Smith, Stevens's father-in-law, who posed as a would-be rancher and succeeded in purchasing the 102-acre farm of Mr. and Mrs. L. S. Evans, ibid., 176.

25. In 1890 Denison had a population of nearly 11,000, almost 4,000 more than Sherman.

26. Philadelphia, 1872.

27. Brit Allan Storey, "William Jackson Palmer, Promoter," 50.

28. Edna Monch Parker, "The Southern Pacific Railroad and Settlement in Southern California," 118.

29. Ibid., 117.

30. Richard Carroll, "The Founding of Salida, Colorado," 125-127.

31. LeRoy R. Hafen and Frank M. Young, "The Mormon Settlement at Pueblo, Colorado, during the Mexican War," 121-136.

32. Animas City *Southwest*, May 1, 1880, as quoted in Mary C. Ayres, "The Founding of Durango, Colorado," 86.

33. December 29, 1880, as quoted in ibid., 86.

34. A plat of Durango filed in April, 1881, is among the records of the La Plata

County Recorder, Durango. The view referred to appeared in *Harper's Weekly*, July 13, 1889, engraved from a photograph by W. H. Jackson and Co.

35. Denver *Weekly Rocky Mountain News*, July 15, 1874, as quoted in Storey, "Palmer," 52.

36. Much of the information in the foregoing paragraphs has been drawn from Quiett, *They Built the West*, 100-112.

XVIII · TRACKS AND TOWNS: RAILROADS AND URBAN GROWTH IN TEXAS AND THE SOUTHWEST

1. Robert Riegel, *The Story of the Western Railroads*, Lincoln, 1964, 119-120.

2. Dallas Department of City Planning, *Dallas Central District* (1958), and *Dallas Central District* (1961).

3. Oliver Knight, *Fort Worth: Outpost on the Trinity*, 46-61.

4. Conditions in Fort Worth during 1873 are vividly described at greater length in ibid., 66-76.

5. This and other exchanges between the two officials are quoted in ibid., 79-80, as reported in the Fort Worth *Democrat* for the period September 10-14, 1874.

6. Ibid., 82.

7. Ibid., 82-85; U.S. Writers' Program, *Texas: A Guide to the Lone Star State*, 260.

8. Katharyn Duff, *Abilene . . . On Catclaw Creek*, 55-57.

9. Ibid., 59-67. See pp. 67-100 and 187-198 for Abilene's development and its later concern with obtaining additional rail service. Growth of the towns in central west Texas is the subject of Robert L. Martin, *The City Moves West*.

10. For descriptions of these settlements in 1854 see Rex W. Strickland, *El Paso in 1854*, 34-37. Some material on the state of early American settlement in the area can also be found in W. W. Mills, *Forty Years at El Paso, 1858-1898*, El Paso, 1962, 5-11. See also John Russell Bartlett, *Personal Narrative of Explorations and Incidents in Texas . . .*, I, 192-194.

11. Clyde Wise, Jr., "The Effects of the Railroad Upon El Paso," 91-101.

12. For a brief note about the Satterthwaite plan see Eugene O. Porter, "Map No. Two of Satterthwaite's Addition to El Paso, 1884," 68-69.

13. John Credgington, "Old Town Amarillo," *Panhandle Plains Historical Review*, XXX (1957), 79-108, is the source of my information about the planning of Amarillo.

14. Seymour V. Connor, "The Founding of Lubbock," in Lawrence L. Graves (ed.), *A History of Lubbock: Part One: Story of a Country Town*, 72-79.

15. Seymour V. Connor, "The New Century," in ibid., 109-110.

16. Llerena Friend, "Wichita Falls, Texas," in Walter Prescott Webb (ed.), *The Handbook of Texas*, II, 903-904; U.S. Writers' Program, *Texas*, 363-370.

17. "Honey Grove, Texas," in Webb, *Handbook of Texas*, I, 831-832.

18. A. W. Neville, "Paris, Texas," in ibid., II, 334.

19. Impressions of all three views are in the Texas State Archives. Most of Fowler's lithographs were of towns in Pennsylvania and adjoining states. The principal collections of his views are those in the Geography and Map Division of the Library of Congress and in the Rare Book Division of the Pennsylvania State University library.

20. Cora Allen Staniforth, "Gainesville, Texas," in Webb, *Handbook of Texas*, I, 660.

21. Eleanor Pace, "Greenville, Texas," in ibid., I, 729-730.

22. For a brief account with plans and views of the planning of Pullman see John W. Reps, *The Making of Urban America*, 421-424. In addition to the sources cited there, two other works deal in part with the planning of the town and the roles of Behman and Barrett: Almont Lindsey, *The Pullman Strike*; and Stanley Buder, *Pullman: An Experiment in Industrial Order and Community Planning, 1880-1930*.

23. Dick King, *Ghost Towns of Texas*, 74-75, quoting from Hattie Joplin Roach, *History of Cherokee County*. King's study contains a summary of the founding, growth, and demise of New Birmingham on which I have drawn.

24. From a prospectus issued by the company quoted in the Dallas *News*, October 11, 1936, the text of which appears in King, *Ghost Towns*, 75.

25. Dormand Winfrey, "New Birmingham, Texas," in Webb, *The Handbook of Texas*, II, 271.

26. As quoted in U.S. Writers' Program, *Texas*, 317. Stilwell's peculiar brand of spiritualism is described in my principal source of information about him and the development of Port Arthur: Keith L. Bryant, Jr., "Arthur E. Stilwell and the Founding of Port Arthur: A Case of Entrepreneurial Error," 19-40. Some additional information appears in Dermot H. Hardy and Ingham S. Roberts (eds.), *Historical Review of South-East Texas*, I, 429-431.

27. For Port Arthur at the end of the 1930s see U.S. Writers' Program, *Port Arthur*.

28. The founding and growth of Beaumont is traced in U.S. Writers' Program, *Beaumont: A Guide to the City and its Environs*. See also Hardy and Roberts, *South-East Texas*, I, 432-433.

29. For an extended extract from the U.S. Weather Bureau's account of the hurricane and an eye-witness report of the devastated city from the Houston *Daily Post* of September 12, 1900, see Ernest Wallace and David M. Vigness, *Documents of Texas History*, 249-252.

30. S. G. Reed, "Indianola, Texas," in Webb, *Handbook of Texas*, I, 883.

31. "Corpus Christi, Texas," in ibid., I, 415. The city's major period of growth took place after the first World War with the successful exploitation of natural gas and, after 1930, of vast oil reserves discovered in the vicinity. From a town of about 8,000 in 1910 it grew to nearly 30,000 twenty years later. By 1950 its population exceeded 100,000. For an extended history of the town see Coleman McCampbell, *Texas Seaport: The Story of the Growth of Corpus Christi and the Coastal Bend Area*.

32. "Laredo, Texas," in Webb, *Handbook of Texas*, II, 28; U.S. Writers' Program, *Texas*, 306-313.

33. Roger N. Conger, *A Pictorial History of Waco with a Reprint of Highlights of Waco History*. On p. 138 Conger reproduces a bird's-eye view of Waco in 1873.

34. Las Vegas began its existence as a tiny fortified *plaza* in 1833. Shortly after the middle of the following decade Dr. A. Wislizenus described it as nothing more than a place of "100 odd houses and poor dirty-looking inhabitants." A. Wislizenus, *Memoir of a Tour to Northern Mexico . . . in 1846 and 1847*, 17. It was from this unimposing spot that General Kearny, Commander of the Army of the West, issued his proclamation claiming the region for the United States. For a brief period during the Civil War the town served as the capital of the territory. F. S. Donnell, "When Las Vegas was the Capital of New Mexico," 265-272. The Santa Fé Railroad chose to follow the Santa Fe Trail to southeastern Colorado and then through the Raton Pass to reach Las Vegas rather than the shorter Cimarron Cut-Off because of the coal fields in the Colorado Rockies.

35. As a condition for running its tracks through Las Vegas, the Santa Fé line demanded and apparently received a cash subsidy of $10,000, 30 acres of land for its depot and related buildings, and a half interest in the 400-acre tract platted as New Las Vegas. Victor Westphall, "Albuquerque in the 1870's," 257.

36. D. W. Meinig, *Southwest: Three Peoples in Geographical Change, 1600-1970*, 47-49; Howard Roberts Lamar, *The Far Southwest, 1846-1912*, 174-175.

37. As quoted in U.S. Writers' Program, *New Mexico: A Guide to the Colorful State*, 235. The guide also provides a partial roll-call of other undesirables of the period, including Dirty-face Mike, Hoodoo Brown, Scar-face Charlie, Hatchet-face Kit, Rattlesnake Sam, Split-nose Mike, Cold-deck George, Stuttering Tom, and Flyspeck Sam.

38. For the events leading up to the planning of New Albuquerque and a lengthy quotation from Judge Hazledine's speech see Westphall, "Albuquerque in the 1870's," 253-268.

39. Clarence A. Miller, "A City in the Old West," 341.

40. A concise summary of the effect of rail transportation in New Mexico and Arizona can be found in Meinig, *Southwest*, 38-52.

41. Another early view of Tucson showing the town in the distance and Mission San Xavier del Bac in the foreground appears in Bartlett, *Personal Narrative*, II. Several nineteenth-century views of buildings and streets of Tucson are reproduced in Andrew Wallace, *The Image of Arizona: Pictures from the Past*, 177-180.

42. U.S. Writers' Program, *Arizona: A State Guide*, 262.

43. Kitty Jo Parker Nelson, "Prescott: Sketch of a Frontier Capital, 1863-1900," 18-19.

44. Chap. LXXX, *U.S. Statutes at Large*, XII, 37th Congress, 3rd Sess.,1863, An Act for increasing the Revenue by Reservation and Sale of Town Sites on Public Lands, Approved March 3, 1863.

45. These decisions were reached at a public meeting on May 30. The proceedings were published in the June 22 edition of the Prescott *Arizona Miner*, the text of which can be found in Pauline Henson, *Founding a Wilderness Capital*, 166-169.

46. The board of commissioners appointed in 1871 modified the original plat slightly, dropping two tiers of blocks on the east and adding two tiers on the west. The omitted portion along the eastern boundary was later added in essentially the same pattern as shown on the 1864 plat under the name of East Prescott Addition. These changes and the difficulties caused by the proceeding under the Act of 1863 are described in Henson, *Wilderness Capital*, 176-180.

47. Prescott *Arizona Miner*, June 22, 1864, as quoted in ibid., 173.

48. *History of Arizona Territory*, 250. A small and not very helpful view of Prescott in 1878 appears as the frontispiece in Richard J. Hinton, *The Hand-Book to Arizona*. This is reproduced with other nineteenth-century illustrations of the town and its buildings in Wallace, *Image of Arizona*, 181-183.

49. Rufus Kay Wyllys, *Arizona: The History of a Frontier State*, 115, 117-118; Wallace, *Image of Arizona*, 191-192; *History of Arizona Territory*, 245-247.

50. Wyllys, *Arizona*, 120, quoting an unidentified contemporary source. See also *History of Arizona Territory*, 247. Brief histories and old photographs of Gila City and the other mining towns of Arizona appear in James E. Sherman and Barbara H. Sherman, *Ghost Towns of Arizona*.

51. *History of Arizona Territory*, 247-248; Sherman, *Ghost Towns of Arizona*, 51.

52. *History of Arizona Territory*, 253; Wyllys, *Arizona*, 218; U.S. Writers' Program, *Arizona: A State Guide*,187-192; George H. Tinker, *Northern Arizona and Flagstaff in 1887*, 3-4.

53. Views of this structure as projected in 1878 are reproduced in Sherman, *Ghost Towns of Arizona*, 18, and Wallace, *Image of Arizona*, 200.

54. *History of Arizona Territory*, 260.

55. For the planning of Nogales see George E. Sites, Jr., "The Bradford Map of Nogales, Arizona," 1-13. A plan of the Mexican and American settlement in 1888 surveyed by Gustavo Cox is in the records of Santa Cruz County at Nogales. The international boundary line passes through the business district. One of the early saloon keepers, John Brickwood, arranged his premises so that the bar was on the American side and the cigar counter in Mexico in order to avoid paying duty. U.S. Writers' Program, *Arizona*, 210. Both Mexican and American Nogales were planned in gridiron fashion, but the Mexican streets were arranged in true north-south and east-west orientations while the American town in 1882 was laid out to conform to magnetic north.

56. James M. Barney, "Phoenix—A History of its Pioneer Days and People," 264-269; *History of Arizona Territory*, 272-275.

57. Letter in the Prescott *Arizona Miner*, January 7, 1871, as quoted in Barney, "Phoenix," 272.

58. Tucson *Arizona Citizen*, June 3, 1871, as quoted in Barney, "Phoenix," 274. A correspondent writing for the San Diego *Union* the following March was equally enthusiastic about the new town, and his now century-old prediction of its future was uncannily accurate: "This is a smart town which had its first house completed about a year ago. Now it contains many houses; also stores, workshops, hotel, butcher shop, bakery, courthouse, jail, and an excellent school, which has been in operation four months. Lately hundreds of ornamental trees have been set out, which, in a few years, will give the town the appearance of a 'forest city' and will add to its beauty and comfort. When it has become the capi-

tal of the Territory, which it will, undoubtedly, at no very distant day, and when the 'iron horse' steams through our country on the Texas Pacific road, Salt River will be the garden of the Pacific slope, and Phoenix the most important inland town." San Diego *Union*, March 5, 1872, as quoted in Frank C. Lockwood, *Pioneer Days in Arizona from the Spanish Occupation to Statehood*, 339.

XIX · RUSHING FOR LAND: OKLAHOMA'S OVERNIGHT CITIES

1. Only minor changes were made in these tribal allotments up to 1889. Small areas were designated to the west of the Osage lands for the Tonkawa, Ponca, and Oto and Missouri tribes, and the Cheyennes and Arapahoes were confined to the southwesterly of the two areas appearing on the map of 1876. Most of the large tract controlled by the Cheyennes and Arapahoes immediately south of the Kansas border became known as the Cherokee Outlet, a hunting area for the Cherokees whose settlements occupied the northeastern corner of Indian Territory. Maps showing the tribal boundaries at various times as well as maps of individual tribal domains can be found in the useful *Historical Atlas of Oklahoma*, compiled by John W. Morris and Edwin C. McReynolds.

2. Diagrams of the Creek communities can be found in Edwin C. McReynolds, *Oklahoma: A History of The Sooner State*, Norman, 1954, 99. McReynolds also provides a full account of the separate Indian cultures, the story of their removal from their homelands, and their life in Oklahoma, all of which I have drawn on in this brief summary. The sources cited by McReynolds provide more detailed and specialized treatment of various aspects of U.S. Indian policy.

3. This line was completed on April 26, 1887, by two subsidiaries of the Santa Fé road—the Southern Kansas Railway Company and the Gulf, Colorado and Santa Fe Railway Company. Berlin B. Chapman, "Oklahoma City, from Public Land to Private Property," 211-215.

4. A. W. Durham, "Oklahoma City before the Run of 1889," *Chronicles of Oklahoma*, 75. A visitor to Muscogee on the Katy line in eastern Oklahoma found that new town similar in character: "I opened my eyes the next morning upon a long, straggling, miserable railroad town, the exact image of a Union Pacific 'city,' in the last stages of decay. Some two hundred yards from the railroad a single street extended for nearly a quarter of a mile; the buildings were rude shanties, frame and canvas tents and long cabins, open to the wind, which blew a hurricane for the thirty-six hours I was there." Joseph B. Thoburn and Muriel H. Wright, *Oklahoma: A History of the State and Its People*, Appendix xxxvii-6, "J. H. Beadle's Story of the New Railway," 882.

5. A map showing the Cherokee Outlet leases can be found in Morris and McReynolds, *Historical Atlas of Oklahoma*, Map 41. For a description of the lease arrangements and other material on the Outlet see Gaston Litton, *History of Oklahoma*, I, 333-340; and McReynolds, *Oklahoma*, 259-266.

6. Litton, *Oklahoma*, I, 241-246; McReynolds, *Oklahoma*, 229-234.

7. Boudinot had served for a time as clerk of the House of Representatives Committee on Private Land Claims. He may also have been secretly employed by one of the western railroads, which would explain his advocacy of white settlement on Indian lands. Litton, *Oklahoma*, I, 356-358, 364-365.

8. Carl Coke Rister, *Land Hunger: David L. Payne and the Oklahoma Boomers*, 62.

9. Ibid., 204.

10. B. B. Chapman, "The Legal Sooners of 1889 in Oklahoma," 368. Chapman's article is a helpful source of information on this group and contains full citations of documents concerned with their land claims.

11. The law of 1867 authorized persons to settle on and enter claims for townsites of up to 1,280 acres if the inhabitants numbered over 1,000. For each additional 1,000 persons, up to 5,000, a further 320 acres could be claimed. The entries were to be made at the nearest land office by the officials of an incorporated town or, if not incorporated, by the judge of the county court. The land office would then sell the townsite at the minimum government price. Theoretically the land was to be held "in trust for the several use and benefit of the occupants thereof, according to their respective interests; the execution of which trust, as to the disposal of the lots in such town, and the proceeds of the sales thereof, to be conducted under such rules and regulations as may be prescribed by the legislative authority of the State or Territory in which the same may be situated." Chap. 177, *U.S. Statutes at Large*, March 2, 1867, 514. The so-called trust arrangement was, in most cases, a fiction, and townsite companies simply proceeded to sell lots for the maximum price and for private benefit rather than for community use. For reasons that are not clear, the act authorizing the opening of the Unassigned Lands limited townsites in the territory to "one-half section of land," or three hundred and twenty acres. Chap. 412, *U.S. Statutes at Large*, March 2, 1889, 1005.

12. Roy Gittinger, *The Formation of the State of Oklahoma (1803-1906)*, 156.

13. Apparently the only study of town founding and the development of municipal institutions on the Unassigned Lands is the short but excellent work by John Alley, *City Beginnings in Oklahoma Territory*. Alley includes reproductions of early photographs of Oklahoma City, Kingfisher, and Norman. The most extensive archive of early photographs of Oklahoma's towns is in the Western History Collection of the University of Oklahoma library at Norman.

14. Litton, *Oklahoma*, I, 384-385.

15. William Willard Howard, "The Rush to Oklahoma," 391. Howard's is one of the most interesting and informative of contemporary accounts of the rush and its aftermath. See also his earlier article for the same journal, "The Oklahoma Movement."

16. Three months after the land rush, a correspondent for the Kansas City *Times* described Orlando as consisting of "a dozen tents and one small frame building." Alfred, however, was "booming like everything else—with twenty or thirty frame buildings and as many tents." Kansas City *Times*, July 22, 1889. The complete dispatch appears under the title, "The Magic City: Guthrie," *Chronicles of Oklahoma*, xxxvi (1958), 65-71.

17. Howard, "Rush to Oklahoma," 391.

18. Ibid., 391.

19. Hamilton S. Wicks, "The Opening of Oklahoma," 466-467.

20. Some of these persons were identified as illegal townsite "sooners" in newspaper dispatches of the time. See the extract from the Kansas City *Daily Journal* of April 24, 1889, quoted in B. B. Chapman, "Guthrie, From Public Land to Private Property," 63; and a dispatch in the New York *Daily Graphic*, XLIX, April 23, 1889.

21. Howard, "Rush to Oklahoma," 391.

22. The quotation is from testimony in the case of *Townsite Settlers of East Guthrie v. Veeder B. Paine et al.*, as quoted in Chapman, "Guthrie," 71. Chapman summarizes the circumstances of the founding of East Guthrie.

23. Howard, "Rush to Oklahoma," 391.

24. Since the community was made up of total strangers, candidates were elected largely on the basis of their appearance. Each man nominated was hoisted aboard a wagon bed and stood before the assembled crowd before a vote was taken. To give some semblance of legality to these proceedings, John M. Galloway, the U.S. commissioner, administered oaths of office to each successful candidate, although no statute existed giving him any authority for this action.

25. The early days of municipal government in the territory are described in Litton, *Oklahoma*, I, 422-432. More extended treatment of individual cities may be found in other works. For El Reno see Berlin B. Chapman, "The Founding of El Reno," 79-108. The circumstances of the founding of Perkins are described in the same author's "Perkins Townsite: An Archival Case Study," 82-91. Material on the founding of Norman, the location of Oklahoma University, appears in Roy Gittinger, *The University of Oklahoma: A History of Fifty Years, 1892-1942*. For Stillwater see B. B. Chapman, *The Founding of Stillwater*. All of these draw on Alley, *City Beginnings*.

26. An extensive summary of the case, with full citations to relevant documents, appears in Chapman, "Guthrie."

27. Kansas City *Times*, July 22, 1889, quoted in "The Magic City," 68.

28. Howard, "Rush to Oklahoma," 391.

29. Kansas City *Times*, July 22, 1889, quoted in "The Magic City," 67, 71.

30. A. W. Durham, "Oklahoma City before the Run of 1889," 77.

31. The text of the charter is included in Chapman, "Oklahoma City," 219-220.

32. Letter from James Layman Brown to the Secretary of the Interior, May 1, 1889, as quoted in ibid., 221.

33. Ibid., 224, 229-230.

34. Ibid., 225 gives the names of those elected and the number of votes they received as recorded in a document in the National Archives. This event is also described in Angelo C. Scott, *The Story of Oklahoma City*, 14. Scott arrived in Oklahoma City on opening day and played a major role in reconciling conflicting demands for town lots. His book is a valuable source of information on the founding of the town. Neither Chapman nor Scott suggests the probable reason for the Oklahoma Town Company's election of "municipal" officers. They in-

tended to file a townsite application of their own for all or part of the area occupied by the Seminole Company. For that purpose they needed to have town officials designated as trustees, and they doubtless hoped that their claim would be recognized as one submitted by a group legally entering the territory. They assumed, as did the Seminole Company, that even though there was no statutory basis for incorporation, land office officials would more readily approve an application that seemed to come from a body with "official" status.

35. Ibid., 19.

36. Scott gives the names of the committee members. None among them appears in the list of officers and leaders of the Seminole Company who signed the minutes of the first meeting of that group. For that list see Chapman, "Oklahoma City," 225.

37. Scott, *Oklahoma City*, 21. The committee probably needed some protection as well from irate claimants who were dispossessed by this procedure. The following month the *Oklahoma Gazette* reflected their unhappiness with this bit of frontier newspaper humor: "When Adam entered Paradise, Satan sent in a lot of surveyors and kept changing the stakes on the corner lots and streets and alleys, and juggling with the ground he made vacant until Adam was willing to eat sour apples and green persimmons and be let out." Oklahoma City, *Oklahoma Gazette*, May 25, 1889, as quoted in Thoburn and Wright, *Oklahoma: A History of the State and Its People*, II, 548, n 10. Four days earlier the same paper carried the following item: "And Satan took him up unto an exceeding high place and showed him the whole valley . . . and said: All these have my deputy marshals staked before noon of April 22, 1889." *Oklahoma Gazette*, May 21, 1889, as quoted in Thoburn and Wright, *Oklahoma*, II, 546, n 6.

38. Scott, *Oklahoma City*, 22.

39. Statement by J. L. Brown, as quoted in Chapman, "Oklahoma City," 333, n 12.

40. An extended account of these early political crises can be found in Scott, *Oklahoma City*, 43-48, 65-74; and Chapman, "Oklahoma City," 338-353.

41. Litton, *Oklahoma*, I, 431; Alley, *City Beginnings*, 91.

42. Ibid., 93-94; U.S. Writers' Program, *Oklahoma: A Guide to the Sooner State*, 200. A more extended treatment of the political maneuvering that won the college for Stillwater and the period of its early development can be found, with many illustrations, in Robert E. Cunningham, *Stillwater: Where Oklahoma Began*, 139-156.

43. Litton, *Oklahoma*, I, 430-431; Alley, *City Beginnings*, 87.

44. Townsite legislation and regulations of Oklahoma under this law and others enacted to 1893 are summarized in Dick T. Morgan, *Morgan's Manual of the U.S. Homestead and Townsite Laws*. Regulations for townsite trustees promulgated by Secretary of the Interior John W. Noble on June 18 and July 10, 1890, may be found in *Annual Report of the Commissioners of the General Land Office for the Fiscal Year Ended June 30, 1890*, Washington, 1890, 223-228.

45. The work of one of these boards is traced in Berlin B. Chapman, "Perkins Townsite: An Archival Case Study," 82-91.

46. Litton, *Oklahoma*, ɪ, 456-458, 524-528. The eventual decision was preceded by a referendum on the matter, with Oklahoma City receiving a large majority of the votes cast over those for Guthrie and Shawnee. Governor Charles Haskell immediately transferred the state seal to an office he established in an Oklahoma City hotel. The state supreme court invalidated the results of the referendum on a technicality, the legislature passed the measure described above, and this was sustained by both the Oklahoma and the U.S. Supreme Courts early in 1911. Some of the details of the fight over the location of Oklahoma's capital can also be found in Gerald Forbes, *Guthrie: Oklahoma's First Capital*. Forbes includes a brief summary of a proposal for an entirely new capital city that was suggested to the constitutional convention held at Guthrie in December, 1906. This was evidently known as the "New Jerusalem" plan. "It suggested that the second session of the state legislature, after approval of the constitution, purchase land near the geographical center of the state (a point not far north and east of the present town of Britton). After the state had reserved sufficient land for all public buildings the lots should be sold at auction. The resulting capital city would bear the name, 'Indiahome.' The streets would be named for the presidents of the United States in chronological order." Ibid., 23-24.

47. Congress on March 3, 1893, ratified an agreement with the Cherokee Indians that had been signed by tribal leaders and the Cherokee Commission on December 19, 1891. The commission had been created by congressional action on March 2, 1889, to acquire for the public domain land previously assigned to the Cherokees. For this and other details concerning the opening of the Cherokee Outlet see Berlin B. Chapman, "Opening the Cherokee Outlet: An Archival Study," 158-181, 253-285.

48. The speculative maneuvering by the railroads and the efforts of federal officials to counter these activities is exhaustively treated in Berlin B. Chapman, "The Enid 'Railroad War': An Archival Study," 126-197. The conflict continued after settlement, for the railroad refused to stop its trains at the government townsite of Enid, hoping by this practice to promote its own settlement at the Rock Island railroad station three miles to the north. Certain citizens of the government townsite took matters into their own hands, and in July 1894 they cut through the timbers of a railroad bridge, the effect of which was to bring one of the Rock Island freight trains to a sudden, unscheduled, and violent halt. Further and less drastic persuasion by the federal government resulted in the construction of a freight and passenger station at Enid in September of that year.

49. Of the four school sites, one is now used for commerical purposes, and a second came to be used by the railroad when the right-of-way was moved sometime after the town's founding. Only the northeast school site is used for its intended purpose. The block at the southeast corner provides the site for Woodward's city hall. The park in front of the courthouse square has survived.

50. The planners of Perry and Newkirk also produced rigid grid plans oriented to section lines rather than the diagonal alignments of the Santa Fé tracks through the two townsites. Each has a courthouse block, a school site, and a block reserved as a public park. At Newkirk, two city blocks were consolidated for the centrally situated courthouse site, the original design for which had a small park at each end. Today the courthouse on that location is flanked by the city hall and the high school. Filed copies of the original plats are in the county records at both towns.

51. The plan of Blackburn shows two blocks set aside as public squares and an area equivalent to nearly four blocks consolidated as a city park at the north end of the irregularly shaped townsite divided into rectangular blocks. The plan of Cleo is of greater interest. In the southwest sector is a public square of just under one acre. It is surrounded by streets 120 feet wide. Streets leading to the square terminate at the midpoints of its sides. An eight-acre park and a two-acre school site were also reserved for public use. Both plats are among the townsite plats of the General Land Office Records, Cartographic Branch, the National Archives.

52. This and other aspects of the founding and planning of Ponca City are described in Louis Seymour Barnes, "The Founding of Ponca City," 154-162.

53. Chapman, "Cherokee Outlet," 285. Chapman quotes the president as stating that the Cherokee run "furnished an exhibition though perhaps in a modified degree of the mad scramble, the violence, and the fraudulent occupation which have accompanied previous openings of public land."

54. Litton, *Oklahoma*, ɪ, 402-404.

55. Ibid., 477-483, provides a summary of the lengthy negotiations of the Dawes Commission with the Indian tribes. For a more detailed study of the commission's work see Loren N. Brown, "The Dawes Commission," 71-105; and Brown, "The Establishment of the Dawes Commission for Indian Territory," 171-184.

56. White domination of the "Indian" towns in the Chickasaw Nation and the system of urban land tenure under tribal jurisdiction are described in Arrell M. Gibson, *The Chicksasaws*, 284-286. For the platting of towns in the former Chickasaw Nation see p. 307.

57. Chap. 517, *U. S. Statutes at Large*, June 28, 1893, 495-505. The act is known as the Curtis Act after its sponsor, Representative Charles Curtis of Kansas.

58. Estimates of population for the area at various dates are provided in Gittinger, *Oklahoma*, 175-188.

59. There are dozens of townsite plats of this period among the records of the Bureau of Indian Affairs, Cartographic Branch, the National Archives. Copies of most of them are on file in the office of the Survey Division, Oklahoma Department of Highways, Oklahoma City.

60. Vinita in the old Cherokee Nation is one exception to this generalization. There, two 10-acre parks were reserved on either side of the Frisco railway tracks.

61. A photograph of what is evidently Main Street in 1893 is reproduced in Angie Debo, *Tulsa: From Creek Town to Oil Capital*, a work on which I have relied for much of the material on Tulsa's origins and development.

1. Henry Gannett, *Statistical Atlas of the United States*, 14.

2. Turner also outlined an essay—never completed—to be called "The Significance of the City in American History." He proposed to address himself to the following topics: "When and how and why did cities become densely populated . . . How did urban (including alien) ideas, interests and ideals react on frontier and section . . . Extent to which the cities were built up by movement from interior rural areas to city. . . . Include editors, teachers, preachers, etc. . . . Its counter influence in modifying frontier and sectional traits." Both quotations are from Turner's notes as transcribed in Ray Allen Billington, *Frederick Jackson Turner: Historian, Scholar, Teacher*, New York, 1973, 458, 493.

3. Richard C. Wade, *The Urban Frontier: Pioneer Life in Early Pittsburgh, Cincinnati, Lexington, Louisville, and St. Louis*, Chicago, 1964, 1. First published in 1959 under a slightly different title, Wade's seminal study was the earliest full-length treatment of urbanization in an important section of the Old West. Its implied challenge to the validity of Turner's hypothesis was obvious. An earlier but briefer study by Bayrd Still of early Buffalo, Cleveland, Detroit, Chicago, and Milwaukee reached a similar conclusion: "On many a frontier the town builder was as conspicuous as the farmer pioneer; the western city, through the efforts of its founders to extend its economic hinterland, actually facilitated the agrarian development of the West; and the opportunities attending city growth as well as those afforded by cheap farm lands contributed to the dynamic sense of economic abundance felt by Americans of the mid-nineteenth century." Bayrd Still, "Patterns of Mid-Nineteenth Century Urbanization in the Middle West," *Mississippi Valley Historical Review*, xxviii (September, 1941), 187.

4. The most comprehensive early survey of the extent of municipal services in American cities dates from 1880. Two volumes of the census for that year deal with this subject in exhaustive detail for the major communities of the nation. These reports include narrative statements concerning the history and development of each city, most of them include maps, and much miscellaneous information is added. The cities of the West are treated in Part II. This special report of the census constitutes a little-known but highly important treasury of comparative urban data. See George E. Waring, Jr. (comp.), *Report on the Social Statistics of Cities*. Useful as a supplement to material in these volumes is the series of entries under the general heading, "Cities, American, Recent Growth of," in the volumes from 1886 through 1894 of *Appletons' Annual Cyclopaedia and Register of Important Events*. The 1880 census data referred to above are analyzed in Lawrence H. Larsen and Robert L. Branyan, "The Development of an Urban Civilization on the Frontier of the American West," 33-50.

5. "Portland," *The West Shore*, January, 1886, 11.

6. This assessment is in virtual total disagreement with that advanced by Turner's biographer and most articulate and persuasive disciple. See Ray Billington, *Westward Expansion: A History of the American Frontier*, New York, 3rd ed., 1967, 6-7.

7. Blake McKelvey, *The Urbanization of America*, 1860-1915, New Brunswick, N.J., 1963, 34.

8. McKelvey in ibid., 32, stresses this point in his discussion of Western city growth.

9. I have chosen to compare city population in 1890 with urbanized area population in 1970 because the latter seems to me a better reflection of the true importance of the urban community than either city population or that of the Standard Statistical Metropolitan Area. As defined in the 1970 Census, an urbanized area consists of a central city of 50,000 or more plus nearby incorporated places exceeding 2,500 and smaller incorporated places having closely settled areas of 100 housing units or more. Added to this are unincorporated areas with a density of 1,000 inhabitants or more per square mile and certain other noncontiguous areas having the required population density and not located more than 1½ miles from the main body of the urbanized area. While some of the western cities in 1890 had suburbs, the bulk of the urban population then resided within their incorporated limits. In Table I data for cities in 1890 is from U.S. Bureau of the Census, *Abstract of the Twelfth Census of the United States, 1900*, Washington, 1904, Table 80. The information on urbanized areas in 1970 is from U.S. Department of Commerce, Bureau of the Census, *1970 Census of Population, General Population Characteristics, United States Summary*, Washington, 1972, Table 66.

10. "Lincoln," *Appletons' Annual Cyclopaedia . . . 1888*, New Series, xiii, 167. As mentioned in Chapter XII, note 46, the population of Lincoln in 1890 as reported by the census was probably inflated. The city's true population was just under 30,000.

11. "Dallas," *Appletons' Annual Cyclopaedia . . . 1890*, New Series, xv, 124-125.

12. "Fort Worth," *Appletons' Annual Cyclopaedia . . . 1889*, New Series, xiv, 146. A slightly earlier view of Fort Worth was published in 1886 showing the city from an identical point. The view reproduced is a revised and updated version. The 1886 view is entitled *Fort Worth, Tex. "The Queen of the Prairies."* It was drawn by Henry Wellge, printed by Beck and Pauli of Milwaukee, and published in that city by Norris, Wellge and Co. An impression is in the Division of Geography and Maps at the Library of Congress. An extensive legend at the bottom identifies important public and private buildings.

13. For a description of Houston in 1889 see "Houston," *Appletons' Annual Cyclopaedia . . . 1889*, New Series, xiv, New York, 1890, 150-151.

14. *Special Supplement to The HemisFair Edition of San Antonio*, 18.

15. For a picture guide to some of the old buildings of San Antonio see the brochure prepared by the San Antonio Chapter of the American Institute of Architects, *Historic San Antonio, 1700-1900*.

16. A summary of conditions in the city in 1890 appears in "Austin," *Appletons' Annual Cyclopaedia . . . 1890*, New Series, xv, 119-120. A revised version of the 1887 view was issued around 1895. The only change seems to be the addition of Hyde Park, a large new subdivision located between the university and the state

hospital. An impression can be found in the Texas State Archives, Map Collection No. 926E. It is entitled *Partial View of Austin, Texas*. A full-scale treatment of Austin's planning and development, including the disposal of the balance of the public urban land domain, would be an important contribution to urban history. There is a wealth of graphic and documentary material available for study and analysis, virtually all of it located in libraries and public archives within the city.

17. Sylvester Baxter, "Along the Rio Grande," 700.

18. "El Paso," *Appletons' Annual Cyclopaedia . . . 1890*, New Series, xv, 126.

19. The swift development of the new town of Albuquerque is described in Baxter, "Along the Rio Grande," 694-697. In 1882 Baxter found the business district to consist of "sturdy ranks" of buildings constructed of "brick, stone, adobe, and timber." He concluded that "Albuquerque had become the most city-like looking town in the Southwest, and a place of bright prospects—'a second Denver,' it was called." Baxter dismissed the original settlement in these words: "The old town . . . has a number of picturesque features, it being pretty thoroughly Mexican, and the entire business of the place having removed to New Albuquerque, it is dull enough."

20. U.S. Writers' Program, *New Mexico: A Guide to the Colorful State*, 204.

21. Clarence A. Miller, "A City in the Old West," 338.

22. A useful descriptive guide to the Tucson of ca. 1880 with a detailed map by Don Bufkin is Ray Brandes, "Guide to the Historic Landmarks of Tucson," 27-38.

23. Ibid., 28.

24. As quoted in Anne Merriman Peck, *The March of Arizona History*, 270.

25. "Phenix, or Phoenix," *Appletons' Annual Cyclopaedia . . . 1889*, New Series, xiv, 156.

26. William M. Thayer, *Marvels of the New West*, 357. Thayer reproduces engravings of several buildings of the Denver he saw and described: the depot, the Windsor hotel, the capitol, the Tabor Grand Opera House, and the high school.

27. Denver is another city crying for a full-scale history with adequate attention to its remarkable record of physical development. Much useful material on the city's early decades can be found in Gunther Barth, *Instant Cities: Urbanization and the Rise of San Francisco and Denver*. In recent years much of the older part of the community near the river has been demolished as part of a huge urban renewal project. Only a small part of old Denver remains—Larimer Square—an imaginative restoration of two blocks of that once historic street that throbbed with mercantile life in the old days and now once again thrives on the tourist trade. During the twentieth century the city created a notable system of parks, boulevards, and other civic improvements in addition to its governmental and cultural center mentioned in the text. None of this seems to have been adequately documented, although much helpful information is contained in Charles A. Johnson, *Denver's Mayor Speer*.

28. James Fullarton Muirhead, *The Land of Contrasts*, 212-213.

29. For descriptions of both towns at this time see "Cheyenne," *Appletons'*

Annual Cyclopaedia . . . 1888, New Series, xiii, 161-162; and "Laramie City," *Appletons' Annual Cyclopaedia . . . 1889*, New Series, xiv, 152.

30. Hubert Howe Bancroft, *History of Washington, Idaho, and Montana*, 755-756. See also "Helena," *Appletons' Annual Cyclopaedia . . . 1889*, New Series, xiv, 149-150.

31. "Salt Lake City," *Appletons' Annual Cyclopaedia . . . 1889*, New Series, xiv, 158.

32. A useful description of the city in 1890 is Will L. Visscher, "Tacoma, Washington," 76-81. See also "Tacoma," *Appletons' Annual Cyclopaedia . . . 1889*, New Series, xiv, 161. The development of the city to the 1930s is traced in Glenn Chesney Quiett, *They Built the West*, 400-438. In 1921 the Northern Pacific abandoned the majestic headquarters building it had occupied since 1886 and moved its western office to Seattle in a belated but final recognition that Tacoma had lost out to its rival as a transportation, shipping, and industrial center.

33. Frederic James Grant, "Seattle: A Chapter from an Uncompleted History," 642.

34. Clarence B. Bagley, *History of Seattle from the Earliest Settlement to the Present Time*, i, 273-275.

35. *Appletons' General Guide to the United States and Canada*, 485. For a long account of Portland six years earlier with many illustrations see "Portland," *West Shore*, January, 1886, 11-18.

36. Charles Dwight Willard, *The Herald's History of Los Angeles City*, 354.

37. *Appletons' General Guide to the United States*, 423.

38. Muirhead, *Land of Contrasts*, 208-209.

39. Daniel H. Burnham, *Report on a Plan for San Francisco*. For a summary and criticism of the plan with reproductions of some of its illustrations see John W. Reps, *The Making of Urban America*, 514-518. A more extended treatment of Burnham's studies in San Francisco can be found in Mel Scott, *The San Francisco Bay Area*, 95-108; and Thomas S. Hines, *Burnham of Chicago: Architect and Planner*, New York, 1974, 174-196.

40. Thayer, *Marvels of the New West*, 1959, 95-108.

41. James Bryce, *The American Commonwealth*, ii, 833. Bryce revised his original work following its first publication in London in 1888, but the chapter on the West remained unchanged through all editions.

42. Ibid., ii, 837.

43. Ibid., ii, 837-838.

44. Ibid., ii, 839.

45. The manuscript for this book was completed in September, 1973. In rewriting the final chapter in the summer of 1975, I discovered an article that had not previously come to my attention: Oliver Knight, "Toward an Understanding of the Western Town," *Western Historical Quarterly*, iv (1973), 27-42. It bristles with questions, all of them pertinent, and which would take a team of historians several working lives to answer. If this had been published by 1966 when my research began, I would have written a different book—or would have aban-

doned the project before its start as a hopeless quest! In my own and rather different way from what Knight suggests, I have addressed myself to only one of many sets of related questions he poses dealing with western towns. For other scholars who wish to study western urbanization but who may feel that there are few important topics left to explore, a reading of Knight's narrative catalogue of potential research issues cannot fail to be rewarding.

SELECTED BIBLIOGRAPHY OF SOURCES CONSULTED ●────────

This bibliography is divided into twenty-one sections: one for general works on the American West and one for each of the twenty chapters. In a study of this scope no bibliography could be exhaustive, but it should prove a useful beginning point for persons wishing to pursue further the subjects treated in this book.

GENERAL WORKS

Allen, James B., *The Company Town in the American West*. Norman: University of Oklahoma Press, 1966.

Bancroft, Hubert Howe, *The Works of Hubert Howe Bancroft*. 39 vols. San Francisco: A. L. Bancroft and Co. and The History Company, 1882-1890.

Barth, Gunther, *Instant Cities: Urbanization and the Rise of San Francisco and Denver*. New York: Oxford University Press, 1975.

Bartlett, Richard A., *Great Surveys of the American West*. Norman: University of Oklahoma Press, 1962.

———, *The New Country: A Social History of the American Frontier, 1776-1890*. New York: Oxford University Press, 1974.

Beebe, Lucius, and Charles Clegg, *The American West: The Pictorial Epic of a Continent*. New York: Dutton, 1955.

Bieber, Ralph P., and Le Roy R. Hafen (eds.), *The Southwest Historical Series: Historical Documents, Hitherto Unpublished or Inaccessible, Depicting Social and Economic Conditions in the Southwest During the 19th Century*. 12 vols. Glendale, California: Arthur H. Clark Co., 1931-1943.

Billington, Ray A., *Frederick Jackson Turner: Historian, Scholar, Teacher*. New York: Oxford University Press, 1973.

———, *The Frontier Thesis: Valid Interpretation of American History?* New York: Holt, Rinehart and Winston, 1966.

———, *Westward Expansion: A History of The American Frontier*. New York: Macmillan, 3rd ed., 1967.

Bender, A. B., "Military Posts in the Southwest, 1848-1860," *New Mexico Historical Review*, XVI (April 1941), 125-147.

Bogue, Allan G.,Thomas D. Phillips, and James E. Wright (eds.), *The West of the American People*. Itasca, Illinois: F. E. Peacock Publishers, Inc., 1970.

Bowles, Samuel, *Across the Continent: A Stage Ride over the Plains, to the Rocky Mountains, the Mormons, and the Pacific States, in the Summer of 1865*. Springfield, Mass.: Samuel Bowles and Co., 1869.

———, *Our New West*. Hartford, Conn.: Hartford Publishing Co., 1869.

Briggs, Harold E., *Frontiers of the Northwest*. New York: Peter Smith, 1950.

Brown, Ralph H., *Historical Geography of the United States*. New York: Harcourt, Brace and Co., 1948.

Carroll, John Alexander, "Broader Approaches to the History of the West: A Descriptive Bibliography," *Arizona and the West*, I (Autumn, 1959), 217-231.

Clark, John G. (ed.), *The Frontier Challenge: Responses to the Trans-Mississippi West*. Lawrence: University Press of Kansas, 1971.

Coman, Katherine, *Economic Beginnings of the Far West: How We Won the Land Beyond the Mississippi*. 2 vols. New York: The Macmillan Company, 1912.

Davis, Ronald L., and Harry D. Holmes, "Studies in Western Urbanization," *Journal of the West*, XIII (July, 1974), 1-5.

Dick, Everett, *The Sod-House Frontier, 1854-1890*. New York: D. Appleton-Century Co., 1937.

———, *Vanguards of the Frontier: A Social History of the Northern Plains and Rocky Mountains from the Earliest White Contacts to the Coming of the Homemaker*. New York: D. Appleton-Century Co., 1941.

Ellis, David M. (ed.), *The Frontier in American Development: Essays in Honor of Paul Wallace Gates*. Ithaca, N.Y.: Cornell University Press, 1969.

Freidel, Frank Burt (ed.), *Harvard Guide to American History*. 2 vols. Cambridge: Harvard University Press, 1974.

Friis, Herman R., and Suzanne Pitzer, *Federal Exploration of the American West before 1880*. Washington: The National Archives, 1963.

Gabriel, Ralph Henry (ed.), *The Pageant of America*. 15 vols. New Haven: Yale University Press, 1926-1929.

Gibson, Arrell Morgan, *The West in the Life of the Nation*. Lexington, Mass.: D. C. Heath & Co., 1976.

Glaab, Charles N., and A. Theodore Brown, *A History of Urban America*. New York: The Macmillan Company, 1967.

Goetzmann, William H., *Exploration and Empire*. New York: Alfred A. Knopf, 1966.

Green, Constance M., *American Cities in the Growth of the Nation*. New York: John DeGraff, 1957.

Hafen, LeRoy R., W. Eugene Hollon, and Carl Coke Rister, *Western America: The Exploration, Settlement, and Development of the Region Beyond the Mississippi*. Englewood Cliffs, N.J.: Prentice-Hall, 3rd ed., 1970.

Hawgood, John A., *America's Western Frontiers*. New York: Alfred A. Knopf, 1967.

Hébert, John R. (comp.), *Panoramic Maps of Anglo-American Cities: A Checklist of Maps in the Collection of the Library of Congress, Geography and Maps Division*. Washington, D. C.: Library of Congress, 1974.

Hine, Robert V., *The American West: An Interpretive History*. Boston: Little, Brown and Company, 1973.

Hine, Robert V., and Edwin R. Bingham (eds.), *The Frontier Experience*: Readings in the Trans-Mississippi West. Belmont, California: Wadsworth Publishing Company, 1963.

Horan, James D., *The Great American West: A Pictorial History from Coronado to the Last Frontier*. New York: Crown, 1959.

Howe, Henry, *Historical Collections of the Great West*. Cincinnati: Henry Howe, 1856.

Jackson, W. Turrentine, *Wagon Roads West: A Study of Federal Road Surveys and Construction in the Trans-Mississippi West, 1846-1849*. New Haven: Yale University Press, 1967.

Knight, Oliver, "Toward an Understanding of the Western Town," *Western Historical Quarterly*, IV (January, 1973), 27-42.

Ladd, Richard S. (ed.), *Maps Showing Explorers' Routes, Trails & Early Roads in the United States: An Annotated List*. Washington: Library of Congress, 1962.

Le Gear, Clara E. (comp.), *United States Atlases: A Catalogue of National, State, County, City, and Regional Atlases in the Library of Congress and Cooperating Libraries*. Washington, D. C.: Division of Geography and Maps, U. S. Library of Congress, 1953.

———, *United States Atlases: A List of National, State, County, City and Regional Atlases in the Library of Congress*. Washington, D. C.: Division of Geography and Maps, U. S. Library of Congress, 1950.

Luckingham, Bradford, "The City in the Westward Movement—A Bibliographical Note," *Western Historical Quarterly*, V (July, 1974), 295-306.

McDermott, John F. (ed.), *The Frontier Re-Examined*. Urbana: University of Illinois Press, 1967.

McManis, Douglas R. (comp.), *Historical Geography of the United States: A Bibliography*. Ypsilanti, Michigan: Division of Field Services, Eastern Michigan University, 1965.

Meany, Edmond S., "The Towns of the Pacific Northwest Were Not Founded on the Fur Trade," American Historical Association, *Annual Report, 1909*, Washington, D.C., 1911, 165-172.

Montêquin, François-Auguste de, "Maps and Plans of Cities and Towns in Colonial New Spain, the Floridas, and Louisiana: Selected Documents from the Archivo General de Indias of Sevilla. Unpublished Ph.D. dissertation, University of New Mexico, Albuquerque, New Mexico, 1974.

Out West on the Overland Train. Palo Alto, California: American West Publishing Company, 1967.

Paullin, Charles O., *Atlas of the Historical Geography of the United States*. Washington: Carnegie Institution of Washington and American Geographical Society of New York, 1932.

Perrigo, Lynn I., *Our Spanish Southwest*. Dallas: Banks, Upshaw & Co., 1960.

Peters, Harry T., *America on Stone*. Garden City, N.Y.: Doubleday, Doran & Co., 1931.

———, *California on Stone*. Garden City, N.Y.: Doubleday, Doran & Co., 1935.

Phillips, Philip L., *A List of Maps of America in the Library of Congress*. Washington, D. C.: Government Printing Office, 1901.

Pinckney, Pauline A., *Painting in Texas: The Nineteenth Century*. Austin: University of Texas Press, 1967.

Pomeroy, Earl, *The Pacific Slope: A History of California, Oregon, Washington, Idaho, Utah, and Nevada*. New York: Alfred A. Knopf, 1965.

Powell, Lawrence Clark, "Resources of Western Libraries for Research in History," *Pacific Historical Review*, XI (September, 1942), 263-280.

Quiett, Glenn Chesney, *They Built the West: An Epic of Rails and Cities*. New York: D. Appleton-Century Co., 1934.

Reps, John W., *The Making of Urban America: A History of City Planning in the United States*. Princeton: Princeton University Press, 1965.

———, *Cities on Stone: Nineteenth Century Lithograph Images of the Urban West*. Fort Worth: Amon Carter Museum of Western Art, 1976.

Richardson, Albert Deane, *Beyond the Mississippi: From the Great River to the Great Ocean, Life and Adventure on the Prairies, Mountains, and Pacific Coast . . . 1857-1867*. Hartford: American Publishing Co., 1867.

Riegel, Robert E., *America Moves West*. New York: Holt, 3rd ed., 1956.

Robbins, Roy, *Our Landed Heritage: The Public Domain, 1776-1936*. Princeton: Princeton University Press, 1942.

Rohrbough, Malcolm, *The Land Office Business: The Settlement and Administration of American Public Lands, 1789-1837*. New York: Oxford University Press, 1968.

Root, Frank A., and William Elsey Connelley, *The Overland Stage to California*. Topeka, Kansas: Crane & Co., 1901.

Sakolski, A. M., *The Great American Land Bubble*. New York: Harper & Brothers, 1932.

Schmitt, Martin, and Dee Brown, *The Settlers' West*. New York: Charles Scribner's Sons, 1955.

Schnell, J. Christopher and Patrick E. McLear, "Why the Cities Grew: A Historiographical Essay on Western Urban Growth, 1850-1880." *Missouri Historical Society Bulletin*, XXVII (April, 1972), 162-177.

Silverberg, Robert, *Ghost Towns of the American West*. New York: Thomas Crowell Co., 1968.

Stokes, I. N. Phelps, and D. C. Haskell (comps.), *American Historical Prints: Early Views of American Cities*. New York: New York Public Library, 1932.

Taft, Robert, *Artists and Illustrators of the Old West. 1850-1900*. New York: Charles Scribner's Sons, 1953.

Thwaites, Reuben Gold (ed.), *Early Western Travels, 1748-1846*. 32 vols. Cleveland: The Arthur H. Clark Co., 1904-1907.

Tucker, Mary, *Books of the Southwest: A General Bibliography*. New York: J. J. Augustin, 1937.

Tunnard, Christopher, and Henry Hope Reed, *American Skyline: The Growth and Form of Our Cities and Towns*. Boston: Houghton Mifflin, 1955.

Turner, Frederick Jackson, *The Frontier in American History*. New York: Holt, 1920.

———, "The Significance of the Frontier in American History," *Annual Report of the American Historical Association, 1893*. Washington, D. C.: Government Printing Office, 1894, 199-227.

U. S. Federal Writers' Program, *American Guide Series*. 153 vols. Various publishers, 1936-1943.

U. S. Library of Congress, *A Guide to the Study of the United States of America*. Prepared under the direction of Roy P. Basler by Donald H. Mugridge and Blanche P. McCrum. Washington, D. C.: Government Printing Office, 1960.

———, *California: The Centennial of the Gold Rush and the First State Constitution*. Washington, D. C.: Government Printing Office, 1949.

———, *Centennial of the Oregon Territory*. Washington, D. C.: Government Printing Office, 1948

———, *Centennial of the Settlement of Utah*. Washington, D. C.: Government Printing Office, 1947.

———, *Colorado: The Diamond Jubilee of Statehood*. Washington, D.C.: Government Printing Office, 1951.

———, *Kansas and Nebraska: Centennial of the Territories, 1854-1954*. Washington, D. C.: Government Printing Office, 1954.

———, *Nevada: Centennial of Statehood*. Washington, D. C.: Government Printing Office, 1965.

———, *Oklahoma: The Semicentennial of Statehood*. Washington, D. C.: Government Printing Office, 1957.

———, *Texas Centennial Exhibition*. Washington, D. C.: Government Printing Office, 1946.

———, *Washington: Centennial of the Territory, 1853-1953*. Washington, D. C.: Government Printing Office, 1953.

Wallace, William S. (comp.), "Bibliography of Published Bibliographies on the History of the Eleven Western States, 1941-1947: a Partial Supplement to the *Writings in American History*," *New Mexico Historical Review*, XXIX (July, 1954), 224-233.

Watson, Douglas S. (ed.), *California in the Fifties. Fifty Views of Cities and Mining Towns in California and the West, Originally Drawn on Stone by Kuchel & Dresel and Other Early San Francisco Lithographers*. San Francisco: John Howell, 1936.

Webb, Walter Prescott, *The Great Plains*. Boston: Ginn & Co., 1931.

West, Ray B. (ed.), *Rocky Mountain Cities*. New York: W. W. Norton, 1949.

Winsor, Justin, *The Westward Movement*. Boston: Houghton Mifflin and Co., 1897.

Winther, Oscar O., *A Classified Bibliography of the Periodical Literature of the Trans-Mississippi West, 1811-1957*. Bloomington, Indiana: Indiana University Press, 1961. *A Supplement (1957-1967)*, with Richard A. Van Orman. Bloomington, Indiana: Indiana University Press, 1970.

———, *The Great Northwest: A History*. New York: A. A. Knopf, 2nd ed., 1950.

———, *The Transportation Frontier: Trans-Mississippi West, 1865-1890*. New York: Holt, Rinehart and Winston, 1964.

Woestemeyer, Ina Faye (ed. and comp.), *The Westward Movement: A Book of Readings on Our Changing Frontiers*. New York: D. Appleton-Century Co., 1939.

Wolle, Muriel Sibell, *The Bonanza Trail: Ghost Towns and Mining Camps of the West*. Bloomington, Indiana: Indiana University Press, 1966.

I · CITIES ON THE WAY WEST: THE BEGINNING OF URBANIZATION IN THE OHIO AND MISSISSIPPI VALLEYS

Andreas, A. T., *History of Chicago*. 3 vols. Chicago: A. T. Andreas, 1884.

Babcock, Charles A., *Venango County Pennsylvania, Her Pioneers and People*. 2 vols. Chicago: J. H. Beers, 1919.

Baily, Francis, *Journal of a Tour in Unsettled Parts of North America in 1796 & 1797*. Jack D. L. Holmes (ed.), Carbondale, Illinois: Southern Illinois University Press, 1969.

Balestier, Joseph N., *The Annals of Chicago*. Chicago: Fergus Printing Co., 1876.

Bausman, Joseph H., *History of Beaver County, Pennsylvania*. 2 vols. New York: The Knickerbocker Press, 1904.

Bingham, Robert W., *Cradle of the Queen City: A History of Buffalo to the Incorporation of the City*. Buffalo: Buffalo Historical Society, 1931.

Bolton, Nathaniel, *Early History of Indianapolis and Central Indiana*. Indianapolis: The Bowen-Merrill Co., 1897.

Brackenridge, H. M., *View of Louisiana; Together with a Journal of a Voyage up the Missouri River, in 1811*. Pittsburgh: Cramer, Spear and Eichbaum, 1814.

Buck, Solon J., and Elizabeth Hawthorn Buck, *The Planting of Civilization in Western Pennsylvania*. Pittsburgh: University of Pittsburgh Press, 1939.

Buckingham, James Silk, *The Eastern and Western States of America*. 3 vols. London: Fisher, Son, & Co., 1842.

Burt, Jesse C., *Nashville: Its Life and Times*. Nashville: Tennessee Book Company, 1949.

Capers, Gerald M., Jr., *The Biography of a River Town: Memphis: Its Heroic Age*. Chapel Hill: University of North Carolina Press, 1939.

Carmony, Donald F., "Genesis and Early History of the Indianapolis Fund, 1816-1826," *Indiana Magazine of History*, XXXVIII (March, 1942), 17-30.

Chapman, Edmund H., "City Planning Under Mercantile Expansion: The Case of Cleveland, Ohio," *Journal of the Society of Architectural Historians*, X (December, 1951), 10-17.

Creekmore, Betsey Beeler, *Knoxville*. Knoxville: University of Tennessee Press, 2nd ed., 1967.

Dick, Everett, *Vanguards of the Frontier*. New York: D. Appleton-Century Co., 1941.

Evans, Paul D., *The Holland Land Company*. Buffalo: Buffalo Historical Society, 1924.

Flint, Timothy, *Recollections of the Last Ten Years in the Valley of the Mississippi*. George R. Brooks (ed.). Carbondale: Southern Illinois University Press, 1968.

Folwell, William Watts, *A History of Minnesota*. 4 vols. St. Paul: Minnesota Historical Society, rev. ed., 1956.

Garwood, Darrell, *Crossroads of America: The Story of Kansas City*. New York: W. W. Norton & Co., 1948.

Glaab, Charles N., "Business Patterns in the Growth of a Midwestern City: The

Kansas City Business Community before the Civil War," *Business History Review*, xxxiii (Summer, 1959), 156-174.

Gregg, Josiah, *Commerce of the Prairies*, Max L. Moorhead (ed.). Norman: University of Oklahoma Press, 1954.

Hatcher, Harlan, *The Western Reserve: The Story of New Connecticut in Ohio*. Indianapolis: Bobbs-Merrill Co., 1942.

Havighurst, Walter, *Land of Promise: The Story of the Northwest Territory*. New York: The Macmillan Co., 1946.

————, *Wilderness for Sale: The Story of the First Western Land Rush*. New York: Hastings House, 1956.

Hildreth, S. P., "History of an Early Voyage on the Ohio and Mississippi Rivers, with Historical Sketches of the Different Points Along Them, &c, &c.," *American Pioneer*, i (March, 1842), 89-145.

Howe, E. W., "A Bit of Weston, Missouri, History," *Missouri Historical Review*, xlvii (October, 1952), 29-36.

Hoyt, Homer, *One Hundred Years of Land Values in Chicago*. Chicago: University of Chicago Press, 1933.

Kirkland, Joseph, *The Story of Chicago*. Chicago: Dibble Publishing Co., 1892.

Latrobe, Charles Joseph, *The Rambler in North America*. 2 vols. London: R. B. Seeley and W. Burnside, 1836.

Lewis, Henry, *The Valley of the Mississippi Illustrated*. A. Hermina Poatgieter (trans.), Bertha L. Heilbron (ed.). St. Paul: Minnesota Historical Society, 1967.

Liscomb, A. A., and A. L. Bergh (eds.), *The Writings of Thomas Jefferson*. 20 vols. Washington: Thomas Jefferson Memorial Association of the U. S., 1903-04.

Lorant, Stefan, *Pittsburgh: The Story of an American City*. Garden City, N.Y.: Doubleday & Co., 1964.

McDougal, H. C., "Historical Sketch of Kansas City from the Beginning to 1909," *Missouri Historical Review*, iv (October, 1909), 1-17.

McKnight, William J., *Pioneer Outline History of Northwestern Pennsylvania*. Philadelphia: J. B. Lippincott, 1905.

McRaven, Henry, *Nashville: "Athens of the South."* Chapel Hill, N.C.: Tennessee Book Company, 1949.

McReynolds, Edwin C., *Missouri: A History of the Crossroads State*. Norman: University of Oklahoma Press, 1962.

Mathews, Catharine Van Cortlandt, *Andrew Ellicott: His Life and Letters*. New York: The Grafton Press, 1908.

Melish, John, *Travels Through the United States of America in the Years 1806 & 1807, and 1809, 1810 & 1811*. 2 vols. Philadelphia: John Melish, 1812.

Miller, Robert E., "State Planned Towns in Pennsylvania: Allegheny, Beaver, Franklin, Waterford, Warren and Erie," unpublished seminar paper, Department of Urban Planning and Development, Cornell University, Ithaca, N.Y., 1973.

Moore, Charles, "Augustus Brevoort Woodward—A Citizen of Two Cities," Columbia Historical Society, *Records*, iv (1901).

Nelson, S. B., *Nelson's Biographical Dictionary and Historical Reference Book of Erie County, Pennsylvania*. Erie, Pa.: S. B. Nelson, 1896.

Pattison, William D., "The Survey of the Seven Ranges," *Ohio Historical Quarterly*, lxviii (April, 1959), 115-140.

Peterson, Charles E., "Colonial Saint Louis," *Missouri Historical Society Bulletin*, iii (April, 1947), 94-111.

Pierce, Bessie Louise, *A History of Chicago*. 3 vols. New York: A. A. Knopf, 1937-1957.

Pittman, Philip, *The Present State of the European Settlements on The Mississippi*. London: J. Nourse, 1770.

Pomeroy, Earl, *The Pacific Slope: A History of California, Oregon, Washington, Idaho, Utah, and Nevada*. New York: A. A. Knopf, 1965.

Reps, John W., "Great Expectations and Hard Times: The Planning of Cairo, Illinois," *Journal of the Society of Architectural Historians*, xvi (December, 1957), 14-21.

————, *Monumental Washington: The Planning and Development of the Capital Center*. Princeton: Princeton University Press, 1967.

————, "New Madrid on the Mississippi: American 18th Century Planning on the Spanish Frontier," *Journal of the Society of Architectural Historians*, xviii (March, 1959), 21-26.

————, *The Making of Urban America: A History of City Planning in the United States*. Princeton: Princeton University Press, 1965.

————, *Tidewater Towns: City Planning in Colonial Virginia and Maryland*. Williamsburg, Virginia: The Colonial Williamsburg Foundation, 1972.

————, "Thomas Jefferson's Checkerboard Towns," *Journal of the Society of Architectural Historians*, xx (October, 1961), 108-114.

————, "Urban Redevelopment in the Nineteenth Century: The Squaring of Circleville," *Journal of the Society of Architectural Historians*, xiv (December, 1955), 23-26.

Robbins, Roy M., *Our Landed Heritage: The Public Domain, 1776-1936*. Lincoln: University of Nebraska Press, 1962.

Robertson, John E. L., "Paducah: Origins to Second Class," *Register of the Kentucky Historical Society*, lxvi (April, 1968), 108-136.

Savelle, Max, *George Morgan, Colony Builder*. New York: Columbia University Press, 1932.

Schaaf, Ida M., "The Founding of Ste Genevieve, Missouri," *Missouri Historical Review*, xxvii (January, 1933), 145-150.

Smith, Alice Elizabeth, *James Duane Doty, Frontier Promoter*. Madison: State Historical Society of Wisconsin, 1954.

Still, Bayard, "Patterns of Mid-Nineteenth Century Urbanization in the Middle West," *Mississippi Valley Historical Review*, xxviii (September, 1941), 187-206.

Treat, Payson Jackson, *The National Land System, 1785-1820*. New York: E. B. Treat & Co., 1910.

Viles, Jonas, "Missouri Capitals and Capitols," *Missouri Historical Review*, xiii (January, 1919), 142-145.

————, "Old Franklin: A Frontier Town of the Twenties," *Mississippi Valley Historical Review*, IX (March, 1923), 269-282.

————, "Population and Extent of Settlement in Missouri before 1804," *Missouri Historical Review*, VI (July, 1911), 189-213.

Wade, Richard C., *The Urban Frontier: The Rise of Western Cities, 1790-1830*. Cambridge: Harvard University Press, 1959.

————, "Urban Life in Western America, 1790-1830," *American Historical Review*, LXIV (October, 1958), 14-30.

Webb, W. L., "Independence, Missouri, A Century Old," *Missouri Historical Review*, XXII (October, 1927), 30-50.

Wild, John Casper, *The Valley of the Mississippi; Illustrated in a Series of Views*. St. Louis: J. Garnier, 1948.

Wood, William A., "Beginnings of the City of St. Joseph," *Magazine of American History*, XXVI (August, 1891), 108-114.

Woodford, Frank B., *Mr. Jefferson's Disciple: A Life of Justice Woodward*. East Lansing: Michigan State University Press, 1953.

Wright, Alfred J., "Joel Wright, City Planner," *Ohio Archaeological and Historical Quarterly*, LVI (July, 1947), 287-294.

II · SPANISH SETTLEMENTS IN THE SOUTHWEST: EVOLUTION OF POLICY, ELEMENTS OF COLONIZATION, AND THE FIRST TOWNS IN NEW MEXICO

Adams, Eleanor B. (ed.), *Bishop Tamarón's Visitation of New Mexico, 1760*. Albuquerque: Historical Society of New Mexico, 1954.

————, "The Chapel and Cofradia of Our Lady of Light in Santa Fe," *New Mexico Historical Quarterly*, XXII (October, 1947), 327-341.

Adams, Eleanor B., and Fray Angelico Chavez (trans. and eds.), *The Missions of New Mexico, 1776: A Description by Fray Francisco Atanasio Dominguez*. Albuquerque: University of New Mexico Press, 1956.

Andrachek, Steven, "Towns of New Mexico: Sante Fe and Albuquerque," unpublished seminar paper, Department of City and Regional Planning, Cornell University, 1970.

Bannon, John Francis, *The Spanish Borderlands Frontier, 1513-1821*. New York: Holt, Rinehart and Winston, 1970.

Blackmar, Frank W., *Spanish Colonization in the Southwest*. Baltimore: Johns Hopkins University Press, 1890.

Bloom, Lansing B., "Alburquerque and Galisteo: Certificate of their Founding, 1706," *New Mexico Historical Review*, X (January, 1935), 48-51.

Bolton, Herbert E. (ed.), *Spanish Exploration in the Southwest, 1542-1706*. New York: Charles Scribner's Sons, 1916.

————, "The Mission as a Frontier Institution in the Spanish American Colonies," *American Historical Review*, XXIII (October, 1917), 42-61.

Brinckerhoff, Sidney B., and Odie B. Faulk (trans.), *Lancers for the King: A Study of the Frontier Military System of Northern New Spain, With A Translation of the Royal Regulations of 1772*. Phoenix: Arizona Historical Foundation, 1965.

Burnett, Hugh and Evelyn, "Madrid Plaza," *Colorado Magazine*, XLII (Summer, 1965), 224-237.

Burrus, Ernest J. (trans.), *Kino's Plan for the Development of Pimería Alta, Arizona & Upper California*. Tucson: Arizona Pioneers' Historical Society, 1961.

Carroll, H. Bailey, and J. Villasana Haggard, (eds.), *Three New Mexico Chronicles*. Albuquerque: The Quivira Society, 1942.

Chaves, Ireneo L. (trans.), "Instructions to Peralta by Viceroy," *New Mexico Historical Review*, IV (April, 1929), 179-187.

Christiansen, Paige W., "The Presidio and the Borderlands: A Case Study," *Journal of the West*, VIII (January, 1969), 29-37.

Chueca Goitia, Fernando, and Leopoldo Torres Balbas, *Planos de Ciudades Iberoamericanas y Filipinas Existentes en el Archivo de Indias*. 2 vols. Madrid: Instituto de Estudios de Administracion Local, 1951.

Columbus, Christopher, *The Journal of Christopher Columbus*. Cecil Jane (trans.). New York: Clarkson N. Potter, 1960.

Crouch, Dora P., and Axel I. Mundigo, "The City Planning Ordinances of the Laws of the Indies Revisited, Part II: Three American Cities," *Town Planning Review*, XLVIII (October, 1977), 397-418.

Cutter, Donald C., *Malaspína in California*. San Francisco: John Howell Books, 1960.

Davis, W.W.H., *El Gringo; or, New Mexico and Her People*. New York: Harper and Brothers, 1857.

Faulk, Odie B., "The Presidio: Fortress or Farce?" *Journal of the West*, VIII (January, 1969), 22-27.

Folmer, Henry, *Franco-Spanish Rivalry in North America, 1524-1763*. Glendale, California: A. H. Clark Co., 1953.

Forrestal, Peter P. (trans.), *Benavides' Memorial of 1630*. Washington: Academy of American Franciscan History, 1954.

Garr, Daniel, "Hispanic Colonial Settlement in California: Planning and Urban Development on the Frontier, 1769-1850," unpublished Ph.D. dissertation, Cornell University, Ithaca, N.Y., 1972.

Greenleaf, Richard E., "The Founding of Albuquerque, 1706: An Historical-Legal Problem," *New Mexico Historical Review*, XXXIX (January, 1964), 1-15.

Hackett, Charles Wilson (ed.), *Historical Documents Relating to New Mexico, Nueva Viscaya, and Approaches Thereto to 1773*. Washington: Carnegie Institution of Washington, 1923.

Hammond, George P., *Don Juan de Oñate and the Founding of New Mexico*. Santa Fe: Historical Society of New Mexico, 1927.

Hammond, George P., and Agapito Rey, *Don Juan de Oñate: Colonizer of New Mexico, 1595-1628*. Albuquerque: University of New Mexico Press, 1953.

Hodge, Frederick Webb, George P. Hammond, and Agapito Rey (eds.), *Fray Alonso de Benavides' Revised Memorial of 1634*. Albuquerque: University of New Mexico Press, 1945.

Jones, O. Garfield, "Local Government in the Spanish Colonies as Provided by the Recopilación de Leyes de Los Reynos de Las Indias," *Southwestern Historical Quarterly*, xix (July, 1915), 66-69.

Kinnaird, Lawrence (ed.), *The Frontiers of New Spain: Nicolas de Lafora's Description, 1766-1768*. Berkeley: The Quivira Society, 1958.

Kubler, George, "Mexican Urbanism in the Sixteenth Century," *The Art Bulletin*, xxiv (June, 1942), 160-171.

Loomis, Sylvia Glidden (ed.), *Old Santa Fe Today*. Santa Fe: The School of American Research, 1966.

Lowery, Woodbury, *The Spanish Settlements within the Present Limits of the United States*. New York: G. P. Putnam's Sons, 1901.

Moorhead, Max L., *The Presidio: Bastion of the Spanish Borderland*. Norman: University of Oklahoma Press, 1975.

Morse, Richard, "Some Characteristics of Latin American Urban History," *American Historical Review*, lxvii (January, 1962), 317-338.

Mundigo, Axel I., and Dora P. Crouch, "The City Planning Ordinances of the Laws of the Indies Revisited, Part I: Their Philosophy and Implications," *Town Planning Review*, xlviii (July, 1977), 247-268.

Nuttall, Zelia, "Royal Ordinances Concerning the Laying Out of New Towns," *Hispanic American Historical Review*, iv (November, 1921), 743-753; v (May, 1922), 249-254.

Oviedo, Gonzalo Fernández de, *Natural History of the West Indies* (Toledo, 1526). Sterling A. Stoudemire (trans. and ed.). Chapel Hill: University of North Carolina Press, 1959.

Powell, Philip Wayne, "Presidios and Towns on the Silver Frontier of New Spain, 1550-1580," *Hispanic American Historical Review*, xxiv (May, 1944), 179-200.

Priestly, Herbert Ingram, "Spanish Colonial Municipalities," *California Law Review*, vii (1918-1919), 397-416.

Reps, John W., *Tidewater Towns: City Planning in Colonial Virginia and Maryland*. Williamsburg, Va.: The Colonial Williamsburg Foundation, 1972.

———, *The Making of Urban America*. Princeton: Princeton University Press, 1965.

Sauer, Carl Ortwin, *The Early Spanish Main*. Berkeley: University of California Press, 1966.

Simmons, Marc, "Settlement Patterns and Village Plans in Colonial New Mexico," *Journal of the West*, viii (January, 1969), 7-21.

———, "Spanish Government and Colonial Land Practices," *New Mexico Quarterly*, xxxviii (Spring, 1968), 37-43.

———, *Spanish Government in New Mexico*. Albuquerque: University of New Mexico Press, 1968.

Sporleder, Louis B., "La Plaza de Los Leones," *Colorado Magazine*, x (January, 1933), 28-38.

Stanislawski, Dan, "Early Spanish Town Planning in the New World," *Geographical Review*, xxxvii (January, 1947), 94-105.

Thomas, Alfred Barnaby (ed. and trans.), *Forgotten Frontiers: a Study of the Spanish Indian Policy of Don Juan Bautista de Anza, Governor of New Mexico, 1777-1787*. Norman: University of Oklahoma Press, 1932.

———, (ed. and trans.), *Teodore de Croix and the Northern Frontier of New Spain, 1776-1783*. Norman: University of Oklahoma Press, 1941.

Tichy, Marjorie F., "New Mexico's First Capital," *New Mexico Historical Review*, xxi (October, 1946), 140-144.

Twitchell, Ralph Emerson, *Old Santa Fe* (1915). Chicago: The Rio Grande Press, 1963.

———, *The Leading Facts of New Mexican History*. 2 vols. Albuquerque: Horn and Wallace, 1963.

U. S. Federal Writers' Program, *California: A Guide to the Golden State*. New York: Hastings House, 1942.

Vitruvius, *The Ten Books of Architecture*. Morris Hicky Morgan (trans. and ed.). Cambridge: Harvard University Press, 1926.

von Wuthenau, A., "The Spanish Military Chapels in Santa Fé and the Reredos of Our Lady of Light," *New Mexico Historical Quarterly*, x (July, 1935), 175-194.

White, Katherine H., "Spanish and Mexican Surveying Terms and Systems," *Password*, vi (Winter, 1961), 24-27.

Wilson, Benjamin Davis, *The Indians of Southern California in 1852*. John Walton Caughey (ed.). San Marino: The Huntington Library, 1952.

Wislizenus, A., *Memoir of a Tour to Northern Mexico, Connected with Col. Doniphan's Expedition, in 1846 and 1847*. Sen. Misc. Doc. 26, 30th Cong., 1st Sess. Washington: Tippin & Streeper, Printers, 1848.

Wyllys, Rufus Kay, "The Spanish Missions of the Southwest," *Arizona Historical Review*, vi (January, 1935), 27-37.

III · SPANISH TOWNS OF THE TEXAS FRONTIER

Austin, Mattie Alice, "The Municipal Government of San Fernando de Bexar, 1730-1800," *Quarterly of the Texas State Historical Association*, viii (April, 1905), 277-352.

Bannon, John Francis, *The Spanish Borderlands Frontier, 1513-1821*. New York: Holt, Rinehart and Winston, 1970.

———, (ed.), *Bolton and the Spanish Borderlands*. Norman: University of Oklahoma Press, 1964.

Blake, R. B., "Locations of the Early Spanish Missions and Presidio in Nacogdoches County," *Southwestern Historical Quarterly*, xli (January, 1938), 212-224.

Bolton, Herbert E., *Texas in the Middle Eighteenth Century*. Berkeley: University of California Press, 1915.

———, "The Location of La Salle's Colony on the Gulf of Mexico," *Mississippi Valley Historical Review*, II (September, 1915), 165-182.

———, "The Spanish Occupation of Texas, 1519-1690," *Southwestern Historical Quarterly*, XVI (July, 1912), 1-26.

———, "Tienda de Cuervo's *Ynspección* of Laredo, 1757," *Quarterly of the Texas State Historical Association*, VI (January, 1903), 187-203.

Brinckherhoff, Sidney B., and Odie B. Faulk (trans.), *Lancers for the King*. Phoenix: Arizona Historical Foundation, 1965.

Buckley, Eleanor Claire, "The Aguayo Expedition into Texas and Louisiana, 1719-1722," *Quarterly of the Texas State Historical Association*, XV (July, 1911), 1-65.

Castañeda, Carlos E., *Our Catholic Heritage in Texas*. 6 vols. Austin: Von Boeckmann-Jones Company, 1936-1950.

Céliz, Francisco, *Dairy of the Alarcón Expedition into Texas, 1718-1719*, Fritz Leo Hoffman (ed. and trans.). Los Angeles: The Quivira Society, 1935.

Chabot, Frederick C., *San Antonio and its Beginnings, 1691-1731*. San Antonio: Naylor Printing Co., 1931.

Chueca Goitia, Fernando, and Leopoldo Torres Balbas, *Planos de Ciudades Iberoamericanas y Filipinas Existentes en el Archivo de Indias*. 2 vols. Madrid: Instituto de Estudios de Administracion Local, 1951.

Clark, Robert C., "Louis Juchereau de Saint-Denis and the Reestablishment of the Tejas Missions," *Texas State Historical Association Quarterly*, VI (July, 1902), 1-26.

Cole, E. W., "La Salle in Texas," *Southwestern Historical Quarterly*, XLIX (April, 1946), 473-500.

Connor, Seymour V., *Texas in 1776: A Historical Description*. Austin: Jenkins Publishing Co., 1975.

Coopwood, Bethel, "Notes on the History of La Bahía del Espíritu Santo," *Quarterly of the Texas State Historical Assocation*, II (October, 1898), 162-169.

Craig, Robert M., "Spanish Texas and the Development of San Antonio," unpublished seminar paper, Department of City and Regional Planning, Cornell University, 1971.

Dabbs, Jack Autrey, "Additional Notes on the Champ-d'Asile," *Southwestern Historical Quarterly*, LIV (January, 1951), 347-358.

Dunn, William E., *Spanish and French Rivalry in the Gulf Region of the United States, 1678-1702: The Beginnings of Texas and Pensacola*. Austin: University of Texas, 1917.

Duty, Tony E., "Champ D'Asile," *Texana*, X (1972), 87-103.

Fathford, Fanny E. (ed.), *The Story of Champ D'Asile*. Austin: Steck-Vaughn Co., 1969.

Faulk, Odie B., *The Last Years of Spanish Texas, 1778-1821*. The Hague: Mouton and Co., 1964.

Gaillardet, Frédéric, *Sketches of Early Texas and Louisiana*. James L. Shepherd (trans.), Austin: University of Texas Press, 1966.

Gilmore, Kathleen, *A Documentary and Archeological Investigation of Presidio San Luis de las Amarillas and Mission Santa Cruz de San Sabá*. Austin: Texas State Building Commission, Archeological Program, Report Number 9, December, 1967.

Habig, Marion A., "Mission San José y San Miguel de Aguayo, 1720-1824," *Southwestern Historical Quarterly*, LXXI (April, 1968), 495-516.

———, *San Antonio's Mission San José*. Chicago: Franciscan Herald Press, 1968.

Hackett, Charles W., "The Marquis of San Miguel de Aguayo and His Recovery of Texas from the French, 1719-1723," *Southwestern Historical Quarterly*, XLIX (October, 1945), 193-214.

———, "Visitador Rivera's Criticisms of Aguayo's Work in Texas," *Hispanic American Historical Review*, XVI (May, 1936), 162-172.

Hamilton, Peter J., *Colonial Mobile*. Boston: Houghton Mifflin Company, rev. ed., 1910.

Hill, Lawrence F., *José de Escandón and the Founding of Nuevo Santander: A Study in Spanish Colonization*. Columbus: Ohio State University Press, 1926.

Kinnaird, Lawrence, *The Frontiers of New Spain: Nicolas de Lafora's Description, 1766-1768*. Berkeley: The Quivira Society, 1958.

Kramer, V. Paul, "The Spanish Borderlands of Texas and Tamaulipas," *Texana*, X (1972), 260-272.

Looscan, Adele B., "The Old Fort on the San Saba River as Seen by Dr. Ferdinand Roemer in 1847," *Quarterly of the Texas State Historical Association*, V (October, 1901), 137-141.

Morfi, Juan Agustín, *History of Texas, 1673-1779*, Carlos Eduardo Castañeda (ed. and trans.). Albuquerque: The Quivira Society, 1935.

O'Connor, Kathryn Stoner, *The Presidio La Bahia del Espiritu Santo de Zuniga, 1721 to 1846*. Austin: Von Boeckmann-Jones Company, 1966.

Perry, Carmen (ed. and trans.), *The Impossible Dream by the Rio Grande*. San Antonio: St. Mary's University Press, 1971.

Phares, Ross, *Cavalier in the Wilderness: The Story of the Explorer and Trader Louis Juchereau de St. Denis*. Baton Rouge: Louisiana State University Press, 1952.

Reeves, Jesse E., *The Napoleonic Exiles in America*. Baltimore: Johns Hopkins University Studies in Historical and Political Science, XXIII (1905), 531-656.

Reps, John W., *The Making of Urban America: A History of City Planning in the United States*. Princeton: Princeton University Press, 1965.

Schuetz, Mardith K., *Historic Background of the Mission San Antonio de Valero*. Austin: Texas State Building Commission, Archeological Program, Report Number 1, November, 1966.

Scott, Florence Johnson, *Historical Heritage of the Lower Rio Grande*. San Antonio: The Naylor Company, 1937.

———, "Spanish Colonization of the Lower Rio Grande, 1747-1767," in Thomas E. Cotner and Carlos E. Castañeda (eds.), *Essays in Mexican History*. Austin: University of Texas, Institute of Latin American Studies, 1958.

Spell, Lota M., "The Grant and First Survey of the City of San Antonio," *Southwestern Historical Review*, LXVI (July, 1962), 73-89.

Thomas, Alfred Barnaby (ed. and trans.), *Teodore de Croix and the Northern Frontier of New Spain, 1776-1783*. Norman: University of Oklahoma Press, 1941.

Vigness, David M., "Nuevo Santander in 1795: A Provincial Inspection by Félix Calleja," *Southwestern Historical Quarterly*, LXXV (April, 1972), 461-506.

Wallace, Ernest, and David M. Vigness, *Documents of Texas History*. Austin: The Steck Company, 1963.

Walters, Paul H., "Secularization of the La Bahia Missions," *Southwestern Historical Quarterly*, LIV (January, 1951), 287-300.

Weddle, Robert S., *The San Sabá Mission: Spanish Pivot in Texas*. Austin: University of Texas Press, 1964.

Wilkinson, J. B., *Laredo and the Rio Grande Frontier*. Austin: Jenkins Publishing Co., 1975.

Willard, James F., and Colin B. Goodykootz (eds.), *The Trans-Mississippi West*. Boulder: University of Colorado Press, 1930.

Wissler, Clark, Constance Lindsay Skinner, and William Wood, *The Pageant of America*, I, *Adventurers in the Wilderness*. New Haven: Yale University Press, 1925.

IV · EXPANSION OF THE SPANISH BORDERLANDS: URBAN SETTLEMENT OF ARIZONA AND CALIFORNIA IN THE HISPANIC ERA

Atherton, Faxon Dean, *California Diary*. Doyce B. Nunis, Jr. (ed.), San Francisco: California Historical Society, 1964.

Bancroft, Hubert Howe, *History of California*. 7 vols. San Francisco: The History Company, 1884-90.

———, *History of Arizona and New Mexico*. San Francisco: The History Company, 1889.

Bannon, John Francis, *The Spanish Borderlands Frontier, 1513-1821*. New York: Holt, Rinehart and Winston, 1970.

Beilharz, Edwin A., *Felipe de Neve: First Governor of California*. San Francisco: California Historical Society, 1971.

Bolton, Herbert E., *Rim of Christendom: A Biography of Eusebio Francisco Kino, Pacific Coast Pioneer*. New York: Macmillan, 1936.

——— (trans. and ed.), *Spanish Exploration in the Southwest, 1542-1706*. New York: Scribner's, 1916.

Bowman, Jacob N., "The Spanish Anchorage in San Francisco Bay," *California Historical Society Quarterly*, XXV (December, 1946), 319-324.

———, "The Third Map of Yerba Buena," *California Historical Society Quarterly*, XXVI (September, 1947), 267-269.

Brandes, Ray, and Andrew Wallace, "A Centennial Checklist of Readings for the Study and Teaching of Arizona History," *Arizoniana*, IV (Spring, 1963), 14-22; (Summer, 1963), 19-27; (Fall, 1963), 9-18; (Winter, 1963), 39-48.

Brinckerhoff, Sidney B. and Odie B. Faulk, *Lancers for the King*. Phoenix: Arizona Historical Foundation, 1965.

Brooks, B. S., "Alcalde Grants in the City of San Francisco," *Pioneer, or California Monthly Magazine*, I (April, 1854), 193-200.

Brown, John Henry, *Early Days of San Francisco*. Oakland: Biobooks, 1949.

Bryant, Edwin, *What I Saw in California: Being the Journal of a Tour . . . in the Years 1846, 1847*. Minneapolis: Ross & Haines, Inc., 1967.

Bynum, Lindley, "Governor Don Felipe de Neve," Historical Society of Southern California, *Annual Publications*, XV (1931), 57-98.

Carter, Charles Franklin (trans.), "Duhaut-Cilly's Account of California in the Years 1827-28," *California Historical Society Quarterly*, VIII (June, 1929), 130-166; (September, 1929), 214-250; (December, 1929), 306-336.

Chapman, Charles E., *The Founding of Spanish California: The Northwestward Expansion of New Spain, 1687-1783*. New York: Macmillan, 1916.

Costansó, Miguel, "The Narrative of the Portolá Expedition of 1769-1770," Adolph Van Hemert-Engert and Frederick J. Teggarts (eds.), Academy of Pacific Coast History, *Publications*, I (March, 1910), 93-159.

Dana, Richard Henry, *Two Years Before the Mast*. New York: The Modern Library, 1936.

Dane, George Ezra (trans.), "The Founding of the Presidio and Mission of Our Father Saint Francis, Being Chapter 45 of Fray Francisco Palóu's Life of the Venerable Padre Fray Junípero Serra, Written at the Mission of San Francisco de Asis, and Newly Translated from the Original Edition of 1787," *California Historical Society Quarterly*, XIV (June, 1935), 102-110.

Davis, William Heath, *Seventy-Five Years in California*. San Francisco: John Howell, 1929.

de Packman, Ana Begue, "Landmarks and Pioneers of Los Angeles in 1853," *Quarterly of the Historical Society of Southern California*, XXVI (June-September, 1944), 57-95.

Duflot de Mofras, Eugène, *Exploration du Territoire de l'Orégon, des Californies, et de la Mer Vermeille*. 2 vols. Paris: A. Bertrand, 1844.

Dunne, Peter Masten, *Black Robes in Lower California*. Berkeley: University of California Press, 1952.

Du Petit-Thouars, Abel Aubert, *Voyage Autour du Monde*. 11 vols. Paris: Gide, 1840-1864.

Dwinelle, John W., *Colonial History of San Francisco*. San Francisco: Town and Bacon, 1866.

Eldredge, Zoeth S., *The Beginnings of San Francisco*. 2 vols. San Francisco: Z. S. Eldredge, 1912.

Emory, W. H., *Notes of a Military Reconoissance from Fort Leavenworth in Missouri, to San Diego in California*. Washington: Wendell and Van Benthuysen, 1848.

Engelhardt, Zephyrin, *The Missions and Missionaries of California*. 4 vols. San Francisco: The James H. Barry Company, 1908-1915.

Essig, E. O., "The Russian Settlement at Ross," *California Historical Society Quarterly*, XII (September, 1933), 191-216.

Ferris, Robert G. (ed.), *Explorers and Settlers: Historic Places Commemorating the Early Exploration and Settlement of the United States*. National Park Service, U. S. Department of the Interior, The National Survey of Historic Sites and Buildings, v. Washington: Government Printing Office, 1968.

Fink, Augusta, *Monterey: The Presence of the Past*. San Francisco: Chronicle Books, 1972.

Ford, Henry Chapman, *Etchings of the Franciscan Missions of California*. New York: n.p., 1883.

Garr, Daniel, "Hispanic Colonial Settlement in California: Planning and Urban Development on the Frontier: 1769-1850," unpublished Ph.D. dissertation, Cornell University, Ithaca, New York, 1972.

———, "Planning, Politics and Plunder: The Missions and Indian Pueblos of Hispanic California," *Southern California Quarterly*, LIV (Winter, 1972), 291-312.

———, "A Rare and Desolate Land: Population and Race in Hispanic California," *The Western Historical Quarterly*, VI (April, 1975), 133-148.

———, "A Frontier Agrarian Settlement: San José de Guadelupe, 1777-1850," *San José Studies*, II (November, 1976), 93-105.

Gerald, Rex E., *Spanish Presidios of the Late Eighteenth Century in Northern New Spain*. Sante Fe: Museum of New Mexico Press, 1968.

Gregory, Thomas, *History of Sonoma County*. Los Angeles: Historic Record Company, 1911.

Guinn, J. M., "From Pueblo to Ciudad: The Municipal and Territorial Expansion of Los Angeles," *Historical Society of Southern California*, *Publications*, VII (1908), 216-221.

———, "The Story of a Plaza," *Historical Society of Southern California*, *Annual Publications*, IV (1898), 247-256.

Hall, Frederick, *The History of San José and Surroundings*. San Francisco: A. L. Bancroft Company, 1871.

Harlow, Neal, "The Maps of San Francisco Bay and the Town of Yerba Buena to 100 Years Ago," *Pacific Historical Review*, XVI (November, 1947), 365-378.

Hart, Herbert M., *Old Forts of the Far West*. New York: Bonanza Books, 1965.

Johnson, John Everett (trans.), *Regulations for Governing the Province of the Californias approved by His Majesty by Royal Order, dated October 24, 1781*. San Francisco: Grabhorn Press, 1929.

Kessell, John L. (ed.), "San Jose de Tumacacori—1773. A Franciscan Reports from Arizona," *Arizona and the West*, VI (Winter, 1964), 303-312.

Kinnaird, Lawrence, *History of the Greater San Francisco Bay Region*. 3 vols. New York: Lewis Historical Publishing Company, 1966.

Lummis, Charles F. (trans.), "Regulations and Instructions for the Garrisons of the Peninsula of California," *Historical Society of Southern California*, *Annual Publications*, XV (1931), 157-188.

Mattison, Ray H., "Early Spanish and Mexican Settlements in Arizona," *New Mexico Historical Review*, XXI (October, 1946), 273-327.

"Padron and Confirmation of Titles to Pueblo Lands," *Historical Society of Southern California*, *Annual Publications*, XV (1931), 150-155.

Palóu, Francisco, *Historical Memoirs of New California*. Herbert E. Bolton (ed.). 4 vols. New York: Russell & Russell, 1966.

Peters, Harry T., *California on Stone*. Garden City, N.Y.: Doubleday, Doran & Co., 1935.

Pierce, Richard A., and John H. Winslow (eds.), *H.M.S. Sulphur At California, 1837 and 1839*. San Francisco: Book Club of California, 1969.

Pourade, Richard F., *The History of San Diego*. 5 vols. San Diego: Union-Tribune Publishing Co., 1960-65.

Richman, Irving Berdine, *California under Spain and Mexico, 1535-1847*. Boston: Houghton Mifflin Company, 1911.

Robinson, W. W., *Los Angeles from the Days of the Pueblo, Together with a Guide to the Historic Old Plaza Area Including the Pueblo de Los Angeles State Historical Monument*. San Francisco: California Historical Society, 1959.

Ruschenberger, William S. W., *A Voyage Round the World . . . in 1835, 1836 and 1837*. Philadelphia: Carey, Lea & Blanchard, 1838.

"San Francisco in 1792," *California Historical Society Quarterly*, XIV (June, 1935), 111-120.

San José, California City Planning Commission, *The Master Plan*. San José: City Planning Commission, 1958.

Simpson, Lesley Byrd, *An Early Ghost Town of California, Branciforte*. San Francisco: H. W. Porte, 1935.

Torchiana, H. A. van Coenen, *Story of the Mission Santa Cruz*. San Francisco: Paul Elder and Co., 1933.

Treutlein, Theodore E., *San Francisco Bay: Discovery and Colonization, 1769-1776*. San Francisco: California Historical Society, 1968.

U. S. Federal Writers' Program, *California: A Guide to the Golden State*. New York: Hastings House, 1942.

Van Nostrand, Jeanne, *A Pictorial and Narrative History of Monterey: Adobe Capital of California, 1770-1847*. San Francisco: California Historical Society, 1968.

Weber, Francis J., "Jesuit Missions in Baja California," *The Americas*, XXIII (April, 1967), 408-422.

Winther, Oscar Osburn, "The Story of San José, 1777-1869, Chapter I: The Spanish Period," *California Historical Society Quarterly*, XIV (March, 1935), 3-27.

"Yerba Buena Biographies," *California Historical Society Quarterly*, XIV (June, 1935), 123-131.

V · TOWNS IN TRANSITION: THE SOUTHWEST DURING THE PERIOD OF MEXICAN CONTROL, TEXAS INDEPENDENCE, AND THE EARLY YEARS OF AMERICAN SETTLEMENT

Adams, Judge F., "Tucson in 1847," *Arizona Historical Review*, I (January, 1929), 83-85.

Banks, C. Stanley, "The Mormon Migration into Texas," *Southwestern Historical Quarterly*, XLIX (October, 1945), 233-244.

Bartlett, John R., *Personal Narrative of Explorations and Incidents in Texas, New*

Mexico, California, Sonora, and Chihuahua . . . during the Years 1850, '51, '52, and '53. 2 vols. New York: D. Appleton and Company, 1854.

Benjamin, Gilbert Giddings, *The Germans in Texas: A Study in Immigration.* New York: D. Appleton & Company, 1910.

Biesele, Rudolph L., "Early Times in New Braunfels and Comal County," *Southwestern Historical Quarterly*, L (July, 1946), 75-92.

————, *History of the German Settlements in Texas, 1831-1861.* Austin: Von Boeckmann-Jones Company, 1930.

Bitton, Davis, "Mormons in Texas: The Ill-Fated Lyman Wight Colony, 1844-1858," *Arizona and the West*, XI (Spring, 1969), 5-26.

Brinckerhoff, Sidney B., and Odie B. Faulk (trans.), *Lancers for the King: A Study of the Frontier Military System of Northern New Spain, With a Translation of the Royal Regulations of 1772.* Phoenix: Arizona Historical Foundation, 1965.

Broussard, Ray, "San Antonio During the Texas Republic," *Southwestern Studies*, V, No. 2, Monograph No. 18, 1967.

Byars, Charles, "Documents of Arizona History: The First Map of Tucson," *Journal of Arizona History*, VII (Winter, 1966), 188-189.

Carroll, B. H. (ed.), *Standard History of Houston, Texas.* Knoxville: H. W. Crew and Co., 1912.

Carroll, H. Bailey, "Texas County Histories," *Southwestern Historical Quarterly*, XLV (July, 1941), 75-98; (October, 1941), 164-188; (January, 1942), 260-276; (April, 1942), 343-362.

Castañeda, Carlos E., *Our Catholic Heritage in Texas, 1519-1936.* 6 vols. Austin: Von Boeckmann-Jones Company, 1936-1950.

City of Galveston, on Galveston Island, in Texas . . . Accompanied with a Plan of the City and Harbor. New Orleans: Hotchkiss and Co., 1837.

Coleman, Marion Moore (trans. and ed.), "New Light on La Réunion," *Arizona and the West*, VI (Spring, 1964), 41-68; (Summer, 1964), 137-154.

Conger, Roger N., *A Pictorial History of Waco with a Reprint of Highlights of Waco History.* Waco: The Texian Press, 2nd ed., 1964.

Cozzens, Samuel Woodworth, *The Marvellous Country; or, Three Years in Arizona and New Mexico, the Apaches' Home.* Minneapolis: Ross and Haines, Inc., 1967.

East, Lorecia, *History and Progress of Jefferson County.* Dallas: Royal Publishing Company, 1961.

Faulk, Odie B., "The Icarian Colony in Texas, 1848: A Problem in Historiography," *Texana*, V (Summer, 1967), 132-140.

————, *The Last Years of Spanish Texas, 1778-1821.* The Hague: Mouton and Co., 1964.

Fehrenbach, T. R., *Lone Star: A History of Texas and the Texans.* New York: The Macmillan Company, 1968.

Flanagan, Sue, *Sam Houston's Texas.* Austin: University of Texas Press, 1964.

Foote, Henry Stuart, *Texas and the Texans.* Austin: The Steck Company, 1935.

Gage, Larry J., "The City of Austin on the Eve of the Civil War," *Southwestern Historical Quarterly*, LXIII (January, 1960), 428-438.

Graf, Leroy P., "Colonizing Projects in Texas South of the Nueces, 1820-1845," *Southwestern Historical Quarterly*, L (April, 1947), 431-448.

Greenleaf, Cameron, and Andrew Wallace, "Tucson: Pueblo, Presidio, and American City, A Synopsis of its History," *Arizoniana*, III (Summer, 1962), 18-27.

Gulick, Charles Adams, Jr., Winnie Allen, Katherine Elliott, and Harriet Smither (eds.), *Papers of Mirabeau Buonaparte Lamar.* 7 vols. Austin: The Pemberton Press, 1968.

Haas, Oscar, *History of New Braunfels and Comal County, Texas, 1844-1946.* Austin: The Steck Company, 1968.

Hammond, William J., and Margaret F. Hammond, *La Réunion, A French Settlement in Texas.* Dallas: Royal Publishing Company, 1958.

Hardy, Dermot H., and Ingham S. Roberts (eds.), *Historical Review of Southeast Texas.* Chicago: Lewis Publishing Co., 1910.

Harnstone, Howard, *The Galveston That Was.* Photographs by Henri Cartier-Bresson and Ezra Stoller. New York: The Macmillan Company, 1966.

Hart, Herbert M., *Old Forts of the Far West.* New York: Bonanza Books, 1965.

Haskew, Corrie Pattison (comp.), *Historical Records of Austin and Waller Counties.* Houston: Premier Printing & Letter Service, Inc., 1969.

Henderson, Mary Virginia, "Minor Empresario Contracts for the Colonization of Texas, 1825-1834," *Southwestern Historical Quarterly*, XXXI (April, 1928), 295-324; and XXXII (July, 1928), 1-29.

Hinton, Richard J., *The Hand-Book to Arizona.* San Francisco: Payot, Upham and Co., 1878.

Holley, Mary Austin, *Texas.* Baltimore: Armstrong and Plaskitt, 1833.

————, *The Texas Diary, 1835-1838.* J. P. Bryan (ed.). Austin: University of Texas, Humanities Research Center, 1965.

Houston, Samuel, *The Writings of Sam Houston.* Amelia W. Williams and Eugene C. Barker (eds.). 8 vols. Austin: University of Texas Press, 1938-1943.

Jenkins, John W. (comp.) *Cracker Barrel Chronicles: A Bibliography of Texas Town and County Histories.* Austin: The Pemberton Press, 1965.

Keeth, Kent, "Sankt Antonius: Germans in the Alamo City in the 1850's," *Southwestern Historical Quarterly*, LXXVI (October, 1972), 183-202.

Knight, Oliver, *Fort Worth: Outpost on the Trinity.* Norman, Oklahoma: University of Oklahoma Press, 1953.

Looscan, Adele B., "Harris County, 1822-1845, IV. The Beginnings of Houston," *Southwestern Historical Quarterly*, XIX (July, 1915), 37-64.

Lubbock, Francis R., *Six Decades in Texas.* C. W. Rains (ed.). Austin: Ben C. Jones & Co., 1900.

McComb, David G., *Houston: The Bayou City.* Austin: University of Texas Press, 1969.

Mattison, Ray H., "Early Spanish and Mexican Settlements in Arizona," *New Mexico Historical Review*, XXI (October, 1946), 273-327.

Meinig, D. W., *Imperial Texas.* Austin: University of Texas Press, 1969.

Moore, Francis, Jr., *Map and Description of Texas*. Philadelphia: H. Tanner, 1840.

Muir, Andrew Forrest, "Railroads Come to Houston, 1857-61," *Southwestern Historical Quarterly*, LXIV (July, 1960), 42-63.

———, "The Municipality of Harrisburg, 1835-1836," *Southwestern Historical Quarterly*, LVI (July, 1953), 36-50.

——— (ed.), *Texas in 1837*. Austin: University of Texas Press, 1958.

Olmsted, Frederick Law, *A Journey Through Texas; or, a Saddle-Trip on the Southwestern Frontier*. New York: Dix, Edwards & Co., 1857.

Oberste, William H., *Texas Irish Empresarios and Their Colonies*. Austin: Von Boeckmann-Jones Company, 1953.

Paddock, B. B., *History of Texas: Fort Worth and the Texas Northwest*. 4 vols. Chicago: Lewis Publishing Co., 1922.

Penninger, Robert, *Fredericksburg, Texas*. Fredricksburg, Texas: Fredericksburg Publishing Co., 1971.

Pokinski, Deborah F., "The Development of the County Courthouse Town Plan: Town Planning on the Texas Frontier, 1836-1860," unpublished seminar paper, Department of City and Regional Planning, Cornell University, 1971.

———, "Town Planning in Colonial Texas: The Mexican Empresario System, 1821-1836," unpublished seminar paper, Department of City and Regional Planning, Cornell University, 1970.

Pratt, W. W. (ed.), *The Journal of Francis Sheridan, 1839-1840*. Austin: University of Texas Press, 1954.

Ramsdell, Charles, *San Antonio, a Historical and Pictorial Guide*. Austin: University of Texas Press, 1959.

Rather, Ethel Zivley, "De Witt's Colony," *Quarterly of the Texas State Historical Association*, VIII (October, 1904), 95-191.

Reinhardt, Louis, "The Communist Colony of Bettina, 1846-8," *Texas Historical Association Quarterly*, III (July, 1899), 33-41.

Reps, John W., "New Madrid on the Mississippi: American 18th Century Planning on the Spanish Frontier," *Journal of the Society of Architectural Historians*, XVIII (March, 1959), 21-26.

Robinson, Willard B., "The Public Square as a Determinant of Courthouse Form in Texas," *Southwestern Historical Quarterly*, LXXV (January, 1972), 339-356.

Roemer, Ferdinand, *Roemer's Texas, 1845 to 1847*. Oswald Mueller (trans.). Waco: The Texian Press, 1967.

Santerre, George H., *Dallas' First Hundred Years, 1856-1956*. Dallas: The Book Craft, 1956.

———, *White Cliffs of Dallas: The Story of La Réunion the Old French Colony*. Dallas: The Book Craft, 1955.

Savelle, Max, *George Morgan, Colony Builder*. New York: Columbia University Press, 1932.

Sayles, John, and Henry Sayles (comps.), *Early Laws of Texas*. 3 vols. St. Louis: Gilbert Book Co., 1888.

Sears, Joan N., "Brunswick, Milledgeville, Macon, Columbus—Four Towns Founded by the State of Georgia," unpublished seminar paper, Department of City and Regional Planning, Cornell University, 1969.

Sher, Steven E., "Austin, Texas and Lincoln, Nebraska," unpublished seminar paper, Department of City and Regional Planning, Cornell University, 1970.

Sibley, Marilyn McAdams, *The Port of Houston: A History*. Austin: University of Texas Press, 1968.

Stieghorst, Junann J., *Bay City and Matagorda County: A History*. Austin, Texas: The Pemberton Press, 1965.

Stiff, Edward, *The Texas Emigrant: Being a Narration of the Adventures of the Author in Texas, and a Description of the Soil, Climate, Productions, Minerals, Towns, Bays, Harbors, Rivers, Institutions, and Manners and Customs of the Inhabitants of that Country*. Cincinnati: George Conclin, 1840.

Suhler, Sam A., "Stephen F. Austin and the City of Austin: An Anomaly," *Southwestern Historical Quarterly*, LXIX (January, 1966), 265-286.

Terrell, Alex. W., "The City of Austin from 1839 to 1865," *Quarterly of the Texas State Historical Association*, XIV (October, 1910), 113-128.

"The City of Galveston, Texas," *De Bow's Review*, III (April, 1847), 348-349.

"Tucson in 1847: Reminiscences of Judge F. Adams," *Arizona Historical Review*, I (January, 1929), 83-85.

Tunnard, Christopher, *The City of Man*. New York: Charles Scribner's Sons, 1953.

U. S. Federal Writers' Program, *Houston: A History and Guide*. Houston: The Anson Jones Press, 1942.

———, *Texas: A Guide to the Lone Star State*. New York: Hastings House, 1940.

Wallace, Ernest, and David M. Vigness (eds.), *Documents of Texas History*. Austin: The Steck Company, 1953.

Waugh, Julia Nott, *Castro-Ville and Henri Castro Empresario*. San Antonio: Standard Printing Co., 1934.

Webb, Walter Prescott (ed.), *The Handbook of Texas*. 2 vols. Austin: Texas State Historical Association, 1952.

Wheeler, Kenneth W., *To Wear A City's Crown: The Beginnings of Urban Growth in Texas, 1836-1865*. Cambridge: Harvard University Press, 1968.

White, Joseph M., *A New Collection of Laws, Charters and Local Ordinances of the Governments of Great Britain, France and Spain, Relating to the Concession of Land in their Respective Colonies; together with the Laws of Mexico and Texas on the Same Subject*. 2 vols. Philadelphia: T. and J. W. Johnson, Law Booksellers, 1839.

Williamson, Roxanne K., *Austin, Texas: An American Architectural History*. San Antonio: Trinity University Press, 1973.

Winkler, Ernest W., "The Seat of Government of Texas: I. Temporary Location of the Seat of Government," *Quarterly of the Texas State Historical Association*, X (October, 1906), 140-171.

———, "The Seat of Government of Texas: II. The Permanent Location of the Seat of Government," *Quarterly of the Texas State Historical Association*, X (January, 1907), 185-245.

Wooster, Ralph, "Texans Choose a Capital Site," *Texana*, IV (Winter, 1966), 351-357.

VI · NORTHERN CALIFORNIA: URBAN PLANNING AND
DEVELOPMENT IN THE POST-HISPANIC YEARS

Baird, Joseph Armstrong, Jr., and Edwin Clyve Evans, *Historic Lithographs of San Francisco*. San Francisco: S. A. Waterson for Burger and Evans, 1972.

Bancroft, Hubert Howe, *History of California*, San Francisco: The History Company, VI, 1888.

Barth, Gunther, *Instant Cities: Urbanization and the Rise of San Francisco and Denver*. New York: Oxford University Press, 1975.

Bowles, Samuel, *Across the Continent . . . in the Summer of 1865*. Springfield, Mass: Samuel Bowles and Co., 1869.

Britzche, Bruno, "San Francisco, 1845-1848: The Coming of the Land Speculator," *California Historical Quarterly*, LI (Spring, 1972), 17-34.

Bryant, Edwin, *What I Saw in California: Being the Journal of a Tour . . . in the Years 1846, 1847*. Minneapolis: Ross and Haines, Inc., 1967.

Buffum, E. Gould, *Six Months in the Gold Mines: From a Journal of Three Years' Residence in Upper and Lower California, 1847-8-9*. Philadelphia: Lea and Blanchard, 1850.

Dwinelle, John W., *The Colonial History of the City of San Francisco*. San Francisco, 4th ed.: Towne and Bacon, 1867.

Elias, Solomon P., *Stories of Stanislaus*. Modesto, California: Sol. P. Elias, 1924.

Fein, Albert, *Frederick Law Olmsted and the American Environmental Tradition*, New York: George Braziller, 1972.

Fritzsche, Bruno, "San Francisco in 1843: A Key to Dr. Sandels' Drawing," *California Historical Quarterly*, L (March, 1971), 3-13.

———, "San Francisco, 1846-1848: The Coming of the Land Speculator," *California Historical Quarterly*, LI (Spring, 1972), 17-34.

Garner, William Robert, *Letters from California, 1846-1847*. Donald Munro Craig (ed.). Berkeley: University of California Press, 1970.

Garr, Daniel, "Hispanic Colonial Settlement in California: Planning and Urban Development on the Frontier: 1769-1850." Unpublished Ph.D. dissertation, Cornell University, Ithaca, N.Y., 1972.

Garrett, Lula May, "San Francisco in 1851 as Described by Eyewitnesses," *California Historical Society Quarterly*, XXII (September, 1943), 253-280.

Gates, Paul, "The California Land Act of 1851," *California Historical Quarterly*, L (December, 1971), 395-430.

George, Henry, "What the Railroad Will Bring Us," *The Overland Monthly*, I (October, 1868), 297-306.

Hall, Frederic, *The History of San José and Surroundings*. San Francisco: A. L. Bancroft and Company, 1871.

Hopkins, H. C., *History of San Diego: Its Pueblo Lands & Water*. San Diego: City Printing Company, 1929.

Kinnaird, Lawrence, *History of the Greater San Francisco Bay Region*. 3 vols. New York: Lewis Historical Publishing Company, 1966.

Kirkland, Joseph, *The Story of Chicago*. Chicago: Dibble Publishing Company, 1892.

Lotchin, Roger W., *San Francisco, 1846-1856: From Hamlet to City*. New York: Oxford University Press, 1974.

Morris, Stephen, "Urban Developmemt and Planning in Early San Francisco," unpublished seminar paper, Department of City and Regional Planning, Cornell University, 1971.

Muscatine, Doris, *Old San Francisco: The Biography of a City from Early Days to the Earthquake*. New York: G. P. Putnam's Sons, 1975.

Nicolay, Kenneth, "San Francisco: Goldrush to Earthquake," unpublished seminar paper, Department of City and Regional Planning, Cornell University, 1971.

Neasham, Aubrey, "The Preservation of Historic Monterey," *Pacific Historical Review*, VIII (June, 1939), 215-224.

Olmsted, Vaux and Company, *Report upon a Projected Improvement of the Estate of the College of California, at Berkeley, Near Oakland*. New York: William C. Bryant and Co, 1866.

Pettitt, George A., *Berkeley: The Town and Gown of it*. Berkeley: Howell-North Books, 1973.

Rather, Lois, *Oakland's Image: A History of Oakland, California*. Oakland: The Rather Press, 1972.

Robinson, W. W., *Maps of Los Angeles*. Los Angeles: Dawson's Bookshop, 1966.

Scott, Mel, *The San Francisco Bay Area: A Metropolis in Perspective*. Berkeley: University of California Press, 1959.

Soulé, Frank, John H. Givon, and James Nisbet, *The Annals of San Francisco* (1855). Pal Alto: Louis Osborne, 1966.

Studer, Jack J., "Julius Kellersberger, A Swiss as Surveyor and City Planner in California, 1851-1857," *California Historical Society Quarterly*, XLVII (March, 1968), 3-14.

———, "The First Map of Oakland, California: An Historical Speculation as Solution to An Enigma," *California Historical Society Quarterly*, XLVIII (March, 1969), 59-71.

Taylor, Bayard, *Eldorado, or Adventures in the Path of Empire*, (1850). New York: Alfred A. Knopf, 1949.

Upton, M. G., "The Plan of San Francisco," *Overland Monthly*, II (February, 1869), 131-137.

U. S. Federal Writers' Program, *San Francisco: The Bay and Its Cities*. New York: Hastings House, 2nd ed., rev., 1947.

Vance, James E., Jr., *Geography and Urban Evolution in the San Francisco Bay Area*. Berkeley: Univrsity of California Press, 1964.

Vandor, Paul E., *History of Fresno County, California*. 2 vols. Los Angeles: Historic Record Company, 1919.

Van Nostrand, Jeanne, *San Francisco, 1806-1906 in Contemporary Paintings, Drawings and Watercolors*. San Francisco: The Book Club of California, 1975.

Van Sicklen, Helen Putnam, "Jasper O'Farrell: His Survey of San Fransicso," *Quarterly of the Society of California Pioneers*, x (1933), 85-100.

Wheeler, Alfred, *Land Titles in San Francisco, and the Laws Affecting the Same, with a Synopsis of All Grants and Sales of Land Within the Limits Claimed by the City*. San Francisco: Alta California Steam Printing Establishment, 1852.

Willard, Charles Dwight, *The Herald's History of Los Angeles City*. Los Angeles: Kingsley-Barnes and Neuner Co., 1901.

Winther, Oscar O., "The Story of San José, 1777-1869: California's First Pueblo. Chapter II: American Conquest and Discovery of Gold." *California Historical Society Quarterly*, xiv (June, 1935), 147-174.

Wooster, Clarence, "Brief History of San Francisco Lands," *Quarterly of the Society of California Pioneers*, i (September, 1924), 5-68.

VII · MINING CAMPS AND TOWNS OF CALIFORNIA AND NEVADA

Baird, Joseph Armstrong, Jr., "Architectural Legacy of Sacramento: A Study of 19th Century Style," *California Historical Society Quarterly*, xxxix (September, 1960), 193-207.

———, *California's Pictorial Letter Sheets, 1849-1869*. San Francisco: David McGee, 1967.

Bancroft, Hubert Howe, *History of California*. vi. San Francisco: The History Company, 1888.

———, *History of Nevada, Colorado, and Wyoming, 1540-1888*. San Francisco: The History Company, 1890.

Bartlett, John Russell, *Personal Narrative of Explorations and Incidents in Texas, New Mexico, California, Sonora, and Chihuahua Connected With the United States and Mexican Boundary Commission, During the Years 1850, '51, '52, and '53*. 2 vols. New York: D. Appleton and Co., 1854.

Bowles, Samuel, *Across the Continent . . . in the Summer of 1865*. Springfield, Mass.: Samuel Bowles & Co., 1869.

Browne, J. Ross, *A Peep at Washoe and Washoe Revisited*. Balboa Island, Calif.: Paisano Press, 1959.

Bryant, Edwin, *What I Saw in California: Being the Journal of a Tour . . . in the Years 1846, 1847*. Minneapolis: Ross and Haines, Inc., 1967.

Buckbee, Edna Bryan, *The Saga of Old Tuolumne*. New York: Press of the Pioneers, 1935.

Buffum, E. Gould, *Six Months in the Gold Mines*. Philadelphia: Lea and Blanchard, 1850,

Burnett, Peter H., *An Old California Pioneer*. Oakland: Biobooks, 1946.

Darnall, Margaretta Jean, "Town Planning of the State Capitals of California During the American Period," unpublished research paper, Department of City and Regional Planning, Cornell University, 1969.

Davis, William Heath, *Seventy-Five Years in California*. San Francisco: John Howell, 1929.

Gay, Theressa, *James W. Marshall: The Discoverer of California Gold: A Biography*. Georgetown, Calif.: The Talisman Press, 1967.

Greever, William S., *The Bonanza West: The Story of the Western Mining Rushes, 1848-1900*. Norman: University of Oklahoma Press, 1963.

Gudde, Erwin G., *Sutter's Own Story*. New York: G. P. Putnam's Sons, 1936.

———, *California Gold Camps: A Geographical and Historical Dictionary of Camps, Towns, and Localities where Gold was Found and Mined, Wayside Stations and Trading Centers*. Berkeley: University of California Press, 1975.

History of Amador County, California. Oakland: Thompson and West, 1881.

Husband, Michael B., "Morton M. McCarver: An Iowa Entrepreneur in the Far West," *Annals of Iowa*, xl (Spring, 1970), 241-254.

Jackson, Joseph H., *Anybody's Gold*. New York: D. Appleton-Century Co., 1941.

———, *Gold Rush Album*. New York: Charles Scribner's Sons, 1949.

Künzel, Heinrich, *Obercalifornien*. Darmstadt: C. W. Leske, 1848.

Letts, John M., *A Pictorial View of California*. New York: Henry Bill, 1853.

Lewis, Oscar, *Sutter's Fort: Gateway to the Gold Fields*. Englewood Cliffs, N.J.: Prentice-Hall, 1966.

Lord, Eliot, *Comstock Mining and Miners*. Monographs of the United States Geological Survey, IV. Washington: Government Printing Office, 1883.

Mack, Effie Mona, *Nevada: A History of the State from the Earliest Times Through the Civil War*. Glendale, Calif.: The Arthur H. Clark Co., 1936.

Morley, Jim, and Doris Foley, *Gold Cities*. Berkeley: Howell-North Books, 1965.

Neasham, V. Aubrey, and James E. Henley, *The City of the Plain: Sacramento in the Nineteenth Century*. Sacramento: Sacramento Pioneer Foundation, 1969.

Paher, Stanley W., *Nevada Ghost Towns & Mining Camps*. Berkeley: Howell North Books, 1970.

Paul, Rodman W., *California Gold: The Beginning of Mining in the Far West*. Cambridge: Harvard University Press, 1947.

Phoenix, John (pseud. for George Horatio Derby), *Phoenixiana; or, Sketches and Burlesques*. New York: D. Appleton and Co., 1855.

Potter, Elizabeth Gray, "Columbia—'Gem of the Southern Mines,' " *California Historical Society Quarterly*, xxiv (September, 1945), 267-270.

Powers, Stephen, "A City of a Day," *The Overland Monthly*, xiii (November, 1874), 430-433.

Ramey, Earl, "The Beginnings of Marysville," *California Historical Society Quarterly*, xiv (September, 1935), 194-229; and (December, 1935), 375-407.

Reps, John W., *The Making of Urban America: A History of City Planning in the United States*. Princeton: Princeton University Press, 1965.

Revere, Joseph Warren, *Naval Duty in California* (1849). Oakland: Biobooks, 1947.

Richardson, Albert D., *Our New States and Territories*. New York: Beadle and Company, 1866.

Sherman, William T., *Memoirs of Gen. William T. Sherman*. 2 vols. New York: D. Appleton and Company, 1891.

Shinn, Charles Howard, *Mining Camps: A Study in American Frontier Government* (1885). Joseph Henry Jackson (ed.). New York: Alfred A. Knopf, 1948.

Stoddart, Thomas Robertson, *Annals of Tuolumne County*. Sonora, Calif.: Tuolumne County Historical Society, 1963.

Taylor, Bayard, *Eldorado, or Adventures in the Path of Empire*. Glass Cleland (ed.), New York: Alfred A. Knopf, 1949.

Twain, Mark, *Roughing It*. Hartford: American Publishing Company, 1872.

U. S. Department of the Interior, National Park Service, *Prospector, Cowhand, and Sodbuster*. Washington: Government Printing Office, 1967.

U. S. War Department, *Reports of Explorations and Surveys, to Ascertain the Most Practicable and Economical Route for a Railroad from the Mississippi River to the Pacific Ocean*, v, California Geology. Washington: Government Printing Office, 1856.

Wheat, Carl I., *Books of the California Gold Rush*. San Francisco: Colt Press, 1949.

Wiltsee, Ernest A., "The City of New York of the Pacific," *California Historical Society Quarterly*, xii (March, 1933), 24-34.

VIII · URBAN GROWTH AND EXPANSION IN SOUTHERN CALIFORNIA DURING THE POST-HISPANIC ERA

Arnold, Benjamin F., and Artilissa Dorland Clark, *History of Whittier*. Whittier, California: Western Printing Corporation, 1933.

Bartlett, John Russell, *Personal Narrative of Explorations and Incidents in Texas, New Mexico, California, Sonora, and Chihuahua Connected with the United States and Mexican Boundary Commission, During the Years 1850, '51, '52 and '53*. 2 vols. New York: D. Appleton and Co., 1854.

Batman, Richard Dale, " 'Anaheim Was an Oasis in a Wilderness,' " *Journal of the West*, iv (January, 1965), 1-19.

Baur, John E., "Los Angeles County in the Health Rush, 1870-1900," *California Historical Society Quarterly*, xxxi (March, 1952), 13-31.

Booth, Larry, Rogert Olmsted, and Richard F. Pourade, "Portrait of a Boom Town: San Diego in the 1880's," *California Historical Quarterly*, l (December, 1971), 363-394.

Dickson, Lucile E., "The Founding and Early History of Anaheim, California," Historical Society of Southern California, *Publications*, xi (1919), 26-37.

Donley, Ward T., "Vision of Greatness (Alonzo E. Horton)," *Journal of San Diego History*, xiii (April, 1967), 21-41.

Dumke, Glenn S., *The Boom of the Eighties in Southern California*. San Marino, California: Huntington Library, 1963.

———, "The Real Estate Boom of 1887 in Southern California," *Pacific Historical Review*, xi (December, 1942), 425-438.

Elliott, Wallace W., *History of San Bernardino and San Diego Counties*. San Francisco: Wallace W. Elliott & Co., 1883.

Fogelson, Robert M., *The Fragmented Metropolis: Los Angeles, 1850-1930*. Cambridge: Harvard University Press, 1967.

Garr, Daniel, "Hispanic Colonial Settlement in California: Planning and Urban Development on the Frontier: 1769-1850." Unpublished Ph.D. dissertation, Cornell University, Ithaca, New York, 1972.

Guinn, J. M., "From Pueblo to Ciudad: The Municipal and Territorial Expansion of Los Angeles," Historical Society of Southern California, *Publications*, vii, No. 3 (1908), 216-221.

———, "The Great Real Estate Boom of 1887," Historical Society of Southern California, *Publications*, i (1890), 13-21.

———, "The Plan of Old Los Angeles and the Story of its Highways and Byways," Historical Society of Southern California, *Publications*, iii, Part 3 (1895), 40-50.

History of Los Angeles County California. Oakland: Thompson & West, 1880.

History of San Luis Obispo County California. Oakland: Thompson & West, 1883.

History of Santa Barbara & Ventura Counties, California. Oakland: Thompson & West, 1883.

Holmes, Elmer W., *History of Riverside County, California*. Los Angeles: Historic Record Company, 1912.

Hopkins, H. C., *History of San Diego: Its Pueblo Lands & Water*. San Diego: City Printing Company, 1929.

Layne, J. Gregg, "Edward Otho Cresap Ord: Soldier and Surveyor," *Historical Society of Southern California Quarterly*, xvii (December, 1935), 139-142.

MacArthur, Mildred Yorba, *Anaheim "The Mother Colony,"* Los Angeles: The Ward Ritchie Press, 1959.

MacPhail, Elizabeth C., *The Story of New San Diego and of its Founder, Alonzo E. Horton*. San Diego: Pioneer Printers, 1969.

Nadeau, Remi A., *City-Makers: The Men Who Transformed Los Angeles from Village to Metropolis During the First Great Boom 1868-76*. Garden City: Doubleday & Company, 1948.

Nerhood, Harry W., "Whittier, California: The Life of a Boom Town of the 'Eighties as Reflected in its First Newspaper," *Pacific Historical Review*, xiv (March, 1945), 36-44.

Netz, Joseph, "The Great Los Angeles Real Estate Boom of 1887," Historical Society of Southern California, *Publications*, x (1915-16), 54-68.

Peterson, J. Harold, *The Coronado Story*. Coronado, California: Coronado Federal Savings and Loan Association, 2nd ed., 1959.

Pflueger, Donald, *Glendora*. Claremont, California: Saunder Press, 1951.

Quiett, Glenn Chesney, *They Built the West: An Epic of Rails and Cities*. New York: D. Appleton-Century Co., 1934.

Raup, Hallock F., "Anaheim: A German Community of Frontier California," *American German Review*, xii (December, 1945), 7-11.

———, "The German Colonization of Anaheim, California," *University of California Publications in Geography*, vi, No. 3 (1932), 123-146.

Robinson, W. W., *Maps of Los Angeles From Ord's Survey of 1849 to the End of the Boom of the Eighties*. Los Angeles: Dawson's Bookshop, 1966.

———, "Story of Ord's Survey as Disclosed by the Los Angeles Archives," *His-*

torical Society of Southern California Quarterly, xix (September-December, 1937), 121-131.

———, The Story of Pershing Square. Los Angeles: Title Guarantee and Trust Co., 1931.

Rolle, Andrew F., "William Heath Davis and the Founding of American San Diego," California Historical Society Quarterly, xxxi (March, 1952), 33-48.

Ruhlen, George, "San Diego Barracks," Journal of San Diego History, xiii (April, 1967), 7-15.

Splitter, Henry W., "Los Angeles as Described by Contemporaries, 1850-90," Historical Society of Southern California Quarterly, xxxvii (June and September, 1955), 125-138, 261-283.

Stonehouse, Merlin, "The Michigan Excursion for the Founding of Riverside, California," Michigan History, xlv (September, 1961), 193-209.

Storke, Yda A., A Memorial and Biographical History of the Counties of Santa Barbara, San Luis Obispo and Ventura, California. Chicago: The Lewis Publishing Co., 1891.

Swanner, Charles D., Santa Ana: A Narrative of Yesterday, 1870-1910. Claremont, California: Saunder Press, 1953.

U. S. Federal Writers' Program, California: A Guide to the Golden State. New York: Hastings House, 1942.

U. S. Federal Writers' Program, Los Angeles: A Guide to the City and Its Environs. New York: Hastings House, 1941.

Van Dyke, Theodore Strong, The City and County of San Diego. San Diego: Leber-thon & Taylor, 1888.

Wiley, John L., History of Monrovia. Pasadena, California: Press of Pasadena Star-News, 1927.

Willard, Charles Dwight, The Herald's History of Los Angeles City. Los Angeles: Kingsley-Barnes & Neuner Co., 1901.

Winther, Oscar Osburn, "The Colony System of Southern California," Agricultural History, xxvii (July, 1953), 94-103.

Wood, J. W. Pasadena, California Historical and Personal: A Complete History of the Organization of the Indiana Colony. Pasadena: published by the author, 1917.

Zink, Orion M., "Places and People in Old Town: Part I—Places in Old Town," Journal of San Diego History, xv (Winter, 1969), 3-21.

IX · CITIES OF ZION: ORIGINS OF THE MORMON WEST

Andreas, A. T., Illustrated Historical Atlas of Hancock County, Illinois. Chicago: A. T. Andreas, 1874.

Arrington, Leonard J., Great Basin Kingdom: An Economic History of the Latter-Day Saints, 1830-1900. Cambridge: Harvard University Press, 1958.

Balestier, Joseph N., The Annals of Chicago: A Lecture Delivered before the Chicago Lyceum. Chicago: Fergus Printing Co., 1876.

The Book of Mormon: An Account Written by the Hand of Mormon upon Plates Taken from the Plates of Nephi. Joseph Smith, Jr. (trans.). Salt Lake City: Church of Jesus Christ of Latter-Day Saints, 1948.

Brodie, Fawn M., No Man Knows My History: The Life of Joseph Smith, the Mormon Prophet. New York: Alfred A. Knopf, 1946.

Brooks, Juanita (ed.), On the Mormon Frontier: The Diary of Hosea Stout, 1844-1861. 2 vols. Salt Lake City: University of Utah Press, 1964.

Burton, Richard, The City of the Saints. London: Longman, Green, Longman & Roberts, 1861.

Clayton, William, William Clayton's Journal. Salt Lake City: Clayton Family Association, 1921.

Creer, Leland Hargrave, The Founding of an Empire: The Exploration and Colonization of Utah, 1776-1856. Salt Lake City: Bookcraft, 1947.

Dyer, Alvin R., The Refiner's Fire. Salt Lake City: Deseret Book Company, 1968.

Flanders, Robert Bruce, Nauvoo: Kingdom on the Mississippi. Urbana: University of Illinois Press, 1965.

Gregg, Thomas, History of Hancock County, Illinois. Chicago: Charles C. Chapman & Co., 1880.

Hayden, Dolores, Seven American Utopias: The Architecture of Communitarian Socialism, 1790-1975. Cambridge, Mass.: The MIT Press, 1976.

History of Caldwell and Livingston Counties, Missouri. St. Louis: St. Louis National Historical Company, 1886.

History of the Church of Jesus Christ of Latter Day Saints 1836-1844. Lamoni, Iowa: Board of Publication of the Reorganized Church of Jesus Christ of Latter Day Saints, 6th ed., 1911.

Hunter, Milton R., Brigham Young the Colonizer. Salt Lake City: The Deseret News Press, 1940.

Illustrated Historical Atlas of Hancock County, Illinois. Chicago: A. T. Andreas, 1874.

Ivins, Stanley S., "Notes on Mormon Polygamy," Western Humanities Review, x (Summer, 1956), 229-239.

Kane, Thomas Leiper, A Friend of the Mormons. Oscar O. Winther (ed.). San Francisco: Gelber-Lilienthal, 1937.

Kenneth, James H., Early Days of Mormonism, Palmyra, Kirtland, Nauvoo. New York: C. Scribner's Sons, 1888.

———, "The Mormon Episode at Kirtland," Annals of the Early Settlers Association of Cuyahoga County, Ohio, iv (1901), 348-365.

Melcher, Marguerite Fellows, The Shaker Adventure. Princeton: Princeton University Press, 1941.

Mulder, William, and A. Russell Mortensen (eds.), Among the Mormons: Historic Accounts by Contemporary Observers. New York: Alfred A. Knopf, 1958.

Nelson, Lowry, The Mormon Village: A Pattern and Technique of Land Settlement. Salt Lake City: University of Utah Press, 1952.

Nibley, Preston, Exodus to Greatness: The Story of the Mormon Migration. Salt Lake City: Deseret News Press, 1947.

Oscarson, R. Don, and Stanley B. Kimball, *The Traveller's Guide to Historic Mormon America*. St. Louis: R. Don Oscarson, 1965.

Piercy, Caroline B., *The Valley of God's Pleasure*. New York: Stratford House, 1951.

Piercy, Frederick Hawkins, *Route from Liverpool to Great Salt Lake Valley* (1855), Fawn M. Brodie (ed.). Cambridge: The Belknap Press of Harvard University Press, 1962.

Pratt, Parley P., *A Voice of Warning*. Liverpool: F. D. Richards, 1854.

———, *The Autobiography of Parley Parker Pratt*. Chicago: Pratt Bros., 1888.

Ricks, Joel Edward, *Forms and Methods of Early Mormon Settlement in Utah and the Surrounding Region, 1847 to 1877*. Logan, Utah: Utah State University Press, 1964.

Roberts, Brigham H., *A Comprehensive History of the Church of Jesus Christ of Latter-Day Saints*. 6 vols. Salt Lake City: Deseret News Press, 1959.

Sellers, Charles L., "Early Mormon Community Planning," *Journal of the American Institute of Planners*, xxviii (February, 1962), 24-30.

Shumway, E. Widtsoe, "Winter Quarters, Nebraska, 1846-1848," *Nebraska History*, xxxv (June, 1954), 115-125; xxxvi (March, 1955), 43-54.

Smith, Henry C., "City Planning," *Journal of History*, xv (January, 1922), 1-17.

Smith, Joseph, *History of the Church of Jesus Christ of Latter-Day Saints*. 7 vols. Introduction and Notes by B. H. Roberts. Salt Lake City: Deseret Book Company, rev. ed. 1948-1961.

Stansbury, Howard, *Exploration and Survey of the Valley of the Great Salt Lake of Utah*. Senate ex. doc. No. 3, Special Session, March 1851. Washington: Robert Armstrong, Public Printer, 1853.

Taylor, Philip A. M., "Recent Writing on Utah and the Mormons," *Arizona and the West*, iv (Autumn, 1962), 249-260.

Tullidge, Edward W., *The History of Salt Lake City and Its Founders*. Salt Lake City: Edward W. Tullidge, 1886.

West, Ray B., Jr., *Kingdom of the Saints: The Story of Brigham Young and the Mormons*. New York: Viking Press, 1957.

Whitney, Orson F., *Life of Heber C. Kimball, An Apostle*. Salt Lake City: Published by the Kimball Family, 1888.

Wood, William A., "An Old Mormon City in Missouri," *Magazine of American History*, xvi (July, 1886), 98-99.

X · CITIES OF THE SAINTS: MORMON TOWN PLANNING IN THE GREAT BASIN KINGDOM

Acts, Resolutions and Memorials . . . *of the Legislative Assembly of the Territory of Utah*. Salt Lake City: Joseph Cain, Public Printer, 1855.

Aikman, Duncan (ed.), *The Taming of the Frontier*. New York: Minton-Balch Company, 1925.

Alexander, Thomas G., and James B. Allen (eds.), "The Mormons in the Mountain West: A Selected Bibliography," *Arizona and the West*, ix (Winter, 1967), 365-384.

Allen, James B., "Ecclesiastical Influence on Local Government in the Territory of Utah," *Arizona and the West*, viii (Spring, 1966), 35-48.

Anderson, Bernice Gibbs, "The Gentile City of Corinne," *Utah Historical Quarterly*, ix (July-October, 1941), 140-154.

Anderson, Nels, *Desert Saints: The Mormon Frontier in Utah*. Chicago: University of Chicago Press, 1942.

Arrington, Leonard J., "Cooperative Community in the North: Brigham City, Utah," *Utah Historical Quarterly*, xxxiii (Summer, 1965), 199-217.

———, "Early Mormon Communitarianism: The Law of Consecration and Stewardship," *Western Humanities Review*, vii (Fall, 1953), 341-369.

———, "Economic History of a Mormon Valley," *Pacific Northwest Quarterly*, xlvi (October, 1955), 97-107.

———, *Great Basin Kingdom*. Cambridge: Harvard University Press, 1958.

———, "Inland to Zion: Mormon Trade on the Colorado River, 1864-1867," *Arizona and the West*, viii (Autumn, 1966), 239-250.

———, "The Mormon Cotton Mission in Southern Utah," *Pacific Historical Review*, xxv (August, 1956), 221-238.

———, and Thomas G. Alexander, "The U. S. Army Overlooks Salt Lake Valley: Fort Douglas, 1862-1965," *Utah Historical Quarterly*, xxxiii (Fall, 1965), 326-350.

Bailey, Paul, *Sam Brannan and the California Mormons*. Los Angeles: California Westernlore Press, 1943.

Bancroft, Hubert Howe, *History of Arizona and New Mexico, 1530-1888*. San Francisco: The History Company, 1889.

Barth, Gunther, *Instant Cities: Urbanization and the Rise of San Francisco and Denver*. New York: Oxford University Press, 1975, 39-60.

———, *History of Utah*. San Francisco: The History Company, 1889.

Beattie, George William, and Helen Pruitt Beattie, *Heritage of the Valley: San Bernardino's First Century*. Oakland: Biobooks, 1951.

Bolton, Herbert E., "The Mormons in the Opening of the Great West," *Utah Genealogical and Historical Magazine*, lxiv (June, 1926), 9-16.

Bowles, Samuel, *Across the Continent . . . in the Summer of 1865*. Springfield, Mass.: Samuel Bowles & Co., 1869.

Cooley, Everett L., "Report of an Expedition to Locate Utah's First Capital," *Utah Historical Quarterly*, xxiii (October, 1955), 329-338.

Creer, Leland H., *Mormon Towns in the Region of the Colorado*. Salt Lake City: University of Utah Anthropological Papers, No. 32, 1958.

———, *Utah and the Nation*. Seattle: University of Washington Press, 1929.

Dumke, Glenn S., "Mission Station to Mining Town: Early Las Vegas," *Pacific Historical Review*, xxii (August, 1953), 257-270.

Dwyer, Robert Joseph, *The Gentile Comes to Utah: A Study in Religious and Social Conflict (1862-1890)*. Washington, D. C.: Catholic University of America Press, 1941.

Elliott, Wallace W., *History of San Bernardino and San Diego Counties California*. Riverside, California: Riverside Museum Press, 1965.

Evans, John Henry, *Charles Coulson Rich: Pioneer Builder of the West*. New York: The Macmillan Company, 1936.

Fox, Feramorz Y., "Experiment in Utopia: The United Order of Richfield, 1874-1877," *Utah Historical Quarterly*, xxxii (Fall, 1964), 355-380.

Furniss, Norman F., *The Mormon Conflict, 1850-1859*. New Haven: Yale University Press, 1960.

Hafen, LeRoy R., *Handcarts to Zion: The Story of a Unique Western Migration, 1856-1860*. Glendale, Calif.: Arthur H. Clark Company, 1960.

Henderson, W. W. (ed.), "The Salmon River Mission: Extract from the Journal of L. W. Shurtliff," *Utah Historical Quarterly*, v (January, 1932), 3-24.

History of Arizona Territory (1884). Flagstaff, Arizona: Northland Press, 1964.

History of Brigham Young, 1847-1867. Berkeley: MassCal Associates, 1964.

Hunter, Milton R., *Brigham Young the Colonizer*. Salt Lake City: The Deseret News Press, 1940.

———, "The Mormon Corridor," *The Pacific Historical Review*, viii (June, 1939), 179-200.

Jensen, J. Marinus, *History of Provo, Utah*. Provo, Utah: published by the Author, 1924.

Jenson, Andrew, "The Founding of Mormon Settlements in the San Luis Valley, Colorado," *Colorado Magazine*, xvii (September, 1940), 174-180.

Judd, B. Ira, "Tuba City: Mormon Settlement," *Journal of Arizona History*, x (Spring, 1969), 37-42.

Lamar, Howard Roberts, *The Far Southwest, 1846-1912: A Territorial History*. New York: W. W. Norton & Co., 1970.

McClintock, James H., *Mormon Settlement in Arizona*. Phoenix: The Author, 1921.

Meinig, D. W., "The Mormon Culture Region: Strategies and Patterns in the Geography of The American West, 1847-1964," *Annals of the Association of American Geographers*, lv (June, 1965), 191-220.

Morgan, Dale L., "The Changing Face of Salt Lake City," *Utah Historical Quarterly*, xxviii (July, 1959), 208-232.

———, "The State of Deseret," *Utah Historical Quarterly*, viii (April, July, and October, 1940), 65-239.

Mortensen, A. R., "Main Street," *Utah Historical Quarterly*, xxvii (July, 1959), 275-283.

Mulder, William, and A. Russell Mortensen (eds.), *Among the Mormons: Historic Accounts by Contemporary Observers*. New York: Knopf, 1958.

Nash, John D., "The Salmon River Mission of 1855," *Idaho Yesterdays*, xi (Spring, 1967), 22-31.

Nelson, Lowry, *The Mormon Village: A Pattern and Technique of Land Settlement*. Salt Lake City: University of Utah Press, 1952.

Pendleton, Mark A., "The Orderville United Order of Zion," *Utah Historical Quarterly*, vii (October, 1939), 141-159.

Peterson, Charles S., *Take Up Your Mission: Mormon Colonizing Along the Little Colorado*. Tucson: University of Arizona Press, 1973.

Raup, H. F., *San Bernardino, California: Settlement and Growth of a Pass-Site City*. Berkeley: University of California Press, 1940.

Remy, Jules, *A Journey to Great Salt-Lake City*. 2 vols. London: W. Jeffs, 1859.

Ricks, Joel E., *Forms and Methods of Early Mormon Settlement in Utah and the Surrounding Region, 1847 to 1877*. Logan, Utah: Utah State University Press, 1964.

Ricks, Joel E. (ed.), *The History of a Valley: Cache Valley, Utah-Idaho*. Logan, Utah: Cache Valley Centennial Commission, 1956.

Roberts, Brigham H., *A Comprehensive History of the Church of Jesus Christ of Latter-day Saints*. 6 vols. Salt Lake City: Deseret News Press, 1930.

Rollins, George W., "Land Policies of the United States as Applied to Utah to 1910," *Utah Historical Quarterly*, xx (July, 1952), 239-251.

"Salt Lake City," *Harper's Weekly*, xxx (October 30, 1886), 706.

Seegmiller, Emma Carroll, "Personal Memories of the United Order of Orderville, Utah," *Utah Historical Quarterly*, vii (October, 1939), 160-200.

Stansbury, Howard, *Exploration and Survey of the Valley of the Great Salt Lake of Utah*. Senate ex. doc. No. 3, Special Session, March 1851. Washington: Robert Armstrong, Public Printer, 1853.

Tullidge, Edward W., *The History of Salt Lake City and Its Founders*. Salt Lake City: Edward W. Tullidge, 1886.

———, *Tullidge's Histories (Volume II) Containing the History of all the Northern, Eastern, and Western Counties of Utah: also the Counties of Southern Idaho*. Salt Lake City: Press of the Juvenile Instructor, 1889.

Utah Historical Records Survey, *A History of Ogden*. Ogden: Ogden City Commission, 1940.

Whitney, Orson F., *History of Utah*, 4 vols. Salt Lake City: George Q. Cannon and Sons,1892-1903.

Black, Lloyd D., "Middle Willamette Valley Population Growth," *Oregon Historical Quarterly*, XLIII (March, 1942), 40-55.

Brown, Arthur J., "The Promotion of Emigration to Washington, 1854-1909," *Pacific Northwest Quarterly*, XXXVI (January, 1945), 3-18.

Buckley, Wallace T., "The Historical Geography of Spokane, an Inland Metropolis," *Bulletin of the Geographical Society of Philadelphia*, XXX (January, 1932), 59-69.

Burnett, Peter H., *Recollections and Opinions of an Old Pioneer*. New York: D. Appleton & Co., 1880.

Butterfield, Grace, and J. H. Horner, "Wallowa Valley Towns and Their Beginnings," *Oregon Historical Quarterly*, XLI (December, 1940), 382-385.

Carey, Charles H., *A General History of Oregon Prior to 1861*. 2 vols. Portland: Metropolitan Press, 1935.

Corning, Howard McKinley (ed.), *Dictionary of Oregon History Compiled from the Research Files of the Former Oregon Writers' Project with Much Added Material*. Portland, Oregon: Binfords & Mort, 1956.

———, "Ghost Towns on the Willamette of the Riverboat Period," *Oregon Historical Quarterly*, XLVIII (June, 1947), 55-67.

Dittrich, Barbara F., "A History of the Planning of Seattle, Washington, and the University of Washington Campus from 1851 to 1911," unpublished seminar paper, Department of Urban Planning and Development, Cornell University, New York, 1971.

Dryden, Cecil, *Dryden's History of Washington*. Portland, Oregon: Binfords & Mort, 1968.

Durham, Nelson Wayne, *History of the City of Spokane and Spokane Country Washington from its Earliest Settlement to the Present Time*. 3 vols. Spokane: S. J. Clarke Publishing Company, 1912.

"Edmund Sylvester's Narrative of the Founding of Olympia," *Pacific Northwest Quarterly*, XXXVI (October, 1945), 331-339.

Fargo, Lucile F., *Spokane Story*. New York: Columbia University Press, 1950.

Franchère, Gabriel, *Adventure at Astoria, 1810-1814*. Hoyt C. Franchère (trans.). Norman: University of Oklahoma Press, 1967.

Gates, Charles M., *The First Century at the University of Washington*. Seattle: University of Washington Press, 1961.

Ghent, W. J., *The Road to Oregon: A Chronicle of the Great Emigrant Trail*. London: Longmans, Green & Co., 1929.

Grant, Frederic James, "Seattle: A Chapter from an Uncompleted History," *Magazine of Western History*, XI (April, 1890), 636-642.

Hastings, Lansford W., *The Emigrant's Guide to Oregon and California*. Cincinnati: George Conclin, 1945.

Hedges, James B., *Henry Villard and the Railways of the Northwest*. New Haven: Yale University Press, 1930.

"Henry Yesler and the Founding of Seattle," *Pacific Northwest Quarterly*, XLII (October, 1951), 271-276.

Husband, Michael B., "Morton M. McCarver: An Iowa Entrepreneur in the Far West," *Annals of Iowa*, XL (Spring, 1970), 241-254.

Hussey, John A., *Champoeg: Place of Transition*. Portland: Oregon Historical Society, 1967.

———, *The History of Fort Vancouver and its Physical Structure*. Tacoma: Washington State Historical Society, 1957.

Iber, Howard John, "Early Town Planning in Oregon's Willamette Valley," unpublished seminar paper, Department of Urban Planning and Development, Cornell University, Ithaca, New York, 1973.

Irving, Washington, *Astoria: or Anecdotes of an Enterprise Beyond the Rocky Mountains*. Edgeley W. Todd (ed.). Norman: University of Oklahoma Press, 1964.

Knuth, Priscilla, " 'Picturesque' Frontier: The Army's Fort Dalles," *Oregon Historical Quarterly*, LXVIII (December, 1966), 293-333; (March, 1967), 5-52.

Lamb, Martha J., "A Glimpse of the Valley of Many Waters: Its Settlement and Development," *Magazine of American History*, XII (September, 1884), 193-210.

Lauridsen, G. M., and A. A. Smith, *The Story of Port Angeles, Clallam County, Washington*. Seattle: Lowman & Hanford Co., 1937.

Lyman, H. S., "The Aurora Community," *Quarterly of the Oregon Historical Society*, II (March, 1901), 78-93.

McArthur, Lewis A., *Oregon Geographic Names*. Portland: Binsfords & Mort, 1952.

McCallum, John, and Lorraine Wilcox Ross, *Port Angeles, U.S.A.* Seattle: Wood & Reber, Inc., 1961.

McDonald, Lucile, and Werner Lenggenhager, *The Look of Old Time Washington*. Seattle: Superior Publishing Co., 1971.

Meany, Edmund S., "First American Settlement on the Puget Sound," *Washington Historical Quarterly*, VII (April, 1916), 135-143.

Meeker, Ezra, *The Busy Life of Eighty-Five Years of Ezra Meeker*. Seattle: Published by the Author, 1916.

Meinig, D. W., *The Great Columbia Plain: A Historical Geography, 1805-1910*. Seattle: University of Washington Press, 1968.

Minter, Harold Avery, *Umpqua Valley, Oregon and its Pioneers*. Portland: Binfords & Mort, 1967.

Mohler, Samuel R., "Boom Days in Ellensburg, 1888-1891," *Pacific Northwest Quarterly*, XXXVI (October, 1945), 289-308.

Montgomery, Richard G., *The White-Headed Eagle: John McLoughlin, Builder of an Empire*. New York: The Macmillan Company, 1935.

Morris, Grace P., "Development of Astoria, 1811-1850," *Oregon Historical Quarterly*, XXXVIII (December, 1937), 413-424.

Nesbit, Robert C., *"He Built Seattle": A Biography of Judge Thomas Burke*. Seattle: University of Washington Press, 1961.

Oliphant, J. Orin, "Notes on Early Settlements and on Geographic Names of Eastern Washington," *Washington Historical Quarterly*, XXII (July, 1931), 172-202.

Phelps, Thomas, *Reminiscences of Seattle, Washington Territory, and of the U. S. Sloop-of-War Decatur during the Indian War of 1855-1856*. Fairfield, Washington: Ye Galleon Press, 1970.

Phillips, James W., *Washington State Place Names*. Seattle: University of Washington Press, 1971.

"Portland, The Metropolis of the Pacific Northwest," *The West Shore* (September, 1883), 201-205.

Powell, Fred Wilbur, "Hall Jackson Kelley—Prophet of Oregon," *Oregon Historical Society Quarterly*, xviii (March, 1917); 1-54; (June, 1917), 93-139; (September, 1917), 167-223; (December, 1917), 271-295.

———, *Hall J. Kelley on Oregon*. Princeton: Princeton University Press, 1932.

Quiett, Glenn Chesney, *They Built the West: An Epic of Rails and Cities*. New York: D. Appleton-Century Co., 1934.

Reps, John W., *The Making of Urban America: A History of City Planning in the United States*. Princeton: Princeton University Press, 1965.

Robertson, Wyndham, Jr., *Oregon, Our Right and Title, Containing an Account of the Condition of the Oregon Territory*. Washington, D.C.: J. & G. S. Gideon, 1846.

Scott, Harvey Whitefield, *History of Portland, Oregon*. Syracuse, N.Y.: D. Mason & Co., 1890.

Snyder, Eugene E., *Early Portland, Stump-Town Triumphant: Rival Towns on the Willamette, 1831-1854*. Portland, Oregon: Binfords & Mort, 1970.

Stewart, Edgar I., *Washington: Northwest Frontier*. 4 vols. New York: Lewis Historical Publishing Company, 1957.

The Portland Directory for the Year Commencing January, 1867. Portland, Oregon: A. G. Walling & Co., 1867.

The Salem Directory; Embracing a Resident and Business Directory, for 1874. Salem, Oregon: E. M. Waite, 1874.

Thornton, J. Quinn, *Oregon and California in 1848*. 2 vols. New York: Harper & Brothers, 1849.

U. S. Federal Writers' Program, *Oregon: End of the Trail*. Portland, Oregon: Binfords & Mort, 1940.

U. S. Federal Writers' Program, *The Oregon Trail: The Missouri River to the Pacific Ocean*. New York: Hastings House, 1939.

U. S. Federal Writers' Program, *Washington: A Guide to the Evergreen State*. Portland, Oregon: Binfords & Mort, 1941.

Victor, Frances Fuller, *All Over Oregon and Washington*. San Francisco: John H. Carmany & Co., 1872.

Warre, Captain H., *Sketches in North America and the Oregon Territory*. London: Dickinson & Co., 1849.

———, *Sketches in North America and the Oregon Territory*. The Imprint Society: Barre, Massachusetts, 1970.

Washington State Historical Society, *Early Washington Communities in Art*. Introd. and Notes by Bruce Le Roy. Tacoma: Washington State Historical Society, 1965.

Winslow, Walter C., "Contests over the Capital of Oregon," *Oregon Historical Society Quarterly*, ix (June, 1908), 173-178.

XII · URBAN PLANNING ON THE CENTRAL PLAINS: THE SETTLEMENT OF NEBRASKA

Abbott, H. C., *Lincoln: Name and Place*. Lincoln: Nebraska State Historical Society, *Publications*, xxi (1930), 1-133.

Andreas, A. T., *History of the State of Nebraska*. 3 vols. Chicago: The Western Historical Company, 1882.

Berry, Myrtle D., (comp.), "Local Nebraska History—A Bibliography," *Nebraska History*, xxvi (April-June, 1945), 104-115.

Burke, Marguerette R., "Henry James Hudson and the Genoa Settlement," *Nebraska History*, xli (September, 1960), 201-236.

Butterfield, Consul Willshire, "Omaha," *Magazine of Western History*, ix (December, 1888), 192-200.

Danker, Donald F., "Columbus, A Territorial Town in the Platte Valley," *Nebraska History*, xxxiv (December, 1953), 275-288.

———, "C. W. Giddings and the Founding of Table Rock," *Nebraska History*, xxxiv (March, 1953), 33-54.

———, (ed.), *Mollie: The Journal of Mollie Dorsey Sanford in Nebraska and Colorado Territories, 1857-1866*. Lincoln: University of Nebraska Press, 1959.

———, "The Nebraska Winter Quarters Company and Florence," *Nebraska History*, xxxvii (March, 1956), 27-50.

Dick, Everett N., "Problems of the Post Frontier Prairie City as Portrayed by Lincoln, Nebraska, 1880-1890," *Nebraska History*, xxviii (April-June, 1947), 132-143.

Fitzpatrick, Lilian L., *Nebraska Place-Names*. Lincoln: University of Nebraska Press, 1960.

Gilmore, G. H., "Ghost Towns in Cass County, Nebraska," *Nebraska History*, xviii (July-September, 1937), 181-191.

Graebner, Norman A., "Nebraska's Missouri River Frontier, 1854-1860," *Nebraska History*, xlii (December, 1961), 213-235.

Hayes, A. B., and Samuel D. Cox, *History of the City of Lincoln*. Lincoln: State Journal Company, 1889.

Jenson, Andrew (comp.), "Latter-Day Saints Emigration from Wyoming, Nebraska—1864-1866," *Nebraska History*, xvii (April-June, 1936), 113-127.

Jensen, Richard E., "Bellevue: The First Twenty Years, 1822-1842," *Nebraska History*, lvi (Fall, 1975), 339-374.

Johnson, J. R., "Covington: Nebraska's Sinful City, *Nebraska History*, xlix (Autumn, 1968), 269-281.

Jones, Alfred D., "Omaha's Early Days," Nebraska State Historical Society, *Transactions and Reports*, IV, Lincoln, 1892, 152-54.

Leighton, George R., "Omaha, Nebraska," *Nebraska History*, XIX (October-December, 1938), 293-329.

Magie, John Q., and Carl H. Jones, *A History and Historic Sites Survey of Johnson, Nemaha, Pawnee, and Richardson Counties in Southeastern Nebraska*. Lincoln: Nebraska State Historical Society, 1969.

Miller, John C., "Ghost Towns in Otoe County," *Nebraska History*, XVIII (July-September, 1937), 185-191.

Morton, J. Sterling, and Albert Watkins, *Illustrated History of Nebraska*. 3 vols. Lincoln: Jacob North & Company, 1907-1913.

Nichols, Roy F., "The Kansas-Nebraska Act: A Century of Historiography," *Mississippi Valley Historical Review*, XLIII (September, 1956), 187-212.

Olson, James C., *History of Nebraska*. Lincoln: University of Nebraska Press, 1955.

———, *J. Sterling Morton*. Lincoln: University of Nebraska Press, 1942.

Savage, James W., and John T. Bell, *History of the City of Omaha, Nebraska*. New York: Munsell & Company, 1894.

Shallcross, William J., *Romance of a Village: Story of Bellevue*. Omaha: Roncka Bros., 1954.

Sheldon, Addison E., *Land Systems and Land Policies in Nebraska*. Lincoln: Nebraska State Historical Society, *Publications*, XXII, 1936.

———, *Nebraska: The Land and the People*. Chicago: Lewis Publishing Company, 1931.

Wakely, Arthur C., *Omaha: The Gate City and Douglas County Nebraska*. 2 vols. Chicago: S. J. Clarke Publishing Company, 1917.

White, John Browning, *Published Sources on Territorial Nebraska: An Essay and Bibliography*. Nebraska Historical Society, *Publications*, XXIII (1950).

Williams, Helen Roberta, "Old Wyoming," *Nebraska History*, XVII (April-June, 1936), 79-90.

Wyman, Walter D., "Omaha: Frontier Depot and Prodigy of Council Bluffs," *Nebraska History*, XVII (July-September, 1936), 143-155.

XIII · THE CENTRAL PLAINS: TOWNS OF KANSAS

Adams, Franklin G., "The Capitals of Kansas," Kansas Historical Society, *Collections*, VIII (1903-04), 331-351.

Anderson, Lorene, and Alan W. Farley (comps.), "A Bibliography of Town and County Histories of Kansas," *Kansas Historical Quarterly*, XXI (Autumn, 1955), 513-551.

Baldinger, Wallace S., "The Amateur Plans a City," *Kansas Historical Quarterly*, XII (February, 1943), 3-13.

Barry, Louise, "The Emigrant Aid Company Parties of 1854," *Kansas Historical Quarterly*, XII (May, 1943), 115-155.

Baughman, Robert W., *Kansas in Maps*. Topeka: Kansas State Historical Society, 1961.

Bentley, Orsemus H., *History of Wichita and Sedwick County, Kansas*. 2 vols. Chicago: C. F. Cooper & Co., 1910.

Blackmer, Frank W. (ed.), *Kansas: A Cyclopedia of State History*. 2 vols. Chicago: Standard Publishing Company, 1912.

Caldwell, Martha B., "When Horace Greeley Visited Kansas in 1859," *Kansas Historical Quarterly*, IX (May, 1940), 115-140.

Carr, E. T., "Reminiscences Concerning Fort Leavenworth in 1855-56," Kansas State Historical Society, *Collections*, XII (1911-12), 375-382.

Cole, Fannie, "Pioneer Life in Kansas," Kansas State Historical Society, *Collections*, XII (1911-12), 353-358.

Colt, Miriam Davis, *Went to Kansas: Being a Thrilling Account of an Ill-Fated Expedition to that Fairy Land and its Sad Results*. Watertown, N.Y.: L. Ingalls & Co., 1862.

[Dana, C. W.], *The Garden of the World, or the Great West . . . by an Old Settler*. Boston: Wentworth and Company, 1856.

Dick, Everett, *The Sod-House Frontier*. Lincoln: Johnsen Publishng Company, 1954.

Giles, F. W., *Thirty Years in Topeka*. Topeka: Geo. W. Crane, 1886.

Gladstone, T. H., *The Englishman in Kansas*. New York: Miller & Company, 1857.

Graham, F. P., *An Introduction to City Planning in Kansas*. Manhattan, Kansas: Kansas State College Engineering Experiment Station Bulletin 76, 1955.

Greeley, Horace, *An Overland Journey, From New York to San Francisco, in the Summer of 1859*. New York: C. M. Saxton, Barker & Co., 1860.

Hickman, Russell K., "The Vegetarian and Octagon Settlement Companies," *Kansas Historical Quarterly*, II (November, 1933), 377-385.

Ingalls, Sheffield, *History of Atchison County, Kansas*. Lawrence: Standard Publishing Company, 1916.

Johnson, Samuel A., *The Battle Cry of Freedom*. Lawrence: University of Kansas Press, 1954.

King, James L. *History of Shawnee County, Kansas*. Chicago: Richmond & Arnold, 1905.

Langsdorf, Edgar, "S. C. Pomeroy and the New England Emigrant Aid Company, 1854-1858," *Kansas Historical Quarterly*, VII (August, 1938), 227-245 (November, 1938), 379-398.

Lovejoy, Julia Louisa, "Letters from Kanzas," *Kansas Historical Quarterly*, XI (February, 1942), 29-44.

Malin, James C., "Emergency Housing at Lawrence, 1854," *Kansas Historical Quarterly*, XXI (Spring, 1954), 34-49.

———, "Housing Experiments in the Lawrence Community, 1855," *Kansas Historical Quarterly*, XXI (Summer, 1954), 95-121.

Martin, George, "Some of the Lost Towns of Kansas," Kansas State Historical Society, *Collections*, XII (1911-12), 426-490.

Miller, George P., "The Historical Aspects of Community Development in Kansas.'' Unpublished master's thesis, Department of Architecture and Allied Arts, Kansas State University, Manhattan, Kansas, 1961.

Miller, Myle H., Edgar Langsdorf, and Robert W. Richmond, *Kansas: A Pictorial History*. Topeka: The Kansas Centennial Commission and the State Historical Society, 1961.

Moore, Ely, Jr., ''The Story of Lecompton,'' Kansas State Historical Society, *Collections*, II (1909-10), 463-479.

Pantle, Alberta, ''The Connecticut Kansas Colony,'' *Kansas Historical Quarterly*, XXII (Spring, 1956), 1-50.

Richardson, Albert D., *Beyond the Mississippi*. Hartford: American Publishing Company, 1867.

Richmond, Robert W., ''The First Capitol of Kansas,'' *Kansas Historical Quarterly*, XXI (Spring, 1955), 321-325.

Robbins, Roy M., *Our Landed Heritage: The Public Domain, 1776-1936*. Lincoln: University of Nebraska Press, 1964.

Shindler, Henry, ''The First Capital of Kansas,'' Kansas State Historical Society, *Collections*, XII (1911-12), 331-337.

''Some of the Lost Towns of Kansas,'' Kansas State Historical Society, *Collections*, XII (1911-12), 426-490.

Taylor, Bayard, *Colorado: A Summer Trip*. New York: G. P. Putnam and Son, 1867.

Taylor, David G., ''Boom Town Leavenworth: The Failure of the Dream,'' *Kansas Historical Quarterly*, XXXVIII (Winter, 1972), 389-415.

Wyandotte County and Kansas City, Kansas. Chicago: Goodspeed Publishing Company, 1890.

Wyman, Walker D., ''Atchison, a Great Frontier Depot,'' *Kansas Historical Quarterly*, XI (August, 1942), 297-308.

Zornow, William Frank, *Kansas: A History of the Jayhawk State*. Norman: University of Oklahoma Press, 1957.

XIV · RUSH TO THE ROCKIES: DENVER AND THE MINING TOWNS OF COLORADO

Bancroft, Caroline, *Gulch of Gold: A History of Central City, Colorado*, Denver, Sage Books, 1958.

Bancroft, Hubert Howe, *History of Nevada, Colorado, and Wyoming, 1540-1888*. San Francisco: The History Company, 1890.

Barney, Libeus, *Letters of the Pike's Peak Gold Rush*. San José: The Talisman Press, 1959.

Barnes, George C., *Denver, The Man*. Wilmington, Ohio: The Author, 1950.

Barth, Gunther, *Instant Cities: Urbanization and the Rise of San Francisco and Denver*. New York: Oxford University Press, 1975.

Bixby, Amos, *History of Clear Creek and Boulder Valleys, Colorado*. Chicago: Baskin & Company, 1880.

Bowles, Samuel, *Our New West*. Hartford: Hartford Publishing Co., 1869.

Crofutt, George A., *Crofutt's Grip-Sack Guide of Colorado*. Omaha: Overland Publishing Co., 1885.

Denver City and Auraria, the Commercial Emporium of the Pike's Peak Gold Regions in 1859. n.p., n.d.

Dorset, Phyllis Flanders, *The New Eldorado: The Story of Colorado's Gold and Silver Rushes*. New York: The Macmillan Company, 1970.

Frink, Maurice, *The Boulder Story: Portrait of a Colorado Town*. Boulder, Colorado: Pruett Press, 1965.

Greever, William S., *The Bonanza West: The Story of the Western Mining Rushes, 1848-1900*. Norman: University of Oklahoma Press, 1963.

Griswold, Don L., and Jean Harvey Griswold, *The Carbonate Camp Called Leadville*. Denver: University of Denver Press, 1951.

History of Clear Creek and Boulder Valleys, Colorado. Chicago: O. L. Baskin & Co., 1880.

Hollenback, Frank R., *Central City and Black Hawk, Colorado Then and Now*. Denver, Sage Books, 1961.

Hunt, Helen, ''To Leadville,'' *Atlantic*, LXXIX (May, 1897), 547-575.

Kohl, Edith Eudora, *Denver's Historic Mansions*. Denver: Sage Books, 1957.

Lamb, Ellen E., ''Colorado Mining Towns,'' unpublished seminar paper, Department of City and Regional Planning, Cornell University, Ithaca, New York, 1970.

Lavender, David, ''This Wondrous Town; This Instant City,'' *The American West*, IV (August, 1967), 4-14, 68-70.

McGaa, William, ''A Statement Regarding the Formation of the St. Charles and Denver Town Companies,'' *Colorado Magazine*, XXII (January, 1945), 125-129.

''Mr. Whitsitt's Letter to Daniel Witter,'' *Colorado Magazine*, I (July, 1893), 283-285.

Mumey, Nolie, *History of the Early Settlements of Denver (1599-1860)*. Glendale, Calif.: The Arthur H. Clark Company, 1942.

———, *Prof. Oscar J. Goldrick and his Denver*. Denver: Sage Books, 1959.

Quiett, Glenn Chesney, *They Built the West: An Epic of Rails and Cities*. New York: D. Appleton-Century Company, 1934

Richardson, Albert D., *Beyond the Mississippi*. Hartford: American Publishing Company, 1867.

———, *Our New States and Territories*. New York: Beadle and Company, 1866.

Robbins, Sara E., *Jefferson County, Colorado: The Colorful Past of a Great Community*. Lakewood, Colo.: Jefferson County Bank, 1962.

Simonin, Louis L., *The Rocky Mountain West in 1867*. Lincoln: University of Nebraska Press, 1966.

Smith, Duane A., *Rocky Mountain Mining Camps: The Urban Frontier*. Bloomington: Indiana University Press, 1967.

———, *Colorado Mining: A Photographic Essay*. Albuquerque: University of New Mexico Press, 1977.

Sprague, Marshall, *Money Mountain: The Story of Cripple Creek Gold*. Boston: Little, Brown and Company, 1953.

Taft, Robert, *Artists and Illustrators of the Old West, 1850-1900*. New York: Charles Scribner's Sons, 1953.

Taylor, Bayard, *Colorado: A Summer Trip*. New York: G. P. Putnam & Son, 1867.

Taylor, Robert Guilford, *Cripple Creek*. Indiana University Geographic Monograph Series, Vol. I. Bloomington: Indiana University, 1966.

U. S. Federal Writers' Program, *Ghost Towns of Colorado*. New York: Hastings House, 1947.

[Vickers, W. B.], *History of the City of Denver, Arapahoe County, and Colorado*. Chicago: O. L. Baskin & Co., 1880.

Villard, Henry, *The Past and Present of the Pike's Peak Gold Regions* (1860). Princeton: Princeton University Press, 1932.

XV · THE EXPANDING MINING FRONTIER: CAMPS AND TOWNS OF IDAHO, MONTANA, AND SOUTH DAKOTA

Bancroft, Hubert Howe, *History of Washington, Idaho, and Montana, 1845-1889*. San Francisco: The History Company, 1890.

Barsness, Larry, *Gold Camp: Alder Gulch and Virginia City, Montana*. New York: Hastings House, 1962.

Beal, Merrill D., and Merle W. Wells, *History of Idaho*. 3 vols. New York: Lewis Historical Publishing Company, 1959.

Bird, Annie Laurie, "A Footnote on the Capital Dispute in Idaho," *Pacific Northwest Quarterly*, XXXVI (October, 1945), 341-346.

"Boise, City of Trees: A Centennial History," *Idaho Historical Series*, No. 12, Idaho Historical Society, June, 1963.

Bradley, James H., "Account of the Attempts to Build a Town at the Mouth of the Musselshell River," Historical Society of Montana, *Contributions*, II (1896), 304-313.

Briggs, Harold E., *Frontiers of the Northwest: A History of the Upper Missouri Valley*. New York: Peter Smith, 1950.

———, "The Black Hills Gold Rush," *North Dakota Historical Quarterly*, V (January, 1931), 71-99.

Burlingame, Merrill G., *The Montana Frontier*. Helena: State Publishing Company, 1942.

———, and K. Ross Toole, A History of Montana. 3 vols. New York: Lewis Historical Publishing Company, 1957.

Chaffee, Eugene B., "Boise: The Founding of a City," *Idaho Yesterdays*, VII (Summer, 1963), 3-7.

———, "The Political Clash Between North and South Idaho over the Capital," *Pacific Northwest Quarterly*, XXIX (July, 1938), 255-267.

Conard, Jane, "Charles Collina: The Sioux City Promotion of the Black Hills," *South Dakota History*, II (Spring, 1972), 131-171.

Craig, Robert Michael, "Montana Mining Towns," unpublished seminar paper, Department of City and Regional Planning, Cornell University, 1971.

"Fabulous Florence," *Idaho Yesterdays*, VI (Summer, 1962), 22-31.

Fletcher, Bob, "Virginia City," *Montana Magazine of History*, III (Summer, 1953), 54-59.

Greever, William S., *The Bonanza West: The Story of the Western Mining Rushes, 1848-1900*. Norman: University of Oklahoma Press, 1963.

Hamilton, James McClellan, *From Wilderness to Statehood: A History of Montana, 1850-1900*. Portland: Binfords and Mort, 1957.

Hughes, Richard B., *Pioneer Years in the Black Hills*, Agnes Wright Spring (ed.). Glendale, Calif.: The Arthur H. Clark Co., 1957.

Idaho Historical Society, *Eleventh Biennial Report, 1927-1928*, Boise: Idaho Historical Society, 1929.

Jennewein, J. Leonard, *Black Hills Booktrails*. Mitchell, South Dakota: Dakota Wesleyan University, 1962.

Larsen, Arthur J. (ed.), "A Journey to the Black Hills in 1880," *North Dakota Historical Quarterly*, VII (October, 1932), 37-53.

"Letters from the Boise Basin, 1864-1865," *Idaho Yesterdays*, VI (Fall, 1962), 26-30.

Miller, James Knox Polk, *The Road to Virginia City*. Norman: University of Oklahoma Press, 1960.

Miller, Joaquin, *An Illustrated History of the State of Montana*. Chicago: The Lewis Publishing Co., 1894.

Parker, Watson, *Gold in the Black Hills*. Norman: University of Oklahoma Press, 1966.

———, "Some Black Hills Ghost Towns and Their Origins," *South Dakota History*, II (Spring, 1972), 89-114.

Pence, Mary Lou, and Lola M. Holmsher, *The Ghost Towns of Wyoming*. New York: Hastings House, 1956.

Porter, Gertrude Illingworth, "An Historical Study of the Establishment of Boise City and Fort Boise," unpublished M.A. Thesis, Univerity of Southern California, 1937.

Richardson, Albert D., *Beyond the Mississippi*. Hartford: American Publishing Company, 1867.

———, *Our New States and Territories*, New York: Beadle and Company, 1866.

Schell, Herbert S., *History of South Dakota*. Lincoln: University of Nebraska Press, 1961.

Sherman, James E., and Barbara H. Sherman, *Ghost Towns and Mining Camps of New Mexico*. Norman, Oklahoma: University of Oklahoma Press, 1974.

Shinn, Charles Howard, *Mining Camps: A Study in American Frontier Government* (1885). New York: Alfred A. Knopf, 1948.

Smith, E. B., "Pioneer Background of Atlanta," MS, Idaho Historical Society.

Spring, Agnes Wright, *The Cheyenne and Black Hills Stage and Express Routes*. Glendale, Calif.: The Arthur H. Clark Company, 1949.

Stuart, Granville, *Forty Years on the Frontier*. Paul C. Phillips (ed.). 2 vols. Cleveland: The Arthur H. Clark Company, 1925.

Taylor, James W., *Report of James W. Taylor, on the Mineral Resources of the United States East of the Rocky Mountains*. Washington, D.C.: Government Printing Office, 1868.

"Those Were the Days: Idaho in 1860," *Idaho Yesterdays*, IV (Spring, 1960), 16-26.

Trimble, William J., *The Mining Advance into the Inland Empire: A Comparative Study of the Beginnings of the Mining Industry in Idaho and Montana, Eastern Washington and Oregon, and the Southern Interior of British Columbia*. Madison: Bulletin of the University of Wisconsin, No. 638, History Series, Vol. IV, No. 2, 1914.

U. S. Federal Writers' Program. *A South Dakota Guide*. Pierre: South Dakota Guide Commission, 1938.

U. S. Federal Writers' Program, *Copper Camp: Stories of the World's Greatest Mining Town, Butte, Montana*. New York: Hastings House, 1943.

U. S. Federal Writers' Program, *The Idaho Encyclopedia*. Caldwell, Idaho: The Caxton Printers, Ltd., 1938.

———, *Montana*. New York: The Viking Press, 1939.

Weiss, Norman D., *Ghost Towns of the Northwest*. Caldwell, Idaho: The Caxton Printers, Ltd., 1971.

" 'We're Off to the Mines': Elk City, Pierce, and the Clearwater Gold Rush," *Idaho Yesterdays*, V (Summer, 1961), 8-15.

White, Helen McCann (ed.), *Ho! For the Gold Fields: Northern Overland Wagon Trains of the 1860's*. St. Paul: Minnesota Historical Society, 1966.

Wolle, Muriel Sibell, *Montana Pay Dirt: A Guide to the Mining Camps of the Treasure State*. Denver: Sage Books, 1963.

XVI · RAILROADS TO THE ROCKIES AND THE URBAN SETTLEMENT OF THE CENTRAL AND NORTHERN GREAT PLAINS

Abbott, Othman A., "Building a City in the Prairie Wilderness," *Nebraska History*, XI (July-September, 1928), 121-132.

Ames, Charles Edgar, *Pioneering the Union Pacific: A Reappraisal of the Builders of the Railroad*. New York: Appleton-Century-Crofts, 1969.

Andreas, A. T., *History of the State of Nebraska*. 3 vols. Chicago: Western Historical Company, 1882.

Armstrong, Moses K., *The Early Empire Builders of the Great West*. St. Paul: E. W. Porter, 1901.

Bell, William A., *New Tracks in North America*. 2 vols. London: Chapman and Hall, 1869.

Bird, George F., and Edwin J. Taylor, Jr., *History of the City of Bismarck, North Dakota: The First 100 Years, 1872-1972*. Bismarck, N.D.: Bismarck Centennial Association, 1972.

Bowles, Samuel, *Our New West*. Hartford: Hartford Publishing Company, 1869.

Briggs, Harold E., *Frontiers of the Northwest*. New York: Peter Smith, 1950.

Brown, Ralph H., *Historical Geography of the United States*. New York: Harcourt, Brace and Company, 1948.

Burlingame, Merrill G., and K. Ross Toole, *A History of Montana*. 3 vols. New York: Lewis Historical Publishing Co., 1957.

Cushman, George L., "Abilene, First of the Kansas Cow Towns," *Kansas Historical Quarterly*, IX (August, 1940), 240-258.

Davis, Thomas M., "Building the Burlington Through Nebraska—A Summary View," *Nebraska History*, XXX (December, 1949), 317-343.

Dodge, Grenville M., *How We Built the Union Pacific Railway*. Denver: Sage Books, 1965.

Dyer, J. E., *Dakota: The Observations of a Tenderfoot*. [Fargo]: Fargo Republican Steam Printing House, 1884.

Dykstra, Robert R., *The Cattle Towns*. New York: Alfred A. Knopf, 1968.

Gates, Paul, *The Illinois Central Railroad and Its Colonization Work*. Cambridge: Harvard University Press, 1934.

Havins, T. R., "Texas Fever," *Southwestern Historical Quarterly*, LII (July, 1948), 147-162.

Hedges, James B., "The Colonization Work of the Northern Pacific Railroad," *Mississippi Valley Historical Review*, XIII (December, 1926), 311-342.

Jones, Mildred McEwen, *Early Beadle County, 1879-1900*. Huron, S.D. (?): n.p., 1961.

Karolevitz, Robert, *Yankton: A Pioneer Past*. Aberdeen, South Dakota: North Plains Press, 1972.

Kingsbury, George W., *History of Dakota Territory*. 5 vols. Chicago: The S. J. Clarke Publishing Co., 1915.

Kliewer, Waldo O., "The Foundations of Billings, Montana," *Pacific Northwest Quarterly*, XXXI (July, 1940), 255-283.

Lamar, Howard Roberts, *Dakota Territory, 1861-1889*. New Haven: Yale University Press, 1956.

Larson, T. A., *History of Wyoming*. Lincoln: University of Nebraska Press, 1965.

Lowther, Charles C., *Dodge City, Kansas*. Philadelphia: Dorrance and Co., 1940.

McCoy, Joseph G., *Historic Sketches of the Cattle Trade of the West and Southwest*. Ralph P. Bieber (ed.). Glendale, Calif.: The Arthur H. Clark Company, 1940.

Mahnken, Norbert R., "Ogallala—Nebraska's Cowboy Capital," *Nebraska History*, XXVIII (April-June, 1947), 85-109.

Morgan, John, "Garland City, Railroad Terminus, 1878," *Colorado Magazine*, XXV (November, 1948), 259-262,.

"Name Origins of North Dakota Cities, Towns, and Counties," *North Dakota History*, XIII (April, 1946), 118-143.

Overton, Richard C., *Burlington West: A Colonization History of the Burlington Railroad*. Cambridge: Harvard University Press, 1941.

Potter, Merle, "The North Dakota Capital Fight," *North Dakota Historical Quarterly*, VII (October, 1932), 25-53.

Richardson, Albert D., *Beyond the Mississippi*. Hartford: American Publishing Company, 1867.

Riegel, Robert, *The Story of the Western Railroads*. New York: The Macmillan Company, 1926.

Robinson, Elwyn B., *History of North Dakota*. Lincoln: University of Nebraska Press, 1966.

Savage, James W., and John T. Bell, *History of the City of Omaha, Nebraska*. New York: Munsell & Company, 1894.

Simonin, Louis L., *The Rocky Mountain West in 1867*. Lilson O. Clough (trans.), Lincoln: University of Nebraska Press, 1966.

Smalley, E. V., "The New North-West," *Century Magazine*, xxiv (September, 1882), 769-779.

————, *History of the Northern Pacific Railroad*. New York, G. P. Putnam's Sons, 1883.

Schell, Herbert S., *History of South Dakota*. Lincoln: University of Nebraska Press, 1961.

Stelter, Gilbert, "The City and Westward Expansion," *Western Historical Quarterly*, iv (April, 1973), 187-202.

Train, George Francis, *My Life in Many States and in Foreign Lands*. London: William Heinemann, 1902.

Triggs, J. H., *History of Cheyenne and Northern Wyoming*. Omaha: Herald Steam Book and Job Printing House, 1876.

U. S. National Park Service, National Survey of Historic Sites and Buildings, Vol. xi, *Prospector, Cowhand, and Sodbuster*. Washington, D.C.: Government Printing Office, 1967.

Vestal, Stanley, *Dodge City: Queen of Cow Towns*. New York: Harper and Brothers, 1952.

XVII · RAILROAD TOWNS OF THE MOUNTAIN STATES AND THE SOUTHERN PLAINS

Athearn, Robert, *Rebel of the Rockies: A History of the Denver and Rio Grande Western Railroad*. New Haven: Yale University Press, 1962.

Ayers, Mary C., "The Founding of Durango, Colorado," *Colorado Magazine*, vii (May, 1930), 85-94.

Briggs, Harold E., *Frontiers of the Northwest: A History of the Upper Missouri Valley*. New York: D. Appleton-Century Company, Inc., 1940.

Burlingame, Merrill G., and K. Ross Toole, *A History of Montana*. 3 vols. New York: Lewis Historical Publishing Company, 1957.

Carroll, Richard, "The Founding of Salida, Colorado," *Colorado Magazine*, xi (July, 1934), 121-133.

Gerard, P., *How to Build a City*. Philadelphia: Review Printing House, 1872.

Hafen, LeRoy R., and Frank M. Young, "The Mormon Settlement at Pueblo, Colorado, during the Mexican War," *Colorado Magazine*, lx (July, 1932), 121-136.

Hamilton, James M., *From Wilderness to Statehood: A History of Montana, 1805-1900*. Portland: Binfords & Mort, 1957.

Hunt, Herbert, *Tacoma: Its History and Its Builders*. 3 vols. Chicago: The S. J. Clarke Publishing Co., 1916.

Husband, Michael B., "Morton M. McCarver: An Iowa Entrepreneur in the Far West," *Annals of Iowa*, xl (Spring, 1970), 242-254.

Kipling, Rudyard, *From Sea to Sea*. 2 vols. New York: Doubleday, Page & Co., 1913.

Larson, T. A., *History of Wyoming*. Lincoln: University of Nebraska Press, 1965.

[Leeson, Michael] (ed.), *History of Montana, 1739-1885*. Chicago: Warner & Co., 1885.

Masterson, V. V., *The Katy Railroad and the Last Frontier*. Norman: University of Oklahoma Press, 1952.

Means, Lawrence G., *Reno: A Criterion for Progress*, [Reno]: n.p., n.d.

Miller, Joaquin, *An Illustrated History of the State of Montana*. Chicago: The Lewis Publishing Co., 1894.

Ormes, Manly Dayton, and Eleanor R. Ormes, *The Book of Colorado Springs*. Colorado Springs, Colorado: The Dentan Printing Co., 1933.

Owen, James, "Reminiscences of Early Pueblo," *Colorado Magazine*, xxii (May, 1945), 97-107.

Parker, Edna Monch, "The Southern Pacific Railroad and Settlement in Southern California," *Pacific Historical Review*, vi (June, 1937), 103-120.

Perkins, J. R., *Trails, Rails and War: The Life of General G. M. Dodge*. Indianapolis: Bobbs-Merrill Company, 1929.

Quiett, Glenn Chesney, *They Built the West: An Epic of Rails and Cities*. New York: D. Appleton-Century Company, Inc., 1934.

Rankin, James H., "The Founding and Early Years of Grand Junction," *Colorado Magazine*, vi (March, 1929), 39-45.

Riegel, Robert E., *The Story of the Western Railroads*. New York: The Macmillan Company, 1926.

Smalley, Eugene V., *History of the Northern Pacific Railroad*. New York: G. P. Putnam's Sons, 1883.

Storey, Brit Allan, "William Jackson Palmer, Promoter," *Colorado Magazine*, xliii (Winter, 1966), 44-55.

Tacoma Land Company, *Tacoma, the Western Terminus of the Northern Pacific Railroad*. Tacoma: n.p., 1889.

Toole, K. Ross, *Montana: An Uncommon Land*. Norman: University of Oklahoma Press, 1959.

Train, George Francis, *My Life in Many States and in Foreign Lands*. London: William Heinemann, 1902.

Worthen, Clifton B., and Oscar O. Mueller, "Central Montana," in Merrill G. Burlingame and K. Ross Toole, *A History of Montana*. New York: Lewis Historical Publishing Company, 1957, ii, 159-166.

Wrigley, Robert L., Jr., "The Early History of Pocatello, Idaho," *Pacific Northwest Quarterly*, xxxiv (October, 1943), 353-365.

XVIII · TRACKS AND TOWNS: RAILROADS AND URBAN GROWTH IN TEXAS AND THE SOUTHWEST

Barney, James M., "Phoenix—A History of its Pioneer Days and People," *Arizona Historical Review*, v (January, 1933), 264-268.

Bartlett, John R., *Personal Narrative of Explorations and Incidents in Texas, New Mexico, California, Sonora, and Chihuahua . . . during the Years 1850, '51, '52 and '53*. 2 vols. New York: D. Appleton and Co., 1854.

Bryant, Keith L., Jr., "Arthur E. Stilwell and the Founding of Port Arthur: A Case of Entrepreneurial Error," *Southwestern Historical Quarterly*, LXXV (July, 1971), 19-40.

———, *Arthur E. Stilwell: Promoter with a Hunch*. Nashville: Vanderbilt University Press, 1971.

Buder, Stanley, *Pullman: An Experiment in Industrial Order and Community Planning, 1880-1930*. New York: Oxford University Press, 1967.

Clark, Ira G., *Then Came the Railroads: The Century from Steam to Diesel in the Southwest*. Norman: University of Oklahoma Press 1958.

Conger, Roger N., *A Pictorial History of Waco with a Reprint of Highlights of Waco History*. Waco, Texas: The Texian Press, 2nd ed., 1964.

Credgington, John, "Old Town Amarillo," *Panhandle Plains Historical Review*, XXX (1957), 79-108.

Dallas Department of City Planning, *Dallas Central District: Its Problems and Needs: A Master Plan Report*. Dallas: Dallas Department of City Planing, 1958.

———, *Dallas Central District: A Master Plan Report*. Dallas: Dallas Department of City Planning, 1961.

Donnell, F. S., "When Las Vegas Was the Capital of New Mexico," *New Mexico Historical Review*, VIII (October, 1933), 265-272.

Duff, Katharyn, *Abilene . . . on Catclaw Creek*. Abilene, Texas: The Reporter Publishing Co., 1970.

Farish, Thomas Edwin, *History of Arizona*. 8 vols. Phoenix: The author, 1915-1918.

Fergusson, Erna, *Albuquerque*. Albuquerque: M. Armitage, 1947.

Garwood, Darrell, *Crossroads of America: The Story of Kansas City*. New York: W. W. Norton & Co., 1948.

Graves, Lawrence L. (ed.), *A History of Lubbock: Part One: Story of a Country Town*. Lubbock, Texas: West Texas Museum Association, 1959.

Greever, William S., "Railway Development in the Southwest," *New Mexico Historical Review*, XXXII (April, 1957), 151-203.

Gregg, Andrew, *New Mexico In the Nineteenth Century: A Pictorial History*. Albuquerque: University of New Mexico Press, 1968.

Hardy, Dermot N., and Ingham S. Roberts (eds.), *Historical Review of South-East Texas*. 2 vols. Chicago: The Lewis Publishing Company, 1910.

Henson, Pauline, *Founding a Wilderness Capital: Prescott, A.T. 1864*. Flagstaff: Northland Press, 1965.

Hinton, Richard J., *The Hand-Book to Arizona*. San Francisco: Payot, Upham & Co., 1878.

History of Arizona Territory. San Francisco: Wallace W. Elliott & Co., 1884.

King, Dick, *Ghost Towns of Texas*. San Antonio: The Naylor Company, 1953.

Knight, Oliver, *Fort Worth: Outpost on the Trinity*. Norman, Oklahoma: University of Oklahoma Press, 1953.

Lamar, Howard Roberts, *The Far Southwest, 1846-1912: A Territorial History*. New York: W. W. Norton & Company, 1970.

Laumbach, Verna, "Las Vegas Before 1850," *New Mexico Historical Review*, VIII (October, 1933), 241-264.

Lindsey, Almont, *The Pullman Strike*. Chicago: University of Chicago Press, 1942.

Lockwood, Frank C., *Pioneer Days in Arizona from the Spanish Occupation to Statehood*. New York: The Macmillan Company, 1932.

McCampbell, Coleman, *Texas Seaport: The Story of the Growth of Corpus Christi and the Coastal Bend Area*. New York: Exposition Press, 1952.

Martin, Robert L., *The City Moves West: Economic and Industrial Growth in Central West Texas*. Austin: University of Texas Press, 1969.

Meinig, D. W., *Southwest: Three Peoples in Geographical Change, 1600-1970*. New York: Oxford University Press, 1971.

Miller, Clarence A., "A City in the Old West," *The Overland Monthly*, IV (2nd Ser. October, 1884), 337-341.

Mills, William Wallace, *Forty Years at El Paso, 1858-1898*. El Paso: C. Hertzog, 1962.

Myers, Sandra L., "Fort Worth, 1870-1900," *Southwestern Historical Quarterly*, LXXII (October, 1968), 200-222.

Nelson, Kitty Jo Parker, "Prescott: Sketch of a Frontier Capital, 1863-1900," *Arizoniana*, IV (Winter, 1963), 17-26.

Peck, Anne Merriman, *The March of Arizona History*. Tucson: Arizona Silhouettes, 1962.

Porter, Eugene O., "Map No. Two of Satterthwaite's Addition to El Paso, 1884," *Password*, I (February, 1956), 68-69.

Reps, John W., *The Making of Urban America: A History of City Planning in the United States*. Princeton: Princeton University Press, 1965.

Riegel, Robert Edgar, *The Story of the Western Railroads from 1852 Through the Reign of the Giants*. Lincoln: University of Nebraska Press, 1964.

Sherman, James E., and Barbara H. Sherman, *Ghost Towns of Arizona*. Norman: University of Oklahoma Press, 1969.

Sites, George E., Jr., "The Bradford Map of Nogales, Arizona," *Journal of Arizona History*, XI (Spring, 1970), 1-13.

Strickland, Rex W., *El Paso in 1854*. El Paso, Texas: Texas Western Press, 1969.

Tinker, George H., *Northern Arizona and Flagstaff in 1887*. Glendale, California: The Arthur H. Clark Company, 1969.

U. S. Federal Writers' Program, *Arizona: A State Guide*. New York: Hastings House, 1940.

———, *Beaumont: A Guide to the City and its Environs*. Houston: The Anson Jones Press, 1939.

———, *New Mexico: A Guide to the Colorful State*. Albuquerque: The University of New Mexico Press, 2nd ed., 1945.

———, *Port Arthur*. Houston: The Anson Press, 1940.

———, *Texas: A Guide to the Lone Star State*. New York: Hastings House, 1940.

Wallace, Andrew, *The Image of Arizona: Pictures from the Past.* Albuquerque: University of New Mexico Press, 1971.

Wallace, Ernest and David M. Vigness (eds.), *Documents of Texas History.* Austin: The Steck Company, 1963.

Webb, Walter Prescott (ed.), *The Handbook of Texas.* 2 vols. Austin: The Texas State Historical Association, 1952.

Westphall, Victor, "Albuquerque in the 1870's," *New Mexico Historical Review,* XXIII (October, 1948), 253-268.

Wise, Clyde, Jr., "The Effects of the Railroad upon El Paso," *Password,* V (July, 1960), 91-101.

Wislizenus, A., *Memoir of a Tour to Northern Mexico, Connected with Col. Doniphan's Expedition, in 1846 and 1847.* Sen. Misc. Doc. 26, 30th Cong., 1st Sess. Washington: Tippin & Streeper, Printers, 1848.

Wyllys, Rufus Kay, *Arizona: The History of a Frontier State.* Phoenix: Hobson & Herr, 1950.

Young, J. H., "Tombstone, Arizona," *The Overland Monthly,* VIII, 2nd ser. (November, 1886), 483-487.

XIX · RUSHING FOR LAND: OKLAHOMA'S OVERNIGHT CITIES

Alley, John, *City Beginnings in Oklahoma Territory.* Norman: University of Oklahoma Press, 1939.

Barnes, Louis Seymour, "The Founding of Ponca City," *Chronicles of Oklahoma,* XXXV (Summer, 1957), 154-162.

Brown, Loren N., "The Dawes Commission," *Chronicles of Oklahoma,* IX (March, 1931), 71-105.

———, "The Establishment of the Dawes Commission for Indian Territory," *Chronicles of Oklahoma,* XVIII (June, 1940), 171-184.

Buck, Solon J., "The Settlement of Oklahoma," Wisconsin Academy of Science, Arts and Letters, *Transactions,* XV, Part II (1907), 325-380.

Chambers, Homer S., "Townsite Promotion in Early Oklahoma," *Chronicles of Oklahoma,* XIX (June, 1941), 162-165.

Chapman, Berlin B., "Guthrie, from Public Land to Private Property," *Chronicles of Oklahoma,* XXXIII (Spring, 1955), 63-86.

———, "Oklahoma City, From Public Land to Private Property," *Chronicles of Oklahoma,* XXXVII (Summer, 1959), 211-237; (Autumn, 1959), 330-352; (Winter, 1959-60), 440-479.

———, "Opening the Cherokee Outlet: An Archival Study," *Chronicles of Oklahoma,* XL (Summer, 1962), 158-181; (Autumn, 1962), 253-285.

———, "Perkins Townsite: An Archival Case Study," *Chronicles of Oklahoma,* XXV (Summer, 1947), 82-91.

———, "The Enid 'Railroad War': An Archival Study," *Chronicles of Oklahoma,* XLIII (Summer, 1965), 126-197.

———, "The Founding of El Reno," *Chronicles of Oklahoma,* XXXIV (Spring, 1956), 79-108.

———, "The Legal Sooners of 1889 in Oklahoma," *Chronicles of Oklahoma,* XXXV (Winter, 1957-58), 382-415.

———, *The Founding of Stillwater.* Oklahoma City: Times-Journal Publishing Co., 1948.

Cunningham, Robert E., *Stillwater: Where Oklahoma Began.* Stillwater, Oklahoma: The Arts and Humanities Council of Stillwater, 1969.

Debo, Angie, *Tulsa: From Creek Town to Oil Capital.* Norman: University of Oklahoma Press, 1943.

Durham, A. W., "Oklahoma City before the Run of 1889," *Chronicles of Oklahoma,* XXXVI (Spring, 1958), 72-78.

Forbes, Gerald, *Guthrie: Oklahoma's First Capital.* Norman: University of Oklahoma Press, 1938.

Furer, Howard B., "The Founding of Oklahoma City and Guthrie," *American Chronicle,* I (February, 1972), 9-15.

Gibson, Arrell M., *The Chickasaws.* Norman: University of Oklahoma Press, 1971.

Gittinger, Roy, *The Formation of the State of Oklahoma (1803-1906).* Berkeley: University of California Press, 1917.

———, *The University of Oklahoma: A History of Fifty Years, 1892-1942.* Norman: University of Oklahoma Press, 1942.

Howard, William Willard, "The Oklahoma Movement," *Harper's Weekly,* XXXIII (May 4, 1889), 350-351.

———, "The Rush to Oklahoma," *Harper's Weekly,* XXXIII (May 18, 1889), 391-394.

Kelley, E. H., "When Oklahoma City was Seymour and Verbeck," *Chronicles of Oklahoma,* XXVII (Winter, 1949-50), 347-353.

Litton, Gaston, *History of Oklahoma at the Golden Anniversary of Statehood.* 4 vols. New York: Lewis Historical Publishing Co., 1957.

McCarty, John L., *Maverick Town: The Story of Old Tascosa.* Norman: University of Oklahoma Press, 1946.

McReynolds, Edwin C., *Oklahoma: A History of the Sooner State.* Norman: University of Oklahoma Press, 1954.

Morgan, Dick T., *Morgan's Manual of the U. S. Homestead and Townsite Laws.* Guthrie: State Capital Printing Co., 1893.

Morris, John W., and Edwin C. McReynolds. *Historical Atlas of Oklahoma.* Norman: University of Oklahoma Press, 1965.

Rister, Carl Coke, *Land Hunger: David L. Payne and the Oklahoma Boomers.* Norman: University of Oklahoma Press, 1942.

Scott, Angelo C., *The Story of Oklahoma City.* Oklahoma City: Times-Journal Publishing Co., 1939.

Squire, C. A., "Old Grand, Ghost Town," *Chronicles of Oklahoma,* XXVIII (Winter, 1950-51), 399-417.

"The Magic City: Guthrie," *Chronicles of Oklahoma,* XXXVI (Spring, 1958), 65-71.

Thoburn, Joseph B., and Muriel H. Wright, *Oklahoma: A History of the State and Its People.* 2 vols. New York: Lewis Historical Publishing Company, 1929.

U. S. Commissioners of the General Land Office, *Annual Report for the Fiscal Year Ended June 30, 1890*. Washington, D.C.: Government Printing Office, 1890.

U. S. Federal Writers' Program, *Oklahoma: A Guide to the Sooner State*. Norman: University of Oklahoma Press, 1941.

White, Robe Carl, "Experiences at the Opening of Oklahoma, 1889," *Chronicles of Oklahoma*, xxvii (Spring, 1949), 56-69.

Wicks, Hamilton S., "The Opening of Oklahoma," *The Cosmopolitan*, vii (September, 1889), 460-470.

XX · THE URBAN WEST AT THE END OF THE FRONTIER ERA

American Institute of Architects, San Antonio Chapter, *Historic San Antonio, 1700-1900*. San Antonio: San Antonio AIA, n.d.

Appletons' Annual Cyclopaedia and Register of Important Events, New Series, xi-xix. New York: D. Appleton and Co., 1886-1894.

Appletons' General Guide to the United States and Canada. New York: D. Appleton and Company, 1892.

Bagley, Clarence B., *History of Seattle from the Earliest Settlement to the Present Time*. 3 vols. Chicago: The S. J. Clarke Publishing Co., 1916.

Bancroft, Hubert Howe, *History of Washington, Idaho, and Montana*, San Francisco: The History Company, 1890.

Barth, Gunther, *Instant Cities: Urbanization and the Rise of San Francisco and Denver*. New York: Oxford University Press, 1975.

Baxter, Sylvester, "Along the Rio Grande," *Harper's New Monthly Magazine*, lxx (April, 1885), 687-700.

Billington, Ray Allen, *Frederick Jackson Turner: Historian, Scholar, Teacher*. New York: Oxford University Press, 1973.

———, *Westward Expansion: A History of the American Frontier*. New York: Macmillan, 3rd ed., 1967.

Brandes, Ray, "Guide to the Historic Landmarks of Tucson," *Arizoniana*, iii (Summer, 1962), 27-38.

Bryce, James, *The American Commonwealth*. 2 vols. New York: The Macmillan Company, 3rd ed., 1907.

Burnham, Daniel H., *Report on a Plan for San Francisco*. San Francisco: Published by the City, 1905.

Gannett, Henry, *Statistical Atlas of the United States, Based upon Results of the Eleventh Census*. Washington, D.C.: Government Printing Office, 1898.

Grant, Frederic James, "Seattle: A Chapter from an Uncompleted History," *Magazine of Western History*, xi (April, 1890), 636-642.

Hines, Thomas S., *Burnham of Chicago: Architect and Planner*. New York: Oxford University Press, 1974.

Johnson, Charles A., *Denver's Mayor Speer*. Denver: Bighorn Books, 1969.

Larsen, Lawrence H., and Robert L. Branyan, "The Development of an Urban Civilization on the Frontier of the American West," *Societas—A Review of Social History*, i (Winter, 1971), 33-50.

Miller, Clarence, "A City in the Old West," *The Overland Monthly*, iv, 2nd series (October, 1884), 337-341.

Muirhead, James Fullarton, *The Land of Contrasts: A Briton's View of His American Kin*. London: John Lane, 1898.

Peck, Anne Merriman, *The March of Arizona History*. Tucson: Arizona Silhouettes, 1962.

Porter, Robert P., *The West: From the Census of 1880*. Chicago: Rand, McNally & Co., 1882.

"Portland," *The West Shore*. (January, 1886), 11-18.

Quiett, Glenn Chesney, *They Built the West: An Epic of Rails and Cities*. New York: D. Appleton-Century Co., 1934.

Reps, John W., *The Making of Urban America: A History of City Planning in the United States*. Princeton: Princeton University Press, 1965.

Scott, Mel, *The San Francisco Bay Area: A Metropolis in Perspective*. Berkeley: University of California Press, 1959.

Special Supplement to The HemisFair Edition of San Antonio: A Historical and Pictorial Guide. Austin: University of Texas Press, 1968.

Still, Bayrd, "Patterns of Mid-Nineteenth Century Urbanization in the Middle West," *Mississippi Valley Historical Review*, xxviii (September, 1941), 187-206.

Thayer, William M., *Marvels of the New West*. Norwich, Conn.: Henry Bill Publishing Co., 1888.

U. S. Federal Writers' Program. *New Mexico: A Guide to the Colorful State*. Albuquerque: University of New Mexico Press, 2nd ed., 1945.

Visscher, Will L., "Tacoma, Washington," *Magazine of Western History*, xii (May, 1890), 76-81.

Waring, George E., Jr. (comp.), *Report on the Social Statistics of Cities*. 2 vols. Washington, D.C.: Government Printing Office, 1887.

Willard, Charles Dwight, *The Herald's History of Los Angeles City*. Los Angeles: Kingsley-Barnes & Neuner Co., 1901.

NOTES ON THE ILLUSTRATIONS

This list contains bibliographic information about the illustrations reproduced in this work. The symbols below indicate locations of originals from which photographs were made.

A	Author's collection.
AAS-W	American Antiquarian Society, Worcester, Massachusetts.
ACMW-FW	The Amon Carter Museum of Western Art, Fort Worth, Texas.
AHS-T	Arizona Historical Society, Tucson, Arizona.
APL-A	Austin-Travis County Collection, Austin Public Library, Austin, Texas.
APS-P	American Philosophical Society, Philadelphia, Pennsylvania.
BM-M	Map Room, The British Library, London, England.
BM-MS	Manuscripts Division, The British Museum, London, England.
BPL-B	Bozeman Public Library, Bozeman, Montana.
CCDC-D	Office of County Clerk, Dallas County, Dallas, Texas.
CC-LA	Office of City Clerk, Los Angeles, California.
CCPC-A	Office of County Clerk, Potter County, Amarillo, Texas.
CC-SA	Office of City Clerk, San Antonio, Texas.
CE-D	Office of City Engineer, City and County of Denver, Colorado.
CHS-C	Chicago Historical Society, Chicago, Illinois.
CHS-SF	California Historical Society, San Francisco, California.
CSA-S	California State Archives, Sacramento, California.
CSL-S	California State Library, Sacramento, California
CSHS-D	Colorado State Historical Society of Colorado, Denver, Colorado.
CU-O	Olin Library, Cornell University, Ithaca, New York.
DCL-H	Dartmouth College Library, Hanover, New Hampshire.
DCP-SL	Department of City Planning, Salt Lake City, Utah.
DHS-D	Dallas Historical Society, Dallas, Texas.
HH-SM	The Henry E. Huntington Library and Art Gallery, San Marino, California.
HLDS-SL	Historical Department, Church of Jesus Christ of Latter-Day Saints, Salt Lake City, Utah.
HSP-P	The Historical Society of Pennsylvania, Philadelphia, Pennsylvania.
IHS-B	Idaho State Historical Society, Boise, Idaho.
ISL-I	Indiana State Library, Indianapolis, Indiana
JAM-O	Joslyn Art Museum, Omaha, Nebraska.
JCB-P	The John Carter Brown Library, Providence, Rhode Island
JSM-SD	Junipero Serra Museum, San Diego, California.
KSHS-T	Kansas State Historical Society, Topeka, Kansas.
LAP-P	Library Association of Portland, Portland, Oregon.
LC-GC	General Collection, Library of Congress, Washington, D.C.
LC-M	Geography and Map Division, Library of Congress, Washington, D.C.
LC-MS	Division of Manuscripts, Library of Congress, Washington, D.C.
LC-P	Prints and Photographs Division, Library of Congress, Washington, D.C.
LC-R	Division of Rare Books, Library of Congress, Washington, D.C.
LPL-L	Lincoln Public Library, Lincoln, Nebraska.
LUO-N	University of Oklahoma Library, Norman, Oklahoma.
MA-A	Museum of Albuquerque, Albuquerque, New Mexico.
MGK-S	Mrs. Gerald Kennedy, Stockton, California.
MHS-H	Montana Historical Society, Helena, Montana.
MHS-SL	Missouri Historical Society, St. Louis, Missouri.
MM-NN	The Mariner's Museum, Newport News, Virginia.
NA-CB	Cartographic Branch, National Archives, Washington, D.C.
NBL-C	Edward D. Graff Collection, The Newberry Library, Chicago, Illinois.
NDHS-B	North Dakota Historical Society, Bismarck, North Dakota.
NHM-LA	History Division, Natural History Museum of Los Angeles County, Los Angeles, California.
NHS-R	Nevada Historical Society, Reno, Nevada.
NMSA-SF	New Mexico State Archives, Santa Fe, New Mexico.
NSHS-L	Nebraska State Historical Society, Lincoln, Nebraska.
NSM-CC	Nevada State Museum, Carson City, Nevada.
NYH-NY	The New-York Historical Society, New York City.
NYP-NY	New York Public Library, Astor, Lenox, and Tilden Foundations, New York City.
OHS-P	Oregon Historical Society, Portland, Oregon.
OKHS-OC	Oklahoma Historical Society, Oklahoma City, Oklahoma.
OM-O	The Oakland Museum, Oakland, California.
PUL-P	Princeton University Library, Princeton, New Jersey.
RBP-SA	Republic Blue Print Co., San Antonio, Texas.
RCC-J	Office of Recorder, Clark County, Jeffersonville, Indiana.
RDC-A	Office of Recorder, Dickinson County, Abilene, Kansas.
RFC-F	Office of Recorder, Fresno County, Fresno, California.
RGC-B	Office of Recorder, Gallatin County, Bozeman, Montana.
RHC-P	Office of Recorder, Hughes County, Pierre, South Dakota.
RKC-S	Office of Recorder, King County, Seattle, Washington.
RLAC-LA	Office of Recorder, Los Angeles County, Los Angeles, California.
RLC-L	Office of Recorder, Lancaster County, Lincoln, Nebraska.

RMC-S   Office of Recorder, Marion County, Salem, Oregon.
RMC-P   Office of Recorder, Maricopa County, Phoenix, Arizona.
RNC-C   Office of Recorder, Natrona County, Casper, Wyoming.
RSBC-SB Office of Recorder, San Bernardino County, San Bernardino, California.
RSC-W   Office of Recorder, Sedgwick County, Wichita, Kansas.
RSLC-SL Office of Recorder, Salt Lake County, Salt Lake City, Utah.
RTC-O   Office of Recorder, Thurston County, Olympia, Washington.
RWWC-WW Office of Recorder, Walla Walla County, Walla Walla, Washington.
RYC-B   Office of Recorder, Yellowstone County, Billings, Montana.
SDHS-P   South Dakota State Historical Society, Pierre, South Dakota.
SDT-SD   Historical Collection, Title Insurance and Trust Company, San Diego, California.
SHS-S   Seattle Historical Society, Seattle, Washington.
SI-DC   The Smithsonian Institution, Washington, D.C.
SPNB-LA Historical Collection, Security Pacific National Bank, Los Angeles, California.
TGLO-A   Texas General Land Office, Austin, Texas.
TPL-T   Tacoma Public Library, Tacoma, Washington.
TSL-A   Archives Division, Texas State Library, Austin, Texas.
UCB-AE   Office of Architects and Engineers, University of California, Berkeley, California.
UCBL-B   Bancroft Library, University of California, Berkeley, California.
UC-LA   Department of Special Collections, University Research Library, University of California, Los Angeles, California.
UHS-SL   Utah State Historical Society, Salt Lake City, Utah.
UT-A   Barker Texas History Center Archives, University of Texas Library, Austin, Texas.
VRL-V   Fort Vancouver Regional Library, Vancouver, Washington.
WHPL-D   Western History Department, Denver Public Library, Denver, Colorado.
WHS-M   Wisconsin Historical Society, Madison, Wisconsin.
WLC-A   William L. Clements Library, University of Michigan, Ann Arbor, Michigan.
WM-SA   Witte Memorial Museum, San Antonio Museum Association, San Antonio, Texas.
WRHS-C   Western Reserve Historical Society, Cleveland, Ohio.
WSA-C   Wyoming State Archives and Historical Department, Cheyenne, Wyoming.
WSD-R   Washoe County School District, Reno, Nevada.
WSHS-T   Washington State Historical Society, Tacoma, Washington.
YUM-NH   Map Collection, Yale University Library, New Haven, Connecticut.

Figure 1.1 *A Map of the United States of America.* Map of the eastern United States in 1813, drawn and published by John Melish, engraved by H. S. Tanner. From John Melish, *Travels Through the United States of America, in the Years 1806 & 1807, and 1809, 1810, & 1811.* Philadelphia, 1815, I. CU-O   4

Figure 1.2 *Plan of the City and Suburbs of Philadelphia.* Plan of Philadelphia, Pennsylvania in 1794, drawn by A. P. Folie, engraved by R. Scot and S. Allardice. HSP-P   5

Figure 1.3 *Plan of the City of Washington in the Territory of Columbia.* Restrike of a plan of Washington, D. C., in 1792, drawn by Andrew Ellicott, engraved by Thackara and Vallance, Philadelphia. CU-O   6

Figure 1.4 *Plan of Pittsburg and Adjacent Country.* Undated plan of Pittsburgh, Pennsylvania, ca. 1815, surveyed by William Darby, engraved by H. S. Tanner, published by R. Patterson and W. Darby, Philadelphia. LC-M   7

Figure 1.5 *Map of the Borough of Erie, Including the Second & Third Sections & Out Lots.* Plan of Erie, Pennsylvania, in 1836, drawn by Thomas Forster, engraved by A. F. Marthens, Pittsburgh, published by Oliver Spafford, Erie. HSP-P   9

Figure 1.6 *Map of the Village of New Amsterdam (now the City of Buffalo).* Village of Buffalo. Plans of Buffalo, New York in 1804 and 1851, based on maps in the offices of the Secretary of State and the Surveyor General of New York State, printed by Richard H. Pease, Albany. From E. B. O'Callaghan (ed.), *The Documentary History of the State of New York,* Albany, 1851, IV. A   10

Figure 1.7 *A Plan of the City of Cleaveland.* Plan of Cleveland, Ohio, in 1796 by Seth Pease as redrawn in 1855 by L. M. Pillsbury. From *Journal of the Association of Engineering Societies, Transactions,* III (1884). LC-M   11

Figure 1.8 *Plat of the Seven Ranges of Townships being Part of the Territory of the United States N.W. of the River Ohio Which by a late act of Congress are directed to be sold.* Map of the first townships in the federal public domain surveyed in eastern Ohio, drawn by Mathew Carey after surveys by Thomas Hutchins, engraved by W. Barker, published by Mathew Carey, Philadelphia, 1796. WLC-A   11

Figure 1.9 *Plan of the City Marietta Laid out at the Confluence of the Rivers Ohio and Muskingum.* Undated plan of Marietta, Ohio, in 1789, drawn by E. Ruggles, Jr. AAS-W   12

Figure 1.10 *Plan of Cincinnati, Including All the late Additions & Subdivisions.* Plan of Cincinnati, Ohio, in 1815, drawn by Thomas Darby. From Daniel Drake, *Natural and Statistical View, or Picture of Cincinnati and the Miami Country,* Cincinnati, 1815. DCL-H   13

Figure 1.11 *Plan of Detroit.* Unsigned and undated plan of Detroit, Michigan, as planned by Judge Augustus Brevoort Woodward in   14

INDEX

Library of Congress Cataloging in Publication Data

Reps, John William.
  Cities of the American West.

  Bibliography: p.
  Includes index.
    1. Cities and towns—The West—History.   2.   Urbaniza-
tion—The West.   I.   Title.
HT123.5.A17R46   301.36'3'0978   78-51187
ISBN 0-691-04648-4